Standard Large Sample Tests and Confidence Intervals for Means and Proportions (*cont.*)

Problem & Parameter	Data & Assumptions	Hypotheses	Test Statistic	α-Level Rejection Region	100(1−α)% Confidence Interval
Two Ind. Samples $\mu_1 - \mu_2$	$x_1, \ldots, x_{n_1} \sim N(\mu_1, \sigma_1^2)$ $y_1, \ldots, y_{n_2} \sim N(\mu_2, \sigma_2^2)$ $\sigma_1^2 \neq \sigma_2^2$ unknown	$H_0: \mu_1 - \mu_2 \leq \delta_0$ vs. $H_1: \mu_1 - \mu_2 > \delta_0$ $H_0: \mu_1 - \mu_2 \geq \delta_0$ vs. $H_1: \mu_1 - \mu_2 < \delta_0$ $H_0: \mu_1 - \mu_2 = \delta_0$ vs. $H_1: \mu_1 - \mu_2 \neq \delta_0$	$t = \dfrac{\bar{x} - \bar{y} - \delta_0}{\sqrt{\frac{s_1^2}{n_1} + \frac{s_2^2}{n_2}}}$ $\nu = \dfrac{(w_1 + w_2)^2}{w_1^2/(n_1-1) + w_2^2/(n_2-1)}$, $w_1 = \frac{s_1^2}{n_1},\; w_2 = \frac{s_2^2}{n_2}$	$t > t_{\nu,\alpha}$ $t < -t_{\nu,\alpha}$ $|t| > t_{\nu,\alpha/2}$	$\mu_1 - \mu_2 \geq \bar{x} - \bar{y} - t_{\nu,\alpha}\sqrt{\frac{s_1^2}{n_1} + \frac{s_2^2}{n_2}}$ $\mu_1 - \mu_2 \leq \bar{x} - \bar{y} + t_{\nu,\alpha}\sqrt{\frac{s_1^2}{n_1} + \frac{s_2^2}{n_2}}$ $\left[\bar{x} - \bar{y} \pm t_{\nu,\alpha/2}\sqrt{\frac{s_1^2}{n_1} + \frac{s_2^2}{n_2}}\right]$
Paired Samples μ_d	$(x_1, y_1), \ldots, (x_n, y_n)$ $d_i = x_i - y_i$ $d_1, \ldots, d_n \sim N(\mu_d, \sigma_d^2)$ σ_d^2 unknown	$H_0: \mu_d \leq \delta_0$ vs. $H_1: \mu_d > \delta_0$ $H_0: \mu_d \geq \delta_0$ vs. $H_1: \mu_d < \delta_0$ $H_0: \mu_d = \delta_0$ vs. $H_1: \mu_d \neq \delta_0$	$t = \dfrac{\bar{d} - \delta_0}{s_d/\sqrt{n}}$	$t > t_{n-1,\alpha}$ $t < -t_{n-1,\alpha}$ $|t| > t_{n-1,\alpha/2}$	$\mu_d \geq \bar{d} - t_{n-1,\alpha}\frac{s_d}{\sqrt{n}}$ $\mu_d \leq \bar{d} + t_{n-1,\alpha}\frac{s_d}{\sqrt{n}}$ $\left[\bar{d} \pm t_{n-1,\alpha/2}\frac{s_d}{\sqrt{n}}\right]$
Single Sample p	$x_1, \ldots, x_n \sim \text{Bern}(p)$	$H_0: p \leq p_0$ vs. $H_1: p > p_0$ $H_0: p \geq p_0$ vs. $H_1: p < p_0$ $H_0: p = p_0$ vs. $H_1: p \neq p_0$	$z = \dfrac{\hat{p} - p_0}{\sqrt{p_0 q_0/n}}$ $\hat{p} = \bar{x},\; \hat{q} = 1 - \hat{p}$	$z > z_\alpha$ $z < -z_\alpha$ $|z| > z_{\alpha/2}$	$p \geq \hat{p} - z_\alpha\sqrt{\frac{\hat{p}\hat{q}}{n}}$ $p \leq \hat{p} + z_\alpha\sqrt{\frac{\hat{p}\hat{q}}{n}}$ $\left[\hat{p} \pm z_{\alpha/2}\sqrt{\frac{\hat{p}\hat{q}}{n}}\right]$
Two Ind. Samples $p_1 - p_2$	$x_1, \ldots, x_{n_1} \sim \text{Bern}(p_1)$ $y_1, \ldots, y_{n_2} \sim \text{Bern}(p_2)$ $\hat{p}_1 = \bar{x}, \hat{q}_1 = 1 - \hat{p}_1$ $\hat{p}_2 = \bar{y}, \hat{q}_2 = 1 - \hat{p}_2$	$H_0: p_1 - p_2 \leq \delta_0$ vs. $H_1: p_1 - p_2 > \delta_0$ $H_0: p_1 - p_2 \geq \delta_0$ vs. $H_1: p_1 - p_2 < \delta_0$ $H_0: p_1 - p_2 = \delta_0$ vs. $H_1: p_1 - p_2 \neq \delta_0$	$z = \dfrac{\hat{p}_1 - \hat{p}_2 - (p_1 - p_2)}{\sqrt{\frac{\hat{p}_1\hat{q}_1}{n_1} + \frac{\hat{p}_2\hat{q}_2}{n_2}}}$	$z > z_\alpha$ $z < -z_\alpha$ $|z| > z_{\alpha/2}$	$p_1 - p_2 \geq \hat{p}_1 - \hat{p}_2 - z_\alpha\sqrt{\frac{\hat{p}_1\hat{q}_1}{n_1} + \cdots}$ $p_1 - p_2 \leq \hat{p}_1 - \hat{p}_2 + z_\alpha\sqrt{\frac{\hat{p}_1\hat{q}_1}{n_1} + \cdots}$ $\left[\hat{p}_1 - \hat{p}_2 \pm z_{\alpha/2}\sqrt{\frac{\hat{p}_1\hat{q}_1}{n_1} + \cdots}\right]$

Library of Congress Cataloging-in-Publication Data

Tamhane, Ajit C.
    Statistics and data analysis : from elementary to intermediate /
    Ajit Tamhane, Dorothy Dunlop.
      p. cm.
    Includes index.
    ISBN 0-13-744426-5 (hardcover)
    1. Statistics. I. Dunlop, Dorothy. II. Title.
    QA276.T25 2000   99-047149
    519.5–dc21   CIP

Acquisitions editor: **Kathleen Boothby Sestak**
Executive project manager: **Ann Heath**
Marketing manager: **Melody Marcus**
Production editor: **Betsy Williams**
Senior managing editor: **Linda Mihatov Behrens**
Executive managing editor: **Kathleen Schiaparelli**
Vice-president and director of manufacturing and production: **David W. Riccardi**
Manufacturing buyer: **Alan Fischer**
Manufacturing manager: **Trudy Pisciotti**
Marketing assistant: **Vince Jansen**
Art director: **Jayne Conte**
Cover designer: **Bruce Kenselaar**
Editorial assistant: **Joanne Wendelken**
Composition: **PreTEX**

© 2000 by Prentice-Hall, Inc.
Upper Saddle River, NJ 07458

Printed in the United States of America
10 9 8 7 6 5 4 3 2

ISBN 0-13-744426-5

Prentice-Hall International (UK) Limited, *London*
Prentice-Hall of Australia Pty. Limited, *Sydney*
Prentice-Hall Canada Inc., *Toronto*
Prentice-Hall Hispanoamericana, S.A., *Mexico*
Prentice-Hall of India Private Limited, *New Delhi*
Prentice-Hall of Japan, Inc., *Tokyo*
Prentice-Hall (Singapore) Pte. Ltd., *Singapore*
Editora Prentice-Hall do Brasil, Ltda., *Rio de Janeiro*

To Our Families
Meena, Shalaka, and Salil
and
John, James, and Robert

CONTENTS

Preface _____ **ix**

▶ **1 INTRODUCTION**   **1**

1.1   What Is Statistics?   1
1.2   The Nature of Statistics   2
1.3   What Is This Book About?   4
1.4   Advice to the Student   5

▶ **2 REVIEW OF PROBABILITY**   **7**

2.1   Basic Ideas   8
2.2   Conditional Probability and Independence   15
2.3   Random Variables and Their Distributions   20
2.4   Expected Value, Variance, and Other Parameters of a Distribution   24
2.5   Jointly Distributed Random Variables   30
2.6   Chebyshev's Inequality and Weak Law of Large Numbers   40
2.7   Selected Discrete Distributions   42
2.8   Selected Continuous Distributions   49
2.9   Normal Distribution   52
2.10   *Transformations of Random Variables   58
2.11   Chapter Summary   62
     Exercises   63

▶ **3 COLLECTING DATA**   **82**

3.1 Types of Statistical Studies   83
3.2 Observational Studies   85
3.3 Basic Sampling Designs   91
3.4 Experimental Studies   95
3.5 Chapter Summary   100
     Exercises   101

▶ **4 SUMMARIZING AND EXPLORING DATA**   **107**

4.1 Types of Data   107
4.2 Summarizing Categorical Data   109
4.3 Summarizing Numerical Data   109
4.4 Summarizing Bivariate Data   128
4.5 Summarizing Time-Series Data   142
4.6 Chapter Summary   149
     Exercises   150

▶ **5 SAMPLING DISTRIBUTIONS OF STATISTICS**   **167**

5.1 Sampling Distribution of the Sample Mean   168
5.2 Sampling Distribution of the Sample Variance   175
5.3 Student's t-Distribution   179
5.4 Snedecor-Fisher's F-Distribution   181
5.5 *Sampling Distributions of Order Statistics   184
5.6 Chapter Summary   187
     Exercises   188

▶ **6 BASIC CONCEPTS OF INFERENCE**   **196**

6.1 Point Estimation   197
6.2 Confidence Interval Estimation   203
6.3 Hypothesis Testing   208
6.4 Chapter Summary   227
     Exercises   228

▶ **7 INFERENCES FOR SINGLE SAMPLES**   **237**

7.1 Inferences on Mean (Large Samples)   237
7.2 Inferences on Mean (Small Samples)   249
7.3 Inferences on Variance   254
7.4 *Prediction and Tolerance Intervals   257
7.5 Chapter Summary   260
     Exercises   262

▶ **8 INFERENCES FOR TWO SAMPLES**   **269**

8.1   Independent Samples and Matched Pairs Designs   269
8.2   Graphical Methods for Comparing Two Samples   271
8.3   Comparing Means of Two Populations   272
8.4   *Comparing Variances of Two Populations   286
8.5   Chapter Summary   289
      Exercises   290

▶ **9 INFERENCES FOR PROPORTIONS AND COUNT DATA**   **299**

9.1   Inferences on Proportion   299
9.2   Inferences for Comparing Two Proportions   307
9.3   Inferences for One-Way Count Data   314
9.4   Inferences for Two-Way Count Data   321
9.5   Chapter Summary   329
      Exercises   330

▶ **10 SIMPLE LINEAR REGRESSION AND CORRELATION**   **346**

10.1 A Probabilistic Model for Simple Linear Regression   347
10.2 Fitting the Simple Linear Regression Model   348
10.3 Statistical Inference for Simple Linear Regression   356
10.4 Regression Diagnostics   365
10.5 *Correlation Analysis   379
10.6 Pitfalls of Regression and Correlation Analyses   384
10.7 Chapter Summary   385
      Exercises   386

▶ **11 MULTIPLE LINEAR REGRESSION**   **401**

11.1 A Probabilistic Model for Multiple Linear Regression   402
11.2 Fitting the Multiple Regression Model   403
11.3 *Multiple Regression Model in Matrix Notation   405
11.4 Statistical Inference for Multiple Regression   407
11.5 Regression Diagnostics   413
11.6 Topics in Regression Modeling   415
11.7 Variable Selection Methods   427
11.8 A Strategy for Building a Multiple Regression Model   437
11.9 Chapter Summary   439
      Exercises   440

▶ **12** ANALYSIS OF SINGLE FACTOR EXPERIMENTS   **457**

12.1   Completely Randomized Design   457
12.2   Multiple Comparisons of Means   467
12.3   *Random Effects Model for a One-Way Layout   480
12.4   Randomized Block Design   482
12.5   Chapter Summary   490
       Exercises   492

▶ **13** ANALYSIS OF MULTIFACTOR EXPERIMENTS   **504**

13.1   Two-Factor Experiments with Fixed Crossed Factors   505
13.2 2^k Factorial Experiments   522
13.3   Other Selected Types of Two-Factor Experiments   540
13.4   Chapter Summary   547
       Exercises   548

▶ **14** NONPARAMETRIC STATISTICAL METHODS   **562**

14.1   Inferences for Single Samples   562
14.2   Inferences for Two Independent Samples   573
14.3   Inferences for Several Independent Samples   580
14.4   Inferences for Several Matched Samples   583
14.5   Rank Correlation Methods   586
14.6   *Resampling Methods   594
14.7   Chapter Summary   603
       Exercises   604

▶ **15** LIKELIHOOD, BAYESIAN, AND DECISION THEORY METHODS   **613**

15.1   Maximum Likelihood Estimation   613
15.2   Likelihood Ratio Tests   631
15.3   Bayesian Inference   646
15.4   Decision Theory   650
15.5   Chapter Summary   657
       Exercises   660

▶ Appendix **A** TABLES   **669**

▶ Appendix **B** ABBREVIATED ANSWERS TO
                 SELECTED ODD-NUMBERED EXERCISES   **686**

Index   713

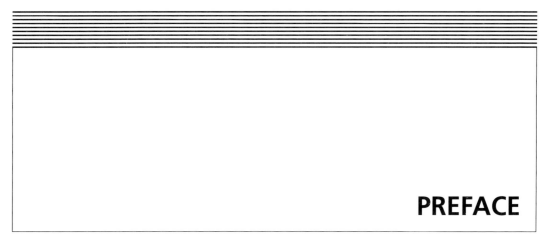

PREFACE

SCOPE AND GOALS

This book provides a one-year calculus-based coverage of statistics and data analysis that spans from the very beginnings of the subject to intermediate level topics in mathematical statistics. We wrote this book with two main goals in mind. The first goal is to introduce the basic concepts and commonly used methods of statistics in a unified manner with sound explanations of when and how to use the methods and why they work (including mathematical derivations given in separate sections marked with asterisks). The second goal is to demonstrate diverse applications of the methods to a wide range of disciplines.

INTENDED AUDIENCE

The book is primarily intended for junior and senior level undergraduates. Some of the more advanced topics in the book, especially the final chapter on the likelihood, Bayesian, and decision theory methods, can form a one-semester survey course for graduate students with good mathematical backgrounds. We have used the preliminary drafts of the book for both such undergraduate and graduate courses at Northwestern University.

UNIQUE FEATURES

1. There is an extensive breadth of coverage ranging from very elementary methods to such advanced methods as logistic regression and multifactor experiments. Thus a thorough study of the book will not only prepare students to do most standard statistical analyses, but will also serve as a reference for the future.

2. The book emphasizes the applicability of statistics to a wide variety of fields (including the biomedical sciences, business, education, engineering, physical and chemical sciences, and the social sciences) by drawing examples from these fields using real data wherever possible. We hope that this cross-disciplinary approach will help students learn to be flexible and adaptive to the ever-changing demands in today's workplace, where they will often be required to deal with problems outside their fields of expertise.

3. The book covers some topics that are not included in most textbooks at this level. For example, methods of collecting data, including sample surveys and designed

experiments, are discussed in an early chapter (Chapter 3). In our view, this topic should be covered before plunging into the details of data analysis. After all, how the data are collected dictates how they should be analyzed. More importantly, the method of data collection affects the quality of the data, and no amount of statistical magic can salvage a poorly designed study. This chapter discusses the important basic notions of sources of biases in data and presents randomization and blocking/matching as devices to avoid some types of biases.

4. Another topic that is not covered in most other textbooks is modern computer-intensive methods; in particular those based on the ideas of resampling and boot-strap. These are covered briefly in the chapter on nonparametric statistics (Chapter 14, Section 14.6). We subscribe to the widespread view that these methods will become increasingly important in the analysis of data as they permit a user to break the traditional shackles of strong distributional assumptions, typically normality and independence.

5. Chapter summaries are provided for a quick review of the main concepts and results. Tabular summaries of the basic formulas for standard probability distributions and tests and confidence intervals for selected parameters are given in respective chapters.

6. Each statistical method is presented and followed by one or two illustrative examples. A mathematical derivation of the method is generally given at the end of the section, and is marked with an asterisk. All advanced sections are marked with asterisks, so that the more elementary courses may skip them without disrupting the flow of the material.

7. In many cases the same examples are developed in steps in each chapter, analyzing the data in more depth as additional techniques are introduced. Some examples are carried across chapters to illustrate the applications of different methods to the same data sets.

8. We have paid particular attention to writing interesting and educational exercises. As far as possible, real data sets with sufficient background information are used. Many of the data sets are taken from the book *A Handbook of Small Data Sets* by Hand et al.[1], all references to this book are abbreviated as *Small Data Sets*. Most exercises guide a student through several steps, each step addressing a different or an additional aspect of analysis. The emphasis is on urging a student to think critically and to interpret the analysis, not just calculate numbers even if they are the "right" answers.

9. Exercises for each chapter are grouped together at the end, but are categorized by chapter sections. A few drill type exercises are given at the beginning of each section, followed by more challenging ones. Advanced exercises are given at the end. They typically involve simple mathematical proofs or generalizations of some results or more extensive data analyses requiring methods from different sections of the chapter. Many of these advanced exercises give students glimpses into topics beyond the scope of the present text. As such, they may be assigned to graduate students or to bright, motivated undergraduates to encourage them to pursue further

---

[1] D. J. Hand, F. Daly, A. D. Lunn, K. J. McConway, and E. Ostrowski (1993), *A Handbook of Small Data Sets*, London: Chapman & Hall, 1993.

studies in statistics. Answers to selected odd-numbered exercises are included at the end of the text.

10. Many exercises require the use of a computer; these exercises are marked by the symbol ■. It is recommended that some of the smaller data sets be analyzed by hand as this experience adds to the understanding of the methods. The diskette packaged in the back of the text contains data sets for all exercises.

SUPPLEMENTARY MATERIALS

The following supplementary materials are available to facilitate the use of this book.

1. **The Instructor's Solution Manual**: The manual gives detailed solutions including mathematical proofs, derivations, and graphical plots for all exercises in the book. It may be requested from the publisher upon adoption of the book.
2. **Data Disk**: The diskette packaged in the back of the text contains data sets for all exercises saved as ASCII, MINITAB, and Microsoft Excel files. Users who prefer to obtain the data files in SAS or SPSS format may download them from the web site.
3. **Web site**: A web site is set up at `http://www.prenhall.com/tamhane` where the following items will be posted as they become available: (i) errata, (ii) supplementary text material, (iii) book reviews, (iv) data files for all exercises, and (v) links to other useful sources of data sets.
4. **Text and Student Version Software Packages**:
   Statistics and Data Analysis: **and SPSS 9.0 Student Version Integrated Package:** A CD-Rom containing the SPSS 9.0 for Windows Student Version and the data files from the text may be purchased as a package with the text book for a small additional charge.
   Statistics and Data Analysis: **and Minitab 12.0 Student Edition Integrated Package:** A CD-Rom containing the Minitab Release 12.0 Student Edition and the data files from the text may be purchased as a package with the text book for a small additional charge.

BACKGROUND AND THE TOOLS NEEDED

Mathematics and probability are the two important tools needed in the study of statistics. Although calculus is used relatively in modicum in this text, a certain mathematical maturity and ability that comes with a calculus background is required. In addition, basic knowledge of matrix algebra is necessary in the chapter on multiple regression. The chapter on probability (Chapter 2) covers the essentials needed to follow the remainder of the text. This chapter is provided for review and reference purposes for those students who have had a previous course in probability. This chapter may be used as a condensed introduction to probability in a combined probability-statistics course.

Another indispensable tool required in modern statistics is a computer. It is useful not just for the tedious task of number crunching, but is equally important for plotting informative graphics in a fast and interactive manner. We assume that a student has access to a desktop computer and a statistical package or a spreadsheet package with statistical capabilities. There are many excellent statistical packages to choose from, MINITAB®, SYSTAT®, SAS®, STATGRAPHICS®, S-PLUS®, and SPSS® to name a few. The Microsoft Excel® spreadsheet package can perform many statistical tasks. It is not the purpose of this text to provide instruction in the use of any of these packages. After all, packages keep evolving, so any software instruction is likely to become obsolete even before the book is published. Fortunately, most of these packages now allow the user to perform complex statistical tasks at the click of a mouse. Also, each package has its strengths and weaknesses, and it is up to the individual instructor to choose the package that best suits the needs of his or her students. We illustrate examples using outputs from several different packages, but mainly from MINITAB, as it is one of the easiest to use.

POSSIBLE COURSE SYLLABI

There is more than enough material in this book for a year-long course in statistics alone (with a probability course as a prerequisite). We realize that most curricula do not have the luxury of such an extensive course. At Northwestern University, we teach a two-quarter undergraduate sequence in statistics (with a quarter-long probability course as a prerequisite), which is taken mainly by industrial engineering (IE) majors with a sprinkling of other majors. For the benefit of IE majors we focus on quality control, reliability, and some business applications primarily through examples. We are able to cover about 70% of the material in this book (excluding Chapters 2 and 15). The optional material is indicated by asterisks which we typically do not cover. Both these courses require student team projects. The project in the first course usually requires a two-group comparison based on a designed experiment or an observational study. The project in the second course requires developing a multiple regression model by using a large archival data base (e.g., marketing, salary, etc.). We also teach a one-quarter graduate course that covers multiple regression (Chapter 11), ANOVA (parts of Chapters 12 and 13), and selected mathematical statistics topics from Chapter 15.

Below we give some suggested syllabi for different undergraduate courses. These assume that lecture hours are not used to give exams. Some instructors may choose not to omit certain indicated sections or cover them through self-reading/homeworks/problem sessions or decide to omit other sections instead. For example, instead of covering Section 4.4 on summarizing bivariate data, one may cover Section 4.5 on summarizing time-series data, or instead of covering Section 14.5 on nonparametric measures of correlation, one may cover Section 14.6 on resampling methods. Also, some instructors may want to give an elementary introduction to the topic of maximum likelihood estimation from the beginning sections of Chapter 15. In any case, we warn the instructor that the following syllabi are quite ambitious and intense in topical coverage, and not much extra material can be added to them. If anything, many of the asterisked sections may need to be omitted.

A ONE-SEMESTER (45 ONE-HOUR LECTURES + 15 ONE-HOUR PROBLEM SESSIONS) PROBABILITY-STATISTICS COURSE

1. Chapter 1:   (*1 lecture*)
2. Chapter 2: Sections 2.1, 2.2 (omit Section 2.2.4), 2.3, 2.4 (omit Sections 2.4.3 −2.4.5), 2.5 (omit Sections 2.5.4, 2.5.7), 2.7 (omit Sections 2.7.3, 2.7.5, 2.7.6), 2.8 (omit Sections 2.8.3, 2.8.4), 2.9   (*12 lectures*)
3. Chapter 3: Sections 3.1, 3.2 (omit Section 3.2.2), 3.3   (*2 lectures*)
4. Chapter 4: Sections 4.1, 4.2, 4.3 (omit Section 4.3.3), 4.4   (*5 lectures*)

5. Chapter 5: Sections 5.1, 5.2   (*3 lectures*)
6. Chapter 6: Sections 6.1 (omit Section 6.1.2), 6.2, 6.3 (omit Section 6.3.4)   (*5 lectures*)
7. Chapter 7: Sections 7.1, 7.2 (discuss Section 5.3 here)   (*3 lectures*)
8. Chapter 8: Sections 8.1 (discuss Section 3.4 here), 8.2, 8.3   (*4 lectures*)
9. Chapter 9: Sections 9.1 (omit Section 9.1.3), 9.2 (omit Section 9.2.2)   (*2 lectures*)
10. Chapter 10: Sections 10.1, 10.2, 10.3 (discuss Section 5.4 here), 10.4   (*6 lectures*)
11. Chapter 11: Sections 11.1, 11.2   (*2 lectures*)

A ONE-QUARTER (30 ONE-HOUR LECTURES + 10 ONE-HOUR PROBLEM SESSIONS) FIRST STATISTICS COURSE WITH A PROBABILITY PREREQUISITE

1. Chapter 1:   (*1 lecture*)
2. Chapter 3: Sections 3.1, 3.2 (omit Section 3.2.2), 3.3   (*2 lectures*)
3. Chapter 4: Sections 4.1, 4.2, 4.3 (omit Section 4.3.3), 4.4   (*5 lectures*)
4. Chapter 5: Sections 5.1, 5.2   (*3 lectures*)
5. Chapter 6: Sections 6.1 (omit Section 6.1.2), 6.2, 6.3 (omit Section 6.3.4)   (*5 lectures*)
6. Chapter 7: Sections 7.1, 7.2 (discuss Section 5.3 here)   (*3 lectures*)
7. Chapter 8: Sections 8.1 (discuss Section 3.4 here), 8.2, 8.3   (*4 lectures*)
8. Chapter 9: Sections 9.1 (omit Section 9.1.3), 9.2 (omit Section 9.2.2)   (*2 lectures*)
9. Chapter 10: Sections 10.1, 10.2, 10.3 (discuss Section 5.4 here)   (*5 lectures*)

A ONE-QUARTER (30 ONE-HOUR LECTURES + 10 ONE-HOUR PROBLEM SESSIONS) SECOND STATISTICS COURSE

1. Chapter 11: Sections 11.1, 11.2, 11.3, 11.4, 11.5 (discuss Section 10.4 here), 11.6 (omit Sections 11.6.4, 11.6.5), 11.7, 11.8   (*10 lectures*)
2. Chapter 12: Sections 12.1, 12.2 (omit Section 12.2.2), 12.4 (omit Section 12.4.5)   (*6 lectures*)
3. Chapter 13: Sections 13.1 (omit Sections 13.1.5, 13.1.6), 13.2 (omit Section 13.2.5)   (*5 lectures*)
4. Chapter 9: Sections 9.3, 9.4 (omit Section 9.4.3)   (*3 lectures*)
5. Chapter 14: Sections 14.1, 14.2 (omit Section 14.2.2), 14.3 (omit Section 14.3.2), 14.4 (omit Section 14.4.2), 14.5 (omit Section 14.5.3)   (*6 lectures*)

ACKNOWLEDGMENTS

First we would like to acknowledge the source of inspiration for this book, which are the following three outstanding texts: *Statistics* by David Freedman, Robert Pisani, Roger Purves and Ani Adhikari, *Introduction to the Practice of Statistics* by David Moore and George McCabe, and *Mathematical Statistics and Data Analysis* by John Rice. Their presentation of the subject is very much in line with our view of how statistics ought to be taught (albeit at increasingly higher mathematical levels). Unfortunately, these texts did not always suit our needs because of the special backgrounds of our students and the topics that we wanted to cover in our courses. We believe we are not unique in this respect. In trying to emulate these texts, we realize that we have set ourselves a very difficult but laudable goal.

We have taken data for exercises and presentation techniques from many other books. It is impossible to list them all, although we have tried to give credit in specific cases. We apologize for any inadvertent omissions. One group whose debt can never be fully repaid is our teachers from whom we have learned a great deal, and whose ideas and thoughts permeate this book.

We thank the following reviewers for their comments and suggestions, which have greatly improved the book: David Allen (University of Kentucky), George Casella (Cornell University), Mahtash Esfandiari (UCLA), Dale Everson (University of Idaho), Chris Franklin (University of Georgia), Robert Gould (UCLA), Steven Jordan (University of Illinois at Chicago), Carl Spruill (Georgia Tech), Gunther Walther (Stanford), and Michael Wolf (UCLA). Joe Feinglass and Yi-Ching Hsieh of the Northwestern University Medical School provided comments on Chapters 3 and 6, respectively. Yi-Cheng Hsieh also helped in writing the solutions for the exercises from Chapter 6.

Brent Logan, a PhD student in the Department of Statistics at Northwestern University, wrote the Instructor's Solution Manual and the answers to selected odd-numbered exercises given in Appendix B and found many errors in the process. All solutions were checked by Priscilla Gathoni. Several batches of students at Northwestern University toiled through early drafts of the book and gave us invaluable feedback. An early draft was also used in a course at UCLA; comments from the instructor and students in that course were very helpful. Despite all the comments and corrections that we received from many individuals, there are bound to be some residual errors for which we take full responsibility.

We thank Professor Bruce Ankenman of the Department of Industrial Engineering and Management Sciences at Nortwestern University, who helped in creating the illustration shown on the cover. We also thank Mark Harms, a research assistant in the Institute for Health Services Research and Policy Studies at Northwestern University, who converted all figures into encapsulated postscript files.

It was a pleasure to work with Ann Heath, Editor, and Betsy Williams, Production Editor, both of Prentice Hall. Ann helped us in the development of the manuscript over several years with patience and encouragement. She also converted all data files into MINITAB and SPSS formats. Betsy efficiently oversaw the transition of the manuscript into the final book form. Last but not the least, we are grateful for the love and support of our respective families. This book is dedicated to them.

Ajit C. Tamhane, Evanston, IL
Dorothy D. Dunlop, Evanston, IL

CHAPTER 1

INTRODUCTION

1.1 WHAT IS STATISTICS?

Statistics is the science of collecting and analyzing data for the purpose of drawing conclusions and making decisions. The key feature of any data is that they are variable. For example, to determine the traffic-signal timings at a busy intersection, data on vehicle flows are gathered. The number of vehicles passing through an intersection varies depending on the time of the day and from day to day; in addition, there could be measurement and recording errors. Statistics provides data collection methods to reduce biases, and analysis methods to identify patterns and draw inferences from noisy data.

Statistics pervades our everyday lives. Everyone is familiar with election and opinion polls that survey samples of people. A controversial proposal by the U. S. Bureau of the Census to make a statistical adjustment for the undercount of people not reached by the usual methods is a major example of statistics affecting public policy. Monthly surveys conducted by federal government agencies report on critical economic statistics such as unemployment rate, consumer price index, balance of trade, and producers' inventories. The Centers for Disease Control monitors and reports data on cases of communicable diseases such as AIDS, and on life expectancies of different demographic groups. Reports on risk and prevention factors for cancer and heart disease appear regularly in the media. TV shows live or die based on the ratings obtained by sampling households; large amounts of advertising dollars ride on these ratings.

Statistics also pervades our working lives. The majority of new statistical methodologies have been developed to solve problems arising in scientific research. In fact, statistics is an integral part of what is known as the scientific method and forms an intellectual basis for testing theories based on empirical studies.[1] Traditionally, agricultural and biological sciences have been the source of many problems requiring innovative statistical methods. Physical and chemical sciences also play an important role in the development of statistics. Engineers use statistically designed experiments to test products for reliability and to determine failure modes. Medical researchers perform controlled clinical trials to test the efficacy of new therapies and drugs. Genetic researchers use statistics for gene mapping and DNA matching. Sales and marketing managers use customer survey data to plan new promotions and advertising strategies. Demand forecasting is an important statistical tool to determine inventory and production quantities. Political and social researchers use data from opinion polls and surveys to model behaviors of individuals and groups of people.

In summary, in today's "information age," one needs an elementary knowledge of statistics to be able to make wise choices in everyday life. To be a successful professional, basic knowledge of statistics is almost essential.

1.2   THE NATURE OF STATISTICS

1.2.1 Three Common Statistical Tasks

Every application of statistics involves one or more of the following three tasks:

- Collecting data.
- Summarizing and exploring data.
- Drawing conclusions and making decisions based on data.

Statistical issues in collecting data concern the design of observational studies (e.g., sample surveys) and experimental studies with a goal to minimize biases and variability in data so that the effects of relevant factors can be estimated accurately. Once the data are obtained, they need to be summarized and explored to detect errors and assess patterns, which involves tabulating overall summaries and making graphical plots of data. This aspect of statistics is referred to as **descriptive statistics** or, in more contemporary terms, as **exploratory data analysis**. In contrast, **confirmatory data analysis** deals with drawing conclusions and making decisions. This type of analysis constitutes a major part of most statistical investigations and is referred to as **inferential statistics**. A very important task related to inferential methods is **fitting models** to data. This includes fitting distributions to data and modeling relationships between variables.

1.2.2 Probability and Statistics

Statistics uses tools of probability to model the variability in the data and to quantify the uncertainty in the conclusions drawn from such data. To understand the relationship

---

[1] G. E. P. Box (1976), "Science and statistics," *Journal of the American Statistical Association*, **71**, pp. 791–799.

between probability and statistics, it is first necessary to explain the basic concepts of population and sample. We discuss these and other related concepts here in an informal way; more formal definitions and explanations are given in Chapters 3 and 6.

A **population** is a collection of all **units** of interest. The units may be people, households, geographic regions, time periods, items produced, etc. A **sample** is a subset of a population that is actually observed. For example, the Nielsen ratings of TV shows are based on a sample of a few thousand households.

We are interested in one or more measurable properties or attributes associated with each unit in the population. These properties or attributes are called **variables**, e.g., the employment status and gender of each adult in the U.S. or the location and sales revenue of each franchise of a fast food chain. Generally, we want to know some numerical characteristic(s) of the population defined for each variable of interest. These population characteristics are called **parameters**. For instance, the Bureau of Labor Statistics wants to know the unemployment rate for the population of all adults in the U.S., or a fast food chain wants to know the median sales revenue for all its franchises, and the distribution of the franchises among urban, suburban, and rural locations.

Why study a sample rather than the complete population? Because most populations are too large, e.g., all households in the U.S. This is the primary reason that a sample is used to draw conclusions about the unknown aspects of the population. In order to avoid a biased sample that differs in systematic ways from the population, usually a **random sample** is required that gives an equal preassigned chance to every unit in the population to enter the sample.

In probability we assume that the population and its parameters are *known* and compute the probability of drawing a particular sample. For example, in a typical probability problem, given that a lot of 100 items (the population) contains 5 defectives, one can compute the probability that a random sample of 10 items drawn from this lot contains no defectives. In statistics, on the other hand, we assume that the population and its parameters are *unknown*, e.g., the number of defectives in the lot is unknown. A typical statistical problem is to estimate the unknown number of defectives in the lot from the observed number of defectives in the sample.

More generally, the distribution of the variable values in a population can be modeled by a probability distribution. For example, one may postulate that the distribution of the number of sick days for a large population of employees of a company follows a Poisson distribution (discussed in Chapter 2). In probability this distribution is assumed to be completely *known*. In statistics, on the other hand, while we may assume some probability distribution as a model for the population, one or more parameters associated with that distribution are assumed to be *unknown*. For example, the mean of the Poisson distribution for the number of sick days would be an unknown parameter, which the human resources department of the company wants to know. The statistical problem is to estimate or make some decision about an unknown parameter based on sample data. A quantity computed from the sample data to make statements about an unknown parameter is called a **statistic**. For example, the mean of the number of sick days for a sample of employees is a statistic used to estimate the corresponding unknown mean for the population of all employees. Because a sample does not in general mirror the population exactly and because different samples from the same population give different results (called **sampling variability**), a statistical estimate or a decision is subject to what is called a **sampling error**. One of the goals in inferential statistics is to quantify this sampling error.

　　To summarize, in probability, given the population we draw inferences about a sample; in other words, we proceed from the general to a particular. In statistics, on the other hand, given a sample we draw inferences about the population; in other words, we proceed from a particular to the general. Thus probability is *deductive* in nature, while statistics is *inductive* in nature. However, as discussed previously, statistics uses the tools of probability. Figure 1.1 shows schematically the symbiotic relationship between these two subjects.

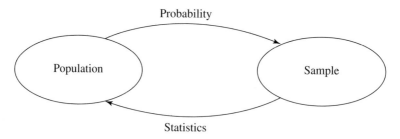

Figure 1.1   Relationship between Probability and Statistics*

1.3   WHAT IS THIS BOOK ABOUT?

The present book is organized according to the three common statistical tasks listed above in Section 1.2. Because of the importance of knowing probability before studying statistics, we begin in Chapter 2 with a review of basic probability and standard distributions. This chapter is primarily intended for someone who has had a previous course in probability; it provides a compendium of basic results for reference. Chapter 3 covers data collection methods, Chapter 4 covers data summary and exploration methods, and Chapters 5 through 15 cover inferential statistical methods, forming the main core of the book.

　　The theoretical underpinnings of statistics reside in probability and mathematics, and yet its motivation stems from applications in many disciplines that use empirical data. In this book, we approach the subject from an applied angle, introducing the methods intuitively. However, the mathematical derivations of the methods are also given in many cases. If a derivation is simple and straightforward, it is integrated in the text; in other cases, it is given in a separate starred section (indicating that it may be skipped without disrupting the flow of the text) following the discussion of the method and examples. An exception to this general rule is Chapter 15, which gives an introduction to mathematical statistics to prepare advanced undergraduates and beginning graduate students for further studies in statistics.

　　Computing is an integral part of modern data analysis. This book primarily covers standard analysis methods that are available in most commercial statistical packages.

---

*Figure adapted from J. L. Devore (1995), *Probability and Statistics for Engineering and the Sciences*, 4th ed., Belmont, CA: Duxbury Press.

There are numerous packages on the market, with a wide range of capabilities and prices. In this book, for the most part, we give outputs from the MINITAB package, since it is easy to use. The data sets used in all exercises are provided in text (ASCII), SAS, SPSS, and MINITAB format as well as Excel spreadsheets to facilitate analyses using other software packages. Exercises requiring use of computers are marked with the symbol ▉.

We have not provided instructions on how to use any statistical packages, since continual evolution of packages quickly makes such instructions obsolete. Also, basic applications of most statistical procedures require nothing more than a few clicks of the mouse after entering the data in a worksheet. Your instructor can help you with the features of the statistical software used for your course.

1.4   ADVICE TO THE STUDENT

Many students approach a required statistics course with trepidation. Prior interest in the subject is usually very low. This colors students' anticipation of the course as being dry and boring, which ultimately affects their performance. (Of course, not all the blame for this impression lies with students; instructors of statistics must share equal blame.) When their "bad" experiences are transmitted to the next generation of students, this vicious cycle repeats itself.

Our first word of advice to the student is to keep an open mind and have a positive attitude. Statistics is an interesting and valuable subject. The mathematics of statistics is not at all difficult at the level of this book. To help you grasp the concepts, we have made every attempt to explain them as clearly as possible with many examples. Please read and digest these explanations. Always focus on the interpretation of results, rather than how to compute them.

One reason for the reputation of statistics as a dull subject was its previous emphasis on formulas and the tedium of calculations. Now we use a computer to do most statistical calculations, so this problem no longer exists. Another advantage of a computer is that it helps us to transform and graph the data quickly and in a variety of ways. Keep this visual analysis of data in mind. It will often add unanticipated insights into data that many calculations cannot.

This book is not devoid of formulas; in fact, there are many. The formulas are important, not so much to show you how to compute, but rather to help you understand what is being computed. They provide a mathematical language for communicating statistical ideas. Although you will use a computer to perform most calculations, it is worthwhile for you to do one or two calculations by hand with each important formula using small data sets. This will help you understand the methods better.

Another common student complaint about statistical formulas is that they don't know which one to use when. Some books provide a decision-tree diagram for guidance, but there is no easy solution to this dilemma apart from doing as many word exercises as you can. Soon you will be able to recognize the structure and the type of the data and the nature of the comparisons to be made. These dictate the statistical method to be used for data analysis.

Statistics do not come alive without the use of real data to answer substantive questions. We have provided real data in many exercises, but no data are as real as your own data. These could be new data that you collect or archival data (e.g., data available in handbooks or on Web sites). Collecting and analyzing data to answer your questions is the best way to learn how statistics is used in practice. Ask your instructor whether you can do a project, if it is not already a part of the course.

Each chapter has a number of starred sections and a number of advanced exercises. These are generally meant for students who want to study in greater depth. If you find the subject matter in unstarred sections of the book easy to follow and interesting, read the starred sections and try some advanced exercises. You will find the additional learning worthwhile, and it may even motivate you to explore topics beyond this book; references for this purpose are provided in footnotes. Best wishes to you on this stimulating and rewarding journey!

CHAPTER 2

REVIEW OF PROBABILITY

People often claim to know nothing about probability, but probabilistic concepts permeate daily life. A physician tells a patient with Hodgkin's disease that there is a 95% cure rate with treatment. A sportscaster gives a football team a 70% chance of winning the next Superbowl. These two situations represent two different approaches to probability.

The **frequentist approach**, illustrated by the cure rate for a disease, assigns a probability that is a long-term relative frequency. The cure rate is based on the experience from observing the outcomes of a large number of treated cases. When an experiment is repeated a large number of times under identical conditions, a regular pattern may emerge. In that case, the relative frequencies with which different outcomes occur will settle down to fixed proportions. These fixed proportions are defined as the probabilities of the corresponding outcomes.

The frequentist approach evolved from the **classical approach** to probability originating in the study of games of chance in the 17th century by Fermat (1601–1665), Pascal (1623 − 1662), and James Bernoulli (1654–1705), among others. The mathematical theory of the classical approach was further developed by de Moivre (1667–1754), Poisson (1781–1840), Laplace (1749–1827), and Gauss (1777–1855). In this approach different elementary outcomes of a game (e.g., head or tail in a toss of a coin or one of six faces in a toss of a die) are assumed to be equally likely. The probabilities of more complex outcomes (e.g., two heads in two tosses of coins or a face value of more than 5 in a toss of a die) are then computed by counting. Although the probabilities of elementary outcomes may be assumed based on the nature of the game, they can also be thought of as long-term relative frequencies (obtained by repeating the game a large number of times).

The **personal** or **subjective approach**, illustrated by the sportscaster's Superbowl forecast, is a personal assessment of the chance that a given outcome will occur. The situations in this case are one-time phenomena that are not repeatable. The accuracy of this probability depends on the information available about the particular situation and a person's interpretation of that information. A probability can be assigned, but it may vary from person to person.

Both the frequentist approach (including the classical approach) and the subjective approach can be addressed within a common mathematical framework of the **axiomatic approach**, in which one starts with a few axioms or postulates, from which all results are derived. This is the modern approach to theoretical probability, which is introduced in Section 2.1.2. Nonetheless, the frequentist approach will be the basis for interpreting probability in this text.

2.1   BASIC IDEAS

2.1.1 Sample Spaces and Events

We begin with the notion of a **random experiment**, which is a procedure or an operation whose outcome is uncertain and cannot be predicted in advance. The collection of all possible outcomes of a random experiment is called a **sample space**. We will use letter S to denote a sample space.

EXAMPLE 2.1

The following are some examples of random experiments and the associated sample spaces.

1. Toss a coin once: $S = \{H, T\}$ where H = Head and T = Tail.
2. Toss a coin twice: $S = \{(H, H), (H, T), (T, H), (T, T)\}$.
3. Roll a single die: $S = \{1, 2, \ldots, 6\}$.
4. Roll two dice: $S = \{(1, 1), (1, 2), \ldots, (6, 6)\}$.
5. Count the number of defective welds in a car body: $S = \{0, 1, 2, \ldots, N\}$, where N = total number of welds.
6. Measure the relative humidity of air: $S = [0, 100]$.
7. Observe the lifetime of a car battery: $S = [0, \infty)$.

In the first five examples, we have **discrete sample spaces**; in the last two, we have **continuous sample spaces**.   ◆

An **event** is a set of outcomes of a random experiment, i.e., a subset of the sample space S.

EXAMPLE 2.2

Here are some events corresponding to the sample spaces given in Example 2.1.

1. Head = {H}.

2. Exactly one head = {(H, T), (T, H)}.

3. The outcome is even = {2, 4, 6}.

4. The sum of the numbers on two dice equals five = {(1, 4), (2, 3), (3, 2), (4, 1)}.

5. The number of defective welds is no more than two = {0, 1, 2}.

6. The relative humidity is at least 90% = [90,100].

7. The car battery fails before 12 months = [0, 12).   ◆

Event Algebra.   Event algebra is a mathematical language to express relationships among events and combinations of events.

The **union** of two events A and B (denoted by $A \cup B$) is the event consisting of all outcomes that belong to A or B or both. For example, if A = {Sum of two dice is a multiple of 3} = {3, 6, 9, 12} and B = {Sum of two dice is a multiple of 4} = {4, 8, 12}, then $A \cup B$ = {3, 4, 6, 8, 9, 12}.

The **intersection** of events A and B (denoted by $A \cap B$ or simply by AB) is the event consisting of all outcomes common to both A and B. For events A and B of the previous example we have $A \cap B$ = {12}.

The **complement** of an event A (denoted by A^c) is the event consisting of all outcomes *not* in A. For events A and B of the previous example, A^c = {2, 4, 5, 7, 8, 10, 11} and B^c = {2, 3, 5, 6, 7, 9, 10, 11}.

If A and B have no outcomes in common, i.e., if $A \cap B = \phi$, then A and B are called **disjoint** or **mutually exclusive** events. For example, if A is the event that the sum of the two dice is even and B is the event that the sum of the two dice is odd, then $A \cap B = \phi$. These relationships can be illustrated by a **Venn diagram**, as shown in Figure 2.1.

An event A is said to be **included** in B (denoted by $A \subset B$) if every outcome in A is also in B. For example, if A is the event that the sum of the two dice is a multiple of 4 and B is the event that the sum of the two dice is a multiple of 2, then $A \subset B$.

Augustus de Morgan (1806–1871) related the union and intersection operations through the complement:

1. $(A \cup B)^c = A^c \cap B^c$.

2. $(A \cap B)^c = A^c \cup B^c$.

These relationships, known as **de Morgan's laws**, can be understood by drawing the appropriate Venn diagrams.

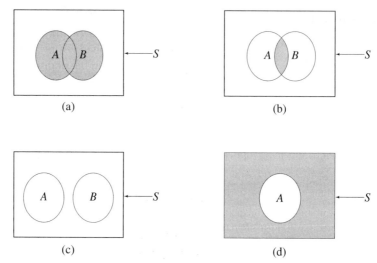

Figure 2.1   Venn Diagrams for (a) Union: $A \cup B$; (b) Intersection: $A \cap B$; (c) Disjoint Events: $A \cap B = \phi$; (d) Complement: A^c

2.1.2 Axioms of Probability and Basic Results

Let S denote the sample space of an experiment. Associated with each event A in S is a number, $P(A)$, called the **probability** of A, which satisfies the following three axioms:

Axiom 1: $P(A) \geq 0$.

Axiom 2: $P(S) = 1$.

Axiom 3: If A and B are mutually exclusive events, then $P(A \cup B) = P(A) + P(B)$.

These three axioms form the basis of all of probability theory. This **axiomatic approach** was developed by Kolmogorov (1903–1987), one of the most prominent Russian mathematicians of the 20th century.

The following basic results (and others) can be derived using event algebra (or Venn diagrams).

Result 1: $P(A^c) = 1 - P(A)$.

Result 2: For any two events A and B, $P(A \cup B) = P(A) + P(B) - P(A \cap B)$.

Result 3: For any two events A and B, $P(A) = P(A \cap B) + P(A \cap B^c)$.

Result 4: If $B \subset A$, then $A \cap B = B$. Therefore $P(A) - P(B) = P(A \cap B^c)$ and $P(A) \geq P(B)$.

Applying Result 1 to de Morgan's laws, we obtain

$$P\left\{(A \cup B)^c\right\} = 1 - P(A \cup B) = P(A^c \cap B^c)$$

and

$$P\left\{(A \cap B)^c\right\} = 1 - P(A \cap B) = P(A^c \cup B^c).$$

EXAMPLE 2.3

Samples of spinal fluid are routinely tested for the presence of tuberculosis (TB) and bacteria. Suppose that 80% of the samples test negative for both TB and bacteria. What is the probability that a random sample tests positive for either TB or bacteria?

Consider the events A = Sample tests positive for TB, B = Sample tests positive for bacteria, A^c = Sample tests negative for TB, and B^c = Sample tests negative for bacteria. Thus $A^c \cap B^c$ = Sample tests negative for both TB *and* bacteria. Using de Morgan's law, the required probability is

$$P(A \cup B) = 1 - P\left\{(A \cup B)^c\right\}$$

$$= 1 - P\left\{A^c \cap B^c\right\}$$

$$= 1 - 0.80 = 0.20. \qquad \blacklozenge$$

From Result 2, we obtain the inequality

$$P(A \cup B) \leq P(A) + P(B),$$

since $P(A \cap B) \geq 0$. This is known as the **Bonferroni inequality**. It provides a useful upper bound on the probability of a union of two events. The following is a generalization of Result 2 to more than two events: Let $A_1, A_2, \ldots, A_n$ be $n \geq 2$ events. Then

$$P(A_1 \cup A_2 \cup \cdots \cup A_n) = \sum_{i=1}^{n} P(A_i) - \sum_{i \neq j} P(A_i \cap A_j)$$

$$+ \sum_{i \neq j \neq k} P(A_i \cap A_j \cap A_k) - \cdots$$

$$+ (-1)^{n-1} P(A_1 \cap A_2 \cap \cdots \cap A_n). \qquad (2.1)$$

This is known as the **inclusion–exclusion principle**. The first term on the right side, namely $\sum_{i=1}^{n} P(A_i)$, provides an upper bound for the probability on the left side, which gives a generalization of the Bonferroni inequality. If the events are mutually exclusive, then their intersections are empty, so all terms except the first term are zero. Therefore the upper bound is actually exact, which is a generalization of Axiom 3. An example of the application of the inclusion–exclusion principle is given in the next section.

2.1.3 How to Calculate Probabilities

Sample Spaces with Equally Likely Outcomes.   If a sample space consists of a finite number of outcomes, say N, and each outcome is equally likely, then it is natural to assign equal probability to each outcome. Thus

$$P(\text{each outcome}) = \frac{1}{N}.$$

If event A consists of M outcomes, then from Axiom 3 it follows that

$$P(A) = \frac{\text{number of outcomes in } A}{\text{number of outcomes in } S} = \frac{M}{N}.$$

EXAMPLE 2.4

If a number is picked at random from the first 1000 integers, what is the probability that it is divisible by either 3 or 5 or 7?

In the first 1000 integers, there are 333 integers divisible by 3, 200 integers divisible by 5, 142 integers divisible by 7, 66 integers divisible by both 3 and 5 (i.e., by 15), 47 integers divisible by both 3 and 7 (i.e., by 21), 28 integers divisible by both 5 and 7 (i.e., by 35), and 9 integers divisible by all three numbers, 3, 5, and 7 (i.e., by 105). Denoting by A_i the event that a randomly chosen number from 1 to 1000 is divisible by i, the desired probability can be evaluated using the inclusion–exclusion principle as follows:

$$P(A_3 \cup A_5 \cup A_7)$$

$$= P(A_3) + P(A_5) + P(A_7) - P(A_3 \cap A_5) - P(A_3 \cap A_7) - P(A_5 \cap A_7)$$

$$+ P(A_3 \cap A_5 \cap A_7)$$

$$= \frac{333}{1000} + \frac{200}{1000} + \frac{142}{1000} - \frac{66}{1000} - \frac{47}{1000} - \frac{28}{1000} + \frac{9}{1000}$$

$$= \frac{543}{1000} = 0.543.$$

Note that the Bonferroni upper bound on this probability is $0.333 + 0.200 + 0.142 = 0.675$.   ◆

It is tedious to list and count every possible outcome if the sample space S is large. There are some counting formulas that provide shortcuts.

Counting Formulas.   We begin by stating a simple rule.

Multiplication Rule: If an operation O consists of a sequence of operations O_1, followed by $O_2, \ldots,$ followed by O_k, and O_1 can result in any one of n_1 outcomes, O_2 can result in any one of n_2 outcomes after performing O_1, and $\ldots,$ O_k can result in any one of n_k outcomes after performing $O_1, O_2 \cdots O_{k-1}$, then the operation O can result in any one of $n_1 n_2 \cdots n_k$ outcomes.

We now derive four counting formulas using this rule.

Counting Formula 1:   A **permutation** is an *ordered arrangement* of distinct items. The total number of permutations of n distinct items is

$$n(n - 1) \cdots (2)(1) = n!$$

where the symbol $n!$ is read as "n factorial" and 0! is defined to be 1. The total number of permutations is obtained by multiplying the number of available choices at each step when creating an arrangement.

EXAMPLE 2.5   (TRAVELING SALESMAN PROBLEM)

This is a well-known, computationally hard optimization problem that can be simply stated as follows: A salesman starting from his origination city has to visit n other cities, each one exactly once, and return home. The distances between all cities are given. Find the shortest path. The reason this problem is hard is that the number of paths increases rapidly with n, which makes complete enumeration impossible for large n, and heuristic practical algorithms do not guarantee the best solution, although some can be shown to come extremely close. Find the number of possible paths for $n = 10$.

There are n choices for the first city to visit, $n - 1$ choices for the second city to visit, and so on. Multiplying these together, we find that there are $n!$ total number of paths. For $n = 10$ the number of paths equals $10! = 3,628,800$. ◆

Counting Formula 2:   The number of permutations of r items out of n distinct items is

$$n(n-1)(n-2)\cdots(n-r+1) = \frac{n(n-1)\cdots(n-r+1)(n-r)\cdots 1}{(n-r)(n-r-1)\cdots 1} = \frac{n!}{(n-r)!}.$$

This expression is obtained by multiplying the number of available choices at each step until the rth choice is made.

EXAMPLE 2.6

Eight swimmers compete for the first, second, and third place titles in the final NCAA National Championship 500-meter freestyle race. The number of different ways that the titles could be awarded is

$$8 \times 7 \times 6 = \frac{8!}{5!} = \frac{40,320}{120} = 336.$$

◆

EXAMPLE 2.7   (BIRTHDAY PROBLEM)

At a gathering of n randomly chosen people, what is the probability that at least two will have the same birthday?

Assume that the birthday of any person has an equal chance of falling on any one of the 365 days of a year. Here the sample space is the collection of all possible choices of birthdays for n people. Since each person's birthday can be any one of 365 days, the sample space has $N = 365^n$ outcomes. We want P(at least two people share a birthday), which equals $1 - P$ (no two people share a birthday) $= 1 - P$ (all n people have different birthdays). Let event $A=\{$all n people have different birthdays$\}$ and $M =$ number of ways to have n different birthdays. Then

$$P(A) = \frac{M}{N}$$

$$= \frac{(365)(364)\cdots(365 - n + 1)}{365^n}$$

$$= \frac{\frac{365!}{(365-n)!}}{(365)^n}.$$

This probability is tabulated below for selected values of n.

n=size of group	2	3	4	$\cdots$	23	$\cdots$	75	$\cdots$	366
P(no two people share a birthday)	.9973	.9918	.9840	$\cdots$	.4927	$\cdots$	.0004	$\cdots$	0

This shows that in a group of 23 people there is at least a 50% chance ($= 1 - 0.4927 = 0.5073$) that at least two will have the same birthday. In fact, 23 is the smallest group size for which this probability exceeds 50%. If you are at a party with 23 or more people and bet that at least two people in the party have the same birthday, your chances of winning are better than 50%. ◆

Counting Formula 3: The number of *unordered* arrangements of r items out of n (called the number of **combinations**) is

$$\frac{n!}{r!(n-r)!} = \binom{n}{r}.$$

The symbol $\binom{n}{r}$ is read as "*n* choose *r*." This expression equals the number of ordered arrangements (from Counting Formula 2) divided by $r!$, the number of duplicates created when the order is disregarded. When the order does not matter, these $r!$ different permutations represent a single selection of r items out of n.

EXAMPLE 2.8

Consider a team of 3 marketing personnel selected from a department of 10 people who will represent a company at a trade show. In counting the number of *distinct* teams that can be selected in this situation, it is the composition of the team that is relevant, not the order in which the names are listed. The number of distinct teams that can be selected from this group is

$$\binom{10}{3} = \frac{10!}{3!(10-3)!} = \frac{10!}{3!7!} = 120.$$

Note that this number also can be obtained by finding the number of different arrangements of 3 people from Counting Formula 2 (which is $\frac{10!}{7!} = 720$) and then dividing by the number of duplicates (which is $3! = 6$). ◆

The quantity $\binom{n}{r}$ appears in the formula for the binomial expansion:

$$(x+y)^n = \sum_{r=0}^{n} \frac{n!}{r!(n-r)!} x^r y^{n-r} = \sum_{r=0}^{n} \binom{n}{r} x^r y^{n-r}$$

where it is referred to as the **binomial coefficient**. This coefficient can be viewed as the number of ways of classifying n objects into two groups so that r of them belong to one group and $n-r$ to the other.

Counting Formula 4: A generalization of the binomial coefficient is required when we need to count the number of ways of classifying n objects into k groups ($k \geq 2$) so that there are r_i in group i ($1 \leq i \leq k$), $r_1 + r_2 + \cdots + r_k = n$. To obtain this number, first consider classifying r_1 items in group 1 and the remaining ones in groups 2 through k. The number of ways of doing this is

$$\binom{n}{r_1} = \frac{n!}{r_1!(n-r_1)!}.$$

Next consider the $n - r_1$ objects in groups 2 through k. The number of ways of classifying these objects so that r_2 of them are in group 2 and the remaining ones are in groups 3 through k is

$$\binom{n - r_1}{r_2} = \frac{(n - r_1)!}{r_2!(n - r_1 - r_2)!}.$$

Continuing in this manner, at each step we obtain that the number of ways of classifying the remaining items so that a specified number of them are in the next group is given by a binomial coefficient. Using the Multiplication Rule, we obtain the total number of ways by multiplying these binomial coefficients, which yields

$$\binom{n}{r_1} \times \binom{n - r_1}{r_2} \times \cdots \times \binom{n - r_1 - \cdots - r_{k-1}}{r_k}$$

$$= \frac{n!}{r_1!(n - r_1)!} \times \frac{(n - r_1)!}{r_2!(n - r_1 - r_2)!} \times \cdots \times \frac{(n - r_1 - \cdots - r_{k-1})!}{r_k!0!}$$

$$= \frac{n!}{r_1!r_2!\cdots r_k!}. \tag{2.2}$$

This is known as the **multinomial coefficient**, which for $k = 2$ reduces to the binomial coefficient.

EXAMPLE 2.9

In bridge, 52 cards in a pack are dealt to four players, with 13 cards to each. Therefore the total number of different bridge hands is the number of ways the 52 cards can be partitioned into four groups of 13 each. Using (2.2), this number is given by

$$\frac{52!}{13!13!13!13!}$$

which is approximately 5.36×10^{28}, an astronomical number indeed.   ◆

2.2   CONDITIONAL PROBABILITY AND INDEPENDENCE

2.2.1 Conditional Probability

Consider two events, A and B. Suppose we know that B has occurred. This knowledge may change the probability that A will occur. We denote by $P(A \mid B)$ the conditional probability of event A given that B has occurred.

As an example, if a card is randomly drawn from a well-shuffled deck of 52 cards, then the probability of drawing a Heart is 1/4. But if additional information is given that the drawn card is red, then the probability of a Heart changes to 1/2, because the sample space is now reduced to just 26 red cards, of which 13 are Hearts. Thus $P(\text{Heart} \mid \text{Red}) = 1/2$. On the other hand, if we are told that the drawn card is black, then $P(\text{Heart} \mid \text{Black}) = 0$.

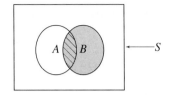

Figure 2.2   Conditional Probability of A Given B

The conditional probability of an event A given an event B with $P(B) > 0$ is defined as

$$P(A \mid B) = \frac{P(A \cap B)}{P(B)}. \tag{2.3}$$

To understand this definition, refer to Figure 2.2. Note that the knowledge that B has occurred effectively reduces the sample space from S to B. Therefore, interpreting the area of an event in the Venn diagram as its probability, $P(A \mid B)$ is the proportion of the area of B occupied by A.

EXAMPLE 2.10   (TOSSING TWO DICE: CONDITIONAL PROBABILITY)

An experiment consists of tossing two fair dice, which has a sample space of $6 \times 6 = 36$ outcomes. Consider two events

$$A = \{\text{Sum of the numbers on the dice is 4 or 8}\}$$

$$= \{(1, 3), (2, 2), (3, 1), (2, 6), (3, 5), (4, 4), (5, 3), (6, 2)\},$$

and

$$B = \{\text{Sum of the numbers on the dice is even}\}$$

$$= \{(1, 1), (1, 3), (1, 5), (3, 1), (3, 3), (3, 5), (5, 1), (5, 3), (5, 5),$$

$$(2, 2), (2, 4), (2, 6), (4, 2), (4, 4), (4, 6), (6, 2), (6, 4), (6, 6)\}.$$

Thus A consists of 8 outcomes, while B consists of 18 outcomes. Furthermore $A = A \cap B$. Assuming that all outcomes are equally likely, the conditional probability of A given B is

$$P(A \mid B) = \frac{P(A \cap B)}{P(B)} = \frac{\frac{8}{36}}{\frac{18}{36}} = \frac{8}{18} = \frac{4}{9}. \qquad \blacklozenge$$

2.2.2 Independence

There are situations in which knowing that an event B has occurred gives no additional information about the occurrence of an event A. The event A is called **independent** of the event B if $P(A \mid B) = P(A)$. In this case, we have

$$P(A \cap B) = P(A \mid B)P(B) = P(A)P(B). \tag{2.4}$$

Since $P(A \cap B)$ can also be expressed as $P(B \mid A)P(A)$, it follows from (2.4) that $P(B \mid A) = P(B)$, showing that B is independent of A. Thus A and B are **mutually independent**.

Independent events are not the same as disjoint events. In fact, there is a strong dependence between disjoint events. If $A \cap B = \phi$ and if A occurs, then B cannot occur. Similarly, if B occurs, then A cannot occur.

EXAMPLE 2.11

Suppose that the proportions shown in the following table (which may be interpreted as probabilities) were obtained from a survey of a large number of college freshmen. The survey asked whether they attended a public or private high school and whether they took any advanced placement (AP) courses during high school. Do the results indicate that taking an AP course is independent of attending a public or private high school among college freshmen?

	High School		
	Private (B)	Public (B^c)	Total
AP Yes (A)	0.12	0.28	0.40
AP No (A^c)	0.18	0.42	0.60
	0.30	0.70	1.00

Define the events A, A^c, B, and B^c as shown in the preceding table. Then $P(A \cap B) = 0.12$, $P(A) = 0.40$, and $P(B) = 0.30$. It follows that $P(A \cap B) = P(A)P(B) = (0.30)(0.40) = 0.12$. Thus A and B are mutually independent. This implies that A^c and B, A and B^c, and A^c and B^c are also mutually independent, as can be easily checked. ◆

EXAMPLE 2.12 (SERIES-PARALLEL SYSTEM RELIABILITY)

Suppose that the probability that a relay is closed is 0.99 in the circuit shown in Figure 2.3. If all the relays function independently, what is the probability that current flows between terminals L and R?

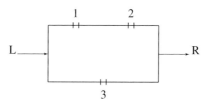

Figure 2.3 Circuit with Components Connected in Parallel and Series

Define the events A_i = Relay i is closed ($i = 1, 2, 3$), and C = Current flows from L to R. Then $C = (A_1 \cap A_2) \cup A_3$. Thus we can write

$$P(C) = P(A_1 \cap A_2) + P(A_3) - P(A_1 \cap A_2 \cap A_3)$$

$$= (0.99)^2 + 0.99 - (0.99)^3 = 0.9998.$$

◆

This example illustrates the calculation of the **reliability** of a system (i.e., the probability that a system functions) assuming that the components fail independently. In this system relays 1 and 2 are connected in series, while relay 3 is connected in parallel with relays 1 and 2. Components are connected in parallel to increase the reliability of a system at the expense of **redundancy**.

2.2.3 Law of Total Probability

Result 3, following the axioms in Section 2.1.2, states that for any two events A and B,

$$P(A) = P(A \cap B) + P(A \cap B^c).$$

Furthermore, if $P(B) > 0$ and $P(B^c) > 0$, then by conditioning on B and B^c we can write

$$P(A) = P(A \mid B)P(B) + P(A \mid B^c)P(B^c).$$

This is known as the **law of total probability**. It is a useful tool when it is difficult to calculate $P(A)$ directly, but it is easier to calculate $P(A \mid B)$ and $P(A \mid B^c)$, as the following example illustrates.

Example 2.13   (Pólya's Urn Scheme)

An urn contains $a > 0$ white balls and $b > 0$ black balls. A ball is drawn at random and its color is noted. The ball is returned to the urn with $c > 0$ additional balls of the same color. Then the next ball is drawn at random and the same procedure is repeated. Show that the probabilities of drawing the balls of the two colors remain unchanged at every step of this scheme, which is called **Pólya's urn scheme** in honor of the mathematician George Pólya (1888–1985).

At the first step, the probabilities of a white and a black ball are $a/(a+b)$ and $b/(a+b)$, respectively. For the second step, using the total probability law, we can write

$$P(\text{2nd ball is white}) = P(\text{2nd ball is white} \mid \text{1st ball is white})P(\text{1st ball is white})$$

$$+ P(\text{2nd ball is white} \mid \text{1st ball is black})P(\text{1st ball is black})$$

$$= \left(\frac{a+c}{a+b+c} \right) \left(\frac{a}{a+b} \right) + \left(\frac{a}{a+b+c} \right) \left(\frac{b}{a+b} \right)$$

$$= \frac{a}{a+b}.$$

Then

$$P(\text{2nd ball is black}) = 1 - \frac{a}{a+b} = \frac{b}{a+b}.$$

The proof of the general step follows by induction.   ◆

For a more general form of the total probability law, consider events $B_1, B_2, \cdots, B_n$, which are mutually exclusive and collectively exhaustive, i.e.,

$$B_i \cap B_j = \phi \text{ for all } i \neq j$$

and

$$B_1 \cup B_2 \cup \cdots \cup B_n = S.$$

We say that $B_1, B_2, \ldots, B_n$ form a **partition** of the sample space S. Then an event A can be expressed as a union of mutually exclusive events as follows:

$$A = (A \cap B_1) \cup (A \cap B_2) \cup \cdots \cup (A \cap B_n).$$

Figure 2.4 shows this in terms of a Venn diagram for $n = 3$. From the preceding expression we obtain the following generalization of the total probability law:

$$P(A) = P(A \cap B_1) + P(A \cap B_2) + \cdots + P(A \cap B_n)$$

$$= P(A \mid B_1)P(B_1) + P(A \mid B_2)P(B_2) + \cdots + P(A \mid B_n)P(B_n)$$

$$= \sum_{j=1}^{n} P(A \mid B_j)P(B_j). \qquad (2.5)$$

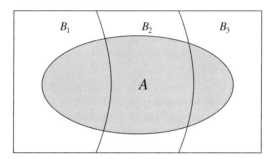

Figure 2.4   Event A as a Union of Its Disjoint Partitions

2.2.4 Bayes' Theorem

For any two events A and B in a sample space, we can write

$$P(A \cap B) = P(A \mid B)P(B) = P(B \mid A)P(A).$$

This leads to a simple formula:

$$P(B \mid A) = \frac{P(A \mid B)P(B)}{P(A)} \qquad (2.6)$$

which is known as **Bayes' theorem** or the **inverse probability law**. It was first used by an 18th century monk named Rev. Thomas Bayes (1702–1761) to draw statistical inferences. It forms the basis of a statistical methodology called **Bayesian statistics**. This methodology is reviewed briefly in Chapter 15. Here we will use some of its terminology.

In Bayesian statistics, $P(B)$ is called the **prior probability** of B, which refers to the probability of B prior to the knowledge of the occurrence of A. We call $P(B \mid A)$ the **posterior probability** of B, which refers to the probability of B after observing A. Thus Bayes' theorem can be viewed as a way of updating the probability of B in light of the knowledge about A.

We can write (2.6) in a more useful form by using the total probability law (2.5):

$$P(B_i \mid A) = \frac{P(A \mid B_i)P(B_i)}{P(A)} = \frac{P(A \mid B_i)P(B_i)}{\sum_{j=1}^{n} P(A \mid B_j)P(B_j)} \qquad (2.7)$$

where $B_1, B_2, \ldots, B_n$ form a partition of the sample space. This result can be used to update the prior probabilities of mutually exclusive events $B_1, B_2, \ldots, B_n$ in light of the new information that A has occurred. The following example illustrates an interesting application of Bayes' theorem.

EXAMPLE 2.14   (MONTE HALL PROBLEM)

A TV game show called *Let's Make a Deal*, hosted by Monte Hall, was popular in the 1960s and 1970s. A contestant in the show was given a choice of three doors. Behind one door was a valuable prize such as a car; behind the other two doors were much less valuable prizes. After a contestant chose a door, say Door 1, the host opened one of the other two doors, say Door 3, showing a less valuable prize. He then gave the contestant the opportunity to switch from Door 1 to Door 2. Would switching from Door 1 to Door 2 increase the contestant's chances of winning the car?

Define the events D_i = {Door i conceals a car} and O_j = {Host opens Door j *after* a contestant chooses Door 1}. When a contestant makes his initial choice, the prior probabilities are $P(D_1) = P(D_2) = P(D_3) = \frac{1}{3}$. After the host shows that the car is not behind Door 3, the chances of winning the car are given by the posterior probabilities $P(D_1 \mid O_3)$ and $P(D_2 \mid O_3)$. These conditional probabilities can be found by using (2.7).

First evaluate $P(O_3 \mid D_1)$, $P(O_3 \mid D_2)$, $P(O_3 \mid D_3)$ in light of the strategy of the show: $P(O_3 \mid D_1) = \frac{1}{2}$ (Door 3 is one of the two doors with lesser prizes that can be opened, given that Door 1 conceals the car).

$P(O_3 \mid D_2) = 1$ (The host can open only Door 3 if Door 2 conceals the car).

$P(O_3 \mid D_3) = 0$ (The host will not open Door 3 if Door 3 conceals the car).

Applying (2.7) gives the following updated (posterior) probabilities:

$$P(D_1 \mid O_3) = \frac{P(O_3 \mid D_1)P(D_1)}{P(O_3 \mid D_1)P(D_1) + P(O_3 \mid D_2)P(D_2) + P(O_3 \mid D_3)P(D_3)}$$

$$= \frac{\frac{1}{2} \times \frac{1}{3}}{(\frac{1}{2} \times \frac{1}{3}) + (1 \times \frac{1}{3}) + (0 \times \frac{1}{3})} = \frac{1}{3}.$$

$$P(D_2 \mid O_3) = \frac{P(O_3 \mid D_2)P(D_2)}{P(O_3 \mid D_1)P(D_1) + P(O_3 \mid D_2)P(D_2) + P(O_3 \mid D_3)P(D_3)}$$

$$= \frac{1 \times \frac{1}{3}}{(\frac{1}{2} \times \frac{1}{3}) + (1 \times \frac{1}{3}) + (0 \times \frac{1}{3})} = \frac{2}{3}.$$

Thus, given the additional knowledge that the car is not behind Door 3, the chances of winning the car are doubled by switching from Door 1 to Door 2.   ◆

2.3   RANDOM VARIABLES AND THEIR DISTRIBUTIONS

A **random variable (r.v.)** associates a unique numerical value with each outcome in the sample space. Formally, an r.v. is a single (real) valued function defined over a sample space. We denote an r.v. by a capital letter (e.g., X or Y) and a particular value taken by an r.v. by the corresponding lower case letter (e.g., x or y).

Here are some examples of random variables.

1. Run a laboratory test. $X = \begin{cases} 1 & \text{if the result is positive} \\ 0 & \text{if the result is negative.} \end{cases}$

2. Toss two dice. $X =$ Sum of the numbers on the dice.

3. Observe how long a transistor lasts. $X =$ Lifetime of the transistor.

An r.v. X may be **discrete** or **continuous**. The r.v.'s in the first two examples are discrete, while the third one is continuous.

2.3.1 Discrete Random Variables

An r.v. is discrete if the number of possible values it can take is finite (e.g., $\{0,1\}$) or countably infinite (e.g., all nonnegative integers $\{0, 1, 2, \ldots\}$). Thus the possible values of a discrete r.v. can be listed as $x_1, x_2, \ldots$. Suppose that we can calculate $P(X = x)$ for every value x that X can take. The collection of these probabilities can be viewed as a function of x. We denote them by $f(x) = P(X = x)$ for each x. The function $f(x)$ is called the **probability mass function (p.m.f.)**.

The p.m.f. satisfies the following conditions:

1. $f(x) \geq 0$ for all x.
2. $\sum_x f(x) = 1$.

The **cumulative distribution function (c.d.f.)** is defined as

$$F(x) = P(X \leq x) = \sum_{k \leq x} f(k).$$

Notice that $F(x)$ is a nondecreasing function with $F(-\infty) = 0$ and $F(\infty) = 1$.

EXAMPLE 2.15 (TOSSING TWO DICE: DISTRIBUTION OF THE SUM)

Let X denote the sum of the numbers on two fair tossed dice (see Example 2.10). The p.m.f. of X can be derived by listing all 36 possible outcomes, which are equally likely, and counting the outcomes that result in $X = x$ for $x = 2, 3, \ldots, 12$. Then

$$f(x) = P(X = x) = \frac{\natural \text{ of outcomes with } X = x}{36}.$$

For example, there are 4 outcomes that result in $X = 5$: $(1, 4), (2, 3), (3, 2), (4, 1)$. Therefore,

$$f(5) = P(X = 5) = \frac{4}{36}.$$

The c.d.f. $F(x)$ is obtained by cumulatively summing the p.m.f. The p.m.f. and c.d.f. are tabulated in Table 2.1 and are graphed in Figure 2.5. ◆

Table 2.1 The p.d.f and c.d.f. of X, the Sum of the Numbers on Two Fair Dice

x	2	3	4	5	6	7	8	9	10	11	12
$f(x) = P(X = x)$	$\frac{1}{36}$	$\frac{2}{36}$	$\frac{3}{36}$	$\frac{4}{36}$	$\frac{5}{36}$	$\frac{6}{36}$	$\frac{5}{36}$	$\frac{4}{36}$	$\frac{3}{36}$	$\frac{2}{36}$	$\frac{1}{36}$
$F(x) = P(X \leq x)$	$\frac{1}{36}$	$\frac{3}{36}$	$\frac{6}{36}$	$\frac{10}{36}$	$\frac{15}{36}$	$\frac{21}{36}$	$\frac{26}{36}$	$\frac{30}{36}$	$\frac{33}{36}$	$\frac{35}{36}$	$\frac{36}{36}$

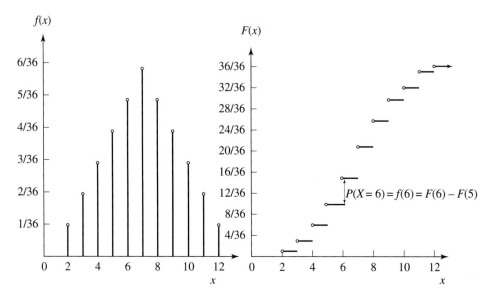

Figure 2.5   Graphs of p.d.f. and c.d.f. of the Sum of Two Fair Dice

We see that if an r.v. takes successive integer values, then the height of the jump in the c.d.f. at x is

$$f(x) = F(x) - F(x - 1).$$

Using this relationship, we obtain the following useful result for integer valued a and b:

$$P(a \leq X \leq b) = f(a) + f(a + 1) + \cdots + f(b)$$
$$= [F(a) - F(a - 1)] + [F(a + 1) - F(a)] + \cdots$$
$$+ [F(b) - F(b - 1)]$$
$$= F(b) - F(a - 1).$$

For example, from Table 2.1 we see that $P(4 \leq X \leq 7) = F(7) - F(3) = \frac{21}{36} - \frac{3}{36} = \frac{18}{36} = 0.5$.

2.3.2 Continuous Random Variables

An r.v. X is continuous if it can assume any value from one or more intervals of real numbers. We cannot use a p.m.f. to describe the probability distribution of X, because its possible values are uncountably infinite. We use a new notion called the **probability density function (p.d.f.)**, still denoted by $f(x)$, such that *areas* (not heights) under the $f(x)$ curve represent probabilities. An example of a p.d.f. is shown in Figure 2.6. The p.d.f. has the following properties:

1. $f(x) \geq 0$ for all x.
2. $\int_{-\infty}^{\infty} f(x)\, dx = 1$.
3. $P(a \leq X \leq b) = \int_{a}^{b} f(x)\, dx$ for any $a \leq b$.

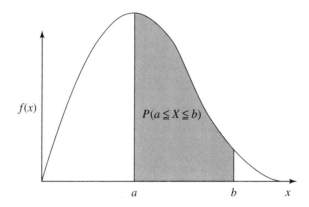

Figure 2.6 $P(a \leq X \leq b)$ = Area under the p.d.f. Curve between a and b

A consequence of Property 3 is that the probability that a continuous r.v. takes a specific value is zero; i.e., $P(X = x) = 0$ for any x. For example, suppose $X =$ the time until the breakdown of a motor. It is not impossible for the breakdown time to be *exactly* 1000 hours, but it is extremely unlikely. In other words, if the time is measured on a sufficiently fine scale, the breakdown time is very likely to be different from 1000 hrs., e.g., 999.92 hrs. This illustrates that a zero-probability event is not necessarily an impossible (empty) event.

The **cumulative distribution function (c.d.f.)**, denoted by $F(x)$, for a continuous r.v. X is given by

$$F(x) = P(X \leq x) = \int_{-\infty}^{x} f(y)\, dy.$$

From this it follows that

$$f(x) = \frac{dF(x)}{dx}.$$

Note that $F(x)$ is the area under the p.d.f. curve to the left of x.

As in the discrete case, $F(x)$ is a nondecreasing function with $F(-\infty) = 0$ and $F(\infty) = 1$. The probabilities of intervals can be obtained directly from the c.d.f.:

$$P(a \leq X \leq b) = F(b) - F(a).$$

This is illustrated graphically in Figure 2.6.

Example 2.16   (Exponential Distribution: Probability Calculation)

The simplest distribution used to model the times to failure (lifetimes) of items or survival times of patients is the **exponential distribution** (see Section 2.8.2). The p.d.f. and c.d.f. of the exponential distribution are given by

$$f(x) = \lambda e^{-\lambda x} \text{ and } F(x) = 1 - e^{-\lambda x} \quad \text{for} \quad x \geq 0 \tag{2.8}$$

where λ is the failure rate (expressed as the average number of failures per unit time). Suppose a certain type of computer chip has a failure rate of once every 15 years ($\lambda = 1/15$), and the time to failure is exponentially distributed. What is the probability that a chip would last 5 to 10 years?

Denote the lifetime of a chip by X. The desired probability is

$$P(5 \leq X \leq 10) = F(10) - F(5) = [1 - e^{-10/15}] - [1 - e^{-5/15}]$$

$$= 0.4866 - 0.2835 = 0.2031.$$

◆

2.4   EXPECTED VALUE, VARIANCE, AND OTHER PARAMETERS OF A DISTRIBUTION

The c.d.f. (or equivalently the p.m.f. or the p.d.f.) completely describes the probabilistic behavior of an r.v. However, certain numerical measures computed from the distribution provide useful summaries. Two common measures (called **parameters**) that summarize the behavior of an r.v. are its **expected value** or **mean** and its **variance**. They are the measures of the center and dispersion, respectively, of the distribution of an r.v. There are other parameters that describe other features of the distribution.

2.4.1 Expected Value

The **expected value** or the **mean** of a discrete r.v. X, denoted by $E(X)$, μ_X, or simply μ, is defined as

$$E(X) = \mu = \sum_x xf(x) = x_1 f(x_1) + x_2 f(x_2) + \cdots. \tag{2.9}$$

This is a weighted average of all possible values, $x_1, x_2, \ldots$, taken by the r.v. X, where the weights are the corresponding probabilities.

The expected value of a continuous r.v. X is defined as

$$E(X) = \mu = \int xf(x) \, dx. \tag{2.10}$$

$E(X)$ can be thought of as the center of gravity of the distribution of X. This is illustrated in Figure 2.7, where a fulcrum placed at μ balances the distribution.

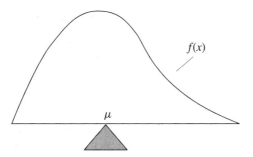

Figure 2.7   The Mean as the Center of Gravity of the Distribution

If the probability distribution of an r.v. X is known, then the expected value of a function of X, say $g(X)$ (e.g., $g(X) = X^2$ or $g(X) = e^{-X}$), equals

$$E[g(X)] = \begin{cases} \sum_x g(x)f(x) & \text{if } X \text{ is discrete} \\ \int g(x)f(x)\ dx & \text{if } X \text{ is continuous.} \end{cases}$$

Some useful relations that can be easily shown are as follows:

1. Suppose that a and b are constants and $g(X) = aX + b$. Then

$$E[g(X)] = \int (ax + b)f(x)\ dx$$

$$= a \underbrace{\int xf(x)\ dx}_{E(X)} + b \underbrace{\int f(x)\ dx}_{1}$$

$$= aE(X) + b.$$

Thus the expected value of a linear function of an r.v. X is the same linear function of the expected value of X.

2. Let X and Y be any r.v.'s. and a and b be constants. Then

$$E(aX + bY) = aE(X) + bE(Y). \tag{2.11}$$

2.4.2 Variance and Standard Deviation

The **variance** of an r.v. X, denoted by $\text{Var}(X)$, σ_X^2, or simply σ^2, is defined as

$$\text{Var}(X) = \sigma^2 = E(X - \mu)^2.$$

The variance is a measure of the dispersion of an r.v. about its mean. The variance of a constant is zero.

An alternative expression for $\text{Var}(X)$ is given by

$$E(X - \mu)^2 = E(X^2 - 2\mu X + \mu^2)$$

$$= E(X^2) - 2\mu E(X) + \mu^2$$

$$= E(X^2) - 2\mu^2 + \mu^2$$

$$= E(X^2) - \mu^2.$$

The **standard deviation (SD)** is the square root of the variance:

$$\text{SD}(X) = \sigma = \sqrt{\text{Var}(X)}.$$

Analogous to the result for the expected value of a linear function of an r.v. X, we have the following result for the variance and SD of a linear function of an r.v. X: If a and b are constants, then

$$\text{Var}(aX + b) = a^2 \, \text{Var}(X), \quad \text{SD}(aX + b) = |a| \text{SD}(X),$$

where $|a|$ is the absolute value of a; see Exercise 2.43. Note that $\text{Var}(aX + b)$ is unaffected by the additive constant b, because adding a constant simply shifts the distribution but does not change its spread. On the other hand, multiplying X by a constant different from ± 1 changes the spread of its distribution.

EXAMPLE 2.17   (TOSSING TWO DICE: MEAN AND VARIANCE OF SUM)

Let $X = $ sum of the numbers on two fair dice (see Example 2.15). From the p.d.f. of X tabulated in Table 2.1, we can calculate $E(X)$ and $\text{Var}(X)$ as follows:

$$E(X) = \mu = \left(2 \times \frac{1}{36}\right) + \left(3 \times \frac{2}{36}\right) + \cdots + \left(12 \times \frac{1}{36}\right)$$

$$= 7.$$

$$\text{Var}(X) = \sigma^2 = E(X - \mu)^2$$

$$= \left[(2 - 7)^2 \times \frac{1}{36}\right] + \left[(3 - 7)^2 \times \frac{2}{36}\right] + \cdots$$

$$+ \left[(12 - 7)^2 \times \frac{1}{36}\right]$$

$$= 5.833.$$

Alternatively, we can find $\text{Var}(X)$ using the relationship

$$\text{Var}(X) = E(X^2) - \mu^2$$

where

$$E(X^2) = \left(2^2 \times \frac{1}{36}\right) + \left(3^2 \times \frac{2}{36}\right) + \cdots + \left(12^2 \times \frac{1}{36}\right)$$

$$= 54.833.$$

Therefore, $\text{Var}(X) = 54.833 - 7^2 = 5.833$. Hence, $\text{SD}(X) = \sqrt{5.833} = 2.415$.   ◆

2.4.3 *Skewness and Kurtosis

The quantities $E(X) = \mu$ and $E(X^2)$ are called the first and second moments of the distribution of X. More generally, $E(X^k)$ is called the **kth moment** of X and $E(X - \mu)^k$ is called the **kth central moment** of X; thus $\text{Var}(X) = E(X - \mu)^2$ is the second central moment of X. Higher moments are useful for characterizing other features of a distribution.

The standardized third central moment given by

$$\beta_3 = \frac{E(X - \mu)^3}{\sigma^3}$$

is called the **skewness** of the distribution of X. It measures the lack of symmetry of the distribution. The skewness is 0 for symmetric distributions and is negative or positive depending on whether the distribution is negatively skewed (has a longer left tail) or positively skewed (has a longer right tail); see Figure 2.8 for a positively skewed distribution.

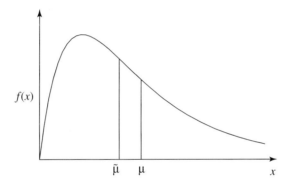

Figure 2.8   A Positively Skewed Distribution

The standardized fourth central moment given by

$$\beta_4 = \frac{E(X - \mu)^4}{\sigma^4}$$

is called the **kurtosis** of the distribution of X. It measures the tail-heaviness (the amount of probability in the tails) of the distribution. For the normal distribution discussed in Section 2.9, β_4 equals 3. The normal distribution is regarded as a light-tailed distribution since the probability in its tails beyond, say, three standard deviations from the mean is negligible. Thus, depending on whether $\beta_4 > 3$ or < 3, a distribution is heavier tailed or lighter tailed than the normal distribution.

EXAMPLE 2.18   (EXPONENTIAL DISTRIBUTION: MOMENTS)

An r.v. X has an exponential distribution given by (2.8). Obtain expressions for the mean, variance, skewness, and kurtosis of the exponential distribution.

To obtain the first four moments of an exponential r.v. X, the following recursive formula for the kth moment (derived using integration by parts) is useful:

$$E(X^k) = \int_0^\infty x^k \lambda e^{-\lambda x}\, dx$$

$$= \left[-x^k e^{-\lambda x}\right]_0^\infty + k \int_0^\infty x^{k-1} e^{-\lambda x}\, dx$$

$$= 0 + \frac{k}{\lambda} \int_0^\infty x^{k-1} \lambda e^{-\lambda x}\, dx$$

$$= \frac{k}{\lambda} E(X^{k-1}).$$

From this formula the following expressions are easily obtained:

$$E(X) = \frac{1}{\lambda}, \; E(X^2) = \frac{2}{\lambda^2}, \; E(X^3) = \frac{6}{\lambda^3}, \; E(X^4) = \frac{24}{\lambda^4}.$$

Then, using simple algebra, the following expressions can be derived:

$$\mu = E(X) = \frac{1}{\lambda},$$

$$\sigma^2 = E(X^2) - \mu^2 = \frac{1}{\lambda^2},$$

$$\beta_3 = \frac{E(X - \mu)^3}{\sigma^3} = \frac{2/\lambda^3}{1/\lambda^3} = 2,$$

$$\beta_4 = \frac{E(X - \mu)^4}{\sigma^4} = \frac{9/\lambda^4}{1/\lambda^4} = 9.$$

The positive value of the skewness indicates that the exponential distribution is positively skewed (see Figure 2.10 on page 50), and $\beta_4 > 3$ indicates that it has heavier tails than the normal distribution. ◆

2.4.4 *Moment Generating Function

As the name implies, the **moment generating function (m.g.f.)** is useful for deriving the moments of an r.v. However, its primary use is to characterize the distribution of an r.v. We will discuss it only briefly here.

The m.g.f. of an r.v. X with p.d.f. (or p.m.f.) $f(x)$ is defined for a real number $t \neq 0$ as

$$M_X(t) = E(e^{tX}) = \begin{cases} \sum_x e^{tx} f(x) & \text{if } X \text{ is discrete} \\ \int_x e^{tx} f(x)\, dx & \text{if } X \text{ is continuous.} \end{cases} \tag{2.12}$$

The m.g.f. $M_X(t)$ is said to exist if and only if $E(e^{tX})$ exists in a neighborhood of $t = 0$.

How can one derive moments of X from its m.g.f.? It can be shown that the first derivative of $M_X(t)$ evaluated at $t = 0$ equals the first moment. Symbolically,

$$M_X'(0) = \frac{d}{dt} (M_X(t)) \Big|_{t=0} = E(X).$$

The second derivative of $M_X(t)$ evaluated at $t = 0$ equals the second moment, and so on. In general,

$$M_X^{(k)}(0) = \left. \frac{d^k}{dt^k} \left(M_X(t) \right) \right|_{t=0} = E(X^k).$$

Another useful result is that if a and b are constants, then

$$M_{aX+b}(t) = e^{at} M_X(bt). \tag{2.13}$$

EXAMPLE 2.19   (EXPONENTIAL DISTRIBUTION: MOMENT GENERATING FUNCTION)

An r.v. X has an exponential distribution given by (2.8). Find the m.g.f. of X and find its first two moments.

For $t < \lambda$, we have

$$M_X(t) = \int_0^\infty e^{tx} \lambda e^{-\lambda x} \, dx$$

$$= \lambda \int_0^\infty e^{-(\lambda - t)x} \, dx$$

$$= \frac{\lambda}{\lambda - t}.$$

The first moment is

$$E(X) = \left. \frac{d}{dt} \left(\frac{\lambda}{\lambda - t} \right) \right|_{t=0} = \left. \frac{\lambda}{(\lambda - t)^2} \right|_{t=0} = \frac{1}{\lambda}.$$

The second moment is

$$E(X^2) = \left. \frac{d^2}{dt^2} \left(\frac{\lambda}{\lambda - t} \right) \right|_{t=0} = \left. \frac{d}{dt} \left[\frac{\lambda}{(\lambda - t)^2} \right] \right|_{t=0} = \left. \frac{2\lambda}{(\lambda - t)^3} \right|_{t=0} = \frac{2}{\lambda^2}.$$

Note that these expressions coincide with those derived in Example 2.18. Higher moments can be obtained in a similar manner. ◆

The distribution characterizing property of the m.g.f. is summarized in the following important result:

Theorem: Consider two r.v.'s X and Y. If the m.g.f.'s $M_X(t)$ and $M_Y(t)$ exist and $M_X(t) = M_Y(t)$ in some neighborhood of $t = 0$, then X and Y have the same distribution, i.e., $F_X(u) = F_Y(u)$ for all u. ■

2.4.5 Quantiles and Percentiles

The other parameters of a distribution that are often of interest are its quantiles (also referred to as percentiles). For $0 \le p \le 1$, the pth **quantile** (or the $100p$th **percentile**), denoted by θ_p, of a continuous r.v. X is defined by the following equation:

$$P(X \le \theta_p) = F(\theta_p) = p. \tag{2.14}$$

A percentile of special interest is the 50th percentile, $\theta_{.5}$, known as the **median** of the distribution because it divides the total area under the p.d.f. curve into two equal halves. We will use $\tilde{\mu}$ as a notation for the median. The median of a distribution always exists, but the mean defined by the sum (2.9) or the integral (2.10) may not exist, since these quantities can diverge for some distributions. If the distribution is symmetric and if the mean exists, then $\mu = \tilde{\mu}$. For a negatively skewed distribution $\mu < \tilde{\mu}$, while for a positively skewed distribution $\mu > \tilde{\mu}$; see Figure 2.8.

EXAMPLE 2.20 (EXPONENTIAL DISTRIBUTION: PERCENTILES)

Obtain an expression for the percentiles of the exponential distribution given by (2.8).

The $100p$th percentile, θ_p, solves the equation

$$F(\theta_p) = 1 - e^{-\lambda \theta_p} = p$$

which yields

$$\theta_p = \frac{1}{\lambda} \log_e \left(\frac{1}{1-p} \right).$$

For $p = 0.5$, the median $\tilde{\mu}$ is given by

$$\tilde{\mu} = \theta_{0.5} = \frac{1}{\lambda} \log_e(2) = \frac{0.6931}{\lambda}.$$

Note that $\tilde{\mu}$ is less than the mean $\mu = 1/\lambda$ found earlier. This is an example of the previously stated fact that $\tilde{\mu} < \mu$ for positively skewed distributions. ◆

2.5 JOINTLY DISTRIBUTED RANDOM VARIABLES

Frequently, more than one random variable is associated with an outcome. An insurance file provides information on a customer's auto and homeowner policy. Vital signs monitored on a hospital patient include the systolic and diastolic blood pressure. The relationship between several variables can be investigated through their **joint probability distribution**.

To illustrate jointly distributed r.v.'s, we consider data on grades (A = 4, B = 3, C = 2, D = 1) in a probability and a statistics course for a sample of 200 Northwestern University undergraduate engineering students. A tabulation of these grades is shown in Table 2.2.

Table 2.2 Probability and Statistics Grades of 200 Students

		Statistics Grade, Y				
		A=4	B=3	C=2	D=1	
Probability	A=4	32	22	8	1	63
Grade	B=3	11	35	25	1	72
X	C=2	3	25	20	2	50
	D=1	0	5	5	5	15
		46	87	58	9	200

Table 2.3 Joint Distribution of Probability and Statistics Grades

		Statistics Grade Y				
		A=4	B=3	C=2	D=1	
Probability	A=4	0.160	0.110	0.040	0.005	0.315
Grade	B=3	0.055	0.175	0.125	0.005	0.360
X	C=2	0.015	0.125	0.100	0.010	0.250
	D=1	0.000	0.025	0.025	0.025	0.075
		0.230	0.435	0.290	0.045	1.000

Suppose the transcript of one of these students is drawn at random. What is the probability that the student received an A in probability and a B in statistics? This probability is simply $\frac{22}{200}$, the proportion of students with this particular combination of grades. Thus $P(X = 4, Y = 3) = 0.110$. The joint p.m.f. of the discrete r.v.'s X and Y is given by Table 2.3, which shows the proportion of students with each combination of probability and statistics grades.

2.5.1 Joint Probability Mass or Density Function

If X and Y are discrete r.v.'s, their joint p.m.f. is $f(x, y) = P(X = x, Y = y)$ for all x, y. The joint p.m.f. satisfies

1. $f(x, y) \geq 0$ for all x and y.
2. $\sum_x \sum_y f(x, y) = 1$.

The joint c.d.f. of X and Y is given by

$$F(x, y) = P(X \leq x, Y \leq y) = \sum_{i \leq x} \sum_{j \leq y} f(i, j).$$

Similarly, the joint p.d.f. of two continuous r.v.'s X and Y is denoted by $f(x, y)$, which satisfies

1. $f(x, y) \geq 0$ for all x and y.
2. $\int \int f(x, y)\, dx\, dy = 1$.

The joint c.d.f. of X and Y is given by

$$F(x, y) = P(X \leq x, Y \leq y) = \int_{-\infty}^{x} \int_{-\infty}^{y} f(u, v)\, du\, dv.$$

2.5.2 Marginal Distribution

Not only does the joint p.m.f. (or p.d.f.) give information about the behavior of the r.v.'s together, it also contains information about the separate behaviors of the individual r.v.'s. In the grades example, by computing the row and column totals of the joint probabilities from Table 2.3, we can find the p.m.f. of X and Y. The row totals give the p.m.f. of X and the column totals give the p.m.f. of Y. The resulting marginal distributions are shown in Table 2.4.

Table 2.4 Marginal Distributions of Probability and Statistics Grades

Marginal Distribution of X (Probability Grade)

x	1	2	3	4
$g(x) = P(X=x)$	0.075	0.250	0.360	0.315

Marginal Distribution of Y (Statistics Grade)

y	1	2	3	4
$h(y) = P(Y=y)$	0.045	0.290	0.435	0.230

Given the joint p.m.f. of two discrete r.v.'s X and Y, the marginal p.m.f. of one r.v. can be found by summing over the values of the other:

$$g(x) = P(X = x) = \sum_y f(x, y) \quad \text{and} \quad h(y) = P(Y = y) = \sum_x f(x, y).$$

Similarly, given the joint p.d.f. of two continuous r.v.'s, the marginal p.d.f. of one r.v. can be found by integrating over the values of the other:

$$g(x) = \int_{-\infty}^{\infty} f(x, y)\, dy \quad \text{and} \quad h(y) = \int_{-\infty}^{\infty} f(x, y)\, dx.$$

2.5.3 Independent Random Variables

The independence of r.v.'s can be defined in terms of independent events. Consider two r.v.'s X and Y and suppose that an event A is defined in terms of X and an event B is defined in terms of Y. Then X and Y are said to be independent if and only if, for all such events A and B,

$$P(A \cap B) = P(A)P(B).$$

This definition is not useful for checking the independence of X and Y, because we cannot check it for all events A and B. However, the following equivalent condition is much easier to verify in practice: Let $f(x, y)$, $g(x)$, and $h(y)$ be the joint and marginal p.d.f.'s (p.m.f.'s in the discrete case) of X and Y, respectively. Then X and Y are independent if and only if

$$f(x, y) = g(x)h(y) \quad \text{for all } x \text{ and } y,$$

i.e., the joint distribution of X and Y factors into their marginal distributions.

EXAMPLE 2.21 (PROBABILITY AND STATISTICS GRADES: INDEPENDENCE)

To check whether the probability and statistics grades are independently distributed, consider the joint p.m.f. of X and Y given in Table 2.3 for, say, $X = 4$ and $Y = 3$:

$$f(4, 3) = P(X = 4, Y = 3) = 0.110.$$

But from Table 2.4, we have

$$g(4)h(3) = P(X = 4)P(Y = 3) = (0.315)(0.435) = 0.137.$$

Thus $f(4, 3) \neq g(4)h(3)$, and therefore the probability and statistics grades are not independently distributed. ◆

*M.G.F. of Sum of Independent Random Variables. If X_1 and X_2 are two independent r.v.'s with p.d.f.'s $f_1(x_1)$ and $f_2(x_2)$, respectively, then the moment generating function (m.g.f.) of their sum is given by

$$M_{X_1+X_2}(t) = \int_{x_1}\int_{x_2} e^{t(x_1+x_2)} f(x_1, x_2)dx_1dx_2$$

$$= \int_{x_1}\int_{x_2} e^{t(x_1+x_2)} f_1(x_1)f_2(x_2)dx_1dx_2$$

$$= \left[\int_{x_1} e^{tx_1} f_1(x_1)dx_1\right]\left[\int_{x_2} e^{tx_2} f_2(x_2)dx_2\right]$$

$$= M_{X_1}(t)M_{X_2}(t).$$

More generally, if $X_1, X_2, \ldots, X_n$ are mutually independent r.v.'s, then the m.g.f. of their sum is the product of their individual m.g.f.'s:

$$M_{X_1+X_2+\cdots+X_n}(t) = M_{X_1}(t)M_{X_2}(t)\cdots M_{X_n}(t).$$

If the X_i's have the same p.d.f., then they have the same m.g.f. Therefore,

$$M_{X_1+X_2+\cdots+X_n}(t) = [M_{X_1}(t)]^n. \tag{2.15}$$

At the end of the chapter we will use this and other results on m.g.f.'s from Section 2.4.4 to derive the distribution of the mean of independent and identically distributed (i.i.d.) observations from a normal distribution.

2.5.4 Conditional Distribution

In the grades example, it might be of interest to determine how well a student is likely to do in statistics, given his/her grade in probability. In other words, we want to calculate the conditional probabilities $P(Y = y \mid X = x)$ for $y = 1, 2, 3, 4$, for a given value $X = x$. These conditional probabilities give the conditional distribution of Y conditioned on $X = x$. A similar problem arises when X and Y are jointly distributed *continuous* r.v.'s and we want the distribution of Y for given $X = x$. For example, we may want the distribution of repair costs for three year old cars of a particular car model from the joint distribution of the repair costs and vehicle age of all cars of that model.

The definition of the conditional distribution follows from the conditional probability definition (2.3). Let $f(x, y)$ be the joint p.m.f. or p.d.f. of r.v.'s X and Y and let $g(x)$ be the marginal p.m.f. or p.d.f. of X. Then for any x for which $g(x) > 0$, the conditional p.m.f. or p.d.f. of Y given $X = x$ is defined as

$$f(y \mid x) = \frac{f(x, y)}{g(x)}. \tag{2.16}$$

Note that if X and Y are independent with respective marginal p.m.f.'s or p.d.f.'s $g(x)$ and $h(y)$, then $f(x, y) = g(x)h(y)$, and hence, $f(y \mid x) = h(y)$. Thus for independent r.v.'s, the conditional distribution of one r.v. given the other is the same as the marginal distribution of the first one.

A conditional distribution is just a probability distribution defined on a reduced sample space. It follows the same rules as does any probability distribution. In particular,

1. $f(y \mid x) \geq 0$ for all y, and
2. For every x, $\sum_y f(y \mid x) = 1$ (in the discrete case), $\int_y f(y \mid x) dy = 1$ (in the continuous case).

EXAMPLE 2.22 (PROBABILITY AND STATISTICS GRADES: CONDITIONAL DISTRIBUTION)

Consider the joint distribution of probability and statistics grades given in Table 2.3. Suppose we wish to find the conditional distribution of the statistics grade, Y, for students earning an A in probability (i.e., $X = 4$). From Table 2.4 we have $g(4) = P(X = 4) = 0.315$. Hence the conditional distribution, $f(y \mid X = 4)$, is given by

y	1	2	3	4
$f(y \mid 4) = P(Y = y \mid X = 4)$	$\frac{0.005}{0.315} = 0.016$	$\frac{0.040}{0.315} = 0.127$	$\frac{0.110}{0.315} = 0.349$	$\frac{0.160}{0.315} = 0.508$

This conditional distribution can also be obtained by restricting attention to the 63 students who got an A in probability and calculating the proportions who got different grades in statistics. Note that the conditional distribution sums to 1. ◆

Since the conditional distribution is just a probability distribution, we can define parameters such as the mean and variance for it. The mean of a conditional distribution is called the **conditional expectation** or the **conditional mean** and is defined by

$$\mu_{Y \mid x} = E(Y \mid X = x) = \begin{cases} \sum_y y f(y \mid x) & \text{in the discrete case} \\ \int_y y f(y \mid x) dy & \text{in the continuous case.} \end{cases} \tag{2.17}$$

When X and Y are independent, $f(y \mid x) = h(y)$ and therefore $\mu_{Y \mid x} = \mu_Y$. Thus the unconditional and conditional means are the same when the r.v.'s are independent. However, in other cases $\mu_{Y \mid x}$ is a function of x and is called the **regression function** of Y on x. Regression analysis deals with the problem of estimating this function from data on X and Y and is covered in Chapter 10 when this function is linear in x.

The unconditional mean of Y, $E(Y)$, can be computed from the conditional means, $E(Y \mid X = x)$, using the formula:

$$E(Y) = \begin{cases} \sum_x E(Y \mid X = x)P(X = x) & \text{in the discrete case} \\ \int_x E(Y \mid X = x)g(x)dx & \text{in the continuous case.} \end{cases} \quad (2.18)$$

This is usually written as $E(Y) = E[E(Y \mid X)]$, where the outside expectation is with respect to the marginal distribution of X.

EXAMPLE 2.23 (GEOMETRIC DISTRIBUTION: MEAN)

Let p be the probability of hitting a slot machine jackpot on a single attempt. Suppose that the outcomes of successive attempts are mutually independent and the chance of winning the jackpot on any attempt is p. What is the expected number of attempts required?

Let Y denote the number of attempts required. The distribution of Y is known as the **geometric distribution** discussed in Section 2.7.5. We can find $E(Y)$ by using (2.18) as follows. Let

$$X = \begin{cases} 0 & \text{if the first attempt is a failure} \\ 1 & \text{if the first attempt is a success.} \end{cases}$$

Then

$$E(Y) = E(Y \mid X = 0)P(X = 0) + E(Y \mid X = 1)P(X = 1)$$

$$= E(Y \mid X = 0)(1 - p) + E(Y \mid X = 1)p.$$

Now, if the first attempt is a failure, then $E(Y \mid X = 0) = 1 + E(Y)$ because one attempt is already made and the expected additional number of attempts is just $E(Y)$, since future attempts are independent of the past and follow the same distribution. On the other hand, if the first attempt is a success, then $E(Y \mid X = 1) = 1$. Therefore,

$$E(Y) = [1 + E(Y)](1 - p) + 1 \times p.$$

Solving this equation for $E(Y)$ yields

$$E(Y) = \frac{1}{p}.$$

$\blacklozenge$

The **conditional variance**, $\text{Var}(Y \mid X = x)$, is defined as the variance of the conditional distribution of Y given $X = x$, i.e.,

$$\sigma_{Y|x}^2 = \text{Var}(Y \mid X = x) = \begin{cases} \sum_y (y - \mu_{Y|x})^2 f(y \mid x) & \text{in the discrete case} \\ \int_y (y - \mu_{Y|x})^2 f(y \mid x)dy & \text{in the continuous case.} \end{cases} \quad (2.19)$$

The unconditional variance of Y can be obtained by applying the unconditioning method:

$$\sigma_Y^2 = \text{Var}(Y) = E(Y^2) - [E(Y)]^2 = E[E(Y^2 \mid X)] - \{E[E(Y \mid X)]\}^2. \quad (2.20)$$

The following example illustrates the use of (2.20) for finding the variance of the geometric distribution.

EXAMPLE 2.24 (GEOMETRIC DISTRIBUTION: VARIANCE)

An r.v. Y has a geometric distribution. (See Example 2.23.) To find $\text{Var}(Y)$, we use similar arguments as before to calculate

$$E(Y^2 \mid X = 0) = E[(1 + Y)^2] \quad \text{and} \quad E(Y^2 \mid X = 1) = 1.$$

Hence,

$$
\begin{aligned}
E(Y^2) &= E[(1 + Y)^2](1 - p) + 1 \times p \\
&= [1 + 2E(Y) + E(Y^2)](1 - p) + p \\
&= 1 - p + 2(1 - p) \times \frac{1}{p} + (1 - p)E(Y^2) + p
\end{aligned}
$$

which, upon solving for $E(Y^2)$, yields

$$E(Y^2) = \frac{2 - p}{p^2}.$$

Therefore

$$\text{Var}(Y) = E(Y^2) - [E(Y)]^2 = \frac{2 - p}{p^2} - \frac{1}{p^2} = \frac{1 - p}{p^2}.$$

◆

2.5.5 Covariance

The covariance of two r.v.'s, X and Y, measures the joint dispersion from their respective means. It is defined as

$$\text{Cov}(X, Y) = \sigma_{XY} = E[(X - \mu_X)(Y - \mu_Y)].$$

Recall the computational formula $\text{Var}(X) = E(X^2) - \mu_X^2$. There is a corresponding formula for the covariance:

$$\text{Cov}(X, Y) = E(XY) - \mu_X \mu_Y = E(XY) - E(X)E(Y).$$

Note that $\text{Cov}(X, Y)$ can be positive or negative. Positive covariance implies that large values of X are associated with large values of Y and vice versa; negative covariance implies that large values of X are associated with small values of Y and vice versa. We will see later that the covariance measures only linear association.

If X and Y are independent, then $E(XY) = E(X)E(Y)$ and hence $\text{Cov}(X, Y) = 0$. However, the converse of this is not true in general. In other words, X and Y may be *dependent* and yet their covariance may be zero. This is illustrated by the following example.

EXAMPLE 2.25

Define Y in terms of X such that

$$
Y = \begin{cases} X & \text{with probability } \frac{1}{2} \\ -X & \text{with probability } \frac{1}{2} \end{cases}
$$

Obviously, Y depends on X; however, $\text{Cov}(X, Y) = 0$, which can be verified as follows:

$$E(XY) = \frac{1}{2}E(X^2) - \frac{1}{2}E(X^2) = 0.$$

$$E(Y) = \frac{1}{2}E(X) - \frac{1}{2}E(X) = 0.$$

Hence, $\text{Cov}(X, Y) = E(XY) - E(X)E(Y) = 0.$

$\blacklozenge$

In the following example, we illustrate the covariance computation by calculating the covariance between the probability and statistics grades given in Table 2.3.

EXAMPLE 2.26   (PROBABILITY AND STATISTICS GRADES: COVARIANCE)

The joint distribution of the probability and statistics grades, X and Y, is given in Table 2.3 and their marginal distributions are given in Table 2.4. To find the covariance, first calculate

$$E(XY) = (4 \times 4 \times 0.160) + (4 \times 3 \times 0.110) + \cdots + (1 \times 1 \times 0.025) = 8.660,$$

$$E(X) = (4 \times 0.315) + \cdots + (1 \times 0.075) = 2.915,$$

$$E(Y) = (4 \times 0.230) + \cdots + (1 \times 0.045) = 2.850.$$

Then,

$$\text{Cov}(X, Y) = E(XY) - \mu_X\mu_Y = 8.660 - (2.915)(2.850) = 0.352.$$

This covariance is positive, indicating that students who do well in probability also tend to do well in statistics and vice versa.

$\blacklozenge$

The following are some useful covariance relationships. In these relationships X and Y are r.v.'s, while a, b, c, d are constants.

1. $\text{Cov}(X, X) = E[(X - \mu_X)(X - \mu_X)] = E(X - \mu_X)^2 = \text{Var}(X).$

2. $\text{Cov}(aX + c, bY + d) = ab\text{Cov}(X, Y).$

3. More generally, suppose that $X_i \ (1 \le i \le m)$ and $Y_j \ (1 \le j \le n)$ are r.v.'s and $a_i \ (1 \le i \le m)$ and $b_j \ (1 \le j \le n)$ are constants. Then

$$\text{Cov}\left(\sum_{i=1}^{m} a_i X_i, \sum_{j=1}^{n} b_j Y_j\right) = \sum_{i=1}^{m}\sum_{j=1}^{n} a_i b_j \ \text{Cov}(X_i, Y_j). \qquad (2.21)$$

A special case of this formula is

$$\text{Var}\left(\sum_{i=1}^{m} a_i X_i\right) = \text{Cov}\left(\sum_{i=1}^{m} a_i X_i, \sum_{j=1}^{m} a_j X_j\right)$$

$$= \sum_{i=1}^{m} a_i^2 \text{Var}(X_i) + 2 \sum_{i=j+1}^{m}\sum_{j=1}^{m-1} a_i a_j \text{Cov}(X_i, X_j). \qquad (2.22)$$

4. $\text{Var}(X \pm Y) = \text{Var}(X) + \text{Var}(Y) \pm 2\,\text{Cov}(X, Y)$.

5. If X and Y are *independent*, then $\text{Cov}(X, Y) = 0$. Therefore the previous expression simplifies to

$$\text{Var}(X \pm Y) = \text{Var}(X) + \text{Var}(Y).$$

2.5.6 Correlation Coefficient

To judge the extent of dependence or association between two r.v.'s, we need to standardize their covariance. The correlation coefficient is simply the covariance standardized so that its range is $[-1, +1]$. The correlation coefficient between two r.v.'s X and Y is defined by

$$\rho_{XY} = \text{Corr}(X, Y) = \frac{\text{Cov}(X, Y)}{\sqrt{\text{Var}(X)\,\text{Var}(Y)}} = \frac{\sigma_{XY}}{\sigma_X \sigma_Y}.$$

Note that ρ_{XY} is a unitless quantity, while $\text{Cov}(X, Y)$ is not. It follows from the covariance relationships that if X and Y are independent, then $\rho_{XY} = 0$; however, $\rho_{XY} = 0$ does not imply that they are independent. It can be shown that $\rho_{XY} = +1$ or -1 if and only if X and Y have a deterministic linear relationship of the form $Y = aX + b$, where $a \neq 0$ and b are constants. Specifically, $\rho_{XY} = +1$ if $a > 0$ and $\rho_{XY} = -1$ if $a < 0$. Thus both covariance and correlation coefficient measure the strength of *linear* association between X and Y.

EXAMPLE 2.27   (PROBABILITY AND STATISTICS GRADES: CORRELATION COEFFICIENT)

We saw that the covariance between the probability and statistics grades is 0.352 in Example 2.26. Although this tells us that the two grades are positively associated, it does not tell us the strength of linear association, since the covariance is not a standardized measure. For this purpose, we calculate the correlation coefficient. Check that $\text{Var}(X) = 0.858$ and $\text{Var}(Y) = 0.678$. Then

$$\rho_{XY} = \frac{\text{Cov}(X, Y)}{\sqrt{\text{Var}(X)\,\text{Var}(Y)}} = \frac{0.352}{\sqrt{(0.858)(0.678)}} = 0.462.$$

This correlation is not very close to 1, which implies that there is not a strong *linear* relationship between X and Y. However, this does not rule out a *nonlinear* relationship.   ◆

EXAMPLE 2.28

Find $\text{Corr}(X, Y)$ if the joint p.d.f. of (X, Y) is given by

$$f(x, y) = \begin{cases} 2, & 0 \leq y \leq x \leq 1 \\ 0, & \text{otherwise.} \end{cases}$$

The marginal distributions of X and Y are, respectively,

$$g(x) = \begin{cases} \int_{-\infty}^{\infty} f(x, y)\,dy = \int_0^x 2\,dy = 2x, & 0 \leq x \leq 1 \\ 0 & \text{otherwise,} \end{cases}$$

and

$$h(y) = \begin{cases} \int_{-\infty}^{\infty} f(x, y)\,dx = \int_y^1 2\,dx = 2 - 2y & 0 \leq y \leq 1 \\ 0 & \text{otherwise.} \end{cases}$$

We need to calculate $\text{Var}(X)$, $\text{Var}(Y)$, and $\text{Cov}(X, Y)$ to find ρ_{XY}. First calculate

$$\mu_X = E(X) = \int_0^1 x(2x)\, dx = \frac{2}{3}$$

and

$$E(X^2) = \int_0^1 x^2(2x)\, dx = \frac{1}{2}.$$

Hence

$$\text{Var}(X) = E(X^2) - \mu_X^2 = \frac{1}{2} - \left(\frac{2}{3}\right)^2 = \frac{1}{18}.$$

Next calculate

$$\mu_Y = E(Y) = \int_0^1 y(2 - 2y)\, dy = \frac{1}{3}$$

and

$$E(Y^2) = \int_0^1 y^2(2 - 2y)\, dy = \frac{1}{6}.$$

Hence

$$\text{Var}(Y) = E(Y^2) - \mu_Y^2 = \frac{1}{6} - \left(\frac{1}{3}\right)^2 = \frac{1}{18}.$$

Next calculate

$$E(XY) = \int_0^1 \int_y^1 xy(2)\, dx\, dy = \int_0^1 \int_0^x xy(2)\, dy\, dx = \frac{1}{4}.$$

Hence

$$\text{Cov}(X, Y) = E(XY) - \mu_X \mu_Y = \frac{1}{4} - \left(\frac{2}{3}\right)\left(\frac{1}{3}\right) = \frac{1}{36}.$$

Therefore the correlation coefficient is

$$\rho_{XY} = \frac{\text{Cov}(X, Y)}{\sqrt{\text{Var}(X)\,\text{Var}(Y)}} = \frac{\frac{1}{36}}{\sqrt{\left(\frac{1}{18}\right)\left(\frac{1}{18}\right)}} = \frac{1}{2}.$$

◆

2.5.7 Multivariate Distributions

The above discussion has been confined to just two r.v.'s. We refer to their joint distribution as a **bivariate distribution**. When more than two r.v.'s, say $X_1, X_2, \ldots, X_k$, are jointly distributed, we can similarly define their joint p.m.f. (in the discrete case) or joint p.d.f. (in the continuous case), denoted by $f(x_1, x_2, \ldots, x_k)$. We refer to this as a **multivariate distribution**. The properties of a multivariate distribution are natural extensions of the bivariate distribution properties. Marginal distributions can also be defined in a similar way. For example, the marginal distribution of X_1 is given by

$$f_1(x_1) = \begin{cases} \sum_{x_2} \cdots \sum_{x_k} f(x_1, x_2, \ldots, x_k) & \text{in the discrete case} \\ \int_{-\infty}^{\infty} \cdots \int_{-\infty}^{\infty} f(x_1, x_2, \ldots, x_k)\, dx_2 \cdots dx_k & \text{in the continuous case.} \end{cases}$$

The r.v.'s $X_1, X_2, \ldots, X_k$ are said to be **mutually independent** if and only if their joint distribution factors into the product of their marginal distributions, i.e.,

$$f(x_1, x_2, \ldots, x_k) = f_1(x_1) f_2(x_2) \cdots f_k(x_k) \quad \text{for all } x_1, x_2, \ldots, x_k.$$

Suppose that the r.v.'s $X_1, X_2, \ldots, X_k$ have variances $\sigma_1^2, \sigma_2^2, \ldots, \sigma_k^2$, respectively, and pairwise covariances

$$\sigma_{ij} = \text{Cov}(X_i, X_j) \quad (1 \leq i \neq j \leq k).$$

If we form a $k \times k$ matrix $\boldsymbol{\Sigma}$, which has the ith diagonal entry equal to $\text{Var}(X_i) = \sigma_i^2$ and the (i, j)th off-diagonal entry equal to $\text{Cov}(X_i, X_j) = \sigma_{ij}$, then

$$\boldsymbol{\Sigma} = \begin{bmatrix} \sigma_1^2 & \sigma_{12} & \cdots & \sigma_{1k} \\ \sigma_{21} & \sigma_2^2 & \cdots & \sigma_{2k} \\ \vdots & \vdots & \ddots & \vdots \\ \sigma_{k1} & \sigma_{k2} & \cdots & \sigma_k^2 \end{bmatrix}$$

is called the **variance-covariance matrix** (or just the **covariance matrix**) of the X_i's. Note that $\boldsymbol{\Sigma}$ is a symmetric matrix, since $\sigma_{ij} = \sigma_{ji}$ for all $i \neq j$.

Analogously, we can define the **correlation matrix** of the X_i's. This matrix, denoted by $\boldsymbol{R}$, has all diagonal entries equal to 1 and the (i, j)th off-diagonal entry equal to $\rho_{ij} = \text{Corr}(X_i, X_j)$ $(1 \leq i \neq j \leq k)$. Thus

$$\boldsymbol{R} = \begin{bmatrix} 1 & \rho_{12} & \cdots & \rho_{1k} \\ \rho_{21} & 1 & \cdots & \rho_{2k} \\ \vdots & \vdots & \ddots & \vdots \\ \rho_{k1} & \rho_{k2} & \cdots & 1 \end{bmatrix}.$$

$\boldsymbol{R}$ is also a symmetric matrix, since $\rho_{ij} = \rho_{ji}$ for all $i \neq j$. It can be thought of as the covariance matrix of the standardized X_i's, i.e., the X_i's divided by their standard deviations σ_i's.

2.6   CHEBYSHEV'S INEQUALITY AND WEAK LAW OF LARGE NUMBERS

The variance σ^2 of an r.v. X measures the dispersion of X about its mean μ. If σ^2 is small, there is a high probability that X takes values close to μ. Can this probability be bounded regardless of the actual distribution of X? An elegant answer to this question was provided by a Russian probabilist named Chebyshev (1821–1894). He proved the following result.

Chebyshev's Inequality: Let $c > 0$ be any constant. Then, irrespective of the distribution of X,

$$P(|X - \mu| \geq c) \leq \frac{\sigma^2}{c^2} \tag{2.23}$$

where $\mu = E(X)$ and $\sigma^2 = \text{Var}(X)$. In other words, the probability that an r.v. X deviates by at least c units from its mean μ is no more than σ^2/c^2. The smaller the σ^2, the smaller is this upper bound for any fixed $c > 0$.   ∎

EXAMPLE 2.29 (TOSSING TWO DICE: APPLICATION OF CHEBYSHEV'S INEQUALITY)

Consider the r.v. X = sum of the numbers on two fair dice. (See Examples 2.15 and 2.17.) Recall that $E(X) = \mu = 7$ and $\text{Var}(X) = \sigma^2 = 5.833$. Suppose we wish to find an upper bound on $P(|X - 7| \geq 5)$. By Chebyshev's inequality this bound is given by

$$P(|X - 7| \geq 5) \leq \frac{5.833}{5^2} = 0.233.$$

The exact value of this probability from Table 2.1 is

$$P(X = 2) + P(X = 12) = \frac{2}{36} = 0.056,$$

which is much smaller than 0.233. The Chebyshev bound is not very sharp, since it does not consider the actual distribution of X. ◆

An important application of Chebyshev's inequality is to prove the **Weak Law of Large Numbers (WLLN)**.[1] The WLLN formalizes our intuition that if we observe independent and identically distributed (i.i.d.) r.v.'s, $X_1, X_2, \ldots, X_n$, from a distribution with a finite mean μ and variance σ^2, then the sample mean $\bar{X} = \frac{X_1 + X_2 + \cdots + X_n}{n}$ should approximate μ very closely if n is large.

To state and prove this result, we first find expressions for $E(\bar{X})$ and $\text{Var}(\bar{X})$:

$$E(\bar{X}) = \frac{1}{n}\{E(X_1) + E(X_2) + \cdots + E(X_n)\}$$

$$= \frac{1}{n}\{\mu + \mu + \cdots + \mu\}$$

$$= \mu \tag{2.24}$$

and

$$\text{Var}(\bar{X}) = \frac{1}{n^2}\{\text{Var}(X_1) + \text{Var}(X_2) + \cdots + \text{Var}(X_n)\}$$

$$= \frac{1}{n^2}\{\sigma^2 + \sigma^2 + \cdots + \sigma^2\}$$

$$= \frac{n\sigma^2}{n^2}$$

$$= \frac{\sigma^2}{n}. \tag{2.25}$$

Note that $E(\bar{X}) = \mu$ does not imply that $\bar{X}$ is close to μ; it implies only that the probability distribution of $\bar{X}$ has mean μ. This can be explained using the frequentist interpretation: If repeated i.i.d. samples of size n (even $n = 1$) are drawn from a

---

[1] The **Strong Law of Large Numbers (SLLN)** is beyond the scope of the present text.

distribution with mean μ, and sample mean $\bar{X}$ is calculated for each sample, then the average of the $\bar{X}$ values will approach μ as the number of samples increases indefinitely. In order that any individual sample mean $\bar{X}$ be close to μ, we must have a large sample size n. This is formalized in the following theorem.

Weak Law of Large Numbers (WLLN): Let $\bar{X}$ be the sample mean of n i.i.d. observations from a population with a finite mean μ and variance σ^2. Then for any fixed $c > 0$,

$$P\left(|\bar{X} - \mu| \geq c\right) \to 0$$

as $n \to \infty$.

Proof: Noting that $E(\bar{X}) = \mu$ and $\text{Var}(\bar{X}) = \sigma^2/n$, we can apply the Chebyshev inequality to conclude that

$$P\left(|\bar{X} - \mu| \geq c\right) \leq \frac{\sigma^2}{nc^2}.$$

As $n \to \infty$, the upper bound on the probability approaches zero for any fixed $c > 0$, thus proving the theorem.   ∎

2.7   SELECTED DISCRETE DISTRIBUTIONS

2.7.1 Bernoulli Distribution

An r.v. that can take only two values, say 0 and 1, is called a **Bernoulli r.v.** The Bernoulli distribution is a useful model for dichotomous outcomes. Some examples are the sex of a baby (male or female), the outcome of an experiment (success or failure), and the toss of a coin (head or tail). An experiment with a dichotomous outcome is called a **Bernoulli trial**.

As an example, suppose that an item drawn at random from a production process can be either defective or nondefective. Let p denote the fraction of the defective items produced by the process. Then the probabilities of the possible outcomes for an item drawn randomly from this process are $P(\text{Defective}) = p$ and $P(\text{Nondefective}) = 1 - p$. A Bernoulli r.v. can be defined as $X = 1$ if the item is defective and 0 if nondefective with the following distribution:

$$f(x) = P(X = x) = \begin{cases} p & \text{if } x = 1 \\ 1 - p & \text{if } x = 0. \end{cases}$$

The mean and variance of a Bernoulli r.v. can be found from their respective definitions:

$$E(X) = 0 \times P(X = 0) + 1 \times P(X = 1)$$
$$= 0(1 - p) + 1(p) = p$$

and

$$\text{Var}(X) = E(X^2) - [E(X)]^2$$
$$= \left[0^2(1 - p) + 1^2(p)\right] - p^2$$
$$= p - p^2 = p(1 - p).$$

2.7.2 Binomial Distribution

Some experiments can be viewed as a sequence of i.i.d. Bernoulli trials, where each outcome is a "success" or a "failure." The *total number* of "successes" from such an experiment is often of interest rather than the individual outcomes. If there is a fixed number n of trials that are independent and each trial has the same probability p of success, then the sum of these i.i.d. Bernoulli r.v.'s is referred to as a binomial r.v.

The general form of the p.m.f. of a binomial r.v. X with parameters n and p (denoted by $X \sim \text{Bin}(n, p)$) is derived as follows: The probability of obtaining x successes and $n - x$ failures in a particular way (e.g., the first x trials resulting in successes and the last $n - x$ trials resulting in failures) is $p^x(1 - p)^{n-x}$, because the trials are independent. There are a total of $\binom{n}{x}$ ways of distributing x successes and $n - x$ failures among n trials. Therefore the p.m.f. is given by

$$f(x) = P(X = x) = \binom{n}{x} p^x (1 - p)^{n-x} \quad \text{for } x = 0, 1, \ldots, n. \qquad (2.26)$$

Note that $f(0) = P(X = 0) = (1 - p)^n$ and $f(n) = P(X = n) = p^n$. This distribution is tabulated for selected values of n and p in Table A.1 in Appendix A.

To find the mean and the variance of $X \sim \text{Bin}(n, p)$, note that $X = Y_1 + Y_2 + \cdots + Y_n$, where the Y_i are i.i.d. Bernoulli r.v.'s with parameter p. From this representation we obtain

$$E(X) = E(Y_1) + E(Y_2) + \ldots + E(Y_n) = np$$

and

$$\text{Var}(X) = \text{Var}(Y_1) + \text{Var}(Y_2) + \cdots + \text{Var}(Y_n) = np(1 - p).$$

EXAMPLE 2.30   (TOOTH CAVITIES: BINOMIAL PROBABILITY)

Suppose that the incidence of tooth cavities in a population of children is known to be 10%. A toothpaste manufacturer tests a newly formulated toothpaste on a random sample of 20 children. The children are examined one year after using the new toothpaste. Only one child in the sample (i.e., 5% of the sample) is found to have new cavities. Based on this test, the manufacturer advertises that the new formula reduces the incidence of tooth cavities by half. Is this claim supported by the test results?

Superficially the claim appears to be valid. However, due to the small sample size of 20, this result could occur simply by chance. How likely is it to find no more than 1 child with cavities if the new toothpaste has in fact no effect (i.e., the incidence rate remains at 10%)? Under the assumption of no effect, X = number of children in a sample of 20 who develop cavities has the $\text{Bin}(n = 20, p = 0.1)$ distribution and this probability is

$$P(X \leq 1) = P(X = 0) + P(X = 1)$$

$$= (0.90)^{20} + \binom{20}{1}(0.10)(0.90)^{19}$$

$$= 0.122 + 0.270 = 0.392.$$

Thus, test results as good or better than what were actually found would have occurred almost 40% of the time even if the toothpaste was ineffective. Therefore the manufacturer's claim is not conclusively supported by the data. ◆

This example illustrates the kind of probabilistic reasoning used in hypothesis testing. This will be studied in detail in Chapter 6.

2.7.3 Hypergeometric Distribution

Two key assumptions underlying the binomial distribution are that (a) the Bernoulli trials are independent, and (b) each Bernoulli trial has the same probability of "success." These assumptions are valid when a random sample is drawn from an infinite or a very large population[2] of items of which a fraction p has a specific attribute. When the population is finite, the assumptions are valid if each randomly sampled item is returned to the population before the next draw. This is called **sampling with replacement**. But in practice we generally use **sampling without replacement**. When the population is finite, sampling without replacement creates dependence among the successive Bernoulli trials, and the probability of success changes as successive items are drawn. We now derive this distribution.

Let N be the size of the population in which M items have a specific attribute. We randomly sample n items from the population without replacement. What is the probability that exactly x of the n sampled items have the attribute? First we find the number of ways to draw x items from the M with the attribute *and* $(n-x)$ items from the remaining $(N-M)$ items without the attribute. This is given by $\binom{M}{x}\binom{N-M}{n-x}$. We then divide it by the number of ways to sample n items from the population of size N without any restriction, which is $\binom{N}{n}$. Thus

$$f(x) = P(X = x) = \frac{\binom{M}{x}\binom{N-M}{n-x}}{\binom{N}{n}}.$$

This is referred to as the hypergeometric distribution with parameters N, M, and n. If the sampling fraction n/N is small (≤ 0.10), then this distribution is well approximated by the binomial distribution (2.26) with parameters n and $p = M/N$.

The mean and variance of a hypergeometric r.v. X with parameters N, M, and n with $p = M/N$ are given by

$$E(X) = np \text{ and } \text{Var}(X) = \left(\frac{N-n}{N-1}\right)np(1-p).$$

---

[2] A common rule of thumb is that the population size must be at least 10 times the sample size.

EXAMPLE 2.31   (ACCEPTANCE SAMPLING)

A furniture warehouse buyer must decide whether or not to accept a shipment of 50 tables. The decision is based on inspecting a random sample of five tables. The shipment will be accepted if no defective tables are found. Suppose that two tables in the shipment are defective. Let $X =$ number of defective tables in the sample. What is the probability that the shipment will be accepted, i.e., $P(X = 0)$?

In terms of the hypergeometic probability formula we have,

$$N = 50, \text{ the shipment size}$$

$$M = 2, \text{ the number of defective tables in the shipment}$$

$$n = 5, \text{ the size of the sample.}$$

Therefore

$$P(\text{Accept Shipment}) = P(X = 0)$$

$$= \frac{\binom{2}{0}\binom{48}{5}}{\binom{50}{5}}$$

$$= \frac{1 \times \frac{48!}{5!43!}}{\frac{50!}{5!45!}}$$

$$= 0.8082. \qquad \blacklozenge$$

2.7.4 Poisson Distribution

The Poisson distribution is a limiting form of the binomial distribution. Recall that the binomial p.m.f. is given by $P(X = x) = \binom{n}{x}p^x(1 - p)^{n-x}$. When $n \to \infty$ and $p \to 0$ in such a way that np approaches a positive constant λ, the limiting binomial p.m.f. can be shown to be

$$f(x) = P(X = x) = \frac{e^{-\lambda}\lambda^x}{x!}, \quad x = 0, 1, 2, \ldots. \tag{2.27}$$

which is the Poisson p.m.f.

The Poisson distribution can be used to model the number of occurrences of a rare event (e.g., the number of defective welds in a car body) when the number of opportunities for the event (the total number of welds) is very large, but the probability that the event occurs in any specific instance is very small. Moreover, the occurrences are i.i.d. Bernoulli trials. Other examples include the number of accidents at an intersection, the number of earthquakes, the number of leukemia cases, etc.

An r.v. X having this distribution is called a Poisson r.v. with parameter λ (denoted by $X \sim \text{Pois}(\lambda)$). This distribution is tabulated in Table A.2 in Appendix A for selected values of λ. The mean and variance of X are given by

$$E(X) = \lambda \text{ and } \text{Var}(X) = \lambda.$$

EXAMPLE 2.32   (TOOTH CAVITIES: POISSON APPROXIMATION TO BINOMIAL)

Let us see how well the Poisson distribution approximates the binomial distribution for the tooth cavity problem, even though $n = 20$ is not very large and $p = 0.10$ is not very small. Calculate $\lambda = np = 20 \times 0.10 = 2.0$. The Poisson approximation to $P(X = 0) + P(X = 1)$ is

$$\frac{e^{-2}2^0}{0!} + \frac{e^{-2}2^1}{1!} = 0.135 + 0.271$$

$$= 0.406$$

which is reasonably close to the binomial probability of 0.392 found in Example 2.30.   ◆

The Poisson distribution is used as a model for the count of random events occurring over time, e.g., the number of jobs arriving at a work station or the number of radioactive particle emissions. If N_t denotes the number of events occurring in time interval $[0, t]$, then the collection of random variables $\{N_t, t \geq 0\}$ is called a **counting process**. The **Poisson process** is a special type of a counting process having the property that $N_0 = 0$, and the probability distribution of N_t for any fixed $t > 0$ is given by

$$P\{N_t = n\} = \frac{e^{-\lambda t}(\lambda t)^n}{n!}, \quad n = 0, 1, 2, \ldots$$

for some $\lambda > 0$, which is called the **rate** of the Poisson process. For example, if the arrival rate of jobs at a work station is $\lambda = 2$ per minute, then the number of jobs arriving in a five-minute interval will be Poisson distributed with a mean of 10.

2.7.5 Geometric Distribution

The geometric distribution models the number of i.i.d. Bernoulli trials needed to obtain the first success. It is an example of a **discrete waiting time distribution**, i.e., the distribution of discrete time to an event. Here the number of required trials is the r.v. of interest. As an example, consider playing on a slot machine until hitting the jackpot. Let the probability of hitting the jackpot on any attempt be p. The sample space is

$$\{S, FS, FFS, FFFS, FFFFS, \ldots\}$$

where S denotes a "success" and F denotes a "failure." Let X be the number of trials required to hit the first jackpot. Assuming that the attempts are independent and p remains constant, the probability of hitting the jackpot on the xth attempt is

$$f(x) = P(X = x) = \underbrace{P(F) \times P(F) \times \cdots \times P(F)}_{x - 1 \text{ unsuccessful attempts}} \times P(S)$$

$$= (1 - p)^{x-1}p, \quad x = 1, 2, \ldots. \tag{2.28}$$

This is a geometric distribution with parameter p. Its c.d.f. is given by

$$F(x) = P(X \leq x) = \sum_{k=1}^{x}(1 - p)^{k-1}p = 1 - (1 - p)^{x}.$$

The formulas for the mean and variance of a geometric r.v. were derived in Examples 2.23 and 2.24, respectively:

$$E(X) = \frac{1}{p} \text{ and } \text{Var}(X) = \frac{1 - p}{p^2}.$$

Memoryless Property. A geometric r.v. has a property of forgetting the past in the following sense: Given that the first success has not occurred by the sth trial, the probability that it will not occur for at least another t trials is the same as if one were to start all over; i.e., it is the probability that the first success will not occur for at least t trials starting at time zero. This property is easy to prove:

$$P(X > s + t \mid X > s) = \frac{P\{(X > s + t) \cap (X > s)\}}{P(X > s)} = \frac{P(X > s + t)}{P(X > s)}$$

$$= \frac{(1 - p)^{s+t}}{(1 - p)^{s}} = (1 - p)^{t}$$

which is the probability $P(X > t)$. The geometric distribution is the only discrete distribution with this property.

 If the geometric distribution is used to model the lifetime of an item that can fail only at discrete times: 1, 2, ..., etc., then the probability that the item will last at least t more time periods given its current age is independent of the age. Thus the item does not age.

EXAMPLE 2.33

Suppose that a system is tested for a fault once every hour. The fault-detection algorithm fails to detect an existing fault with probability 0.05. What is the probability that a fault will be detected in exactly 3 hours? in 3 hours or more? in more than 3 hours, given that it has not been detected for 2 hours? What is the average time to detection of a fault?

 Let X be the time to detection of a fault. Then X has a geometric distribution with $p = 1 - 0.05 = 0.95$. The first probability is

$$P(X = 3) = (0.05)^2(0.95) = 0.002375.$$

The second probability is

$$P(X \geq 3) = P(X > 2) = (0.05)^2 = 0.0025.$$

The third probability is (using the memoryless property)

$$P(X > 3 \mid X > 2) = P(X > 1) = 0.05.$$

The average time to detection of a fault is

$$E(X) = \frac{1}{0.95} = 1.053 \text{ hours.}$$

◆

2.7.6 Multinomial Distribution

The binomial distribution applies when we have a fixed number of independent Bernoulli trials with constant probabilities p and $1 - p$ for the two outcomes. In some situations there are more than two possible outcomes in each trial; e.g., a respondent's ethnic group may be classified as Caucasian, African-American, Hispanic, Native American, Asian, or other. For such trials we need a generalization of the binomial distribution to model the frequencies of different outcomes. Consider a fixed number n of trials where each trial can result in one of $k \geq 2$ outcomes, and the probabilities of the outcomes, $p_1, p_2, \ldots, p_k$, are the same from trial to trial, with $p_1 + p_2 + \cdots + p_k = 1$. Let $X_1, X_2, \ldots, X_k$ be the frequencies of different outcomes with $X_1 + X_2 + \cdots + X_k = n$. The joint multivariate distribution of $X_1, X_2, \ldots, X_k$ is called the multinomial distribution and is given by

$$f(x_1, x_2, \ldots, x_k) = P(X_1 = x_1, X_2 = x_2, \ldots, X_k = x_k)$$

$$= \frac{n!}{x_1! x_2! \cdots x_k!} \, p_1^{x_1} p_2^{x_2} \cdots p_k^{x_k} \tag{2.29}$$

where $x_i \geq 0$ for all i and $x_1 + x_2 + \cdots + x_k = n$. This formula can be derived by using the same argument that was used in deriving the formula for the binomial distribution. Specifically, $p_1^{x_1} p_2^{x_2} \cdots p_k^{x_k}$ gives the probability that outcome 1 occurs x_1 times, outcome 2 occurs x_2 times, etc., in a specific order. This probability is multiplied by the multinomial coefficient (see (2.2)), which counts the number of these different orders.

Note that the multinomial distribution is a discrete $(k - 1)$-variate distribution (since any $k - 1$ of the X_i's fix the remaining one). The binomial distribution is a special case of the multinomial distribution for $k = 2$. The means, variances, and covariances of multinomial r.v.'s are given by the following:

$$
\begin{aligned}
E(X_i) &= np_i & (1 \leq i \leq k), \\
\mathrm{Var}(X_i) &= np_i(1 - p_i) & (1 \leq i \leq k), \\
\mathrm{Cov}(X_i, X_j) &= -np_i p_j & (1 \leq i \neq j \leq k).
\end{aligned}
$$

EXAMPLE 2.34

In a large population of voters, 50% favor candidate A, 40% favor candidate B, and 10% are undecided. What is the probability that in a random sample of 10 voters, the same proportions would be found? What about in a sample of 20 voters?

Let X_1, X_2, and X_3 be the numbers in the sample who favor A, B and who are undecided, respectively. Then X_1, X_2, X_3 have a trinomial distribution with $p_1 = 0.5$, $p_2 = 0.4$, $p_3 = 0.1$, and $n = 10$. The required probability is given by

$$P(X_1 = 5, X_2 = 4, X_3 = 1) = \frac{10!}{5!4!1!} \, (0.5)^5 (0.4)^4 (0.1)^1$$

$$= 0.1008.$$

If the sample size is $n = 20$, then the probability is

$$P(X_1 = 10, X_2 = 8, X_3 = 2) = \frac{20!}{10!8!2!} (0.5)^{10}(0.4)^8(0.1)^2$$

$$= 5.912 \times 10^{-4}.$$

Notice the much smaller probability for $n = 20$. ◆

2.8   SELECTED CONTINUOUS DISTRIBUTIONS

This section discusses some important continuous distributions. The normal distribution, which is perhaps the most important continuous distribution, is discussed separately in Section 2.9.

2.8.1 Uniform Distribution

A uniform distribution arises in situations where all values are "equally likely" over an interval. Specifically, the p.d.f. of a uniform distribution is constant over an interval. An r.v. X has a uniform distribution over the interval $[a, b]$ (denoted by $X \sim U[a, b]$) if the p.d.f. (shown in Figure 2.9) is given by

$$f(x) = \begin{cases} \frac{1}{b-a}, & a \leq x \leq b \\ 0, & \text{otherwise.} \end{cases}$$

The c.d.f. of a uniform r.v. is given by

$$F(x) = \begin{cases} 0, & x < a \\ \frac{x-a}{b-a}, & a \leq x \leq b \\ 1, & x > b. \end{cases}$$

The mean and variance of $X \sim U[a, b]$ are given by

$$E(X) = \frac{a+b}{2} \quad \text{and} \quad \text{Var}(X) = \frac{(b-a)^2}{12}.$$

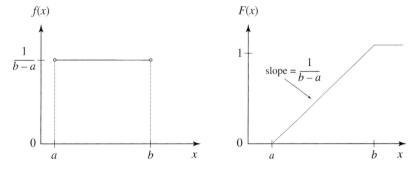

Figure 2.9   Uniform Distribution p.d.f. and c.d.f.

2.8.2 Exponential Distribution

The exponential distribution is a continuous analog of the geometric distribution; as such it is an example of a continuous **waiting time distribution**. The p.d.f. of an exponential r.v. X with parameter $\lambda > 0$ was given in (2.8), which is

$$f(x) = \lambda e^{-\lambda x} \quad \text{for } x \geq 0.$$

This p.d.f. is pictured in Figure 2.10. The c.d.f. of an exponential r.v. is given by

$$F(x) = \int_0^x \lambda e^{-\lambda y} \, dy = 1 - e^{-\lambda x} \quad \text{for } x \geq 0.$$

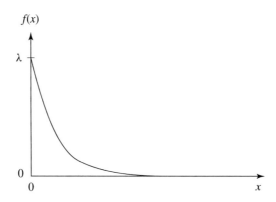

Figure 2.10   Exponential Distribution p.d.f.

A shorthand notation $X \sim \text{Exp}(\lambda)$ will denote that X is exponentially distributed with parameter λ. The following formulas for the mean and variance of $X \sim \text{Exp}(\lambda)$ were obtained in Example 2.18:

$$E(X) = \frac{1}{\lambda} \quad \text{and} \quad \text{Var}(X) = \frac{1}{\lambda^2}.$$

Since $1/\lambda$ is the average time between two events, λ can be interpreted as the rate at which events occur. It can be shown that if events occur according to a Poisson process with rate λ, then the interevent times are exponentially distributed with mean $1/\lambda$ and vice versa.

Memoryless Property.   The exponential distribution shares the memoryless property with the geometric distribution, and it is the only continuous distribution having this property. The proof of the property is simple:

$$P(X > s + t \mid X > s) = \frac{P\{(X > s + t) \cap (X > s)\}}{P(X > s)} = \frac{P(X > s + t)}{P(X > s)}$$

$$= \frac{e^{-\lambda(s+t)}}{e^{-\lambda s}} = e^{-\lambda t}$$

which is the probability $P(X > t)$.

EXAMPLE 2.35

Suppose that airport shuttle buses arrive at a terminal at the rate of one every 10 minutes with exponentially distributed interarrival times. If a person arrives at the bus stop and sees a bus leaving, what is the probability that he must wait for more than 10 minutes for the next bus? What if the person does not see a bus leaving?

Let X be the time between arrivals of buses; $X \sim \text{Exp}(\lambda = 1/10)$. The first probability is

$$P(X > 10) = e^{-10/10} = 0.368.$$

One might think that the second probability should be smaller, since the person arrived after the previous bus had left and so there is a smaller chance that he will have to wait for more than 10 minutes. However, because of the memoryless property of the exponential distribution this probability is also 0.368. ◆

2.8.3 Gamma Distribution

An r.v. X is said to have a gamma distribution with parameters $\lambda > 0$ and r if its p.d.f. is given by

$$f(x) = \frac{\lambda^r x^{r-1} e^{-\lambda x}}{\Gamma(r)} \quad \text{for } x \geq 0,$$

where the **gamma function**, $\Gamma(r)$, is defined by

$$\Gamma(r) = \int_0^\infty u^{r-1} e^{-u} du \quad \text{for } r > 0. \tag{2.30}$$

For positive integer values of r, it can be shown that $\Gamma(r) = (r-1)!$. This special case of the gamma distribution, known as the **Erlang distribution**, is used in queuing theory to model waiting times. A shorthand notation $X \sim \text{Gamma}(\lambda, r)$ denotes that X has a gamma distribution with parameters λ and r.

The mean and variance of $X \sim \text{Gamma}(\lambda, r)$ are given by

$$E(X) = \frac{r}{\lambda} \quad \text{and} \quad \text{Var}(X) = \frac{r}{\lambda^2}.$$

The sum of n i.i.d. exponential r.v.'s, each with parameter λ, can be shown to have the $\text{Gamma}(\lambda, n)$ distribution. As an illustration, consider a project that requires completing n independent successive tasks; each task has a processing time that is exponentially distributed with the same parameter λ. Then the total processing time has the $\text{Gamma}(\lambda, n)$ distribution.

EXAMPLE 2.36

Suppose that customers arrive at a bank teller's counter at the rate of one every two minutes on the average, and their interarrival times are exponentially distributed. What is the probability that at least 5 customers will arrive in 10 minutes?

Let T_i denote the interarrival time between customer $i-1$ and customer i ($i = 1, \ldots, 5$). Then $X = T_1 + \cdots + T_5$ has a gamma distribution with $n = 5$ and $\lambda = 1/2$. We want $P(X \leq 10)$, which is calculated to be 0.560 using MINITAB. ◆

2.8.4 Beta Distribution

The beta distribution provides a flexible way to model many types of measurements that have finite ranges. An r.v. X has a beta distribution on the interval $[0, 1]$ with parameters a and b (denoted by $X \sim \text{Beta}(a, b)$) if its p.d.f. is given by

$$f(x) = \frac{1}{B(a, b)} x^{a-1}(1-x)^{b-1} \quad \text{for } 0 \le x \le 1,$$

where $B(a, b)$ is the **beta function** defined by

$$B(a, b) = \frac{\Gamma(a)\Gamma(b)}{\Gamma(a+b)}.$$

Note that an r.v. having a finite range other than $[0, 1]$ can always be transformed to the $[0, 1]$ range.

The $U[0, 1]$ distribution is a special case of the beta distribution when $a = b = 1$, in which case the above p.d.f. reduces to $f(x) = \frac{1}{B(1,1)} = 1$.

The mean and variance of $X \sim \text{Beta}(a, b)$ are given by

$$E(X) = \frac{a}{a+b} \quad \text{and} \quad \text{Var}(X) = \frac{ab}{(a+b)^2(a+b+1)}.$$

2.9   NORMAL DISTRIBUTION

The normal distribution is used to model many real-life phenomena such as measurements of blood pressure, weight, dimensions, etc. This distribution was first discovered by de Moivre (1667–1754) in 1733 and later rediscovered by Laplace (1749–1827) and Gauss (1777–1855) in their studies of errors in astronomical measurements. It is often referred to as the **Gaussian distribution**. The German ten Deutsche Mark bill (see Fig 2.11) has Gauss's picture on it along with the familiar bell-shaped normal p.d.f. curve and its formula (2.31). A large body of statistics is based on the assumption that the data follow the normal distribution.

A continuous r.v. X has a normal distribution with parameters μ and σ^2 (denoted by $X \sim N(\mu, \sigma^2)$), if its p.d.f. is given by

$$f(x) = \frac{1}{\sigma\sqrt{2\pi}} e^{-\frac{(x-\mu)^2}{2\sigma^2}} \quad \text{for } -\infty < x < \infty \qquad (2.31)$$

where $-\infty < \mu < \infty$ and $\sigma > 0$. The normal p.d.f. curve shown in Figure 2.12 is centered at μ, and σ is the distance from μ to the inflection point of the curve. It can be shown that the mean and variance of $X \sim N(\mu, \sigma^2)$ are given by

$$E(X) = \mu \quad \text{and} \quad \text{Var}(X) = \sigma^2.$$

The bivariate generalization of the normal distribution is discussed in Chapter 10.

Figure 2.11 A Ten Deutsche Mark Bill with a Picture of Gauss and the Normal Distribution.

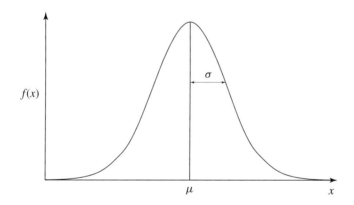

Figure 2.12 Normal Distribution p.d.f.

2.9.1 Standard Normal Distribution

A normal r.v. Z with a zero mean and unit variance ($Z \sim N(0, 1)$) is called a standard normal r.v., and its distribution is called the standard normal distribution. Any normal r.v. can be transformed to a standard normal r.v. by subtracting its mean and then dividing by its standard deviation. This is called **standardizing**. If $X \sim N(\mu, \sigma^2)$ then

$$Z = \frac{X - \mu}{\sigma} \sim N(0, 1).$$

This is a useful technique, since any probability involving $X \sim N(\mu, \sigma^2)$ can be expressed in terms of $Z \sim N(0, 1)$.

We will use special notations for the p.d.f. and c.d.f. of $Z \sim N(0, 1)$, since they occur frequently. The p.d.f. of Z is denoted by

$$\phi(z) = \frac{1}{\sqrt{2\pi}}e^{-z^2/2}, \quad -\infty < z < \infty,$$

and the c.d.f. of Z is denoted by

$$\Phi(z) = P(Z \leq z) = \int_{-\infty}^{z} \phi(y) \, dy.$$

Since the standard normal p.d.f. curve is symmetric about zero, it is easy to see from Figure 2.13 that the area to the left of $-z$ is equal to the area to the right of $+z$. Since the total area under a p.d.f. curve is 1, the standard normal c.d.f. satisfies the relation

$$\Phi(-z) = 1 - \Phi(z).$$

For $z = 0$, we get $\Phi(0) = 1 - \Phi(0)$ or $\Phi(0) = 1/2$. This result is, of course, obvious from the symmetry of this curve about zero.

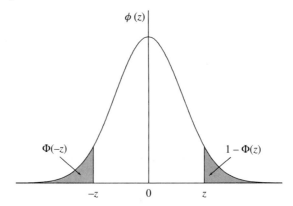

Figure 2.13 $\Phi(-z) = 1 - \Phi(z)$

Unfortunately, there is no closed-form expression for $\Phi(z)$. However, values of $\Phi(z)$ can be numerically computed and are provided in Table A.3 of Appendix A. This table can be used to find the probabilities associated with *any* normal r.v. by simply transforming it into a standardized form. Thus, if $X \sim N(\mu, \sigma^2)$, then

$$P(X \leq x) = P\left(Z = \frac{X - \mu}{\sigma} \leq \frac{x - \mu}{\sigma}\right) = \Phi\left(\frac{x - \mu}{\sigma}\right).$$

EXAMPLE 2.37

Suppose that the breaking strength (in pounds) of a rope has an $N(205, 5^2)$ distribution. A rope is considered defective if the breaking strength is less than 200 pounds. What proportion of ropes are defective?

The proportion p is given by the probability that a randomly chosen rope has strength $X < 200$ pounds. Then

$$p = P(X < 200) = P\left(Z = \frac{X - 205}{5} < \frac{200 - 205}{5}\right) = \Phi(-1) = 0.1587.$$

Thus nearly 16% of the ropes are defective.   ◆

EXAMPLE 2.38

When the data are normally distributed, σ is often used as a standard measure of distance from the mean μ of the distribution. Let us calculate the proportion of the population that falls within one, two, and three standard deviations from μ. In general, when $X \sim N(\mu, \sigma^2)$ and a is a positive constant, the proportion of the population that falls within a standard deviations from μ is

$$P(\mu - a\sigma \leq X \leq \mu + a\sigma) = P\left(-a \leq Z = \frac{X - \mu}{\sigma} \leq +a\right)$$

$$= \Phi(a) - \Phi(-a)$$

$$= 2\Phi(a) - 1.$$

Using this relationship, we find

$$P(\mu - 1\sigma \leq X \leq \mu + 1\sigma) = 2\Phi(1) - 1 = 2(0.8413) - 1 = 0.6826$$

$$P(\mu - 2\sigma \leq X \leq \mu + 2\sigma) = 2\Phi(2) - 1 = 2(0.9772) - 1 = 0.9544$$

$$P(\mu - 3\sigma \leq X \leq \mu + 3\sigma) = 2\Phi(3) - 1 = 2(0.9987) - 1 = 0.9973.$$

These calculations show that approximately 68% of a normal population lies within $\pm 1\sigma$ of μ, approximately 95% lies within $\pm 2\sigma$ of μ and nearly 100% lies within $\pm 3\sigma$ of μ.

Note that the Chebyshev *lower* bounds on the above probabilities are given by $1 - \frac{1}{1^2} = 0, 1 - \frac{1}{2^2} = 0.75$, and $1 - \frac{1}{3^2} = 0.8889$, respectively. This again illustrates that the Chebyshev bound is not very sharp. ◆

2.9.2 Percentiles of the Normal Distribution

Suppose that the scores on a standardized test are normally distributed with $\mu = 500$ and $\sigma = 100$. What is the 75th percentile score for this test? By definition, the 75th percentile is the value such that 75% of the scores are below it and 25% are above it. This percentile can be found using the standard normal distribution as follows. Let $X \sim N(500, 100^2)$ and let x denote its 75th percentile. We require that

$$P(X \leq x) = P\left(Z = \frac{X - 500}{100} \leq \frac{x - 500}{100}\right) = 0.75.$$

Now the 75th percentile of the standard normal distribution can be found from Table A.3 to be approximately 0.675, i.e., $\Phi(0.675) = 0.75$. Setting

$$\frac{x - 500}{100} = 0.675$$

we find that the 75th percentile score is $x = 500 + (0.675)(100) = 567.5$.

This idea is easily generalized. Denote by z_α the number such that the area to its right (called the **upper tail area**) under the $N(0, 1)$ p.d.f. curve is α, i.e.,

$$P(Z > z_\alpha) = 1 - \Phi(z_\alpha) = \alpha. \tag{2.32}$$

The upper tail area is shown in Figure 2.14. We refer to z_α as the **upper α critical point** or the **$100(1 - \alpha)$th percentile** of the standard normal distribution. Due to the symmetry of

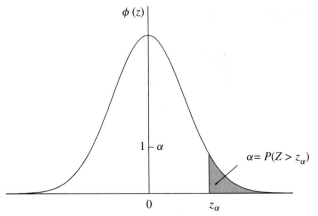

Figure 2.14 $100(1 - \alpha)$ Percentile (Upper α Critical Point) of the Standard
Normal Distribution

the $N(0, 1)$ distribution, the point $-z_\alpha$ has a **lower tail area** equal to $\alpha = P(Z \le -z_\alpha)$,
as shown in Figure 2.15, and is referred to as the **lower α critical point**.

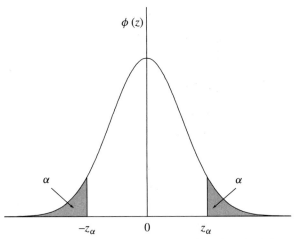

Figure 2.15   Upper and Lower α Critical Points of the Standard Normal
Distribution

Some commonly used critical points are

α	.005	.01	.025	.05	.10
z_α	2.576	2.326	1.960	1.645	1.282

If $X \sim N(\mu, \sigma^2)$, then its $100(1-\alpha)$th percentile can be found by using the relationship
$X = \mu + \sigma Z$, where $Z \sim N(0, 1)$. The required percentile is

$$x_\alpha = \mu + \sigma z_\alpha.$$

EXAMPLE 2.39

A distribution commonly used to model lifetimes is the **lognormal distribution**. The lifetime T of an item has a lognormal distribution if $X = \log T$ has a normal distribution. Suppose that T is measured in hours, and $X = \log_{10} T \sim N(4, 0.5^2)$. Determine the warranty period for the item so that no more than 5% of the items would fail before the warranty period.

Let w be the required warranty period. Then w must satisfy the equation

$$P(T \leq w) = P(X = \log_{10} T \leq \log_{10} w) = P\left(Z = \frac{X - 4}{0.5} \leq \frac{\log_{10} w - 4}{0.5}\right)$$

$$= 0.05.$$

Solving this equation yields

$$\frac{\log_{10} w - 4}{0.5} = -z_{.05} = -1.645$$

or

$$\log_{10} w = 4 - 1.645 \times 0.5 = 3.1775.$$

Therefore,

$$w = 10^{3.1775} = 1504.$$

Thus the manufacturer may specify 1500 hours as the warranty period with the assurance that there will be only about 5% warranty claims. ◆

2.9.3 Linear Combinations of Normal Random Variables

A convenient property of normal r.v.'s is that their linear combination has a normal distribution. Specifically, consider $X_i \sim N(\mu_i, \sigma_i^2)$ for $i = 1, \ldots, n$ and $\text{Cov}(X_i, X_j) = \sigma_{ij}$ for $i \neq j$. Let

$$X = a_1 X_1 + a_2 X_2 + \cdots + a_n X_n$$

where $a_1, a_2, \ldots, a_n$ are constants. Then the r.v. X will have a normal distribution with mean

$$E(X) = a_1 \mu_1 + a_2 \mu_2 + \cdots + a_n \mu_n$$

and variance

$$\text{Var}(X) = \sum_{i=1}^{n} a_i^2 \sigma_i^2 + 2 \sum \sum_{1 \leq i < j \leq n} a_i a_j \sigma_{ij}.$$

The preceding expressions for the mean and variance follow from (2.11) and (2.22), respectively. This property can be used to find the distribution of the sample mean $\bar{X}$ when the data consist of n i.i.d. observations from an $N(\mu, \sigma^2)$ distribution. Because $\bar{X}$ is a linear combination of independent normal r.v.'s, it follows that

$$\bar{X} \sim N\left(\mu, \frac{\sigma^2}{n}\right) \tag{2.33}$$

where the expressions for the mean and variance of the distribution of $\bar{X}$ follow from (2.24) and (2.25), respectively.

*Proof of Result (2.33) Using Moment Generating Functions.   First, let us derive the m.g.f. of the normal distribution. If $Z \sim N(0, 1)$, then

$$M_Z(t) = \int_{-\infty}^{\infty} e^{tz} \frac{1}{\sqrt{2\pi}} e^{-\frac{1}{2}z^2} dz$$

$$= \int_{-\infty}^{\infty} \frac{1}{\sqrt{2\pi}} e^{-\frac{1}{2}(z^2 - 2tz + t^2)} e^{\frac{t^2}{2}} dz$$

$$= e^{\frac{t^2}{2}} \int_{-\infty}^{\infty} \frac{1}{\sqrt{2\pi}} e^{-\frac{1}{2}(z-t)^2} dz$$

$$= e^{\frac{t^2}{2}}.$$

The last step follows from the fact that $\frac{1}{\sqrt{2\pi}} e^{-\frac{1}{2}(z-t)^2}$ is a normal p.d.f. with mean t and variance 1, and every p.d.f. integrates to 1.

Next, if $X \sim N(\mu, \sigma^2)$, then we know that X can be expressed as $X = \mu + \sigma Z$. Using the result (2.13), we can write

$$M_X(t) = e^{\mu t} M_Z(\sigma t) = e^{\mu t + \frac{1}{2}\sigma^2 t^2}. \tag{2.34}$$

If the X_i are i.i.d. $N(\mu, \sigma^2)$, then using (2.15), we get

$$M_{X_1 + \cdots + X_n}(t) = \left(e^{\mu t + \frac{1}{2}\sigma^2 t^2} \right)^n = e^{n\mu t + \frac{1}{2}n\sigma^2 t^2}.$$

Since the m.g.f. characterizes a distribution according to the theorem stated at the end of Section 2.4.4 and since this is the m.g.f. of the $N(n\mu, n\sigma^2)$ distribution, it follows that $X_1 + \cdots + X_n \sim N(n\mu, n\sigma^2)$. Finally, since $\bar{X} = (X_1 + \cdots + X_n)/n$, once again using (2.13) we obtain

$$M_{\bar{X}}(t) = e^{\mu t + \frac{1}{2}(\sigma^2 t^2 / n)}$$

which is the m.g.f. of the $N(\mu, \sigma^2/n)$ distribution from which the result (2.33) follows.

■

The key facts about the distributions (i.e., the formulas for the p.d.f. or p.m.f., the mean and the variance) discussed in Sections 2.7–2.9 and a few distributions introduced in exercises are summarized in Table 2.5.

2.10   ***TRANSFORMATIONS OF RANDOM VARIABLES**

Suppose that we are given the distribution of an r.v. X. Then the distribution of a function of X can be found by using the change-of-variables technique from calculus. Specifically, suppose X is a continuous r.v. with p.d.f. $f(x)$ and c.d.f. $F(x)$. Let $Y = \phi(X)$, where ϕ is an invertible (i.e., a one-to-one) function. Let $\psi = \phi^{-1}$, so that $X = \psi(Y)$. Furthermore, suppose ψ is differentiable. Then the p.d.f. of Y is

Table 2.5 Selected Probability Distributions

Name and Parameter(s)	p.m.f./p.d.f.	Mean	Variance
Discrete Distributions			
Bernoulli (p)	$f(0) = 1 - p,$ $f(1) = 0$	p	$p(1-p)$
Binomial (n, p)	$f(x) = \binom{n}{x} p^x (1-p)^{n-x},$ $x = 0, 1, \cdots, n$	np	$np(1-p)$
Hypergeometric (N, M, n),	$f(x) = \dfrac{\binom{M}{x}\binom{N-M}{n-x}}{\binom{N}{n}}$	np, where $p = \dfrac{M}{N}$	$\left(\dfrac{N-n}{N-1}\right) np(1-p)$
Poisson (λ)	$f(x) = \dfrac{e^{-\lambda}\lambda^x}{x!},$ $x = 0, 1, 2, \ldots$	λ	λ
Geometric (p)	$f(x) = (1-p)^{x-1} p,$ $x = 1, 2, \ldots$	$\dfrac{1}{p}$	$\dfrac{1-p}{p^2}$
Negative Binomial (p, r)	$f(x) = \binom{x-1}{r-1} p^r (1-p)^{x-r},$ $x = r, r+1, \ldots$	$\dfrac{r}{p}$	$\dfrac{r(1-p)}{p^2}$
Uniform (N)	$f(x) = \dfrac{1}{N},$ $x = 1, \ldots, N$	$\dfrac{N+1}{2}$	$\dfrac{N^2-1}{12}$
Continuous Distributions			
Uniform (a, b)	$f(x) = \dfrac{1}{b-a},$ $a \le x \le b$	$\dfrac{a+b}{2}$	$\dfrac{(b-a)^2}{12}$
Normal (μ, σ^2)	$f(x) = \dfrac{1}{\sigma\sqrt{2\pi}} e^{-\frac{(x-\mu)^2}{2\sigma^2}},$ $-\infty < x < \infty$	μ	σ^2
Exponential (λ)	$f(x) = \lambda e^{-\lambda x}, x \ge 0$	$\dfrac{1}{\lambda}$	$\dfrac{1}{\lambda^2}$
Gamma (λ, r)	$f(x) = \dfrac{1}{\Gamma(r)} \lambda^r x^{r-1} e^{-\lambda x},$ $x \ge 0$	$\dfrac{r}{\lambda}$	$\dfrac{r}{\lambda^2}$
Beta (a, b)	$f(x) = \dfrac{\Gamma(a+b)}{\Gamma(a)\Gamma(b)} x^{a-1}(1-x)^{b-1},$ $0 \le x \le 1$	$\dfrac{a}{a+b}$	$\dfrac{ab}{(a+b)^2(a+b+1)}$
Lognormal (μ, σ^2)	$f(x) = \dfrac{1}{x\sigma\sqrt{2\pi}} e^{-\frac{\left(\ln(x)-\mu\right)^2}{2\sigma^2}},$ $x \ge 0$	$e^{\mu+\sigma^2/2}$	$e^{2\mu+\sigma^2}\left(e^{\sigma^2}-1\right)$

$$g(y) = f(\psi(y)) \left| \frac{dx}{dy} \right| \qquad (2.35)$$

where $x = \psi(y)$. The proof of this result is straightforward. Let $G(y)$ denote the c.d.f. of Y. First suppose that ϕ is a strictly increasing function. Then $\psi = \phi^{-1}$ is also a strictly increasing function and $d\psi(y)/dy > 0$. Therefore

$$G(y) = P\{Y \leq y\} = P\{\phi(X) \leq y\} = P\{X \leq \phi^{-1}(y)\} = F(\psi(y)).$$

Differentiating $G(y)$ by using the chain rule, it follows that

$$g(y) = \frac{dG(y)}{dy} = \frac{dF(\psi(y))}{dy} = f(\psi(y)) \frac{d\psi(y)}{dy} = f(\psi(y)) \frac{dx}{dy}.$$

Next suppose that ϕ is a strictly decreasing function. Then $\psi = \phi^{-1}$ is also a strictly decreasing function and $d\psi(y)/dy < 0$. Therefore

$$G(y) = P\{Y \leq y\} = P\{\phi(X) \leq y\} = P\{X \geq \phi^{-1}(y)\} = 1 - F(\psi(y)).$$

Differentiating $G(y)$ by using the chain rule, it follows that

$$g(y) = \frac{dG(y)}{dy} = -\frac{dF(\psi(y))}{dy} = -f(\psi(y)) \frac{d\psi(y)}{dy} = f(\psi(y)) \left| \frac{dx}{dy} \right|.$$

Therefore the result (2.35) follows. The following example illustrates the use of this formula.

EXAMPLE 2.40

Suppose that $X \sim U[0, 1]$. Find the distribution of $Y = -(1/\lambda) \ln X$, where $\lambda > 0$ is a given constant.

The p.d.f. of X is $f(x) = 1$ for $0 \leq x \leq 1$. The range of the function $y = -(1/\lambda) \ln x$ is 0 to ∞. Expressing $x = \exp(-\lambda y)$, we get

$$\frac{dx}{dy} = -\lambda e^{-\lambda y}.$$

Therefore the p.d.f. of Y equals

$$g(y) = 1 \times \left| -\lambda e^{-\lambda y} \right| = \lambda e^{-\lambda y},$$

which is the exponential density function. Thus $Y \sim \text{Exp}(\lambda)$.   ◆

The formula (2.35) can be generalized to two variables. Suppose that X_1, X_2 are jointly distributed continuous r.v.'s with joint p.d.f. $f(x_1, x_2)$. Consider r.v.'s $Y_1 = \phi_1(X_1, X_2)$ and $Y_2 = \phi_2(X_1, X_2)$. Assume that the following conditions hold:

1. The functions $y_1 = \phi_1(x_1, x_2)$ and $y_2 = \phi_2(x_1, x_2)$ are one-to-one, so that we can express $x_1 = \psi_1(y_1, y_2)$ and $x_2 = \psi_2(y_1, y_2)$ for some functions ψ_1 and ψ_2.
2. The first partial derivatives of $x_1 = \psi_1(y_1, y_2)$ and $x_2 = \psi_2(y_1, y_2)$ are continuous.

3. The **Jacobian** of the transformation, defined as the determinant

$$\begin{vmatrix} \frac{\partial x_1}{\partial y_1} & \frac{\partial x_1}{\partial y_2} \\ \frac{\partial x_2}{\partial y_1} & \frac{\partial x_2}{\partial y_2} \end{vmatrix} = \frac{\partial x_1}{\partial y_1} \times \frac{\partial x_2}{\partial y_2} - \frac{\partial x_1}{\partial y_2} \times \frac{\partial x_2}{\partial y_1}$$

and denoted by J, is nonzero.

Then the p.d.f. of Y_1, Y_2 is given by

$$g(y_1, y_2) = f(\psi_1(y_1, y_2), \psi_2(y_1, y_2)) |J|. \tag{2.36}$$

The above result generalizes in a straightforward way to more than two variables.

Example **2.41**

Suppose that X_1, X_2 are i.i.d. $U[0, 1]$ r.v.'s and let

$$Y_1 = \cos(2\pi X_1)\sqrt{-2 \ln X_2} \quad \text{and} \quad Y_2 = \sin(2\pi X_1)\sqrt{-2 \ln X_2}. \tag{2.37}$$

Find the joint distribution of Y_1, Y_2.

First note that $f(x_1, x_2) = 1$ for $0 < x_1, x_2 < 1$ because X_1, X_2 are i.i.d. $U(0, 1)$ r.v.'s. Next, solving for x_1, x_2 from the equations

$$y_1 = \phi_1(x_1, x_2) = \cos(2\pi x_1)\sqrt{-2 \ln x_2} \quad \text{and} \quad y_2 = \phi_2(x_1, x_2) = \sin(2\pi x_1)\sqrt{-2 \ln x_2}$$

we get

$$x_1 = \psi_1(y_1, y_2) = \frac{1}{2\pi} \arctan\left(\frac{y_2}{y_1}\right) \quad \text{and} \quad x_2 = \psi_2(y_1, y_2) = e^{-\frac{1}{2}(y_1^2 + y_2^2)}.$$

Also note that $-\infty < y_1, y_2 < \infty$ for $0 < x_1, x_2 < 1$.

The partial derivatives are as follows:

$$\frac{\partial x_1}{\partial y_1} = \frac{-y_2}{2\pi(y_1^2 + y_2^2)}$$

$$\frac{\partial x_1}{\partial y_2} = \frac{y_1}{2\pi(y_1^2 + y_2^2)}$$

$$\frac{\partial x_2}{\partial y_1} = y_1 e^{-\frac{1}{2}(y_1^2 + y_2^2)}$$

$$\frac{\partial x_2}{\partial y_2} = y_2 e^{-\frac{1}{2}(y_1^2 + y_2^2)}.$$

Therefore the Jacobian equals

$$J = \begin{vmatrix} \dfrac{-y_2}{2\pi(y_1^2 + y_2^2)} & \dfrac{y_1}{2\pi(y_1^2 + y_2^2)} \\ y_1 e^{-\frac{1}{2}(y_1^2 + y_2^2)} & y_2 e^{-\frac{1}{2}(y_1^2 + y_2^2)} \end{vmatrix} = -\frac{y_2^2 e^{-\frac{1}{2}(y_1^2 + y_2^2)}}{2\pi(y_1^2 + y_2^2)} - \frac{y_1^2 e^{-\frac{1}{2}(y_1^2 + y_2^2)}}{2\pi(y_1^2 + y_2^2)}$$

$$= -\frac{1}{2\pi} e^{-\frac{1}{2}(y_1^2 + y_2^2)}.$$

Since $f(x_1, x_2) = f(\psi_1(y_1, y_2), \psi_2(y_1, y_2)) = 1$ for $-\infty < y_1, y_2 < \infty$, the joint p.d.f. of Y_1, Y_2 is given by

$$g(y_1, y_2) = 1 \times |J| = \frac{1}{2\pi} e^{-\frac{1}{2}(y_1^2 + y_2^2)} = \left[\frac{1}{\sqrt{2\pi}} e^{-\frac{1}{2}y_1^2} \right] \times \left[\frac{1}{\sqrt{2\pi}} e^{-\frac{1}{2}y_2^2} \right].$$

Note that each term in square brackets is the p.d.f. of an $N(0, 1)$ r.v. So if we integrate $g(y_1, y_2)$ with respect to y_2, since the second term integrates to 1, we get just the first term, which is the marginal p.d.f. of Y_1. Similarly, the marginal p.d.f. of Y_2 is just the second term. Therefore Y_1 and Y_2 are i.i.d. $N(0, 1)$ r.v.'s.

The transformation (2.37) is called the **Box-Müller transformation**, which yields a pair of i.i.d. $N(0, 1)$ r.v.s from a pair of i.i.d. $U(0, 1)$ r.v.s (which are relatively easy to generate on a computer using a pseudorandom number generator). ◆

2.11   CHAPTER SUMMARY

This chapter reviews basic ideas of probability, random variables, and probability distributions. The **axiomatic approach** is followed to define probabilities of **events** in a **sample space**, which is the collection of all possible outcomes of an experiment. When the outcomes are equally likely, the probability of an event is just the ratio of the number of outcomes in the event to the number of outcomes in the sample space. Combinatorial formulas are useful for counting the outcomes.

The **conditional probability** of an event A given that an event B has occurred, $P(A \mid B)$, is defined as $P(A \cap B)/P(B)$. Events A and B are **independent** if $P(A \mid B) = P(A)$ or equivalently if $P(A \cap B) = P(A)P(B)$. The **Bayes theorem** is a reexpression of the conditional probability formula to find $P(B \mid A)$ in terms of $P(A \mid B)$, $P(A)$ and $P(B)$.

A **random variable (r.v.)** X assigns a unique numerical value x to each outcome in the sample space. Random variables are classified as discrete or continuous. The **probability distribution** of a discrete r.v. is given by its **probability mass function (p.m.f.)** $f(x) = P(X = x)$ for all values x that the r.v. X can take. For a continuous r.v., the corresponding function is the **probability density function (p.d.f.)**, also denoted by $f(x)$, which has the property that $P(a \leq X \leq b)$ is given by the area under the p.d.f. curve between a and b for any interval $[a, b]$. The **cumulative distribution function (c.d.f.)**, defined as $F(x) = P(X \leq x)$ for all x, unifies these two concepts.

Two **parameters** useful for summarizing a symmetrically distributed r.v. X are the **mean** or the **expected value**, $E(X) = \mu$, which is a measure of center of the distribution, and the **variance**, $\sigma^2 = E[(X - \mu)^2]$, which is a measure of dispersion of the distribution about its mean. The **median**, $\tilde{\mu}$, defined by $F(\tilde{\mu}) = 1/2$ for a continuous distribution, is a preferred measure of center for a skewed distribution.

The above concepts can be generalized to two (or more) r.v.'s, say, X and Y. The **joint probability distribution** (p.d.f. or p.m.f.) of X and Y is denoted by $f(x, y)$. The **marginal distribution** $g(x)$ of X is just the p.m.f. (or p.d.f.) of X, which is obtained by summing (or integrating) $f(x, y)$ over y for fixed x; the marginal distribution $h(y)$ of Y is defined similarly. The **conditional distribution** of Y given $X = x$ is defined as $f(y \mid x) = f(x, y)/g(x)$. The r.v.'s X and Y are **independent** if $f(y \mid x) = h(y)$ or equivalently $f(x, y) = g(x)h(y)$ for all x and y. The **covariance** $\sigma_{XY} =$

$E[(X - \mu_X)(Y - \mu_Y)]$ of X and Y measures their joint dispersion from their respective means. The **correlation coefficient** ρ_{XY} standardizes the covariance to the range $[-1, +1]$. Both are measures of *linear* relationship between X and Y.

It is useful to have standard probability models for certain types of r.v.'s that are common in practice. Standard distributions for discrete r.v.'s include **Bernoulli** (for binary r.v's, e.g., success or failure), **binomial** (for the number of successes in n independent Bernoulli trials with a common success probability p), **hypergeometric** (for the number of successes in n dependent Bernoulli trials when sampling without replacement from a finite collection of successes and failures), **Poisson** (the limiting form of the binomial distribution, obtained by letting $n \to \infty$, $p \to 0$, and $np \to \lambda$, which is used to model the number of occurrences of rare events; here $\lambda > 0$ is the mean number of events per unit time), **geometric** (for the number of trials required to obtain the first success in a sequence of independent Bernoulli trials with a common success probability p), and **multinomial** (a generalization of the binomial for more than two outcomes).

Standard distributions for continuous r.v.'s include **uniform** (to model situations where all outcomes over an interval $[a, b]$ are equally likely), **exponential** (a continuous counterpart of the geometric distribution, used to model the time to an event), **gamma** (obtained by summing n i.i.d. exponential r.v.'s) and **beta** (a generalization of the uniform distribution).

The **normal distribution** is the most important and extensively used continuous distribution. The mean μ and variance σ^2 completely characterize a normal distribution, denoted by $N(\mu, \sigma^2)$. A normal distribution with $\mu = 0$ and $\sigma^2 = 1$ is called the **standard normal distribution**. All normal distributions are the same when measurements are made in the units of σ from the mean. Therefore the probabilities involving $X \sim N(\mu, \sigma^2)$ can be expressed and calculated in terms of $Z = \frac{X-\mu}{\sigma} \sim N(0, 1)$. An especially useful result is that if $X_1, X_2, \ldots, X_n$ are i.i.d. $N(\mu, \sigma^2)$ r.v.'s, then their mean $\bar{X} \sim N(\mu, \sigma^2/n)$.

The final section of the chapter discusses how to obtain the distribution of transformed r.v.'s. The primary tool here is the **Jacobian** of the transformation.

■ EXERCISES

Section 2.1

2.1   Consider an experiment that uses a fair die and a fair coin. First toss the die. Next toss the coin as many times as the number on the face of the die.

   (a) Make a table of the sample space. In each row of the table, list one outcome from the die and the corresponding possible outcomes from the coin toss(es). If there are many possible outcomes from the coin tosses, only list two or three sample outcomes in that row. How many outcomes are in this sample space?

   (b) Repeat part (a) but modify the outcomes so that only the *number* of heads from the set of coin tosses is of interest. Make a table of the sample space, listing all outcomes. How many outcomes are in this sample space?

2.2 A survey is made of sources of news for people in a metropolitan area. It is of interest whether people obtain their news from television (Event T), a newspaper (Event N), or radio (Event R). Express the following events in terms of T, N, or R in set theoretic notation.

    (a) News is obtained from television, but *not* newspapers.

    (b) News is not obtained from either television or radio.

    (c) None of these three sources is used to obtain news.

2.3 Derive Results 1 to 4 from Axioms 1 to 3 given in Section 2.1.2.

2.4 For two events A and B show that

$$P(A \cap B) \geq P(A) + P(B) - 1.$$

(*Hint*: Apply de Morgan's law and then the Bonferroni inequality.)

2.5 Two cards are drawn at random without replacement from a standard deck of 52 cards.

    (a) What is the number of ways two cards can be drawn?

    (b) What is number of ways two aces can be drawn?

    (c) What is the number of ways at least one ace can be drawn?

2.6 In a state lottery game you must match all 6 numbers drawn at random from 1 to 54 without replacement to win the grand prize, 5 out of 6 numbers to win the second prize, and 4 out of 6 numbers to win the third prize. The order of the numbers is irrelevant. Find the probability of winning each prize.

2.7 Consider a uniform lattice (grid) in a plane where the lattice points are indexed using the usual Cartesian coordinates. How many paths connect points $(0, 0)$ and (m, n) (where $m, n > 0$ are integers) if you can only move one unit to the right or one unit up at each step?

2.8 Show that

$$\binom{n}{r} = \sum_{i=\max(0,r-n_2)}^{\min(n_1,r)} \binom{n_1}{i}\binom{n_2}{r-i}$$

where n_1 and n_2 are positive integers with $n_1 + n_2 = n$. (*Hint*: The right hand side represents a different way of counting the number of ways of choosing r things out of n by dividing the n things into two groups of n_1 and n_2.)

2.9 Show that

$$\binom{n}{r} = \binom{n-1}{r-1} + \binom{n-1}{r}.$$

Make a triangle of numbers starting at the apex $(n = 0)$ with $\binom{0}{0} = 1$ and the next row $(n = 1)$ consisting of two numbers, $\binom{1}{0} = 1$ and $\binom{1}{1} = 1$. Find the entries of the next four rows $(n = 2, 3, 4,$ and $5)$ using the above relation. Notice that the entries are the binomial coefficients. This triangle (continued for all $n > 1$) is called **Pascal's triangle**.

2.10 Without actually expanding, find the coefficients of the indicated terms in the following expansions:

    (a) The coefficient of x^2y^5 in the expansion of $(x + y)^7$.

    (b) The coefficient of x^2y^5 in the expansion of $(2x - 3y)^7$.

    (c) The coefficient of $x^2y^2z^3$ in the expansion of $(x + y + z)^7$.

2.11   A team of three people to assess computer needs of a company is randomly formed from a group of 2 managers, 12 analysts, and 20 technicians.

    (a) Find the probability that the team is composed only of analysts.

    (b) Find the probability that both managers are on the team.

    (c) Find the probability that two team members are from the same job category and the third member is from a different category.

    (d) Find the probability that at least two team members are from the same job category.

2.12   An Internal Review Service (IRS) examiner has a file of 30 returns to examine. Unknown to him, 5 of the returns have errors. Suppose he randomly selects returns to examine from the file.

    (a) What is the probability that the first return does not have an error, but the second return does?

    (b) What is the probability that the second return has an error?

    (c) What is the probability that each of the first three returns has an error?

2.13   Refer to Exercise 2.2. Suppose that 77% of people obtain news from television, 63% from newspapers, 47% from radio, 45% from television and newspapers, 29% from television and radio, 21% from newspapers and radio, and 6% from television, newspapers, and radio.

    (a) Find the proportion who obtain news from television, but *not* newspapers.

    (b) Find the proportion who do not obtain news from either television or radio.

    (c) Find the proportion who do not obtain news from any of these three sources.

2.14   A mathematics contest is held among four high schools. Each school enters a team of three students. The twelve contestants are ranked from 1 (best performance) to 12 (worst performance). The team that has the overall best performance (i.e., the lowest sum of ranks of the three students in the team) gets an award. In how many ways can the 12 ranks be assigned among the four teams without distinguishing between the individual ranks of the students in each team (since only the sum of their ranks matters)?

2.15   Find the probability that all four suits are represented in a poker hand of five cards.

Section 2.2

2.16   Given the following probabilities:

$$P(A) = 0.5 \qquad P(B) = 0.6 \qquad P(C) = 0.6$$
$$P(A \cap B) = 0.3 \quad P(A \cap C) = 0.2 \quad P(B \cap C) = 0.3 \quad P(A \cap B \cap C) = 0.1$$

find the conditional probabilities $P(A \mid B)$, $P(B \mid C)$, $P(A \mid B^c)$, and $P(B^c \mid A \cap C)$.

2.17   Let A and B be two events. Suppose that $P(A) = 0.4$, $P(B) = p$, and $P(A \cup B) = 0.8$.

    (a) For what value of p will A and B be mutually exclusive?

    (b) For what value of p will A and B be independent?

2.18   Refer to Exercise 2.13.

    (a) Given that radio is a news source, what is the probability that a newspaper is also a news source?

    (b) Given that TV is a news source, what is the probability that radio is not a news source?

    (c) Given that both newspaper and radio are news sources, what is the probability that TV is not a news source?

2.19 Suppose that the IRS examiner of Exercise 2.12 correctly detects and flags 90% of all erroneous returns that he reviews. In addition, he mistakenly flags 2% of correct returns. Consider again his file of 30 tax returns, of which 5 contain errors.

 (a) What is the probability that the first return has an error and is flagged?

 (b) What is the probability that the first return is flagged?

 (c) What is the probability that the second return has an error and is flagged?

2.20 A card is drawn successively at random and with replacement from a pack of 52 cards until an ace or a face card (king, queen, or jack) is drawn. What is the probability that an ace is drawn before a face card?

2.21 Each hereditary trait in an offspring depends on a pair of genes, one contributed by the father and the other by the mother. A gene is either recessive (denoted by a) or dominant (denoted by A). The hereditary trait is A if one gene in the pair is dominant (AA, Aa, aA) and the trait is a if both genes in the pair are recessive (aa). Suppose that the probabilities of the father carrying the pairs AA, Aa (which is the same as aA), and aa are p_0, q_0, and r_0, respectively, where $p_0 + q_0 + r_0 = 1$. The same probabilities hold for the mother.

 (a) Assume that the matings are random and the genetic contributions of the father and mother are independent. Show that the corresponding probabilities for a first-generation offspring are

$$p_1 = (p_0 + q_0/2)^2, q_1 = 2(p_0 + q_0/2)(r_0 + q_0/2), r_1 = (r_0 + q_0/2)^2.$$

 Find the probabilities that the offspring has hereditary trait A and trait a.

 (b) Show that the above probabilities remain unchanged for all future generations of offspring, i.e., $p_n = p_1, q_n = q_1, r_n = r_1$ for all $n > 1$. This is known as the **Hardy-Weinberg law**. (*Hint*: Show for $n = 2$, using algebra. Then use induction.)

2.22 In a survey, 1000 adults were asked whether they favored an increase in the state income tax if the additional revenues went to education. In addition it was noted whether the person lived in a city, suburb, or rural part of the state. Do the results indicate that the place of residence and the opinion about tax increase are independent?

Increase Income Tax

	Yes	No	Total
City	100	300	400
Suburb	250	150	400
Country	50	150	200
	400	600	1000

2.23 Suppose that $n \geq 2$ components are connected in parallel. The components operate independently of each other, and the reliability of each one is p. Let A_i denote the event that the ith component functions. Show that the system reliability is given by

$$P(A_1 \cup A_2 \cup \cdots \cup A_n) = 1 - (1 - p)^n.$$

Find this probability for $p = 0.9$ and $n = 2, 3$, and 4. What do you conclude?

2.24 The following figure shows a circuit with five independently operating relays. Suppose that the probability that any relay is closed is 0.9.

   (a) Express the event that current flows from A to C in terms of the union and intersection of the elementary events R_i that the ith relay is closed.

   (b) What is the probability that current flows from A to C?

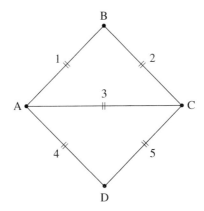

2.25 Two plants, A and B, ship appliances to a warehouse. Plant A produces 63% of the warehouse's inventory with a 4% defect rate. Plant B produces 37% of the warehouse's inventory with an 8% defect rate.

   (a) A warehouse inspector randomly selects an appliance. What is the probability that it is a defective appliance from Plant B?

   (b) What is the probability that a randomly selected appliance is defective?

   (c) Suppose that an appliance is defective. What is the probability that it came from Plant B?

2.26 Computer screening of tax returns is used to flag tax forms that need to be investigated further. The method correctly flags 85% of all erroneous returns and incorrectly flags 5% of error-free returns. The pool of tax returns submitted for computer screening contains 15% with errors.

   (a) A tax return is randomly screened. What is the probability that it is flagged by the computer and has an error?

   (b) What is the probability that a random tax form is flagged by the computer?

   (c) If a tax return is not flagged by the computer, what is the probability that it is correct?

2.27 The accuracy of a medical diagnostic test, in which a positive result indicates the presence of a disease, is often stated in terms of its **sensitivity**, the proportion of diseased people that test positive or $P(+\,|\,\text{Disease})$, and its **specificity**, the proportion of people without the disease who test negative or $P(-\,|\,\text{No Disease})$. Suppose that 10% of the population has the disease (called the **prevalence rate**). A diagnostic test for the disease has 99% sensitivity and 98% specificity. Therefore

$$P(+\,|\,\text{ Disease}) = 0.99,\ P(-\,|\,\text{ No Disease}) = 0.98,$$
$$P(-\,|\,\text{ Disease}) = 0.01,\ P(+\,|\,\text{ No Disease}) = 0.02.$$

(a) A person's test result is positive. What is the probability that the person actually has the disease?

(b) A person's test result is negative. What is the probability that the person actually does not have the disease? Considering this result and the result from (a), would you say that this diagnostic test is reliable? Why or why not?

(c) Now suppose that the disease is rare with a prevalence rate of 0.1%. Using the same diagnostic test, what is the probability that the person who tests positive actually has the disease?

(d) The results from (a) and (c) are based on the same diagnostic test applied to populations with very different prevalence rates. Does this suggest any reason why mass screening programs should not be recommended for a rare disease? Explain.

Section 2.3

2.28 Consider the following function.

$$f(x) = P(X = x) = \begin{cases} c(\frac{1}{2})^x & \text{for } x = 1, 2, 3, 4 \\ 0 & \text{otherwise.} \end{cases}$$

(a) Find the constant c so that $f(x)$ is a p.m.f.

(b) Find the c.d.f. of X.

2.29 Two fair dice are rolled. Let X be the absolute difference between the outcomes of the dice. For example, if the outcomes are 2 and 6, then $X = 4$.

(a) Find the p.m.f. and c.d.f of X.

(b) Find $P(0 < X \le 3)$ and $P(1 \le X < 3)$.

2.30 Consider the following function.

$$f(x) = P(X = x) = \frac{1}{x(x + 1)}, \quad x = 1, 2, \ldots.$$

(a) Show that $f(x)$ is a p.m.f.

(b) Find the c.d.f. of X.

2.31 A box contains N chips, marked $1, 2, \ldots, N$. A random sample of n chips is drawn and the maximum number, X, is noted. Show that the p.m.f. of X is

$$f(x) = P(X = x) = \frac{\binom{x-1}{n-1}}{\binom{N}{n}} \quad \text{for } x = n, n + 1, \ldots, N.$$

2.32 Consider the following function.

$$f(x) = \begin{cases} 0.5, & \text{if } 0 < x < 1 \\ 0.5 + c(x - 1), & \text{if } 1 \le x < 3 \\ 0, & \text{otherwise.} \end{cases}$$

(a) Find the constant c so that $f(x)$ is a p.d.f.

(b) Find the c.d.f. corresponding to $f(x)$.

2.33   Suppose a random variable X has the following c.d.f. (figure not to scale)

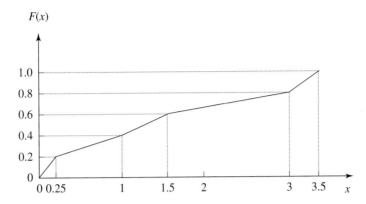

   (a) Is the r.v. X discrete or continuous?
   (b) What is the probability that $1 \leq X \leq 3$?
   (c) What is the probability that $X \geq 1$?

2.34   Suppose a random variable X has the following c.d.f.

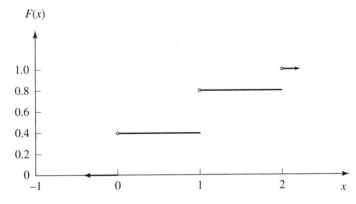

   (a) Is the r.v. X discrete or continuous?
   (b) What is the probability that $1 \leq X < 2$?
   (c) What is the probability that $X \geq 1$?

Section 2.4

2.35   Let X be the outcome of a random draw from integers 1 to N.
   (a) What is the p.m.f. of X?
   (b) Show that $E(X) = (N + 1)/2$ and $\text{Var}(X) = (N^2 - 1)/12$.
   (c) Find the mean and variance of the outcome of a single die from the above formulas.

2.36   The distribution of the number of children in a family is given below.

No. Children	0	1	2	3	4	5	6	7	8
Probability	0.10	0.20	0.30	0.15	0.10	0.05	0.05	0.03	0.02

(a) Find the expected number of children per family and the standard deviation of the number of children.

(b) Which way is the distribution skewed? Verify by calculating the skewness coefficient.

2.37 Refer to Exercise 2.31.

(a) Show that

$$E(X) = \frac{n(N + 1)}{n + 1}$$

by using the result that

$$\sum_{x=n}^{N} \binom{x}{n} = \binom{N + 1}{n + 1}.$$

(b) Suppose that N, the number of chips in the box, is unknown. Having observed X, the maximum number on n randomly drawn chips, how will you estimate N?

2.38 Refer to Exercise 2.30. Show that $E(X) = \infty$.

2.39 **(Newsboy Problem)** A young boy, who is a budding entrepreneur, starts his career by selling newspapers. He wants to know how many newspapers to order from the wholesaler every day to maximize his expected net profit. He buys newspapers for $1 each and sells them at $1.50 each, making a cool profit of $0.50 per newspaper sold. For every unsold newspaper he loses $1. If the demand exceeds his stock of newspapers, then he incurs a penalty cost of $0.75 for each extra newspaper because of customer dissatisfaction. The demand for newspapers is uncertain and follows the distribution given below.

Demand (x)	1	2	3	4	5	6	7	8	9	10
Probability ($f(x)$)	0.01	0.04	0.05	0.10	0.15	0.20	0.20	0.10	0.10	0.05

(a) Find the expected demand.

(b) Let n denote the number of newspapers that the boy orders. Write the net profit as a function of n and random demand X. (*Hint*: The profit function has different formulas for $X \leq n$ and $X > n$.)

(c) Find the value of n that maximizes the expected net profit. You may limit your search for optimum n to $n = 5, 6$, and 7.

2.40 An r.v. X has the following p.d.f.:

$$f(x) = \begin{cases} 1/(1 + x)^2, & \text{if } x \geq 0 \\ 0, & \text{otherwise.} \end{cases}$$

(a) Find the c.d.f. of X.

(b) Give a formula for the pth quantile of X and use it to find the median of X.

(c) Show that $E(\sqrt{X}) = \pi/2$.

2.41 An r.v. X has the following p.d.f.:

$$f(x) = \begin{cases} 2x^{-3}, & \text{if } x \geq 1 \\ 0, & \text{otherwise.} \end{cases}$$

(a) Find the c.d.f. of X.

(b) Give a formula for the pth quantile of X and use it to find the median of X.

(c) Find the mean and variance of X.

2.42 An r.v. X has the following p.d.f.:

$$f(x) = \begin{cases} cx(1-x), & \text{if } 0 \le x < 1 \\ 0, & \text{otherwise.} \end{cases}$$

    (a) Find the constant c so that $f(x)$ is a p.d.f.

    (b) Find the c.d.f. of X.

    (c) Find the mean and variance of X.

2.43 For an r.v. X and constants a, b show that

$$\text{Var}(aX + b) = a^2 \text{Var}(X).$$

(*Hint:* Let $Y = aX + b$. Then use the results that $E(Y) = aE(X) + b$ and $\text{Var}(Y) = E[Y - E(Y)]^2$.)

2.44 For nonnegative integer-valued r.v.'s the following method of computing the expected value is sometimes convenient.

    (a) Let $f(x)$ and $F(x)$ be the p.m.f. and c.d.f. of a nonnegative integer-valued r.v. X; note that $F(x)$ has jumps only at $x = 0, 1, 2, \ldots$. Show that the expected value of X equals the sum of its upper tail probabilities (i.e., $1 - F(x)$):

$$E(X) = \sum_{x=0}^{\infty} [1 - F(x)].$$

    (*Hint:* Consider X having a finite range: $0, 1, 2, \ldots, N$, so that $F(N) = 1$. Express $E(X) = \sum_{x=0}^{N} xf(x)$ as a telescopic series using $f(x) = F(x) - F(x-1)$, which yields the result for finite N. Now let $N \to \infty$.)

    (b) For the geometric distribution defined in Section 2.7.5, $F(x) = 1 - (1-p)^x$ for $x = 0, 1, 2, \ldots$, where $0 < p < 1$. Show that $E(X) = 1/p$. (Example 2.23 uses a different method to show this result.)

2.45 The method of the previous exercise extends to nonnegative continuous r.v.'s.

    (a) Let $f(x)$ and $F(x)$ be the p.d.f. and c.d.f. of a continuous nonnegative-valued r.v. X. Show that

$$E(X) = \int_0^{\infty} [1 - F(x)]\, dx.$$

    (*Hint:* Consider X having a finite range: $[0, A]$. Integrate $E(X) = \int_0^A xf(x)\, dx$ by parts, which yields the result for finite A. Now let $A \to \infty$.)

    (b) For the exponential distribution, $F(x) = 1 - e^{-\lambda x}$ according to equation (2.8). Show that $E(X) = 1/\lambda$. (Example 2.18 uses a different method to show this result.)

2.46 **(a)** Show that the m.g.f. of a Bin(n, p) r.v. is given by

$$\psi_X(t) = (pe^t + q)^n$$

    where $q = 1 - p$. (*Hint:* First find the m.g.f. of a Bernoulli r.v. with parameter p. Then use the fact that a Bin(n, p) r.v. is the sum of n i.i.d. Bernoulli r.v.'s.)

    (b) Find the mean and variance of a Bin(n, p) r.v. from its m.g.f.

2.47   **(a)** Show that the m.g.f. of a Poisson r.v. X with parameter λ is

$$\psi_X(t) = \exp(\lambda(e^t - 1)).$$

Find the mean and variance of X from its m.g.f.

(b) Show that if the X_i are independent $\text{Pois}(\lambda_i)$ r.v.'s for $i = 1, 2, \ldots, n$, then their sum is also Poisson distributed with parameter $\sum_{i=1}^{n} \lambda_i$.

Section 2.5

2.48   Show the following relationships:

(a) $\text{Cov}(aX + b, cY + d) = ac\,\text{Cov}(X, Y)$, where a, b, c, and d are constants.

(b) $\text{Var}(X \pm Y) = \text{Var}(X) + \text{Var}(Y) \pm 2\,\text{Cov}(X, Y)$.

(c) If X and Y are independent then $\text{Cov}(X, Y) = 0$. (*Hint*: Use the fact that $f(x, y) = g(x)h(y)$ due to independence and the definition of covariance in terms of expected values.)

2.49   Let X_1, X_2 be uncorrelated r.v.'s, each with variance σ^2. Show that $Y_1 = X_1 + X_2$ and $Y_2 = X_1 - X_2$ are uncorrelated.

2.50   Let X_0, X_1, X_2 be three uncorrelated r.v.'s with variances $\sigma_0^2, \sigma_1^2, \sigma_2^2$, respectively. Find the correlation between $Y_1 = X_0 - X_1$ and $Y_2 = X_0 - X_2$.

2.51   Let $X_1, X_2, \ldots, X_n$ be independent and identically distributed r.v's, each with variance σ^2. Let $\bar{X}$ be the sample mean. Show that

$$\text{Cov}(\bar{X}, X_i - \bar{X}) = 0 \text{ for } i = 1, 2, \ldots, n.$$

Thus the sample mean $\bar{X}$ and the differences $X_i - \bar{X}$ of the individual observations from the sample mean are uncorrelated.

2.52   An elderly patient is examined for heart and lung problems using scores X and Y, respectively. A score has a value of 0 if there is no impairment, 1 if there is mild impairment, and 2 if there is severe impairment. Suppose that the distributions of X and Y in the population are as follows:

$$P(X = 0) = 0.6, \quad P(X = 1) = 0.3, \quad P(X = 2) = 0.1;$$

$$P(Y = 0) = 0.5, \quad P(Y = 1) = 0.3, \quad P(Y = 2) = 0.2.$$

Let $T = X + Y$ be the total score for heart and lung impairment for a patient.

(a) List each of the 9 possible heart and lung score combinations. For each outcome compute the value of the total impairment score T and the associated probability, assuming independence between X and Y.

(b) Obtain the distribution of T.

(c) Find $E(T)$ and $\text{Var}(T)$.

(d) Suppose that the heart and lung problems are not independent but are positively correlated. Would it change $E(T)$? Would it change $\text{Var}(T)$? Explain.

2.53   A husband and wife invest their \$2000 IRAs in two different portfolios. After one year, the husband's portfolio has 0.2 probability of losing \$200 and 0.8 probability of gaining \$400. The wife's portfolio has 0.1 probability of losing \$100 and 0.9 probability of gaining \$300.

(a) Let X denote the husband's gain. Find $E(X)$ and $SD(X)$.

(b) Let Y denote the wife's gain. Find $E(Y)$ and $SD(Y)$.

(c) Make a table of possible values of $U = X + Y$ (the couple's total gain) and $V = X - Y$ (the difference between the husband's and the wife's gain). Assuming that X and Y are independent, find the distributions of U and V.

(d) Use the distributions of U and V to compute $E(U)$, $E(V)$, $SD(U)$, and $SD(V)$.

(e) Verify the formulas $E(X \pm Y) = E(X) \pm E(Y)$ and $SD(X \pm Y) = \sqrt{\text{Var}(X) + \text{Var}(Y)}$.

2.54 Consider an insurance agency with 15,000 customers who have both auto and homeowners policies. Let X and Y be discrete r.v.'s, where X = the deductible amount on the auto policy and Y = the deductible amount on the homeowner policy. A summary of these policies is shown below.

		Number of Customers			
		Y (Home	Policy	Deductible)	
		\$0	\$100	\$200	
	\$100	3000	1500	3000	7500
X (Auto Policy Deductible)					
	\$250	750	2250	4500	7500
		3750	3750	7500	15,000

(a) Find the marginal p.m.f.'s of X and Y. Are X and Y statistically independent?

(b) Find the conditional distribution of Y given X.

(c) Find the covariance of X and Y.

2.55 Suppose that the joint p.d.f. of X and Y is given by

$$f(x, y) = 8xy \quad \text{for } 0 \le x < y \le 1.$$

(a) Find the marginal p.d.f.'s of X and Y. Are X and Y independent?

(b) Find the conditional distribution of Y given X.

(c) Find $\text{Cov}(X, Y)$.

Section 2.6

2.56 An r.v. X can have values of -1 or 1, each with probability of $\frac{1}{2}$. Let $Y = X_1 + \cdots + X_{10}$, where $X_1, \ldots X_{10}$ are independent observations on X.

(a) Find $E(Y)$ and $\text{Var}(Y)$.

(b) Find an upper bound on $P(|Y| \ge 4)$ using the Chebyshev inequality.

(c) Find an upper bound on $P(|\bar{X}| \ge 4)$ using the Chebyshev inequality.

2.57 An r.v. X has mean μ and variance $\sigma^2 = 1$. Let $\bar{X}$ denote the mean of a random sample of size n.

(a) Use the Chebyshev inequality to find a lower bound on $P\{|\bar{X} - \mu| \le c\}$.

(b) Find the value of n to assure a probability of at least 0.95 that $\bar{X}$ falls within c units of μ for $c = 0.1, 1.0$, and 2.0.

2.58 A certain item is sold in lots of 1000. On the average, a lot has 20 defective items with SD = 4.4. Use the Chebychev inequality to find a lower bound on the probability that a lot contains between 15 and 25 defectives.

Section 2.7

2.59 A grocery store has 10 checkout lanes. During a busy hour the probability that any given lane is occupied (has at least one customer) is 0.75. Assume that the lanes are occupied or not occupied independently of each other.

 (a) What is the probability that a customer will find at least one lane unoccupied?

 (b) What is the expected number of occupied lanes? What is the standard deviation of the number of occupied lanes?

2.60 In a shotgun seminar, the topic is announced 1 week in advance, but the speaker is randomly chosen when the seminar begins. Suppose that you attend 12 seminars with 10 other participants.

 (a) What is the expected number of times you will be selected as speaker?

 (b) What is the probability that you will be selected twice?

 (c) Suppose that the 10 participants are divided into five teams of two for preparation. What is the probability that your *team* (i.e., either you or your partner) will be selected twice?

2.61 Suppose that X has a hypergeometric distribution with $N = 40$, $M = 10$, and $n = 4$.

 (a) Find $P(X \leq 2)$.

 (b) Find the binomial approximation to the probability in (a) by ignoring that N is finite and taking $p = M/N = 0.25$. Is the approximation accurate?

2.62 An office supply warehouse receives an order for three computers. The warehouse has 50 computers in stock, two of which are defective. The order is filled by randomly drawing from the computers in stock. Let X be the number of defective computers in the order.

 (a) Give the formula for the probability distribution of X.

 (b) What is the probability that the customer is not sent any of the defective computers?

 (c) Use the binomial distribution to approximate the probability that no defective computers are sent. Is the approximation accurate?

2.63 An experiment measures the number of particle emissions from a radioactive substance. The number of emissions has a Poisson distribution with rate $\lambda = 0.25$ per week.

 (a) What is the probability of at least one emission in a week?

 (b) What is the probability of at least one emission in a year?

2.64 A typist makes a typographical error at the rate of 1 every 20 pages. Let X be the number of errors in a manuscript of 200 pages.

 (a) Write the binomial distribution model for X and show how you will calculate the exact binomial probability that the manuscript has at least 5 errors.

 (b) Why is it reasonable to assume that X has a Poisson distribution? Calculate the Poisson approximation to the probability in (a).

2.65 A communication channel can carry up to 10 messages at a time. The channel capacity is designed assuming that the number of messages to be transmitted at any given time is Poisson distributed with a mean of 5.

    (a) What is the probability that a message cannot be transmitted because the channel is busy?

    (b) What is the probability distribution of the *actual* number of messages transmitted at any given time? What is the expected value of this distribution? (*Hint:* This is a **truncated Poisson distribution** conditional on the number being less than or equal to 10.)

2.66 Suppose that X_1, X_2, X_3, X_4 have a multinomial distribution with $p_1 = 0.1, p_2 = 0.2$, $p_3 = 0.3, p_4 = 0.4$, and $n = 20$.

    (a) Find the expected values of X_1, X_2, X_3, X_4.

    (b) Find the variance-covariance matrix of X_1, X_2, X_3, X_4.

    (c) Find the correlation matrix of X_1, X_2, X_3, X_4.

    (d) Find $P(X_1 = 2, X_2 = 4, X_3 = 6, X_4 = 8)$.

2.67 A marketing researcher surveys shoppers at a large shopping mall. The geographic area served by the mall is 30% low income, 45% middle income, and 25% high income. In the first hour the researcher randomly interviews four people.

    (a) What is the probability that the four interviewed include 1 with low, 1 with middle, and 2 with high income?

    (b) What is the probability that all four are middle income?

    (c) What is the probability that this group has no one with high income?

2.68 Suppose that there are $c \geq 2$ independent sources of events (e.g., new AIDS cases in c geographic regions) and that the number of events in the ith source, denoted by N_i, has a Poisson distribution with mean λ_i ($1 \leq i \leq c$). From Exercise 2.47(b) we know that $N = N_1 + N_2 + \cdots + N_c$ has a Poisson distribution with mean $\lambda = \sum_{i=1}^{c} \lambda_i$. Show that the conditional joint distribution of $N_1, N_2, \ldots, N_c$, conditioned on $N = n$, is multinomial:

$$P(N_1 = n_1, N_2 = n_2, \ldots, N_c = n_c \mid N = n) = \frac{n!}{n_1! n_2! \cdots n_c!} p_1^{n_1} p_2^{n_2} \cdots p_c^{n_c}$$

for $n_1 + n_2 + \cdots + n_c = n$, where $p_i = \lambda_i / \lambda$.

2.69 The **negative binomial distribution** is a generalization of the geometric distribution. It is the distribution of the r.v. $X =$ the number of independent Bernoulli trials, each with success probability p, required to obtain $r \geq 1$ successes. It is used as an alternative to the Poisson distribution to model count data.

    (a) Show that the distribution of X is given by

$$\binom{x-1}{r-1} p^r (1-p)^{x-r}, \quad x = r, r+1, \ldots.$$

    (b) Show that the mean and variance of a negative binomial r.v. are

$$E(X) = \frac{r}{p} \quad \text{and} \quad \text{Var}(X) = \frac{r(1-p)}{p^2}.$$

(*Hint:* Express X as the sum of r i.i.d. geometric r.v.'s.)

2.70 The NBA final is a seven-game series, and the team that wins four games first wins the series. Denote by p the probability that the Eastern Conference team wins a game and by $q = 1 - p$ the probability that the Western Conference team wins a game. Assume that these probabilities remain constant from game to game and that the outcomes of the games are mutually independent.

(a) Find the probability that the Eastern Conference team wins the series.

(b) Show that the probability that the series ends in j games is

$$\binom{j-1}{3}[p^4 q^{j-4} + q^4 p^{j-4}], \quad j = 4, 5, 6, 7.$$

Section 2.8

2.71 Suppose that the daily high temperature in a particularly temperate place varies uniformly from day to day over the range $70°F$ to $100°F$. Further assume that the daily temperatures are independently distributed.

(a) What proportion of the days does the daily high temperature exceed $90°F$?

(b) Which temperature is exceeded only 10% of the time?

2.72 A car travels between two cities A and C which are 75 miles apart. If the car has a breakdown, the distance X from the breakdown to city A is distributed as $U[0, 75]$. The driver is a member of an automobile service that has contracts with garages in cities A, B, and C, where city B is between cities A and C, 25 miles from city A. If the car breaks down, it is towed to the closest garage.

(a) Find the probability that the car is towed more than 10 miles.

(b) Find the probability that the car is towed more than 20 miles.

(c) Find the probability that the car is towed more than 10 miles given that it is more than 20 miles from city A.

2.73 Let $X =$ the time between the jobs arriving at a workstation. Assume that X is exponential with a mean of 10 minutes.

(a) Find an expression for the pth quantile and use it to find the median and the 75th percentile of the distribution of time between job arrivals.

(b) What is the probability that no jobs arrive in a 15-minute interval?

2.74 Let $X =$ the time to failure of a light bulb. Assume that X is exponentially distributed.

(a) If the mean time to failure is 10,000 hours, what is the median time to failure?

(b) What is the probability that the bulb will last at least 1000 hours?

(c) What is the probability that the bulb will burn an additional 1000 hours if it has already burned for 1000 hours?

2.75 Refer to the previous exercise. Suppose that a light bulb is replaced immediately after it burns out by an identical one (i.e., one that has the same failure distribution). Let T denote the total time until the failure of the fifth bulb. Assuming that the failures are independent, what is the distribution of T? What are $E(T)$ and $\text{Var}(T)$?

2.76 Find the parameters of a beta distribution over the interval $[0, 1]$ so that the mean = 3/4 and variance = 3/32.

2.77 Refer to Exercise 2.71. Suppose that the standardized temperature $X = (T - 70)/(100 - 70)$ has a beta distribution over $[0, 1]$ with parameters $a = 3$ and $b = 1$. What are the mean and variance of T?

Section 2.9

2.78   Let $Z \sim N(0, 1)$. Find the following probabilities.

    (a) $P(Z \le 1.68)$, $P(Z > 0.75)$, $P(Z \le -2.42)$, $P(Z > -1)$.

    (b) $P(1 \le Z \le 2)$, $P(-2 \le Z \le -1)$, $P(-1.5 \le Z \le 1.5)$, $P(-1 \le Z \le 2)$.

    (c) $P(Z \le z_{.10})$, $P(Z > -z_{.05})$, $P(z_{.25} \le Z \le z_{.01})$, $P(-z_{.25} \le Z \le z_{.01})$.

2.79   **(a)** Find $z_{.30}, z_{.15}, z_{.075}$.

    (b) Let $X \sim N(4, 3^2)$. Find $x_{.30}, x_{.15}, x_{.075}$.

2.80   The weight of coffee in a can is normally distributed with a mean of 16.1 oz. and standard deviation of 0.5 oz.

    (a) According to the label, a can contains 16 oz. of coffee. What is the probability that there is less than 16 oz. of coffee in a can?

    (b) What is the probability that a can contains 16 to 16.5 oz. of coffee?

    (c) What is the lower 10th percentile of the distribution of the coffee weight? (Ten percent of the cans contain coffee less than this weight.)

2.81   The weight U of a man is normally distributed with mean 160 lb. and standard deviation 30 lb. The weight V of a woman is normally distributed with mean 120 lb. and standard deviation 25 lb. A man and woman are randomly selected. Let $W = U - V$.

    (a) What is the distribution of W?

    (b) What are the mean and variance of W?

    (c) What is the probability that the man is at least 50 lb. heavier than the woman?

2.82   In a shaft and bearing assembly, the diameters of the bearings, X, are normally distributed with mean $= 0.526$ inches and standard deviation $= 3.0 \times 10^{-4}$ inches. The diameters of the shafts, Y, are also normally distributed with mean $= 0.525$ inches and standard deviation $= 4.0 \times 10^{-4}$ inches.

    (a) What is the distribution of the clearance, $X - Y$? What is its mean and standard deviation?

    (b) What is the probability that a shaft will fit inside a bearing?

    (c) What is the probability that out of ten shaft-bearing pairs, at least nine will fit properly?

2.83   Suppose that the monthly phone bills of a population of households are normally distributed with a mean of \$90 and standard deviation of \$20. A random sample of 25 households is taken from this population.

    (a) What is the distribution of the average of their monthly phone bills?

    (b) What is the probability that this average will exceed \$100?

    (c) What dollar amount will this average exceed with probability 0.10?

Section 2.10

2.84   Show that if $X \sim U[0, 1]$, then the c.d.f. and p.d.f. of $Y = \ln\left(\frac{X}{1-X}\right)$ are given by

$$G(y) = \frac{e^y}{1 + e^y} \quad \text{and} \quad g(y) = \frac{e^y}{(1 + e^y)^2}.$$

This distribution is known as the standard **logistic distribution**.

2.85   Show that if X has a $U[-\pi/2, \pi/2]$ distribution then $Y = \tan(X)$ has a **Cauchy distribution**, whose p.d.f. is given by

$$f(y) = \frac{1}{\pi(1 + y^2)} \quad \text{for } -\infty < y < \infty.$$

This distribution is symmetric about 0 but has the pathological properties that its mean and variance do not exist (its median equals 0).

2.86   Suppose that X has a **Pareto distribution** with the p.d.f.

$$f(x) = \lambda x^{-(\lambda+1)} \text{ for } x \geq 1.$$

Show that $Y = \ln X$ has the $\text{Exp}(\lambda)$ distribution.

2.87   Let X_1, X_2 be independent $N(0, 1)$ r.v.'s.

(a) Find the joint distribution of $Y_1 = X_1/X_2$ and $Y_2 = X_2$.

(b) Show that Y_1 has a Cauchy distribution whose p.d.f. is given in Exercise 2.85.

2.88   Let X_1, X_2 be independent $\text{Exp}(1/2)$ r.v.'s. Show that $Y_1 = \frac{1}{2}(X_1 - X_2)$ has a **double exponential distribution** with p.d.f. given by

$$g(y_1) = \frac{1}{2} e^{-|y_1|}, \quad -\infty < y_1 < \infty,$$

and $Y_2 = \frac{1}{2}(X_1 + X_2)$ has a $\text{Gamma}(2, \frac{1}{2})$ distribution with p.d.f. given by

$$h(y_2) = y_2 e^{-y_2}, \quad y_2 \geq 0.$$

Are Y_1 and Y_2 independent?

Advanced Exercises

2.89   **(Matching Game Problem)** In a party game, n men and women, who are husbands and wives, are randomly paired. What is the probability that at least one man-woman pair is a husband-wife pair?

(a) Let A_i be the event that the ith man is paired with his wife. Then the probability that we want to compute is $P(A_1 \cup A_2 \cup \cdots \cup A_n)$. We will compute this probability using the inclusion-exclusion formula (2.1). Toward this end, first show that

$$P(A_i) = \frac{(n-1)!}{n!}, \quad P(A_i \cap A_j) = \frac{(n-2)!}{n!}, \quad P(A_i \cap A_j \cap A_k) = \frac{(n-3)!}{n!}, \text{ etc.}$$

(b) Hence show, using the inclusion-exclusion formula, that

$$P(A_1 \cup A_2 \cup \cdots \cup A_n) = n\frac{(n-1)!}{n!} - \binom{n}{2}\frac{(n-2)!}{n!} + \binom{n}{3}\frac{(n-3)!}{n!} - \cdots$$

$$+ (-1)^{n-1}\binom{n}{n}\frac{1}{n!}$$

$$= 1 - \frac{1}{2!} + \frac{1}{3!} - \cdots + (-1)^{n-1}\frac{1}{n!}.$$

(c) Show that as $n \to \infty$, the above probability approaches $1 - e^{-1} \simeq 0.632$.

2.90 **(Banach's Matchbox Problem)** This is an apocryphal story about a mathematician named Stefan Banach (1892–1945), who carries two matchboxes, one in his left pocket and one in his right. When he wants to light a cigarette, he selects a pocket at random and takes out a match from the box. Suppose that initially each matchbox contains n matches. What is the probability that when Mr. Banach discovers that one matchbox is empty, the other matchbox contains exactly m matches, $m = 0, 1, 2, \ldots, n$?

  (a) The left matchbox will be found empty with m matches remaining in the right matchbox on the $n + (n - m) + 1 = (2n - m + 1)$st trial. Show that the probability of this happening is

$$\binom{2n - m}{n} \left(\frac{1}{2}\right)^{n+1} \left(\frac{1}{2}\right)^{n-m}.$$

  (b) Hence show that the probability of either matchbox being found empty with m matches remaining in the other matchbox is

$$\binom{2n - m}{n} \left(\frac{1}{2}\right)^{2n-m}.$$

2.91 **(Gambler's Ruin Problem)** Two players, A and B, play a game of "heads or tails." A fair coin is successively tossed. If the coin comes up heads, then A gets one dollar from B; if the coin comes up tails, then B gets one dollar from A. If A begins with a dollars and B begins with b dollars, what is the probability that A will be ruined before B?

  (a) Let p_i denote the probability of A's ruin, given that he has i dollars and B has $a + b - i$ dollars. Note that $p_0 = 1$ (because A is already ruined) and $p_{a+b} = 0$ (because B is already ruined). Show, using the total probability law, that

$$p_i = \frac{1}{2} p_{i+1} + \frac{1}{2} p_{i-1} \text{ or } p_{i+1} - p_i = p_i - p_{i-1} = \delta \text{ (say)}.$$

  (b) Solve the recursive system of equations $p_1 = p_0 + \delta$, $p_2 = p_1 + \delta$, ... to show that $\delta = -1/(a + b)$ and $p_a = b/(a + b)$. Therefore the probability that A will be ruined before B is $b/(a + b)$.

  (c) Similarly show that the probability that B will be ruined before A is $a/(a + b)$. Therefore the probability that the game goes on forever without either player getting ruined is 0.

2.92 Consider an r.v. X which has p.d.f. (or p.m.f.) $f_1(x)$ with probability p_1 and p.d.f. (or p.m.f.) $f_2(x)$ with probability p_2, where $p_1 + p_2 = 1$. We can think of first observing a Bernoulli r.v. Y which equals 1 with probability p_1 and 2 with probability $p_2 = 1 - p_1$. If $Y = 1$, then $X = X_1 \sim f_1(x)$, and if $Y = 2$, then $X = X_2 \sim f_2(x)$. We say that X has a **mixture distribution**. This is used to model samples drawn from a heterogeneous population formed by a mixture of two different populations and to model data contaminated by outliers.

  (a) Show that the p.d.f. (or p.m.f.) of X is

$$f(x) = p_1 f_1(x) + p_2 f_2(x).$$

  (b) Let μ_1 and μ_2 be the means of $f_1(x)$ and $f_2(x)$, respectively. Show that

$$E(X) = \mu = p_1 \mu_1 + p_2 \mu_2.$$

(c) Let σ_1^2 and σ_2^2 be the variances of $f_1(x)$ and $f_2(x)$, respectively. Show that

$$\text{Var}(X) = \sigma^2 = p_1\sigma_1^2 + p_2\sigma_2^2 + p_1\mu_1^2 + p_2\mu_2^2 - (p_1\mu_1 + p_2\mu_2)^2.$$

2.93 Suppose X and Y are jointly distributed.

(a) Show that

$$\text{Var}(X) = E[\text{Var}(X \mid Y)] + \text{Var}[E(X \mid Y)].$$

To find $\text{Var}(X)$, first find the conditional variance and conditional expectation of X, given Y. Then find the expected value of the former and the variance of the latter by unconditioning on Y, and add the two results.

(b) Use the above formula to derive the result from part (c) of the previous exercise.

2.94 The exponential and Poisson distributions are closely related: If the times between events (e.g., arrivals of customers at a service facility) are i.i.d. exponential, then the number of events occurring in any fixed time span is Poisson distributed. Show this result by following the steps below.

(a) Let $T_1, T_2, \ldots, T_n, T_{n+1}$ be i.i.d. interevent times having an exponential distribution with an event rate λ. Let $X = T_1 + T_2 + \cdots + T_n$. For fixed $t > 0$, let N_t be the number of events. We want to show that N_t has a Poisson distribution with mean λt. First show that

$$\{N_t = n\} \equiv \{X \le t; X + T_{n+1} > t\}.$$

(b) Use the facts that X has a gamma distribution with p.d.f.

$$f(x) = \frac{\lambda^n x^{n-1} e^{-\lambda x}}{\Gamma(n)} \quad \text{for } x \ge 0,$$

and T_{n+1} is independent of X with an exponential p.d.f.

$$f(y) = \lambda e^{-\lambda y} \quad \text{for } y \ge 0$$

to show that

$$P\{N_t = n\} = \int_{x=0}^{t} \frac{\lambda^n x^{n-1} e^{-\lambda x}}{\Gamma(n)} e^{-\lambda(t-x)} \, dx$$

$$= \frac{e^{-\lambda t}(\lambda t)^n}{n!}.$$

Therefore N_t is Poisson with mean λt.

2.95 **(a)** Use the result from the previous exercise to show that

$$P\{T_1 + T_2 + \cdots + T_n \le t\} = \frac{\lambda^n}{\Gamma(n)} \int_0^t x^{n-1} e^{-x} dx = P\{N_t \ge n\} = \sum_{i=n}^{\infty} \frac{e^{-\lambda t}(\lambda t)^i}{i!}.$$

(b) In Example 2.36 we calculated the probability that at least 5 customers arrive in 10 minutes when the mean arrival rate is 1 customer every 2 minutes, using the gamma distribution. Use the Poisson distribution to calculate the same probability.

2.96 The results of Exercises 2.46 and 2.47 can be combined to obtain the distribution of the number of Poisson-distributed arrivals which are counted using a Bernoulli screen (i.e., each arrival is counted with probability p and not counted with probability $1 - p$). The resulting distribution is called the **compound Poisson distribution**. As an example, suppose that the number of radioactive particles emitted, N, follows the Poisson distribution with parameter λ. The counter registers each particle with probability p. Show that the number of counted particles, X, follows the Poisson distribution with parameter λp.

   (a) Let $N \sim \text{Pois}(\lambda)$ and let $Y_1, Y_2, \ldots, Y_N$ be i.i.d. Bernoulli r.v.'s with success probability p which are independent of N. Here Y_i is an indicator variable of whether the ith particle is counted or not. Then $X = Y_1 + Y_2 + \cdots + Y_N$. Show that, conditioned on N, the m.g.f. of X is

$$\psi_X(t \mid N) = (pe^t + q)^N.$$

   (b) Show that the unconditional m.g.f. of X is

$$\psi_X(t) = E[(pe^t + q)^N] = \exp(\lambda p(e^t - 1)),$$

   which is the m.g.f. of a Poisson r.v. with parameter λp.

2.97 Let T have a lognormal distribution with $X = \log_e T \sim N(\mu, \sigma^2)$.

   (a) Show that

$$E(T) = e^{\mu + \frac{1}{2}\sigma^2} \quad \text{and} \quad \text{Var}(T) = e^{2\mu + \sigma^2}\left(e^{\sigma^2} - 1\right).$$

   (*Hint*: Use the formula (2.34) for the m.g.f. of X to find $E(T)$ and $E(T^2)$.)

   (b) In Example 2.39 we had $X = \log_{10} T \sim N(4, (0.5)^2)$. Show that

$$E(T) = \exp\left(4 \log_e 10 + \frac{1}{2}(0.5 \log_e 10)^2\right) = 19{,}400 \text{ hr.}$$

CHAPTER 3

COLLECTING DATA

Data are used to answer questions, to make decisions, and to gain a deeper understanding of some phenomena. For example, does lowering the speed limit reduce the number of fatal traffic accidents? How many women are abused by their spouses? Will denying benefits to teenage welfare mothers lower the birth rate among these women? What fraction of books in a library are missing or damaged? To answer questions such as these and make informed decisions we need factual data.

Before data collection begins, two important questions must be answered:

1. What are the specific goals of the study?
2. Which variables should be measured and how?

Strictly speaking, the first question is not within the realm of statistics. However, a statistician can help in making the study goals precise by requiring measurable criteria.

The second question is concerned with deciding which characteristics are of interest and how to measure them. The measured characteristics are called **variables**; their measured values constitute the **data**. Sometimes it is not possible to directly measure a variable of interest, and some proxy variable must be used instead. For example, the Weschler Adult Intelligence Scale (commonly known as IQ) is used as a proxy to measure intelligence. It is important to obtain instruments which provide consistent and reliable measurement scales. A statistician can help provide answers to these aspects of the second question.

To assure the validity of the findings and conclusions drawn from data, it is extremely important that the data be pertinent, free of bias, and of good quality. In order to obtain such data, proper planning is necessary. Even the most sophisticated statistical analyses cannot salvage a poorly planned study. In this chapter we study sound principles of data collection.

3.1   TYPES OF STATISTICAL STUDIES

Sometimes **historical data** available in archival sources, such as the Dow Jones Information Service, decennial census data, almanacs, and journal articles, are sufficient to address the study goals. An advantage of using historical data is that they are relatively inexpensive. However, often relevant historical data are not available. Even if available, they may not be pertinent because of different measurement methods used or different conditions under which they were obtained. Then we need to collect new data. In this section we give a classification of statistical studies used to collect new data; in later sections we discuss the different types of studies in more detail.

A study whose purpose is to compare two or more alternative methods or groups distinguished by some attribute is called a **comparative (analytical) study**. For example, studies to compare the effectiveness of different management training methods or the cost effectiveness of different health care programs are comparative studies. A study whose purpose is to learn about the characteristics of a group(s), but not necessarily to make comparisons, is called a **noncomparative (descriptive) study**. For example, studies to estimate the number of illiterate Americans or the rate of defective parts produced by a manufacturing process or the proportion of expectant mothers who receive prenatal care are noncomparative studies.

A study may be observational or experimental. An **observational study** records data without interfering with the course of events. Essentially, the researcher is a passive observer who documents the process. In contrast, in an **experimental study** the researcher actively intervenes to control the study conditions and records the responses. Observational and experimental studies can be either comparative or noncomparative. For example, consider a study to compare the effectiveness of two software training methods. An observational comparative study could be done by identifying two groups of programmers trained by the two methods and measuring their performance. An experimental comparative study could be done by assigning half the programmers to each training method and measuring their performance at a later time.

Stronger conclusions are possible in an experimental study than in an observational study, since the researcher is better able to control the conditions of an experiment. Therefore *causation* can be established in an experiment by systematically varying one or more variables (called **predictor** or **explanatory variables**) and measuring their effects on **outcome** or **response variables**. It should be emphasized, however, that there is no such thing as a fully controlled study; control is a matter of degree.

In an observational, study only *association* between the predictor and response variables can be established, because, unknown to the investigator, the response variables may also be affected by other variables which are not controlled. Therefore the effects of predictor variables cannot be separated from the effects of the uncontrolled variables; this is called **confounding**. The variables that cause confounding of the predictor variables are called **confounding variables**. Sometimes the presence of these variables is not recognized or only recognized after the fact, in which case they are referred to as **lurking variables**. We see such studies reported in popular media all the time. For example, a recent study found that listening to Mozart *makes* people smarter. Even if Mozart listeners *were* generally smarter, this does not prove a cause-effect relationship, because there are confounding variables present: smarter people may have preference for Mozart, or Mozart listeners may also like to engage in brain-stimulating activities such as puzzles, reading, etc., which make them smarter.

3.1.1 Importance of a Control Group in a Comparative Study

The goal of the simplest and most common comparative studies is to evaluate how a "change" from a "baseline" or "normal" condition affects a response variable. The changed condition is called a **treatment** or an **intervention** and the normal condition is called a **control**. In a well-planned experimental study, if a relationship is found, it can be attributed to the treatment. For example, treatment/control studies can address questions such as: Do people who regularly exercise (treatment) live longer than people who don't (control)? Does a new workplace design (treatment) improve worker productivity compared to the current design (control)?

These studies compare the outcomes under the treatment condition with outcomes under the control condition. The study units that receive the treatment constitute a **treatment group**; those that do not receive the treatment constitute a **control group**. The two groups should be similar in all other respects to provide a valid comparison. (A method for ensuring similarity of the groups is **random allocation**, which is discussed in Section 3.4.1.) Although all comparative studies use a treatment group, not all use a control group. For example, in some laboratory investigations there are well-established standards which can be used as benchmarks for comparison.

Experimental studies that lack a control group are of one of the following types:

1. Pretest Only Design:
   Intervention → **Observation.**
2. Pretest–Posttest Design:
   Observation → **Intervention** → **Observation.**

The pretest–posttest design is preferred to the pretest only design because it looks at *changes* in the response variable after the intervention is introduced. Nevertheless, both these designs are flawed when there is no valid basis for comparison. This is because any changes in the response variable could be due to confounding variables rather than the intervention. If a control group is used, then the confounding variables would affect the two groups similarly, and the differences in the outcomes could be attributed to the intervention. The following example illustrates the danger of claiming a treatment effect in the absence of a control group.

Example 3.1

In the early 1960's a clinical trial was carried out to study the efficacy of a technique known as gastric freezing to treat ulcer patients. The treatment required patients to swallow a balloon, which was positioned in the stomach. A coolant was then passed through the balloon. It was reported[1]

---

[1] O. H. Wangensteen, E. T. Peter, D. M. Nicoloff, et al. (1962), "Achieving 'physiologic gastrectomy' by gastric freezing: A preliminary report of an experimental and chemical study," *Journal of the American Medical Association*, **180**, pp. 439–444.

that the patients given this treatment experienced relief of the symptoms, and the treatment was recommended for ulcer patients. But is the claim of "success" of this treatment valid, given that there was no control group to provide a benchmark for comparison?

Subsequently, clinical trials were conducted which included a control group. The control group patients swallowed the balloon, but freezing was not done. This intervention, which is identical to the treatment except for the active component, is called a **placebo**. In these trials no long term benefit was found from gastric freezing compared with the placebo.[2] As a result, gastric freezing (which would have been expensive and highly invasive, as well as ineffective) was abandoned as a possible treatment for ulcer patients. ◆

This example illustrates a phenomenon called the **placebo effect**. Although the placebo is inactive, the feeling of being treated causes a temporary improvement in as many as two-thirds of the patients.[3,4] To account for the placebo effect, clinical researchers include a control group of patients who receive a placebo treatment. To further remove possible psychological effects due to patients' knowledge of their group assignment, a **single blind** study may be designed in which the patients are kept unaware of the treatment that they receive. This is easily done when the treatment is in the form of a pill, in which case the placebo is the proverbial "sugar pill." Recently, placebo controls have been used in a clinical trial to evaluate the efficacy of implanting human fetal tissue in brains of Parkinson disease patients; the control patients got a "sham surgery" involving drilling of holes in the skull but no implants.[5]

In addition, the evaluating physician may also introduce bias if he/she is aware of the treatment group that the patient belongs to. If both the patient and the evaluating physician are kept unaware of the treatment, then the study is referred to as **double blind**. With more complex treatments involving surgical and other procedures, it is often difficult to blind patients and/or physicians.

Sometimes, due to the difficulty of obtaining a **concurrent control group**, researchers use past data to form a **historical control group**. However, a comparison with past data often leads to invalid results, especially in studies involving people. The problem is that environmental influences change over time, so that the present is often different from the past. Also, there are other problems with historical data, as mentioned at the beginning of this section. As a result, present results can differ from past results without any experimental intervention.

3.2 OBSERVATIONAL STUDIES

Observational studies are of three basic types. A **sample survey** provides a snapshot of the population based on a sample observed at a point in time, while the other two types

---

[2] L. L. Miao (1977), "Gastric freezing: An example of the evaluation of medical therapy by randomized clinical trials," in J. P. Bunker, B. A. Barnes, and F. Mosteller, (eds.): *Costs, Risks and Benefits of Surgery*, New York: Oxford University Press, pp. 198–211.

[3] "Placebo effect is shown to be twice as powerful as expected," *The New York Times*, Science Times, Tuesday, August 12, 1993.

[4] J. A. Turner, R. A. Deyo, J. D. Loeser, M. Von Korff, and W. E. Fordyce (1994), "The importance of placebo effects in pain treatment and research," *Journal of the American Medical Association*, **271**, pp. 1609–1814.

[5] "Sham surgery is used to test effectiveness of novel operations," *Wall Street Journal*, December 12, 1998.

of studies track changes in a population by following a sample over time. A **prospective study** follows a sample *forward* in time, while a **retrospective study** follows a sample *backward* in time.

3.2.1 Sample Surveys

Sample surveys are pervasive in our daily and professional lives. Examples of sample surveys are preelection polls, consumer attitude and preference surveys conducted by market research firms, acceptance sampling procedures used in industry, and field surveys used to estimate agricultural output.

Population and Sample.   Two basic elements of a sample survey are a population and a sample. A **population** is a collection of all objects, items, or human/animal subjects (referred to as **sampling units** or just **units**) about which information is sought. A **sample** is a part or subset of the population that is actually observed. Our focus is on the values of some variable associated with the units in the population rather than the units themselves. Therefore it is convenient to define the population as the collection of the values of the variable for all units. Then a sample consists of the values of the variable (i.e., data) that are actually observed for a subset of the units.

A numerical characteristic of a population defined for a specific variable is called a **parameter**. Some examples are the percent of unemployed adults in the U.S., the median household income in the city of Chicago, and the mean time to failure of a particular brand of a kitchen appliance. Because a population is generally not fully observed, a parameter is an unknown quantity. A numerical function of the sample data, called a **statistic**, is used to estimate an unknown population parameter. For example, the monthly current population survey conducted by the Bureau of Labor Statistics uses the percent unemployed adults in the sample (a *statistic*) to estimate the corresponding percentage in the population (a *parameter*).

A national preelection poll, such as a Gallup poll, typically uses a sample of about 1000 to 2000 persons drawn from the population of all adults over 18 years of age. In **acceptance sampling**, a sample of items from a shipment is inspected to estimate the proportion of defectives in the shipment and to decide whether to accept or reject the shipment. Accountants sample account book entries for audit purposes to estimate accounts receivable that are overdue.

If the sample equals the population so that all members of the population are observed, then we have a **census**. The most familiar example is the decennial population census, which is mandated by the U.S. Constitution. However, even here only the most essential information is obtained from the entire population; other information is obtained on a sampling basis.

Why is sampling used so widely instead of a census? Here are some reasons:

1. In many applications the population is so large that sampling is the only practical and feasible option.
2. Some tests used in engineering inspection are destructive or alter the units irrevocably. In that case sampling is the sole available option, even if the population is small.

3. Sampling involves less work than a census, which generally leads to a higher measurement accuracy. Observing the whole population means more work, which leads to more measurement errors (e.g., due to fatigue). For this reason sampling is often employed to estimate a warehouse inventory rather than counting every item.

There are two types of populations. If it is possible to list all units in a population (at least in principle), then we refer to it as a **finite population**. A list of all units in a finite population is called a **sampling frame**. If there is no upper limit on the number of units in a population, making it impossible to list them, then it is an **infinite population**. Even though the population of all adults or the population of all households in the U.S. are both very large and their sampling frames cannot be constructed, they still are finite populations. An example of an infinite population is all patients with a certain disease. Here the population includes not only the current patients but also those who would contract the disease in future. Many finite populations are so large that for all practical purposes they can be regarded as infinite.

The population of interest, called the **target population**, should be carefully defined in the study goals. This requires that clear inclusion and exclusion criteria be stated for the membership of the target population. Consider a poll to address the question of whether "people" support U.S. military intervention to diffuse an international crisis. Are the "people" registered voters? U.S. citizens 18 years or older? Men registered for selective service? Different populations can have different views on this question.

Sometimes the target population is difficult to study, so sampling is done using another easily accessible population, called the **sampled population**. If the sampled population differs from the target population in important ways, then conclusions drawn from the sample may not extend to the target population. For example, a treatment successfully tested in a university hospital with experienced research personnel and state-of-the-art equipment may not be equally effective in a community hospital.

EXAMPLE 3.2

Marketing and other researchers often draw samples from telephone directories because of convenience. However, the population of residences listed in directories differs from the target population of all households, since the directories do not include residences with unlisted numbers or without telephones. The problem of unlisted numbers is solved by random digit dialing, but this still excludes residences without phones, which are more likely to belong to low income people. On the other hand, high income people may have more than one phone line.   ◆

EXAMPLE 3.3

This example illustrates the pitfall of extending conclusions to a population different from the one that is sampled. Gayle et al. (1990)[6] reported a study of almost 17,000 blood specimens tested for HIV virus from 19 university health centers. The results indicated that 0.2% tested positive. Press reports on the study extrapolated the results to estimate that 25,000 U.S. college students may be infected with the virus. This conclusion is faulty, because the sampled population consists

---

[6] H. D. Gayle, R. P. Keeling, M. Garcia-Tunon, et al. (1990), "Prevalence of the human immunodeficiency virus among university students," *New England Journal of Medicine*, **323**, pp. 1538–1541.

of college students who took blood tests at their health centers, while the target population is the population of all college students. Students with a problem that causes them to visit the clinic and take a blood test are more likely to be at risk of exposure to sexually transmitted diseases and HIV than healthy students. Therefore the HIV rate for this population is likely to be higher than the rate for the population of all college students.   ◆

Sampling and Nonsampling Errors.   A sample gives only partial information about the population, since it is only a part of the population. Therefore the sample estimate is rarely exactly equal to the population parameter value. The deviation between a sample estimate and the true parameter value is called the **sampling error**. The sampling error can be driven down to zero, at least in theory, by taking a census. But **nonsampling errors** often are present, even if a census is taken. These errors cause **bias**, which is a systematic deviation between the sample estimate and the population parameter value. Often, bias is a more serious problem than sampling errors, because it doesn't go away just by increasing the sample size. For example, **measurement bias** affects all measurements. Measuring instruments such as mail questionnaires and telephone or personal interviews are often subject to biases due to improper and unclear wording, slanted questions, and lack of rapport between the interviewer and the respondent. For instance, it was reported[7] that when the Roper Poll changed the wording of a question from a confusing double negative, the sample percentage of Americans who think that Holocaust never happened dropped from 22% to 1%. This shows how important it is to have clear, simple, and neutral wording. A story in *U.S. News & World Report*[8] discusses many examples of nonsampling errors. A cartoon from this article is shown in Figure 3.1.

Other sources of nonsampling errors are refusals or nonresponse and untruthful or faulty responses. People often refuse to answer a sensitive or an embarrassing question (e.g., Have you ever used cocaine?).[9] People who choose to participate in a survey are motivated by factors that make them different from nonrespondents. This results in **self-selection bias**. Sometimes faulty recall of the past events is to be blamed (e.g., people tend to overestimate how frequently they exercise). Untruthful or faulty reponses result in **response bias**.

The following example illustrates biases caused by undercoverage of the population and self-selection of the sample.

EXAMPLE 3.4   (LITERARY DIGEST POLL)

In the 1936 U.S. presidential election, the *Literary Digest* magazine (since gone defunct) conducted a preelection poll. The Republican party candidate was Alfred E. Landon and the Democratic party candidate was Franklin D. Roosevelt. The magazine selected its sample mainly from telephone directories, lists of auto registrations, and the magazine's subscribers. Questionnaire forms were sent to more than 2 million people, of whom about 250,000 responded. Based on this

---

[7] "The Numbers Game," *Newsweek*, 25 July 1994, pp. 56–58.

[8] "Consulting the Oracle: Everyone loves polls. But can you trust them?" *U.S. News & World Report*, 4 December 1995, pp. 52–58.

[9] See Exercise 6.33 for an interesting technique to elicit honest responses to potentially sensitive and stigmatizing questions in a survey.

Figure 3.1 The Princess and the Poll (STEVE BENSON reprinted by permission of United Feature Syndicate, Inc.)

survey, the magazine predicted that Landon would win with a 57% majority. The final result was that Roosevelt won with a 62% majority. What caused this 19% reversal in the final result in spite of such a large sample?

The problem was that the sample was not representative of the target population of all adults who were eligible and were likely to vote on the election day. First, in the Depression era many people could not afford telephones and cars. Thus the sample overrepresented affluent people, who were more likely to be Republicans. Second, the sample was voluntary and had only a 12.5% response rate. Generally, respondents are more likely than nonrespondents to be vocal, better educated, and from higher socioeconomic strata. The majority of respondents, in this case, happened to be Republicans.   ◆

From these examples we see that in order to generalize from the sample to the population, we must have a **representative sample**, i.e., a sample that does not differ systematically from the population. Otherwise the results of the sample cannot be readily extended to the population. In Section 3.3 we discuss some sampling designs for selecting a representative sample.

3.2.2 Prospective and Retrospective Studies

A **prospective study** begins in the present with a sample survey and follows the sample forward in time to record the occurrence of specific outcomes over the study period. A **retrospective study**, on the other hand, begins and ends in the present but takes a look back in time to collect data about things in the past.

Both prospective and retrospective studies are often comparative. Comparative studies are important in epidemiology for identifying risk factors related to a disease. They can be **cohort studies**, which follow a group of people forward in time to observe and compare characteristics of people who do and who do not develop disease. Or they can be **case-control studies**, which identify a case group of people with the disease and a control group of people without the disease, then look back in time for risk factors associated with the disease. Typically cohort studies are prospective, but they can begin with questions concerning earlier experiences and then follow the subsequent disease development, thus providing both backward and forward looks in time.

Consider the question: Is obesity related to hypertension? A prospective cohort study is designed to identify two groups of people without hypertension, but one group is obese while the other is nonobese. The groups are followed for a specified period (e.g., five years). At the end of the study the proportions of hypertensive people in the two groups are compared. For a disease where strong risk factors are not known, a prospective cohort study begins with a single cohort of disease-free people, and a record of potential risk factors is maintained. At the end of the study period it is noted whether each person does or does not have the disease. The risk factor exposures of the two groups are then compared. For example, a preliminary study to determine risk factors associated with hypertension identifies a group of people without hypertension and then collects data on their weight, diet, smoking, exercise, and stress. The rates of hypertension at the end of the study among people with different exposures to risk factors are then compared.

Alternatively, a case-control study could be used to evaluate association between hypertension and obesity by sampling people with ("cases") and without ("controls") hypertension and dividing them into obese and nonobese groups. One could then compare the proportion of obese people among cases and controls. To make this comparison more accurate, cases and controls are usually matched on confounding variables such as smoking, exercise, and stress. If a larger proportion of hypertensive people are obese in this comparison, then it is flagged as a possible risk factor.

Retrospective cohort studies are cheaper and timely to do, but they are more problematic for several reasons. First, recall of past events can be inaccurate and selective. Second, since the events occurred in the past, no control over the course of the study is possible. In the hypertension example, it would be difficult to gather reliable past data on potentially confounding variables such as frequency of exercise, work related stress, use of medication, etc. In prospective studies subjects can keep diaries of their daily activities, thus giving more trustworthy data. Also, subjects can be asked to avoid certain practices which might bias the study. In conclusion, prospective studies are more costly but provide better information.

It is important to note that even the prospective studies are observational and the potential influences of confounding variables cannot be completely controlled. It is possible to remove some of the bias introduced by confounding variables by restricting comparisons to matched subsamples (e.g., among smokers compare the rates of hypertension among obese and nonobese people). Even if the two groups are equal on these confounding variables, one could argue that a common lurking factor is responsible for the differences in the outcomes. For example, in the hypertension-obesity study, one could argue that a common gene causes both obesity and hypertension.

3.3 BASIC SAMPLING DESIGNS

The discussion and examples in Section 3.2.1 on sample surveys show that a **representative sample**, i.e., a sample that does not differ in systematic and important ways from the population, is needed to help assure valid and unbiased conclusions about the population. Unfortunately, some commonly used sampling methods are subject to bias resulting in nonrepresentative samples. The simplest among these is **haphazard sampling**, or **convenience sampling**, where one chooses a sample that is easily available. For example, a news reporter may interview people on the street to get their reaction to some important event. However, people on the street do not represent the general population because the sample misses people at work, people at home, and so on. To estimate the proportion of damaged fruits in a carton, if a convenience sample is taken only from the top layer, then we miss fruits in the lower layers, which are more likely to be damaged.

To obtain more reliable results, **judgment sampling** may be used, in which the interviewers or inspectors are trained to exercise their judgment in selecting a representative sample. A systematic method to do this is **quota sampling**, where an interviewer is given quotas of interviews for specified categories. The categories and their quotas are determined to reflect the general population. For example, if the population has 40% Caucasians, 30% African-Americans, 20% Hispanics, and 10% other ethnic groups, then the sample is required to have the same percentages for these categories. The categories can be broken down further, (e.g., males/females, white/blue collar workers, etc.). Given the quotas, it is up to the interviewer to select the persons who fit those categories. Although this is an improvement over the previous methods, it still does not guarantee a truly representative sample for the following reasons:

1. There is a possibility of an interviewer bias. For example, an interviewer may approach only friendly people to fill quotas. This personality trait and related characteristics would then be overrepresented in the sample.
2. Only a limited number of categories can be designated. There are always other categories, some known and others unknown, on which the sample will not match the population.

This discussion and Example 3.4 illustrate that bias is possible whether a researcher selects people to enter the sample or people self-select themselves. The problem of a nonrepresentative sample is especially serious when sampling from human populations, but it is present in other populations as well. What method should one use, then, to avoid bias? The answer is: Use a chance mechanism! This is called **simple random sampling (SRS)**, where each unit in the population has the same chance of being selected into the sample. Note that *random* does not mean *haphazard*. Random sampling is fair to all units in the population because it does not systematically favor certain subsets of the population.

Random sampling has another equally important consequence. As we shall see in later chapters, statistics computed from a random sample (e.g., the sample mean, median, standard deviation) have well-defined probability distributions, which form the basis for statistical inference. This is not possible with a nonrandom sample, even if it is representative of the population.

3.3.1 Simple Random Sampling

A **simple random sample** (**SRS**) of size n from a population of size N is drawn *without replacement* in such a way that each possible sample of size n (there are $\binom{N}{n}$ of them) has the same chance of being chosen. This implies that each unit in the population also has the same selection probability, which is n/N. For example, if $N = 1000$ and $n = 100$, then the selection probability is 0.1 for each unit. This is called the **sampling rate** or **sampling fraction**. All statistical inference methods discussed in this book assume simple random sampling; they also ignore the effect of finiteness of populations, i.e., they assume that the sampling fraction is negligibly small.

How do we select an SRS? First we need a sampling frame. The units in the population can then be labeled by numbers $1, 2, \ldots, N$. One way to select an SRS is to randomly draw one number at a time *without replacement* from the available numbers until n numbers are selected. This is much more practical than listing all possible $\binom{N}{n}$ samples and picking one at random. But how do you ensure randomness of selection at each stage? Most physical mixing schemes to achieve randomness are far from perfect, as the following example illustrates.

EXAMPLE 3.5   (THE 1970 DRAFT LOTTERY)

The first random selection method for drafting American young men into military service was used in 1970. Paper slips with 31 January dates written on them were inserted into capsules, which were placed in a wooden box and mixed. Next the capsules for February were prepared the same way, added to the box, and mixed with the January dates. This procedure was repeated for the subsequent months, giving a total of 366 capsules (to allow for an extra day in a leap year). The box was shut and the contents were given a final thorough mix. Then the capsules were drawn one at a time, with the first capsule receiving draft number 1, the next one 2, and so on.[10] A statistical analysis[11] showed that this lottery was biased, because men born later in the year generally received lower draft numbers. (See Table 4.14 for the summary data on average lottery numbers by month.) What went wrong?

---

[10] Note that here we have an ordered sample drawn from the population of all birthdates with $n = N = 366$.

[11] S. E. Fienberg (1971), "Randomization and social affairs: The 1970 draft lottery," *Science*, **171**, pp. 255–261.

With hindsight it is easy to see why this sampling was not random. Since the capsules were added to the box beginning with the month of January, the later birthdates were near the top due to inadequate mixing (the January capsules were mixed with others 11 times, the February capsules were mixed 10 times, and so on). A more sophisticated scheme was devised for the 1971 draft lottery.[12] ◆

To avoid problems with physical randomizing devices, a table of random digits or computer generated random numbers are used to draw an SRS. Many statistical packages can generate an SRS of a specified size from a sampling frame.

EXAMPLE 3.6

Suppose that we have a population of size $N = 500$ and we want to draw an SRS of size $n = 10$. The sampling units are labeled as $001, 002, \ldots, 500$. Random numbers are generated on a scientific calculator, keeping only the first three digits and discarding any repeats or numbers greater than 500, until 10 numbers are obtained, resulting in the following sequence: 232, 337, 404, 259, 103, 147, 291, 413, 305, 203. The sampling units with these labels form an SRS of size $n = 10$. ◆

A common misconception is that the larger the population, the larger the sample size needed to obtain the same amount of information. In fact, the amount of information in a sample depends more on the absolute sample size n and less on the relative sample size n/N, as long as n is not too large relative to N (e.g., $n/N \le 0.10$). Therefore, it is not necessary to draw a proportionately larger sample from a larger population. Thus, whether the population size is 500 or 5000, an SRS of size 50 is almost equally informative.

Simple random sampling is not a practical method except for rather small populations for which sampling frames are available. However, it forms a basic building block of more complicated sampling schemes used in practice, as we will see next.

3.3.2 Stratified Random Sampling

If a population is highly diverse, then simple random sampling is not an efficient method, because it can require a very large sample size in order for a sample to be representative. But if a population can be divided into homogeneous subpopulations (having similar units), a small SRS can be drawn from each one, resulting in a sample that is representative of the population. As an extreme example, if each subpopulation consists of identical units, then we need to sample only one unit from each subpopulation. The subpopulations are called **strata**, and the sampling design is called **stratified random sampling**.

Two other reasons for employing stratified random sampling are:

1. Separate estimates for subpopulations are obtained without additional work. For example, separate demographic and economic statistics are often required for different population groups, such as urban and rural or Caucasian, African-American, and Hispanic.

2. Sampling from subpopulations is generally more economical because of administrative convenience.

---

[12] J. R. Rosenblatt and J. J. Filliben (1971), "Randomization and the draft lottery," *Science*, **171**, pp. 306–308.

EXAMPLE 3.7

Suppose the Internal Revenue Service wants to estimate the median amounts of deductions taxpayers claim in different categories, e.g., property taxes, charitable donations, etc. These amounts vary greatly over the taxpayer population. Therefore an SRS will not be very efficient. The taxpayers can be divided into strata based on their adjusted gross incomes, and separate SRS can be drawn from the individual strata. Because the deductions generally increase with incomes, the resulting stratified random sample would require a much smaller total sample size to provide equally precise estimates. ◆

3.3.3 Multistage Cluster Sampling

Both simple and stratified random samples require a sampling frame, which is generally not available for large scale surveys, e.g., for sampling individuals or households from the whole U.S. Even if a sampling frame were available, an SRS would be too geographically scattered to be administratively feasible. **Multistage cluster sampling** is generally used to survey large populations. In the case of a national sample this may be done as follows: First, draw an SRS of states. Second, draw an SRS of counties from each selected state. Third, draw an SRS of towns from each selected county. At the fourth stage, draw an SRS of wards from each selected town. Finally, prepare a sampling frame of households for each selected ward and draw an SRS of households as the actual sample. Notice that the sampling units are different at each stage.

Many variations are possible on this basic design. For example, unequal selection probabilities may be assigned to sampling units. One scheme commonly used is called **probability proportional to size (PPS) sampling**, in which larger units are assigned proportionately larger selection probabilities and vice versa.

3.3.4 Systematic Sampling

As mentioned above, an SRS is practical only for small populations. Even when a sampling frame for a large population exists, drawing and measuring an SRS is not easy. Systematic sampling provides a practical alternative when a sequential list of sampling units exists (e.g., a telephone directory or a computer file of library books). It can also be used when the sampling units become available sequentially (e.g., items coming off an assembly line or cars entering a toll booth on a highway). Notice that a sampling frame does not exist in this latter case.

A 1-in-k **systematic sample** consists of selecting one unit at random from the first k units and selecting every kth unit thereafter. For example, if we want a 4% sample from a telephone directory, then one name out of the first 25 is selected at random and every 25th name is selected thereafter. If the first number drawn is 17, then the selected sample consists of entries numbered 17, 42, 67, 92, 117, etc. Notice that for a finite population of size N, systematic sampling assigns each sampling unit the same selection probability, namely $\frac{n}{N}$, as in an SRS; however, not all $\binom{N}{n}$ possible samples are equally likely.

Systematic sampling gives a representative sample as long as there are no regular cyclic variations in the population (e.g., seasonal variation in temperature or business cycles in sales). Because of its simplicity, systematic sampling is widely used.

3.4   EXPERIMENTAL STUDIES

The subject of design of experiments was established by Sir R. A. Fisher (1890–1962) as a methodology for planning agricultural experiments while he was serving at the Rothamstead Agricultural Experimental Station in England. Many of the basic concepts, designs, and data analysis methods are due to him.

3.4.1 Terminology and Basic Concepts

The primary purpose of an experiment is to evaluate how a set of predictor variables (called **factors** in experimental design jargon) affect a response variable. Further objectives may be to

1. Screen the factors to weed out the unimportant ones.
2. Select the best combination of the factor values to optimize the response.
3. Fit a model that can be used to make predictions and/or to adjust controllable factors to keep the response on target.

Factors are of two types. **Treatment factors** are controlled in an experiment, and their effects on the response variable are of primary interest. **Nuisance factors**, or **noise factors**, are all the other factors that might affect the response variable. The different possible values of a factor are called its **levels**. Each **treatment** is a particular combination of the levels of different treatment factors. (If there is only one factor, then its levels are the treatments.) The treatments are applied to subjects or items, whose responses are then measured. These subjects or items are called **experimental units**. All experimental units receiving the same treatment form a **treatment group**. A **run** is an observation made on an experimental unit under a particular treatment condition. A **replicate** is another independent run carried out under identical treatment conditions. Note that replicates are not just **repeat measurements** of the same response; see the following example to distinguish between the two.

EXAMPLE 3.8   (HEAT TREATMENT OF STEEL: TREATMENT FACTORS)

A metallurgical engineer designing a heat treatment procedure wants to study the effects of furnace temperature (High and Low) and quench bath temperature (High and Low) on the surface hardness of steel. Twenty steel samples are available. Identify the key features of this experiment.

   The response variable is the surface hardness, and the steel samples are the experimental units which are heat treated using different methods. The treatment factors are furnace temperature and quench bath temperature, each with 2 levels. This gives $2 \times 2 = 4$ treatments. The nuisance factors include ambient temperature, variation between steel samples, etc. With 20 steel samples, five replicate runs can be made with each treatment combination. If the surface hardness of each treated steel sample is measured twice, then we have two repeat measurements per replicate.   ◆

3.4.2 Strategies to Reduce Experimental Error Variation

The main purpose of an experiment is to evaluate the **effects** of treatment factors on a response variable. However, if there is excessive **experimental error**, then even large treatment effects may be masked, thus defeating the purpose. We need to minimize the experimental error to make the experiment sufficiently sensitive to detect factor effects of practically important magnitudes. To understand how to do this, let us look at the main components of experimental error:

- **Systematic error** is caused by the differences between experimental units. The nuisance factors on which the experimental units differ are said to **confound** or **bias** the treatment comparisons. This is similar to the bias introduced in observational studies because of nonrepresentative samples or because the treatment and control groups differ on some confounding variables.

- **Random error** is caused by the inherent variability in the responses of similar experimental units given the same treatment.

- **Measurement error** is caused by imprecise measuring instruments.

We first discuss how to account for the effects of nuisance factors in order to reduce the systematic error. Keep in mind that not all nuisance factors are specified or even known. Nuisance factors that are specified and measured may or may not be controllable.

EXAMPLE 3.9   (HEAT TREATMENT OF STEEL: NUISANCE FACTORS)

Refer to Example 3.8. Suppose that the 20 steel samples come from five different batches of steel, four per batch. The differences between batches are not of primary interest. Thus the batch is a nuisance factor; however, it is controllable, since the batches can be identified before the experiment begins. On the other hand, the ambient temperature at which the steel samples are finally cooled may not be controlled and may not even be measured.   ◆

Strategies to reduce the systematic error differ, depending on which type of nuisance factor we are dealing with. Some strategies are discussed below.

- **Blocking:** When a nuisance factor is controllable or its value for each experimental unit is known before the treatments are applied, its effect can be separated from the treatment effects as follows. Divide the sample into groups of similar experimental units (i.e., units having the same or similar values for the nuisance factor). These groups are called **blocks**, and the nuisance factor used to form the blocks is called a **blocking factor**. All treatments are assigned on the experimental units within each block; thus the effect of the nuisance factor is the same across all treatments within each block and cancels out when these treatments are compared to each other. In Example 3.9, the batch can be used as a blocking factor.

- **Regression Analysis:** Normally, only a few nuisance factors can be used for blocking. Some nuisance factors cannot be used as blocking factors because they are not controllable. Such nuisance factors are called **covariates**, assuming they are measured. In Example 3.9, ambient temperature may be regarded as a covariate. It is often possible to model the effects of covariates by a data analysis technique called **regression analysis**; see Chapters 10 and 11. Note that a covariate should be measured before the treatments are applied to experimental units, because it could also be affected by the treatment, and so regression analysis could give biased results.

- **Randomization:** What about additional nuisance factors, whether known or unknown? The experimental units may well differ on these factors, thus biasing the results. To make the treatment groups equal on every single nuisance factor is an impossible task. Fisher's brilliant solution to this problem was to make the treatment groups *probabilistically* equal on *all* nuisance factors by *randomly assigning* experimental units to different treatments. Randomization does not imply that experimental units are equal for each treatment, but that no one treatment is favored.

In summary, the basic strategy for dealing with nuisance factors is:

**Block over those nuisance factors that can be
easily controlled, randomize over the rest.**

Note that in both sample surveys and experiments, the chance element is introduced intentionally to reduce bias. As in the case of random sampling, another important consequence of randomization is that it makes statistical inference possible, because the sample statistics calculated from the resulting data have well-defined probability distributions.

The effect of random error can be reduced by replicating the experimental runs, i.e., by making multiple independent runs under identical treatment conditions. The effect of measurement error can be reduced by making repeat measurements, including having different persons make the measurements. In both cases, some average of the readings is used. Another benefit of replicates and repeat measurements is that variation within each group of measurements can be used to estimate random and measurement errors, respectively.

To summarize, the following four strategies are useful to improve the precision of an experiment:

1. Blocking
2. Randomization
3. Replication
4. Repeat measurements

The first two are smart strategies, since they do not require larger samples. The last two are more costly but are necessary if random and measurement errors must be estimated and controlled.

3.4.3 Basic Experimental Designs

Completely Randomized Design.   In a **completely randomized design (CRD)** *all* experimental units are assigned at random to the treatments. The following examples provide some illustrations.

EXAMPLE 3.10   (HEAT TREATMENT OF STEEL: COMPLETELY RANDOMIZED DESIGN)

Refer to Example 3.8. A CRD consists of randomly assigning the 20 samples to the 4 treatment combinations (labeled A, B, C, and D) without regard to the batches that the samples came from; see Figure 3.2(a). It is not necessary to assign an equal number to each treatment, although randomization is often done under this restriction.   ◆

EXAMPLE 3.11   (CHEMICAL PROCESS YIELD: COMPLETELY RANDOMIZED DESIGN)

The yield of a chemical process is to be compared under 3 different operating conditions: A, B, C. Suppose that 6 runs can be made in a day, allowing 2 runs per treatment. The CRD would randomize the order of runs so as to neutralize any confounding effect of the time of the day. One possible random order is {B, C, B, A, A, C}. A practical difficulty in using a completely random order is that the operating conditions may not be easy to change. Then it may be necessary to make the 2 runs for each process condition consecutively; the resulting design is *not* a CRD.   ◆

EXAMPLE 3.12   (MEMORY EXPERIMENT: COMPLETELY RANDOMIZED DESIGN)

Two ways of memorizing words are to be compared. Thirty persons are randomly divided into two groups of 15 persons each. One group is given printed instructions for memorization and a list of 50 words; the other group is given different instructions but the same 50 words. After reviewing the instructions and the list of words, people return the cards and then write down as many words from the list as they can recall within a specified time limit. The average number of words recalled in each group is used to compare the two methods of memorization.   ◆

Randomized Block Design.   A CRD exploits the benefits of randomization, but fails to use information on any blocking factors. The result is that the experimental error is not minimized which could make it difficult to detect treatment differences. A more precise comparison between treatments can be made by forming blocks of units which are similar (in terms of chosen blocking factors) and then randomly assigning the treatments to the units within each block. The resulting design is called a **randomized block design (RBD)**.

The relationship between a CRD and an RBD is analogous to the relationship between an SRS and a stratified random sample, with the blocks playing the role of strata. In an SRS a random sample is drawn from the entire population. Similarly, in a CRD randomization is done over *all* experimental units. In a stratified random sample the population is divided into homogeneous strata and an SRS is drawn separately from each stratum. Similarly, in an RBD the experimental units are divided into homogeneous blocks and randomization is done separately within each block. The objective of both an RBD and a stratified random sample is to achieve greater precision by exploiting the similarity of experimental or sampling units within subgroups (blocks or strata).

EXAMPLE 3.13   (HEAT TREATMENT OF STEEL: RANDOMIZED BLOCK DESIGN)

Refer to Example 3.8. The steel samples from the same batch are likely to be similar. Therefore we can form blocks of 4 samples from each batch and randomly assign them to the 4 treatments. We then have 1 replicate per treatment from each batch. The resulting design is shown in Figure 3.2(b).   ◆

(a) Completely Randomized Design

Batch 1	Batch 2	Batch 3	Batch 4	Batch 5
A	C	D	D	B
B	A	A	C	D
C	D	B	A	C
B	C	D	B	A

(b) Randomized Block Design

Batch 1	Batch 2	Batch 3	Batch 4	Batch 5
A	D	C	D	B
C	A	B	C	C
B	C	D	B	A
D	B	A	A	D

Figure 3.2 Completely Randomized and Randomized Block Designs for Heat Treatment of Steel Samples

EXAMPLE 3.14 (CHEMICAL PROCESS YIELD: RANDOMIZED BLOCK DESIGN)

Refer to Example 3.11. Suppose it is known from past experience that the morning (AM) runs are different from the afternoon (PM) runs in terms of the yield obtained. Then the CRD given in Example 3.11, namely

$$\{B, C, B, A, A, C\},$$
$$\underbrace{}_{AM} \underbrace{}_{PM}$$

is not balanced with respect to this nuisance factor, since both B runs are done in the morning, while both A runs are done in the afternoon. Therefore the A vs. B difference is confounded with the AM vs. PM difference. An RBD that uses the AM and PM runs as blocks provides the required balance. An example is

$$\{B, C, A, A, B, C\}.$$
$$\underbrace{}_{AM} \underbrace{}_{PM}$$

◆

EXAMPLE 3.15 (MEMORY TESTING: RANDOMIZED BLOCK DESIGN)

Refer to Example 3.12. If data are available on nuisance factors such as educational level, age, etc., then a more precise experiment can be done by forming pairs of persons who are matched on these nuisance factors. Persons from each pair are randomly assigned to the two methods of memorization. The resulting design is called a **matched pairs design**, which is a special case of an RBD for blocks of size two.

Another option is to use each person as his or her own match, which gives an ideal balance between the treatment groups. One way to do this is as follows: Randomly divide the 30 persons into two groups of 15 each and conduct the experiment in two stages. The first stage, described in Example 3.12, assigns each group a different set of instructions, and the subjects then recall as many words as possible from the word list. In the second stage each group receives the other set of the instructions and a new word list (which is the same for both groups) and is asked to recall words using the new method. Thus each person is tested using both memorization methods. The difference in the number of words recalled by each person may be used to compare the two methods. This variation on the matched pairs design is called a **cross-over design**. ◆

There are practical difficulties in using a cross-over design, and in some situations it cannot be used at all, e.g., if the experimental units can be given only one treatment. In the above example, notice that we needed to use a new word list in the second stage, which could introduce bias; however, that bias is likely to affect the two methods equally. The order in which the methods are administered may also introduce bias due to the learning effect.

3.4.4 Iterative Nature of Experimentation

Experimentation is often an iterative process that cycles through the steps given below:

1. Recognize and state the problem.
2. Review literature and determine what has been previously done.
3. Plan an experiment to answer the questions.
4. Conduct the experiment and collect data.
5. Analyze the data to find the answers.
6. Redefine the problem in light of the results of the experiment.

The ideas of experimental designs introduced in this section apply mainly to step 3 of this iterative cycle.

3.5 CHAPTER SUMMARY

This chapter discusses principles of designing studies for collecting data. Studies are broadly divided into **comparative** or **descriptive**, and **observational** or **experimental**. The goal in a comparative study is to *compare* the characteristics of two or more groups, while that in a descriptive study is to *estimate* the characteristics of groups. In an observational study the investigator passively records data on the groups. In an experimental study the investigator actively controls the study conditions and records the results. A **control group** is essential in a comparative study to avoid biases in results.

A study group is generally a **sample** from a larger **population**. The numerical value of a characteristic for the population is called a **parameter**, which is unknown because the population is rarely studied in its entirety. A numerical value calculated from sample data is called a **statistic**. A statistic used as an **estimate** of a population parameter generally differs from it for the following reasons: (a) The **sampling error**, caused because a sample is only a part of the population and different samples give different estimates, and (b) the **nonsampling error**, caused when a sample differs in systematic ways from the population, i.e., when a sample is not a **representative sample**.

An observational study can be a **sample survey** (in which the sample is observed at one point in time), a **prospective study** (in which the sample is tracked forward in time), or a **retrospective study** (in which the sample is tracked backward in time). **Simple random sampling** is a basic design used in surveys to produce a representative sample by giving each population member an equal chance of being selected. **Stratified random sampling**, **systematic sampling**, and **multistage cluster sampling** are more complex designs that address some of the practical difficulties of using simple random sampling.

An experimental study consists of systematically varying selected variables, called **treatment factors**, and measuring their effects on a **response variable**. Other factors that also affect the response variable, and which if not properly controlled can **confound** the effects of the treatment factors, are called **nuisance factors**. The combinations of the levels of the treatment factors used in an experiment are called **treatments**, which are applied to **experimental units**. The simplest comparative experiment involves a single treatment factor with two nominal levels: present and absent; the experimental units subjected to the treatment form the **treatment group**, while those not subjected form the **control group**.

Treatment effects can be masked by **experimental error** resulting from three common sources: **systematic error** caused because treatment groups differ in systematic ways on nuisance factors, **random error** inherent in the variability of the responses of identical experimental units to a treatment, and **measurement error** in assessing the response. Basic strategies to reduce systematic error are **blocking** and **randomization**. One first forms blocks of experimental units that are similar on key nuisance factors. Treatments are then randomly assigned to units within each block. **Replicating** treatments reduces the effect of random error, and **repeat measurements** on the same response reduce the effect of measurement error. An experiment that randomizes treatments to all experimental units without separating them into blocks is called a **completely randomized design**. An experiment that first forms blocks of experimental units and then carries out treatment randomization separately within each block is called a **randomized block design**.

■ EXERCISES

Section 3.1

3.1   In each of the following instances (i) tell whether the study is experimental or observational, (ii) tell whether the study is comparative or descriptive, and (iii) if the study is comparative, identify the response and explanatory variables.

(a) Teenage students from suburban schools are interviewed to estimate the proportion with a gang affiliation.

(b) A study from hospital records found that women who had low weight gain during their pregnancy were more likely to have low birth weight babies than women who had high weight gains.

(c) A study monitors the occurrence of heart disease over a 5 year period in men randomized to eat high fiber or low fiber diets.

(d) Annual rates of return on investment are compared among different groups of mutual funds.

3.2   In each of the following instances (i) tell whether the study is experimental or observational, (ii) tell whether the study is comparative or descriptive, and (iii) if the study is comparative, identify the response and explanatory variables.

(a) A biologist examines fish in a river to determine the proportion that show signs of problems due to pollutants poured in the river upstream.

(b) In a pilot phase of fund-raising campaign, a university randomly contacts half of a group of alumni by telephone and the other half by a personal letter from the chair of the alumnae's department to determine which method results in a larger proportion of contributors.

(c) To analyze possible problems from the by-products of gas combustion, women with respiratory problems (e.g., wheezing, asthma) are matched by age to women without respiratory problems and then asked whether or not they cook on a gas stove.

(d) An industrial pump manufacturer monitors warranty claims and surveys customers to assess the failure distribution of its pumps.

3.3 Confounding is present in each of the following situations. Explain the nature of the confounding and why the conclusions drawn may not be valid.

    (a) An emergency room institutes a new screening procedure to identify people suffering from life threatening heart problems so that treatment can be initiated quickly. The procedure is credited with saving lives, because in the first year after its initiation, there is a lower death rate due to heart failure compared to the previous year among patients seen in the emergency room.

    (b) A study on proofreading compares the percent of missed errors when there is a high rate of errors (1 error in every 5 lines of text) and a low rate (1 error in every 20 lines of text). A document is prepared in which the first part has a high error rate and the second part a low error rate. Twenty people who proofread the document have an average missed error rate which is similar on both parts of the document. It is concluded that there is not a relationship between the error rate in a document and the proofreading accuracy.

3.4 Confounding is present in each of the following situations. Explain the nature of the confounding and why the conclusions drawn may not be valid.

    (a) A cross-country coach thinks that a particular technique will improve the times of his runners. As an experiment he offers an extra daily practice to work on this technique for runners who want to participate. At the end of the season the coach concludes that the technique is effective, because runners who participated in the extra practices have faster average times than those who did not.

    (b) In a geriatric study samples of people over 65 from a general community and from a retirement community are followed. At the end of two years it is found that a larger proportion of the people continue to reside in the retirement community than in the general community. It is concluded that the retirement community living allows elderly to maintain their independence longer than does the general community living.

3.5 A study was done to evaluate the benefits of an exercise program to reduce mortality among patients who have survived a heart attack. Mortality among volunteers who enrolled in an exercise program was compared with that among controls selected from medical records of eligible patients who chose not to join the exercise program.[13] Reasons given for not exercising included physician disapproval, shift work, and lack of interest. The study results showed that the patients in the exercise program had half as many deaths as those in the control group. What are the response, explanatory and confounding variables in this study? Explain why the chosen control group is not appropriate and how it could influence the study results.

3.6 A study monitored women from 1980 to 1990 and found that those who were moderate coffee drinkers in 1980 (up to six cups of coffee daily) were not at an increased risk of heart disease over non-coffee drinkers after adjustment for smoking and other known risk factors.[14] In contrast, some observational studies which studied the effects of coffee consumption on heart disease have not accounted for the fact that many heavy coffee

---

[13] P. A. Rechnitzer, H. A. Pickard, A. U. Paivio, et al. (1972), "Long-term follow-up study of survival and recurrence rates following myocardial infarction in exercising and control subjects," *Circulation*, **45**, pp. 853–857.

[14] W. C. Willett, M. J. Stampfer, J. E. Mason, et al. (1996), "Coffee consumption and coronary heart disease in women," *Journal of the American Medical Association*, **285**, pp. 486–462.

drinkers are also smokers, a known risk factor for heart disease. Identify the response, explanatory, and confounding variables in these studies.

Section 3.2

3.7 In each of the following instances (i) tell whether the study is a survey, a prospective study or a retrospective study, (ii) tell whether the study is comparative or descriptive, and (iii) if the study is comparative, identify the response and explanatory variable.

   (a) A sample of members listed in the directory from a professional organization is used to estimate the proportion of female members.

   (b) To assess the effect of smoking during pregnancy on premature delivery, mothers of preterm infants are matched by age and number of previous pregnancies to mothers of full term infants and then both are asked about their smoking habits during pregnancy.

   (c) A sociologist interviews juvenile offenders to find out what proportion live in foster care.

   (d) A marketing study uses the registration card mailed back to the company following the purchase of a VCR to gauge the percentage of purchasers who learned about that brand from advertising on radio, television, periodicals, or by word of mouth.

3.8 The Nationwide Food Consumption Survey is the only survey on U.S. household food consumption and individual diets. Done once a decade, it is the basis for decisions regarding food programs such as the multibillion dollar Food Stamps program. The survey conducted for the U.S. Department of Agriculture in 1987–1988 did extensive interviews that required from 80 minutes to over 5 hours to complete in exchange for a $2 reimbursement. As a result, only about one-third of the people contacted participated. In addition, interviewers were inadequately trained, there was a high interviewer turnover, and the survey design was disrupted. The combination of low response rate and poor execution of the survey resulted in data with low credibility, prompting the General Accounting Office to question whether or not the data were usable.[15]

   (a) What are some potential sources of bias in this survey?

   (b) Explain how the problems you listed in (a) could influence the survey results.

3.9 A Chicago radio station frequently broadcasts an opinion question during the afternoon rush hour and gives a telephone number to call for a "Yes" response and another for a "No" response. Poll results are announced at the end of afternoon rush hour. Why are such call-in polls likely to be biased?

3.10 The Longitudinal Study on Aging (LSOA)[16] surveyed community dwelling people aged 70 and over in 1984 and reinterviewed them biannually through 1990. By the final 1990 LSOA interview, over 30% of those interviewed in 1984 had died. If an estimate of nursing home admission rates is based only on people responding to all four interviews, is bias likely to be a problem? Explain.

3.11 Early studies on Alzheimer's disease (AD), which sampled patients treated by a medical specialist in neurology, found that people with more education were more likely to have AD. However, later studies based on community surveys found that people with more

---

[15] "Nutrition Monitoring: Mismanagement of nutrition survey has resulted in questionable data," General Accounting Office/RCED–91–117.

[16] M. G. Kovar, J. E. Fitti, and M. M. Chyba (1992), "The Longitudinal Study of Aging: 1984–1990" *Vital Health Statistics*: [1]; 28. Hyattsville, MD: National Center for Health Statistics.

education were less likely to have AD. Explain how a selection bias from people who decide to consult a medical specialist in neurology could show a different relationship between education and AD than the community sample studies.

Section 3.3

3.12   A large school district plans to survey 1000 out of 50,000 parents or guardians with enrolled children regarding their preferences on options to deal with growth in student enrollment. A complete alphabetical list of parent/guardian names is available. In each of the following instances name the sampling method used.

   (a) One of the first 50 names on the complete list is randomly chosen; that person and every 50th person on the list after that person are surveyed.

   (b) The complete list of names is divided into separate lists by their oldest child's year in school (K through 12). Random numbers are assigned to names, and each list is ordered by the assigned random numbers. The first 2% of the ordered names in each list are surveyed.

   (c) A random number is assigned to each name using a computer random number generator. Names are ordered by the random numbers, and the first 1000 are surveyed.

   (d) A 50% SRS is taken of the high schools (grades 9–12) and of the elementary schools (grades K–8) from the district. Within each selected school a 50% SRS of grades is chosen. A sampling frame is composed of parents or guardians of children in the selected grades and an SRS of those people is surveyed.

3.13   Comment on the advantages and disadvantages associated with the sampling plans (a) through (d) of Exercise 3.12.

3.14   One strategy to develop and test a statistical model is to divide the data into a training set used to fit the model and a test set used to assess the fitted model's accuracy. In each of the following situations name the sampling method used to divide the data from a list of subjects into a training set and a test set with an allocation of 2/3 and 1/3, respectively.

   (a) A random number between 1 and 3 is chosen. Starting with that subject, every third subject is assigned to the test set. All others are assigned to the training set.

   (b) A random number is assigned to each subject on the list using a computer random number generator. Subjects are ordered by their random number, and the first 2/3 are assigned to the training set. All others are assigned to the test set.

   (c) Subjects assigned random numbers in (b) are divided into two lists by gender. Within each list, the first 2/3 of the subjects ordered by random number are assigned to the training set. All others are assigned to the test set.

3.15   A survey of 10 million residential telephone customers in a state with 15 geographic "local" calling areas is planned to estimate the market share of long distance phone companies. One of the local calling areas is a major city in the state with 20% of the total customers. A list of residential phone numbers for each calling area is available. Describe how you would select a sample of 1,000 residential customers using SRS, systematic sampling, stratified random sampling, and multistage cluster sampling. Comment on the advantages and disadvantages associated with each sampling plan.

3.16   A professional society plans to survey 1000 of its 500,000 members to estimate its ethnic composition (Caucasian, African-American, Hispanic, Other). The society is organized by local chapters within each state. Each local chapter maintains its own membership list. Describe how you would select the sample based on SRS, systematic sampling, stratified random sampling, and multistage cluster sampling. Comment on the advantages and disadvantages associated with each sampling plan.

3.17 A company employs 2000 men and 1500 women, of whom 100 men and 50 women are in management positions. A survey is planned to study employee attitudes towards the company options on retirement contributions. Attitudes appear to differ by gender and by management/regular employee status. Describe a sampling plan that would provide attitude information for each subgroup defined by gender and management status as well as companywide based on a total sample of 700 people.

3.18 Tell which sampling design you would use and why in each of the following instances.

(a) You need to collect statistics on types of software applications (e.g., for word processing, spreadsheets, e-mail, internet, number crunching, etc.) used by employees of a company. Separate lists of employees are available classified by job categories (e.g., managerial, engineers, R & D scientists, workers, and secretarial staff).

(b) Patients arriving at an emergency room facility are to be sampled to study their demographics, type of ailment, time until triage, etc. It is decided to sample 10% of the patients.

(c) An engineering school plans to conduct a mail survey of its alumni who graduated after 1980 to collect data on their current employment status. A complete alphabetical list of the alumni is available.

(d) A national sample of college students is to be taken, but a comprehensive list of all college students doesn't exist. A list of all colleges (private and public) exists. For any particular college, a list of all students can be obtained.

Section 3.4

3.19 A study tests two chemical agents (A and B) to strengthen a particular fabric. The agents can be applied using different wash times (short and medium). A Martindale wear tester is used, which can test four materials at a time. The outcome is the loss in fabric weight. Fabric from four bolts, which may vary slightly, is used for testing. Name the response variable; list the treatment factors and a possible blocking factor.

3.20 To determine whether or not the artificial sweetener aspartame (Nutrasweet) causes headaches, researchers gave capsules containing aspartame or placebo to subjects with a history of headaches and observed their response.[17] After a period which allowed subjects to rid their bodies of chemicals, those originally given placebo were given aspartame and vice versa. Similar incidence rates of headaches were reported following placebo and aspartame.

(a) What are the response and explanatory variables in this study?

(b) What are the control and treatment groups in this study?

(c) This is a cross-over design in which each person is assigned both treatments in a random order. What advantage does this design have over a study in which people are randomized to receive only one treatment, either placebo or aspartame?

3.21 Three types of gasoline additives (A, B, and C) in two concentrations (Low and High) are tested for mileage performance. Six test cars of two different makes (a total of 12 cars) are available for testing. Name the response variable, the treatment factors, and a possible blocking factor.

[17] S. S. Schiffman, C. E. Buckley, H. A. Samson, et al. (1987), "Aspartame and susceptibility to headache," *New England Journal of Medicine*, **317**, pp. 1181–1185.

3.22 Erythromycin, an antibiotic used to treat strep infections, is tested using two different dosing schedules (3 times per day and 4 times per day) and two forms of administration (timed release and regular release). The outcome of interest is whether or not patients experience stomach irritation over a 10 day course. The drug is tested on patients with sore throats who test positive for strep but have no other known health problem. These people may vary in the severity of their infection, weight, age, etc. Name the response variable and list the treatment factors and any confounding variables.

3.23 Three different techniques of forming handmade soft pretzels are tested to determine if one technique is faster. A large batch of dough is divided into nine equal portions. The outcome is the total time used to form each portion into 50 pretzel shapes.

    (a) Diagram a completely randomized design for this experiment.

    (b) Three people work at making the pretzels. It is recognized that there are differences in how fast each person works. Diagram a randomized block design using the people as blocks.

3.24 An experiment is planned to determine whether students can add 5 digits more rapidly when the problem is written as a column sum or a row sum. The same set of 25 problems are given to all 20 students in a fourth grade class, but half the papers present the problems as row sums and the other half as column sums. The outcome is the time a student takes to solve the 25 problems.

    (a) Diagram a completely randomized design for this experiment.

    (b) Recognizing that the students may differ in their ability to do basic arithmetic, they are first given a timed test on basic addition facts. Diagram a randomized block design. How can the results from the basic facts test be used to form blocks?

3.25 A study is planned to determine if a three month exercise program can increase endurance in elderly people. Three treatment groups are to be compared: aerobic exercise, muscle strengthening exercise, and normal (control) activity. The outcome is the prestudy to poststudy difference in the distance a person can walk in 5 minutes. A pilot study is done using 24 people over 65 years of age from a senior citizens center to determine if the experiment can be done on a large scale.

    (a) Diagram a completely randomized design for this experiment.

    (b) Recognizing that functional ability often decreases with age, the pilot study enrolled equal numbers in two age groups: 65–79 and 80 or older. Diagram a randomized block design using the age groups as blocks.

3.26 A researcher compares the precision of two assay methods, a standard method and a new method. A solution is prepared and divided into 30 samples. The variance of the concentration readings from the two methods is compared.

    (a) Diagram a completely randomized design for this experiment.

    (b) Three technicians perform the assays who have slightly individualized techniques in running the assays. Diagram a randomized block design using the technicians as blocks.

CHAPTER 4

SUMMARIZING AND EXPLORING DATA

We live in the midst of an information explosion. Data banks have become a basic resource. Marketing executives rely on Dunn and Bradstreet computer tapes for timely business information. National disease registries allow epidemiologists to learn characteristics of a disease process. Census data are a crucial ingredient for remapping congressional districts and allocating public funds. The computerization of daily business transactions allows up to the minute feedback on inventories, cash flow, service times, etc. Properly collected data are an invaluable resource for problem solving and decision making.

We learned about methods of data collection in the previous chapter. In order to use the data in making informed decisions, it is necessary to first get a sense of the data by summarizing and displaying them in a concise form. In this chapter we will study some simple numerical and graphical methods to do this. There are many other methods that are not covered here; a book by Tufte[1] is an excellent reference.

4.1 TYPES OF DATA

All numbers are not created equal. Different statistical methods are required to analyze different types of data. The **data** are the result of observing or measuring selected characteristics of the study units, called **variables**. A variable's type, determined by its measurement scale, governs the appropriate statistical treatment of the resulting data.

---

[1] E. R. Tufte (1992), *The Visual Display of Quantitative Information*, Cheshire, CT: Graphics Press.

Broadly speaking, variables can be classified into two types: **categorical** and **numerical**. Each type can be further classified into two subtypes, as shown in Figure 4.1. We now explain these types and subtypes.

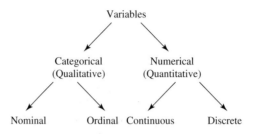

Figure 4.1   Types of Variables

A **categorical variable** (also called a **qualitative variable**) classifies each study unit into one of several distinct categories. When the categories simply represent distinct labels (e.g., Red, Green, Black), the variable is **nominal**. When the categories can be ordered or ranked (e.g., Disagree, Neutral, Agree), the variable is **ordinal**. Categories can be represented by symbols or numbers. As an example, the Moody bond rating (an ordinal variable) is coded by symbols: Aaa, Aa, A, Baa, Ba, B, Caa, Ca, C. Equivalently, these ratings could be coded by numbers: 1, 2, 3, . . . , 9. When numbers are used to represent nominal data, distinct numbers must be used for each category. Ordinal data should be coded so that the ordered numbers or symbols correspond to the ordered categories. Although ordinal data are often represented by successive integers, this is not essential since the actual numbers are not meaningful—only their order. Therefore arithmetic operations such as averaging are not meaningful for categorical data.[2]

A **numerical variable** (also called a **quantitative variable**) takes values from a set of numbers. A **continuous variable** takes values from a continuous set of numbers (at least in principle). Some examples of a continuous variable are time, weight, and distance. A **discrete variable** takes values from a discrete set of numbers, typically integers. Some examples of a discrete variable are number of children in a family and count of absent employees in a company.

These four different kinds of variables are illustrated in the next example.

EXAMPLE 4.1

The following data are collected on newborns as part of a birth registry database.

$$
\text{Ethnic Background:} \begin{cases} \text{African-American} \\ \text{Hispanic} \\ \text{Native American} \\ \text{Caucasian} \\ \text{Other} \end{cases} \quad \textbf{Nominal Variable}
$$

---

[2] This dictum is often ignored in practice for ordinal data (e.g., when computing a grade point average), thus implicitly assuming numerical scale for the data.

$$
\text{Infant's Condition:} \begin{cases} \text{Excellent} \\ \text{Good} \\ \text{Fair} \\ \text{Poor} \end{cases} \quad \textbf{Ordinal Variable}
$$

Birthweight: in grams   **Continuous Variable**

Number of Prenatal Visits: [0, 1, 2, ...] **Discrete Variable**

◆

Sometimes numerical variables are classified in an alternative way. If two measurements on a variable can be meaningfully compared by their difference, but not by their ratio, then it is called an **interval variable**. On the other hand, if both the difference and the ratio are meaningful, it is called a **ratio variable**. An example of an interval variable is temperature. If the average winter temperature is $20°$F and the average summer temperature $80°$F, it is meaningful to say that the difference in average temperatures is $60°$F, but we cannot say that the summer months are four times hotter than the winter months. An example of a ratio variable is count data, e.g., number of crimes. Suppose there were 100 crimes in January and 300 in July. It is meaningful to say that there were 200 more crimes in July. It is also meaningful to say that July had three times as many crimes as January.

A unique property of the ratio scale is that it has a natural zero, while the interval scale does not. For example, zero distance has an absolute meaning regardless of the unit of measurement used (e.g., miles or kilometers), but a zero on a temperature scale is arbitrary and depends on the unit of measurement. Thus $0°$ is defined differently on the Fahrenheit and Celsius scales. The ratio scale is the strongest scale of measurement.

4.2 SUMMARIZING CATEGORICAL DATA

A natural way to summarize a batch of categorical data is a **frequency table**, which shows the number of occurrences of each category. Table 4.1 is an example of a frequency table summarizing the breakdown of 573 rejected alumininum castings over a three-month period by the cause of rejection.[3] The **relative frequency** is the proportion in each category. Such frequency data are often displayed graphically as a **bar chart** or a **pie chart**. A bar chart with categories arranged from the highest to the lowest frequency is called a **Pareto chart**. Figure 4.2 shows a Pareto chart of the frequencies given in Table 4.1. The Pareto chart is a simple graphical technique to distinguish "the vital few from the trivial many." In Figure 4.2, the first three causes account for more than 75% of all the rejections. Therefore effort should be targeted to remove those three causes, especially the first (sand), which accounts for more than half the rejections. The Pareto chart has gained wide acceptance as a simple graphical tool to improve quality in manufacturing and service industries.

4.3 SUMMARIZING NUMERICAL DATA

To gain an understanding of a set of numerical data, it is convenient to summarize it by a few key numbers that represent its major features. For example, most people feel

---

[3] G. A. Hunt (1989), "A training program becomes a 'clinic,'" *Quality Engineering*, **19**, pp. 113–117.

Table 4.1 Causes of Rejection of Aluminum Castings

Cause of Rejection	Frequency	Relative Frequency (%)
Sand	299	52.2
Mis-run	27	4.7
Blow	1	0.2
Shift	30	5.2
Cut	1	0.2
Broken	63	11.0
Drop	33	5.8
Corebreak	82	14.3
Run-out	15	2.6
Core Missing	7	1.2
Crush	15	2.6
Total	573	100

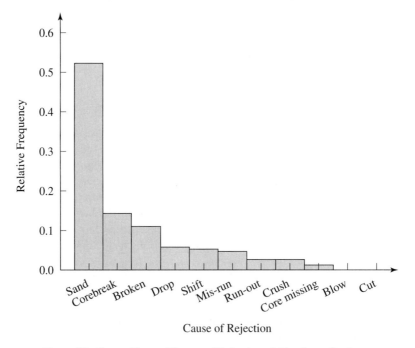

Figure 4.2   Pareto Chart of Causes of Rejection of Aluminum Castings

that the Dow Jones Industrial average is easier to monitor than the 30 individual stock prices that comprise that index.

Consider the data in Table 4.2, showing the Environmental Protection Agency's (EPA) highway mileage ratings (in miles per gallon (MPG)) for twenty-four 1992 model cars.[4] Such data are notationally represented by $x_1, x_2, \ldots, x_n$ where n is the sample size. In this section we study the use of summary statistics (Section 4.3.1–Section 4.3.3) and graphical methods (Section 4.3.4) to display the main features of numerical data.

If the data are obtained by drawing a random sample from some well-defined population, then the summary statistics can be regarded as sample estimates of appropriate parameters of that population. In the following discussion we have noted for some summary statistics the corresponding population parameters. Such use of summary statistics falls under the topic of statistical inference, which is covered in detail from Chapter 6 onward. The present chapter focuses on their use as descriptive measures of the main features and trends in a data set. This is their sole use when the data are not a random sample from an identifiable population or when the sample itself is the population. In other words, it is not of interest to extend or generalize the conclusions to some larger population, e.g., when summarizing the numerical grades of students in a course to help in assigning letter grades.

Table 4.2 EPA 1992 Highway Gas Mileage Ratings (in MPG) for 24 Cars

Model	Mileage	Model	Mileage
Acura NSX	24	Lincoln Capri	31
BMW M5	23	Mazda MX–3	32
Chevy Cavalier	36	Mitsubishi Galant	30
Chrysler LeBaron	27	Nissan Stanza	29
Daihatsu Charade	38	Peugot 405	28
Dodge Ramcharger	13	Plymouth Sundance	25
Eagle Summit	31	Pontiac Sunbird	28
Ferrari F40	17	Porsche 911 Turbo	21
Ford Escort FS	40	Saturn SL	35
Geo Metro LSi	50	Toyota Celica	31
Honda Civic	37	Volvo 240	25
Isuzu Amigo	20	VW Jetta	40

4.3.1 Summary Statistics: Measures of Location

Mean and Median. A measure of location is a statistic that represents a central or typical value in the data. The most familiar way to summarize data by a central value is to compute the **sample mean**, denoted by $\bar{x}$:

$$\bar{x} = \frac{x_1 + x_2 + \cdots + x_n}{n} = \frac{\sum_{i=1}^{n} x_i}{n}.$$

[4] Jack Gillis (1991), *The Car Book*, Washington, D.C.: Tilden Press

The mean is the center of the data in the sense that it is the closest point to all the data values in terms of the total of the squared distances. Specifically,

$$\sum_{i=1}^{n}(x_i - m)^2$$

is minimized when $m = \bar{x}$. Just as the population mean μ is the center of gravity of the population distribution, as illustrated in Figure 2.7, the sample mean $\bar{x}$ is the center of gravity of the sample distribution. In fact, $\bar{x}$ is used to estimate μ.

Another well-known central value is the **sample median**, denoted by $\tilde{x}$, which is the middle value in the ordered sample. The ordered (ranked) data values (called the **order statistics**) are denoted by

$$x_{\min} = x_{(1)} \leq x_{(2)} \leq \cdots \leq x_{(n)} = x_{\max}.$$

The sample median is the closest point to all the data values in terms of the total of the absolute distances. Specifically,

$$\sum_{i=1}^{n}|x_i - m|$$

is minimized when $m = \tilde{x}$. The sample median $\tilde{x}$ is used to estimate the population median $\tilde{\mu}$.

If n is odd, then there is a unique middle value, $x_{(\frac{n+1}{2})}$. If n is even, then there are two middle values, $x_{(\frac{n}{2})}$ and $x_{(\frac{n}{2}+1)}$. The common convention is to average these two values. Thus the median is given by

$$\tilde{x} = \begin{cases} x_{(\frac{n+1}{2})} & \text{if } n \text{ is odd} \\ \frac{1}{2}\left[x_{(\frac{n}{2})} + x_{(\frac{n}{2}+1)} \right] & \text{if } n \text{ is even.} \end{cases} \tag{4.1}$$

Table 4.3 lists the ordered gas mileage data from Table 4.2. The mean of the mileage data is $\bar{x} = 29.625$. The median of the mileage data is the average of the two middle values $x_{(\frac{n}{2})} = x_{(12)} = 29$ and $x_{(\frac{n}{2}+1)} = x_{(13)} = 30$; thus $\tilde{x} = \frac{1}{2}(29+30) = 29.5$. The mean and median are quite close in this example.

Table 4.3 Ordered Highway Gas Mileage Ratings

$x_{(1)} = 13$	$x_{(2)} = 17$	$x_{(3)} = 20$	$x_{(4)} = 21$	$x_{(5)} = 23$	$x_{(6)} = 24$
$x_{(7)} = 25$	$x_{(8)} = 25$	$x_{(9)} = 27$	$x_{(10)} = 28$	$x_{(11)} = 28$	$x_{(12)} = 29$
$x_{(13)} = 30$	$x_{(14)} = 31$	$x_{(15)} = 31$	$x_{(16)} = 31$	$x_{(17)} = 32$	$x_{(18)} = 35$
$x_{(19)} = 36$	$x_{(20)} = 37$	$x_{(21)} = 38$	$x_{(22)} = 40$	$x_{(23)} = 40$	$x_{(24)} = 50$

Which should be used to describe the center of the data, the mean or the median? The mean is appropriate when the data follow a **symmetric distribution** with **light tails** (i.e., a relatively small proportion of observations lie away from the center of the data). Extreme data values that are far removed from the main body of the data are called **outliers**. Often the outliers are erroneous observations. The mean and median are close for symmetrically distributed data uncorrupted by outliers. If a distribution has **heavy tails** (i.e., a relatively large proportion of observations lie away from the center of the data) or is **asymmetric** (also called **skewed**), then the observations in the tail have a strong influence on the mean but not on the median. Therefore the median is a better measure of the center of data than the mean for heavy-tailed or skewed distributions. When a distribution has a long right tail (referred to as a **positively skewed** or **right skewed** distribution), the mean is greater than the median; see Figure 4.3. Annual household incomes and lifetimes of items are two common examples of positively skewed variables. When a distribution is **negatively skewed** or **left skewed**, the mean is less than the median.

The outliers in the data also influence the mean much more than the median. We say that the median is a **robust** or **resistant** measure of center, because large changes in a few data values change the median very little. In contrast, the mean is *not* resistant to such changes, since it gives equal weight to all observations. Consider a sample consisting of five numbers: 10, 20, 30, 40, and 50. For this sample, the mean and median both equal 30. But suppose that the number 50 was misrecorded as 500. Then the mean would jump to 120, while the median would remain at 30.

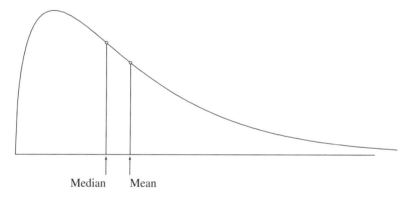

Figure 4.3   Median and Mean of a Positively Skewed Distribution

A resistant version of the mean is a **trimmed mean**. An α-trimmed mean, denoted by $\bar{x}^{(\alpha)}$, refers to the mean computed after trimming away an α fraction of the observations from each end of the ordered data set. Consider a 10%-trimmed mean for the mileage data. The number of observations removed from each end of the ordered data set is the integer part of $n\alpha = 24 \times 0.10 = 2.4$, which is 2. Therefore the 10%-trimmed mean is

$$\bar{x}^{(.10)} = \frac{x_{(3)} + x_{(4)} + \cdots + x_{(22)}}{20} = 29.55,$$

which is very close to the untrimmed mean $\bar{x} = 29.625$. This indicates a possible lack of outliers in the data.

4.3.2 Summary Statistics: Measures of Dispersion

Another important feature of a set of numerical data is the dispersion or spread. Two data sets may have the same center but quite different dispersions around it. For example, consider two data sets consisting of the ages of persons at a large family reunion and the ages of students at a college cafeteria. Although both data sets may have approximately the same center (about 20 years), the family reunion data set will have a higher variation than the college students data set.

One way to summarize the variability in a data set is to give additional "milestones" which divide the ordered sample into several equal parts. Another way is to compute a single-number summary, such as the range between the maximum and the minimum. We next discuss these two ways.

Quartiles and Percentiles.   The median $\tilde{x}$ divides the sample into two equal parts. For this reason it is also referred to as the 50th percentile. The 25th and 75th percentiles together with the median divide the sample into four equal parts. These percentiles are called **quartiles**. In general, the $100p$th **percentile** (also called the pth **quantile**) is the value $\tilde{x}_p$ which divides the ordered sample so that a fraction p $(0 < p < 1)$ of the data values are less than or equal to $\tilde{x}_p$ and the remaining fraction $(1 - p)$ are greater than $\tilde{x}_p$. Using this notation, the first (or lower) quartile (Q_1) is $\tilde{x}_{.25}$, the second (or middle) quartile (Q_2) is $\tilde{x}_{.50} = \tilde{x}$, and the third (or upper) quartile (Q_3) is $\tilde{x}_{.75}$.

The formula (4.1) suggests that the median $\tilde{x} = \tilde{x}_{.5}$ can be thought of as the $0.5(n+1)$th order statistic. The value $0.5(n+1)$ is an integer if n is odd and a fraction if n is even. When n is even, the median is computed by averaging $x_{(\frac{n}{2})}$ and $x_{(\frac{n}{2}+1)}$, which can be viewed as a linear interpolation between the two observations with ranks closest to $0.5(n+1)$. Generalizing this idea, we can take $\tilde{x}_p$ to be the $p(n+1)$th order statistic. If $p(n+1)$ is an integer, then $\tilde{x}_p = x_{(p(n+1))}$; if $p(n+1)$ is a fraction, then we linearly interpolate between the two observations with ranks closest to that number. Thus

$$\tilde{x}_p = \begin{cases} x_{(p(n+1))} & \text{if } p(n+1) \text{ is an integer} \\ x_{(m)} + [p(n+1) - m]\left(x_{(m+1)} - x_{(m)}\right) & \text{if } p(n+1) \text{ is a fraction} \end{cases} \quad (4.2)$$

where m denotes the integer part of $p(n+1)$.

We can use (4.2) to calculate Q_1 and Q_3. Alternatively, a quick approximate method to find Q_1 and Q_3 is to use the medians of the lower and upper halves of the ordered sample.

The three quartiles together with the sample minimum and maximum, $\{x_{\min}, Q_1, Q_2, Q_3, x_{\max}\}$, are together referred to as the **five number summary**. This is used to summarize the major milestones and the extent of variation in the data.

Example 4.2   (Gas Mileage Data: Five Number Summary)

For the gas mileage data from Table 4.2, the five number summary is as follows:

$$x_{\min} = x_{(1)} = 13$$

$$Q_1 = x_{(6.25)} = x_{(6)} + 0.25\left(x_{(7)} - x_{(6)}\right)$$

$$= 24 + 0.25\,(25 - 24) = 24.25$$

$$Q_2 = x_{(12.5)} = x_{(12)} + 0.5\left(x_{(13)} - x_{(12)}\right)$$

$$= 29 + 0.5\,(30 - 29) = 29.5$$

$$Q_3 = x_{(18.75)} = x_{(18)} + 0.75(x_{(19)} - x_{(18)})$$

$$= 35 + 0.75(36 - 35) = 35.75$$

$$x_{\max} = x_{(24)} = 50.$$

Using the quick approximate method to calculate Q_1 and Q_3, we find Q_1 is the median of the 12 smallest observations, $Q_1 = x_{(6.5)} = 24.5$. Similarly, Q_3 is the median of the 12 largest observations, $Q_3 = x_{(18.5)} = 35.5$. These values are not much different from Q_1 and Q_3 found above. Notice that Q_1 and Q_3 are nearly equidistant from Q_2. This suggests that these data are symmetrically distributed. ◆

Range, Interquartile Range, and Standard Deviation.   Statistics to summarize variation are especially useful if the data are symmetrically distributed. The simplest measure of dispersion is the **range**, which equals $x_{\max} - x_{\min}$. A limitation of the range is that it is a function only of the extreme observations; thus for large samples it ignores much information. Also the extreme observations may be outliers which may exaggerate the variability in the data. The range is commonly used in some quality control charts, partly because it is easy to compute[5] and partly because these charts employ small samples (thus not much information is lost).

A trimmed version of the range that is resistant to outliers is the **interquartile range (IQR)**:

$$\text{IQR} = Q_3 - Q_1.$$

The IQR covers the middle half of the ordered sample.

The average distance of the data points from their center can be used to measure dispersion. The sample **variance**, denoted by s^2, is such a measure, given by

$$s^2 = \frac{1}{n-1} \sum_{i=1}^{n} (x_i - \bar{x})^2 = \frac{1}{n-1} \left[\sum_{i=1}^{n} x_i^2 - n\bar{x}^2 \right]. \tag{4.3}$$

The sample variance is the average of the squared distances of the data points from $\bar{x}$. The average is computed by dividing by $n-1$ rather than n, because there are only $n-1$ independent differences, $x_i - \bar{x}$, since $\sum_{i=1}^{n}(x_i - \bar{x}) = 0$. We shall see another reason for this in Example 6.3. The second expression for s^2 above is obtained from the first expression by expanding the square inside the summation and simplifying. It is sometimes useful for hand computation.

The square root of the sample variance,

$$s = \sqrt{\frac{1}{n-1} \sum_{i=1}^{n} (x_i - \bar{x})^2} \tag{4.4}$$

is called the sample **standard deviation (SD)**. Note that s and s^2 are the sample analogs, respectively, of the population standard deviation σ and population variance σ^2 introduced in Section 2.4.2. The SD is more convenient to use than the variance because

---

[5] This was an important consideration in the days when pocket calculators and on-line computers were nonexistent.

it has the same units as the original measurements (the x_i's). It should be emphasized that just as the sample mean should be used as a measure of center only for symmetrically distributed data, the sample variance, or SD, should be used as a measure of dispersion only for symmetrically distributed data. For skewed data, a more detailed breakup of the dispersion must be given in terms of the quartiles.

How is the standard deviation related to the scatter of the data around the sample mean? If the data come from a normal distribution, then, using the results of Example 2.38, we can answer this question as follows: For a large sample, approximately

$$50\% \text{ of the data values fall between } \quad \bar{x} \pm 0.67s$$

$$68\% \text{ of the data values fall between } \quad \bar{x} \pm 1s$$

$$95\% \text{ of the data values fall between } \quad \bar{x} \pm 2s$$

$$99.7\% \text{ of the data values fall between } \quad \bar{x} \pm 3s.$$

From the above, we see that for normally distributed data,

$$\text{IQR} \simeq (\bar{x} + 0.67s) - (\bar{x} - 0.67s) = 1.34s. \tag{4.5}$$

This relationship provides an approximate method to calculate s from the quartiles.

The **coefficient of variation (CV)** is a relative measure of dispersion that expresses the sample SD in terms of the sample mean, $CV = s/\bar{x}$. Thus the CV provides a unitless measure of dispersion. As an example, body-composition studies[6] on a group of children showed a mean arm circumference of $\bar{x} = 138$ mm and $s = 9$ mm, yielding $CV = 9/138 = 6.5\%$, while body water constituted a mean of $\bar{x} = 60\%$ of total body weight and $s = 4\%$, yielding $CV = 4/60 = 6.7\%$. Although the units and scales of these measures are very different, the CV's show that their dispersions relative to their respective means are similar.

EXAMPLE 4.3   (GAS MILEAGE DATA: MEASURES OF DISPERSION)

The measures of dispersion calculated for the gas mileage data are as follows:

$$\text{Range} = 50 - 13 = 37$$

$$\text{IQR} = 35.75 - 24.25 = 11.5$$

$$s^2 = \frac{(13 - 29.625)^2 + (17 - 29.625)^2 + \cdots + (50 - 29.625)^2}{24 - 1} = 68.245$$

$$s = \sqrt{68.245} = 8.261$$

$$\text{CV} = \frac{8.261}{29.625} = 27.88\%.$$

Notice that for the mileage data, relationship (4.5) for a normally distributed sample is approximately satisfied, since $\text{IQR}/1.34 = 11.5/1.34 = 8.58 \simeq s = 8.261$.   ◆

---

[6] C. R. Field, D. A. Schoeller, and K. H. Brown (1989), "Body composition of children recovering from severe protein-energy malnutrition," *American Journal of Clinical Nutrition*, **50**, pp. 1266–1275.

Example 4.4   (Gas Mileage Data: Summary Statistics)

The various measures of location and dispersion discussed here can be obtained in MINITAB. The following is a sample output for the gas mileage data from Table 4.2.

	N	MEAN	MEDIAN	TRMEAN	STDEV	SEMEAN
MPG	24	29.63	29.50	29.45	8.26	1.69

	MIN	MAX	Q1	Q3
MPG	13.00	50.00	24.25	35.75

Here the TRMEAN is the 20% trimmed mean and SEMEAN $= s/\sqrt{n}$ refers to the standard error of the mean, which is explained in Chapter 6.   ◆

Standardized z-Scores.   Often it is useful to express the data on a standardized scale. One way to do this is by computing z-scores of the data values, obtained by subtracting the mean and dividing by the standard deviation:

$$z_i = \frac{x_i - \bar{x}}{s} \quad (i = 1, 2, \ldots, n). \tag{4.6}$$

The z-score tells us how many standard deviations that data value is above or below the sample mean. The z-scores are unitless quantities and are standardized to have mean $= 0$ and SD $= 1$. Obviously, they are useful mainly for symmetrically distributed data. Here are some of their uses.

- They can be used to flag outliers (i.e., extreme observations). For example, a z-score greater than 3 in magnitude corresponds to a data value that is more than 3 standard deviations away from the mean and therefore may be an outlier.

- They provide a way to compare two or more batches of data (possibly measured in different units) on the same scale. For example, consider two sets of test scores. On the first test the mean is 70 and SD $= 8$, while on the second the mean is 80 and SD $= 6$. Then a score of 86 on the first test has a z-score of 2, while a score of 86 on the second has a z-score of 1. Thus 86 on the first test is twice as high compared to the mean than 86 on the second. Therefore, while 86 on the first test might be an A, 86 on the second might be a B. This is the basic idea behind "grading on a curve."

- If a sample follows a normal distribution, then, using Table A.3 in Appendix A, the z-scores can be converted into corresponding percentiles. For example, a z-score of 2 corresponds to the 97.72th percentile of the $N(0, 1)$ distribution, while a z-score of 1 corresponds to the 84.13th percentile. Conversely, a score corresponding to a given percentile can be found from Table A.3. For example, the 95th percentile corresponds to a z-score of 1.645, and hence the 95th percentile on the first test is $70 + 1.645 \times 8 = 83.16$.

4.3.3 *Summary Statistics: Skewness and Kurtosis

The sample mean, $\bar{x} = \sum x_i / n$, is an average of the first powers of the data values and is sometimes referred to as the **first moment**. The sample variance, $s^2 = \sum (x_i - \bar{x})^2 / (n-1)$, is an average of the second powers of the data values after centering them about the mean and is sometimes referred to as the **second central moment**. We have used these two moments to describe the location and spread, respectively, of the distribution of the data values. Two higher moments of the data are useful for describing other features of the distribution.

The third central moment (standardized by dividing by the cube of the standard deviation so that the result is unitless) is called the **sample skewness** and is given by

$$b_1 = \frac{\sum_{i=1}^{n}(x_i - \bar{x})^3 / n}{s^3}.$$

We can think of b_1 as a sample estimate of the population skewness β_1 defined in Section 2.4.3. From the properties of β_1 it follows that $b_1 \simeq 0$ indicates a symmetric distribution, $b_1 \gg 0$ indicates a positively skewed distribution, while $b_1 \ll 0$ indicates a negatively skewed distribution.

The fourth central moment (standardized by dividing by the fourth power of the standard deviation so that the result is unitless) is called the **sample kurtosis** and is given by

$$b_2 = \frac{\sum_{i=1}^{n}(x_i - \bar{x})^4 / n}{s^4}.$$

We can think of b_2 as a sample estimate of the population kurtosis β_2 defined in Section 2.4.3. Since the fourth powers of the differences from the mean are much larger for the observations in the tails of a distribution than for the observations closer to the mean, the kurtosis can be regarded as a measure of the **tail heaviness** of the distribution. The heavier the tails of the distribution, the greater is the kurtosis. The normal distribution is regarded as a light tail distribution (because it has very little probability in its tails, e.g., beyond three standard deviations from the mean) and has $\beta_2 = 3$. Thus $b_2 \gg 3$ indicates a distribution with heavier tails than the normal distribution, while $b_2 \ll 3$ indicates a distribution with lighter tails than the normal distribution.

Many texts and statistical packages use $g_1 = \sqrt{b_1}$ and $g_2 = b_2 - 3$ as the definitions of skewness and kurtosis, respectively. It should be noted that the sample skewness and especially kurtosis are not very reliable estimates unless the sample size is sufficiently large, say at least 50.

EXAMPLE 4.5   (GAS MILEAGE DATA: SKEWNESS AND KURTOSIS)

The skewness and kurtosis measures for the gas mileage data from Table 4.2 are computed to be $b_1 = 0.0671$ ($g_1 = 0.259$) and $b_2 = 3.173$ ($g_2 = 0.173$), respectively. These values are fairly close to those expected for the normal distribution. Therefore the data appear to be approximately normally distributed. ◆

4.3.4 Graphical Techniques

Summary statistics provide key numerical features of the data. However, a picture is invaluable for revealing characteristics such as the shape of the distribution. Some graphical methods for this purpose are presented in this section.

Histogram.   A **histogram** may be regarded as a bar chart for numerical data. The first step in making a histogram is to divide the range of the data into **class intervals**. The number of class intervals is usually between 5 and 50, depending on the sample size n. A rough rule is to group the data into $\sqrt{n}$ class intervals. According to this rule, we need $\sqrt{24} \simeq 5$ intervals for the mileage data. Because a histogram requires grouping the data into intervals, the sample size should be at least modestly large ($n \geq 20$) and preferably larger ($n \geq 50$). The class interval width is approximately the range divided by the number of intervals. For the gas mileage data we use a class interval width of $\frac{50-13}{5} \simeq 8$, which gives the following intervals: 10–18, 18–26, 26–34, 34–42, and 42–50. When a data value falls on the boundary between two class intervals, we will arbitrarily count it in the lower interval. The resulting frequency table is given in Table 4.4. The corresponding histogram, shown in Figure 4.4, is a bar chart for this frequency table with the bars centered over the midpoints of the class intervals. The area of each bar represents the fraction of data values in that interval; the total area of the histogram is 1. In this histogram all the class intervals have equal width, and so the bar heights are proportional to the corresponding relative frequencies. However, if the data are widely scattered, it may be necessary to use unequal width class intervals and adjust the bar heights so that the *bar areas* are proportional to the relative frequencies.

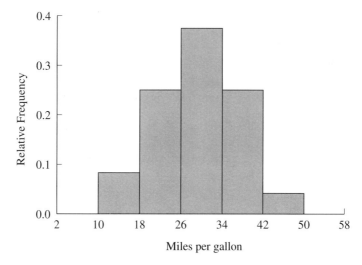

Figure 4.4   Histogram for Highway Gas Mileage Data

The following are some of the uses of a histogram.

- A histogram gives a picture of the distribution of the data. In fact, it may be viewed as a sample estimate of the probability density function (p.d.f.) of the

Table 4.4 Frequency Table for Highway Gas Mileage Data

Class Interval	Frequency	Relative Frequency
10–18	2	0.083
18–26	6	0.250
26–34	9	0.375
34–42	6	0.250
42–50	1	0.042
Total	24	1.000

population from which the sample is drawn. (While the areas under a p.d.f. curve represent probabilities, the areas under a histogram represent sample proportions, which are sample estimates of the corresponding probabilities.) It shows whether the distribution is symmetric or skewed, whether the distribution has a single mode (called a **unimodal distribution**) or multiple modes, and other features of the distribution. For example, a distribution with two modes (called a **bimodal distribution**) may indicate that the sample is drawn from a mixture of two distinct populations.

- Any gaps or valleys in a histogram may indicate a problem with the measurement process. W. Edwards Deming[7] (1900–1993), who was a leading figure in the modern quality movement based on statistics, cites an example of a histogram for diameters of steel rods. The histogram shows an unexpected gap immediately below the lower specification limit on the diameter. This suggests that the inspector may have fudged the data to pass the parts that fell just below the lower specification limit.

- A histogram is useful for detecting outliers.

Stem and Leaf Plot. A histogram provides a visual summary of the data, but the individual data points cannot be distinguished once they are grouped into class intervals. A **stem and leaf plot** is an alternative graphical technique for modest size data sets ($n \simeq$ 20 to 50) that preserves the original data and yet displays the sample distribution.

The first step in making a stem and leaf plot is to divide each observation into two parts (ignoring the decimal point if present): a stem consisting of leading digits and a leaf consisting of trailing digits. Stems play the role of class intervals in a histogram. A stem may have as many digits as necessary, but leaves must have an equal number of digits. (Most statistical packages use only single digit leaves; additional trailing digits are dropped.) To construct the plot, draw a vertical line and write the stem values down the left side of the line in increasing order. Write the leaves horizontally on the right side of the line next to the appropriate stem from left to right.

This technique is best understood by going through an illustration. A stem and leaf plot of the gas mileage data for the 24 cars is shown in Figure 4.5. The original data can be read from the display. The stem in this display is the "tens" part and the leaf is the "ones" part. Thus, the first value, 13, is represented as stem = 1 and leaf = 3. Note

---

[7] W. E. Deming (1986), *Out of the Crisis,* Boston: MIT Press, p. 266.

Stem	Leaf
1	37
2	0134557889
3	011125678
4	00
5	0

Figure 4.5 Stem and Leaf Plot of Highway Gas Mileage Data

that if the stem and leaf plot of Figure 4.5 were laid on its side, it would have a shape similar to the histogram in Figure 4.4.

If only a few stems can be formed relative to the size of the data set, then it may be necessary to split each stem into several substems. For example, if we had 100 cars (say) in the highway gas mileage data set, then five stems would be too few. We can double the number of stems by splitting each stem into two substems: the first substem of 1 would include the data values from 10 to 14, while the second substem would include the data values from 15 to 19, etc.

Box and Whiskers Plot. A **box and whiskers plot** (also known as a **box plot**) is constructed from the five-number summary. First, a rectangle (called a **box**) is drawn extending from Q_1 to Q_3 and divided at the median, Q_2; Q_1 and Q_3 are referred to as **hinges** of the box plot. The width of the box is unimportant. Next, two numbers, called **fences**, are calculated:

$$\text{Lower Fence} = Q_1 - 1.5 \times \text{IQR}$$

$$\text{Upper Fence} = Q_3 + 1.5 \times \text{IQR}.$$

Finally, two lines, called **whiskers**, are drawn extending from the ends of the box to the most extreme data values that are still *inside* the fences. Observations which fall outside the fences are regarded as *possible* outliers and are indicated by asterisks.

From a box plot one can easily see whether the data are symmetrically distributed or not and whether the distribution has long tails (whiskers). It also helps to identify outliers.

EXAMPLE 4.6 (GAS MILEAGE DATA: BOX AND WHISKERS PLOT)

Figure 4.6 shows a box and whiskers plot for the gas mileage data from Table 4.2. The lower and upper fences are calculated as follows: First calculate IQR = $Q_3 - Q_1 = 35.75 - 24.25 = 11.5$. Then calculate

$$\text{Lower Fence} = 24.25 - 1.5 \times 11.5 = 7.0$$

$$\text{Upper Fence} = 35.75 + 1.5 \times 11.0 = 53.0.$$

The whiskers extend from the ends of the box out to 13 and 50, the extreme data points that are still within the fences. Thus, all the data points fall within the fences and none are marked as outliers. The symmetric distribution of the data is indicated by the fact that the box is divided into approximately equal parts by the median, and the whiskers are roughly the same length. ◆

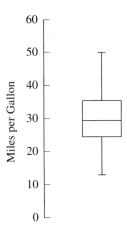

Figure 4.6 Box and Whiskers Plot for Highway Gas Mileage Data

Box plots are especially useful for comparing two or more samples. These are made by placing the plots side by side on the same scale. The locations and spreads of the samples can then be visually compared. The following example illustrates this use of box plots.

EXAMPLE 4.7 (HOSPITALIZATION COSTS: SIDE-BY-SIDE BOX PLOTS)

A pilot study was carried out in 1991 at the Northwestern Memorial Hospital in Chicago to compare two different methods of care management of geriatric patients who were transferred from the emergency room to the geriatric ward. The two methods were "usual care" and "geriatric team care." The assignment of patients to the two groups was done at random; 58 patients were assigned to the "usual care" group (control group) and 50 to the "geriatric team care" group (treatment group). The two groups were compared on various outcome measures. Table 4.5 gives data on the hospitalization costs for a subsample of 30 patients from each group.[8]

Table 4.5 Hospitalization Costs (in $) for Geriatric Patients Cared for by Two Different Methods

Control Group	478	605	626	714	818	1203	1204	1323	2150	2700
	2969	3151	3565	3626	3739	4148	4382	4576	6953	6963
	7062	7284	7829	8681	9319	12,664	17,539	23,237	26,677	32,913
Treatment Group	528	650	912	1130	1289	1651	1706	1708	1882	1998
	2391	2432	2697	2829	3039	3186	3217	3345	3590	4153
	5928	6018	6267	6790	7365	8635	9615	13,890	15,225	19,083

Figure 4.7 gives side-by-side box plots for the two samples, which show that the control group costs are generally higher than those for the treatment group. Also, the control group costs are more variable than those for the treatment group. Another point to note from the box plots is that both samples are skewed to the right, and each has three outliers at the high end. (One outlier in the control group is marked with an open circle instead of an asterisk. This outlier is "too extreme," being beyond $Q_3 + 3 \times$ IQR.) ◆

[8] Data courtesy of Dr. Bruce Naughton, formerly of the Northwestern Memorial Hospital.

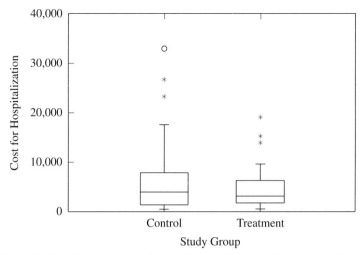

Figure 4.7   Box Plots for Hospitalization Costs of Geriatric Patients Cared for by Two Different Methods

Normal Plot.   Many of the techniques discussed in this book assume that the data are normally distributed. Real data almost never follow the normal distribution exactly, because the normal distribution is an idealized mathematical model. Yet, it is important to know how close the approximation is for a given set of data. One can make a histogram of the data for this purpose. However, for small samples a histogram is not very sensitive, since it requires that the data to be grouped first. The same is true for the stem and leaf plot. Even for large samples these techniques are only sufficient to determine if the data are grossly nonnormal. This is because it is difficult for a human eye to judge whether a plot approximates the theoretical normal density function *curve*.[9] It is much easier for a human eye to judge whether a plot approximates a *straight line*. The **normal plot** is based on this principle and gives a much more accurate assessment of normality. It is one of the most frequently used tools in the kit of an applied statistician.

If the data follow an $N(\mu, \sigma^2)$ distribution, then the percentiles of that normal distribution should plot linearly against the sample percentiles, except for sampling variations. The parameters μ and σ^2 of the theoretical normal distribution are unknown, but it can be shown (see below) that to check the linearity of the plot it is sufficient to take $\mu = 0$ and $\sigma^2 = 1$, i.e., use the standard normal distribution percentiles. For the sample percentiles we use the ordered data values themselves, the ith ordered data value being the $100\left(\frac{i}{n+1}\right)$th sample percentile, where n is the sample size. The corresponding standard normal percentiles are called **normal scores**. The plot of these normal scores against the ordered data values is the normal plot. Usually a computer package is used to make this plot, but in the following example we show the detailed calculations.

---

[9] Also, there are other distributions that have the familiar bell shaped density function, e.g., the family of Student's t distributions discussed in Section 5.3.

EXAMPLE 4.8   (GAS MILEAGE DATA: NORMAL PLOT)

The previous examples in this chapter have suggested that the gas mileage data from Table 4.2 are approximately normally distributed. Let us verify this by making a normal plot. Table 4.6 gives the calculations necessary to make the normal plot. In these calculations we have defined $x_{(i)}$ as the $\left(\frac{i}{n+1}\right)$th quantile. Thus $x_{(1)} = 13$ is the $\left(\frac{1}{24+1}\right) = .04$th quantile, and the corresponding normal score is the .04th quantile of the standard normal distribution, which is -1.751.

Table 4.6 Calculations for the Normal Plot of Highway Gas Mileage Data

i	$x_{(i)}$	$\dfrac{i}{n+1}$	Normal Score	i	$x_{(i)}$	$\dfrac{i}{n+1}$	Normal Score
1	13	0.04	-1.751	13	30	0.52	0.050
2	17	0.08	-1.405	14	31	0.56	0.151
3	20	0.12	-1.175	15	31	0.60	0.253
4	21	0.16	-0.995	16	31	0.64	0.358
5	23	0.20	-0.842	17	32	0.68	0.468
6	24	0.24	-0.706	18	35	0.72	0.583
7	25	0.28	-0.583	19	36	0.76	0.706
8	27	0.32	-0.468	20	37	0.80	0.842
9	28	0.36	-0.358	21	38	0.84	0.995
10	28	0.40	-0.253	22	40	0.88	1.175
11	28	0.44	-0.151	23	40	0.92	1.406
12	29	0.48	-0.050	24	50	0.96	1.751

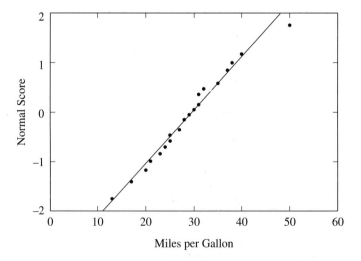

Figure 4.8   Normal Plot for the Highway Gas Mileage Data

The resulting normal plot is shown in Figure 4.8. It appears to be quite linear, thus supporting the normality assumption.   ◆

To emphasize the fact that sampling variations can mask linearity of a normal plot, which makes it difficult to assess normality for small sample sizes, we give in Figure 4.9 normal plots for random samples of four different sample sizes drawn from an $N(0, 1)$ distribution. Note that for sample sizes of 10 and 25 the plots are quite choppy, even though the samples are drawn from a normal distribution. Only when the sample size is about at least 50 does the linearity of the plot and hence the normality of the data become evident.

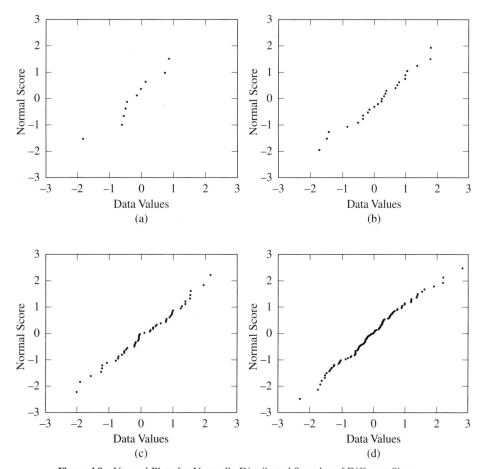

Figure 4.9   Normal Plots for Normally Distributed Samples of Different Sizes: (a) 10 values from a standard normal distribution; (b) 25 values from a standard normal distribution; (c) 50 values from a standard normal distribution; (d) 100 values from a standard normal distribution

A normal plot can be used as a diagnostic tool to check for the type of departure from normality as well as to detect outliers in the data. Figure 4.10 shows normal plots exhibiting different kinds of departures from normality.

Normalizing Transformations.   Data can be nonnormal in any number of ways, e.g., the distribution may not be bell shaped or may be heavier tailed than the normal dis-

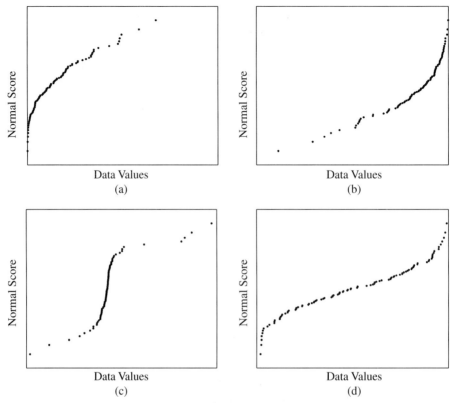

Figure 4.10 Normal Plots for Non-Normally Distributed Samples: (a) Right skewed distribution; (b) Left skewed distribution; (c) Heavy tailed distribution; (d) Light tailed distribution

tribution or may not be symmetric. Only the departure from symmetry can be easily corrected by transforming the data. If the distribution is positively skewed, then its right tail needs to be shrunk inward. The most common transformation used for this purpose is the logarithmic transformation, i.e., $x \rightarrow \log(x)$. The square-root transformation $(x \rightarrow \sqrt{x})$ provides a weaker shrinking effect; it is frequently used for count data. For negatively skewed distributions the inverses of the above transformations should be used. The inverse of the logarithmic transformation is the exponential transformation $(x \rightarrow e^x)$, while the inverse of the square-root transformation is the square transformation $(x \rightarrow x^2)$. In practice, different transformations must be tried to determine which one gives the most symmetric distribution.

EXAMPLE 4.9 (HOSPITALIZATION COSTS: NORMAL PLOTS)

The normal plot for the treatment group hospitalization cost data given in Table 4.7 is shown in Figure 4.11(a). It is clear from the curving nature of the plot (steep at the lower end, plateauing at the upper end) that the data are positively skewed. Figure 4.11(b) shows the normal plots for the logs of the hospitalization cost data. Note that the logarithmically transformed data are nearly normally distributed. The plots for the control group cost data are similar.   ◆

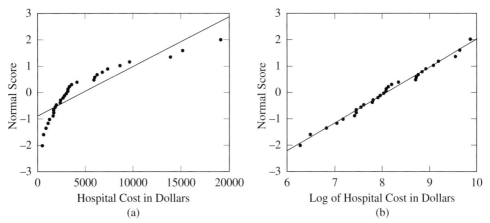

Figure 4.11   Normal Plots for the Treatment Group Hospitalization Costs and for Their Logs

A drawback of data transformation is that, although it may facilitate statistical analyses, the transformed scale may not have a physical meaning. Moreover, the same results are not obtained by transforming back to the original scale as by performing the same statistical analyses on the raw data. For instance, the average of the logs does not equal the log of the average. This can cause difficulties if the results must be reported in the original scale.

*Derivation of the Normal Plot.   Let $x_{(1)} \leq x_{(2)} \leq \cdots \leq x_{(n)}$ be the ordered values of a sample of n observations. Suppose we want to check whether this sample follows an $N(\mu, \sigma^2)$ distribution. Recall from equation (4.2) that the $100p$th sample percentile or the pth sample quantile is the $p(n+1)$th ordered data value. By letting $p = \frac{i}{n+1}$, we see that $x_{(i)}$ is the $\left(\frac{i}{n+1}\right)$th sample quantile.[10] Denote the $\left(\frac{i}{n+1}\right)$th quantile of an $N(0, 1)$ distribution by $\Phi^{-1}\left(\frac{i}{n+1}\right)$, where $\Phi(z)$ is the standard normal c.d.f. The normal scores $\Phi^{-1}\left(\frac{i}{n+1}\right)$ can be obtained from Table A.3 in Appendix A. Then the corresponding quantile of an $N(\mu, \sigma^2)$ distribution, denoted by $q_{(i)}$, is given by

$$q_{(i)} = \mu + \sigma \Phi^{-1}\left(\frac{i}{n+1}\right). \tag{4.7}$$

If the data in fact follow an $N(\mu, \sigma^2)$ distribution, then $x_{(i)} \simeq q_{(i)}$ and the plot of $x_{(i)}$ vs. $q_{(i)}$ should be approximately linear with slope $= 1$.

---

[10] Statistical packages use slightly different definitions for the sample quantile when making a normal plot. For example, in SYSTAT $x_{(i)}$ is defined to be the $\left(\frac{i-1/2}{n}\right)$th sample quantile, while in MINITAB $x_{(i)}$ is defined to be the $\left(\frac{i-3/8}{n+1/4}\right)$th sample quantile.

The $q_{(i)}$ values depend on μ and σ, which are unknown. However, since we are interested only in checking the linearity of the plot, we can simply plot the $x_{(i)}$ against the normal scores themselves, because they are linearly related to the $q_{(i)}$. The resulting plot is called the **normal plot** (more specifically, the **normal quantile plot**). The common practice is to plot the normal scores on the vertical axis and the $x_{(i)}$ on the horizontal axis. If the data are sampled from a normal distribution, this plot will be approximately linear with a slope of $1/\sigma$, if the sample size is sufficiently large.

Sometimes the normal plot comes in a slightly different form, in which the vertical axis is labeled with the cumulative probabilities corresponding to the normal scores (i.e., $\frac{i}{n+1}$). This is called a **normal probability plot**.

Run Chart.   The graphical techniques described above are inappropriate for **time-series data** (i.e., data collected sequentially over time), because they ignore the time sequence. Hence they mask patterns that are related to time. A **run chart** graphs the data points against time. A run chart enables us to see time related patterns such as trends, cycles, etc. Time-series data are discussed in more detail in Section 4.5.

EXAMPLE **4.10**

Consider the run chart in Figure 4.12(a) reported by Deming[11] for elongation measurements on 50 springs made sequentially over time. It is evident that there is a decreasing time trend in these data. A histogram of the same data (Figure 4.12(b)) masks this time trend and gives a misleading picture that suggests a stable process with normally distributed output. In fact, the process does not have a stable distribution, so the summary statistics such as the mean and standard deviation have no predictive value.   ◆

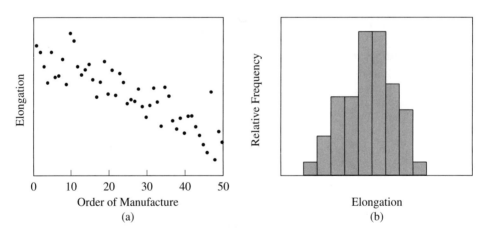

Figure 4.12   (a) Run Chart and (b) Histogram of Time-Series Data

4.4   SUMMARIZING BIVARIATE DATA

Frequently, two or more variables are measured on each sampling unit. For example, in a cardiac study, each patient's age, sex, height, weight, cardiac output, heart rate,

---

[11] W. E. Deming (1986), *Out of the Crisis,* Boston: MIT Press, p. 313.

and blood pressure are recorded. The resulting data are referred to as **multivariate**. If only two variables are measured, the data are referred to as **bivariate**. For example, a financial analyst may monitor the internal rate of return and the net present value of each investment in a portfolio.

Denote n paired observations by $(x_1, y_1), (x_2, y_2), \ldots, (x_n, y_n)$. We can summarize the data on the x or y variables separately using methods of Section 4.3 and Section 4.4. However, these methods do not answer questions concerning *relationship* between x and y, for example,

- What is the nature of relationship (if any) between x and y?
- How strong is this relationship?
- How well can one variable be predicted from the other?

In the present section we give some simple methods that help answer these questions.

4.4.1 Summarizing Bivariate Categorical Data

As we saw in Section 4.2, data on one categorical variable can be summarized using a frequency table. This approach can be extended to bivariate data when both variables are categorical. The basic idea is to display the frequency (count) for each possible *combination* of categories; the resulting table is called a **two-way table**. For example, Table 4.7 gives frequencies for a sample of 901 individuals cross-classified according to their incomes (four categories) and the level of their job satisfaction (four categories).[12]

Table 4.7 Individuals Cross-Classified by Income and Job Satisfaction

	y: Job Satisfaction				
x: Income (US $)	Very Dissatisfied	Little Dissatisfied	Moderately Satisfied	Very Satisfied	Row Sum
< 6000	20	24	80	82	206
6000–15,000	22	38	104	125	289
15,000–25,000	13	28	81	113	235
> 25,000	7	18	54	92	171
Column Sum	62	108	319	412	901

It is useful to convert the frequencies in Table 4.7 into percentages with respect to the overall total to assess the joint distribution of the two variables. The row and column percentages give the separate (marginal) distributions of the row and column variables, respectively. Table 4.8 gives these percentages for data in Table 4.7. From this table we see that although 55% of the individuals made less than $15,000, more than 80% were either moderately or very satisfied with their jobs.

---

[12] 1984 General Survey of the National Data Program as quoted by Norusis (1988), *SPSS^X Advanced Statistics Guide*, 2d ed., New York: McGraw-Hill.

Table 4.8 Overall Percentages for Income and Job Satisfaction Data

Income (US $)	Job Satisfaction				Row Percent
	Very Dissatisfied	Little Dissatisfied	Moderately Satisfied	Very Satisfied	
< 6000	2.2	2.7	8.9	9.1	22.9
6000–15,000	2.4	4.2	11.5	13.9	32.1
15,000–25,000	1.4	3.1	9.0	12.5	26.1
> 25,000	0.8	2.0	6.0	10.2	19.0
Column Percent	6.9	12.0	35.4	45.7	100.0

In many situations it is informative to compute percentages with respect to the row or column totals. For example, if it is of interest to know the distribution of job satisfaction for each income level, then we would compute row percentages. On the other hand, if it is of interest to know the distribution of income levels for each category of job satisfaction, then we would compute column percentages. Table 4.9 gives the row percentages for data in Table 4.7. From this table we see that the percentage of the people who are very dissatisfied with their jobs decreases as income level increases, while the percentage of the people who are very satisfied with their jobs increases. This indicates that income and job satisfaction are positively associated.

Table 4.9 Row Percentages for Income and Job Satisfaction Data

Income (US $)	Job Satisfaction				Row Sum
	Very Dissatisfied	Little Dissatisfied	Moderately Satisfied	Very Satisfied	
< 6000	9.7	11.7	38.8	39.8	100.0
6000–15,000	7.6	13.1	36.0	43.3	100.0
15,000–25,000	5.5	11.9	34.5	48.1	100.0
> 25,000	4.1	10.5	31.6	53.8	100.0

In some cases, the sampling method used to collect the data provides a guideline as to how the percentages should be computed. When a sample is drawn and then cross-classified according to the row and column variables, overall percentages should be reported, since the total sample size is predetermined. In the example discussed above, 901 individuals were sampled and then cross-classified according to their income and job satisfaction; thus, overall percentages are meaningful.

When a sample is drawn by using predetermined sample sizes for the rows (or columns), the row (or column) percentages should be reported. For example, suppose that a respiratory problem is studied by first finding 50 smokers and 50 nonsmokers and then determining whether or not each individual has the problem, with the following results:

| | Respiratory Problem? | | Row |
	Yes	No	Total
Smokers	25	25	50
Nonsmokers	5	45	50
Column Total	30	70	100

In this example, the row totals of smokers and nonsmokers were fixed by the design of the study; thus row percentages are meaningful. Statements in this situation can be made only relative to the smokers or nonsmokers. It would be misleading to conclude from this table that the smokers account for 25/30 or 83% of the people with a respiratory problem, because the proportion of the smokers in this sample does not reflect the proportion of the smokers in the population. However, it would be meaningful to say that 25/50 or 50% of the smokers have a respiratory problem, while only 5/50 or 10% of the nonsmokers do.

Simpson's Paradox.   Often each item in the sample can be cross-classified using more than two categorical variables, but to find association between two particular variables, a two-way table is made by aggregating the counts on other variables. This can lead to misleading conclusions, especially if the data are observational and the effects of aggregated variables are not controlled. These are the **lurking variables** which confound the association between displayed variables.

A classic example of this is provided by the sex-bias study in graduate admissions at the University of California, Berkeley.[13] The summary statistics for the number admitted and the number denied broken down by the gender are given in Table 4.10.

Table 4.10 Aggregate Totals of Men and Women Admitted or Denied Admission

	Admitted	Denied	Total	% Admitted
Men	3738	4704	8442	44.3
Women	1494	2827	4321	34.6

These numbers strongly suggest bias against women. However, if the data are further broken down by the major to which the admission was sought then a completely different picture emerges. Table 4.11 gives the number of men and women who applied to the six largest majors (which account for over one-third of the total number of applicants) and the corresponding admission rates. This table shows that the admission rates for men and women are roughly equal for majors B through F; for major A the admission rate for women is actually higher. Yet, the overall admission rate for women is much lower. The explanation lies in the fact that far fewer women than men apply to majors A and B, which have the highest admission rates. Thus the choice of major con-

---

[13] P. J. Bickel, E. A. Hammel, and J. W. O'Connell (1975), "Sex bias in graduate admissions: Data from Berkeley," *Science*, **187**, pp. 398–404, as quoted in D. Freedman, R. Pisani, R. Purves, and A. Adhikari (1991), *Statistics*, 2d ed., New York: Norton, p. 17.

founds the results. Aggregating the data over the choice of major results in a misleading conclusion. This phenomenon is known as **Simpson's paradox**.

Table 4.11 Men and Women Applicants and Admission Rates for Six Largest Majors at the University of California, Berkeley in Fall 1973

Major	Men		Women		Total	
	No. of Applicants	Percent Admitted	No. of Applicants	Percent Admitted	No. of Applicants	Percent Admitted
A	825	62	108	82	933	64
B	560	63	25	68	585	67
C	325	37	593	34	918	35
D	417	33	375	35	792	34
E	191	28	393	24	584	25
F	373	6	341	7	714	6
Total	2691	44	1835	30	4526	39

How can we make a fair comparison between the admission rates of men and women? One way to do this is to calculate the overall admission rates for men and women, assuming that the *same* number of men and women apply to each major but experience the observed gender specific admission rates shown in Table 4.11. Let us use, for the common number of applicants, the total number of applicants to each major as shown in Table 4.11. The resulting overall admission rates are called **adjusted (standardized) rates**. They are as follows:

Men:

$$\frac{0.62 \times 933 + 0.63 \times 585 + 0.37 \times 918 + 0.33 \times 792 + 0.28 \times 584 + 0.06 \times 714}{4526} = 39\%,$$

Women:

$$\frac{0.82 \times 933 + 0.68 \times 585 + 0.34 \times 918 + 0.35 \times 792 + 0.24 \times 584 + 0.07 \times 714}{4526} = 43\%.$$

We see that the adjusted admission rate is higher for women than for men, suggesting that bias if any is in favor of women.

4.4.2 Summarizing Bivariate Numerical Data

Scatter Plot.   When both x and y are numerical variables, the first step in analyzing their relationship is to plot the data points (x_i, y_i). This plot is called a **scatter plot**. A scatter plot helps to visualize the relationship between x and y (e.g., a straight line or a curve or a random scatter indicating no relationship).

Example 4.11   (Cardiac Output Data: Scatter Plot)

A medical researcher wanted to compare two different methods, A and B, for measuring cardiac output. Method A is the "gold standard" but is invasive (involves inserting a catheter into the main heart artery). Method B is less accurate but is noninvasive. The researcher wanted to find out how well the two methods correlate and whether method B can be calibrated with respect to method A. For this purpose, cardiac outputs of 26 subjects were measured by the two methods. The data are given in Table 4.12.[14] The first step in the analysis is to make a scatter plot, which is shown in Figure 4.13. The appearance of this plot indicates a fairly strong linear relationship between the two methods of measurement of cardiac output, suggesting that it should be possible to calibrate method B with respect to method A.   ◆

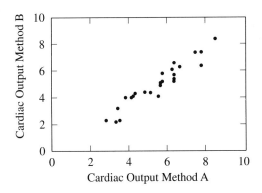

Figure 4.13   Scatter Plot of Two Measurements of Cardiac Output

Table 4.12 Cardiac Output (liters/min.) Measured by Two Methods

No.	Method A (x_i)	Method B (y_i)	No.	Method A (x_i)	Method B (y_i)
1	6.3	5.2	14	7.7	7.4
2	6.3	6.6	15	7.4	7.4
3	3.5	2.3	16	5.6	4.9
4	5.1	4.4	17	6.3	5.4
5	5.5	4.1	18	8.4	8.4
6	7.7	6.4	19	5.6	5.1
7	6.3	5.7	20	4.8	4.4
8	2.8	2.3	21	4.3	4.3
9	3.4	3.2	22	4.2	4.1
10	5.7	5.2	23	3.3	2.2
11	5.6	4.9	24	3.8	4.0
12	6.2	6.1	25	5.7	5.8
13	6.6	6.3	26	4.1	4.0

Sometimes the sampling units on which bivariate measurements are made belong to different groups. In other words, three variables are measured on each sampling

[14] Data courtesy of Dr. James Hasty, Vascular Care Technology, Inc., Glenview, IL.

unit (x, y, z), where x and y are numerical variables and z is a categorical (grouping) variable. For example, for employees of a company define three variables: x = years of experience, y = salary, and z = department. We could make separate scatter plots for similarly qualified employees of different departments such as sales, purchase, marketing, manufacturing, etc. However, it may be more informative to make a single scatter plot in which the data points for different departments are indicated by different symbols. Then it is easier to visualize how the departments differ in their salary vs. experience relationships. This is called a **labeled scatter plot**.

EXAMPLE 4.12

Table 4.13 gives life expectancies of white males and females and black males and females for the years 1920–1990 on a decennial basis.[15] Figure 4.14 shows a labeled run chart for the four demographic groups. We see that the greatest gains have been made by black females; after starting out with the lowest life expectancy, they have achieved a near parity with white females, who have had the highest life expectancy over the entire time period.   ◆

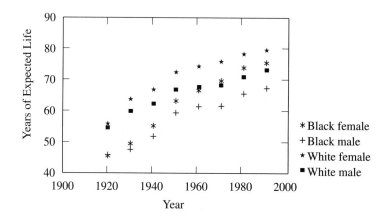

Figure 4.14   Life Expectancies of White and Black Males and Females

Table 4.13 Years of Life Expected at Birth

Year	White Male	White Female	Black Male	Black Female
1920	54.4	55.6	45.5	45.2
1930	59.7	63.5	47.3	49.2
1940	62.1	66.6	51.5	54.9
1950	66.5	72.2	59.1	62.9
1960	67.4	74.1	61.1	66.3
1970	68.0	75.6	61.3	69.4
1980	70.7	78.1	65.3	73.6
1990	72.9	79.4	67.0	75.2

---

[15] *The World Almanac and Book of Facts* (1994), Mahwah, NJ: Funk & Wagnalls Corporation, p. 972.

Correlation Coefficient.   Often it is informative to give a simple numerical summary statistic which measures the strength of a *linear* relationship between x and y. The **sample correlation coefficient** measures how well a straight line fits the points (x_i, y_i) from n paired observations.[16] The sample correlation coefficient between x and y, denoted by r_{xy} or simply by r, is the sample analog of the population correlation coefficient ρ defined in Chapter 2:

$$r = \frac{s_{xy}}{s_x s_y} \tag{4.8}$$

where

$$s_{xy} = \frac{1}{n-1} \sum_{i=1}^{n} (x_i - \bar{x})(y_i - \bar{y}) = \frac{1}{n-1} \left[\sum_{i=1}^{n} x_i y_i - n\bar{x}\bar{y} \right]$$

is the **sample covariance** between x and y, and s_x and s_y are the sample standard deviations of x and y, respectively. It is useful to note that r is the average of the products of the standardized scores (z-scores) of the x_i and y_i by writing it as follows:

$$r = \frac{1}{n-1} \sum_{i=1}^{n} \left(\frac{x_i - \bar{x}}{s_x} \right) \left(\frac{y_i - \bar{y}}{s_y} \right).$$

The sample correlation coefficient r has properties similar to those of the population correlation coefficient ρ. In particular, r is a unitless quantity and takes values between -1 and $+1$. These extreme values are attained if and only if the points (x_i, y_i) fall *exactly* on a straight line[17] ($r = -1$ for a line with a negative slope and $r = +1$ for a line with a positive slope). The value of r is negative if the scatter plot has a negative slope, positive if the scatter plot has a positive slope, and is close to zero if the scatter plot exhibits purely random noise. Figure 4.15 shows different scatter plots and the corresponding r's. Inspection of these plots should give you an idea of the extent of linear relationship represented by different values of r.

The value of r can also be close to zero if the scatter plot is curved. This is not surprising, since r measures the strength only of linear relationship. In this case, r is not a suitable measure of association. Figure 4.16(a) illustrates this case. Figures 4.16(b), (c), and (d) illustrate additional cases where r is close to zero despite linear relationships between x and y. In (b), the linear relationship is marred by two outliers. In (c) and (d) the data form two clusters, each exhibiting a separate linear relationship. These figures demonstrate the importance of always plotting the data first. As a general rule, check outliers carefully for their validity before including them in the analysis. If the data form clusters, then the reason for the clusters should be investigated, and possibly the data should be analyzed separately for each cluster.

---

[16] There are other correlation coefficients that measure the strength of a monotone (increasing or decreasing) but not necessarily linear relationship between two variables; see Chapter 14.

[17] However, r is undefined if the points fall exactly on a horizontal line (i.e., if y_i's are constant) or on a vertical line (i.e., if x_i's are constant).

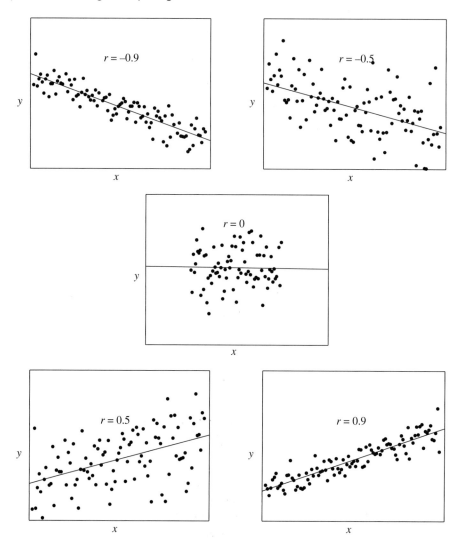

Figure 4.15   Scatter Plots with Different Values of Correlation Coefficient r

Another point to keep in mind is that if the data on (x, y) are averaged over subsets of the sample, then the correlation coefficient is usually larger than the correlation coefficient for the raw data. The reason is that averaging smooths out variations in the raw data. For example, the daily closes of the S & P 500 stock index and the S & P bond index exhibit less correlation than the monthly averages of the daily closes of these indexes. Therefore prediction of one index from the other is not as reliable as one would think based on the correlation between the monthly averages. As another example, consider the 1970 draft lottery of Example 3.5.[18]   The scatter plot of draft

[18] S. E. Fienberg (1971), "Randomization and social affairs: The 1970 draft lottery," *Science*, **171**, pp. 255–261.

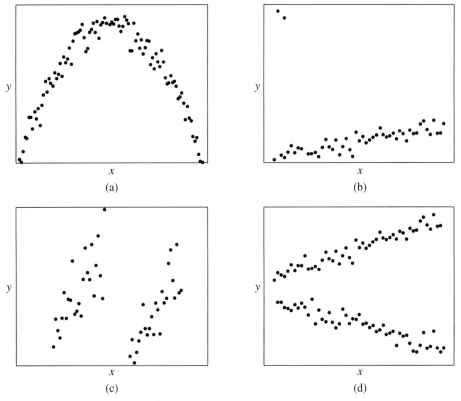

Figure 4.16 Scatter Plots with $r = 0$: (a) $r = 0$ due to curved relationship;
(b) $r = 0$ due to outliers; (c) $r = 0$ due to two parallel linear trends; (d) $r = 0$
due to two different linear trends

selection number (1 to 366) vs. birth date (1 to 366) is shown in Figure 4.17(a). This
scatter plot looks quite random; the correlation coefficient between these two variables
is $r = -0.226$. Now consider these same data, but averaged over each month. The
averaged data are given in Table 4.14 and are plotted in Figure 4.17(b). Notice that this
scatter plot appears far more linear and has a correlation coefficient of -0.866.

Table 4.14 Average Lottery Number for Each Birth Month for 1970 Draft
Lottery

Month	Avg. Lottery Number	Month	Avg. Lottery Number
January	201.2	July	181.5
February	203.0	August	173.5
March	225.8	September	157.3
April	203.7	October	182.5
May	208.0	November	148.7
June	195.7	December	121.5

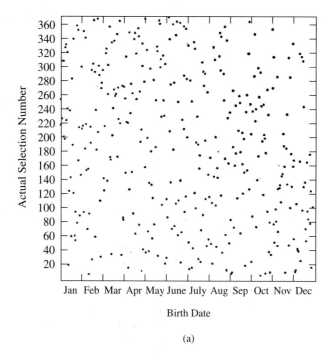

(a)

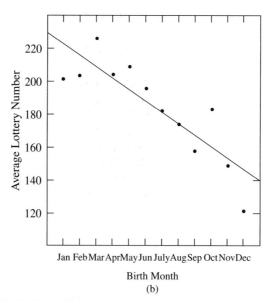

Birth Month
(b)

Figure 4.17   (a) Scatter Plot of Actual Selection Number vs. Birth Date; (b) Scatter Plot of Average Lottery Number vs. Birth Month (*Source*: S. E. Fienberg (1971), "Randomization and social affairs: The 1970 draft lottery," *Science*, **171**, pp. 255–261)

EXAMPLE 4.13   (CARDIAC OUTPUT DATA: CORRELATION COEFFICIENT)

For the cardiac output data in Table 4.12 we have

$$\bar{x} = 5.469, \bar{y} = 5.015, s_x = 1.486, s_y = 1.582.$$

To calculate the correlation coefficient between x and y we next calculate

$$s_{xy} = \frac{1}{26-1}\{(6.3-5.469)(5.2-5.015) + \cdots + (4.1-5.469)(4.0-5.015)\} = 2.238.$$

Therefore

$$r = \frac{2.238}{(1.486)(1.582)} = 0.952.$$

This value of r suggests a high degree of positive linear association between the two methods of measurement of cardiac output, agreeing with the impression obtained from the scatter plot in Figure 4.13. ◆

Correlation and Causation.   High correlation is commonly mistaken for a cause and effect relationship. Such a conclusion may not be valid in observational studies, where the variables are not controlled. Any correlation between x and y could occur because these two variables are both affected by a lurking variable that is not controlled and whose existence may not be recognized. Therefore we can only claim *association* in these cases, unless there is convincing nonstatistical justification for *causation*.

As an example,[19] a high fat diet is found to be a risk factor for breast and colon cancer in several epidemiological studies. Does it mean that it is the cause of these cancers? The evidence is far from clear. Usually high fat diets are found in richer, developed countries which also have other dietary, lifestyle, and environmental differences (e.g., higher pollution levels). These could be the lurking variables that explain the correlation between a high fat diet and the incidence of these cancers. Similar explanations can be given for association that some observational studies have found between coffee drinking and heart disease.

A common lurking variable in many studies is the time order. The time effects such as aging, wear, learning, etc. can affect many variables simultaneously. For example, as people age, their health problems often increase as well as their accumulated wealth. But from this one cannot conclude that health affects wealth or vice versa.

In extreme cases two variables may be completely unrelated (i.e., there are not even plausible lurking variables) and still have a high spurious correlation. For example, significant correlation has been found between cycles of sunspot activity and economic cycles. Explanations based on sunspot cycles affecting weather patterns and hence agricultural production and resulting economic cycles would appear rather far-fetched.

Straight Line Regression.   It is convenient to summarize the relationship between two numerical variables, x and y, by an equation. Such an equation can be used for a

---

[19] D. Freedman, R. Pisani, R. Purves, and A. Adhikari (1991), *Statistics*, 2nd ed., New York: W. W. Norton, pp. 143–144.

variety of purposes, e.g., to predict or interpolate y for given x. The simplest equation is that of a straight line.

A common method for fitting a straight line is the **least squares method**. This method will be developed in detail in Chapter 10. Here we present only the final equation of the least squares line:

$$\frac{y - \bar{y}}{s_y} = r \left[\frac{x - \bar{x}}{s_x} \right]. \tag{4.9}$$

This equation predicts that if the x value is one standard deviation (s_x) away from $\bar{x}$, then the corresponding y value will be r standard deviations (rs_y) away from $\bar{y}$. The direction of the departure of y from $\bar{y}$ is determined by the sign of the correlation coefficient r (i.e., $y - \bar{y}$ has the same sign as $x - \bar{x}$ if $r > 0$ and opposite sign if $r < 0$). Thus the "effect" of change in x on y is modulated by a factor of r when both are measured on the standardized scale.

Equation (4.9) can be written in the common form of a straight line equation as follows:

$$y = a + bx \quad \text{where} \quad b = r\frac{s_y}{s_x} \quad \text{and} \quad a = \bar{y} - b\bar{x}. \tag{4.10}$$

In this equation a is the intercept and b is the slope of the straight line.

EXAMPLE 4.14   (CARDIAC OUTPUT DATA: STRAIGHT LINE FIT)

A least squares straight line can be fitted to the scatter plot in Figure 4.13 as follows. Substitute in equation (4.10) from the calculations made in Example 4.13 to obtain

$$b = r\frac{s_y}{s_x} = 0.952 \times \frac{1.582}{1.486} = 1.014$$

and

$$a = \bar{y} - b\bar{x} = 5.015 - 1.014 \times 5.469 = -0.528.$$

Therefore the equation of the least squares straight line is

$$y = -0.528 + 1.014x.$$

◆

Regression Toward the Mean.   "Regression" means falling back. The use of this word in the context of fitting equations to data comes from a phenomenon called **regression toward the mean** discovered by two great British statisticians, Sir Francis Galton (1822–1911) and Karl Pearson (1857–1936). They found that many hereditary traits tend to fall back toward the mean in successive generations, higher values being followed by lower, and vice versa. This is best illustrated by Galton's data on the heights of 1078 pairs of fathers and sons. Denote a father's height by x and a son's height by y. The following are the summary statistics for these data:[20]

$$\bar{x} \simeq 68", \bar{y} \simeq 69", s_x \simeq 2.7", s_y \simeq 2.7", r \simeq 0.5.$$

---

[20] This discussion is taken from D. Freedman, R. Pisani, R. Purves, and A. Adhikari (1991), *Statistics*, 2nd ed., New York: Norton, pp. 160–163.

Based on these statistics, it is natural to think that the line $y = x + 1$ would give good predictions, i.e., on the average, a son would be taller than his father by 1 inch. However, from (4.9) we find that the least squares line is

$$y - 69 = 0.5(x - 68).$$

From this equation we find that the sons of 72 inch tall fathers are only 71 inches tall on the average, while the sons of 64 inch tall fathers are 67 inches tall on the average. Thus, the sons of taller fathers are shorter than expected, while the sons of shorter fathers are taller than expected. This is the **regression effect**.

The raw data with the straight lines $y = x + 1$ (dashed) and the least squares straight line (solid) are shown in Figure 4.18. As you can see, the dashed straight line overestimates the heights of sons of taller fathers and understimates the heights of sons of shorter fathers. The solid line is closer to target in the sense that for each thin strip of x values (father heights) there are roughly an equal number of points (son heights) above and below it.

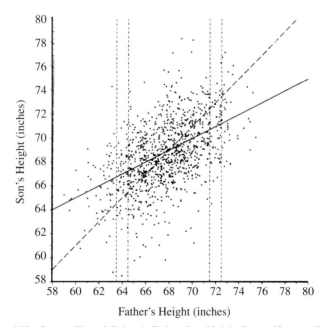

Figure 4.18 Scatter Plot of Galton's Father–Son Height Data. (*Source*: D. Freedman et al. (1991), *Statistics*, 2nd ed., New York: Norton, pp. 160–163)

The same phenomenon occurs in pretest posttest situations. Subjects who do better than expected on the pretest tend to do not so well on the posttest, and vice versa. Therefore one should be cautious in attributing changes from the pretest to posttest necessarily to any interventions. Misleading conclusions of this kind are the result of regression toward the mean, and the resulting fallacy is called the **regression fallacy**. An example is provided by an incident cited in an article in the *Discover* magazine[21] on two

---

[21] K. McKean (1985), "Decisions," *Discover*, June 1985, pp. 22–31.

eminent psychologists, Daniel Kahneman and Amos Tversky. A flight instructor in the Israeli air force claimed to Kahneman that when pilots are praised for well-executed maneuvers, invariably they do worse on the next maneuver. On the other hand, if they are criticized for poorly executed maneuvers, by and large they improve. Kahneman explained that this is just the regression toward the mean phenomenon. The conclusion that "praise spoils, criticism improves" is unwarranted in this case.

4.5   *SUMMARIZING TIME-SERIES DATA

Data obtained at successive time points for the same sampling unit(s) are referred to as **time-series data**. Such data arise in various applications, e.g., circadian-rhythm type biological data, hourly traffic data, and monthly or quarterly economic data. As noted in the discussion of the run chart in Section 4.3.4, standard data summary techniques are not useful for time-series data because they do not capture the time trends. In this section we introduce a few basic techniques for this purpose.

A time series typically consists of the following components.

1. **Stable Component:** This represents an underlying constant component.
2. **Trend Component:** This represents an overall or persistent long-term pattern. A trend could be linear, quadratic, or some other nonlinear type.
3. **Seasonal Component:** This represents short-term periodic fluctuations, e.g., hourly, daily, weekly, monthly, or quarterly.
4. **Random Component:** This represents random fluctuations present in any statistical data.

In economic data there may be an additional **cyclic component**, representing long-term aperiodic fluctuations (economic cycles).

We denote a univariate time series by $\{x_t, t = 1, 2, \ldots, T\}$, where t is the time index and T is the length of the time period for which the data are available. The first step in the analysis is always to plot the data vs. time to visually examine the trends and patterns. This is called a **time-series plot**. If the time variable is just the sequential number of each observation instead of a calendar time (e.g, week or month), then the plot is called a **run chart**, which is discussed in Section 4.3.4.

EXAMPLE 4.15   (DOMESTIC CAR SALES: TIME-SERIES PLOT)

Table 4.15 gives the domestic retail car sales in the U.S.[22] during 1980–1995 (expressed in millions of units sold, rounded to the third decimal place). The time-series plot for this data set is shown in Figure 4.19. From the plot we see that these data do not show any persistent trend or cyclic variations. ◆

4.5.1 Data Smoothing and Forecasting Techniques

Two types of *sequences* of averages are often computed for time-series data. They are called (i) moving averages and (ii) exponentially weighted moving averages. These

---

[22] *Source: The World Almanac and Book of Facts 1997*, World Almanac Books, Mahwah, NJ, p. 246.

Table 4.15 Domestic Retail Car Sales
(in Millions of Units Sold)
in the U.S., 1980–1995

Year	Sales	Year	Sales
1980	6.581	1988	7.526
1981	6.208	1989	7.073
1982	5.759	1990	6.879
1983	6.795	1991	6.137
1984	7.951	1992	6.277
1985	8.205	1993	6.742
1986	8.215	1994	7.255
1987	7.081	1995	7.129

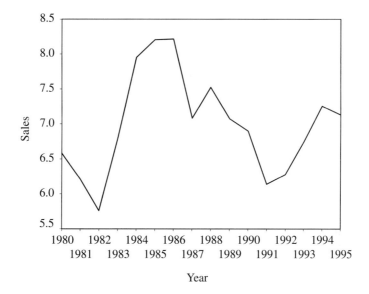

Figure 4.19   Time-Series Plot for Domestic Car Sales Data

averages are used to smooth out the local variations in the data and to make forecasts. However, they should be used only when the mean of the time-series is constant or varies slowly, i.e., there are no trend or seasonal components. Such a time series is called **stationary**. Trends in the data can be modeled using regression techniques; e.g., linear trend can be modeled by fitting a straight line, as discussed in Section 4.4.2, to the time-series plot. To model seasonality and dependence between successive observations, more advanced techniques are needed, for which we refer the reader to the book by Box and Jenkins (1976).[23]

---

[23] G. E. P. Box and G. M. Jenkins (1976), *Time Series analysis: Forecasting and Control*, San Francisco: Holden-Day.

Moving Averages.   A **moving average (MA)** is the average of a set of successive data values (called the **window**); to calculate a sequence of moving averages the window is shifted to the right by one observation for each new moving average. The window size, denoted by w, is assumed to be fixed. Thus, the moving average at time t is given by

$$\text{MA}_t = \frac{x_{t-w+1} + \ldots + x_t}{w} \quad \text{for } t = w, w+1, \ldots, T. \tag{4.11}$$

For the first $w - 1$ observations, the moving average either is not computed or may be computed by just averaging the previous observations:

$$\text{MA}_t = \frac{x_1 + \ldots + x_t}{t} \quad \text{for } t = 1, 2, \ldots, w-1.$$

The larger the window size w, the greater is the extent of data smoothing but the less sensitive then is the moving average to local trends. Typically, a window size of three or four time periods is chosen. For quarterly data, a window size of four is convenient to use.

Aside from data smoothing, an important use of the moving average is as a forecast of the next observation. At time $t - 1$, the one-period-ahead **MA forecast** of x_t is given by $\hat{x}_t = \text{MA}_{t-1}$. The corresponding **forecast error** equals

$$e_t = x_t - \hat{x}_t = x_t - \text{MA}_{t-1} \quad (t = 2, \ldots, T).$$

Note that there is no forecast available for x_1. Various measures can be used to judge how well the time-series is smoothed or forecasted by the moving average. We use the **mean absolute percent error (MAPE)**, defined as

$$\text{MAPE} = \left(\frac{1}{T-1} \sum_{t=2}^{T} \left| \frac{e_t}{y_t} \right| \right) \times 100\%. \tag{4.12}$$

EXAMPLE 4.16   (DOMESTIC CAR SALES: MOVING AVERAGE)

For the data in Table 4.15, compute the moving averages using a window size of three, the associated forecast errors, and the mean absolute percent error.

Table 4.16 summarizes all calculations, which were done using MINITAB. For the first two moving averages, we used

$$\text{MA}_1 = x_1 = 6.581 \text{ and MA}_2 = \frac{x_1 + x_2}{2} = \frac{6.581 + 6.209}{2} = 6.395.$$

The subsequent moving averages are computed using (4.11). For example,

$$\text{MA}_3 = \frac{x_1 + x_2 + x_3}{3} = \frac{6.581 + 6.209 + 5.759}{3} = 6.183$$

and

$$\text{MA}_4 = \frac{x_2 + x_3 + x_4}{3} = \frac{6.209 + 5.759 + 6/795}{3} = 6.254.$$

Figure 4.20 shows a time-series plot of the raw data and the moving-average smoothed data.

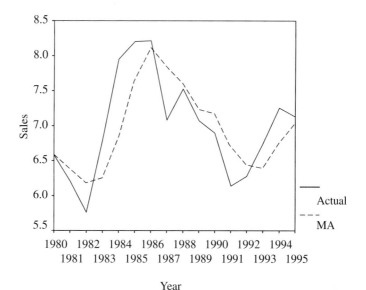

Figure 4.20   Time-Series Plot of Raw and MA Smoothed Domestic Car Sales Data

Table 4.16 Moving Averages and Forecast Errors for Domestic Retail Car Sales Data

Year	Sales	Moving Average	Forecast Error	Year	Sales	Moving Average	Forecast Error
1980	6.581	6.581	—	1988	7.526	7.607	−0.308
1981	6.209	6.395	−0.372	1989	7.073	7.227	−0.534
1982	5.759	6.183	−0.636	1990	6.897	7.165	−0.330
1983	6.795	6.254	0.612	1991	6.137	6.702	−1.028
1984	7.951	6.835	1.697	1992	6.277	6.437	−0.425
1985	8.205	7.650	1.370	1993	6.742	6.385	0.305
1986	8.215	8.124	0.565	1994	7.255	6.758	0.870
1987	7.081	7.834	−1.043	1995	7.129	7.042	0.371

The first four forecast errors are

$$e_2 = x_2 - \text{MA}_1 = 6.209 - 6.581 = -0.372, \quad e_3 = x_3 - \text{MA}_2 = 5.759 - 6.395 = -0.636$$

$$e_4 = x_4 - \text{MA}_3 = 6.795 - 6.183 = 0.612, \quad e_5 = x_5 - \text{MA}_4 = 7.591 - 6.254 = 1.697.$$

The MAPE is computed to be

$$\text{MAPE} = \left(\frac{1}{15} \left[\frac{0.372}{6.209} + \frac{0.636}{5.759} + \ldots + \frac{0.371}{7.129} \right] \right) \times 100\% = 9.824\%.$$

◆

Exponentially Weighted Moving Averages.   While the moving average drops old data values, the **exponentially weighted moving average (EWMA)** (also called **expo-**

nential smoothing) takes all previous data values into account but weights them differentially, putting less weight on old data and more weight on recent data.

The EWMA at time t is defined as

$$\text{EWMA}_t = wx_t + (1 - w)\text{EWMA}_{t-1} \tag{4.13}$$

where $0 < w < 1$ is a **smoothing constant** that determines the rate at which the weights on previous data values decrease. The larger the value of the smoothing constant w, the greater the weight put on the most current observation and the less the weight put on the past data.

Notice that this definition of EWMA_t is recursive; i.e., EWMA_t is defined in terms of EWMA_{t-1}. It is a weighted average of the current observation x_t and EWMA_{t-1}, which is a summary of the past data. To initialize the calculation we need the value of EWMA_0, which may be taken to be x_1 or some suitable constant.

To see that EWMA_t is a weight average of all past data with decreasing weights, write

$$\text{EWMA}_t = wx_t + (1 - w)\text{EWMA}_{t-1}$$
$$= wx_t + (1 - w)[wx_{t-1} + (1 - w)\text{EWMA}_{t-2}]$$
$$= w[x_t + (1 - w)x_{t-1}] + (1 - w)^2[wx_{t-2} + (1 - w)\text{EWMA}_{t-3}]$$
$$\vdots$$
$$= w[x_t + (1 - w)x_{t-1} + (1 - w)^2 x_{t-2} +$$
$$\ldots + (1 - w)^{t-1}x_1] + (1 - w)^t\text{EWMA}_0.$$

Notice that the weights decrease geometrically as the data values get older. The weights can be shown to sum to 1. Typically w is chosen between 0.2 and 0.3. For example, if $w = 0.3$, then for $t = 4$ we have

$$\text{EWMA}_4 = 0.3x_4 + 0.21x_3 + 0.147x_2 + 0.1029x_1 + 0.2401\text{EWMA}_0.$$

At time $t - 1$, the one-period ahead **EWMA forecast** of x_t is given by $\hat{x}_t = \text{EWMA}_{t-1}$. The corresponding **forecast error** equals

$$e_t = x_t - \hat{x}_t = x_t - \text{EWMA}_{t-1}.$$

Then equation (4.13) for EWMA_t can be written as

$$\text{EWMA}_t = w(x_t - \text{EWMA}_{t-1}) + \text{EWMA}_{t-1} = we_t + \text{EWMA}_{t-1}.$$

This gives an alternative explanation of $\text{EWMA}_t = \hat{x}_{t+1}$ as the previous period's forecast plus a fraction w times that period's forecast error. If the forecast error is positive, i.e., if the forecast underestimated the actual data value, then the next period's forecast is adjusted upward by a fraction of the forecast error. Similarly, if the forecast overestimated the actual data value, then the next period's forecast is adjusted downward by a fraction of the forecast error.

EXAMPLE 4.17   (DOMESTIC CAR SALES: EXPONENTIALLY WEIGHTED MOVING AVERAGE)

For the data in Table 4.15 compute EWMA with smoothing coefficient $w = 0.2$, the associated forecast errors, and the mean absolute percent error.

Table 4.17 summarizes all calculations, which were done using MINITAB. For illustration purposes we show the calculation of the first few EWMA values. We begin with $\text{EWMA}_0 = \text{EWMA}_1 = x_1 = 6.581$. Then

$$\text{EWMA}_2 = 0.2x_2 + 0.8\text{EWMA}_1 = (0.2)(6.209) + (0.8)(6.581) = 6.507$$

$$\text{EWMA}_3 = 0.2x_3 + 0.8\text{EWMA}_2 = (0.2)(5.759) + (0.8)(6.507) = 6.357.$$

etc.

Figure 4.21 shows a time-series plot of the raw data and the EWMA smoothed data.

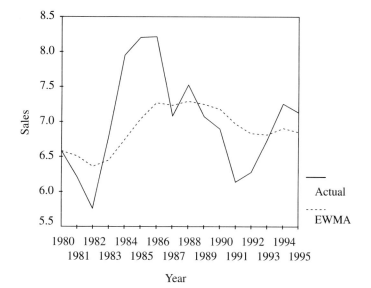

Figure 4.21   Time-Series Plot of Raw and EWMA Smoothed Domestic Car Sales Data

The first four forecast errors are

$$e_2 = x_2 - \text{EWMA}_1 = 6.209 - 6.581 = -0.372, \quad e_3 = x_3 - \text{EWMA}_2 = 5.759 - 6.507 = -0.748$$

$$e_4 = x_4 - \text{EWMA}_3 = 6.795 - 6.357 = 0.438, \quad e_5 = x_5 - \text{EWMA}_4 = 7.951 - 6.445 = 1.506.$$

The MAPE is computed to be

$$\text{MAPE} = \left(\frac{1}{15} \left[\frac{0.372}{6.209} + \frac{0.748}{5.759} + \cdots + \frac{0.227}{7.129} \right] \right) \times 100 = 8.066\%.$$

Note that this is less than the MAPE $= 9.824\%$ for moving averages computed in Example 4.16. Generally, EWMA gives more accurate forecasts than does the moving average method.   ◆

Table 4.17 Exponentially Weighted Moving Averages and Forecast Errors for Domestic Retail Car Sales Data

Year	Sales	EWMA	Forecast Error	Year	Sales	EWMA	Forecast Error
1980	6.581	6.581	—	1988	7.526	7.293	0.291
1981	6.209	6.507	−0.372	1989	7.073	7.249	−0.220
1982	5.759	6.357	−0.748	1990	6.897	7.179	−0.352
1983	6.795	6.445	0.438	1991	6.137	6.970	−1.042
1984	7.951	6.746	1.506	1992	6.277	6.832	−0.693
1985	8.205	7.038	1.459	1993	6.742	6.814	−0.090
1986	8.215	7.273	1.177	1994	7.255	6.902	0.441
1987	7.081	7.235	−0.192	1995	7.129	6.947	0.227

4.5.2 Autocorrelation Coefficients

In Section 4.4.2, we learned about the correlation coefficient as a measure of dependence for a paired set of data. For time-series data we need a similar measure for observations separated by specified time periods, called the **lag**. The first order **autocorrelation coefficient** or the **serial correlation coefficient** between the observations with lag $= 1$ is of particular interest. In analogy with formula (4.8) for the ordinary correlation coefficient, it is given by

$$r_1 = \frac{\sum_{t=2}^{T}(x_{t-1} - \bar{x})(x_t - \bar{x})}{\sum_{t=1}^{T}(x_t - \bar{x})^2}. \tag{4.14}$$

where $\bar{x}$ is the sample mean of all T observations. Note that the above formula involves two approximations. First, the numerator is the sum of $T - 1$ terms, while the denominator is the sum of T terms. Thus their ratio should be multiplied by the factor $\left(\frac{T}{T-1}\right)$ to obtain a ratio of the corresponding averages. However, this factor is approximately 1 for large T and hence is ignored. Second, $\bar{x}$ is used as if it were the sample mean of the first $T - 1$ as well as the last $T - 1$ observations in computing the numerator.

The above formula can be generalized to compute the kth-order autocorrelation coefficient:

$$r_k = \frac{\sum_{t=k+1}^{T}(x_{t-k} - \bar{x})(x_t - \bar{x})}{\sum_{t=1}^{T}(x_t - \bar{x})^2}.$$

The different order autocorrelation coefficients are useful in assessing the dependence structure of the time series.

EXAMPLE 4.18   (DOMESTIC CAR SALES: AUTOCORRELATION COEFFICIENTS)

Using MINITAB the first three autocorrelation coefficients for the data in Table 4.15 are calculated to be

$$r_1 = 0.633, r_2 = 0.142, \text{ and } r_3 = -0.302.$$

These coefficients indicate that sales in successive years are modestly positively correlated, but removed two years apart they are nearly uncorrelated, and removed three years apart they are in fact slightly negatively correlated.   ◆

4.6   CHAPTER SUMMARY

This chapter discusses ways to summarize different types of data. **Variables** that the data are collected on can be classified as either **categorical** or **numerical**. A categorical variable is either **nominal**, if the categories represent distinct labels, or **ordinal**, if the categories can be ordered. A numerical variable is either **discrete**, taking a finite collection of values, or **continuous**, taking all values (at least in principle) in an interval of real numbers.

Categorical data can be summarized in a **frequency table** showing the frequency or count and the relative frequency (percent or proportion) of the occurrence of each value of the categorical variable. A **bar chart** is a graphical summary in which the heights of bars represent the proportions or counts in different categories. A **Pareto chart** is a bar chart with the categories ordered from the most to the least frequent. It is used in quality control applications to identify major causes of defects.

The main summary statistics for numerical data are measures of center and dispersion (or spread). The **mean** and **median** are the two common measures of center. The mean is appropriate for symmetrically distributed data that are free of **outliers**. The median is preferred for **skewed** data or data contaminated by outliers. The sample standard deviation, s, is a suitable measure of dispersion for symmetrically distributed data. For skewed data, the dispersion can be described by the **five number summary**, consisting of the minimum and maximum data values and the three **quartiles** that divide the distribution into four equal parts.

A **histogram** and a **stem and leaf plot** are graphical summaries of numerical data which are useful for representing the shape of the distribution. A **box plot** is obtained from the five number summary; it gives a quick visual assessment of the extent of symmetry of the data and identifies any outliers. It is also useful for visually comparing two or more batches of data. A **normal plot** is a graphical technique for assessing the normality of data. When the data are normally distributed, this plot is roughly linear.

Multivariate data result when two or more variables are measured on each sampling unit. **Bivariate** categorical data are summarized by a **two-way table** of frequencies or relative frequencies. **Simpson's paradox** occurs when the relationship between two categorical variables is in the same direction for each level of a third variable, but is reversed when the data are aggregated over the levels of that variable. If this variable is not recognized or is suppressed when reporting the data (therefore referred to as a **lurking variable**), misleading conclusions can result.

Bivariate numerical data on two variables, x and y, are graphically summarized by a **scatter plot** of the y vs. the x values. The sample **correlation coefficient** r measures the strength of a linear relationship between x and y. The closer r is to -1 or $+1$, the more tightly the scatter plot approximates a straight line with a negative or a positive slope, respectively. An r close to zero indicates either no relationship, a nonlinear relationship, or the more complex situations shown in Figure 4.16. It is important to remember that correlation does not imply causation.

A **regression line** fitted to a scatter plot predicts that if x is one standard deviation, s_x, from its mean, $\bar{x}$, then the corresponding y value will be r standard deviations, rs_y, from $\bar{y}$. This modulation of the effect of change in x on y causes the **regression toward the mean** phenomenon.

A **time-series** typically consists of four components: (1) stable, (2) trend, (3) seasonal, and (4) random. If a time-series does not have a significant trend or a seasonal component, i.e., if the mean of the time-series is constant or varies slowly, then the **moving average (MA)** or the **exponentially weighted moving average (EWMA)** can be used to smooth the series and forecast future values. **Autocorrelation coefficients** are used to summarize the dependence structure of the time-series.

■ EXERCISES

Section 4.1

4.1   For the following variables, indicate whether the data are best considered categorical (nominal or ordinal) or numerical (discrete or continuous).

(a) Grade of meat: prime, choice, good.

(b) Type of house: split-level, ranch, colonial, other.

(c) Income.

(d) Highest political office held by a candidate.

4.2   Information collected to compare new car models includes engine size in liters, number of cylinders, size of car (subcompact, compact, mid size, full size), type of transmission (automatic, lockup, or manual), gas guzzler tax (yes/no), dealer cost, and theft rate index (1–1200).

(a) Classify each variable as categorical (nominal or ordinal) or numerical (discrete or continuous).

(b) Classify the numerical variables as ratio scale or interval scale.

4.3   A handbook lists the following information on accredited U.S. colleges and universities: enrollment, required entrance tests (ACT, SAT, none), annual tuition, fields of study, selectivity (high, moderate, low), and percent of applicants accepted.

(a) Classify each variable as categorical (nominal or ordinal) or numerical (discrete or continuous).

(b) Classify the numerical variables as ratio scale or interval scale.

4.4   A survey collected the following information on new college graduates: sex, age at graduation, time to complete degree, future plans (graduate school, employment, indefinite), citizenship, class rank, and grade point average.

(a) Classify each variable as categorical (nominal or ordinal) or numerical (discrete or continuous).

(b) Classify the numerical variables as ratio scale or interval scale.

Section 4.2

4.5   A cause analysis of 100 customer complaints in a fast food restaurant showed the following distribution. The numbers in the last row are the demerit ratings per complaint and represent the seriousness of the complaint. (A = stale/spoiled meat, B = stale/spoiled veggies, C = excessive wait, D = unclean eating area/rest rooms, E = surly/incompetent order takers.)

Cause	A	B	C	D	E
No. of Complaints	5	15	25	10	45
Demerit Rating	5	4	3	2	1

Make a Pareto chart for no. of complaints and total demerit score. List in order the causes which account for at least 80% of the problems in each case, and hence should be addressed first.

4.6   The numbers of doctorate degrees awarded in the U.S. in 1991 were as follows: 6276 in physical sciences, 5212 in engineering, 6928 in life sciences, 6127 in social sciences, 4094 in humanities, 6397 in education, and 2417 in other professional fields.[24] Make a Pareto chart to summarize these results. Comment on the distribution of degrees in these fields of study.

4.7   In Exercise 4.6 the percentages of doctoral degrees awarded to women in each field were as follows: 14.6% in physical sciences, 8.7% in engineering, 38.6% in life sciences, 49.4% in social sciences, 46.5% in humanities, 58.1% in education, and 34.6% in other professional fields.

(a) Calculate the number of degrees awarded to women and make a Pareto chart. Make the same chart for men.

(b) What do these charts show regarding the degrees awarded to men and women?

4.8   The number of foreign acquisitions and the value of those acquisitions for 1992 are tabulated below for selected countries.[25]

Country	Number	Value in Billion $	Country	Number	Value in Billion $
Britain	291	6.2	Italy	82	5.3
Canada	77	1.6	Japan	79	3.5
France	180	9.9	Mexico	8	3.2
Germany	140	4.0	Switzerland	82	3.8
Hong Kong	17	7.8	U.S.	342	13.3

(a) Make a Pareto chart summarizing the number of acquisitions. Comment on what the chart shows.

(b) Make a Pareto chart summarizing the acquisition values. Comment on what the chart shows.

---

[24] National Research Council, Survey of Earned Doctorates.

[25] *Time*, January 25, 1993, p. 22.

Section 4.3

4.9   A large sample is taken from an asymmetric distribution with a long left tail.

(a) Which one will be larger—mean or median?

(b) Will the sample skewness be positive, negative, or zero?

(c) Which quartile (Q_1 or Q_3) do you expect to be farther from the median (Q_2)? Why?

4.10   The following is a stem-and-leaf plot (made using SYSTAT) of the cost of grocery purchases in dollars from a sample of 50 shoppers.[26]

```
              0   2
              0     6689
              1 H 0112233444
              1     556788899
              2 M 00013
              2     6789
              3 H 012334
              3     679
              4     03
              4     5
              5     2
              5
              6     1
         ***OUTSIDE VALUES***
              6     249
```

(a) Which way is the distribution skewed?

(b) Which quartile (Q_1 or Q_3) do you expect to be farther from the median (Q_2)? Why?

(c) Check your answer in (b) by computing the three quartiles.

(d) Will the mean for these data be greater or smaller than the median? Why?

(e) The stem containing the median is marked with M, and the stems containing the quartiles, Q_1 and Q_3, are marked with H (for **hinges**, another name for quartiles). The "outside values" (outliers) shown in the plot are values less than $Q_1 - 1.5 \times$ IQR or greater than $Q_3 + 1.5 \times$ IQR. What are the outside values in this display? Verify that they are outliers.

4.11   ■ Body temperatures (in °F) were measured on 30 healthy individuals, resulting in the following data:[27]

97.0, 97.2, 97.3, 97.6, 97.6, 97.7, 97.9, 98.2, 98.2, 98.4,

98.4, 98.5, 98.6, 98.6, 98.6, 98.6, 98.6, 98.7, 98.8, 98.9,

99.0, 99.0, 99.1, 99.2, 99.3, 99.4, 99.5, 99.5, 99.7, 99.8

---

[26] Data taken from Moore, D. S. and McCabe, G. P. (1993), *Introduction to the Practice of Statistics*, New York: W. H. Freeman and Co., p. 9.

[27] C. K. Amy and A. Strong (1995), "Teaching the concepts and tools of variation using body temperatures," *Quality Progress*, **28**, p. 168.

(a) Calculate the mean, median, SD, and quartiles.

(b) Are there any outliers? If you think that the range of variation is excessive, note that medical studies have found that normal body temperature actually varies between individuals up to 4.8°F and for the same individual up to 1.09°F.[28]

(c) Make a histogram or a stem and leaf plot. Comment on the shape of the distribution.

4.12 ⬛ Daily rainfall in millimeters was recorded over a 47 year period in Turramurra, Sydney, Australia. For each year, the day with the greatest rainfall was identified. The most rainfall in a day in each year is shown below.[29]

1468	909	841	475	846	452
3830	1397	556	978	1715	747
909	2002	1331	1227	2543	2649
1781	1717	2718	584	1859	1138
2675	1872	1359	1544	1372	1334
955	1849	719	1737	1389	681
1565	701	994	1188	962	1564
1800	580	1106	880	850	

(a) Calculate the five number summary of these data. Does this summary suggest a symmetric or a skewed distribution?

(b) Calculate a rough estimate of SD from IQR and compare it with the sample SD.

(c) How does a 10% trimmed mean compare with the sample mean? Does this comparison suggest any outliers?

4.13 ⬛ Refer to the rainfall data from Exercise 4.12.

(a) Make a stem and leaf plot. Comment on the shape of the distribution and the number of modes and outliers.

(b) Make a box plot. Are there any outliers in the data using the $1.5 \times$ IQR rule?

(c) Make a normal plot. Comment on its shape.

4.14 ⬛ The following are the pH measurements on 50 soil samples a landscaper took from ground adjacent to a new building.

6.10 6.74 6.22 5.65 6.38 6.70 7.00 6.43 7.00 6.70 6.70 5.94 6.28
6.34 6.62 6.55 2.92 6.10 6.20 6.70 7.00 6.85 6.31 6.26 6.36 6.28
6.38 6.70 6.62 7.00 6.45 6.31 2.86 6.31 6.09 6.17 6.64 6.45
7.00 6.18 6.58 5.38 6.34 7.00 5.70 6.65 6.56 6.00 6.70 6.45

(a) Calculate the five number summary of these data. Does this summary suggest a symmetric or a skewed distribution? Explain.

(b) Calculate a rough estimate of SD from IQR and compare it with the sample SD.

(c) How does a 10% trimmed mean compare with the sample mean? Does this comparison suggest any outliers?

[28] J. Raloff (1992), "Body temperature: Don't look for 98.6°F," *Science News*, **142**, p. 196.

[29] J. C. W. Rayner and D. J. Best (1989), *Smooth Tests of Goodness of Fit*, Oxford: Oxford University Press. Reprinted in *Small Data Sets*, p. 123.

4.15 ⬛ Refer to the soil sample data from Exercise 4.14.

(a) Make a stem and leaf plot. Comment on the shape of the distribution and the number of modes and outliers.

(b) Make a box plot. Are there any outliers in the data using the $1.5 \times$ IQR rule?

(c) Make a normal plot. Comment on its shape.

4.16 ⬛ The following are the numbers per thousand of "deadbeat" parents (who are delinquent in paying child support) from each state.[30]

45	40	28	51	18	35	29	21	29	22	38	24	34	37	43	44	48
28	9	41	31	40	24	17	15	37	33	35	28	25	25	31	29	44
41	43	29	25	45	17	61	94	51	39	50	37	40	64	34	20	

(a) Calculate the five number summary of rates of deadbeat parents. Does this summary suggest a symmetric or a skewed distribution? Why?

(b) Calculate a rough estimate of SD from IQR and compare it with the sample SD.

(c) How does a 10% trimmed mean compare with the sample mean? Does this comparison suggest any outliers?

4.17 ⬛ Refer to the rates of deadbeat parents from Exercise 4.16.

(a) Make a stem and leaf plot. Comment on the shape of the distribution and the number of modes and any outliers.

(b) Make a box plot. Are there any outliers in the data using the $1.5 \times$ IQR rule?

(c) Make a normal plot. Comment on its shape.

4.18 ⬛ The following table gives average city mileage ratings and average fuel cost per 15,000 miles (city and highway) for a sample of 1992 model cars.[31]

City Gas Mileage and Fuel Cost from EPA 1992 Ratings

Model	City mpg	Dollars/ 15,000 mi	Model	City mpg	Dollars/ 15,000 mi
Acura NSX	18	964	Lincoln Capri	25	666
BMW M5	12	1351	Mazda Eclipse	20	921
Chevy Cavalier	25	621	Mitsubishi Galant	23	693
Chrysler LeBaron	20	783	Nissan Stanza	22	720
Daihatsu Charade	35	500	Peugot 405	21	783
Dodge Ramcharger	9	1800	Plymouth Sundance	26	921
Eagle Summit	28	599	Pontiac Sunbird	20	783
Ferrari F40	12	1446	Porsche 911 Turbo	13	1266
Ford Escort FS	32	515	Saturn SL	26	621
Geo Metro LSi	46	383	Toyota Celica	24	693
Honda Civic	30	545	Volvo 240	20	819
Isuzu Amigo	16	1001	VW Jetta	37	473

[30] *Time*, June 19, 1995, p. 18.

[31] Jack Gillis (1991), *The Car Book*, Wahsington, DC: Tilden Press

(a) Calculate the five number summary of the city mileage data. Does this summary suggest a symmetric or a skewed distribution?

(b) How does a 10% trimmed mean compare with the sample mean? Does this comparison suggest any outliers?

4.19 ◼ Refer to the city mileage data from Exercise 4.18.

(a) Make a stem and leaf plot. Comment on the shape of the distribution, the number of modes and outliers.

(b) Make a box plot. Are there any outliers in the data using the $1.5 \times$ IQR rule?

4.20 ◼ Refer to the fuel cost data from Exercise 4.18.

(a) Calculate the five number summary of the fuel cost (dollars/15,000 miles) data. Does this summary suggest a symmetric or a skewed distribution?

(b) Find the mean, standard deviation, skewness, and kurtosis. What do these statistics suggest about the shape of the distribution?

(c) How does a 10% trimmed mean compare with the sample mean? Does this comparison suggest any outliers?

4.21 ◼ Refer to the fuel cost data from Exercise 4.18.

(a) Make a histogram. Comment on the shape of the distribution and the number of modes and outliers.

(b) Make a box plot. Are there any outliers in the data using the $1.5 \times$ IQR rule?

4.22 ◼ One theory about the cause of schizophrenia involves a change in the activity of a substance called dopamine in the central nervous system. To test this theory, dopamine activity (in units of b-hydroxylase in nmol/(ml)(h)/(mg)) was measured for samples of psychotic and nonpsychotic patients. The data for the two groups of patients were as follows:[32]

Nonpsychotic: .0104 .0105 .0112 .0116 .0130 .0145 .0154 .0156
.0170 .0180 .0200 .0200 .0210 .0230 .0252

Psychotic: .0150 .0204 .0208 .0222 .0226 .0245 .0270 .0275
.0306 .0320

Make side-by-side box plots for the two groups and compare the central values and dispersions.

4.23 The following are the lifetimes in months of a sample of nine electrical motors.

12.5, 14.4, 4.7, 26.6, 18.0, 7.3, 9.8, 36.2, 20.1

(a) Calculate the normal scores using Table A.3 for the standard normal distribution.

(b) Plot the normal scores against the data values. Comment on the shape of the plot.

[32] D. E. Sternberg, D. P. Van Kammen, and W. E. Bunney (1982), "Schizophrenia: dopamine b-hydroxylase activity and treatment response," *Science*, **216**, pp. 1423–1425. Reprinted in *Small Data Sets*, p. 37.

4.24 ■ In order to interpret normal plots, it helps to see the plots for samples drawn from a normal and some nonnormal distributions.

(a) Simulate 50 observations from a normal distribution with mean 0 and standard deviation 1. Make a normal plot. Comment on the shape of the plot.

(b) Repeat the simulation of (a) but use an exponential distribution with mean = 1. How does the shape of the plot compare to the plot using normal data?

(c) Repeat the simulation of (a) but use a uniform distribution on [0, 1]. How does the shape of the plot compare to the plot using normal data?

4.25 ■ Make normal plots for the hospitalization cost data from Table 4.5 and their logs for the control group. What do you conclude?

4.26 ■ The severity of arthritis can be measured using a score that reflects impairment over all joints. The following table gives the initial joint impairment scores for a random sample of 33 elderly people with arthritis.[33]

6	5	10	9	13	8	8	22	9	18	3
12	11	14	8	32	9	12	17	6	14	9
4	18	18	14	22	9	2	5	3	3	29

(a) Make a normal plot. Do the data appear to be normally distributed? If not, how do they deviate from normality?

(b) Find a suitable normalizing transformation of the data.

4.27 ■ The time required to complete a hand performance test (HPT) is related to the risk of nursing home admission in older populations. The following table gives the seconds required by a random sample of 50 people to complete the HPT.[34]

96	91	104	89	106	100	90	146	106	127	565	595	188
93	154	115	99	77	90	114	123	134	117	136	82	139
152	142	79	83	354	84	132	112	377	138	47	82	
223	113	195	782	250	154	159	187	177	154	156	129	

(a) Make a normal probability plot. Do the data appear to be normally distributed? If not, how do they deviate from normality?

(b) Transform the data in three ways: $\sqrt{HPT}$, log(HPT), and 1/HPT. Which transformation gives the most nearly normal distribution?

---

[33] Data courtesy of Dr. Susan Hughes, Center for Research on Aging, School of Public Health, University of Illinois at Chicago, Chicago, IL.

[34] Data courtesy of Dr. Susan Hughes, Center for Research on Aging, School of Public Health, University of Illinois at Chicago, Chicago, IL.

4.28   ▣ The monthly sales of pairs of jeans (in 1000's) over six years in the United Kingdom are shown in the table below.[35]

Month	1980	1981	1982	1983	1984	1985
January	1998	1924	1969	2149	2319	2137
February	1968	1959	2044	2200	2352	2130
March	1937	1889	2100	2294	2476	2154
April	1827	1819	2103	2146	2296	1831
May	2027	1824	2110	2241	2400	1899
June	2286	1979	2375	2369	3126	2117
July	2484	1919	2030	2251	2304	2266
August	2266	1845	1744	2126	2190	2176
September	2107	1801	1699	2000	2121	2089
October	1690	1799	1591	1759	2032	1817
November	1808	1952	1770	1947	2161	2162
December	1927	1956	1950	2135	2289	2267

(a) Make a histogram of these data. Comment on the shape of the distribution and any outliers.

(b) Make a run chart of the jeans sales for all 72 months. Comment on trends and outliers.

(c) Plot separate run charts for different years on the same sheet. Does this make it easier to detect trends and outliers?

(d) What is evident from the run charts that is missed by the histogram? For which displays was the value of 3126 an outlier?

(e) Which of these three displays would be most useful for forecasting future sales?

Section 4.4

4.29   A marketing manager for a grocery store chain wants to know the customer usage of store coupons in newspaper ads for food versus nonfood items. He hopes to use the resulting data to plan future marketing strategies. He takes a random sample of 50 purchases each of advertised food and nonfood items and notes whether a coupon was used in each case. The data are as follows:

	Coupon Used?		Row
	Yes	No	Total
Food Item	20	30	50
Nonfood Item	10	40	50
Column Total	30	70	100

In (a)–(d) below state whether the statement is true or false.

(a) About 50% of the advertised item purchases are food and 50% are nonfood.

---

[35] S. Conrand (1989), *Assignments in Applied Statistics*, Chichester: John Wiley & Sons, p. 78. Reprinted in *Small Data Sets*, p. 314.

(b) About 30% of the advertised item purchases use coupons and 70% do not use coupons.

(c) About 40% of the advertised food purchases use coupons, while 20% of the advertised nonfood purchases do.

(d) About 20% of all advertised item purchases are food using coupons.

4.30 A university surveyed 200 recent graduates from its liberal arts school and 300 from its engineering school. The frequency of low and high income earners classified by gender is shown below.

Gender	Liberal Arts Degree		Engineering Degree	
	Low Income	High Income	Low Income	High Income
Female	90	60	20	30
Male	30	20	100	150

(a) Within each type of degree, compare rates of high income earners for males and females. What do these rates indicate?

(b) Combine the frequencies over the two schools to construct a 2×2 table of income level (columns) by gender (rows). Compare the proportion of male and female high income earners. What does this table indicate? Explain any differences from the results found in (a).

4.31 The number of NCAA Division I student athletes who were college freshmen in 1984 or 1985 and graduated within 5 years are as follows: 54 of 143 black females, 498 of 796 white females, 197 of 660 black males, and 878 of 1625 white males.[36]

(a) Make a $2 \times 2 \times 2$ frequency table to show frequencies for graduates and nongraduates by ethnic group and gender.

(b) Within each ethnic group compare rates of graduation for males and females. What do these graduation rates indicate?

(c) Combine the frequencies across ethnic groups to construct a 2×2 table of graduation status (columns) by gender (rows). Compare the proportion of male and female graduates. How do these results compare to the results found in (b)? Is the graduation rate independent of gender?

4.32 A park district surveyed teenagers in a large metropolitan area regarding participation in a preteen soccer program and subsequent teenage drug use. The results are classified by family income as shown in the following table.

Family Income	Played Soccer	Drug Use	
		Yes	No
Low	Yes	10	40
	No	30	120
Medium	Yes	10	90
	No	10	90
High	Yes	6	144
	No	2	48

---

[36] J. J. McArdle and F. Hamagami (1994), "Logit and multilevel logit modeling of college graduation for 1984–1985 freshman student-athletes," *Journal of the American Statistical Association*, **89**, pp. 1124–1134.

(a) For each income level, compare the proportion of drug users among teenagers who did and did not play soccer. What do these proportions indicate?

(b) Combine the income levels to construct a 2 × 2 table of drug use (columns) by soccer participation (rows). Compare the proportion of drug users among the teenagers who did and did not participate in soccer.

(c) Why would it be misleading to conclude from this table that involvement in soccer lowers the rate of teenage drug use? Why is it inappropriate to conclude a causal relationship from this type of survey?

4.33 Hospitals are graded based on their success rates in treating different categories of patients. We want to compare two hospitals—A, which is a university affiliated research hospital, and B, which is a general community hospital—with respect to success rates for a certain complicated surgery. The data classified by low risk patients and high risk patients are shown in the following table.

	Low Risk				High Risk		
	Success	Failure	Total		Success	Failure	Total
Hospital A	400	100	500	Hospital A	160	640	800
Hospital B	300	200	500	Hospital B	20	180	200
Total	700	300	1000	Total	180	820	1000

(a) Calculate the success rates for each category of patients for both hospitals. Which hospital is better?

(b) Aggregate the data over the two categories of patients and calculate the overall success rates for both hospitals. Now which hospital is better?

(c) Explain the discrepancy between the results obtained in (a) and (b).

4.34 In 1972–74 a one-in-six survey of electoral roll was conducted in Whickham, U.K. Twenty years later a follow-up survey was conducted. The following table reports data on 1314 women on their smoking status and age at the first survey, and whether they were dead or alive at the follow-up survey.[37]

Age Group	Smokers Dead	Smokers Alive	Nonsmokers Dead	Nonsmokers Alive
18–24	2	53	1	61
25–34	3	121	5	152
35–44	14	95	7	114
45–54	27	103	12	66
55–64	51	64	40	81
65–74	29	7	101	28
75+	13	0	64	0

[37] D. R. Appleton, J. M. French, and M. P. J. Vanderpump (1997), "Ignoring a covariate: An example of Simpson's paradox," *The American Statistician*, **50**, pp. 340–341.

(a) Aggregate the data over age groups and calculate the overall death rates for smokers and nonsmokers. Which group has the higher death rate?

(b) Now calculate the adjusted (for age) death rates for smokers and nonsmokers. Which group has the higher death rate?

(c) What does the fact that there were far few smokers in higher age groups suggest about the effect of smoking? This exercise illustrates what can go wrong if a covariate (age) is correlated with the risk factor (smoking) and outcome variable (survival).

4.35   ▣   The numbers of goals scored in 340 full matches in the two professional soccer divisions in the Netherlands in the 1991–1992 season are classified by 15-minute intervals of play.[38]

Time Interval (min)	0–15	16–30	31–45	46–60	61–75	76–90
Number of Goals	128	140	147	169	170	198

(a) Using the midpoint of each time interval, make a scatter plot of time–interval of play by the number of goals scored. What kind of relationship is indicated by the scatter plot?

(b) Calculate the correlation coefficient. Does it correspond to the relationship indicated by the scatter plot?

4.36   ▣   The following table provides data on the annual snowfall in Amherst, MA, and the U.S. unemployment rate for the years 1973 to 1982.

Year	1973	1974	1975	1976	1977	1978	1979	1980	1981	1982
Snowfall (inches)	45	59	82	80	71	60	55	69	79	95
Unemployment (%)	4.9	5.6	8.5	7.7	7.1	6.1	5.8	7.1	7.6	9.7

(a) Make a scatter plot of unemployment rate vs. snowfall. What relationship is indicated by the scatter plot?

(b) Calculate the correlation coefficient. Is there a strong linear relationship between snowfall and unemployment?

(c) Does this relationship mean that the Amherst annual snowfall influences the national unemployment rates or vice versa?

4.37   ▣   Refer to the city mileage and fuel cost data from Exercise 4.18.

(a) Make a scatter plot of fuel cost vs. city mileage. What kind of relationship is indicated by the scatter plot?

(b) Calculate the correlation coefficient. Does it correspond to the relationship indicated by the scatter plot?

4.38   The correlation coefficient between the midterm scores and final scores in a course is 0.75. A student scored two standard deviations below the mean on the midterm. How many standard deviations above/below the mean would that student be predicted to score on the final? If the final mean and SD are 75 (out of 100) and 12, respectively, what is that student's predicted score on the final?

---

[38] G. Ridder, J. S. Cramer, and P. Hopstaken (1994), "Down to ten: Estimating the effect of the red card in soccer," *Journal of the American Statistical Association*, **89**, pp. 1124–1134.

4.39   A survey in a large metropolitan city found that the commuting times to work and time spent with the family on a working day are negatively correlated with $r = -0.6$. A person commutes one and one-half standard deviations longer than the average. How many standard deviations more/less would that person's family time be predicted to be compared to the average? If the average family time is 60 minutes with SD = 20 minutes, what is that person's predicted family time?

4.40   A computer network manager wants to model how access time in milliseconds (y) for data files varies with the number of simultaneous users (x) accessing the files. Based on 50 paired observations, the following summary statistics are obtained:

$$\bar{x} = 8.7, s_x = 2.5, \bar{y} = 15.3, s_y = 3.8, r = 0.8.$$

Give the equation of the least-squares straight line to estimate the access time as a function of the number of simultaneous users. What is the estimated access time if there are 10 simultaneous users?

4.41   ◾ The following table gives the average math and verbal SAT scores from 1985 through 1992 for Illinois.

Year	1985	1986	1987	1988	1989	1990	1991	1992
Math	522	519	521	520	520	528	535	537
Verbal	468	466	463	464	462	466	471	473

(a) Make a run chart of math scores. What kind of trend is indicated by the run chart?

(b) Calculate the least squares regression line for the run chart in (a). (Note that the years can be relabeled 1 through 8.)

(c) Repeat (a) and (b) for the verbal scores.

(d) In which case (math scores or verbal scores) does the calculated regression line reflect the actual trend better? (*Hint*: Note that the verbal scores are up only in the last two years.)

Section 4.5

4.42   ◾ The following table gives quarterly sales (in millions of cans) of a soft drink.

Year	Quarter	Sales	Year	Quarter	Sales
1	Fall	41.2	3	Fall	54.7
	Winter	50.2		Winter	74.2
	Spring	54.5		Spring	79.4
	Summer	41.3		Summer	62.7
2	Fall	44.6	4	Fall	62.7
	Winter	59.9		Winter	79.9
	Spring	69.0		Spring	83.6
	Summer	53.3		Summer	65.6

Make a time-series plot of Sales vs. Quarter. Is this time-series stationary or are there evident trend and seasonal components present?

4.43 ■ Examples 4.15 –4.18 analyzed the domestic car sales for 1980–1995. Here are the data for import sales.

Year	Sales	Year	Sales
1980	2.398	1988	3.004
1981	2.327	1989	2.699
1982	2.224	1990	2.403
1983	2.387	1991	2.038
1984	2.439	1992	1.937
1985	2.838	1993	1.776
1986	3.245	1994	1.735
1987	3.196	1995	1.606

(a) Make a time-series plot of the data. Does the time-series appear to be stationary?

(b) Calculate the moving averages and the associated mean absolute percent error of prediction. Use window size $= 3$.

(c) Calculate the exponentially weighted moving averages and the associated mean absolute percent error of prediction. Use smoothing parameter $= 0.2$.

(d) Calculate lag–1, lag–2, and lag–3 autocorrelation coefficients. What conclusions do you draw?

4.44 ■ The monthly U.S. consumer price index (CPI) data for 1997–98 are given in the following table.[39]

Month	CPI 1997	CPI 1998
January	159.1	161.6
February	159.6	161.9
March	160.0	162.2
April	160.2	162.5
May	160.1	162.8
June	160.3	163.0
July	160.5	163.2
August	160.8	163.4
September	161.2	163.6
October	161.6	164.0
November	161.5	164.0
December	161.3	163.9

[39] *Source*: The U.S. Bureau of Labor Statistics Web site: http://www.bls.gov.

(a) Make a time-series plot of the data. Does the time-series appear to be stationary?

(b) Calculate the moving averages and the associated mean absolute percent error of prediction. Use window size = 3.

(c) Calculate the exponentially weighted moving averages and the associated mean absolute percent error of prediction. Use smoothing parameter = 0.2.

(d) Calculate lag–1, lag–2, and lag–3 autocorrelation coefficients. What conclusions do you draw?

4.45 ▣ The monthly U.S. composite index of leading indicators for 1996–97 is given in the following table.[40]

	Composite Index	
Month	1996	1997
January	100.6	102.8
February	101.3	103.3
March	101.5	103.4
April	101.8	103.3
May	102.0	103.6
June	102.2	103.6
July	102.3	103.9
August	102.3	104.1
September	102.4	104.3
October	102.5	104.4
November	102.6	104.5
December	102.6	104.5

(a) Make a time-series plot of the data. Does the time-series appear to be stationary?

(b) Calculate the exponentially weighted moving averages and the associated mean absolute percent error (MAPE) of prediction using four different smoothing parameters $w = 0.1, 0.2, 0.3$, and 0.4. Which value of w gives the smallest MAPE?

4.46 ▣ The monthly average unleaded gasoline prices per gallon (for the 55 largest cities in U.S.) for 1996 −97 are given in the following table.[41]

[40] *Source: Standard and Poor's Statistical Service*, April 1999.

[41] *Source: Standard and Poor's Statistical Service*, April 1999.

	Price Per Gallon in U.S. cents	
Month	1996	1997
January	112.9	126.1
February	112.4	125.5
March	116.2	123.5
April	125.1	123.1
May	132.3	122.6
June	129.9	122.9
July	127.2	120.5
August	124.0	125.3
September	123.4	127.7
October	122.7	124.2
November	125.0	121.3
December	126.0	117.7

(a) Make a time-series plot of the data. Does the time-series appear to be stationary?

(b) Calculate the exponentially weighted moving averages and the associated mean absolute percent error (MAPE) of prediction using four different smoothing parameters $w = 0.1, 0.2, 0.3$, and 0.4. Which value of w gives the smallest MAPE?

Advanced Exercises

4.47 Here is a variation on Simpson's paradox. A small college has two undergraduate schools, A and B. School A admits 1000 students with an average SAT score of 1300. School B admits 1000 students with an average SAT score of 1200. Thus the average SAT score for all admitted students is 1250. Each school loses some top admitted students to other colleges and universities. Of the admitted students in School A, 600 enroll with an average SAT score of 1270 and in School B, 900 enroll with an average SAT score of 1170. Thus the "loss" in average SAT scores for each school is 30 points.[42]

(a) Calculate the average SAT score for all enrolled students. What is the overall "loss" in average SAT scores?

(b) Explain to a concerned admissions officer why the overall "loss" is greater than the individual "loss" for each school.

4.48 Here is the same variation on Simpson's paradox, but using real data.[43] The following table gives the total incomes and federal taxes for different income groups for the years 1974 and 1978.

---

[42] This is a much simplified version of a similar problem that was brought to us for resolution by Mr. Alan Wolff, Manager of Information Services, Northwestern University Enrollment Office.

[43] C. H. Wagner (1982), "Simpson's paradox in real life," *The American Statistician*, **36**, pp. 46–48.

Adjusted	1974		1978	
Gross Income	Income	Tax	Income	Tax
Under $5000	$41,651,643	$2,244,467	$19,879,622	$689,318
$5000 to $9999	$146,400,740	$13,646,348	$122,853,315	$8,819,461
$10,000 to $14,999	$192,688,922	$21,449,597	$171,858,024	$17,155,758
$15,000 to $99,999	$470,010,790	$75,038,230	$865,037,814	$137,860,951
$100,000 or more	$29,427,152	$11,311,672	$62,806,159	24,051,698
Total	$880,179,247	$123,690,314	$1,242,434,934	$188,577,186

(a) Calculate the tax rate for each income group and the overall tax rate for both the years.

(b) Why did the overall tax rate go up from 1974 to 1978?

4.49 For doing hand calculations, (and even for some computer calculations) it is convenient to code some types of data by subtracting (or adding) a common constant from all observations and then dividing (or multiplying) by another common constant so that the resulting numbers are on a manageable scale, preferably integers. How can we find the mean and SD of the raw data from coded data?

(a) Suppose the data values $x_1, x_2, \ldots, x_n$ are coded by subtracting a constant a from each x_i and then dividing by a constant $b > 0$. Denote the coded data by $y_1, y_2, \ldots, y_n$, where $y_i = (x_i - a)/b$. Show that the mean and SD of the x's are related to those of the y's by

$$\bar{x} = b\bar{y} + a \text{ and } s_x = bs_y.$$

(b) The following are the measurements of atomic weights of carbon (the nominal atomic weight is 12) made by one method.[44]

12.0129	12.0072	12.0064	12.0054	12.0016
11.9853	11.9949	11.9985	12.0077	12.0061

Find the mean and SD by coding the data first. What values of a and b are convenient to use?

(c) The z-scores defined in Section 4.3.2 are a particular way of coding the data. Use the formulae from (a) to show that $\bar{z} = 0$ and $s_z = 1$.

4.50 ■ The idea of a normal plot can be extended to other distributions. Let $x_1, x_2, \ldots, x_n$ be a random sample. To check if a specified (continuous) distribution with c.d.f. F fits this sample, we need to plot the theoretical quantiles against the sample quantiles. The order statistic $x_{(i)}$ is the $\left(\frac{i}{n+1}\right)$th sample quantile and $F^{-1}\left(\frac{i}{n+1}\right)$ is the corresponding theoretical quantile. Let us apply this method to check the exponentiality of a data set. The resulting plot is called the **exponential plot**.

---

[44] D. J. Best and J. C. W. Rayner (1987), "Welch's approximate solution for the Behrens-Fisher problem," *Technometrics*, **29**, pp. 205–210.

(a) For the exponential distribution with c.d.f. $F(x) = 1 - \exp(-\lambda x)$ show that the $\left(\frac{i}{n+1}\right)$th theoretical quantile is given by

$$F^{-1}\left(\frac{i}{n+1}\right) = \frac{1}{\lambda}\log_e\left(\frac{n+1}{n+1-i}\right).$$

(b) Explain why, although λ is not known, it suffices to use $\lambda = 1$ when making the plot. The corresponding quantiles are called the **unit exponential scores**.

(c) Make an exponential plot for the cost of hospitalization data from Table 4.5 for the control group. Does the exponential distribution fit well?

4.51 ◼ The **Weibull distribution** is often used to model reliability data in engineering applications. It is a generalization of the exponential distribution with c.d.f. given by

$$F(t) = 1 - \exp\left\{-\left(\frac{t}{\alpha}\right)^\beta\right\} \quad \text{for } t \geq 0.$$

Here $\beta > 0$ is called the shape parameter; for $\beta = 1$, the Weibull distribution reduces to the exponential distribution with $\alpha = 1/\lambda$.

(a) Show that

$$\log_e\log_e(1 - F(t))^{-1} = \beta\log_e t - \beta\log_e \alpha.$$

(b) Suppose $t_{(1)} < t_{(2)} < \cdots < t_{(n)}$ are the ordered failure times of n items. The **Weibull plot** is made by plotting $\log_e\log_e\left(1 - \frac{i}{n+1}\right)^{-1}$ against $\log_e t_{(i)}$ by regarding $t_{(i)}$ as the $\left(\frac{i}{n+1}\right)$th sample quantile. A linear plot indicates that the lifetime distribution is Weibull. The parameters α and β can be estimated from the slope and the intercept of the line. Use this method to check whether the following data[45] on the failure times of 22 transformers follow the Weibull distribution:

Operating Hours Until Failure of 22 Transformers

10	314	730	740	990	1046	1570	1870	2020	2040	2096
2110	2177	2306	2690	3200	3360	3444	3508	3770	4042	4186

(c) There were 158 other transformers that did not fail during the course of the study. All we can say is that their lifetimes exceeded 4186 hours. Such data are said to be **censored** or **truncated**. If one were interested in estimating the mean lifetime of transformers, what kind of bias would be introduced by ignoring the censored data?

---

[45] W. Nelson (1982), *Applied Life Data Analysis*, New York: Wiley, p. 138.

CHAPTER 5

SAMPLING DISTRIBUTIONS OF STATISTICS

In Chapter 3 we learned about the dichotomy between a population and a sample, and between a parameter and a statistic. A sample statistic used to estimate an unknown population parameter is called an **estimate**. Given an estimate of a parameter, we need to assess its accuracy. After all, because of sampling variation, the estimate that we compute from the data is generally off from the true parameter value. This discrepancy is known as the **sampling error**. For example, in an election poll the parameter is the population proportion, p, of voters who plan to vote for a particular candidate. Suppose that in a random sample of 1000 voters 560 said that they would vote for the candidate, so our estimate of p is 56%. How far is this estimate likely to be from the true value of p? Methods to answer questions such as this are developed in later chapters of this book. The purpose of the present chapter is to present some mathematical tools required by these methods.

In this book we mostly follow the **frequentist approach**, which assesses the accuracy of a sample estimate by considering how the estimate would vary around the true parameter value if repeated samples were drawn from the same population. In the election poll example, if more samples were drawn from the same voter population, the resulting sample fractions would generally be different from the 56% that we initially got. Each of the sample fractions would also be an estimate of the same true p. In other words, a statistic is a random variable (r.v.) with a probability distribution. This probability distribution is called the **sampling distribution** of the statistic. The numerical value that was actually observed (namely 56%) is a particular realization from this sampling distribution.

We will use the sampling distribution of a statistic to assess the sampling error in our estimate (by putting probabilistic bounds on the error). This chapter presents the sampling distributions of two important statistics, namely, the sample mean and sample variance. We will also study the sampling distributions of order statistics of which the sample median is an example.

5.1   SAMPLING DISTRIBUTION OF THE SAMPLE MEAN

Consider a **random sample** (i.e., independent and identically distributed or i.i.d. observations) $X_1, X_2, \ldots, X_n$ drawn from a (population) distribution with mean $\mu = E(X_i)$ and variance $\sigma^2 = \text{Var}(X_i)$. The question of interest is: How does the sample mean $\bar{X} = \frac{1}{n}\sum_{i=1}^{n} X_i$ vary in repeated random samples of size n drawn from the same population distribution? This is called the sampling distribution of $\bar{X}$. The following example shows how to derive this distribution when all possible samples can be enumerated.

EXAMPLE 5.1   (ROLLING TWO DICE: DISTRIBUTION OF $\bar{X}$)

The outcomes of the rolls of two fair dice, represented by (X_1, X_2), can be viewed as a random sample of size 2 from a uniform distribution on integers $1, 2, \ldots, 6$. The mean and variance of this distribution are

$$\mu = \frac{1}{6}(1 + 2 + \cdots + 6) = 3.5$$

and

$$\sigma^2 = E(X^2) - \mu^2 = \frac{1}{6}(1^2 + 2^2 + \cdots + 6^2) - (3.5)^2 = 2.9166.$$

These values can also be obtained directly from the formulas $\mu = (N + 1)/2$ and $\sigma^2 = (N^2 - 1)/12$ derived in Exercise 2.35 for a uniform distribution on integers $1, 2, \ldots, N$; here $N = 6$.

There are 36 possible samples of size 2 from this distribution, which are listed in Table 5.1. For each sample (x_1, x_2), the sample mean $\bar{x}$ and sample variance s^2 are calculated. We can construct the sampling distribution of $\bar{X}$ as shown in Table 5.2, using the fact that each of the 36 samples is equally likely (with probability $\frac{1}{36}$). The mean and variance of the sampling distribution can be calculated as follows:

$$E(\bar{X}) = 1.0 \times \frac{1}{36} + 2.0 \times \frac{2}{36} + \cdots + 6.0 \times \frac{1}{36} = 3.5$$

and

$$\text{Var}(\bar{X}) = (1.0 - 3.5)^2 \times \frac{1}{36} + (2.0 - 3.5)^2 \times \frac{2}{36} + \cdots + (6.0 - 3.5)^2 \times \frac{1}{36}$$

$$= 1.4583 = 2.9166/2.$$

These values are consistent with the formulas

$$E(\bar{X}) = \mu \quad \text{and} \quad \text{Var}(\bar{X}) = \frac{\sigma^2}{n} \qquad (5.1)$$

derived in Chapter 2.   ◆

Table 5.1 All Possible Samples of Size 2 from a Uniform Distribution on 1, 2, ..., 6 and Associated Sample Means and Variances

(x_1, x_2)	$\bar{x}$	s^2	(x_1, x_2)	$\bar{x}$	s^2
(1, 1)	1.0	0.0	(4, 1)	2.5	4.5
(1, 2)	1.5	0.5	(4, 2)	3.0	2.0
(1, 3)	2.0	2.0	(4, 3)	3.5	0.5
(1, 4)	2.5	4.5	(4, 4)	4.0	0.0
(1, 5)	3.0	8.0	(4, 5)	4.5	0.5
(1, 6)	3.5	12.5	(4, 6)	5.0	2.0
(2, 1)	1.5	0.5	(5, 1)	3.0	8.0
(2, 2)	2.0	0.0	(5, 2)	3.5	4.5
(2, 3)	2.5	0.5	(5, 3)	4.0	2.0
(2, 4)	3.0	2.0	(5, 4)	4.5	0.5
(2, 5)	3.5	4.5	(5, 5)	5.0	0.0
(2, 6)	4.0	8.0	(5, 6)	5.5	0.5
(3, 1)	2.0	2.0	(6, 1)	3.5	12.5
(3, 2)	2.5	0.5	(6, 2)	4.0	8.0
(3, 3)	3.0	0.0	(6, 3)	4.5	4.5
(3, 4)	3.5	0.5	(6, 4)	5.0	2.0
(3, 5)	4.0	2.0	(6, 5)	5.5	0.5
(3, 6)	4.5	4.5	(6, 6)	6.0	0.0

Table 5.2 Sampling Distribution of $\bar{X}$ for Samples of Size 2 from a Uniform Distribution on 1, 2, ..., 6

$\bar{x}$	1.0	1.5	2.0	2.5	3.0	3.5	4.0	4.5	5.0	5.5	6.0
$f(\bar{x})$	$\frac{1}{36}$	$\frac{2}{36}$	$\frac{3}{36}$	$\frac{4}{36}$	$\frac{5}{36}$	$\frac{6}{36}$	$\frac{5}{36}$	$\frac{4}{36}$	$\frac{3}{36}$	$\frac{2}{36}$	$\frac{1}{36}$

For small problems (finite discrete distributions), the *exact* sampling distribution of $\bar{X}$ can be derived by listing all possible samples, as illustrated above. There are other special cases where the exact distribution of $\bar{X}$ can be derived. We saw three specific cases in Chapter 2:

1. If the X_i's are i.i.d. Bernoulli r.v.'s with $P(X_i = 1) = p$, then the distribution of the sample mean $\bar{X} = \frac{1}{n} \sum_{i=1}^{n} X_i$ can be expressed in terms of the binomial distribution:

$$P\left[\bar{X} = \frac{x}{n}\right] = P\left[\sum_{i=1}^{n} X_i = x\right] = \binom{n}{x} p^x (1-p)^{n-x} \quad \text{for } x = 0, 1, \ldots, n.$$

2. If the X_i's are i.i.d. $N(\mu, \sigma^2)$ r.v.'s, then $\bar{X}$ has an $N(\mu, \sigma^2/n)$ distribution.

3. If the X_i's are i.i.d. exponential r.v.'s with parameter λ, then the X_i/n are i.i.d. exponential r.v.'s with parameter $n\lambda$. Therefore $\bar{X} = \sum_{i=1}^{n} X_i/n$ has a gamma distribution with parameters n and $n\lambda$ (see Section 2.8.2). Hence the p.d.f. of $\bar{X}$ can be expressed as

$$f(\bar{x}) = \frac{(n\lambda)^n}{\Gamma(n)}(\bar{x})^{n-1} e^{-n\lambda\bar{x}} \quad \text{for } \bar{x} \geq 0.$$

What can be said about the distribution of $\bar{X}$ when the sample is drawn from an arbitrary population? Generally, the exact distribution of $\bar{X}$ is difficult to derive, and if the population distribution is unspecified, it is not possible to derive the exact distribution of $\bar{X}$ at all. The good news is that, in many cases, we can approximate the distribution of $\bar{X}$ when n is large by a normal distribution. This important result is discussed in the next section.

5.1.1 Central Limit Theorem

The problem of approximating the sampling distribution of $\bar{X}$ for large n has concerned mathematicians for centuries. The earliest results were obtained by Laplace (1749–1827), de Morgan (1806–1871), and Gauss (1777–1855). From these investigations, a rather surprising result emerged, which is called the **central limit theorem**. Loosely speaking, it states that for sufficiently large n, the sample mean $\bar{X}$ has an approximately normal distribution regardless of the form of the population distribution.

Central Limit Theorem (CLT): Let $X_1, X_2, \ldots, X_n$ be a random sample drawn from an arbitrary distribution with a finite mean μ and variance σ^2. As $n \to \infty$, the sampling distribution of $\frac{(\bar{X}-\mu)}{\sigma/\sqrt{n}}$ converges to the $N(0, 1)$ distribution. ■

Note from (5.1) that $E(\bar{X}) = \mu_{\bar{X}} = \mu$ and $\text{Var}(\bar{X}) = \sigma_{\bar{X}}^2 = \sigma^2/n$. The CLT tells us that if n is sufficiently large, the standardized sample mean,

$$\frac{\bar{X} - \mu_{\bar{X}}}{\sigma_{\bar{X}}} = \frac{(\bar{X} - \mu)}{\sigma/\sqrt{n}}$$

is approximately distributed as $N(0, 1)$. The CLT is sometimes expressed in terms of the sum of r.v.'s. Specifically,

$$\frac{\sum_{i=1}^{n} X_i - n\mu}{\sigma\sqrt{n}} \approx N(0, 1)$$

for sufficiently large n. Here the notation $\approx$ stands for "approximately distributed."

EXAMPLE 5.2

We illustrate the central limit theorem for random samples drawn from a uniform distribution over the interval [0, 10]. Figure 5.1(a) shows a histogram of 500 single observations that were randomly drawn from this uniform distribution. This histogram has a flat shape, reflecting the shape of the uniform distribution. The single observations may be viewed as sample means with $n = 1$. Figure 5.1(b) is a histogram of sample means of $n = 2$ observations drawn from a uniform distribution. It is impressive that although only two observations are averaged, the distribution of those means is much lighter in the tails and heavier in the middle than is the distribution of single observations. Figure 5.1(c) is a histogram of sample means of $n = 10$ observations which resembles the normal bell shape. As the sample size increases to $n = 30$, as shown in Figure 5.1(d), the shape of the distribution is very close to the normal distribution. ◆

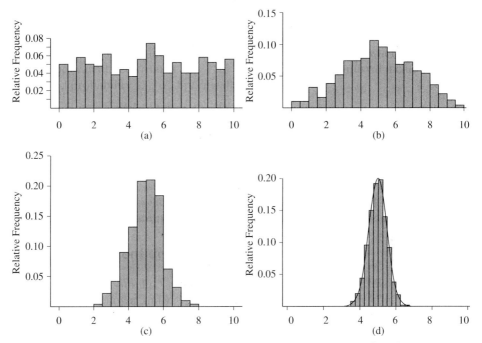

Figure 5.1 Histograms of Means of 500 Random Samples from a $U[0, 10]$ Distribution: (a) Single observations from a uniform distrbution; (b) Sample means from $n = 2$ observations; (c) Sample means from $n = 10$ observations; (d) Sample means from $n = 30$ observations.

What is the relationship between the CLT and the law of large numbers (LLN) stated in Chapter 2? Both are asymptotic results about $\bar{X}$. The LLN says that, as $n \to \infty$, the *unstandardized* $\bar{X}$ converges (in probability) to μ, a constant, with no variation around it; equivalently $(\bar{X} - \mu)$ converges to zero. The CLT states that the rate of this convergence is $1/\sqrt{n}$. So the right constant to multiply the difference $\bar{X} - \mu$ is $\sqrt{n}$ in order that, as $n \to \infty$, the resulting asymptotic distribution is nontrivial (not converging to a constant or diverging to infinity). In fact, the CLT makes a stronger statement that this asymptotic distribution is $N(0, \sigma^2)$.

How large an n do you need to obtain a good normal approximation using the CLT? The answer depends on the shape of the population distribution and how accurate an approximation is required. Next, we will explore this question when the population distribution is Bernoulli.

5.1.2 Normal Approximation to the Binomial Distribution

Probabilities involving the binomial distribution are laborious to compute when n is large. However, recognizing that a binomial r.v. is the sum of i.i.d. Bernoulli r.v.'s permits us to apply the CLT to obtain a good approximation under certain circumstances. Suppose X is a Bin(n, p) r.v. The mean of X is np and the variance is $np(1 - p)$. When n is large, the CLT can be applied giving the approximation

$$\frac{X - np}{\sqrt{np(1 - p)}} \approx N(0, 1).$$

A key issue is to determine how large n must be so that the CLT can be applied to obtain a good approximation. The answer depends on the value of p and the accuracy needed. To appreciate the magnitude of n needed to obtain a good normal approximation, consider the binomial distributions for $p = 0.5$ and for $p = 0.1$ shown in Figures 5.2 and 5.3, respectively, for selected values of n.[1] We see in Figure 5.2 that when $p = 0.5$, the distribution resembles a "normal" bell-shaped curve for n as small as 10. However, from Figure 5.3 we see that when $p = 0.1$, the distribution is right skewed for $n = 10$; only when n is as large as 100 does the distribution become nearly symmetric and bell-shaped.

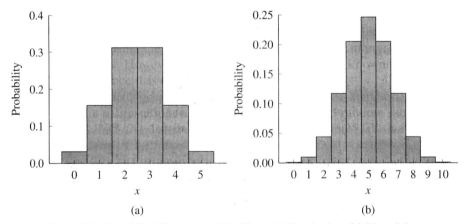

Figure 5.2   Probability Histograms of the Binomial distrubution: (a) Binomial distribution with $p = 0.5$, $n = 5$; (b) Binomial distribution with $p = 0.5$, $n = 10$.

---

[1] In these figures, the probabilities at discrete points, 0, 1, 2, ..., are shown as bars spread over unit intervals around these points. Because of the resemblance of the resulting diagrams to sample histograms, they are called **probability histograms**.

Thus, we see that when p is close to 0 or 1, a much larger n is required than when p is near $\frac{1}{2}$. The recommendations in the statistical literature differ somewhat. One rule of thumb is that n is large enough to apply the CLT if both

$$np \geq 10 \quad \text{and} \quad n(1 - p) \geq 10.$$

Thus n must be at least 20 if $p = 0.5$ and at least 100 if $p = 0.1$ or 0.9.

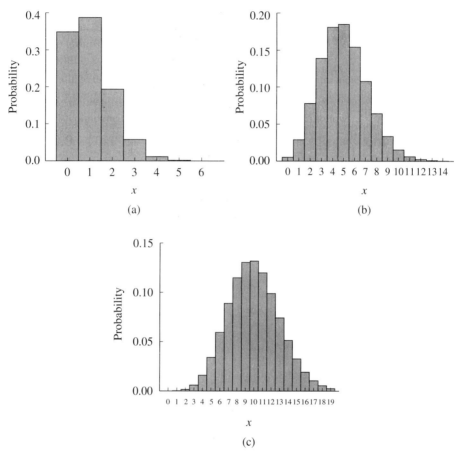

Figure 5.3   Probability Histograms of the Binomial Distribution: (a) Binomial distribution with $p = 0.1, n = 10$; (b) Binomial distribution with $p = 0.1, n = 50$; (c) Binomial distribution with $p = 0.1, n = 100$.

Example 5.3

In a noisy communication channel there is a 2% chance that each transmitted bit (0 or 1) will be corrupted. If 1000 bits are transmitted, what is the probability that no more than 10 will be corrupted?

Let $X =$ the number of corrupted bits. Then X has a binomial distribution with $n = 1000$ and $p = 0.02$. The required probability is

$$P(X \leq 10) = \sum_{x=0}^{10} \binom{1000}{x} (0.02)^x (0.98)^{1000-x}.$$

This probability is tedious to compute by hand. Using a computer package, we obtain the answer as 0.0102. The normal approximation can be computed more easily. We regard X as approximately normally distributed with $\mu = np = (1000)(0.02) = 20$ and $\sigma = \sqrt{np(1-p)} = \sqrt{(1000)(0.02)(0.98)} = 4.427$. Therefore

$$P(X \leq 10) = P\left(Z = \frac{X - \mu}{\sigma} \leq \frac{10 - 20}{4.427}\right) \simeq \Phi(-2.259) = 0.0118.$$

This approximate probability is quite close to the exact binomial probability.   ◆

5.1.3 Continuity Correction

We now describe a method to improve the accuracy of the normal approximation to the binomial distribution. Consider a binomial r.v. X with $n = 20$ and $p = 0.5$. Suppose we want to approximate $P(X \leq 8)$. The probability histogram for this binomial distribution is shown in Figure 5.4. The desired probability includes all the area in the bars over 0, 1, . . . , 8.

Exact Binomial Probability:

$$P(X \leq 8) = P(X = 0) + P(X = 1) + \cdots + P(X = 8) = 0.2517.$$

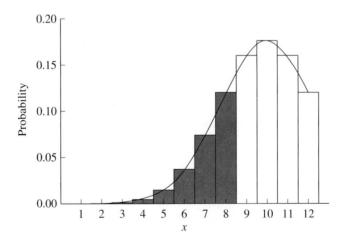

Figure 5.4   Normal Approximation to the Binomial Distribution

If we use the CLT to approximate $P(X \leq 8)$, this misses the area inside the bar over 8 approximately between 8 and 8.5. To include that area, we need to apply the CLT to $P(X \leq 8.5)$. This correction to the normal approximation is called the **continuity correction**, so termed because it is used to approximate a discrete (binomial) distribution by a continuous (normal) distribution. The two approximations compare as follows:

Normal Approximation without Continuity Correction:

$$P(X \leq 8) = P\left(Z = \frac{X - np}{\sqrt{np(1-p)}} \leq \frac{8 - 10}{\sqrt{20(0.5)(0.5)}}\right) \simeq \Phi(-0.8944) = 0.1867.$$

Normal Approximation with Continuity Correction:

$$P(X \leq 8.5) = P\left(Z = \frac{X - np}{\sqrt{np(1-p)}} \leq \frac{8.5 - 10}{\sqrt{20(0.5)(0.5)}}\right) \simeq \Phi(-0.6708) = 0.2514.$$

Thus the continuity correction gives a much better approximation to the exact binomial probability.

In general, the continuity corrected normal approximation to the lower and upper tail binomial probabilities are given by

$$P(X \leq x) \simeq \Phi\left(\frac{x + 0.5 - np}{\sqrt{np(1-p)}}\right)$$

and

$$P(X \geq x) \simeq 1 - \Phi\left(\frac{x - 0.5 - np}{\sqrt{np(1-p)}}\right),$$

respectively.

5.2   SAMPLING DISTRIBUTION OF THE SAMPLE VARIANCE

The population variance σ^2 can be estimated from a random sample $X_1, X_2, \ldots, X_n$ by the sample variance

$$S^2 = \frac{\sum_{i=1}^{n}(X_i - \bar{X})^2}{n - 1}. \tag{5.2}$$

The sampling distribution of S^2 can be derived if all possible samples can be listed, as in the case of the distribution of $\bar{X}$. Let us return to the two dice example for an illustration.

EXAMPLE 5.4   (ROLLING TWO DICE: SAMPLING DISTRIBUTION OF S^2)

Using the values of s^2 for all possible samples in Table 5.1, we obtain the distribution given in Table 5.3. Note that the distribution of S^2 is skewed to the right, in contrast to the distribution of $\bar{X}$ given in Table 5.2, which is symmetric. This is quite typical; in general, the distribution of $\bar{X}$ is approximately symmetric for modestly large n even if the population distribution is not symmetric (and exactly symmetric for any n if the population distribution is symmetric), while the distribution of S^2 is always skewed to the right. The mean of the distribution of S^2 is

$$E(S^2) = \frac{6}{36}(0) + \frac{10}{36}(0.5) + \frac{8}{36}(2.0) + \frac{6}{36}(4.5) + \frac{4}{36}(8.0) + \frac{2}{36}(12.5) = 2.9166,$$

which verifies that $E(S^2) = \sigma^2$.   ◆

Table 5.3 Sampling Distribution of S^2 for Samples of Size 2 from a Uniform Distribution on $1, 2, \ldots, 6$

s^2	0.0	0.5	2.0	4.5	8.0	12.5
$f(s^2)$	$\frac{6}{36}$	$\frac{10}{36}$	$\frac{8}{36}$	$\frac{6}{36}$	$\frac{4}{36}$	$\frac{2}{36}$

The distribution of S^2 is difficult to derive in the general case. Also, there is no analog of the CLT which gives an approximation to this distribution for large samples when the population distribution is arbitrary. However, the exact distribution of S^2 can be derived for the important case when $X_1, X_2, \ldots, X_n$ are i.i.d. normal. In this case, the distribution of S^2 is related to the **chi-square (χ^2) distribution** (see (5.8) below). We first introduce this new distribution.

Chi-Square Distribution. For $\nu \geq 1$, let $Z_1, Z_2, \ldots, Z_\nu$ be i.i.d. $N(0, 1)$ r.v.'s and let

$$X = Z_1^2 + Z_2^2 + \cdots + Z_\nu^2. \tag{5.3}$$

Then the probability density function (p.d.f.) of X can be shown to be

$$f(x) = \frac{1}{2^{\nu/2}\Gamma(\nu/2)} \, x^{(\nu/2)-1} e^{-x/2} \qquad \text{for } x \geq 0. \tag{5.4}$$

This is known as the χ^2-distribution with ν degrees of freedom (d.f.), abbreviated as $X \sim \chi_\nu^2$. Note that (5.4) is a special case of the gamma distribution (see Section 2.8.2) with $\lambda = 1/2$ and $r = \nu/2$.

The shape of the density function $f(x)$ is different for each value of ν; thus there is a family of chi-square distributions, one for each value of ν ($\nu = 1, 2, \ldots$). Graphs of $f(x)$ for $\nu = 5$ and 10 are shown in Figure 5.5. Observe that the density function curves are positively skewed. The curves shift to the right as the d.f. increase. The d.f. reflect the number of Z_i^2 terms summed to obtain X; as the d.f. increase, the value of X tends to increase and the density function curves shift to the right.

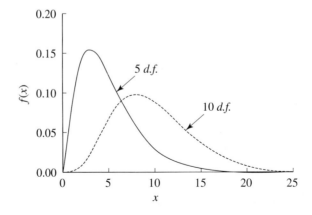

Figure 5.5 Chi-Square Density Function Curves for $\nu = 5$ and 10

We denote by $\chi^2_{v,\alpha}$ the upper α critical point of the χ^2_v distribution, which is the value that cuts off an area α in the upper tail of the χ^2_v distribution. Similarly, let $\chi^2_{v,1-\alpha}$ denote the lower α critical point. These upper and lower α critical points are shown in Figure 5.6 and are tabulated in Table A.5 in Appendix A for selected values of v and α.

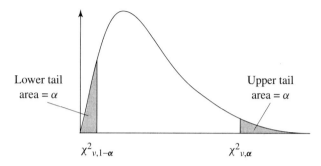

Figure 5.6 Lower and Upper α Critical Points of a Chi-Square Distribution

Applying the definition (5.3) that the χ^2_v r.v. is a sum of v i.i.d. squared $N(0, 1)$ r.v.'s, it follows that if $Z \sim N(0, 1)$ then

$$Z^2 \sim \chi^2_1. \tag{5.5}$$

From this relationship it is easy to show that

$$z^2_{\alpha/2} = \chi^2_{1,\alpha}; \tag{5.6}$$

see Exercise 5.19. For example, $z^2_{.025} = (1.960)^2 = 3.84 = \chi^2_{1,.05}$.

It can be shown that (see the derivation given at the end of this section)

$$\frac{(n-1)S^2}{\sigma^2} \sim \chi^2_{n-1} \tag{5.7}$$

or equivalently

$$S^2 \sim \frac{\sigma^2 \chi^2_{n-1}}{n-1}. \tag{5.8}$$

From the expressions for the mean and variance of the gamma distribution given in Section 2.8.2, we obtain

$$E(\chi^2_v) = v$$

and

$$\mathrm{Var}(\chi^2_v) = 2v.$$

From this it follows that

$$E(S^2) = E\left(\frac{\sigma^2 \chi^2_{n-1}}{n-1}\right) = \frac{\sigma^2}{n-1} E(\chi^2_{n-1}) = \frac{\sigma^2}{n-1} \times (n-1) = \sigma^2 \tag{5.9}$$

and

$$\text{Var}(S^2) = \text{Var}\left(\frac{\sigma^2 \chi_{n-1}^2}{n-1}\right) = \frac{\sigma^4}{(n-1)^2}\text{Var}(\chi_{n-1}^2) = \frac{\sigma^4}{(n-1)^2} \times 2(n-1) = \frac{2\sigma^4}{n-1}.$$

$$(5.10)$$

EXAMPLE 5.5

The precision of an instrument refers to its ability to make repeat measurements that closely agree. One measure of precision is the variance among the repeat measurements; the smaller the variance the greater the precision. Suppose that an advertised claim for a thermometer is $\sigma = .01°F$, but it is suspected that the true $\sigma > .01°F$. To verify this claim, 10 repeat measurements are taken on a controlled temperature bath using this thermometer. If the observed sample variance s^2 is significantly larger than the claimed variance $\sigma^2 = (.01)^2$, this casts doubt on the advertised claim. In other words, if $s^2 > c(.01)^2$ for sufficiently large $c > 0$, then it is unlikely that $\sigma^2 = (.01)^2$. How large a value of c should be required to confidently reject the claim that the true $\sigma^2 = (.01)^2$?

One commonly used approach is to determine c so that there is only a 5% chance that S^2 will be larger than $c(.01)^2$ when in fact $\sigma^2 = (.01)^2$. Using this approach there is only a 5% chance of incorrectly concluding that the claim is unjustified, so we can be "95% confident" (this phrase is defined rigorously in the next chapter) in our rejection of the claim. Thus we need to find a value of c that satisfies

$$P\{S^2 > c(.01)^2\} = 0.05$$

when the claim $\sigma^2 = (.01)^2$ is true. We use the relationship

$$\frac{(n-1)S^2}{\sigma^2} = \frac{9S^2}{(.01)^2} \sim \chi_9^2$$

to write the above equation as

$$P\left\{\frac{9S^2}{(.01)^2} > \frac{9c(.01)^2}{(.01)^2}\right\} = P\{\chi_9^2 > 9c\} = 0.05.$$

Therefore $9c = \chi_{9,.05}^2 = 16.92$ or $c = \frac{16.92}{9} = 1.88$. Thus, if s^2 exceeds $1.88(.01)^2$, we decide that the advertised claim is not supported by the data.   ◆

*Derivation of the Distribution of S^2 in the Normal Case.   Define the following r.v.'s:

$$U = \frac{(n-1)S^2}{\sigma^2}$$

$$V = \left[\frac{\sqrt{n}\,(\bar{X} - \mu)}{\sigma}\right]^2$$

$$W = \sum_{i=1}^{n}\left(\frac{X_i - \mu}{\sigma}\right)^2.$$

First note that $W \sim \chi_n^2$, because $Z_i = \frac{X_i - \mu}{\sigma}$ are i.i.d. $N(0, 1)$ for $i = 1, 2, \ldots, n$.

Also, since $\frac{\sqrt{n}(\bar{X}-\mu)}{\sigma} \sim N(0, 1)$, it follows that $V \sim \chi_1^2$. Furthermore,

$$
\begin{aligned}
W &= \sum_{i=1}^{n} \left(\frac{X_i - \bar{X} + \bar{X} - \mu}{\sigma} \right)^2 \\
&= \sum_{i=1}^{n} \left(\frac{X_i - \bar{X}}{\sigma} \right)^2 + 2(\bar{X} - \mu) \underbrace{\sum_{i=1}^{n} \left(\frac{X_i - \bar{X}}{\sigma} \right)}_{=0} + \frac{n(\bar{X} - \mu)^2}{\sigma^2} \\
&= U + V.
\end{aligned}
\tag{5.11}
$$

To obtain the distribution of U from the above information, we use the following results from mathematical statistics.

- *Result 1:* Let $U \sim \chi_a^2$ and $V \sim \chi_b^2$ be two independent r.v.'s and let $W = U + V$. Then $W \sim \chi_{a+b}^2$. Conversely, if $W = U + V \sim \chi_{a+b}^2$, $V \sim \chi_b^2$, and U and V are independent, then $U \sim \chi_a^2$.

- *Result 2:* The sample mean $\bar{X}$ and sample variance S^2 are statistically independent for a random sample from a normal distribution. This result follows from Exercise 2.51, which shows that $\text{Cov}(\bar{X}, X_i - \bar{X}) = 0$, i.e., $\bar{X}$ and $X_i - \bar{X}$ are uncorrelated for $i = 1, 2, \ldots, n$. If the X_i's are normally distributed, this implies that $\bar{X}$ and $X_i - \bar{X}$ are also independent. Therefore $\bar{X}$ and S^2, which is a function only of the $X_i - \bar{X}$, are also independent.

Apply the converse part of Result 1 to expression (5.11) (with $a + b = n$ and $b = 1$) combined with Result 2. Then we get the conclusion that for normally distributed data, the distribution of the sample variance S^2 is given by (5.7). ◆

5.3   STUDENT'S t-DISTRIBUTION

Consider a random sample, $X_1, X_2, \ldots, X_n$ drawn from an $N(\mu, \sigma^2)$ distribution. It is known that $\frac{(\bar{X}-\mu)}{\sigma/\sqrt{n}}$ is *exactly* distributed as $N(0, 1)$ for any n. However, when σ in the denominator is replaced by the sample standard deviation S, the distribution of the new r.v.:

$$
T = \frac{(\bar{X} - \mu)}{S/\sqrt{n}}
\tag{5.12}
$$

is no longer standard normal because of the sampling variation introduced by S. This distribution was investigated by the Irish chemist William Sealy Gosset (1876–1937), who worked for Guiness Breweries and published his statistical research under the pseudonym "Student." The distribution of T is named **Student's t-distribution** in his honor.

The r.v. T in (5.12) can be expressed as

$$T = \frac{\frac{(\bar{X}-\mu)}{\sigma/\sqrt{n}}}{\sqrt{S^2/\sigma^2}} = \frac{Z}{\sqrt{U/\nu}} \tag{5.13}$$

where $Z = \frac{(\bar{X}-\mu)}{\sigma/\sqrt{n}} \sim N(0,1)$ and $U = \frac{\nu S^2}{\sigma^2} \sim \chi_\nu^2$ for $\nu = n-1$. This provides a general definition of T as a ratio of a standard normal r.v. to the square root of an independently distributed chi-square r.v. divided by its d.f. The p.d.f. of T can be shown to be

$$f(t) = \frac{\Gamma\left(\frac{\nu+1}{2}\right)}{\sqrt{\pi\nu}\,\Gamma\left(\frac{\nu}{2}\right)}\left(1 + \frac{t^2}{\nu}\right)^{-\frac{\nu+1}{2}} \qquad \text{for } -\infty < t < \infty \tag{5.14}$$

where ν is referred to as the d.f. of the t-distribution. We say that T has a t-distribution with ν d.f. (abbreviated as $T \sim T_\nu$). The density function (5.14) has a different shape for each value of ν; thus there is a family of t-distributions, one for each value of $\nu = 1, 2, \dots$. It is symmetric around zero and is bell-shaped for every ν. When $\nu \to \infty$, one can reason from (5.13) that T approaches a standard normal r.v. Z, using the fact that $E(U) = \nu$ and hence $U/\nu \to 1$.

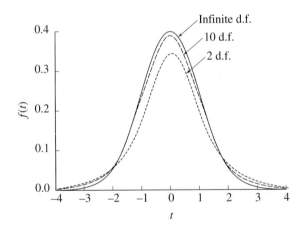

Figure 5.7   Student's t Density Function Curves for $\nu = 2, 10$ and ∞

Graphs of the density function (5.14) for $\nu=2, 10$, and ∞ are shown in Figure 5.7. Observe that as ν increases (i.e., as σ^2 is estimated from larger samples), the density curve becomes more peaked and its tails become lighter, eventually approaching (as $\nu \to \infty$) the standard normal p.d.f. We will denote the upper α critical point of the t-distribution with ν d.f. by $t_{\nu,\alpha}$. The upper α critical points are tabulated in Table A.4 in Appendix A for selected values of ν and α. Notice that the last row of the table for $\nu = \infty$ gives the critical points $t_{\infty,\alpha} = z_\alpha$ for the standard normal distribution. Due to the symmetry of the t-distribution around zero, the lower α critical point is simply $-t_{\nu,\alpha}$.

Example **5.6**

Half-pint (8 oz.) milk cartons are filled at a dairy by a filling machine. To provide a check on the machine, a sample of 10 cartons is periodically measured. If the sample mean $\bar{x}$ deviates by more than a certain amount d from the nominal value of 8 oz., i.e., if $|\bar{x} - 8| > d$, then the machine setting is adjusted. The chance of a false alarm indicating an unnecessary adjustment is to be limited to 1%. Find a formula for d.

   If the true mean amount of milk, denoted by μ, equals 8 oz. then no adjustment is required. Therefore the probability of a false alarm is given by

$$P\left(|\bar{X} - 8| > d|\mu = 8\right) = 0.01.$$

Divide both sides of the inequality in the probability statement by $S/\sqrt{n}$, where $n = 10$, and use the fact that $\frac{\bar{X}-8}{S/\sqrt{10}}$ has a t-distribution with $10 - 1 = 9$ d.f. when $\mu = 8$. Therefore the above equation becomes

$$P\left(|T_9| > \frac{d}{S/\sqrt{10}}\right) = 0.01.$$

Let

$$c = \frac{d}{S/\sqrt{10}} \quad \text{or} \quad d = \frac{cS}{\sqrt{10}}.$$

Then c must cut off an area $0.01/2 = 0.005$ in each tail of the t-distribution with 9 d.f., i.e., $c = t_{9,.005} = 3.250$ from Table A.4. Thus the decision rule decides that the machine needs adjustment if

$$|\bar{x} - 8| > d = 3.250 \frac{s}{\sqrt{10}}. \qquad \blacklozenge$$

5.4   SNEDECOR-FISHER'S F-DISTRIBUTION

In Example 5.5 we saw an application of the chi-square distribution for comparing the variance of a measuring instrument to a claimed nominal value. Another common problem is to compare the unknown variances of two measuring instruments. The same problem arises in quality control applications where the unknown variabilities associated with different alternatives (e.g., manufacturing processes, suppliers, product designs) are compared. If sample data from two alternatives are available, then comparisons can be based on the ratio of their sample variances. George W. Snedecor (1881–1974) and Sir R. A. Fisher (1890–1962) derived the distribution of this ratio, and it is called Snedecor-Fisher's F-**distribution**.

   Specifically, consider two independent random samples, $X_1, X_2, \ldots, X_{n_1}$ from an $N(\mu_1, \sigma_1^2)$ distribution and $Y_1, Y_2, \ldots, Y_{n_2}$ from an $N(\mu_2, \sigma_2^2)$ distribution. Let

$$S_1^2 = \frac{\sum (X_i - \bar{X})^2}{n_1 - 1} \quad \text{and} \quad S_2^2 = \frac{\sum (Y_i - \bar{Y})^2}{n_2 - 1}$$

be the sample variances calculated from these two samples. From Section 5.2 we know that

$$\frac{S_1^2}{\sigma_1^2} \sim \frac{\chi_{n_1-1}^2}{n_1 - 1} \quad \text{and} \quad \frac{S_2^2}{\sigma_2^2} \sim \frac{\chi_{n_2-1}^2}{n_2 - 1}.$$

We consider the distribution of the ratio

$$\frac{S_1^2/\sigma_1^2}{S_2^2/\sigma_2^2}.$$

When $\sigma_1^2 = \sigma_2^2$, this ratio reduces to the ratio of the two sample variances, S_1^2/S_2^2.
Now,

$$\frac{S_1^2/\sigma_1^2}{S_2^2/\sigma_2^2} \sim \frac{\chi_{n_1-1}^2/(n_1 - 1)}{\chi_{n_2-1}^2/(n_2 - 1)} \tag{5.15}$$

where the two chi-square r.v.'s are independent. The r.v. on the right hand side of (5.15) is called an F r.v. with $n_1 - 1$ d.f. in the numerator and $n_2 - 1$ d.f. in the denominator. Note that the distribution of this r.v. is free of unknown parameters σ_1^2 and σ_2^2 (as well as μ_1 and μ_2).

More generally, let U and V be two independent r.v.'s, $U \sim \chi_{\nu_1}^2$ and $V \sim \chi_{\nu_2}^2$. Then

$$W = \frac{U/\nu_1}{V/\nu_2}$$

has an F-distribution with ν_1 d.f. in the numerator and ν_2 d.f. in the denominator (denoted by $W \sim F_{\nu_1,\nu_2}$). The p.d.f. of W can be shown to be

$$f(w) = \frac{\Gamma[(\nu_1 + \nu_2)/2]}{\Gamma(\nu_1/2)\Gamma(\nu_2/2)} \left(\frac{\nu_1}{\nu_2}\right)^{\nu_1/2} w^{\nu_1/2-1} \left(1 + \frac{\nu_1}{\nu_2}w\right)^{-(\nu_1+\nu_2)/2} \quad \text{for } w \geq 0. \tag{5.16}$$

There is a family of F-distributions, each characterized by its numerator d.f. ν_1 and denominator d.f. ν_2. Exchanging the two d.f. results in a different F-distribution unless $\nu_1 = \nu_2$; in particular, it is easy to see that

$$F_{\nu_1,\nu_2} \sim \frac{1}{F_{\nu_2,\nu_1}}. \tag{5.17}$$

Figure 5.8 shows a typical F_{ν_1,ν_2} density function curve. This figure also shows the upper and lower α critical points of this distribution, denoted by $f_{\nu_1,\nu_2,\alpha}$ and $f_{\nu_1,\nu_2,1-\alpha}$, respectively. The upper α critical points are given for $\alpha = .10, .05, .025, .01$ and for selected values of ν_1 and ν_2 in Table A.6 in Appendix A. The lower α critical points can be found from the relationship

$$f_{\nu_1,\nu_2,1-\alpha} = \frac{1}{f_{\nu_2,\nu_1,\alpha}}. \tag{5.18}$$

This result can be proved using (5.17); see Exercise 5.31.

EXAMPLE 5.7

A company tests samples of electrical resistors made by two different suppliers to determine whether the variabilities in their resistances (measured in ohms) are different, and if so, which is smaller. Samples of 10 resistors from Supplier 1 and 16 resistors from Supplier 2 are tested. Let s_1^2 and s_2^2 denote the sample variances computed from the test data with $\nu_1 = 9$ and $\nu_2 = 15$ d.f., respectively. Using an approach similar to that in Example 5.5, the chance of declaring that the true variances of the two suppliers, σ_1^2 and σ_2^2, are different when in fact they are the same is to be limited to no more than 10%. Give an appropriate decision rule.

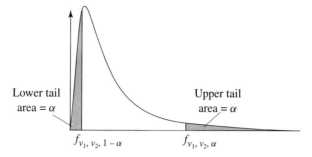

Figure 5.8   Lower and Upper α Critical Points of an F-Distribution

Consider a decision rule that declares the two variances different if their ratio is too large or too small, i.e., if

$$\frac{s_1^2}{s_2^2} < c_1 \quad \text{or} \quad \frac{s_1^2}{s_2^2} > c_2$$

for some constants $c_1 < 1$ and $c_2 > 1$. To determine the constants c_1, c_2 so that the error probability of 10% is maintained, we use the result mentioned earlier: Under the condition $\sigma_1^2 = \sigma_2^2$ the ratio S_1^2/S_2^2 has an $F_{9,15}$ distribution. One way to choose c_1 and c_2 would be to make c_1 equal to the lower 5% critical point and c_2 equal to the upper 5% critical point of the $F_{9,15}$ distribution, i.e., $c_1 = f_{9,15,.95}$ and $c_2 = f_{9,15,.05}$. With this choice, the probability of deciding that $\sigma_1^2 < \sigma_2^2$ or $\sigma_1^2 > \sigma_2^2$ when, in fact, $\sigma_1^2 = \sigma_2^2$, is each 0.05 (so that the total probability is 0.10). These critical points can be found from Table A.6 as follows:

$$c_1 = f_{9,15,.95} = \frac{1}{f_{15,9,.05}} = \frac{1}{3.01} = 0.332$$

and

$$c_2 = f_{9,15,.05} = 2.59.$$

Note that $f_{15,9,.05} \neq f_{9,15,.05}$, because $F_{15,9}$ and $F_{9,15}$ have different distributions.

Thus, if the ratio s_1^2/s_2^2 is less than 0.332 or greater than 2.59, the two variances would be declared different. In the former case we would choose Supplier 1 and in the latter case Supplier 2.   ◆

A relationship exists between the t-distribution and the F-distribution. Using the representation

$$T_\nu = \frac{Z}{\sqrt{U/\nu}}$$

where Z and U are independently distributed as $N(0, 1)$ and χ_ν^2 r.v.'s, respectively, we can write

$$T_\nu^2 = \frac{Z^2/1}{U/\nu}.$$

But from (5.5) we know that $Z^2 \sim \chi_1^2$. Hence T_ν^2 is a ratio of two independent chi-square r.v.'s divided by their d.f. with the numerator d.f. $= 1$ and the denominator d.f. $= \nu$. Hence we get the result that

$$T_\nu^2 \sim F_{1,\nu}. \tag{5.19}$$

From this relationship it can be shown that

$$t_{\nu,\alpha/2}^2 = f_{1,\nu,\alpha}; \tag{5.20}$$

see Exercise 5.32. For example, $t_{10,.025}^2 = (2.228)^2 = 4.96 = f_{1,10,.05}$. The results (5.19) and (5.20) are analogous to the corresponding results (5.5) and (5.6) for the standard normal and the chi-square distributions.

5.5   *SAMPLING DISTRIBUTIONS OF ORDER STATISTICS

Most of the sampling distribution results discussed above apply to samples drawn from normal populations. In fact, most of this book is devoted to normal theory methods, which are statistical methods based on the normality assumption. In many situations, however, the assumption that a population can be modeled by a normal distribution may not be valid. In such cases statistical methods can be used that do not make strong assumptions about the distributional form of the data. These are called distribution-free or nonparametric methods and are discussed in Chapter 14. Nonparametric methods are often based on ordered data values (called **order statistics**) or just their ranks. Therefore it is useful to study the sampling distributions of order statistics.

5.5.1 Distribution of the Sample Minimum and Maximum

Let $X_1, X_2, \ldots, X_n$ be i.i.d. observations from a continuous distribution with cumulative distribution function (c.d.f.) $F(x)$ and p.d.f. $f(x)$. Let $X_{(1)} < X_{(2)} < \cdots < X_{(n)}$ be the corresponding order statistics. Note that we can ignore the possibility of ties (i.e., two or more X_i's being equal) since ties occur with zero probability for continuous r.v.'s. We first consider the sampling distributions of $X_{(1)} = X_{\min}$ and $X_{(n)} = X_{\max}$. The c.d.f. $F_{(n)}(x)$ of $X_{(n)}$ can be found as follows:

$$\begin{aligned}
F_{(n)}(x) &= P\{X_{\max} \leq x\} \\
&= P\{X_1 \leq x, X_2 \leq x, \ldots, X_n \leq x\} \\
&= P\{X_1 \leq x\} \times P\{X_2 \leq x\} \times \cdots \times P\{X_n \leq x\} \\
&= F(x) \times F(x) \times \cdots \times F(x) \\
&= \{F(x)\}^n. \tag{5.21}
\end{aligned}$$

The p.d.f. $f_{(n)}(x)$ is obtained by differentiating $F_{(n)}(x)$:

$$f_{(n)}(x) = \frac{d F_{(n)}(x)}{dx} = n\{F(x)\}^{n-1} f(x). \tag{5.22}$$

The c.d.f. $F_{(1)}(x)$ and p.d.f. $f_{(1)}(x)$ of $X_{(1)} = X_{\min}$ can be similarly derived:

$$F_{(1)}(x) = 1 - P\{X_{\min} > x\}$$

$$= 1 - P\{X_1 > x, X_2 > x, \ldots, X_n > x\}$$

$$= 1 - P\{X_1 > x\} \times P\{X_2 > x\} \times \cdots \times P\{X_n > x\}$$

$$= 1 - \{1 - F(x)\} \times \{1 - F(x)\} \times \cdots \times \{1 - F(x)\}$$

$$= 1 - \{1 - F(x)\}^n \tag{5.23}$$

and

$$f_{(1)}(x) = \frac{d F_{(1)}(x)}{dx} = n\{1 - F(x)\}^{n-1} f(x). \tag{5.24}$$

EXAMPLE 5.8

A system consists of n identical components connected in series. Each component's lifetime is exponentially distributed with failure rate λ, and the failures are independent. What is the lifetime distribution of the system?

Let the component lifetimes be $T_1, T_2, \ldots, T_n$ and let T be the system lifetime. Then $T = \min(T_1, T_2, \ldots, T_n)$, since a series system fails when any component fails. The exponential c.d.f. of each T_i is given by $1 - \exp(-\lambda t)$; see equation (2.8). Using (5.23), the c.d.f. of T is given by

$$1 - \{1 - (1 - e^{-\lambda t})\}^n = 1 - e^{-n\lambda t}$$

which is the c.d.f. of the exponential distribution with parameter $n\lambda$. From this it follows that T has an exponential distribution with failure rate $n\lambda$ or mean $1/n\lambda$.

The same technique can be applied to find the strength distribution of a system consisting of components connected in series where the strength of the system depends on the weakest link. ◆

EXAMPLE 5.9

Let $\tilde{\mu}$ denote the median of a continuous distribution F, i.e., $F(\tilde{\mu}) = 0.5$. Let $X_1, X_2, \ldots, X_n$ denote a random sample from this distribution, and let $X_{\min}$ and $X_{\max}$ represent the smallest and the largest order statistics. What is the probability that $\tilde{\mu}$ is included in the random interval $[X_{\min}, X_{\max}]$?

At first sight it appears that this probability must be 1. However, we will see that the correct answer is $1 - (0.5)^{n-1}$. The wrong answer is due to the confusion between the *population* median $\tilde{\mu}$ and the *sample* median $\tilde{X}$ ($\tilde{X}$ must, of course, fall between $X_{\min}$ and $X_{\max}$). First calculate the probability that $\tilde{\mu}$ is outside the interval $[X_{\min}, X_{\max}]$:

$$P\left(X_{\min} > \tilde{\mu} \quad \text{or} \quad X_{\max} < \tilde{\mu}\right) = P\left(X_{\min} > \tilde{\mu}\right) + P\left(X_{\max} < \tilde{\mu}\right)$$

$$= \{1 - F_{(1)}(\tilde{\mu})\} + \{F_{(n)}(\tilde{\mu})\}$$

$$= \{1 - F(\tilde{\mu})\}^n + \{F(\tilde{\mu})\}^n$$

$$= (0.5)^n + (0.5)^n$$

$$= 2(0.5)^n = (0.5)^{n-1}.$$

Therefore $P\{X_{\min} \le \tilde{\mu} \le X_{\max}\} = 1 - (0.5)^{n-1}$. ◆

5.5.2 Distribution of the rth Order Statistic

The expressions for the sampling distributions of $X_{\min}$ and $X_{\max}$ are simple enough. How can they be generalized to provide the sampling distribution of the rth order statistic, $X_{(r)}$, for any r $(1 \leq r \leq n)$? For example, the sample median $\tilde{X}$ is $\left(\frac{n+1}{2}\right)$th order statistic when n is odd. The c.d.f. $F_{(r)}(x)$ can be derived as follows:

$$
\begin{aligned}
F_{(r)}(x) &= P\{X_{(r)} \leq x\} \\
&= P\{\text{at least } r \text{ of the } X_i\text{'s are } \leq x\} \\
&= \sum_{j=r}^{n} P\{\text{exactly } j \text{ of the } X_i\text{'s are } \leq x \text{ and } n - j \text{ of the } X_i\text{'s are } > x\} \\
&= \sum_{j=r}^{n} \binom{n}{j} \{F(x)\}^j \{1 - F(x)\}^{n-j}.
\end{aligned}
\tag{5.25}
$$

If we substitute $p = F(x)$, the c.d.f. of the rth order statistic is seen to be the tail sum of a binomial distribution:

$$
F_{(r)}(x) = \sum_{j=r}^{n} \binom{n}{j} p^j (1 - p)^{n-j} = P\{\text{Bin}(n, p) \geq r\}.
$$

The p.d.f. $f_{(r)}(x)$ can be obtained by differentiating the expression in (5.25) for $F_{(r)}(x)$, but the algebra is messy. A simpler approach is as follows:

$$
\begin{aligned}
f_{(r)}(x)dx &= P\{x \leq X_{(r)} \leq x + dx\} \\
&= P\{r - 1 \ X_i\text{'s are } < x, \text{ one } X_i \text{ is in } [x, x + dx], \\
&\qquad \text{and } n - r \ X_i\text{'s are } > x\}.
\end{aligned}
$$

The X_i that falls in the infinitesimal interval $[x, x + dx]$ can be chosen from n X's in n ways; the probability that it falls in this interval is $f(x)\,dx$. Having chosen this X_i, the $r - 1$ smaller X_i's can be chosen from the remaining $n - 1$ X's in $\binom{n-1}{r-1}$ ways; the probability that they are all less than x is $\{F(x)\}^{r-1}$. Finally, the probability that the remaining $n - r$ X_i's are all greater than x is $\{1 - F(x)\}^{n-r}$. Multiplying these three terms together, we obtain

$$
\begin{aligned}
f_{(r)}(x)dx &= n \binom{n-1}{r-1} \{F(x)\}^{r-1} \{1 - F(x)\}^{n-r} f(x)\,dx \\
&= n \times \frac{(n-1)!}{(r-1)!(n-r)!} \{F(x)\}^{r-1} \{1 - F(x)\}^{n-r} f(x)\,dx \\
&= \frac{n!}{(r-1)!(n-r)!} \{F(x)\}^{r-1} \{1 - F(x)\}^{n-r} f(x)\,dx
\end{aligned}
$$

$$= \frac{\Gamma(n+1)}{\Gamma(r)\Gamma(n-r+1)} \{F(x)\}^{r-1}\{1 - F(x)\}^{n-r} f(x)\,dx$$

$$= \frac{1}{B(r, n-r+1)} \{F(x)\}^{r-1}\{1 - F(x)\}^{n-r} f(x)\,dx \qquad (5.26)$$

where $B(r, n-r+1)$ is the beta function defined in Section 2.8.4, viz. $B(r, s) = \Gamma(r)\Gamma(s)/\Gamma(r+s)$. Cancelling dx from both sides of the equation gives the final expression for the p.d.f. of $X_{(r)}$.

A connection between (5.26) and the beta distribution discussed in Section 2.8.4 can be made as follows. Make a change of variables $y = F(x)$ so that $dy = f(x)dx$. This is equivalent to transforming the r.v.'s X_i to $Y_i = F(X_i)$. It can be shown that the Y_i's are i.i.d. $U[0, 1]$ r.v.'s; see Exercise 5.43. Since F is a nondecreasing function, the Y_i's will be ordered in the same way as the X_i's. Let $Y_{(r)}$ denote the corresponding rth order statistic and let $g_{(r)}(y)$ denote its p.d.f. Then from (5.26) we see that

$$g_{(r)}(y) = \frac{1}{B(r, n-r+1)} y^{r-1}(1-y)^{n-r} \quad \text{for } 0 \le y \le 1. \qquad (5.27)$$

Thus the rth order statistic in a random sample of size n from a $U[0, 1]$ distribution has the beta distribution with parameters r and $n - r + 1$.

5.6 CHAPTER SUMMARY

The **sampling distribution** of a **statistic** is its probability distribution, obtained by considering how the statistic value varies in repeated random samples drawn from the same population distribution. The sampling distribution of a statistic is useful for assessing the **sampling error** in the inferences based on that statistic about a population parameter.

For a random sample of size n (i.e., n i.i.d. observations) from any population with mean μ and variance σ^2, the mean and variance of the distribution of the sample mean, $\bar{X}$, equal

$$E(\bar{X}) = \mu \quad \text{and Var}(\bar{X}) = \frac{\sigma^2}{n}.$$

The **central limit theorem (CLT)** states that for large n, $\bar{X}$ is approximately distributed as $N(\mu, \sigma^2/n)$. Equivalently, the standardized sample mean

$$\frac{(\bar{X} - \mu)}{\sigma/\sqrt{n}}$$

is approximately distributed as $N(0, 1)$. If the population distribution is normal, then this result is exactly true for any n as shown in Chapter 2. One application of the CLT is to approximate the $\text{Bin}(n, p)$ distribution by a normal distribution with mean np and variance $np(1 - p)$. This approximation is made more accurate by applying the **continuity correction**.

The **chi-square distribution** with ν d.f. (denoted by χ_ν^2) is defined as the distribution of the sum of ν i.i.d. squared $N(0, 1)$ r.v.'s. The distribution of the sample variance,

S^2, calculated from a random sample of size n from an $N(\mu, \sigma^2)$ distribution, is related to the χ^2_{n-1} distribution as follows:

$$\frac{(n-1)S^2}{\sigma^2} \sim \chi^2_{n-1}.$$

This distribution is useful to draw inferences on the population variance σ^2 based on the sample variance S^2. There is no analog of the CLT to approximate the distribution of S^2 when the data are not normal.

Let $Z \sim N(0, 1)$ and $U \sim \chi^2_{\nu}$ be independent r.v.'s. Then the r.v.

$$T_\nu = \frac{Z}{\sqrt{U/\nu}}$$

has **Student's t-distribution** with ν d.f. The standardized sample mean when standardization is done by using S as an estimate of σ has a t-distribution with $n-1$ d.f.:

$$\frac{(\bar{X} - \mu)}{S/\sqrt{n}} \sim T_{n-1}.$$

This distribution is useful to draw inferences on population mean μ when the population standard deviation σ is not known.

The **F-distribution** with ν_1 and ν_2 d.f. (denoted by F_{ν_1, ν_2}) is defined as the ratio of independent $\chi^2_{\nu_1}$ and $\chi^2_{\nu_2}$ r.v.'s, each divided by its own d.f.:

$$F_{\nu_1, \nu_2} = \frac{\chi^2_{\nu_1}/\nu_1}{\chi^2_{\nu_2}/\nu_2}.$$

This distribution arises when comparing the ratio of sample variances, S_1^2 and S_2^2, based on independent random samples of sizes n_1 and n_2 from $N(\mu_1, \sigma_1^2)$ and $N(\mu_2, \sigma_2^2)$ populations, respectively. It follows that

$$\frac{S_1^2/\sigma_1^2}{S_2^2/\sigma_2^2} \sim F_{n_1-1, n_2-1}.$$

The final section of the chapter discusses distributions of the **order statistics** from a random sample. These distributions are useful in nonparametric and ranking problems.

■ EXERCISES

Section 5.1

5.1   A box contains five chips marked $1, 2, \ldots, 5$. One chip is drawn at random, the number on it is noted, and the chip is replaced. The process is repeated with another chip. Let X_1, X_2 be the outcomes of the two draws.

   (a) What is the population from which this random sample is drawn? Find the mean μ and variance σ^2 of this population.

(b) List all possible (25 in all) samples and calculate the value of the sample mean $\bar{X}$ for each sample.

(c) Obtain the sampling distribution of $\bar{X}$ from this list.

(d) Find $E(\bar{X})$ and $\text{Var}(\bar{X})$. Check that they equal μ and $\sigma^2/2$, respectively.

5.2 ▣ Simulate 100 rolls of two fair dice. (Generate 100 pairs of observations from a discrete uniform distribution on integers $1, 2, \ldots, 6$ by using a computer package.) Compute the sample mean $\bar{X}$ for each sample.

(a) For the 11 distinct observed values of the sample mean make a bar chart which gives the empirical distribution of $\bar{X}$. How closely does this empirical distribution compare with the theoretical distribution of $\bar{X}$ given in Table 5.2?

(b) Using the empirical distribution obtained in (a), compute the average and the variance of the 100 sample means. How closely do they estimate the corresponding population values $\mu = 3.5$ and $\sigma^2/2 = 1.4583$?

5.3 ▣ Simulate 100 rolls of ten fair dice. Let $X_1, \ldots, X_{10}$ be the outcomes. Compute the sample mean $\bar{X}$ for each sample.

(a) For the distinct observed values of the sample mean, make a bar chart which gives the empirical distribution of $\bar{X}$.

(b) Using the empirical distribution obtained in (a), compute the average and the variance of the 100 sample means. How closely do they estimate the corresponding population values $\mu = 3.5$ and $\sigma^2/10 = 0.2916$?

(c) Compare your results from (a) and (b) with those of Exercise 5.2. Note and explain any differences.

5.4 A soft drink company uses a filling machine to fill cans. Each 12 oz. can is to contain 355 milliliters of beverage. In fact, the amount varies according to a normal distribution with mean $\mu = 355.2$ ml and standard deviation $\sigma = 0.5$ ml.

(a) What is the probability that an individual can contains less than 355 ml?

(b) What is the probability that the mean content of a six-pack of cans is less than 355 ml?

5.5 A random sample $X_1, \ldots, X_{150}$ is drawn from a population with mean $\mu = 40$ and standard deviation $\sigma = 15$ but an unknown distribution. Let $U = (X_1 + \cdots + X_{50})/50$ represent the sample mean of the first 50 observations and $V = (X_{51} + \cdots + X_{150})/100$ the sample mean of the last 100 observations.

(a) What are the approximate distributions of U and V?

(b) Which probability would you expect to be larger, $P(35 \leq U \leq 45)$ or $P(35 \leq V \leq 45)$? Why?

(c) Find $P(35 \leq U \leq 45)$ and $P(35 \leq V \leq 45)$ using the normal approximation.

5.6 A truck can carry a maximum load of 4000 lb. A manufacturer wants to ship an order of 50 boxes. The weights of the boxes are normally distributed with mean $\mu = 78$ lb. and standard deviation $\sigma = 12$ lb. What is the probability that all 50 boxes can be sent in one shipment? If the weights are not normally distributed, will the answer be still approximately correct? Why or why not?

5.7 ▣ To estimate the average number of years an employee stays with a company, a random sample of 25 employees is drawn from the company's past employee records and the sample mean $\bar{X}$ is calculated. Suppose that the true but unknown distribution of the length of stay of an employee is exponential with a mean of 5 years.

(a) What is the exact distribution of $\bar{X}$? What is its mean and standard deviation?

(b) Simulate 100 random samples of size 25 from this exponential distribution. Compute the sample mean for each sample and make a normal plot of the 100 sample means. Does the normal plot suggest that the sample means are approximately normally distributed?

(c) Use the normal approximation to find the probability that the sample mean will estimate the true mean of 5 years within a margin of error of ± 0.5 years, i.e., $P(-0.5 \le \bar{X} - 5 \le 0.5)$.

5.8   The lifetime of disc brake pads varies according to a normal distribution with mean $\mu = 50{,}000$ miles and standard deviation $\sigma = 3000$ miles. Suppose that a sample of nine brake pads is tested.

(a) What is the distribution of the sample mean $\bar{X}$? Give the mean and standard deviation of this distribution.

(b) Does your answer in (a) require the use of the central limit theorem? Why or why not?

(c) Suppose that a sample mean less than 47,000 miles is considered evidence that $\mu < 50{,}000$ miles. What is the probability that this will happen even when the true mean $\mu = 50{,}000$, leading to an incorrect conclusion?

5.9   Consider an r.v. $X \sim \text{Bin}(n = 25, p = 0.4)$. Find the probability that $X \le 10$ using the following methods and compare the results.

(a) Exact binomial probability from Table A.1.

(b) Normal approximation without a continuity correction.

(c) Normal approximation with a continuity correction.

5.10   Repeat Exercise 5.9 using $p = 0.2$ and find the probability that $X \le 5$. Compare the results. Is the normal approximation more accurate for $p = 0.4$ or $p = 0.2$? Why?

5.11   A buyer must decide whether or not to accept a large lot of items which, unknown to him, contains 5% defectives. The lot will be accepted if there are only 0 or 1 defective items in a sample of 20 items randomly drawn from the lot.

(a) Calculate the exact probability that the lot will be accepted.

(b) Use the Poisson distribution to approximate the acceptance probability.

(c) Use the normal distribution with a continuity correction to approximate the acceptance probability.

(d) Which approximation gives the better result: Poisson or normal? Why?

5.12   The quality control department of a company that makes computer backup tapes tests a sample of 25 tapes from each production run. An investigation for production problems is initiated if 2 or more tapes are defective. Suppose that a production run contains 30% defective tapes.

(a) Calculate the probability that the production problems will be investigated. Use the exact binomial formula.

(b) Calculate the normal approximation without a continuity correction.

(c) Calculate the normal approximation with a continuity correction. Does this improve the accuracy?

5.13 A university considers giving only pass/fail grades to freshmen to reduce competition and stress. The student newspaper interviews faculty members and reports their opinions of the proposed policy. Suppose that 70% of the faculty favor the pass/fail proposal.

   (a) If 10 faculty members are interviewed, find the exact probability that a majority (6 or more) will favor the policy.

   (b) If 50 faculty members are interviewed, find the probability that a majority (26 or more) will favor the proposal. Check if the normal approximation will give accurate results. If so, use it with a continuity correction.

5.14 In an extrasensory perception (ESP) experiment, five choices are offered for each question. Assume that a person without ESP guesses randomly and thus correctly answers with probability 1/5. Further assume that the responses are independent. Suppose that 100 questions are asked.

   (a) What are the mean and standard deviation of the number of correct answers?

   (b) What are the mean and standard deviation of the proportion of correct answers?

   (c) What is the probability that a person without ESP will correctly answer at least 30 of the 100 questions? Check if the normal approximation will give accurate results. If so use it with a continuity correction.

Section 5.2

5.15 Refer to Exercise 5.1.

   (a) List all possible (25 in all) samples and calculate the value of the sample variance S^2 for each sample.

   (b) Obtain the sampling distribution of S^2 using this list.

   (c) Find $E(S^2)$. Check that it equals σ^2.

5.16 Using Table A.5, find the following values: $\chi^2_{5,.01}$, $\chi^2_{10,.05}$, $\chi^2_{10,.95}$, $\chi^2_{10,.75}$.

5.17 Consider the chi-square distribution with 8 degrees of freedom.

   (a) What are the mean and variance of a χ^2_8 r.v.?

   (b) Using Table A.5, find constants a, b, c, d and e so that $P(\chi^2_8 > a) = .05$, $P(\chi^2_8 > b) = .99$, $P(\chi^2_8 < c) = .90$, and $P(d < \chi^2_8 < e) = .95$.

   (c) Express the constants from (b) in terms of the notation $\chi^2_{\nu,\alpha}$.

   (d) Sketch each of the probabilities from (b) as an area under the χ^2_8 p.d.f. curve.

5.18 Consider the chi-square distribution with 14 degrees of freedom.

   (a) What are the mean and variance of a χ^2_{14} r.v.?

   (b) Using Table A.5, find constants a, b, c, d and e so that $P(\chi^2_{14} > a) = .95$, $P(\chi^2_{14} > b) = .05$, $P(\chi^2_{14} < c) = .99$ and $P(d < \chi^2_{14} < e) = .90$.

   (c) Express the constants from (b) in terms of the notation $\chi^2_{\nu,\alpha}$.

   (d) Sketch each of the probabilities from (b) as an area under the χ^2_{14} p.d.f. curve.

5.19 Show the result (5.6) that $z^2_{\alpha/2} = \chi^2_{1,\alpha}$. (*Hint*: Note that $P(-z_{\alpha/2} \leq Z \leq z_{\alpha/2}) = P(Z^2 \leq z^2_{\alpha/2}) = 1 - \alpha$ and use (5.5).)

5.20 Let S^2 denote the sample variance computed from a random sample of size n from an $N(\mu, \sigma^2)$ distribution. Using Table A.5 for the percentiles of the χ^2-distribution, for sample sizes $n = 8, 17$, and 21, find approximately the probability that the sample variance S^2 exceeds the true variance σ^2 by a factor of two, i.e., $P(S^2 > 2\sigma^2)$. Comment on the results.

5.21   ■ If a random sample of size n is drawn from a normal distribution, we know from equation (5.7) that the standardized sample variance, $U = (n-1)S^2/\sigma^2$, has a χ^2_{n-1}-distribution. Conduct a simulation to look at this relationship.

(a) Generate 100 random samples of size five from an $N(10, 3^2)$ distribution. Calculate S^2 for each sample. Standardize the S^2 values by calculating $U = (n-1)S^2/\sigma^2 = 4S^2/9$.

(b) Find the 25th, 50th, and 90th percentiles of the simulated sample. How do these percentiles compare to the corresponding percentiles of the χ^2_4-distribution?

5.22   ■ This exercise uses simulation to illustrate definition (5.3) that the sum $X = Z_1^2 + Z_2^2 + \cdots + Z_\nu^2$ is distributed as χ^2_ν where $Z_1, Z_2, \ldots, Z_\nu$ are i.i.d. $N(0, 1)$ r.v.'s.

(a) Generate 100 random samples of size four, $Z_1, \ldots, Z_4$, from an $N(0, 1)$ distribution and calculate $X = Z_1^2 + Z_2^2 + Z_3^2 + Z_4^2 \sim \chi^2_4$.

(b) Find the 25th, 50th, and 90th percentiles of the simulated sample. How do these percentiles compare to the corresponding percentiles of the χ^2_4-distribution?

5.23   An engineer suspects that the temperature inside an oven is not as uniform as when it was new, at which time the temperature varied $\pm 10°$F around its setting. (Taking the range of a normal distribution to be roughly $\pm 2\sigma$, this translates into $\sigma = 5°$F.) To verify his suspicion, he takes 20 measurements in different parts of the oven. He wants a rule which decides that the true $\sigma > 5$ if the sample standard deviation of the measurements exceeds $5c$, where $c > 0$ is a suitably chosen constant. The rule must not have more than a 10% chance of making a wrong decision, i.e., deciding that $\sigma > 5$ when, in fact, $\sigma = 5$.

(a) Find the value of c.

(b) Based on this value of c, does the rule decide that $\sigma > 5$ if the sample standard deviation of the engineer's measurements is $s = 7.5°$F?

Section 5.3

5.24   Using Table A.4, find the following values: $t_{5,.05}, t_{10,.10}, t_{10,.90}, t_{20,.01}$.

5.25   Consider the Student's t-distribution with 10 degrees of freedom.

(a) Using Table A.4, find constants a, b, c, d so that $P(T_{10} > a) = .05$, $P(T_{10} > b) = .99$, $P(T_{10} < c) = .90$ and $P(|T_{10}| < d) = .95$.

(b) Express the constants from (a) in terms of the notation $t_{\nu,\alpha}$.

(c) Sketch each of the probabilities from (a) as an area under the T_{10} p.d.f. curve.

5.26   Find the following probabilities:

$$P(-t_{8,.10} \le T_8 \le t_{8,.10}), \quad P(-t_{8,.05} \le T_8 \le t_{8,.01}), \quad P(t_{8,.05} \le T_8 \le t_{8,.01}), \quad P(T_8 > -t_{8,.05}).$$

Sketch these probabilities as areas under the T_8 p.d.f. curve.

5.27   ■ In this exercise we use simulation to verify that the standardized sample mean $T = (\bar{X} - \mu)\sqrt{n}/S$ has a t_{n-1}-distribution for a random sample of size n from an $N(\mu, \sigma^2)$ distribution.

(a) Generate 100 random samples of size five from an $N(10, 3^2)$ distribution. (If your computer package generates $Z \sim N(0, 1)$, then compute $X = 3Z + 10$ to obtain $X \sim N(10, 3^2)$.) Calculate $\bar{X}$ and S for each sample and then $T = (\bar{X} - \mu)\sqrt{n}/S$.

(b) Find the 25th, 50th, and 90th percentiles of the simulated sample. How do these percentiles compare to the corresponding percentiles of the t_4-distribution?

5.28 ■ In this exercise we simulate the t-distribution with 4 d.f. using the general definition (5.13), $T = \frac{Z}{\sqrt{U/\nu}}$, where $Z \sim N(0, 1)$ and $U \sim \chi_\nu^2$.

    (a) Generate 100 i.i.d. standard normal r.v.'s (Z's) and 100 i.i.d. χ_4^2 r.v.'s (U's) and compute $T = Z/\sqrt{U/4} = 2Z/\sqrt{U}$.

    (b) Find the 25th, 50th, and 90th percentiles of the simulated sample of the T values. How do these percentiles compare to the corresponding percentiles of the t_4-distribution?

Section 5.4

5.29 Using Table A.6, find the following values: $f_{10,10,.025}$, $f_{10,10,.975}$, $f_{5,10,.10}$, $f_{5,10,.90}$, $f_{10,5,.90}$.

5.30 Consider the F-distribution with 8 and 12 degrees of freedom.

    (a) Using Table A.6, find constants a, b, c, d, e so that $P(F_{8,12} > a) = .05$, $P(F_{8,12} > b) = .99$, $P(F_{8,12} < c) = .90$, and $P(d < F_{8,12} < e) = .95$.

    (b) Express the constants from (a) in terms of the notation $f_{\nu_1,\nu_2,\alpha}$.

    (c) Sketch each of the probabilities from (a) as an area under the $F_{8,12}$ p.d.f. curve.

5.31 Show the result (5.18) that $f_{\nu_1,\nu_2,1-\alpha} = \frac{1}{f_{\nu_2,\nu_1,\alpha}}$. (*Hint*: Begin with the probability statement $P(F_{\nu_1,\nu_2} \leq f_{\nu_1,\nu_2,1-\alpha}) = \alpha$ and use (5.17).)

5.32 Show the result (5.20) that $t_{\nu,\alpha/2}^2 = f_{1,\nu,\alpha}$. (*Hint*: Note that $P(-t_{\nu,\alpha/2} \leq T_\nu \leq t_{\nu,\alpha/2}) = P(T_\nu^2 \leq t_{\nu,\alpha/2}^2) = 1 - \alpha$ and use (5.19).)

5.33 Two independent random samples of sizes n_1 and n_2 are drawn from $N(\mu_1, \sigma_1^2)$ and $N(\mu_2, \sigma_2^2)$ distributions, respectively, and sample variances S_1^2 and S_2^2 are computed. If σ_1^2 and σ_2^2 are equal, use Table A.6 to find $P(S_1^2/S_2^2 > 4)$ for the following pairs of sample sizes: $(n_1 = 7, n_2 = 5)$, $(n_1 = 13, n_2 = 7)$, and $(n_1 = 9, n_2 = 16)$.

Section 5.5

5.34 Let $X_1, \ldots X_9$ be a random sample drawn from the $U[0, 1]$ distribution. Find the p.d.f.'s of $X_{\min}$, $X_{\max}$, and the sample median $\tilde{X}$.

5.35 Let $X_1, \ldots X_9$ be a random sample drawn from an exponential distribution with $\lambda = 0.10$. Find the p.d.f.'s of $X_{\min}$, $X_{\max}$, and the sample median $\tilde{X}$.

5.36 A calculator runs on three batteries. The time to failure of any battery is exponentially distributed with a mean of 6 months.

    (a) Suppose the calculator fails to function properly if *any* battery fails. Let T be the time to failure of the calculator. What is the c.d.f. of T?

    (b) Suppose the calculator fails to function properly only if *all* batteries fail. Let T be the time to failure of the calculator. What is the c.d.f. of T?

Advanced Exercises

5.37 ■ A photolithographic process etches contact windows through an oxide layer deposited on a silicon wafer used in integrated circuit fabrication. For each wafer the r.v. of interest is the number of windows that are not properly formed (unopened or too small or too large). Suppose that the distribution of this r.v. is as follows:

No. defective widows	0	1	2	3	4	5
Probability	0.5	0.2	0.1	0.1	0.05	0.05

(a) Compute the mean μ and standard deviation σ of this distribution.

(b) To estimate the average number of defective windows per wafer, a random sample of five wafers is inspected periodically. To find the distribution of the sample mean, simulate 500 samples of size five, compute their sample means, and plot a histogram. (In your computer package use a discrete distribution on integers 0 through 5 with the above probabilities to simulate the data.) Also calculate the average and the standard deviation of the means.

(c) Comment on the shape of the empirical distribution of $\bar{X}$. Does it look close to the normal distribution? Repeat the simulation for a sample of size 10. Do you see any difference in the shape?

(d) How close are the average of the sample means and their standard deviation calculated in (b) to their theoretical values μ and $\sigma/\sqrt{n}$, where μ and σ are calculated in (a) and $n = 5$?

5.38 The sampling scheme used in Exercise 5.1 is called **sampling with replacement**. When **sampling without replacement**, the chips are not replaced. Suppose that two chips are drawn at random in this way. Let X_1, X_2 be the outcomes of the two draws.

(a) List all possible (20 in all) samples and calculate the value of the sample mean $\bar{X}$ for each sample.

(b) Obtain the sampling distribution of $\bar{X}$ using this list.

(c) Find $E(\bar{X})$ and $\text{Var}(\bar{X})$. Are their values different from those obtained for sampling with replacement?

(d) For sampling without replacement, $\text{Var}(\bar{X})$ equals $(\frac{N-n}{N-1})\frac{\sigma^2}{n}$, where n is the sample size and N is the population size. Check your answer from (c) with this formula.

5.39 ■ Refer to Exercise 5.22. Another way to simulate a χ_ν^2 r.v. uses the fact that the χ_ν^2-distribution is the same as the gamma distribution with $\lambda = 1/2$ and $r = \nu/2$. If ν is an even number, then by generating $r = \nu/2$ i.i.d. exponential r.v.'s with $\lambda = 1/2$ and adding them up we get a χ_ν^2 r.v.

(a) Use this method to generate a random sample of size 100 from the χ_4^2-distribution.

(b) Find the 25th, 50th, and 90th percentiles of the sample generated in (a). How do these percentiles compare to the corresponding percentiles of the χ_4^2-distribution?

5.40 As noted in equation (5.3), a χ_ν^2 r.v. can be represented as the sum of n i.i.d. $\chi_1^2 = (N(0, 1))^2$ r.v.'s. Therefore we can apply the central limit theorem to conclude that for large ν, the distribution of χ_ν^2 can be approximated by a normal distribution with $\mu = E(\chi_\nu^2) = \nu$ and $\sigma^2 = \text{Var}(\chi_\nu^2) = 2\nu$. Check the accuracy of this approximation by comparing the lower and upper 10th, 5th, and 1st percentiles of the two distributions for $\nu = 40$. The χ_{40}^2 percentiles can be read from Table A.5, while the upper and lower α quantiles of an $N(\mu, \sigma^2)$ distribution are given by $\mu + z_\alpha \sigma$ and $\mu - z_\alpha \sigma$, respectively.

5.41 Show that a T_1 r.v. can be expressed as a ratio of two independent $N(0, 1)$ r.v.'s. Using the fact that $\Gamma(\frac{1}{2}) = \sqrt{\pi}$, show that the p.d.f. (5.14) of a T_1 r.v. simplifies to

$$f(t) = \frac{1}{\pi(1 + t^2)} \quad \text{for} \quad -\infty < t < \infty.$$

This is known as the **Cauchy distribution**, which is derived in Exercises 2.85 and 2.87 by different methods.

5.42 Show that as $\nu \to \infty$, the p.d.f. (5.14) of the t_ν distribution approaches the standard normal p.d.f. (*Hint*: Use **Stirling's approximation** that as $n \to \infty$, $\Gamma(n + 1) \sim \sqrt{2\pi n} n^n e^{-n}$, i.e., the ratio of these two quantities approaches 1.)

5.43 Let X be an r.v. with a continuous c.d.f. F and consider the r.v. $Y = F(X)$.

(a) Show that Y has a uniform distribution over the interval $[0, 1]$. (*Hint*: If G denotes the c.d.f. of Y, then show that $G(y) = P(Y \leq y) = y$, which is the c.d.f. of a $U[0, 1]$ r.v.)

(b) The transform $Y = F(X)$ is known as the **probability integral transform**, which is a useful technique for simulating an r.v. X from any continuous distribution if F^{-1} can be obtained in a closed form: Generate Y from a $U[0, 1]$ distribution (which is easy to do using a random number generator) and find $X = F^{-1}(Y)$. Show how you will use this method to generate an observation from an exponential distribution with parameter λ (mean = $1/\lambda$). (*Hint*: F^{-1} for the exponential distribution is derived in Exercise 4.50.)

5.44 Consider n identical components whose lifetimes, $T_1, T_2, \ldots, T_n$ are i.i.d. uniform r.v.'s over the interval $[0, \theta]$, where θ is an upper limit on the lifetime.

(a) Suppose that the components are connected in series. Show that the lifetime of the system is $T_{(1)} = T_{\min}$ with p.d.f.

$$f_{(1)} = n\left(1 - \frac{t}{\theta}\right)^{n-1} \frac{1}{\theta}.$$

Use this p.d.f. to show that the **mean time to failure (MTTF)** of the system is

$$E(T_{\min}) = \frac{\theta}{n + 1}.$$

(b) Suppose that the components are connected in parallel. Show that the lifetime of the system is $T_{(n)} = T_{\max}$ with p.d.f.

$$f_{(n)} = n\left(\frac{t}{\theta}\right)^{n-1} \frac{1}{\theta}.$$

Use this p.d.f. to show that the MTTF of the system is

$$E(T_{\max}) = \frac{n}{n + 1} \theta.$$

(c) Compare the MTTF's of the series and parallel systems as n increases.

CHAPTER 6

BASIC CONCEPTS OF INFERENCE

Statistical inference deals with methods for making statements about a population based on a sample drawn from that population. There are two common types of inference problems. The first is *estimating* an unknown population parameter. The second is making a decision by *testing* a hypothesis about an unknown population parameter. The following example illustrates these two types of inference.

A food company wants to estimate the mean package weight of a cereal box filled during a production shift. To do this, a random sample of 25 boxes of cereal is taken from the production process and the contents are weighed. The mean of this sample can be used to estimate the mean package weight of the population of all boxes filled during the shift. This is an of example of **estimation** where the sample mean is used to estimate the unknown population mean. In addition, the sample data could also be used to address the question: Do the cereal boxes meet the minimum mean weight specification of 16 oz.? This is a two-decision problem (with "yes" or "no" as possible decisions) which is usually formulated as a **hypothesis testing** problem.

Inferences are often made informally using summary statistics or graphical displays that we studied in Chapter 4. However, informal inferences lack statements about statistical accuracy or sampling errors. In the above example, suppose we require the mean weight for the sample to be at least 16.10 oz. to assure that the weight specification is met. Because of the sampling error (caused by the variability in the filling process and other sources of variation), it is possible that even when the population mean is less than 16 oz., the sample mean may exceed 16.10 oz. Conversely, it is also possible that the population mean is greater than 16 oz. and yet the sample mean is less than 16.10 oz.

How confident can we be in the correctness of a decision made by this rule? Can we quantify the chance of making an error? In this chapter we study formal aspects of estimation and hypothesis testing which use methods of probability and sampling distributions (studied in Chapters 2 and 5, respectively) to develop measures of statistical accuracy.

6.1   POINT ESTIMATION

We consider two types of estimation problems. The first is to estimate an unknown population parameter by a single statistic calculated from sample data. This is referred to as **point estimation**, which is discussed in the present section. The second is to calculate an interval from sample data that includes the parameter with a preassigned probability. This is referred to as **confidence interval estimation**, which is discussed in Section 6.2.

Let $X_1, X_2, \ldots, X_n$ be a random sample from a population with an unknown parameter θ. A **point estimator** $\hat{\theta}$ of θ is a statistic computed from sample data (i.e., $\hat{\theta}$ is a function of $X_1, X_2, \ldots, X_n$). For example, if θ is the population mean, then we can use the sample mean, $\bar{X} = \sum_{i=1}^{n} X_i / n = \hat{\theta}$, as an estimator of θ. If θ is the population variance, then we can use the sample variance, $S^2 = \sum_{i=1}^{n} (X_i - \bar{X})^2 / (n-1) = \hat{\theta}$, as an estimator of θ.

The statistic $\hat{\theta}$ is a random variable (r.v.) because it is a function of the X_i's which are r.v.'s. Generally, we will use the term **estimator** to refer to the r.v. $\hat{\theta}$ and the term **estimate** to refer to a numerical value of $\hat{\theta}$ calculated from the observed sample data $X_1 = x_1, \ldots, X_n = x_n$. Think of an estimator as a rule to compute the desired value from the data and an estimate as the specific numerical value obtained using that rule. The following two examples illustrate these concepts.

EXAMPLE 6.1

An alternative estimator of the population mean θ is the **midrange**, defined as $\hat{\theta} = \frac{1}{2}(X_{\min} + X_{\max})$. Suppose a sample of size five is observed with $x_1 = 2.3$, $x_2 = 3.3$, $x_3 = 1.9$, $x_4 = 2.8$, and $x_5 = 2.4$. Then $x_{\min} = 1.9$, $x_{\max} = 3.3$, and the midrange estimate equals $\hat{\theta} = \frac{1}{2}(1.9+3.3) = 2.6$. The sample mean estimate equals $\hat{\theta} = \bar{x} = \frac{1}{5}(2.3 + 3.3 + 1.9 + 2.8 + 2.4) = 2.54$.   ◆

EXAMPLE 6.2

A random sample of 100 transistors from a large shipment is inspected to estimate the proportion of defectives in the shipment. Let θ be the fraction of defective transistors in the shipment and $\hat{\theta}$ be the proportion of defectives in the sample. Suppose that four independent samples are drawn with replacement from the shipment, yielding the following results.

Sample	1	2	3	4
Proportion defectives $\hat{\theta}$	0.02	0.00	0.01	0.04

Although each value of $\hat{\theta}$ in this table is an estimate of the proportion of defectives θ in the shipment, the estimate varies from sample to sample. Thus the population parameter θ is a constant, but the point estimator $\hat{\theta}$ is an r.v.   ◆

6.1.1 Bias, Variance, and Mean Square Error

Although an estimator is a random variable, we want it to be as close to the true parameter value as possible. This idea is quantified through two properties of an estimator: bias and variance. The **bias** of an estimator $\hat{\theta}$ is defined as

$$\text{Bias}(\hat{\theta}) = E(\hat{\theta}) - \theta$$

where θ is the true parameter value and $E(\hat{\theta})$ is the mean of the distribution of $\hat{\theta}$. The bias measures the average *accuracy* of an estimator: the lower the bias, the more accurate the estimator. An estimator whose bias is zero is called **unbiased**; i.e., $\hat{\theta}$ is unbiased if $E(\hat{\theta}) = \theta$ regardless of the true value of θ. In other words, if $\hat{\theta}$ is computed from repeated independent random samples drawn from the same distribution, the average of those estimates converges to the true θ as the number of samples becomes large.

An estimator $\hat{\theta}$ may be unbiased and yet fluctuate greatly from sample to sample. It is little consolation to know that an estimator is unbiased if it is likely that the estimate from your particular sample (which is often the only sample available) might be far from the target. A measure of the *precision* or *reliability* of an estimator is its variance:

$$\text{Var}(\hat{\theta}) = E[\hat{\theta} - E(\hat{\theta})]^2;$$

the lower the variance, the more precise (reliable) the estimator.

The two measures, bias and variance, can be illustrated by a dart game.[1] The bull's-eye in Figure 6.1 represents the true parameter value θ. The $\times$'s are darts thrown at the target which represent estimates from repeated samples. A good estimator with low variability and low bias is illustrated by Figure 6.1(a), where darts are tightly clustered around the bull's-eye. Darts that are widely dispersed around the bull's-eye, as shown in Figure 6.1(b), represent high variability, but low bias. Darts that systematically hit in a tight cluster far from the bull's-eye, as shown in Figure 6.1(c), represent low variability, but high bias. Finally, darts that generally hit systematically far from the bull's-eye and are widely dispersed, as shown in Figure 6.1(d), represent high variability and high bias.

A "good" estimator should have low bias as well as low variance. Among unbiased estimators, the one with the smallest variance should be chosen. To choose among all estimators (biased or unbiased) we use a measure that combines both bias and variance. It is called the **mean square error (MSE)** and is defined as:

$$\text{MSE}(\hat{\theta}) = E(\hat{\theta} - \theta)^2. \tag{6.1}$$

The MSE may be viewed as the **expected squared error loss**. This means that if the loss from estimating the true value θ by $\hat{\theta}$ is measured by the square of the sampling error, $(\hat{\theta} - \theta)^2$, then the MSE is the expected value of this loss.

---

[1] D. S. Moore (1985), *Statistics: Concepts & Controversies*, 2nd ed., New York: W. H. Freeman and Co., p. 17.

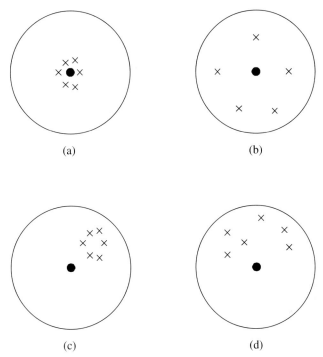

(a)   (b)

(c)   (d)

Figure 6.1   Illustration of Bias and Variance of an Estimator: (a) Low bias, low variance; (b) Low bias, high variance; (c) High bias, low variance; (d) High bias, high variance

To see more clearly how the MSE combines the variance and bias of an estimator, write (6.1) as follows:

$$\text{MSE}(\hat{\theta}) = E\left[\hat{\theta} - E(\hat{\theta}) + E(\hat{\theta}) - \theta\right]^2$$

$$= E[\hat{\theta} - E(\hat{\theta})]^2 + [E(\hat{\theta}) - \theta]^2 + 2\{E[\hat{\theta} - E(\hat{\theta})][E(\hat{\theta}) - \theta]\}$$

$$= \text{Var}(\hat{\theta}) + [\text{Bias}(\hat{\theta})]^2 + \underbrace{2E[\hat{\theta} - E(\hat{\theta})][E(\hat{\theta}) - \theta]}_{=0}$$

$$= \text{Var}(\hat{\theta}) + [\text{Bias}(\hat{\theta})]^2. \tag{6.2}$$

Thus the MSE is the sum of the variance and the bias-squared terms.

EXAMPLE 6.3

Let $X_1, X_2, \ldots, X_n$ be a random sample from any distribution with a finite mean μ and variance σ^2. Show that the sample variance $S^2 = \left[\sum_{i=1}^{n}(X_i - \bar{X})^2\right]/(n-1)$ is an unbiased estimator of σ^2.

First write $\sum_{i=1}^{n}(X_i - \bar{X})^2$ in the following way:

$$\sum_{i=1}^{n}(X_i - \bar{X})^2 = \sum_{i=1}^{n}[(X_i - \mu) - (\bar{X} - \mu)]^2$$

$$= \sum_{i=1}^{n}(X_i - \mu)^2 - 2(\bar{X} - \mu)\sum_{i=1}^{n}(X_i - \mu) + n(\bar{X} - \mu)^2$$

$$= \sum_{i=1}^{n}(X_i - \mu)^2 - 2(\bar{X} - \mu)(\sum_{i=1}^{n}X_i - n\mu) + n(\bar{X} - \mu)^2$$

$$= \sum_{i=1}^{n}(X_i - \mu)^2 - 2(\bar{X} - \mu)(n\bar{X} - n\mu) + n(\bar{X} - \mu)^2$$

$$= \sum_{i=1}^{n}(X_i - \mu)^2 - 2n(\bar{X} - \mu)^2 + n(\bar{X} - \mu)^2$$

$$= \sum_{i=1}^{n}(X_i - \mu)^2 - n(\bar{X} - \mu)^2.$$

Using the facts that $E(X_i - \mu)^2 = \text{Var}(X_i) = \sigma^2$ and $E(\bar{X} - \mu)^2 = \text{Var}(\bar{X}) = \sigma^2/n$, we see that

$$E\left[\sum_{i=1}^{n}(X_i - \bar{X})^2\right] = \underbrace{\sum_{i=1}^{n}E(X_i - \mu)^2}_{n\sigma^2} - n\underbrace{E(\bar{X} - \mu)^2}_{\frac{\sigma^2}{n}}$$

$$= n\sigma^2 - \sigma^2$$

$$= (n-1)\sigma^2.$$

Therefore,

$$E(S^2) = E\left[\frac{\sum_{i=1}^{n}(X_i - \bar{X})^2}{n-1}\right] = \frac{(n-1)\sigma^2}{n-1} = \sigma^2.$$

◆

The MSE can be used as a criterion to compare competing estimators. The following example illustrates this.

EXAMPLE 6.4

Let $X_1, X_2, \ldots, X_n$ be a random sample from an $N(\mu, \sigma^2)$ distribution. Compare the following two estimators of σ^2 in terms of their MSE's:

$$S_1^2 = \frac{\sum_{i=1}^{n}(X_i - \bar{X})^2}{n-1} \quad \text{and} \quad S_2^2 = \frac{\sum_{i=1}^{n}(X_i - \bar{X})^2}{n}.$$

First note that $\text{Bias}(S_1^2) = 0$ from Example 6.3 and $\text{Var}(S_1^2) = 2\sigma^4/(n-1)$ from equation (5.10). Hence,

$$\text{MSE}(S_1^2) = \text{Var}(S_1^2) + \text{Bias}(S_1^2) = \frac{2\sigma^4}{n-1}.$$

Next, write $S_2^2 = \frac{n-1}{n}S_1^2$. Hence,

$$\text{Var}(S_2^2) = \frac{(n-1)^2}{n^2}\text{Var}(S_1^2) = \frac{(n-1)^2}{n^2} \cdot \frac{2\sigma^4}{n-1} = \frac{2(n-1)\sigma^4}{n^2}$$

and

$$\text{Bias}(S_2^2) = E(S_2^2) - \sigma^2 = E\left(\frac{n-1}{n}S_1^2\right) - \sigma^2 = \frac{n-1}{n}\sigma^2 - \sigma^2 = -\frac{\sigma^2}{n}.$$

Therefore,

$$\text{MSE}(S_2^2) = \frac{2(n-1)\sigma^4}{n^2} + \frac{\sigma^4}{n^2}$$

$$= \frac{2n-1}{n^2}\sigma^4.$$

Simple algebra shows that $\text{MSE}(S_1^2) > \text{MSE}(S_2^2)$ when $n > 1$. Although S_2^2 is *biased*, it has a smaller MSE! However, the difference is very slight and approaches zero as n becomes large. In practice, S_1^2 is almost universally used.   ◆

Suppose that an estimator is chosen and the value of $\hat{\theta}$ is calculated from the sample. How precise is this estimate? Can we assess the discrepancy between the estimate and the true value? To answer these questions, it is customary to report the standard deviation of $\hat{\theta}$, which is referred to as its **standard error (SE)**. Usually the standard error also must be estimated from the sample; for convenience, we will refer to the **estimated standard error** also as **SE**. For example, the observed sample mean $\bar{x}$ based on a random sample of size n from a population with mean μ and variance σ^2 is an unbiased estimate of μ. $\text{SD}(\bar{X}) = \sigma/\sqrt{n}$ is itself estimated from the sample by $s/\sqrt{n}$, where s is the observed sample standard deviation. Therefore

$$\text{SE}(\bar{x}) = \frac{s}{\sqrt{n}}.$$

This is commonly referred to as the **standard error of the mean (SEM)**. For another example, the sample proportion $\hat{p}$ of successes in a Bernoulli sample of size n is an estimate of the success probability p, and its estimated standard error is

$$\text{SE}(\hat{p}) = \sqrt{\frac{\hat{p}(1-\hat{p})}{n}}.$$

The next question is how to interpret the SE of an estimate. A precise estimate has a small standard error, but exactly how are the precision and standard error related? We can answer this question if the sampling distribution of an estimator $\hat{\theta}$ is normal with mean equal to the true value θ. Then we know that about 95% of the time the estimator will be within two SE's from θ. This idea will be used in Section 6.2 to obtain a confidence interval for θ.

6.1.2 *Methods of Estimation

In the previous subsection we discussed some properties of estimators. The problem of finding estimators with good properties is a difficult one in general. One method used for this purpose is that of **maximum likelihood estimation**, which is discussed in Chapter 15, Section 15.1. For estimating parameters in regression models the method of **least squares estimation** is useful and is discussed in Chapters 10 and 11. Here we present a simple intuitive method, called the **method of moments**, which gives reasonable estimators in many problems.

Method of Moments.   To estimate the unknown mean μ of a population, it is common to use the sample mean $\bar{X} = \sum_{i=1}^{n} X_i/n$ calculated from a random sample $X_1, X_2, \ldots, X_n$ from that population. The population is modeled by a probability distribution involving one or more unknown parameters. If X denotes an r.v. from this distribution, then $\mu = E(X)$ is the first population moment (see Section 2.4.2) and $\hat{\mu} = \bar{X}$ is the first sample moment. This is the simplest application of the method of moments.

More generally, suppose the distribution used to model the population involves m unknown parameters, $\theta_1, \theta_2, \ldots, \theta_m$. To find the moments estimators of these parameters, we express the first m population moments, $\mu_k = E(X^k)$, $k = 1, 2, \ldots, m$, in terms of $\theta_1, \theta_2, \ldots, \theta_m$. Then we estimate the population moments by the corresponding sample moments:

$$\hat{\mu}_k = \frac{1}{n} \sum_{i=1}^{n} X_i^k, \quad k = 1, 2, \ldots, m$$

and solve the resulting m simultaneous equations for the m unknown θ's, thus obtaining their estimators $\hat{\theta}_1, \hat{\theta}_2, \ldots, \hat{\theta}_m$.

EXAMPLE 6.5

Let $X_1, X_2, \ldots, X_n$ be a random sample from a uniform distribution on the interval $[0, \theta]$. Find the method of moments estimator of θ.

The mean of the $U[0, \theta]$ distribution equals $\mu = \theta/2$. Set $\hat{\mu} = \bar{X} = \hat{\theta}/2$, which yields $\hat{\theta} = 2\bar{X}$. ◆

EXAMPLE 6.6

Let $X_1, X_2, \ldots, X_n$ be a random sample from a uniform distribution on the interval $[\theta_1, \theta_2]$. Find the method of moments estimators of θ_1 and θ_2.

The first two moments of the $U[\theta_1, \theta_2]$ distribution equal

$$\mu_1 = \int_{\theta_1}^{\theta_2} \frac{x\,dx}{\theta_2 - \theta_1} = \frac{\theta_1 + \theta_2}{2} \quad \text{and} \quad \mu_2 = \int_{\theta_1}^{\theta_2} \frac{x^2\,dx}{\theta_2 - \theta_1} = \frac{\theta_2^3 - \theta_1^3}{3(\theta_2 - \theta_1)} = \frac{\theta_1^2 + \theta_1\theta_2 + \theta_2^2}{3}.$$

These moments can also be derived from the expressions for $E(X) = (\theta_1 + \theta_2)/2$ and $\mathrm{Var}(X) = E(X^2) - [E(X)]^2 = (\theta_2 - \theta_1)^2/12$ for the uniform distribution given in Section 2.8.1.

Let $\hat{\mu}_1 = \bar{X}$ and $\hat{\mu}_2 = \sum_{i=1}^{n} X_i^2/n$ be the first two sample moments. Then the equations for $\hat{\theta}_1$ and $\hat{\theta}_2$ are:

$$\hat{\mu}_1 = \frac{\hat{\theta}_1 + \hat{\theta}_2}{2} \quad \text{and} \quad \hat{\mu}_2 = \frac{\hat{\theta}_1^2 + \hat{\theta}_1\hat{\theta}_2 + \hat{\theta}_2^2}{3}.$$

Solving these two equations yields

$$\hat{\theta}_1 = \hat{\mu}_1 - \sqrt{3(\hat{\mu}_2 - \hat{\mu}_1^2)} \quad \text{and} \quad \hat{\theta}_2 = \hat{\mu}_1 + \sqrt{3(\hat{\mu}_2 - \hat{\mu}_1^2)}.$$

Note that the same solution is obtained by equating the population mean and variance to the sample mean and variance, respectively, as follows:

$$\hat{\mu} = \frac{\hat{\theta}_1 + \hat{\theta}_2}{2} \quad \text{and} \quad \hat{\sigma}^2 = \hat{\mu}_2 - \hat{\mu}_1^2 = \frac{(\hat{\theta}_2 - \hat{\theta}_1)^2}{12}.$$

◆

6.2   CONFIDENCE INTERVAL ESTIMATION

As in the previous section, let θ be an unknown parameter to be estimated based on a random sample $X_1, X_2, \ldots, X_n$ from a distribution with that parameter θ. But now instead of a point estimator $\hat{\theta}$, we want an interval $[L, U]$, where L and U are two statistics calculated from $X_1, X_2, \ldots, X_n$, such that the interval includes θ with a preassigned probability $1 - \alpha$. Specifically, we want

$$P\{L \leq \theta \leq U\} \geq 1 - \alpha$$

regardless of the true value of θ. Note that L and U are r.v.'s, being functions of $X_1, X_2, \ldots, X_n$, so $[L, U]$ is a random interval. It is called a $100(1 - \alpha)\%$ **confidence interval (CI)**, and $1 - \alpha$ is called the **confidence level**. After observing the data $X_1 = x_1, X_2 = x_2, \ldots, X_n = x_n$, the **confidence limits** $L = \ell$ and $U = u$ can be calculated. We now give a specific application of this general definition of a CI for estimating the mean of a normal population. We also give the interpretation of the confidence level.

6.2.1 Two-Sided Confidence Intervals

Consider a random sample $X_1, X_2, \ldots, X_n$ from an $N(\mu, \sigma^2)$ distribution, where σ^2 is assumed to be known and μ is an unknown parameter to be estimated. A natural estimator of μ is the sample mean $\bar{X}$. From Chapter 2, Section 2.9.3, and also Chapter 5, Section 5.1, we know that $\bar{X}$ is normally distributed with mean μ and standard deviation $\sigma/\sqrt{n}$. If the sample size is large, then by the central limit theorem (CLT) it follows that, even if the population distribution is not normal, $\bar{X}$ is approximately $N(\mu, \sigma^2/n)$. From the properties of the normal distribution it follows that there is 95% probability that $\bar{X}$ falls within a distance of $1.96\sigma/\sqrt{n}$ from μ:

$$P\left[\mu - 1.96\frac{\sigma}{\sqrt{n}} \leq \bar{X} \leq \mu + 1.96\frac{\sigma}{\sqrt{n}}\right] = 0.95.$$

But $\bar{X}$ is within a distance of $1.96\sigma/\sqrt{n}$ from μ if and only if μ is within a distance of $1.96\sigma/\sqrt{n}$ from $\bar{X}$. Therefore

$$P\left[L = \bar{X} - 1.96\frac{\sigma}{\sqrt{n}} \leq \mu \leq U = \bar{X} + 1.96\frac{\sigma}{\sqrt{n}}\right] = 0.95.$$

Therefore the interval

$$\ell = \bar{x} - 1.96\frac{\sigma}{\sqrt{n}} \leq \mu \leq u = \bar{x} + 1.96\frac{\sigma}{\sqrt{n}} \tag{6.3}$$

based on the observed sample mean $\bar{x}$ is a 95% confidence interval (CI) for μ. Because both the lower and upper limits are calculated, this CI is called **two-sided**.

EXAMPLE 6.7   (AIRLINE REVENUES: 95% CONFIDENCE INTERVAL)

Airlines use sampling to estimate their mean share of the revenue for passengers traveling on two or more airlines.[2] Suppose that the revenues for a certain airline are normally distributed with $\sigma = 50$ dollars. To estimate its mean share per ticket, the airline uses a sample of 400 tickets resulting in sample mean $\bar{x} = 175.60$ dollars. Calculate a 95% CI for the true mean share μ.

A 95% CI for μ is

$$\left[175.60 - 1.96 \times \frac{50}{\sqrt{400}}, 175.60 + 1.96 \times \frac{50}{\sqrt{400}} \right] = [170.70, 180.50].$$

This can be considered as a plausible set of values for the true mean share of revenue that is consistent with the observed sample mean $\bar{x} = 175.60$.   ◆

Note that *before* this CI was calculated, one could make the statement that the probability is 0.95 that the *random* interval $[\bar{X} \pm 1.96 \times \frac{\sigma}{\sqrt{n}}]$ will include μ, which is fixed but unknown. However, *after* the limits of the interval are calculated, the interval is *no longer random* because its limits are now fixed numbers. Either μ does or does not lie in the calculated interval. Thus $P(170.70 \leq \mu \leq 180.50)$ is either 1 or 0, but not 0.95. Therefore it is *incorrect* to say that the probability is 0.95 that the true μ is in [170.70,180.50].

What then exactly is meant by the statement that the confidence level is 95%? The answer lies in the **frequentist interpretation** of a CI: In an infinitely long series of trials in which repeated samples of size n are drawn from the same population and 95% CI's for μ are calculated using the same method, the proportion of intervals that actually include μ will be 95%. However, for any particular CI, it is not known whether or not that CI includes μ (since μ is unknown).

To understand this concept better, look at the sample means and the corresponding 95% CI's in Figure 6.2 resulting from 25 computer generated random samples of size 10 drawn from an $N(5, 2^2)$ distribution. We see that 24 of the 25 CI's include $\mu = 5$. In the long run, about 95% of the CI's will include μ.

The 95% CI for the mean of a normal population derived in (6.3) can be easily generalized to any confidence level $1 - \alpha$. Let $X_1, X_2, \ldots, X_n$ be a random sample from an $N(\mu, \sigma^2)$ distribution with known σ^2. Then we know that

$$Z = \frac{(\bar{X} - \mu)}{\sigma/\sqrt{n}} \sim N(0, 1). \tag{6.4}$$

In addition, we know that an area equal to $1 - \alpha$ lies under the standard normal density

---

[2] J. Neter (1972),"How accountants save money by sampling," *Statistics: A Guide to the Unknown*, (ed. J. M. Tanur et al.), New York: Holden-Day, pp. 203–211.

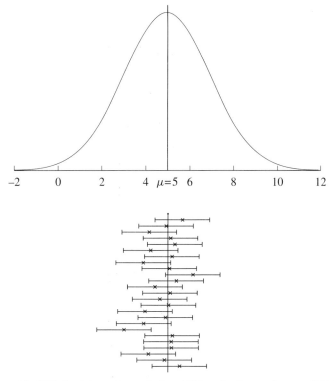

Figure 6.2   95% Confidence Intervals from 25 Samples Drawn from an $N(5, 2^2)$ Distribution

function curve in the interval $[-z_{\alpha/2}, z_{\alpha/2}]$ (see Figure 6.3). It follows that

$$1 - \alpha = P\left[-z_{\alpha/2} \leq Z = \frac{(\bar{X} - \mu)}{\sigma/\sqrt{n}} \leq z_{\alpha/2}\right]$$

$$= P\left[\bar{X} - z_{\alpha/2}\frac{\sigma}{\sqrt{n}} \leq \mu \leq \bar{X} + z_{\alpha/2}\frac{\sigma}{\sqrt{n}}\right].$$

Thus a $100(1 - \alpha)\%$ CI for μ based on an observed sample mean $\bar{x}$ is given by

$$\bar{x} - z_{\alpha/2}\frac{\sigma}{\sqrt{n}} \leq \mu \leq \bar{x} + z_{\alpha/2}\frac{\sigma}{\sqrt{n}}. \tag{6.5}$$

This CI is referred to as a $(1 - \alpha)$-level **z-interval**.

The r.v. Z of (6.4) has the following properties:

1. It is a function of the unknown parameter μ to be estimated, but of no other unknown parameters. (Remember that σ is assumed to be known.)
2. The distribution of Z (which is $N(0, 1)$) is free of any unknown parameters.

An r.v. having these two properties is called a **pivotal r.v.** This technique of using a pivotal r.v. to derive a CI for an unknown parameter is exploited in many problems, as we shall see in later chapters.

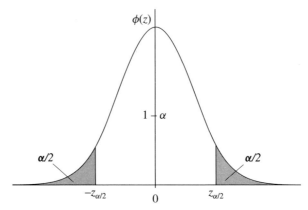

Figure 6.3   Critical Values Corresponding to an Area $1 - \alpha$ under the Standard Normal Curve.

EXAMPLE 6.8   (AIRLINE REVENUES: 99% CONFIDENCE INTERVAL)

Calculate a 99% CI for the airline's mean share of revenue using data from Example 6.7.

Here $1 - \alpha = 0.99$, hence $\alpha = 0.01$ and $\alpha/2 = 0.005$. From Table A.3 we have $z_{.005} = 2.576$. The required CI is

$$\left[175.60 - 2.576 \times \frac{50}{\sqrt{400}}, \, 175.60 + 2.576 \times \frac{50}{\sqrt{400}} \right] = [169.16, 182.04].$$

We are 99% confident that the mean revenue μ is between \$169.16 and \$182.04, but we do not know for sure whether μ is actually in this interval.   ◆

Note that the 99% CI is wider than the 95% CI calculated in Example 6.7 from the same data. The price paid for a higher confidence level is a wider and therefore a less informative CI when the sample size is fixed. One way to simultaneously control both the confidence level and the CI width is by designing a sufficiently large study. The problem of sample size determination is discussed in Chapter 7.

6.2.2 One-Sided Confidence Intervals

In some applications only one confidence bound is required. For example, only a **lower confidence bound** on the mean shear strength of a steel pin is required to ensure that the minimum design specification is met. Similarly, only an **upper confidence bound** on the mean impurity level of a batch of chemical is required to ensure that the maximum allowable level is not exceeded. When only one confidence bound is used, the CI is called **one-sided**.

One-sided CI's on μ are derived by following the same method used to derive the two-sided CI (6.5). The $100(1 - \alpha)\%$ one-sided CI's on μ are given by

$$\mu \geq \bar{x} - z_\alpha \frac{\sigma}{\sqrt{n}} \quad \text{(Lower One-Sided CI)} \tag{6.6}$$

and

$$\mu \leq \bar{x} + z_\alpha \frac{\sigma}{\sqrt{n}} \quad \text{(Upper One-Sided CI).} \tag{6.7}$$

Note that these one-sided CI's use the upper α critical point z_α instead of the upper $\alpha/2$ critical point $z_{\alpha/2}$ used by the two-sided CI (6.5). This is because one-sided confidence bounds cut off probability α only in one tail of the distribution of $\bar{X}$; see Figure 6.4.

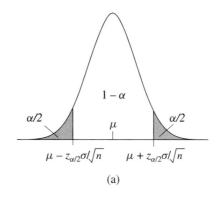

(a)

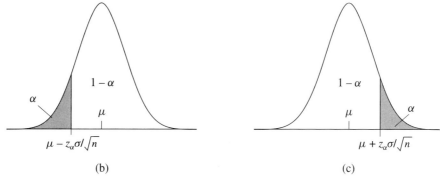

(b)   (c)

Figure 6.4   Tails of the Distribution of $\bar{X}$ with Probability α: (a) Two tails with probability α; (b) Lower tail with probability α; (c) Upper tail with probability α

EXAMPLE 6.9   (AIRLINE REVENUES: ONE-SIDED CONFIDENCE INTERVALS)

Calculate *separate* 95% lower and upper one-sided confidence bounds for the airline's mean share of revenue using data from Example 6.7.

The lower 95% confidence bound is given by

$$\mu \geq \bar{x} - z_{.05} \frac{\sigma}{\sqrt{n}} = 175.60 - 1.645 \frac{50}{\sqrt{400}} = 171.49.$$

The upper 95% confidence bound is given by

$$\mu \leq \bar{x} + z_{.05} \frac{\sigma}{\sqrt{n}} = 175.60 + 1.645 \frac{50}{\sqrt{400}} = 179.71.$$

These one-sided confidence bounds are sharper than the two-sided confidence bounds computed in Example 6.7 because $z_{.05}$ is smaller than $z_{.025}$. It must be emphasized, however, that only one of these bounds, upper or lower, is actually used depending on the application. If both the bounds are used simultaneously then it is equivalent to making a 90% two-sided CI.   ◆

The assumptions that the sample is drawn from a normal population and the variance is known can be relaxed for large samples. First, the central limit theorem (CLT) from Chapter 5 allows us to regard the distribution of $\bar{X}$ as approximately $N(\mu, \sigma^2/n)$, even though the sample comes from a nonnormal distribution. Second, when n is large, the sample variance S^2 can be regarded as an accurate estimator of σ^2, and its sampling variability can be ignored. Thus the estimated SEM = $s/\sqrt{n}$ can be used in place of $\sigma/\sqrt{n}$ in the formulas (6.5)–(6.7).

6.3   HYPOTHESIS TESTING

Many problems in business, industry, and public policy require making a decision or choosing an alternative based on information gathered from a sample. For example, it may be necessary to decide among several suppliers of a product or among different braking system designs for an automobile. A closely related problem is to assess whether sample data support a claim or a theory. For example, the Environmental Protection Agency may take air samples to verify a manufacturer's claim that emission levels from the factory smokestack meet regulatory standards. Problems that require a data-based decision or an assessment of evidence are usually formulated as hypothesis testing problems.

The 1954 Salk vaccine trial provides another illustration of hypothesis testing to assess the efficacy of the vaccine against polio. A part of this large experiment was a controlled clinical trial. A sample of grade school students was randomly divided into two groups, each with about 200,000 children. The treatment group received the vaccine, while the control group received placebo (i.e., a medication containing no active ingredient). The trial tested the claim that the population of vaccinated children would have a lower rate of new polio cases than the population of unvaccinated children. The rates of new polio cases were 2.84 and 7.06 per 10,000 children in the vaccine and control groups, respectively. Is this sufficiently strong evidence to support the efficacy claim for the Salk vaccine? If the vaccine were actually ineffective, what would be the probability of finding such a large difference merely by chance? We will return to this example in Chapter 9, where we will see that this probability is less than one in million. Thus chance alone does not adequately explain these results: it would be improbable (but not impossible) to have results this extreme if the vaccine were truly ineffective. Therefore the trial provides strong evidence that the vaccine is effective against polio. This is the type of statistical argument used in hypothesis testing.

6.3.1 Null and Alternative Hypotheses

A **hypothesis** is a statement of a theory or a claim. The objective in a hypothesis testing problem is to assess the validity of a claim against a counterclaim using sample data. The two competing claims are called the null and alternative hypotheses, denoted by H_0 and H_1, respectively. The classical approach to hypothesis testing designates the claim to be proved as H_1, the **alternative hypothesis**. The competing claim is then designated as H_0, the **null hypothesis**.

In the classical approach, we begin with the assumption that H_0 is true. If the data fail to contradict H_0 beyond a reasonable doubt, then H_0 is not rejected. However, failing to reject H_0 does not mean that we accept it as true; it simply means that H_0 cannot be ruled out as a possible explanation for the observed data. Only when the data strongly contradict H_0, is it rejected and H_1 accepted. Thus the proof of H_1 is by contradiction of H_0.

The U.S. justice system provides an analogy to the logic of hypothesis testing. An accused person is presumed innocent until proven guilty. The burden of proof is on the prosecution to show that the accused is guilty. Thus the hypotheses are H_0: Accused person is not guilty vs. H_1: Accused person is guilty. The evidence plays the role of data. Only when the evidence strongly contradicts the person's innocence is a "guilty" verdict rendered. If the evidence is insufficient to establish guilt, then the "not guilty" verdict is rendered. A "not guilty" verdict does not prove that the accused person is innocent, but it gives him the benefit of doubt.

Formally, the hypotheses must be formulated as statements concerning unknown parameters of populations from which the data are sampled. We give three examples below.

EXAMPLE 6.10   (ACCEPTANCE SAMPLING: FORMULATION OF HYPOTHESES)

An electrical parts manufacturer receives a large lot of fuses from a vendor. The lot is regarded as "satisfactory" if the fraction defective p is no more than 1%; otherwise it is regarded as "unsatisfactory." Since it is not feasible to inspect all the fuses in the lot, p is an unknown parameter. Therefore sampling inspection is done to decide the fate (accept/reject) of the lot. There are two hypotheses: (i) the lot is "satisfactory" ($p \leq 1\%$) and (ii) the lot is "unsatisfactory" ($p > 1\%$). If the vendor has an established quality record, then he is given the benefit of doubt, and the hypotheses are set up as $H_0: p \leq 1\%$ vs. $H_1: p > 1\%$. On the other hand, if the vendor is new, then the burden of proof is on him to show that the quality standard is met. Therefore the hypotheses are set up as $H_0: p \geq 1\%$ vs. $H_1: p < 1\%$.[3]   ◆

EXAMPLE 6.11   (SAT COACHING: FORMULATION OF HYPOTHESES)

There is considerable debate about the effectiveness of various coaching programs in improving the SAT scores. Powers[4] reviewed the literature on this subject. Here we consider only the verbal part (SAT-V) of the test. Based on the 1990–91 test data, it is known that the *changes* in the test scores for the general population of high school juniors and seniors retaking the test without any special coaching have a mean μ of about 15 points and a standard deviation (SD) σ of about 40 points.[5] The changes in the test scores are approximately normally distributed. Thus 15 points represent the average improvement due to the learning effect and the natural increase in the verbal ability that occurs over time. If a coaching program does not improve the test scores by more than 15 points on average, then we say that the coaching program has no effect.

Suppose that an SAT coaching company claims that its coaching program will improve the test scores, on the average, by more than 15 points, i.e., the coaching program is effective. (The advertised claim may be much stronger, e.g., improvement by at least 40 points.) Let μ denote

---

[3] It is a common convention in hypothesis testing to include the equality under H_0 and to state H_1 as a strict inequality.

[4] D. E. Powers (1993), "Coaching for the SAT: Summary of summaries and update," *Educational Measurement: Issues and Practices*, Summer 1993, pp. 24–39.

[5] This is the SD of the *change* in the score between two tests. The SD of the scores on a *single* test is about 100.

the mean *change* in the test scores for the population of students who are coached. Since the company's claim requires proof, the hypotheses are set up as $H_0: \mu = 15$ (the coaching program has no effect) vs. $H_1: \mu > 15$.

At this point one may ask, why not set up H_0 as $\mu \leq 15$ rather than as $\mu = 15$, because it is possible that the coaching program may actually reduce the mean score? We will see later in this chapter that we can replace $H_0: \mu = 15$ by $H_0: \mu \leq 15$ without any loss. Until then we will continue to use the formulation $H_0: \mu = 15$. ◆

EXAMPLE 6.12   (SALK POLIO VACCINE TRIAL: FORMULATION OF HYPOTHESES)

In the Salk vaccine trial, we can imagine two infinite populations of children. The control population consists of all children who will not be vaccinated; the treatment population consists of all children who will be vaccinated. Let p_1 and p_2 be the proportions of children who would develop polio in the control and treatment populations, respectively. The claim requiring proof is that the incidence rate of polio is reduced for vaccinated children; the counterclaim is that the vaccine is ineffective, i.e., the incidence rate of polio is not changed by the vaccine. Therefore the hypotheses are set up as $H_0: p_1 = p_2$ vs. $H_1: p_1 > p_2$. We can replace $H_0: p_1 = p_2$ by $H_0: p_1 \leq p_2$. ◆

Since the classical approach to hypothesis testing demands a proof beyond a reasonable doubt before H_0 is rejected, it protects H_0. If H_0 is rejected despite this protection, then we have a proof of H_1 with a preassigned degree of confidence. Why not set up the claim to be proved as H_0? The reason is that it does not allow us to decide in favor of the claim with a specified degree of confidence. It is possible that H_0 is not rejected merely due to lack of sufficient data. A proof by insufficient data is no proof at all!

6.3.2 Hypothesis Tests

A **hypothesis test** is a data-based rule to decide between H_0 and H_1. A **test statistic** calculated from data is used to make this decision. The values of the test statistic for which the test rejects H_0 comprises the **rejection region** of the test; the complement of the rejection region is called the **acceptance region**. The boundaries of the rejection region are defined by one or more **critical constants**. A test rejects H_0 when the test statistic value falls above (or below) the critical constants.

EXAMPLE 6.13   (ACCEPTANCE SAMPLING: A HYPOTHESIS TEST)

Refer to Example 6.10. Suppose that the hypotheses are set up as $H_0: p \leq 1\%$ (the lot is satisfactory) vs. $H_1: p > 1\%$ (the lot is not satisfactory), where p is the unknown fraction defective in the lot. A sample of 100 items is inspected. The decision rule is to accept the lot if the number of defectives in the sample is 0 or 1, otherwise reject the lot. The number of defectives in the sample, denoted by x, is the test statistic. The rejection region of the test is $x > 1$. ◆

EXAMPLE 6.14 (SAT COACHING: A HYPOTHESIS TEST)

Refer to Example 6.11. Consider conducting the following experiment: A sample of 20 students take the SAT before and after participating in the coaching program.[6] Let $\bar{x}$ be the sample mean of changes in the test scores of the 20 students and let μ be the corresponding unknown population mean. The hypothesis test is: Reject $H_0: \mu = 15$ in favor of $H_1: \mu > 15$ if $\bar{x} > 25$. The test statistic is $\bar{x}$ and the rejection region is $\bar{x} > 25$. ◆

Historically, the formulation of a hypothesis test as a **two-decision problem** is due to two great statisticians, Jerzy Neyman (1894–1981) and Egon Pearson[7] (1895–1980). However, many statisticians prefer to think of a hypothesis test as a method to weigh evidence in the data against H_0 rather than as a decision procedure. Typically, H_0 is a hypothesis of no difference (hence the name "null" hypothesis) between a new method and an existing method or no effect of an intervention under study (e.g., $H_0: \mu = 15$ in Example 6.11 represents no improvement due to coaching, or $H_0: p_1 = p_2$ in Example 6.12 represents no effect of vaccine). The truth of H_0 is never seriously entertained; it is set up simply as a "straw man." Therefore H_0 is never formally accepted. The purpose of the test is to determine if the observed data can be reasonably explained by chance alone, assuming that H_0 is true. If not, then we have a **statistically significant** proof of the research claim (H_1). When a hypothesis test is used in this fashion, it is called a **significance test**.

6.3.3 Type I and Type II Error Probabilities

When a hypothesis test is viewed as a decision procedure, two types of error are possible, depending on which hypothesis, H_0 or H_1, is actually true. If a test rejects H_0 (and accepts H_1) when H_0 is true, it is called a **type I error**. If a test fails to reject H_0 when H_1 is true, it is called a **type II error**. Table 6.1 shows the results of the different decisions.

Table 6.1 Decisions in a Hypothesis Test

		Decision	
		Do not reject H_0	Reject H_0
H_0	True	Correct Decision	Type I Error
	False	Type II Error	Correct Decision

EXAMPLE 6.15

A diagnostic test for a disease can be viewed as a hypothesis test. There are two hypotheses: (i) the person being tested does not have the disease and (ii) the person has the disease. If it is known that the person's a priori chances of having the disease are small, and/or the costs (economic, emotional, side effects) of treating a misdiagnosed disease-free person are high, then

---

[6] As discussed in Chapter 3, the experiment should include a parallel control group of students who do not undergo coaching and who are also tested twice. Assignment of students to control and coaching groups should be done at random. Here a simpler experiment is considered for ease of explanation.

[7] Egon Pearson was the son of another great statistician, Karl Pearson, whom we met in Chapter 4.

strong evidence is needed before concluding that the person has the disease. Thus the hypotheses are set up as H_0: The person does not have the disease vs. H_1: The person has the disease. In that case, a **false positive** outcome (the person does not have the disease, but the test is positive) is a type I error; a **false negative** outcome (the person has the disease, but the test is negative) is a type II error. ◆

Since we do not know in fact whether H_0 is true or H_1 is true, we cannot tell whether a test has made a correct decision or not. If a test rejects H_0, we do not know whether the decision is correct or a type I error is made. If a test fails to reject H_0, we do not know whether the decision is correct or a type II error is made. We can only assess the long term accuracy of decisions made by a test by adopting the same **frequentist approach** that we used to interpret the confidence intervals.

Consider a long series of trials in which the same decision rule is applied to repeated samples drawn under identical conditions (either under H_0 or under H_1). The limiting proportion of trials in which H_0 is rejected when H_0 is true is the **probability of a type I error**, also called the **α-risk**. Similarly, the limiting proportion of trials in which H_0 is not rejected when H_1 is true is the **probability of a type II error**, also called the **β-risk**. This frequentist interpretation of error probabilities leads to the following definitions:

$$\alpha = P\{\text{Type I error}\} = P\{\text{Reject } H_0 \text{ when } H_0 \text{ is true}\}$$
$$= P\{\text{Reject } H_0 \mid H_0\} \tag{6.8}$$

and

$$\beta = P\{\text{Type II error}\} = P\{\text{Fail to reject } H_0 \text{ when } H_1 \text{ is true}\}$$
$$= P\{\text{Fail to reject } H_0 \mid H_1\}. \tag{6.9}$$

Instead of β it is common to work with

$$\pi = 1 - \beta = P\{\text{Reject } H_0 \mid H_1\}. \tag{6.10}$$

This is called the **power** of the test, which is the probability that the test correctly rejects H_0. Keeping in mind that H_1 is the research hypothesis to be proved, the power of a test measures its ability to "prove" H_1 when H_1 is true. A test with high power is preferred.

The error probabilities are calculated using the sampling distribution of the test statistic. This sampling distribution depends on the population distribution from which the sample is drawn. The null and alternative hypotheses each specify different population distributions. Therefore the sampling distribution of the test statistic is different under the two hypotheses. We now illustrate the calculation of the error probabilities.

EXAMPLE 6.16 (ACCEPTANCE SAMPLING: α- AND β-RISKS)

Refer to Example 6.13. Suppose that the long run average defective rate for the lots supplied by a vendor is 1% and we are testing $H_0: p = .01$ vs. $H_1: p > .01$ where p is the unknown fraction defective of the current lot. The fate of each lot is based on an inspection of a random sample of 100 items drawn from it. The decision rule is: Do not reject H_0 (accept the lot) if the number of defectives x in a sample of 100 is 0 or 1, otherwise reject H_0 (reject the lot). The r.v. X has a Bin(100, p) distribution. The α-risk of this decision rule is

$$\alpha = P\{\text{Type I error}\} = P\{\text{Reject } H_0 \mid H_0: p = .01\}$$

$$= 1 - P\{X = 0 \text{ or } 1 \mid H_0: p = .01\}$$

$$= 1 - \sum_{i=0}^{1} \binom{100}{i}(.01)^i(.99)^{100-i} = 0.264.$$

Next suppose that if the fraction defective in the lot is as high as .03, then the lot is regarded as clearly unsatisfactory. So it is of interest to calculate the β-risk for $p = .03$:

$$\beta = P\{\text{Type II error}\} = P\{\text{Fail to reject } H_0 \mid H_1: p = .03\}$$

$$= P\{X = 0 \text{ or } 1 \mid H_1: p = .03\}$$

$$= \sum_{i=0}^{1} \binom{100}{i}(.03)^i(.97)^{100-i} = 0.195.$$

The power is

$$\pi = 1 - \beta = 1 - 0.195 = 0.805.$$

Note that the α- and β-risks do not add up to 1, although they are probabilities of complementary events. This is because the two probabilities are calculated under different population distributions (binomial with $p = .01$ and $p = .03$).

In acceptance sampling, where H_0 corresponds to accepting the lot and H_1 corresponds to rejecting the lot, the α- and β-risks are called the **producer's risk** and the **consumer's risk**, respectively. In this example, the producer's risk is the probability 0.264 that a satisfactory lot (with $p = .01$) will be rejected and the consumer's risk is the probability 0.195 that an unsatisfactory lot (with $p = .03$) will be accepted.   ◆

EXAMPLE 6.17   (SAT COACHING: α- AND β-RISKS)

Refer to Example 6.14. The hypotheses $H_0: \mu = 15$ (coaching program is ineffective) vs. $H_1: \mu > 15$ (coaching program improves SAT-V scores) are tested by rejecting H_0 if $\bar{x} > 25$, where $\bar{x}$ is the mean change in SAT-V scores for a sample of 20 students. Calculate the error probabilities of this decision rule.

Note that the r.v. $\bar{X}$ is normally distributed with mean = μ and SD = $\sigma/\sqrt{n} = 40/\sqrt{20}$. Therefore, $\frac{\bar{X}-\mu}{40/\sqrt{20}} = Z \sim N(0, 1)$. Using this fact, we can write

$$\alpha = P\{\text{Type I error}\} = P\{\bar{X} > 25 \mid \mu = 15\}$$

$$= P\left\{ Z = \frac{\bar{X} - 15}{40/\sqrt{20}} > \frac{25 - 15}{40/\sqrt{20}} \,\middle|\, \mu = 15 \right\}$$

$$= P\{Z > 1.118\} = 1 - \Phi(1.118) = 0.132.$$

Thus there is a 13% chance that this test will conclude that the coaching program is effective when in fact it is not.

Next suppose that the coaching company claims that the actual mean improvement is at least 40 points. The β-risk for $\mu = 40$ is the probability that the test will fail to prove this claim even if it is in fact true. It is calculated as follows:

$$\beta = P\{\text{Type II error}\} = P\{\bar{X} \leq 25 \mid \mu = 40\}$$

$$= P\left\{Z = \frac{\bar{X} - 40}{40/\sqrt{20}} \leq \frac{25 - 40}{40/\sqrt{20}} \,\middle|\, \mu = 40\right\}$$

$$= P\{Z \leq -1.677\} = 0.047.$$

The power, which is the probability that the claim will be proved when $\mu = 40$, equals $\pi = 1 - \beta = 1 - 0.047 = 0.953.$ ◆

The above two examples show how to calculate the error probabilities of a test when exactly one parameter value (i.e., one probability distribution) is specified under each hypothesis. Such a hypothesis is called a **simple hypothesis**, e.g., H_0: $p = .01$ and H_1: $p = .03$ or H_0: $\mu = 15$ and H_1: $\mu = 40$. If a hypothesis specifies more than one probability distribution, then it is called a **composite hypothesis**, e.g., H_1: $p > .01$ or H_1: $\mu > 15$.

We next show how to calculate the error probabilities as *functions* of the test parameters for composite hypotheses. These functions are monotone (i.e., increasing or decreasing) in the test parameters for many standard testing problems. This enables us to specify H_0 more naturally as a composite hypothesis rather than as a simple hypothesis (as we have done thus far for mathematical convenience), e.g., H_0: $p \leq .01$ instead of H_0: $p = .01$ or H_0: $\mu \leq 15$ instead of H_0: $\mu = 15$. The reason is that the maximum type I error probability of the tests we use occurs at the boundary parameter value of H_0; see the discussion in the following two sections. Since we are concerned with controlling this maximum type I error probability, we may as well assume from now on, that both H_0 and H_1 are specified as composite hypotheses.

6.3.4 *Operating Characteristic and Power Functions

When H_0 and H_1 are composite, the two error probabilities are not just single *numbers* but are *functions* of the test parameter. For instance, in Example 6.16 they are functions of p and in Example 6.17 they are functions of μ. Instead of dealing with these functions separately, we can combine them into a single function called the **operating characteristic (OC) function** of the test. In general, if θ denotes the test parameter, then the OC function is the probability of failing to reject H_0 as a function of θ:

$$\text{OC}(\theta) = P\{\text{Test fails to reject } H_0 \mid \theta\}. \tag{6.11}$$

Note that for θ values under H_1 the OC function is simply the β-risk. The **power function** is

$$\pi(\theta) = P\{\text{Test rejects } H_0 \mid \theta\} = 1 - \text{OC}(\theta). \tag{6.12}$$

The following examples show how the OC function can be used to compute the error probabilities.

EXAMPLE **6.18**   (ACCEPTANCE SAMPLING: OC FUNCTION)

Consider the test that rejects $H_0: p \leq .01$ if $x > 1$, where x is the number of defective items in a sample of 100. Since the r.v. X is distributed as $\text{Bin}(100, p)$, the OC function is given by

$$OC(p) = P\{X \leq 1\} = \sum_{i=0}^{1} \binom{100}{i} p^i (1-p)^{100-i} = (1-p)^{100} + 100p(1-p)^{99}.$$

A plot of $OC(p)$ is called the **OC curve** and is shown in Figure 6.5. Now consider a lot with fraction defective $p = .01$ (H_0 is true). The probability of accepting this lot can be read directly from the OC curve as $OC(p = .01) = 0.736$, which gives $\alpha = 1 - OC(p = .01) = 0.264$. On the other hand, the probability of accepting a lot with fraction defective $p = .03$ (H_1 is true) is $\beta = OC(p = .03) = 0.195$. These are the same α- and β-risks calculated in Example 6.16. For an intermediate value, say the proportion defective $p = .02$ (H_1 is true), the β-risk equals $OC(p = .02) = 0.403$; the corresponding power equals $\pi = 1 - OC(p = .02) = 0.597$.   ◆

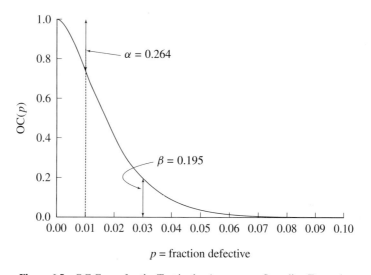

Figure 6.5   OC Curve for the Test in the Acceptance Sampling Example

EXAMPLE **6.19**   (SAT COACHING: OC FUNCTION)

Consider the test that rejects $H_0: \mu \leq 15$ if $\bar{x} > 25$, where $\bar{x}$ is the mean change in IQ scores for a sample of 20 students. Since the r.v. $\bar{X}$ is normally distributed with SD = $40/\sqrt{20}$, the OC function is given by

$$OC(\mu) = P\{\bar{X} \leq 25 \mid \mu\}$$

$$= P\left\{ Z = \frac{\bar{X} - \mu}{40/\sqrt{20}} \leq \frac{25 - \mu}{40/\sqrt{20}} \Big| \mu \right\}$$

$$= \Phi\left(\frac{25 - \mu}{40/\sqrt{20}} \right)$$

where $\Phi(\cdot)$ is the standard normal distribution function. A plot of this OC function is shown in Figure 6.6.

We shall illustrate the use of this OC curve to assess the performance of the test under three different situations: the coaching program has no effect ($\mu = 15$), a moderate effect ($\mu = 25$), and a large effect ($\mu = 40$). If there is no effect, the probability of rejecting H_0 is $\alpha = 1 - \text{OC}(\mu = 15) = 0.132$. If there is a moderate effect, the probability of failing to reject H_0 is $\beta = \text{OC}(\mu = 25) = 0.5$. If there is a large effect, the probability of failing to reject H_0 decreases to $\text{OC}(\mu = 40) = 0.047$.   ◆

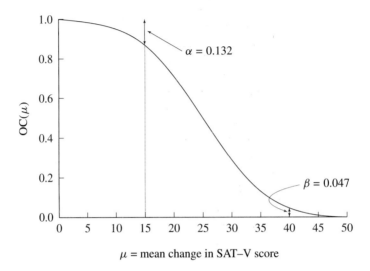

Figure 6.6   OC Curve for the Test in the SAT Coaching Example

A good hypothesis test has small type I and type II error probabilities; i.e., its OC function falls steeply as the parameter value changes from H_0 to H_1. A test with this property is said to *discriminate* between H_0 and H_1. Due to sampling variation, no statistical test can be perfectly discriminating.

6.3.5 Level of Significance

The error probabilities of a test are like two sides of a see-saw; if one goes down, the other goes up. It is not possible to simultaneously reduce both if the sample size is fixed. A traditional approach to this dilemma is to put an upper bound on $P(\text{Type I error})$ and, subject to that constraint, find a test with the lowest possible $P(\text{Type II error})$, i.e., the highest possible power. The upper bound on $P(\text{Type I error})$, which is usually a small number like $0.01, 0.05$, or 0.10, is called the **level of significance** and is denoted by α. The test is required to satisfy

$$P\{\text{Type I error}\} = P\{\text{Test rejects } H_0 \mid H_0\} \leq \alpha \qquad (6.13)$$

for all parameter values under H_0. Note that α is now used to denote an *upper bound* on $P(\text{Type I error})$; previously α was used to denote the $P(\text{Type I error})$ itself. A hypothesis test with a significance level α is called an **α-level test**.

Notice from Figures 6.5 and 6.6 that the OC functions are monotone. A consequence is that if $P(\text{Type I error}) = \alpha$ at the boundary of H_0, then the inequality (6.13) is satisfied. Therefore we can test composite hypotheses such as $H_0: p \leq .01$ and $H_0: \mu \leq 15$ using tests that give $P(\text{Type I error}) = \alpha$ for $H_0: p = .01$ and $H_0: \mu = 15$, respectively. This monotone behavior is common in many hypothesis testing problems.

By specifying the level of significance we control $P(\text{Type I error})$, but $P(\text{Type II error})$ is not controlled. This approach is motivated by the fact that generally the type I error is the more serious of the two errors. Referring to the U.S. justice system analogy, a type I error corresponds to convicting an innocent person. This is regarded as a far more serious error than failing to convict a guilty person because of lack of evidence, a type II error. In scientific research, H_0 is often the status quo hypothesis that protects the current method. A type I error corresponds to the decision to adopt the new method when in fact it is not better than the current. An unwarranted change to the new method is unnecessarily costly and is generally regarded as a more serious error. Note that if an α-level test is used, then there is at most a $100\alpha\%$ chance that a false claim is made. Thus we can place $100(1-\alpha)\%$ confidence in a research finding when the null hypothesis is rejected by an α-level test.

EXAMPLE 6.20 (ACCEPTANCE SAMPLING: 0.10-LEVEL TEST)

Suppose that we want a 0.10-level test of $H_0: p \leq .01$ vs. $H_1: p > .01$. We saw in Example 6.16 that if x denotes the number of defectives in a sample of 100 fuses, then the test that rejects H_0 when $x > 1$ has $P\{\text{Type I error}\} = 0.264$, which is too high. If we change the rejection region to $x > 2$, we get

$$P\{\text{Type I error}\} = P\{\text{Test rejects } H_0 \mid H_0\} = P\{X > 2 \mid p = .01\}$$

$$= 1 - \sum_{i=0}^{2} \binom{100}{i}(.01)^i(.99)^{100-i} = 0.079,$$

which is less than the upper bound $\alpha = 0.10$. In fact, this test has $\alpha = 0.079$.[8] The $P\{\text{Type II error}\}$ for this test can be computed to be 0.420, which is greater than $P\{\text{Type II error}\} = 0.195$ that we obtained in Example 6.16 for the test with $\alpha = 0.264$. ◆

EXAMPLE 6.21 (SAT COACHING: 0.05-LEVEL TEST)

Suppose we want a 0.05-level test of $H_0: \mu \leq 15$ vs. $H_1: \mu > 15$. Consider the test that rejects H_0 if $\bar{x} > c$, where the critical value c is to be determined so that the test will have level $\alpha = 0.05$. Thus we need to solve the equation

$$P\{\text{Type I error}\} = P\{\bar{X} > c \mid \mu = 15\} = 0.05.$$

The solution c can be obtained by standardizing $\bar{X}$. This results in the equation

$$P\left\{Z = \frac{\bar{X}-15}{40/\sqrt{20}} > \frac{c-15}{40/\sqrt{20}}\right\} = 0.05$$

---

[8] A test having an *exact* significance level of 0.10 cannot be obtained in this example because of the discreteness of the binomial distribution.

which is satisfied when

$$\frac{c - 15}{40/\sqrt{20}} = z_{.05} = 1.645 \quad \text{or} \quad c = 15 + 1.645 \times \frac{40}{\sqrt{20}} = 29.71.$$

Thus a 0.05-level test of $H_0: \mu \le 15$ vs. $H_1: \mu > 15$ rejects H_0 when $\bar{x} > 29.71$.

If an actual experiment resulted in a mean improvement of $\bar{x} = 35$, then that result would be significant at $\alpha = 0.05$ and the coaching program would be declared to be effective. ◆

The above test can be alternatively expressed in terms of the standardized test statistic

$$z = \frac{\bar{x} - 15}{\sigma/\sqrt{n}} = \frac{\bar{x} - 15}{40/\sqrt{20}}$$

as follows:

$$\text{Reject } H_0 \text{ if } z > z_{.05} = 1.645.$$

In the above example

$$z = \frac{35 - 15}{40/\sqrt{20}} = 2.236 > 1.645,$$

so H_0 is rejected at $\alpha = .05$.

More generally, an α-level test of

$$H_0: \mu \le \mu_0 \text{ vs. } H_1: \mu > \mu_0 \tag{6.14}$$

where μ_0 is a specified number ($\mu_0 = 15$ in the above example) is:

$$\text{Reject } H_0 \text{ if } z > z_\alpha \text{ or equivalently if } \bar{x} > \mu_0 + z_\alpha \frac{\sigma}{\sqrt{n}} \tag{6.15}$$

where z is the standardized test statistic,

$$z = \frac{\bar{x} - \mu_0}{\sigma/\sqrt{n}}. \tag{6.16}$$

Here we are able to obtain an exact test for any level α, because the test statistic $\bar{X}$ (or equivalently Z) has a continuous distribution.

Choice of Significance Level.   What α level should one use? We have seen that when $P(\text{Type I error})$ decreases, $P(\text{Type II error})$ increases and the power of the test decreases. A proper choice of α should take into account the relative costs of type I and type II errors. Unfortunately, in most practical problems these costs cannot be accurately determined. Conventionally, $\alpha = 5\%$ is used following Sir R. A. Fisher's[9] recommendation:

---

[9] R. A. Fisher (1929), "The statistical method in psychical research," *Proceedings of the Society for Psychical Research*, **39**, 189–192.

It is a common practice to judge a result significant, if it is of such a magnitude that it would have been produced by chance not more frequently than once in every twenty experiments. This is an arbitrary, but convenient level of significance for the practical investigator . . .

Another convention is to use $\alpha = 10\%$ for research claims requiring a liberal standard of proof, $\alpha = 5\%$ for a normal standard, and $\alpha = 1\%$ for a stringent standard. Strong evidence (small α) is needed for a decision to change from a well-accepted current standard (H_0) to a new alternative (H_1).

Although significance levels of 1%, 5%, and 10% are commonly used, it should be pointed out that they are relics from the days when hypotheses tests relied on tables of critical constants published for a few selected α values. Easy access to computers and statistical packages has largely obviated the need for such tables. For most hypothesis testing problems, it is now possible to calculate the exact (observed) α-level at which H_0 can be rejected. This observed α-level is the topic of the next section.

6.3.6 Observed Level of Significance or P-Value

Simply rejecting or not rejecting H_0 at a specified α does not fully convey the information in the data. It is more useful to report the *smallest* α-level at which the observed test result is significant. This smallest α-level is called the **observed level of significance** or the **P-value**. The smaller the P-value, the more significant is the test result. Once the P-value is computed, a test at any specified α can be conducted by rejecting H_0 if P-value $< \alpha$. An alternative definition of the P-value is that it is the probability under H_0 of obtaining a test statistic at least as "extreme" as the observed value. This definition will become apparent from the following two examples.

EXAMPLE 6.22   (ACCEPTANCE SAMPLING: P-VALUE)

We want to test $H_0: p \leq .01$ vs. $H_1: p > .01$ based on a random sample of 100 fuses which has $x = 1$ defectives. The smallest α at which this outcome will result in the rejection of H_0 is the α-level of the test that rejects when $X \geq 1$. The α-level of this test, which is the P-value, is computed as follows:

$$
\begin{aligned}
P\text{-value} &= P\{X \geq 1 \mid p = .01\} \\
&= 1 - P\{X = 0 \mid p = .01\} \\
&= 1 - (0.99)^{100} \\
&= 0.634.
\end{aligned}
$$

Since the P-value > 0.10, H_0 is not rejected at $\alpha = 0.10$. ◆

EXAMPLE 6.23   (SAT COACHING: *P*-VALUE)

We want to test $H_0: \mu \leq 15$ vs. $H_1: \mu > 15$ based on $\bar{x} = 35$, where $\bar{x}$ is the observed mean increase in test scores for a sample of 20 students in the coaching program. The smallest α at which H_0 will be rejected for this outcome is the α-level of the test which rejects H_0 when $\bar{X} \geq 35$. This α-level, which is the *P*-value, is computed as follows:

$$P\text{-value} = P\{\bar{X} \geq 35 \mid \mu = 15\}$$

$$= P\left\{ Z = \frac{\bar{X} - 15}{40/\sqrt{20}} \geq z = \frac{35 - 15}{40/\sqrt{20}} \middle| \mu = 15 \right\}$$

$$= P\{Z \geq 2.236\}$$

$$= 1 - \Phi(2.236)$$

$$= 0.013.$$

Alternatively, we can obtain this *P*-value directly as the α corresponding to the observed $z = 2.236 = z_\alpha$. This is the smallest α at which H_0 can be rejected, since at this α we are on the borderline of rejection of H_0. Using Table A.3, this α is found as the area under the standard normal curve to the right of 2.236, which is 0.013. Since the *P*-value < 0.05, H_0 is rejected at $\alpha = 0.05$.   ◆

In each of the above examples the *P*-value is computed as the probability under H_0 of obtaining a result at least as large as the observed one ($X \geq 1$ in Example 6.22 and $\bar{X} \geq 35$ in Example 6.23). This illustrates the alternative definition of the *P*-value given above. A small *P*-value indicates that the observed result is rare under the assumption of H_0. For instance, in Example 6.23, there is only 1.3% chance of obtaining a mean increase in test scores of 35 or greater if the coaching program were ineffective ($\mu = 15$). This probability is quite small, indicating that an outcome as extreme as $\bar{x} = 35$ is *possible*, but *not probable* under H_0. In other words, chance by itself does not adequately explain a mean increase of at least 35. So we can reject H_0 as a plausible explanation of the observed outcome. On the other hand, in Example 6.22, the *P*-value $= 0.634$ is very large, indicating that an outcome as extreme as $x = 1$ can occur with high probability even when $H_0: p = .01$ holds. So we cannot reject H_0 as a plausible explanation of the observed outcome.

6.3.7 One-Sided and Two-Sided Tests

In both Example 6.10 and Example 6.11 the alternative hypothesis specifies that the parameter is greater than the values specified under H_0, e.g., $H_1: \mu > 15$. Such a hypothesis is called **upper one-sided**. The corresponding test is an **upper one-sided test**. A **lower one-sided** alternative states that the parameter is less than the values specified under H_0. The corresponding test is a **lower one-sided test**. A **two-sided test** addresses a **two-sided alternative** hypothesis, which states that the parameter is not equal to (i.e., either greater than or less than) the specified value under H_0, e.g., $H_0: \mu = \mu_0$ vs. $H_1: \mu \neq \mu_0$.

Example 6.24 (Chemical Impurities: Lower One-Sided Test)

The impurity level in a chemical used in a manufacturing process must not exceed 50 parts per million (ppm). Each batch of the chemical purchased from a vendor is tested to see if this requirement is met. The hypotheses are set up as $H_0: \mu \geq 50$ vs. $H_1: \mu < 50$, where μ is the mean impurity level. This is a lower one-sided alternative.

Suppose that 10 samples are tested from each batch, and the impurity measurements are normally distributed with mean μ and standard deviation $\sigma = 2$ ppm. The chance of accepting a batch of chemical that does not meet the standard is to be limited to no more than 1%. The lower one-sided test is of the form "Reject H_0 if $\bar{x} < c$," where $\bar{x}$ is the mean of 10 measurements. The critical value c is determined so that $P(\text{Type I error}) = \alpha = 0.01$. We use the fact that when H_0 is true, the r.v. $\bar{X}$ is normally distributed with mean $\mu = 50$ and SD $= \sigma/\sqrt{n} = 2/\sqrt{10}$. The equation for c is then

$$P\{\text{Type I error}\} = P\{\bar{X} < c \mid \mu = 50\}$$

$$= P\left\{ Z = \frac{\bar{X} - 50}{2/\sqrt{10}} < \frac{c - 50}{2/\sqrt{10}} \middle| \mu = 50 \right\}$$

$$= 0.01.$$

This is satisfied when

$$\frac{c - 50}{2/\sqrt{10}} = -z_{.01} = -2.326 \quad \Longleftrightarrow \quad c = 50 - 2.326 \times \frac{2}{\sqrt{10}} = 48.53.$$

Thus the 1% level lower one-sided test rejects H_0 if the observed sample mean $\bar{x} < 48.53$. Alternatively, this test can be expressed in terms of the standardized test statistic

$$z = \frac{\bar{x} - 50}{\sigma/\sqrt{n}} = \frac{\bar{x} - 50}{2/\sqrt{10}}$$

as follows: Reject H_0 if

$$z < -z_{.01} = -2.326.$$

◆

For the general problem of testing

$$H_0: \mu \geq \mu_0 \text{ vs. } H_1: \mu < \mu_0,$$

an α-level test is:

$$\text{Reject } H_0 \text{ if } z < -z_\alpha \text{ or equivalently if } \bar{x} < \mu_0 - z_\alpha \frac{\sigma}{\sqrt{n}} \qquad (6.17)$$

where $z = \frac{\bar{x} - \mu_0}{\sigma/\sqrt{n}}$.

This test can also be applied by first calculating the P-value in a similar manner to the upper one-sided test, and comparing the P-value with designated α. This is illustrated in the following example.

EXAMPLE 6.25 (CHEMICAL IMPURITIES: P-VALUE)

Measurements on 10 samples from a batch of the chemical resulted in a sample mean of $\bar{x} = 48.7$ ppm of impurities. Calculate the P-value for testing $H_0: \mu \geq 50$ vs. $H_1: \mu < 50$. Will H_0 be rejected, i.e., will the batch be accepted, using $\alpha = 0.01$? $\alpha = 0.05$?

First calculate

$$z = \frac{\bar{x} - \mu_0}{\sigma/\sqrt{n}} = \frac{48.7 - 50}{2/\sqrt{10}} = -2.055.$$

Therefore,

$$P\text{-value} = P\{\bar{X} \leq 48.7 \mid \mu = 50\} = P\left\{Z = \frac{\bar{X} - 50}{2/\sqrt{10}} \leq -2.055 \,\middle|\, \mu = 50\right\} = 0.020.$$

Since the P-value is less than 0.05 but greater than 0.01, H_0 can be rejected at $\alpha = 0.05$ but not at $\alpha = 0.01$. Of course, we know from Exaple 6.24 that $\bar{x} = 48.7$ does not fall in the rejection region "$\bar{x} < 48.53$" for $\alpha = 0.01$. ◆

EXAMPLE 6.26 (CONTROL CHART: TWO-SIDED TEST)

The nominal package weight of a box of a breakfast cereal is 16 oz. If the mean filled weight μ deviates (in either direction) from 16 oz., this fact must be detected as soon as possible to take a corrective action. Therefore the hypotheses are set up as $H_0: \mu = 16$ vs. $H_1: \mu \neq 16$.

A graphical method commonly used in quality control applications to monitor the process mean and keep it on target is the $\bar{X}$ **control chart**.[10] A sample of $n = 5$ boxes is taken from the filling process every hour and the contents are weighed. Assume that the package weights are normally distributed with mean μ and $\sigma = 0.1$ oz. Then the sample mean $\bar{X}$ of these measurements is normally distributed with mean μ and SD $= \sigma/\sqrt{n} = 0.1/\sqrt{5}$. The $\bar{X}$-chart can be viewed as a graphical way of applying the test that rejects H_0 if any observed $\bar{x}$ deviates more than three standard deviations from the target mean in either direction. In other words, an alarm is sounded if

$$\bar{x} < 16 - 3\frac{\sigma}{\sqrt{n}} = 16 - 3 \times \frac{0.1}{\sqrt{5}} = 15.866 \quad \text{or} \quad \bar{x} > 16 + 3\frac{\sigma}{\sqrt{n}} = 16 + 3 \times \frac{0.1}{\sqrt{5}} = 16.134.$$
$$(6.18)$$

This is a two-sided test, which is graphically implemented, as shown in Figure 6.7, by drawing two horizontal lines at 15.866 and 16.134 called the lower and upper **three-sigma control limits**, respectively. The $\bar{x}$ value for each sample is plotted on the chart. As long as the plotted points fall within the control limits, the process is assumed to be *in control* (H_0 is not rejected) and no corrective action is taken. If a plotted point falls beyond the control limits, then the process is regarded to be *out of control* (H_0 is rejected), resulting in a hunt for a cause of the disturbance. Of course, this could be a false alarm, i.e., a type I error.

---

[10] Control charts are used in a much broader manner than just doing a hypothesis test. See any book on quality control, e.g., D. C. Montgomery (1996), *Introduction to Statistical Quality Control*, 3rd ed., New York: John Wiley.

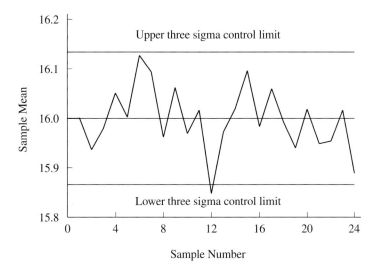

Figure 6.7 $\bar{X}$ Control Chart

The α level of this test is the **false alarm probability**, which is given by

$$\alpha = P\{\bar{X} > 16.134 \mid \mu = 16\} + P\{\bar{X} < 15.866 \mid \mu = 16\}$$

$$= P\left\{Z = \frac{\bar{X} - 16}{0.1/\sqrt{5}} > \frac{16.134 - 16}{0.1/\sqrt{5}} = 3\right\} + P\left\{Z = \frac{\bar{X} - 16}{0.1/\sqrt{5}} < \frac{15.866 - 16}{0.1/\sqrt{5}} = -3\right\}$$

$$= [1 - \Phi(3)] + \Phi(-3) = 0.00135 + 0.00135 = 0.0027.$$

This means that there is a false alarm every $1/0.0027 = 370.4$ samples on the average.   ◆

The test (6.18) can be written in the following equivalent form:

$$|z| = \frac{|\bar{x} - 16|}{\sigma/\sqrt{n}} > 3 = z_{.00135} \iff |\bar{x} - 16| > z_{.00135}\frac{\sigma}{\sqrt{n}} = 3 \times \frac{0.1}{\sqrt{5}} = 0.134.$$

This suggests the following general two-sided α-level test for

$$H_0 : \mu = \mu_0 \text{ vs. } H_1 : \mu \neq \mu_0$$

where μ_0 is a specified value ($\mu_0 = 16$ in Example 6.26). Compute $z = \frac{\bar{x} - \mu}{\sigma/\sqrt{n}}$.

$$\text{Reject } H_0 \text{ if } \quad |z| > z_{\alpha/2} \text{ or equivalently if } |\bar{x} - \mu_0| > z_{\alpha/2}\frac{\sigma}{\sqrt{n}}. \qquad (6.19)$$

EXAMPLE 6.27   (SAT COACHING: TWO-SIDED TEST)

To show that the coaching program improves the mean SAT-V score, an upper one-sided test was used in Example 6.21. This use of a one-sided test is based on the assumption that the only anticipated effect of the coaching program is to improve the average test score. However, this does not allow for the unanticipated possibility that it may actually reduce the average test score. If this possibility must be accounted for, then the alternative hypothesis must be set up as two-sided: $H_0: \mu = 15$ vs. $H_1: \mu \neq 15$.

Using (6.19) and $\sigma = 40$, $n = 20$, a 0.05-level two-sided test rejects H_0 if

$$|z| > z_{.025} = 1.96 \quad \Longleftrightarrow \quad |\bar{x} - 15| > 1.96 \times \frac{\sigma}{\sqrt{n}} = 1.96 \times \frac{40}{\sqrt{20}} = 17.53$$

i.e., if

$$\bar{x} < -2.53 \quad \text{or} \quad \bar{x} > 32.53.$$

If H_0 is rejected in the upper tail ($\bar{x} > 32.53$), then we can conclude that $\mu > 15$. Conversely, if H_0 is rejected in the lower tail ($\bar{x} < -2.53$), then we can conclude that $\mu < 15$. Compare this with the one-sided 0.05-level test of Example 6.21 that rejects H_0 when $\bar{x} > 29.71$, and notice that for the same α, the two-sided rejection rule makes it harder to reject H_0.   ◆

EXAMPLE 6.28   (SAT COACHING: *P*-VALUE FOR TWO-SIDED TEST)

In the above example where the alternative hypothesis is set up as two-sided, $H_1: \mu \neq 15$, calculate the P-value of the test statistic if the observed sample mean is $\bar{x} = 35$. Take $\sigma = 40$ and $n = 20$ as before.

Corresponding to $\bar{x} = 35$, we calculate the z-statistic to be 2.236 as in Example 6.21, where H_1 was one-sided. The value of the z-statistic does not change when H_1 is two-sided. So how does the P-value change? To see this, recall from Example 6.23 that the **one-sided P-value** = 0.013 was calculated as the α-level for which $z = 2.236 = z_\alpha$. Similarly, the **two-sided P-value** can be calculated as the α-level for which $z = 2.236 = z_{\alpha/2}$. Therefore $\alpha/2 = 0.013$ and $\alpha = 0.026$. Therefore the two-sided P-value equals 0.026.   ◆

We see that the two-sided P-value is simply twice the corresponding one-sided P-value for the same data. Thus if the alternative hypothesis is two-sided instead of one-sided, the same experimental outcome appears less significant. For example, if the one-sided P-value is 0.03, then the two-sided P-value is 0.06. Thus, at $\alpha = .05$, the one-sided test result is significant, but not the two-sided test result.

Which Test to Use—One-Sided or Two-Sided?   In Example 6.27 we saw that a two-sided alternative makes it more difficult to reject H_0. Equivalently, the same observed outcome appears less significant when a two-sided alternative is used instead of a one-sided alternative. Which alternative hypothesis should one use?

It is clear that a two-sided alternative should be used when the deviation in either direction from H_0 is worth detecting. This is the case in the control chart example above. Another situation where a two-sided alternative should be used is when a priori there is no reason to expect deviation from the null value to be in a particular direction. When the deviation is expected to be in a particular direction, there is some debate as to which alternative should be used. It seems logical to use a one-sided alternative, because then we can use a one-sided test, which has a higher power than a two-sided test. However, some statisticians feel that this gives an unfair advantage to the claim to be proved. In addition, if there is little previous experience with a research claim, an unanticipated effect in the opposite direction cannot be ruled out. A claim that passes the tougher hurdle of a two-sided test has a stronger supporting proof.

6.3.8 Relation Between Confidence Intervals and Hypothesis Tests

A careful inspection of the formulas for the confidence intervals and hypothesis tests for μ indicates that these two methods of inference are related. We now clarify this relation.

First consider the two-sided test (6.19) for μ which does not reject $H_0: \mu = \mu_0$ if and only if

$$|\bar{x} - \mu_0| \leq z_{\alpha/2} \frac{\sigma}{\sqrt{n}} \iff -z_{\alpha/2} \frac{\sigma}{\sqrt{n}} \leq \bar{x} - \mu_0 \leq z_{\alpha/2} \frac{\sigma}{\sqrt{n}}$$

$$\iff \bar{x} - z_{\alpha/2} \frac{\sigma}{\sqrt{n}} \leq \mu_0 \leq \bar{x} + z_{\alpha/2} \frac{\sigma}{\sqrt{n}}.$$

Therefore the two-sided α-level test (6.19) does not reject $H_0: \mu = \mu_0$ if and only if μ_0 is included in the $(1 - \alpha)$-level two-sided CI (6.5) for μ. Equivalently, that test rejects $H_0: \mu = \mu_0$ at level α if and only if μ_0 falls outside the $(1 - \alpha)$-level two-sided CI (6.5).

A similar relationship holds between one-sided CI's and one-sided tests. In order to reject $H_0: \mu \leq \mu_0$ in favor of $H_1: \mu > \mu_0$ at level α, the lower $(1 - \alpha)$ confidence bound, $\bar{x} - z_\alpha \sigma / \sqrt{n}$, on μ must be greater than μ_0. Similarly, to reject $H_0: \mu \geq \mu_0$ in favor of $H_1: \mu < \mu_0$ at level α, the upper $(1 - \alpha)$ confidence bound, $\bar{x} + z_\alpha \sigma / \sqrt{n}$, on μ must be less than μ_0. In both cases we reject H_0 at level α if and only if μ_0 falls outside the appropriate $(1 - \alpha)$-level CI for μ.

6.3.9 Use and Misuse of Hypothesis Tests in Practice

It is not an exaggeration to say that, for better or worse, hypothesis testing is the most widely used statistical tool in practice. However, user beware! A tool that is widely used can be abused. Be alert to possible misuses of hypothesis tests.

Difficulties of Interpreting Tests on Nonrandom Samples and Observational Data. The methods of formal statistical inference, including estimation and hypothesis testing, are based in probability theory. They assume that the data are a random sample from some distribution. Valid hypothesis tests in comparative studies require that the experimental units be randomly assigned to the treatment groups. These conditions are often violated. Observational studies are especially problematic because, as we saw in Chapter 3, they do not use randomization. Therefore the probability calculations in these studies (e.g., of confidence levels or P-values) are tenuous and may at best be taken only as rough indicators of statistical confidence or significance.

Observational studies also invite the pitfall of drawing a cause-effect conclusion from the test results. Although a test may reject H_0, this does not necessarily "prove" H_1, because some other uncontrolled confounding factor could have influenced the test results. For instance, in pretest/posttest studies, any observed change may simply be due to a time trend (e.g., a learning curve effect) rather than due to an intervention (e.g., a coaching program). To account for the possible effect of a time trend, a controlled experiment with a parallel control group must be used.

Statistical Significance vs. Practical Significance. A common mistake is to equate statistical significance with practical significance. A result can be statistically significant but not practically significant or vice versa. For instance, consider the hypothesis test in Example 6.21 to evaluate the coaching program. Suppose that the coaching program increases the mean SAT-V scores by $\mu = 15.5$ points, which is only half a point more than the natural retest gain. This is a practically insignificant improvement. However, if we have a very large sample, say a sample of one million students, then $\bar{x}$ will estimate μ quite accurately: $\bar{x} \simeq 15.5$. Therefore,

$$z = \frac{\bar{x} - 15}{\sigma/\sqrt{n}} \simeq \frac{15.5 - 15}{40/\sqrt{1,000,000}} = 12.5$$

which is highly statistically significant.

It is evident from this example that statistical significance is a function of the sample size. With a very large sample size, even a small, practically unimportant difference can be shown to be statistically significant. On the other hand, with a small sample size, a test may lack power to show even a large, practically important difference to be statistically significant.

In practice, an *estimate* of the difference between two alternatives is usually much more useful than a *test* for its statistical significance. A confidence interval provides such an estimate. A practically meaningful difference can be compared with a confidence interval to see whether a new alternative merits consideration. For example, if the lower confidence limit on the difference exceeds a certain minimum threshold, then we can claim that the new alternative is significantly better both in statistical and practical terms. Another advantage of a confidence interval is that it permits you to test any hypothesis that you want, as explained in Section 6.3.8. Therefore confidence intervals should be used more widely.

What is practically significant cannot be determined by statistical methods; this is for the subject matter expert to decide in the context of a specific problem. For instance, if there is no existing drug available to treat a life-threatening disease, then a new drug that offers even a small chance of saving lives may merit consideration. On the other hand, if a drug has undesirable side effects, then only a large improvement may make it practically viable, especially if other, safer drugs are available.

Perils of Searching for Significance. Significance at the 5% level has become almost mandatory for publication of research findings in many applied fields. This has resulted in the unfortunate practice of "data dredging" or "fishing expeditions" in quest of statistical significance. For example, a sociologist may measure many characteristics on each person in a sample and test all pairwise correlations to see which characteristics are significantly correlated. For another example, the protocol of a controlled clinical trial to evaluate an experimental drug may call for many outcome variables to be measured on each patient. The treatment and control groups are then compared on all variables, and the significant differences are reported. It is clear that if enough hypotheses are tested, you are almost sure to find at least one significant result even if no real relationships or differences exist. As a saying goes, "If you torture the data long enough they will confess." In fact, the very meaning of doing 5% level tests is that if you do 100 tests, then on the average 5 tests will show significance even if the null hypothesis holds in all cases. Therefore it is incorrect to highlight only a few significant results, which could easily have been obtained by a mere chance. Yet, this is commonly done!

The problem of obtaining spurious positive results due to data dredging is called the problem of **multiple comparisons**. Of course, no one would deny a researcher complete freedom to explore the data in various ways to see if any interesting patterns or differences emerge; this is how scientific discoveries are often made. But any such findings must be regarded as exploratory, and the process by which they are arrived at should be fully described. Follow-up studies should be done to confirm these findings. Alternatively, there are statistical methods which adjust for the effect of multiple testing. One simple but crude method is the **Bonferroni method**. It allocates the allowable type I error probability α equally among the tests and performs each test at level α/k, where k is the number of tests. This and other methods are described in Chapter 12.

Ignoring Lack of Significance. The flip side of reporting only the significant results is that nonsignificant results go mostly unreported, although they may be equally important. If an experiment is designed to have sufficient power to detect a specified difference, but does not detect it, that is an important finding and should be reported so that other researchers will not follow that false lead. For instance, in an epidemiological study it is important to know that a suspected risk factor is not associated with a disease.

Scientific Research and Hypothesis Testing. In scientific research, a single experiment generally does not make or break a theory. Therefore the purpose of a hypothesis test in such experiments is not to make a decision, but to quantify the evidence in support of a theory. Usually, what makes or breaks a theory is the reproducibility of results from independently replicated experiments by several investigators. There are situations, however, where a single scientific experiment is used to make a critical decision. Some examples are: (i) the experiment is prohibitively costly to repeat, (ii) the results of the experiment overwhelmingly support (or refute) a theory, and (iii) the problem that the experiment addresses requires immediate solution. The Salk Polio vaccine trial had all three elements present, and resulted in an enormously important health policy decision of vaccinating all young children. The drug AZT for AIDS was approved by the Food and Drug Administration of U.S. in 1987 based on a rather small trial before the trial was even completed.

6.4 CHAPTER SUMMARY

This chapter discusses basic concepts of three types of statistical inference, namely, point estimation, confidence interval estimation, and hypothesis testing. A statistic $\hat{\theta}$ used to estimate an unknown population parameter θ is called an **estimator**. Two important properties of an estimator $\hat{\theta}$ are its **accuracy** and **precision**. The average accuracy of $\hat{\theta}$ is measured by its **bias**, defined as $\text{Bias}(\hat{\theta}) = E(\hat{\theta}) - \theta$. An **unbiased estimator** has zero bias, i.e., $E(\hat{\theta}) = \theta$. The precision of an estimator is measured by its **variance**, $\text{Var}(\hat{\theta})$. The **mean square error (MSE)**, defined as $\text{MSE}(\hat{\theta}) = E(\hat{\theta}-\theta)^2 = \text{Var}(\hat{\theta}) + [\text{Bias}(\hat{\theta})]^2$, combines both measures. The estimated standard deviation of an estimator $\hat{\theta}$ is referred to as its **standard error (SE)** and is denoted by $\text{SE}(\hat{\theta})$.

A $100(1-\alpha)\%$ **confidence interval (CI)** for an unknown parameter θ is a random interval computed from sample data that will contain the true θ with probability $1-\alpha$; this probability is called the **confidence level**. A CI is **two-sided** if both its lower and upper limits are finite; a CI is **one-sided** if only the lower or the upper limit is finite.

In hypothesis testing, the claim or the conjecture to be proved is set up as the **alternative hypothesis**, denoted by H_1, and the counterclaim to be disproved is set up as the **null hypothesis**, denoted by H_0. The hypotheses are stated on an unknown parameter of the distribution from which the data are sampled. A **hypothesis test** is a method for judging the evidence in the data against H_0 and in favor of H_1 and deciding when to reject or not reject H_0. This decision is based on a **test statistic** calculated from the data. Two possible errors can result in a hypothesis test. A **type I error** occurs if H_0 is rejected when in fact it is true. A **type II error** occurs if H_0 is *not* rejected when in fact it is false and H_1 is true. The probabilities of these two errors are known as the **α-risk** and **β-risk**, respectively. They can be combined into a single function, called the **operating characteristic (OC) function**, which gives the probability of not rejecting H_0 for all parameter values (both under H_0 and under H_1). The **power** of a test equals $1-\beta$, which is the probability of correctly rejecting H_0 when it is false.

The conventional approach in hypothesis testing is to use a test that has its type I error probability controlled at or below a specified value α, called the **significance level**. One way of carrying out this test uses the **critical point** of the sampling distribution of the test statistic under H_0 such that the probability is α that the test statistic has values more extreme (which values are extreme depends on the direction specified on the parameter under H_1) than this critical point. The **α-level test** rejects H_0 when the test statistic is more extreme than the critical point. The second way is to calculate the **P-value** of the test statistic, which is the probability that the test statistic will be at least as extreme as what is actually observed assuming H_0 is true. The α-level test rejects H_0 if P-value is $<\alpha$. In fact, the P-value can be defined as the smallest α-level at which H_0 can be rejected given the value of the test statistic.

A **one-sided alternative** refers to H_1 that specifies a certain direction for the population parameter, e.g., $H_0: \mu \leq \mu_0$ vs. $H_1: \mu > \mu_0$; the corresponding test is called a **one-sided test**. A **two-sided alternative** refers to H_1 that specifies that the parameter is not equal to (i.e., either greater than or less than) a specified value, e.g., $H_0: \mu = \mu_0$ vs. $H_1: \mu \neq \mu_0$; the corresponding test is called a **two-sided test**. In addition to the two ways of carrying out α-level tests of H_0 given above, a $100(1-\alpha)\%$ CI (one-sided or two-sided depending on the alternative hypothesis) can also be used in the following manner: reject H_0 if the parameter values specified under H_0 are not in the CI.

Misuses of hypothesis tests are common in practice and should be avoided. Some common misuses are: (i) equating statistical significance with practical significance, (ii) hunting for significance, (iii) ignoring nonsignificant results, and (iv) drawing conclusions from nonrandom and/or observational data.

■ EXERCISES

Section 6.1

6.1   State whether each boldfaced number is a parameter or a statistic.

(a) A shipment of 1000 fuses contains **3** defective fuses. A sample of 25 fuses contained **0** defectives.

(b) The speed of 100 vehicles was monitored. It was found that **63** vehicles exceeded the posted speed limit.

(c) A telephone poll of registered voters one week before a statewide election showed that **48%** would vote for the current governor, who was running for reelection. The final election returns showed that the incumbent won with **52%** of the votes cast.

6.2 Let X_1, X_2, X_3, X_4 be i.i.d. observations from a distribution with mean μ and variance σ^2. Consider the following four estimators of μ:

$$\hat{\mu}_1 = X_1, \hat{\mu}_2 = \frac{X_2 + X_3}{2}, \hat{\mu}_3 = 0.1X_1 + 0.2X_2 + 0.3X_3 + 0.4X_4, \hat{\mu}_4 = \bar{X}.$$

(a) Show that all four estimators are unbiased.

(b) Calculate the variance of each estimator. Which one has the smallest variance?

(c) More generally, for a random sample of size n, show that if an estimator $\hat{\mu} = a_1 X_1 + a_2 X_2 + \cdots + a_n X_n$, where $a_1, a_2, \ldots, a_n$ are constants, is unbiased, then its variance is minimum when $a_1 = a_2 = \cdots = a_n = 1/n$, i.e., $\hat{\mu} = \bar{X}$. (*Hint:* Subject to $\sum a_i = 1$, $\sum a_i^2$ is minimized by choosing $a_1 = a_2 = \cdots = a_n = 1/n$.)

6.3 Let $X_1, X_2, \ldots, X_n$ be a random sample from a $U[0, \theta]$ distribution. Use the result of Exercise 5.44 to show the following.

(a) $X_{\max}$ is a biased estimator of θ. What is its bias?

(b) $X_{\min} + X_{\max}$ is an unbiased estimator of θ. From this it follows that the **midrange**, defined as $(X_{\min} + X_{\max})/2$, is an unbiased estimator of $\theta/2$, which is the mean of the $U[0, \theta]$ distribution.

6.4 Let $X_1, X_2, \ldots, X_n$ be a random sample from a distribution with mean μ and variance σ^2. Show that $\bar{X}^2$ is a biased estimator of μ^2. What is its bias? (*Hint:* $E(\bar{X}^2) - \mu^2 = \text{Var}(\bar{X}) = \sigma^2/n$.)

6.5 Suppose we have n independent Bernoulli trials with true success probability p. Consider two estimators of p: $\hat{p}_1 = \hat{p}$ where $\hat{p}$ is the sample proportion of successes and $\hat{p}_2 = 1/2$, a fixed constant.

(a) Find the expected value and bias of each estimator.

(b) Find the variance of each estimator. Which estimator has the lower variance?

(c) Find the MSE of each estimator and compare them by plotting against the true p. Use $n = 4$. Comment on the comparison.

6.6 Denote by $\hat{\theta}_1$ and $\hat{\theta}_2$ two independent unbiased estimators of θ. Suppose that $\text{Var}(\hat{\theta}_1) = \sigma_1^2$ and $\text{Var}(\hat{\theta}_2) = \sigma_2^2$. Consider a pooled estimator $\hat{\theta} = w_1 \hat{\theta}_1 + w_2 \hat{\theta}_2$, where w_1 and w_2 are fixed "weights."

(a) Show that $\hat{\theta}$ is unbiased if and only if $w_1 + w_2 = 1$.

(b) Show that $\text{Var}(\hat{\theta}) = w_1^2 \sigma_1^2 + w_2^2 \sigma_2^2$ is minimized when

$$w_1 = \frac{\sigma_2^2}{\sigma_1^2 + \sigma_2^2}, w_2 = 1 - w_1 = \frac{\sigma_1^2}{\sigma_1^2 + \sigma_2^2}.$$

What does this say about how $\hat{\theta}_1$ and $\hat{\theta}_2$ should be weighted?

6.7   A random sample of 10 coffee cans is taken from a production line and the contents are weighed. The weights (in oz.) are as follows:

$$26.3, 25.9, 26.9, 26.7, 25.8, 25.3, 26.4, 25.7, 26.3, 26.2$$

Calculate the sample mean as an estimate of the process mean, and the standard error of the mean (SEM).

6.8   At the beginning of Bill Clinton's presidential administration, he spoke on proposed economic reforms. A sample of people who heard the speech ($n = 611$) were asked if they favored higher taxes on all forms of energy; 43% responded Yes.[11] Considering this sample percentage as an estimate of the population percentage (what is the population here?), calculate its standard error.

6.9   Find the method of moments estimators of the parameters θ_1 and θ_2 in the gamma distribution with the probability density function:

$$f(x) = \frac{\theta_1^{\theta_2} x^{\theta_2 - 1} e^{-\theta_1 x}}{\Gamma(\theta_2)} \text{ for } x \geq 0$$

based on a random sample $X_1, X_2, \ldots, X_n$. (*Hint*: Equate the mean and variance of the gamma distribution, the formulas for which are given in Section 2.8.3, to the corresponding sample quantities, $\hat{\mu}_1$ and $\hat{\mu}_2 - \hat{\mu}_1^2$, respectively, and solve.)

6.10   Find the method of moments estimators of the parameters θ_1 and θ_2 in the beta distribution with the probability density function:

$$f(x) = \frac{\Gamma(\theta_1 + \theta_2)}{\Gamma(\theta_1)\Gamma(\theta_2)} x^{\theta_1 - 1}(1 - x)^{\theta_2 - 1} \text{ for } 0 \leq x \leq 1$$

based on a random sample $X_1, X_2, \ldots, X_n$. (*Hint*: Equate the mean and variance of the beta distribution, the formulas for which are given in Section 2.8.4, to the corresponding sample quantities, $\hat{\mu}_1$ and $\hat{\mu}_2 - \hat{\mu}_1^2$, respectively, and solve.)

Section 6.2

6.11   Consider the probability

$$P\left[-1.645 \leq Z = \frac{\bar{X} - \mu}{\sigma/\sqrt{n}} \leq +1.645\right]$$

where $\bar{X}$ is the mean of a random sample of size n drawn from an $N(\mu, \sigma^2)$ distribution.

   (a) Use this statement to find a CI for μ. What is the confidence level of this CI?

   (b) A sample of $n = 100$ is taken from a normal population with $\sigma = 10$. The sample mean is 30. Calculate the CI for μ using the result from (a).

   (c) What is the probability that μ is included in the CI calculated in (b)?

6.12   ■ Simulate 25 samples of size 20 from an $N(50, 6^2)$ distribution and find a 95% CI for each sample.

   (a) How many of the intervals contain the true mean 50? the wrong mean 53?

   (b) If the sample size were increased to $n = 100$, what would happen to the width of the 95% CI? Would you expect more or less of these intervals to contain the true mean 50? the wrong mean 53?

---

[11] *Time*, March 1, 1993, p. 26.

    (c) If you did not know that the true mean is 50, could you tell for any particular CI whether it included the true μ?

6.13 Suppose that 100 random samples of size 9 are generated from an $N(70, 3^2)$ distribution and the associated 95% CI is calculated for each sample.

    (a) How many of these 100 intervals would you expect to contain the true $\mu = 70$?

    (b) Let X be the number of intervals out of 100 that contain the true μ. What is the distribution of the r.v. X?

6.14 A random sample of size 25 from an $N(\mu, 6^2)$ distribution has mean $\bar{x} = 16.3$.

    (a) Calculate CI's for μ for three levels of confidence: 80%, 90%, and 99%. How do the CI widths change?

    (b) How would the CI widths change if n is increased to 100?

6.15 We want to estimate the mean output voltage of a batch of electrical power supply units. A random sample of 10 units is tested, and the sample mean is calculated to be 110.5 volts. Assume that the measurements are normally distributed with $\sigma = 3$ volts.

    (a) Calculate a two-sided 95% CI on the mean output voltage. Suppose that the specifications on the true mean output voltage are 110 ± 2.5 volts. Explain how the CI can be used to check whether these specifications are met.

    (b) Suppose that only the lower specification is applicable, since the main concern is that too low a voltage may cause malfunction of the equipment. Calculate an appropriate one-sided 95% confidence bound on the mean output voltage and explain how it can be used to check whether the lower specification limit is met.

    (c) Suppose that only the upper specification is applicable, since the main concern is that too high a voltage may cause malfunction of the equipment. Calculate an appropriate one-sided 95% confidence bound on the mean output voltage and explain how it can be used to check whether the upper specification limit is met.

6.16 Let $X_1, X_2, \ldots, X_n$ be a random sample from a continuous distribution with median $\tilde{\mu}$. If $[X_{\min}, X_{\max}]$ is used as a CI for $\tilde{\mu}$, what is its confidence level? What is the confidence level if $n = 10$? (*Hint*: See Example 5.9.)

Section 6.3

6.17 In each of the following cases, state the null hypothesis H_0 and the alternative hypothesis H_1 about the population proportion p under test. Interpret p in each instance.

    (a) The winner in the last congressional election received 54% of the vote. One year before the next election, the congressman hired a polling agency to conduct a sample survey of voters to determine if this proportion has changed.

    (b) The proportion of overdue books in a library is 5%. It is proposed to raise the fine for overdue books from 5 cents to 10 cents per day. It is felt that this would reduce the proportion of overdue books.

    (c) The scrap rate in making of a composite material is as high as 40%. A new production process is proposed which is claimed to reduce the scrap rate.

    (d) Gatorade and All Sport are two drinks popular among athletes. A marketing firm wants to determine whether a greater proportion of people like the taste of Gatorade or All Sport. For this purpose, a blind test is conducted in which the two drinks are offered in a random order to a group of tasters, who are then asked to indicate preference for one or the other drink.

6.18 In each of the following cases, state the null hypothesis H_0 and the alternative hypothesis H_1 about the population mean μ under test. Interpret μ in each instance.

   (a) A consumer watchdog group suspects that a yogurt advertised to be 98% fat free has actually a higher fat content. The group plans to measure the fat contents of 25 yogurt cups (each containing 170 grams) to verify its suspicion that the true mean fat content per cup is more than 2%, i.e., 3.4 grams.

   (b) The engineering specification on the shear strength for a fastener used in a mechanical assembly is 10,000 psi. A random sample of fasteners from a large lot supplied by a vendor is tested to see whether the mean shear strength of the lot meets the specification. Consider two situations: (i) The vendor is new, so little past history on the quality of his lots is available. (ii) The vendor is old, and past history shows that his lots have generally met the specification.

   (c) A commuter's average commuting time from home to work is 25 minutes. He wants to try a different route for a month to see if it would cut down the average commuting time.

   (d) Refer to part (d) of the previous exercise, but now instead of simply indicating preference suppose that the tasters assign a numerical score on a scale of 1 to 10 to each drink. The difference between the Gatorade score and the the All Sport score for each taster forms the data set.

6.19 In each of the following cases, explain which hypothesis should be set up as the null and which should be set up as the alternative by deciding which hypothesis, if incorrectly rejected, would result in a more serious error. This is the hypothesis that should be set up as the null. State any assumptions that you make.

   (a) A chemical compound used as a food additive is a suspected carcinogen. The two hypotheses are: (i) it is safe, (ii) it is not safe in the amount normally consumed.

   (b) A new analgesic has been developed by a pharmaceutical company. The two hypotheses are: (i) it is effective, (ii) it is not effective.

   (c) In order for a new generic drug to be approved by the regulatory agency, it must be demonstrated, among other things, that it is biologically equivalent to the original drug. The two hypotheses are: (i) it is bioequivalent, (ii) it is not bioequivalent.

   (d) It is claimed that cloud seeding is an effective technique to increase precipitation. The two hypotheses are: (i) it is effective, (ii) it is not effective.

6.20 Let X be a Bernoulli r.v. with $P(X = 1) = p$ and $P(X = 0) = 1 - p$. We want to test $H_0\colon p = 1/4$ vs. $H_1\colon p = 3/4$.

   (a) Suppose that based on a single observation X the decision rule is: do not reject H_0 if $X = 0$; reject H_0 if $X = 1$. Find the probabilities of type I and type II errors for this rule.

   (b) Suppose that based on two i.i.d. observations X_1 and X_2 the decision rule is: do not reject H_0 if $X_1 + X_2 = 0$ or 1; otherwise reject H_0. Find the probabilities of type I and type II errors for this rule.

6.21 ■ Consider an acceptance sampling plan which takes a random sample of 50 items from a large lot and accepts the lot if the number of defectives is no more than 2; otherwise it rejects the lot. Let p be the unknown fraction defective in the lot. The lot is regarded as "satisfactory" if $p = 0.02$ or less, and "unsatisfactory" if $p = 0.1$ or greater. Plot the OC curve of this rule by calculating the probability of accepting H_0 for $p = 0.01$ to 0.05 in steps of 0.01 and $p = 0.05$ to 0.20 in steps of 0.05. (You may use a software package that gives the binomial c.d.f. values to calculate these probabilities.) What are the α- and β-risks of this rule for $p = 0.02$ and $p = 0.1$, respectively? What is the power for $p = 0.15$?

6.22 Refer to Exercise 6.17, part (d). Let p be the proportion of people in the population who prefer Gatorade over All Sport. We want to decide if more people prefer Gatorade. The hypotheses are set up as $H_0: p \leq 1/2$ vs. $H_1: p > 1/2$. Fifteen tasters participated in the taste-testing experiment.

    (a) Suppose that 11 of the 15 tasters preferred Gatorade over All Sport. What is the P-value? Can you reject H_0 at $\alpha = .10$?

    (b) Suppose that a priori there is no reason to claim that one drink is preferred over the other. We want the taste-testing experiment to tell us if there is a significant difference, and if so, in which direction. Therefore the alternative hypothesis is now two-sided. What is the P-value? Can you reject H_0 at $\alpha = .10$?

6.23 ▐ The purpose of this exercise is to give you a feel for the α- and β-risks of a test as proportions of type I and type II errors in a long series of application of the same test when H_0 is true and when H_1 is true, respectively. Consider testing $H_0: \mu = 0$ vs. $H_1: \mu > 0$ at the 5% level of significance based on a sample of size 9 from a normal distribution with unknown mean μ and known $\sigma = 1$.

    (a) What is the α-risk of this rule? What is the β-risk of this rule if $\mu = 1$?

    (b) Simulate this test 100 times for $\mu = 0$ (by drawing 100 samples of size 9 from an $N(0, 1)$ distribution and performing the test) and count the proportion of times a type I error is committed (H_0 is rejected). Repeat for $\mu = 1$ and count the proportion of times a type II error is committed (H_0 is not rejected). How close are these proportions to the α- and β-risks?

6.24 A company buys metal fasteners in large lots. The mean shear strength must be at least 10,000 psi in order for the lot to be acceptable. This may be formulated as a hypothesis testing problem with $H_0: \mu \leq 10,000$ vs. $H_1: \mu > 10,000$. A sample of 10 fasteners is tested, and if the sample mean exceeds 10,500 psi, then H_0 is rejected and the lot is accepted. Assume $\sigma = 1000$ psi. Calculate the α- and β-risks for this rule if the true $\mu = 10,000$ and 11,000 psi, respectively.

6.25 ▐ Refer to the previous exercise. Plot the OC curve of this rule by calculating the probability of not rejecting H_0 for μ-values from 9600 to 11,600 in steps of 200. (You may use a software package that gives the normal c.d.f. values to calculate these probabilities.)

6.26 Refer to Exercise 6.25. Suppose the company wants to control the α-risk at .01. What is the decision rule in terms of $\bar{x}$? What is its β-risk and power when $\mu = 11,000$ psi? Repeat the calculations assuming a sample size of 20. What do you conclude?

6.27 In order to shorten the cycle time of an assembly process, an industrial engineer has simplified the operations and designed a new fixture. With the old method, the average time for assembly is 10 minutes. To test his claim an experiment is conducted in which 15 workers trained in the new method participate.

    (a) Set up the hypotheses to show that the average assembly time with the new method is less than 10 minutes.

    (b) Suppose that the sample mean for the 15 workers is 8.7 minutes. If $\sigma = 2$ minutes, is there statistically significant evidence that the average time is reduced? Use $\alpha = .05$.

    (c) The industrial engineer claims that the new method will reduce the average time by at least 1.5 minutes. What chance (power) does this experiment have of detecting the claimed improvement?

6.28   In 1993 a typical American family spent 22% of its after-tax income on clothing, entertainment, and other activities, while the remaining 78% was spent on essentials like housing, food, transportation, health care, and insurance/pensions. It is suggested that because of the increase in the cost of essentials since 1993, the mean percentage income spent on the first three items has decreased. To test this proposition a random sample of 50 households is taken and the percentage spent on these three items is determined. Assume that this percentage varies across families according to a normal distribution with unknown mean μ and known $\sigma = 5\%$. (Note that this percentage is not a binomial proportion.)

   (a) Set up the hypotheses on μ.

   (b) If the average percentage for 50 families is 20.5%, would you conclude that this is a significant decrease compared to the 1993 level? Use $\alpha = .01$.

   (c) Carry out the test in (b) by calculating the P-value.

6.29   Example 6.26 uses a 3-sigma control chart for controlling the mean of a process. In some countries 2.5-sigma control charts are used, i.e., the control limits are $\mu_0 - 2.5\sigma/\sqrt{n}$ and $\mu_0 + 2.5\sigma/\sqrt{n}$, where μ_0 is the target value for the process mean μ, σ is the process standard deviation, and n is the sample size.

   (a) Use the data from Example 6.26 to calculate the control limits and the α-risk for the 2.5-sigma control chart. Compare the results with those for the 3-sigma control chart and comment.

   (b) Calculate the β-risks for both the charts if the mean shifts by 0.1 oz. from the target value of 16 oz. Compare the results and comment.

6.30   A researcher desperate to find a statistically significant difference between two groups has data on 20 variables from each group. He tests 20 null hypotheses, each null hypothesis being that the two group means of a given variable are equal, hoping to find a significant difference on at least one variable.

   (a) Suppose that the 20 tests are mutually independent and are conducted individually at the 5% significance level. What is the probability that at least one null hypothesis will be incorrectly rejected even if all null hypotheses are true?

   (b) What does the above calculation tell you about the perils of searching for significance by multiple testing?

6.31   Consider testing $H_0: \mu = 0$ vs. $H_1: \mu > 0$ based on a random sample of size n from an $N(\mu, 1^2)$ distribution. Calculate the P-values for the following three cases: (i) $\bar{x} = 0.1, n = 100$, (ii) $\bar{x} = 0.1, n = 400$, (iii) $\bar{x} = 0.1, n = 900$. What do you conclude?

Advanced Exercises

6.32   Let $X_1, X_2, \ldots, X_n$ be a random sample from a uniform distribution on the interval $[0, \theta]$, which has mean $\mu = \theta/2$ and variance $\sigma^2 = \theta^2/12$. Consider two estimators of θ: $\hat{\theta}_1 = X_{max}$ and $\hat{\theta}_2 = 2\bar{X}$.

   (a) Use the result of Exercise 5.44(b) to find $E(\hat{\theta}_1)$, $Var(\hat{\theta}_1)$, and $MSE(\hat{\theta}_1)$.

   (b) Find $E(\hat{\theta}_2)$, $Var(\hat{\theta}_2)$, and $MSE(\hat{\theta}_2)$.

   (c) Compare $MSE(\hat{\theta}_1)$ and $MSE(\hat{\theta}_2)$.

6.33   In sample surveys, if people are asked a sensitive or a potentially stigmatizing question (e.g., "Have you ever shoplifted?" or "Do you take drugs?"), they often give an evasive answer or refuse to answer at all, which introduces a bias in the estimate of the proportion p of people in the population belonging to the sensitive group. To avoid this bias and to still protect the privacy of the survey respondents, Warner[12] introduced a technique called **randomized response**. In its simplest form, the respondent chooses one of the following two questions using a random device such as a spinner:

1. I belong to the sensitive group: Answer "Yes" or "No."

2. I *do not* belong to the sensitive group: Answer "Yes" or "No."

The interviewer does not see the outcome of the random device and hence does not know which question is answered, thus protecting the respondent's privacy.

Let $\theta \neq 1/2$ denote the *known* probability that the random device chooses question 1 and let π denote the probability of a "Yes" response. The population proportion to be estimated is p.

(a) Assuming that the respondent answers truthfully, show that

$$\pi = P(\text{Yes}) = p\theta + (1 - p)(1 - \theta).$$

(b) Suppose $\hat{\pi}$ is the sample proportion of "Yes" responses in a simple random sample of n people. Show that

$$\hat{p} = \frac{\hat{\pi} - (1 - \theta)}{2\theta - 1}$$

is an unbiased estimator of p.

(c) Show that

$$\text{Var}(\hat{p}) = \frac{[p(2\theta - 1) + (1 - \theta)][\theta - p(2\theta - 1)]}{n(2\theta - 1)^2}.$$

(*Hint*: Since $\hat{\pi}$ is a binomial proportion, $\text{Var}(\hat{\pi}) = \pi(1 - \pi)/n$. Substitute for π in terms of p and θ.)

(d) Simplify the above expression to the following:

$$\text{Var}(\hat{p}) = \frac{p(1 - p)}{n} + \frac{\theta(1 - \theta)}{n(2\theta - 1)^2}.$$

The first term is the usual binomial variance of $\hat{p}$, while the second term is the variance due to randomization. Analyze and interpret the contribution from the second term as θ moves away from 1/2 toward 0 or 1.

6.34 Assume the following result: Let $T_1, T_2, \ldots, T_n$ be i.i.d. $\text{Exp}(\lambda)$ r.v.'s, and let $T_{(1)} \leq T_{(2)} \leq \cdots \leq T_{(n)}$ be their order statistics. The **exponential spacings** are defined as

$$S_1 = T_{(1)}, S_2 = T_{(2)} - T_{(1)}, \ldots, S_n = T_{(n)} - T_{(n-1)}.$$

Then the $S_i \sim \text{Exp}((n - i + 1)\lambda)$; also, the S_i are independently distributed. In this exercise we use this result to show that an estimator used for the mean lifetime in censored life-testing is unbiased.

Consider a life-testing experiment in which n identical items are put on test. The experiment is terminated when the first $m < n$ (where m is fixed) items have failed (called **type I censoring**). The failure times of these items are the m smallest order statistics, $T_{(1)} \leq T_{(2)} \leq \cdots \leq T_{(m)}$, from the common lifetime distribution of the items, which we

---

[12] S. L. Warner (1965), "Randomized response: A survey technique for eliminating evasive answer bias," *Journal of the American Statistical Association*, **60**, pp. 63–69.

assume to be exponential with failure rate λ and mean $\mu = 1/\lambda$. The total time on test (TTT) is defined as

$$\text{TTT} = T_{(1)} + T_{(2)} + \cdots + T_{(m)} + (n - m)T_{(m)}$$

where the first m terms add up the times on test (failure times) of the m failed items and the last term is the total time on test of the $n - m$ items that were still functional when the test was terminated.

(a) Show that

$$\hat{\mu} = \frac{\text{TTT}}{m}$$

is an unbiased estimator of μ. (*Hint:* Express $T_{(i)} = S_1 + S_2 + \cdots + S_i$, collect the terms in each S_i, and use the fact that $E(S_i) = 1/(n - i + 1)\lambda = \mu/(n - i + 1)$.)

(b) In **type II censoring** the time of the test (denoted by t^*) is fixed; thus the number of failures before time t^* is now a random variable. The total time on test is defined as TTT $= T_{(1)} + T_{(2)} + \cdots + T_{(m)} + (n - m)t^*$, and the same estimator $\hat{\mu}$ is used. Explain why the same proof of unbiasedness will not work here. (In fact, $\hat{\mu}$ is *not* unbiased in this case.)

6.35 Let $\bar{X}$ be the mean of a random sample of size n from an $N(\mu, \sigma^2)$ distribution and suppose that σ^2 is known.

(a) Show that

$$[\bar{X} - z_{\alpha_1} \frac{\sigma}{\sqrt{n}}, \bar{X} + z_{\alpha_2} \frac{\sigma}{\sqrt{n}}]$$

is a $(1 - \alpha)$-level CI for μ if α_1 and α_2 satisfy $\alpha_1 + \alpha_2 = \alpha$.

(b) Show that $\alpha_1 = \alpha, \alpha_2 = 0$ yields the lower one-sided confidence bound (6.6) for μ, while $\alpha_1 = 0, \alpha_2 = \alpha$ yields the upper one-sided confidence bound (6.7).

CHAPTER 7

INFERENCES FOR SINGLE SAMPLES

Many statistical problems address questions about some characteristic of a population based on a sample drawn from that population. For example, it may be important to monitor the *mean* of a manufacturing process to determine if the process is under control. Or it may be necessary to evaluate the precision of a laboratory instrument measured by the *variance* of its readings. This chapter applies the basic concepts of confidence intervals and hypothesis tests that we learned in the previous chapter to make inferences about the mean and variance of a normal population. By using the central limit theorem (CLT), inference procedures for the mean of a normal population can be extended to the mean of a nonnormal population when a large sample is available. The chapter concludes with a discussion of prediction intervals and tolerance intervals, which are methods for estimating future observations from a population.

7.1 INFERENCES ON MEAN (LARGE SAMPLES)

A common problem is to estimate by a confidence interval (CI) or to test a hypothesis on the unknown mean μ of a population using a random sample $X_1, X_2, \ldots, X_n$ from that population. Initially we will assume that the population is normal with *known* variance σ^2. Inferences on μ will be based on the sample mean $\bar{X}$, which is an unbiased estimator of μ with variance σ^2/n. For a large sample size n, the CLT tells us that $\bar{X}$ is approximately $N(\mu, \sigma^2/n)$ distributed, even if the population is not normal. Also, for large n, the sample variance S^2 may be taken as an accurate estimator of σ^2 with negligible sampling error. Thus the methods given below can be applied even if the sample comes from a nonnormal population with unknown variance, as long as the sample size is large enough (say ≥ 30); the only change required is that in the formulas for the tests and CI's, replace σ by the sample standard deviation $s \simeq \sigma$. In Chapter 9 we will apply these large sample methods to make inferences on proportions for binary data.

7.1.1 Confidence Intervals on Mean

Recall from Chapter 6 that

$$Z = \frac{\bar{X} - \mu}{\sigma/\sqrt{n}} \sim N(0, 1) \tag{7.1}$$

is a pivotal r.v. for μ. The probability statement

$$P\left[-z_{\alpha/2} \leq Z = \frac{\bar{X} - \mu}{\sigma/\sqrt{n}} \leq z_{\alpha/2}\right] = 1 - \alpha$$

leads to the following two-sided $100(1 - \alpha)\%$ CI for μ:

$$\bar{x} - z_{\alpha/2}\frac{\sigma}{\sqrt{n}} \leq \mu \leq \bar{x} + z_{\alpha/2}\frac{\sigma}{\sqrt{n}} \quad \text{(Two-Sided CI)} \tag{7.2}$$

where $z_{\alpha/2}$ is the upper $\alpha/2$ critical point of the $N(0, 1)$ distribution, $\bar{x}$ is the observed sample mean, and $\sigma/\sqrt{n}$ is the standard error of the mean (SEM). Similarly, the formulas for one-sided $100(1 - \alpha)\%$ CI's on μ (derived in Chapter 6) are

$$\mu \leq \bar{x} + z_{\alpha}\frac{\sigma}{\sqrt{n}} \quad \text{(Upper One-Sided CI)} \tag{7.3}$$

and

$$\mu \geq \bar{x} - z_{\alpha}\frac{\sigma}{\sqrt{n}} \quad \text{(Lower One-Sided CI).} \tag{7.4}$$

These CI's are known as **z-intervals**.

Sample Size Determination for a z-Interval. The formula (7.2) shows that a two-sided CI on μ can be computed for any confidence level $1 - \alpha$, no matter how small the sample size n is. The price paid for a small sample size is, of course, a wide CI. To obtain a CI with a specified width, we need a certain minimum sample size n. Suppose that we require a $(1 - \alpha)$-level two-sided CI for μ of the form $[\bar{x} - E, \bar{x} + E]$ with a specified **width** $2E$ or **margin of error** E. We set

$$E = z_{\alpha/2}\frac{\sigma}{\sqrt{n}}$$

and solve for n, obtaining

$$n = \left[\frac{z_{\alpha/2}\sigma}{E}\right]^2, \tag{7.5}$$

which is rounded up to the next integer.

Note that n increases as σ and the confidence level $1 - \alpha$ (through $z_{\alpha/2}$) increase, and as E decreases. Thus the greater the underlying variation in the data or the greater the confidence level or the smaller the margin of error allowed, the greater the sample size required. Since this sample size calculation is made at the design stage, a sample estimate of σ is not available. An approximate estimate of σ can be obtained as follows. It is often possible to approximately anticipate the range of the observations (barring any outliers). Divide this range by four and use the resulting number as an approximate estimate of σ. This estimate is based on the normal distribution property that 95% of the observations are expected to fall in the range $[\mu - 2\sigma, \mu + 2\sigma]$.

EXAMPLE 7.1   (AIRLINE REVENUE: SAMPLE SIZE DETERMINATION)

Refer to Example 6.7. Suppose that the airline wants to estimate the mean share of its revenue per ticket within \$5 using a 99% CI. The anticipated range of the airline's share of the revenue per ticket is estimated to be \$200. How many tickets should be sampled?

Here $E = 5, \alpha = 0.01, z_{\alpha/2} = z_{.005} = 2.576$, and an approximate estimate of σ equals $200/4 = 50$. Substituting these values in (7.5), we obtain

$$n = \left[\frac{2.576 \times 50}{5} \right]^2 = 664. \qquad \blacklozenge$$

7.1.2 Hypothesis Tests on Mean

In Chapter 6 we derived one-sided and two-sided α-level z-tests on the mean of a normal population. These tests are summarized in Table 7.1. The test statistic used in these tests is

$$z = \frac{\bar{x} - \mu_0}{\sigma/\sqrt{n}} \qquad (7.6)$$

which is obtained from the pivotal r.v. Z of (7.1).

As we saw in Chapter 6, a P-value is more informative than a reject/do not reject decision based on an arbitrarily chosen level of significance α. Once the P-value is calculated, a test at any level α can be conducted by simply rejecting H_0 if the P-value is $< \alpha$. This avoids a table look-up of critical constants.

The P-value is the probability under H_0 of obtaining a test statistic at least as extreme as the one actually observed. Which values of the test statistic are "extreme" depends on the alternative hypothesis H_1. For example, if H_1 specifies $\mu > \mu_0$, then values greater than or equal to the observed test statistic z are extreme. The pivotal r.v. Z has an $N(0, 1)$ distribution when H_0 holds. Using these facts, the formulas for the P-values for the three hypothesis testing problems in Table 7.1 can be easily derived; they are summarized in Table 7.2.

Recall also from Chapter 6 the relationship between tests and CI's. An α-level test on μ rejects H_0 if μ_0 falls outside the corresponding $(1 - \alpha)$-level CI. A two-sided α-level hypothesis test on μ is illustrated in the following example using a z-test, a P-value, and a CI.

Table 7.1 Level α Tests on μ When σ^2 Is Known (Test Statistic: $z = \frac{\bar{x}-\mu_0}{\sigma/\sqrt{n}}$)

Testing Problem	Hypotheses	Reject H_0 if	Pictorial Representation
Upper One-Sided	$H_0\colon \mu \le \mu_0$ vs. $H_1\colon \mu > \mu_0$	$z > z_\alpha$ $\Longleftrightarrow$ $\bar{x} > \mu_0 + z_\alpha \frac{\sigma}{\sqrt{n}}$	
Lower One-sided	$H_0\colon \mu \ge \mu_0$ vs. $H_1\colon \mu < \mu_0$	$z < -z_\alpha$ $\Longleftrightarrow$ $\bar{x} < \mu_0 - z_\alpha \frac{\sigma}{\sqrt{n}}$	
Two-Sided	$H_0\colon \mu = \mu_0$ vs. $H_1\colon \mu \ne \mu_0$	$|z| > z_{\alpha/2}$ $\Longleftrightarrow$ $|\bar{x} - \mu_0| > z_{\alpha/2}\frac{\sigma}{\sqrt{n}}$	

EXAMPLE 7.2

A change in the manufacturing process of steel beams is suggested. The manufacturer wants to know if the mean strength μ of the beams made by the new process is different from 42,000 psi, which is the mean strength of the beams made by the present process. A two-sided hypothesis test on μ is appropriate to answer this question. Breaking strengths are measured for a test sample of $n = 32$ beams made by the new process. The sample mean for this test sample is $\bar{x} = 42{,}196$ psi and the sample SD is $s = 500$ psi. Assume that the observations are normally distributed and that the sample size is large enough so that $s \approx \sigma$. Perform a two-sided test of the hypotheses $H_0\colon \mu = 42{,}000$ vs. $H_1\colon \mu \ne 42{,}000$ at the 10% level of significance.

The test can be done in three ways:

Table 7.2 P-Values for Hypothesis Tests on μ When σ^2 Is Known (Test Statistic: $z = \frac{\bar{x}-\mu_0}{\sigma/\sqrt{n}}$)

Testing Problem	Hypotheses	P-Value	Pictorial Representation
Upper One-Sided	$H_0: \mu \le \mu_0$ vs. $H_1: \mu > \mu_0$	$P(Z \ge z \mid H_0)$ $=$ $1 - \Phi(z)$	
Lower One-Sided	$H_0: \mu \ge \mu_0$ vs. $H_1: \mu < \mu_0$	$P(Z \le z \mid H_0)$ $=$ $\Phi(z)$	
Two-Sided	$H_0: \mu = \mu_0$ vs. $H_1: \mu \ne \mu_0$	$P(\lvert Z\rvert \ge \lvert z\rvert \mid H_0)$ $=$ $2[1 - \Phi(\lvert z\rvert)]$	

1. Calculate the z-statistic (7.6):

$$z = \frac{\bar{x} - \mu_0}{\sigma/\sqrt{n}} = \frac{42196 - 42000}{500/\sqrt{32}} = 2.217.$$

Here $\alpha = 0.10$, so $z_{\alpha/2} = z_{.05} = 1.645$. Since $\lvert z\rvert = 2.217 > 1.645$, we reject H_0 and conclude that the mean breaking strength of the beams made by the new process is different. In fact, we can make a stronger claim that $\mu > 42{,}000$.

2. Calculate the P-value:

$$P\text{-value} = 2[1 - \Phi(\lvert z\rvert)] = 2[1 - \Phi(2.217)] = 2[1 - 0.987] = 0.026.$$

This tells us that if the true process mean is $\mu = 42{,}000$ psi, the probability of obtaining a sample mean that is different by at least 196 psi (which is 2.217 standard deviation units) from the true mean is only 0.026. Since this probability is less than $\alpha = 0.10$, we reject H_0. In fact, we can reject H_0 even at $\alpha = 0.05$, but not at $\alpha = 0.01$.

3. Calculate a 90% CI for μ:

$$\left[\bar{x} \pm z_{\alpha/2}\frac{\sigma}{\sqrt{n}}\right] = \left[42196 \pm 1.645\frac{500}{\sqrt{32}}\right] = [42051, 42341].$$

Since $\mu_0 = 42{,}000$ does not fall in this CI, we reject H_0. Again, we can make a stronger claim that $\mu > 42{,}000$, since the lower confidence limit exceeds 42,000.   ◆

Power Calculation for One-Sided z-Tests.   As we saw in Chapter 6, the power function[1] of a test gives the probability of rejecting H_0 as a function of the true value of the test parameter. For z-tests, the power is a function of μ:

$$\pi(\mu) = P(\text{Test rejects } H_0 \mid \mu),$$

where the notation $P(A \mid \mu)$ means that the probability of event A is calculated assuming that the true mean $= \mu$. The power function is useful for assessing whether the test has sufficiently high probability to reject H_0 when H_1 is true.

Consider the problem of testing $H_0\colon \mu \leq \mu_0$ vs. $H_1\colon \mu > \mu_0$. The power function of the α-level upper one-sided z-test for this problem can be derived as follows:

$$\pi(\mu) = P\left(\bar{X} > \mu_0 + z_\alpha\frac{\sigma}{\sqrt{n}} \,\middle|\, \mu\right)$$

$$= P\left(Z = \frac{\bar{X} - \mu}{\sigma/\sqrt{n}} > z_\alpha + \frac{\mu_0 - \mu}{\sigma/\sqrt{n}} \,\middle|\, \mu\right)$$

$$= 1 - \Phi\left[z_\alpha + \frac{(\mu_0 - \mu)\sqrt{n}}{\sigma}\right]$$

$$= \Phi\left[-z_\alpha + \frac{(\mu - \mu_0)\sqrt{n}}{\sigma}\right]. \tag{7.7}$$

In the last step we have used the normal c.d.f. property that $1 - \Phi(x) = \Phi(-x)$, which follows from the symmetry of the normal distribution about 0; see Section 2.9.1. Figure 7.1 shows the p.d.f. curves of $\bar{X} \sim N(\mu, \sigma^2/n)$ for two different values of μ: $\mu = \mu_0$ (when H_0 holds) and $\mu = \mu_1 > \mu_0$ (when H_1 holds). The rejection region, namely $\bar{x} > \mu_0 + z_\alpha \sigma/\sqrt{n}$, is also shown. For the top p.d.f. curve (the null distribution), the shaded area in the rejection region represents the probability of *incorrectly* rejecting H_0 when $\mu = \mu_0$ is true (the type I error probability); note that $\pi(\mu_0) = \alpha$. For the bottom p.d.f. curve (the alternative distribution), the shaded area in the rejection region represents $\pi(\mu_1)$, the probability of *correctly* rejecting H_0 when $\mu = \mu_1$ is true.

---

[1] The power function and the operating characteristic (OC) function discussed in Section 6.3.6 are simply related by $\pi(\mu) = 1 - \text{OC}(\mu)$.

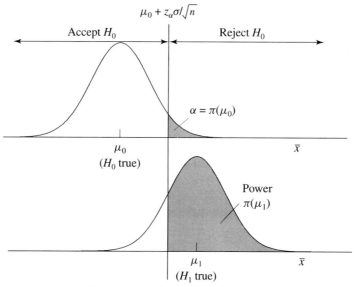

Figure 7.1   Level of Significance and Power of the Upper One-Sided α-Level z-Test Shown as Areas under the Density Function Curves of $\bar{X}$ under H_0: $\mu = \mu_0$ and under H_1: $\mu = \mu_1 > \mu_0$

Figure 7.2 shows the power function curves for two sample sizes, n and $n' > n$. We see that the larger sample size n' yields greater power for $\mu > \mu_0$, while for both sample sizes we have $\pi(\mu_0) = \alpha$.

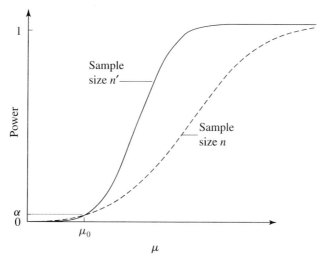

Figure 7.2   Power Function Curves for the Upper One-Sided α-Level z-Test with Two Different Sample Sizes, n and $n' > n$

From Figures 7.1 and 7.2 we can intuitively see the following properties of the power function.[2]

1. Note that $\pi(\mu) > \pi(\mu_0) = \alpha$ for $\mu > \mu_0$. Hence the power is greater than α in the alternative hypothesis region.

2. Furthermore, $\pi(\mu) \leq \alpha$ for all $\mu \leq \mu_0$. This justifies (as alluded to at the end of Section 6.3.3 in Chapter 6) replacing the simple null hypothesis $H_0\colon \mu = \mu_0$ by a composite null hypothesis $H_0\colon \mu \leq \mu_0$, which still guarantees that $P(\text{Type I error}) = \pi(\mu) \leq \alpha$ for all μ under the composite null hypothesis H_0.

3. As the distribution of $\bar{X}$ moves further to the right (i.e., as μ increases), more of the distribution lies in the rejection region, thus increasing the power. This means that the greater the difference $\mu - \mu_0$, the greater the power to detect it. In mathematical terms, the power is an increasing function of $\mu - \mu_0$.

4. For fixed $\mu - \mu_0$, σ, and α, the power increases monotonically with sample size n.

EXAMPLE 7.3   (SAT COACHING: POWER CALCULATION)

In Example 6.21 we considered the problem of testing the hypothesis that μ, the mean improvement in the SAT verbal (SAT-V) scores due to the coaching program, is more than 15 points. A 0.05-level test of $H_0\colon \mu \leq 15$ vs. $H_1\colon \mu > 15$ based on a sample of 20 students was derived assuming that the changes in the test scores are normally distributed with $\sigma = 40$. This test rejects H_0 if $\bar{x} > 29.71$, where $\bar{x}$ is the sample mean of changes in the test scores. What is the power of this test if the true mean change in SAT-V scores after coaching is 30 points?

Substitute $\mu_0 = 15$, $\mu = 30$, $z_\alpha = z_{.05} = 1.645$, $\sigma = 40$ and $n = 20$ in (7.7) to obtain

$$\pi(30) = \Phi\left[-1.645 + \frac{(30-15)\sqrt{20}}{40}\right] = \Phi(0.032) = 0.513.$$

Thus there is only a 51.3% chance to detect a coaching effect of 30 points.   ◆

The power function of the α-level lower one-sided z-test of $H_0 : \mu \geq \mu_0$ vs. $H_1 : \mu < \mu_0$ can be derived in a similar manner, and is given by

$$\pi(\mu) = \Phi\left[-z_\alpha + \frac{(\mu_0 - \mu)\sqrt{n}}{\sigma}\right]. \tag{7.8}$$

Power Calculation for Two-Sided z-Tests.   Next consider the problem of testing $H_0\colon \mu = \mu_0$ vs. $H_1\colon \mu \neq \mu_0$. The power function of the α-level two-sided z-test for this problem is given by

$$\pi(\mu) = P\left(\bar{X} < \mu_0 - z_{\alpha/2}\frac{\sigma}{\sqrt{n}}\,\middle|\,\mu\right) + P\left(\bar{X} > \mu_0 + z_{\alpha/2}\frac{\sigma}{\sqrt{n}}\,\middle|\,\mu\right)$$

$$= P\left(Z = \frac{\bar{X}-\mu}{\sigma/\sqrt{n}} < -z_{\alpha/2} + \frac{\mu_0 - \mu}{\sigma/\sqrt{n}}\right) + P\left(Z = \frac{\bar{X}-\mu}{\sigma/\sqrt{n}} > z_{\alpha/2} + \frac{\mu_0 - \mu}{\sigma/\sqrt{n}}\right)$$

---

[2] These properties can also be deduced analytically from the power function expression (7.7).

$$= \Phi\left[-z_{\alpha/2} + \frac{(\mu_0 - \mu)\sqrt{n}}{\sigma}\right] + 1 - \Phi\left[z_{\alpha/2} + \frac{(\mu_0 - \mu)\sqrt{n}}{\sigma}\right]$$

$$= \Phi\left[-z_{\alpha/2} + \frac{(\mu_0 - \mu)\sqrt{n}}{\sigma}\right] + \Phi\left[-z_{\alpha/2} + \frac{(\mu - \mu_0)\sqrt{n}}{\sigma}\right]. \tag{7.9}$$

Figure 7.3 shows the distributions of $\bar{X}$ under $H_0: \mu = \mu_0$ and under $H_1: \mu = \mu_1 \neq \mu_0$. Note that the rejection region of the two-sided test is in both the tails. The total shaded area in the two tails under the null distribution equals $\pi(\mu_0) = \alpha$. The corresponding shaded area under the alternative distribution equals $\pi(\mu_1)$, which is the power to correctly reject H_0 when $\mu = \mu_1$. Figure 7.4 gives the plots of the power function for the two-sided test for two different sample sizes, n and $n' > n$. The following properties of the power function of the two-sided test can be summarized from these two figures.

1. The power function is symmetric about μ_0.

2. The power increases as $|\mu - \mu_0|$ increases. The lowest value is $\pi(\mu_0) = \alpha$.

3. For fixed $\mu - \mu_0$, σ, and α, the power increases monotonically with sample size n.

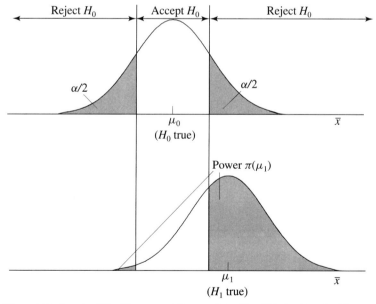

Figure 7.3   Level of Significance and Power of the Two-Sided α-Level z-Test Shown as Areas under the Density Function Curves of $\bar{X}$ under $H_0: \mu = \mu_0$ and under $H_1: \mu = \mu_1 \neq \mu_0$

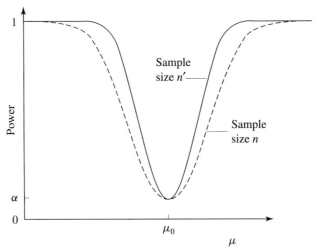

Figure 7.4   Power Function Curves for the α-Level Two-Sided z-Test with Two Different Sample Sizes, n and $n' > n$

EXAMPLE 7.4   (CONTROL CHART: POWER CALCULATION)

Recall the three-sigma control chart from Example 6.26 to control the mean of a filling process at the target level of 16 oz. based on hourly samples of size $n = 5$. The filling weights were assumed to be distributed $N(\mu, 0.1^2)$. This control chart can be viewed as a graphical method to test $H_0: \mu = 16$ vs. $H_1: \mu \neq 16$ using the rejection region $\bar{x} < 16 - 3\sigma/\sqrt{n} = 15.866$ or $\bar{x} > 16 + 3\sigma/\sqrt{n} = 16.134$. This corresponds to using $z_{\alpha/2} = 3$ or $\alpha = 0.0027$. Calculate the power of this test to detect a shift of 0.1 oz. (i.e., of one standard deviation) in the process mean.

Since the power function is symmetric around $\mu_0 = 16$, the power is the same for an equal shift in the mean in either direction. In the following we use (7.9) to calculate the power for $\mu = 16.1$ (i.e., upward shift of 0.1 oz.):

$$\pi(16.1) = \Phi\left[-3 + \frac{(16 - 16.1)\sqrt{5}}{0.1}\right] + \Phi\left[-3 + \frac{(16.1 - 16)\sqrt{5}}{0.1}\right]$$

$$= \Phi(-5.236) + \Phi(-0.764)$$

$$= 0.000 + 0.223 = 0.223.$$

The average number of samples needed to detect this shift in the mean is $1/0.223 = 4.494$, i.e., between 4 to 5 samples.   ◆

Table 7.3 summarizes the power function formulas for the three testing situations given in Table 7.1.

Sample Size Determination for a One-Sided z-Test.   A central problem in designing an observational or experimental study is to determine the sample size so that the study will have sufficient power to detect an effect of practically important magnitude. If the goal of the study is to show that the mean response μ under a treatment is higher

Table 7.3 Power Function Formulas for α-Level z-Tests

Testing Problem	Power Function $\pi(\mu)$	Pictorial Representation
Upper One-Sided	$\Phi\left[-z_\alpha + \frac{(\mu-\mu_0)\sqrt{n}}{\sigma}\right]$	
Lower One-Sided	$\Phi\left[-z_\alpha + \frac{(\mu_0-\mu)\sqrt{n}}{\sigma}\right]$	
Two-Sided	$\Phi\left[-z_{\alpha/2} + \frac{(\mu_0-\mu)\sqrt{n}}{\sigma}\right] + \Phi\left[-z_{\alpha/2} + \frac{(\mu-\mu_0)\sqrt{n}}{\sigma}\right]$	

than the mean response μ_0 without the treatment, then $\mu - \mu_0$ is called the **treatment effect**. For example, the effect of SAT-V coaching in Example 7.3 can be defined as $\mu - 15$, which represents the mean increase in SAT-V scores due to the coaching program over and above the average increase of 15 points that occurs on retesting without any coaching. Let $\delta > 0$ denote a practically important treatment effect and let $1 - \beta$ denote the minimum power required to detect it. The goal is to find the minimum sample size n which would guarantee that an α-level z-test of H_0 has at least $1 - \beta$ power to reject H_0 when the treatment effect is at least δ. Because the power is an increasing function of $\mu - \mu_0$, it is only necessary to find n that makes the power equal to $1 - \beta$ at $\mu = \mu_0 + \delta$. From (7.7) we obtain

$$\pi(\mu_0 + \delta) = \Phi\left(-z_\alpha + \frac{\delta\sqrt{n}}{\sigma}\right) = 1 - \beta.$$

Using the fact that $\Phi(z_\beta) = 1 - \beta$ gives the relation

$$-z_\alpha + \frac{\delta\sqrt{n}}{\sigma} = z_\beta.$$

Solving for n, we obtain

$$n = \left[\frac{(z_\alpha + z_\beta)\sigma}{\delta} \right]^2, \qquad (7.10)$$

which is rounded up to the next integer. Note that n increases with an increase in σ, z_α (reflecting a smaller α), or z_β (reflecting a greater power, $1 - \beta$) or a decrease in δ. Thus the greater the measurement variation, the smaller the significance level, the greater the power required, or the smaller the meaningful difference to be detected, the larger the sample size needed.

Example 7.5 (SAT Coaching: Sample Size Determination)

Refer to Example 7.3. Calculate the number of students that must be tested in order to have at least 90% power for detecting an increase of 30 points or more in the mean SAT-V scores due to the coaching program.

We have $\alpha = 0.05$, $z_\alpha = 1.645$, $\beta = 0.10$, $z_\beta = 1.282$, $\sigma = 40$, and $\delta = \mu - \mu_0 = 30 - 15 = 15$. Substituting these values in (7.10), we obtain

$$n = \left[\frac{(1.645 + 1.282)40}{15} \right]^2 = 60.92 \quad \text{or} \quad 61.$$

Therefore at least 61 students must be tested. ◆

Similar reasoning is used to determine the sample size for the lower one-sided α-level z-test of $H_0: \mu \geq \mu_0$ vs. $H_1: \mu < \mu_0$. Here the treatment effect is defined as $\mu_0 - \mu$. Then the sample size that guarantees at least $1 - \beta$ power when the treatment effect is at least $\delta > 0$ is given by the same formula (7.10) for the upper one-sided case. This is easy to verify by using the fact that the power function curves for the upper and lower one-sided cases given by (7.7) and (7.8), respectively, are mirror images of each other.

Sample Size Determination for a Two-Sided z-Test. For a two-sided α-level z-test of $H_0: \mu = \mu_0$ vs. $H_1: \mu \neq \mu_0$, we have the analogous problem of determining the minimum sample size n required to guarantee $1 - \beta$ power when the treatment effect $|\mu - \mu_0|$ is at least $\delta > 0$. Because the power function (7.9) for the two-sided case is increasing and symmetric in $|\mu - \mu_0|$, it is only necessary to find n that makes the power equal to $1 - \beta$ when $\mu = \mu_0 + \delta$ or when $\mu = \mu_0 - \delta$. The resulting equation is

$$\pi(\mu_0 + \delta) = \pi(\mu_0 - \delta) = \Phi\left(-z_{\alpha/2} - \frac{\delta\sqrt{n}}{\sigma}\right) + \Phi\left(-z_{\alpha/2} + \frac{\delta\sqrt{n}}{\sigma}\right) = 1 - \beta.$$

There is not a simple closed form solution in n to this equation. However, a simple approximation is obtained by noting that for $\delta > 0$, the term $\Phi\left(-z_{\alpha/2} - \frac{\delta\sqrt{n}}{\sigma}\right)$ is negligible. Similarly, for $\delta < 0$, the term $\Phi\left(-z_{\alpha/2} + \frac{\delta\sqrt{n}}{\sigma}\right)$ is negligible. Hence,

$$\Phi\left(-z_{\alpha/2} + \frac{\delta\sqrt{n}}{\sigma}\right) \simeq 1 - \beta.$$

Using the fact that $\Phi(z_\beta) = 1 - \beta$ gives

$$-z_{\alpha/2} + \frac{\delta\sqrt{n}}{\sigma} \simeq z_\beta.$$

Solving for n, we obtain

$$n = \left[\frac{(z_{\alpha/2} + z_\beta)\sigma}{\delta}\right]^2, \qquad (7.11)$$

which is rounded up to the next integer. Notice that this sample size formula is the same as (7.10) for the one-sided case except that z_α is replaced by $z_{\alpha/2}$.

EXAMPLE 7.6 (CONTROL CHART: SAMPLE SIZE DETERMINATION)

In Example 7.4 we found that using a sample size of 5 to monitor the cereal filling process gave only 22% power to detect a shift of one standard deviation (0.1 oz.) from the target mean weight of 16 oz. What is the minimum sample size required to guarantee at least 75% power?

We have $\alpha = 0.0027, z_{\alpha/2} = z_{.00135} = 3.0, 1 - \beta = 0.75, z_\beta = z_{.25} = 0.675$, and $\delta/\sigma = 1.0$. Substituting these values in (7.11), we obtain

$$n = \left[\frac{(3.0 + 0.675)}{1}\right]^2 = 13.51 \quad \text{or} \quad 14. \qquad \blacklozenge$$

7.2 INFERENCES ON MEAN (SMALL SAMPLES)

The population variance is generally unknown and is estimated by the sample variance S^2. The sampling variability of S^2 may be sizeable if the sample size is small (less than about 30). Therefore inference methods must take into account the fact that σ^2 is unknown, and its estimator S^2 is an r.v.

We assume that $X_1, \ldots, X_n$ is a random sample from an $N(\mu, \sigma^2)$ distribution, but now σ^2 is unknown. We saw in Section 5.3 that the pivotal r.v. for making inferences on μ in this case is obtained by replacing σ in the formula (7.1) for Z by S. This pivotal r.v. is

$$T = \frac{\bar{X} - \mu}{S/\sqrt{n}} \qquad (7.12)$$

which has a t-distribution with $n - 1$ degrees of freedom (d.f.).

7.2.1 Confidence Intervals on Mean

Using the pivotal r.v. T, we can write the probability statement

$$1 - \alpha = P\left[-t_{n-1,\alpha/2} \leq T = \frac{\bar{X} - \mu}{S/\sqrt{n}} \leq t_{n-1,\alpha/2}\right]$$

$$= P\left[\bar{X} - t_{n-1,\alpha/2}\frac{S}{\sqrt{n}} \leq \mu \leq \bar{X} + t_{n-1,\alpha/2}\frac{S}{\sqrt{n}}\right]$$

where $t_{n-1,\alpha/2}$ is the upper $\alpha/2$ critical point of the t-distribution with $n - 1$ d.f. These critical points are given in Table A.4. It follows that a $100(1 - \alpha)\%$ CI for μ is

$$\bar{x} - t_{n-1,\alpha/2}\frac{s}{\sqrt{n}} \leq \mu \leq \bar{x} + t_{n-1,\alpha/2}\frac{s}{\sqrt{n}} \quad \text{(Two-Sided CI)} \qquad (7.13)$$

where $\bar{x}$ is the observed sample mean and s is the observed sample standard deviation. This CI is referred to as a **two-sided t-interval**. Note that it is of the same form as the z-interval (7.2), namely sample mean $\pm$(critical constant) $\times$ SEM, except that the critical constant $t_{n-1,\alpha/2}$ replaces $z_{\alpha/2}$ and s replaces σ in SEM. Since $t_{n-1,\alpha/2} > z_{\alpha/2}$, the t-interval is wider on the average than the corresponding z-interval. This is the price paid for not knowing σ. For $n > 30$, the z-interval may be used as a good approximation to the t-interval.

EXAMPLE 7.7

Table 7.4 gives 29 measurements of the density of earth (expressed as multiples of the density of water, i.e., in grams/cc) made in 1798 by the British scientist Henry Cavendish.[3] Estimate the density of earth from these measurements using a 95% CI.

Table 7.4 Measurements of the Density of Earth

5.50	5.61	4.88	5.07	5.26	5.55	5.36	5.29	5.58	5.65
5.57	5.53	5.62	5.29	5.44	5.34	5.79	5.10	5.27	5.39
5.42	5.47	5.63	5.34	5.46	5.30	5.75	5.86	5.85	

The box plot and normal plot for these data are shown in Figure 7.5. Both plots are satisfactory and no outliers are indicated. Therefore we proceed with formal calculations. For these data, the sample mean $\bar{x} = 5.448$, the sample standard deviation $s = 0.221$, and hence the SEM, $s/\sqrt{n} = 0.221/\sqrt{29} = 0.041$. The d.f. are $29 - 1 = 28$, and the required critical point is $t_{28,.025} = 2.048$ from Table A.4. The 95% CI is calculated to be

$$[5.448 - 2.048 \times 0.041, 5.420 + 2.048 \times 0.041] = [5.363, 5.532]. \qquad \blacklozenge$$

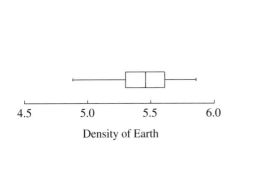

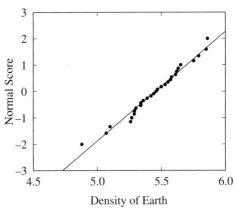

Figure 7.5   Box Plot and Normal Plot of the Cavendish Data on the Density of Earth

---

[3] K. A. Brownlee (1965), *Statistical Theory and Methodology in Science and Engineering*, 2nd ed., New York: Wiley.

One-Sided Intervals.   One-sided $100(1-\alpha)\%$ t-intervals for μ when σ^2 is unknown are derived in a similar manner to the two-sided t-interval. These CI's are:

$$\mu \leq \bar{x} + t_{n-1,\alpha}\frac{s}{\sqrt{n}} \quad \text{(Upper One-Sided CI)}, \qquad (7.14)$$

and

$$\mu \geq \bar{x} - t_{n-1,\alpha}\frac{s}{\sqrt{n}} \quad \text{(Lower One-Sided CI)}. \qquad (7.15)$$

EXAMPLE 7.8   (TEAR STRENGTH OF RUBBER: LOWER 95% CONFIDENCE LIMIT ON THE MEAN)

The following are the measurements made on the tear strengths of 16 sample sheets of a silicone rubber used in a high voltage transformer. Calculate a 95% lower confidence limit on the mean tear strength μ.

Tear Strength in PSI

33.74	34.40	32.62	32.57	34.69	33.78	36.76	34.31
37.61	33.78	35.43	33.22	33.53	33.68	33.24	32.98

The box plot and the normal plot for these data are shown in Figure 7.6. The box plot indicates that the measurements 36.76 and 37.61 are possible outliers. Generally, the outliers should be examined further to see if they can be corrected or modified or whether they can be explained; they should not be automatically discarded. Not having any additional information on the source of these outliers, we omit them for the purpose of this example. However, we caution the reader that discarding of outliers may result in loss of useful information. Also, the presence of outliers may indicate nonnormality. In such a case one of the nonparametric or robust methods from Chapter 14 should be used, or expert help sought.

The two plots obtained after omitting these two measurements are shown in Figure 7.7, and they indicate that the remainder of the data are better behaved and are approximately normally distributed.

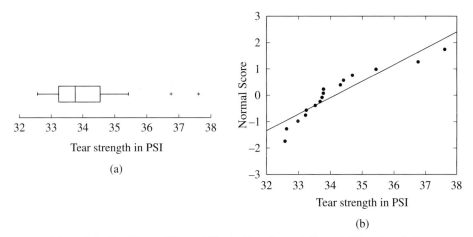

Figure 7.6   Box Plot and Normal Plot for Tear Strength Data: (a) Box plot of all observations ($n = 16$); (b) Normal plot of all observations ($n = 16$)

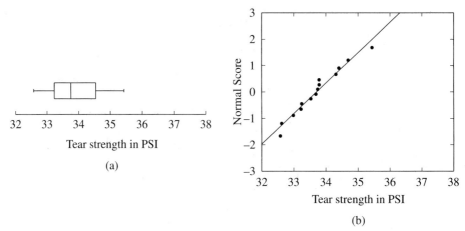

Figure 7.7   Box Plot and Normal Plot for Tear Strength Data after Omitting Outliers: (a) Box plot omitting outliers ($n = 14$); (b) Normal plot omitting outliers ($n = 14$);

The summary statistics for the data after omitting the two outliers are $\bar{x} = 33.712$, $s = 0.798$, and $n = 14$. Therefore a lower 95% confidence limit calculated using $t_{13,.05} = 1.771$ is

$$\mu \geq 33.712 - 1.771 \frac{0.798}{\sqrt{14}} = 33.334. \qquad \blacklozenge$$

7.2.2 Hypothesis Tests on Mean

The one-sided and two-sided hypothesis tests in this case are known as the **t-tests** and are analogous to the corresponding z-tests. The test statistic obtained from the pivotal r.v. (7.12) is given by

$$t = \frac{\bar{x} - \mu_0}{s/\sqrt{n}} \qquad (7.16)$$

where $\bar{x}$ is the observed sample mean, s is the observed sample standard deviation, and μ_0 is the postulated value of μ under H_0. The formulas for the t-tests and P-values are summarized in Table 7.5. The P-values cannot be directly obtained from Table A.4, because that table gives the percentiles of the t-distribution rather than the areas under its density function curve. The percentiles can be used to place bounds on P-values (e.g., $.01 < P\text{-value} < .05$). A computer package must be used to obtain exact P-values.

EXAMPLE 7.9   (TEAR STRENGTH OF RUBBER: UPPER ONE-SIDED t-TEST)

For the data (after omitting the outliers) of Example 7.8, test whether the mean tear strength exceeds a lower specification limit of 33 psi.

The hypotheses are formulated as $H_0\colon \mu \leq 33$ vs. $H_1\colon \mu > 33$. From the 95% lower confidence limit of 33.334 psi calculated in Example 7.8 we know that $\mu > 33$, and so H_0 can be rejected at $\alpha = .05$. Let us calculate the t- statistic (7.16) to check that we get the same result.

Table 7.5 Level α Tests on μ When σ^2 Is Unknown (Test Statistic: $t = \frac{\bar{x}-\mu_0}{s/\sqrt{n}}$)

Testing Problem	Hypotheses	Reject H_0 if	P-value
Upper One-Sided	$H_0\!: \mu \le \mu_0$ vs. $H_1\!: \mu > \mu_0$	$t > t_{n-1,\alpha}$ $\Longleftrightarrow$ $\bar{x} > \mu_0 + t_{n-1,\alpha}\frac{s}{\sqrt{n}}$	$P(T_{n-1} \ge t)$
Lower One-Sided	$H_0\!: \mu \ge \mu_0$ vs. $H_1\!: \mu < \mu_0$	$t < -t_{n-1,\alpha}$ $\Longleftrightarrow$ $\bar{x} < \mu_0 - t_{n-1,\alpha}\frac{s}{\sqrt{n}}$	$P(T_{n-1} \le t)$
Two-Sided	$H_0\!: \mu = \mu_0$ vs. $H_1\!: \mu \ne \mu_0$	$\lvert t\rvert > t_{n-1,\alpha/2}$ $\Longleftrightarrow$ $\lvert \bar{x} - \mu_0\rvert > t_{n-1,\alpha/2}\frac{s}{\sqrt{n}}$	$P(\lvert T_{n-1}\rvert \ge \lvert t\rvert)$ = $2P(T_{n-1} \ge \lvert t\rvert)$

We are given $\bar{x} = 33.712$, $s = 0.798$, and $n = 14$. Therefore the t-statistic is

$$ t = \frac{33.712 - 33}{0.798/\sqrt{14}} = 3.343. $$

Since the calculated t exceeds the critical value $t_{13,.05} = 1.771$, we reject H_0 and conclude that the minimum specification of 33 psi is met. The calculated $t = 3.343$ falls between $t_{13,.005} = 3.012$ and $t_{13,.0025} = 3.372$; therefore the exact P-value is bounded between .0025 and .005. ◆

*Power Calculation and Sample Size Determination for t-Tests.   The power function and sample size formulas for the t-tests are not easy to obtain, and the calculations require the use of special charts. We shall illustrate the difficulty for the upper one-sided testing problem. In this case, the power $\pi(\mu)$ of the α-level t-test is given by

$$ \pi(\mu) = P\left\{ \frac{\bar{X} - \mu_0}{S/\sqrt{n}} > t_{n-1,\alpha} \,\middle|\, \mu \right\} $$

where μ is the true mean. When $\mu > \mu_0$, i.e., $\mu - \mu_0 = \delta > 0$, the r.v. $\frac{\bar{X}-\mu_0}{S/\sqrt{n}}$ does not have a t-distribution. To see this, express the r.v. as

$$ \frac{(\bar{X} - \mu_0)\sqrt{n}/\sigma}{S/\sigma}. $$

In this expression, the numerator is distributed as $N(\delta\sqrt{n}/\sigma, 1)$, the denominator is distributed as $\sqrt{\chi^2_{n-1}/(n-1)}$, and the two are independent. Thus all the components of a t-distribution as defined in (5.13) are present, except that the numerator does not have a zero mean. In this case, the resulting distribution is called a **noncentral t-distribution** with **noncentrality parameter** $\delta\sqrt{n}/\sigma$ and d.f. $n-1$. The power is an increasing function of the noncentrality parameter. When $H_0 : \mu = \mu_0$ is true, the noncentrality parameter equals 0, reducing the noncentral t-distribution to the familiar Student's (central) t-distribution, and the power equals α.

Areas under the noncentral t-distribution are required when making the power and sample size calculations. For this purpose, one must use special charts (or computer programs) which are given in standard texts on design of experiments.[4] Reasonably good approximations to the power of the t-test and to the required sample size can be obtained from the corresponding formulas for the z-test. The estimated power is slightly on the high side and the sample size is on the low side.

Robustness of Inference Methods for Mean.   The confidence intervals and hypothesis tests for means based on z and t statistics assume normality of the sample data. This assumption is often violated in practice. Another problem with real data is the presence of outliers. What effect do these disturbing influences have on these methods? For instance, is the actual confidence level of a 95% CI close to the nominal level of 95%? If not, then we cannot put much trust in probability calculations such as the confidence level and the P-value.

An outlier can have a strong effect on the results because these methods are based on the sample mean, which is not a resistant statistic (see Section 4.3). Lack of normality of data has less effect because the CLT ensures that the sample mean is approximately normally distributed even if the raw data are not.

7.3   INFERENCES ON VARIANCE

In contrast to the inference procedures for means in the previous two sections, the procedures in this section are strongly dependent on the assumption of normality of the data. Therefore these procedures should be used with caution, especially since nonnormality is very difficult to detect for small or moderate sample sizes.

Assume that $X_1, \cdots, X_n$ is a random sample from an $N(\mu, \sigma^2)$ distribution. The sample variance S^2 is an unbiased estimator of σ^2. Recall from Chapter 5 that

$$\chi^2 = \frac{(n-1)S^2}{\sigma^2}$$

has a chi-square distribution with $n-1$ d.f. (χ^2_{n-1} distribution). This is a pivotal r.v. for σ^2, since it is not a function of any unknown parameters other than σ^2 and its distribution is free of all unknown parameters. This pivotal r.v. is used to develop CI's and hypothesis tests on σ^2.

---

[4] See, e.g., D. C. Montgomery (1997), *Design and Analysis of Experiments*, 4th ed, New York: Wiley.

7.3.1 Confidence Interval on Variance

Let $\chi^2_{n-1,1-\frac{\alpha}{2}}$ and $\chi^2_{n-1,\frac{\alpha}{2}}$ be the lower and upper $\alpha/2$ critical points of the χ^2_{n-1} distribution, respectively. As shown in Figure 7.8, the area under the χ^2_{n-1} density function between these two critical points is $1 - \alpha$. This can be used to write the probability statement

$$1 - \alpha = P\left[\chi^2_{n-1,1-\frac{\alpha}{2}} \leq \frac{(n-1)S^2}{\sigma^2} \leq \chi^2_{n-1,\frac{\alpha}{2}}\right]$$

$$= P\left[\frac{(n-1)S^2}{\chi^2_{n-1,\frac{\alpha}{2}}} \leq \sigma^2 \leq \frac{(n-1)S^2}{\chi^2_{n-1,1-\frac{\alpha}{2}}}\right].$$

It follows that the $100(1-\alpha)\%$ CI for σ^2 has the form:

$$\frac{(n-1)s^2}{\chi^2_{n-1,\frac{\alpha}{2}}} \leq \sigma^2 \leq \frac{(n-1)s^2}{\chi^2_{n-1,1-\frac{\alpha}{2}}} \quad \text{(Two-Sided CI)}, \qquad (7.17)$$

where s^2 is the observed value of the sample variance. A $100(1-\alpha)\%$ CI for σ is

$$s\sqrt{\frac{n-1}{\chi^2_{n-1,\frac{\alpha}{2}}}} \leq \sigma \leq s\sqrt{\frac{n-1}{\chi^2_{n-1,1-\frac{\alpha}{2}}}} \quad \text{(Two-Sided CI)}. \qquad (7.18)$$

Using similar reasoning, one-sided $100(1-\alpha)\%$ CI's for σ^2 are given by

$$\sigma^2 \geq \frac{(n-1)s^2}{\chi^2_{n-1,\alpha}} \quad \text{(Lower One-Sided CI)} \qquad (7.19)$$

and

$$\sigma^2 \leq \frac{(n-1)s^2}{\chi^2_{n-1,1-\alpha}} \quad \text{(Upper One-Sided CI)}. \qquad (7.20)$$

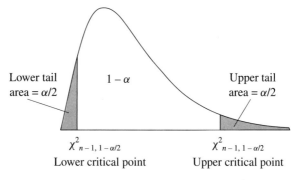

Figure 7.8   Lower and Upper $\alpha/2$ Critical Points of a χ^2_{n-1} Distribution

EXAMPLE 7.10   (THERMOMETER PRECISION: CONFIDENCE INTERVAL)

Refer to Example 5.5 concerning verification of the advertised precision of $\sigma = .01°$F for a thermometer. Verification is done by taking 10 repeat measurements of a controlled temperature bath. Suppose that the sample variance of these 10 measurements is $s^2 = 2.0 \times 10^{-4}$. Then a 90% CI for σ is

$$\left[\sqrt{\frac{9s^2}{\chi^2_{9,.05}}}, \sqrt{\frac{9s^2}{\chi^2_{9,.95}}} \right] = \left[\sqrt{\frac{9 \times 2 \times 10^{-4}}{16.92}}, \sqrt{\frac{9 \times 2 \times 10^{-4}}{3.325}} \right] = [0.0103, 0.0233].$$

The claimed value, $\sigma = 0.01$, does not lie in this interval. Hence the data do not support the claim at the 10% level of significance. Since the lower confidence limit is greater than 0.01, we conclude that $\sigma > 0.01$.   ◆

7.3.2 Hypothesis Tests on Variance

In the previous example, a CI was used to test hypotheses of the form

$$H_0: \sigma^2 = \sigma_0^2 \text{ vs. } H_1: \sigma^2 \neq \sigma_0^2.$$

The same test can be performed directly using the **chi-square statistic**:

$$\chi^2 = \frac{(n-1)s^2}{\sigma_0^2}. \tag{7.21}$$

When H_0 is true, this statistic has a χ^2_{n-1} distribution. This leads to the following α-level two-sided test:

$$\text{Reject } H_0 \text{ if } \chi^2 > \chi^2_{n-1,\alpha/2} \text{ or if } \chi^2 < \chi^2_{n-1,1-\alpha/2}.$$

One-sided tests can be derived in the same manner. These tests are summarized in Table 7.6.

The P-value of the χ^2-statistic can be obtained by finding the appropriate tail area under the chi-square density function curve. To find the P-value for the two-sided test, the smaller of the lower and upper tail areas corresponding to the observed χ^2-statistic is first found, and then multiplied by two. As in the case of the t-statistic, only bounds on these P-values can be obtained from Table A.5. To obtain exact P-values, one must use a computer package.

EXAMPLE 7.11   (THERMOMETER PRECISION: HYPOTHESIS TEST)

In Example 7.10, we tested $H_0: \sigma = 0.01$ vs. $H_1: \sigma \neq 0.01$ at $\alpha = 0.10$ using a 90% CI for σ. Equivalently, we can use a 0.10-level two-sided χ^2-test as follows.

Calculate

$$\chi^2 = \frac{(n-1)s^2}{\sigma_0^2} = \frac{9 \times 2 \times 10^{-4}}{1 \times 10^{-4}} = 18.0.$$

Since this is greater than $\chi^2_{n-1,\alpha/2} = \chi^2_{9,.05} = 16.92$, we reject H_0 and conclude that $\sigma > 0.01$. MINITAB was used to find the c.d.f. value of the χ^2_9-distribution at 18.0, which is 0.965. Therefore the two-sided P-value is $2(1 - 0.965) = 0.070$. Since the P-value < 0.10, H_0 is rejected at $\alpha = 0.10$.   ◆

Table 7.6 Level α Tests on σ^2 (Test Statistic: $\chi^2 = \frac{(n-1)s^2}{\sigma_0^2}$)

Testing Problem	Hypotheses	Reject H_0 if	P-value
Upper One-Sided	$H_0: \sigma^2 \le \sigma_0^2$ vs. $H_1: \sigma^2 > \sigma_0^2$	$\chi^2 > \chi_{n-1,\alpha}^2$ $\Longleftrightarrow$ $s^2 > \frac{\sigma_0^2 \chi_{n-1,\alpha}^2}{n-1}$	$P_U = P(\chi_{n-1}^2 \ge \chi^2)$
Lower One-Sided	$H_0: \sigma^2 \ge \sigma_0^2$ vs. $H_1: \sigma^2 < \sigma_0^2$	$\chi^2 < \chi_{n-1,1-\alpha}^2$ $\Longleftrightarrow$ $s^2 < \frac{\sigma_0^2 \chi_{n-1,1-\alpha}^2}{n-1}$	$P_L = P(\chi_{n-1}^2 \le \chi^2)$
Two-Sided	$H_0: \sigma^2 = \sigma_0^2$ vs. $H_1: \sigma^2 \ne \sigma_0^2$	$\chi^2 > \chi_{n-1,\alpha/2}^2$ or $\chi^2 < \chi_{n-1,1-\alpha/2}^2$ $\Longleftrightarrow$ $s^2 > \frac{\sigma_0^2 \chi_{n-1,\alpha/2}^2}{n-1}$ or $s^2 < \frac{\sigma_0^2 \chi_{n-1,1-\alpha/2}^2}{n-1}$	$2\min\{P_U, P_L = 1 - P_U\}$

7.4   *PREDICTION AND TOLERANCE INTERVALS

7.4.1 Prediction Intervals

Many practical applications call for an interval estimate of an *individual* (future) observation sampled from a population rather than of the mean of the population. For example, a company buying a new machine would like to estimate the performance of *that* machine—not the average performance of all similar machines. An important difference is that an individual observation is an r.v., while the population mean is a fixed unknown parameter. An interval estimate for an individual observation is called a **prediction interval (PI)**.

Suppose that a random sample $X_1, X_2, \ldots, X_n$ from an $N(\mu, \sigma^2)$ distribution is available. Based on this random sample we want to find a $100(1-\alpha)\%$ PI for a future observation X from the same distribution, i.e., an interval that would include X with probability $1 - \alpha$.

Let $\bar{X}$ be the sample mean and S be the sample SD. Note that the future observation X is independent of $\bar{X}$. Since $X \sim N(\mu, \sigma^2)$ and $\bar{X} \sim N(\mu, \sigma^2/n)$, we have

$$X - \bar{X} \sim N\left(0, \sigma^2(1 + 1/n)\right).$$

Since S^2 is distributed as $\frac{\sigma^2 \chi_{n-1}^2}{n-1}$ and is independent of both X and $\bar{X}$, it follows that

$$\frac{X - \bar{X}}{S\sqrt{1 + \frac{1}{n}}}$$

has a t_{n-1}-distribution. Hence we can write

$$P\left\{ -t_{n-1,\alpha/2} \leq \frac{X - \bar{X}}{S\sqrt{1 + \frac{1}{n}}} \leq t_{n-1,\alpha/2} \right\} = 1 - \alpha.$$

Rewriting this probability statement to find bounds on X yields

$$P\left\{ \bar{X} - t_{n-1,\alpha/2} S\sqrt{1 + \frac{1}{n}} \leq X \leq \bar{X} + t_{n-1,\alpha/2} S\sqrt{1 + \frac{1}{n}} \right\} = 1 - \alpha.$$

Therefore, a $100(1 - \alpha)\%$ PI for a future observation $X \sim N(\mu, \sigma^2)$ is given by

$$\bar{x} - t_{n-1,\alpha/2} s\sqrt{1 + \frac{1}{n}} \leq X \leq \bar{x} + t_{n-1,\alpha/2} s\sqrt{1 + \frac{1}{n}} \qquad (7.22)$$

where $\bar{x}$ and s are the observed sample mean and sample SD, respectively. Note that this PI for X is generally much wider than the CI (7.13) for μ. This is explained by the fact that a PI is meant to include an r.v., while a CI is meant to include a fixed unknown parameter. In the limiting case as $n \to \infty$, the CI converges to a single point μ, while the PI (7.22) converges to $[\mu - z_{\alpha/2}\sigma, \mu + z_{\alpha/2}\sigma]$.

7.4.2 Tolerance Intervals

A related problem is to find an interval that will contain at least a specified fraction $1-\gamma$ of all future observations from a given population with some preassigned probability $1-\alpha$. Such an interval is called a **tolerance interval (TI)**. One common use of a TI is to check whether a specified large fraction of a product made by a manufacturing process would fall within the specification limits for the product. For example, suppose that the specification limits on the contents of a beverage can are [12.00, 12.30] oz., and that a 95% TI that includes at least 99% of the cans is [11.95, 12.35] oz. Since the TI does not fall entirely within the specification limits, there is a high probability that a significant fraction of cans will not meet the specification limits, signaling that the variability in the filling process needs to be reduced.

The standard form of a TI based on a random sample from an $N(\mu, \sigma^2)$ distribution is

$$[\bar{x} - Ks, \bar{x} + Ks] \qquad (7.23)$$

where $\bar{x}$ and s are the observed sample mean and sample SD, respectively, and K is a constant that depends on the sample size n and specified values of $1 - \alpha$ and $1 - \gamma$. To determine K, consider the fraction of the population captured by the interval (7.23). This fraction is given by

$$\Phi\left(\frac{\bar{x} + Ks - \mu}{\sigma}\right) - \Phi\left(\frac{\bar{x} - Ks - \mu}{\sigma}\right)$$

where Φ denotes the standard normal c.d.f. Therefore K solves the equation:

$$P\left\{\Phi\left(\frac{\bar{X} + KS - \mu}{\sigma}\right) - \Phi\left(\frac{\bar{X} - KS - \mu}{\sigma}\right) \geq 1 - \gamma\right\} = 1 - \alpha.$$

Note that the probability expression in this equation is independent of the unknown parameters μ and σ because the distributions of $\frac{\bar{X}-\mu}{\sigma} \sim N(0, 1/n)$ and $\frac{S}{\sigma} \sim \sqrt{\frac{\chi^2_{n-1}}{n-1}}$ are free of these unknown parameters. Solutions K for selected values of n, $1 - \alpha$, and $1 - \gamma$ are given in Table A.12 in Appendix A.

EXAMPLE 7.12   (TEAR STRENGTH OF RUBBER: TWO-SIDED CONFIDENCE, PREDICTION, AND TOLERANCE INTERVALS)

Suppose that the 14 measurements on the tear strength of silicone rubber (after omitting the two outliers) from Example 7.8 are regarded as measurements on 14 successive batches of rubber coming from a stable process with a constant mean μ and SD $= \sigma$. A run chart in Figure 7.9 indicates that there are no obvious patterns and the assumption of a stable process appears to be valid. Calculate a two-sided 95% CI for the mean tear strength of the process and compare it with a 95% PI for the tear strength of the next batch of rubber made by the same manufacturing process and a 95% TI for the tear strengths of 90% of all future batches.

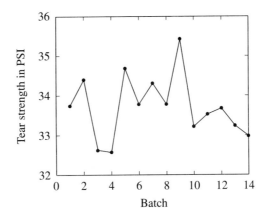

Figure 7.9   Run Chart of Tear Strength Measurements

We are given $\bar{x} = 33.712$, $s = 0.798$, and $n = 14$. Calculation of both a 95% CI and a 95% PI requires the critical point $t_{13, .025} = 2.160$. Using (7.13), we obtain the following 95% CI for the mean tear strength μ:

$$\left[33.712 - 2.160 \times \frac{0.798}{\sqrt{14}}, 33.712 + 2.160 \times \frac{0.798}{\sqrt{14}}\right] = [33.252, 34.172].$$

Using (7.22), we obtain the following 95% PI for the tear strength of a future batch:

$$\left[33.712 - 2.160 \times 0.798\sqrt{1 + \frac{1}{14}}, \, 33.712 + 2.160 \times 0.798\sqrt{1 + \frac{1}{14}} \right] = [31.928, 35.496].$$

Note that the PI is almost four times wider than the CI.

From Table A.12 we obtain $K = 2.529$ for $1 - \alpha = 0.95$, $1 - \gamma = 0.90$, and $n = 14$. Using (7.23), we obtain the following 95% TI for the tear strengths of 90% of all future batches:

$$[33.712 - 2.529 \times 0.798, \, 33.712 + 2.529 \times 0.798] = [31.694, 35.730].$$

Note that the TI is slightly wider than even the PI. $\blacklozenge$

7.5   CHAPTER SUMMARY

This chapter discusses confidence intervals (CI's) and hypothesis tests on the mean μ and variance σ^2 of a normal population based on a random sample of size n. Inferences on μ use the result that

$$Z = \frac{\bar{X} - \mu}{\sigma/\sqrt{n}} \sim N(0, 1)$$

where $\bar{X}$ is the sample mean. Because the same result holds for any population asymptotically according to the CLT, these inferences are approximately correct (**robust**) even for nonnormal populations if n is large. However, the inferences are not robust if the data contain outliers.

When σ^2 is known, Z can be used as a **pivotal r.v.** to derive a $100(1 - \alpha)\%$ two-sided CI (z-**interval**) on μ:

$$\left[\bar{x} \pm z_{\alpha/2} \frac{\sigma}{\sqrt{n}} \right].$$

An α-level two-sided test (z-**test**) of $H_0: \mu = \mu_0$ vs. $H_1: \mu \neq \mu_0$, rejects H_0 when

$$|z| = \frac{|\bar{x} - \mu_0|}{\sigma/\sqrt{n}} > z_{\alpha/2}.$$

One-sided CI's and tests are obtained in a similar manner. The rejection regions, P-value expressions, and power expressions for the z-tests are summarized in Tables 7.1–7.3.

The sample sizes for the CI and the hypothesis tests can be calculated given the appropriate requirements. For the above two-sided testing problem, if the power is required to be at least $1 - \beta$ if μ differs from μ_0 by at least an amount $\delta > 0$, then the required sample size is given by

$$n = \left[\frac{(z_{\alpha/2} + z_\beta)\sigma}{\delta} \right]^2.$$

The sample size for a one-sided test is obtained by replacing $z_{\alpha/2}$ in this formula by z_α.

When σ^2 is unknown and is estimated by the sample variance S^2, the pivotal r.v. Z is replaced by

$$T = \frac{\bar{X} - \mu}{\sigma/\sqrt{n}}$$

which has a Student's t-distribution with $n-1$ degrees of freedom (d.f.). A $100(1-\alpha)\%$ two-sided CI (***t*-interval**) for μ equals

$$\left[\bar{x} \pm t_{n-1,\alpha/2} \frac{s}{\sqrt{n}} \right].$$

An α-level two-sided test (***t*-test**) of $H_0: \mu = \mu_0$ vs. $H_1: \mu \neq \mu_0$ rejects H_0 when

$$|t| = \frac{|\bar{x} - \mu_0|}{s/\sqrt{n}} > t_{n-1,\alpha/2}.$$

One-sided CI's and tests are obtained in a similar manner. Table 7.5 summarizes the t-tests.

Hypothesis tests and confidence intervals on σ^2 are based on the sample variance S^2. The pivotal r.v. in this case is

$$\frac{(n-1)S^2}{\sigma^2}$$

which has a chi-square distribution with $n-1$ d.f. A two-sided $100(1-\alpha)\%$ CI on σ^2 is given by

$$\left[\frac{(n-1)s^2}{\chi^2_{n-1,\frac{\alpha}{2}}}, \frac{(n-1)s^2}{\chi^2_{n-1,1-\frac{\alpha}{2}}} \right].$$

An α-level two-sided test of $H_0: \sigma^2 = \sigma_0^2$ vs. $H_1: \sigma^2 \neq \sigma_0^2$ uses the test statistic

$$\chi^2 = \frac{(n-1)s^2}{\sigma_0^2}$$

and rejects H_0 when either $\chi^2 > \chi^2_{n-1,\alpha/2}$ or $\chi^2 < \chi^2_{n-1,1-\alpha/2}$. One-sided CI's and tests are obtained in a similar manner. Table 7.6 summarizes the tests on the variance. In contrast to inferences on the mean, inferences on the variance are *not* robust to the assumption of normality. Therefore these methods should not be used for nonnormal data.

Prediction and tolerance intervals are given for normal data. These intervals are designed to include future random observations with a preassigned probability, whereas a confidence interval is designed to include a fixed unknown parameter, e.g., the mean, with a preassigned probability.

■ EXERCISES

Section 7.1

7.1 An EPA researcher wants to design a study to estimate the mean lead level of fish in a lake located near an industrial area. Based on past sample data, the researcher estimates that σ for the lead level in the fish population is approximately 0.016 mg/g. He wants to use a 98% CI having a margin of error no greater than 0.005 mg/g.

  (a) How many fish does he need to catch?

  (b) If 100 fish are actually caught, by what factor will the margin of error be reduced?

7.2 A textile engineer wants to know how many fabric fibers to test to obtain a 90% confidence interval for the mean tensile strength having a margin of error of no more than 0.5 psi. From past experience it is known that the range of measurements is approximately ±5 psi around the mean.

  (a) Calculate the necessary sample size. Use a rough estimate of σ obtained from the range of measurements.

  (b) Suppose that a sample of the size determined in (a) had a mean of 50 psi and SD = 2.45 psi. Calculate the 90% confidence interval.

7.3 The personnel department of a firm wants to estimate the average number of days lost to absenteeism per year for its professional employees. Based on past experience it is believed that $\sigma = 5$ days.

  (a) How many employee files should be sampled in order to find a 95% confidence interval having a margin of error of no more than 1 day?

  (b) Suppose that a sample of the size determined in (a) has a mean of 6.30 days and SD = 4.57 days. Calculate the 95% confidence interval.

7.4 The mail-order division of a large clothing company wants to estimate its loss due to incorrectly filled orders. It plans to sample incorrect orders and determine the associated cost for each one. It is estimated that the loss from an incorrectly filled order ranges from $10 to $350.

  (a) How many incorrect orders should be sampled to estimate the average loss within $10 using a 95% confidence interval? Use a rough estimate of σ obtained from the range of losses.

  (b) Repeat (a) if a 99% confidence interval is to be used.

7.5 The mean yield of corn in the U.S. is about 120 bushels per acre. A survey of 50 farmers from Illinois yielded a sample mean of $\bar{x} = 123.6$ bushels per acre. Assume that the standard deviation of the yield for this population is $\sigma = 10$ bushels per acre. Determine if the mean yield for Illinois differs from the national mean.[5]

  (a) Set up the hypotheses assuming that there was no a priori reason to suspect that the Illinois mean would be higher than the national mean.

  (b) Calculate the P-value of the test. Can you conclude that the mean yield for Illinois differs from the national mean? Use $\alpha = 0.01$.

  (c) Which assumption is more important to the validity of the conclusion drawn from this test: the assumption that the 50 farmers form a random sample from the population

---

[5] This exercise is adapted from Exercise 6.29 in Moore, D. S. and McCabe, G. P. (1993), *Introduction to the Practice of Statistics*, 2nd Ed., New York: W. H. Freeman and Co.

of all Illinois farmers or the assumption that the yields in this population are normally distributed? Explain.

7.6   Coffee cans are to be filled with 16 oz. of coffee. The mean content of cans filled on a production line is monitored. It is known from past experience that the standard deviation of the contents is 0.1 oz. A sample of 9 cans is taken every hour and their mean content is measured.

   (a) Set up the hypotheses to test whether the mean content is 16 oz. Should the alternative be one-sided or two-sided? Why?

   (b) Give a decision rule in terms of the sample mean $\bar{x}$ for a 0.05-level test.

   (c) If the *true* mean content during a particular period is 16.1 oz., what is the probability that the test derived in (b) will correctly detect this deviation from the target value of 16 oz.?

   (d) How many cans should be sampled to assure 90% power in (c)?

7.7   A tire company has developed a new tread design. To determine if the newly designed tire has a mean life of 60,000 miles or more, a random sample of 16 prototype tires is tested. The mean tire life for this sample is 60,758 miles. Assume that the tire life is normally distributed with unknown mean μ and standard deviation $\sigma = 1500$ miles. Test the hypothesis $H_0: \mu = 60,000$ vs. $H_1: \mu > 60,000$.

   (a) Compute the test statistic and its P-value. Based on the P-value, state whether H_0 can be rejected at $\alpha = 0.01$.

   (b) What is the power of the 0.01-level test in (a) if the true mean life for the new tread design is 61,000 miles?

   (c) Suppose that at least 90% power is needed to identify a tread design that has the mean life of 61,000 miles. How many tires should be tested?

7.8   The mean pH value of a certain chemical is to be controlled at 5. Deviation from this target value in either direction is to be detected with high probability. For this purpose it is proposed to measure a certain number of samples from each batch and decide that the mean pH is different from 5 if the sample mean differs significantly from 5 at the 10% level of significance.

   (a) State the hypotheses tested by the above decision rule. Interpret the test parameter μ.

   (b) What sample size is needed if the probability of *not* detecting a change of one standard deviation is to be no more than 1%?

   (c) Suppose that 16 samples are measured. The sample mean $\bar{x}$ is 4.915 and the sample standard deviation s is 0.2. Ignoring that we have a small sample and assuming that $s \approx \sigma$, calculate the P-value. Do you conclude that the mean pH has changed from the target value of 5? Use $\alpha = 0.10$.

7.9   A consumer watchdog group suspects that a yogurt that is advertised to be 98% fat free has in fact a higher mean fat content. The group will take action against the company if it can substantiate its suspicion with factual data. For this purpose, the group takes a sample of 25 yogurt cups (each containing 170 grams) and measures the fat contents. If the company's claim is correct, then the mean fat content should be no more than 2%, i.e., 3.4 grams.

   (a) Set up the hypotheses to be tested. Explain why you set up the hypotheses the way you did.

   (b) Suppose that the mean fat content for 25 sample cups was 3.6 grams. Also suppose that σ of fat contents is 0.5 grams. Do a 0.01-level test of the hypotheses. Is there enough statistical evidence to support the consumer group's suspicion?

(c) If the true mean fat content per cup is 3.7 grams, what is the probability that this test will detect it? How many yogurt cups should be tested if this probability must be at least 0.95?

7.10   In order to test the accuracy of speedometers purchased from a subcontractor, the purchasing department of an automaker orders a test of a sample of speedometers at a controlled speed of 55 mph. At this speed, it is estimated that the readings will range ± 2 mph around the mean.

(a) Set up the hypotheses to detect if the speedometers have any bias.

(b) How many speedometers need to be tested to have a 95% power to detect a bias of 0.5 mph or greater using a 0.01-level test? Use the rough estimate of σ obtained from the range.

(c) A sample of the size determined in (b) has a mean of $\bar{x} = 55.2$ and $s = 0.8$. Can you conclude that the speedometers have a bias?

(d) Calculate the power of the test if 50 speedometers are tested and the actual bias is 0.5 mph. Assume $\sigma = 0.8$.

Section 7.2

7.11   Suppose that 100 random samples of size 25 are drawn from a normal distribution with $\mu = 12$ and $\sigma = 2$.

(a) If a 95% z-interval is calculated for each sample, how many of the intervals would you expect to contain the true $\mu = 12$?

(b) If a 95% t-interval is calculated for each sample, will the answer be different from (a)? Why or why not?

7.12   A random sample of size 16 is drawn from a normal distribution with $\mu = 70$ and $\sigma = 3$. The mean of the sample is 68.45 and $s = 2.73$.

(a) Calculate a 90% z-interval for μ assuming that you know $\sigma = 3$.

(b) Calculate a 90% t-interval for μ assuming that you do not know σ.

(c) Which interval is shorter for this sample? Which interval would be shorter on the average if a large number of samples are drawn from this normal distribution, and z and t intervals are calculated for each sample? Explain.

7.13   ▣ A gasoline company tested 20 samples of gasoline produced during a day to check whether the day's production meets the nominal octane rating of 87. The results were as follows:

87.5	86.9	86.6	87.3	87.9	88.0	86.7	87.5	87.2	87.0
88.1	87.5	86.5	87.7	88.0	87.1	87.0	87.6	87.5	88.3

(a) Find a lower 95% confidence limit on the mean octane rating. Use this confidence limit to determine if the mean octane rating exceeds 87.

(b) Set up the hypotheses to show that the mean octane rating exceeds 87. Calculate the t-statistic and find bounds on its P-value. Is the result significant at $\alpha = .005$? at $\alpha = .001$?

7.14   Refer to Exercise 7.8, part (c). Take into account the fact that the sample size is small, and redo the test. Has your conclusion changed? Why?

7.15 ◼ In response to student complaints and financial considerations, a high school decides to close its kitchen and contract a food service to provide school lunches. The previous year, when food was prepared in the high school kitchen, about 60% of the students purchased lunch on a daily basis. The daily proportions of students using the food service during the fourth month of the contract are given below.

68	61	65	74	68	80	78	63	74	65
70	53	65	70	78	65	74	68	61	70

Compared to the previous year, is there an increase in the average proportion of students purchasing lunches provided by the food service?

(a) The hypotheses are set up as $H_0: \mu \leq 60$ vs. $H_1: \mu > 60$. Explain the meaning of μ, the parameter under test.

(b) Perform a test of the hypotheses in (a) using $\alpha = 0.01$. Interpret your results.

(c) The food service set a goal of attracting at least 70% of the students to purchase lunches. Set up the hypotheses to test whether the food service has met its goal.

(d) Calculate the P-value for the test of the hypotheses in (c). Is the result significant at $\alpha = 0.10$?

7.16 ◼ A thermostat used in an electrical device is to be checked for the accuracy of its design setting of $200°$ F. Ten thermostats were tested to determine their actual settings, resulting in the following data:

202.2	203.4	200.5	202.5	206.3	198.0	203.7	200.8	201.3	199.0

Perform the t-test to determine if the mean setting is different from $200°$ F. Use $\alpha = .05$.

Section 7.3

7.17 ◼ Diabetic patients monitor their blood sugar levels with a home glucose monitor which analyzes a drop of blood from a finger stick. Although the monitor gives precise results in a laboratory, the results are too variable when it is used by patients. A new monitor is developed to improve the precision of the assay results under home use. Home testing on the new monitor is done by 25 persons using drops from a sample having a glucose concentration of 118 mg/dl. If $\sigma < 10$ mg/dl, then the precision of the new device under home use is better than the current monitor. The readings from 25 tests are as follows.

125	123	117	123	115
112	128	118	124	111
116	109	125	120	113
123	112	118	121	118
122	115	105	118	131

The sample mean is $\bar{x} = 118.5$ and the sample standard deviation is $s = 6.2$.

(a) Make a normal probability plot of these readings. Is it reasonable to assume that the data follow a normal distribution?

(b) Test $H_0: \sigma \geq 10$ vs. $H_1: \sigma < 10$ at the 0.10 level.

    (c) Find an upper one-sided 90% confidence interval for σ. Use this interval to test the hypotheses in (b).

7.18 A bottling company uses a filling machine to fill bottles. A bottle is to contain 475 milliliters (about 16 oz.) of beverage. The actual amount is normally distributed with a standard deviation of 1.0 ml. The purchase of a new machine is contemplated. Based on a sample of 16 bottles filled by the new machine, the sample mean is 476.4 ml and the standard deviation is $s = 0.7$ ml. Does the new machine have a significantly less variation than the current machine?

    (a) To answer the question posed, test the hypotheses $H_0: \sigma \geq 1.0$ vs. $H_1: \sigma < 1.0$, where σ is the standard deviation of the new machine. Find the exact P-value of the test if you have a program available for computing the tail areas of a chi-square distribution; otherwise find bounds on the P-value using Table A.5.

    (b) Find an appropriate one-sided 95% confidence interval for σ which can be used to test the hypotheses in (a).

7.19 The durability of upholstery fabric is measured in double rubs (DR), which simulates a person getting in and out of a chair. The manufacturing label on one fabric gives its durability range as 68,000–82,000 DR. The company's quality control department independently evaluated the fabric by testing 25 one-yard samples. The sample mean was 74,283 DR and the sample standard deviation was 4676 DR. Although the mean is acceptable, is the standard deviation consistent with the labeled range? Assume that the DR measurements are normally distributed.

    (a) Set up the hypotheses to check whether the actual standard deviation is different from the value of σ obtained by dividing the range by four.

    (b) Test the hypotheses by calculating a 95% confidence interval for σ. Is the value of σ obtained from the range in the interval? What about a 99% confidence interval? Summarize your findings.

Section 7.4

7.20 The SAT scores (math plus verbal) for a freshman class of 200 at a private college averaged 1250 with $s = 120$. Assume that this class represents a random sample of all future students.

    (a) Find a 95% confidence interval for the mean SAT score of all future students.

    (b) Find a 95% prediction interval for the SAT score of a future student.

    (c) Find a 95% tolerance interval that will include 90% of the SAT scores of all future students.

7.21 Refer to the data of Exercise 7.18 for the sample of 16 bottles filled by the new filling machine. Suppose that specifications on the contents of a bottle are 476 ± 1 ml of beverage.

    (a) Find a 95% confidence interval for the mean amount of beverage in all bottles.

    (b) Find a 95% prediction interval for the amount of beverage in a bottle.

    (c) Find a 95% tolerance interval that will include the amounts of beverage in 95% of all bottles. Does the tolerance interval fall within the specification limits? What does this indicate?

7.22 Refer to the fabric durability data of Exercise 7.19.

    (a) Find a 95% prediction interval for the durability of this fabric. If an office is buying this fabric to cover furniture in a waiting room and requires a fabric with durability of at least 70,000 DR, would this be a good purchase?

(b) Find a 95% tolerance interval that would include the DR values for 99% of all fabric made by the same manufacturing process. Does this tolerance interval fall within the manufacturing specifications of 68,000–82,000 DR?

Advanced Exercises

7.23 Let $X_1, X_2, \ldots, X_n$ be a random sample from an $N(\mu, \sigma^2)$ distribution where both μ and σ^2 are unknown, and consider the problem of testing $H_0: \mu = \mu_0$ vs. $H_1: \mu > \mu_0$. In Section 7.2.2 we saw that the power of the α-level t-test at the alternative $\mu = \mu_1 > \mu_0$ can be expressed in terms of the noncentral t-distribution with noncentrality parameter $\delta\sqrt{n}/\sigma$, where $\delta = \mu_1 - \mu_0$. If only δ is specified, then the power cannot be evaluated, since σ is unknown. One must specify the ratio δ/σ; that is, δ must be specified in the units of σ (e.g., $\delta = 0.5\sigma$). Similarly, one cannot determine the sample size n to guarantee a given power, say $1 - \beta$, if only δ is specified. However, this is possible if the test is done in two stages. Charles Stein[6] derived such a **two-stage test** which operates as follows.

At the first stage take a random sample $X_1, X_2, \ldots, X_n$ as above. Calculate the sample variance S^2 from this sample and the overall sample size N as the smallest integer greater than or equal to

$$\max\left\{ n, \left[\frac{(t_{n-1,\alpha} + t_{n-1,\beta})^2 S^2}{\delta^2} \right] \right\}.$$

If $N = n$, stop sampling. Otherwise take a second stage sample, $X_{n+1}, \ldots, X_N$. In either case, calculate the overall sample mean $\bar{X}$ and reject H_0 at level α if

$$\frac{\bar{X} - \mu_0}{S/\sqrt{N}} > t_{n-1,\alpha}$$

where S is the first stage sample SD. It can be shown that under $H_0: \mu = \mu_0$ the above test statistic has a t_{n-1} distribution. (This is not obvious, since the sample size N is now an r.v., being a function of S^2.)

(a) Show that the power of this test when $\mu = \mu_1$ can be written as

$$P\left\{ T_{n-1} > t_{n-1,\alpha} - \frac{\delta\sqrt{N}}{S} \right\}$$

where T_{n-1} is a t r.v. with $n - 1$ d.f.

(b) Use the fact that $N \geq \left[\frac{(t_{n-1,\alpha} + t_{n-1,\beta})^2 S^2}{\delta^2} \right]$ to show that a lower bound on the power is

$$P\left\{ T_{n-1} > -t_{n-1,\beta} \right\} = 1 - \beta.$$

(c) Compare the similarity of the formula for N with the formula (7.10) for the sample size when σ^2 is known. Also note that N is an increasing function of the preliminary sample variance S^2.

(d) Refer to Exercise 7.7 where the hypotheses are $H_0: \mu = 60,000$ vs. $H_1: \mu > 60,000$, but now assume that σ is unknown and the preliminary sample of 16 tires yielded $s = 1500$ miles. Find the overall sample size N required to guarantee 90% power if

---

[6] C. Stein (1945), "A two-sample test for a linear hypothesis whose power is independent of the variance," *Annals of Mathematical Statistics*, **16**, pp. 243–258.

the true mean tire life is 61,000 miles. Compare your answer with that obtained in part (c) of that exercise.

7.24 Under the setting of Section 7.3 consider the problem of testing $H_0: \sigma^2 = \sigma_0^2$ vs. $H_1: \sigma^2 > \sigma_0^2$ at level α using the test that rejects H_0 if

$$\frac{(n-1)S^2}{\sigma_0^2} > \chi^2_{n-1,\alpha}$$

where S^2 is the sample variance.

(a) Find an expression for the power of this test in terms of the χ^2_{n-1} distribution if the true $\sigma^2 = c\sigma_0^2$, where $c > 1$.

(b) Use Table A.5 to find the power of this test if $\alpha = .05$, $n = 16$, and $c = 4$; that is, the true σ^2 is four times the value being tested under H_0.

7.25 In this exercise we will see how to use the chi-square distribution to make inferences on the mean of an exponential distribution. Let $X_1, X_2, \ldots, X_n$ be a random sample (e.g., the times to failure of n items) from an exponential distribution with p.d.f.

$$f(x) = \lambda \exp(-\lambda x) \text{ for } x \geq 0.$$

The mean of this distribution is $\mu = 1/\lambda$, referred to as the **mean time between failures (MTBF)** in reliability applications. We want to construct a CI for μ.

(a) From Section 2.8.2 we know that $Y = \sum_{i=1}^{n} X_i$ has a gamma distribution with p.d.f. given by

$$g(y) = \frac{1}{\Gamma(n)} \lambda^n y^{n-1} \exp(-\lambda y).$$

Show that $Z = 2\lambda Y = 2Y/\mu$ has the p.d.f.

$$h(z) = \frac{1}{2^n \Gamma(n)} z^{n-1} \exp(-z/2).$$

Compare this p.d.f. with the formula (5.4) for the chi-square distribution to conclude that $Z \sim \chi^2_{2n}$.

(b) Show that

$$\frac{2Y}{\chi^2_{2n,\alpha/2}} \leq \mu \leq \frac{2Y}{\chi^2_{2n,1-\alpha/2}}$$

is a $(1 - \alpha)$-level CI for μ.

(c) Suppose that 10 identical batteries are tested for the number of hours of continuous operation with the following results: 4.6, 5.8, 10.6, 12.5, 13.4, 14.3, 20.6, 21.9, 22.1, 23.0. Assuming an exponential distribution for the failure times, find a 95% CI for the mean lifetime of the batteries.

CHAPTER 8

INFERENCES FOR TWO SAMPLES

A majority of statistical studies, whether experimental or observational, are comparative in nature. For example, R & D engineers conduct an experiment to compare the reliabilities of different product designs by putting the prototypes on a life test. An investment counselor compares the net rates of return for a sample of load versus no load mutual funds for the last ten years. The simplest type of a comparative study compares two populations based on samples drawn from them.

In this chapter we study statistical methods to compare two populations. First we review two principal designs for comparative studies using independent samples and matched pairs. Next we present some graphical methods for informal comparisons. This is followed by inferential methods for formal comparisons of means and variances of two normal populations via confidence intervals and hypothesis tests. By the use of the central limit theorem (CLT) the methods for comparing means can be applied to nonnormal populations if the sample sizes are large.

8.1 INDEPENDENT SAMPLES AND MATCHED PAIRS DESIGNS

Consider a research project to compare two methods of teaching spelling to grade school children, a new method and an old method. The researcher first gives a pretest to all children participating in the study. They are then randomly divided into two groups. One using the old method (the **control group**) and the other using the new method (the **treatment group**). To keep the design simple, let us assume that the confounding effect of a teacher is eliminated by having the same teacher teach both groups. Finally, the researcher gives a posttest to all children and calculates the changes from the pretest to the posttest scores. The changes are compared for the control and treatment groups. This is an **independent samples design**, because the data for the two groups are statistically independent.

The data from an independent samples design are of the following form:

Sample 1: $x_1, x_2, \ldots, x_{n_1}$

Sample 2: $y_1, y_2, \ldots, y_{n_2}$.

The sample sizes of the two groups, n_1 and n_2, need not be equal. In the teaching method example, the x_i's and y_i's are the changes in the test scores for the control and the treatment group children, respectively.

The independent samples design relies upon randomization to make the two groups equal (on the average) on all attributes except for the treatment used. In the teaching method example, the two groups would be expected to be roughly equal with regard to all characteristics—in particular, the pretest scores. They differ only in terms of the teaching method used, which is called a **treatment factor**.

An alternative method to assure that the two groups are relatively equal on pretest scores is to pair children who have similar scores and then randomly assign one child from each pair to the control group and the other to the treatment group. This is called a **matched pairs design**. The pretest score is called a **blocking factor**. Other attributes such as gender, age, IQ, etc. may also be used as blocking factors when forming matched pairs.

The data from a matched pairs design arc of the following form:

Pair:	1	2	...	n
Sample 1:	x_1	x_2	...	x_n
Sample 2:	y_1	y_2	...	y_n

where n is the number of matched pairs. For the ith pair, x_i is the change in the test score of the child taught by the old method and y_i the change in the score of the child taught by the new method.

Each design has its pros and cons. In an independent samples design the two groups may not be quite equal on some attributes, especially if the sample sizes are small, because randomization assures equality only on average. If the groups are not quite equal on all attributes, then the conclusions can become vitiated. For example, if one group has higher pretest scores than the other group, then a competing explanation for the differences in the results for the two groups could be the differences in the pretest scores rather than the differences in the teaching methods. In a matched pairs design, however, the two groups are nearly matched with respect to the blocking factors used in matching. Therefore the results are less likely to be caused by factors other than the treatment factor and any differences in the results for the two groups can be attributed with greater confidence to the teaching methods. The matched pairs design enables more precise comparisons to be made between treatment groups because of smaller experimental error.

On the other hand, it can be difficult to form matched pairs, especially when dealing with human subjects, unless the experimental units come naturally in pairs, e.g., two eyes, two arms, twins, the same person observed under two different conditions (thus serving as his/her own match), etc.

These two designs can also be used in observational studies, although the groups are not formed by randomization. For example, samples of smokers and nonsmokers may be compared with respect to the incidence rates of respiratory problems. This design is analogous to the independent samples design. The form of the data and the methods of analysis are similar. The only difference is that, due to lack of randomization, a cause-effect relationship cannot be established between smoking and respiratory problems.

As an example of a matched pairs design in an observational study, consider an investigation of a possible salary "gap" between men and women workers in a company, based on existing data. An equitable comparison of the salaries of men and women should take into account the type of job, qualification, and experience. One way to do this would be to match men and women on these attributes and compare the salaries within each matched pair. A practical difficulty is to form matched pairs with the data at hand. One may have to discard data on some persons because suitable matches cannot be found.

8.2 GRAPHICAL METHODS FOR COMPARING TWO SAMPLES

A first step in data analysis is to summarize and plot the data. Some of the techniques we learned in Chapter 4 can be applied to compare the two samples. First consider the independent samples design. **Side-by-side box plots** are especially useful for visually comparing the two sample distributions in terms of their centers, dispersions, and skewnesses. An illustration was given in Chapter 4, Example 4.7.

Another useful technique is called the **quantile-quantile (Q-Q) plot** in which the quantiles of the two samples are plotted against each other. If the two distributions are approximately the same, then their quantiles would be roughly equal and would plot along the 45° line. Depending on how the plot deviates from this line, one can draw inferences about how the two samples differ from each other.

If the two sample sizes are equal, then the Q-Q plot is obtained by just plotting the order statistics $x_{(i)}$ and $y_{(i)}$ (which are the $\left(\frac{i}{n+1}\right)$th quantiles of the respective samples) against each other. This is illustrated in the following example. If the two sample sizes are unequal, the following procedure can be followed to make the Q-Q plot: Suppose that $n_1 > n_2$. Then plot the $\left(\frac{i}{n_1+1}\right)$th quantiles of the two samples against each other. For the larger sample, they are just the order statistics, $x_{(1)} \leq x_{(2)} \leq \cdots \leq x_{(n_1)}$. For the smaller sample, the corresponding quantiles can be computed using the interpolation formula (4.2).

EXAMPLE 8.1 (HOSPITALIZATION COSTS: Q-Q PLOT)

Refer to the hospitalization cost data for two groups of geriatric patients given in Table 4.5 and reproduced here in Table 8.1. The Q-Q plot for these data is shown in Figure 8.1. The Q-Q plot lies mostly below the 45° line, indicating that the quantiles for the control group (plotted on the x-axis) are generally greater than those for the treatment group (plotted on the y-axis). ◆

Table 8.1 Hospitalization Costs (in $) for Geriatric Patients Cared for by Two Different Methods

Control Group	478	605	626	714	818	1203	1204	1323	2150	2700
	2969	3151	3565	3626	3739	4148	4382	4576	6953	6963
	7062	7284	7829	8681	9319	12,664	17,539	23,237	26,677	32,913
Treatment Group	528	650	912	1130	1289	1651	1706	1708	1882	1998
	2391	2432	2697	2829	3039	3186	3217	3345	3590	4153
	5928	6018	6267	6790	7365	8635	9615	13,890	15,225	19,083

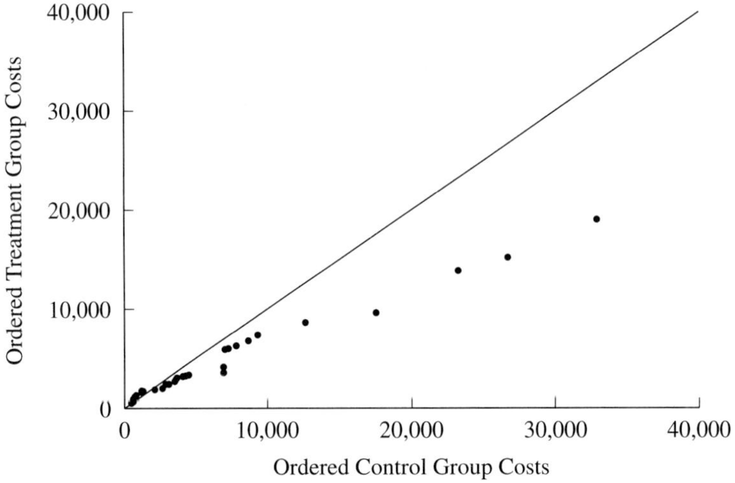

Figure 8.1 Q-Q Plot of Hospitalization Costs for Geriatric Patients Cared for by Two Different Methods

Finally, consider graphical displays of data from a matched pairs design. Since the within pair comparisons are of interest here, it is natural to plot the pairs (x_i, y_i), i.e., to make a scatter plot. Using the 45° line as a reference, one can judge whether the two sets of sample values are similar or whether one set tends to be larger than the other. Additional plots, e.g., plots of the differences $d_i = x_i - y_i$ or the ratios $r_i = x_i/y_i$ vs. x_i, may also prove useful. Note that a Q-Q plot is meaningless for paired data because the same quantiles based on the ordered observations do not, in general, come from the same pair.

8.3   COMPARING MEANS OF TWO POPULATIONS

8.3.1 Independent Samples Design

Inferences for Large Samples.   Suppose that the observations $x_1, x_2, \ldots, x_{n_1}$ and $y_1, y_2, \ldots, y_{n_2}$ are random samples from two populations with means μ_1 and μ_2 and variances σ_1^2 and σ_2^2, respectively. Both the means and variances of the populations are assumed to be unknown, but the interest is focused on the means. The goal is to compare μ_1 and μ_2 in terms of their difference $\mu_1 - \mu_2$. Initially we assume that the sample sizes n_1 and n_2 are large (say ≥ 30).

The first step in computing a confidence interval (CI) or doing a hypothesis test on $\mu_1 - \mu_2$ is to calculate the sample means,

$$\bar{x} = \frac{\sum x_i}{n_1}, \quad \bar{y} = \frac{\sum y_i}{n_2}$$

and the sample variances,

$$s_1^2 = \frac{\sum(x_i - \bar{x})^2}{n_1 - 1}, \quad s_2^2 = \frac{\sum(y_i - \bar{y})^2}{n_2 - 1}.$$

Let $\bar{X}, \bar{Y}, S_1^2$, and S_2^2 denote the random variables (r.v.'s) corresponding to the observed sample quantities $\bar{x}, \bar{y}, s_1^2$, and s_2^2, respectively. Note that

$$E(\bar{X} - \bar{Y}) = E(\bar{X}) - E(\bar{Y}) = \mu_1 - \mu_2$$

and

$$\text{Var}(\bar{X} - \bar{Y}) = \text{Var}(\bar{X}) + \text{Var}(\bar{Y}) = \frac{\sigma_1^2}{n_1} + \frac{\sigma_2^2}{n_2}.$$

Therefore the standardized r.v.

$$Z = \frac{\bar{X} - \bar{Y} - (\mu_1 - \mu_2)}{\sqrt{\sigma_1^2/n_1 + \sigma_2^2/n_2}} \tag{8.1}$$

has mean = 0 and variance = 1. If n_1 and n_2 are large, then Z is approximately $N(0, 1)$ by the central limit theorem (CLT). (See Section 5.1.1.) For large samples, σ_1^2 and σ_2^2 can be replaced by their unbiased estimators S_1^2 and S_2^2. This does not affect the large sample distribution of Z. Using these facts, a large sample (approximate) $100(1-\alpha)\%$ CI for $\mu_1 - \mu_2$ can be derived to be

$$\bar{x} - \bar{y} - z_{\alpha/2}\sqrt{s_1^2/n_1 + s_2^2/n_2} \leq \mu_1 - \mu_2 \leq \bar{x} - \bar{y} + z_{\alpha/2}\sqrt{s_1^2/n_1 + s_2^2/n_2} \tag{8.2}$$

where $z_{\alpha/2}$ is the upper $\alpha/2$ critical point of the standard normal distribution. One-sided CI's can be derived in a similar manner.

Next consider the problem of testing the hypotheses

$$H_0: \mu_1 - \mu_2 = \delta_0 \quad \text{vs.} \quad H_1: \mu_1 - \mu_2 \neq \delta_0 \tag{8.3}$$

where δ_0 is the specified value of $\mu_1 - \mu_2$ under H_0. Typically, $\delta_0 = 0$ is used, which corresponds to testing $H_0: \mu_1 = \mu_2$. A large sample (approximate) α-level z-test uses the test statistic

$$z = \frac{\bar{x} - \bar{y} - \delta_0}{\sqrt{s_1^2/n_1 + s_2^2/n_2}}$$

and rejects H_0 if

$$|z| > z_{\alpha/2} \quad \text{or equivalently if} \quad |\bar{x} - \bar{y} - \delta_0| > z_{\alpha/2}\sqrt{s_1^2/n_1 + s_2^2/n_2}. \quad (8.4)$$

One-sided tests can be carried out in a similar manner. The different tests are summarized in Table 8.2.

Table 8.2 Level α Tests on $\mu_1 - \mu_2$ for Large Samples $\left(\text{Test Statistic} : z = \frac{\bar{x} - \bar{y} - \delta_0}{\sqrt{s_1^2/n_1 + s_2^2/n_2}} \right)$

Testing Problem	Hypotheses	Reject H_0 if	P-value
Upper One-Sided	$H_0: \mu_1 - \mu_2 \leq \delta_0$ vs. $H_1: \mu_1 - \mu_2 > \delta_0$	$z > z_\alpha$ $\Longleftrightarrow$ $\bar{x} - \bar{y} > \delta_0 + z_\alpha\sqrt{s_1^2/n_1 + s_2^2/n_2}$	$P(Z \geq z)$
Lower One-Sided	$H_0: \mu_1 - \mu_2 \geq \delta_0$ vs. $H_1: \mu_1 - \mu_2 < \delta_0$	$z < -z_\alpha$ $\Longleftrightarrow$ $\bar{x} - \bar{y} < \delta_0 - z_\alpha\sqrt{s_1^2/n_1 + s_2^2/n_2}$	$P(Z \leq z)$
Two-Sided	$H_0: \mu_1 - \mu_2 = \delta_0$ vs. $H_1: \mu_1 - \mu_2 \neq \delta_0$	$\|z\| > z_{\alpha/2}$ $\Longleftrightarrow$ $\|\bar{x} - \bar{y} - \delta_0\| > z_{\alpha/2}\sqrt{s_1^2/n_1 + s_2^2/n_2}$	$P(\|Z\| \geq \|z\|)$ = $2P(Z \geq \|z\|)$

EXAMPLE 8.2

Two large calculus classes, each consisting of 150 students, are taught at the same time by two different professors, who use the same text and give the same tests. On the final exam, out of a maximum total of 100 points, class 1 had a mean of 75 points and SD of 15 points, while class 2 had a mean of 70 points and SD of 12 points. Is there a statistically significant difference between the two means at $\alpha = .01$?

In order to perform a formal test, we assume that each class represents a random sample from a population of students taught by that professor using the same text and the same exams. Let μ_1 and μ_2 be the respective population means and σ_1^2 and σ_2^2 be the population variances. The hypotheses are $H_0: \mu_1 = \mu_2$ vs. $H_1: \mu_1 \neq \mu_2$. Since both sample sizes exceed 30, we can use the large sample methods given above. The z-statistic equals

$$z = \frac{75 - 70}{\sqrt{(15)^2/150 + (12)^2/150}} = 3.188$$

which has a two-sided P-value $= 2[1 - \Phi(3.188)] = .0014$. Since this P-value is less than .01, the difference is statistically significant at $\alpha = .01$.

We can also answer this question by calculating a 99% CI for $\mu_1 - \mu_2$ (using $z_{.005} = 2.576$):

$$\left[(75 - 70) - 2.576\sqrt{\frac{(15)^2}{150} + \frac{(12)^2}{150}}, (75 - 70) + 2.576\sqrt{\frac{(15)^2}{150} + \frac{(12)^2}{150}} \right] = [0.960, 9.040].$$

Since 0 is not in this interval, we conclude that the difference is statistically significant at $\alpha = .01$.

$\blacklozenge$

Inferences for Small Samples.   When n_1 and n_2 are small, we cannot invoke the CLT to claim that the pivotal r.v. Z of (8.1) is approximately standard normal. However, if we assume that the populations themselves are normal, then, as in Chapter 7, we can use the t-distribution to make the inferences. From now on in this section, we assume that

Sample 1: $x_1, x_2, \ldots, x_{n_1}$ is a random sample from an $N(\mu_1, \sigma_1^2)$ distribution

Sample 2: $y_1, y_2, \ldots, y_{n_2}$ is a random sample from an $N(\mu_2, \sigma_2^2)$ distribution

and the two samples are independent. The parameters $\mu_1, \mu_2, \sigma_1^2, \sigma_2^2$ are unknown.

We consider two separate cases under this distributional setup. Case 1 assumes that σ_1^2 and σ_2^2 are equal. (A test to check this assumption is given in Section 8.4.) This case has the mathematical advantage that a pivotal r.v. which has an exact t-distribution can be obtained. Case 2 does not assume that σ_1^2 and σ_2^2 are equal. This is a more common practical situation. However, only approximate inferences are possible in this case.

Case 1: Variances σ_1^2 and σ_2^2 Equal.   Let us denote the common value of σ_1^2 and σ_2^2 by σ^2, which is unknown. The two normal populations under comparison are shown in Figure 8.2. The parameter of interest is $\mu_1 - \mu_2$. An unbiased estimator of this parameter is the sample mean difference $\bar{X} - \bar{Y}$. The sample variances from the two samples,

$$S_1^2 = \frac{\sum(X_i - \bar{X})^2}{n_1 - 1} \quad \text{and} \quad S_2^2 = \frac{\sum(Y_i - \bar{Y})^2}{n_2 - 1}$$

are both unbiased estimators of σ^2. It is natural to pool these two independent estimators. A good way to pool is to use the weighted average of the two estimators, where the weights are the corresponding degrees of freedom (d.f.). This pooled estimator is given by

$$S^2 = \frac{(n_1 - 1)S_1^2 + (n_2 - 1)S_2^2}{(n_1 - 1) + (n_2 - 1)} = \frac{\sum(X_i - \bar{X})^2 + \sum(Y_i - \bar{Y})^2}{n_1 + n_2 - 2} \tag{8.5}$$

which has $n_1 + n_2 - 2$ d.f. It can be shown that a pivotal r.v. for $\mu_1 - \mu_2$ is

$$T = \frac{\bar{X} - \bar{Y} - (\mu_1 - \mu_2)}{S\sqrt{1/n_1 + 1/n_2}} \tag{8.6}$$

which has a t-distribution with $n_1 + n_2 - 2$ d.f.; see the proof at the end of the discussion of Case 1.

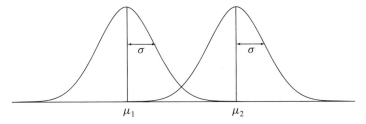

Figure 8.2 Two Normal Populations with Unequal Means But Equal Variances

Using this result, t-intervals and t-tests can be derived for the parameter $\mu_1 - \mu_2$. For example, a two-sided $100(1-\alpha)\%$ CI is given by

$$\bar{x} - \bar{y} - t_{n_1+n_2-2,\alpha/2} s \sqrt{\frac{1}{n_1} + \frac{1}{n_2}} \leq \mu_1 - \mu_2 \leq \bar{x} - \bar{y} + t_{n_1+n_2-2,\alpha/2} s \sqrt{\frac{1}{n_1} + \frac{1}{n_2}}.$$

$$(8.7)$$

Next consider the problem (8.3) of testing hypotheses $H_0: \mu_1 - \mu_2 = \delta_0$ vs. $H_1: \mu_1 - \mu_2 \neq \delta_0$. We use the test statistic

$$t = \frac{\bar{x} - \bar{y} - \delta_0}{s\sqrt{\frac{1}{n_1} + \frac{1}{n_2}}}.$$

$$(8.8)$$

The corresponding α-level two-sided test is:

Reject H_0 if $|t| > t_{n_1+n_2-2,\alpha/2}$ or equivalently if $|\bar{x} - \bar{y} - \delta_0| > t_{n_1+n_2-2,\alpha/2} s \sqrt{\frac{1}{n_1} + \frac{1}{n_2}}.$

$$(8.9)$$

One-sided CI's and hypothesis tests can be obtained in a similar manner. The different tests are summarized in Table 8.3.

EXAMPLE 8.3 (HOSPITALIZATION COSTS: INFERENCES USING A POOLED VARIANCE)

Compare the mean hospitalization costs from Table 8.1 for the control group and the treatment group using a two-sample t-test and a CI.

As seen in Examples 4.7 and 4.9, the raw data do not satisfy the assumptions of normality and equal variances that are needed to apply the methods of this section. For example, the sample SD's for the control group and the treatment group are, respectively, $s_1 = 8101$ and $s_2 = 4558$, which are quite different. Also, there are outliers in both the data sets. These difficulties can be resolved if we use the logarithmic transformation.[1] The log-transformed costs are given in Table 8.4.

Figure 8.3 shows side-by-side box plots for the log-transformed data. Note that the log transformation has made the distributions more symmetric and normal and the variances more equal. Also, there are no outliers in the log-transformed data.

---

[1] However, note that inferences on the *difference* in the means for the log-transformed data roughly correspond to inferences on the *ratio* of the means of the raw data.

Table 8.3 Level α Tests on $\mu_1 - \mu_2$ for Small Samples When $\sigma_1^2 = \sigma_2^2$ $\Big($ Test Statistic:

$t = \dfrac{\bar{x}-\bar{y}-\delta_0}{s\sqrt{1/n_1+1/n_2}}$ where $s^2 = \dfrac{(n_1-1)s_1^2+(n_2-1)s_2^2}{(n_1-1)+(n_2-1)}$ $\Big)$

Testing Problem	Hypotheses	Reject H_0 if	P-value
Upper One-Sided	$H_0: \mu_1-\mu_2 \le \delta_0$ vs. $H_1: \mu_1-\mu_2 > \delta_0$	$t > t_{n_1+n_2-2,\alpha}$ $\Longleftrightarrow$ $\bar{x}-\bar{y} > \delta_0 + t_{n_1+n_2-2,\alpha}s\sqrt{1/n_1+1/n_2}$	$P(T_{n_1+n_2-2} \ge t)$
Lower One-Sided	$H_0: \mu_1-\mu_2 \ge \delta_0$ vs. $H_1: \mu_1-\mu_2 < \delta_0$	$t < -t_{n_1+n_2-2,\alpha}$ $\Longleftrightarrow$ $\bar{x}-\bar{y} < \delta_0 > t_{n_1+n_2-2,\alpha}s\sqrt{1/n_1+1/n_2}$	$P(T_{n_1+n_2-2} \le t)$
Two-Sided	$H_0: \mu_1-\mu_2 = \delta_0$ vs. $H_1: \mu_1-\mu_2 \ne \delta_0$	$\|t\| > t_{n_1+n_2-2,\alpha/2}$ $\Longleftrightarrow$ $\|\bar{x}-\bar{y} > \delta_0\| > t_{n_1+n_2-2,\alpha/2}s\sqrt{1/n_1+1/n_2}$	$P(\|T_{n_1+n_2-2}\| \ge \|t\|)$ $=$ $2P(T_{n_1+n_2-2} \ge \|t\|)$

Table 8.4 Log_e (Hospitalization Costs) for Geriatric Patients Cared for by Two Different Methods

Control Group:	6.170	6.405	6.439	6.571	6.707	7.093	7.093	7.188	7.673	7.901
	7.996	8.056	8.179	8.196	8.227	8.330	8.385	8.429	8.847	8.848
	8.863	8.893	8.966	9.069	9.140	9.447	9.772	10.054	10.192	10.402
Treatment Group	6.269	6.477	6.816	7.030	7.162	7.409	7.442	7.443	7.540	7.600
	7.779	7.796	7.900	7.948	8.019	8.067	8.076	8.115	8.186	8.332
	8.687	8.703	8.743	8.823	8.904	9.064	9.171	9.539	9.631	9.857

The means and SD's for the log-transformed data are:

$$\bar{x} = 8.251, \quad \bar{y} = 8.084, \quad s_1 = 1.167, \quad s_2 = 0.905.$$

The sample SD's each have 29 d.f. They are not too different, so they can be pooled to give

$$s = \sqrt{\frac{29(1.167)^2 + 29(0.905)^2}{58}} = \sqrt{\frac{(1.167)^2 + (0.905)^2}{2}} = 1.045 \quad \text{with 58 d.f.}$$

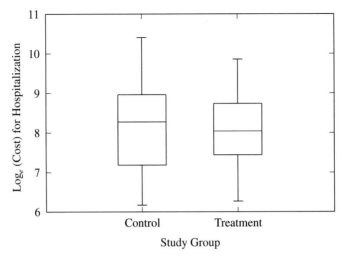

Figure 8.3   Box Plots of $\log_e$(Cost) for Geriatric Patients Cared for by Two Different Methods

A 95% CI for the difference in the means of the control and treatment populations can be computed from (8.7) with $t_{58,.025} = 2.002$:

$$\left[(8.251 - 8.084) \pm 2.002 \times 1.045 \sqrt{\frac{2}{30}} \right] = [-0.373, 0.707].$$

Since the value $\mu_1 - \mu_2 = 0$ falls in this CI, the difference in the means (on the logarithmic scale) of the two samples is not statistically significant at $\alpha = 0.05$. This can also be checked by calculating the t-statistic from (8.8):

$$t = \frac{8.251 - 8.084}{1.045\sqrt{1/30 + 1/30}} = 0.619$$

which has a two-sided P-value = 0.538. Thus the result is clearly not significant.   ◆

*The Proof of the t-Distribution Property of the r.v. T of (8.6)   The sampling distribution of $\bar{X} - \bar{Y}$ follows from the facts that $\bar{X} \sim N(\mu_1, \sigma^2/n_1)$, $\bar{Y} \sim N(\mu_2, \sigma^2/n_2)$, and the two are independent. Therefore $\bar{X} - \bar{Y}$ is normally distributed with

$$E(\bar{X} - \bar{Y}) = E(\bar{X}) - E(\bar{Y}) = \mu_1 - \mu_2$$

and

$$\text{Var}(\bar{X} - \bar{Y}) = \text{Var}(\bar{X}) + \text{Var}(\bar{Y}) = \frac{\sigma^2}{n_1} + \frac{\sigma^2}{n_2} = \sigma^2 \left(\frac{1}{n_1} + \frac{1}{n_2} \right).$$

In the standardized form,

$$Z = \frac{\bar{X} - \bar{Y} - (\mu_1 - \mu_2)}{\sigma\sqrt{1/n_1 + 1/n_2}} \sim N(0, 1).$$

We cannot use Z as a pivotal r.v., since σ is unknown. From Chapter 5, Section 5.2 we know that

$$\frac{(n_1-1)S_1^2}{\sigma^2} \sim \chi^2_{n_1-1}, \quad \frac{(n_2-1)S_2^2}{\sigma^2} \sim \chi^2_{n_2-1}$$

and the two are independent. Also recall from Result 1 in Chapter 5, Section 5.2, that if χ_a^2 and χ_b^2 are independent, then $\chi_a^2 + \chi_b^2 \sim \chi^2_{a+b}$. Hence

$$\frac{(n_1-1)S_1^2}{\sigma^2} + \frac{(n_2-1)S_2^2}{\sigma^2} = \frac{(n_1+n_2-2)S^2}{\sigma^2} \sim \chi^2_{n_1+n_2-2}.$$

Note that S^2 is independent of both $\bar{X}$ and $\bar{Y}$ because S_1^2 and S_2^2 are independent of $\bar{X}$ and $\bar{Y}$. Using the definition (5.12) of a T r.v., we conclude that

$$T = \frac{\bar{X}-\bar{Y}-(\mu_1-\mu_2)}{S\sqrt{1/n_1+1/n_2}} = \frac{\frac{\bar{X}-\bar{Y}-(\mu_1-\mu_2)}{\sigma\sqrt{1/n_1+1/n_2}}}{\frac{S}{\sigma}} = \frac{Z}{\sqrt{\frac{S^2}{\sigma^2}}} \sim \frac{N(0,1)}{\sqrt{\frac{\chi^2_{n_1+n_2-2}}{n_1+n_2-2}}}$$

has a t-distribution with n_1+n_2-2 d.f.   ∎

Case 2: Variances σ_1^2 and σ_2^2 Not Equal.   The two normal populations under comparison in this case are shown in Figure 8.4. It is natural to try to use

$$T = \frac{\bar{X}-\bar{Y}-(\mu_1-\mu_2)}{\sqrt{S_1^2/n_1+S_2^2/n_2}} \tag{8.10}$$

as a pivotal r.v. to derive CI's and hypothesis tests on $\mu_1-\mu_2$. Unfortunately, T does not have a Student's t-distribution. In fact, it can be shown that the distribution of T depends on the ratio of the *unknown* variances σ_1^2 and σ_2^2. Thus T is not a valid pivotal r.v. and no other pivotal r.v. exists.

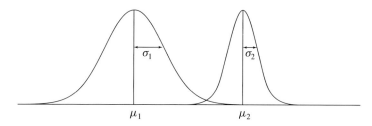

Figure 8.4   Two Normal Populations with Unequal Means and Unequal Variances

As we saw earlier, when n_1 and n_2 are large, T is approximately $N(0,1)$ distributed and large-sample methods can be used. For small n_1 and n_2, the distribution of T can be approximated by Student's t with d.f. ν, computed as follows. Denote the standard errors of the means (SEM's) by $SEM_1 = SEM(\bar{x}) = s_1/\sqrt{n_1}$ and

$SEM_2 = SEM(\bar{y}) = s_2/\sqrt{n_2}$. Let

$$w_1 = SEM_1^2 = \frac{s_1^2}{n_1} \quad \text{and} \quad w_2 = SEM_2^2 = \frac{s_2^2}{n_2}.$$

Then the d.f. are given by

$$\nu = \frac{(w_1 + w_2)^2}{w_1^2/(n_1 - 1) + w_2^2/(n_2 - 1)}. \tag{8.11}$$

Note two things about this formula:

1. The d.f. are *estimated* from data and are not a function of the sample sizes alone.
2. The d.f. are generally fractional. For convenience, we will truncate them down to the nearest integer.

Using this result, the approximate $100(1 - \alpha)\%$ two-sided CI for $\mu_1 - \mu_2$ is given by

$$\bar{x} - \bar{y} - t_{\nu,\alpha/2}\sqrt{\frac{s_1^2}{n_1} + \frac{s_2^2}{n_2}} \le \mu_1 - \mu_2 \le \bar{x} - \bar{y} + t_{\nu,\alpha/2}\sqrt{\frac{s_1^2}{n_1} + \frac{s_2^2}{n_2}}. \tag{8.12}$$

To test the hypotheses (8.3) we first compute

$$t = \frac{\bar{x} - \bar{y} - \delta_0}{\sqrt{s_1^2/n_1 + s_2^2/n_2}}. \tag{8.13}$$

An approximate α-level t-test is given by

$$\text{Reject } H_0 \text{ if } |t| > t_{\nu,\alpha/2} \quad \text{or equivalently if} \quad |\bar{x} - \bar{y} - \delta_0| > t_{\nu,\alpha/2}\sqrt{\frac{s_1^2}{n_1} + \frac{s_2^2}{n_2}}. $$
$$\tag{8.14}$$

One-sided CI's and hypothesis tests follow in a similar manner. This method of obtaining approximate CI's and hypothesis tests based on the approximate t-distribution of r.v. T of (8.10) is known as the **Welch-Satterthwaite method**. The different tests are summarized in Table 8.5.

EXAMPLE 8.4   (HOSPITALIZATION COSTS: INFERENCES USING SEPARATE VARIANCES)

We shall redo Exaple 8.3 without making the equal variances assumption. First note that since $n_1 = n_2 = n$,

$$\frac{s_1^2}{n_1} + \frac{s_2^2}{n_2} = \frac{s_1^2 + s_2^2}{2}\left(\frac{1}{n} + \frac{1}{n}\right) = \frac{2s^2}{n}$$

where s^2 is the pooled sample variance. Therefore the t-statistic is the same as that calculated using the pooled variance estimate, i.e., $t = 0.619$.

To calculate the estimated d.f. for this t-statistic, first calculate

$$w_1 = \frac{(1.167)^2}{30} = 0.0454, \quad w_2 = \frac{(0.905)^2}{30} = 0.0273.$$

Table 8.5 Level α Tests on $\mu_1 - \mu_2$ for Small Samples When $\sigma_1^2 \neq \sigma_2^2$ $\left(\text{Test Statistic:} \right.$

$\left. t = \frac{\bar{x}-\bar{y}-\delta_0}{\sqrt{s_1^2/n_1+s_2^2/n_2}} \right)$

Testing Problem	Hypotheses	Reject H_0 if	P-value
Upper One-Sided	$H_0: \mu_1 - \mu_2 \leq \delta_0$ vs. $H_1: \mu_1 - \mu_2 > \delta_0$	$t > t_{v,\alpha}$ $\Longleftrightarrow$ $\bar{x} - \bar{y} > \delta_0 + t_{v,\alpha}\sqrt{s_1^2/n_1 + s_2^2/n_2}$	$P(T_v \geq t)$
Lower One-Sided	$H_0: \mu_1 - \mu_2 \geq \delta_0$ vs. $H_1: \mu_1 - \mu_2 < \delta_0$	$t < -t_{v,\alpha}$ $\Longleftrightarrow$ $\bar{x} - \bar{y} < \delta_0 - t_{v,\alpha}\sqrt{s_1^2/n_1 + s_2^2/n_2}$	$P(T_v \leq t)$
Two-Sided	$H_0: \mu_1 - \mu_2 = \delta_0$ vs. $H_1: \mu_1 - \mu_2 \neq \delta_0$	$\|t\| > t_{v,\alpha/2}$ $\Longleftrightarrow$ $\|\bar{x} - \bar{y} - \delta_0\| > t_{v,\alpha/2}\sqrt{s_1^2/n_1 + s_2^2/n_2}$	$P(\|T_v\| \geq \|t\|)$ = $2P(T_v \geq \|t\|)$

Here $v = \dfrac{(w_1+w_2)^2}{w_1^2/(n_1-1)+w_2^2/(n_2-1)}$ where $w_1 = s_1^2/n_1$ and $w_2 = s_2^2/n_2$.

Then calculate

$$v = \frac{(0.0454 + 0.0273)^2}{(0.0454)^2/29 + (0.0273)^2/29} = 54.6$$

which is truncated down to 54. Notice that we lost only 4 d.f. by using separate variance estimates in this example. The final result is essentially the same as that obtained by pooling the sample variances. ◆

In this example, the pooled d.f. and the separate variance estimates d.f. using the Welch-Satterthwaite formula (8.11) do not differ much for two reasons:

1. The two sample variances are not too different.

2. The two sample sizes are equal.

In other cases, there can be a considerable loss in d.f. as a result of using separate variance estimates. For instance, suppose that s_1^2 and s_2^2 are the same as in the above example, but $n_1 = 50$ and $n_2 = 10$. The d.f. of the t-statistic based on the pooled variance is still 58, but the d.f. of the t-statistic based on separate variance estimates is only 15.66 (computed from (8.11)).

Which method should one use in practice—the pooled variance or the separate variances? It might appear that there is a gain in d.f. due to pooling. However, this gain is illusory, because if the assumption of equal variances is not valid, then pooling could give misleading results (the actual confidence level can be much less than the nominal level). In other words, the pooled variance method is not robust. This is especially true when $n_1 \neq n_2$ and the larger variance is paired with the smaller sample size (inverse pairing). If the sample sizes are equal or if the larger variance is paired with the larger sample size (direct pairing), then the pooled variance method gives satisfactory results. The assumption of equal variances is often not valid in practical settings. Therefore a safer approach is to use the separate variances method.

Sample Size Determination.   We consider only Case 1: $\sigma_1^2 = \sigma_2^2 = \sigma^2$. (Case 2 is considered in Exercise 8.26.) For design purposes, we assume that σ^2 is known. Under the assumption of equal variances, one should take equal size samples from both groups, i.e., $n_1 = n_2 = n$. We derive an approximation to the common sample size n required by the independent samples t-test by using the power function of the large sample z-test (see Section 7.1.2 of Chapter 7). This approximation[2] slightly underestimates the sample size, because it is obtained by treating σ^2 as exactly known, when actually it is estimated from data.

Consider the one-sided testing problem,

$$H_0: \mu_1 - \mu_2 \leq 0 \quad \text{vs.} \quad H_1: \mu_1 - \mu_2 > 0.$$

An α-level z-test rejects H_0 if

$$z = \frac{\bar{x} - \bar{y}}{\sigma\sqrt{2/n}} > z_\alpha.$$

The power function of this test is easily derived to be

$$\pi(\mu_1 - \mu_2) = P\{\text{Test rejects } H_0\} = \Phi\left(-z_\alpha + \frac{\mu_1 - \mu_2}{\sigma}\sqrt{\frac{n}{2}}\right).$$

We want to find the sample size n necessary to guarantee at least $1 - \beta$ power when $\mu_1 - \mu_2 = \delta$, where δ is the smallest difference of practical importance. The necessary sample size is obtained by equating

$$\Phi\left(-z_\alpha + \frac{\delta}{\sigma}\sqrt{\frac{n}{2}}\right) = 1 - \beta.$$

Since $1 - \beta = \Phi(z_\beta)$, we have $-z_\alpha + \frac{\delta}{\sigma}\sqrt{\frac{n}{2}} = z_\beta$ or

$$n = 2\left[\frac{\sigma(z_\alpha + z_\beta)}{\delta}\right]^2. \tag{8.15}$$

The same formula is applicable to the lower one-sided testing problem. For the two-sided testing problem the only change required is to replace z_α by $z_{\alpha/2}$.

---

[2] For an exact determination of the sample size, the use of the noncentral t-distribution is required as discussed in Chapter 7.

EXAMPLE 8.5   (HOSPITALIZATION COSTS: SAMPLE SIZE DETERMINATION)

Let μ_1 and μ_2 be the mean hospitalization costs on the logarithmic scale for the control and treatment groups, respectively. Although the new method of geriatric care management is expected to lower the cost, we consider a two-sided test of $H_0: \mu_1 = \mu_2$ vs. $H_1: \mu_1 \neq \mu_2$ with $\alpha = 0.05$. Assume a common $\sigma = 1.0$ for log-transformed costs in each group. (This assumed value of σ is consistent with $s_1 = 1.167$ and $s_2 = 0.905$ that we obtained in Example 8.3.) If the mean costs (on the untransformed scale) for the two methods differ by a factor of two, then we want the test to have power $1 - \beta = 0.90$ or higher. What is the minimum sample size needed in each group?

If the mean costs differ by a factor of 2 on the original scale, then they would differ roughly by $\log_e(2) = 0.693$ on the logarithmic scale; therefore we take $\delta = 0.693$. We also have $\sigma = 1.0$, $z_{\alpha/2} = z_{.025} = 1.960$, and $z_\beta = z_{.10} = 1.282$. Substituting these values in (8.15), we obtain

$$n = 2 \left[\frac{1.0(1.960 + 1.282)}{0.693} \right]^2 = 43.75.$$

Therefore at least 44 patients are required in each group. ◆

8.3.2 Matched Pairs Design

The clinical study to compare two methods of measuring cardiac output discussed in Example 4.11 is a matched pairs design. Method A is invasive, because it involves inserting a catheter into the main heart artery, while method B is noninvasive. To control for differences between persons, both methods are used on each person participating in the study to allow the two measurements to be directly compared. Here our purpose is to compare the two methods in terms of the mean difference.[3] The data from that example are reproduced in Table 8.6.

Let X_i and Y_i denote the measurements on the ith matched pair using methods A and B, respectively. As in the case of the independent samples design, we assume that $X_i \sim N(\mu_1, \sigma_1^2)$ and $Y_i \sim N(\mu_2, \sigma_2^2)$, but now because X_i and Y_i are measurements on the same matched pair, they are in general correlated. Let $\mathrm{Corr}(X_i, Y_i) = \rho$. Further assume that the pairs (X_i, Y_i) are mutually independent. Then it follows that the differences $D_i = X_i - Y_i$ are independent normal r.v.'s with

$$\mu_D = E(D_i) = E(X_i - Y_i) = E(X_i) - E(Y_i) = \mu_1 - \mu_2$$

and

$$\sigma_D^2 = \mathrm{Var}(D_i) = \mathrm{Var}(X_i - Y_i) = \mathrm{Var}(X_i) + \mathrm{Var}(Y_i) - 2\mathrm{Cov}(X_i, Y_i)$$

$$= \sigma_1^2 + \sigma_2^2 - 2\rho\sigma_1\sigma_2.$$

We see from this expression that if $\rho > 0$, i.e., if matching induces positive correlation between the measurements on matched units, then the variance of the difference of the measurements is reduced as compared to the independent samples case. This is what makes the matched pairs comparison more precise; see Exercise 8.24 for more details.

---

[3] In Example 4.5 the purpose of the analysis was to *calibrate* method B with respect to method A by fitting a straight line. The purpose of the present analysis is to *compare* the two methods in terms of the means. Which analysis is appropriate depends on the research question of interest.

Let x_i, y_i, and $d_i = x_i - y_i$ be the observed values of the r.v.'s X_i, Y_i, and D_i, respectively. Once the paired data are reduced to differences, we have a single sample setting which allows application of the inference methods learned in the previous chapter. For example, a $100(1 - \alpha)\%$ CI on $\mu_D = \mu_1 - \mu_2$ is

$$\bar{d} - t_{n-1,\alpha/2}\frac{s_d}{\sqrt{n}} \leq \mu_1 - \mu_2 \leq \bar{d} + t_{n-1,\alpha/2}\frac{s_d}{\sqrt{n}} \tag{8.16}$$

where

$$\bar{d} = \frac{\sum d_i}{n} \quad \text{and} \quad s_d = \sqrt{\frac{\sum(d_i - \bar{d})^2}{n - 1}}.$$

To test a null hypothesis $H_0: \mu_D = \mu_1 - \mu_2 = \delta_0$ (where δ_0 is a specified number) against a one-sided or a two-sided alternative, we use the t-statistic

$$t = \frac{\bar{d} - \delta_0}{s_d/\sqrt{n}}. \tag{8.17}$$

The rejection regions of α-level tests are the same as given in Table 7.5 for the one sample problem, and the corresponding tests are called **paired t-tests**. In particular, the rejection region for the two-sided test is

Reject H_0 if $|t| > t_{n-1,\alpha/2}$ or equivalently if $|\bar{d} - \delta_0| > t_{n-1,\alpha/2}\frac{s_d}{\sqrt{n}}.$ (8.18)

The P-values are also obtained in the same way as for a single sample t-test.

EXAMPLE 8.6

For the data in Table 8.6, calculate a 95% CI on the mean difference in cardiac outputs measured by the two methods. Also assess the statistical significance of the difference in the means by calculating the P-value.

Before we calculate various statistics, let us look at the data graphically. A scatter plot of the data was given in Chapter 4, Figure 4.13. Although the relationship between Method A and Method B measurements is linear, if a 45° line is superimposed on that plot, we see that most points fall below the line. In fact, 20 of the 26 method A measurements are greater than the corresponding method B measurements, as seen from Table 8.6. To check for normality and outliers, a normal plot of the differences is created, as shown in Figure 8.5. This plot appears satisfactory, and we may proceed with formal calculations.

The summary statistics for the differences are:

$$\bar{d} = \bar{x} - \bar{y} = 0.454, \quad s_d = 0.485 \text{ with 25 d.f.}$$

Hence a 95% CI for $\mu_1 - \mu_2$ from (8.16) with $t_{25,.025} = 2.060$ is

$$\left[0.454 \pm 2.060 \times \frac{0.485}{\sqrt{26}}\right] = [0.258, 0.650].$$

This interval is on the positive side of zero, indicating that the method A mean is significantly higher than the method B mean. Alternatively, this can be checked by calculating the t-statistic (8.17):

$$t = \frac{0.454 - 0}{0.485/\sqrt{26}} = 4.773$$

which has a two-sided P-value < 0.0001.   ◆

Table 8.6 Cardiac Output (liters/min.) Measured by Methods A and B

No.	Method A	Method B	Difference	No.	Method A	Method B	Difference
i	x_i	y_i	d_i	i	x_i	y_i	d_i
1	6.3	5.2	1.1	14	7.7	7.4	0.3
2	6.3	6.6	−0.3	15	7.4	7.4	0.0
3	3.5	2.3	1.2	16	5.6	4.9	0.7
4	5.1	4.4	0.7	17	6.3	5.4	0.9
5	5.5	4.1	1.4	18	8.4	8.4	0.0
6	7.7	6.4	1.3	19	5.6	5.1	0.5
7	6.3	5.7	0.9	20	4.8	4.4	0.4
8	2.8	2.3	0.5	21	4.3	4.3	0.0
9	3.4	3.2	0.2	22	4.2	4.1	0.1
10	5.7	5.2	0.5	23	3.3	2.2	1.1
11	5.6	4.9	0.7	24	3.8	4.0	−0.2
12	6.2	6.1	0.1	25	5.7	5.8	−0.1
13	6.6	6.3	0.3	26	4.1	4.0	0.1

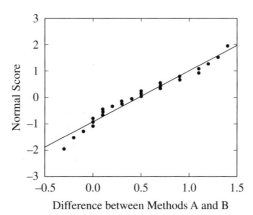

Figure 8.5 Normal Plot of the Differences between Method A and Method B Cardiac Output Readings

Sample Size Determination.   To determine the sample size n for the matched pairs design, the same formulas as for the one sample case derived in Chapter 7 for z-tests can be used as approximations. Thus, for an α-level paired t-test with power $1 - \beta$ to detect a threshold mean difference of δ, the necessary sample sizes can be calculated using

$$n = \left[\frac{(z_\alpha + z_\beta)\sigma_D}{\delta} \right]^2$$

for a one-sided test, and

$$n = \left[\frac{(z_{\alpha/2} + z_\beta)\sigma_D}{\delta} \right]^2$$

for a two-sided test. Here σ_D is a prior estimate of the standard deviation of the differences D_i. When σ_D is estimated from the data, these formulas yield slight underestimates.

8.4   *COMPARING VARIANCES OF TWO POPULATIONS

We now turn to the problem of comparing the variances of two distributions. This problem arises when comparing instrument precisions or uniformities of products. Another application is to check the assumption of equal variances used for the pooled variances (Case 1) methods in Section 8.3.1.

The methods that we discuss below are applicable only under the assumption of normality of the data. They are highly sensitive to even modest departures from normality and therefore must be used only when the data strongly support the normality assumption. In case of nonnormal data there are nonparametric and other robust tests available which should be used.

We consider only the independent samples design. Assume that

Sample 1: $x_1, x_2, \ldots, x_{n_1}$ is a random sample from an $N(\mu_1, \sigma_1^2)$ distribution
Sample 2: $y_1, y_2, \ldots, y_{n_2}$ is a random sample from an $N(\mu_2, \sigma_2^2)$ distribution.

To compare the two population variances we use the ratio σ_1^2/σ_2^2. This ratio is estimated by s_1^2/s_2^2, where s_1^2 and s_2^2 are the sample variances calculated in the usual way with $n_1 - 1$ and $n_2 - 1$ d.f., respectively.

To obtain a CI for σ_1^2/σ_2^2 we use the pivotal r.v.

$$F = \frac{S_1^2/\sigma_1^2}{S_2^2/\sigma_2^2}.$$

We saw in Chapter 5 that this r.v. has an F-distribution with $n_1 - 1$ and $n_2 - 1$ d.f. (denoted by $F \sim F_{n_1-1,n_2-1}$). Let $f_{n_1-1,n_2-1,\alpha/2}$ and $f_{n_1-1,n_2-1,1-\alpha/2}$ denote the upper and lower $\alpha/2$ critical points of this F-distribution. Then we can write the following probability statement:

$$P\left\{ f_{n_1-1,n_2-1,1-\alpha/2} \leq \frac{S_1^2/\sigma_1^2}{S_2^2/\sigma_2^2} \leq f_{n_1-1,n_2-1,\alpha/2} \right\} = 1 - \alpha.$$

A rearrangement of the terms leads to the equation

$$P\left\{ \frac{1}{f_{n_1-1,n_2-1,\alpha/2}} \frac{S_1^2}{S_2^2} \leq \frac{\sigma_1^2}{\sigma_2^2} \leq \frac{1}{f_{n_1-1,n_2-1,1-\alpha/2}} \frac{S_1^2}{S_2^2} \right\} = 1 - \alpha.$$

This yields the following $(1 - \alpha)$-level two-sided CI:

$$\frac{1}{f_{n_1-1,n_2-1,\alpha/2}} \frac{s_1^2}{s_2^2} \leq \frac{\sigma_1^2}{\sigma_2^2} \leq \frac{1}{f_{n_1-1,n_2-1,1-\alpha/2}} \frac{s_1^2}{s_2^2}. \tag{8.19}$$

The critical point needed for the upper confidence limit can be obtained from Table A.6 using the relation

$$\frac{1}{f_{n_1-1,n_2-1,1-\alpha/2}} = f_{n_2-1,n_1-1,\alpha/2}$$

from Chapter 5, equation (5.18). One-sided CI's can be obtained in a similar manner.

Next consider the problem of testing

$$H_0: \sigma_1^2 = \sigma_2^2 \quad \text{vs.} \quad H_1: \sigma_1^2 \neq \sigma_2^2.$$

An α-level test can be obtained by rejecting H_0 if the ratio $\sigma_1^2/\sigma_2^2 = 1$ falls outside the $(1 - \alpha)$-level CI (8.19), i.e., if the lower confidence limit is greater than 1 or the upper confidence limit is less than 1. Equivalently, we can conduct the test by using the statistic

$$F = \frac{s_1^2}{s_2^2}$$

and rejecting H_0 if

$$F > f_{n_1-1,n_2-1,\alpha/2} \quad \text{or} \quad F < f_{n_1-1,n_2-1,1-\alpha/2}. \tag{8.20}$$

An easier way to apply this test is to label the samples so that $s_1^2 \geq s_2^2$. Then only the first part of the above rejection rule needs to be checked. One-sided tests can be obtained in a similar manner. These are called **F-tests** for variances and are summarized in Table 8.7.

Table 8.7 Level α Tests for Equality of σ_1^2 and σ_2^2 $\left(\text{Test Statistic: } F = s_1^2/s_2^2\right)$

Testing Problem	Hypotheses	Reject H_0 if
Upper One-Sided	$H_0: \sigma_1^2 \leq \sigma_2^2$ vs. $H_1: \sigma_1^2 > \sigma_2^2$	$F > f_{n_1-1,n_2-1,\alpha}$
Lower One-Sided	$H_0: \sigma_1^2 \geq \sigma_2^2$ vs. $H_1: \sigma_1^2 < \sigma_2^2$	$F < f_{n_1-1,n_2-1,1-\alpha}$
Two-Sided	$H_0 : \sigma_1^2 = \sigma_2^2$ vs. $H_1: \sigma_1^2 \neq \sigma_2^2$	$F < f_{n_1-1,n_2-1,1-\alpha/2}$ or $F > f_{n_1-1,n_2-1,\alpha/2}$

EXAMPLE 8.7   (HOSPITALIZATION COSTS: TEST OF EQUALITY OF VARIANCES)

In Example 8.3 the sample SD's of log-transformed costs for the two groups of geriatric patients were judged to be nearly equal. Verify this heuristic judgment by applying the F-test (8.20) for the equality of variances.

The sample SD's were $s_1 = 1.167$ for the control group and $s_2 = 0.905$ for the treatment group. Therefore the F-ratio is

$$F = \frac{s_1^2}{s_2^2} = \frac{(1.167)^2}{(0.905)^2} = 1.663.$$

Since $n_1 = n_2 = 30$, the d.f. for the F-distribution are (29, 29). For a two-sided 0.05-level test the critical constant is $f_{29,29,.025} = 2.101$. The F-ratio does not exceed this critical constant. Therefore our heuristic judgment is supported by the F-test. The same F-test cannot reliably be used to test the equality of variances for the untransformed costs because they are not normally distributed.   ◆

EXAMPLE 8.8

This example illustrates the calculation of the CI for the ratio of two population variances when their estimates are obtained by pooling separate estimates from several samples.

A manufacturing company conducted a study to compare the accuracy and consistency of thermal conductivity measurements made by two testing labs on silicone rubber samples. Random samples from three batches of rubber were sent to each lab (12 samples from each batch to Lab 1 and 6 samples to Lab 2). The sample means and SD's are summarized in Table 8.8. Find a 95% CI for the ratio of the true variances of the two labs.

Table 8.8 Sample Means and SD's of Thermal
Conductivity Measurements by
Two Testing Labs

	Batch 1	Batch 2	Batch 3
Lab 1	$\bar{x} = 1.032$	$\bar{x} = 1.038$	$\bar{x} = 1.056$
	$s_1 = 0.019$	$s_1 = 0.018$	$s_1 = 0.021$
	$n_1 = 12$	$n_1 = 12$	$n_1 = 12$
Lab 2	$\bar{y} = 0.929$	$\bar{y} = 0.934$	$\bar{y} = 0.951$
	$s_2 = 0.006$	$s_2 = 0.036$	$s_2 = 0.025$
	$n_2 = 6$	$n_2 = 6$	$n_2 = 6$

Eyeballing the data suggests that Lab 2 measurements are lower on the average but more variable. Here we focus only on the variances. First we pool the three sample variances by weighting them by their individual d.f. ($n_1 - 1$ and $n_2 - 1$) to obtain a single pooled sample variance for each lab. In doing so, we implicitly assume that the true variability did not change between the three batches for each lab. Denote the true variances by σ_1^2 and σ_2^2, which are estimated by the pooled sample variances s_1^2 and s_2^2 calculated below:

$$\text{Lab 1: } s_1^2 = \frac{11(0.019)^2 + 11(0.018)^2 + 11(0.021)^2}{33} = (0.0194)^2 \text{ with 33 d.f.}$$

and

$$\text{Lab 2: } s_2^2 = \frac{5(0.006)^2 + 5(0.036)^2 + 5(0.025)^2}{15} = (0.0255)^2 \text{ with 15 d.f.}$$

The critical points needed to compute a 95% CI for σ_1^2/σ_2^2 using (8.19) are $f_{33,15,.025} = 2.623$ and $f_{15,33,.025} = 2.261$. Therefore a 95% CI for σ_1^2/σ_2^2 is

$$\left[\frac{1}{2.623} \frac{(0.0194)^2}{(0.0255)^2}, 2.261 \frac{(0.0194)^2}{(0.0255)^2} \right] = [0.221, 1.309].$$

Since this CI includes the value $\sigma_1^2/\sigma_2^2 = 1$, we cannot reject $H_0: \sigma_1^2 = \sigma_2^2$ at $\alpha = 0.05$; so we do not have sufficient evidence to conclude that the Lab 2 measurements are more variable than the Lab 1 measurements. ◆

8.5   CHAPTER SUMMARY

This chapter discusses methods for comparing two populations in terms of their means and variances. The data may be obtained using an **independent samples design** or a **matched pairs design**. Graphical methods for comparing data from an independent samples design include a **side-by-side box plot** and a **quantile-quantile (Q-Q) plot**. The data from a matched pairs design may be compared graphically by a **scatter plot**.

First consider an independent samples design with random samples of sizes n_1 and n_2 from populations with means μ_1 and μ_2, and variances σ_1^2 and σ_2^2, respectively. Let $\bar{x}$ and $\bar{y}$ denote the sample means, and s_1^2 and s_2^2 denote the sample variances of the two samples. The sample estimate of $\mu_1 - \mu_2$ is $\bar{x} - \bar{y}$ with the estimated standard error equal to $\sqrt{s_1^2/n_1 + s_2^2/n_2}$. If the populations are not normal but n_1 and n_2 are large, then the central limit theorem (CLT) can be applied to obtain approximate inferences on $\mu_1 - \mu_2$. For example, a large sample $100(1 - \alpha)\%$ confidence interval (CI) on $\mu_1 - \mu_2$ is given by

$$\left[\bar{x} - \bar{y} \pm z_{\alpha/2}\sqrt{s_1^2/n_1 + s_2^2/n_2} \right],$$

where $z_{\alpha/2}$ is the upper $\alpha/2$ critical point of the standard normal distribution. An α-level two-sided test on $\mu_1 - \mu_2$ can be obtained from this CI in the usual manner. One-sided CI's and tests also follow similarly.

Since the CLT does not apply when the sample sizes are small, the inference methods for $\mu_1 - \mu_2$ described in this chapter strictly hold in that case only when the populations are normal. If we can assume that $\sigma_1^2 = \sigma_2^2 = \sigma^2$, but the common σ^2 is unknown (Case 1), then exact inferences on $\mu_1 - \mu_2$ can be based on the t-distribution as follows: Estimate the common σ^2 by the pooled sample variance

$$s^2 = \frac{(n_1 - 1)s_1^2 + (n_2 - 1)s_2^2}{n_1 + n_2 - 2},$$

with $n_1 + n_2 - 2$ degrees of freedom (d.f.). Then an exact $100(1 - \alpha)\%$ CI on $\mu_1 - \mu_2$ is given by

$$\left[\bar{x} - \bar{y} \pm t_{n_1+n_2-2,\alpha/2} s\sqrt{1/n_1 + 1/n_2} \right],$$

where $s\sqrt{1/n_1 + 1/n_2}$ is the estimated standard error of $\bar{x} - \bar{y}$ and $t_{n_1+n_2-2,\alpha/2}$ is the upper $\alpha/2$ critical point of the t-distribution with $n_1 + n_2 - 2$ d.f.

If $\sigma_1^2 \neq \sigma_2^2$ and both variances are unknown (Case 2) then exact inferences on $\mu_1 - \mu_2$ are not possible. Approximate inferences can be based on the t-distribution with estimated d.f. as follows. Let $w_1 = s_1^2/n_1$ and $w_2 = s_2^2/n_2$. Calculate the d.f. using the formula

$$\nu = \frac{(w_1 + w_2)^2}{w_1^2/(n_1 - 1) + w_2^2/(n_2 - 1)}$$

and rounding off to the next lower integer. Then an approximate $100(1 - \alpha)\%$ CI on $\mu_1 - \mu_2$ is given by

$$\left[\bar{x} - \bar{y} \pm t_{\nu,\alpha/2}\sqrt{s_1^2/n_1 + s_2^2/n_2} \right].$$

When the samples are obtained from a matched pairs design, the difference of each matched pair is first calculated, which produces a single sample. The difference between the population means is then analyzed by applying one-sample procedures to the differences from the pairs. A **paired t-test** is simply a single sample t-test applied to the paired differences.

These procedures for comparing the means are fairly robust even when the data are non-normal, but they are not robust if the data contain outliers.

To compare the unknown variances σ_1^2 and σ_2^2 of normal populations when using an independent samples design, we use the sample variances s_1^2 and s_2^2, which have $n_1 - 1$ and $n_2 - 1$ d.f., respectively. A two-sided $100(1 - \alpha)\%$ CI on the ratio σ_1^2/σ_2^2 is given by

$$\left[\frac{1}{f_{n_1-1,n_2-1,\alpha/2}} \frac{s_1^2}{s_2^2}, \frac{1}{f_{n_1-1,n_2-1,1-\alpha/2}} \frac{s_1^2}{s_2^2} \right],$$

where $f_{n_1-1,n_2-1,\alpha/2}$ is the upper $\alpha/2$ critical point of the F-distribution with $n_1 - 1$ and $n_2 - 1$ d.f. An α-level test of $H_0 : \sigma_1^2 = \sigma_2^2$ vs. $H_1 : \sigma_1^2 \neq \sigma_2^2$ rejects H_0 when either $F = s_1^2/s_2^2 > f_{n_1-1,n_2-1,\alpha/2}$ or $F = s_1^2/s_2^2 < f_{n_1-1,n_2-1,1-\alpha/2}$. The procedures for comparing the variances are highly sensitive to the normality assumption and should not be used when that assumption is in doubt.

■ EXERCISES

Section 8.1

8.1   Tell in each of the following instances whether the study uses an independent samples or a matched pairs design.

   (a) Two computing algorithms are compared in terms of the CPU times required to do the same six test problems.

(b) A survey is conducted of teens from inner city schools and suburban schools to compare the proportion who have tried drugs.

(c) A psychologist measures the response times of subjects under two stimuli; each subject is observed under both the stimuli in a random order.

(d) An agronomist compares the yields of two varieties of soybean by planting each variety in 10 separate plots of land (a total of 20 plots).

8.2   Tell in each of the instances of Exercise 8.1 whether the study is experimental or observational.

8.3   Tell in each of the following instances whether the study uses an independent samples or a matched pairs design.

(a) Military test pilots who had at least one accident are matched by length of experience to pilots without accidents. The two groups are then surveyed about the number of childhood accidents to determine if the former group of pilots is "accident prone."

(b) Lung cancer patients admitted in a hospital over a 12 month period are each matched with a noncancer patient by age, sex, and race. To determine whether or not smoking is a risk factor for lung cancer, it is noted for each patient if he or she is a smoker.

(c) A survey is conducted of college bound and noncollege bound high school seniors to compare the proportion who have at least one parent who attended college.

(d) An advertising agency has come up with two different TV commercials for a household detergent. To determine which one is more effective, a test is conducted in which a sample of 100 adults is randomly divided into two groups. Each group is shown a different commercial, and the people in the group are asked to score the commercial.

8.4   Tell in each of the instances of Exercise 8.3 whether the study is experimental or observational.

Section 8.2

8.5   ▣ The effect of unseeded vs. seeded clouds on rainfall was compared by randomly seeding 26 of 52 clouds with silver nitrate and measuring the rainfall; the other 26 clouds were unseeded to serve as controls. The rainfall measured to the nearest unit (in acre-feet) yielded the following results:[4]

Unseeded	1203	830	372	346	321	244	163	148	95	87	81	69	47
	41	37	29	29	26	26	24	23	17	12	5	5	1
Seeded	2746	1698	1656	978	703	489	430	334	303	275	275	255	243
	201	199	130	119	118	115	92	41	33	31	18	8	4

(a) Explain why these samples are independent.

(b) Make a Q-Q plot of the data. What does this plot tell you about the rainfall from the two groups?

---

[4] From DAZL "Clouds" data file available on the Web site `http://lib.stat.cmu.edu/~DAZL`

8.6   ■ Production lines in a manufacturing plant are set to make steel ball bearings with a diameter of 1 micron. Ten ball bearings were randomly selected from two production lines. The diameters of the ball bearings measured in microns were as follows:[5]

First line	1.18 1.42 0.69 0.88 1.62 1.09 1.53 1.02 1.19 1.32
Second line	1.72 1.62 1.69 0.79 1.79 0.77 1.44 1.29 1.96 0.99

(a) Explain why these samples are independent.

(b) Make a Q-Q plot of the data. Does one set of ball bearing diameters tend to be larger than the other?

8.7   ■ To determine whether glaucoma affects the corneal thickness, measurements were made in 8 people affected by glaucoma in one eye but not in the other. The corneal thicknesses (in microns) were as follows:[6]

Person	1	2	3	4	5	6	7	8
Eye affected by glaucoma	488	478	480	426	440	410	458	460
Eye not affected by glaucoma	484	478	492	444	436	398	464	476

(a) Explain why these samples are matched pairs.

(b) Make a scatter plot of the corneal thicknesses. Do the pairs tend to lie above or below the 45° line through the origin? Do eyes affected by glaucoma tend to have either thicker or thinner corneas than unaffected eyes?

8.8   ■ The effect of two types of viruses on tobacco leaves was studied by rubbing a preparation containing each virus onto a different half of each of 8 tobacco leaves. The number of lesions counted on the two halves of these leaves were as follows:[7]

Tobacco Leaf	1	2	3	4	5	6	7	8
Treated by virus 1	31	20	18	17	9	8	10	7
Treated by virus 2	18	17	14	11	10	7	5	6

(a) Explain why these samples are matched pairs.

(b) Make a scatter plot of the numbers of lesions. Do the pairs tend to lie above or below the 45° line through the origin? Does one virus tend to produce more lesions than the other?

---

[5] A. Romano (1977), *Applied Statistics for Science and Industry*, Boston: Allyn and Bacon. Reprinted in *Small Data Sets*, p. 131.

[6] N. Ehlers, "On corneal thickness and introcular pressure," *Acta Opthalmologica*, **48**, pp. 1107–1112. Reprinted in *Small Data Sets*, p. 127.

[7] W. J. Youden and H. P. Beale (1964), *Contrib. Boyce Thompson Inst.*, **6**, p. 437. Reprinted in *Small Data Sets*, p. 308.

Section 8.3

8.9   Two brands of water filters are to be compared in terms of the mean reduction in impurities measured in parts per million (ppm). Twenty-one water samples were tested with each filter and reduction in the impurity level was measured, resulting in the following data:

$$\text{Filter 1:} \quad n_1 = 21 \quad \bar{x} = 8.0 \quad s_1^2 = 4.5$$
$$\text{Filter 2:} \quad n_2 = 21 \quad \bar{y} = 6.5 \quad s_2^2 = 2.0$$

(a) Calculate a 95% confidence interval for the mean difference $\mu_1 - \mu_2$ between the two filters, assuming $\sigma_1^2 = \sigma_2^2$. Is there a statistically significant difference at $\alpha = .05$ between the two filters?

(b) Repeat (a) without assuming $\sigma_1^2 = \sigma_2^2$. Compare the results.

8.10   ◼ Refer to the data from Exercise 4.22. Calculate a 95% confidence interval for the mean difference $\mu_1 - \mu_2$ between the dopamine levels of the two groups of patients, assuming $\sigma_1^2 = \sigma_2^2$. Is there a statistically significant difference at $\alpha = .05$ between the two groups?

8.11   ◼ Two methods of measuring atomic weight of carbon (the nominal atomic weight is 12) yielded the following results:[8]

Method 1	12.0129	12.0072	12.0064	12.0054	12.0016
	11.9853	11.9949	11.9985	12.0077	12.0061
Method 2	12.0318	12.0246	12.0069	12.0006	12.0075

(a) Test $H_0: \mu_1 = \mu_2$ vs. $H_1: \mu_1 \neq \mu_2$ at $\alpha = .05$, assuming $\sigma_1^2 = \sigma_2^2$. What is your conclusion?

(b) Repeat (a) without assuming $\sigma_1^2 = \sigma_2^2$. Compare the results.

8.12   ◼ Refer to the data from Exercise 8.5 on the effects of cloud seeding on rainfall.

(a) Make normal plots of the raw data and log-transformed data. State why log-transformed data should be used for formal comparisons. Use the log-transformed data in the following analyses.

(b) Test $H_0: \mu_1 = \mu_2$ vs. $H_1: \mu_1 \neq \mu_2$ at $\alpha = .05$, assuming $\sigma_1^2 = \sigma_2^2$. What is your conclusion?

(c) Repeat (a) without assuming $\sigma_1^2 = \sigma_2^2$. Compare the results.

8.13   ◼ Refer to the data from Exercise 8.6 on the diameters of ball bearings from two production lines.

(a) Calculate a 95% confidence interval for the difference between the mean diameters of ball bearings from the two production lines, assuming $\sigma_1^2 = \sigma_2^2$. Is there a statistically significant difference at $\alpha = .05$?

(b) Repeat (a) without assuming assuming $\sigma_1^2 = \sigma_2^2$. Compare the results.

8.14   A food store maintains statistics on customer sales during a week in August which reflects regular grocery volume and a week in December which reflects higher grocery volume due to the holiday season. Records on the number of items processed per minute (IPM)

---

[8] D. J. Best and J. C. W. Rayner (1987), "Welch's approximate solution for the Behrens-Fisher problem," *Technometrics*, **29**, pp. 205–210.

and the percent of idle time (PIT) were available for both weeks for 25 employees.[9] The difference (August minus December) for each employee was calculated.

(a) The August average of IPM was 27.5; the December average was 25.5. The standard deviation of the differences was $s_d = 2.0$. Compare the IPM for the two seasons, using a 95% confidence interval.

(b) The August average of PIT was 37.3; the December average was 30.6. The standard deviation of the differences was $s_d = 13.0$. Compare the PIT for the two seasons, using a 95% confidence interval.

(c) What can you conclude about the performance differences in handling regular volume compared to high holiday volume?

8.15 ▣ To study the effectiveness of wall insulation in saving energy for home heating, the energy consumption (in MWh) for 10 houses in Bristol, England, was recorded for two winters; the first winter was before insulation and the second winter was after insulation.[10]

House	1	2	3	4	5	6	7	8	9	10
Before insulation	12.1	11.0	14.1	13.8	15.5	12.2	12.8	9.9	10.8	12.7
After insulation	12.0	10.6	13.4	11.2	15.3	13.6	12.6	8.8	9.6	12.4

(a) Set up hypotheses to test if insulation has reduced the average energy consumption. Perform the test using $\alpha = .10$ and state your conclusion.

(b) Note that this is an observational study, and many factors that could affect the difference are uncontrolled. Name two such factors and indicate how they could have affected the result.

8.16 ▣ Refer to the data from Exercise 8.7 which show the corneal thicknesses of eyes with and without glaucoma.

(a) Test $H_0: \mu_1 = \mu_2$ against a two-sided alternative using $\alpha = .10$. What do you conclude?

(b) Calculate a 90% confidence interval for the mean difference in thickness.

8.17 ▣ Refer to the data from Exercise 8.8 giving the number of lesions on tobacco leaves treated with two viruses.

(a) Test $H_0: \mu_1 = \mu_2$ against a two-sided alternative using $\alpha = .05$. What do you conclude?

(b) Calculate a 95% confidence interval for the mean difference in the number of lesions caused by the two viruses.

---

[9] Data courtesy of Mr. David Sparks, Director of Store Operations Services, Jewel Food Stores, Chicago, IL. Certain details are simplified.

[10] The Open University (1983), *MDST242 Statistics in Society, Unit A10: Introduction*, 1st ed., Figure 2.9. Reprinted in *Small Data Sets*, p. 68.

Section 8.4

8.18 A restaurant adds a new commercial oven to its kitchen. It is hoped that the new oven has more evenly distributed heat than the current oven. The ovens are heated to $350°F$, using a thermostat control, and temperature readings are obtained from thermometers placed at 9 locations in each oven, yielding the following data:

$$\text{Current oven:} \quad n_1 = 9 \quad \bar{x} = 352.4 \quad s_1 = 2.3$$
$$\text{New oven:} \quad n_2 = 9 \quad \bar{y} = 350.2 \quad s_2 = 1.1$$

Test $H_0: \sigma_1^2 = \sigma_2^2$ vs. $H_1: \sigma_1^2 > \sigma_2^2$ using $\alpha = .05$. Do the data indicate that the new oven provides more even heating than the current one?

8.19 ◼ Refer to Exercise 8.12, in which you log-transformed the rainfall data from Exercise 8.5. Use those log-transformed data to test for the equality of variances of the rainfall at $\alpha = .05$ by calculating the corresponding 95% confidence interval for the ratio of the variances.

8.20 Refer to Exercise 8.9, which gives statistics on two brands of water filters. Test for the equality of variances at $\alpha = .10$. If the equality of the means is tested, would you recommend using a t-test calculated from pooled variances or separate variances?

8.21 ◼ Refer to Exercise 8.11, which gives data on two carbon measurement methods. Calculate a 90% confidence interval for the ratio of the variances of the two methods. Does this confidence interval indicate that the two variances are different? If the equality of the means is tested, would you recommend using a t-test calculated from pooled variances or separate variances?

8.22 Life threatening heart arrhythmias can be predicted from an electrocardiogram by measuring the lengths of QT intervals (the distances from the starts of the Q-waves to the starts of the T-waves). Two different calipers, A and B, were used to measure a set of 10 QT intervals. The sample variances for the two calipers were 831 and 592, respectively. Do these data suggest that the calipers A and B have different variability? Use $\alpha = .05$.

Advanced Exercises

8.23 A study to compare the effects of high fiber and low fiber diet supplements on the serum cholesterol was done at a Boston hospital.[11] Twenty subjects participated. During the baseline period of one week all subjects ate their normal diets. Serum cholesterol levels were measured at baseline for all subjects. For the following six weeks half the subjects received high fiber diet supplement in the form of oat bran, while the other half received low fiber diet supplement in the form of wheat bran. At the end of this period cholesterol levels were again measured. Then the subjects switched their diets. (This is called a **crossover design**.) At the end of six more weeks the measurements were again made. Subjects as well as the physicians were not told about which diet each subject was receiving. (This is called a **double blind design**.) The sample means and sample standard deviations for the 20 subjects were as follows:

---

[11] J. F. Swain, I. L. Rouse, C. B. Curley, and F. M. Sacks (1990), "Comparison of the effects of oat bran and low-fiber wheat on serum lipoprotein levels and blood pressure," *New England Journal of Medicine*, **322**, pp. 147–152.

	Baseline	High Fiber (Oat Bran)	Low Fiber (Wheat Bran)
Mean	4.80	4.44	4.46
SD	0.80	0.73	0.64

Total Cholesterol (mmol/liter)

(a) Compute a 95% confidence interval for the difference between the mean cholesterol levels for high fiber and low fiber diets. Assume that the two samples are independent (with $n_1 = n_2 = 20$). What do you conclude about the difference between the high and low fiber diets?

(b) The samples are really matched, because each person received both the diets in two different periods. To analyze the data correctly, we need the sample standard deviation of the differences of the cholesterol levels of the 20 subjects. This standard deviation was $s_d = 0.40$. Recalculate the confidence interval. Compare the result with that obtained in (a) and comment.

(c) Calculate a 95% confidence interval to compare the cholesterol levels under high fiber diet with baseline measurements. Use $s_d = 0.40$.

(d) Summarize the results by stating whether high or low fiber diets reduce the cholesterol level and whether any additional benefit is derived from high vs. low fiber diet.

8.24 This exercise compares an independent samples design with a matched pairs design in terms of their statistical precisions. For the independent samples design, assume that X_1, $X_2, \ldots, X_n$ and $Y_1, Y_2, \ldots, Y_n$ are mutually independent random samples from $N(\mu_1, \sigma^2)$ and $N(\mu_2, \sigma^2)$ distributions, respectively. (Note that we are confining attention to the special case $\sigma_1^2 = \sigma_2^2 = \sigma^2$ and $n_1 = n_2 = n$.) For the matched pairs design, assume also that $\text{Corr}(X_i, Y_i) = \rho$ and let $D_i = X_i - Y_i$. To estimate $\mu_1 - \mu_2$, we use $\bar{X} - \bar{Y}$ for the independent samples design and $\bar{D} = \bar{X} - \bar{Y}$ for the matched pairs design; thus we use the same estimator for both designs.

(a) Show that the ratio of the variances of $\bar{X} - \bar{Y}$ for the two designs equals

$$\frac{\text{Var}_{\text{matched}}(\bar{X} - \bar{Y})}{\text{Var}_{\text{independent}}(\bar{X} - \bar{Y})} = 1 - \rho.$$

Hence the ratio of the margins of errors of the confidence intervals for $\mu_1 - \mu_2$ equals $\sqrt{1 - \rho}$, assuming σ^2 is known.

(b) Discuss in each of the following cases: $\rho < 0, = 0$, and > 0, how the matched pairs design compares with the independent samples design in terms of the precision. Give practical situations where matching would result in these values of ρ.

8.25 To compare salaries of people in two types of occupations, 72 advertisements in the newspaper *The Guardian* were sampled for (i) creative, media, and marketing occupations and (ii) occupations in education.[12]

(a) To investigate the salary distribution, examine the box plots in Figure 8.6 of salary and $\log_e(\text{salary})$ by occupation. Comment on the shapes of the distributions and outliers in each case. If a test of the means is planned, what are the advantages and disadvantages of using the raw data on salaries vs. log-transformed data?

---

[12] *The Guardian*, 6 April 1992. Reprinted in *Small Data Sets*, p. 317.

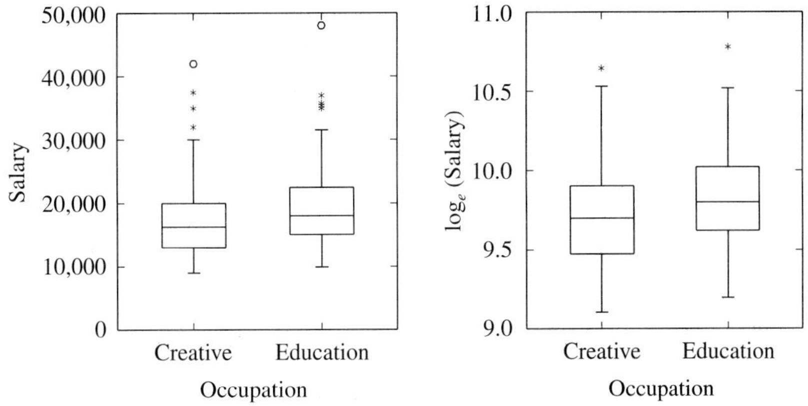

Figure 8.6   Box Plots of Salaries for Two Types of Occupations

(b) Set up and test hypotheses to determine if there is a statistically significant difference between the two occupational groups based on the actual data. Use the following summary statistics for salary. Interpret your findings.

Occupation Group	Sample Size	Sample Mean	Sample SD
Creative, media, marketing	72	17,410	6423
Education	72	19,817	7123

(c) Set up and test hypotheses to determine if there is a statistically significant difference between the two occupational groups based on the transformed data. Use the following summary statistics for $\log_e$(salary). Interpret your findings.

Occupation Group	Sample Size	Sample Mean	Sample SD
Creative, media, marketing	72	9.709	0.325
Education	72	9.840	0.325

(d) Compare the results from (b) and (c) and comment.

8.26 In this exercise we derive formulas to determine the sample sizes for testing $H_0: \mu_1 = \mu_2$ vs. $H_1: \mu_1 > \mu_2$ (the results are similar for lower one-sided and two-sided tests) when the samples are independently drawn from two normal populations, $N(\mu_1, \sigma_1^2)$ and $N(\mu_2, \sigma_2^2)$, and σ_1^2 and σ_2^2 are assumed known for design purposes. Let n_1 and n_2 be the sample sizes and $\bar{x}$ and $\bar{y}$ be the sample means. The α-level test of H_0 rejects if

$$z = \frac{\bar{x} - \bar{y}}{\sqrt{\sigma_1^2/n_1 + \sigma_2^2/n_2}} > z_\alpha.$$

(a) Show that the power of the α-level test as a function of $\mu_1 - \mu_2$ is given by

$$\pi(\mu_1 - \mu_2) = \Phi\left[-z_\alpha + \frac{\mu_1 - \mu_2}{\sqrt{\sigma_1^2/n_1 + \sigma_2^2/n_2}}\right].$$

(b) For detecting a specified difference, $\mu_1 - \mu_2 = \delta > 0$, show that for a fixed total sample size $n_1 + n_2 = N$, the power is maximized when

$$n_1 = \frac{\sigma_1}{\sigma_1 + \sigma_2} N \quad \text{and} \quad n_2 = \frac{\sigma_2}{\sigma_1 + \sigma_2} N$$

i.e., the optimum values of the n_i are proportional to the σ_i (ignoring the integer restrictions on the n_i).

(c) Show that the smallest total sample size N required to guarantee at least $1 - \beta$ power when $\mu_1 - \mu_2 = \delta > 0$ is given by

$$N = \left[\frac{(z_\alpha + z_\beta)(\sigma_1 + \sigma_2)}{\delta} \right]^2.$$

(d) Calculate the sample sizes n_1 and n_2 for $\alpha = .05$, $\beta = .10$, $\delta = 2.0$, $\sigma_1 = 2.0$, $\sigma_2 = 4.0$. Note that you must round n_1 and n_2 up to the nearest integers.

8.27 Consider the setting of Section 8.4. Derive an expression in terms of the F-distribution for the power of an α-level test of $H_0: \sigma_1^2 = \sigma_2^2$ vs. $H_1: \sigma_1^2 > \sigma_2^2$ when $\sigma_1^2 = c^2 \sigma_2^2$ for $c > 1$. Find the power for $\alpha = .05$, $n_1 = n_2 = 16$, and $c = 2.40$. (*Hint:* Recall from (5.18) that $f_{v_1, v_2, 1-\alpha} = 1/f_{v_2, v_1, \alpha}$.)

CHAPTER 9

INFERENCES FOR PROPORTIONS AND COUNT DATA

As we have seen in Chapter 4, tables of counts are quite common in practice. The simplest example of count or frequency data arises when we have a single categorical variable with two outcomes, generically labeled as a "success" and a "failure." Each sample observation is regarded as an independent and identically distributed (i.i.d.) Bernoulli trial, which leads to the assumption that the number of successes follows a binomial distribution. The parameter of interest is the success probability (population proportion) of the binomial distribution, which is estimated by the sample proportion of successes. Inferences for a single proportion are discussed in Section 9.1; those for comparing two proportions are discussed in Section 9.2.

Count data for more than two outcomes arise in a variety of situations. One-way count data can be modeled by a multinomial distribution. Inferences for multinomial data are discussed in Section 9.3. Two-way count data result when sample units are cross-classified according to two categorical variables. For example, consider the income–job satisfaction data in Chapter 4, Table 4.7. Inferences for two-way count data are also based on the multinomial model; they are discussed in Section 9.4.

9.1 INFERENCES ON PROPORTION

9.1.1 Large Sample Confidence Interval for Proportion

Binary data indicating the presence or absence of a specific attribute are often modeled as a random sample from a Bernoulli distribution with parameter p, where p is the proportion in the population with that attribute. In this section we study how to calculate a confidence interval (CI) for p and determine the sample size necessary to obtain a CI with a preassigned margin of error.

Consider a large population in which an unknown proportion p of the units have a specific attribute. A random sample, $X_1, X_2, \ldots, X_n$, is drawn from this population, where $X_i = 1$ if the attribute is present ("success") and 0 if the attribute is absent ("failure") for the ith unit in the sample. We assume that the X_i's are i.i.d. with $P(X_i = 1) = p$ and $P(X_i = 0) = 1 - p$. Let $Y = \sum_{i=1}^{n} X_i$ be the sample total; then Y has a binomial distribution with sample size n and success probability p (abbreviated as $Y \sim \text{Bin}(n, p)$).

The sample proportion

$$\hat{p} = \frac{Y}{n} = \frac{\sum_{i=1}^{n} X_i}{n}$$

is an unbiased estimator of p. From Chapter 5, Section 5.1.2, we know that by applying the central limit theorem (CLT), $\hat{p}$ is approximately $N(p, pq/n)$ distributed for large n, where $q = 1 - p$. The guideline for treating n as large is

$$n\hat{p} \geq 10 \text{ and } n(1 - \hat{p}) \geq 10.$$

We can estimate $\text{Var}(\hat{p})$ by $\hat{p}\hat{q}/n$. Using the results on large sample CI's for the mean of a population (here p is the mean of the Bernoulli population) from Chapter 7, Section 7.1.1, it follows that an approximate $(1 - \alpha)$-level CI for p is

$$\hat{p} - z_{\alpha/2}\sqrt{\frac{\hat{p}\hat{q}}{n}} \leq p \leq \hat{p} + z_{\alpha/2}\sqrt{\frac{\hat{p}\hat{q}}{n}}. \tag{9.1}$$

A more accurate CI for p can be obtained by using

$$\frac{(\hat{p} - p)}{\sqrt{pq/n}} \approx N(0, 1). \tag{9.2}$$

as a pivotal random variable (r.v.). We can write the probability statement

$$P\left[-z_{\alpha/2} \leq \frac{(\hat{p} - p)}{\sqrt{pq/n}} \leq z_{\alpha/2}\right] \simeq 1 - \alpha.$$

The CI is comprised of the values of p which satisfy this equation. This CI is a bit complicated to compute because the unknown parameter p appears in the numerator as well as the denominator of the pivotal r.v. (9.2). Exercise 9.39 shows how to find the interval of values of p which satisfies the inequality in the above probability statement. This interval is

$$\frac{\hat{p} + \frac{z^2}{2n} - \sqrt{\frac{\hat{p}\hat{q}z^2}{n} + \frac{z^4}{4n^2}}}{\left(1 + \frac{z^2}{n}\right)} \leq p \leq \frac{\hat{p} + \frac{z^2}{2n} + \sqrt{\frac{\hat{p}\hat{q}z^2}{n} + \frac{z^4}{4n^2}}}{\left(1 + \frac{z^2}{n}\right)} \tag{9.3}$$

where $z = z_{\alpha/2}$.

For small n, the formula (9.3) gives a more accurate answer than (9.1) at the cost of some extra computation. For large n, the two formulas give nearly the same CI for p as the following example illustrates. We will use the simpler formula (9.1) in most cases.

EXAMPLE 9.1

Time magazine reported[1] a telephone poll survey of 800 adults, of whom 45% stated that they had guns in their homes. The margin of error for this sample estimate was reported as 3.5%. This means that a 95% CI for the proportion p of homes in the population that have guns is $45\% \pm 3.5\% = [41.5\%, 48.5\%]$. Verify the calculation of this CI.

Here $\hat{p} = 0.45, \hat{q} = 0.55, n = 800, z_{\alpha/2} = z_{.025} = 1.960$. Substituting these values in (9.1) yields

$$\left[0.45 \pm 1.960\sqrt{\frac{(0.45)(0.55)}{800}} \right] = [0.415, 0.485]$$

which is the desired CI with a margin of error of 3.5%.

The 95% confidence limits using (9.3) can be calculated as follows:

$$\text{Lower limit} = \frac{0.45 + \frac{(1.96)^2}{1600} - \sqrt{\frac{(0.45)(0.55)(1.96)^2}{800} + \frac{1}{4}\left(\frac{(1.96)^2}{800}\right)^2}}{1 + \frac{(1.96)^2}{800}} = 0.416.$$

$$\text{Upper limit} = \frac{0.45 + \frac{(1.96)^2}{1600} + \sqrt{\frac{(0.45)(0.55)(1.96)^2}{800} + \frac{1}{4}\left(\frac{(1.96)^2}{800}\right)^2}}{1 + \frac{(1.96)^2}{800}} = 0.485.$$

These limits are almost the same as the approximate limits.   ◆

One-sided CI's can be obtained in a similar manner. They are as follows:

$$p \geq \hat{p} - z_\alpha \sqrt{\frac{\hat{p}\hat{q}}{n}} \quad \text{(Lower One-Sided CI)}$$

and

$$p \leq \hat{p} + z_\alpha \sqrt{\frac{\hat{p}\hat{q}}{n}} \quad \text{(Upper One-Sided CI)}.$$

Sample Size Determination for a Confidence Interval on Proportion.   Suppose that we want to estimate p by a $(1 - \alpha)$-level two-sided CI with a specified margin of error E. To determine the necessary sample size, we note that the CI for p in (9.1) is of the form $\hat{p} \pm E$, where the margin of error is

$$E = z_{\alpha/2} \sqrt{\frac{\hat{p}\hat{q}}{n}}.$$

Solving this equation for n gives

$$n = \left(\frac{z_{\alpha/2}}{E}\right)^2 \hat{p}\hat{q}.$$

---

[1] *Time*, March 29, 1993, p. 30.

However, this expresses n in terms of $\hat{p}$, which is unknown at the design stage (when the data are yet to be collected). If a prior guess p^* for the proportion p is available, then the necessary sample size can be computed using

$$n = \left(\frac{z_{\alpha/2}}{E}\right)^2 p^* q^* \qquad (9.4)$$

where $q^* = 1 - p^*$. If a reasonable prior guess p^* is not available, a conservative upper bound on the required sample size can be obtained by setting $p^* = q^* = 1/2$, which maximizes the product $p^* q^*$ and hence the required sample size. This maximum sample size is

$$n = \left(\frac{z_{\alpha/2}}{E}\right)^2 \frac{1}{4}. \qquad (9.5)$$

Note that $p^* q^*$ viewed as a function of p^* is quite flat around $p^* = 1/2$; e.g., $p^* q^* = 0.25$ for $p^* = 1/2$, while $p^* q^* = 0.24$ for $p^* = 0.6$ or 0.4. Therefore the above upper bound is not too conservative, unless the correct p^* is close to 0 or 1.

EXAMPLE 9.2

Suppose that a nationwide survey is planned to estimate the proportion p of people who have a favorable approval rating of the President. This proportion is to be estimated within a margin of error of three percentage points, using a 95% CI. What sample size should be planned for the survey?

If reliable information is not available to make a prior guess p^*, then, using (9.5), the required sample size is

$$n = \left(\frac{1.96}{0.03}\right)^2 \frac{1}{4} = 1067.11 \quad \text{or} \quad 1068.$$

If a prior guess $p^* = 0.65$ is available from the previous survey, then, using (9.4), the required sample size is

$$n = \left(\frac{1.96}{0.03}\right)^2 (0.65)(0.35) = 971.07 \quad \text{or} \quad 972.$$

Note from formula (9.5) that the sample size varies inversely with the square of the margin of error E. Thus if E is specified to be 1%, then the sample size would increase ninefold to $n = 9604$. Many nationwide surveys use sample sizes in the range of 1000 to 10,000, which roughly correspond to a margin of error between 3% to 1%, respectively, for a 95% CI.   ◆

9.1.2 Large Sample Hypothesis Tests on Proportion

In this section we present approximate large sample tests on the proportion p for a Bernoulli population. Analogous to approximate large sample CI's of the previous section, these tests are based on the asymptotic normality of $\hat{p}$. Exact small sample tests on p are presented in the following section.

First consider the two-sided testing problem, $H_0: p = p_0$ vs. $H_1: p \neq p_0$, where p_0 is specified. For example, a control chart (called the **p-chart**) used to monitor the proportion of defective items produced by a manufacturing process essentially tests whether the current defective rate p has shifted from the historical defective rate p_0.

When H_0 is true,

$$\hat{p} \approx N\left(p_0, \frac{p_0 q_0}{n}\right) \quad \text{or} \quad Y = n\hat{p} \approx N(np_0, np_0 q_0)$$

for large n; here $q_0 = 1 - p_0$. Therefore the test can be based on the standardized statistic:

$$z = \frac{\hat{p} - p_0}{\sqrt{p_0 q_0/n}} = \frac{y - np_0}{\sqrt{np_0 q_0}}. \tag{9.6}$$

The r.v. Z corresponding to this z-statistic is approximately $N(0, 1)$ under H_0. An α-level test of H_0 is:

$$\text{Reject } H_0 \text{ if } |z| > z_{\alpha/2} \quad \text{or equivalently if} \quad |\hat{p} - p_0| > z_{\alpha/2}\sqrt{\frac{p_0 q_0}{n}}.$$

Note that this test uses $\sqrt{p_0 q_0/n}$ for the standard error of $\hat{p}$ and not $\sqrt{\hat{p}\hat{q}/n}$ used in the formula (9.1) for the CI. As a result, the dual relationship between CI's and hypothesis tests discussed in Section 6.3.8 does not hold here. However, if we use the test statistic

$$z = \frac{\hat{p} - p_0}{\sqrt{\hat{p}\hat{q}/n}} = \frac{y - np_0}{\sqrt{n\hat{p}\hat{q}}} \tag{9.7}$$

then the α-level two-sided z-test of H_0: $p = p_0$ is equivalent to rejecting H_0 when p_0 falls outside the $(1-\alpha)$-level CI (9.1). Both statistics (9.6) and (9.7) are asymptotically standard normal when H_0 is true and either statistic may be used, although (9.6) is more common.

Tests for one-sided testing problems can be derived analogously. Once the z-statistic is calculated, the usual formulas for the z-test can be applied. These tests are summarized in Table 9.1.

EXAMPLE 9.3

A professional basketball player has been a 70% free throw shooter (i.e., he has a long run average of making 70% of the attempted free throws). In the current season he made 300 of the 400 (75%) attempted free throws. Has his free throw percentage really improved, or can this increase be attributed to chance?

We view the 400 free throws as a random sample of i.i.d. Bernoulli trials with success probability p, which is the player's "true" shooting percentage. The hypotheses are formulated as H_0: $p = 0.70$ (the player's true free throw shooting percentage has stayed the same) vs. H_1: $p > 0.70$ (the player's true free throw shooting percentage has improved). The z-statistic for testing H_0 is

$$z = \frac{0.75 - 0.70}{\sqrt{(0.70)(0.30)/400}} = \frac{300 - (400)(0.70)}{\sqrt{400(0.70)(0.30)}} = 2.182.$$

Thus his observed free throw shooting percentage this season is 2.182 standard deviations higher than his past percentage. The chance that an improvement this large or larger will be observed even if the true percentage for the current season had stayed the same (= 0.70) is given by the P-value $= 1 - \Phi(2.182) = 0.015$. This probability is small enough ($< \alpha = 0.05$ but

Table 9.1 Level α Tests on a Proportion (Test Statistic: $z = \frac{\hat{p} - p_0}{\sqrt{p_0 q_0 / n}} = \frac{y - np_0}{\sqrt{np_0 q_0}}$)

Testing Problem	Hypotheses	Reject H_0 if	Power Function $\pi(p)$
Upper One-Sided	$H_0: p \le p_0$ vs. $H_1: p > p_0$	$z > z_\alpha$ $\Longleftrightarrow$ $\hat{p} > p_0 + z_\alpha \sqrt{\frac{p_0 q_0}{n}}$	$\Phi \left[\frac{(p - p_0)\sqrt{n} - z_\alpha \sqrt{p_0 q_0}}{\sqrt{pq}} \right]$
Lower One-Sided	$H_0: p \ge p_0$ vs. $H_1: p < p_0$	$z < -z_\alpha$ $\Longleftrightarrow$ $\hat{p} < p_0 - z_\alpha \sqrt{\frac{p_0 q_0}{n}}$	$\Phi \left[\frac{(p_0 - p)\sqrt{n} - z_\alpha \sqrt{p_0 q_0}}{\sqrt{pq}} \right]$
Two-Sided	$H_0: p = p_0$ vs. $H_1: p \ne p_0$	$\|z\| > z_{\alpha/2}$ $\Longleftrightarrow$ $\|\hat{p} - p_0\| > z_{\alpha/2} \sqrt{\frac{p_0 q_0}{n}}$	$\Phi \left[\frac{(p - p_0)\sqrt{n} - z_{\alpha/2} \sqrt{p_0 q_0}}{\sqrt{pq}} \right]$ $+$ $\Phi \left[\frac{(p_0 - p)\sqrt{n} - z_{\alpha/2} \sqrt{p_0 q_0}}{\sqrt{pq}} \right]$

not $< \alpha = 0.01$) to conclude that the improved free throw shooting percentage this season is probably real and not attributable to chance. $\blacklozenge$

*Power Calculation and Sample Size Determination for Large Sample Tests on Proportion.   The formulas for the power and sample size can be derived in an analogous manner to those for the z-test of the mean of a normal population. Consider the upper one-sided testing problem, $H_0: p \le p_0$ vs. $H_1: p > p_0$. The r.v. Z corresponding to the test statistic (9.6) is approximately $N(0, 1)$ for large n when H_0 holds. If the true proportion p is not equal to p_0, then the mean and variance of Z change to the following:

$$E(Z) = \frac{(p - p_0)\sqrt{n}}{\sqrt{p_0 q_0}} \quad \text{and} \quad \text{Var}(Z) = \frac{pq}{p_0 q_0}.$$

Using these formulas, we can derive an expression for power as follows:

$$\pi(p) = P\{Z > z_\alpha \mid p\}$$

$$= P\left\{ \frac{Z - E(Z)}{\sqrt{\text{Var}(Z)}} > \frac{(p_0 - p)\sqrt{n}}{\sqrt{pq}} + z_\alpha \sqrt{\frac{p_0 q_0}{pq}} \,\Big|\, p \right\}$$

$$= 1 - \Phi \left[\frac{(p_0 - p)\sqrt{n} + z_\alpha \sqrt{p_0 q_0}}{\sqrt{pq}} \right]$$

$$= \Phi\left[\frac{(p - p_0)\sqrt{n} - z_\alpha\sqrt{p_0 q_0}}{\sqrt{pq}}\right].$$ (9.8)

The power expressions for the lower one-sided and two-sided tests can be derived similarly. They are summarized in Table 9.1. If the test statistic (9.7) is used instead of (9.6), then the corresponding power expressions are obtained by replacing $\sqrt{p_0 q_0}$ by $\sqrt{pq}$.

By using (9.8) we can determine the minimum sample size necessary to guarantee a specified power requirement. Suppose that the power for rejecting H_0 must be at least $1 - \beta$ when the true proportion $p = p_1 > p_0$. Let $\delta = p_1 - p_0$. To find the necessary sample size, equate

$$\pi(p_1) = \Phi\left[\frac{(p_1 - p_0)\sqrt{n}}{\sqrt{p_1 q_1}} - z_\alpha\sqrt{\frac{p_0 q_0}{p_1 q_1}}\right] = 1 - \beta.$$

Using the fact that $\Phi(z_\beta) = 1 - \beta$ and solving for n gives the formula:

$$n = \left[\frac{z_\alpha\sqrt{p_0 q_0} + z_\beta\sqrt{p_1 q_1}}{\delta}\right]^2.$$ (9.9)

The sample size formula for the lower one-sided test is the same. The formula for the two-sided test is obtained by replacing z_α by $z_{\alpha/2}$. If the test statistic (9.7) is used instead of (9.6), then the corresponding sample size formulas are obtained by replacing $\sqrt{p_0 q_0}$ by $\sqrt{p_1 q_1}$.

EXAMPLE 9.4 (PIZZA TASTING: POWER CALCULATION AND SAMPLE SIZE DETERMINATION)

A frozen pizza maker wants to conduct a taste-testing experiment to find out which of the two preparations of pizza sauce, A or B, is preferred by more people. A panel of 100 expert tasters will judge the sauces. Each taster will taste a piece of pizza made using each sauce (the tasters will be blinded as to the sauce they are tasting) in a random order and indicate the preference. Let p be the true fraction in the population that prefers A and $1 - p$ be the fraction that prefers B. Since a priori it is not known whether A or B is more preferred, the hypotheses are set up in a two-sided manner, $H_0: p = 0.5$ (equal preference) vs. $H_1: p \neq 0.5$ (unequal preference). If H_0 is rejected, then the sauce preferred by more tasters will be chosen. What is the power of the 0.10-level test if the true p differs from 0.5 by 0.1 in either direction? How many expert tasters are needed if the power must be at least 0.75?

The two-sided 0.10-level test rejects H_0 if

$$|z| = \frac{|\hat{p} - 0.5|\sqrt{100}}{\sqrt{(0.5)(0.5)}} = \frac{|y - 100(0.5)|}{\sqrt{100(0.5)(0.5)}} > z_{.05} = 1.645$$

where $\hat{p}$ is the sample proportion of tasters and y is the observed number of tasters out of 100 who prefer A. This test is equivalent to rejecting H_0 when $y \geq 59$ or $y \leq 41$. The power of this test when the true $p = 0.6$ is obtained from the formula given in Table 9.1:

$$\pi(0.6) = \Phi\left[\frac{(0.6 - 0.5)\sqrt{100} - 1.645\sqrt{(0.5)(0.5)}}{\sqrt{(0.6)(0.4)}}\right]$$

$$+ \Phi\left[\frac{(0.5 - 0.6)\sqrt{100} - 1.645\sqrt{(0.5)(0.5)}}{\sqrt{(0.6)(0.4)}}\right]$$

$$= \Phi(0.362) + \Phi(-3.720)$$

$$= 0.641 + 0.000 = 0.641.$$

Thus using 100 tasters provides 64.1% power to detect $p = 0.5 \pm 0.1$. The minimum sample size necessary to guarantee $1 - \beta = 0.75$ is found from (9.9) (with z_α replaced by $z_{\alpha/2} = z_{.05} = 1.645$ and $z_\beta = z_{0.25} = 0.675$):

$$n = \left[\frac{1.645\sqrt{(0.5)(0.5)} + 0.675\sqrt{(0.6)(0.4)}}{0.1}\right]^2 = 132.98 \quad \text{or} \quad 133.$$

So at least 133 tasters are needed.   ◆

9.1.3 *Small Sample Hypothesis Tests on Proportion

Large sample hypothesis tests on p are based on the asymptotic normal distribution of the sample proportion $\hat{p}$ or equivalently of $n\hat{p} = Y$, which is the sample sum. Exact small sample tests can be easily obtained by using the result that $Y \sim \text{Bin}(n, p)$. In fact, we used this test in Example 6.20 of Chapter 6.

   Consider the problem of testing $H_0: p \leq p_0$ vs. $H_1: p > p_0$. A test that rejects $H_0: p \leq p_0$ when the sample proportion $\hat{p}$ is large is equivalent to rejecting H_0 when Y is large. The P-value, which is the probability of getting a sample total Y at least as large as the observed value y when $p = p_0$ is true, is

$$P\text{-value} = P(Y \geq y \mid p = p_0) = \sum_{i=y}^{n} \binom{n}{i} p_0^i (1 - p_0)^{n-i} \quad \text{(Upper One-Sided)}.$$

Similar reasoning is used to obtain the P-value for the lower one-sided test of $H_0: p \geq p_0$ vs. $H_1: p < p_0$:

$$P\text{-value} = P(Y \leq y \mid p = p_0) = \sum_{i=0}^{y} \binom{n}{i} p_0^i (1 - p_0)^{n-i} \quad \text{(Lower One-Sided)}.$$

The P-value for the two-sided test of $H_0: p = p_0$ vs. $H_1: p \neq p_0$ is given by

$$P\text{-value} = 2 \min\left[P(Y \geq y \mid p = p_0), P(Y \leq y \mid p = p_0)\right] \quad \text{(Two-Sided)}.$$

   An α-level test is obtained by rejecting H_0 if the P-value $\leq \alpha$. These tests are *exact* because they are based on the exact binomial distribution of the test statistic Y. For large n, the tests discussed in the previous section provide a good approximation and are easier to apply. Examples of P-value calculations for small sample tests are given in Chapter 2, Example 2.30, and Chapter 6, Example 6.22.

9.2   INFERENCES FOR COMPARING TWO PROPORTIONS

In this section we consider the problem of comparing the proportions or rates in two populations with binary outcomes. For example, the Salk polio vaccine trial discussed in Chapter 6 compared the incidence rates of polio in the placebo and the vaccine groups using an independent samples design. A psychometric study that compares the proportions of subjects who respond under two different conditions is an example of a matched pairs design with a binary outcome (respond/do not respond).

9.2.1 Independent Samples Design

Consider two Bernoulli populations with parameters p_1 and p_2. Independent random samples of sizes n_1 and n_2 are available from these two populations. Let $X \sim \text{Bin}(n_1, p_1)$ and $Y \sim \text{Bin}(n_2, p_2)$ be the corresponding numbers of "successes." The problem is to compare p_1 and p_2 using a CI or a hypothesis test based on the observed data $X = x$ and $Y = y$. Different measures can be used to compare the success probabilities p_1 and p_2. The most common measure is the difference $p_1 - p_2$. Two other measures are p_1/p_2 (called the **relative risk**) and $\{p_1/(1 - p_1)\}/\{p_2/(1 - p_2)\}$ (called the **odds ratio**). In this section we use the difference measure. The odds ratio is discussed in Section 9.4.3.

Inferences for Large Samples.   Inference on $p_1 - p_2$ will be based on its sample estimate $\hat{p}_1 - \hat{p}_2$, where $\hat{p}_1 = x/n_1$ and $\hat{p}_2 = y/n_2$ are the sample proportions of successes. We will assume that n_1 and n_2 are large. As before, the guideline for this purpose is

$$n_1\hat{p}_1, n_1(1 - \hat{p}_1) \geq 10 \quad \text{and} \quad n_2\hat{p}_2, n_2(1 - \hat{p}_2) \geq 10.$$

We can then use the CLT to conclude that the r.v.'s $\hat{p}_1$ and $\hat{p}_2$ are approximately normally distributed with

$$E(\hat{p}_1) = p_1, \quad \text{Var}(\hat{p}_1) = \frac{p_1 q_1}{n_1}, \quad E(\hat{p}_2) = p_2, \quad \text{Var}(\hat{p}_2) = \frac{p_2 q_2}{n_2}$$

where $q_i = 1 - p_i$ $(i = 1, 2)$. It follows that $\hat{p}_1 - \hat{p}_2$ is approximately normally distributed with

$$E(\hat{p}_1 - \hat{p}_2) = E(\hat{p}_1) - E(\hat{p}_2) = p_1 - p_2,$$

and

$$\text{Var}(\hat{p}_1 - \hat{p}_2) = \text{Var}(\hat{p}_1) + \text{Var}(\hat{p}_2) = \frac{p_1 q_1}{n_1} + \frac{p_2 q_2}{n_2}.$$

An estimate of this variance is given by

$$\frac{\hat{p}_1 \hat{q}_1}{n_1} + \frac{\hat{p}_2 \hat{q}_2}{n_2}$$

where $\hat{q}_i = 1 - \hat{p}_i$ $(i = 1, 2)$. Thus, for large n_1, n_2,

$$Z = \frac{\hat{p}_1 - \hat{p}_2 - (p_1 - p_2)}{\sqrt{\frac{\hat{p}_1 \hat{q}_1}{n_1} + \frac{\hat{p}_2 \hat{q}_2}{n_2}}} \approx N(0, 1)$$

and can be used as a pivotal r.v.

Using this pivotal r.v., a large sample approximate $(1 - \alpha)$-level two-sided CI for $p_1 - p_2$ is:

$$\hat{p}_1 - \hat{p}_2 - z_{\alpha/2}\sqrt{\frac{\hat{p}_1\hat{q}_1}{n_1} + \frac{\hat{p}_2\hat{q}_2}{n_2}} \le p_1 - p_2 \le \hat{p}_1 - \hat{p}_2 + z_{\alpha/2}\sqrt{\frac{\hat{p}_1\hat{q}_1}{n_1} + \frac{\hat{p}_2\hat{q}_2}{n_2}}. \quad (9.10)$$

An α-level two-sided test of $H_0\colon p_1 - p_2 = \delta_0$ can be performed by rejecting H_0 if δ_0 falls outside this CI. Equivalently, a large sample z-test can be used to reject H_0 at level α if $|z| > z_{\alpha/2}$, where the test statistic is

$$z = \frac{\hat{p}_1 - \hat{p}_2 - \delta_0}{\sqrt{\frac{\hat{p}_1\hat{q}_1}{n_1} + \frac{\hat{p}_2\hat{q}_2}{n_2}}}. \quad (9.11)$$

The P-value is given by $2[1 - \Phi(|z|)]$. One-sided tests and CI's can be obtained in a similar manner.

Often, the null hypothesis to be tested is $H_0\colon p_1 = p_2$ (i.e., $\delta_0 = 0$). In that case, the following alternative test is generally used. If H_0 is true, then $\hat{p}_1$ and $\hat{p}_2$ both estimate the same true proportion, which we denote by p. A pooled estimate of p is given by

$$\hat{p} = \frac{n_1\hat{p}_1 + n_2\hat{p}_2}{n_1 + n_2} = \frac{x + y}{n_1 + n_2}$$

which is just the overall sample proportion of "successes." We can use $\hat{p}$ to estimate the variance of $\hat{p}_1 - \hat{p}_2$ resulting in an alternative test statistic

$$z = \frac{\hat{p}_1 - \hat{p}_2}{\sqrt{\hat{p}\hat{q}\left(\frac{1}{n_1} + \frac{1}{n_2}\right)}}. \quad (9.12)$$

When $H_0\colon p_1 = p_2$ is true, the distribution of the corresponding r.v. Z is also approximately $N(0, 1)$ in large samples. Therefore this test statistic can be used to perform the z-tests in the usual manner. However, the statistic (9.11) has certain advantages, such as its dual relation with the CI (9.10), ability to test for a nonzero $p_1 - p_2$ difference (i.e., $\delta_0 \neq 0$), and better power in many cases.[2] The following example illustrates both these tests.

---

[2] K. R. Eberhardt and M. A. Fligner (1977), "A comparison of two tests for equality of two proportions," *The American Statistician*, **31**, pp. 151–155.

EXAMPLE 9.5 (SALK POLIO VACCINE TRIAL)

In this trial there were 201,229 children in the placebo group and 200,745 children in the vaccine group. There were 142 new polio cases in the placebo group, which gives $\hat{p}_1 = \frac{142}{201,229} = 7.06 \times 10^{-4}$ or an incidence rate of 7.06 cases per 10,000 children. There were 57 new polio cases in the vaccine group, which gives $\hat{p}_2 = \frac{57}{200,745} = 2.84 \times 10^{-4}$ or an incidence rate of 2.84 cases per 10,000 children. Test H_0: $p_1 = p_2$ vs. H_1: $p_1 \neq p_2$ by computing a 95% CI for $p_1 - p_2$. Also assess the statistical significance of the observed difference $\hat{p}_1 - \hat{p}_2$.

The sample sizes in this example are obviously very large, so we can use the large sample methods given above. The estimated standard error of $(\hat{p}_1 - \hat{p}_2)$ is

$$\sqrt{\frac{7.06 \times 10^{-4}(1 - 7.06 \times 10^{-4})}{201,229} + \frac{2.84 \times 10^{-4}(1 - 2.84 \times 10^{-4})}{200,745}} = 0.69 \times 10^{-4}.$$

Therefore the 95% CI for $p_1 - p_2$ is

$$[7.06 - 2.84 \pm 1.960 \times 0.69] \times 10^{-4} = [2.85 \times 10^{-4}, 5.59 \times 10^{-4}].$$

This interval does not include the value $p_1 - p_2 = 0$, so H_0: $p_1 = p_2$ can be rejected at the .05 level.

To assess the statistical significance of the observed difference, we calculate the P-value. First consider the z-statistic (9.11):

$$z = \frac{7.06 \times 10^{-4} - 2.84 \times 10^{-4}}{\sqrt{\frac{7.06 \times 10^{-4}(1 - 7.06 \times 10^{-4})}{201,229} + \frac{2.84 \times 10^{-4}(1 - 2.84 \times 10^{-4})}{200,745}}} = 6.116$$

which is highly significant (P-value $< 10^{-6}$). Thus, there is a less than 1 in one million chance that $(\hat{p}_1 - \hat{p}_2)$ would be at least as large as $(7.06 - 2.84)10^{-4}$ if in fact the vaccine were actually ineffective.

Alternatively, we could compute the z-statistic using (9.12). We first calculate the pooled estimate of the common p:

$$\hat{p} = \frac{142 + 57}{201,229 + 200,745} = 4.95 \times 10^{-4}.$$

Then,

$$z = \frac{7.06 \times 10^{-4} - 2.84 \times 10^{-4}}{\sqrt{4.95 \times 10^{-4}(1 - 4.95 \times 10^{-4})(1/201,229 + 1/200,745)}} = 6.014$$

which gives essentially the same result as the previous calculation. ◆

EXAMPLE 9.6 (COMPARING TWO LEUKEMIA THERAPIES: z-TEST)

O'Brien and Fleming[3] give data for a randomized clinical trial for comparing Prednisone and Prednisone+VCR drug therapies for leukemia. The data are shown in Table 9.2. Test if the success and failure probabilities are the same for the two drugs.

---

[3] P. C. O'Brien and T. R. Fleming (1979), "A multiple testing procedure for clinical trials," *Biometrics*, **35**, pp. 549–556.

Table 9.2 Leukemia Trial Data

Drug Group	Success	Failure	Row Total
Prednisone	14	7	21
Prednisone+VCR	38	4	42
Column Total	52	11	63

The hypotheses are formulated as $H_0: p_1 = p_2$ vs. $H_1: p_1 \neq p_2$, where p_1 is the success probability of Prednisone and p_2 is the success probability of Prednisone+VCR. We will use the statistic (9.12). First calculate

$$\hat{p}_1 = \frac{14}{21} = 0.667, \hat{p}_2 = \frac{38}{42} = 0.905, \hat{p} = \frac{14 + 38}{21 + 42} = 0.825, \quad \text{and} \quad \hat{q} = 1 - 0.825 = 0.175.$$

Therefore

$$z = \frac{0.667 - 0.905}{\sqrt{(0.825)(0.175)\left(\frac{1}{21} + \frac{1}{42}\right)}} = -2.347.$$

The two-sided P-value of the z-test equals $2[1 - \Phi(2.347)] = 0.019$, which is significant at the .05 level but not at the .01 level.   ◆

*Inferences for Small Samples.   Approximate tests based on the asymptotic normality of $\hat{p}_1 - \hat{p}_2$ do not apply when small size samples are used to compare p_1 and p_2. However, the null hypothesis $H_0: p_1 = p_2$ can still be tested using **Fisher's exact test**.

Let $X \sim \text{Bin}(n_1, p_1)$ and $Y \sim \text{Bin}(n_2, p_2)$ be the numbers of successes from two independent Bernoulli samples, and let x and y be the corresponding observed values. Let $n = n_1 + n_2$ be the total sample size and $m = x + y$ be the total observed number of successes. Table 9.3 presents the data in the form of a 2×2 table.

Table 9.3 A 2×2 Table for Data from Two Independent Bernoulli Samples

	Outcome		Row
	Success	Failure	Total
Sample 1	x	$n_1 - x$	n_1
Sample 2	y	$n_2 - y$	n_2
Column Total	m	$n - m$	n

Fisher's exact test uses X, the number of successes from sample 1, as the test statistic. The test is derived by regarding the total number of successes m as *fixed*, i.e., by conditioning on $X + Y = m$. There are some theoretical reasons for this conditioning, which we do not wish to go into here, but one reason is mathematical convenience, since it gives a simple form for the exact null distribution of the test statistic X. This null distribution is the hypergeometric distribution (see Section 2.7.3), which is obtained as follows: When H_0 is true, the successes are equally likely from the two samples.

Therefore the probability that i successes come from sample 1 and the remaining $m - i$ successes come from sample 2 is given by

$$P\{X = i \mid X + Y = m\} = \frac{\binom{n_1}{i}\binom{n_2}{m-i}}{\binom{n}{m}}.$$

First consider the upper one-sided testing problem:

$$H_0: p_1 = p_2 \quad \text{vs.} \quad H_1: p_1 > p_2.$$

The P-value is the probability that at least x of the total m successes come from sample 1 when H_0 is true:

$$\text{Upper One-Sided } P\text{-value} = P_U = P(X \geq x \mid X + Y = m) = \sum_{i \geq x} \frac{\binom{n_1}{i}\binom{n_2}{m-i}}{\binom{n}{m}};$$

here the summation extends over $i = x, x + 1, \ldots$ to an upper limit which is either n_1 or m, whichever is smaller. For a lower one-sided alternative $H_1: p_1 < p_2$ the corresponding lower tail probability gives the P-value:

$$\text{Lower One-Sided } P\text{-value} = P_L = P(X \leq x \mid X + Y = m) = \sum_{i \leq x} \frac{\binom{n_1}{i}\binom{n_2}{m-i}}{\binom{n}{m}};$$

here the summation extends over $i = x, x - 1, \ldots$ to a lower limit which is either zero or $m - n_2$, whichever is larger. For a two-sided alternative $H_1: p_1 \neq p_2$,

$$\text{Two-sided } P\text{-value} = 2\min(P_L, P_U).$$

EXAMPLE 9.7

Table 9.4 gives data[4] concerning an age discrimination suit brought against Transco Services of Milwaukee. Test whether a significantly larger proportion of old employees were terminated compared to young employees.

Table 9.4 Age Discrimination Data

Age Group	No. Fired	No. Kept	Row Total
Young	1	24	25
Old	10	17	27
Column Total	11	41	52

Let p_1 be the probability that a young employee will be terminated, and let p_2 be the same probability for an old employee. We want to test

$$H_0: p_1 = p_2 \quad \text{vs.} \quad H_1: p_1 < p_2.$$

---

[4] *StatXact–3 for Windows User Manual* (1995), Cytel Software Corporation, Cambridge, MA, p. 434.

To apply Fisher's exact test, we condition on the total number of fired employees: $m = 1 + 10 = 11$. Therefore,

$$P\text{-value} = \sum_{i=0}^{1} \frac{\binom{25}{i}\binom{27}{11-i}}{\binom{52}{11}} = \frac{\binom{25}{0}\binom{27}{11}}{\binom{52}{11}} + \frac{\binom{25}{1}\binom{27}{10}}{\binom{52}{11}}.$$

The hypergeometric probabilities are not easy to compute by hand, but Fisher's exact test is available in many statistical packages. Using SYSTAT, we obtain the P-value = .005. Thus significantly more old employees were terminated than young employees. ◆

EXAMPLE 9.8 (COMPARING TWO LEUKEMIA THERAPIES: FISHER'S EXACT TEST)

Perform Fisher's exact test on the leukemia data in Table 9.2 to determine if there is a significant difference between Prednisone and Prednisone+VCR drug therapies.

Here $n_1 = 21, n_2 = 42, n = 21 + 42 = 63, m = 52$, and $x = 14$. The lower one-sided P-value is given by

$$P_L = P(X \le 14 | X + Y = 52) = \sum_{i=10}^{14} \frac{\binom{21}{i}\binom{42}{52-i}}{\binom{63}{52}}$$

where the lower limit in the summation equals $\max(0, 52 - 42) = 10$. Using SYSTAT, we obtain the P-value = .016. The upper one-sided P-value is clearly larger. Therefore the two-sided P-value is $2(.016) = .032$. So the difference is significant at the .05 level but not at the .01 level.

Note that this P-value is substantially larger than the P-value = .019 calculated in Example 9.6 for the large sample approximate test. This generally holds true; i.e., Fisher's exact test gives a less significant result than does the large sample test for the same data. ◆

9.2.2 *Matched Pairs Design

A matched pairs design with binary outcomes is illustrated by a psychometric study to determine how people respond under two different conditions. For each person we have four possible outcomes, depending on whether the person does or does not respond under each of the two conditions. The data from such a study can be presented in the form of a 2×2 table as shown in Table 9.5, where a, b, c, d are the observed counts of (Yes, Yes), (Yes, No), (No, Yes), (No, No) responses, respectively, and $a+b+c+d = n$ is the total sample size.

Table 9.5 A 2×2 Table for Data from Two Matched Pairs Bernoulli Samples

		Condition 2 Response	
		Yes	No
Condition 1	Yes	a	b
Response	No	c	d

Denote by A, B, C, D the r.v.'s corresponding to the observed counts a, b, c, d with $A + B + C + D = n$ and the probabilities of the four possible outcomes on a single trial by p_A, p_B, p_C, p_D with $p_A + p_B + p_C + p_D = 1$. Then A, B, C, D have a multinomial distribution with sample size $= n$ and the given outcome probabilities. The response (success) probability under condition 1 is $p_1 = p_A + p_B$ and under condition 2 is $p_2 = p_A + p_C$.

Note that $p_1 - p_2 = p_B - p_C$, irrespective of p_A and p_D. Therefore only the untied responses, (Yes, No) and (No, Yes), are useful for testing the difference between p_1 and p_2.[5]

Consider $H_0: p_1 = p_2$ (no difference between the response probabilities under the two conditions), which is equivalent to $H_0: p_B = p_C$. Suppose that the number of untied responses is $b + c = m$. By conditioning on $B + C = m$, we can use B as the test statistic. It is easy to show that

$$B \sim \text{Bin}\left(m, p = \frac{p_B}{p_B + p_C}\right).$$

Also, $H_0: p_B = p_C$ becomes $H_0: p = \frac{1}{2}$, which can be tested by using this binomial distribution. The resulting test is called **McNemar's test**.

Consider the upper one-sided testing problem:

$$H_0: p = \frac{1}{2} \quad \text{vs.} \quad H_1: p > \frac{1}{2}.$$

The P-value corresponding to the observed test statistic b is given by

$$P\text{-value} = P(B \geq b \mid B + C = m) = \left(\frac{1}{2}\right)^m \sum_{i=b}^{m} \binom{m}{i}.$$

If m is large, then the large sample z-statistic given in (9.6) (with $p_0 = \frac{1}{2}$) with a continuity correction (discussed in Section 5.1.3) can be applied by calculating

$$z = \frac{b - mp_0 - \frac{1}{2}}{\sqrt{mp_0(1 - p_0)}} = \frac{b - \frac{m}{2} - \frac{1}{2}}{\sqrt{\frac{m}{4}}} = \frac{b - c - 1}{\sqrt{b + c}}$$

and finding the upper one-sided P-value $= 1 - \Phi(z)$. The lower one-sided P-value can be similarly computed using either the exact binomial distribution or the normal approximation to it when m is large. The two-sided P-value is given by $2\min(P_L, P_U)$, where P_L and P_U are the lower and upper one-sided P-values.

EXAMPLE 9.9

A preference poll of a panel of 75 voters was conducted before and after a TV debate during the campaign for the 1980 Presidential election between Jimmy Carter and Ronald Reagan. The resulting data are shown in Table 9.6.[6] Test whether there was a significant shift away from Carter as a result of the TV debate.

---

[5] However, the tied responses contain information concerning similarity of the two conditions. For example, the occurrence of many tied responses suggests that the conditions are similar.

[6] S. Siegel and N. J. Castellan (1988), *Nonparametric Statistics for the Behavioral Sciences*, 2nd ed., New York: McGraw-Hill.

Table 9.6 Preference for Presidential Candidates

Preference Before TV Debate	Preference After TV Debate	
	Carter	Reagan
Carter	28	13
Reagan	7	27

The same persons are surveyed before and after the TV debate, so this is a matched pairs design with binary outcomes (prefer Carter or prefer Reagan). Let p_1 and p_2 be the population proportions favoring Carter before and after the TV debate, respectively. We want to test

$$H_0: p_1 = p_2 \quad \text{vs.} \quad H_1: p_1 > p_2.$$

Of the 75 respondents, only the 20 who switched their preference after the TV debate can be used to test this hypothesis. Of these 20 respondents, 13 switched from Carter to Reagan while 7 switched from Reagan to Carter. Therefore the one-sided P-value is given by

$$P\text{-value} = \left(\frac{1}{2}\right)^{20} \sum_{i=13}^{20} \binom{20}{i} = 0.132.$$

This is a rather large P-value, indicating that there is not a significant shift (cannot reject H_0 in favor of H_1).

The large sample z-test can be carried out as follows: Calculate

$$z = \frac{13 - \frac{20}{2} - \frac{1}{2}}{\sqrt{\frac{20}{4}}} = 1.118.$$

Therefore the large sample one-sided P-value $= 1 - \Phi(1.118) = 0.132$, which is the same as the exact P-value obtained above. ◆

9.3   INFERENCES FOR ONE-WAY COUNT DATA

9.3.1 A Test for the Multinomial Distribution

The multinomial distribution introduced in Chapter 2, Section 2.7.6, is a generalization of the binomial distribution when the outcome of each trial can be from one of $c \geq 2$ categories (called **cells**). The trials are assumed to be independent and identically distributed (i.i.d.). The number of trials, n, is fixed. Denote the **cell probabilities** by $p_1, p_2, \ldots, p_c$, the observed **cell counts** by $n_1, n_2, \ldots, n_c$, and the corresponding r.v.'s by $N_1, N_2, \ldots, N_c$ with $\sum_{i=1}^{c} p_i = 1$ and $\sum_{i=1}^{c} n_i = \sum_{i=1}^{c} N_i = n$. The joint distribution of the N_i then is the multinomial distribution given by

$$P\{N_1 = n_1, N_2 = n_2, \ldots, N_c = n_c\} = \frac{n!}{n_1! n_2! \cdots n_c!} p_1^{n_1} p_2^{n_2} \cdots p_c^{n_c}.$$

We consider the problem of testing

$$H_0: p_1 = p_{10}, p_2 = p_{20}, \ldots, p_c = p_{c0} \quad \text{vs.} \quad H_1: \text{At least one } p_i \neq p_{i0} \quad (9.13)$$

where the p_{i0} are specified and sum to 1. For example, consider a market survey of n people to find out what proportions use different detergents. Suppose there are $c \geq 2$ detergents. Let $p_1, p_2, \ldots, p_c$ be the unknown population proportions who use these detergents (current market shares), and let $n_1, n_2, \ldots, n_c$ be the corresponding numbers in the sample. Suppose the p_{i0} are the past market shares of the detergents. Then the hypotheses are set up to test whether the current market shares differ from the past.

To test H_0 we construct a test statistic as follows: Calculate the expected cell counts e_i assuming that H_0 is true, using

$$e_i = n p_{i0} \quad (i = 1, 2, \ldots, c).$$

Next calculate a measure of discrepancy (denoted by χ^2) between the observed cell counts and the expected cell counts under H_0 using

$$\chi^2 = \sum_{i=1}^{c} \frac{(n_i - e_i)^2}{e_i}. \tag{9.14}$$

It can be shown that when H_0 is true, the large sample (as $n \to \infty$) distribution of the r.v. corresponding to (9.14) is chi-square with $c - 1$ degrees of freedom (d.f.). Therefore H_0 can be rejected at level α if

$$\chi^2 > \chi^2_{c-1,\alpha}$$

where $\chi^2_{c-1,\alpha}$ is the upper α critical point of the χ^2-distribution with $c - 1$ d.f. Alternatively, the P-value can be computed by finding the upper tail area under the χ^2_{c-1}-distribution to the right of the observed χ^2 value. The d.f. for χ^2 are $c - 1$ because the c parameters, $p_1, \ldots, p_c$, under test are subject to one constraint—that they add up to 1; thus there are only $c - 1$ independent parameters.

When $c = 2$, the multinomial distribution reduces to the binomial distribution. In that case the χ^2 test of $H_0: p_1 = p_{10}, p_2 = p_{20}$, where $p_{20} = 1 - p_{10}$, can be shown to be identical to the two-sided z-test of a binomial proportion discussed in Section 9.1.2 based on the z-statistic (9.6); see Exercise 9.43.

A comment about the notation is in order. First, χ^2 without any subscripts denotes the observed value of the test statistic (9.14). Second, χ^2_{c-1} denotes a chi-square r.v. with $c - 1$ d.f. Third, $\chi^2_{c-1,\alpha}$ denotes the upper α critical point of the chi-square distribution with $c - 1$ d.f.

EXAMPLE 9.10   (TESTING THE UNIFORMITY OF RANDOM DIGITS)

Algorithms are used in computers to generate random digits. Many tests are available to test for randomness of the digits, e.g., no systematic runs or cyclic patterns. We consider a very simple test that checks whether all 10 digits occur with equal probability. This is equivalent to checking whether the digits follow a uniform distribution on the integers $0, 1, \ldots, 9$. The following counts are observed from 100 successive random digits:

Digit	0	1	2	3	4	5	6	7	8	9
Observed Count	12	7	12	7	13	13	7	13	6	10

Test, using $\alpha = .10$, whether these counts are in agreement with the uniform distribution model.
Denote by p_i the probability of occurrence of digit i $(i = 0, 1, \ldots, 9)$. The null hypothesis corresponding to the uniform distribution model is

$$H_0: p_0 = p_1 = \cdots = p_9 = \frac{1}{10}.$$

The expected counts under H_0 are

$$e_i = 100 \times \frac{1}{10} = 10 \quad \text{for all } i.$$

The χ^2-statistic equals

$$\chi^2 = \frac{(12 - 10)^2}{10} + \frac{(7 - 10)^2}{10} + \cdots + \frac{(10 - 10)^2}{10} = 7.40$$

which is compared with the chi-square distribution with $10 - 1 = 9$ d.f. The upper 10% critical point of this distribution is $\chi^2_{9,.10} = 14.684$. Since the observed $\chi^2 = 7.40 < 14.684$, we cannot reject H_0 at $\alpha = 0.10$; in fact, the P-value is 0.596. Thus the observed digit counts exhibit no significant deviation from the uniform distribution model; any deviations (e.g., only 6 occurrences of digit 8 compared to 10 expected occurrences) can be attributed to chance. We say that the uniform distribution fits the data well. Even though this is true, there are numerous other ways in which the digits can be nonrandom. Can you think of some ways which the above test will not detect? ◆

EXAMPLE 9.11   (MENDEL'S GENETIC EXPERIMENTS USING GARDEN PEAS)

Gregor Mendel (1822–1884) was an Austrian monk whose genetic theory is one of the greatest scientific discoveries of all time. Based on the experiments done using garden pea plants, he proposed a genetic model that explains the occurrence of hereditary characteristics. In particular, he studied how the shape (smooth or wrinkled) and color (yellow or green) of pea seeds are transmitted through generations. He postulated that there is a shape *allele* which has two forms, S and W. The actual expressed shape, the *phenotype*, is determined by a pair of alleles (SS, SW, WS, or SS) called a *genotype*. The S form is *dominant*; therefore a smooth pea results when the genotype is SS, SW, or WS. The W form is *recessive* and governs the shape only if it is paired with another recessive W allele. Therefore a wrinkled pea results only when the genotype is WW. Similarly, the color allele has two forms, Y and G. The Y form is dominant and G is recessive. Therefore the genotypes YY, YG, and GY result in yellow color, while the genotype GG results in green color. When pollen from one plant fertilizes ovules on another plant, each plant contributes one allele at random (each with probability 1/2) for each trait, forming independent pairs.

Mendel bred a pure smooth-yellow strain with SS and YY genotypes and a pure wrinkled-green strain with WW and GG genotypes. When these two strains were crossed, the first generation (hybrid) seeds were all smooth-yellow (since they only had SW and YG genotypes); wrinkled-green seeds were totally absent. When the first generation plants were crossed with each other, both the wrinkled shape and green color reappeared in the second generation (since they had all four genotypes for both traits). This model is diagrammed in Figure 9.1, which shows that in the second generation, smooth shaped seeds occur with probability 3/4 and wrinkled shaped seeds occur with probability 1/4. Similarly yellow color seeds occur with probability 3/4 and green color seeds occur with probability 1/4. Furthermore, since the two characteristics are independent, the four combinations: smooth-yellow, smooth-green, wrinkled-yellow, and wrinkled-green occur with probabilities $3/4 \times 3/4 = 9/16, 3/4 \times 1/4 = 3/16, 1/4 \times 3/4 = 3/16$, and $1/4 \times 1/4 = 1/16$, respectively.

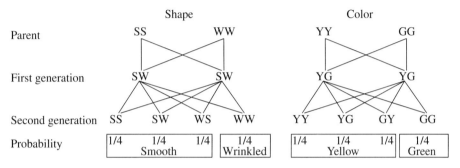

Figure 9.1   Mendel's Genetic Model for the Shape and Color of Pea Seeds

Test how well this model fits the following data obtained by Mendel on the counts observed in 556 second generation hybrids.

Category	1	2	3	4
Type	Smooth-Yellow	Smooth-Green	Wrinkled-Yellow	Wrinkled-Green
Observed Count	315	108	102	31

The null hypothesis to be tested corresponding to Mendel's model is

$$H_0: p_1 = 9/16, \quad p_2 = 3/16, \quad p_3 = 3/16, \quad p_4 = 1/16$$

where p_i is the probability of the ith category ($i = 1, 2, 3, 4$). The expected counts for the four categories are, respectively,

$$e_1 = 556 \times \frac{9}{16} = 312.75, e_2 = 556 \times \frac{3}{16} = 104.25, e_3 = 556 \times \frac{3}{16} = 104.25, e_4 = 556 \times \frac{1}{16} = 34.75.$$

The χ^2-statistic equals

$$\chi^2 = \frac{(315 - 312.75)^2}{312.75} + \frac{(108 - 104.25)^2}{104.25} + \frac{(102 - 104.75)^2}{104.75} + \frac{(31 - 34.75)^2}{34.75} = 0.604$$

which is compared with the chi-square distribution with $4 - 1 = 3$ d.f. The P-value is 0.895, indicating that the deviation of the data from the model is highly nonsignificant. In fact, the fit is almost too good to be true. Similar results in other Mendel's experiments led Sir R. A. Fisher to suspect that the data were fudged to fit the model.   ◆

Several points are worth noting about this chi-square test.

1. Here H_0 represents the model whose validity is to be tested. Contrast this formulation with the conventional formulation of H_0 as the hypothesis that is to be disproved. The goal here is not to disprove the model, but rather to see whether the data are consistent with the model and whether any deviations can be attributed to chance.

2. The chi-square statistic in (9.14) can be expressed in a generic form that extends to all the tests for count data discussed in this chapter. This general form is known as the **Pearson chi-square statistic** and is given by

$$\chi^2 = \sum \frac{(\text{observed} - \text{expected})^2}{\text{expected}} \tag{9.15}$$

where "observed" and "expected" refer to the observed and expected (under H_0) cell counts, and the sum is over all cells of the table.

3. The null distribution of the statistic (9.15) is approximately chi-square only when the sample size is large. Whether or not the sample size is large enough to use this approximation is determined from the expected cell counts, $e_i = np_{i0}$. A rule of thumb is that all the e_i must be ≥ 1 and no more than 1/5th of the e_i must be < 5. If this rule is not satisfied, then an alternative is to combine the sparse cells (having small e_i values) with adjacent cells. Unfortunately, this has the drawback of losing some information.

4. The d.f. of the chi-square distribution equal the number of *independent* parameters under test minus the number of *independent* parameters estimated from data. For the test on the multinomial cell probabilities, the number of independent parameters under test is $c - 1$, as we saw before, and no parameters are estimated, since H_0 completely specifies the values of the $p_i = p_{i0}$. The following sections deal with problems where H_0 does not completely specify the values of the multinomial cell probabilities, which must be estimated from data under the constraints imposed by H_0.

9.3.2 Chi-Square Goodness of Fit Test

A common problem is to determine whether a specified distribution fits a set of data. The above test on the cell probabilities of a multinomial distribution can be adapted to this problem. We shall consider only discrete data, for which this adaptation is straightforward. In this case, the categories of the specified discrete distribution can be used as the cells of a multinomial distribution. For continuous data, it is necessary to group the data into intervals, as in a histogram, and then treat the grouped data as multinomially distributed with cell probabilities equal to the corresponding interval probabilities under the specified continuous distribution (e.g., normal).

Example 9.10 illustrated a goodness of fit test for the uniform distribution on integers $0, 1, \ldots, 9$. In that example, the probability distribution was completely specified. More generally, however, only the functional form of the distribution is specified, but not all of its parameters. For example, we may want to test if a Poisson distribution with an unknown parameter λ fits a set of count data. The general principle for testing whether some member of a specified family of distributions (e.g., Poisson) fits the data is to find the best fitting member of that family by estimating the unknown parameters from the data, and to test the goodness of fit of that member. The test procedure must be adjusted to account for estimating unknown parameters from the data. As stated at the end of the previous subsection, the appropriate adjustment is to deduct degrees of freedom equal to the number of independent estimated parameters.

EXAMPLE 9.12 (RADIOACTIVE DECAY OF POLONIUM: GOODNESS OF FIT OF THE POISSON DISTRIBUTION)

Two great physicists, Rutherford and Geiger, made measurements[7] on the number of scintillations in 1/8th minute intervals caused by radioactive decay of polonium. These data are shown in Table 9.7. The first column gives the number of scintillations i, and the second column gives the count of 1/8th minute intervals, n_i, during which exactly i scintillations were witnessed. The total number of time intervals is $n = \sum n_i = 2608$. Test whether the number of scintillations follows a Poisson distribution.

Before we perform a formal hypothesis test, it is useful to get a graphical picture of the histogram of the scintillation counts superimposed on the probability histogram of the Poisson distribution having the same mean (calculated as $\hat{\lambda}$ on the next page). This graph based on the computations given in Table 9.7 is shown in Figure 9.2. We see that the two histograms agree fairly closely, so the Poisson distribution will likely provide a good fit.

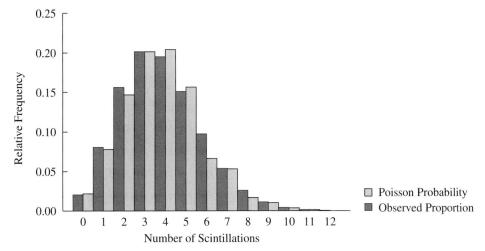

Figure 9.2 Histograms of the Scintillation Counts and the Poisson Distribution with Matching Mean

The hypotheses are H_0: The number of scintillations in a 1/8th minute interval follows a Poisson distribution vs. H_1: the number of scintillations follows a different distribution. If p_i denotes the probability that exactly i scintillations occur in a 1/8th minute interval, then H_0 can

---

[7] E. Rutherford and H. Geiger (1910), "The probability variations in the distribution of α particles," *The Philosophical Magazine*, 6th Ser., **20**, pp. 698–704. Reprinted in D. C. Hoaglin (1980), "A Poissonness plot," *The American Statistician*, **34**, pp. 146–149.

be rewritten in a form similar to (9.13):

$$H_0: p_i = p_{i0} = \frac{e^{-\lambda}\lambda^i}{i!} \quad (i = 0, 1, 2, \ldots).$$

To fit this into the multinomial framework, we truncate the Poisson distribution at $i = 14$.

Table 9.7 Observed and Expected Counts of the Number of Scintillations Assuming a Poisson Distribution with λ Estimated from Data

No. Scintillations i	No. Time Intervals n_i	Poisson Prob. $\hat{p}_{i0} = e^{-\hat{\lambda}}\hat{\lambda}^i/i!$	Expected No. Time Intervals $\hat{e}_i = n\hat{p}_{i0}$
0	57	0.0208	54.317
1	203	0.0806	210.289
2	383	0.1561	407.066
3	525	0.2014	525.319
4	532	0.1950	508.443
5	408	0.1510	393.687
6	273	0.0974	254.027
7	139	0.0539	140.495
8	45	0.0261	67.991
9	27	0.0112	29.247
10	10	0.0043	11.323
11	4	0.0015	3.985
12	0	0.0005	1.286
13	1	0.0001	0.383
14	1	0.00004	0.106

To test H_0 we first estimate λ (which is the mean of the Poisson distribution) by the sample mean. We use the Poisson distribution with this estimated λ as the specific Poisson distribution to be tested, and then apply the chi-square test. Since λ is estimated from the data, we deduct one extra degree of freedom. So we refer the test statistic to the chi-square distribution with $c - 2$ d.f. instead of $c - 1$.

The mean number of scintillations equals

$$\hat{\lambda} = \frac{0 \times 57 + 1 \times 203 + 2 \times 383 + \cdots + 14 \times 1}{2608} = 3.872.$$

Columns 3 and 4 of Table 9.7 give the $\hat{p}_{i0} = e^{-\hat{\lambda}}\hat{\lambda}^i/i!$ and the $\hat{e}_i = n\hat{p}_{i0}$ calculations based on the Poisson distribution with $\hat{\lambda} = 3.872$. Since $\hat{e}_{13}$ and $\hat{e}_{14}$ are both less than 1, we combine the last three cells, which gives $n_{12} = 0 + 1 + 1 = 2$ and $\hat{e}_{12} = 1.286 + 0.383 + 0.106 = 1.775$. The rule of thumb for applying the large sample χ^2-test is satisfied, since all $\hat{e}_i$ are > 1 and only two out of 13 $\hat{e}_i$'s (less than 1/5th) are < 5.

The chi-square statistic equals

$$\chi^2 = \frac{(57 - 54.317)^2}{54.317} + \frac{(203 - 210.289)^2}{210.289} + \cdots + \frac{(2 - 1.775)^2}{1.775} = 12.983$$

and has $13 - 2 = 11$ d.f. The corresponding P-value equals 0.294. Thus H_0 cannot be rejected at conventional values of α, and we conclude that the Poisson distribution fits these data well.   ◆

9.4   INFERENCES FOR TWO-WAY COUNT DATA

9.4.1 Sampling Models

One example of a two-way count data is income vs. job satisfaction survey data (see Table 4.7), reproduced here in Table 9.8.[8]   A second example is the leukemia drug (Prednisone vs. Prednisone+VCR) trial data from Example 9.6.

Table 9.8 Individuals Cross-Classified by Income and Job Satisfaction

Income (U.S. $)	Job Satisfaction				Row Total
	Very Dissatisfied	Little Dissatisfied	Moderately Satisfied	Very Satisfied	
< 6000	20	24	80	82	206
6000–15,000	22	38	104	125	289
15,000–25,000	13	28	81	113	235
> 25,000	7	18	54	92	171
Column Total	62	108	319	412	901

These two examples represent two different study designs. The study design of the survey data in Table 9.8 fixed the *total* sample size $n = 901$, while that of the leukemia data in Table 9.2 fixed the sample size in each drug group (i.e., in each row). In the first example we have a sample from a single population, which is then cross-classified. The investigators did not a priori fix the numbers in each income group (the row totals) or in each job satisfaction group (the column totals); thus both the row and column totals are r.v.'s. In contrast, in the leukemia study the numbers of patients to be treated by each therapy were determined in advance; as a result, the row totals were fixed a priori. The second design can be viewed as independent random samples from the two row populations. Two different probability models apply to these two different sampling designs.

Sampling Model 1 (Total Sample Size Fixed):   A random sample of size n is drawn from a single population, and sample units are cross-classified into r row categories and c column categories resulting in an $r \times c$ table of observed counts n_{ij} ($i = 1, \ldots, r; j =$

---

[8] 1984 General Survey of the National Data Program as quoted by Norusis (1988), *SPSS*[X] *Advanced Statistics Guide*, 2nd ed., New York: McGraw-Hill.

$1, \ldots, c$). Let p_{ij} be the probability that a sample unit will be classified into cell (i, j) $(\sum_{i=1}^{r} \sum_{j=1}^{c} p_{ij} = 1)$, and let N_{ij} be the r.v. corresponding to n_{ij} $(\sum_{i=1}^{r} \sum_{j=1}^{c} N_{ij} = n)$. Then the joint distribution of the N_{ij} is the multinomial distribution given by

$$P\{N_{ij} = n_{ij} \ (i = 1, \ldots, r; j = 1, \ldots, c)\} = \frac{n!}{\prod_{i=1}^{r} \prod_{j=1}^{c} n_{ij}!} \prod_{i=1}^{r} \prod_{j=1}^{c} p_{ij}^{n_{ij}}.$$

The p_{ij} are unknown parameters.

The data can be summarized in the form shown in Table 9.9. In this table the $n_{i \cdot} = \sum_{j=1}^{c} n_{ij}$ are the row totals, the $n_{\cdot j} = \sum_{i=1}^{r} n_{ij}$ are the column totals, and $n_{\cdot \cdot} = n$ is the overall total. The cell probabilities p_{ij} can be represented in a similar table with the same notational convention and with $p_{\cdot \cdot} = 1$. This is called the **multinomial sampling model**.

Table 9.9 A Two-Way Table of Observed Counts

		Column						Row
		1	2	$\ldots$	j	$\ldots$	c	Total
	1	n_{11}	n_{12}	$\ldots$	n_{1j}	$\ldots$	n_{1c}	$n_{1 \cdot}$
	2	n_{21}	n_{22}	$\ldots$	n_{2j}	$\ldots$	n_{2c}	$n_{2 \cdot}$
	$\vdots$	$\ldots$	$\ldots$	$\ldots$	$\ldots$	$\ldots$	$\ldots$	$\vdots$
Row	i	n_{i1}	n_{i2}	$\ldots$	n_{ij}	$\ldots$	n_{ic}	$n_{i \cdot}$
	$\vdots$	$\ldots$	$\ldots$	$\ldots$	$\ldots$	$\ldots$	$\ldots$	$\vdots$
	r	n_{r1}	n_{r2}	$\ldots$	n_{rj}	$\ldots$	n_{rc}	$n_{r \cdot}$
Column Total		$n_{\cdot 1}$	$n_{\cdot 2}$	$\ldots$	$n_{\cdot j}$	$\ldots$	$n_{\cdot c}$	$n_{\cdot \cdot} = n$

Sampling Model 2 (Row Totals Fixed): In this model random samples of sizes n_1, n_2, $\ldots$, n_r are drawn independently from $r \geq 2$ row populations. The data can be represented as in Table 9.9 with row totals $n_{i \cdot} = n_i$ $(i = 1, \ldots, r)$. The counts from each row can be modeled by a multinomial distribution as follows: For the ith row let $(p_{i1}, p_{i2}, \ldots, p_{ic})$ be the vector of cell probabilities, where $\sum_{j=1}^{c} p_{ij} = 1$ for each row, $i = 1, 2, \ldots, r$. The distribution for the ith row is given by

$$P\{N_{i1} = n_{i1}, N_{i2} = n_{i2}, \ldots, N_{ic} = n_{ic}\} = \frac{n_i!}{n_{i1}! \cdots n_{ic}!} p_{i1}^{n_{i1}} \cdots p_{ic}^{n_{ic}}.$$

The multinomial distributions for different rows are assumed to be independent, so that the joint distribution of all the rows is the product of the individual multinomial distributions. This is called the **product multinomial sampling model**.

9.4.2 Hypothesis Tests

The inferential goal is to show that the row variable and the column variable are associated. The null hypothesis is that no association exists between the two. How the hypotheses are mathematically formulated depends on how the study is designed and hence which sampling model is applicable.

Sampling Model 1 (Total Sample Size Fixed): If we denote the row variable by X and the column variable by Y, then the cell probabilities p_{ij} represent the joint bivariate distribution of X and Y:

$$p_{ij} = P(X = i, Y = j).$$

Furthermore, the $p_{i\cdot} = \sum_{j=1}^{c} p_{ij} = P(X = i)$ give the marginal distribution of X and the $p_{\cdot j} = \sum_{i=1}^{r} p_{ij} = P(Y = j)$ give the marginal distribution of Y.

The null hypothesis is that X and Y are *statistically independent*, i.e.,

$$H_0: p_{ij} = P(X = i, Y = j) = P(X = i)P(Y = j) = p_{i\cdot}p_{\cdot j} \quad \text{for all } i, j. \quad (9.16)$$

This is called the **hypothesis of independence**. The alternative hypothesis is $H_1: p_{ij} \neq p_{i\cdot}p_{\cdot j}$ for some i, j.

Sampling Model 2 (Row Totals Fixed): Here X is held fixed and the response Y is observed. Therefore the p_{ij} represent the conditional probabilities:

$$p_{ij} = P(Y = j \mid X = i).$$

The null hypothesis is that the probability of response j is the same, regardless of the row population:

$$H_0: p_{ij} = P(Y = j \mid X = i) = p_j \quad \text{for all } i, j = 1, 2, \ldots, c$$

or equivalently

$$H_0: (p_{i1}, p_{i2}, \ldots, p_{ic}) = (p_1, p_2, \ldots, p_c) \quad \text{for all } i. \quad (9.17)$$

This is called the **hypothesis of homogeneity**, since it postulates the equality of r multinomial cell probability vectors. The alternative hypothesis is $H_1: (p_{i1}, p_{i2}, \ldots, p_{ic})$ are not the same for all i.

Although the hypotheses to be tested are different for the two sampling models, the chi-square test turns out to be identical. To calculate the χ^2-statistic we first compute the "estimated" expected frequencies:

$$\hat{e}_{ij} = \frac{n_{i\cdot}n_{\cdot j}}{n}. \quad (9.18)$$

Using the general form (9.15) of the chi-square statistic, we then calculate

$$\chi^2 = \sum_{i=1}^{r} \sum_{j=1}^{c} \frac{(n_{ij} - \hat{e}_{ij})^2}{\hat{e}_{ij}}. \quad (9.19)$$

For both the sampling models this chi-square statistic can be shown to have an asymptotic χ^2-distribution under H_0 with $(r-1)(c-1)$ d.f. Therefore, an α-level test of H_0 of both (9.16) and (9.17) is:

$$\text{Reject } H_0 \text{ if } \chi^2 > \chi^2_{(r-1)(c-1),\alpha}. \quad (9.20)$$

The derivation of this χ^2-test is given following the two examples below.

EXAMPLE 9.13

Test if the income and job satisfaction are associated based on the data in Table 9.8.

As discussed before, these data follow sampling model 1, so we test the hypothesis of independence. The first step in calculating the χ^2-statistic is to calculate the estimated expected frequencies $\hat{e}_{ij}$. Table 9.10 summarizes both the observed frequencies n_{ij} (upper entry), and the estimated expected frequencies $\hat{e}_{ij}$ (lower entry). For example, $\hat{e}_{11}$ is calculated as

$$\hat{e}_{11} = \frac{n_{1.}n_{.1}}{n} = \frac{206 \times 62}{901} = 14.18.$$

Next, the χ^2-statistic is calculated as

$$\chi^2 = \frac{(20 - 14.18)^2}{14.18} + \frac{(24 - 24.69)^2}{24.69} + \frac{(80 - 72.93)^2}{72.93} + \frac{(82 - 94.20)^2}{94.20}$$

$$+ \frac{(22 - 19.89)^2}{19.89} + \frac{(38 - 34.64)^2}{34.64} + \frac{(104 - 102.32)^2}{102.32} + \frac{(125 - 132.15)^2}{132.15}$$

$$+ \frac{(13 - 16.17)^2}{16.17} + \frac{(28 - 28.17)^2}{28.17} + \frac{(81 - 83.20)^2}{83.20} + \frac{(113 - 107.46)^2}{107.46}$$

$$+ \frac{(7 - 11.77)^2}{11.77} + \frac{(18 - 20.50)^2}{20.50} + \frac{(54 - 60.54)^2}{60.54} + \frac{(92 - 78.19)^2}{78.19}$$

$$= \mathbf{2.393} + 0.019 + 0.684 + \mathbf{1.579}$$

$$+ 0.225 + 0.326 + 0.028 + 0.387$$

$$+ 0.622 + 0.001 + 0.058 + 0.286$$

$$+ \mathbf{1.931} + 0.304 + 0.707 + \mathbf{2.438}$$

$$= 11.989.$$

The d.f. for this χ^2-statistic is $(4 - 1)(4 - 1) = 9$. For a 0.05-level test, the critical value is $\chi^2_{9,.05} = 16.919$. Since the calculated $\chi^2 = 11.989 < 16.919$ (the P-value = 0.214), there is not sufficient evidence to reject the independence hypothesis. Thus we cannot conclude that income and job satisfaction are associated.

Although the χ^2-statistic is nonsignificant, it is interesting that most of the contribution to it comes from the four corner cells (shown by bold numbers). These cells are associated with the lowest and highest levels of income and job satisfaction. The residuals $n_{ij} - \hat{e}_{ij}$ for these four cells are shown in Table 9.11. This table clearly shows that there are more people with low incomes and low satisfaction, and high incomes and high satisfaction, than expected under H_0. Similarly, there are fewer people with low incomes and high satisfaction, and high incomes and low satisfaction, than expected under H_0. Thus the two variables are positively associated. The reason for nonsignificant χ^2 are the two middle categories for each variable, where independence approximately holds. If we analyze the 2×2 subtable of corner cells, we obtain $\chi^2 = 6.794$ with 1 d.f., which is highly significant with a P-value = 0.009. ◆

Table 9.10 Observed and Expected Frequencies for Income-Job Satisfaction Data

Income (U.S. $)	Job Satisfaction				Row Total
	Very Dissatisfied	Little Dissatisfied	Moderately Satisfied	Very Satisfied	
< 6000	20	24	80	82	206
	14.18	24.69	72.93	94.20	
6000–15,000	22	38	104	125	289
	19.89	34.64	102.32	132.15	
15,000–25,000	13	28	81	113	235
	16.17	28.17	83.20	107.46	
> 25,000	7	18	54	92	171
	11.77	20.50	60.54	78.19	
Column Total	62	108	319	412	901

Table 9.11 Residuals for Corner Cells for Income-Job
Satisfaction Data

		Job Satisfaction	
		V. Dissatisfied	V. Satisfied
Income	< $6000	+5.82	−12.20
	> $25,000	−4.77	+13.81

Example 9.14 (Comparison of Two Drugs for Leukemia: χ^2-Test)

Test if the success and failure probabilities are the same for Prednisone and Prednisone+VCR drugs based on the leukemia trial data in Table 9.2.

Since these data follow sampling model 2, we test the hypothesis of homogeneity. There are only two outcomes (success and failure), so the hypothesis of homogeneity of the cell probability vectors can be stated in a simplified form as follows: Let p_1 and $1 - p_1$ be the success and failure probabilities for the Prednisone group, and p_2 and $1 - p_2$ be the corresponding probabilities for the Prednisone+VCR group. Then the hypotheses to be tested are

$$H_0: p_1 = p_2 \quad \text{vs.} \quad H_1: p_1 \neq p_2.$$

Table 9.12 shows the observed frequencies n_{ij} (upper entries) and the estimated expected frequencies $\hat{e}_{ij}$ (lower entries) computed using (9.18). The χ^2-statistic is calculated as

$$\chi^2 = \frac{(14 - 17.33)^2}{17.33} + \frac{(7 - 3.67)^2}{3.67} + \frac{(38 - 34.67)^2}{34.67} + \frac{(4 - 7.33)^2}{7.33}$$

$$= (3.33)^2 \left[\frac{1}{17.33} + \frac{1}{3.67} + \frac{1}{34.67} + \frac{1}{7.33} \right]$$

$$= 5.507$$

which has $(2 - 1)(2 - 1) = 1$ d.f. The P-value equals 0.019, which indicates a statistically significant difference between the success rates for the drug groups, with a higher success rate for the Prednisone+VCR group ($p_2 > p_1$).

Table 9.12 Observed and Expected Frequencies for the Leukemia Trial Data

	Success	Failure	Row Total
Prednisone	14	7	21
	17.33	3.67	
Prednisone+VCR	38	4	42
	34.67	7.33	
Column Total	52	11	63

Observe that the same P-value was obtained in Example 9.6, where we used a two-sided z-test to analyze this data set. In fact, $\chi^2 = 5.507 = z^2 = (-2.347)^2$. The equivalence between these two tests is shown in general in Exercise 9.43. The advantage of the z-test is that it can be used to test a one-sided or a two-sided alternative hypothesis, while the chi-square test always tests a two-sided alternative hypothesis.

Also note that $(n_{ij} - \hat{e}_{ij}) = \pm 3.33$ for all four cells. For any 2×2 table, it is always true that $(n_{ij} - \hat{e}_{ij}) = \pm d$ for some common value $d \geq 0$, because the n_{ij} and the $\hat{e}_{ij}$ must sum to the same row and column totals. ◆

*Derivation of the Chi-Square Test for Two-Way Tables.   First consider the hypothesis testing problem (9.16) for sampling model 1 (total sample size fixed). The expected frequencies under H_0 are given by

$$e_{ij} = np_{ij} = np_{i \cdot} p_{\cdot j}.$$

We cannot use this equation to calculate the e_{ij}, since the $p_{i \cdot}$ and $p_{\cdot j}$ are unknown. However, they can be estimated using

$$\hat{p}_{i \cdot} = \frac{n_{i \cdot}}{n} \quad \text{and} \quad \hat{p}_{\cdot j} = \frac{n_{\cdot j}}{n}.$$

Substituting these estimates in the formula for e_{ij}, we obtain the formula (9.18).

Next consider the hypothesis testing problem (9.17) for sampling model 2 (row totals fixed). Under H_0, the expected frequencies are given by

$$e_{ij} = n_i p_{ij} = n_i p_j$$

where p_j is the common value of the p_{ij} for $i = 1, 2, \ldots, r$ under H_0. We cannot use this equation to calculate the e_{ij}, since the p_j are unknown. However, they can be estimated using

$$\hat{p}_j = \frac{n_{\cdot j}}{n}.$$

Substituting these estimates in the formula for e_{ij}, we obtain the same formula (9.18).

How do we get d.f. $= (r-1)(c-1)$? As stated before, the d.f. for the χ^2-statistic is given by the number of *independent* parameters under test minus the number of *independent* parameters estimated from data. In sampling model 1 there are $rc - 1$ independent parameters, since the rc p_{ij}'s are subject to one constraint, $\sum_{i=1}^{r} \sum_{j=1}^{c} p_{ij} = 1$. The p_{ij}'s are estimated using the equation $\hat{p}_{ij} = \hat{p}_{i\cdot} \hat{p}_{\cdot j}$, which requires estimates of $r-1$ independent $p_{i\cdot}$ (since they are subject to one constraint, $\sum_{i=1}^{r} p_{i\cdot} = 1$) and $c-1$ independent $p_{\cdot j}$ (since they are subject to one constraint, $\sum_{j=1}^{c} p_{\cdot j} = 1$). Thus the number of *independent* parameters estimated from data is $(r-1) + (c-1)$. Therefore the d.f. are:

$$\text{d.f.} = (rc - 1) - [(r - 1) + (c - 1)] = (r - 1)(c - 1).$$

In sampling model 2 there are $r(c - 1)$ independent parameters, since for each row i, the c cell probabilities, $p_{i1}, p_{i2}, \ldots, p_{ic}$, sum to 1, and there are r rows. The p_{ij}'s are estimated using the equation $\hat{p}_{ij} = \hat{p}_j$, which requires estimates of $c - 1$ independent $p_{\cdot j}$ (since they are subject to one constraint, $\sum_{j=1}^{c} p_{\cdot j} = 1$). Therefore the d.f. are:

$$\text{d.f.} = r(c - 1) - (c - 1) = (r - 1)(c - 1). \qquad \blacklozenge$$

9.4.3 *Odds Ratio as a Measure of Association

The χ^2-test tells us whether statistically significant association exists between the row and the column variable. However, it does not give us an idea of the magnitude of association. It is possible to have a significant χ^2-statistic although magnitude of association is small, if the sample size is large. The reverse could be true if the sample size is small. Measures of the magnitude of association for general $r \times c$ tables are beyond the scope of the present text. We consider only 2×2 tables.

The most common measure of association for a 2×2 table is the **odds ratio**, ψ, defined as

$$\psi = \frac{p_{11}/p_{12}}{p_{21}/p_{22}} \text{ for sampling model 1 and } \psi = \frac{p_1/(1 - p_1)}{p_2/(1 - p_2)} \text{ for sampling model 2.}$$
$$(9.21)$$

Note that for sampling model 1, the numerator is the odds of column 1 outcome vs. column 2 outcome for row 1, and the denominator is the same odds for row 2, hence the name "odds ratio." For sampling model 2, if the two column outcomes are labeled as "success" and "failure," then ψ is the ratio of the odds of success for the row 1 population vs. the odds of success for the row 2 population. Note that when the row and column variables are unrelated (i.e., when H_0 of independence holds in (9.16) or when H_0 of row homogeneity holds in (9.17)), $\psi = 1$. Furthermore, $\psi > 1$ corresponds to positive association between the row and the column variable (the odds of column 1 outcome are higher for row 1 than for row 2) and $\psi < 1$ corresponds to negative association.

A natural estimate of ψ is

$$\hat{\psi} = \frac{n_{11}/n_{12}}{n_{21}/n_{22}} = \frac{n_{11}n_{22}}{n_{21}n_{12}} \tag{9.22}$$

assuming all n_{ij}'s are positive. For sampling model 1, this estimate follows because each p_{ij} is estimated by n_{ij}/n. For sampling model 2, this estimate follows because p_1 and $1 - p_1$ are estimated by $n_{11}/n_{1\cdot}$ and $n_{12}/n_{1\cdot}$, respectively; similarly p_2 and $1 - p_2$ are estimated by $n_{21}/n_{2\cdot}$ and $n_{22}/n_{2\cdot}$, respectively.

To obtain a CI or to perform a hypothesis test on ψ, the following result is used. For sampling model 1, if n_{ij}'s are large, $\log_e \hat{\psi}$ is approximately distributed as a normal r.v. with

$$E(\log_e \hat{\psi}) \simeq \log_e \psi \quad \text{and} \quad \text{Var}(\log_e \hat{\psi}) \simeq \frac{1}{np_{11}} + \frac{1}{np_{12}} + \frac{1}{np_{21}} + \frac{1}{np_{22}}.$$

For sampling model 2 the same result holds, but the variance formula is

$$\text{Var}(\log_e \hat{\psi}) \simeq \frac{1}{n_1 p_1} + \frac{1}{n_1(1 - p_1)} + \frac{1}{n_2 p_2} + \frac{1}{n_2(1 - p_2)}.$$

For the derivation of this variance formula, see Exercise 15.14. For both sampling models, $\text{Var}(\log_e \hat{\psi})$ can be estimated by

$$\widehat{\text{Var}}(\log_e \hat{\psi}) \simeq \frac{1}{n_{11}} + \frac{1}{n_{12}} + \frac{1}{n_{21}} + \frac{1}{n_{22}}.$$

This gives the following approximate $100(1 - \alpha)\%$ CI on $\log_e \psi$:

$$\left[\log_e \hat{\psi} - z_{\alpha/2}\sqrt{\frac{1}{n_{11}} + \frac{1}{n_{12}} + \frac{1}{n_{21}} + \frac{1}{n_{22}}}, \quad \log_e \hat{\psi} + z_{\alpha/2}\sqrt{\frac{1}{n_{11}} + \frac{1}{n_{12}} + \frac{1}{n_{21}} + \frac{1}{n_{22}}} \right]. \tag{9.23}$$

Denoting this CI by $[\ell, u]$, it follows that the CI for ψ is $[e^\ell, e^u]$. A hypothesis test on ψ or equivalently on $\log_e \psi$ can be based on this result.

EXAMPLE 9.15   (COMPARING TWO LEUKEMIA THERAPIES: ODDS RATIO)

Calculate a 95% CI on ψ for the leukemia trial data in Table 9.2. Also perform a test of significance on $\hat{\psi}$.

From the data in Table 9.2 we first calculate

$$\hat{\psi} = \frac{14 \times 4}{38 \times 7} = 0.2105 \quad \text{and} \quad \log_e \hat{\psi} = -1.558.$$

Therefore a 95% CI on $\log_e \psi$ is

$$\left[-1.558 \pm 1.960\sqrt{\frac{1}{14} + \frac{1}{7} + \frac{1}{38} + \frac{1}{4}} \right] = [-1.558 \pm 1.960 \times 0.700] = [-2.931, -0.185].$$

A 95% CI on ψ is then

$$[e^{-2.931}, e^{-0.185}] = [0.053, 0.831].$$

Since this CI excludes 1 (or equivalently the CI on $\log_e \psi$ excludes 0), it is clear that $\hat{\psi}$ is significantly different from 1 at the 5% significance level. This tells us that $H_0: \psi = 1$ can be rejected at $\alpha = 0.05$ in favor of a two-sided alternative, and we can conclude that $\psi < 1$. Thus the odds of success with Prednisone are less than those with Prednisone+VCR.

To find the P-value associated with this test, we calculate the z-statistic (corresponding to $H_0: \log_e \psi = 0$) as follows:

$$z = \frac{\log_e \hat{\psi}}{\sqrt{\frac{1}{n_{11}} + \frac{1}{n_{12}} + \frac{1}{n_{21}} + \frac{1}{n_{22}}}} = \frac{-1.558}{\sqrt{\frac{1}{14} + \frac{1}{7} + \frac{1}{38} + \frac{1}{4}}} = -2.226.$$

Notice that this is nearly the same as -2.347 obtained in Example 9.6. The two-sided P-value is $2[1 - \Phi(2.226)] = 0.026$.

9.5 CHAPTER SUMMARY

This chapter begins with inference procedures for an unknown proportion p in a Bernoulli population. The sample proportion $\hat{p}$ from a random sample of size n is an unbiased estimate of p. Inferences on p are based on the central limit theorem (CLT) result that for large n, the sample proportion $\hat{p}$ is approximately normal with mean $= p$ and standard deviation $= \sqrt{pq/n}$. A large sample two-sided $100(1-\alpha)\%$ confidence interval for p is given by

$$\left[\hat{p} \pm z_{\alpha/2} \sqrt{\frac{\hat{p}\hat{q}}{n}} \right]$$

where $\hat{q} = 1 - \hat{p}$ and $z_{\alpha/2}$ is the upper $\alpha/2$ critical point of the standard normal distribution. A large sample test on p to test $H_0: p = p_0$ can be based on the test statistic

$$z = \frac{\hat{p} - p_0}{\sqrt{\hat{p}\hat{q}/n}} \quad \text{or} \quad z = \frac{\hat{p} - p_0}{\sqrt{p_0 q_0/n}}.$$

Both these statistics are asymptotically standard normal under H_0.

Next we consider the problem of comparing two Bernoulli proportions, p_1 and p_2, based on two independent random samples of sizes n_1 and n_2. The basis for inferences on $p_1 - p_2$ is the result that for large n_1 and n_2, the difference in the sample proportions, $\hat{p}_1 - \hat{p}_2$, is approximately normal with mean $= p_1 - p_2$ and standard deviation $= \sqrt{p_1 q_1/n_1 + p_2 q_2/n_2}$. A large sample two-sided $100(1-\alpha)\%$ confidence interval for $p_1 - p_2$ is given by

$$\left[\hat{p}_1 - \hat{p}_2 \pm z_{\alpha/2} \sqrt{\frac{\hat{p}_1 \hat{q}_1}{n_1} + \frac{\hat{p}_2 \hat{q}_2}{n_2}} \right].$$

A large sample two-sided z-test can be used to test $H_0: p_1 = p_2$ vs. $H_1: p_1 \neq p_2$ by using the test statistic

$$z = \frac{\hat{p}_1 - \hat{p}_2}{\sqrt{\frac{\hat{p}_1 \hat{q}_1}{n_1} + \frac{\hat{p}_2 \hat{q}_2}{n_2}}} \quad \text{or} \quad z = \frac{\hat{p}_1 - \hat{p}_2}{\sqrt{\hat{p}\hat{q}\left(\frac{1}{n_1} + \frac{1}{n_2}\right)}}$$

where $\hat{p} = (n_1 \hat{p}_1 + n_2 \hat{p}_2)/(n_1 + n_2)$ is the pooled sample proportion. Small sample tests to compare p_1 and p_2 are also given for independent samples and matched pairs designs.

A generalization of the test on the binomial proportion p is a test on the cell probabilities of a multinomial distribution. Based on a random sample of size n from a c-cell multinomial distribution (one-way count data) with cell probabilities $p_1, p_2, \ldots, p_c$, the test of

$$H_0: p_1 = p_{10}, p_2 = p_{20}, \ldots, p_c = p_{c0} \quad \text{vs.} \quad H_1: \text{At least one } p_i \neq p_{i0}$$

is based on the **chi-square statistic** having the general form:

$$\chi^2 = \sum \frac{(\text{observed} - \text{expected})^2}{\text{expected}}$$

where "observed" refers to the observed cell counts n_i and "expected" refers to the expected cell counts $e_i = np_{i0}$ under H_0. The degrees of freedom (d.f.) of the chi-square statistic are $c - 1$. The primary use of this statistic is for the **goodness of fit test** of a specified distribution to a set of data. If any parameters of the distribution are estimated from the data, then one d.f. is deducted for each independent estimated parameter from the total d.f. $c - 1$.

Two-way count data result when (i) a single sample is cross-classified based on two categorical variables into r rows and c columns (**multinomial sampling**), or (ii) independent samples are drawn from r multinomial distributions with the same c categories (**product multinomial sampling**). In both cases, the data are summarized in the form of an $r \times c$ **contingency table** of counts. In case (i), the null hypothesis of interest is the **independence hypothesis** between the row and column variables; in case (ii), it is the **homogeneity hypothesis**. In both cases, the chi-square statistic has the same general form given above, with the expected count for the (i, j)th cell (under H_0) being the ith row total times the proportion of all observations falling in the jth column. The d.f. of the chi-square statistic equal $(r-1)(c-1)$. Thus association between the row and the column variable is demonstrated at level α if $\chi^2 > \chi^2_{(r-1)(c-1),\alpha}$.

■ EXERCISES

Section 9.1

9.1   A business journal publisher plans to survey a sample of the subscribers to estimate the proportion p with annual household incomes over $100,000.

(a) How many subscribers must be surveyed to obtain a 99% CI for p with a margin of error no greater than 0.05? Assume that no prior estimate of p is available.

(b) The marketing department thinks that $p = 0.30$ would be a reasonable guess. What is the corresponding sample size?

(c) Refer to the sample size obtained in (b). If a 40% nonresponse rate is anticipated, how many surveys need to be mailed? How may such a high nonresponse rate cause bias in the estimate?

9.2 While imprisoned by the Germans during World War II, the English mathematician John Kerrich tossed a coin 10,000 times and obtained 5067 heads. Let p be the probability of a head on a single toss. We wish to check if the data are consistent with the hypothesis that the coin was fair.

(a) Set up the hypotheses. Why should the alternative be two-sided?

(b) Calculate the P-value. Can you reject H_0 at the .05 level?

(c) Find a 95% CI for the proportion of heads for Kerrich's coin.

9.3 Calls to technical support service of a software company are monitored on a sampling basis for quality assurance. Each monitored call is classified as satisfactory or unsatisfactory by the supervisor in terms of the quality of help offered. A random sample of 100 calls was monitored over one month for a new trainee; 8 calls were classified as unsatisfactory.

(a) Calculate a 95% CI for the actual proportion of unsatisfactory calls during the month. Use both formulas (9.1) and (9.3) and compare the results.

(b) This CI is used to test $H_0: p = 0.10$ vs. $H_1: p \neq 0.10$. If H_0 is not rejected, then monitoring of the trainee is continued at the same frequency; if H_0 is rejected in the lower tail, then monitoring frequency is reduced; and if H_0 is rejected in the upper tail, then the trainee is provided additional training. Based on the CI calculated in (a), what action should be taken on this trainee?

9.4 The fraction defective in a high volume production process is to be estimated using a 95% CI with a margin of error of 0.2%.

(a) If the a priori guess at the fraction defective is 1%, how many parts should be sampled? Compare this number with the sample size that you would need if no a priori information regarding the true fraction defective is assumed.

(b) One problem with estimating a very low fraction defective is that no defectives may be obtained in the sample, making it impossible to calculate a CI. What sampling method would you use to ensure that there will be sufficient number of defectives in the sample to provide reliable information on the true fraction defective?

9.5 A quarterback from a Big Ten college football team worked to improve his proportion of completed passes. His career average had been 46.5% completed passes. His record halfway into the new season is 82 completed passes out of 151 attempted.

(a) Set up the hypotheses to test whether his proportion of completed passes has improved. Should the alternative be one-sided or two-sided? Explain.

(b) Perform a test at $\alpha = .05$. Is there a significant improvement?

(c) At least how many passes out of 151 should he have completed in order to demonstrate significant improvement at $\alpha = .025$?

9.6   A blood test intended to identify patients at "high risk" of cardiac disease gave positive results on 80 out of 100 known cardiac patients, but also on 16 out of 200 known normal patients.

(a) Find a 90% CI for the **sensitivity** of the test, which is defined as the probability that a cardiac patient is correctly identified.

(b) Find a 90% CI for the **specificity** of the test, which is defined as the probability that a normal patient is correctly identified.

9.7   People at high risk of sudden cardiac death can be identified using the change in a signal averaged electrocardiogram before and after prescribed activities. The current method is about 80% accurate. The method was modified, hoping to improve its accuracy. The new method is tested on 50 people and gave correct results on 46 patients. Is this convincing evidence that the new method is more accurate?

(a) Set up the hypotheses to test that the accuracy of the new method is better than that of the current method.

(b) Perform a test of the hypotheses at $\alpha = .05$. What do you conclude about the accuracy of the new method?

9.8   Refer to the previous exercise.

(a) If the new method actually has 90% accuracy, what power does a sample of 50 have to demonstrate that the new method is better, using a .05-level test?

(b) How many patients should be tested in order for this power to be at least 0.75?

9.9   A preelection poll is to be planned for a senatorial election between two candidates. Previous polls have shown that the election is hanging in delicate balance. If there is a shift (in either direction) by more than 2 percentage points since the last poll, then the polling agency would like to detect it with probability of at least 0.80 using a .05-level test. Determine how many voters should be polled. If actually 2500 voters are polled, what is the value of this probability?

Section 9.2

9.10   To gauge a change in opinion regarding the public view on bilingual education, a telephone poll was taken in September 1993 and again in September 1995.[9] The results based on the survey of 1000 American adults contacted in each poll were that 40% from the 1993 poll and 48% from the 1995 poll favored teaching all children in English over bilingual alternatives. Has there been a significant change in opinion? Answer by doing a two-sided test for the significance of the difference in two proportions at $\alpha = .05$. Why is a two-sided alternative appropriate here?

9.11   A high school had 17 students receive National Merit recognition (semifinalist or commendation) out of 482 seniors in 1992 and 29 students out of 503 seniors in 1995. Does this represent a significant change in the proportion recognized at this school? Answer by doing a two-sided test for the significance of the difference in two proportions at $\alpha = .10$. Why is a two-sided alternative appropriate here?

---

[9] *Source: Time*, October 9, 1995, p. 49.

9.12   The following data set[10] from a study by the well-known chemist and Nobel Laureate Linus Pauling (1901–1994) gives the incidence of cold among 279 French skiers who were randomized to the Vitamin C and Placebo groups.

Group	Cold		Total
	Yes	No	
Vitamin C	17	122	139
Placebo	31	109	140

Is there a significant difference in the incidence rates for cold between the Vitamin C and Placebo groups at $\alpha = .05$? What do you conclude about the effectiveness of Vitamin C in preventing cold?

9.13   The graduate degrees of faculty from a research group within a medical school were tabulated by gender, giving the following results.

		Degree	
		M.D.	Ph.D.
Gender	Male	5	1
	Female	3	6

(a) Set up the hypotheses to determine whether the proportion of male M.D.'s differs from the proportion of female M.D.'s. Which statistical test is appropriate to test the hypotheses?

(b) Calculate the P-value of the test. What is your conclusion using $\alpha = .05$?

9.14   A study evaluated the urinary-thromboglobulin excretion in 12 normal and 12 diabetic patients.[11] Summary results are obtained by coding values of 20 or less as "low" and values above 20 as "high," as shown in the following table.

	Excretion	
	Low	High
Normal	10	2
Diabetic	4	8

(a) Set up the hypotheses to determine whether there is a difference in the urinary-thromboglobulin excretion between normal and diabetic patients. Which statistical test is appropriate to test the hypotheses?

(b) Calculate the P-value of the test. What is your conclusion using $\alpha = .05$?

---

[10] L. Pauling (1971) "The significance of the evidence about ascorbic acid and the common cold," *Proceedings of the National Academy of Sciences*, **68**, pp. 2678–2681.

[11] B. A. van Oost, B. Veldhayzen, and A. P. M. Timmermans (1983), "Increased urinary β-thromboglobulin excretion in diabetes assayed with a modified RIA kit-technique," *Thrombosis and Haemostasis*, **9**, pp. 18–20. Reprinted in *Small Data Sets*, p. 249.

9.15 A matched pairs study[12] was conducted to compare two topical anesthetic drugs for use in dentistry. The two drugs were applied on the oral mucous membrane of the two sides of each patient's mouth, and after a certain period of time it was noted whether or not the membrane remained anesthetized. Data on 45 patients showed the following responses.

Drug 2 Response

		Anesthetized	Not Anesthetized
Drug 1	Anesthetized	15	13
Response	Not Anesthetized	3	14

(a) Set up the hypotheses to determine whether there is a statistically significant difference between the two drugs. Which statistical test is appropriate to test the hypotheses?

(b) Calculate the P-value of the test. What is your conclusion using $\alpha = .05$?

9.16 In a speech class two persuasive speeches, one pro and the other con, were given by two students on requiring guest lists for fraternity/sorority parties. The opinions of the other 52 students in the class were obtained on this issue before and after the speeches with the following responses.

After

		Pro	Con
Before	Pro	2	8
	Con	26	16

(a) Set up the hypotheses to determine whether or not there is a change in opinion of the students. Which statistical test is appropriate to test the hypotheses?

(b) Calculate the P-value of the test. What is your conclusion using $\alpha=.05$?

Section 9.3

9.17 Use the following data to test the hypothesis that a horse's chances of winning are unaffected by its position on the starting lineup. The data give the starting position of each of 144 winners, where position 1 is closest to the inside rail of the race track.[13]

Starting Position	1	2	3	4	5	6	7	8
Number of Wins	29	19	18	25	17	10	15	11

State the hypotheses and perform a test at $\alpha = .05$.

---

[12] J. W. Fertig, N. W. Chilton, and A. O. Varma (1964), "Studies in the design and analysis of dental experiments, 9: Sequential analysis (sign test)," *Journal of Oral and Therapeutical Pharmacology*, **1**, pp. 45–56.

[13] *New York Post*, August 30, 1955, p. 42. Reprinted in *Small Data Sets*, p. 36.

9.18 The number of first births to 700 women are shown by month from the University Hospital of Basel, Switzerland.[14]

Month	Jan	Feb	Mar	Apr	May	June	July	Aug	Sept	Oct	Nov	Dec
Births	66	63	64	48	64	74	70	59	54	51	45	42

State the hypotheses to test that births are spread uniformly through the year. Perform a test of the hypotheses at $\alpha = .05$.

9.19 The Hutterite Brethren is a religious group that is essentially a closed population with almost all marriages within the group. The following table shows the distribution of sons in families with 7 children whose mothers were born between 1879 and 1936.[15]

Number of Sons in Families with Seven Children								
Sons	0	1	2	3	4	5	6	7
Count	0	6	14	25	21	22	9	1

(a) State the hypotheses to test that the number of sons follows a binomial distribution with $p = 0.5$, where p is the probability that a child is male. Conduct a test of the hypotheses using a χ^2-test at $\alpha = .10$.

(b) State the hypotheses to test that the number of sons follows a binomial distribution (with unspecified p). Conduct a test of the hypotheses using a χ^2-test at $\alpha = .10$. How does the result of this test compare with the result from part (a)?

9.20 A genetics experiment on characteristics of tomato plants provided the following data on the numbers of offspring expressing four phenotypes.[16]

Phenotype	Frequency
Tall, cut-leaf	926
Dwarf, cut-leaf	293
Tall, potato-leaf	288
Dwarf, potato-leaf	104
Total	1611

(a) State the hypotheses to test that theoretically the four phenotypes will appear in the proportion 9:3:3:1.

(b) Test the hypotheses. Use $\alpha = .05$.

---

[14] P. Walser (1969), "Untersuchung über die Verteilung der Gerburtsermine bei der mehrgebärenden Frau," *Helvetica Paediatrica Acta*, Suppl. XX ad vol. 24, fasc 3, pp. 1–30. Reprinted in *Small Data Sets*, p. 77.

[15] P. Guttorp (1991), *Statistical Inference for Branching Processes*, New York: John Wiley & Sons, p. 194. Reprinted in *Small Data Sets*, p. 77.

[16] J. W. MacArthur (1931), "Linkage studies with the tomato, III. Fifteen factors in six groups," *Transactions of the Royal Canadian Institute*, **18**, pp. 1–19. Reprinted in *Small Data Sets*, p. 34.

9.21   During World War II, a 36 sq. km area of South London was gridded into 0.25 km squares to record bomb hits. The following data[17] give the number of squares receiving 0 hits, 1 hit, etc. If hits were random, a Poisson model would fit the data. Test using $\alpha = .05$ to see if this is the case.

Number of Hits	0	1	2	3	4	5	6	7
Number of 0.25 km Squares	229	211	93	35	7	0	0	1

9.22   Studies were made to estimate the number of passengers (other than the driver) per car in urban traffic. The numbers of passengers carried in 1011 cars traveling through the Wilshire and Bundy boulevard intersection in Los Angeles between 10:00 A.M. and 10:20 A.M. on March 24, 1959, are given below.[18]

Number of Passengers	0	1	2	3	4	≥ 5
Frequency	678	227	56	28	8	14

(a) The average number of passengers per car is 0.519. Test to see if the number of passengers follows a Poisson distribution.

(b) Consider a geometric distribution for the number of occupants. (The number of occupants = 1 + the number of passengers). Recall that the geometric distribution is given by

$$P(X = x) = (1 - p)^{x-1}p, \quad x = 1, 2, \ldots$$

where $p = 1/\mu$. Estimate p using $\hat{\mu} = 1.519$ occupants. Test to see if the number of occupants follows a geometric distribution.

(c) Which distribution fits the data better?

9.23   Consider the problem of testing $H_0: p = p_0$ vs. $H_1: p \neq p_0$, where p is the success probability of a Bernoulli population from which we have a random sample of size n. Equation (9.6) gives the following test statistic for this problem:

$$z = \frac{y - np_0}{\sqrt{np_0(1 - p_0)}}$$

where y is the number of successes.

(a) Show that $z^2 = \chi^2$, where the χ^2-statistic is given by (9.14). This χ^2-statistic has 1 d.f.

(b) Show that the two-sided z-test and the χ^2-test are equivalent.

9.24   The NBA final is a seven game series, and the first team to win four games wins the series. Denote by p the probability that the Eastern Conference team wins a game and by $q = 1 - p$ that the Western Conference team wins a game. Assume that these probabilities remain constant from game to game and that the outcomes of the games are mutually

---

[17] R. D. Clarke (1946), "An application of the Poisson distribution," *Journal of the Institute of Actuaries*, **72**, p. 48. Reprinted in *Small Data Sets*, p. 232.

[18] F. A. Haight (1970), "Group size distributions with applications to vehicle occupancy," in G. P. Patil ed., *Random Counts in Physical Science, Geo Science, and Business*, **3**, pp. 95–105. Reprinted in I. Olkin, L. J. Gleser, and C. Derman, (1980), *Probability Models and Applications*, New York: Macmillan, p. 204.

independent. Assume the result from Exercise 2.70 that the probability that the series ends in j games is given by

$$\binom{j-1}{3}[p^4 q^{j-4} + q^4 p^{j-4}], \quad j = 4, 5, 6, 7.$$

There have been 52 finals in NBA's history (from 1947 to 1998). The number of finals that have gone for 4, 5, 6 and 7 games has been as follows:

4 games: 6 finals,   5 games: 11 finals,   6 games: 21 finals,   7 games: 14 finals.

Suppose we assume that the two finalists are evenly matched, so that $p = q = 1/2$. Show that the above model fits these data well.

Section 9.4

9.25 Tell in each of the following instances whether sampling is multinomial or product multinomial. State mathematically the null hypothesis of no association between the two categorical variables under study.

(a) A sample of 500 people is cross-classified according to each person's religious affiliation (Christian, Jewish, Agnostic, Other) and political party affiliation (Republican, Democrat, Independent, Other).

(b) To compare the performances of different types of mutual funds, five groups of funds are sampled (municipal bond fund, corporate bond fund, equity income fund, blue chip stock fund, and aggressive growth fund) with 20 funds from each group. The sampled funds are classified according to whether the fund's return over a five year period is low (less than 5%), medium (5% to 10%), or high (greater than 10%).

9.26 Tell in each of the following instances whether sampling is multinomial or product multinomial. State mathematically the null hypothesis of no association between the two categorical variables under study.

(a) To see if there is an association between age and willingness to use internet grocery ordering services, 100 people are surveyed in each of four age groups (21–35, 36–50, 50–65, and over 65). The people surveyed are asked whether or not they would use the service, if they had the software.

(b) A sample of 1000 traffic accidents is cross-classified according to the severity of injury (none, minor, disabling, death) and the use of a safety restraint (none, seat belt, seat and shoulder belt).

9.27 Evidence for authorship of a document can be based on the distribution of word lengths. In 1861 the *New Orleans Crescent* published a set of ten letters signed Quintus Curtius Snodgrass. It has been claimed that the author was Mark Twain. A way to test this claim is to see if the word length distribution of the Q.C.S. letters matches the distribution of the word lengths in a sample of Mark Twain's writing. Here are the data for the two distributions.[19]

---

[19] C. S. Brinegar (1963), "Mark Twain and the Q.C.S. letters—a statistical test of authorship," *Journal of the Royal Statistical Association*, **58**, pp. 85–96. Reprinted in *Small Data Sets*, pp. 280–281.

Word Length	1	2	3	4	5	6	7	8	9	10	11	12	13+
Mark Twain	312	1146	1394	1177	661	442	367	231	181	109	50	24	12
Q.C.S.	424	2685	2752	2302	1431	992	896	638	465	276	152	101	61

(a) Which type of sampling is used here—multinomial or product multinomial?

(b) Do the appropriate test at $\alpha = .01$. State your conclusion.

9.28 *Reader's Digest* conducted an experiment to find out how honest people are in different cities.[20] Three cities of each type were selected: big cities (Atlanta, GA, Seattle, WA, and St. Louis, MO), suburbs (Boston, MA, Houston, TX, and Los Angeles, CA), medium cities (Dayton, OH, Greensboro, PA, and Las Vegas, NV) and small cities (Cheyenne, WY, Concord, NH, and Meadville, PA). In each selected city 10 wallets were left in public places. Each wallet contained $50 cash and a telephone number and an address where the owner could be reached. A record was kept of the number of wallets returned by people who found the wallets. The data are summarized in the table below.

	Wallet		
Type of Cities	Returned	Kept	Row Total
Big Cities	21	9	30
Suburbs	18	12	30
Medium Cities	17	13	30
Small Cities	24	6	30
Column Total	80	40	120

(a) Which type of sampling is used here—multinomial or product multinomial?

(b) Set up the hypotheses to check whether there are significant differences between the percentages of people who returned the wallets in different types of cities.

(c) Do a χ^2-test of the hypotheses. Can you conclude that there are significant differences among the return rates in different types of cities? Use $\alpha = .10$.

9.29 Biologists studying sandflies at a site in eastern Panama looked at the relationship between gender and the height at which the flies were caught in a light trap, resulting in the following data.[21]

	Height above Ground		Row
Gender	3 feet	35 feet	Total
Males	173	125	298
Females	150	73	223
Column Total	323	198	521

[20] R. K. Bennett (1995), "How honest are we?" *Reader's Digest*, December 1995, pp. 49–55.

[21] H. A. Christensen, A. Herrer, and S. R. Telford (1972), "Enzootic cutaneous leishmaniasis in Eastern Panama. 2. Entomological investigations," *Annals of Tropical Medicine and Parasitology*, **66**, pp. 56–66. Reprinted in *Small Data Sets*, p. 96.

(a) Which type of sampling is used here—multinomial or product multinomial?

(b) Set up the hypotheses to test whether the gender of the sandflies and trap height are associated.

(c) Do a chi-square test of the hypotheses. Use $\alpha = .05$.

9.30 The drug Dramamine was tested for its effectiveness to prevent airsickness compared to placebo. A total of 216 volunteers were randomly assigned to receive treatment (Dramamine) or control (placebo). Of the 108 volunteers receiving treatment, 31 became airsick; of the 108 volunteers receiving placebo, 60 became airsick.[22]

(a) Make a 2 × 2 table displaying the results.

(b) Set up the hypotheses to test whether Dramamine is effective in reducing the chances of airsickness.

(c) Do a chi-square test of the hypotheses. Use $\alpha = .05$.

9.31 The Western Collaborative Group Study investigated the risk of coronary heart disease in 3154 men. From these data, the 40 heaviest men were classified by their cholesterol measurements (mg per 100 ml) and behavior (Type A or Type B). Broadly speaking, Type A behavior is competitive, while Type B behavior is noncompetitive. There were 20 Type A men, of whom 8 had cholesterol levels above 250 mg per 100 ml. There were 20 Type B men, of whom 3 had cholesterol levels above 250 mg per 100 ml.[23]

(a) Make a 2 × 2 table displaying the personality type by cholesterol levels (≤ 250 vs. > 250).

(b) Set up the hypotheses to test whether or not personality type is associated with cholesterol level. Conduct a test of the hypotheses. Use $\alpha = .10$.

9.32 The following table gives the eye color and hair color of 592 students.[24]

Eye	Hair Color				Row
Color	Black	Brown	Red	Blond	Total
Brown	68	119	26	7	220
Blue	20	84	17	94	215
Hazel	15	54	14	10	93
Green	5	29	14	16	64
Column Total	108	286	71	127	592

(a) Which type of sampling is used here—multinomial or product multinomial?

(b) Set up the hypotheses to test that the eye color and hair color are associated. Do a chi-square test at $\alpha = .05$. What do you conclude?

[22] B. A. Strickland and J. L. Han (1949), "Effectiveness of Dramamine in prevention of airsickness," *Science*, **109**, p. 359. Reprinted in A. K. Bahn (1972), *Basic Medical Statistics*, New York: Grune & Stratton, p. 68.

[23] S. Selvin (1991), *Statistical Analysis of Epidemiological Data*, New York: Oxford University Press, Table 2.1. Reprinted in *Small Data Sets*, p. 39.

[24] R. D. Snee, (1974), "Graphical display of two-way contingency tables," *The American Statistician*, **28**, pp. 9–12.

9.33 Following the nuclear mishap at Three Mile Island near Harrisburg, PA, a sample of 150 households was surveyed. One question asked was: "Should there have been a full evacuation of the immediate area?" The following table classifies the responses according to the distance from the accident.[25]

Full Evacuation	Distance (in miles) from Three Mile Island						Row Total
	1–3	4–6	7–9	10–12	13–15	15+	
Yes	7	11	10	5	4	29	66
No	9	11	13	6	6	39	84
Column Total	16	22	23	11	10	68	150

(a) Set up the hypotheses to test whether distance from the accident and evacuation attitudes are associated.

(b) Conduct a test of the hypotheses. Use $\alpha = .10$.

9.34 To investigate whether there is a relationhip between tonsil size and carriers of a particular bacterium, *Streptococcus pyrogenes*, 1398 school children were examined. The following table classifies the children according to tonsil size and carrier status.[26]

Tonsil Size	Carrier Status		Row Total
	Carrier	Noncarrier	
Normal	19	497	516
Large	29	560	589
Very Large	24	269	293
Column Total	72	1326	1398

(a) Set up the hypotheses to test whether tonsil size and carrier status are associated.

(b) Conduct a test of the hypotheses. Can you conclude that tonsil size and carrier status are associated? Use $\alpha = .05$.

9.35 A study was done to investigate the association between the age at which breast cancer was diagnosed and the frequency of breast self-examination. The following table classifies the women in the sample according to these two criteria.[27]

---

[25] S. Brown et al. (1979), "Final report on a survey of Three Mile Island area residents," Department of Geography, Michigan State University. Reprinted in W. Mendenhall and T. Sincich (1984), *Statistics for the Engineering and Computer Sciences*, Upper Saddle River, NJ: Prentice Hall, p. 701.

[26] W. J. Dranowski (1988), *Principles of Multivariate Analysis*, Oxford: Oxford University Press, p. 269. Reprinted in *Small Data Sets*, pp. 96–97.

[27] R. T. Senie, P. P. Rosen, M. Lesser, and D. W. Kinne (1981), "Breast self-examinations and medical examination relating to breast cancer stage," *American Journal of Public Health*, **71**, pp. 583–590. Reprinted in *Small Data Sets*, p. 307.

Age at Diagnosis	Frequency of Breast Self-examination		
of Breast Cancer	Monthly	Occasionally	Never
< 45	91	90	51
45–59	150	200	155
60+	109	198	172

    (a) Set up the hypotheses to test that frequency of self-examination is related to the age of breast cancer diagnosis.

    (b) Conduct a test of the hypotheses. Can you conclude association using $\alpha = .10$?

9.36 Refer to Exercise 9.30. Calculate a 95% CI for the odds ratio. What does this say about the odds of airsickness if Dramamine is used?

9.37 Refer to Exercise 9.31. Calculate a 90% CI for the odds ratio. What does this say about the odds of higher cholesterol levels for a Type A personality?

Advanced Exercises

9.38 A sample of employed men aged 18 to 67 were asked if they had carried out work on their home in the preceding year for which they would have previously employed a craftsman. The following table gives the summary of responses of 906 homeowners.[28]

Work	Home Repair	Age			Row Total
		< 30	31–45	46+	
Skilled	Yes	56	56	35	147
	No	12	21	8	41
Unskilled	Yes	23	52	49	124
	No	9	31	51	91
Office	Yes	54	191	102	347
	No	19	76	61	156
	Column Totals	173	427	306	906

    (a) For each category of work, set up the hypotheses to test that frequency of home repair is related to the age. Conduct the test using $\alpha = .05$.

    (b) Create a table of home repair by age summing across all types of work. Test for association between the frequency of home repair and age group using $\alpha = .05$.

    (c) Compare the results in (a) and (b). What information is missed in (b)?

9.39 In this exercise we will derive the more accurate large sample CI (9.3) for the binomial proportion p.

    (a) Begin with the probability statement

$$P\left[-z_{\alpha/2} \le \frac{(\hat{p} - p)}{\sqrt{pq/n}} \le z_{\alpha/2}\right] = P\left[(\hat{p} - p)^2 \le z_{\alpha/2}^2 \frac{pq}{n}\right] \simeq 1 - \alpha$$

---

[28] D. E. Edwards and S. Kreiner (1983), "The analysis of contingency tables by graphical models," *Biometrika*, **70**, pp. 553–565. Reprinted in *Small Data Sets*, p. 24.

and simplify it to the form

$$P\{Ap^2 + Bp + C \le 0\} \simeq 1 - \alpha.$$

(b) Find the two roots of the quadratic equation $Ap^2 + Bp + C = 0$, and show that they are given by

$$p_L = \frac{\hat{p} + \frac{z^2}{2n} - \sqrt{\frac{\hat{p}\hat{q}z^2}{n} + \frac{z^4}{4n^2}}}{\left(1 + \frac{z^2}{n}\right)}, \quad p_U = \frac{\hat{p} + \frac{z^2}{2n} + \sqrt{\frac{\hat{p}\hat{q}z^2}{2n} + \frac{z^4}{4n^2}}}{\left(1 + \frac{z^2}{n}\right)}$$

where $z = z_{\alpha/2}$.

(c) Show that $Ap^2 + Bp + C \le 0$ is equivalent to $p_L \le p \le p_U$. (*Hint:* Sketch the quadratic function $Ap^2 + Bp + C$ and note that it falls below zero when p falls between its two roots, p_L and p_U.) Therefore $P\{p_L \le p \le p_U\} \simeq 1 - \alpha$, and thus $[p_L, p_U]$ is an approximate $(1 - \alpha)$-level CI for p. Why is this CI more accurate than that given in (9.1)?

(d) Show that if the terms of the order of $1/n$ are ignored in comparison to the terms of the order of $1/\sqrt{n}$ when n is large, the CI $[p_L, p_U]$ simplifies to (9.1).

9.40 Consider three categorical variables, X, Y, and Z, with r, c, and t categories, respectively. A three-way $r \times c \times t$ frequency table is obtained by randomly sampling n units and cross-classifying them with respect to X, Y, and Z. Denote the observed count in cell (i, j, k) by n_{ijk} and the cell probability by p_{ijk}.

(a) Write the null hypothesis of independence between the X, Y, and Z in terms of the p_{ijk}.

(b) Give a formula for the estimates of the expected frequencies e_{ijk} under the null hypothesis.

(c) Give a formula for the chi-square statistic. What are its degrees of freedom?

9.41 The following table[29] gives the racial characteristics of 326 individuals convicted of homicide in 20 Florida counties during 1976–1977, racial characteristics of their victims, and whether they received the death penalty or not.

Defendant's Race	Victim's Race			
	White		Black	
	Death Penalty		Death Penalty	
	Yes	No	Yes	No
White	19	132	0	9
Black	11	52	6	97

(a) Create a 2 × 2 table of Defendant's Race vs. Death Penalty by summing over the Victim's Race. Is there a racial difference between the proportions of White and Black convicts who received the death penalty? Do a large sample z-test at $\alpha = .05$.

(b) Now consider two separate 2 × 2 tables for White victims and Black victims. In each case repeat the test in (a).

---

[29] M. Radelet (1981), "Racial characteristics and the imposition of death penalty," *American Sociological Review*, **46**, pp. 918–927.

(c) Does it appear that the death penalty depends on the victim's race? Explain.

9.42 Exercise 9.39 derived a large sample CI for the binomial proportion p. The same method can be applied to derive large sample CI's for the parameters of many other distributions. In this exercise we will do this for the Poisson distribution. Suppose that $X_1, X_2, \ldots, X_n$ are the counts of defective items produced on n different days. The number of defectives on any given day is modeled as a Poisson random variable with parameter λ, which is the unknown population mean defectives per day. Since $E(X_i) = \mu = \lambda$ and $\text{Var}(X_i) = \sigma^2 = \lambda$ for the Poisson distribution, it follows that $E(\bar{X}) = \lambda$ and $\text{Var}(\bar{X}) = \lambda/n$. Furthermore, by the central limit theorem,

$$\frac{\bar{X} - \lambda}{\sqrt{\lambda/n}} \approx N(0, 1).$$

(a) Beginning with the probability statement

$$P\left[-z_{\alpha/2} \leq \frac{\bar{X} - \lambda}{\sqrt{\lambda/n}} \leq z_{\alpha/2} \right] \simeq 1 - \alpha$$

show that $[\lambda_L, \lambda_U]$ is a large sample $(1 - \alpha)$-level CI for λ, where

$$\lambda_L = \bar{X} + \frac{z^2}{2n} - \sqrt{\frac{\bar{X}z^2}{n} + \frac{z^4}{4n^2}} \quad \text{and} \quad \lambda_U = \bar{X} + \frac{z^2}{2n} + \sqrt{\frac{\bar{X}z^2}{n} + \frac{z^4}{4n^2}}$$

where $z = z_{\alpha/2}$.

(b) Show that if the terms of the order of $1/n$ are ignored in comparison to the terms of the order of $1/\sqrt{n}$ when n is large, the CI $[\lambda_L, \lambda_U]$ simplifies to

$$\left[\bar{X} - z_{\alpha/2}\sqrt{\frac{\bar{X}}{n}}, \bar{X} + z_{\alpha/2}\sqrt{\frac{\bar{X}}{n}} \right].$$

9.43 Consider the problem of comparing two Bernoulli populations based on samples of sizes n_1 and n_2, respectively, with the following outcomes.

	Success	Failure	Row Total
Population 1	n_{11}	n_{12}	n_1
Population 2	n_{21}	n_{22}	n_2
Column Total	m	$n - m$	n

We want to test $H_0: p_1 = p_2$ vs. $H_1: p_1 \neq p_2$. The large sample z-test for this problem uses the test statistic

$$z = \frac{\hat{p}_1 - \hat{p}_2}{\sqrt{\hat{p}(1 - \hat{p})\left(\frac{1}{n_1} + \frac{1}{n_2} \right)}}$$

where $\hat{p}_1 = n_{11}/n_1$, $\hat{p}_2 = n_{21}/n_2$, and $\hat{p} = m/n$.

(a) Show that $z^2 = \chi^2$, where the χ^2-statistic is given by (9.19). This χ^2-statistic has 1 d.f.

(b) Show that the two-sided z-test and the χ^2-test are equivalent.

9.44 The National Revenue Service of Canada used a psychological and general intelligence test to make promotion decisions. In this test 59% of the males passed and 27% of the females passed, as shown in the following table:[30]

	Pass	Fail	Row Total	Percent Pass
Male	68	47	115	59%
Female	68	183	251	27%
Column Total	136	230	366	37%

The test was challenged in the court as being discriminatory against females. The Revenue Service defended the test by arguing that the test results are in line with the college education of the males and females, as shown in the following table:

	Some College	No College	Row Total	Percent College
Male	60	55	115	52%
Female	63	188	251	25%
Column Total	123	243	366	34%

The Appeals Board accepted this explanation and denied the discrimination suit.

(a) Do you accept the explanation offered by the Revenue Service? Why or why not?

(b) Let p_{cm} and p_{cf} be the true pass rates for college educated males and females, respectively, and let p_{nm} and p_{nf} be the corresponding rates for non-college educated males and females. We want to test two hypotheses simultaneously—$H_{0c}: p_{cm} = p_{cf}$ and $H_{0n}: p_{nm} = p_{nf}$. The Appeals Board was never offered the pass/fail data for males and females stratified by college education. However, we can consider two extreme cases—in one case college educated males and females have nearly the same pass rate and in the other case non-college educated males and females have nearly the same pass rate—and see if the explanation still holds. For the first case consider the following $2 \times 2 \times 2$ table.

	College Pass	College Fail	No College Pass	No College Fail	Row Total
Male	56	4	12	43	115
Female	60	3	8	180	251
Column Total	116	7	20	223	366

Show that in this case non-college educated males have a significantly higher pass rate than females, although there is no significant difference between college educated males and females.

---

[30] J. Gastwirth, A. Krieger, and P. Rosenbaum (1994), "How a court accepted an impossible decision," *The American Statistician*, **48**, pp. 313–315.

For the second case, consider the following $2 \times 2 \times 2$ table.

| | College | | No College | | Row |
	Pass	Fail	Pass	Fail	Total
Male	56	4	12	43	115
Female	27	36	41	147	251
Column Total	83	40	53	190	366

Show that in this case college educated males have a significantly higher pass rate than females, although there is no significant difference between non-college educated males and females.

Thus in both extreme cases, males have a higher pass rate than females in one of the education categories. Hence the Revenue Service's argument is not valid.

9.45 We saw in Section 9.2.1 that the exact distribution of Fisher's test statistic is hypergeometric under $H_0 \colon p_1 = p_2$. In this exercise we derive the exact distribution under $H_1 \colon p_1 \neq p_2$, which is useful for evaluating the power of the test. We use the same notation as in the text.

(a) Show that

$$P(X = x \mid X + Y = m) = \frac{\binom{n_1}{x}\binom{n_2}{m-x}\psi^x}{\sum_i \binom{n_1}{i}\binom{n_2}{m-i}\psi^i}$$

where

$$\psi = \frac{p_1/(1 - p_1)}{p_2/(1 - p_2)}$$

is the odds ratio and where the summation over i extends from $\max(0, m - n_2)$ to $\min(n_1, m)$. (*Hint:* Substitute the binomial probabability formulas for $X \sim \mathrm{Bin}(n_1, p_1)$ and $Y \sim \mathrm{Bin}(n_2, p_2)$ in the expression for $P(X = x \mid X + Y = m)$, simplify the resulting expression and cancel the common terms from the numerator and denominator.)

(b) State H_0 and H_1 in terms of ψ. Explain how the above expression for $P(X = x \mid X + Y = m)$ can be used to evaluate the power of Fisher's exact test as function of ψ.

(c) Show that the above distribution reduces to the hypergeometric distribution when $\psi = 1$. (*Hint:* Use the combinatorial identity from Exercise 2.8 that $\sum_i \binom{n_1}{i}\binom{n_2}{m-i} = \binom{n}{m}$, where $n = n_1 + n_2$.)

CHAPTER 10

SIMPLE LINEAR REGRESSION AND CORRELATION

A primary goal in many studies is to understand and quantify relationships between variables. In the previous chapter we studied methods to evaluate the relationship between two categorical variables. In the present and the next chapter we study corresponding methods for two or more numerical variables.

Often, one of the variables is regarded as a **response** or **outcome** or **dependent** variable and the others as **predictor** or **explanatory** or **independent** variables. In certain laws of natural sciences and engineering, a **theoretical model** between the variables is *exactly* known. An example is Boyle's law, which relates the pressure and volume of an ideal gas at a constant temperature. A characteristic feature of these models is that they have a *deterministic* relationship between the response and predictor variables. Unfortunately, theoretical models exist only in rare and idealized situations. Even when they exist, they often involve unknown parameters (e.g., the gravitational constant in Newton's gravity law) and the variables are subject to measurement errors. In all other applications, the actual relationships are never exactly known. There are various sources of random errors that cannot be fully accounted for and/or modeled. As a result, the relationships are *probabilistic*. In such cases, a general approach is to fit an **empirical model** that *approximately* captures the main features of the relationship between the response variable and the key predictor variables.

Regression analysis is a statistical methodology to estimate the relationship (using a theoretical or an empirical model) of a response variable to a set of predictor variables. In this chapter we consider only two variables, which we label as x and y. When it is clear which variable is a predictor and which is a response, we use x to denote

346

the predictor variable and y to denote the response variable. For example, consider an energy planner who predicts the demand for gas for home heating (y) from the average daily temperature (x). In other situations, it is not always clear which variable represents a response and which is a predictor. For example, consider a financial analyst who studies the relationship between a stock market index and a bond market index or a pediatrician who studies the relationship between the head size and the body size of a newborn. **Correlation analysis**, which is closely related to regression analysis, is a statistical methodology used in this case to assess the strength of relationship between x and y.

The simplest relationship between x and y is linear. In Chapter 4 we used the method of **linear regression** to fit a straight line of the form $y = a + bx$ to paired data on (x, y). In this chapter we go beyond the use of linear regression as a merely descriptive tool to summarize bivariate data and study methods of statistical inference, so that we can answer questions such as "How strongly is y related to x?" We begin by giving a probabilistic model for linear regression and then present the least squares method to estimate the equation of the "best fitting" straight line. We also discuss other important aspects, including model diagnostics and data transformations to find a better fitting model. The final section discusses correlation analysis.

10.1   A PROBABILISTIC MODEL FOR SIMPLE LINEAR REGRESSION

Let $x_1, x_2, \ldots, x_n$ be specific settings of the predictor variable chosen by the investigator and let $y_1, y_2, \ldots, y_n$ be the corresponding values of the response variable. We assume that y_i is the observed value of the random variable (r.v.) Y_i, which depends on x_i according to the following model:

$$Y_i = \beta_0 + \beta_1 x_i + \epsilon_i \quad (i = 1, 2, \ldots, n). \tag{10.1}$$

Here ϵ_i is a **random error** with $E(\epsilon_i) = 0$ and $\text{Var}(\epsilon_i) = \sigma^2$. Thus,

$$E(Y_i) = \mu_i = \beta_0 + \beta_1 x_i \tag{10.2}$$

represents the true but unknown mean of Y_i. This relationship between $E(Y_i)$ and x_i is referred to as the **true regression line**, with β_0 being its unknown intercept and β_1 being its unknown slope.[1] We further assume that the ϵ_i are independent and identically distributed (i.i.d.) r.v.'s. These random errors may arise due to a variety of causes (e.g., measurement error, error due to other variables affecting Y_i not being included in the model, etc.). The assumption $E(\epsilon_i) = 0$ means that there is no systematic bias due to these causes. Usually we assume that the ϵ_i are normally distributed with unknown variance σ^2. Then the Y_i are independent $N(\mu_i = \beta_0 + \beta_1 x_i, \sigma^2)$ r.v.'s. Notice that the predictor variable is regarded as *nonrandom* because it is assumed to be set by the investigator.

---

[1] In Chapter 4 we used a and b to denote the intercept and slope, respectively, simply as sample summary statistics with no notion of their being estimates of some population parameters. Here we use Greek letters for two reasons: (i) we want to denote that they are unknown population parameters, and (ii) this notation extends naturally when we have multiple predictors.

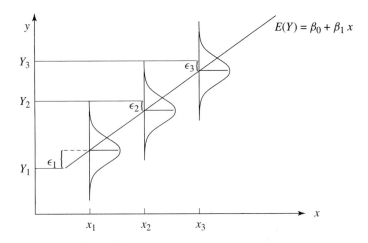

Figure 10.1   Simple Linear Regression Model

This linear regression model, which is represented graphically in Figure 10.1, has four basic assumptions.

1. The mean of Y_i is a linear function of x_i.
2. The Y_i have a common variance σ^2, which is the same for all values of x.
3. The errors ϵ_i (and hence the observations Y_i) are normally distributed.
4. The errors ϵ_i (and hence the observations Y_i) are independent.

In Section 10.4 we shall study graphical and other methods to check whether the data satisfy these assumptions, and if not, how to correct for them.

The following comments about these assumptions should be noted.

1. As will become evident later, the above model is called "linear" not because it is linear in x, but rather because it is linear in the parameters β_0 and β_1. In other words, a model such as $E(Y) = \beta_0 + \beta_1 \log x$ is also a linear model because we can relabel $\log x$ as x.
2. In many cases the predictor variable is not set at predetermined fixed values, but is random (denoted by X) along with Y. An example is height (X) and weight (Y) measurements on a sample of children with the objective of predicting a child's weight given his/her height. In this case we use the model $E(Y \mid X = x) = \beta_0 + \beta_1 x$, which is the **conditional expectation** of Y given $X = x$. Recall from Chapter 2 that this is called the **regression function**. (See equation (2.17).)

10.2   FITTING THE SIMPLE LINEAR REGRESSION MODEL

10.2.1 Least Squares (LS) Fit

Before attempting to fit the linear regression model (10.1) to the data (x_1, y_1), (x_2, y_2), ..., (x_n, y_n), it is advisable to first make a **scatter plot**, as suggested in Chapter 4, and see if the plot is approximately linear.

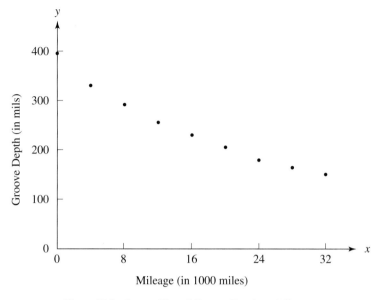

Figure 10.2   Scatter Plot of Groove Depth vs. Mileage

EXAMPLE 10.1   (TIRE TREAD WEAR VS. MILEAGE: SCATTER PLOT)

A laboratory tested tires for tread wear by running the following experiment.[2] Tires of a certain brand were mounted on a car. The tires were rotated from position to position every 1000 miles, and the groove depth was measured in mils (.001 inches) initially and after every 4000 miles. Measurements were made at six equiangular positions on each of six grooves around the circumference of every tire. Table 10.1 gives the averages of the six equiangular measurements on the outside groove of one tire after every 4000 miles up to 32,000 miles. The scatter plot for these data is shown in Figure 10.2. It looks fairly linear, and therefore it is reasonable to fit a straight line to the data.   ◆

Table 10.1 Mileage and Groove Depth of a Car Tire

Mileage (in 1000 miles)	Groove Depth (in mils)
0	394.33
4	329.50
8	291.00
12	255.17
16	229.33
20	204.83
24	179.00
28	163.83
32	150.33

---

[2] Experimental details and data courtesy of Mr. Doug Domeck, Smithers Scientific Services, Inc., Akron, OH. Certain experimental details are simplified for expository purposes.

We will use the **least squares (LS) method** to fit the model (10.1). The LS method was proposed by the famous German mathematician Gauss (1777–1855), whom we met in Chapter 2 when discussing the normal (Gaussian) distribution. To understand the method, consider fitting a straight line

$$y = \beta_0 + \beta_1 x$$

to the tread wear data with trial values $\beta_0 = 375$ for the intercept and the slope $\beta_1 = -(394.33 - 150.33)/32 = -7.625$, which is determined from the first and the last point. This straight line is plotted on the scatter plot for the tread wear data in Figure 10.3.

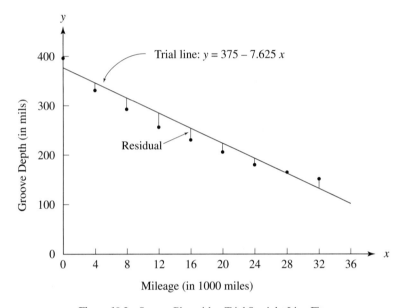

Figure 10.3 Scatter Plot with a Trial Straight Line Fit

How well does this straight line fit the data? To answer this question, we look at the deviations between the observed y_i's and the corresponding points on the straight line $y = \beta_0 + \beta_1 x$:

$$y_i - (\beta_0 + \beta_1 x_i) \quad (i = 1, 2, \ldots, n).$$

For the fit to be good, these deviations should be small. We use the sum of squared deviations:

$$Q = \sum_{i=1}^{n} [y_i - (\beta_0 + \beta_1 x_i)]^2 \tag{10.3}$$

as an overall measure of distance of the data points from the fitted line; the smaller the value of Q, the better the fit. For the trial straight line we compute $Q = 3350.80$. The LS method gives the "best" fitting straight line in the sense of minimizing Q. The values of β_0 and β_1 that minimize Q are referred to as the **least squares (LS) estimates** and denoted by $\hat{\beta}_0$ and $\hat{\beta}_1$, respectively.

It should be pointed out that minimizing the sum of squared deviations is done partly for mathematical convenience. As we shall see below, the LS estimates are easy to compute and have rather simple distributions. Other criteria are possible, e.g., minimizing the sum of absolute deviations, but the resulting estimates are more difficult to compute and do not have simple distributions.

One way to find the LS estimates $\hat{\beta}_0$ and $\hat{\beta}_1$ is to set the first partial derivatives of Q with respect to β_0 and β_1 equal to zero, and solve the resulting equations for β_0 and β_1.[3] We have

$$\frac{\partial Q}{\partial \beta_0} = -2 \sum_{i=1}^{n} [y_i - (\beta_0 + \beta_1 x_i)]$$

and   (10.4)

$$\frac{\partial Q}{\partial \beta_1} = -2 \sum_{i=1}^{n} x_i [y_i - (\beta_0 + \beta_1 x_i)].$$

Setting these partial derivatives equal to zero and simplifying, we obtain a pair of equations called the **normal equations**:

$$\beta_0 n + \beta_1 \sum_{i=1}^{n} x_i = \sum_{i=1}^{n} y_i$$

and   (10.5)

$$\beta_0 \sum_{i=1}^{n} x_i + \beta_1 \sum_{i=1}^{n} x_i^2 = \sum_{i=1}^{n} x_i y_i.$$

Since the normal equations are simultaneous *linear* equations,[4] they can be easily solved for β_0 and β_1. The solutions are:

$$\hat{\beta}_0 = \frac{(\sum x_i^2)(\sum y_i) - (\sum x_i)(\sum x_i y_i)}{n \sum x_i^2 - (\sum x_i)^2}, \quad \hat{\beta}_1 = \frac{n \sum x_i y_i - (\sum x_i)(\sum y_i)}{n \sum x_i^2 - (\sum x_i)^2}. \quad (10.6)$$

We introduce the following notation to simplify the above formulas as well as for later use. Let

$$S_{xy} = \sum_{i=1}^{n} (x_i - \bar{x})(y_i - \bar{y}) = \sum_{i=1}^{n} x_i y_i - \frac{1}{n} \left(\sum_{i=1}^{n} x_i \right) \left(\sum_{i=1}^{n} y_i \right)$$

$$S_{xx} = \sum_{i=1}^{n} (x_i - \bar{x})^2 = \sum_{i=1}^{n} x_i^2 - \frac{1}{n} \left(\sum_{i=1}^{n} x_i \right)^2$$

---

[3] Q can be shown to be a bowl-shaped ("convex") function of β_0 and β_1, and hence $\hat{\beta}_0$ and $\hat{\beta}_1$ yield a global minimum.

[4] That the normal equations are linear in β_0 and β_1 is a consequence of choosing the criterion function Q as the sum of *squared* deviations.

$$S_{yy} = \sum_{i=1}^{n}(y_i - \bar{y})^2 = \sum_{i=1}^{n} y_i^2 - \frac{1}{n}\left(\sum_{i=1}^{n} y_i\right)^2.$$

The meaning of this notation is as follows: S_{xy} gives the sum of cross-products of the x_i's and y_i's around their respective means. This can be seen from the first expression for S_{xy}; the second expression is more convenient for hand calculation. S_{xx} and S_{yy} give the sums of squares of the differences between the x_i and $\bar{x}$, and the y_i and $\bar{y}$, respectively. This can be seen in each case from the first expression, while the second expression is more convenient for hand calculation. Using this notation, the expressions (10.6) for the LS estimates can be simplified to

$$\hat{\beta}_0 = \bar{y} - \hat{\beta}_1\bar{x}, \quad \hat{\beta}_1 = \frac{S_{xy}}{S_{xx}}. \tag{10.7}$$

The sign of the slope coefficient $\hat{\beta}_1$ is the same as the sign of the cross-product sum S_{xy}, since S_{xx} is positive. What determines the sign of S_{xy}? See Figure 10.4(a), which shows a positively sloping scatter plot. By regarding the point $(\bar{x}, \bar{y})$ as the origin, we see that most points fall in the first and the third quadrants. For the points in the first quadrant, both $x_i - \bar{x}$ and $y_i - \bar{y}$ are positive, so $(x_i - \bar{x})(y_i - \bar{y}) > 0$. For the points in the third quadrant both $x_i - \bar{x}$ and $y_i - \bar{y}$ are negative, so again $(x_i - \bar{x})(y_i - \bar{y}) > 0$. Thus a majority of the cross-products are positive making their sum positive. Similarly, for the negatively sloping scatter plot shown in Figure 10.4(b), a majority of the points fall in the second and the fourth quadrants; hence the corresponding cross-products $(x_i - \bar{x})(y_i - \bar{y}) < 0$, making their sum negative.

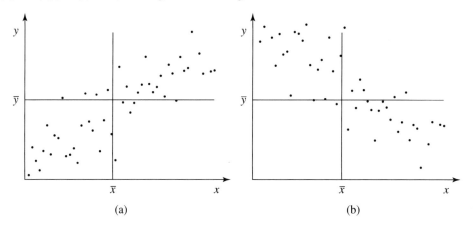

Figure 10.4   Scatter Plots with (a) Positive slope and (b) Negative slope

The equation

$$\hat{y} = \hat{\beta}_0 + \hat{\beta}_1 x \tag{10.8}$$

is known as the **least squares (LS) line**, which is an estimate of the true regression line. If we substitute $x = \bar{x}$, the corresponding fitted value is $\hat{\beta}_0 + \hat{\beta}_1\bar{x} = \bar{y} - \hat{\beta}_1\bar{x} + \hat{\beta}_1\bar{x} = \bar{y}$. This shows that the LS line passes through the point $(\bar{x}, \bar{y})$, the "centroid" of the scatter plot.

EXAMPLE 10.2 (TIRE TREAD WEAR VS. MILEAGE: LS LINE FIT)

Find the equation of the LS line for the tire tread wear data from Table 10.1.

We have $\sum x_i = 144$, $\sum y_i = 2197.32$, $\sum x_i^2 = 3264$, $\sum y_i^2 = 589{,}887.08$, $\sum x_i y_i = 28{,}167.72$, and $n = 9$. From these we calculate $\bar{x} = 16$, $\bar{y} = 244.15$,

$$S_{xy} = \sum_{i=1}^{n} x_i y_i - \frac{1}{n}\left(\sum_{i=1}^{n} x_i\right)\left(\sum_{i=1}^{n} y_i\right) = 28{,}167.72 - \frac{1}{9}(144 \times 2197.32) = -6989.40$$

and

$$S_{xx} = \sum_{i=1}^{n} x_i^2 - \frac{1}{n}\left(\sum_{i=1}^{n} x_i\right)^2 = 3264 - \frac{1}{9}(144)^2 = 960.$$

The slope and intercept estimates are

$$\hat{\beta}_1 = \frac{-6989.40}{960} = -7.281 \quad \text{and} \quad \hat{\beta}_0 = 244.15 + 7.281 \times 16 = 360.64.$$

Therefore the equation of the LS line is

$$\hat{y} = 360.64 - 7.281x.$$

From the fitted equation we conclude that, on the average, there is a loss of 7.281 mils in the tire groove depth for every 1000 miles of driving. This "best" fitting line has $Q_{\min} = 2531.53$, while for the trial line we had $Q = 3350.80$.

The fitted equation can be used to estimate the mean groove depth for a given mileage. For example, the mean groove depth for all tires driven for 25,000 miles under the experimental conditions is estimated to be

$$\hat{y} = 360.64 - 7.281 \times 25 = 178.62 \text{ mils.}$$

Note that the groove depth of individual tires will vary around the mean value. The problem of *predicting* the groove depth of an individual tire after a given mileage is discussed in Section 10.3.3. ◆

10.2.2 Goodness of Fit of the LS Line

Coefficient of Determination and Correlation. Denote the **fitted values** of the y_i by $\hat{y}_i$ given by

$$\hat{y}_i = \hat{\beta}_0 + \hat{\beta}_1 x_i, \quad i = 1, 2, \ldots, n.$$

The **residuals**

$$e_i = y_i - \hat{y}_i = y_i - (\hat{\beta}_0 + \hat{\beta}_1 x_i), \quad i = 1, 2, \ldots, n$$

are used to evaluate the goodness of fit of the LS line. The $Q_{\min} = \sum e_i^2$ obtained using the LS method is called the **error sum of squares (SSE)**. For the tire tread wear data, SSE $= Q_{\min} = 2531.53$. Although this is the minimum possible value of Q, is it small enough? In other words, is the best fit provided by the LS method good enough? To answer this question we need to compare SSE with some benchmark. This benchmark is provided by the $Q_{\min}$ that is obtained if we fit the simplest possible model: $Y_i = \beta_0 + \epsilon_i$ ($i = 1, 2, \ldots, n$). In this model the x_i's are ignored and all Y_i's have the same mean, $\mu = \beta_0$. It is easily seen that the LS estimate of the common mean is $\hat{\mu} = \hat{\beta}_0 = \bar{y}$. Therefore the corresponding $Q_{\min}$ equals

$$\sum_{i=1}^{n}(y_i - \bar{y})^2 = \sum_{i=1}^{n} y_i^2 - \frac{1}{n}\left(\sum_{i=1}^{n} y_i\right)^2 = S_{yy}.$$

We refer to this as the **total sum of squares (SST)**, which measures the variability of the y_i's around $\bar{y}$.

The SST can be decomposed into two components as follows. First write

$$y_i - \bar{y} = (\hat{y}_i - \bar{y}) + (y_i - \hat{y}_i).$$

Square both sides and sum over $i = 1$ to n, yielding

$$\text{SST} = \underbrace{\sum_{i=1}^{n}(y_i - \bar{y})^2}_{} = \underbrace{\sum_{i=1}^{n}(\hat{y}_i - \bar{y})^2}_{\text{SSR}} + \underbrace{\sum_{i=1}^{n}(y_i - \hat{y}_i)^2}_{\text{SSE}} + \underbrace{2\sum_{i=1}^{n}(y_i - \hat{y}_i)(\hat{y}_i - \bar{y})}_{=0}.$$

The first term is nonnegative, the second term is simply the SSE, and the third term can be shown to be zero (see Exercise 10.33). Therefore $\text{SST} \geq \text{SSE}$. The first term represents the variation in y that is accounted for by regression on x; it is called the **regression sum of squares (SSR)**. This yields the identity

$$\text{SST} = \text{SSR} + \text{SSE}. \tag{10.9}$$

The ratio

$$r^2 = \frac{\text{SSR}}{\text{SST}} = 1 - \frac{\text{SSE}}{\text{SST}}$$

represents the proportion of variation in y that is accounted for by regression on x; it is called the **coefficient of determination**. Note that r^2 is always between 0 and 1.

The **sample correlation coefficient** r that we used in Chapter 4 (see equation (4.8)) to measure linear association between x and y can be shown to be the square root of r^2; see the proof given below. Thus, $r = 0.7$ implies that $r^2 = (0.7)^2 = 0.49$, or almost 50% of the variation in y is accounted for by x. The sign of r is the same as the sign of $\hat{\beta}_1$; $r > 0$ indicates a positive slope and $r < 0$ indicates a negative slope for the LS line. See Section 4.4.2 for further interpretation of r.

EXAMPLE 10.3 (TIRE TREAD WEAR VS. MILEAGE: COEFFICIENT OF DETERMINATION AND CORRELATION)

For the tire tread wear data, calculate r^2 and r using the results from Example 10.2.

We have

$$\text{SST} = S_{yy} = \sum_{i=1}^{n} y_i^2 - \frac{1}{n}\left(\sum_{i=1}^{n} y_i\right)^2 = 589{,}887.08 - \frac{1}{9}(2197.32)^2 = 53{,}418.73.$$

Next calculate SSR = SST − SSE = $53{,}418.73 - 2531.53 = 50{,}887.20$. Therefore

$$r^2 = \frac{50{,}887.20}{53{,}418.73} = 0.953 \quad \text{and} \quad r = \sqrt{0.953} = -0.976$$

where the sign of r follows from the sign of $\hat{\beta}_1 = -7.281$. Since 95.3% of the variation in tread wear is accounted for by linear regression on mileage, the relationship between the two is strongly linear with a negative slope. ◆

*Derivation of Formulas for r^2 and r.   The formulas for r^2 and r are obtained from the formulas for SSR and SST. Since $\bar{y} = \hat{\beta}_0 + \hat{\beta}_1 \bar{x}$, we can write

$$
\begin{aligned}
\text{SSR} &= \sum_{i=1}^{n} (\hat{y}_i - \bar{y})^2 \\
&= \sum_{i=1}^{n} \left[\hat{\beta}_0 + \hat{\beta}_1 x_i - (\hat{\beta}_0 + \hat{\beta}_1 \bar{x}) \right]^2 \\
&= \hat{\beta}_1^2 \sum_{i=1}^{n} (x_i - \bar{x})^2 \\
&= \hat{\beta}_1^2 S_{xx}.
\end{aligned}
\tag{10.10}
$$

Therefore,

$$
r^2 = \frac{\text{SSR}}{\text{SST}} = \frac{\hat{\beta}_1^2 S_{xx}}{S_{yy}} = \frac{S_{xy}^2}{S_{xx} S_{yy}}
\tag{10.11}
$$

by substituting $\hat{\beta}_1 = S_{xy}/S_{xx}$ from (10.7).

Let

$$
r = \sqrt{r^2} = \frac{S_{xy}}{\sqrt{S_{xx} S_{yy}}}.
$$

To see that this equals the sample correlation coefficient

$$
r = \frac{s_{xy}}{s_x s_y}
$$

defined in (4.8), where s_{xy} is the sample covariance between x and y, and s_x and s_y are the sample standard deviations of x and y, simply note that

$$
s_{xy} = \frac{S_{xy}}{n-1}, \quad s_x = \sqrt{\frac{S_{xx}}{n-1}}, \quad \text{and} \quad s_y = \sqrt{\frac{S_{yy}}{n-1}}.
$$

An alternative formula for r is

$$
r = \hat{\beta}_1 \frac{s_x}{s_y}
\tag{10.12}
$$

which shows that r is a standardized form of $\hat{\beta}_1$.

10.2.3 Estimation of σ^2

The variance σ^2 measures the scatter of the Y_i around their means $\mu_i = \beta_0 + \beta_1 x_i$. A large scatter of the data points around this straight line indicates a large σ^2, while data points that fall tightly around it indicate a small σ^2. This true straight line is, of course, unknown but is estimated by the LS line. Thus it is not surprising that the information to estimate σ^2 is contained in the residuals $e_i = y_i - \hat{y}_i$, which represent the scatter of the observed y_i's around the LS line. In fact, it can be shown that an unbiased estimate of σ^2 is given by

$$s^2 = \frac{\sum e_i^2}{n-2} = \frac{\text{SSE}}{n-2}. \tag{10.13}$$

This estimate of σ^2 has $n-2$ degrees of freedom (d.f.); 2 is subtracted from n because two unknown parameters, β_0 and β_1, are estimated. Another way to explain the d.f. is that although n residuals are available to estimate σ^2, they are subject to two linear constraints as shown later in (10.21); thus only $n-2$ residuals are linearly independent.

EXAMPLE 10.4   (TIRE TREAD WEAR VS. MILEAGE: ESTIMATE OF σ^2)

Find the estimate of σ^2 for the tread wear data using the results from Example 10.3.
We have SSE = 2531.53 and $n-2 = 7$, therefore

$$s^2 = \frac{2531.53}{7} = 361.65$$

which has 7 d.f. The estimate of σ is $s = \sqrt{361.65} = 19.02$ mils.   ◆

10.3   STATISTICAL INFERENCE FOR SIMPLE LINEAR REGRESSION

10.3.1 Statistical Inference on β_0 and β_1

To make statistical inferences on the parameters β_0 and β_1, we need to know the sampling distributions of their LS estimates $\hat{\beta}_0$ and $\hat{\beta}_1$. These are the distributions that would result if $\hat{\beta}_0$ and $\hat{\beta}_1$ were estimated from repeated samples of Y_i's drawn using the model (10.1) with *fixed* values of $x_1, x_2, \ldots, x_n$. A mathematical derivation of the sampling distributions of $\hat{\beta}_0$ and $\hat{\beta}_1$ is given later. The final result is that $\hat{\beta}_0$ and $\hat{\beta}_1$ are both normally distributed with their means and standard deviations given by

$$E(\hat{\beta}_0) = \beta_0, \quad \text{SD}(\hat{\beta}_0) = \sigma\sqrt{\frac{\sum x_i^2}{nS_{xx}}}$$

and

$$E(\hat{\beta}_1) = \beta_1, \quad \text{SD}(\hat{\beta}_1) = \frac{\sigma}{\sqrt{S_{xx}}}.$$

In the standardized form we have

$$\frac{\hat{\beta}_0 - \beta_0}{\text{SD}(\hat{\beta}_0)} \sim N(0,1) \quad \text{and} \quad \frac{\hat{\beta}_1 - \beta_1}{\text{SD}(\hat{\beta}_1)} \sim N(0,1). \tag{10.14}$$

EXAMPLE 10.5

An experiment is to be designed to estimate the coefficient of thermal expansion of a metal rod. Suppose that 10 readings on the temperature (x) and the length of the rod (y) are to be taken, and the temperature is to be varied over the range $100°$F to $300°$F. The coefficient of thermal expansion will then be estimated as the slope coefficient $\hat{\beta}_1$ of the fitted LS line. How should the settings of temperature be spaced in order to estimate the coefficient most precisely, i.e., to minimize $\text{Var}(\hat{\beta}_1)$?

To minimize $\text{Var}(\hat{\beta}_1) = \sigma^2/S_{xx}$, we need to choose the temperature settings x_i so that S_{xx} is maximum, i.e., the x_i's must be dispersed as much as possible.[5] It is easy to check that this maximum is achieved when five observations are taken at $100°$F and the other five at $300°$F; none are taken at intermediate values of x.

This solution may seem nonsensical. However, it makes perfect theoretical sense if we assume that the straight line model is correct, in which case the slope is estimated most precisely if half the observations are taken at each end of the range of x. In practice, the validity of the straight line model is often in doubt. To check any departures from the linear relationship, some observations must be taken at intermediate temperatures. ◆

Let S^2 be the r.v. corresponding to the estimate s^2 of σ^2 given in (10.13). It can be shown that

$$\frac{(n-2)S^2}{\sigma^2} = \frac{\text{SSE}}{\sigma^2} \sim \chi^2_{n-2}$$

independently of $\hat{\beta}_0$ and $\hat{\beta}_1$. This result is analogous to the single sample case, where the corresponding r.v. has the χ^2_{n-1}-distribution. It follows that if we replace $\text{SD}(\hat{\beta}_0)$ and $\text{SD}(\hat{\beta}_1)$ in (10.14) by the respective estimated SE's, namely,

$$\text{SE}(\hat{\beta}_0) = s\sqrt{\frac{\sum x_i^2}{nS_{xx}}} \quad \text{and} \quad \text{SE}(\hat{\beta}_1) = \frac{s}{\sqrt{S_{xx}}}, \tag{10.15}$$

each resulting r.v. will have a t_{n-2}-distribution. These are the pivotal r.v.'s (see Chapter 6) for β_0 and β_1 that can be used to compute confidence intervals (CI's) or to test hypotheses on β_0 and β_1. For example, $100(1-\alpha)\%$ CI's on β_0 and β_1 are given by

$$\hat{\beta}_0 \pm t_{n-2,\alpha/2}\text{SE}(\hat{\beta}_0) \quad \text{and} \quad \hat{\beta}_1 \pm t_{n-2,\alpha/2}\text{SE}(\hat{\beta}_1) \tag{10.16}$$

respectively.

For a specified value β_1^0 we can test the hypotheses

$$H_0: \beta_1 = \beta_1^0 \quad \text{vs.} \quad H_1: \beta_1 \neq \beta_1^0$$

by using the t-test: Reject H_0 at level α if

$$|t| = \frac{|\hat{\beta}_1 - \beta_1^0|}{\text{SE}(\hat{\beta}_1)} > t_{n-2,\alpha/2}.$$

---

[5] On the other hand, if the x_i's are clustered together, then S_{xx} is small, which makes $\text{Var}(\hat{\beta}_1)$ large. In the extreme case, when all the x_i's are equal, $S_{xx} = 0$ and the slope cannot be estimated at all.

A useful application of this test is to show that there is a linear relationship between x and y. Since the slope β_1 of the true regression line is nonzero when there is a linear relationship, the hypotheses for this test are

$$H_0: \beta_1 = 0 \quad \text{vs.} \quad H_1: \beta_1 \neq 0.$$

The t-statistic to test this hypothesis is

$$t = \frac{\hat{\beta}_1}{\mathrm{SE}(\hat{\beta}_1)} \qquad (10.17)$$

and H_0 is rejected at level α if $|t| > t_{n-2,\alpha/2}$. Hypotheses on β_0 can be tested in the same manner. One-sided alternative hypotheses can be tested using one-sided t-tests.

EXAMPLE 10.6   (TIRE TREAD WEAR VS. MILEAGE: INFERENCE ON WEAR RATE)

Refer to Examples 10.2 and 10.4. Suppose the objective of the experiment is to evaluate a new tire design. The tread wear rate for the old design is 8 mils for every 1000 miles. Do a one-sided test to see if the new design has a significantly lower wear rate than the old design at $\alpha = .05$. Also calculate a 95% CI on the wear rate.

Ignoring the negative sign of β_1, the hypotheses are set up as

$$H_0: \beta_1 \geq 8 \quad \text{vs.} \quad H_1: \beta_1 < 8.$$

The estimated standard error of $\hat{\beta}_1$ is

$$\mathrm{SE}(\hat{\beta}_1) = \frac{s}{\sqrt{S_{xx}}} = \frac{19.02}{\sqrt{960}} = 0.614.$$

Therefore the t-statistic for testing H_0 is

$$t = \frac{\hat{\beta}_1 - \beta_1^0}{\mathrm{SE}(\hat{\beta}_1)} = \frac{7.281 - 8}{0.614} = -1.171$$

which is clearly nonsignificant (one-sided P-value = 0.140). Thus there is not a statistically significant improvement in the wear rate. However, it must be remembered that this result is based on the data from only one tire. If this improvement persists after testing many tires, then it might be practically significant.

From (10.16), a 95% CI on the wear rate is calculated as (using $t_{7,.025} = 2.365$)

$$[7.281 \pm 2.365 \times 0.614] = [5.289, 8.733].$$

Note that this CI includes the wear rate values greater than 8 mils per 1000 miles among the plausible values. ◆

*Derivation of the Sampling Distributions of $\hat{\beta}_0$ and $\hat{\beta}_1$.   To obtain the distribution of $\hat{\beta}_1$, regard the Y_i's as random but the x_i's as fixed, and write $\hat{\beta}_1$ as:

$$\hat{\beta}_1 = \frac{\sum(x_i - \bar{x})(Y_i - \bar{Y})}{S_{xx}} = \frac{\sum(x_i - \bar{x})Y_i}{S_{xx}} = \sum_{i=1}^{n} \frac{(x_i - \bar{x})Y_i}{S_{xx}} = \sum_{i=1}^{n} c_i Y_i.$$

In the above, we have put $c_i = (x_i - \bar{x})/S_{xx}$ and used the fact that $\sum(x_i - \bar{x})\bar{Y} = \bar{Y}\sum(x_i - \bar{x}) = 0$. This shows that $\hat{\beta}_1$ is a linear combination of the Y_i's with coefficients

c_i where $\sum c_i = 0$. In Section 2.9.3 we stated the result that a linear combination of normal r.v.'s is normally distributed. It follows therefore that $\hat{\beta}_1$ is normally distributed.

It is easy to calculate $E(\hat{\beta}_1)$ and $\text{Var}(\hat{\beta}_1)$, given that the model (10.1) is correct. First we show that $\hat{\beta}_1$ is an unbiased estimator of β_1 by showing that $E(\hat{\beta}_1) = \beta_1$:

$$
\begin{aligned}
E(\hat{\beta}_1) &= \sum_{i=1}^{n} c_i E(Y_i) \\[2mm]
&= \sum_{i=1}^{n} c_i (\beta_0 + \beta_1 x_i) \\[2mm]
&= \beta_0 \underbrace{\sum_{i=1}^{n} c_i}_{=0} + \beta_1 \sum_{i=1}^{n} c_i x_i = \beta_1 \sum_{i=1}^{n} \frac{(x_i - \bar{x}) x_i}{S_{xx}} \\[2mm]
&= \frac{\beta_1}{S_{xx}} \sum_{i=1}^{n} (x_i - \bar{x})^2 \\[2mm]
&= \beta_1
\end{aligned}
$$

which is obtained by using the fact that $\sum (x_i - \bar{x}) x_i = \sum (x_i - \bar{x})^2 = S_{xx}$. Next,

$$
\begin{aligned}
\text{Var}(\hat{\beta}_1) &= \sum_{i=1}^{n} c_i^2 \text{Var}(Y_i) \\[2mm]
&= \sigma^2 \sum_{i=1}^{n} c_i^2 \\[2mm]
&= \sigma^2 \sum_{i=1}^{n} \frac{(x_i - \bar{x})^2}{S_{xx}^2} = \frac{\sigma^2}{S_{xx}^2} \sum_{i=1}^{n} (x_i - \bar{x})^2 \\[2mm]
&= \frac{\sigma^2 S_{xx}}{S_{xx}^2} = \frac{\sigma^2}{S_{xx}}.
\end{aligned}
$$

Analogously, we can show that $\hat{\beta}_0$ is normally distributed with $E(\hat{\beta}_0) = \beta_0$ and

$$
\begin{aligned}
\text{Var}(\hat{\beta}_0) &= \text{Var}(\bar{Y} - \hat{\beta}_1 \bar{x}) = \text{Var}(\bar{Y}) + \bar{x}^2 \text{Var}(\hat{\beta}_1) \\[2mm]
&= \frac{\sigma^2}{n} + \frac{\bar{x}^2 \sigma^2}{S_{xx}} = \sigma^2 \left(\frac{1}{n} + \frac{\bar{x}^2}{S_{xx}} \right) = \frac{\sigma^2 \sum x_i^2}{n S_{xx}}.
\end{aligned}
$$

When writing $\text{Var}(\bar{Y} - \hat{\beta}_1\bar{x}) = \text{Var}(\bar{Y}) + \bar{x}^2\text{Var}(\hat{\beta}_1)$, we have used the fact that $\bar{Y}$ and $\hat{\beta}_1$ are independent (see Exercise 10.14).

10.3.2 Analysis of Variance for Simple Linear Regression

The **analysis of variance (ANOVA)** is a statistical technique to decompose the total variability in the y_i's into separate variance components associated with specific sources. We will learn more about ANOVA in Chapters 12 and 13.

For simple linear regression recall the identity (10.9): SST = SSR + SSE. Thus the total variability is decomposed into the variability accounted for by regression on x plus the error variability. The degrees of freedom (d.f.) can also be similarly decomposed. The total d.f. for SST $= \sum(y_i - \bar{y})^2$ is taken to be $n - 1$, because it is the sum of n squared differences, $y_i - \bar{y}$, which are subject to one linear constraint: $\sum(y_i - \bar{y}) = 0$. As we have seen, the error d.f. is $n - 2$. This leaves 1 d.f. due to regression, which corresponds to the fact that there is one predictor.

A sum of squares divided by its d.f. is called a **mean square**. The quantities

$$\text{MSR} = \frac{\text{SSR}}{1} \quad \text{and} \quad \text{MSE} = \frac{\text{SSE}}{n - 2}$$

are called the **mean square regression** and **mean square error**, respectively. The MSE is the same as the unbiased estimate s^2 of σ^2 given by (10.13).

The ratio of MSR to MSE provides an equivalent to the t- statistic of (10.17) to test the significance of the linear relationship between x and y. This can be seen as follows:

$$\frac{\text{MSR}}{\text{MSE}} = \frac{\text{SSR}}{s^2} = \frac{\hat{\beta}_1^2 S_{xx}}{s^2} = \left(\frac{\hat{\beta}_1}{s/\sqrt{S_{xx}}}\right)^2 = \left(\frac{\hat{\beta}_1}{\text{SE}(\hat{\beta}_1)}\right)^2 = t^2$$

using the formula (10.10) for SSR. Thus $\frac{\text{MSR}}{\text{MSE}}$ is the square of the t-statistic in (10.17). In Chapter 5 we learned that the square of a T_ν r.v. is an $F_{1,\nu}$ r.v. (see equation (5.19)). Therefore the F r.v. corresponding to the ratio

$$F = \frac{\text{MSR}}{\text{MSE}} = t^2$$

has an F-distribution with 1 and $n - 2$ d.f. when $H_0: \beta_1 = 0$ is true. Knowing that $f_{1,n-2,\alpha} = t^2_{n-2,\alpha/2}$ (see equation (5.20)), we can test

$$H_0: \beta_1 = 0 \quad \text{vs.} \quad H_1: \beta_1 \neq 0$$

at level α by rejecting H_0 if $F > f_{1,n-2,\alpha}$, since this is equivalent to rejecting H_0 if $|t| > t_{n-2,\alpha/2}$. The above calculations are conveniently presented in a tabular form, called the **analysis of variance (ANOVA) table**, shown in Table 10.2.

Table 10.2 ANOVA Table for Simple Linear Regression

Source of Variation (Source)	Sum of Squares (SS)	Degrees of Freedom (d.f.)	Mean Square (MS)	F
Regression	SSR	1	$\text{MSR} = \frac{\text{SSR}}{1}$	$F = \frac{\text{MSR}}{\text{MSE}}$
Error	SSE	$n - 2$	$\text{MSE} = \frac{\text{SSE}}{n-2}$	
Total	SST	$n - 1$		

EXAMPLE 10.7   (TIRE TREAD WEAR VS. MILEAGE: ANOVA TABLE)

Give the ANOVA table for the tire tread wear data. Test the significance of the linear relationship between tread wear and mileage.

Using the calculations made in Example 10.3, we can complete the ANOVA table shown in Table 10.3. The F-statistic value of 140.71 is highly significant (P-value = .000). From (10.17), it can be checked that $t = -11.862$ and $F = 140.71 = (-11.862)^2 = t^2$. This t-statistic has the same two-sided P-value as the P-value of the F-statistic. ◆

Table 10.3 ANOVA Table for Tire Tread Wear Data

Source	SS	d.f.	MS	F
Regression	50,887.20	1	50,887.20	140.71
Error	2531.53	7	361.65	
Total	53,418.73	8		

10.3.3 Prediction of Future Observations

A common use of a regression model is to predict the value of the response variable Y when the predictor variable x is set at a specified value x^*. Let us denote this future value of Y by Y^*. Note that Y^* is an r.v. Actually, there are two different, but related, inference problems here. One is to *predict* the value of the r.v. Y^*; the other is to *estimate* the fixed unknown mean of Y^*, denoted by $\mu^* = E(Y^*) = \beta_0 + \beta_1 x^*$. For instance, in the tire wear example, the prediction problem arises when we have a particular tire in mind: what will be the groove depth of this tire when it has 25,000 miles on it? The estimation problem arises when we want to estimate the mean groove depth for the population of all tires with a mileage of 25,000. In this example, the prediction problem is important to an individual who purchases a tire, while the estimation problem is important to the company that makes the tires or a dealer who purchases large quantities of the tires.

Denote the predicted value of Y^* by $\hat{Y}^*$ and the estimate of μ^* by $\hat{\mu}^*$. Both are given by

$$\hat{Y}^* = \hat{\mu}^* = \hat{\beta}_0 + \hat{\beta}_1 x^*.$$

To reflect the precision of an estimate of a fixed parameter such as μ^* we report a confidence interval (CI). The corresponding interval when predicting an r.v. such as Y^*

is called a **prediction interval (PI)**.[6] A $100(1 - \alpha)\%$ PI for Y^* has the property that it includes the future observation Y^* with probability $1 - \alpha$.

A $100(1 - \alpha)\%$ CI for μ^* is given by

$$\hat{\mu}^* - t_{n-2,\alpha/2}s\sqrt{\frac{1}{n} + \frac{(x^* - \bar{x})^2}{S_{xx}}} \leq \mu^* \leq \hat{\mu}^* + t_{n-2,\alpha/2}s\sqrt{\frac{1}{n} + \frac{(x^* - \bar{x})^2}{S_{xx}}} \quad (10.18)$$

where $\hat{\mu}^* = \hat{\beta}_0 + \hat{\beta}_1 x^*$ and $s = \sqrt{\text{MSE}}$ is the estimate of σ.

A $100(1 - \alpha)\%$ PI for Y^* is given by

$$\hat{Y}^* - t_{n-2,\alpha/2}s\sqrt{1 + \frac{1}{n} + \frac{(x^* - \bar{x})^2}{S_{xx}}} \leq Y^* \leq \hat{Y}^* + t_{n-2,\alpha/2}s\sqrt{1 + \frac{1}{n} + \frac{(x^* - \bar{x})^2}{S_{xx}}}$$
$$(10.19)$$

where $\hat{Y}^* = \hat{\beta}_0 + \hat{\beta}_1 x^*$. The derivation of these formulas is given later.

Notice that the two formulas differ only in the quantity under the square root sign; the formula for the PI[7] has an additional term of 1, which makes the PI much wider than the CI. For the same $1 - \alpha$ coverage probability, the PI must be wider than the CI, because there is more uncertainty associated with predicting an r.v. than with estimating a fixed parameter.

EXAMPLE 10.8 (TIRE TREAD WEAR VS. MILEAGE: CONFIDENCE AND PREDICTION INTERVALS)

Calculate a 95% CI for the mean groove depth for the population of all tires and a 95% PI for the groove depth of a single tire with a mileage of 25,000.

In Example 10.2 we calculated $\hat{\beta}_0 + \hat{\beta}_1 x^* = 178.62$ mils for $x^* = 25$. In Examples 10.3, 10.4, and 10.6 the following quantities have been calculated: $s = 19.02$, $S_{xx} = 960$, $\bar{x} = 16$, $n = 9$, and $t_{7,.025} = 2.365$. Substituting these quantities in (10.18), we obtain the following 95% CI for μ^*:

$$\left[178.62 \pm 2.365 \times 19.02\sqrt{\frac{1}{9} + \frac{(25 - 16)^2}{960}} \right] = [158.73, 198.51].$$

A 95% PI for Y^* is

$$\left[178.62 \pm 2.365 \times 19.02\sqrt{1 + \frac{1}{9} + \frac{(25 - 16)^2}{960}} \right] = [129.44, 227.80].$$

Notice that the PI is nearly two and one-half times wider than the CI. The MINITAB output of the regression analysis of the tire wear data is shown on the next page.

---

[6] In Chapter 7, Section 7.5, we discussed the prediction interval for a future observation in the context of a single sample with no predictor variables.

[7] Refer to Example 7.12, where the same extra term of 1 occurs in the formula for the PI for a future observation compared to that for the CI for the mean.

```
The regression equation is
wear = 361 - 7.28 miles
Predictor          Coef        Stdev      t-ratio        p
Constant         360.64        11.69        30.85     0.000
miles           -7.2806        0.6138      -11.86     0.000
s = 19.02        R-sq = 95.3%      R-sq(adj) = 94.6%
Analysis of Variance
SOURCE           DF           SS           MS         F         p
Regression        1         50887        50887     140.71    0.000
Error             7          2532         362
Total             8         53419
Unusual Observations
Obs.    miles     wear       Fit      Stdev.Fit   Residual    St.Resid
  1      0.0     394.33    360.64      11.69       33.69       2.25R
R denotes an obs. with a large st. resid.
    Fit   Stdev.Fit          95% C.I.           95% P.I.
 178.62      8.41     ( 158.73, 198.51)   ( 129.44, 227.80)
```

Note that the output gives a 95% CI for μ^* and a 95% PI for Y^* for $x^* = 25{,}000$ miles. The term "Unusual Observations" is explained in Example 10.11. ◆

Both the CI and PI have the shortest widths when $x^* = \bar{x}$. The intervals become wider as x^* deviates from $\bar{x}$ on either side. Figure 10.5 shows this pattern graphically. For x^* values far away from $\bar{x}$, prediction of Y^* or estimation of μ^* becomes even less precise than that indicated by the PI or the CI, because the assumed linear model may not hold. Therefore **extrapolation** beyond the range of the data is a risky business and should be avoided.

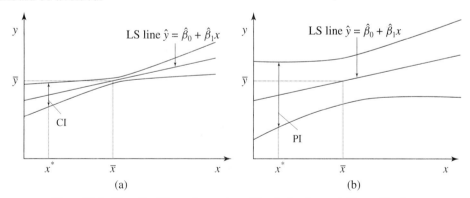

Figure 10.5 How Confidence Intervals and Prediction Intervals Vary with x^*: (a) Confidence interval; (b) Prediction interval

*Derivation of Formulas (10.18) and (10.19).   To derive the formulas (10.18) and (10.19), we first note that the sampling distribution of $\hat{\mu}^* = \hat{Y}^* = \hat{\beta}_0 + \hat{\beta}_1 x^*$ is normal, since this quantity is a linear function of $\hat{\beta}_0$ and $\hat{\beta}_1$, both of which are normally distributed, as seen in Section 10.3.1. To find the mean of $\hat{\mu}^* = \hat{Y}^*$, we use the fact that $E(\hat{\beta}_0) = \beta_0$ and $E(\hat{\beta}_1) = \beta_1$, which yields

$$E(\hat{\mu}^*) = E(\hat{Y}^*) = E(\hat{\beta}_0 + \hat{\beta}_1 x^*) = \beta_0 + \beta_1 x^* = \mu^*.$$

To find its variance, using $\hat{\beta}_0 = \bar{Y} - \hat{\beta}_1 \bar{x}$ we can express

$$\hat{\mu}^* = \hat{Y}^* = \hat{\beta}_0 + \hat{\beta}_1 x^* = \bar{Y} + \hat{\beta}_1(x^* - \bar{x}).$$

As noted in Section 10.3.1, $\bar{Y}$ and $\hat{\beta}_1$ are statistically independent. Therefore

$$\text{Var}(\hat{\mu}^*) = \text{Var}(\hat{Y}^*) = \text{Var}(\bar{Y} + \hat{\beta}_1(x^* - \bar{x}))$$

$$= \text{Var}(\bar{Y}) + (x^* - \bar{x})^2 \text{Var}(\hat{\beta}_1)$$

$$= \frac{\sigma^2}{n} + (x^* - \bar{x})^2 \frac{\sigma^2}{S_{xx}}.$$

The CI for μ^* is derived from the r.v. $\hat{\mu}^* - \mu^*$. Its mean and variance are:

$$E(\hat{\mu}^* - \mu^*) = E(\hat{\mu}^*) - \mu^* = 0$$

and

$$\text{Var}(\hat{\mu}^* - \mu^*) = \text{Var}(\hat{\mu}^*) = \sigma^2 \left[\frac{1}{n} + \frac{(x^* - \bar{x})^2}{S_{xx}}\right].$$

Similarly, the PI for Y^* is derived from the r.v. $\hat{Y}^* - Y^*$. Its mean and variance are:

$$E(\hat{Y}^* - Y^*) = E(\hat{Y}^*) - E(Y^*) = \mu^* - \mu^* = 0$$

and

$$\text{Var}(\hat{Y}^* - Y^*) = \text{Var}(Y^*) + \text{Var}(\hat{Y}^*) = \sigma^2 + \text{Var}(\hat{Y}^*) = \sigma^2\left[1 + \frac{1}{n} + \frac{(x^* - \bar{x})^2}{S_{xx}}\right];$$

the additional σ^2 is the variance of the future observation Y^*, which is assumed to be independent of the past data on which $\hat{Y}^* = \hat{\beta}_0 + \hat{\beta}_1 x^*$ is based. Furthermore, both $\hat{\mu}^* - \mu^*$ and $\hat{Y}^* - Y^*$ are normally distributed. Therefore,

$$\frac{\hat{\mu}^* - \mu^*}{\sigma\sqrt{\frac{1}{n} + \frac{(x^* - \bar{x})^2}{S_{xx}}}} \sim N(0, 1) \quad \text{and} \quad \frac{\hat{Y}^* - Y^*}{\sigma\sqrt{1 + \frac{1}{n} + \frac{(x^* - \bar{x})^2}{S_{xx}}}} \sim N(0, 1).$$

Replacing σ by its estimate $S = \sqrt{\text{MSE}}$ and using the fact that $(n - 2)S^2/\sigma^2 \sim \chi^2_{n-2}$ is independent of both $\hat{\beta}_0 + \hat{\beta}_1 x^*$ and Y^* results in the following t-distributed pivotal r.v.'s:[8]

$$\frac{\hat{\mu}^* - \mu^*}{S\sqrt{\frac{1}{n} + \frac{(x^* - \bar{x})^2}{S_{xx}}}} \sim T_{n-2} \quad \text{and} \quad \frac{\hat{Y}^* - Y^*}{S\sqrt{1 + \frac{1}{n} + \frac{(x^* - \bar{x})^2}{S_{xx}}}} \sim T_{n-2}.$$

---

[8] Independence between $\hat{\beta}_0 + \hat{\beta}_1 x^*$ and S^2 holds because S^2 is independent of both $\hat{\beta}_0$ and $\hat{\beta}_1$. Independence between Y^* and S^2 holds because S^2 is based on the past data, while Y^* is a future observation which is assumed to be independent of the past data.

Finally, substituting the above pivotal r.v.'s in place of T_{n-2} in the probability statement

$$P\{-t_{n-2,\alpha/2} \le T_{n-2} \le t_{n-2,\alpha/2}\} = 1 - \alpha$$

yields the CI and PI formulas (10.18) and (10.19), respectively.

10.3.4 Calibration (Inverse Regression)

We have looked at the problem of estimating μ^* for given x^*. The opposite problem is to estimate x^* for given μ^*. This is called the **calibration** or **inverse regression** problem.

The formula for an estimate of x^* is obtained by solving for x^* from $\mu^* = \hat{\beta}_0 + \hat{\beta}_1 x^*$, which yields

$$\hat{x}^* = \frac{\mu^* - \hat{\beta}_0}{\hat{\beta}_1}.$$

The problem of finding a CI for x^* is more complicated and is addressed in Exercise 10.38.

EXAMPLE 10.9   (TIRE TREAD WEAR VS. MILEAGE: INVERSE REGRESSION)

Estimate the mean life of a tire at wearout (62.5 mils remaining) using the results from Example 10.2.

We want to estimate x^* when $\mu^* = 62.5$. Substituting $\hat{\beta}_0 = 360.64$ and $\hat{\beta}_1 = -7.281$ in the above formula we obtain

$$\hat{x}^* = \frac{62.5 - 360.64}{-7.281} \times 1000 = 40{,}947.67 \text{ miles.}$$

Caution should be exercised in using this projection, since we do not have any data past 32,000 miles. ◆

10.4   REGRESSION DIAGNOSTICS

The four basic assumptions of linear regression stated in Section 10.1 need to be verified from the data to assure that the analysis is valid. We now introduce some graphical plots to check these assumptions.

10.4.1 Checking the Model Assumptions

The residuals $e_i = y_i - \hat{y}_i$ can be viewed as the "leftovers" after the model is fitted. If the model is correct, then the e_i can be viewed as the "estimates" of the random errors ϵ_i's. As such, the residuals are vital for checking the model assumptions. First, they can be used to check the assumptions regarding the form of the model (10.2) (namely, that $E(Y)$ is linear in x). If the assumed model form is correct, then they can be used to check the assumptions concerning the distribution of the ϵ_i's. **Residual plots** are the primary tool in this analysis.[9] Most statistical packages allow you to save the residuals from a regression analysis and plot them in various ways.

---

[9] Although some formal statistical tests are available for this purpose, we will not discuss them, since the graphical plots are usually simpler and more informative.

Before proceeding with residual plots, it is useful to summarize the basic distributional results concerning the e_i's: If the assumed regression model is correct, then the e_i's are normally distributed with $E(e_i) = 0$ and

$$\text{Var}(e_i) = \sigma^2 \left[1 - \frac{1}{n} - \frac{(x_i - \bar{x})^2}{S_{xx}} \right] \simeq \sigma^2. \tag{10.20}$$

The approximate equality holds for large n because $1/n + (x_i - \bar{x})^2 / S_{xx}$ is much smaller in comparison to 1.

The e_i's are not independent (even though the ϵ_i's are independent) because they are subject to the following two linear constraints:

$$\sum_{i=1}^{n} e_i = 0, \quad \sum_{i=1}^{n} x_i e_i = 0. \tag{10.21}$$

These constraints follow from setting the partial derivatives in (10.4) equal to zero and noting that $\hat{\beta}_0$ and $\hat{\beta}_1$ are the solutions to the resulting equations. Thus we get

$$\sum_{i=1}^{n} [y_i - (\hat{\beta}_0 + \hat{\beta}_1 x_i)] = \sum_{i=1}^{n} (y_i - \hat{y}_i) = \sum_{i=1}^{n} e_i = 0$$

and

$$\sum_{i=1}^{n} x_i [y_i - (\hat{\beta}_0 + \hat{\beta}_1 x_i)] = \sum_{i=1}^{n} x_i (y_i - \hat{y}_i) = \sum_{i=1}^{n} x_i e_i = 0.$$

However, the dependence introduced by these constraints is negligible if n is modestly large, say greater than 20 or so. The basic principle underlying the residual plots is that *if the assumed model is correct* then the residuals should be randomly scattered around 0 and should show no obvious systematic pattern.

Checking for Linearity.   If regression of y on x is linear, then the plot of e_i vs. x_i should exhibit random scatter around zero. Any systematic pattern indicates a corresponding deviation from linearity. For example, a parabolic plot indicates that a second degree term in x should be added to the regression equation, i.e., a quadratic model, $E(Y) = \beta_0 + \beta_1 x + \beta_2 x^2$, should be fitted. This residual plot reveals a nonlinear relationship more vividly than the scatter plot of y vs. x, since it shows only the "leftovers" on a magnified scale after filtering out the linear component of the relationship.

EXAMPLE 10.10   (TIRE TREAD WEAR VS. MILEAGE: RESIDUAL PLOT TO CHECK LINEARITY)

Check for the goodness of the linearity of the fit of the groove depth vs. mileage obtained in Example 10.2.

Table 10.4 gives the observed y_i, fitted $\hat{y}_i$, and the residuals $e_i = y_i - \hat{y}_i$ for the tire wear data. Most packages will compute these quantities for you. You can verify that the constraints (10.21): $\sum e_i = 0$ and $\sum x_i e_i = 0$ are satisfied.

Table 10.4 The x_i, y_i, $\hat{y}_i$, and e_i for the Tire Wear Data

i	x_i	y_i	$\hat{y}_i$	e_i
1	0	394.33	360.64	33.69
2	4	329.50	331.51	−2.01
3	8	291.00	302.39	−11.39
4	12	255.17	273.27	−18.10
5	16	229.33	244.15	−14.82
6	20	204.83	215.02	−10.19
7	24	179.00	185.90	−6.90
8	28	163.83	156.78	7.05
9	32	150.33	127.66	22.67

The e_i are plotted against the x_i in Figure 10.6. The plot is clearly parabolic, indicating that after filtering out the linear component, there still is a nonlinear component left. So the linear regression does not fit the data adequately, even though the linear slope coefficient $\hat{\beta}_1$ is significant. An important lesson to learn here is that a significant $\hat{\beta}_1$ does *not* necessarily mean that the relationship is linear, but only that there is a significant linear component.

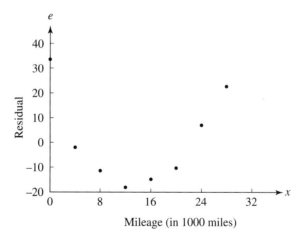

Figure 10.6 Plot of Residuals e_i vs. x_i for the Linear Fit for Tire Wear Data

To rectify this problem, one solution is to fit a second degree model, $y = \beta_0 + \beta_1 x + \beta_2 x^2$; this is done in the next chapter in Example 11.1. Another solution is to fit an exponential model, $y = \alpha \exp(-\beta x)$; this is done in Example 10.13. ◆

Checking for Constant Variance.   To check this assumption it is most convenient to plot the residuals e_i against the fitted values $\hat{y}_i$, which are estimates of the $\mu_i = E(Y_i)$. It should be noted, however, that since the $\hat{y}_i$ are linear functions of the x_i, one could as well plot the e_i against the x_i. If the constant variance assumption is correct, the dispersion of the e_i's is approximately constant (since $\text{Var}(e_i) \simeq \sigma^2$) with respect to the $\hat{y}_i$'s. If the assumption is incorrect, often $\text{Var}(Y)$ is some function of $E(Y) = \mu$. This plot helps us to see the nature of this functional relationship. Figure 10.7 shows the residual plots (a) when $\text{Var}(Y)$ is constant, (b) when $\text{Var}(Y) \propto \mu^2$ (i.e., $\text{SD}(Y) \propto \mu$), and (c) when $\text{Var}(Y) \propto \mu$ (i.e., $\text{SD}(Y) \propto \sqrt{\mu}$).

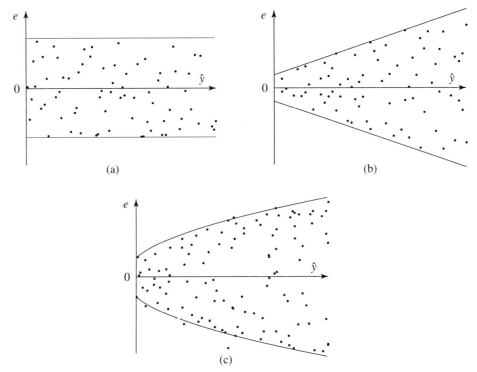

Figure 10.7   Plots of Residuals e_i vs. $\hat{y}_i$ Corresponding to Different Functional Relationships Between $\text{Var}(Y)$ and $E(Y)$: (a) Constant variance; (b) Variance proportional to μ^2; (c) Variance proportional to μ

Checking for Normality.   As we saw in Chapter 4, the preferred way to check normality of the data is to make a normal plot. The normal plot requires that the observations form a random sample with a common mean and variance. The y_i do not form such a random sample, because the $\mu_i = E(Y_i)$ depend on the x_i and hence are not equal. Therefore, even if the independence and the common variance assumptions hold, a normal plot of the y_i could be misleading. The residuals should be used to make a normal plot, since they have a zero mean and an *approximately* constant variance (assuming, of course, that the other assumptions about the model are correct).

If the normality assumption is not satisfied, the usual corrective action is to transform the y_i's, but by no means this is a panacea. The same transformations discussed in Section 4.6 may be employed here. A normal plot of residuals is shown in Example 10.13 where an exponential model is fitted to the tire tread wear data.

Checking for Independence.   The assumption of independence is violated for time-series data due to correlation introduced by time order, called **serial correlation** or **autocorrelation** (see Section 4.5.2). Even cross-sectional data (i.e., data collected on different units at about the same time) may be correlated because of spatial proximity, family relationships, or other reasons.

A simple way to check for serial correlation is to make a run chart of the residuals. For positively autocorrelated data, the run chart of residuals shows a few long cycles. For negatively autocorrelated data, the run chart has a sawtooth pattern with many short cycles. A well-known statistical test for autocorrelation is the Durbin-Watson test.[10]

Correcting for serial correlation involves time-series modeling. This is beyond the scope of the present text. The interested reader is referred to Box and Jenkins (1976).[11]

Consequences of Violation of Assumptions.   Not all assumptions are equally critical for the theory of least squares inference to be valid. The normality assumption is the least critical for large n, since in that case a version of the central limit theorem (CLT) can be applied to show that the LS estimates are still approximately normally distributed; therefore the t-tests and CI's are still approximately valid. The other assumptions are more critical. If the true model is nonlinear in x, then the LS estimates $\hat{\beta}_0$ and $\hat{\beta}_1$ as well as $\hat{\sigma}^2 = S^2$ are biased. If the variances are not constant, then the formulas for $\mathrm{Var}(\hat{\beta}_0)$ and $\mathrm{Var}(\hat{\beta}_1)$ do not hold. If the observations are not independent, then also the formulas for $\mathrm{Var}(\hat{\beta}_0)$ and $\mathrm{Var}(\hat{\beta}_1)$ do not hold; therefore the t-tests and CI's based on them are not valid.

10.4.2 Checking for Outliers and Influential Observations

Checking for Outliers.   An outlier is an observation that does not follow the general pattern of the relationship between y and x. It is important to detect outliers, because the LS estimates are not resistant to them, just as the sample mean is not resistant to outliers, as we saw in Chapter 4.

A large residual indicates an outlier. To gauge the largeness of a residual, we need to standardize it. An estimate of $\mathrm{Var}(e_i)$ is obtained by replacing σ^2 in (10.20) by s^2. Thus the **standardized residuals** are given by

$$e_i^* = \frac{e_i}{\mathrm{SE}(e_i)} = \frac{e_i}{s\sqrt{1 - \frac{1}{n} - \frac{(x_i-\bar{x})^2}{S_{xx}}}} \simeq \frac{e_i}{s}, \quad i = 1, 2, \ldots, n. \tag{10.22}$$

If $|e_i|$ exceeds two standard deviations, i.e., if $|e_i^*| > 2$, then the corresponding observation may be regarded an outlier. Graphical plots, such as a box plot, may also be used to reveal outliers.

---

[10] See, e.g., N. R. Draper and H. Smith (1981), *Applied Regression Analysis*, 2nd ed., New York: Wiley, pp. 162–169.

[11] G. E. P. Box and G. M. Jenkins (1976), *Time Series Analysis: Forecasting and Control*, San Francisco: Holden-Day.

EXAMPLE 10.11   (TIRE TREAD WEAR VS. MILEAGE: OUTLIER DETECTION)

Identify any outliers in the tire tread wear data using the results from Example 10.10.

Table 10.5 gives the standardized residuals for the tire wear data. Note that $|e_1^*| = 2.25$ exceeds 2 and hence is a possible outlier. The MINITAB output in Example 10.8 also identified this observation as an outlier (termed an "Unusual Observation" in MINITAB).

Table 10.5 Standardized Residuals for Tire Wear Data

i	e_i^*
1	2.25
2	−0.12
3	−0.66
4	−1.02
5	−0.83
6	−0.57
7	−0.40
8	0.43
9	1.51

There are two reasons for the groove depth of a new tire to be much higher than the fitted value: (i) it is difficult to accurately measure the initial groove depth due to mold vents on the tire surface, and (ii) the tire wear rate is higher at the beginning. Therefore it may be advisable to omit the first observation and refit the model. You should try doing this and compare your results with the above. You will find that the linear fit is still unsatisfactory, but the quadratic and exponential fits alluded to at the end of Example 10.10 are quite good.   ◆

Checking for Influential Observations.   The LS fit can be excessively influenced by an observation that is not necessarily an outlier as defined above, but has an extreme x-value. See Figure 10.8 for two such examples. Note the dramatic differences between the LS lines with and without the influential points. In summary, an observation can be influential because it has an extreme x-value, an extreme y-value, or both.

How can we identify influential observations? In the next chapter we show that the fitted value $\hat{y}_i$ can be expressed as a linear combination of all the y_j as follows:

$$\hat{y}_i = \sum_{j=1}^{n} h_{ij} y_j$$

where the h_{ij} are some functions of the x's. We can think of h_{ij} as the **leverage** exerted by y_j on the fitted value $\hat{y}_i$. If $\hat{y}_i$ is largely determined by y_i with a very small contribution from the other y_j, then we say that the ith observation is **influential** (also called **high leverage**). Since h_{ii} determines how much $\hat{y}_i$ depends on y_i, it is used as a measure of the leverage of the ith observation. It can be shown that $\sum_{i=1}^{n} h_{ii} = k+1$ or the average h_{ii} is $(k+1)/n$, where k is the number of predictor variables. A rule of thumb is to regard any $h_{ii} > 2(k+1)/n$ as high leverage. In the present case, $k = 1$,

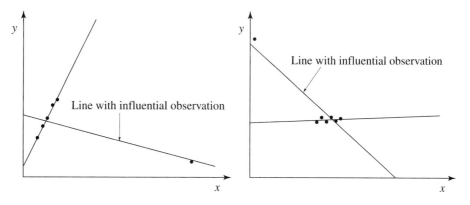

Figure 10.8   Illustration of Influential Observations

and so $h_{ii} > 4/n$ is regarded as high leverage. The formula for h_{ii} for $k = 1$ is given by

$$h_{ii} = \frac{1}{n} + \frac{(x_i - \bar{x})^2}{S_{xx}}. \tag{10.23}$$

Note that if x_i deviates greatly from $\bar{x}$, then h_{ii} is large. Also note that the standardized residual defined in (10.22) equals

$$e_i^* = \frac{e_i}{\text{SE}(e_i)} = \frac{e_i}{s\sqrt{1 - h_{ii}}};$$

thus for the same value of e_i, the standardized residual will be large for a high leverage observation.

EXAMPLE 10.12

The following is a part of the data set[12] given in Exercise 10.22. Show that the observation no. 8 is influential, but not an outlier.

No.	1	2	3	4	5	6	7	8	9	10	11
x	8	8	8	8	8	8	8	19	8	8	8
y	6.58	5.76	7.71	8.84	8.47	7.04	5.25	12.50	5.56	7.91	6.89

In this data set, all x values are equal to 8 except observation no. 8, for which $x = 19$. That observation determines the slope of the LS line, which passes through the midpoint of the y values of the remaining ten observations and y_8; see Figure 10.9. Thus $e_8 = y_8 - \hat{y}_8 = 0$. So the observation is not an outlier, but it is highly influential.

The leverage h_{88} can be calculated as follows. Here $\bar{x} = 9$, $S_{xx} = 110$. Therefore,

$$h_{88} = \frac{1}{n} + \frac{(x_8 - \bar{x})^2}{S_{xx}} = \frac{1}{11} + \frac{(19 - 9)^2}{110} = 1.$$

This far exceeds $4/n = 4/11$, and so by the rule of thumb, observation no. 8 is influential.

---

[12] F. J. Anscombe (1973), "Graphs in statistical analysis," *The American Statistician* **27**, pp. 17–21.

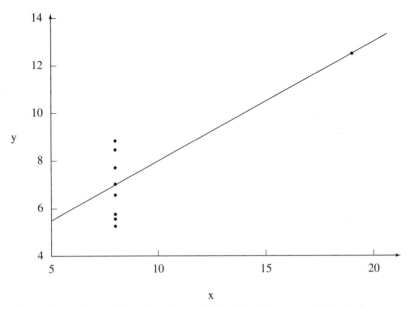

Figure 10.9 Scatter Plot of the Anscombe Data Illustrating an Influential Observation

The MINITAB regression output is shown below.

```
The regression equation is
y = 3.00 + 0.500 x
Predictor        Coef        Stdev      t-ratio         p
Constant        3.002       1.124         2.67     0.026
x               0.4999      0.1178        4.24     0.002
s = 1.236        R-sq = 66.7%      R-sq(adj) = 63.0%
Analysis of Variance
SOURCE          DF            SS          MS          F          p
Regression       1        27.490      27.490      18.00     0.002
Error            9        13.742       1.527
Total           10        41.232
Unusual Observations
Obs.      x        y          Fit    Stdev.Fit   Residual     St.Resid
  8     19.0    12.500      12.500      1.236      0.000          * X
X denotes an obs. whose X value gives it large influence.
```

Notice that observation no. 8 is marked as having a large influence. Its standardized residual is undefined because $e_8 = 0$, and SE(e_8) is also zero because $h_{88} = 1$. ◆

How to Deal with Outliers and Influential Observations. As discussed above, it is important to detect outliers and influential observations because they can give a misleading picture of the relationship between y and x. After detecting such observations, their source should be investigated to determine if they are erroneous observations and whether they can be easily corrected. If the erroneous observations cannot be corrected, then they should be discarded. If the observations are valid (not erroneous), then they should be included in the analysis. Because the LS method of analysis is sensitive to such observations, two separate analyses may be done, one with and one without the outliers and influential observations, to bring forth the differences in the results. Alternatively a more robust method of analysis should be used.

One such robust method was mentioned earlier which finds the best fit by minimizing the sum of the absolute deviations: $\sum_{i=1}^{n} |y_i - (\beta_0 + \beta_1 x_i)|$. The resulting estimates are analogous to the sample median (which, as we know from Chapter 4, is not very sensitive to outliers), whereas the LS estimates are analogous to the sample mean (which, as we know from Chapter 4, is very sensitive to outliers).[13]

10.4.3 Data Transformations

Linearizing Transformations.   Sometimes it is possible to linearize the relationship between x and y by transforming either x or y or both. It is simpler to fit a straight line to transformed data than to fit a nonlinear model to raw data. We study some standard linearizing transformations in this section.

If the functional relationship between x and y is known, then it may be possible to find a linearizing transformation analytically. For example, if the functional relationship between x and y is of the power form: $y = \alpha x^{\beta}$, then taking the log of both sides transforms this to a linear form: $\log_e y = \log_e \alpha + \beta \log_e x$. The transformed data $y \to \log_e y$ and $x \to \log_e x$ can be modeled by a straight line whose intercept is $\beta_0 = \log_e \alpha$ and slope is $\beta_1 = \beta$. Similarly, if the relationship is exponential: $y = \alpha \exp(\beta x)$, then taking the log of both sides transforms this to a linear form: $\log_e y = \log_e \alpha + \beta x$. The transformed data $y \to \log_e y$ and $x \to x$ can be modeled by a straight line whose intercept is $\beta_0 = \log_e \alpha$ and slope is $\beta_1 = \beta$.

If we are fitting an empirical model, then a linearizing transformation can be found by trial and error using the scatter plot as a guide. Figure 10.10 shows some typical shapes of scatter plots and the corresponding linearizing transformations for x and y.[14]

The following example illustrates how to fit an exponential model.

EXAMPLE 10.13   (TIRE TREAD WEAR VS. MILEAGE: EXPONENTIAL MODEL)

One may hypothesize that tire wear follows an exponential law of the form $y = \alpha \exp(-\beta x)$. Fit this model to the tire wear data from Table 10.1.

As noted above, fitting this exponential model is equivalent to doing a straight line regression of the log of tread wear on mileage. The MINITAB output for this regression is shown on the next page. The resulting model is $\log_e(\text{WEAR}) = 5.93 - 0.0298\text{MILES}$ or $\text{WEAR} = 376.15 \exp(-0.0298\text{MILES})$.

---

[13] See D. C. Montgomery and E. Peck (1982), *Introduction to Linear Regression Analysis*, New York: Wiley, pp. 364–383, for a discussion of some robust regression methods.

[14] Adapted from R. L. Ott, (1993), *An Introduction to Statistical Methods and Data Analysis*, 4th ed., Belmont, CA: Duxbury Press, p. 459.

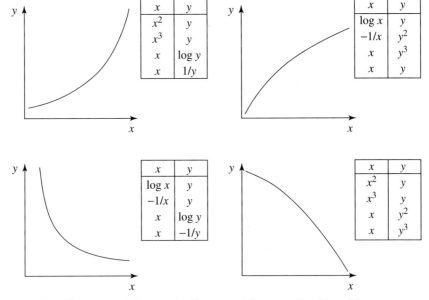

Figure 10.10   Typical Scatter Plot Shapes and Corresponding Linearizing Transformations

```
The regression equation is
logwear = 5.93 - 0.0298 miles

Predictor        Coef        Stdev      t-ratio        p
Constant      5.92595      0.01815      326.58      0.000
miles        0.0297720   0.0009528      -31.25      0.000

s = 0.02952      R-sq = 99.3%      R-sq(adj) = 99.2%

Analysis of Variance

SOURCE          DF          SS          MS          F          p
Regression      1        0.85092     0.85092     976.29     0.000
Error           7        0.00610     0.00087
Total           8        0.85702

Unusual Observations
Obs.    miles  logwear      Fit    Stdev.Fit   Residual    St.Resid
  1      0.0   5.97719   5.92595    0.01815     0.05123       2.20R

R denotes an obs. with a large st. resid.
```

This fit appears to be better than the linear fit in terms of the t- and F-statistics and r^2. A more objective comparison is obtained by backtransforming the fitted values from the exponential model to the original scale and calculating the SSE. This calculation is shown in Table 10.6. We see that SSE $= \sum e_i^2 = 531.36$, which is about one-fifth of the SSE $= 2531.53$ obtained with the best straight line fit. However, the residual plot shown in Figure 10.11 is still slightly curved, mainly because observation no. 1 is an outlier. This also affects the normal plot of the residuals, as seen in Figure 10.12. You can check for yourself that the fit of the exponential model is vastly improved if observation no. 1 is omitted. ◆

Table 10.6 Calculation of Fitted Values and Residuals from the Exponential Model for Tire Tread Wear vs. Mileage

Obs. No.	y_i	$\widehat{\log_e y_i}$	$\hat{y}_i = \exp(\widehat{\log_e y_i})$	$e_i = y_i - \hat{y}_i$
1	394.33	5.926	374.64	19.69
2	329.50	5.807	332.58	−3.08
3	291.00	5.688	295.24	−4.24
4	255.17	5.569	262.09	−6.92
5	229.33	5.450	232.67	−3.34
6	204.83	5.331	206.54	−1.71
7	179.00	5.211	183.36	−4.36
8	163.83	5.092	162.77	1.06
9	150.33	4.973	144.50	5.83

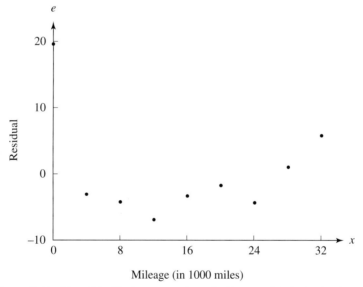

Figure 10.11   Plot of Residuals e_i vs. x_i from the Exponential Fit for the Tire Wear Data

Here is another example of a linearizing transformation.

EXAMPLE **10.14**

Table 10.7 gives data analyzed by Henderson and Velleman,[15] on the weights and gasoline mileages of 38 1978–79 model cars. The column WT gives the weight in thousands of pounds and the

---

[15] H. V. Henderson and P. F. Velleman (1981), "Building multiple regression models interactively," *Biometrics* **37**, pp. 391–411.

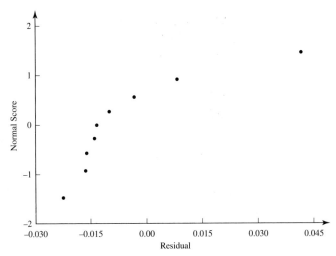

Figure 10.12   Normal Plot of Residuals from the Exponential Fit for the Tire Wear Data

column MPG gives the mileage per gallon of gasoline. Figure 10.13 gives the scatter plot of MPG vs. weight. The scatter plot shows a curved relationship with a negative trend. How should this relationship be linearized?

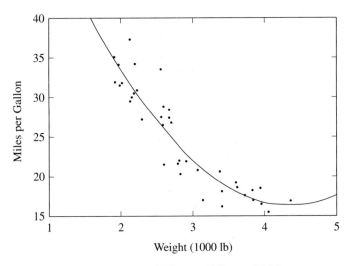

Figure 10.13   Plot of Miles per Gallon vs. Weight

Henderson and Velleman noted that the hyperbolic shape ($xy \simeq$ constant) of the scatter plot can be straightened by making the transformation $y \to \frac{100}{y}$. The new y variable has the units of gallons per 100 miles (GPM). The plot of GPM vs. weight is shown in Figure 10.14. This plot is more linear and has a physical interpretation: GPM represents the amount of chemical

Table 10.7 Weights and Gas Mileages of 38 1978–79 Model
Year Cars

WT (1000 lb.)	MPG	WT (1000 lb.)	MPG
4.360	16.9	3.830	18.2
4.054	15.5	2.585	26.5
3.605	19.2	2.910	21.9
3.940	18.5	1.975	34.1
2.155	30.0	1.915	35.1
2.560	27.5	2.670	27.4
2.300	27.2	1.990	31.5
2.230	30.9	2.135	29.5
2.830	20.3	2.670	28.4
3.140	17.0	2.595	28.8
2.795	21.6	2.700	26.8
3.410	16.2	2.556	33.5
3.380	20.6	2.200	34.2
3.070	20.8	2.020	31.8
3.620	18.6	2.130	37.3
3.410	18.1	2.190	30.5
3.840	17.0	2.815	22.0
3.725	17.6	2.600	21.5
3.955	16.5	1.925	31.9

energy in gasoline required to move the car 100 miles. From physics it is known that this energy is proportional to the mass of the car, hence the positive linear relationship between GPM and WT. This relationship is not perfect, because many other variables, e.g., aerodynamic shape of the car, engine size, type of transmission, road friction, etc., also affect the mileage.

The LS straight line fit to the scatter plot in Figure 10.14 gives the equation GPM = -0.006 + 1.515WT with $r^2 = 85.8\%$. Thus for an increase in weight of 1000 lb, a car requires roughly an additional one and one-half gallons of gasoline to go 100 miles. ◆

*Variance Stabilizing Transformations.   Typically, the constant variance assumption is violated because Var(Y) is a function of $E(Y) = \mu$. In particular, suppose that Var(Y) = $g^2(\mu)$ or SD(Y) = $g(\mu)$, where the function $g(\cdot)$ is known. We want to find a (differentiable) function $h(\cdot)$ so that the transformed r.v. $h(Y)$ will have a variance which is approximately independent of its mean $E[h(Y)]$.

The **delta method** (based on the first order Taylor series expansion of $h(Y)$ around μ) discussed in Section 15.1.5 of Chapter 15 yields the following approximation:

$$\text{Var}(h(Y)) \simeq [h'(\mu)]^2 g^2(\mu).$$

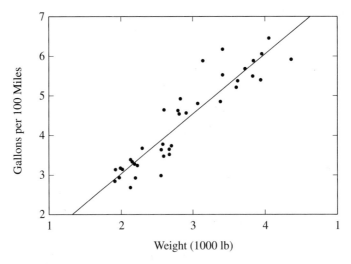

Figure 10.14   Plot of Gallons per 100 Miles vs. Weight

We want to find a function $h(\cdot)$ such that the transformed r.v. $h(Y)$ will have a variance which is approximately independent of its mean $E[h(Y)]$. To make $\mathrm{Var}[h(Y)]$ approximately constant (say, equal to 1), set

$$[h'(\mu)]^2 g^2(\mu) = 1 \quad \text{or} \quad h'(\mu) = \frac{1}{g(\mu)}$$

from which we get

$$h(\mu) = \int \frac{d\mu}{g(\mu)}.$$

Thus an observed y should be transformed to $h(y)$, where

$$h(y) = \int \frac{dy}{g(y)}.$$

EXAMPLE 10.15

Find the variance stabilizing transformations if (i) $\mathrm{Var}(Y) = c^2 \mu^2$ and (ii) $\mathrm{Var}(Y) = c^2 \mu$ where $c > 0$ is a constant.

In case (i) we have $g(\mu) = c\mu$. So

$$h(y) = \int \frac{dy}{cy} = \frac{1}{c} \int \frac{dy}{y} = \frac{1}{c} \log_e(y).$$

This is just the **logarithmic transformation** (the constant $1/c$ can be ignored).[16]

In case (ii) we have $g(\mu) = c\sqrt{\mu}$. So

$$h(y) = \int \frac{dy}{c\sqrt{y}} = \frac{1}{c} \int \frac{dy}{\sqrt{y}} = \frac{2}{c}\sqrt{y}.$$

---

[16] If some of the y_i are negative, then a suitable positive constant may be added to all the y_i to make them positive before applying this transformation.

This is just the **square root transformation** (the constant $2/c$ can be ignored). This transformation is commonly used when the responses are counts (e.g., counts of traffic accidents), which are often modeled as Poisson r.v.'s. If Y has a Poisson distribution, then $\mathrm{Var}(Y) = E(Y) = \mu$. Therefore the square root transformation should be applied to Poisson count data before regressing them on relevant predictor variables. ♦

It should be noted that a variance stabilizing transformation does not necessarily induce normality, although it often does. For example, the square root transformation $(y \rightarrow \sqrt{y})$ stabilizes the variance for Poisson distributed data, but the normalizing transformation is $y \rightarrow y^{2/3}$.

10.5   *CORRELATION ANALYSIS

Regression analysis is used to model the relationship between two variables when it is clear which is the predictor variable and which is the response variable. When there is no such distinction and both the variables are random, correlation analysis is used to study the strength of the relationship. In this section we first present the bivariate normal distribution as a probability model for the joint distribution of two r.v.'s. Next we discuss statistical inference methods for the correlation coefficient.

10.5.1 Bivariate Normal Distribution

The bivariate normal distribution is a generalization of the familiar univariate normal distribution for a single r.v. X. Let μ_X and σ_X be the mean and standard deviation of X, μ_Y and σ_Y those of Y, and

$$\rho = \mathrm{Corr}(X, Y) = \frac{\mathrm{Cov}(X, Y)}{\sqrt{\mathrm{Var}(X)\mathrm{Var}(Y)}}$$

be the correlation coefficient between X and Y. Then the bivariate normal probability density function (p.d.f.) of (X, Y) is given by

$$f(x, y) = \frac{1}{2\pi \sigma_X \sigma_Y \sqrt{1 - \rho^2}} \exp\left\{ -\frac{1}{2(1 - \rho^2)} \left[\left(\frac{x - \mu_X}{\sigma_X}\right)^2 + \left(\frac{y - \mu_Y}{\sigma_Y}\right)^2 \right. \right.$$
$$\left. \left. - 2\rho \left(\frac{x - \mu_X}{\sigma_X}\right)\left(\frac{y - \mu_Y}{\sigma_Y}\right) \right] \right\}$$
$$(10.24)$$

for $-\infty < x, y < +\infty$. Some properties of the bivariate normal distribution are as follows:

1. The p.d.f. $f(x, y)$ is defined for $-1 < \rho < +1$. A plot of $f(x, y)$ against (x, y) produces a bell (mound) shaped surface centered at (μ_X, μ_Y), as shown in Figure 10.15. This is a two-dimensional generalization of the bell shaped curve for the univariate normal p.d.f.

2. The p.d.f. $f(x, y)$ is undefined if $\rho = -1$ or $+1$. In these two cases, $f(x, y)$ is said to be degenerate, as Y depends *deterministically* on X in a linear way:

$Y = a + bX$ for some constants a and $b \neq 0$. The p.d.f. $f(x, y)$ is concentrated along this line rather than being spread over the entire x-y plane.

3. As is true with all bivariate p.d.f.'s, $f(x, y) \geq 0$ and the probability $P(a \leq X \leq b, c \leq Y \leq d)$ for any fixed constants a, b, c, d is given by the volume under the surface $f(x, y)$ above the region $a \leq x \leq b, c \leq y \leq d$. The total volume under the surface is 1.

4. The marginal p.d.f. of X,

$$g(x) = \int_{-\infty}^{\infty} f(x, y) dy$$

is $N(\mu_X, \sigma_X^2)$. Similarly the marginal p.d.f. of Y,

$$h(y) = \int_{-\infty}^{\infty} f(x, y) dx$$

is $N(\mu_Y, \sigma_Y^2)$.

5. The conditional distribution of Y given $X = x$ defined by $f(x, y)/g(x)$ is normal with mean and variance as follows:

$$E(Y \mid x) = \mu_Y - \frac{\rho \sigma_Y}{\sigma_X} \mu_X + \frac{\rho \sigma_Y}{\sigma_X} x, \quad \text{Var}(Y \mid x) = (1 - \rho^2)\sigma_Y^2. \quad (10.25)$$

6. Note that the regression function $E(Y \mid x)$ is linear in x with intercept and slope equal to

$$\beta_0 = \mu_Y - \frac{\rho \sigma_Y}{\sigma_X} \mu_X \quad \text{and} \quad \beta_1 = \frac{\rho \sigma_Y}{\sigma_X}, \quad (10.26)$$

respectively. Also, $\text{Var}(Y \mid x)$ is constant and equals

$$\sigma^2 = (1 - \rho^2)\sigma_Y^2.$$

Therefore, if (X, Y) have a bivariate normal distribution, then the linear regression model of Section 10.1 is the correct model to study the behavior of Y conditioned on x.

7. The conditional variance, $\text{Var}(Y \mid x) = \sigma^2 = (1 - \rho^2)\sigma_Y^2$, is always less than or equal to the unconditional variance, $\text{Var}(Y) = \sigma_Y^2$. The fractional reduction in the variance due to conditioning on x is equal to ρ^2. Thus there is 100% reduction if $\rho = -1$ or $+1$ and no reduction if $\rho = 0$.

8. Bivariate normal r.v.'s X and Y are independent if and only if $\rho = 0$. In this case $E(Y \mid x) = \mu_Y$ and $\text{Var}(Y \mid x) = \sigma_Y^2$. Thus the conditional mean and variance are unaffected by conditioning on x and are the same as the unconditional mean and variance, respectively. In other words, the knowledge of X gives no additional information about Y.

10.5.2 Statistical Inference on the Correlation Coefficient

Earlier we used the sample correlation coefficient r merely as a descriptive measure of the linear relationship. We now view it as a *sample estimate* of the population correlation coefficient ρ between two r.v.'s X and Y on which we have n i.i.d. observations: (x_1, y_1), $(x_2, y_2), \ldots, (x_n, y_n)$ from a bivariate normal distribution.

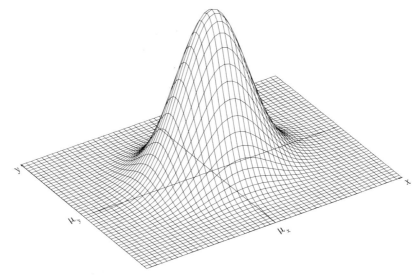

Figure 10.15   Bell Shaped Surface Defined by the Bivariate Normal Density Function

Define the r.v. R corresponding to r:

$$R = \frac{\sum(X_i - \bar{X})(Y_i - \bar{Y})}{\sqrt{\sum(X_i - \bar{X})^2 \sum(Y_i - \bar{Y})^2}}. \tag{10.27}$$

The distribution of R is quite complicated. Figure 10.16 shows the pictures of the p.d.f. $f(r)$ of R for selected values of the true correlation coefficient ρ. Note that the modes of the distributions are equal to the true ρ, but the distributions are skewed except when $\rho = 0$. Inference on ρ based on the exact distribution of R is extremely difficult, except for the problem of testing $H_0: \rho = 0$. We first consider this simpler problem, for which there is an exact test available. Then we discuss approximate CI's and tests for ρ in the general case.

Test of $H_0: \rho = 0$.   When $\rho = 0$, the distribution of R is symmetric about 0 over the interval $[-1, +1]$. The transformation

$$T = \frac{R\sqrt{n-2}}{\sqrt{1-R^2}}$$

changes the range to $[-\infty, +\infty]$ while still maintaining the symmetry of the distribution around 0. But more importantly, we can express this as the t-statistic (10.17) for testing $\beta_1 = 0$ in linear regression. Testing $\beta_1 = 0$ is equivalent to testing $\rho = 0$, since from (10.26) we have $\beta_1 = \rho\sigma_Y/\sigma_X$. Therefore $T \sim t_{n-2}$ when $H_0: \rho = 0$. The derivation of this result is given below. The statistic

$$t = \frac{r\sqrt{n-2}}{\sqrt{1-r^2}} \tag{10.28}$$

is used to test H_0, as illustrated in the following example.

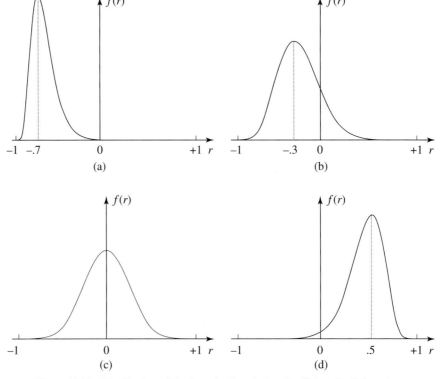

Figure 10.16   Distribution of the Sample Correlation Coefficient for Selected Values of ρ: (a) $\rho = -.7$; (b) $\rho = -.3$; (c) $\rho = 0$; (d) $\rho = .5$

EXAMPLE 10.16   (CORRELATION BETWEEN TEST INSTRUMENTS: AN EXACT TEST OF SIGNIFICANCE)

A researcher wants to determine if two test instruments (e.g., standardized tests) give similar results. The two test instruments are administered to a sample of 15 students. The correlation coefficient between the two sets of scores is found to be 0.7. Is this correlation statistically significant at the .01 level?

We test $H_0: \rho = 0$ vs. $H_1: \rho \neq 0$. Using (10.28), calculate

$$t = \frac{0.7\sqrt{15 - 2}}{\sqrt{1 - 0.7^2}} = 3.534.$$

For $\alpha = .01$, we compare this t-statistic with $t_{13,.005} = 3.012$ and conclude that the observed correlation is significantly different from zero.   ◆

*Derivation of the Result That $T \sim T_{n-2}$.   To derive this result, we first show that the two t-statistics (10.17) and (10.28) are algebraically identical. Substitute

$$r = \hat{\beta}_1 \frac{s_x}{s_y} = \hat{\beta}_1 \sqrt{\frac{S_{xx}}{S_{yy}}} = \hat{\beta}_1 \sqrt{\frac{S_{xx}}{\text{SST}}} \quad \text{and} \quad 1 - r^2 = \frac{\text{SSE}}{\text{SST}} = \frac{(n-2)s^2}{\text{SST}}$$

(from (10.12) and (10.11), respectively). Therefore (10.28) equals

$$t = \hat{\beta}_1 \sqrt{\frac{S_{xx}}{\text{SST}}} \sqrt{\frac{(n-2)\text{SST}}{(n-2)s^2}} = \frac{\hat{\beta}_1}{s/\sqrt{S_{xx}}} = \frac{\hat{\beta}_1}{\text{SE}(\hat{\beta}_1)}$$

which is the t-statistic (10.17) for testing $H_0: \beta_1 = 0$.

If we condition on the $X_i = x_i$, then T has a t_{n-2} distribution when $\rho = 0$ (i.e., when $\beta_1 = 0$). Since this conditional distribution of T does not depend on the x_i's, it follows that the unconditional distribution of T is also t_{n-2}.

Approximate Inference on ρ. As noted above, the exact distribution of R is not very useful for making inferences on ρ. R. A. Fisher showed that the following transformation of R is approximately normally distributed even for n as small as 10:

$$\tanh^{-1} R = \frac{1}{2} \log_e \left(\frac{1+R}{1-R}\right) \approx N\left(\frac{1}{2}\log_e\left(\frac{1+\rho}{1-\rho}\right), \frac{1}{n-3}\right); \quad (10.29)$$

see Exercise 10.26 for a derivation of this transformation. This result can be used to test hypotheses of the form

$$H_0: \rho = \rho_0 \quad \text{vs.} \quad H_1: \rho \neq \rho_0$$

as follows. Define a new parameter:

$$\psi = \frac{1}{2}\log_e\left(\frac{1+\rho}{1-\rho}\right) \quad \text{which corresponds to} \quad \rho = \frac{e^{2\psi}-1}{e^{2\psi}+1}. \quad (10.30)$$

Since ψ is a one-to-one strictly increasing function of ρ, the above hypotheses are equivalent to

$$H_0: \psi = \psi_0 = \frac{1}{2}\log_e\left(\frac{1+\rho_0}{1-\rho_0}\right) \quad \text{vs.} \quad H_1: \psi \neq \psi_0.$$

A sample estimate of ψ is

$$\hat{\psi} = \frac{1}{2}\log_e\left(\frac{1+r}{1-r}\right).$$

Compute the z-statistic

$$z = \sqrt{n-3}(\hat{\psi} - \psi_0) \quad (10.31)$$

and then perform the usual two-sided z-test. This approximate test is not needed when $\rho_0 = 0$, in which case the exact t-test presented previously should be used.

An approximate CI for ρ can be obtained as follows: First calculate an approximate $(1-\alpha)$-level z-interval for ψ:

$$\hat{\psi} - z_{\alpha/2}\frac{1}{\sqrt{n-3}} \leq \psi \leq \hat{\psi} + z_{\alpha/2}\frac{1}{\sqrt{n-3}}.$$

If we denote the lower limit of this CI by ℓ and the upper limit by u, then the corresponding confidence limits on ρ are given by

$$\frac{e^{2\ell} - 1}{e^{2\ell} + 1} \leq \rho \leq \frac{e^{2u} - 1}{e^{2u} + 1}.$$

EXAMPLE 10.17   (CORRELATION BETWEEN TEST INSTRUMENTS: AN APPROXIMATE TEST AND CI)

Refer to Example 10.16. From a practical standpoint, it is usually not sufficient to know whether $\rho > 0$. Rather it may be useful to know whether, e.g., $\rho > 0.5$. Therefore test the hypotheses

$$H_0: \rho \leq 0.5 \quad \text{vs.} \quad H_1: \rho > 0.5.$$

Also calculate a 95% CI for ρ.

The above hypotheses are equivalent to

$$H_0: \psi \leq \psi_0 \quad \text{vs.} \quad H_1: \psi > \psi_0$$

where ψ is defined in (10.30) and

$$\psi_0 = \frac{1}{2} \log_e \left(\frac{1 + 0.5}{1 - 0.5} \right) = 0.549.$$

To test these hypotheses, first calculate

$$\hat{\psi} = \frac{1}{2} \log_e \left(\frac{1 + 0.7}{1 - 0.7} \right) = 0.867.$$

Then the z-statistic equals

$$z = \sqrt{15 - 3}(0.867 - 0.549) = 1.102$$

which is clearly nonsignificant (one-sided P-value = 0.146). Thus we have insufficient evidence to reject H_0. Therefore we cannot conclude that $\rho > 0.5$.

To calculate a 95% CI for ρ, we first calculate a 95% CI for ψ:

$$\left[0.867 \pm 1.960 \frac{1}{\sqrt{15 - 3}} \right] = [0.301, 1.432].$$

From this we obtain a 95% CI for ρ as

$$\left[\frac{e^{2 \times 0.301} - 1}{e^{2 \times 0.301} + 1}, \frac{e^{2 \times 1.432} - 1}{e^{2 \times 1.432} + 1} \right] = [0.292, 0.892].$$

Note that this CI includes the values of $\rho < 0.5$. Also note that this CI is not symmetric about $\hat{\rho} = r = 0.7$, but the CI for ψ is symmetric about $\hat{\psi}$.   ◆

10.6   PITFALLS OF REGRESSION AND CORRELATION ANALYSES

In Section 4.4.2 we discussed cautions that should be exercised when interpreting results from regression and correlation analyses. In particular, we discussed regression fallacy and the perils of equating correlation with causation. In happenstance data, for which these analyses are often used, any observed relationship between two variables could be purely coincidental. Or it could be due to a third unobserved variable (called a

lurking variable), which influences the two observed variables. Often the time order is a lurking variable, since time affects everything. In one of the examples given by Joiner[17] the vitamin B_2 content of turnip greens is "explained" (in terms of r^2) better by the order of observations than by a multiple regression model on three predictor variables (radiation, moisture content, and temperature). Surmising that this order represents the time order, it is likely that the turnips decayed over time, thus causing a drop in the vitamin B_2 content. Even if the data are obtained from a well-controlled and randomized experiment, the possibility of lurking variables cannot be completely ruled out.

Another issue is that extrapolations beyond the range of the data can be off target. In most applications the linear relationship between x and y is true only approximately and often only over a limited range. Globally, most relationships are nonlinear. Although the data may support the assumption of linearity, this does not guarantee that the relationship is linear beyond the range of the data.

10.7   CHAPTER SUMMARY

Linear regression analysis begins by fitting a straight line, $y = \beta_0 + \beta_1 x$, to a set of paired data $\{(x_i, y_i),\ i = 1, 2, \ldots, n\}$ on two numerical variables x and y. The **least squares (LS) estimates** $\hat{\beta}_0$ and $\hat{\beta}_1$ minimize $Q = \sum_{i=1}^{n} [y_i - (\beta_0 + \beta_1 x_i)]^2$ and are given by

$$\hat{\beta}_0 = \bar{y} - \hat{\beta}_1 \bar{x}, \hat{\beta}_1 = \frac{S_{xy}}{S_{xx}}$$

where $S_{xy} = \sum_{i=1}^{n}(x_i - \bar{x})(y_i - \bar{y})$ and $S_{xx} = \sum_{i=1}^{n}(x_i - \bar{x})^2$. The **fitted values** are given by $\hat{y}_i = \hat{\beta}_0 + \hat{\beta}_1 x_i$ and the **residuals** by $e_i = y_i - \hat{y}_i$.

The total sum of squares (SST), regression sum of squares (SSR) and error sum of squares (SSE) are defined as SST $= \sum_{i=1}^{n}(y_i - \bar{y})^2$, SSR $= \sum_{i=1}^{n}(\hat{y}_i - \bar{y})^2$, and SSE $= \sum_{i=1}^{n}(y_i - \hat{y}_i)^2$. These sums of squares satisfy the identity SST $=$ SSR $+$ SSE. A measure of goodness of fit of the least squares line is the **coefficient of determination**,

$$r^2 = \frac{\text{SSR}}{\text{SST}} = 1 - \frac{\text{SSE}}{\text{SST}}$$

which represents the proportion of variation in y that is accounted for by regression on x. The **correlation coefficient** r equals $\pm\sqrt{r^2}$, where $\text{sign}(r) = \text{sign}(\hat{\beta}_1)$. In fact, $r = \hat{\beta}_1(s_x/s_y)$, where s_x and s_y are the sample standard deviations of x and y, respectively.

The **probabilistic model** for linear regression assumes that y_i is the observed value of r.v. $Y_i \sim N(\mu_i, \sigma^2)$, where $\mu_i = \beta_0 + \beta_1 x_i$ and the Y_i are independent. An unbiased estimate of σ^2 is provided by $s^2 = \text{SSE}/(n-2)$ with $n-2$ d.f. The estimated standard errors of $\hat{\beta}_0$ and $\hat{\beta}_1$ equal

$$\text{SE}(\hat{\beta}_0) = s\sqrt{\frac{\sum x_i^2}{n S_{xx}}} \quad \text{and} \quad \text{SE}(\hat{\beta}_1) = \frac{s}{\sqrt{S_{xx}}}.$$

---

[17] B. L. Joiner (1981), "Lurking variables: Some examples," *The American Statistician*, **35**, pp. 227–233.

These are used to construct confidence intervals and perform hypothesis tests on β_0 and β_1. For example, a $100(1 - \alpha)\%$ confidence interval on β_1 is given by

$$\hat{\beta}_1 \pm t_{n-2,\alpha/2}\text{SE}(\hat{\beta}_1).$$

A common use of the fitted regression model is to *predict* Y^* for specified $x = x^*$ or to *estimate* $\mu^* = E(Y^*)$. In both cases we have

$$\hat{Y}^* = \hat{\mu}^* = \hat{\beta}_0 + \hat{\beta}_1 x^*.$$

However, a $100(1 - \alpha)\%$ **prediction interval** for Y^* is wider than a $100(1 - \alpha)\%$ confidence interval for μ^* because Y^* is an r.v., while μ^* is a fixed constant.

Residuals are key to checking the model assumptions such as normality of the Y_i, linearity of the regression model, constant variance σ^2, and independence of the Y_i. Residuals are also useful for detecting **outliers** and **influential observations**. Many of these diagnostic checks are done by plotting residuals in appropriate ways.

Correlation analysis assumes that the data $\{(x_i, y_i), \ i = 1, 2, \ldots, n\}$ form a random sample from a **bivariate normal distribution** with correlation coefficient ρ. An estimate of ρ is the sample correlation coefficient r. An exact test of $H_0: \rho = 0$ is a t-test with $n - 2$ d.f. based on the test statistic

$$t = \frac{r\sqrt{n-2}}{\sqrt{1-r^2}}.$$

This equals $t = \hat{\beta}_1/\text{SE}(\hat{\beta}_1)$ which is used to test $H_0: \beta_1 = 0$ in the related regression model. In other cases only approximate large sample inferences are available. These inferences use the parameterization

$$\psi = \frac{1}{2}\log_e\left(\frac{1+\rho}{1-\rho}\right).$$

The sample estimate $\hat{\psi}$ of ψ, obtained by substituting $\hat{\rho} = r$ in the above expression, is approximately normally distributed with mean $= \frac{1}{2}\log_e\left(\frac{1+\rho}{1-\rho}\right)$ and variance $= \frac{1}{n-3}$.

■ EXERCISES

Section 10.1

10.1 Tell whether the following mathematical models are theoretical and deterministic or empirical and probabilistic.

(a) Maxwell's equations of electromagnetism.

(b) An econometric model of the U.S. economy.

(c) A credit scoring model for the probability of a credit applicant being a good risk as a function of selected variables, e.g., income, outstanding debts, etc.

10.2 Tell whether the following mathematical models are theoretical and deterministic or empirical and probabilistic.

  (a) An item response model for the probability of a correct response to an item on a "true–false" test as a function of the item's intrinsic difficulty.

  (b) The Cobb–Douglas production function, which relates the output of a firm to its capital and labor inputs.

  (c) Kepler's laws of planetary motion.

10.3 Give an example of an experimental study in which the explanatory variable is controlled at fixed values, while the response variable is random. Also, give an example of an observational study in which both variables are uncontrolled and random.

Section 10.2

10.4 ◼ The time between eruptions of Old Faithful geyser in Yellowstone National Park is random but is related to the duration of the last eruption. The table below shows these times for 21 consecutive eruptions.[18]

Old Faithful Eruptions: Duration and Time Between Eruptions (in min.)

Obs. No.	Duration of Eruption (LAST)	Time Between Eruptions (NEXT)	Obs. No.	Duration of Eruption (LAST)	Time Between Eruptions (NEXT)
1	2.0	50	12	3.8	70
2	1.8	57	13	4.5	85
3	3.7	55	14	4.7	75
4	2.2	47	15	4.0	77
5	2.1	53	16	4.0	70
6	2.4	50	17	1.7	43
7	2.6	62	18	1.8	48
8	2.8	57	19	4.9	70
9	3.3	72	20	4.2	79
10	3.5	62	21	4.3	72
11	3.7	63			

Let us see how well we can predict the time to next eruption, given the length of time of the last eruption.

  (a) Make a scatter plot of NEXT vs. LAST. Does the relationship appear to be approximately linear?

  (b) Fit a least squares regression line. Use it to predict the time to the next eruption if the last eruption lasted 3 minutes.

[18] L. Denby and D. Pregibon (1987), "An example of the use of graphics in regression," *The American Statistician*, **41**, pp. 33–38.

(c) What proportion of variability in NEXT is accounted for by LAST? Does it suggest that LAST is a good predictor of NEXT?

(d) Calculate the mean square error estimate of σ.

10.5 ◼ The data below show Olympic triple jump winning distances for men in meters for the years 1896 to 1992 (there were no Olympic games in 1916, 1940, and 1944).[19]

Men's Olympic Triple Jump Winning Distance (in meters)

Year	Distance	Year	Distance	Year	Distance
1896	13.71	1932	15.72	1968	17.39
1900	14.47	1936	16.00	1972	17.35
1908	14.92	1948	15.40	1976	17.29
1912	14.64	1952	16.22	1980	17.35
1920	14.50	1956	16.35	1984	17.25
1924	15.53	1960	16.81	1988	17.61
1928	15.21	1964	16.85	1992	18.17

(a) Make a scatter plot of the length of the jump by year. Does the relationship appear to be approximately linear?

(b) Fit a least squares regression line.

(c) Calculate the mean square error estimate of σ.

10.6 ◼ The following data give the barometric pressure (in inches of mercury) and the boiling point (in °F) of water in the Alps.[20]

Boiling Point of Water in the Alps

Pressure	Boil. Pt.	Pressure	Boil. Pt.	Pressure	Boil. Pt.
20.79	194.5	23.89	200.9	28.49	209.5
20.79	194.3	23.99	201.1	27.76	208.6
22.40	197.9	24.02	201.4	29.04	210.7
22.67	198.4	24.01	201.3	29.88	211.9
23.15	199.4	25.14	203.6	30.06	212.2
23.35	199.9	26.57	204.6		

(a) Make a scatter plot of the boiling point by barometric pressure. Does the relationship appear to be approximately linear?

(b) Fit a least squares regression line. What proportion of variation in the boiling point is accounted for by linear regression on the barometric pressure?

(c) Calculate the mean square error estimate of σ.

---

[19] *World Almanac and Book of Facts* (1995), Mahwah, NJ: Funk & Wagnalls Corporation, p. 860.

[20] A. C. Atkinson (1985), *Plots, Transformations and Regression*, Oxford: Clarendon Press, p. 4. Reprinted in *Small Data Sets*, pp. 270–271.

10.7   ◼ The following table shows Olympic 100 meter backstroke winning times for women for the years 1924 to 1992 (there were no Olympic games in 1940 and 1944).[21]

Women's Olympic 100 Meter Backstroke Winning Times (in seconds)

Year	Time	Year	Time	Year	Time	Year	Time
1924	83.2	1948	74.4	1964	67.7	1980	60.9
1928	82.2	1952	74.3	1968	66.2	1984	62.6
1932	79.4	1956	72.9	1972	65.8	1988	60.9
1936	78.9	1960	69.3	1976	61.8	1992	60.7

(a) Make a scatter plot of the winning times by year. Does the relationship appear to be approximately linear?

(b) Fit a least squares regression line.

(c) Calculate the mean square error estimate of σ.

10.8   Often the conditions of the problem dictate that the intercept coefficient β_0 must be zero, e.g., the sales revenue as a function of the number of units sold or the gas mileage of a car as a function of the weight of the car. This is called **regression through the origin**. Show that the LS estimate of the slope coefficient β_1 when fitting the straight line $y = \beta_1 x$ based on the data $(x_1, y_1), (x_2, y_2), \ldots, (x_n, y_n)$ is

$$\hat{\beta}_1 = \frac{\sum x_i y_i}{\sum x_i^2}.$$

Section 10.3

10.9   ◼ Refer to Exercise 10.5.

(a) Is there a significant increasing linear trend in the triple jump distance? Test at $\alpha = .05$.

(b) Calculate a 95% PI for the winning jump in 2004. Do you think this prediction is reliable? Why or why not? Would a 95% CI for the winning jump in 2004 have a meaningful interpretation? Explain.

10.10   ◼ Refer to Exercise 10.6.

(a) Calculate a 95% CI for the boiling point if the barometric pressure is 28 inches of mercury. Interpret your CI.

(b) Calculate a 95% CI for the boiling point if the barometric pressure is 31 inches of mercury. Compare this with the CI of (a).

10.11   ◼ Refer to the Old Faithful data in Exercise 10.4.

(a) Calculate a 95% PI for the time to the next eruption if the last eruption lasted 3 minutes.

(b) Calculate a 95% CI for the *mean* time to the next eruption for a last eruption lasting 3 minutes. Compare this CI with the PI obtained in (a).

(c) Repeat (a) if the last eruption lasted 1 minute. Do you think this prediction is reliable? Why or why not?

---

[21] *The World Almanac and Book of Facts* (1995), Mahwah, NJ: Funk & Wagnalls Corporation, p. 864.

10.12 ■ Refer to Exercise 10.7.

   (a) Calculate a 95% PI for the winning time in 2004. Do you think this prediction is reliable? Why or why not?

   (b) Use the regression equation to find the year in which the winning time would break 1 minute. Given that the Olympics are every four years, during which Olympics would this happen?

10.13 The U.S. infant mortality rates (IMR) (per 1000 live births) for both sexes and all races for the years 1981–1990 (coded as years 1–10) were as follows:[22]

Year	1	2	3	4	5	6	7	8	9	10
Infant Mortality Rate (IMR)	11.9	11.5	11.2	10.8	10.6	10.4	10.1	10.0	9.8	9.2

The MINITAB regression output is shown below.

```
MINITAB Output for Regression of Infant Mortality Rate Versus
Year
MTB  regress 'IMR' 1 'Year'
The regression equation is
IMR = 12.0 - 0.270 Year
Predictor        Coef        Stdev       t-ratio         p
Constant       12.0333       0.0851       141.35       0.000
Year           -0.26970      0.01372      -19.66       0.000
s = 0.1246      R-sq = 98.0%      R-sq(adj) = 97.7%
Analysis of Variance
SOURCE         DF          SS          MS          F          p
Regression      1        6.0008      6.0008      386.39      0.000
Error           8        0.1242      0.0155
Total           9        6.1250
```

Answer the following questions based on this output.

   (a) What was the average rate of decrease in the infant mortality rate per year during 1981–1990? Suppose that for the rest of the Western world the rate of decrease in IMR was 0.3 deaths per year per 1000 live births. Was the U.S. rate of decrease significantly less than that for the rest of the Western world? Use $\alpha = .05$.

   (b) Predict the IMR for the year 1995. Calculate a 95% prediction interval. (Note that S_{xx} can be obtained from the values of $\text{Stdev}(\hat{\beta}_1)$ and s given in the MINITAB output.)

10.14 For the linear regression model (10.1) show that the sample mean $\bar{Y}$ and the LS slope estimator $\hat{\beta}_1$ are statistically independent. (*Hint:* Write $\bar{Y} = \frac{1}{n} \sum Y_i$ and $\hat{\beta}_1 = \sum c_i Y_i$, where $c_i = (x_i - \bar{x})/S_{xx}$ and satisfy $\sum c_i = 0$. Then show that $\text{Cov}(\bar{Y}, \hat{\beta}_1) = 0$ by using formula (2.21) for the covariance between two sets of linear combinations of r.v.'s. Finally, use the result that if two normal r.v.'s are uncorrelated, then they are independent.)

---

[22] *The World Almanac and Book of Facts* (1994), Mahwah, NJ: Funk & Wagnalls Corporation, p. 956.

Section 10.4

10.15   Often, the probability of response p $(0 \leq p \leq 1)$ is modeled as a function of a stimulus x by the **logistic function**:

$$p = \frac{\exp(\beta_0 + \beta_1 x)}{1 + \exp(\beta_0 + \beta_1 x)}.$$

For example, the stimulus is the dose level of a drug and the response is cured or is not cured. Find the linearizing transformation $h(p)$ so that $h(p) = \beta_0 + \beta_1 x$.

10.16   ◨ A prime is a positive integer that has no integer factors other than 1 and itself (1 is not regarded as a prime). The number of primes in any given interval of whole numbers is highly irregular. However, the proportion of primes less than or equal to any given number x (denoted by $p(x)$) follows a regular pattern as x increases. The following table gives the number and proportion of primes for $x = 10^n$ for $n = 1, 2, \ldots, 10$. The objective of the present exercise is to discover this pattern.[23]

x	No. of Primes	Proportion of Primes ($p(x)$)
10^1	4	0.400000
10^2	25	0.250000
10^3	168	0.168000
10^4	1,229	0.122900
10^5	9,592	0.095920
10^6	78,498	0.078498
10^7	664,579	0.066458
10^8	5,761,455	0.057615
10^9	50,847,534	0.050848
10^{10}	455,052,512	0.045505

(a) Plot the proportion of primes, $p(x)$, against $10{,}000/x$, $1000/\sqrt{x}$, and $1/\log_{10} x$. Which relationship appears most linear?

(b) Estimate the slope of the line $p(x) = \beta_0 + \beta_1 \frac{1}{\log_{10} x}$ and show that $\hat{\beta}_1 \approx \log_{10} e = 0.4343$.

(c) Explain how the relationship found in (b) roughly translates into the **prime number theorem**: For large x, $p(x) \approx 1/\log_e x$.

10.17   ◨ In a memory retention experiment subjects were asked to memorize a list of disconnected items, and then were asked to recall them at various times up to a week later. The proportion p of items recalled at times t (in minutes) is given below.[24]

t	1	5	15	30	60	120	240	480	720	1440	2880	5760	10080
p	0.84	0.71	0.61	0.56	0.54	0.47	0.45	0.38	0.36	0.26	0.20	0.16	0.08

---

[23] This exercise is based on the article by F. Mosteller (1970), "Transformations for linearity," in *Statistics by Example: Detecting Patterns* (ed. F. Mosteller et al.), Reading, MA: Addison-Wesley, pp. 99–108. The data are taken from W. Dunham (1994), *The Mathematical Universe*, New York: Wiley, p. 196.

[24] F. Mosteller, R. E. K. Rourke, and G. B. Thomas (1970), *Probability with Statistical Applications*, 2nd ed., Reading, MA: Addison-Wesley. Reprinted in *Small Data Sets*, p. 128.

(a) Note that t increases almost geometrically throughout. This suggests that a logarithmic transformation of t might linearize the relationship. Plot p vs. $\log_e t$. Is the relationship approximately linear?

(b) Fit a trend line to the plot in (b). From the trend line estimate the time for 50% retention.

10.18   ■ The following are the average distances of the planets in the solar system from the sun:[25]

Planet No.	Planet	Distance (millions of miles)
1	Mercury	47.163
2	Venus	67.235
3	Earth	92.960
4	Mars	141.61
5	Asteroids	313.00
6	Jupiter	483.60
7	Saturn	886.70
8	Uranus	1783.0
9	Neptune	2794.0
10	Pluto	3666.0

(a) How does the distance of a planet from the sun increase with the planet number? Find a transformation of the distance that gives a linear relationship with respect to the planet number.

(b) Fit a least squares straight line after linearizing the relationship.

(c) It is speculated that there is a planet beyond Pluto, called Planet X. Predict its distance from the sun.

10.19   ■ The following are the speeds of the planets in the solar system as they revolve around the sun:

Planet No.	Planet	Speed (miles per hour)
1	Mercury	107,376
2	Venus	78,295
3	Earth	67,109
4	Mars	53,687
5	Jupiter	29,080
6	Saturn	21,600
7	Uranus	15,212
8	Neptune	12,080
9	Pluto	10,515

---

[25] This exercise is based on Example 6, Ch. 3 of F. Mosteller, S. E. Fienberg, and R. E. K. Rourke (1983), *Beginning Statistics with Data Analysis*, Reading, MA: Addison-Wesley.

What relationship do you notice between the distances of the planets from the sun given in the previous exercise and planet speeds? Find a transformation of the speed that linearizes its relationship with the planet distance, and fit this relationship.

10.20 ▣ To relate the stopping distance of a car to its speed, ten cars were tested at five different speeds, two cars at each speed. The following data were obtained.[26]

Speed x (mph)	20	20	30	30	40	40	50	50	60	60
Stop. Dist. y (ft)	16.3	26.7	39.2	63.5	65.7	98.4	104.1	155.6	217.2	160.8

(a) Fit an LS straight line to these data. Plot the residuals against the speed.

(b) Comment on the goodness of the fit based on the overall F-statistic and the residual plot. Which two assumptions of the linear regression model seem to be violated?

(c) Based on the residual plot, what transformation of stopping distance should be used to linearize the relationship with respect to speed? A clue to find this transformation is provided by the following engineering argument: In bringing a car to a stop, its kinetic energy is dissipated as its braking energy, and the two are roughly equal. The kinetic energy is proportional to the square of the car's speed, while the braking energy is proportional to the stopping distance, assuming a constant braking force.

(d) Make this linearizing transformation and check the goodness of fit. What is the predicted stopping distance according to this model if the car is traveling at 40 mph?

10.21 ▣ The direct current output from a windmill (y) was measured against the wind velocity (x) in miles per hour. The following data were obtained.[27]

Wind Velocity (mph)	DC Output (amp)	Wind Velocity (mph)	DC Output (amp)
2.45	0.123	6.20	1.866
2.70	0.500	6.35	1.930
2.90	0.653	7.00	1.800
3.05	0.558	7.40	2.088
3.40	1.057	7.85	2.179
3.60	1.137	8.15	2.166
3.95	1.144	8.80	2.112
4.10	1.194	9.10	2.303
4.60	1.562	9.55	2.294
5.00	1.582	9.70	2.386
5.45	1.501	10.00	2.236
5.80	1.737	10.20	2.310
6.00	1.822		

[26] This exercise is based on Example 2A, Ch. 12 of F. Mosteller, S. E. Fienberg and R. E. K. Rourke, *op. cit.*

[27] G. Joglekar, J. H. Schuenemeyer, and V. LaRicca (1989), "Lack of fit testing when replicates are not available," *The American Statistician*, **43**, pp. 135–143. Reprinted in *Small Data Sets*, p. 271.

(a) Make a scatter plot of the DC output vs. wind velocity. Describe the relationship. Refer to Figure 10.10. Find a transformation that linearizes the relationship. Fit the LS line.

(b) Check the goodness of fit by making residual plots. Do the assumptions of linear regression seem to be satisfied?

(c) What is the predicted output if the wind velocity is 8 mph?

10.22 ■ This data set[28] illustrates the importance of graphical plotting in regression analysis.

No.	x_1	y_1	y_2	y_3	x_2	y_4
1	10	8.04	9.14	7.46	8	6.58
2	8	6.95	8.14	6.77	8	5.76
3	13	7.58	8.74	12.74	8	7.71
4	9	8.81	8.77	7.11	8	8.84
5	11	8.33	9.26	7.81	8	8.47
6	14	9.96	8.10	8.84	8	7.04
7	6	7.24	6.13	6.08	8	5.25
8	4	4.26	3.10	5.39	19	12.50
9	12	10.84	9.13	8.15	8	5.56
10	7	4.82	7.26	6.42	8	7.91
11	5	5.68	4.74	5.73	8	6.89

(a) Make four scatter plots: y_1 vs. x_1, y_2 vs. x_1, y_3 vs. x_1, and y_4 vs. x_2. Comment on their appearances—in particular, the linearity of the relationship exhibited by the plots.

(b) Fit LS straight lines to the four plots and compute the usual statistics that accompany the LS fits. Note that the numerical results are identical.

(c) Why do you think the LS fits are identical even though the scatter plots are quite different? What does this say about the importance of plotting the data before fitting a model?

(d) What does this say about r^2 or the t-statistic for testing the significance of $\hat{\beta}_1$ as measures of the linearity of relationships?

10.23 ■ The approximate gestation time and birthweights are given in the following table for selected mammals.[29] The gestation time t (between fertilization and birth) for a mammal is related to the birthweight w by the relationship $t = ab^w$, where a and b are constants. Regression methods can be used to estimate a and b by transforming this relationship into a linear model.

(a) Apply the log transformation to obtain a linear model of the form $y = \beta_0 + \beta_1 w$, where $y = \log t$. How are β_0 and β_1 related to a and b, respectively?

(b) Plot log(gestation time) vs. weight. Is this relationship approximately linear?

---

[28] F. J. Anscombe (1973), "Graphs in statistical analysis," *The American Statistician*, **27**, pp. 17–21.

[29] Adapted from W. Keienburg, D. Heinemann, and S. Schmitz eds. (1990), *Grizmek's Encyclopedia of Mammals*, New York: McGraw-Hill.

(c) Fit the linear model $y = \beta_0 + \beta_1 w$ to the transformed data.

(d) Using the fitted model in (c), estimate the gestation time of a lion which weighs approximately 1.2 kg at birth.

Mammal	Birthweight (kg)	Gestation (days)	Mammal	Birthweight (kg)	Gestation (days)
Goat	2.75	155	Horse	30	340
Sheep	4.00	175	Camel	40	380
Deer	0.48	190	Zebra	40	390
Porcupine	1.50	210	Giraffe	98	457
Bear	0.37	213	Elephant	113	670
Hippopotamus	50	243			

10.24 Hospitalization cost (h) that is reimbursed by insurance is approximately related to the length of stay ℓ in the hospital by the relationship $h = a\ell^b$, where a and b are constants. Regression methods can be used to estimate a and b by transforming this relationship into a linear model by making the log transformation. The reimbursed hospital cost and associated length of stay are given for a sample of 33 elderly people.[30]

h	13,728	8062	4805	5099	14,963	4295	4046	3193	15,486	9413	9034
ℓ	13	8	13	6	33	2	9	13	16	11	19
h	8939	17,596	1884	1763	1233	6286	2849	2818	2265	1652	1846
ℓ	20	26	3	5	1	30	4	4	2	9	4
h	25,460	4570	12,213	5870	24,484	4735	13,334	35,381	5681	7161	10,592
ℓ	18	16	10	12	52	19	9	85	8	20	41

(a) Apply the log transformation to obtain a linear model of the form $y = \beta_0 + \beta_1 x$, where $x = \log \ell$ and $y = \log h$. How are β_0 and β_1 related to a and b, respectively?

(b) Plot $y = \log h$ vs. $x = \log \ell$. Is this relationship approximately linear?

(c) Fit the linear model $y = \beta_0 + \beta_1 x$ to the transformed data.

(d) Use the fitted model from (c) to estimate the average reimbursed cost for a 3-day hospital stay by an elderly person.

10.25 **(a)** Recall that for a binomial proportion $\hat{p}$ based on a sample of size n we have $E(\hat{p}) = p$ and $\text{Var}(\hat{p}) = p(1-p)/n$. Show that the variance stabilizing transformation for $\hat{p}$ is

$$2\sqrt{n} \sin^{-1} \sqrt{\hat{p}}.$$

This is the so-called **arcsin transformation** for a binomial proportion. (*Hint:* $\int \frac{dx}{\sqrt{x(1-x)}} = 2 \sin^{-1} \sqrt{x}$.)

---

[30] Data courtesy of Professor Susan Hughes, School of Public Health, University of Illinois, Chicago.

(b) Explain how you will use this transformation in the following problem: In a toxico-logical study k doses, $x_1 < x_2 < \cdots < x_k$, of a chemical compound are evaluated for tumorogenicity by treating n_i mice with dose x_i ($i = 1, 2, \ldots, k$). Let $\hat{p}_i$ be the proportion of mice treated with dose level x_i who developed tumors. It is desired to model the probability p of developing a tumor as a function of the dose x of the compound.

10.26 In equation (10.29), the following **arctan hyperbolic transformation** of the sample corre-lation coefficient R is used to achieve approximate normality of its sampling distribution:

$$\tanh^{-1} R = \frac{1}{2} \log_e \left(\frac{1 + R}{1 - R} \right).$$

Show that this is an approximate variance stabilizing transformation by using the results that $E(R) \simeq \rho$ and $\mathrm{Var}(R) \simeq (1 - \rho^2)^2$, where ρ is the population correlation coefficient.

10.27 The **inverse transformation**, $h(y) = 1/y$, is also common in practice. To use this trans-formation how must $\mathrm{Var}(Y)$ be related to $E(Y)$?

Section 10.5

10.28 The following are the heights and weights of 30 eleven year old girls.[31]

Height (cm)	Weight (kg)	Height (cm)	Weight (kg)
135	26	133	31
146	33	149	34
153	55	141	32
154	50	164	47
139	32	146	37
131	25	149	46
149	44	147	36
137	31	152	47
143	36	140	33
146	35	143	42
141	28	148	32
136	28	149	32
154	36	141	29
151	48	137	34
155	36	135	30

(a) Plot weights vs. heights.

(b) Calculate the correlation coefficient. Test if it is significantly greater than 0.7.

[31] The Open University (1983), *MDST242 Statisics in Society, Unit C3: Is my child normal?*, Milton Keynes: The Open University, Figure 3.12. Reprinted in *Small Data Sets*, p. 75.

10.29 Counts of the numbers of finger ridges for 12 pairs of identical twins are given in the following table.[32]

Pair	Twin 1	Twin 2	Pair	Twin 1	Twin 2
1	71	71	7	114	113
2	79	82	8	57	44
3	105	99	9	114	113
4	115	114	10	94	91
5	76	70	11	75	83
6	83	82	12	76	72

(a) Make a scatter plot of the ridges of Twin 2 vs. Twin 1.

(b) Calculate the correlation coefficient and a 95% confidence interval on ρ.

10.30 Times of U.K. male sprinters in 1988 for 200 meters and 100 meters without wind resistence are given in the following table.[33]

Athlete	Best Time (sec)		Athlete	Best Time (sec)	
	200 m	100 m		200 m	100 m
L. Christie	20.09	9.97	A. Mafe	20.94	10.64
J. Regis	20.32	10.31	D. Reid	21.00	10.54
M. Rosswess	20.51	10.40	P. Snoddy	21.14	10.85
A. Carrott	20.76	10.56	L. Stapleton	21.17	10.71
T. Bennett	20.90	10.92	C. Jackson	21.19	10.56

(a) Make a scatter plot of the 200 m vs. 100 m times. Does there appear to be a strong or weak correlation? Explain.

(b) Calculate the correlation coefficient and a 95% confidence interval on ρ. Test if the correlation coefficient is significantly greater than 0.5.

10.31 The United Nations Children's Fund (UNICEF) publishes an annual report which includes statistical tables on 96 variables related to child health and the status of women and children from 129 different countries. The annual death rate of children under 5 (per 1000 live births) and the female literacy rate (for women aged 10 or over) are given for a sample of these countries.[34]

---

[32] H. H. Newman, F. Freeman, and K. J. Holzinger (1937), *Twins*, Chicago: University of Chicago Press. Reprinted in *Small Data Sets*, p. 309.

[33] The Open University (1993), *MDST242 Statistics in Society Unit A4: Relationships*, 2nd ed., Milton Keynes: The Open University, Table 2.1. Reprinted in *Small Data Sets*, p. 83.

[34] The Open University (1993) *MDST242 Statistics in Society Unit A5: Review*, 3rd ed., Milton Keynes: The Open University, Tables 3.1–3.3. Reprinted in *Small Data Sets*, pp. 74–75.

Country	Child Deaths per 10^3	Female Literacy Rate (%)	Country	Child Deaths per 10^3	Female Literacy Rate (%)	Country	Child Deaths per 10^3	Female Literacy Rate (%)
Guinea -Bissau	246	24	Peru	116	79	Argentina	35	95
Rwanda	198	37	El Salvador	87	70	Panama	31	88
Sudan	172	12	Honduras	84	71	Chile	27	93
Guatemala	94	47	Ecuador	83	84	Uruguay	25	96
Turkey	80	71	Brazil	83	80	Costa Rica	22	93
Viet Nam	65	84	Paraguay	60	88	Yemen	187	21
Oman	22	93	Colombia	50	86	Saudi Arabia	91	48
Bolivia	160	71	Venezeula	43	90	Iraq	86	49
Syria	59	51	Iran	59	43	Lebanon	56	73
Jordan	52	70	United Arab	30	38	Kuwait	19	67

(a) Make a scatter plot of the childhood mortality rate vs. the female literacy rate. Comment on the relationship.

(b) Calculate the correlation coefficient and a 95% confidence interval on ρ. Test if the correlation coefficient is significantly greater than 0.7. Interpret the results.

10.32 Show that the sample correlation coefficient between two variables is unchanged except possibly for the sign if they are linearly transformed. Thus the correlation coefficient between the New York and Chicago daily temperatures is the same whether the temperatures are measured in °F or °C. (*Hint*: Suppose r_{xy} is the correlation coefficient for the data $(x_1, y_1), (x_2, y_2), \ldots, (x_n, y_n)$. Let $u_i = ax_i + b$ and $v_i = cy_i + d$ for $i = 1, 2, \ldots, n$ be the linearly transformed data where $a, c \neq 0$. Show that $r_{uv} = \pm r_{xy}$ with a + sign if $ac > 0$ and a − sign if $ac < 0$.)

Advanced Exercises

10.33 Show that

$$\sum_{i=1}^{n}(y_i - \hat{y}_i)(\hat{y}_i - \bar{y}) = 0.$$

(*Hint*: Substitute $\hat{y}_i = \hat{\beta}_0 + \hat{\beta}_1 x_i = \bar{y} + \hat{\beta}_1(x_i - \bar{x})$ and simplify.)

10.34 The problem of comparing the means of two independent samples (see Chapter 8, Section 8.3) can be formulated as a regression problem as follows: Denote n_1 i.i.d. observations from a $N(\mu_1, \sigma^2)$ population by $y_1, y_2, \ldots, y_{n_1}$ and n_2 i.i.d. observations from a $N(\mu_2, \sigma^2)$ population by $y_{n_1+1}, y_{n_1+2}, \ldots, y_{n_1+n_2}$. Define an indicator variable $x_i = 1$ for $i = 1, 2, \ldots, n_1$ and $x_i = 0$ for $i = n_1 + 1, n_1 + 2, \ldots, n_1 + n_2$. Thus if $x_i = 1$, then y_i comes from the first population, and if $x_i = 0$, then y_i comes from the second population.

(a) Show that the regression model (10.1) corresponds to $\beta_0 = \mu_2$ and $\beta_1 = \mu_1 - \mu_2$.

(b) Apply the formulas for the LS estimates $\hat{\beta}_0$ and $\hat{\beta}_1$ to show that $\hat{\beta}_0 = \bar{y}_2$ and $\hat{\beta}_1 = \bar{y}_1 - \bar{y}_2$.

(c) Show that the MSE for regression is the same as the pooled estimate s^2 of σ^2 with $n_1 + n_2 - 2$ d.f.

(d) Show that the regression t-test of $\beta_1 = 0$ is the same as the pooled variances t-test of $\mu_1 = \mu_2$.

10.35 Consider an experiment in which the values of an explanatory variable x are $x_1, x_2, \ldots, x_k$ for $k \geq 2$. For each fixed value x_i, n_i independent replicates, $y_{i1}, y_{i2}, \ldots, y_{in_i}$, are observed, where $n_i \geq 2$. The total sample size is $n_1 + n_2 + \cdots + n_k = n$. Assume that the standard linear regression model holds (with obvious changes in notation necessitated by the replicate observations).

(a) Let $\bar{y}_i$ and s_i^2 be the sample mean and variance, respectively, of the y_{ij} for given x_i:

$$\bar{y}_i = \frac{\sum_{j=1}^{n_i} y_{ij}}{n_i}, \quad s_i^2 = \frac{\sum_{j=1}^{n_i} (y_{ij} - \bar{y}_i)^2}{n_i - 1} \quad (1 \leq i \leq k).$$

Argue that an unbiased estimate of σ^2 with $n - k$ d.f. is obtained by pooling the sample variances of the y_{ij} at each level of $x = x_i$. This estimate is given by

$$s^2 = \frac{\sum_{i=1}^{k} (n_i - 1)s_i^2}{n - k} = \frac{\sum_{i=1}^{k} \sum_{j=1}^{n_i} (y_{ij} - \bar{y}_i)^2}{n - k}.$$

Notice that this estimate does not depend on the particular model (e.g., straight line or nonlinear) fitted to the data. Hence it is called a **pure error estimate** of σ^2 or **pure error mean square (MSPE)**.

(b) A least squares straight line can be fitted to the data as usual. Let $\hat{y}_{ij} = \hat{\beta}_0 + \hat{\beta}_1 x_i$ be the fitted value corresponding to all y_{ij} at $x = x_i$ and let

$$\text{SSE} = \sum_{i=1}^{k} \sum_{j=1}^{n_i} (y_{ij} - \hat{y}_{ij})^2$$

be the error sum of squares with $n - 2$ d.f. Show that SSE can be partitioned as

$$\text{SSE} = \sum_{i=1}^{k} n_i (\bar{y}_i - \hat{y}_{ij})^2 + \sum_{i=1}^{k} \sum_{j=1}^{n_i} (y_{ij} - \bar{y}_i)^2.$$

(*Hint:* $\sum_{j=1}^{n_i} (y_{ij} - \bar{y}_i) = \sum_{j=1}^{n_i} e_{ij} = 0$.)

The first term in this decomposition is called the **lack of fit sum of squares (SSLOF)** and the second term is called the **pure error sum of squares (SSPE)**. Note that MSPE = SSPE/$(n - k)$. The d.f. for lack of fit are $(n - 2) - (n - k) = k - 2$.

(c) Define MSLOF = SSLOF/$(k - 2)$. It can be shown that

$$F = \frac{\text{MSLOF}}{\text{MSPE}}$$

has an F-distribution with $k - 2$ and $n - k$ d.f. when there is no lack of fit. Explain how you will use this statistic to test for lack of fit.

10.36 The data set[35] for this exercise involves replicate observations and can be analyzed using the method outlined in the previous exercise. Tear factor of paper (defined as the percentage of a standard force required to tear the paper) was measured for four sheets taken from each of five batches of paper made at different pressures. The data are presented below.

Pressure Applied During Pressing	Tear Factor			
35.0	112	119	117	113
49.5	108	99	112	118
70.0	120	106	102	109
99.0	110	101	99	104
140.0	100	102	96	101

(a) The pressures are roughly equispaced on the log scale. Therefore make the logarithmic transformation of pressure and plot the data. Is the relationship approximately linear?

(b) Fit a straight line to the data. Produce the analysis of variance table in which the SSE is partitioned into SSPE and SSLOF. Test for lack of fit of the straight line.

10.37 Do the lack of fit test for the model fitted in part (d) of Exercise 10.20 after making the linearizing transformation.

10.38 In this exercise we derive a CI for the calibration (inverse regression) problem. For specified mean response, $\mu = \mu^*$, let $x = x^* = (\mu^* - \beta_0)/\beta_1$ be the corresponding value of x. To derive a CI for x^* proceed as follows. Note that

$$\frac{\hat{\beta}_0 + \hat{\beta}_1 x^* - \mu^*}{S\sqrt{\frac{1}{n} + \frac{(x^* - \bar{x})^2}{S_{xx}}}} = T \sim T_{n-2}.$$

(a) Use this fact to write the probability statement

$$P(-t_{n-2,\alpha/2} \leq T \leq t_{n-2,\alpha/2}) = P(T^2 \leq t_{n-2,\alpha/2}^2) = 1 - \alpha.$$

(b) Solve the quadratic inequality $T^2 \leq t_{n-2,\alpha/2}^2$ for the unknown x^*. The range of x^* for which the inequality is satisfied gives a $(1-\alpha)$-level CI for x^*. (*Hint*: Find the two roots of the corresponding quadratic equation. Check under what conditions the roots are real and form an interval.)

---

[35] E. J. Williams (1959), *Regression Analysis*, New York: Wiley, p. 17. Reprinted in *Small Data Sets*, p. 4.

CHAPTER 11

MULTIPLE LINEAR REGRESSION

In the last chapter we studied how to fit a linear relationship between a response variable y and a predictor variable x. Sometimes a straight line does not provide an adequate fit to the data, and a quadratic or a cubic model is needed. Another type of problem which cannot be handled using simple linear regression arises when there are two or more predictor variables, and their simultaneous "effects" on a response variable are to be modeled. For example, the salary of a company employee may depend on his/her job category, years of experience, education, and performance evaluations. To estimate more complex relationships we need to extend the simple linear regression model to the case of two or more predictor variables. **Multiple linear regression** (or simply **multiple regression**) is the statistical methodology used to fit such models.

In multiple regression we fit a model of the form (excluding the error term)

$$y = \beta_0 + \beta_1 x_1 + \beta_2 x_2 + \cdots + \beta_k x_k$$

where $x_1, x_2, \ldots, x_k$ are $k \geq 2$ predictor variables and $\beta_0, \beta_1, \ldots, \beta_k$ are $k + 1$ unknown parameters. As noted in the previous chapter, this model is called "linear" because it is linear in the β's, not necessarily in the x's. For example, as a special case, this model includes the kth degree polynomial model in a single variable x, namely,

$$y = \beta_0 + \beta_1 x + \beta_2 x^2 + \cdots + \beta_k x^k$$

since we can put $x_1 = x, x_2 = x^2, \ldots, x_k = x^k$; the case $k = 2$ corresponds to a quadratic model and the case $k = 3$ to a cubic model. More generally, we can have a polynomial in two or more variables. For example, the first degree equation

$$y = \beta_0 + \beta_1 x_1 + \beta_2 x_2$$

defines a planar surface as shown in Figure 11.1(a), while the second degree equation

$$y = \beta_0 + \beta_1 x_1 + \beta_2 x_2 + \beta_3 x_1 x_2 + \beta_4 x_1^2 + \beta_5 x_2^2$$

defines a quadratic surface as shown in Figure 11.1(b).

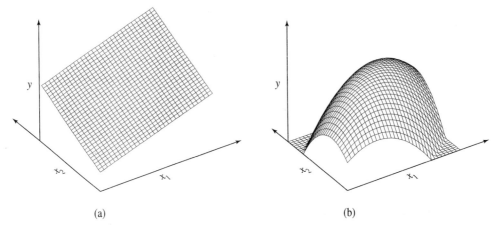

(a)   (b)

Figure 11.1   A Planar Surface and a Quadratic Surface: (a) Planar surface; (b) Quadratic surface

The statistical methods that we learned in the previous chapter for simple linear regression generalize in a natural way to multiple linear regression. The derivation of many of the mathematical results is best approached using a matrix notation formulation. This formulation is presented in Section 11.3. This section may be skipped by those unfamiliar with matrix algebra. Although the following sections use matrix notation in some of the formulas, computations are almost always done using a statistical package on a computer.

11.1   A PROBABILISTIC MODEL FOR MULTIPLE LINEAR REGRESSION

As in the previous chapter, we shall regard the response variable as random and the predictor variables as nonrandom. The data for multiple regression consist of n vectors of observations $(x_{i1}, x_{i2}, \ldots, x_{ik}; y_i)$ for $i = 1, 2, \ldots, n$. For example, the response variable y_i may be the salary of the ith person in the sample, and the predictor variables, x_{i1} and x_{i2}, his/her years of experience and years of education, respectively. For another example, if we wish to fit a kth degree polynomial to data $\{(x_i, y_i), i = 1, 2, \ldots, n\}$ then $x_{ij} = x_i^j$ for $j = 1, 2, \ldots, k$. We regard y_i as the observed value of the random variable (r.v.) Y_i which depends on *fixed* predictor values $x_{i1}, x_{i2}, \ldots, x_{ik}$ according to the following model:

$$Y_i = \beta_0 + \beta_1 x_{i1} + \beta_2 x_{i2} + \cdots + \beta_k x_{ik} + \epsilon_i, \quad i = 1, 2, \ldots, n \tag{11.1}$$

where ϵ_i is a **random error** with $E(\epsilon_i) = 0$, and $\beta_0, \beta_1, \ldots, \beta_k$ are unknown parameters. Usually we assume that the ϵ_i are independent $N(0, \sigma^2)$ r.v.'s. Then the Y_i are independent $N(\mu_i, \sigma^2)$ r.v.'s with

$$\mu_i = E(Y_i) = \beta_0 + \beta_1 x_{i1} + \beta_2 x_{i2} + \cdots + \beta_k x_{ik}.$$

11.2 FITTING THE MULTIPLE REGRESSION MODEL

11.2.1 Least Squares (LS) Fit

To fit the model (11.1) we use the same **least squares (LS) method** introduced in the previous chapter. The LS estimates of the unknown parameters $\beta_0, \beta_1, \ldots, \beta_k$ minimize

$$Q = \sum_{i=1}^{n} [y_i - (\beta_0 + \beta_1 x_{i1} + \beta_2 x_{i2} + \cdots + \beta_k x_{ik})]^2. \tag{11.2}$$

The LS estimates can be found by setting the first partial derivatives of Q with respect to $\beta_0, \beta_1, \ldots, \beta_k$ equal to zero and solving the resulting equations.[1] These equations can be written as

$$\frac{\partial Q}{\partial \beta_0} = -2 \sum_{i=1}^{n} [y_i - (\beta_0 + \beta_1 x_{i1} + \beta_2 x_{i2} + \cdots + \beta_k x_{ik})] = 0 \tag{11.3}$$

$$\frac{\partial Q}{\partial \beta_j} = -2 \sum_{i=1}^{n} [y_i - (\beta_0 + \beta_1 x_{i1} + \beta_2 x_{i2} + \cdots + \beta_k x_{ik})] x_{ij} = 0 \quad (j = 1, 2, \ldots, k).$$

Simplification leads to the following **normal equations**:

$$\beta_0 n + \beta_1 \sum_{i=1}^{n} x_{i1} + \cdots + \beta_k \sum_{i=1}^{n} x_{ik} = \sum_{i=1}^{n} y_i \tag{11.4}$$

$$\beta_0 \sum_{i=1}^{n} x_{ij} + \beta_1 \sum_{i=1}^{n} x_{i1} x_{ij} + \cdots + \beta_k \sum_{i=1}^{n} x_{ik} x_{ij} = \sum_{i=1}^{n} y_i x_{ij} \quad (j = 1, 2, \ldots, k).$$

---

[1] It can be shown that Q is a bowl-shaped ("convex") function of $\beta_0, \beta_1, \ldots, \beta_k$. Hence setting the first partials of Q with respect to these parameters equal to zero yields a global minimum.

These are simultaneous linear equations in $(k+1)$ unknowns and can be solved on a computer or otherwise. The resulting solutions are the **least squares (LS) estimates** of $\beta_0, \beta_1, \ldots, \beta_k$ and are denoted by $\hat{\beta}_0, \hat{\beta}_1, \ldots, \hat{\beta}_k$, respectively.

11.2.2 Goodness of Fit of the Model

To assess the goodness of fit of the LS model we use the **residuals** defined by

$$e_i = y_i - \hat{y}_i \quad (i = 1, 2, \ldots, n)$$

where the $\hat{y}_i$ are the **fitted values**:

$$\hat{y}_i = \hat{\beta}_0 + \hat{\beta}_1 x_{i1} + \cdots + \hat{\beta}_k x_{ik} \quad (i = 1, 2, \ldots, n).$$

In Section 11.5.1 we will discuss how the residuals can be plotted in various ways to check the goodness of fit of the multiple regression model. However, as an overall measure of the goodness of fit, we can use the **error sum of squares** as in Chapter 10:

$$\text{SSE} = \sum_{i=1}^{n} e_i^2$$

which is the minimum value of Q defined in (11.2). We compare this SSE to the **total sum of squares**, $\text{SST} = \sum (y_i - \bar{y})^2$. The reason for using SST as a benchmark of comparison is the same as in the case of simple linear regression, viz., SST is the SSE obtained when fitting the model $Y_i = \beta_0 + \epsilon_i$, which ignores all the x's. As in Chapter 10, define the **regression sum of squares** given by SSR = SST − SSE. The ratio of SSR to SST is called the **coefficient of multiple determination**:

$$r^2 = \frac{\text{SSR}}{\text{SST}} = 1 - \frac{\text{SSE}}{\text{SST}}.$$

It represents the proportion of variation in the y_i's that is accounted for by regression on $x_1, x_2, \ldots, x_k$. Note that r^2 ranges between 0 and 1, with values closer to 1 representing better fits. However, adding more predictor variables to a model never decreases and generally increases r^2. Thus r^2 can be made to approach 1 by increasing the number of predictors. Therefore one must balance the concept of better fit with the number of predictors. This issue is addressed in Section 11.7.2.

The positive square root of r^2, $r = +\sqrt{r^2}$, is called the **multiple correlation coefficient**. Only the positive square root is used here by convention, since it is not meaningful to assign a sign to the association between y and multiple x's. This is in contrast to simple linear regression, where it is meaningful to say whether the association between y and x is positive or negative.

EXAMPLE 11.1 (TIRE WEAR DATA: QUADRATIC FIT USING MINITAB)

Consider the tire wear data of Example 10.1, to which we fitted a straight line. Although the linear fit was found to be statistically significant, Figure 10.6 showed that there is a quadratic component to the relationship that should be included in the model. We now fit the quadratic model

$$y = \beta_0 + \beta_1 x + \beta_2 x^2$$

to the tire wear data, where $y = $ the groove depth and $x = $ the mileage (in 1000 miles).

The following is the MINITAB output of quadratic regression of tire groove depth on the number of miles.

```
The regression equation is
wear = 386 - 12.8 miles + 0.172 miles**2
Predictor        Coef       Stdev     t-ratio        p
Constant      386.265       4.800       80.47    0.000
miles        -12.7724      0.6995      -18.26    0.000
miles**2      0.17162     0.02103        8.16    0.000
s = 5.906        R-sq = 99.6%      R-sq(adj) = 99.5%
Analysis of Variance
SOURCE          DF          SS          MS         F        p
Regression       2       53209       26605    762.83    0.000
Error            6         209          35
Total            8       53419
SOURCE          DF      SEQ SS
miles            1       50887
miles**2         1        2322
Unusual Observations
Obs.   miles       wear       Fit Stdev.Fit  Residual   St.Resid
  1      0.0     394.33    386.26      4.80      8.07      2.34R
```

Note that r^2 = SSR/SST = 53,209/53,419 = 99.6% is quite a bit higher than r^2 = 95.3% obtained with a straight line fit. Thus including the quadratic term in the model has improved the fit. However, the first observation is still an outlier. Residual plots should be examined in order to determine whether the quadratic fit is satisfactory or not. ◆

11.3   *MULTIPLE REGRESSION MODEL IN MATRIX NOTATION

The multiple regression model (11.1) and the formulas for its estimation can be presented in a compact form if we use matrix notation. Let

$$Y = \begin{bmatrix} Y_1 \\ Y_2 \\ \vdots \\ Y_n \end{bmatrix}, \quad y = \begin{bmatrix} y_1 \\ y_2 \\ \vdots \\ y_n \end{bmatrix}, \quad \text{and} \quad \epsilon = \begin{bmatrix} \epsilon_1 \\ \epsilon_2 \\ \vdots \\ \epsilon_n \end{bmatrix}$$

be the $n \times 1$ vectors of the r.v.'s Y_i's, their observed values y_i's, and random errors ϵ_i's, respectively. Next let

$$X = \begin{bmatrix} 1 & x_{11} & x_{12} & \cdots & x_{1k} \\ 1 & x_{21} & x_{22} & \cdots & x_{2k} \\ \vdots & \vdots & \vdots & \ddots & \vdots \\ 1 & x_{n1} & x_{n2} & \cdots & x_{nk} \end{bmatrix}$$

be the $n \times (k+1)$ matrix of the values of predictor variables. Note that the first column of X of all 1's corresponds to the constant term β_0 in the model (11.1), which we could think of as $\beta_0 x_{i0}$ with $x_{i0} \equiv 1$. Finally let

$$
\beta = \begin{bmatrix} \beta_0 \\ \beta_1 \\ \vdots \\ \beta_k \end{bmatrix} \quad \text{and} \quad \hat{\beta} = \begin{bmatrix} \hat{\beta}_0 \\ \hat{\beta}_1 \\ \vdots \\ \hat{\beta}_k \end{bmatrix}
$$

be the $(k+1) \times 1$ vectors of unknown parameters and their LS estimates, respectively. Using this notation, the model (11.1) can be written as

$$
Y = X\beta + \epsilon. \tag{11.5}
$$

The simultaneous linear equations (11.4) whose solution yields the LS estimates can be written in matrix notation as

$$
X'X\beta = X'y.
$$

If the inverse of the matrix $X'X$ exists, then the solution is given by

$$
\hat{\beta} = (X'X)^{-1}X'y. \tag{11.6}
$$

Example 11.2 (Tire Wear Data: Quadratic Fit Using Hand Calculations)

Refer to Example 11.1. Calculate the LS estimates of the parameters of the quadratic regression model using the matrix approach.

For the quadratic model to be fitted, the X matrix is a 9×3 matrix in which the first column is the column of all 1's (corresponding to the constant term β_0), the second column is the column of the x's (corresponding to the linear term), and the third column is the column of the x^2's (corresponding to the quadratic term). Thus

$$
X = \begin{bmatrix} 1 & 0 & 0 \\ 1 & 4 & 16 \\ 1 & 8 & 64 \\ 1 & 12 & 144 \\ 1 & 16 & 256 \\ 1 & 20 & 400 \\ 1 & 24 & 576 \\ 1 & 28 & 784 \\ 1 & 32 & 1024 \end{bmatrix} \quad \text{and} \quad y = \begin{bmatrix} 394.33 \\ 329.50 \\ 291.00 \\ 255.17 \\ 229.33 \\ 204.83 \\ 179.00 \\ 163.83 \\ 150.33 \end{bmatrix} .
$$

First calculate

$$
X'X = \begin{bmatrix} 9 & 144 & 3264 \\ 144 & 3264 & 82,944 \\ 3264 & 82,944 & 2,245,632 \end{bmatrix} .
$$

Inverting this matrix yields (to four decimal place accuracy)

$$
(X'X)^{-1} = \begin{bmatrix} 0.6606 & -0.0773 & 0.0019 \\ -0.0773 & 0.0140 & -0.0004 \\ 0.0019 & -0.0004 & 0.0000 \end{bmatrix} .
$$

Finally, the vector of LS estimates is given by

$$\hat{\boldsymbol{\beta}} = \begin{bmatrix} \hat{\beta}_0 \\ \hat{\beta}_1 \\ \hat{\beta}_2 \end{bmatrix}$$

$$= (\boldsymbol{X}'\boldsymbol{X})^{-1}\boldsymbol{X}'\boldsymbol{y}$$

$$= \begin{bmatrix} 0.6606 & -0.0773 & 0.0019 \\ -0.0773 & 0.0140 & -0.0004 \\ 0.0019 & -0.0004 & 0.0000 \end{bmatrix} \begin{bmatrix} 1 & 1 & 1 & 1 & 1 & 1 & 1 & 1 & 1 \\ 0 & 4 & 8 & 12 & 16 & 20 & 24 & 28 & 32 \\ 0 & 16 & 64 & 144 & 256 & 400 & 576 & 784 & 1024 \end{bmatrix} \begin{bmatrix} 394.33 \\ 329.50 \\ 291.00 \\ 255.17 \\ 229.33 \\ 204.83 \\ 179.00 \\ 163.83 \\ 150.33 \end{bmatrix}$$

$$= \begin{bmatrix} 386.265 \\ -12.772 \\ 0.172 \end{bmatrix}.$$

Therefore, the LS quadratic model is

$$\hat{y} = 386.265 - 12.772x + 0.172x^2.$$

This is the same model that we obtained using MINITAB in Example 11.1.   ◆

11.4   STATISTICAL INFERENCE FOR MULTIPLE REGRESSION

11.4.1 Statistical Inference on β's

After fitting a multiple regression model, often the next step is to determine which predictor variables have statistically significant effects on the response variable. This can be done by testing the hypotheses $H_{0j}: \beta_j = 0$ vs. $H_{1j}: \beta_j \neq 0$ for each β_j. If $H_{0j}: \beta_j = 0$ is *not* rejected (i.e., if $\hat{\beta}_j$ is not significantly different from zero), this indicates that the corresponding variable x_j is not a useful predictor of y and may be dropped from the model. A simplified final model can be refitted with the remaining variables. A confidence interval (CI) for each β_j in the final model can be calculated to assess the effect of each x_j on the response variable. To obtain these tests and CI's we need to know the sampling distributions of the $\hat{\beta}_j$'s (regarded as r.v.'s).

It can be shown that each $\hat{\beta}_j$ is normally distributed with mean β_j and variance $\sigma^2 v_{jj}$ where v_{jj} is the jth diagonal entry ($j = 0, 1, \ldots, k$) of the matrix

$$V = (X'X)^{-1}.$$

The error variance σ^2 is unknown, but its unbiased estimate is given by

$$S^2 = \frac{\text{SSE}}{n - (k + 1)} = \frac{\sum_{i=1}^{n} e_i^2}{n - (k + 1)}.$$

This ratio is referred to as the **error mean square (MSE)** and $n - (k + 1)$ as the **error degrees of freedom** (d.f.). It can be shown that

$$\frac{(n - (k + 1))S^2}{\sigma^2} = \frac{\text{SSE}}{\sigma^2} \sim \chi^2_{n-(k+1)}$$

and S^2 and the $\hat{\beta}_j$ are statistically independent. Hence $(\hat{\beta}_j - \beta_j)/S\sqrt{v_{jj}}$ follows a t-distribution with $n - (k + 1)$ d.f.; this is denoted by

$$\frac{\hat{\beta}_j - \beta_j}{S\sqrt{v_{jj}}} \sim T_{n-(k+1)} \quad (j = 0, 1, \ldots, k).$$

We can use this result to make inferences on β_j as follows.

A $100(1 - \alpha)\%$ CI on β_j is given by

$$\hat{\beta}_j \pm t_{n-(k+1),\alpha/2}\text{SE}(\hat{\beta}_j) \quad (j = 0, 1, \ldots, k),$$

where $t_{n-(k+1),\alpha/2}$ is the upper $\alpha/2$ critical point of the t-distribution with $n - (k + 1)$ d.f., and $\text{SE}(\hat{\beta}_j) = s\sqrt{v_{jj}}$ is the estimated standard error of $\hat{\beta}_j$. An α-level test of

$$H_{0j} : \beta_j = \beta_j^0 \quad \text{vs.} \quad H_{1j} : \beta_j \neq \beta_j^0$$

rejects H_{0j} if

$$|t_j| = \frac{|\hat{\beta}_j - \beta_j^0|}{\text{SE}(\hat{\beta}_j)} > t_{n-(k+1),\alpha/2}. \tag{11.7}$$

A special case is the test of significance of $\hat{\beta}_j$, which is a test of $H_{0j}: \beta_j = 0$ vs. $H_{1j}: \beta_j \neq 0$. An α-level test rejects H_{0j} if

$$|t_j| = \frac{|\hat{\beta}_j|}{\text{SE}(\hat{\beta}_j)} > t_{n-(k+1),\alpha/2}. \tag{11.8}$$

Another hypothesis often tested as a first step in fitting a multiple regression model is

$$H_0: \beta_1 = \cdots = \beta_k = 0 \quad \text{vs.} \quad H_1: \text{At least one } \beta_j \neq 0.$$

Here H_0 is the overall null hypothesis, which states that none of the x variables are related to y since all the regression coefficients are zero. The alternative hypothesis states that at least one of the x variables is related to y. It can be shown that when

H_0: $\beta_1 = \cdots = \beta_k = 0$ is true, the statistic $F = \text{MSR}/\text{MSE}$ follows an F-distribution with k and $n - (k + 1)$ d.f. Therefore an α-level test rejects H_0 if

$$F = \frac{\text{MSR}}{\text{MSE}} > f_{k,n-(k+1),\alpha} \qquad (11.9)$$

where $f_{k,n-(k+1),\alpha}$ is the upper α critical point of the F-distribution with k and $n - (k + 1)$ d.f. Alternatively, many computer programs calculate the P-value of the test. Rejecting H_0 if this P-value is less than α gives an equivalent α-level test. A statistically significant F-statistic does not pinpoint which β_j's are nonzero. The t-tests given by (11.8) can be used to probe this question.

By using the fact that $\text{SSR} = r^2\text{SST}$ and $\text{SSE} = (1 - r^2)\text{SST}$, it follows that (11.9) can be written as

$$F = \frac{r^2\{n - (k + 1)\}}{k(1 - r^2)}.$$

F is an increasing function of r^2, and in this form it is used to test the statistical significance of r^2, which is equivalent to testing H_0: $\beta_1 = \cdots = \beta_k = 0$.

These calculations can be conveniently presented in the form of an **analysis of variance (ANOVA) table** shown in Table 11.1. The identity

$$\text{SST} = \text{SSR} + \text{SSE}$$

derived in Chapter 10 (see (10.9)) holds also in the case of multiple regression. Here

$$\text{SST} = \sum_{i=1}^{n}(y_i - \bar{y})^2, \quad \text{SSR} = \sum_{i=1}^{n}(\hat{y}_i - \bar{y})^2, \quad \text{and} \quad \text{SSE} = \sum_{i=1}^{n}(y_i - \hat{y}_i)^2.$$

The corresponding decomposition of the degrees of freedom (d.f.) is:

$$\underbrace{n - 1}_{\text{total d.f.}} = \underbrace{k}_{\text{regression d.f.}} + \underbrace{n - (k + 1)}_{\text{error d.f.}}.$$

The regression d.f. correspond to the k predictor variables in the model. The error d.f. correspond to the difference between n, the total sample size, and $k + 1$, the number of unknown parameters β_j.

Table 11.1 ANOVA Table for Multiple Regression

Source of Variation (Source)	Sum of Squares (SS)	Degrees of Freedom (d.f.)	Mean Square (MS)	F
Regression	SSR	k	$\text{MSR} = \dfrac{\text{SSR}}{k}$	$F = \dfrac{\text{MSR}}{\text{MSE}}$
Error	SSE	$n - (k + 1)$	$\text{MSE} = \dfrac{\text{SSE}}{n-(k+1)}$	
Total	SST	$n - 1$		

EXAMPLE 11.3 (TIRE WEAR DATA: TESTS OF SIGNIFICANCE FOR THE QUADRATIC FIT)

Test for the overall significance of the fit of the quadratic model $y = \beta_0 + \beta_1 x + \beta_2 x^2$ and separately test for the significance of the linear and quadratic terms using the MINITAB output from Example 11.1.

From the MINITAB output we see that the F-statistic for testing $H_0 : \beta_1 = \beta_2 = 0$ equals 762.83 with 2 and 6 d.f. and has a P-value = 0.000. This result indicates that one or both of β_1 and β_2 are nonzero. Next we want to assess the significance of individual terms. The t-statistics to test $H_{01} : \beta_1 = 0$ and $H_{02} : \beta_2 = 0$ are -18.26 and 8.16, respectively, with 6 d.f. each. Since both of their P-values = 0.000, both the linear and quadratic terms are statistically significant. We can compute 95% CI's for β_1 and β_2 as follows:

CI for β_1 : $[\hat{\beta}_1 \pm t_{6,.025} \text{SE}(\hat{\beta}_1)] = [-12.7724 \pm 2.447 \times 0.6995] = [-14.484, -11.061]$

CI for β_2 : $[\hat{\beta}_2 \pm t_{6,.025} \text{SE}(\hat{\beta}_2)] = [0.17162 \pm 2.447 \times 0.02103] = [0.120, 0.223]$.

◆

Extra Sum of Squares Method for Testing Subsets of Parameters.   Above we have given two-sided tests on the individual β_j's and a simultaneous test on all β_j's $(j = 1, 2, \ldots, k)$. Both are F-tests (the tests on the individual β_j's, being two-sided t-tests, are equivalent to F-tests with a single d.f. for the numerator), and they can be derived using a general method called the **extra sum of squares method**. This method is useful for comparing "nested models," where one regression model uses a subset of the predictor variables of the other model. We call the former model a "partial" model and the latter the "full" model.

Consider the *full model*:

$$Y_i = \beta_0 + \beta_1 x_{i1} + \cdots + \beta_k x_{ik} + \epsilon_i \quad (i = 1, 2, \ldots, n),$$

and the *partial model*:

$$Y_i = \beta_0 + \beta_1 x_{i1} + \cdots + \beta_{k-m} x_{i,k-m} + \epsilon_i \quad (i = 1, 2, \ldots, n).$$

The last m $(1 \leq m \leq k)$ terms are dropped in the partial model by setting the corresponding regression coefficients equal to zero. To determine whether the fit of the full model is significantly better than that of the partial model we test

$$H_0: \beta_{k-m+1} = \cdots = \beta_k = 0 \quad \text{vs.} \quad H_1: \text{At least one of } \beta_{k-m+1}, \ldots, \beta_k \neq 0. \quad (11.10)$$

Let SSR_{k-m} and SSE_{k-m} be the regression and error sums of squares for the partial model (which has $k - m$ predictor variables) and let SSR_k and SSE_k be the corresponding sums of squares for the full model (which has k predictor variables). Note that SSR_k and SSE_k are the usual SSR and SSE. Since SST is fixed regardless of the particular model, we have

$$\text{SST} = \text{SSR}_{k-m} + \text{SSE}_{k-m} = \text{SSR}_k + \text{SSE}_k.$$

Since there are more terms in the full model than in the partial model, we have $SSR_k \geq SSR_{k-m}$ and $SSE_k \leq SSE_{k-m}$. The "extra sum of squares" accounted for by the m predictor variables, $x_{k-m+1}, \ldots, x_k$, is

$$SSE_{k-m} - SSE_k = SSR_k - SSR_{k-m}.$$

The α-level F-test rejects $H_0 : \beta_{k-m+1} = \cdots = \beta_k = 0$ if

$$F = \frac{(SSE_{k-m} - SSE_k)/m}{SSE_k/[n - (k+1)]} > f_{m,n-(k+1),\alpha}. \tag{11.11}$$

The numerator d.f. for this statistic is m, which is the number of β's set equal to zero by H_0, and the denominator d.f. is $n - (k+1)$, which is the error d.f. for the full model. The intuitive idea behind this test is that the extra sum of squares in the numerator represents the part of the variation in y that is accounted for by regression on the m predictors, $x_{k-m+1}, \ldots, x_k$, over and above that accounted for by $x_1, \ldots, x_{k-m}$; this is divided by m to get an average contribution per term. The MSE in the denominator is the normalizing factor, which is an estimate of σ^2 for the full model. If the ratio of these two quantities is large, then we reject H_0.

The null hypothesis on an individual coefficient, e.g., $H_{0k} : \beta_k = 0$, and the null hypothesis on all coefficients, i.e., $H_0 : \beta_1 = \cdots = \beta_k = 0$, are special cases of H_0 in (11.10) for $m = 1$ and $m = k$, respectively. To test the null hypothesis on a single regression coefficient, e.g., $H_{0j} : \beta_j = 0$, the F-statistic obtained using the extra sum of squares method can be shown to be equal to $F_j = t_j^2$, where t_j is the t-statistic defined in (11.8); the numerator d.f. of F_j equals $m = 1$. To test the overall null hypothesis $H_0 : \beta_1 = \cdots = \beta_k = 0$, we can show that the extra sum of squares method yields the F-statistic (11.9) of the ANOVA as follows. Here the partial model is $Y_i = \beta_0 + \epsilon_i$ and $m = k$. The LS estimate of β_0 is $\hat{\beta}_0 = \bar{y}$ under the partial model. Therefore $SSE_0 = \sum_{i=1}^{n}(y_i - \bar{y})^2 = SST$. Under the full model, $SSE_k = SSE$, which yields the extra sum of squares as

$$SSE_0 - SSE_k = SST - SSE = SSR$$

with $m = k$ d.f. Hence the F-ratio equals

$$F = \frac{SSR/k}{SSE/[n - (k+1)]} = \frac{MSR}{MSE}$$

with k and $n - (k+1)$ d.f.

EXAMPLE 11.4   (TIRE WEAR DATA: TEST OF SIGNIFICANCE OF QUADRATIC COEFFICIENT)

Refer to Example 11.1. Conduct a test of significance of the coefficient of the quadratic term by using the extra sum of squares method.

From the MINITAB output we see that the so-called sequential sum of squares (labeled as SEQ SS) for the quadratic term is 2322. This is the extra sum of squares, i.e., the increase in SSR due to the addition of the quadratic term to the model that already includes the linear term.

This extra sum of squares can also be obtained by subtracting the SSR for the straight-line model (which is 50,887) from the SSR for the quadratic model (which is 53,209). The SSE for the full (quadratic) model is 209. The d.f. for the extra sum of squares is 1 (since only one term is added to the model), and the d.f. for the SSE for the full model is 6. Therefore the F-ratio is

$$F = \frac{2322/1}{209/6} = 66.66$$

which is highly significant (P-value = 0.000). Note from the MINITAB output that the t-statistic for the quadratic coefficient is 8.16 and $F = 66.66 = t^2 = (8.16)^2$.   ◆

11.4.2 Prediction of Future Observations

Having fitted a multiple regression model, suppose that we wish to predict the future value of Y for a specified vector of predictor variables, $x^* = (x_0^*, x_1^*, \ldots, x_k^*)'$, where we have included $x_0^* = 1$ as the first component of the vector to correspond to the constant term β_0 in the model. Let Y^* denote this value of Y. For example, suppose that a regression model for the selling price of a house includes the following predictor variables: floor area (x_1), number of bedrooms (x_2), number of bathrooms (x_3), the age of the house (x_4), the lot size (x_5), the garage size (x_6), and the property tax rate (x_7). Using this model, a real estate agency wants to predict the selling price of a house with 3000 sq. ft. floor area, 4 bedrooms, 2.5 baths, 10 years age, 10,000 sq. ft. lot size, 2 car garage, and the property tax rate of 2% of the assessed value of the house. Then $x^* = (1, 3000, 4, 2.5, 10, 10000, 2, .02)'$.

As seen in Chapter 10, actually there are two distinct but related problems. One is to *estimate* $\mu^* = E(Y^*)$ by a **confidence interval (CI)**. The other is to *predict* Y^* by a **prediction interval (PI)**. In both cases we have

$$\hat{\mu}^* = \hat{Y}^* = \hat{\beta}_0 + \hat{\beta}_1 x_1^* + \cdots + \hat{\beta}_k x_k^* = x^{*'}\hat{\beta}.$$

It can be shown that

$$\text{Var}(x^{*'}\hat{\beta}) = x^{*'}\text{Cov}(\hat{\beta})x^* = \sigma^2 x^{*'} V x^* = \sigma^2 \sum_{i=0}^{k}\sum_{j=0}^{k} x_i^* x_j^* v_{ij}$$

where $V = (X'X)^{-1}$ has elements v_{ij}. Replacing σ^2 by its estimate $s^2 = \text{MSE}$, which has $n - (k+1)$ d.f., and using the same methods as in Chapter 10, it can be shown that a $(1-\alpha)$-level CI for μ^* is given by

$$\hat{\mu}^* - t_{n-(k+1),\alpha/2}s\sqrt{x^{*'} V x^*} \le \mu^* \le \hat{\mu}^* + t_{n-(k+1),\alpha/2}s\sqrt{x^{*'} V x^*} \qquad (11.12)$$

and a $(1-\alpha)$-level PI for Y^* is given by

$$\hat{Y}^* - t_{n-(k+1),\alpha/2}s\sqrt{1 + x^{*'} V x^*} \le Y^* \le \hat{Y}^* + t_{n-(k+1),\alpha/2}s\sqrt{1 + x^{*'} V x^*}. \quad (11.13)$$

Most statistical packages compute these intervals when x^* is provided as an input.

11.5   REGRESSION DIAGNOSTICS

11.5.1 Residual Analysis

As in Chapter 10, many of the regression diagnostics are based on a graphical examination of the residuals. Before presenting these techniques, it is useful to derive some properties of the vectors of residuals and fitted values. The fitted value vector is given by

$$\hat{y} = X\hat{\beta} = X(X'X)^{-1}X'y = Hy$$

where

$$H = X(X'X)^{-1}X'$$

is called the **hat matrix** with elements h_{ij} ($1 \leq i, j \leq n$). Thus we get the relation

$$\hat{y}_i = \sum_{j=1}^{n} h_{ij} y_j \quad (i = 1, 2, \ldots, n)$$

given in Section 10.4.2 of Chapter 10. Using some linear algebra, it is not difficult to show that $\sum_{i=1}^{n} h_{ii} = k + 1$, which leads to the rule of thumb that the ith observation is **influential** if

$$h_{ii} > \frac{2(k+1)}{n}$$

i.e., h_{ii} is more than twice their average value. The ith observation is regarded as having an excessive influence or leverage in this case because y_i puts more than its due weight on its own fitted value $\hat{y}_i$.

The residual vector is given by

$$e = y - \hat{y} = y - X(X'X)^{-1}X'y = (I - H)y$$

where I is the identity matrix of order n. The n residuals e_i are subject to $k+1$ linear constraints:

$$\sum_{i=1}^{n} e_i = 0$$

$$\sum_{i=1}^{n} x_{ij} e_i = 0 \quad (j = 1, 2, \ldots, k).$$

These constraints follow from the equation (11.3). Thus, although there are n residuals, only $n - (k+1)$ of them are linearly independent. This explains why the error d.f. equal $n - (k+1)$. It can be also shown that the e_i are individually normally distributed with zero means and

$$\mathrm{Var}(e_i) = \sigma^2(1 - h_{ii}).$$

Therefore $\mathrm{SE}(e_i) = s\sqrt{1 - h_{ii}}$. **Standardized residuals** are given by

$$e_i^* = \frac{e_i}{\mathrm{SE}(e_i)} = \frac{e_i}{s\sqrt{1 - h_{ii}}}.$$

Some computer packages use $e_i^* \simeq e_i/s$ as an approximation, since the h_{ii} are negligible in comparison to 1 if n is large. Large $|e_i^*|$ values indicate **outlier observations,** e.g., MINITAB uses $|e_i^*| > 2$ as a criterion to identify outliers.

Similar residual plots as those discussed in Chapter 10 can be made to evaluate the goodness of fit of the model and to check if the underlying assumptions are met. A summary of these plots is as follows:

1. *Plots of the residuals against individual predictor variables*: These are used to check linearity with respect to the x_j's. Each plot should be random. A systematic pattern indicates the necessity for adding nonlinear terms in the corresponding x_j to the model.

2. *A plot of the residuals against fitted values*: This is used to check the assumption of constant variance. Variability in the e_i should be roughly constant over the range of the $\hat{y}_i$; otherwise a transformation of the response variable is indicated, as discussed in Section 10.4.3. A systematic pattern in this plot also suggests the need for a linearizing transformation of the response variable.

3. *A normal plot of the residuals*: This is used to check the normality assumption.

4. *A run chart of the residuals*: If the data are obtained sequentially over time, this plot should be used to check whether the random errors are autocorrelated and/or if there are any time trends.

5. *Plots of the residuals against any omitted predictor variables*: This is used to check if any of the omitted predictor variables should be included in the model. If a plot shows a systematic pattern, then inclusion of that omitted variable in the model is indicated.

11.5.2 Data Transformations

As discussed in Chapter 10, transformations of the variables (both y and the x's) are often necessary to satisfy the assumptions of linearity, normality, and constant error variance. Many seemingly nonlinear models can be written in the multiple linear regression model form after making a suitable transformation. For example, the model

$$y = \beta_0 x_1^{\beta_1} x_2^{\beta_2}$$

where β_0, β_1 and β_2 are unknown parameters, can be written in the multiple linear regression model form if we take logarithms of both sides. This results in the equation

$$\log y = \log \beta_0 + \beta_1 \log x_1 + \beta_2 \log x_2$$

or

$$y^* = \beta_0^* + \beta_1^* x_1^* + \beta_2^* x_2^*$$

where $y^* = \log y$, $x_1^* = \log x_1$, $x_2^* = \log x_2$, and $\beta_0^* = \log \beta_0$, $\beta_1^* = \beta_1$, $\beta_2^* = \beta_2$. This is a linear model because it is linear in the unknown parameters. Therefore the methods of this chapter can be employed to fit this model and the results can be transformed back to the original model.

A model that can be transformed so that it becomes linear in its unknown parameters is called **intrinsically linear**; otherwise it is called a **nonlinear model**. If a theoretical model exists that is intrinsically linear, then the necessary transformations should be made to convert it into a linear form before fitting it. If a theoretical model does not exist, then scatter plots of y against each of the x's should be made to see what transformations are needed to linearize the relationships. Unless a common transformation of y linearizes its relationship with all x's, effort should be focused on transforming the x's, leaving y untransformed, at least initially. It is usually assumed that the random error enters additively into the final linear form of the model.

The residual plots from the fitted linear model should then be examined as outlined above to see whether the assumptions of normality, linearity, and constant variance are satisfied, and if not, how y should be transformed. One should also check for outliers and influential observations, and see if the fit is considerably improved if these data points are omitted and/or suitably modified. As you can see, model fitting is an iterative trial and error process.

11.6 TOPICS IN REGRESSION MODELING

11.6.1 Multicollinearity

Multicollinearity is present in multiple regression when the columns of the X matrix are exactly or approximately linearly dependent. In practical terms this means that the predictor variables are linearly related. This is often (but not always) manifested by high correlations between the predictor variables.

Multicollinearity can cause serious numerical and statistical difficulties in fitting the regression model unless "extra" predictor variables are deleted. For example, if income, expenditure, and saving are used as predictor variables, then there is an obvious linear relationship between them, namely, saving = income − expenditure. Therefore only two of them should be considered for inclusion in the regression model. For another example, suppose that a regression equation is to be developed to model the cleaning effectiveness of a laundry detergent as a function of the percentages of different ingredients used. The individual percentages add up to 100%, so one of the ingredients should not be included in the model.

What are the difficulties caused by multicollinearity? Recall that $\hat{\boldsymbol{\beta}}$ is the solution to the equation $(X'X)\boldsymbol{\beta} = X'y$. Thus $X'X$ must be invertible (i.e., nonsingular) in order for $\hat{\boldsymbol{\beta}}$ to be unique and computable. If the columns of X are approximately linearly dependent, then $X'X$ is nearly singular, which makes $\hat{\boldsymbol{\beta}}$ numerically unstable. Furthermore, the matrix $V = (X'X)^{-1}$ has very large elements. Therefore $\text{Var}(\hat{\beta}_j) = \sigma^2 v_{jj}$ are large, which makes the $\hat{\beta}_j$ statistically nonsignificant.

To summarize, multicollinearity leads to the following problems:

1. The estimates $\hat{\beta}_j$ are subject to numerical errors and are unreliable. This is reflected in large changes in their magnitudes with small changes in data. Sometimes, the signs of the $\hat{\beta}_j$ are reversed.

2. Most of the coefficients have very large standard errors and as a result are statistically nonsignificant even if the overall F-statistic is significant.

EXAMPLE **11.5** (CEMENT DATA: ILLUSTRATION OF MULTICOLLINEARITY)

Table 11.2 gives data[2] on the heat evolved in calories during hardening of cement on a per gram basis (y) along with the percentages of four ingredients: tricalcium aluminate (x_1), tricalcium silicate (x_2), tetracalcium alumino ferrite (x_3), and dicalcium silicate (x_4). We will illustrate the multicollinearity present in these data and its consequences on fitting the regression model.

Table 11.2 Cement Data

No.	x_1	x_2	x_3	x_4	y
1	7	26	6	60	78.5
2	1	29	15	52	74.3
3	11	56	8	20	104.3
4	11	31	8	47	87.6
5	7	52	6	33	95.9
6	11	55	9	22	109.2
7	3	71	17	6	102.7
8	1	31	22	44	72.5
9	2	54	18	22	93.1
10	21	47	4	26	115.9
11	1	40	23	34	83.8
12	11	66	9	12	113.3
13	10	68	8	12	109.4

First, note that x_1, x_2, x_3, and x_4 add up to approximately 100% for all observations. This approximate linear relationship among the x's results in multicollinearity. The correlation matrix among all five variables is as follows.

```
        x1        x2        x3        x4
x2     0.229
x3    -0.824    -0.139
x4    -0.245    -0.973     0.030
y      0.731     0.816    -0.535    -0.821
```

Note that x_2 and x_4 have a high negative correlation. (If x_2 is high, x_4 is low and vice versa, since the total of all x's is fixed, of which x_2 and x_4 account for nearly 80% of the ingradients.) Similarly x_1 and x_3 have a high negative correlation.

---

[2] A. Hald (1952), *Statistical Theory with Engineering Applications*, New York: Wiley.

The following is the MINITAB output for multiple regression.

```
The regression equation is
y = 62.4 + 1.55 x1 + 0.510 x2 + 0.102 x3 - 0.144 x4
```

Predictor	Coef	Stdev	t-ratio	p
Constant	62.41	70.07	0.89	0.399
x1	1.5511	0.7448	2.08	0.071
x2	0.5102	0.7238	0.70	0.501
x3	0.1019	0.7547	0.14	0.896
x4	-0.1441	0.7091	-0.20	0.844

```
s = 2.446      R-sq = 98.2%     R-sq(adj) = 97.4%
```

Analysis of Variance

SOURCE	DF	SS	MS	F	p
Regression	4	2667.90	666.97	111.48	0.000
Error	8	47.86	5.98		
Total	12	2715.76			

All the coefficients in the fitted equation are nonsignificant (only the coefficient of x_1 has a P-value $< .10$), although the overall $F = 111.48$ is highly significant (P-value $= .000$). We will see in Examples 11.9 and 11.10 that the "best" model includes only x_1 and x_2.   ◆

*Measures of Multicollinearity.   Several measures of multicollinearity are available. The simplest is the correlation matrix R between the predictor variables. If some bivariate correlations are high (as in the cement data example), linear relationships between the corresponding pairs of predictor variables are indicated. However, linear relationships between more than two predictor variables are not always manifested by large bivariate correlations and so are difficult to detect from the correlation matrix.

The extent of singularity of $X'X$ can be used to judge multicollinearity. If the x_j's are suitably standardized (see Section 11.6.4), then $(n-1)^{-1}X'X = R$, where R is the correlation matrix of the x_j's. A measure of multicollinearity is the determinant of R, which ranges between 0 (if R is singular) and 1 (if all correlations are zero, so that R is an identity matrix).

A more direct measure of multicollinearity is the diagonal elements of R^{-1}. These are called **variance inflation factors (VIF)**, since the larger they are, the larger are the variances of the $\hat{\beta}_j$. It can be shown that

$$\text{VIF}_j = \frac{1}{1 - r_j^2}, \quad j = 1, 2, \ldots, k,$$

where r_j^2 is the coefficient of multiple determination when regressing x_j on the remaining $k-1$ predictor variables. If x_j is approximately linearly dependent on other predictor variables, then r_j^2 will be close to 1 and VIF_j will be large. Generally, VIF_j values greater than 10, corresponding to $r_j^2 > .9$, are regarded as unacceptable.

11.6.2 Polynomial Regression

As seen at the beginning of this chapter, polynomial regression is a special case of a linear model. Some special considerations apply when fitting a polynomial model. Suppose that a kth degree polynomial in a single predictor variable is to be fitted:

$$y = \beta_0 + \beta_1 x + \cdots + \beta_k x^k.$$

Two problems arise in this case. The first is that the powers of x, i.e., $x, x^2, \ldots, x^k$, tend to be highly correlated. The second is that if k is large, say more than 3 or 4, the magnitudes of these powers tend to vary over a rather wide range. Both these problems lead to numerical errors in least squares fitting. To avoid them one should limit to a cubic ($k = 3$) if at all possible, and generally to no more than a quintic ($k = 5$).

A simple solution to these problems is to center the x-variable. In other words, fit the model

$$y = \beta_0^* + \beta_1^* (x - \bar{x}) + \cdots + \beta_k^* (x - \bar{x})^k$$

where $\bar{x}$ is the sample mean of $x_1, x_2, \ldots, x_n$. **Centering** has the effect of removing the non-essential multicollinearity in the data. The β coefficients from the uncentered and centered model are linearly related. These relationships can be found by equating the coefficients of the powers of x from the two models. For example, when fitting a quadratic model ($k = 2$), the relationship between the β coefficients for the uncentered model and the β^* coefficients for the centered model can be obtained by expanding the terms in the centered model and collecting the terms, which results in

$$\beta_0 = \beta_0^* - \beta_1^* \bar{x} + \beta_2^* \bar{x}^2, \quad \beta_1 = \beta_1^* - 2\beta_2^* \bar{x}, \text{ and } \beta_2 = \beta_2^*.$$

Using these relationships, the LS estimates for the uncentered model can be calculated from the LS estimates for the centered model, which are easier to compute.

In addition to centering, one could also scale the x variable by dividing by its standard deviation, s_x, thus **standardizing** it to have a zero mean and a unit standard deviation. One could then use the powers of this standardized x variable, $\left(\frac{x-\bar{x}}{s_x}\right)$, in the polynomial model in place of the powers of x. Standardizing x helps to alleviate the second problem mentioned above, viz., the powers of x varying over a wide range.

Next consider fitting a polynomial in two variables, x_1 and x_2. A common example is a second degree polynomial:

$$y = \beta_0 + \beta_1 x_1 + \beta_2 x_2 + \beta_3 x_1 x_2 + \beta_4 x_1^2 + \beta_5 x_2^2.$$

If $\beta_3 \neq 0$, then the change in y for a given change in x_1 for fixed x_2 depends on the value of x_2 (and vice versa). On the other hand, if $\beta_3 = 0$, then the change in y for a given change in x_1 is the same regardless of the fixed value of x_2. In the former case we say that x_1 and x_2 interact with respect to their effects on y, while in the latter case they do not interact. **Interaction** between two predictor variables is present when the effect on the response variable of one predictor variable depends on the value of the other.

11.6.3 Dummy Predictor Variables

Many applications involve categorical predictor variables, e.g., the sex of a person, the season of a year, the prognosis of a patient (poor, average, good), etc. The first two variables are nominal, while the third is ordinal. The categories of an ordinal variable could be assigned suitable numerical scores, effectively treating it as a numerical variable. A common choice for scores is positive integers. Thus one could assign scores 1, 2, and 3 for the prognosis categories poor, average, and good, respectively (implicitly assuming that the response, e.g., survival rate, changes linearly with prognosis).

A nominal variable with $c \geq 2$ categories can be coded using $c - 1$ indicator variables, $x_1, \ldots, x_{c-1}$, called **dummy variables**, where $x_i = 1$ for the ith category and 0 otherwise; for the cth category we have $x_1 = \cdots = x_{c-1} = 0$. If we use indicator variables for all c categories, then there will be a linear dependency among them (since $x_1 + x_2 + \cdots + x_c = 1$) which will cause multicollinearity. Therefore we do not need to code one of the categories (say, the last one in this case). For example, the sex of a person can be coded by a single variable x, where $x = 0$ for females and $x = 1$ for males. Similarly, the four seasons of a year can be coded using three variables, x_1, x_2, x_3, where x_1 is an indicator for Winter, x_2 is an indicator for Spring, and x_3 is an indicator for Summer. With this coding $(x_1, x_2, x_3) = (1, 0, 0)$ for Winter, $(x_1, x_2, x_3) = (0, 1, 0)$ for Spring, $(x_1, x_2, x_3) = (0, 0, 1)$ for Summer, and $(x_1, x_2, x_3) = (0, 0, 0)$ for Fall.

Let us see what different models mean when there are two predictor variables: one nominal and one numerical. Consider modeling the weight of a person as a function of his/her sex and height, with the sex variable coded as $\text{SEX} = 0$ for females and $\text{SEX} = 1$ for males. A simple model is

$$E(\text{WEIGHT}) = \beta_0 + \beta_1 \text{SEX} + \beta_2 \text{HEIGHT}.$$

This can be written as two separate models for females and males as follows:

$$E(\text{WEIGHT}) = \begin{cases} \beta_0 + \beta_2 \text{HEIGHT} & \text{for females} \\ (\beta_0 + \beta_1) + \beta_2 \text{HEIGHT} & \text{for males} \end{cases}$$

These two straight lines are plotted in Figure 11.2(a). Notice that according to this model there is a constant difference β_1 between the average weights of males and females for any given height, the slope of the weight vs. height relationship being the same for both sexes. Using the terminology introduced previously, we say that there is no interaction between SEX and HEIGHT with respect to their effects on WEIGHT. Interaction can be modeled by including the product term SEX*HEIGHT in the equation as follows:

$$E(\text{WEIGHT}) = \beta_0 + \beta_1 \text{SEX} + \beta_2 \text{HEIGHT} + \beta_3 \text{SEX*HEIGHT}.$$

Once again we can write this model as two separate models:

$$E(\text{WEIGHT}) = \begin{cases} \beta_0 + \beta_2 \text{HEIGHT} & \text{for females} \\ (\beta_0 + \beta_1) + (\beta_2 + \beta_3) \text{HEIGHT} & \text{for males} \end{cases}$$

These two straight lines are plotted in Figure 11.2(b). We see that they not only have different intercepts, they also have different slopes. Interaction between SEX and HEIGHT means that the rate of change of weight with respect to height is different for the two sexes.

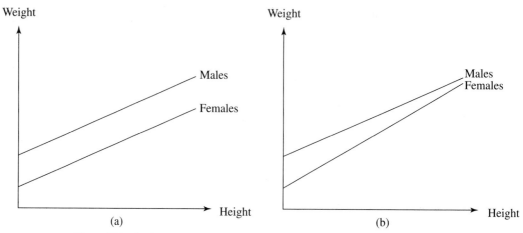

Figure 11.2 Weight-Height Relationships for Sexes: (a) No sex-height interaction;
(b) Sex-height interaction

EXAMPLE 11.6 (SODA CAN SALES)

Four years of quarterly sales data (from Exercise 4.42) of a certain brand of soda cans are shown in Table 11.3. Model the time trend by fitting a multiple regression equation.

Table 11.3 Quarterly Sales of Soda Cans (in
millions of cans)

Quarter	Year	Season	Sales
1	1	Winter	41.2
2	1	Spring	50.2
3	1	Summer	54.5
4	1	Fall	41.3
5	2	Winter	44.6
6	2	Spring	59.9
7	2	Summer	69.0
8	2	Fall	53.3
9	3	Winter	54.7
10	3	Spring	74.2
11	3	Summer	79.4
12	3	Fall	62.7
13	4	Winter	62.7
14	4	Spring	79.9
15	4	Summer	83.6
16	4	Fall	65.6

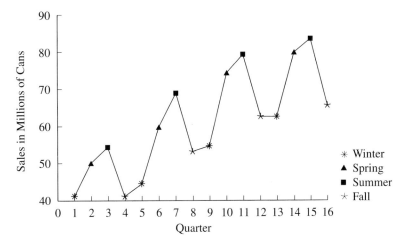

Figure 11.3 The Run Chart for Soda Can Sales

From the run chart of the sales data shown in Figure 11.3 two trends are evident. There is a linearly increasing trend over time; superimposed on it is a cyclic seasonal trend with low sales in Fall and Winter and high sales in Spring and Summer. To model the linear trend we use the Quarter as a predictor variable x_1. To model the seasonal trend we use indicator variables x_2, x_3, and x_4 for Winter, Spring, and Summer, respectively. For Fall, all three equal zero; thus Fall is used as a baseline reference from which changes in the other seasons are measured. The model fitted is:

$$Y_i = \beta_0 + \beta_1 x_{i1} + \beta_2 x_{i2} + \beta_3 x_{i3} + \beta_4 x_{i4} + \epsilon_i \quad (i = 1, \ldots, 16).$$

The data are coded as follows:

Quarter	Sales	Winter	Spring	Summer
1	41.2000	1	0	0
2	50.2000	0	1	0
3	54.5000	0	0	1
4	41.3000	0	0	0
5	44.6000	1	0	0
6	59.9000	0	1	0
7	69.0000	0	0	1
8	53.3000	0	0	0
9	54.7000	1	0	0
10	74.2000	0	1	0
11	79.4000	0	0	1
12	62.7000	0	0	0
13	62.7000	1	0	0
14	79.9000	0	1	0
15	83.6000	0	0	1
16	65.6000	0	0	0

The MINITAB output is shown in Figure 11.4. From this output we see that the coefficient of Quarter is significant, implying that there is a significant linear trend. Also, the coefficients of Spring and Summer are statistically significant, but that of Winter is not. Thus, adjusted for the linear trend, the Spring and Summer sales differ significantly from the Fall sales, but those of Winter do not.

This fitted model may be used to make sales predictions for the next four quarters (i.e., Year 5) for which the predictor variable values are as shown below.

Quarter	Winter	Spring	Summer
17	1	0	0
18	0	1	0
19	0	0	1
20	0	0	0

Sales predictions for these values with 95% prediction intervals (PI's) are also shown in the MINITAB output. (Note that the CI's are not meaningful here, since only the actual future sales are of interest.) The predicted sales for Year 5 are 73.175, 88.425, 94.000, and 78.100 million cans for Winter, Spring, Summer, and Fall, respectively. ◆

```
The regression equation is
Sales = 33.3 + 2.24 Quarter + 1.79 Winter + 14.8 Spring + 18.1 Summer
```

Predictor	Coef	StDev	T	P
Constant	33.350	2.225	14.99	0.000
Quarter	2.2375	0.1658	13.49	0.000
Winter	1.788	2.156	0.83	0.425
Spring	14.800	2.124	6.97	0.000
Summer	18.138	2.104	8.62	0.000

S = 2.966   R-Sq = 96.5%   R-Sq(adj) = 95.3%

Analysis of Variance

Source	DF	SS	MS	F	P
Regression	4	2683.04	670.76	76.23	0.000
Error	11	96.80	8.80		
Total	15	2779.84			

Source	DF	Seq SS
Quarter	1	1684.10
Winter	1	264.10
Spring	1	80.99
Summer	1	653.85

Fit	StDev Fit	95.0% CI	95.0% PI
73.175	2.225	(68.277, 78.073)	(65.012, 81.338)
88.425	2.225	(83.527, 93.323)	(80.262, 96.588)
94.000	2.225	(89.102, 98.898)	(85.837, 102.163)
78.100	2.225	(73.202, 82.998)	(69.937, 86.263)

Figure 11.4 MINITAB Regression Results for Soda Can Sales Data

11.6.4 *Standardized Regression Coefficients

Given a fitted multiple regression model, a user typically wants to compare predictors in terms of the magnitudes of their effects on the response variable. For example, given a model for gas consumption of a car with the car weight and engine horsepower as the predictors, an automobile engineer wants to know which predictor has a larger effect on the fuel consumption. However, the magnitudes of the $\hat{\beta}_j$'s cannot be compared directly, since they depend on the units of measurements of the predictors. Recall that the units of $\hat{\beta}_j$ are (units of y)/(units of x_j). Since weight and horsepower are measured in different units, their relative effects cannot be judged by comparing their regression coefficients.

Standardized regression coefficients may be used to judge the importance of different predictors. They are the LS parameter estimates obtained by running a regression on standardized variables, defined as follows:

$$y_i^* = \frac{y_i - \bar{y}}{s_y} \quad (i = 1, 2, \dots, n),$$

and

$$x_{ij}^* = \frac{x_{ij} - \bar{x}_j}{s_{x_j}} \quad (i = 1, 2, \dots, n; \, j = 1, 2, \dots, k)$$

where s_y and s_{x_j} are the sample SD's of y and x_j, respectively. Note that the standardized variables are unitless. Let $\hat{\beta}_0^*, \hat{\beta}_1^*, \dots, \hat{\beta}_k^*$ be the LS estimates. Since the standardized variables have zero means, it follows that $\hat{\beta}_0^* = 0$. The other $\hat{\beta}_j^*$ can be obtained from the unstandardized regression coefficients $\hat{\beta}_j$ simply by scaling:

$$\hat{\beta}_j^* = \hat{\beta}_j \left(\frac{s_{x_j}}{s_y}\right) \quad (j = 1, 2, \dots, k). \tag{11.14}$$

The magnitudes of the $\hat{\beta}_j^*$ can be directly compared to judge the relative effects of the x_j on y.

It may be noted that since $\hat{\beta}_0^* \equiv 0$, the constant term may be dropped from the model for standardized variables. Let $\boldsymbol{y}^*$ be the vector of the y_i^*'s and $\boldsymbol{X}^*$ be the $k \times k$ matrix (without the column of 1's corresponding to the constant term) of the standardized predictors x_j^*'s. It can be shown that

$$\frac{1}{n-1}\boldsymbol{X}^{*'}\boldsymbol{X}^* = \boldsymbol{R} = \begin{bmatrix} 1 & r_{x_1 x_2} & r_{x_1 x_3} & \cdots & r_{x_1 x_k} \\ r_{x_2 x_1} & 1 & r_{x_2 x_3} & \cdots & r_{x_2 x_k} \\ \vdots & \vdots & \vdots & \ddots & \vdots \\ r_{x_k x_1} & r_{x_k x_2} & r_{x_k x_3} & \cdots & 1 \end{bmatrix}$$

is the correlation matrix between the predictor variables and

$$\frac{1}{n-1}X^{*'}y^* = r = \begin{bmatrix} r_{yx_1} \\ r_{yx_2} \\ \vdots \\ r_{yx_k} \end{bmatrix}$$

is the vector of correlations between y and the x_j's. Thus computation of the standardized regression coefficients requires only the pairwise correlations between all the variables, since

$$\hat{\boldsymbol{\beta}}^* = \begin{bmatrix} \hat{\beta}_1^* \\ \vdots \\ \hat{\beta}_k^* \end{bmatrix} = (X^{*'}X^*)^{-1}X^{*'}y^* = R^{-1}r. \tag{11.15}$$

The unstandardized regression coefficients can be computed from the standardized ones, given the sample SD's of all the variables, using equation (11.14). This method of computing $\hat{\beta}_j$'s is numerically more stable than computing $\hat{\beta}_j$'s directly, because all entries of R and r are between -1 and 1.

EXAMPLE 11.7   (INDUSTRIAL SALES: STANDARDIZED REGRESSION COEFFICIENTS)

Consider the following data on the number of salespeople (x_1), amount of sales expenditures in millions of dollars (x_2), and the amount of sales revenues in millions of dollars (y) for 10 sales territories of an industrial products company. Calculate the standardized regression coefficients for x_1 and x_2, and comment on their relative effects on y.

Table 11.4 Industrial Sales Data

No.	x_1	x_2	y
1	31	1.85	4.20
2	46	2.80	7.28
3	40	2.20	5.60
4	49	2.85	8.12
5	38	1.80	5.46
6	49	2.80	7.42
7	31	1.85	3.36
8	38	2.30	5.88
9	33	1.60	4.62
10	42	2.15	5.88

We calculate standardized regression coefficients in two ways. First we run a regression of y on x_1 and x_2, which gives unstandardized regression coefficients, and then use equation (11.14). The MINITAB output is shown in Figure 11.5. From this output we obtain $\hat{\beta}_1 = 0.19224$ and

```
The regression equation is
y = - 2.61 + 0.192 x1 + 0.341 x2
```

Predictor	Coef	Stdev	t-ratio	p
Constant	-2.6062	0.8042	-3.24	0.014
x1	0.19224	0.04806	4.00	0.005
x2	0.3406	0.7117	0.48	0.647

s = 0.4013   R-sq = 94.4%   R-sq(adj) = 92.8%

Analysis of Variance

SOURCE	DF	SS	MS	F	p
Regression	2	19.1410	9.5705	59.43	0.000
Error	7	1.1273	0.1610		
Total	9	20.2684			

SOURCE	DF	SEQ SS
x1	1	19.1041
x2	1	0.0369

Figure 11.5 MINITAB Output for Regression of y on x_1, x_2 for Industrial Sales Data

$\hat{\beta}_2 = 0.3406$. The sample standard deviations of x_1, x_2, and y are, respectively, $s_{x_1} = 6.830$, $s_{x_2} = 0.461$, and $s_y = 1.501$. Therefore,

$$\hat{\beta}_1^* = 0.19224 \left(\frac{6.830}{1.501} \right) = 0.875 \quad \text{and} \quad \hat{\beta}_2^* = 0.3406 \left(\frac{0.461}{1.501} \right) = 0.105.$$

To compute the standardized regression coefficients using (11.15) we compute the correlation matrix between x_1, x_2, and y shown below:

```
        x1        x2
x2     0.913
y      0.971     0.904
```

Thus we have

$$R = \begin{bmatrix} 1 & 0.913 \\ 0.913 & 1 \end{bmatrix} \quad \text{and} \quad r = \begin{bmatrix} 0.971 \\ 0.904 \end{bmatrix}.$$

Next calculate

$$R^{-1} = \frac{1}{1 - r_{x_1 x_2}^2} \begin{bmatrix} 1 & -r_{x_1 x_2} \\ -r_{x_1 x_2} & 1 \end{bmatrix} = \begin{bmatrix} 6.009 & -5.486 \\ -5.486 & 6.009 \end{bmatrix}.$$

Hence,

$$\begin{bmatrix} \hat{\beta}_1^* \\ \hat{\beta}_2^* \end{bmatrix} = R^{-1} r = \begin{bmatrix} 6.009 & -5.486 \\ -5.486 & 6.009 \end{bmatrix} \begin{bmatrix} 0.971 \\ 0.904 \end{bmatrix} = \begin{bmatrix} 0.875 \\ 0.105 \end{bmatrix}.$$

Note that $|\hat{\beta}_1^*| > |\hat{\beta}_2^*|$ although $|\hat{\beta}_1| < |\hat{\beta}_2|$. Thus x_1 has a much larger effect than x_2 on y.

◆

11.6.5 *Logistic Regression Model

Frequently the response variable is binary, e.g., a patient survives or dies, a mortgage loan is good or bad, etc. It is of interest to model the probability of one of the two outcomes as a function of predictor variables (covariates), e.g., a patient's survival depends on the patient's age, medical condition, the treatment given, and so on. The creditworthiness of a mortgage loan depends on the borrower's income, debts, and so on. The **logistic regression model** is generally used for binary responses. We explain the model below, but the methods for fitting it are discussed in Chapter 15.

Consider a response variable $Y = 0$ or 1 and a single predictor variable x. We want to model $E(Y|x) = P(Y = 1|x)$ as a function of x. The logistic regression model expresses the **logistic transform** of $P(Y = 1 \mid x)$, given by the left hand side of the following equation, as a linear model:

$$\ln\{\text{Odds of } Y = 1|x\} = \ln\left\{\frac{P(Y = 1|x)}{1 - P(Y = 1|x)}\right\} = \ln\left\{\frac{P(Y = 1|x)}{P(Y = 0|x)}\right\} = \beta_0 + \beta_1 x$$

where β_0 and β_1 are unknown parameters. This model may be rewritten as

$$P(Y = 1|x) = \frac{\exp(\beta_0 + \beta_1 x)}{1 + \exp(\beta_0 + \beta_1 x)}.$$

Some properties of this model are as follows.

1. $P(Y = 1|x)$ is bounded between 0 and 1 for all values of x. This is not true if we use the model: $P(Y = 1|x) = \beta_0 + \beta_1 x$.

2. In ordinary regression, the regression coefficient of a predictor x has the interpretation that it is the expected change in the mean of Y for a unit change in x. Here β_1 has the interpretation that it is the log of the odds ratio of success for a unit change in x. This can be seen as follows:

$$\ln\left\{\frac{P(Y = 1|x + 1)/P(Y = 0|x + 1)}{P(Y = 1|x)/P(Y = 0|x)}\right\} = \{\beta_0 + \beta_1(x + 1)\} - \{\beta_0 + \beta_1 x\} = \beta_1.$$

For multiple covariates, $x_1, x_2, \ldots, x_k$, the logistic regression model is

$$\ln\left\{\frac{P(Y = 1|x_1, x_2, \ldots, x_k)}{P(Y = 0|x_1, x_2, \ldots, x_k)}\right\} = \beta_0 + \beta_1 x_1 + \cdots + \beta_k x_k.$$

The properties listed above extend to this model as well.

Some models cannot be transformed into a linear form. An example is

$$y = \beta_0\{\exp(-\beta_1 x_1) - \exp(-\beta_2 x_2)\}.$$

These models are called **nonlinear models**. One can use the least squares (LS) method to fit these models, but closed form solutions for the LS estimates are generally not available and numerical algorithmic methods must be used. Furthermore, the distribution theory of the resulting estimates is not simple, and only asymptotic inferences are possible. Methods for nonlinear models are not covered in the present text.

11.7   VARIABLE SELECTION METHODS

Thus far we have assumed that the set of predictor variables to be included in the regression model is fixed. In practice, a common problem is that there is a large set of candidate variables. One wants to choose a small subset from this set so that the resulting regression model is simple and has good predictive ability. For example, possible predictor variables to model a company employee's salary could include education, job category, starting salary, years of experience, past performance evaluations, sex, and ethnicity. All of these variables may not be necessary to predict a person's salary. We need methods to systematically screen the variables to arrive at a good parsimonious model.

Two classes of methods are used to select variables in a regression model: (i) stepwise regression and (ii) best subsets regression. We discuss them in turn.

11.7.1 Stepwise Regression

As the name suggests, the idea behind stepwise regression is to enter or remove variables one at a time. This is done by taking into account the marginal contribution of each variable to the model controlling for the contribution of the other variables already present in the model. How is this marginal contribution evaluated? This is discussed next.

Partial F-Tests.   Let us suppose that variables $x_1, x_2, \ldots, x_{p-1}$ are in the model and we want to evaluate the marginal contribution of the variable x_p in order to decide whether to include it in the model or not. Thus we want to compare two models:

$(p-1)$**-Variable model:** $Y_i = \beta_0 + \beta_1 x_{i1} + \cdots + \beta_{p-1} x_{i,p-1} + \epsilon_i \ (i = 1, 2, \ldots, n)$

vs.

p**-Variable model:** $Y_i = \beta_0 + \beta_1 x_{i1} + \cdots + \beta_{p-1} x_{i,p-1} + \beta_p x_{ip} + \epsilon_i \ (i = 1, 2, \ldots, n)$.

As seen in Section 11.4.1, the significance of x_p can be concluded (i.e., $H_{0p}: \beta_p = 0$ can be rejected in favor of $H_{1p}: \beta_p \neq 0$) at level α if

$$F_p = \frac{(\text{SSE}_{p-1} - \text{SSE}_p)/1}{\text{SSE}_p/[n - (p+1)]} > f_{1,n-(p+1),\alpha}. \tag{11.16}$$

This is called a **partial F-test**.

Let

$$t_p = \frac{\hat{\beta}_p}{\text{SE}(\hat{\beta}_p)}$$

be the usual t-statistic for testing the significance of $\hat{\beta}_p$ in the p-variable model. It can be shown that $F_p = t_p^2$. Thus the above partial F-test is equivalent to the α-level two-sided t-test that rejects H_{0p} when

$$|t_p| > t_{n-(p+1),\alpha/2}.$$

As we will see shortly, in stepwise regression this partial F-test is applied sequentially to decide whether to keep or delete variables from a regression equation.

Partial Correlation Coefficients.   Recall that r^2 for simple linear regression is defined as the ratio SSR/SST, which is the proportion of total variation in y that is accounted for by a linear regression on x. Write SST as SSE_0, which is the SSE with no variables in the model, and $\text{SSR} = \text{SSE}_0 - \text{SSE}_1$, where SSE_1 is the SSE with a single variable x in the model. When evaluating the marginal contribution of x_p to a model that already includes $x_1, x_2, \ldots, x_{p-1}$, the term corresponding to SST is SSE_{p-1} and the term corresponding to SSE_1 is SSE_p. Thus the term corresponding to SSR is $\text{SSE}_{p-1} - \text{SSE}_p$. The ratio of $\text{SSE}_{p-1} - \text{SSE}_p$ to SSE_{p-1} gives the square of the partial correlation coefficient between y and x_p controlling for $x_1, x_2, \ldots, x_{p-1}$:

$$r^2_{yx_p|x_1,\ldots,x_{p-1}} = \frac{\text{SSE}_{p-1} - \text{SSE}_p}{\text{SSE}_{p-1}} = \frac{\text{SSE}(x_1, \ldots, x_{p-1}) - \text{SSE}(x_1, \ldots, x_p)}{\text{SSE}(x_1, \ldots, x_{p-1})},$$

(11.17)

where the notation $\text{SSE}_p = \text{SSE}(x_1, \ldots, x_p)$ makes it explicit that the p variables used in regression are $x_1, \ldots, x_p$. The partial correlation coefficient, $r_{yx_p|x_1,\ldots,x_{p-1}}$, is the square root of the above ratio, its sign being the same as that of $\hat{\beta}_p$ in the regression of y on $x_1, x_2, \ldots, x_p$. It follows that $-1 \leq r_{yx_p|x_1,\ldots,x_{p-1}} \leq 1$.

The partial F-test can be viewed as a test of significance of $r_{yx_p|x_1,\ldots,x_{p-1}}$ by expressing

$$F_p = t_p^2 = \frac{r^2_{yx_p|x_1,\ldots,x_{p-1}}[n - (p+1)]}{1 - r^2_{yx_p|x_1,\ldots,x_{p-1}}}.$$

Note the similarity of this formula with that of (10.28) for the t-statistic for a sample correlation coefficient. One should add x_p to the regression equation that includes $x_1, x_2, \ldots, x_{p-1}$ only if F_p is large enough, i.e., only if $r_{yx_p|x_1,\ldots,x_{p-1}}$ is statistically significant.

EXAMPLE 11.8   (INDUSTRIAL SALES: PARTIAL CORRELATIONS AND F-TESTS)

For the data given in Table 11.4 on the number of salespeople (x_1), the amount of sales expenditure (x_2), and sales revenues (y), we saw in Example 11.7 that both x_1 and x_2 are individually highly correlated with y ($r_{yx_1} = 0.971$, $r_{yx_2} = 0.904$), but they also are highly correlated with each other ($r_{x_1x_2} = 0.913$). Furthermore, in the regression of y on x_1 and x_2, only x_1 has a significant relationship with y. Calculate the partial correlations $r_{yx_1|x_2}$ and $r_{yx_2|x_1}$, and conduct the corresponding partial F-tests at $\alpha = .05$ to confirm this finding.

From the regression of y on both x_1 and x_2 shown in Figure 11.5, we have $\text{SSE}(x_1, x_2) = 1.127$. Figures 11.6 and 11.7 show the MINITAB outputs for regressions of y on x_1 and y on x_2, respectively, from which we obtain $\text{SSE}(x_1) = 1.164$ and $\text{SSE}(x_2) = 3.704$. Therefore, using formula (11.17),

$$r^2_{yx_1|x_2} = \frac{\text{SSE}(x_2) - \text{SSE}(x_1, x_2)}{\text{SSE}(x_2)} = \frac{3.704 - 1.127}{3.704} = 0.696$$

and $r_{yx_1|x_2} = \sqrt{0.696} = 0.834$. Similarly,

$$r_{yx_2|x_1}^2 = \frac{\text{SSE}(x_1) - \text{SSE}(x_1, x_2)}{\text{SSE}(x_1)} = \frac{1.164 - 1.127}{1.164} = 0.032$$

and $r_{yx_2|x_1} = \sqrt{0.032} = 0.178$. The signs of the partial correlations follow from the signs of the corresponding regression coefficients in the fitted equation $\hat{y} = -2.61 + 0.192x_1 + 0.341x_2$; both are positive. Notice the much smaller magnitude of $r_{yx_2|x_1}$ compared to $r_{yx_1|x_2}$, although both r_{yx_1} and r_{yx_2} are large.

```
The regression equation is
y = - 2.68 + 0.213 x1
Predictor        Coef        Stdev      t-ratio         p
Constant      -2.6840       0.7487       -3.58      0.007
x1             0.21325      0.01861      11.46       0.000
s = 0.3815        R-sq = 94.3%      R-sq(adj) = 93.5%
Analysis of Variance
SOURCE         DF           SS          MS          F          p
Regression      1        19.104      19.104     131.28      0.000
Error           8         1.164       0.146
Total           9        20.268
```

Figure 11.6 MINITAB Output for Regression of y on x_1 for Industrial Sales Data

```
The regression equation is
y = - 0.75 + 2.94 x2
Predictor        Coef        Stdev      t-ratio         p
Constant      -0.745        1.112        -0.67      0.522
x2             2.9403       0.4916        5.98      0.000
s = 0.6804        R-sq = 81.7%      R-sq(adj) = 79.4%
Analysis of Variance
SOURCE         DF           SS          MS          F          p
Regression      1        16.564      16.564      35.78      0.000
Error           8         3.704       0.463
Total           9        20.268
```

Figure 11.7 MINITAB Output for Regression of y on x_2 for Industrial Sales Data

The partial F-statistics are as follows:

$$F_1 = \frac{\text{SSE}(x_2) - \text{SSE}(x_1, x_2)}{\text{SSE}(x_1, x_2)/(n-3)} = \frac{3.704 - 1.127}{0.161} = 16.00 > f_{1,7,.05} = 5.59$$

and

$$F_2 = \frac{\text{SSE}(x_1) - \text{SSE}(x_1, x_2)}{\text{SSE}(x_1, x_2)/(n-3)} = \frac{1.164 - 1.127}{0.161} = 0.23 < f_{1,7,.05} = 5.59.$$

Thus only the marginal contribution of x_1 is significant at $\alpha = 0.05$. In other words, the contribution of sales expenditures (x_2) to sales revenues (y) is already accounted for by the number of salespeople (x_1); therefore once x_1 is in the equation, x_2 is not needed. Note from the MINITAB output in Figure 11.5 that $t_1 = 4.00 = \sqrt{16.00} = \sqrt{F_1}$ and $t_2 = 0.48 = \sqrt{0.23} = \sqrt{F_2}$. ◆

Stepwise Regression Algorithm.   There are several different stepwise regression algorithms. Here we present only the **forward stepping algorithm**, in which we start with no variables in the regression equation and, at each step, enter or remove variables until no more variables can be entered or removed. Notice that this algorithm allows for removal of the variables entered at earlier steps, since such variables may become nonsignificant because of the addition of other variables at later steps. We shall see an example of this later.

First one needs to specify two critical constants, which we label as FIN and FOUT (called FENTER and FREMOVE in MINITAB) with FIN $\geq$ FOUT. The partial F-statistics are compared with these critical constants to make the enter/remove decisions. The flow chart of the algorithm is presented in Figure 11.8. In this flow chart p denotes the number of predictor variables in the regression equation at the current step ($0 \leq p \leq k$).

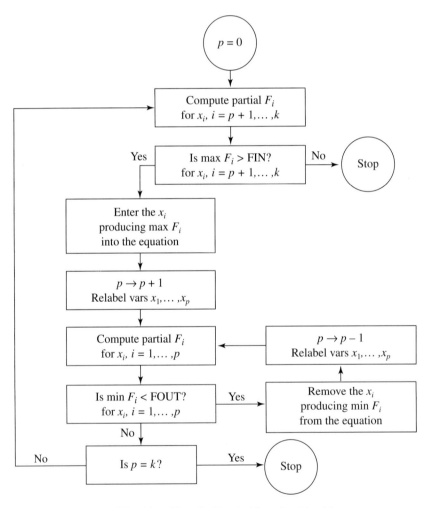

Figure 11.8   Flow Chart for Forward Stepping Algorithm

Why is it necessary to have FIN $\geq$ FOUT? If FIN < FOUT, then it could happen that the partial F-statistic for a variable is greater than FIN, which causes the variable to be entered into the equation, but is less than FOUT, which causes the variable to be removed from the equation, resulting in an infinite loop.

FIN and FOUT values need not be chosen from the F-distribution tables because no rigorous meaning can be attached to the α-level here due to the multiplicity of interdependent partial F-tests. Also, the error d.f. changes at each step. Different packages use different default values, e.g., MINITAB uses FIN = FOUT = 4.0. These values can be changed if desired. Setting smaller values permits more variables to enter and remain in the equation, while larger values imply stricter criteria, leading to a more parsimonious model.

EXAMPLE 11.9 (CEMENT DATA: STEPWISE REGRESSION)

Stepwise regression is used on the cement data given in Table 11.2 to find good predictors of the calories of heat evolved during hardening per gram of cement (y). The candidate predictors are percentages of four ingredients: x_1 =tricalcium aluminate, x_2 = tricalcium silicate, x_3 = tetracalcium alumino ferrite, and x_4 = dicalcium silicate. A summary of the SAS run is shown in Figure 11.9. A detailed output is shown in Figure 11.10.

```
         Summary of Stepwise Procedure for Dependent Variable Y
         Variable          Number   Partial    Model
Step   Entered Removed      In      R**2       R**2      C(p)         F      Prob>F
 1     X4                    1      0.6745     0.6745   138.7308   22.7985   0.0006
 2     X1                    2      0.2979     0.9725     5.4959  108.2239   0.0001
 3     X2                    3      0.0099     0.9823     3.0182    5.0259   0.0517
 4             X4            2      0.0037     0.9787     2.6782    1.8633   0.2054
```

Figure 11.9 Summary SAS Output of Stepwise Regression on Cement Data

At the first step x_4 is entered into the equation, as it is the best individual predictor, of y having the largest (in absolute value) correlation with y among all four predictors and the corresponding F-statistic equals 22.80, which exceeds FIN = 4.0. At the second step x_1 is selected, since it has the highest partial correlation with y (compared to that of x_2 and x_3) controlling for x_4, and the corresponding partial $F = 108.22$ exceeds FIN = 4.0. The third step adds x_2 rather than x_3 to a model containing x_4 and x_1, since $r_{yx_2|x_4,x_1}$ is greater than $r_{yx_3|x_4,x_1}$ in absolute value, and the corresponding partial $F = 5.03$ exceeds FIN = 4.0. However, at this step the partial F-statistic for x_4 equals 1.86, which falls below FOUT = 4.0. Therefore, at the fourth step, x_4 is removed from the model. This is not surprising, since we know from Example 11.5 that x_4 is highly correlated with x_2. Note that the total $r^2 = 0.9787$ of the two variable model of step 4 is slightly higher than the total $r^2 = 0.9725$ of the two variable model of Step 2. Thus, even though x_4 is the best single predictor of y, the pair (x_1, x_2) is a better predictor than the pair (x_1, x_4).   ◆

11.7.2 Best Subsets Regression

A stepwise regression algorithm consists of a set of intuitively reasonable rules to make enter/remove decisions about the predictor variables; the final model is not guaranteed to be optimal in any specified sense. In best subsets regression, a subset of variables

```
                   Stepwise Procedure for Dependent Variable Y
Step 1    Variable X4 Entered           R-square = 0.67454196

                Parameter        Standard        Type II
Variable        Estimate          Error      Sum of Squares        F      Prob>F
INTERCEP       117.56793118     5.26220651    40108.47690796    499.16    0.0001
X4              -0.73816181     0.15459600     1831.89616002     22.80    0.0006
-------------------------------------------------------------------------------
Step 2    Variable X1 Entered           R-square = 0.97247105   C(p) =   5.49585082

                Parameter        Standard        Type II
Variable        Estimate          Error      Sum of Squares        F      Prob>F
INTERCEP       103.09738164     2.12398361    17614.67006622   2356.10    0.0001
X1               1.43995828     0.13841664      809.10480474    108.22    0.0001
X4              -0.61395363     0.04864455     1190.92463664    159.30    0.0001
-------------------------------------------------------------------------------
Step 3    Variable X2 Entered           R-square = 0.98233545   C(p) =   3.01823347

                Parameter        Standard        Type II
Variable        Estimate          Error      Sum of Squares        F      Prob>F
INTERCEP        71.64830697    14.14239348      136.81003409     25.67    0.0007
X1               1.45193796     0.11699759      820.90740153    154.01    0.0001
X2               0.41610976     0.18561049       26.78938276      5.03    0.0517
X4              -0.23654022     0.17328779        9.93175378      1.86    0.2054
-------------------------------------------------------------------------------
Step 4    Variable X4 Removed           R-square = 0.97867837   C(p) =   2.67824160

                Parameter        Standard        Type II
Variable        Estimate          Error      Sum of Squares        F      Prob>F
INTERCEP        52.57734888     2.28617433     3062.60415609    528.91    0.0001
X1               1.46830574     0.12130092      848.43186034    146.52    0.0001
X2               0.66225049     0.04585472     1207.78226562    208.58    0.0001
-------------------------------------------------------------------------------
```

Figure 11.10 SAS Output of Stepwise Regression on Cement Data

is chosen (from the collection of all subsets of k predictor variables) that optimizes a well-defined objective criterion.

Another drawback of stepwise regression is that it yields a *single* final model. In practice there are often several almost equally good models, and the choice of the final model may depend on side considerations such as the number of variables, the ease of observing and/or controlling variables, etc. The best subsets regression algorithm permits determination of a specified number of best subsets of size $p = 1, 2, \ldots, k$ from which the choice of the final model can be made by the investigator. There are 2^k possible subsets including the empty subset. This can be a very large number (e.g., for $k = 10$, it equals 1024), so efficient computing algorithms are needed to search for the optimum subset.

The next question is "What optimality criterion to use?" The following criteria are commonly employed (subscript p is added to the criterion function to indicate the number of variables in the model).

Optimality Criteria.

1. r_p^2-*Criterion*: For a p-variable model,

$$r_p^2 = \frac{SSR_p}{SST} = 1 - \frac{SSE_p}{SST}.$$

Since SSR increases and SSE decreases (so that SST = SSR + SSE remains constant) as more variables are added to a model, it is clear that r_p^2 is maximized when $p = k$, i.e., when all the variables are included in the model. This solution is not very useful, since the goal of variable selection is to find a parsimonious but good model. Therefore the r_p^2-criterion must be employed with an additional consideration, e.g., find the best subset such that adding more variables does not increase r_p^2 significantly.

Another problem with the r_p^2-criterion is that it gives only a measure of the goodness of the *fit* of the model (note that including more variables in the model always gives a better fit, sometimes by a miniscule amount)—not how well the model will *predict* future observations. Some of the criteria discussed below aim to quantify the predictive power of the model.

2. *Adjusted r_p^2-Criterion*: The adjusted r_p^2-criterion is defined as

$$r_{\text{adj},p}^2 = 1 - \frac{SSE_p/(n - (p + 1))}{SST/(n - 1)} = 1 - \frac{MSE_p}{MST}. \qquad (11.18)$$

It charges a penalty for the number of variables in the model as follows: as more variables are added to a model, SSE_p decreases but the error d.f., $n - (p+1)$, also decreases; thus MSE_p may actually increase if the reduction in SSE caused by the additional variables does not compensate for the loss in error d.f. On the other hand, $SST/(n - 1) = MST$ is constant. Therefore adding variables to a model may actually decrease $r_{\text{adj},p}^2$, whereas r_p^2 always increases. In practice, initially (for small values of p) $r_{\text{adj},p}^2$ increases and then begins to decrease as more variables are added to a model, since the marginal decrease in SSE loses pace with the loss in error d.f. Therefore $r_{\text{adj},p}^2$ is a valid criterion for maximization.

The following relation between r_p^2 and $r_{\text{adj},p}^2$ should be noted:

$$r_{\text{adj},p}^2 = 1 - \left[\frac{n - 1}{n - (p + 1)}\right]\frac{SSE_p}{SST} = 1 - \left[\frac{n - 1}{n - (p + 1)}\right](1 - r_p^2).$$

Since $\left[\frac{n-1}{n-(p+1)}\right] > 1$ for $p \geq 1$, it follows that $r_{\text{adj},p}^2 < r_p^2$ except when both equal unity. Note that $r_{\text{adj},p}^2$ can be *negative* if r_p^2 is very small.

3. *MSE$_p$ Criterion*: Some programs use minimization of MSE$_p$ as an optimization criterion. However, from the definition (11.18) of $r_{\text{adj},p}^2$ it is clear that minimizing MSE$_p$ is equivalent to maximizing $r_{\text{adj},p}^2$. Thus MSE$_p$ is not an independent criterion.

4. C_p-*Criterion*: This criterion is based on Mallows' C_p-statistic.[3] It is a measure of the predictive ability of a fitted model. To develop this measure we must choose some predictor variable vectors x for which we want to predict the Y-values. Which x-vectors should we choose for this purpose? The answer to this question is far from clear. The data vectors x_i used to fit the model are chosen for this purpose. One rationale for this choice is that they represent the region over which future predictions would be made. Denote by $\hat{Y}_{ip}$ the predicted value of Y_i for $x = x_i$ using a p-variable model (say, with variables $x_1, x_2, \ldots, x_p$). The total **standardized mean square error of prediction** is defined as

$$\Gamma_p = \frac{1}{\sigma^2} \sum_{i=1}^{n} E[\hat{Y}_{ip} - E(Y_i)]^2$$

which equals

$$\Gamma_p = \frac{1}{\sigma^2} \left\{ \sum_{i=1}^{n} [E(\hat{Y}_{ip}) - E(Y_i)]^2 + \sum_{i=1}^{n} \mathrm{Var}(\hat{Y}_{ip}) \right\}.$$

The first term is the $(\text{bias})^2$ term and the second term is the prediction variance term.[4] The bias term decreases as more variables are added to the model. If we assume that the full model (which includes all k variables) is the true model, then $E(\hat{Y}_{ik}) - E(Y_i) = 0$ and the bias is zero. On the other hand, it can be shown that the prediction variance increases as more variables are added to the model. A trade-off between the two is achieved by minimizing Γ_p.

Unfortunately, Γ_p involves unknown parameters such as the β_j's. Therefore we minimize a sample estimate of Γ_p. Mallows' C_p-statistic, given by

$$C_p = \frac{\mathrm{SSE}_p}{\hat{\sigma}^2} + 2(p + 1) - n$$

provides an almost unbiased estimate of Γ_p, i.e., $E(C_p) \simeq \Gamma_p$. In the above expression, $\hat{\sigma}^2$ is an estimate of σ^2, which is usually taken to be MSE_k, the MSE from the full model. Note that as more variables are added to a model, SSE_p decreases but $2(p + 1)$ increases. Thus minimum C_p for each p (i.e., among all models of size p) first decreases and then increases, as shown in Figure 11.11. The overall minimum C_p is usually attained at some intermediate value of p.

---

[3] C. L. Mallows (1973), "Some comments on C_p," *Technometrics*, **15**, pp. 661–675.

[4] This decomposition into the $(\text{bias})^2$ and variance components is similar to the decomposition of the mean square error of an estimator into its $(\text{bias})^2$ and variance as derived in (6.2).

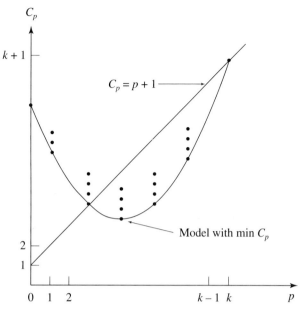

Figure 11.11   Plot of C_p against p

Since the full model is assumed to yield zero bias, let us see what the value of C_p is when $p = k$:

$$C_k = \frac{\text{SSE}_k}{\text{MSE}_k} + 2(k + 1) - n = [n - (k + 1)] + 2(k + 1) - n = k + 1.$$

More generally, it can be shown that if a p-variable model has zero bias (i.e., if $E(\hat{Y}_{ip}) - E(Y_i) = 0$ for $i = 1, 2, \ldots, n$), then $\Gamma_p = p + 1$. Thus if a model with low bias is desired, one could choose a partial model with $C_p \simeq p + 1$, if such a model exists. The line $C_p = p + 1$ is drawn in Figure 11.11 to help in this choice. The C_p-criterion charges a stiffer penalty for adding variables to a model than does the adjusted r_p^2-criterion and so puts more weight on the parsimony of a model.

5. *PRESS$_p$ Criterion*: The PRESS$_p$ criterion[5] evaluates the predictive ability of a postulated model by omitting one observation at a time, fitting the model based on the remaining observations and computing the predicted value for the omitted

---

[5] D. M. Allen (1974), "The relationship between variable selection and data augmentation and a method for prediction," *Technometrics*, **16**, pp. 125–127.

observation. Suppose that we wish to evaluate a p-variable model with variables $x_1, x_2, \ldots, x_p$. We fit this model a total of n times by omitting the ith observation for $i = 1, 2, \ldots, n$, each time using only the remaining $n-1$ observations. Denote the LS estimates that result when the ith observation is omitted by $\hat{\beta}_{(i)0}, \cdots, \hat{\beta}_{(i)p}$. Then the predicted value for the omitted observation is $\hat{y}_{(i)p} = \hat{\beta}_{(i)0} + \hat{\beta}_{(i)1}x_{i1} + \cdots + \hat{\beta}_{(i)p}x_{ip}$. The total **prediction error sum of squares (PRESS)** is given by

$$\text{PRESS}_p = \sum_{i=1}^{n} (\hat{y}_{(i)p} - y_i)^2.$$

This quantity is evaluated for each contending model, and the one associated with the minimum value of PRESS_p is chosen.

The PRESS_p criterion is intuitively easier to grasp than the C_p-criterion, but it is computationally much more intensive and is not available in many packages.

Our recommendation is to use the C_p-criterion because of its ease of computation and its ability to judge the predictive power of a model. In our experience it often gives a good parsimonious model.

EXAMPLE 11.10   (CEMENT DATA: BEST SUBSETS REGRESSION)

The subset of best predictors of the calories of heat evolved during hardening of cement are explored using the data from Table 11.2. The following SAS output shows the values of C_p, r_p^2, adjusted r_p^2, and MSE_p. The models are, sorted by the C_p-values.

C(p)	R-square	In	Adjusted R-square	MSE	Variables in Model
2.67824	0.97867837	2	0.97441405	5.79045	X1 X2
3.01823	0.98233545	3	0.97644727	5.33030	X1 X2 X4
3.04128	0.98228468	3	0.97637957	5.34562	X1 X2 X3
3.49682	0.98128109	3	0.97504146	5.64846	X1 X3 X4
5.00000	0.98237562	4	0.97356343	5.98295	X1 X2 X3 X4
5.49585	0.97247105	2	0.96696526	7.47621	X1 X4
7.33747	0.97281996	3	0.96375995	8.20162	X2 X3 X4
22.37311	0.93528964	2	0.92234757	17.57380	X3 X4
62.43772	0.84702542	2	0.81643050	41.54427	X2 X3
138.22592	0.68006041	2	0.61607249	86.88801	X2 X4
138.73083	0.67454196	1	0.64495487	80.35154	X4
142.48641	0.66626826	1	0.63592901	82.39421	X2
198.09465	0.54816675	2	0.45780010	122.70721	X1 X3
202.54877	0.53394802	1	0.49157966	115.06243	X1
315.15428	0.28587273	1	0.22095207	176.30913	X3

The best subset which minimizes the C_p-criterion is x_1, x_2 which is the same model selected using stepwise regression in Example 11.9. The subset which maximizes $r^2_{\text{adj}, p}$ or equivalently minimizes MSE_p is x_1, x_2, x_4. However, $r^2_{\text{adj}, p}$ increases only from 0.9744 to 0.9763 by the addition of x_4 to the model already containing x_1 and x_2. Thus, the simpler model chosen by the C_p-criterion is preferred. Note that the largest r^2_p-value = 0.9824 is associated with the full model, as one would expect.   ◆

11.8   A STRATEGY FOR BUILDING A MULTIPLE REGRESSION MODEL

In this chapter we have covered much ground dealing with various aspects of multiple regression. The time has come to put together what we have learned so far into a coherent strategy for building a multiple regression model. The strategy outlined below need not be followed exactly in the same sequence, but the spirit of the overall approach and the major steps should be followed. It is also worth repeating that modeling is an iterative process, and several cycles of the steps may be needed before arriving at the final model.

1. *Decide the Type of Model Needed*: Different types of models are:

    - *Predictive*: A model used to predict the response variable from a chosen set of predictor variables.

    - *Theoretical*: A model based on a theoretical relationship between a response variable and predictor variables.

    - *Control*: A model used to control a response variable by manipulating predictor variables.

    - *Inferential*: A model used to explore the strength of relationships between a response variable and individual predictor variables.

    - *Data Summary*: A model used primarily as a device to summarize a large set of data by a single equation.

    Often a model is used for more than one purpose.

    The type of model dictates the type of data needed (e.g., experimental or observational, the type of variables, etc.). For predictive models that we have focused on in this chapter, the data could be observational or experimental; furthermore, the predictor variables need not be causally related to the response variable. As an extreme example, if sunspot activity helps to predict the economic cycles, then it is a perfectly valid predictor variable. However, to fit a control model, the predictor variables must be causally related to the response variable (and easy to manipulate), so that changing their values would directly affect the response variable. Moreover, the data must be experimental so that the effects of any confounding variables do not bias the effects of the predictor variables.

2. *Collect the Data*: Decide the variables (predictor and response) on which to collect data. Consult subject matter experts to identify these variables and how to measure them. See Chapter 3 for precautions necessary to obtain relevant, bias-free data.

3. *Explore the Data*: The data should be examined for outliers, gross errors, missing values, etc. on a univariate basis using the techniques (e.g., summary statistics, box plots) discussed in Chapter 4. Outliers must be dealt with cautiously; it is not advisable to simply discard them (unless they are obviously erroneous observations), because much useful information can be lost. See the section on "How to Deal with Outliers and Influential Observations" from Chapter 10, Section 10.4.2.

   Next, it is useful to study bivariate relationships between the response variable and each of the predictor variables by making scatter plots. These scatter plots can help reveal additional outliers or influential observations which are not detected by univariate techniques. They are also useful for suggesting possible transformations to linearize the relationships. At this point, unless a common transformation of the response variable helps to linearize most of the scatter plots, it is better to restrict any transformations to individual predictor variables. A correlation matrix between all the variables should be computed after making these preliminary transformations to see if there is a possible multicollinearity problem.

4. *Divide the Data into Training and Test Sets*: Only a subset of the data, called the **training set**, should be used to fit the model (steps 5 and 6); the remainder, called the **test set**, should be used for **cross-validation** of the fitted model (step 7). The reason for using an independent data set to test the model is that if the same data are used for both fitting and testing, then an overoptimistic estimate of the predictive ability of the fitted model is obtained. The result is that the "best" model overfits the data (tends to follow even the random wiggles in the data by overparameterization) but does a poor job of prediction for new data. This is exactly the problem with the r_p^2-criterion.

   The training set should have enough observations to leave sufficient error d.f. (at least 15–20) to carry out reliable statistical inferences. The split into the training and test set should be done randomly. A 50:50 split can be used if the sample size is large enough; otherwise more data may be needed to be put into the training set to meet the minimum sample size requirement.

5. *Fit Several Candidate Models*: Generally several equally good models can be identified using the training data set. Best subsets regression is particularly convenient to identify candidate models, since it gives a specified number of best models of each size p. Stepwise regression does not offer a choice of candidate models unless one conducts several runs by varying FIN and FOUT values.

6. *Select and Evaluate a Few "Good" Models*: From the list of candidate models we are now ready to select two or three good models based on criteria such as the C_p-statistic, the number of predictors (p), and the nature of predictors (are they justified on substantive grounds? are they easily measured?). These selected models should be checked for violation of model assumptions using standard diagnostic techniques, in particular, residual plots. At this point, further transformations in the response variable and/or some of the predictor variables may be necessary to improve model fits. Also, inclusion of interaction terms may be contemplated.

Candidate interactions should be carefully chosen with input from subject matter experts to assure that they make sense on substantive grounds. One should not try to include all possible interactions with the hope that a model selection algorithm will weed out the unnecessary ones. Generally, interactions of order higher than two are not needed.

It may turn out that none of the models provides a satisfactory fit. In that case a fresh approach may become necessary. A different class of models (e.g., nonlinear) may be tried, or new data may need to be collected on some omitted predictors that are deemed important in light of this modeling effort.

7. *Select the Final Model*: This is the step where we compare competing models by cross-validating them against the test data. The model with a smaller cross-validation SSE (or equivalently r^2) is a better predictive model. The final selection of the model is based on a number of considerations, both statistical and nonstatistical. These include residual plots, outliers, parsimony, relevance, and ease of measurement of predictors. A final test of any model is that it makes practical sense and the client is willing to buy it.

11.9   CHAPTER SUMMARY

The **multiple regression model** $y = \beta_0 + \beta_1 x_1 + \beta_2 x_2 + \cdots + \beta_k x_k$ extends the simple linear regression model to two or more predictor variables. The **least squares (LS) estimate** of the parameter vector $\boldsymbol{\beta}$ based on n complete sets of observations on all variables equals $\hat{\boldsymbol{\beta}} = (X'X)^{-1} X' y$, where X is the $n \times (k+1)$ matrix of observations on the predictor variables and y is the $n \times 1$ vector of observations on y. The **fitted vector** equals $\hat{y} = X\hat{\boldsymbol{\beta}}$ and the **residual vector** equals $e = y - \hat{y}$. The **error sum of squares (SSE)** equals SSE $= \sum_{i=1}^{n}(y_i - \hat{y}_i)^2 = \sum_{i=1}^{n} e_i^2$. The **multiple coefficient of determination**, r^2, is defined as the ratio of the **regression sum of squares (SSR)** to the **total sum of squares (SST)**, where SST $= \sum_{i=1}^{n}(y_i - \bar{y})^2$, and SSR $=$ SST $-$ SSE. The positive square root of r^2 is called the **multiple correlation coefficient**.

The **probabilistic model** for multiple regression assumes independent $N(0, \sigma^2)$ random errors. It follows that the $\hat{\beta}_j$ are normally distributed with means β_j and variances $\sigma^2 v_{jj}$ where v_{jj} is the jth diagonal term of the matrix $V = (X'X)^{-1}$. Furthermore, $S^2 = \text{SSE}/(n - (k+1))$ is an unbiased estimate of σ^2 and has a $\sigma^2 \chi^2_{n-(k+1)}/(n - (k+1))$ distribution independent of the $\hat{\beta}_j$. From these results we can draw inferences on the β_j based on the t-distribution with $(n - (k+1))$ d.f. For example, a $100(1 - \alpha)\%$ confidence intervals on β_j is given by

$$\hat{\beta}_j \pm t_{n-(k+1),\alpha/2} s \sqrt{v_{jj}}.$$

The **extra sum of squares method** is useful for deriving F-tests on subsets of the β_j's. To test the hypothesis that a specified subset of $m \le k$ of the β_j's equal to zero, we fit the full model which includes all the terms and the partial model which omits the terms corresponding to the β_j's set equal to zero. Let SSE_k and SSE_{k-m} denote the error sum of squares for the two models, respectively. Then the F-statistic is given by

$$F = \frac{(\text{SSE}_{k-m} - \text{SSE}_k)/m}{\text{SSE}_k/[n - (k+1)]}$$

with m and $n - (k+1)$ d.f. Two special cases of this method are the test of significance on a single β_j which is just a t-test, and the test of significance on all β_j's (not including β_0), the F-statistic for which is given by

$$F = \frac{\text{SSR}/k}{\text{SSE}/[n - (k+1)]} = \frac{\text{MSR}}{\text{MSE}}$$

with k and $n - (k+1)$ d.f.

The fitted vector can be written as $\hat{\mathbf{y}} = \mathbf{H}\mathbf{y}$ where $\mathbf{H} = \mathbf{X}(\mathbf{X}'\mathbf{X})^{-1}\mathbf{X}'$ is called the **hat matrix**. If $h_{ii} > 2(k+1)/n$, where h_{ii} is the ith diagonal element of $\mathbf{H}$, then the ith observation is regarded as **influential** because it has high leverage on the model fit. Residuals are used to check the model assumptions like normality and constant variance by making appropriate **residual plots**. If the **standardized residual** $e_i^* = e_i/s\sqrt{1 - h_{ii}}$ is large in absolute value (e.g., $|e_i^*| > 2$) then the ith observation is regarded as an **outlier**.

The **multicollinearity problem** occurs when the columns of $\mathbf{X}$ are approximately linearly dependent which makes $\mathbf{X}'\mathbf{X}$ approximately singular. Multicollinearity makes the parameter estimates numerically unstable (or impossible to calculate) as well as statistically unstable because of large variances. One cause of multicollinearity is predictor variables that are highly correlated with each other. Two general methods are available for selecting a subset of good predictors from the set of all, possibly highly correlated, predictors. Stepwise regression algorithm selects and deletes variables based on their marginal contributions to the model, as measured by their **partial F-statistics** and **partial correlation coefficients**. The **best subsets regression** method chooses a subset of predictor variables so that the corresponding fitted regression model optimizes some criterion function such as $r_{\text{adj}, p}^2$ or the C_p-statistic.

Fitting a multiple regression model in practice involves a number of iterative steps that combine graphical plots of data, fitting the model using a **training data set**, analyzing residuals, data transformations and refitting of the model, and a final **cross-validation** check using a **test data set**.

■ EXERCISES

Section 11.2

11.1   Derive the normal equations for fitting a quadratic equation $y = \beta_0 + \beta_1 x + \beta_2 x^2$ to a set of data $\{(x_i, y_i), \ i = 1, 2, \ldots, n\}$.

11.2   ◼ Develop a model to predict the college GPA of matriculating freshmen based on their college entrance verbal and mathematics test scores. Data for a random sample of 40 graduating seniors on their college GPA (y) along with their college entrance verbal test score (x_1) and mathematics test score (x_2) expressed as percentiles are shown below.[6]

Verbal x_1	Mathematics x_2	GPA y	Verbal x_1	Mathematics x_2	GPA y	Verbal x_1	Mathematics x_2	GPA y
81	87	3.49	83	76	3.75	97	80	3.27
68	99	2.89	64	66	2.70	77	90	3.47
57	86	2.73	83	72	3.15	49	54	1.30
100	49	1.54	93	54	2.28	39	81	1.22
54	83	2.56	74	59	2.92	87	69	3.23
82	86	3.43	51	75	2.48	70	95	3.82
75	74	3.59	79	75	3.45	57	89	2.93
58	98	2.86	81	62	2.76	74	67	2.83
55	54	1.46	50	69	1.90	87	93	3.84
49	81	2.11	72	70	3.01	90	65	3.01
64	76	2.69	54	52	1.48	81	76	3.33
66	59	2.16	65	79	2.98	84	69	3.06
80	61	2.60	56	78	2.58			
100	85	3.30	98	67	2.73			

Use a computer package to fit the model $y = \beta_0 + \beta_1 x_1 + \beta_2 x_2$ to these data. What proportion of variability in the college GPA is accounted for by verbal and mathematics test scores?

11.3   ◼ Are a person's brain size and body size predictive of his/her intelligence? Data on the intelligence (y) based on the performance IQ (PIQ) scores from the Wechsler Adult Intelligence Scale (revised), brain size (x_1) based on the count from MRI scans (given as count/10,000), and body size measured by height (x_2) in inches and weight (x_3) in pounds on 38 college students are shown on the next page.[7]

Use a computer package to fit the model $y = \beta_0 + \beta_1 x_1 + \beta_2 x_2 + \beta_3 x_3$ to these data. What proportion of variability in PIQ is accounted for by a person's brain size, height, and weight?

---

[6] J. T. McClave and F. H. Dietrich, II (1994), *Statistics*, 6th ed., New York: Dellen-MacMillan, p. 811.

[7] L. Willerman, R. Schultz, J. N. Rutledge, and E. Bigler (1991), "In vivo brain size and intelligence," *Intelligence*, **15**, p. 223–228.

Performance IQ	MRI	Height	Weight	Performance IQ	MRI	Weight	Weight
y	x_1	x_2	x_3	y	x_1	x_2	x_3
124	81.69	64.50	118	86	88.91	70.00	180
150	103.84	73.30	143	84	90.59	76.50	186
128	96.54	68.80	172	134	79.06	62.00	122
134	95.15	65.00	147	128	95.50	68.00	132
110	92.88	69.00	146	102	83.18	63.00	114
131	99.13	64.50	138	131	93.55	72.00	171
98	85.43	66.00	175	84	79.86	68.00	140
84	90.49	66.30	134	110	106.25	77.00	187
147	95.55	68.80	172	72	79.35	63.00	106
124	83.39	64.50	118	124	86.67	66.50	159
128	107.95	70.00	151	132	85.78	62.50	127
124	92.41	69.00	155	137	94.96	67.00	191
147	85.65	70.50	155	110	99.79	75.50	192
90	87.89	66.00	146	86	88.00	69.00	181
96	86.54	68.00	135	81	83.43	66.50	143
120	85.22	68.50	127	128	94.81	66.50	153
102	94.51	73.50	178	124	94.94	70.50	144
84	80.80	66.30	136	94	89.40	64.50	139
74	93.00	74.00	148	89	93.59	75.50	179

11.4   ■ Mercury contamination of edible fish poses a health threat. Large mouth bass were studied in Florida lakes to examine factors that influence the amount of mercury contamination. Water samples were collected and analyzed from 38 lakes. Also, samples of fish were taken from each lake and the mercury concentration in their muscle tissue was measured. Since fish absorb mercury over time (older fish tend to have higher concentrations), standardized mercury levels in three year old fish were calculated for each lake. The standardized mercury levels in parts per million (ppm), and the alkalinity (x_1), calcium (x_2) and pH of the water (x_3) are given on the next page.[8]

   (a) Make scatter plots of the standardized mercury level y vs. x_1, x_2 and x_3. It should be evident from the scatter plots that there is curvature in the relationships between y and x_1, and y and x_2. Do the scatter plots of $\log y$ vs. $\log x_1$ and $\log y$ vs. $\log x_2$ indicate linear relationships? Use natural logs.

   (b) Use a computer package to fit the model $\log y = \beta_0 + \beta_1 \log x_1 + \beta_2 \log x_2 + \beta_3 x_3$ to these data. What proportion of variability in mercury is explained by this model?

[8] Data extracted from T. R. Lang, H. E. Royals, and L. L. Connor (1993), "Influence of water chemistry on mercury concentration in large mouth bass from Florida lakes," *Transactions of the American Fisheries Society*, **122**, pp. 74–84.

Std. Mercury (ppm in 3 yr. old fish)	Alkalinity (mg/l)	Calcium (mg/l)	pH	Std. Mercury (ppm in 3 yr. old fish)	Alkalinity (mg/l)	Calcium (mg/l)	pH
y	x_1	x_2	x_3	y	x_1	x_2	x_3
1330	2.5	2.9	4.6	250	67.0	58.6	7.8
250	19.6	4.5	7.3	410	28.8	10.2	7.4
450	5.2	2.8	5.4	160	119.1	38.4	7.9
160	71.4	55.2	8.1	160	25.4	8.8	7.1
720	26.4	9.2	5.8	230	106.5	90.7	6.8
810	4.8	4.6	6.4	560	8.5	2.5	7.0
710	6.6	2.7	5.4	890	87.6	85.5	7.5
510	16.5	13.8	7.2	180	114.0	72.6	7.0
1000	7.1	5.2	5.8	190	97.5	45.5	6.8
150	83.7	66.5	8.2	440	11.8	24.2	5.9
190	108.5	35.6	8.7	160	66.5	26.0	8.3
1020	6.4	4.0	5.8	670	16.0	41.2	6.7
450	7.5	2.0	4.4	550	5.0	23.6	6.2
590	17.3	10.7	6.7	580	25.6	12.6	6.2
810	7.0	6.3	6.9	980	1.2	2.1	4.3
420	10.5	6.3	5.5	310	34.0	13.1	7.0
530	30.0	13.9	6.9	430	15.5	5.2	6.9
310	55.4	15.9	7.3	280	17.3	3.0	5.2
470	6.3	3.3	5.8	250	71.8	20.5	7.9

Section 11.3

11.5 ■ For fitting a multiple linear regression model $y = \beta_0 + \beta_1 x$ based on the following set of 7 observations, write down $\mathbf{y}$, $\mathbf{X}$, $\mathbf{X'X}$, $(\mathbf{X'X})^{-1}$, $\mathbf{X'y}$, $\hat{\boldsymbol{\beta}}$, and $\mathbf{e}$. You may use a computer package to do the matrix calculations; MINITAB has matrix capabilities or you may use a general purpose package like MAPLE® or MATLAB®. For hand calculation purposes the following formula for the inverse of a 2×2 matrix is useful:

$$\begin{bmatrix} a & b \\ c & d \end{bmatrix}^{-1} = \frac{1}{ad - bc} \begin{bmatrix} d & -b \\ -c & a \end{bmatrix}.$$

y	11	18	18	10	7	-2	-13
x	3	2	1	0	-1	-2	-3

11.6 ■ For fitting a multiple linear regression model $y = \beta_0 + \beta_1 x_1 + \beta_2 x_2$ based on the following set of 8 observations, write down $\mathbf{y}$, $\mathbf{X}$, $\mathbf{X'X}$, $(\mathbf{X'X})^{-1}$, $\mathbf{X'y}$, $\hat{\boldsymbol{\beta}}$, and $\mathbf{e}$. Use a computer package to do the matrix calculations.

y	2	2	6	1	6	9	8	1
x_1	0	0	0	0	1	1	1	1
x_2	-3	-1	2	2	1	3	0	-4

11.7 Suppose that based on data $\{(x_i, y_i), i = 1, \ldots, n\}$ we wish to fit a regression line through the origin model $y = \beta x$.

  (a) Write down the the matrices X, $X'X$, and $(X'X)^{-1}$ for this model.

  (b) Find the LS estimate of the slope coefficient β using the matrix approach.

  (c) Find $\mathrm{Var}(\hat{\beta})$ from $V = (X'X)^{-1}$.

11.8 Suppose that based on data $\{(x_i, y_i), i = 1, \ldots, n\}$, we wish to fit the linear regression model $y = \beta_0 + \beta_1 x$.

  (a) Write down the the matrices X, $X'X$, and $(X'X)^{-1}$ for this model.

  (b) Calculate $\hat{\beta}_0$ and $\hat{\beta}_1$.

  (c) Find $\mathrm{Var}(\hat{\beta}_0)$ and $\mathrm{Var}(\hat{\beta}_1)$ from $V = (X'X)^{-1}$.

11.9 Consider the previous exercise, but suppose that the model is written in a slightly different form as $y = \beta_0 + \beta_1(x - \bar{x})$, where $\bar{x} = \sum x_i/n$, i.e., the x's are centered.

  (a) Write down the the matrices X, $X'X$,   and $(X'X)^{-1}$ for this model.

  (b) Calculate $\hat{\beta}_0$ and $\hat{\beta}_1$. How are they related to the LS estimates $\hat{\beta}_0$ and $\hat{\beta}_1$ from the previous exercise?

  (c) Find $\mathrm{Var}(\hat{\beta}_0)$ and $\mathrm{Var}(\hat{\beta}_1)$ from $V = (X'X)^{-1}$.

  (d) What do you see as an advantage of centering the x's?

11.10 Data on blood pressure levels of patients are classified by age (young/old) and by sex (male/female). The following regression model is to be fitted to the data:

$$y = \beta_0 + \beta_1 x_1 + \beta_2 x_2 + \beta_3 x_1 x_2$$

where $x_1 = -1$ if the patient is young and $+1$ if the patient is old. Similarly, $x_2 = -1$ if the patient is a male and $+1$ if the patient is a female.

  (a) Suppose there are 4 patients, one in each group: young male, young female, old male, and old female. Denote their observed blood pressures by y_1, y_2, y_3, and y_4, respectively. Write down the X matrix for these data.

  (b) Calculate $X'X$. What makes this matrix easy to invert? Find $(X'X)^{-1}$.

  (c) Calculate $X'y$. Use $\hat{\boldsymbol{\beta}} = (X'X)^{-1}X'y$ to obtain the formulas for the LS estimates of β_0, β_1, β_2, and β_3.

  (d) How many degrees of freedom are available for estimating error in this model?

  (e) Suppose there are $n > 1$ patients in each of four groups. How will the formulas for the LS estimates of β_0, β_1, β_2, and β_3 change in this case? How many degrees of freedom will be available for estimating error?

Section 11.4

11.11 A multiple linear regression model $y = \beta_0 + \beta_1 x_1 + \beta_2 x_2 + \beta_3 x_3$ is fitted to a set of 34 observations. The total sum of squares is SST = 218.60 and the error sum of squares is SSE = 180.90. Write down the ANOVA table and conduct a test of the hypothesis $H_0 : \beta_1 = \beta_2 = \beta_3 = 0$ at $\alpha = .05$.

11.12 A multiple linear regression model $y = \beta_0 + \beta_1 x_1 + \beta_2 x_2$ is fitted to a set of 25 observations. The resulting least squares estimates are $\hat{\beta}_1 = 0.11$, $\hat{\beta}_2 = 1.40$, and their standard errors are $\mathrm{SE}(\hat{\beta}_1) = 0.055$, $\mathrm{SE}(\hat{\beta}_2) = 0.64$. Construct two-sided 95% confidence intervals for β_1 and β_2. Should x_1 or x_2 be removed from the model?

11.13 A multiple linear regression model $y = \beta_0 + \beta_1 x_1 + \beta_2 x_2 + \beta_3 x_3$ is fitted to a set of 32 observations. The resulting least squares estimates are $\hat{\beta}_1 = 0.06$, $\hat{\beta}_2 = 1.84$, and $\hat{\beta}_3 = 0.65$, and their standard errors are $\mathrm{SE}(\hat{\beta}_1) = 0.05$, $\mathrm{SE}(\hat{\beta}_2) = 0.89$, and $\mathrm{SE}(\hat{\beta}_3) = 0.11$. Test the significance of $\hat{\beta}_1$, $\hat{\beta}_2$, and $\hat{\beta}_3$ separately at $\alpha = .05$. Should any of the variables, x_1, x_2, x_3, be removed from the model?

11.14 A multiple linear regression model $y = \beta_0 + \beta_1 x_1 + \beta_2 x_2$ is fitted to a set of 34 observations resulting in parameter estimates $\hat{\beta}_0 = 5.62$, $\hat{\beta}_1 = 0.82$, $\hat{\beta}_2 = -1.327$, and $s^2 = 2.82$. It is also given that

$$V = (X'X)^{-1} = \begin{bmatrix} .160 & -.110 & -.022 \\ -.110 & .170 & -.009 \\ -.022 & -.009 & .014 \end{bmatrix}.$$

(a) What is the fitted value of the response when $x_1 = 1$ and $x_2 = 2$. Calculate its standard error.

(b) Construct a 95% CI for the mean outcome when $x_1 = 1$ and $x_2 = 2$.

(c) Construct a 95% PI for an actual outcome when $x_1 = 1$ and $x_2 = 2$.

11.15 ■ The life expectancy of the United States population (in thousands) from 1920–1990 is given in the following table.[9]

Life Expectancy in Years		
Year	Males	Females
1920	53.6	54.6
1930	58.1	61.6
1940	60.8	65.2
1950	65.6	71.1
1960	66.6	73.1
1970	67.1	74.7
1980	70.0	77.5
1990	71.8	78.8

(a) Fit a quadratic $y = \beta_0 + \beta_1 t + \beta_2 t^2$, where y is the male life expectancy and t is the time index beginning with 0 for the year 1920.

(b) Test $H_0: \beta_2 = 0$ vs. $H_1: \beta_2 \neq 0$ at $\alpha = .01$. Should the quadratic term be retained in the model?

(c) Repeat (a) and (b) using the female life expectancy data.

11.16 ■ Refer to the fitted equation for GPA obtained in Exercise 11.2. Calculate 95% CI's for the coefficients of the verbal and mathematics test scores.

[9] *World Almanac & Book of Facts* (1996), Mahwah: N. J., Funk & Wagnalls, p. 974.

11.17 ◨ A linear equation was fitted to the GPA data in Exercise 11.2. Determine if the quadratic equation $y = \beta_0 + \beta_1 x_1 + \beta_2 x_2 + \beta_3 x_1^2 + \beta_4 x_2^2 + \beta_5 x_1 x_2$ offers a significantly improved fit by performing an extra sum of squares F-test of $H_0 : \beta_3 = \beta_4 = \beta_5 = 0$. The SSE for the linear fit is 5.9876 and that for the quadratic fit is 1.1908.

11.18 ◨ Refer to the fitted equations for the PIQ data obtained in Exercise 11.3.

   (a) Calculate 95% CI's for the coefficients of brain size, height, and weight. Based on the CI's, should any of the variables be excluded from the model?

   (b) Refit the model excluding the indicated variable(s). What proportion of variation in PIQ is accounted for by the reduced model? How does this compare with that accounted for by the larger model of Exercise 11.3? What does this indicate about the excluded variable(s)?

11.19 ◨ Refer to the fitted equations for the mercury data obtained in Exercise 11.4.

   (a) Calculate 95% CI's for the coefficients of log(alkalinity), log(calcium), and pH. Based on the CI's, should any of the variables be excluded from the model?

   (b) Refit the model by excluding the indicated variable(s). What proportion of variation in mercury is accounted for by the reduced model? How does this compare with that accounted for by the larger model of Exercise 11.4? What does this indicate about the excluded variable(s)?

Section 11.5

11.20 Refer to Exercise 11.7 on fitting a straight line through the origin.

   (a) Show that the entries of the hat matrix $H = X(X'X)^{-1}X'$ are

$$h_{ij} = \frac{x_i x_j}{\sum x_i^2} \quad (1 \le i, j \le n).$$

   (b) Interpret $h_{ii} = x_i^2 / \sum x_i^2$ as the relative distance of x_i from the origin. Explain why a large value of this distance implies that the observation is influential.

11.21 Refer to Exercise 11.8. Show that the entries of the hat matrix $H = X(X'X)^{-1}X'$ for simple linear regression are

$$h_{ij} = \frac{1}{n} + \frac{(x_i - \bar{x})(x_j - \bar{x})}{S_{xx}} \quad (1 \le i, j \le n).$$

How does h_{ii} depend on the distance between x_i and $\bar{x}$? Explain why a large value of this distance implies that the observation is influential.

11.22 ◨ The following table gives data on the specific gravity (x_1), moisture content (x_2), and strength (y) of wood beams.[10]

---

[10] D. C. Hoaglin and R. E. Welsch (1978), "The hat matrix in regression and ANOVA," *The American Statistician*, **32**, pp. 17–22.

Beam Number	Specific Gravity	Moisture Content	Strength
1	0.499	11.1	11.14
2	0.558	8.9	12.74
3	0.604	8.8	13.13
4	0.441	8.9	11.51
5	0.550	8.8	12.38
6	0.528	9.9	12.60
7	0.418	10.7	11.13
8	0.480	10.5	11.70
9	0.406	10.5	11.02
10	0.467	10.7	11.41

(a) Make a scatter plot of the two predictors. Which observation appears to be influential?

(b) Use a computer package to calculate the hat matrix for these data. Check if the same observation found influential in part (a) is identified as influential using the rule $h_{ii} > 2(k+1)/n$.

(c) Fit the equation $y = \beta_0 + \beta_1 x_1 + \beta_2 x_2$ based on all data, and compare it with the fit obtained after omitting the influential observation. Does the fit change much? Which fitted equation would you use to predict the wood beam strength?

11.23 ◼ The average SAT math scores for college bound seniors from 1980–1995 are given in the following table.[11]

Year	Men	Women	Year	Men	Women
1980	491	443	1990	499	455
1985	499	452	1991	497	453
1987	500	453	1992	499	456
1988	498	455	1993	502	457
1989	500	454	1994	501	460
			1995	503	463

(a) Plot the men's scores by year. What trend is evident from this graph?

(b) Fit a straight line $y = \beta_0 + \beta_1 t$, where y is the average men's score and t is the number of years since 1980.

(c) Plot the residuals $e = y - \hat{y}$ against t. Are there any visually evident outliers or patterns?

(d) Obtain the standardized residuals. Do they indicate any outliers?

---

[11] *World Almanac & Book of Facts* (1996), Mahwah: N. J., Funk & Wagnalls, p. 221.

(e) The h_{ii} values are given in the following table.

i	1	2	3	4	5	6	7	8	9	10	11
h_{ii}	0.56	0.20	0.12	0.10	0.09	0.09	0.10	0.13	0.16	0.20	0.25

Which observations, if any, are influential? If any observations are influential, refer to the graph from (a) to explain why.

11.24 ◼ Repeat Exercise 11.23 using the women's average SAT math scores.

11.25 ◼ Refer to Exercise 11.2, where a linear model $y = \beta_0 + \beta_1 x_1 + \beta_2 x_2$ was fitted to the GPA data.

(a) Plot the residuals from this linear fit against x_1 and x_2. Do these plots suggest the need to fit a quadratic model of Exercise 11.17?

(b) Plot the residuals from the quadratic fit against x_1, x_2, and $\hat{y}$. Suggest a suitable transformation to remove the variance heterogeneity exhibited in the plot of residuals against $\hat{y}$.

11.26 ◼ Refer to the PIQ data from Exercise 11.3.

(a) Fit the linear model $y = \beta_0 + \beta_1 x_1 + \beta_2 x_2$. Plot the residuals from this linear fit against x_1, x_2, and $\hat{y}$. What do these plots indicate about the fit of the model and the assumption of constant variance?

(b) Note that variable x_3 has been omitted from this model. Plot the residuals against x_3. Explain if this plot indicates whether x_3 should be included. Is this result consistent with the conclusion from Exercise 11.18 regarding which variables should be included?

11.27 ◼ Refer to the mercury data from Exercise 11.4.

(a) Fit the linear model $\log y = \beta_0 + \beta_1 \log x_1 + \beta_2 \log x_2$ using natural logs. Plot the residuals from this linear fit against $\log x_1$, $\log x_2$, and $\hat{y}$. Comment on the shapes of these plots. Do any plots suggest that a transformation is needed? Explain.

(b) Note that variable $x_3 = $ pH has been omitted from this model. Plot the residuals against x_3. Explain if this plot indicates whether pH should be included in the model. Is this result consistent with the conclusion from Exercise 11.19 regarding which variables should be included in the model?

11.28 ◼ The annual cost of raising a child born in 1990 in a low income family projected through age 17 (the year 2007) is shown below.[12]

Age (years)	0	1	2	3	4	5	6	7	8
Cost in $	4330	4590	4870	5510	5850	6200	6550	6950	7360
Age (years)	9	10	11	12	13	14	15	16	17
Cost in $	7570	8020	8500	10,360	10,980	11,640	13,160	13,950	14,780

(a) Plot the annual cost by the age of the child. Is this graph best described by a straight line or a curve?

(b) Fit a straight line $y = \beta_0 + \beta_1 t$, where y is the annual cost of raising a child and t is the child's age. What is the r^2 for this fit?

---

[12] T. Exter (1991), "The cost of growing up," *American Demographics Magazine*, **13**, p. 59.

(c) Plot the residuals against t. What does the residual plot indicate about the linear fit?

(d) Now fit a quadratic $y = \beta_0 + \beta_1 t + \beta_2 t^2$. Compare the r^2 for this fit with the r^2 for the straight line fit from (b). How much additional variation in y is accounted for by the quadratic term?

(e) Plot the residuals from the quadratic fit against t. How good is the quadratic fit? Are there any outliers?

Section 11.6

11.29 The cigarette consumption in the U.S. since 1950 can be modeled by $y = \beta_0 + \beta_1 t + \beta_2 t^2$, where y is the average annual consumption of cigarettes per person and t is the number of years since 1950. What is the annual rate of change in cigarette consumption? Is it constant? What does β_2 represent? If β_2 is negative what does this indicate?

11.30 Four scatter plots are shown in Figure 11.12. The model $y = \beta_0 + \beta_1 x + \beta_2 z + \beta_3 xz$ is fitted to each data set, where z is an indicator variable coded as 0 for Group A and 1 for Group B. Answer the following questions for each scatter plot:

(a) If this model is fitted to the data set, which fitted coefficients, if any, would you expect to be significantly different from zero? What would be the signs of those nonzero coefficients?

(b) If terms with nonsignificant coefficients are removed from the model, what resulting equation describes Group A? Group B?

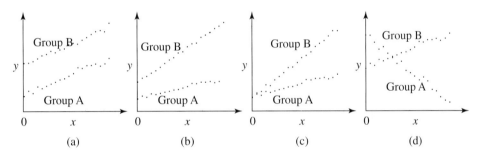

Figure 11.12   Plots of y vs. x for four different data sets

11.31 ■ Refer to the GPA data from Exercise 11.2. Calculate the standardized regression co-efficients $\hat{\beta}_1^*$ and $\hat{\beta}_2^*$ using two different methods: (i) From the unstandardized regression coefficients $\hat{\beta}_1$ and $\hat{\beta}_2$, and the sample SD's of y, x_1, and x_2: $s_y = 0.694$, $s_{x_1} = 16.10$, and $s_{x_2} = 13.15$, and (ii) from the correlation coefficients: $r_{yx_1} = 0.529$, $r_{yx_2} = 0.573$, and $r_{x_1 x_2} = -0.107$. Check that you get the same answers. How do the relative effects of verbal and mathematics test scores compare for predicting GPA?

11.32 ■ Refer to the PIQ model $y = \beta_0 + \beta_1 x_1 + \beta_2 x_2 + \beta_3 x_3$ fitted in Exercise 11.3. Calculate the standardized regression coefficients $\hat{\beta}_1^*$, $\hat{\beta}_2^*$, and $\hat{\beta}_3^*$ from the unstandardized regression coefficients $\hat{\beta}_1$, $\hat{\beta}_2$, and $\hat{\beta}_3$ and the sample SD's $s_y = 22.60$, $s_{x_1} = 7.25$, $s_{x_2} = 3.99$, and $s_{x_3} = 23.48$. How do the relative effects of MRI brain size, height, and weight compare for predicting PIQ?

11.33 ■ Refer to the mercury data model $\log y = \beta_0 + \beta_1 \log x_1 + \beta_2 \log x_2 + \beta_3 x_3$ fitted in Exercise 11.4. Calculate the standardized regression coefficients $\hat{\beta}_1^*$, $\hat{\beta}_2^*$, and $\hat{\beta}_3^*$ from the unstandardized regression coefficients, and the sample SD's of y, $\log x_1$, $\log x_2$, and x_3: $s_{\log y} = 0.627$, $s_{\log x_1} = 1.199$, $s_{\log x_2} = 1.173$, and $s_{x_3} = 1.095$. How do the relative effects of log(alkalinity), log(calcium), and pH compare for predicting mercury content in fish?

11.34 ■ Refer to the PIQ data of Exercise 11.3. The height and weight of a person are often strongly related, which suggests that multicollinearity may be a problem when both variables are in the model. To check for multicollinearity, first calculate the correlation matrix of x_1, x_2, and x_3. Which pair gives the highest correlation? Next calculate the VIF's for these predictors (e.g., find r_1^2 by regressing x_1 on x_2 and x_3, and then $\text{VIF}_1 = 1/(1 - r_1^2)$, etc.). What do these VIF's tell you?

11.35 ■ Refer to the mercury data of Exercise 11.4. Check for multicollinearity in this model due to possible correlations among $\log x_1$, $\log x_2$, and x_3. Calculate the VIF's for these predictors. What do these VIF's tell you?

11.36 The yield y from a chemical process obtained using two methods performed at different temperature settings x is modeled by $y = \beta_0 + \beta_1 x + \beta_2 z$, where z is an indicator variable coded as 0 for the standard method and 1 for the new method.

(a) What is the interpretation of β_0, β_1, and β_2 in this model?

(b) Draw the relationship between the yield and the temperature for the two methods on the same graph if β_0, β_1, and β_2 are all positive. Indicate the equation associated with each method on the graph.

(c) It is felt that temperature influences the effect of the methods on the yield y. This is modeled by $y = \beta_0 + \beta_1 x + \beta_2 z + \beta_3 xz$. Draw the relationship between the yield and temperature for the two methods on the same graph when β_0, β_1, β_2, and β_3 are all positive. Indicate the equation associated with each method on your graph.

11.37 ■ Refer to the annual cost data for raising a child from Exercise 11.28.

(a) One interpretation of the residual plot made in Exercise 11.28(c) is that these cost data can be modeled by two lines: one line for ages 0–11 and a second line for ages 12–17. This can be done by creating a dummy variable and using an interaction term in the following way. Define a new variable z which equals 0 if age < 12 and 1 if age ≥ 12. Write this new model as $y = \beta_0 + \beta_1 t + \beta_2 z + \beta_3 tz$. Fit this model and compare it with the fit from Exercise 11.28(b).

(b) Perform the extra sum of squares F-test of $H_0 : \beta_2 = \beta_3 = 0$. Does this indicate that the terms involving z significantly improve the fit of the model?

(c) Use the final model to write separate equations for younger and older children.

11.38 ■ Refer to the average SAT math scores for men and women tabled in Exercise 11.23. Consider the following model: $y = \beta_0 + \beta_1 t + \beta_2 z + \beta_3 tz$, where z is an indicator variable coded as $z = 0$ for men and $z = 1$ for women, and t is the time index beginning with 0 in 1980. Fit this model and test the significance of the appropriate coefficient at $\alpha = .05$ to see if the rate of improvement is the same for men and women. Explain your results.

11.39 ■ The following table gives data for 19 stocks on the following variables: profit margin (x_1), growth rate (x_2), type of industry (x_3), and price to earnings (P/E) ratio (y). The type of industry is a nominal variable coded as 1 = oil, 2 = drug/health care, and 3 = computers/electronics.[13]

---

[13] D. R. Anderson, D. J. Sweeney, and T. A. Williams (1993), *Statistics for Business and Economics*, 5th ed., St. Paul, MN: West Publishing Co., p. 579.

Company	Profit Margin	Growth Rate	Industry	P/E Ratio
Exxon	6.5	10	1	11.3
Chevron	7.0	5	1	10.0
Texaco	3.9	5	1	9.9
Mobil	4.3	7	1	9.7
Amoco	9.8	8	1	10.0
Pfizer	14.7	12	2	11.9
Bristol Meyers	13.9	14	2	16.2
Merck	20.3	16	2	21.0
American Home Products	16.9	11	2	13.3
Abbott Laboratories	15.2	18	2	15.5
Eli Lilly	18.7	11	2	18.9
Upjohn	12.8	10	2	14.6
Warner-Lambert	8.7	7	2	16.0
Amdahl	11.9	4	3	8.4
Digital	9.8	19	3	10.4
Hewlett-Packard	8.1	18	3	14.8
NCR	7.3	6	3	10.1
Unisys	6.9	6	3	7.0
IBM	9.2	6	3	11.8

(a) Explain why the above coding of the type of industry is not appropriate. Recode the data by defining dummy variables for the type of industry, using the computers/electronics industry as a baseline.

(b) Fit a linear model to predict the P/E ratio as a function of the profit margin, growth rate, and dummy variables for the type of industry. Which predictors are statistically significant at the .05 level? Interpret the coefficients of the dummy variables.

(c) Suppose we choose the drug/health care industry as the baseline. How will the coefficients in the new equation be related to those fitted in (b)?

Section 11.7

11.40 ◼ Refer to the GPA data from Exercise 11.2. The following are the SSE values when y (GPA) is regressed on x_1 (verbal score) alone, on x_2 (mathematics score) alone, and on both x_1 and x_2: $SSE(x_1) = 13.5186$, $SSE(x_2) = 12.6063$, and $SSE(x_1, x_2) = 5.9876$.

(a) Calculate partial correlation coefficients $r_{yx_1|x_2}$ and $r_{yx_2|x_1}$.

(b) Calculate the t (or F) statistics for testing the significance of these partial correlation coefficients. Check that they coincide with the t (or F) statistics for testing the significance of $\hat{\beta}_1$ and $\hat{\beta}_2$ of the linear fit from Exercise 11.2.

11.41   ◼ Refer to the PIQ data from Exercise 11.3.

   (a) Calculate the correlations of y with x_1, x_2, and x_3. Which variable would be the first to enter the equation in stepwise regression?

   (b) Partial correlations can be used to determine the best two variable model, assuming that x_1 = brain size is included in the model. The following are the SSE values when y (PIQ) is regressed on x_1 (brain size) alone, on both x_1 and x_2 (height), and on both x_1 and x_3 (weight): $\text{SSE}(x_1) = 16{,}198$, $\text{SSE}(x_1, x_2) = 13{,}322$, and $\text{SSE}(x_1, x_3) = 15{,}258$. Calculate the partial correlation coefficients $r_{yx_2|x_1}$ and $r_{yx_3|x_1}$.

   (c) Calculate the t (or F) statistics for testing the significance of these partial correlation coefficients. Which variable (height or weight) is the better predictor, given that the brain size is included the model?

11.42   ◼ Refer to the mercury data from Exercise 11.4.

   (a) Calculate the correlations of y with $\log x_1$, $\log x_2$, and x_3. Which variable would be the first to enter the equation in stepwise regression?

   (b) Partial correlations can be used to determine the best two variable model assuming that $\log x_1$ is included in the model. The following are the SSE values when $\log y$ is regressed on $\log x_1$ alone, on both $\log x_1$ and $\log x_2$, and on both $\log x_1$ and x_3: $\text{SSE}(\log x_1) = 6.112$, $\text{SSE}(\log x_1, \log x_2) = 5.815$ and $\text{SSE}(\log x_1, x_3) = 6.053$. Calculate the partial correlation coefficients $r_{\log y, \log x_2|\log x_1}$ and $r_{\log y, x_3|\log x_1}$.

   (c) Calculate the t (or F) statistics for testing the significance of these partial correlation coefficients. Which variable ($\log x_2$ or x_3) is the better predictor, given that $\log(x_1)$ is included the model?

11.43   Show that the partial F-statistic of (11.16) can be expressed in terms of the partial correlation coefficient as follows

$$F_p = \frac{(\text{SSE}_{p-1} - \text{SSE}_p)/1}{\text{SSE}_p/[n - (p + 1)]} = \frac{r^2_{yx_p|x_1,\dots,x_{p-1}}[n - (p + 1)]}{1 - r^2_{yx_p|x_1,\dots,x_{p-1}}}.$$

From this conclude that F_p is an increasing function of the absolute value of $r_{yx_p|x_1,\dots,x_{p-1}}$.

11.44   ◼ Refer to the stocks data from Exercise 11.39.

   (a) Do a stepwise regression with FIN = 2 and FOUT = 2 to find a model to predict the P/E ratio. Which variables are included in this model? Are they significant at the .05 level?

   (b) Perform a best subsets regression with the C_p criterion. Compare with the results from (a).

11.45   ◼ Refer to the mercury data in Exercise 11.4 with $\log y$ as the response variable and $\log x_1$, $\log x_2$, and x_3 as the predictor variables. Perform a best subsets regression with the C_p criterion. Which predictor variables are included in this model? Are they significant at the .05 level?

11.46   The following are the error sums of squares obtained by fitting different models involving three predictor variables, x_1, x_2, x_3, based on a total of $n = 20$ observations. (The constant term is included in all models.)

Variables in Model	SSE_p	p	Error d.f.	MSE_p	Adj. r_p^2	C_p
None	950					
x_1	720					
x_2	630					
x_3	540					
x_1, x_2	595					
x_1, x_3	425					
x_2, x_3	510					
x_1, x_2, x_3	400					

(a) Complete the above table by filling in the values of p (the number of variables in the model), error d.f., MSE_p, adjusted r_p^2 and C_p statistics.

(b) Which models would be selected as the best using the adjusted r_p^2 and the C_p criteria? Which model would you choose and why?

(c) Suppose that stepwise regression is to be carried out with FIN = FOUT = 4.0. Which would be the first variable to enter the model? What is its F-to-enter value?

(d) Which would be the second variable to enter the model? What is its F-to-enter value? What is its partial r^2 with respect to y controlling for the first variable that entered the model?

(e) Will the first variable that entered the model be removed upon the entry of the second variable? Check by doing the partial F-test.

(f) Would stepwise regression enter the third variable in the model, i.e., will it choose the full model? Check by doing the partial F- test.

Advanced Exercises

11.47 In the least squares (LS) estimation we minimize

$$Q = \sum_{i=1}^{n}[y_i - (\beta_0 + \beta_1 x_{i1} + \cdots + \beta_k x_{ik})]^2 = (y - X\beta)'(y - X\beta).$$

This is sometimes called the **ordinary least squares (OLS)** estimation. A more general form of LS estimation minimizes

$$Q = \sum_{i=1}^{n} w_i[y_i - (\beta_0 + \beta_1 x_{i1} + \cdots + \beta_k x_{ik})]^2 = (\boldsymbol{y} - \boldsymbol{X\beta})'\boldsymbol{W}(\boldsymbol{y} - \boldsymbol{X\beta})$$

where $w_i > 0$ is the weight put on the ith observation and $\boldsymbol{W}$ is an $n \times n$ diagonal matrix with the w_i as the diagonal entries. This is called the **weighted least squares (WLS)** estimation.

(a) Show that the WLS estimate of $\boldsymbol{\beta}$ is $\hat{\boldsymbol{\beta}}_W = (\boldsymbol{X'WX})^{-1}\boldsymbol{X'Wy}$.

(b) For the model $y_i = \beta x_i$ (regression through the origin), find the WLS estimate of β.

(c) The WLS estimation is usually used when the variances of the observations are unequal and of the form σ^2/w_i, where the w_i are known constants (e.g., each y_i could be the average of w_i observations). Explain the role of weights in this case.

11.48 The ordinary least squares estimator (OLS) $\hat{\boldsymbol{\beta}}$ of $\boldsymbol{\beta}$ has an optimality property that in the class of all unbiased estimators of $\boldsymbol{\beta}$ that are linear functions of the observation vector $\boldsymbol{y}$, $\mathrm{Cov}(\hat{\boldsymbol{\beta}}) = \sigma^2 \boldsymbol{V}$ is the smallest in the sense of positive semidefiniteness. In particular, if $\hat{\boldsymbol{\beta}}^*$ is any other estimator in this class, then the matrix difference $\mathrm{Cov}(\hat{\boldsymbol{\beta}}^*) - \mathrm{Cov}(\hat{\boldsymbol{\beta}})$ is always positive semidefinite. This is known as the **Gauss–Markov Theorem** and is sometimes stated as "the OLS estimator is the **best linear unbiased estimator (BLUE)**". Prove this theorem by carrying out the following steps.

(a) We know that $\hat{\boldsymbol{\beta}} = (\boldsymbol{X'X})^{-1}\boldsymbol{X'y}$. Write $\hat{\boldsymbol{\beta}}^* = [(\boldsymbol{X'X})^{-1}\boldsymbol{X'} + \boldsymbol{C}]\boldsymbol{y} = \hat{\boldsymbol{\beta}} + \boldsymbol{Cy}$, where $\boldsymbol{C}$ is any $(k+1) \times n$ matrix of constants (so that $\hat{\boldsymbol{\beta}}^*$ is a linear function of $\boldsymbol{y}$). Show that for $\hat{\boldsymbol{\beta}}^*$ to be unbiased, we must have $\boldsymbol{CX}$ equal to a matrix of all zeros (null matrix).

(b) Show that $\mathrm{Cov}(\hat{\boldsymbol{\beta}}^*) = \sigma^2(\boldsymbol{V} + \boldsymbol{CC'})$. Hence $\mathrm{Cov}(\hat{\boldsymbol{\beta}}^*) - \mathrm{Cov}(\hat{\boldsymbol{\beta}})$ is positive semidefinite.

(c) Show that for estimating any linear function of the β's, say $\boldsymbol{c'\beta}$, where $\boldsymbol{c} = (c_0, c_1, \ldots, c_k)'$ is a vector of constants, the estimators $\boldsymbol{c'}\hat{\boldsymbol{\beta}}$ and $\boldsymbol{c'}\hat{\boldsymbol{\beta}}^*$ are both unbiased and $\mathrm{Var}(\boldsymbol{c'}\hat{\boldsymbol{\beta}}) \leq \mathrm{Var}(\boldsymbol{c'}\hat{\boldsymbol{\beta}}^*)$. This is consequence of $\mathrm{Cov}(\hat{\boldsymbol{\beta}}^*) - \mathrm{Cov}(\hat{\boldsymbol{\beta}})$ being positive semidefinite, and means that the OLS estimator gives unbiased estimates with the smallest variance for any linear function of the β's.

11.49 ■ An alternative way of defining a partial correlation coefficient, $r_{yx_p|x_1,\ldots,x_{p-1}}$, between y and x_p controlling for the effects of $x_1, \ldots, x_{p-1}$ is as a correlation coefficient between two sets of residuals: the first set of residuals is from the regression of y on $x_1, x_2, \ldots, x_{p-1}$ and the second is from the regression of x_p on $x_1, x_2, \ldots, x_{p-1}$. In other words, it is the correlation between the "leftovers" in y and x_p after the effects of $x_1, x_2, \ldots, x_{p-1}$ on both have been filtered out. Apply this method to the industrial sales data of Example 11.8, where we obtained $r_{yx_1|x_2} = 0.834$, and check that you get the same value by carrying out the following steps.

(a) Regress y on x_2 and obtain the residuals e_{yx_2}.

(b) Regress x_1 on x_2 and obtain the residuals $e_{x_1x_2}$.

(c) Find the correlation coefficient between e_{yx_2} and $e_{x_1x_2}$ and show that it equals $r_{yx_1|x_2} = 0.834$.

11.50 Still another formula for computing a partial correlation coefficient is

$$r_{yx_1|x_2} = \frac{r_{yx_1} - r_{yx_2}r_{x_1x_2}}{\sqrt{(1 - r_{yx_2}^2)(1 - r_{x_1x_2}^2)}}.$$

This formula computes first order partial correlations (defined when a single variable is conditioned on, e.g., the variable x_2) in terms of ordinary bivariate correlations (which may be thought of as zeroth order partial correlations). It can be applied recursively to obtain higher order partial correlations in terms of the next lower order partial correlations. For example,

$$r_{yx_1|x_2,x_3} = \frac{r_{yx_1|x_3} - r_{yx_2|x_3}r_{x_1x_2|x_3}}{\sqrt{(1 - r_{yx_2|x_3}^2)(1 - r_{x_1x_2|x_3}^2)}}.$$

Verify that $r_{yx_1|x_2} = 0.834$ with the bivariate correlation values, $r_{yx_1} = 0.971$, $r_{yx_2} = 0.904$, and $r_{x_1x_2} = 0.913$ obtained for the industrial sales data from Example 11.7.

11.51 ▣ The following table gives data on conversion of n-heptane to acetylene (y) as observed by varying three reaction conditions: reactor temperature (x_1), ratio of H_2 to n-heptane (x_2), and contact time (x_3).[14]

x_1 Reactor Temperature (°C)	x_2 Ratio of H_2 to n-heptane (mole ratio)	x_3 Contact Time (sec)	y Conversion of n-heptane to Acetylene (%)
1300	7.5	0.0120	49.0
1300	9.0	0.0120	50.2
1300	11.0	0.0115	50.5
1300	13.5	0.0130	48.5
1300	17.0	0.0135	47.5
1300	23.0	0.0120	44.5
1200	5.3	0.0400	28.0
1200	7.5	0.0380	31.5
1200	11.0	0.0320	34.5
1200	13.5	0.0260	35.0
1200	17.0	0.0340	38.0
1200	23.0	0.0410	38.5
1100	5.3	0.0840	15.0
1100	7.5	0.0980	17.0
1100	11.0	0.0920	20.5
1100	17.0	0.0860	29.5

[14] D. W. Marquardt and R. D. Snee (1975), "Ridge regression in practice," *The American Statistician*, **29**, pp. 3–20.

We want to fit a full second degree model:

$$y = \beta_0 + \beta_1 x_1 + \beta_2 x_2 + \beta_3 x_3 + \beta_{12} x_1 x_2 + \beta_{13} x_1 x_3 + \beta_{23} x_2 x_3 + \beta_{11} x_1^2 + \beta_{22} x_2^2 + \beta_{33} x_3^2.$$

(a) Plot the three predictor variables against each other. Also calculate the correlation coefficients between them. Do you see any indications of multicollinearity?

(b) Using a computer package, calculate the VIF's for all the terms in the above model. Comment on your results.

(c) Center the variables x_1, x_2, x_3 by subtracting their respective means from them, and then calculate their products $x_i x_j$ and squares x_i^2. Find the VIF's for all the terms for this second degree model. Compare the results with those from (b). Has centering made the multicollinearity problem less severe?

(d) Do you think the least squares fit of the above model will give reliable results? Explain.

11.52 ◉ An alternative measure for detecting influential observations, which many statistical packages use, is called **Cook's distance**. It is a measure of distance between $\hat{\boldsymbol{\beta}}$, the LS estimate of $\boldsymbol{\beta}$ based on all n observations, and $\hat{\boldsymbol{\beta}}_{(i)}$, the same estimate computed by omitting the ith observation. It is defined as

$$d_i = \frac{(\hat{\boldsymbol{\beta}}_{(i)} - \hat{\boldsymbol{\beta}})' X' X (\hat{\boldsymbol{\beta}}_{(i)} - \hat{\boldsymbol{\beta}})}{(k+1)s^2} \quad (i = 1, 2, \ldots, n).$$

It is related to the h_{ii} as follows:

$$d_i = \left(\frac{e_i^*}{\sqrt{k+1}} \right)^2 \left(\frac{h_{ii}}{1 - h_{ii}} \right) \quad (i = 1, 2, \ldots, n),$$

where e_i^* is the ith standardized residual. Note that while the hat matrix depends only on the x's, Cook's distance also takes into account the y's through the standardized residuals. A value of $d_i > 1$ is usually regarded as an indication of an influential observation. Use this criterion on the wood beam strength data in Exercise 11.22 to detect influential observation(s).

CHAPTER 12

ANALYSIS OF SINGLE FACTOR EXPERIMENTS

In Chapter 8 we studied techniques for comparing two treatments. In this chapter we extend those techniques to compare more than two treatments. The treatments are the levels of a treatment factor. (For the terminology of experimental designs, see Chapter 3). The present chapter considers experiments with a single treatment factor. The next chapter considers multifactor experiments.

As an example of a single factor experiment, consider a study to compare the average flight distances for three types of golf balls differing in the shape of dimples on them: circular, fat elliptical, and thin elliptical. The treatment factor is the type of ball, and the three types of balls are the treatments.

Recall from Chapter 8 that to compare two treatments we considered two different designs: the independent samples design and the matched pairs design. The generalizations of these two designs to compare more than two treatments are called the **completely randomized (CR) design** and the **randomized block (RB) design**, respectively. These designs were discussed in Chapter 3. We will study the methods of analysis for them in the present chapter.

12.1 COMPLETELY RANDOMIZED DESIGN

Suppose that we want to compare $a \geq 2$ treatments, which are the levels of a treatment factor labeled A. In a completely randomized (CR) design, the available experimental units are randomly assigned to each treatment. The number of experimental units in different treatment groups may be equal, say n, or may be unequal with n_i in the i th

Table 12.1 Data from a One-Way Layout Experiment

	Treatment			
	1	2	$\cdots$	a
	y_{11}	y_{21}	$\cdots$	y_{a1}
	y_{12}	y_{22}	$\cdots$	y_{a2}
	$\vdots$	$\vdots$	$\vdots$	$\vdots$
	y_{1n_1}	y_{2n_2}	$\cdots$	y_{an_a}
Sample Mean	$\bar{y}_1$	$\bar{y}_2$	$\cdots$	$\bar{y}_a$
Sample SD	s_1	s_2	$\cdots$	s_a

group ($i = 1, \ldots, a$). The total sample size is $N = \sum_{i=1}^{a} n_i$. On each experimental unit we measure a response variable y. Let y_{ij} denote the observed value of y on the jth unit in the ith treatment group ($i = 1, 2, \ldots, a; j = 1, 2, \ldots, n_i$). The data can be tabulated as shown in Table 12.1.

For example, in the golf ball experiment, suppose we have $n = 10$ balls of each type for a total of $N = 30$ balls. In a CR experiment a golfer would hit the 30 balls in a random order. The flight distance for the jth hit using the ith type of ball is y_{ij} ($i = 1, 2, 3, j = 1, 2, \ldots, 10$).

Because the data are classified according to the levels of a single treatment factor, this design is also referred to as a **one-way layout**. If the sample sizes are equal (to n) in the different treatment groups, then the design is **balanced**; otherwise the design is **unbalanced**.

Similar data arise also in observational studies where the study units are not assigned to different groups by the investigator. For example, a sociologist may wish to compare the family sizes of samples of households from different ethnic groups to see if there are significant differences. As discussed in Chapter 8, the same methods of analysis are used for experimental as well as observational data, but stronger conclusions are possible from experimental data.

The first step in data analysis is computing summary statistics and making graphical plots. The summary statistics include the sample means or medians and standard deviations (SD's). Side-by-side box plots are convenient for visually comparing the centers and spreads of the data from different treatment groups.

EXAMPLE 12.1 (PLASTIC CONTAINER WEIGHTS: BOX PLOTS AND SUMMARY STATISTICS)

Plastic containers for motor oil are blow molded in a machine that has two feeders, each feeding into three molding stations (a total of six stations). Plastic is extruded through the feeders into continuous cylinders between two halves of each mold. As the molds close, the cylinders are pinched off and air is blown into them to form the container shapes. The production engineer is concerned that the weights of the molded containers at different stations are not uniform and a substantial fraction of the containers are not close to the design weight of 51.5 grams. To investigate the causes behind this and to identify the problematic stations, a random sample of

Table 12.2 Weights of Plastic Containers (in Grams)

	Station 1	Station 2	Station 3	Station 4	Station 5	Station 6
	51.28	51.46	51.07	51.70	51.82	52.12
	51.63	51.15	51.44	51.69	51.70	52.29
	51.06	51.21	50.91	52.12	51.25	51.42
	51.66	51.07	51.11	51.23	51.68	51.88
	52.20	51.84	50.77	51.51	51.76	52.00
	51.27	51.46	51.86	52.02	51.63	51.84
	52.31	51.50	51.22	51.35	51.61	51.57
	51.87	50.99	51.54	51.36	52.14	51.74
Sample Mean	51.660	51.335	51.240	51.623	51.699	51.858
Sample SD	0.450	0.281	0.357	0.322	0.247	0.284

eight containers is taken from each station, resulting in data shown in Table 12.2. Analyze the data graphically and by summary statistics to help in the investigation.[1]

Side-by-side box plots of the data are shown in Figure 12.1. Station 5 has two outliers, but they are retained for the purpose of this analysis. The box plots show that the average container weights differ between stations; station 6 appears to be especially on the high side. Also, the dispersions of the data vary somewhat between stations. These qualitative impressions are confirmed by the sample means and sample SD's shown in Table 12.2.

An interesting fact is that stations 4, 5, and 6, which are supplied by feeder 2, have mean container weights > 51.5 grams, while of stations 1, 2, and 3, which are supplied by feeder 1, only station 1 has a mean container weight > 51.5 grams. We shall investigate this fact further in Examples 12.7 and 12.9. ◆

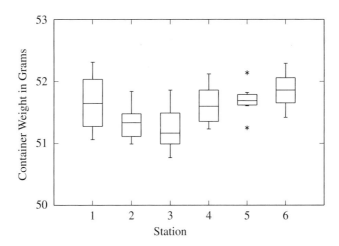

Figure 12.1 Box Plots of Plastic Container Weights

---

[1] This example is courtesy of Professor Bruce Ankenman, Department of Industrial Engineering, Northwestern University, from his consulting project. The experimental set up has been simplified and the data are simulated in order to suit the exposition.

12.1.1 Model and Estimates of Its Parameters

Numerical and graphical summaries can be used to draw informal inferences, as illustrated in the above example. Formal statistical inference to compare the treatment means requires specifying a probability model for the data. We assume that the data on the ith treatment are a random sample from an $N(\mu_i, \sigma^2)$ population. In other words, if Y_{ij} denotes the random variable (r.v.) corresponding to the observed value y_{ij} then

$$Y_{ij} = \mu_i + \epsilon_{ij} \quad (i = 1, 2, \ldots, a; j = 1, 2, \ldots, n_i)$$

where the ϵ_{ij} are independent and identically distributed (i.i.d.) $N(0, \sigma^2)$ random errors. The treatment means μ_i and the error variance σ^2 are unknown parameters. The primary interest is in comparing the means.

A pictorial representation of this model for $a = 4$ treatments is shown in Figure 12.2. You can see by comparison with Figure 8.2 that this is a generalization of the model for two independent samples with equal variances.

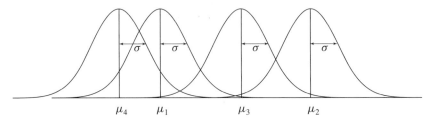

Figure 12.2 Normal Populations Corresponding to Treatments in a One-Way Layout

Frequently, we write $\mu_i = \mu + \tau_i$, where μ is the "grand mean" defined as the weighted average of the μ_i: $\mu = \sum_{i=1}^{a} n_i \mu_i / \sum_{i=1}^{a} n_i$, and $\tau_i = \mu_i - \mu$ is the deviation of the ith treatment mean from this grand mean. We refer to τ_i as the ith **treatment effect**. The τ_i are subject to the constraint $\sum_{i=1}^{a} n_i \tau_i = 0$; when the n_i's are equal, the constraint becomes $\sum_{i=1}^{a} \tau_i = 0$. Thus there are only $a - 1$ linearly independent τ_i's. In this reparameterized form the above model can be written as

$$Y_{ij} = \mu + \tau_i + \epsilon_{ij} \quad (i = 1, 2, \ldots, a; j = 1, 2, \ldots, n_i). \tag{12.1}$$

First we find estimates of the μ_i and σ^2. A natural estimate of μ_i (which also is the **least squares (LS) estimate**) is the sample mean $\bar{y}_i$. Equivalently, the LS estimates of the parameters in the model (12.1) are

$$\hat{\mu} = \bar{\bar{y}} \quad \text{and} \quad \hat{\tau}_i = \bar{y}_i - \bar{\bar{y}},$$

where $\bar{\bar{y}} = \frac{\sum_{i=1}^{a} \sum_{j=1}^{n_i} y_{ij}}{\sum_{i=1}^{a} n_i} = \frac{\sum_{i=1}^{a} n_i \bar{y}_i}{\sum_{i=1}^{a} n_i}$ is the grand sample mean. This yields

$$\hat{\mu}_i = \hat{\mu} + \hat{\tau}_i = \bar{\bar{y}} + (\bar{y}_i - \bar{\bar{y}}) = \bar{y}_i.$$

The $\hat{\tau}_i$ satisfy the same linear constraint that the τ_i do, namely,

$$\sum_{i=1}^{a} n_i \hat{\tau}_i = \sum_{i=1}^{a} n_i (\bar{y}_i - \bar{\bar{y}}) = 0.$$

Since each sample variance, $s_i^2 = \sum_{j=1}^{n_i}(y_{ij} - \bar{y}_i)^2/(n_i - 1)$, is an independent estimate of the common σ^2, we can find a pooled estimate of σ^2 by computing the weighted average of the s_i^2 with respective d.f. as weights:

$$
\begin{aligned}
s^2 &= \frac{(n_1 - 1)s_1^2 + (n_2 - 1)s_2^2 + \cdots + (n_a - 1)s_a^2}{(n_1 - 1) + (n_2 - 1) + \cdots + (n_a - 1)} \\
&= \frac{\sum_{j=1}^{n_1}(y_{1j} - \bar{y}_1)^2 + \cdots + \sum_{j=1}^{n_a}(y_{aj} - \bar{y}_a)^2}{N - a} \\
&= \frac{\sum_{i=1}^{a}\sum_{j=1}^{n_i}(y_{ij} - \bar{y}_i)^2}{N - a}
\end{aligned}
\tag{12.2}
$$

where $N = \sum_{i=1}^{a} n_i$ is the total sample size. This pooled estimate is based on $\nu = N - a$ degrees of freedom (d.f.). Note that this formula is a generalization to $a \geq 2$ samples of the formula (8.5) from Chapter 8 for the pooled estimate of the common variance for two samples.

Using these estimates, a $(1 - \alpha)$-level confidence interval (CI) can be calculated for each μ_i:

$$
\bar{y}_i - t_{\nu,\alpha/2}\frac{s}{\sqrt{n_i}} \leq \mu_i \leq \bar{y}_i + t_{\nu,\alpha/2}\frac{s}{\sqrt{n_i}}
$$

where $t_{\nu,\alpha/2}$ is the upper $\alpha/2$ critical point of the t-distribution with ν d.f. Usually we are more interested in comparing the μ_i with each other than estimating them separately. Methods to do this are discussed in Section 12.2.

EXAMPLE 12.2   (PLASTIC CONTAINER WEIGHTS: ESTIMATES OF PARAMETERS)

Compute estimates of parameters of the model (12.1) for the plastic container weight data from Table 12.2.

The sample means computed in Example 12.1 provide the LS estimates of the μ_i:

$$\hat{\mu}_1 = 51.660, \hat{\mu}_2 = 51.335, \hat{\mu}_3 = 51.240, \hat{\mu}_4 = 51.623, \hat{\mu}_5 = 51.699, \hat{\mu}_6 = 51.858.$$

The LS estimate of the grand mean is $\hat{\mu} = \bar{\bar{y}} = 51.569$. Hence the LS estimates of the station effects are

$$\hat{\tau}_1 = 51.660 - 51.569 = +0.091, \hat{\tau}_2 = 51.335 - 51.569 = -0.234, \hat{\tau}_3 = 51.240 - 51.569 = -0.329,$$

$$\hat{\tau}_4 = 51.623 - 51.569 = +0.054, \hat{\tau}_5 = 51.699 - 51.569 = +0.130, \hat{\tau}_6 = 51.858 - 51.569 = +0.289.$$

Note that $\sum_{i=1}^{a} \hat{\tau}_i = 0$ except for roundoff error.

The estimate of σ^2 can be computed by pooling the sample variances from the six stations:

$$s^2 = \frac{7(0.450)^2 + 7(0.281)^2 + 7(0.357)^2 + 7(0.322)^2 + 7(0.247)^2 + 7(0.284)^2}{42} = 0.109$$

yielding

$$s = \sqrt{0.109} = 0.330.$$

This estimate has 42 d.f. We will instead use the nearest d.f. = 40, for which the critical constants are tabulated. Using $t_{40,.025} = 2.021$ and the common standard error of the mean (SEM), $s/\sqrt{n} = 0.330/\sqrt{8} = 0.117$, the 95% CI's for the six station means are:

$$
\begin{array}{lll}
\textit{Station 1:} & 51.660 \pm (2.021)(0.117) = [51.424, 51.896] \\[4pt]
\textit{Station 2:} & 51.335 \pm (2.021)(0.117) = [51.099, 51.571] \\[4pt]
\textit{Station 3:} & 51.240 \pm (2.021)(0.117) = [51.004, 51.476] \\[4pt]
\textit{Station 4:} & 51.623 \pm (2.021)(0.117) = [51.387, 51.859] \\[4pt]
\textit{Station 5:} & 51.699 \pm (2.021)(0.117) = [51.463, 51.935] \\[4pt]
\textit{Station 6:} & 51.858 \pm (2.021)(0.117) = [51.622, 52.094].
\end{array}
$$

We see that the Station 3 CI falls below the design weight of 51.5 grams, while the Station 6 CI falls above it, indicating that at these two stations the mean container weights differ significantly from the design weight.   ◆

12.1.2 Analysis of Variance

The next step in the analysis of one-way layout data is usually to test the hypotheses

$$H_0: \mu_1 = \mu_2 = \cdots = \mu_a \quad \text{vs.} \quad H_1: \text{Not all the } \mu_i \text{ are equal.} \tag{12.3}$$

The null hypothesis H_0, called the **homogeneity hypothesis**, states that all treatments are the same. Rejection of H_0 implies that there are statistically significant differences between the treatments. In terms of the treatment effects τ_i, the above hypotheses are equivalent to

$$H_0: \tau_1 = \tau_2 = \cdots = \tau_a = 0 \quad \text{vs.} \quad H_1: \text{At least some } \tau_i \neq 0.$$

To test the equality of the μ_i we begin by computing an overall measure of the variability of the $\hat{\mu}_i = \bar{y}_i$ around $\hat{\mu} = \bar{\bar{y}}$. The variability of $\bar{y}_i$ around $\bar{\bar{y}}$ is $(\bar{y}_i - \bar{\bar{y}})^2$. The weighted sum of these quantities, where the weights are the sample sizes n_i, is called the **treatment sum of squares (SS$_{\text{treatments}}$)** or the **factor A sum of squares (SSA)**. It is given by

$$SSA = \sum_{i=1}^{a} n_i (\bar{y}_i - \bar{\bar{y}})^2.$$

A large value of SSA would indicate that H_0 is false. To adjust for the number of treatments, we divide SSA by $a - 1$.[2] The quantity SSA/$(a - 1)$ is called the **mean square treatment (MS$_{\text{treatments}}$)** or the **factor A mean square (MSA)**, and $a - 1$ is called the **treatment d.f.**

Next, MSA needs to be standardized so that we can judge whether it is large or not. The appropriate unit for standardization is the estimate of σ^2 given by (12.2), also

---

[2] The reason for dividing by $a - 1$ and not by a is similar to using $n - 1$ as the degrees of freedom and not n when computing the sample variance. Essentially, only $a - 1$ of the differences, $(\bar{y}_i - \bar{\bar{y}})$'s, are linearly independent, since they satisfy the linear constraint $\sum_{i=1}^{a} n_i (\bar{y}_i - \bar{\bar{y}}) = 0$.

called the **error mean square (MSE)**. The quantity in the numerator of s^2 is called the **error sum of squares (SSE)**, and $v = N - a$ is called the **error d.f.** Thus,

$$s^2 = \text{MSE} = \frac{\text{SSE}}{N - a} = \frac{\sum_{i=1}^{a} \sum_{j=1}^{n_i} (y_{ij} - \bar{y}_i)^2}{v}.$$

It can be shown that the ratio $F = \text{MSA}/\text{MSE}$ has an F-distribution with $a - 1$ and $v = N - a$ d.f. when H_0 is true. Therefore an α-level test rejects H_0 if

$$F = \frac{\text{MSA}}{\text{MSE}} > f_{a-1, v, \alpha} \tag{12.4}$$

where $f_{a-1, v, \alpha}$ is the upper α critical point of the F-distribution with $a - 1$ and v d.f. The P-value is given by the tail area beyond the observed value of the F-statistic under the $F_{a-1, v}$ density function curve. The derivation of this F-test by the extra sum of squares method is given at the end of this subsection.

The total variability of the y_{ij} around their grand mean $\bar{\bar{y}}$, as measured by $\sum_{i=1}^{a} \sum_{j=1}^{n_i} (y_{ij} - \bar{\bar{y}})^2$, is called the **total sum of squares (SST)**. It is shown at the end of this subsection that SST can be partitioned into two components: SSA, which measures the variability of the data *between* treatments, and SSE, which measures the variability of the data *within* treatments. The equation

$$\text{SST} = \text{SSA} + \text{SSE} \tag{12.5}$$

is known as the **analysis of variance (ANOVA) identity**. There is a corresponding decomposition of the degrees of freedom:

$$\underbrace{N - 1}_{\text{(Total d.f.)}} = \underbrace{a - 1}_{\text{(Treatments d.f.)}} + \underbrace{N - a}_{\text{(Error d.f.)}}$$

These calculations can be presented in a tabular form called the **analysis of variance (ANOVA) table** shown in Table 12.3.

Table 12.3 ANOVA Table for One-Way Layout

Source of Variation (Source)	Sum of Squares (SS)	Degrees of Freedom (d.f.)	MeanSquare (MS)	F
Treatments	$\text{SSA} = \sum n_i (\bar{y}_i - \bar{\bar{y}})^2$	$a - 1$	$\text{MSA} = \frac{\text{SSA}}{a-1}$	$F = \frac{\text{MSA}}{\text{MSE}}$
Error	$\text{SSE} = \sum \sum (y_{ij} - \bar{y}_i)^2$	$N - a$	$\text{MSE} = \frac{\text{SSE}}{N-a}$	
Total	$\text{SST} = \sum \sum (y_{ij} - \bar{\bar{y}})^2$	$N - 1$		

EXAMPLE 12.3   (PLASTIC CONTAINER WEIGHTS: ANALYSIS OF VARIANCE)

Give the ANOVA table for the plastic container weight data from Table 12.2. Test if the mean weights for the six stations differ significantly from each other at $\alpha = .05$.

The ANOVA table computed using MINITAB is shown in Figure 12.3. Since $F = 4.03$ exceeds the critical point $f_{5,40,.05} = 2.45$, we reject H_0 that all the station means are equal at $\alpha = .05$. In fact, MINITAB gives the P-value of the F-statistic as $.004 < .05$. ◆

```
Analysis of Variance for Weight
Source     DF        SS        MS       F        P
Station     5      2.194     0.439    4.03    0.004
Error      42      4.577     0.109
Total      47      6.771
```

Figure 12.3 MINITAB Output for the ANOVA of the Plastic Container Data

*Derivation of the ANOVA Identity and the F-statistic.   Each observation y_{ij} can be decomposed into three separate components according to the model (12.1) by replacing the parameters μ and τ_i by their LS estimates and the residual denoted by e_{ij}:

$$y_{ij} = \hat{\mu} + \hat{\tau}_i + e_{ij} = \bar{\bar{y}} + (\bar{y}_i - \bar{\bar{y}}) + (y_{ij} - \bar{y}_i)$$

or

$$y_{ij} - \bar{\bar{y}} = (\bar{y}_i - \bar{\bar{y}}) + (y_{ij} - \bar{y}_i).$$

Square both sides and sum over all i and j, yielding

$$\underbrace{\sum_{i=1}^{a}\sum_{j=1}^{n_i}(y_{ij}-\bar{\bar{y}})^2}_{\text{SST}}=\sum_{i=1}^{a}\sum_{j=1}^{n_i}[(\bar{y}_i-\bar{\bar{y}})+(y_{ij}-\bar{y}_i)]^2$$

$$=\sum_{i=1}^{a}\sum_{j=1}^{n_i}(\bar{y}_i-\bar{\bar{y}})^2+\sum_{i=1}^{a}\sum_{j=1}^{n_i}(y_{ij}-\bar{y}_i)^2+\underbrace{2\sum_{i=1}^{a}\sum_{j=1}^{n_i}(\bar{y}_i-\bar{\bar{y}})(y_{ij}-\bar{y}_i)}_{=0}$$

$$=\underbrace{\sum_{i=1}^{a}n_i(\bar{y}_i-\bar{\bar{y}})^2}_{\text{SSA}}+\underbrace{\sum_{i=1}^{a}\sum_{j=1}^{n_i}(y_{ij}-\bar{y}_i)^2}_{\text{SSE}}.$$

This proves the identity (12.5): SST = SSA + SSE. The cross-product term,

$$2\sum_{i=1}^{a}\sum_{j=1}^{n_i}(\bar{y}_i - \bar{\bar{y}})(y_{ij} - \bar{y}_i) = 2\sum_{i=1}^{a}(\bar{y}_i - \bar{\bar{y}})\sum_{j=1}^{n_i}(y_{ij} - \bar{y}_i)$$

equals 0 because $\sum_{j=1}^{n_i}(y_{ij} - \bar{y}_i) = 0$ for $i = 1, 2, \ldots, a$.

To derive the F-statistic we apply the **extra sum of squares method** of Chapter 11.[3] The LS estimates of the μ_i are $\bar{y}_i$; therefore the **fitted values** are $\hat{y}_{ij} = \bar{y}_i$. The LS **residuals** equal $e_{ij} = y_{ij} - \hat{y}_{ij} = y_{ij} - \bar{y}_i$ and

$$\sum_{i=1}^{a}\sum_{j=1}^{n_i} e_{ij}^2 = \sum_{i=1}^{a}\sum_{j=1}^{n_i}(y_{ij} - \bar{y}_i)^2 = \text{SSE}$$

under the full model. Next, under $H_0 : \mu_1 = \cdots = \mu_a = \mu$, we fit the partial model $Y_{ij} = \mu + \epsilon_{ij}$. The LS estimate of μ is $\bar{\bar{y}}$, which is the common fitted value $\hat{y}_{ij}$. Therefore, under H_0 the LS residuals equal $e_{ij} = y_{ij} - \bar{\bar{y}}$ and

$$\sum_{i=1}^{a}\sum_{j=1}^{n_i} e_{ij}^2 = \sum_{i=1}^{a}\sum_{j=1}^{n_i}(y_{ij} - \bar{\bar{y}})^2 = \text{SST}.$$

The full model has a parameters, μ_i, while the partial model has only 1 parameter, μ. Therefore $a - 1$ parameters are effectively set equal to zero under H_0.[4] Hence the F-statistic is given by

$$F = \frac{(\text{SST} - \text{SSE})/(a-1)}{\text{SSE}/(N-a)} = \frac{\text{SSA}/(a-1)}{\text{SSE}/N-a} = \frac{\text{MSA}}{\text{MSE}}.$$

It can be shown that

$$E(\text{MSE}) = \sigma^2 \quad \text{and} \quad E(\text{MSA}) = \sigma^2 + \frac{\sum_{i=1}^{a} n_i \tau_i^2}{a-1}. \tag{12.6}$$

When H_0 is false, $E(\text{MSA}) > E(\text{MSE})$ because some $\tau_i \neq 0$. When H_0 is true, $\tau_i = 0$ for all i and $E(\text{MSA}) = E(\text{MSE}) = \sigma^2$. In fact, it can be shown that

$$\frac{\text{MSE}}{\sigma^2} \sim \frac{\chi_\nu^2}{\nu}$$

regardless of whether H_0 is true or not, and independently of MSE,

$$\frac{\text{MSA}}{\sigma^2} \sim \frac{\chi_{a-1}^2}{a-1}$$

when H_0 is true. Therefore, under H_0, MSA and MSE provide independent estimates of σ^2, and their ratio

$$F = \frac{\text{MSA}}{\text{MSE}}$$

has an $F_{a-1,\nu}$ distribution. Thus we reject H_0 at level α if $F > f_{a-1,\nu,\alpha}$.

---

[3] Implicit here is the fact that the ANOVA model (12.1) can be written as a regression model. This fact will be explained more fully in the context of multifactor experiments in the next chapter.

[4] Another way to see this is to note that $\tau_1 = \cdots = \tau_{a-1} = 0$ implies that $\tau_a = 0$ because $\sum_{i=1}^{a} n_i \tau_i = 0$.

12.1.3 Model Diagnostics Using Residual Plots

The residuals $e_{ij} = y_{ij} - \bar{y}_i$ can be plotted in a variety of ways to check the model assumptions as in the case of regression analysis; see Section 10.4 and Section 11.5. In particular, a normal plot of the residuals is useful to check the normality assumption. A plot of the residuals against the fitted values $\bar{y}_i$ is useful to check the constant variance assumption. If the data show departures from the constant variance or the normality assumption, then an appropriate **variance stabilizing transformation** should be used, as discussed in Section 10.4.3. The standardized residuals $e_{ij}^* = e_{ij}/s$ can be used to identify outliers. If the time order of data collection is available, then the plot of the residuals against the time order can be made to see if autocorrelation is present.

EXAMPLE 12.4 (PLASTIC CONTAINER WEIGHTS: RESIDUAL PLOTS)

Make residual plots to check the normality and constant variance assumptions for the plastic container weight data from Table 12.2.

The normal plot of the residuals is shown in Figure 12.4. The plot appears fairly linear, suggesting no reason to doubt the normality assumption. The residual plot against the fitted values in Figure 12.5 shows some variation in dispersions, but probably not enough to reject the assumption of equality of variances. Formal tests are available to test this assumption. Bartlett's test[5] is perhaps the most popular among these. It yields a nonsignificant result in the present case. Unfortunately Bartlett's test is very sensitive to the normality assumption (like the F-test for the equality of two variances given in Section 8.4) and therefore is not generally recommended. ◆

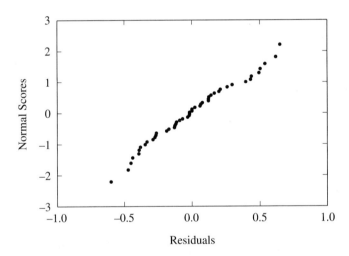

Figure 12.4 Normal Plot of Residuals for Plastic Container Weight Data

---

[5] See, e.g., D. C. Montgomery (1997), *Design and Analysis of Experiments*, 4th ed. New York: Wiley, p. 86.

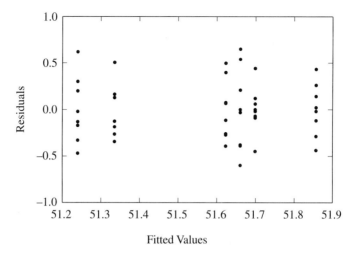

Figure 12.5   Plot of Residuals vs. Fitted Values for Plastic Container Weight Data

12.2   MULTIPLE COMPARISONS OF MEANS

If $H_0: \mu_1 = \cdots = \mu_a$ is rejected, all we can say is that the treatment means are not equal. The F-test does not pinpoint which treatment means are significantly different from each other. To find this out, we need to perform more detailed comparisons among the means, which involves making multiple tests. However, a risk in making multiple tests is that the chance of declaring false significances gets inflated. We discussed this **multiple comparisons problem** in Section 6.3.9.[6] The same problem arises if we do data-snooping and test those differences that appear large in the hope of showing them to be statistically significant.

To determine which treatment means differ from each other, we could test all pairwise equality hypotheses $H_{0ij}: \mu_i = \mu_j$ using two-sided t-tests at level α:[7]

$$\text{Reject } H_{0ij} \text{ if } |t_{ij}| = \frac{|\bar{y}_i - \bar{y}_j|}{s\sqrt{1/n_i + 1/n_j}} > t_{\nu, \alpha/2} \iff |\bar{y}_i - \bar{y}_j| > t_{\nu, \alpha/2} s \sqrt{\frac{1}{n_i} + \frac{1}{n_j}}.$$

The critical value, $t_{\nu, \alpha/2} s \sqrt{1/n_i + 1/n_j}$, that the difference $|\bar{y}_i - \bar{y}_j|$ must exceed in order to be significant at level α is called the **least significant difference (LSD)**. Since in this method each test is done at level α, it is clear that the type I error probability of declaring *at least* one pairwise difference to be falsely significant will exceed α. We define this probability as the **familywise error rate (FWE)**:

$$\text{FWE} = P\{\text{Reject at least one true null hypothesis}\}$$

where the **family** refers to the collection of all pairwise null hypotheses H_{0ij}. For $a = 6$

---

[6] A comprehensive coverage of this topic is given in the book by Y. Hochberg and A. C. Tamhane (1987), *Multiple Comparison Procedures*, New York: Wiley. Additional details and references for the methods discussed in the present section can be found in this book.

[7] Note that these are the usual two sample t-tests except that they use a common pooled estimate $s^2 = \text{MSE}$ of σ^2 based on ν d.f.

treatments, there are $\binom{6}{2} = 15$ comparisons. We will see in Example 12.5 that if all six means are actually equal, then for a balanced one-way layout with $n = 8$, the overall FWE is 0.350 when each LSD test is done at the .05 level.

A popular solution to this problem is to apply the LSD test only if the overall F-test of the ANOVA is significant at the specified α level. This is called **Fisher's protected LSD method**. However, the F-test can be significant with probability approaching 1 if $a - 1$ of the population means are equal, but the remaining one is greatly different. When the LSD test is applied to compare the $a - 1$ equal means, the FWE can still exceed the nominal level α.[8] Therefore the protected LSD does not control the FWE at level α under all configurations of the means. Hence it is not a generally recommended method.

Sometimes we want to make **simultaneous confidence intervals (SCI's)** on the parameters of interest, e.g., the pairwise differences among the treatment means. If each CI has a confidence level $1 - \alpha$, then the probability that *all* CI's include their respective true parameters is less than $1 - \alpha$. This simultaneous coverage probability is called the **simultaneous confidence level (SCL)**. It is the complement of the FWE for the corresponding multiple testing problem.

We shall discuss some standard statistical methods which control the FWE $\leq \alpha$ or equivalently control the SCL $\geq 1 - \alpha$. The flip side of controlling the FWE is that the powers of the tests are reduced compared to the LSD method, which tests each pairwise null hypothesis separately at level α.

12.2.1 Pairwise Comparisons of Means

Bonferroni Method.   The Bonferroni method is based on a very simple idea: to perform k tests simultaneously, divide the familywise error rate α among the k tests. If the error rate is allocated equally among the k tests, as is the common practice, then each test is done at level α/k. For example, if $\alpha = .05$ and $k = 10$, then each test is done at level $.05/10 = .005$. Thus the Bonferroni test declares any pairwise difference, $|\bar{y}_i - \bar{y}_j|$, significant if

$$|t_{ij}| = \frac{|\bar{y}_i - \bar{y}_j|}{s\sqrt{1/n_i + 1/n_j}} > t_{\nu,\alpha/2k}$$

where $k = \binom{a}{2}$. The critical values $t_{\nu,\alpha/2k}$ can be found by interpolation in Table A.4 or by using a computer package.

If the problem is to compute SCI's, then to achieve an SCL of $1-\alpha$, each individual CI should have a level of $1 - \alpha/k$. For example, to achieve an SCL of 95% for 10 CI's, each CI should have a confidence level of $1 - .05/10 = 99.5\%$.

It should be noted that the actual FWE of the Bonferroni method can be much less than the nominal level α (or equivalently the SCL can be much greater than $1 - \alpha$) if k is large. This makes the method conservative, i.e., it has low power. However, for many multiple comparison problems the Bonferroni method provides a reasonable

---

[8] The only exception is $a = 3$, in which case there is just one comparison between the remaining two means.

practical (and sometimes the only) solution as long as k is not too large and the test statistics are not highly correlated. For the pairwise comparisons problem there is an exact method, which we now present.

Tukey Method.   To allow all pairwise differences $\bar{y}_i - \bar{y}_j$ to be tested for significance at FWE $= \alpha$, we consider the problem of testing the significance of $\bar{y}_{max} - \bar{y}_{min}$. If we can test this extreme difference at level α, then we can test all pairwise differences at FWE $= \alpha$. For convenience, assume a balanced one-way layout with a common sample size n per treatment.

The difference $\bar{y}_{max} - \bar{y}_{min}$ is declared significant at level α if, after dividing by the standardizing factor $\mathrm{SE}(\bar{y}_i) = s/\sqrt{n}$, it exceeds the upper α critical point of the distribution of the r.v.

$$Q = \frac{\bar{Y}_{max} - \bar{Y}_{min}}{S/\sqrt{n}}$$

under $H_0\colon \mu_1 = \cdots = \mu_k$. The distribution of Q is called the **Studentized range distribution**. It depends on the number of means a and the error d.f. $\nu = N - a$. Denote its upper α critical point by $q_{a,\nu,\alpha}$. Table A.7 tabulates $q_{a,\nu,\alpha}$ for selected values of a, ν and $\alpha = .01, .05$, and $.10$.

The Tukey method, based on the above test of significance of the extreme difference, rejects *any* pairwise null hypothesis $H_{0ij}\colon \mu_i - \mu_j$ at FWE $= \alpha$ if

$$\frac{|\bar{y}_i - \bar{y}_j|}{s/\sqrt{n}} > q_{a,\nu,\alpha} \quad \text{or equivalently if} \quad |t_{ij}| = \frac{|\bar{y}_i - \bar{y}_j|}{s\sqrt{2/n}} > \frac{q_{a,\nu,\alpha}}{\sqrt{2}}$$

where t_{ij} is the usual pairwise t-statistic. If the design is unbalanced, then $\mathrm{SE}(\bar{y}_i - \bar{y}_j) = s\sqrt{1/n_i + 1/n_j}$ replaces $s\sqrt{2/n}$ in the t_{ij} statistic. The Tukey method can also be presented as $100(1 - \alpha)\%$ SCI's on all pairwise differences $\mu_i - \mu_j$:

$$\bar{y}_i - \bar{y}_j - \frac{q_{a,\nu,\alpha}}{\sqrt{2}}s\sqrt{\frac{1}{n_i} + \frac{1}{n_j}} \le \mu_i - \mu_j \le \bar{y}_i - \bar{y}_j + \frac{q_{a,\nu,\alpha}}{\sqrt{2}}s\sqrt{\frac{1}{n_i} + \frac{1}{n_j}}. \quad (12.7)$$

Note that the critical constants used by the LSD test, the Tukey Test, and the Bonferroni test are ordered as follows:

$$t_{\nu,\alpha/2} \le \frac{q_{a,\nu,\alpha}}{\sqrt{2}} \le t_{\nu,\alpha/2k}$$

where $k = \binom{a}{2}$; equality holds only for $a = 2$. Thus the LSD method has the highest power for detecting pairwise differences; however, it does not control the FWE. The Tukey and Bonferroni methods both control the FWE, but the Bonferroni method is more conservative (less powerful). Of the three, the Tukey method is recommended. It is exact when the n_i are equal and is slightly conservative (i.e., the actual FWE is $< \alpha$ or the SCL is $> 1 - \alpha$) when the n_i are unequal.

EXAMPLE 12.5   (PLASTIC CONTAINER WEIGHTS: PAIRWISE COMPARISONS OF MEANS)

Apply the LSD, Bonferroni, and Tukey methods to the plastic container weight data from Table 12.2 to determine which stations differ significantly from each other at FWE $= .05$.

For these data we have $a = 6$, $k = \binom{6}{2} = 15$, $v = N - a = 42$, and $s = 0.330$. Because the critical constants for $v = 42$ are not tabulated, we use those for $v = 40$, which are as follows:

$$t_{40,.05/2} = 2.021, t_{40,.05/2(15)} = 3.122 \quad \text{and} \quad q_{6,40,.05} = 4.23.$$

The critical values that a pairwise difference must exceed in order to be significant at the .05 level for these three methods are:

$$\text{LSD:} \qquad t_{40,.05/2}s\sqrt{\tfrac{2}{n}} = (2.021)(0.330)\sqrt{\tfrac{2}{8}} = 0.333.$$

$$\text{Bonferroni:} \qquad t_{40,.05/2(15)}s\sqrt{\tfrac{2}{n}} = (3.122)(0.330)\sqrt{\tfrac{2}{8}} = 0.515.$$

$$\text{Tukey:} \qquad \tfrac{q_{6,40,.05}}{\sqrt{2}}s\sqrt{\tfrac{2}{n}} = \tfrac{4.23}{\sqrt{2}}(0.330)\sqrt{\tfrac{2}{8}} = 0.494.$$

By comparing the differences between the ordered sample means:

Station 3	Station 2	Station 4	Station 1	Station 5	Station 6
51.240	51.335	51.623	51.660	51.699	51.858

and the critical values just calculated, we find that the three methods identify the following differences as significant:

LSD:	Stations 3 & 6, Stations 3 & 5, Stations 3 & 1, Stations 3 & 4,
	Stations 2 & 6, Stations 2 & 5.
Bonferroni:	Stations 3 & 6, Stations 2 & 6.
Tukey:	Stations 3 & 6, Stations 2 & 6.

We see that the LSD identifies six significant differences, while the Bonferroni and Tukey each identify only two significant differences.

The MINITAB output for the LSD and the Tukey method is shown in Figure 12.6. Each entry in the matrix is a 95% CI (separate CI for the LSD method, simultaneous CI's for the Tukey method) for a pairwise difference between the corresponding station means. For example, the entry (1, 2) is a CI for $\mu_1 - \mu_2$, which is $[-0.0081, 0.6581]$ for the LSD and $[-0.1675, 0.8175]$ for the Tukey method. If a CI includes 0, then the difference is not statistically significant; otherwise it is significant. Notice that the FWE of LSD is 0.350, although the individual error rate 0.05. On the other hand, the FWE of Tukey's method is 0.05, but its individual error rate is only 0.00471. ◆

*Stepwise Methods.   Both the Bonferroni and Tukey methods can be used to obtain SCI's as well as tests for the differences between pairs of treatment means. However, if only tests are needed, then a more powerful method is to do the tests in a stepwise manner. We now discuss these stepwise testing methods for the balanced one-way layout set up.

Suppose that the treatments are labeled so that the sample means are in ascending order. Write them as $\bar{y}_1 \leq \bar{y}_2 \leq \cdots \leq \bar{y}_a$. At the first step, the significance of the difference between the largest and the smallest sample means, $\bar{y}_a$ and $\bar{y}_1$, is tested. If this difference is not significant, then all a sample means are declared not significantly different from each other by implication, and testing stops. Otherwise, $\bar{y}_a$ and

Fisher's pairwise comparisons

   Family error rate = 0.350
Individual error rate = 0.0500

Critical value = 2.018

Intervals for (column level mean) - (row level mean)

	1	2	3	4	5
2	-0.0081 0.6581				
3	0.0869 0.7531	-0.2381 0.4281			
4	-0.2956 0.3706	-0.6206 0.0456	-0.7156 -0.0494		
5	-0.3718 0.2943	-0.6968 -0.0307	-0.7918 -0.1257	-0.4093 0.2568	
6	-0.5306 0.1356	-0.8556 -0.1894	-0.9506 -0.2844	-0.5681 0.0981	-0.4918 0.1743

Tukey's pairwise comparisons

   Family error rate = 0.0500
Individual error rate = 0.00471

Critical value = 4.22

Intervals for (column level mean) - (row level mean)

	1	2	3	4	5
2	-0.1675 0.8175				
3	-0.0725 0.9125	-0.3975 0.5875			
4	-0.4550 0.5300	-0.7800 0.2050	-0.8750 0.1100		
5	-0.5313 0.4538	-0.8563 0.1288	-0.9513 0.0338	-0.5688 0.4163	
6	-0.6900 0.2950	-1.0150 -0.0300	-1.1100 -0.1250	-0.7275 0.2575	-0.6513 0.3338

Figure 12.6 MINITAB Results of the Fisher LSD and Tukey Methods for Plastic Container Weight Data

$\bar{y}_1$ are declared significantly different. At the next step, the differences between the next pairs of extreme means, $(\bar{y}_a, \bar{y}_2)$ and $(\bar{y}_{a-1}, \bar{y}_1)$, are tested. Testing continues in this manner. If at any step the difference between the two extreme sample means is found nonsignificant, then the intermediate sample means are also declared to be not significantly different, and testing stops on that group of means. A line may be drawn connecting those means to indicate that they are not significantly different from each other. The critical constants used to test the significance of successively smaller ranges of means become successively smaller at each step, which results in higher power.

The α-level used to test the significance of the range of p means (e.g., the first step tests the range of $p = a$ sample means, the second step tests the range of $p = a - 1$ sample means, etc.) depends, in general, on p; we denote it by α_p. The critical value to compare the range of p sample means is therefore

$$c_p = q_{p,v,\alpha_p} \frac{s}{\sqrt{n}}$$

where q_{p,v,α_p} is the upper α_p critical point of the Studentized range distribution with parameter p and d.f. v. Note that $c_2 \leq c_3 \leq \cdots \leq c_a$. For example, at the first step, $\bar{y}_a - \bar{y}_1$ is compared to c_a. At the second step, $\bar{y}_{a-1} - \bar{y}_1$ and $\bar{y}_a - \bar{y}_2$ are compared with c_{a-1}, etc.

Some choices for α_p resulting in different stepwise methods are:

Newman-Keuls Method: $\alpha_p = \alpha$ $(p = 2, \ldots, a)$.

Duncan Method: $\alpha_p = 1 - (1 - \alpha)^{p-1}$ $(p = 2, \ldots, a)$.

Ryan Method: $\alpha_p = p\alpha/a$ $(p = 2, \ldots, a - 2)$, $\alpha_{a-1} = \alpha_a = \alpha$.

It can be shown that the Newman-Keuls and Duncan methods do not control the FWE at level α; the Duncan method is especially lax in this regard. The Ryan method does control the FWE and is therefore recommended.[9]

EXAMPLE 12.6   (PLASTIC CONTAINER WEIGHTS: PAIRWISE COMPARISONS OF MEANS USING THE RYAN METHOD)

Apply the Ryan method to the plastic container weight data from Table 12.2 to find the stations that differ significantly from each other at $\alpha = .05$.

The critical constants for the Ryan method are not tabulated, and they need to be found by interpolation in α (because of the nonstandard α_p-values). This interpolation is done linearly in $-\log\alpha$. E.g., for $p = 4$ we have $\alpha_4 = 4(.05)/6 = .033$ and $-\log_{10}(.033) = 1.478$. The Studentized range critical points are tabulated for $\alpha = .01$ and .05. We have $-\log_{10}(.01) = 2$ and $-\log_{10}(.05) = 1.301$. From Table A.7 we read $q_{4,40,.01} = 4.70$ and $q_{4,40,.05} = 3.79$. Therefore,

$$q_{4,40,.033} = 3.79 + (4.70 - 3.79) \left(\frac{1.478 - 1.301}{2 - 1.301} \right) = 4.02.$$

Other critical points are interpolated in the same manner. The c_p-values are found by multiplying the $q_{p,40,\alpha_p}$ constants by SEM $= s/\sqrt{n} = 0.117$. The results are summarized in the following table.

p	2	3	4	5	6
α_p	.017	.025	.033	.05	.05
$q_{p,40,\alpha_p}$	3.51	3.84	4.02	4.04	4.23
$c_p = q_{p,40,\alpha_p}s/\sqrt{n}$	0.410	0.448	0.469	0.471	0.494

---

[9] There is a slightly more powerful version of the Ryan method which uses $\alpha_p = 1 - (1 - \alpha)^{p/k}$ for $p = 2, \ldots, a - 2$ and $\alpha_{a-1} = \alpha_a = \alpha$.

Station 3	Station 2	Station 4	Station 1	Station 5	Station 6
51.240	51.335	51.623	51.660	51.699	51.858

Figure 12.7 Results of the Ryan Method Applied to the Plastic Container Weight Data

Now write the station means in ascending order as shown in Figure 12.7. Begin by testing the station 6 vs. station 3 difference: $51.858 - 51.240 = 0.618$ against $c_6 = 0.494$. Since $0.618 > 0.494$, this difference is significant. At the next step, test the station 6 vs. station 2 difference: $51.858 - 51.335 = 0.523$, and the station 5 vs. station 3 difference: $51.699 - 51.240 = 0.459$, against $c_5 = 0.471$. The first difference is significant, but because the second difference is not, we can declare stations 3, 2, 4, 1, and 5 as *not* significantly different from each other. We draw a line connecting these stations as shown in Figure 12.7. The next difference to be tested is the station 6 vs. station 4 (note that stations 6 and 4 are not yet connected by a common line): $51.858 - 51.623 = 0.235$. Since this difference is $< c_4 = 0.469$, we draw a line connecting stations 4, 1, 5, and 6, and declare them to be *not* significantly different from each other. There are no more differences to be tested and the procedure terminates. Thus the only significant differences are stations 3 & 6 and stations 2 & 6, which are the same differences found significant by the Tukey method in Example 12.5. In general, the Ryan method finds more significant differences (is more powerful) because it uses smaller critical constants for $p < k$ than does the Tukey method. The drawback of the Ryan method (or for that matter of any stepwise method) is that it does not give SCI's, while the Tukey method does. ◆

12.2.2 *Other Comparisons Among the Means

Sometimes comparisons other than pairwise are of interest. For example, suppose that calibration test data are available from five different laboratories. Labs 1 and 2 use one method of testing, while labs 3, 4, and 5 use another. We want to make comparisons between the two groups of labs. Denoting by μ_i the true mean for the ith lab, the parameter of interest is the difference in the average means for the two groups:

$$\frac{1}{2}(\mu_1 + \mu_2) - \frac{1}{3}(\mu_3 + \mu_4 + \mu_5).$$

The parameters for such general comparisons are linear functions of the μ_i with coefficients summing to zero. A linear function $c_1\mu_1 + \cdots + c_a\mu_a = \sum_{i=1}^{a} c_i\mu_i$, where $c_1 + \cdots + c_a = 0$, is called a **contrast**. A pairwise difference, $\mu_i - \mu_j$, is the simplest contrast.

A sample estimate of a contrast is $\sum_{i=1}^{a} c_i\bar{Y}_i$. It is easy to show that this sample estimate is normally distributed with mean and variance given by

$$E\left(\sum_{i=1}^{a} c_i\bar{Y}_i\right) = \sum_{i=1}^{a} c_i\mu_i \quad \text{and} \quad \text{Var}\left(\sum_{i=1}^{a} c_i\bar{Y}_i\right) = \sigma^2 \sum_{i=1}^{a} \frac{c_i^2}{n_i}.$$

Therefore the t-statistic for testing $H_0 : \sum_{i=1}^{a} c_i \mu_i = 0$ is given by

$$t = \frac{\sum_{i=1}^{a} c_i \bar{y}_i}{s \sqrt{\sum_{i=1}^{a} (c_i^2 / n_i)}} \tag{12.8}$$

which has $\nu = N - a$ d.f. The null hypothesis H_0 is rejected in favor of a two-sided alternative at level α if

$$|t| > t_{\nu, \alpha/2}.$$

EXAMPLE 12.7 (PLASTIC CONTAINER WEIGHTS: COMPARISON OF MEAN WEIGHTS FOR TWO FEEDERS USING A t-TEST)

At the end of Example 12.1 it was noted that stations 4, 5, and 6 fed by feeder 2 have sample means > 51.5 grams, but only station 1 fed by feeder 1 has sample mean > 51.5 grams. Therefore it would be of interest to compare the average of the mean weights for the first three stations with the average of the mean weights for the last three stations. Do this comparison using a t-test at $\alpha = .10$.

The contrast of interest is

$$\frac{1}{3}(\mu_1 + \mu_2 + \mu_3) - \frac{1}{3}(\mu_4 + \mu_5 + \mu_6) \quad \text{or equivalently} \quad (\mu_1 + \mu_2 + \mu_3) - (\mu_4 + \mu_5 + \mu_6).$$

The sample estimate of this contrast is

$$(\bar{y}_1 + \bar{y}_2 + \bar{y}_3) - (\bar{y}_4 + \bar{y}_5 + \bar{y}_6) = (51.660 + 51.335 + 51.240) - (51.623 + 51.699 + 51.858) = -0.945.$$

Its estimated standard error equals

$$s \sqrt{\frac{\sum c_i^2}{n}} = 0.330 \sqrt{\frac{\sum_{i=1}^{6} (\pm 1)^2}{8}} = 0.330 \sqrt{\frac{6}{8}} = 0.286.$$

Therefore the t-statistic equals

$$t = \frac{-0.945}{0.286} = -3.304$$

and has 42 d.f. It exceeds the critical constant $t_{40, .10/2} = 1.684$ in absolute value, and therefore the contrast is significant. Thus we conclude that feeder 2 stations have a higher mean container weight than feeder 1 stations, and an investigation of disparities between the container weights should begin with the two feeders.

The t-test used here ignores the fact that this contrast caught our attention after we looked at the data; it was not specified a priori. Since the contrast was data-snooped, an adjustment ought to be made by using an appropriate multiple comparison test. This is done in Example 12.8. ◆

Suppose we want to simultaneously test $k \geq 2$ contrasts. For example, suppose an experiment is conducted to compare two new treatments with a standard treatment. Denote the mean of the standard treatment by μ_1 and the means of the new treatments by μ_2 and μ_3. If the researcher wants to determine if one of the new treatments is "better" than the standard treatment, then the contrasts of interest are $\mu_2 - \mu_1$ and $\mu_3 - \mu_1$. Alternatively, if the researcher wants to compare the standard treatment with the average of the new treatments and also compare the new treatments with each other, then the contrasts of interest are $\mu_1 - (1/2)(\mu_2 + \mu_3)$ and $\mu_2 - \mu_3$.

Let $t_1, t_2, \ldots, t_k$ be the t-statistics for testing these contrasts. Denote by $T_1, T_2, \ldots, T_k$ the corresponding r.v.'s. The joint distribution of $T_1, T_2, \ldots, T_k$ is known as the **multivariate t-distribution**. This distribution depends on the error d.f. ν, the number of r.v.'s k and the correlations between the contrasts. We shall only consider contrasts having a common correlation $\rho = 1/2$. To perform k one-sided tests on the contrasts at FWE $= \alpha$ we need to compare each t_i-statistic with the upper α critical point of the distribution of the maximum of the r.v.'s, $T_1, T_2, \ldots, T_k$, when H_0 is true. In other words, if this critical point is denoted by $t_{k,\nu,\alpha}$ then

$$P\left\{ \max_{1 \le i \le k} T_i \le t_{k,\nu,\alpha} \right\} = 1 - \alpha.$$

We refer to $t_{k,\nu,\alpha}$ as the upper one-sided α equicoordinate critical point of the multivariate t-distribution. Similarly, to perform k two-sided tests on the contrasts at FWE $= \alpha$ we need to compare each $|t_i|$-statistic with the upper α critical point of the distribution of the maximum of the r.v.'s, $|T_1|, |T_2|, \ldots, |T_k|$, when H_0 is true. The corresponding critical point is denoted by $|t|_{k,\nu,\alpha}$. We refer to $|t|_{k,\nu,\alpha}$ as the upper two-sided α equicoordinate critical point of the multivariate t- distribution. These critical points are tabulated in Tables A.8 and A.9, respectively, for $\alpha = .01, .05, .10$ and for selected values of k and ν. We will now give an application where these critical points are used for comparing several treatments with a control group.

Dunnett Method for Comparisons with a Control.   As discussed in Chapter 3, well-planned experiments and observational studies generally include a control group as a benchmark for comparison. Suppose that group 1 is the control with which groups $2, \ldots, a$ are to be compared. Assume a balanced one-way layout with n observations on each treatment as well as the control. The method for computing SCI's and testing hypotheses on the contrasts: $\mu_2 - \mu_1, \mu_3 - \mu_1, \ldots, \mu_a - \mu_1$ is known as the Dunnett method.

The LS estimates of the contrasts are $\bar{y}_2 - \bar{y}_1, \bar{y}_3 - \bar{y}_1, \ldots, \bar{y}_a - \bar{y}_1$. Their common estimated standard error is $s\sqrt{2/n}$, where $s = \sqrt{\text{MSE}}$, based on $\nu = a(n-1)$ d.f. Their common correlation can be shown to be $\rho = 1/2$. Then $100(1-\alpha)\%$ (lower) one-sided simultaneous confidence bounds on $\mu_i - \mu_1$ are given by

$$\mu_i - \mu_1 \ge \bar{y}_i - \bar{y}_1 - t_{a-1,\nu,\alpha} s \sqrt{\frac{2}{n}} \quad (i = 2, \ldots, a). \tag{12.9}$$

The corresponding two-sided SCI's are given by

$$\bar{y}_i - \bar{y}_1 - |t|_{a-1,\nu,\alpha} s \sqrt{\frac{2}{n}} \le \mu_i - \mu_1 \le \bar{y}_i - \bar{y}_1 + |t|_{a-1,\nu,\alpha} s \sqrt{\frac{2}{n}} \quad (i = 2, \ldots, a). \tag{12.10}$$

These SCI's can be used to test hypotheses (one-sided or two-sided) at FWE $= \alpha$ in the usual way.

Example **12.8**

Table 12.4 gives data from Kirk[10] on the reaction times of subjects in four sleep-deprived groups to the onset of light. There are eight subjects per group, and the 12 hour sleep-deprived group is the control. Make one-sided and two-sided comparisons between the 18, 24, and 30 hour sleep-deprived groups with the 12 hour group to determine at what additional levels of sleep deprivation there is a statistically significant effect on the reaction time.

Table 12.4 Reaction Times (in Hundredths of a Second) of Sleep-Deprived Subjects

	Sleep Deprivation			
	12 Hours	18 Hours	24 Hours	30 Hours
	20	21	25	20
	20	20	23	27
	17	21	22	24
	19	22	23	27
	20	20	21	25
	19	20	22	28
	21	23	22	26
	19	19	23	27
Sample Mean	19.375	20.750	22.625	26.250
Sample SD	1.188	1.282	1.188	1.282

The analysis of variance of the data yields $\text{MS}_{\text{groups}} = 71.083$ with 3 d.f., $\text{MSE} = 1.527$ with 28 d.f., and $F = 46.56$, which is highly significant ($P < .001$). Thus there are significant differences between the four sleep-deprived groups. First let us a priori assume that sleep-deprivation will not decrease the reaction time. In that case, one-sided comparisons should be made. To compute the one-sided 95% lower simultaneous confidence bounds we use the one-sided critical point for 30 d.f., $t_{3,30,.05} = 2.147$, from Table A.8. Also, $s = \sqrt{1.527} = 1.236$. Therefore the confidence bounds are:

18 hours vs. 12 hours: $\mu_2 - \mu_1 \geq 20.750 - 19.375 - (2.147)(1.236)\sqrt{\frac{2}{8}} = 0.048.$

24 hours vs. 12 hours: $\mu_3 - \mu_1 \geq 22.625 - 19.375 - (2.147)(1.236)\sqrt{\frac{2}{8}} = 1.923.$

30 hours vs. 12 hours: $\mu_4 - \mu_1 \geq 26.250 - 19.375 - (2.147)(1.236)\sqrt{\frac{2}{8}} = 5.548.$

Since all three lower confidence bounds are positive, it follows that all three groups show a significant increase in the mean reaction times over the 12 hour group, although the 18 hour group shows only a negligible increase.

Now suppose that the a priori assumption stated is not necessarily valid. In that case, two-sided comparisons should be made. To compute 95% two-sided SCI's we use the critical point

---

[10] R. E. Kirk (1995), *Experimental Design: Procedures for the Behavioral Sciences*, 3rd ed., Pacific Grove, CA: Brooks/Cole, p. 207.

$|t|_{3,30,.05} = 2.474$ from Table A.9. Therefore the SCI's are:

18 hours vs. 12 hours: $[20.750 - 19.375 \pm (2.474)(1.236)\sqrt{\frac{2}{8}}] = [-0.154, 2.904]$.

24 hours vs. 12 hours: $[22.625 - 19.375 \pm (2.474)(1.236)\sqrt{\frac{2}{8}}] = [1.721, 4.779]$.

30 hours vs. 12 hours: $[26.250 - 19.375 \pm (2.474)(1.236)\sqrt{\frac{2}{8}}] = [5.346, 8.404]$.

These SCI's show that the mean reaction times increase significantly for the 24 hour and 30 hour groups, but the 18 hour group does not differ significantly from the 12 hour group.   ◆

Scheffé Method for General Contrasts.   More generally, one can think of the family of *all* contrasts $\sum_{i=1}^{a} c_i \mu_i$ among the treatment means. This is useful for exploring if there are *any* contrasts (typically involving several treatment means) that are significant in light of the data. Based on the differences that one might find, this may lead to unexpected insights or avenues for future investigations. The Scheffé method can be used for this purpose. It gives the following formula for $100(1 - \alpha)\%$ SCI's for all contrasts among the μ_i:

$$\sum_{i=1}^{a} c_i \bar{y}_i - d \leq \sum_{i=1}^{a} c_i \mu_i \leq \sum_{i=1}^{a} c_i \bar{y}_i + d \qquad (12.11)$$

where

$$d = \sqrt{(a-1) f_{a-1,\nu,\alpha}} \sqrt{\frac{s^2}{n} \sum_{i=1}^{a} c_i^2}.$$

Note that the family of all contrasts is infinite in size, and Scheffé's method guarantees that the probability that every one of these infinitely many contrasts, $\sum_{i=1}^{k} c_i \mu_i$, is included in its respective CI is $1 - \alpha$. This may seem impossible to achieve, but it is indeed mathematically possible.

The price of the license for such unlimited exploration of the data is the much larger critical constant $\sqrt{(a-1) f_{a-1,\nu,\alpha}}$ than that used by other methods. For example, for $a = 6$, $\nu = 40$, and $\alpha = .05$, the Tukey method uses $q_{a,\nu,\alpha}/\sqrt{2} = 4.23/\sqrt{2} = 2.991$, while the Scheffé method uses $\sqrt{(a-1) f_{a-1,\nu,\alpha}} = \sqrt{5(2.45)} = 3.500$. But the Tukey method is only applicable to pairwise contrasts. Because of the lower power, the Scheffé method should be used only for data-snooped general contrasts.

EXAMPLE 12.9   (PLASTIC CONTAINER WEIGHTS: COMPARISON OF MEAN WEIGHTS FOR TWO FEEDERS BY THE SCHEFFÉ METHOD)

In Example 12.8 we compared the averages of the mean container weights from the three molding stations supplied by each of the two feeders. Since that comparison was suggested by data and not specified a priori, use Scheffé's method to analyze it. Use $\alpha = .10$.

In Example 12.8 we calculated the estimate of the contrast $(\mu_1 + \mu_2 + \mu_3) - (\mu_4 + \mu_5 + \mu_6)$ as

$$(\bar{y}_1 + \bar{y}_2 + \bar{y}_3) - (\bar{y}_4 + \bar{y}_5 + \bar{y}_6) = -0.945,$$

its estimated standard error as 0.286, and the corresponding t-statistic as -3.304. To account for the fact that this contrast was chosen by data-snooping out of all possible contrasts, we compare the t-statistic with Scheffé's critical constant:

$$\sqrt{(a-1)f_{a-1,\nu,\alpha}} = \sqrt{5f_{5,40,.10}} = \sqrt{5(2.45)} = 3.500.$$

The absolute value of the t-statistic exceeds this constant, and so the contrast passes the much stiffer Scheffé's test of significance. A 90% CI for this data-snooped contrast equals

$$[-0.945 \pm (3.163)(0.286)] = [-1.849, -0.041].$$

Therefore the average mean container weight for feeder 1 stations is lower than that for feeder 2 stations. ◆

Hsu Method for Comparisons with the Best. Frequently, the goal of a single factor experiment is to select the "best" treatment from the several available. For example, select the manufacturing process with the highest mean yield of a product or the algorithm that requires the least mean computing time for a class of optimization problems. We define the best treatment, which is unknown, as the one associated with $\mu_{\max} = \max(\mu_1, \mu_2, \ldots, \mu_a)$. A natural solution is to declare the treatment that produces the largest sample mean, $\bar{y}_{\max}$, as the best. However, this rule does not take account of the uncertainty due to sampling variability. If the sample sizes are small, it is highly probable for a non-best treatment to produce the largest sample mean, especially if the mean of that non-best treatment is close to $\mu_{\max}$. Therefore we need a method that will tell us, with specified confidence, which treatments are non-best and which treatments are close to the best. Hsu's method enables us to draw such conclusions.

Hsu's method gives the following $100(1-\alpha)\%$ SCI's for parameters $\mu_i - \max_{j\neq i}\mu_j$, i.e., the difference between each treatment mean and the mean of the best of the rest, in a balanced one-way layout setting:

$$\left(\bar{y}_i - \max_{j\neq i}\bar{y}_j - d\right)^- \leq \mu_i - \max_{j\neq i}\mu_j \leq \left(\bar{y}_i - \max_{j\neq i}\bar{y}_j + d\right)^+ \quad (i=1, 2, \ldots, a) \quad (12.12)$$

where

$$d = t_{a-1,\nu,\alpha}s\sqrt{\frac{2}{n}}.$$

Here $(x)^-$ denotes the negative part of x (i.e., $(x)^- = x$ if x is negative and $(x)^- = 0$ if x is positive); similarly $(x)^+$ denotes the positive part of x and $t_{a-1,\nu,\alpha}$ denotes the upper one-sided α critical point of the maximal component of an $(a-1)$-variate t-distribution with ν d.f. and common correlation $= 1/2$. Denote the lower and upper confidence limits in (12.12) by ℓ_i and u_i, respectively. If $\ell_i = 0$ for some i (there can be at most one such i), then we can conclude that $\mu_i \geq \max_{j\neq i}\mu_j$, so the ith treatment is the "unique" best treatment (discounting the possibility of equal μ's). On the other hand, if $u_i = 0$, then we can conclude that $\mu_i \leq \max_{j\neq i}\mu_j$, so the ith treatment is not a candidate for the best treatment (again discounting the possibility of equal μ's). If $\ell_i < 0$ and $u_i > 0$, then the ith treatment is a possible candidate for being the best.

EXAMPLE 12.10

An experiment was done to compare four different methods of teaching the concept of percentage to sixth graders.[11] Experimental units were 28 classes which were randomly assigned to the four methods, seven classes per method. A 45 item test was given to all classes. The average test scores of the classes are summarized in Table 12.5. Use Hsu's method to determine which method(s) are close to or uniquely "best" and which method(s) are not "best" at the 90% confidence level.

Table 12.5 Average Test Scores for Each Class

	Case Method	Formula Method	Equation Method	Unitary Analysis Method
	14.59	20.27	27.82	33.16
	23.44	26.84	24.92	26.93
	25.43	14.71	28.68	30.43
	18.15	22.34	23.32	36.43
	20.82	19.49	32.85	37.04
	14.06	24.92	33.90	29.76
	14.26	20.20	23.42	33.88
Mean	18.679	21.240	27.844	32.519
SD	4.667	3.962	4.302	3.679

The ANOVA of the data yields MSE = 17.364 with 24 d.f. and $F = 15.94$, which is highly significant ($P < 0.001$). To calculate 90% SCI's using (12.12) we need the critical point $t_{3,24,.10} \simeq 1.796$ from Table A.8. Also $s = \sqrt{17.364} = 4.167$. Thus we have

$$d = (1.796)(4.167)\sqrt{\frac{2}{7}} = 4.000.$$

The calculations of the intervals are shown in the following table.

Method	$\ell_i = (\bar{y}_i - \max_{j \neq i} \bar{y}_j - d)^-$	$u_i = (\bar{y}_i - \max_{j \neq i} \bar{y}_j + d)^+$
Case	$(18.679-32.519-4.000)^- = -17.840$	$(18.679-32.519+4.000)^+ = 0.000$
Formula	$(21.240-32.519-4.000)^- = -15.279$	$(21.240-32.519+4.000)^+ = 0.000$
Equation	$(27.844-32.519-4.000)^- = -8.675$	$(27.844-32.519+4.000)^+ = 0.000$
Unitary analysis	$(32.519-27.844-4.000)^- = 0.000$	$(32.519-27.844+4.000)^+ = 8.675$

Thus we see that the case, formula, and equation methods are non-best, and the unitary analysis method is the uniquely best method, beating the second best method by up to 8.675 points on the average. ◆

---

[11] J. N. Sparks (1963), "Expository notes on the problem of making multiple comparisons on a completely randomized design," *Journal of Experimental Education*, **31**, pp. 343–349.

12.3   *RANDOM EFFECTS MODEL FOR A ONE-WAY LAYOUT

In previous sections we have assumed that the treatments are fixed by the investigator. Usually this is the case because they are the only treatments of interest. In the container weights example, the six molding stations are the only ones of interest. However, there are practical situations where the treatments studied in an experiment are chosen *at random* from a larger population. It is intended to extend the inferences to all treatments in this population and not restrict to those treatments that *happened* to be chosen for the study. For example, to study the variation between the production outputs of workers in a factory, an industrial engineer may take a random sample of workers and record their outputs over a period of one week. The goal in such a study is not to make comparisons between the specific workers participating in the study, because, after all, they were randomly chosen. Rather the goal is to see what this sample says about the population of *all* workers in the factory.

When the treatments are fixed by an investigator, the treatment factor is called a **fixed factor** and the model studied in Section 12.1.2 is called the **fixed effects model**. When the treatments are randomly chosen from the levels of a treatment factor, it is called a **random factor**. In the above example, the workers are a random factor. The model that we use for this case is called the **random effects model**.

The consequence of selecting the treatments at random is that their means, μ_1, $\mu_2, \ldots, \mu_a$, are random variables (r.v.'s). In contrast, in the fixed effects model the means are fixed parameters. We assume that the population of the levels of the random factor is infinite and has a normal distribution with mean μ and variance σ_A^2, where A is the label of the factor (e.g., "Workers"). We further assume that $\mu_1, \mu_2, \ldots, \mu_a$ is a random sample from this normal population, i.e., they are independent and identically distributed (i.i.d.) $N(\mu, \sigma_A^2)$ r.v.'s. Equivalently, the treatment effects $\tau_i = \mu_i - \mu$ are i.i.d. $N(0, \sigma_A^2)$ r.v.'s. The final model for the observations made on each treatment is

$$Y_{ij} = \mu_i + \epsilon_{ij} = \mu + \tau_i + \epsilon_{ij} \quad (i = 1, 2, \ldots, a; j = 1, 2, \ldots, n_i) \quad (12.13)$$

where the the ϵ_{ij} are i.i.d. $N(0, \sigma^2)$ r.v.'s, which are distributed independently of the τ_i.

Note that while σ^2 is the variance of the observations within each treatment group, σ_A^2 represents the variance of the population of the treatment factor (e.g., the variance between all workers in the factory). Moreover, because of the independence assumption, we can write

$$\sigma_Y^2 = \text{Var}(Y_{ij}) = \text{Var}(\mu_i) + \text{Var}(\epsilon_{ij}) = \sigma_A^2 + \sigma^2. \quad (12.14)$$

This is called the **variance components model** since it expresses the variance σ_Y^2 of the observations as a sum of two components: the variance σ_A^2 between the levels of the treatment factor and the error variance σ^2. By estimating these two components in the workers example, we can say what proportion of the total variation in the daily output can be attributed to the variation between different workers and to the day-to-day variation of individual workers. Note that for the fixed effects model $\text{Var}(\mu_i) = 0$, since the μ_i are fixed; therefore $\sigma_Y^2 = \sigma^2$.

In the random effects model, inferences (estimates or hypothesis tests) on the μ_i are not meaningful, since they are not fixed parameters. For example, the homogeneity hypothesis $H_0: \mu_1 = \mu_2 = \cdots = \mu_a$ or the the pairwise null hypotheses $H_{0ij}: \mu_i = \mu_j$ are not meaningful anymore. However, the ANOVA table is still computed exactly the same way as before and is given in Table 12.3. The F-test can also be carried out the same way, but it now tests the hypotheses

$$H_0: \sigma_A^2 = 0 \quad \text{vs.} \quad H_1: \sigma_A^2 > 0.$$

In other words, the null hypothesis now states that all treatments in the treatment population (not just those chosen for the experiment) have identical means, e.g., all workers in the factory have identical mean daily outputs. The F-ratio = MSA/MSE can be used to perform a test of this null hypothesis just the same way as in (12.4) for the fixed effects model. However, in most situations, since it is recognized that the treatment means vary, it is more useful to estimate σ_A^2 than to test it. Therefore we focus on estimation of the variance components.

We assume a balanced one-way layout with n observations per treatment for the remainder of this section. Analogous to (12.6), it can be shown that

$$E(\text{MSE}) = \sigma^2 \quad \text{and} \quad E(\text{MSA}) = \sigma^2 + n\sigma_A^2. \qquad (12.15)$$

By solving for σ_A^2 from these equations we obtain the following unbiased estimates of the two variance components:

$$\hat{\sigma}^2 = \text{MSE} \quad \text{and} \quad \hat{\sigma}_A^2 = \frac{\text{MSA} - \text{MSE}}{n}.$$

One problem with these estimates is that $\hat{\sigma}_A^2$ will be negative if MSA < MSE, i.e., if $F < 1$. The usual solution in this case is to set $\hat{\sigma}_A^2 = 0$ and conclude that the treatment population variance is much less than the error variance. More complex estimation methods are available that constrain the variance estimates to be nonnegative.

Example 12.11

Table 12.6 gives the measurements on the compressive modulus of silicone rubber used in high voltage transformers. Ten sample sheets of rubber from each batch were tested. It is of interest to compare the between batch variation with the within batch variation. Estimate the two variance components.

Batches are a random factor if we consider the five batches as a random sample from the population of all batches. The following is the ANOVA table.

ANOVA Table for the Compressive Modulus of Rubber Data

Source of Variation	Sum of Squares	Degrees of Freedom	Mean Square	F	P-value
Batches	30,373.0	4	7593.0	3.58	.013
Error	95,518.0	45	2123.0		
Total	125,891.0	49			

Table 12.6 Compressive Modulus (in lb./in.^{2}) of Silicone Rubber Samples

	Batch 1	Batch 2	Batch 3	Batch 4	Batch 5
	997.5	870.1	1018.7	973.0	1018.6
	972.4	1064.1	993.6	1048.7	1061.3
	1064.2	925.9	939.6	1058.3	1066.5
	972.0	906.2	1006.3	961.9	969.0
	994.4	969.8	1027.0	1002.2	1063.9
	1044.5	982.4	877.1	973.3	955.7
	982.6	936.0	926.4	967.6	967.9
	956.3	930.0	980.2	992.3	1018.1
	991.3	927.2	966.6	956.1	925.4
	1001.5	924.5	925.0	973.5	1088.4
Sample Mean	997.7	943.6	966.0	990.7	1013.5
Sample SD	33.2	52.4	48.2	35.8	56.2

We see that the variability between batches is significant ($P = .013$). The variance component estimates are as follows:

$$\hat{\sigma}^2 = 2123.0 \quad \text{and} \quad \hat{\sigma}^2_{\text{batch}} = \frac{7593.0 - 2123.0}{10} = 547.0.$$

Hence $\hat{\sigma}^2_Y = 2123.0 + 547.0 = 2670.0$. The batch-to-batch variation accounts for about 20% of the total variation. ◆

12.4 RANDOMIZED BLOCK DESIGN

12.4.1 Model and Estimates of Its Parameters

More precise comparisons between treatments are possible when an experiment is conducted as a **randomized block (RB) design**. As we saw in Chapter 3, blocking helps to reduce the experimental error variation caused by the differences between the experimental units by grouping them into homogeneous sets (called **blocks**). Treatments are randomly assigned within each block.

In addition to the treatment factor A with $a \geq 2$ levels we now have a blocking factor B with $b \geq 2$ levels. Suppose that each block consists of a experimental units (called **plots**) and the a treatments are randomly assigned to them within each block. Let y_{ij} denote the observation on the ith treatment in the jth block.

For example, reconsider the golf ball experiment mentioned at the beginning of this chapter, but now suppose that to eliminate the confounding caused due to fatigue to a single golfer, we use 10 golfers to hit the 30 balls. To control for golfers' skills, each golfer hits the three types of balls in a random order (determined separately for each golfer). This is an RB design in which the ball type is the treatment factor with $a = 3$ levels and the golfer is the blocking factor with $b = 10$ levels. The flight distance for the ith type of ball hit by the jth golfer is y_{ij}, $i = 1, 2, 3$, $j = 1, 2, \ldots, 10$.

We assume that the r.v.'s Y_{ij} corresponding to the observed values y_{ij} are independently distributed as $N(\mu_{ij}, \sigma^2)$, where the μ_{ij} are the unknown "cell means" and σ^2 is an unknown error variance common to all observations. We introduce the following "dot" notation, where a dot in place of a subscript denotes that an average is taken over that subscript. Thus let $\bar{\mu}_{..} = (\sum_{i=1}^{a} \sum_{j=1}^{b} \mu_{ij})/ab$ be the grand average of all μ_{ij}'s, $\bar{\mu}_{i.} = (\sum_{i=1}^{a} \mu_{ij})/a$ be the average of μ_{ij}'s for the ith treatment, and $\bar{\mu}_{.j} = (\sum_{j=1}^{b} \mu_{ij})/b$ be the average of μ_{ij}'s for the jth block. Next let

$$\mu = \bar{\mu}_{..}, \; \tau_i = \bar{\mu}_{i.} - \bar{\mu}_{..}, \; \beta_j = \bar{\mu}_{.j} - \bar{\mu}_{..}.$$

We write $\mu_{ij} = \mu + \tau_i + \beta_j$ and the **RB design model** as

$$Y_{ij} = \mu + \tau_i + \beta_j + \epsilon_{ij} \qquad (12.16)$$

where the ϵ_{ij} are i.i.d. $N(0, \sigma^2)$ random errors. The interpretation of these parameters is as follows: μ is the **grand mean**; τ_i is called the ith **treatment effect**, which is the difference between the mean response of the ith treatment over all blocks and the grand mean; β_j is called the jth **block effect**, which is the difference between the mean response of the jth block over all treatments and the grand mean. Since the treatment and block effects are defined so that $\sum_{i=1}^{a} \tau_i = 0$ and $\sum_{j=1}^{b} \beta_j = 0$, there are $a - 1$ independent τ_i's and $b - 1$ independent β_j's. Counting the grand mean μ, the model (12.16) has a total of $1 + (a - 1) + (b - 1) = a + b - 1$ unknown parameters and $N = ab$ observations. Thus there are $\nu = ab - (a + b - 1) = (a - 1)(b - 1)$ d.f. for error.

In this model each μ_{ij} is written as

$$\mu_{ij} = \mu + \tau_i + \beta_j = \bar{\mu}_{..} + (\bar{\mu}_{i.} - \bar{\mu}_{..}) + (\bar{\mu}_{.j} - \bar{\mu}_{..}) = \bar{\mu}_{i.} + \bar{\mu}_{.j} - \bar{\mu}_{..}.$$

This means that the terms $\mu_{ij} - \bar{\mu}_{i.} - \bar{\mu}_{.j} + \bar{\mu}_{..}$, which are the contributions due to the particular treatment $\times$ block combinations, are assumed to be zero. We refer to these terms as treatment $\times$ block **interactions**. Assuming no interactions implies that the difference in the mean responses between *any* two treatments is the same across all blocks. To see this, consider two treatments i and i', and note that the difference in their mean responses in the jth block is

$$\mu_{ij} - \mu_{i'j} = (\mu + \tau_i + \beta_j) - (\mu + \tau_{i'} + \beta_j) = \tau_i - \tau_{i'}$$

which is independent of the particular block j. As an example, consider an agricultural trial for comparing several fertilizers where the blocks represent different fields. Then no interaction implies that the difference in the mean yields between any two fertilizers is the same for all fields. We will study models for two factors with interactions in the next chapter.

It is easy to show that the **LS estimates** of the parameters in the model (12.16) are as follows:

$$\hat{\mu} = \bar{y}_{..}, \quad \hat{\tau}_i = \bar{y}_{i.} - \bar{y}_{..}, \quad \hat{\beta}_j = \bar{y}_{.j} - \bar{y}_{..}$$

Note that the estimates $\hat{\tau}_i$ and $\hat{\beta}_j$ satisfy the respective constraints on the τ_i and β_j, namely $\sum_{i=1}^{a} \hat{\tau}_i = 0$ and $\sum_{j=1}^{b} \hat{\beta}_j = 0$. The **fitted values** of the y_{ij} are given by

$$\hat{y}_{ij} = \hat{\mu}_{ij} = \hat{\mu} + \hat{\tau}_i + \hat{\beta}_j = \bar{y}_{..} + (\bar{y}_{i.} - \bar{y}_{..}) + (\bar{y}_{.j} - \bar{y}_{..}) = \bar{y}_{i.} + \bar{y}_{.j} - \bar{y}_{...} \quad (12.17)$$

The **residuals** are

$$e_{ij} = y_{ij} - \hat{y}_{ij} = y_{ij} - \bar{y}_{i.} - \bar{y}_{.j} + \bar{y}_{...} \quad (12.18)$$

EXAMPLE 12.12   (DRIP LOSS IN MEAT LOAVES: PARAMETER ESTIMATES)

Ryan and Joiner[12] give data, shown in Table 12.7, on the percentage drip loss in meat loaves (i.e., the amount of liquid that dripped out of a meat loaf during baking divided by the original weight of the loaf). The goal was to compare the eight oven positions, which might differ due to temperature variations. Three batches of loaves were baked in turn, each batch consisting of eight loaves. The loaves from each batch were randomly placed in the eight positions. This is an RB design with oven positions as treatments and batches of loaves as blocks. Estimate the position and batch effects.

Table 12.7 Drip Loss in Meat Loaves

Oven	Batch			Position
Position	1	2	3	Mean
1	7.33	8.11	8.06	7.833
2	3.22	3.72	4.28	3.740
3	3.28	5.11	4.56	4.317
4	6.44	5.78	8.61	6.943
5	3.83	6.50	7.72	6.017
6	3.28	5.11	5.56	4.650
7	5.06	5.11	7.83	6.000
8	4.44	4.28	6.33	5.017
Batch Mean	4.610	5.465	6.619	5.565

The oven position means and the batch means are given in the margins of Table 12.7. The overall mean is 5.565. From these means we can calculate the position and batch effects as follows:

$\hat{\tau}_1 = 7.833 - 5.565 = +2.268$ $\hat{\tau}_5 = 6.017 - 5.565 = +0.452$ $\hat{\beta}_1 = 4.610 - 5.565 = -0.955$
$\hat{\tau}_2 = 3.740 - 5.565 = -1.825$ $\hat{\tau}_6 = 4.650 - 5.565 = -0.915$ $\hat{\beta}_2 = 5.465 - 5.565 = -0.100$
$\hat{\tau}_3 = 4.317 - 5.565 = -1.248$ $\hat{\tau}_7 = 6.000 - 5.565 = +0.435$ $\hat{\beta}_3 = 6.619 - 5.565 = +1.054$
$\hat{\tau}_4 = 6.943 - 5.565 = +1.378$ $\hat{\tau}_8 = 5.017 - 5.565 = -0.548$.

[12] B. F. Ryan and B. L. Joiner (1994), *MINITAB Handbook*, 3rd ed., Belmont, CA: Duxbury Press, p. 268.

We see that positions 1 and 4 have substantially higher than average drip loss, while position 2 has substantially lower than average drip loss. It turns out that the five positions with the highest average drip losses (positions 1, 4, 5, 7, and 8) had thermometers inserted into the loaves to measure temperature. Since the oven positions are confounded by inserted thermometers, these observed differences cannot be attributed to the positions. ◆

12.4.2 Analysis of Variance

Decompose each y_{ij} into four components by substituting in (12.16) the LS estimates of μ, τ_i and β_j and the residual:

$$y_{ij} = \bar{y}_{..} + (\bar{y}_{i.} - \bar{y}_{..}) + (\bar{y}_{.j} - \bar{y}_{..}) + e_{ij}$$

or equivalently

$$y_{ij} - \bar{y}_{..} = (\bar{y}_{i.} - \bar{y}_{..}) + (\bar{y}_{.j} - \bar{y}_{..}) + e_{ij}.$$

Squaring both sides and summing over $i = 1, 2, \ldots, a$ and $j = 1, 2, \ldots, b$ gives

$$\sum_{i=1}^{a}\sum_{j=1}^{b}(y_{ij} - \bar{y}_{..})^2 = \sum_{i=1}^{a}\sum_{j=1}^{b}\left[(\bar{y}_{i.} - \bar{y}_{..}) + (\bar{y}_{.j} - \bar{y}_{..}) + e_{ij}\right]^2.$$

Expanding the square in the right side of the equation results in three cross-product terms, all of which sum to zero:

$$2\sum_{i=1}^{a}\sum_{j=1}^{b}(\bar{y}_{i.} - \bar{y}_{..})(\bar{y}_{.j} - \bar{y}_{..}) = 0, \quad 2\sum_{i=1}^{a}\sum_{j=1}^{b}(\bar{y}_{.j} - \bar{y}_{..})e_{ij} = 0,$$

$$\text{and} \quad 2\sum_{i=1}^{a}\sum_{j=1}^{b}(\bar{y}_{i.} - \bar{y}_{..})e_{ij} = 0.$$

For example, the first cross-product term sums to zero because $\sum_{j=1}^{b}(\bar{y}_{.j} - \bar{y}_{..}) = 0$. Therefore the expression simplifies to

$$\underbrace{\sum_{i=1}^{a}\sum_{j=1}^{b}(y_{ij} - \bar{y}_{..})^2}_{\text{SST}} = \sum_{i=1}^{a}\sum_{j=1}^{b}(\bar{y}_{i.} - \bar{y}_{..})^2 + \sum_{i=1}^{a}\sum_{j=1}^{b}(\bar{y}_{.j} - \bar{y}_{..})^2 + \sum_{i=1}^{a}\sum_{j=1}^{b}e_{ij}^2$$

$$= b\underbrace{\sum_{i=1}^{a}\hat{\tau}_i^2}_{\text{SSA}} + a\underbrace{\sum_{j=1}^{b}\hat{\beta}_j^2}_{\text{SSB}} + \underbrace{\sum_{i=1}^{a}\sum_{j=1}^{b}e_{ij}^2}_{\text{SSE}}. \tag{12.19}$$

In (12.19) the left hand side of the equation is just the total sum of squares (denoted by SST or SS_{total}), the first term on the right hand side is the sum of squares between the treatment means, $\bar{y}_{i.}$ (denoted by SSA or $\text{SS}_{\text{treatments}}$), the second term is the sum of squares between the block means, $\bar{y}_{.j}$ (denoted by SSB or SS_{blocks}), and the last term is the SSE. Thus we get the **ANOVA identity** for the RB design:

$$SST = SSA + SSB + SSE.$$

The corresponding partitioning of the d.f. is

$$\underbrace{ab - 1}_{\text{(Total d.f.)}} = \underbrace{a - 1}_{\text{(Treatments d.f.)}} + \underbrace{b - 1}_{\text{(Blocks d.f.)}} + \underbrace{(a - 1)(b - 1)}_{\text{(Error d.f.)}}.$$

The mean squares are computed in the usual way by dividing the sums of squares by their degrees of freedom:

$$MSA = \frac{SSA}{a - 1}, \quad MSB = \frac{SSB}{b - 1}, \quad \text{and} \quad MSE = \frac{SSE}{(a - 1)(b - 1)}.$$

MSE provides an unbiased estimate of σ^2 (assuming that the no interaction model is correct). The ratio $F_A = MSA/MSE$ can be used to perform an F-test of the null hypothesis of no treatment effects, $H_{0A}: \tau_1 = \cdots = \tau_a = 0$: Reject H_{0A} at level α if

$$F_A = \frac{MSA}{MSE} > f_{a-1,v,\alpha}$$

where $v = (a - 1)(b - 1)$ is the error d.f. This test can be derived by using the extra sum of squares method.

The test of no block effects, $H_{0B}: \beta_1 = \cdots = \beta_b = 0$, based on $F_B = MSB/MSE$ can also be carried out the same way: reject H_{0B} at level α if

$$F_B = \frac{MSB}{MSE} > f_{b-1,v,\alpha}.$$

This test may be used to check whether blocking is effective or not. If the block effects are not significantly large then blocking is not effective and may perhaps be dispensed with in future experiments.

Table 12.8 summarizes the above calculations.

Table 12.8 ANOVA Table for a Randomized Block Design

Source of Variation (Source)	Sum of Squares (SS)	Degrees of Freedom (d.f.)	Mean Square (MS)	F
Treatments (A)	$SSA = b \sum \hat{\tau}_i^2$	$a - 1$	$MSA = \frac{SSA}{a-1}$	$F_A = \frac{MSA}{MSE}$
Blocks (B)	$SSB = a \sum \hat{\beta}_j^2$	$b - 1$	$MSB = \frac{SSB}{b-1}$	$F_B = \frac{MSB}{MSE}$
Error	$SSE = \sum\sum e_{ij}^2$	$(a - 1)(b - 1)$	$MSE = \frac{SSE}{(a-1)(b-1)}$	
Total	$SST = \sum\sum(y_{ij} - \bar{y}_{..})^2$	$ab - 1$		

EXAMPLE 12.13   (DRIP LOSS IN MEAT LOAVES: ANALYSIS OF VARIANCE)

Give the ANOVA table for the meat loaf drip loss data from Table 12.7. Conduct the F-test for the significance of the position differences.

The ANOVA table including the F-statistic for the position effects is shown in Table 12.9. Since $F_{positions} = 8.70 > f_{7,14,.01} = 4.28$, the positions are significantly different from each other at $\alpha = .01$. Similarly, since $F_{batches} = 12.24 > f_{2,14,.01} = 6.51$, the batches also differ significantly from each other. Thus blocking by batches has been effective.   ◆

Table 12.9 ANOVA Table for the Meat Loaf Data

Source	SS	d.f.	MS	F
Position	40.396	7	5.771	8.70
Batch	16.259	2	8.130	12.24
Error	9.290	14	0.664	
Total	65.945	23		

12.4.3 Model Diagnostics Using Residual Plots

To check the normality assumption we make a normal plot of the residuals. To check the constant variance assumption we plot the residuals against the fitted values.

EXAMPLE 12.14   (DRIP LOSS IN MEAT LOAVES: RESIDUAL PLOTS)

Check the normality and the constant variance assumptions for the meat loaf data from Table 12.7.

The residuals and fitted values can be calculated, stored, and plotted using a computer package. They are shown in Table 12.10. As an illustration of formulas (12.17) and (12.18) we calculate

$$\hat{y}_{11} = \bar{y}_{1.} + \bar{y}_{.1} - \bar{y}_{..} = 7.833 + 4.610 - 5.565 = 6.878 \quad \text{and} \quad e_{11} = y_{11} - \hat{y}_{11} = 7.330 - 6.878 = 0.452.$$

Table 12.10 Fitted Values and Residuals for the Meat Loaf Data

Position	Fitted Values Batch			Residuals Batch		
	1	2	3	1	2	3
1	6.878	7.738	8.888	0.452	0.376	−0.828
2	2.785	3.640	4.794	0.435	0.080	−0.514
3	3.362	4.217	5.371	−0.082	0.893	−0.811
4	5.989	6.844	7.998	0.451	−1.064	0.613
5	5.062	5.917	7.071	−1.232	0.583	0.649
6	3.695	4.550	5.704	−0.415	0.560	−0.144
7	5.045	5.900	7.054	0.015	−0.790	0.776
8	4.062	4.917	6.071	0.378	−0.637	0.259

The normal plot and the plot of residuals against fitted values are shown in Figures 12.8 and 12.9, respectively. We see that the normal plot is not quite linear; thus the normality assumption appears to be violated. The residual plot against the fitted values also has a somewhat conical pattern, suggesting that the error variance may be increasing with the cell mean. There are no obvious outliers in the data. ◆

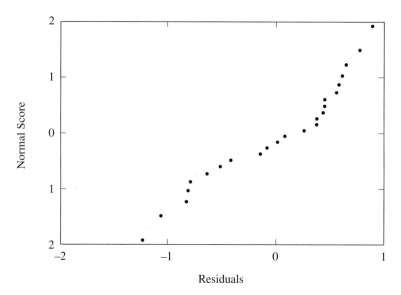

Figure 12.8   Normal Plot of Residuals for the Meat Loaf Data

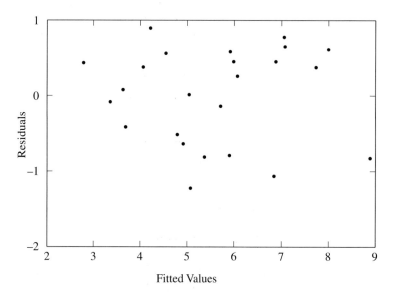

Figure 12.9   Plot of Residuals vs. the Fitted Values for the Meat Loaf Data

12.4.4 Multiple Comparisons of Treatment Effects

For the purpose of making multiple comparisons between the treatments, the RB design can be treated the same as the CR design, except that $s = \sqrt{\text{MSE}}$ is now based on $v = (a-1)(b-1)$ d.f. and the common sample size per treatment is the number of blocks b. Thus, e.g., the Tukey intervals are:

$$\bar{y}_{i\cdot} - \bar{y}_{j\cdot} - q_{a,v,\alpha}\frac{s}{\sqrt{b}} \leq \tau_i - \tau_j \leq \bar{y}_{i\cdot} - \bar{y}_{j\cdot} + q_{a,v,\alpha}\frac{s}{\sqrt{b}}.$$

Treatments i and j are declared significantly different from each other at FWE $= \alpha$ if

$$|\bar{y}_{i\cdot} - \bar{y}_{j\cdot}| > q_{a,v,\alpha}\frac{s}{\sqrt{b}}.$$

Stepwise methods can also be used in the same way.

EXAMPLE 12.15   (DRIP LOSS IN MEAT LOAVES: PAIRWISE COMPARISONS BETWEEN POSITIONS)

Refer to Example 12.13. Apply the Tukey method to determine the oven positions that differ significantly from each other at $\alpha = .05$.

The critical value that any pairwise difference between the position means must exceed in order to be significant using the Tukey method is

$$q_{a,v,\alpha}\frac{s}{\sqrt{b}} = q_{8,14,.05}\frac{0.664}{\sqrt{3}} = (4.99)\frac{0.664}{\sqrt{3}} = 1.913.$$

Pairwise comparisons between the positions are facilitated if the position means are written in ascending order, and then comparisons are carried out as in a stepwise method except that a constant critical value = 1.913 is used. The results of these comparisons can be summarized as shown below, where any two means that are not connected by a common line are significantly different from each other.

Position 2	Position 3	Position 6	Position 8	Position 7	Position 5	Position 4	Position 1
3.740	4.317	4.650	5.017	6.000	6.017	6.943	7.833

Thus positions 1 and 4 differ significantly from positions 2, 3, 6, and 8; also positions 5 and 7 differ significantly from position 2.   ◆

12.4.5 Mixed Effects Model for the RB Design

Thus far we have treated both the treatment and the blocking factor as fixed. However, the blocking factor is random in many applications; e.g., in the meat loaf example discussed above the batches are random. When the treatment factor is fixed and the blocking factor is random, the corresponding model is called a **mixed effects model**. In model (12.16) the treatment effects τ_i have the same interpretation as before, but the block effects β_j are assumed to be i.i.d. $N(0, \sigma_B^2)$ r.v.'s, which are independent of the $\epsilon_{ij} \sim N(0, \sigma^2)$, where σ_B^2 is the variance component for the blocks. The variance of the Y_{ij} can be expressed as the sum of two variance components: $\sigma_Y^2 = \sigma_B^2 + \sigma^2$.

Even if the blocks are random, the analysis of fixed treatment effects remains the same as before. Specifically, it can be shown that

$$E(\text{MSA}) = \sigma^2 + \frac{b \sum_{i=1}^{a} \tau_i^2}{a - 1}, \quad E(\text{MSB}) = \sigma^2 + a\sigma_B^2, \quad \text{and} \quad E(\text{MSE}) = \sigma^2.$$

The unbiased estimates of the variance components are given by

$$\hat{\sigma}^2 = \text{MSE} \quad \text{and} \quad \hat{\sigma}_B^2 = \frac{\text{MSB} - \text{MSE}}{a}.$$

EXAMPLE 12.16   (DRIP LOSS IN MEAT LOAVES: VARIANCE COMPONENT ESTIMATES)

Assuming that the batches are random, estimate the variance components for batches and error for the data in Table 12.2.

From Example 12.13 we have that MSB = 8.130 and MSE = 0.664. Also, $a = 8$. Therefore,

$$\hat{\sigma}^2 = 0.664 \quad \text{and} \quad \hat{\sigma}_B^2 = \frac{8.130 - 0.664}{8} = 0.993.$$

Hence $\hat{\sigma}_Y^2 = 0.993 + 0.664 = 1.597$. The variability due to batches accounts for about 62% of the total variability.   ◆

12.5   CHAPTER SUMMARY

This chapter discusses design and analysis of single factor experiments. The levels of the factor are called **treatments**. A **completely randomized (CR) design** randomizes $N = \sum_{i=1}^{a} n_i$ experimental units to a treatments with n_i units on the ith treatment. We assume that the observations y_{ij} $(j = 1, 2, \ldots, n_i)$ from the ith treatment are a random sample from an $N(\mu_i, \sigma^2)$ distribution and the samples from the a treatments are mutually independent. The parameters $\tau_i = \mu_i - \mu$, where $\mu = \sum n_i \mu_i / N$ is the grand mean, are called the **treatment effects**. They are subject to the side condition: $\sum_{i=1}^{a} n_i \tau_i = 0$.

The **one-way analysis of variance (ANOVA)** partitions the **total sum of squares (SST)** into two components: the **treatment sum of squares (SSA)** and the **error sum of squares (SSE)**. There is a corresponding partition of the degrees of freedom (d.f.):

$$\underbrace{N - 1}_{\text{(Total d.f.)}} = \underbrace{a - 1}_{\text{(Treatments d.f.)}} + \underbrace{N - a}_{\text{(Error d.f.)}}$$

The ratio of a sum of squares to its d.f. is called a mean square. The **error mean square (MSE)** gives an unbiased estimate of σ^2 with $\nu = N - a$ d.f. The overall null hypothesis

$H_0: \mu_1 = \mu_2 = \cdots = \mu_a$ or equivalently $H_0: \tau_1 = \tau_2 = \cdots = \tau_a = 0$ is tested using the statistic

$$F = \frac{\text{MSA}}{\text{MSE}}$$

which has an F-distribution with $a - 1$ and $N - a$ d.f.

Multiple comparison methods are useful for identifying the treatments that differ from each other. Multiple tests can result in excessive false significances. Therefore we control the type I **familywise error rate (FWE)** of finding at least one false significant difference at a specified level α. The **LSD method**, which does pairwise two-sample t-tests each at level α, does not control the FWE. The **Bonferroni method** controls the FWE conservatively at level α by doing each pairwise t-test at level α/k, where $k = \binom{a}{2}$ is the number of pairwise comparisons. The **Tukey method** is exact under $H_0: \mu_1 = \mu_2 = \cdots = \mu_a$ when the sample sizes n_i are equal (and slightly conservative when the n_i are unequal). Stepwise multiple testing methods are less conservative (and hence more powerful). Multiple comparison methods are also available for more general comparisons, called **contrasts**.

If the experimental treatments are selected at random from a large population of treatments, and the results of the experiment are to be generalized to this population, then a **random effects model** is applicable. This model differs from the **fixed effects model** used in the above analysis in that it assumes that the treatment effects τ_i are not fixed unknown constants, but are r.v.'s with an $N(0, \sigma_A^2)$ distribution, where σ_A^2 is the variance of the treatment population. The variance of the individual observations is the sum of the treatment variance σ_A^2 and the error variance σ^2. These variances are called the **variance components**. The main goal in a random effects ANOVA is the estimation of the variance components. For a balanced design, the estimates are given by

$$\hat{\sigma}^2 = \text{MSE} \quad \text{and} \quad \hat{\sigma}_A^2 = \frac{\text{MSA} - \text{MSE}}{n}.$$

In a **randomized block (RB) design**, the a treatments are randomly assigned within b blocks, each consisting of a similar experimental units. The objective of blocking is to enable more precise comparisons between the treatments. An **additive model** is assumed, i.e., the treatment $\times$ block interactions are ignored. The ANOVA partitions the **total sum of squares (SST)** into three components: the **treatment sum of squares (SSA)**, the **block sum of squares (SSB)**, and the **error sum of squares (SSE)**. The corresponding partitioning of the d.f. is

$$\underbrace{ab - 1}_{\text{(Total d.f.)}} = \underbrace{a - 1}_{\text{(Treatments d.f.)}} + \underbrace{b - 1}_{\text{(Blocks d.f.)}} + \underbrace{(a - 1)(b - 1)}_{\text{(Error d.f.)}}.$$

The ratios of mean squares, namely,

$$F_A = \frac{\text{MSA}}{\text{MSE}} \quad \text{and} \quad F_B = \frac{\text{MSB}}{\text{MSE}}$$

provide the F-statistics for testing the hypotheses of no treatment effects and no block effects, respectively.

■ EXERCISES

Section 12.1

12.1   A sample of 20 different types of cereals was taken from each of three grocery store shelves (1, 2, and 3, counting from the floor). A summary of the sugar content (grams per serving) and dietary fiber (grams per serving) of the cereals is given below.[13]

Location	n	Sugar Mean	Sugar SD	Fiber Mean	Fiber SD
Shelf 1	20	4.80	2.138	1.68	1.166
Shelf 2	20	9.85	1.985	0.95	1.162
Shelf 3	20	6.10	1.865	2.17	1.277

(a) Calculate 95% CI's for the sugar and fiber contents of the cereals on the three shelves. Are there any obvious differences among the sugar content or the fiber content?

(b) Construct an ANOVA table and test whether there are significant differences in sugar content between the three shelves. Use $\alpha = .05$. Interpret your results. Repeat for fiber content.

(c) It is noted that Shelf 2 is at the eye level of grade school age children. What does this say about the grocery store strategy for locating cereals on shelves?

12.2   ■ The effect of caffeine levels on performing a simple finger tapping task was investigated in a double blind study. Thirty male college students were trained in finger tapping and randomly assigned to receive three different doses of caffeine (0, 100, or 200 mg) with 10 students per dose group. Two hours following the caffeine treatment, students were asked to finger tap and the numbers of taps per minute were counted.[14] The data are tabulated below.

Caffeine Dose	Finger Taps per Minute
0 mg	242 245 244 248 247 248 242 244 246 242
100 mg	248 246 245 247 248 250 247 246 243 244
200 mg	246 248 250 252 248 250 246 248 245 250

(a) Make side-by-side box plots for the three groups. Do these plots indicate any obvious differences between the groups?

(b) Construct an ANOVA table and test whether there are significant differences in finger tapping between the students treated with different doses of caffeine. Use $\alpha = .10$. Interpret your results.

(c) Check the normality and constant variance assumptions by making residual plots.

---

[13] Adapted from DAZL "Healthy Breakfast" data file from the Web site http://www.cmu.stat.edu/~DAZL

[14] N. R. Draper and H. Smith (1981), *Applied Regression Analysis*, 2nd ed., New York: Wiley, p. 425. Reprinted in *Small Data Sets*, p. 40.

12.3 ■ Three genetic types of fruit flies were compared in terms of the average number of eggs a female lays per day over the first 14 days of life.[15] The resistant type was bred for resistance to DDT, the susceptible type was bred for susceptibility to DDT, and the control type was a nonselected control strain. The data are given below.

Type	Average Eggs Laid per Day												
Control	35.4	27.4	19.3	41.8	20.3	37.6	36.9	37.3	28.2	23.4	33.7	29.2	41.7
	22.6	40.4	34.4	30.4	14.9	51.8	33.8	37.9	29.5	42.4	36.6	47.4	
Resistant	12.8	21.6	14.8	23.1	34.6	19.7	22.6	29.6	16.4	20.3	29.3	14.9	27.3
	22.4	27.5	20.3	38.7	26.4	23.7	26.1	29.5	38.6	44.4	23.2	23.6	
Susceptible	38.4	32.9	48.5	20.9	11.6	22.3	30.2	33.4	26.7	39.0	12.8	14.6	12.2
	23.1	29.4	16.0	20.1	23.3	22.9	22.5	15.1	31.0	16.9	16.1	10.8	

  (a) Make side-by-side box plots for the three types. Do these plots indicate any obvious differences between the groups?

  (b) Construct an ANOVA table and test whether there are significant differences in fecundity (as measured by the number of eggs laid per day) among the three types. Use $\alpha = .05$. Interpret your results.

  (c) Check the normality and constant variance assumptions by making residual plots.

12.4 ■ The salinity of water samples taken from three separate sites in the Bimini Lagoon, Bahamas, was measured.[16] The data are given below.

Site I	37.54	37.01	36.71	37.03	37.32	37.01	37.03	37.70	37.36	36.75	37.45	38.85
Site II	40.17	40.80	39.76	39.70	40.79	40.44	39.79	39.38				
Site III	39.04	39.21	39.05	38.24	38.53	38.71	38.89	38.66	38.51	40.08		

  (a) Make side-by-side box plots for the three sites. Do these plots indicate any obvious differences between the salinity of the sites?

  (b) Construct an ANOVA table and test whether there are significant differences in the salinity at the different sites of the lagoon. Use $\alpha = .01$. Interpret your results.

  (c) Check the normality and constant variance assumptions by making residual plots.

12.5 ■ The hemoglobin levels were measured on patients with three different types of sickle cell disease: classic sickle cell disease with two S genes (HB SS), the combined problem of sickle cell trait with thalassemia (HB S/-thalassemia), and the variant of sickle cell disease which has one S and one C gene (HB SC). The purpose was to investigate whether hemoglobin levels differ with the type of disease.[17] The data are given below.

---

[15] R. R. Sokal and F. J. Rohlf (1981), *Biometry*, San Francisco: W.H. Freeman, p. 239. Reprinted in *Small Data Sets*, p. 16.

[16] R. Till (1974), *Statistical Methods for the Earth Scientist*, London: Macmillan, p. 104. Reprinted in *Small Data Sets*, p. 201.

[17] E. Anionwu, D. Watford, M. Brozovic, and B. Kirkwood (1981), "Sickle cell disease in a British urban community," *British Medical Journal*, **282**, pp. 283–286. Reprinted in *Small Data Sets*, p. 247.

HB SS	7.2	7.7	8.0	8.1	8.3	8.4	8.4	8.5
	8.6	8.7	9.1	9.1	9.1	9.8	10.1	10.3
HB S/-thalassemia	8.1	9.2	10.0	10.4	10.6	10.9	11.1	11.9
	12.0	12.1						
HB SC	10.7	11.3	11.5	11.6	11.7	11.8	12.0	12.1
	12.3	12.6	12.6	13.3	13.3	13.8	13.9	

(a) Make side-by-side box plots for the three groups. Do these plots indicate any obvious differences between the groups?

(b) Construct an ANOVA table and test whether there are significant differences in hemoglobin levels between patients with different types of sickle cell disease. Use $\alpha = .01$. Interpret your results.

(c) Check the normality and constant variance assumptions by making residual plots.

12.6 ◨ Members of the New York Choral Society are organized according to vocal range. Among male singers, the parts from lowest to highest pitch are Bass 1, Bass 2, Tenor 1, and Tenor 2. The heights of male singers are given below.[18]

Part	Heights in Inches												
Tenor 1	69	72	71	66	76	74	71	66	68	67	70	65	72
	70	68	64	73	66	68	67	64					
Tenor 2	68	73	69	71	69	76	71	69	71	66	69	71	71
	71	69	70	69	68	70	68	69					
Bass 1	72	70	72	69	73	71	72	68	68	71	66	68	71
	73	73	70	68	70	75	68	71	70	74	70	75	75
	69	72	71	70	71	68	70	75	72	66	72	70	69
Bass 2	72	75	67	75	74	72	72	74	72	72	74	70	66
	68	75	68	70	72	67	70	70	69	72	71	74	75

(a) Make side-by-side box plots for the four groups. Do these plots indicate any obvious differences between the groups?

(b) Construct an ANOVA table and test whether there are significant differences in height among singers of different pitch. Use $\alpha = .05$. Interpret your results.

(c) Check the normality and constant variance assumptions by making residual plots.

12.7 ◨ Anorexia in young girls was treated using three approaches to help them gain weight: control (standard) treatment, cognitive behavioral treatment, and family therapy. The following table provides the weights of the girls before treatment was initiated and their weight change (posttreatment minus pretreatment) after a fixed period of time.[19]

---

[18] J. M. Chambers, W. S. Cleveland, B. Kleiner, and P. A. Tukey (1983), *Graphical Methods for Data Analysis*, Boston: Duxbury Press, p. 350. Reprinted in *Small Data Sets*, p. 276.

[19] B. Everitt (private communication). Adapted from data reprinted in *Small Data Sets*, p. 229. Although the unit of weight is given as kg in this reference, it appears that the correct unit should be lb.

Treatment Group	Weight before Treatment
Control	80.7 89.4 91.8 74.0 78.1 88.3 87.3 75.1 80.6 78.4
	77.6 88.7 81.3 78.1 70.5 77.3 85.2
Behavioral	80.5 84.9 81.5 82.6 79.9 88.7 94.9 76.3 81.0 80.5
	85.0 89.2 81.3 76.5 70.0 80.4 83.3
Family	83.8 83.3 86.0 82.5 86.7 79.6 76.9 94.2 73.4 80.5
	81.6 82.1 77.6 83.5 89.9 86.0 87.3

Treatment Group	Weight Change (Post − Pre) after Treatment
Control	−0.5 −9.3 −5.4 12.3 −2.0 −10.2 −12.2 11.6 −7.1 6.2
	−0.2 −9.2 8.3 3.3 11.3 0.0 −1.0
Behavioral	1.7 0.7 −0.1 −0.7 −3.5 14.9 3.5 17.1 −7.6 1.6
	11.7 6.1 1.1 −4.0 20.9 −9.1 2.1
Family	11.4 11.0 5.5 9.4 13.6 −2.9 −0.1 7.4 21.5 −5.3
	−3.8 13.4 13.1 9.0 3.9 5.7 10.7

(a) The purpose of random treatment assignment is to ensure that the groups are equal in all respects except the treatment intervention. To check the adequacy of the random assignments, make side-by-side box plots of pretreatment weights for the three groups. Do these plots indicate any differences between the groups?

(b) Construct an ANOVA table and test whether there are significant differences in the pretreatment weights. Use $\alpha = .05$.

(c) To evaluate the effectiveness of treatment interventions, make side-by-side box plots of the changes in weights for the three groups. Do these plots indicate any differences between the groups?

(d) Construct an ANOVA table and test whether there are significant differences in the weight changes. Use $\alpha = .05$.

Section 12.2

12.8 Refer to the cereal data of Exercise 12.1. Make pairwise comparisons using the Bonferroni and Tukey methods to determine which shelf cereals differ in sugar content at $\alpha = .05$. Repeat for fiber content.

12.9 Refer to the water sample data of Exercise 12.4. Make pairwise comparisons using the Tukey and Ryan methods to determine which sites differ in water salinity at $\alpha = .05$. Compare the results.

12.10 Refer to the sickle cell disease data of Exercise 12.5. Calculate 99% simultaneous confidence intervals using the Bonferroni and Tukey methods for the mean differences of hemoglobin levels between different types of sickle cell disease. Compare these intervals with separate 99% t-intervals (LSD method). Summarize the results.

12.11 Refer to the height data of Exercise 12.6. Calculate 90% simultaneous confidence intervals using the Tukey method for the mean differences of heights of different groups (Tenor 1, Tenor 2, Bass 1, and Bass 2).

12.12   Refer to the caffeine data of Exercise 12.2. Compare finger tap rates of the 100 mg and 200 mg caffeine groups with the control group using Dunnett's method with $\alpha = .10$. Interpret the results.

12.13   Refer to the fruit-fly data of Exercise 12.3.

    (a) Which strains differ from each other in terms of the average number of eggs laid? Use Tukey's method at $\alpha = .05$ to address this question.

    (b) Which of the selected strains differ from the control in terms of the average number of eggs laid? Use Dunnett's method at $\alpha = .05$ to address this question.

    (c) Generally, only one of these two questions is of primary interest. If the primary question is to compare the two selected strains with the control group, why would it be inefficient to use Tukey's method for all pairwise comparisons?

12.14   Refer to the anorexia data of Exercise 12.7. Calculate 95% simultaneous confidence intervals using Dunnett's method to compare the weight changes of the two treatment groups with the control group. What do your results indicate about the effectiveness of the treatments?

12.15   Three groups are compared in a one-way layout experiment with sample sizes $n_1 = 8, n_2 = 6, n_3 = 10$. To compare the first group with the other two groups, we use the contrast $2\bar{y}_1 - (\bar{y}_2 + \bar{y}_3)$. Find the standard error of this contrast if MSE = 25.

12.16   ◼ Uniformly strong cables are needed to transmit high voltage electricity. In one design, each cable was composed of 12 wires. Wires in a sample of 9 cables were tested for tensile strength (measured in kg). The results are given below.[20]

Cable 1	Cable 2	Cable 3	Cable 4	Cable 5	Cable 6	Cable 7	Cable 8	Cable 9
329	340	345	328	341	339	347	339	342
327	330	327	344	340	340	341	340	346
332	325	335	342	335	342	345	347	347
348	328	338	350	336	341	340	345	348
337	338	330	335	339	336	350	350	355
328	332	334	332	340	342	346	348	351
328	335	335	328	342	347	345	341	333
330	340	340	340	345	345	342	342	347
345	336	337	335	341	341	340	337	350
334	339	342	337	338	340	339	346	347
328	335	333	337	346	336	330	340	348
330	329	335	340	347	342	338	345	341

    (a) Construct an ANOVA table and test whether there are significant differences between the mean tensile strengths of the cables. Use $\alpha = .05$.

    (b) Cables 1–4 were made from one lot of raw material, while cables 5–9 were made from another lot. Calculate a 95% confidence interval for the difference between

---

[20] A. Hald (1952), *Statistical Theory with Engineering Applications*, New York: Wiley, p. 434. Reprinted in *Small Data Sets*, p. 105.

the average mean tensile strengths of cables 1–4 vs. cables 5–9, i.e., for the contrast $\frac{1}{4}(\mu_1+\mu_2+\mu_3+\mu_4)-\frac{1}{5}(\mu_5+\mu_6+\mu_7+\mu_8+\mu_9)$. Is there a significant difference at $\alpha = .05$?

12.17 The Chicago Bulls was one of the best professional basketball teams of the 1990s. Below are some statistics on their five main starters from December 1997, based on 11 games in which they all played.

Player		Jordan	Rodman	Kukoc	Longley	Harper
Points:	Mean	28.46	5.73	14.73	11.91	13.00
	SD	8.84	2.65	4.86	4.85	5.20
Rebounds:	Mean	6.45	17.55	4.18	5.73	4.73
	SD	3.27	6.11	2.11	2.37	2.05
Assists:	Mean	3.54	2.55	5.82	3.09	2.82
	SD	1.37	1.86	2.71	0.83	1.47

(a) It is evident that Michael Jordan is the highest scorer for the Bulls. However, among the remaining four starters, does one score significantly more points than others? Use Hsu's method to answer this question using $\alpha = .05$.

(b) Dennis Rodman is without question the top rebounder for the Bulls. However, among the remaining four starters, does one get significantly more rebounds than others? Use Hsu's method to answer this question using $\alpha = .05$.

(c) Use Hsu's method with $\alpha = .05$ to determine if Kukoc has significantly more assists than the other starters.

Section 12.3

12.18 ■ Different batches of rubber made by a manufacturing process are checked for tear strength by testing 12 samples from each batch. The sample means and SD's for 10 batches are as follows:

				Tear Strength (lb./in.^{2})						
Batch	1	2	3	4	5	6	7	8	9	10
Mean	36.76	34.31	37.61	33.78	35.43	33.22	33.53	33.68	33.24	32.98
SD	1.81	4.92	2.83	5.32	1.95	4.08	1.19	1.58	1.22	3.96

(a) Construct an ANOVA table from the sample means and SD's of the batches.

(b) Estimate σ^2_{Batch} and σ^2_{Error}. What percent of the total error variation is attributable to differences between batches?

12.19 We want to use the data from Exercise 12.18 to construct a control chart to monitor the mean tear strength of batches of rubber. Sample means of $n = 12$ samples from each batch will be plotted on the chart. The control limits should take into account the natural batch-to-batch variability in addition to the error variability.

(a) Show that

$$\text{Var}(\bar{Y}) = \sigma^2_{\bar{Y}} = \sigma^2_{Batch} + \frac{\sigma^2_{Error}}{n}.$$

(b) The three sigma control limits are given by $\bar{\bar{y}} \pm 3\hat{\sigma}_{\bar{y}}$. Use the estimates of σ^2_{Batch} and σ^2_{Error} from part (b) of Exercise 12.18 to calculate these limits. Check if the sample means of the 10 batches fall within these limits, indicating that the process is under control.

12.20   Refer to the data on tensile strengths of wires in nine cables from Exercise 12.16. In fact, the nine cables should be treated as a random sample from a population of all cables, i.e., the cables is a random factor. Estimate the variance components, σ^2, between cables and σ^2 between wires in a cable. What percent of the total error variation is attributable to differences between cables?

Section 12.4

12.21   ◼ Four methods of manufacturing penicillin were compared in a randomized block design. The blocks are blends of the raw material, corn steep liquor, known to be quite variable. The yield of each method for five blends is given below.[21]

	Method			
Blend	A	B	C	D
1	89	88	97	94
2	84	77	92	79
3	81	87	87	85
4	87	92	89	84
5	79	81	80	88

(a) Estimate the method effects and blend effects.

(b) Construct an ANOVA table. Are there significant differences between the methods? Are there significant differences between the blends? Use $\alpha = .10$ for both tests.

(c) Check the normality and constant variance assumptions by making residual plots.

12.22   ◼ In baseball, it is often thought that it is tougher to play the outfield in domed stadiums because a player cannot take his eyes off the ball. A player's ability to track down balls in his fielding area or "zone" is measured by a zone rating. The higher the rating, the more skillful the fielder. Zone ratings of Minnesota Twins outfielders for their Metrodome, other domed stadiums, and outdoor stadiums are given below for the 1995 season.[22]

---

[21] G. E. P. Box, W. G. Hunter, and J. S. Hunter (1978), *Statistics for Experimenters*, New York: Wiley, Table 7.1.

[22] J. Dewan and D. Zimda (1996), *1996 Baseball Scoreboard*, Skokie, IL: STATS, INC., p. 27.

Player	Home Dome	Other Domes	Outdoors
Alex Cole	0.797	0.789	0.789
Pedro Munoz	0.769	0.767	0.777
Marty Cordova	0.834	0.848	0.867
Kirby Puckett	0.780	0.774	0.793
Shane Mack	0.829	0.826	0.856
Rich Becker	0.795	0.808	0.848

(a) Analyze the data as an RB design where players are blocks. Construct an ANOVA table and test whether there are significant differences between stadiums at the $\alpha = .05$ level.

(b) Use Tukey's method to identify the differences in zone ratings among the three types of stadiums using $\alpha = .05$.

12.23 Refer to the data from the previous exercise. Compare the average of the mean zone ratings in domed stadiums (home and others) vs. the mean zone rating in outdoor stadiums for the particular players. Use $\alpha = .05$.

12.24 🔳 Cork deposits were collected on the north, east, south, and west sides of each of 28 trees.[23] Trees are a blocking factor in this RB design. The weights of cork deposits collected for each tree are given below.

Tree	Direction N	E	S	W	Tree	Direction N	E	S	W
1	72	66	76	77	15	91	79	100	75
2	60	53	66	63	16	56	68	47	50
3	56	57	64	58	17	79	65	70	61
4	41	29	36	38	18	81	80	68	58
5	32	32	35	36	19	78	55	67	60
6	30	35	34	26	20	46	38	37	38
7	39	39	31	27	21	39	35	34	37
8	42	43	31	25	22	32	30	30	32
9	37	40	31	25	23	60	50	67	54
10	33	29	27	36	24	35	37	48	39
11	32	30	34	28	25	39	36	39	31
12	63	45	74	63	26	50	34	37	40
13	54	46	60	52	27	43	37	39	50
14	47	51	52	43	28	48	54	57	43

---

[23] C. R. Rao (1948), "Tests of significance in multivariate analysis," *Biometrika*, **35**, pp. 58–79. Reprinted in *Small Data Sets*, p. 45.

(a) It is of interest to determine if the weight of the cork deposit is influenced by direction. Estimate the direction effects.

(b) Construct an ANOVA table and test whether there are significant differences in cork weight among the four directions. Use $\alpha = .10$.

(c) Check the normality and constant variance assumptions by making residual plots.

12.25 Refer to the data from the previous exercise. Determine which sides of the trees differ significantly from each other using the Tukey, Ryan, and Newman-Keuls methods at $\alpha = .10$. Compare the results.

12.26 ▪ Blood samples from ten subjects taken over 12 hours at three hour intervals were analyzed for plasma citrate concentrations (micromols/liter).[24] The data are given below.

Person	Time				
	8 am	11 am	2 pm	5 pm	8 pm
1	93	121	112	117	121
2	116	135	114	98	135
3	125	137	119	105	102
4	144	173	148	124	122
5	105	119	125	91	133
6	109	83	109	80	104
7	89	95	88	91	116
8	116	128	122	107	119
9	151	149	141	126	138
10	137	139	125	109	107

Technically, the plasma levels of each person at different times are correlated, but for the purpose of this exercise, analyze the measurements as though they are independent. Determine if the concentrations vary over time.

(a) Plot the plasma levels over time, connecting the measurements for each person to make a profile plot. Are there any times at which plasma levels tend to be higher or lower?

(b) Construct an ANOVA table and test whether there are significant differences between times at $\alpha = .05$ level?

(c) Use the Tukey method to determine which sampling times are significantly different from each other using $\alpha = .05$.

12.27 ▪ Home runs were cranked out at a record pace in 1996. To investigate whether this was due to stronger hitters or more home-run friendly ballparks, the home run per game ratio (HR/G = total home runs divided by total games played) was calculated for 8 new major league baseball parks and 12 parks that were unchanged between 1989 and 1996. If the new parks do not influence the number of home runs hit, then the HR/G ratio of

---

[24] A. H. Anderson, E. B. Jensen, and G. Schou (1981), "Two-way analysis of variance with correlated errors," *International Statistical Review*, **49**, pp. 153–167. Reprinted in *Small Data Sets*, p. 235.

these parks will not differ significantly from the HR/G ratio for the unchanged parks. A summary of these data is given below.[25]

	Major League Parks	
Year	New	Not Changed
1989	1.53	1.57
1990	2.16	1.67
1991	1.85	1.76
1992	1.64	1.36
1993	1.95	1.77
1994	2.20	2.05
1995	2.27	2.00
1996	2.38	2.15

(a) Plot the HR/G ratios over time for the new and unchanged parks, connecting the values for the type of park to make two profile plots. What do these plots tell you about the HR/G ratios for the new vs. unchanged parks?

(b) Analyze the data as an RB design where each year is a block. Construct an ANOVA table and test whether there are significant differences between the new and unchanged parks at the $\alpha = .05$ level.

12.28 This exercise examines how the analysis would change if one were to ignore the effect of a blocking factor in an RB design and treat it as a CR design. Consider the meat loaf data from Table 12.7 for which the analysis of variance is given in Table 12.9.

(a) If the batches are ignored as a blocking factor, what happens to the SS and d.f. for the batches? What happens to the error SS and d.f.? (*Hint:* The total SS, the SS for the positions, and their d.f. remain unchanged.)

(b) Give the ANOVA table that results when the batches are ignored as a blocking factor. Are the differences between the positions now significant at the .01 level using the F-test?

(c) Explain why a nonsignificant result is obtained in (b). Will the statistical significance of the differences between the treatment effects be always reduced if the blocks are ignored in an RB design?

12.29 Duncan (1955)[26] analyzed the data from a field experiment conducted using an RB design with six blocks to compare the mean yields of seven varieties of barley. The sample means are shown in the following table.

Mean Yields of Varieties of Barley (in bushels per acre)							
Variety	A	B	C	D	E	F	G
Sample Mean	49.6	71.2	67.6	61.5	71.3	58.1	61.0

[25] J. Dewan and D. Zimda (1997), *1997 Baseball Scoreboard*, Skokie, IL: STATS, INC., p. 110.

[26] D. B. Duncan (1955), "Multiple range and multiple F tests," *Biometrics*, **11**, pp. 1–42.

The MSE from the ANOVA was 79.64 with 30 d.f. Apply Hsu's method at $\alpha = .10$ to classify the varieties as non-best and possible candidates for the best. Is there one variety that is clearly best?

Advanced Exercises

12.30   In the model (12.1) the treatment effects, τ_i, are defined so that they satisfy the linear constraint $\sum_{i=1}^{a} n_i \tau_i = 0$. Suppose that we define the parameters of the model differently as follows:

$$\mu = \frac{\sum_{i=1}^{a} \mu_i}{a} \quad \text{and} \quad \tau_i = \mu_i - \mu$$

so that the τ_i satisfy the linear constraint $\sum_{i=1}^{a} \tau_i = 0$. Find the LS estimates of μ and the τ_i for this parameterization. How do these LS estimates differ from those given for the model (12.1)? Are the LS estimates of the μ_i the same or different?

12.31   Derive the ANOVA identity (12.5) by expressing the three sums of squares as follows:

$$\text{SST} = \sum_{i=1}^{a} \sum_{j=1}^{n_i} y_{ij}^2 - N\bar{\bar{y}}^2, \quad \text{SSA} = \sum_{i=1}^{a} n_i \bar{y}_i^2 - N\bar{\bar{y}}^2, \quad \text{SSE} = \sum_{i=1}^{a} \sum_{j=1}^{n_i} y_{ij}^2 - \sum_{i=1}^{a} n_i \bar{y}_i^2.$$

12.32   Derive the formula (12.6)

$$E(\text{MSA}) = \sigma^2 + \frac{\sum_{i=1}^{a} n_i \tau_i^2}{a - 1}$$

using the formula for SSA derived in the previous exercise. (*Hint:* Use $E(\bar{Y}_i^2) = \text{Var}(\bar{Y}_i) + [E(\bar{Y}_i)]^2 = \sigma^2/n_i + \mu_i^2$, $E(\bar{\bar{Y}}^2) = \text{Var}(\bar{\bar{Y}}) + [E(\bar{\bar{Y}})]^2 = \sigma^2/N + \mu^2$, and simplify. Note that $\tau_i = \mu_i - \mu$.)

12.33   For $a = 2$ show that the one-way ANOVA F-test is equivalent to the two-sided independent samples t-test of $H_0: \mu_1 = \mu_2$ given in (8.9) by carrying out the following steps.

(a) Show that

$$\text{SSA} = \text{MSA} = n_1(\bar{y}_1 - \bar{\bar{y}})^2 + n_2(\bar{y}_2 - \bar{\bar{y}})^2 = \frac{n_1 n_2}{n_1 + n_2}(\bar{y}_1 - \bar{y}_2)^2.$$

(b) Show that

$$F = \frac{\text{MSA}}{\text{MSE}} = \left(\frac{\bar{y}_1 - \bar{y}_2}{s\sqrt{1/n_1 + 1/n_2}}\right)^2 = t^2.$$

(c) Finally show that the α-level F-test of H_0 rejects whenever the α-level two-sided t-test of H_0 rejects by showing that

$$F > f_{1,\nu,\alpha} \iff |t| > t_{\nu,\alpha/2}.$$

(*Hint:* Use the result that $t_{\nu,\alpha/2}^2 = f_{1,\nu,\alpha}$ from Exercise 5.32.)

12.34   For $a = 2$ show that the ANOVA F-test for an RB design is equivalent to the two-sided t-test of equality of means for a matched pairs design by carrying out the following steps.

(a) Using part (a) of the previous exercise show that

$$\text{SSA} = \text{MSA} = b\{(\bar{y}_{1.} - \bar{y}_{..})^2 + (\bar{y}_{2.} - \bar{y}_{..})^2\} = \left(\frac{\bar{y}_{1.} - \bar{y}_{2.}}{\sqrt{2/b}}\right)^2 = \frac{b\bar{d}^2}{2}$$

where $\bar{d}$ is the mean of the $d_j = y_{1j} - y_{2j}$.

(b) Show that

$$(y_{1j} - \bar{y}_{1.} - \bar{y}_{.j} + \bar{y}_{..})^2 = (y_{2j} - \bar{y}_{2.} - \bar{y}_{.j} + \bar{y}_{..})^2 = \frac{1}{4}(d_j - \bar{d})^2.$$

Hence

$$\text{MSE} = \frac{\sum_{i=1}^{a}\sum_{j=1}^{b}(y_{ij} - \bar{y}_{i.} - \bar{y}_{.j} + \bar{y}_{..})^2}{(a-1)(b-1)} = \frac{\sum_{j=1}^{b}(d_j - \bar{d})^2}{2(b-1)} = \frac{s_d^2}{2}$$

where s_d is the standard deviation of the d_j's based on $b-1$ d.f. (*Hint:* Write $\bar{y}_{.j} = (y_{1j} + y_{2j})/2$ and $\bar{y}_{..} = (\bar{y}_{1.} + \bar{y}_{2.})/2$.)

(c) Finally show that

$$F = \frac{\text{MSA}}{\text{MSE}} = \left(\frac{\bar{d}}{s_d/\sqrt{b}}\right)^2 = t^2.$$

Furthermore,

$$F > f_{1,b-1,\alpha} \Longleftrightarrow |t| > t_{b-1,\alpha/2}$$

and hence the desired result follows.

12.35 The Dunnett method given in Section 12.2.2 for many-to-one contrasts is for balanced one-way layouts, and the common correlation $\rho = 1/2$ between the contrasts is the result of equal sample size for all treatments. When the sample sizes are unequal, the correlations are unequal. Show that

$$\text{Corr}(\bar{Y}_i - \bar{Y}_1, \bar{Y}_j - \bar{Y}_1) = \rho_{ij} = \sqrt{\frac{n_i n_j}{(n_1 + n_i)(n_1 + n_j)}}.$$

12.36 Show that

$$\frac{q_{2,\nu,\alpha}}{\sqrt{2}} = t_{\nu,\alpha/2}.$$

Check this relationship from Tables A.4 and A.7 for $\alpha = .05$ and $\nu = 20$. (*Hint:* Note that

$$\frac{|\bar{Y}_1 - \bar{Y}_2|}{S}\sqrt{\frac{n}{2}} = \frac{\bar{Y}_{\max} - \bar{Y}_{\min}}{S\sqrt{2/n}}.$$

Under $H_0: \mu_1 = \mu_2$, the left hand side is a T_ν r.v. while the right hand side is a Studentized range r.v. divided by $\sqrt{2}$ with $a = 2$ and ν d.f.)

CHAPTER 13

ANALYSIS OF MULTIFACTOR EXPERIMENTS

The previous chapter discussed the methods of design and analysis of single factor experiments. In this chapter we extend those methods to experiments involving multiple factors. In Section 13.1 we study two factor experiments where each factor can have two or more levels, and the levels of the two factors are **crossed** with each other. We focus on **factorial experiments**, which are experiments that study *all* factor level combinations (called the **treatment combinations** or simply the **treatments**).

The methods developed for two factors can be generalized to three or more factors. We restrict this generalization to the case where each factor has only two levels. Thus in Section 13.2 we study k-factor experiments ($k \geq 2$) having 2^k treatment combinations. These experiments are useful for screening a large number of factors to determine those that have significant effects on the response variable. Only two levels of each factor are used in these **screening experiments** in order to keep the number of experimental runs within practical limits.

In Section 13.3 we discuss two other types of two-factor designs, primarily to illustrate different experimental settings encountered in practice. In the first design one of the factors is random (see Section 12.3 for discussion of random factors), while the other is fixed. In the second design the levels of one factor, instead of being crossed with the levels of other factor, are **nested** inside it. Examples in Section 13.3 illustrate these concepts.

13.1   TWO-FACTOR EXPERIMENTS WITH FIXED CROSSED FACTORS

13.1.1 Model and Estimates of Its Parameters

Consider two fixed factors, A with $a \geq 2$ levels and B with $b \geq 2$ levels. The two factors are crossed so that there are ab treatment combinations. We consider a completely randomized design in which a total of $abn = N$ experimental units are randomly allocated to the ab treatments with n per treatment. The n observations obtained under each treatment combination are called **replicates**. This design is referred to as a **balanced two-way layout**.

For example, consider a heat treatment experiment to evaluate the effects of a quenching medium (with two levels: oil and water) and quenching temperature (with three levels: low, medium, and high) on the surface hardness of steel. In a factorial experiment all $2 \times 3 = 6$ treatment combinations are studied. The quenching medium has $a = 2$ levels and the quenching temperature has $b = 3$ levels. If $n = 3$ steel samples are treated at each quench medium and temperature combination, then there will be a total of $N = (2)(3)(3) = 18$ observations.

Let y_{ijk} be the kth observation on the (i, j)th treatment combination, $i = 1, 2, \ldots, a$, $j = 1, 2, \ldots, b$, and $k = 1, 2, \ldots, n$. A tabular layout of the data is shown in Table 13.1. We will refer to A as the **row factor** and B as the **column factor**.

Denote by Y_{ijk} the random variable (r.v.) corresponding to the observed outcome y_{ijk}. The basic model assumes that the Y_{ijk} are independent $N(\mu_{ij}, \sigma^2)$ r.v.'s. In other words, the observations from cell (i, j) are normally distributed with mean μ_{ij} for that cell and variance σ^2, which is common for all cells. It is customary to write this model as

$$Y_{ijk} = \mu_{ij} + \epsilon_{ijk} \qquad (13.1)$$

where the ϵ_{ijk} are independent and identically distributed (i.i.d.) $N(0, \sigma^2)$ random errors.

Table 13.1 Data from a Balanced Two-Way Layout

Factor A	Factor B Levels					
Levels	1	2	$\cdots$	j	$\cdots$	b
1	$y_{111}, \ldots, y_{11n}$	$y_{121}, \ldots, y_{12n}$	$\cdots$	$y_{1j1}, \ldots, y_{1jn}$	$\cdots$	$y_{1b1}, \ldots, y_{1bn}$
2	$y_{211}, \ldots, y_{21n}$	$y_{221}, \ldots, y_{22n}$	$\cdots$	$y_{2j1}, \ldots, y_{2jn}$	$\cdots$	$y_{2b1}, \ldots, y_{2bn}$
$\vdots$	$\vdots$	$\vdots$	$\vdots$	$\vdots$	$\vdots$	$\vdots$
i	$y_{i11}, \ldots, y_{i1n}$	$y_{i21}, \ldots, y_{i2n}$	$\cdots$	$y_{ij1}, \ldots, y_{ijn}$	$\cdots$	$y_{ib1}, \ldots, y_{ibn}$
$\vdots$	$\vdots$	$\vdots$	$\vdots$	$\vdots$	$\vdots$	$\vdots$
a	$y_{a11}, \ldots, y_{a1n}$	$y_{a21}, \ldots, y_{a2n}$	$\cdots$	$y_{aj1}, \ldots, y_{ajn}$	$\cdots$	$y_{ab1}, \ldots, y_{abn}$

We now define the **main effects** of A and B and their joint effects (referred to as AB **interactions**) on the response variable. Using the dot notation introduced in Section 12.4, denote the grand average of all the μ_{ij} by $\bar{\mu}_{..}$, the average of the μ_{ij} for the ith row by $\bar{\mu}_{i.}$, and the average of the μ_{ij} for the jth column by $\bar{\mu}_{.j}$. Next let

$$\mu = \bar{\mu}_{..}, \tau_i = \bar{\mu}_{i.} - \bar{\mu}_{..}, \beta_j = \bar{\mu}_{.j} - \bar{\mu}_{..}$$

and   (13.2)

$$(\tau\beta)_{ij} = \mu_{ij} - \mu - \tau_i - \beta_j = \mu_{ij} - \bar{\mu}_{i.} - \bar{\mu}_{.j} + \bar{\mu}_{...}$$

The interpretation of these parameters is as follows: μ is the **grand mean**, τ_i is called the ith **row main effect**, which is the difference between the average of the mean responses of the ith level of factor A (averaged over all levels of factor B) and the grand mean, and β_j is called the jth **column main effect**, which is the difference between the average of the mean responses of the jth level of factor B (averaged over all levels of factor A) and the grand mean. Finally, $(\tau\beta)_{ij}$ is called the (i, j)th **row-column interaction**, which is the part of μ_{ij} that is over and above the separate contributions from the grand mean, the row main effect, and the column main effect. We have the decomposition $\mu_{ij} = \mu + \tau_i + \beta_j + (\tau\beta)_{ij}$. Therefore the model (13.1) can be rewritten as

$$Y_{ijk} = \mu + \tau_i + \beta_j + (\tau\beta)_{ij} + \epsilon_{ijk}. \qquad (13.3)$$

The τ_i, β_j, and the $(\tau\beta)_{ij}$ satisfy the following side conditions:

$$\sum_{i=1}^{a} \tau_i = 0, \sum_{j=1}^{b} \beta_j = 0, \sum_{i=1}^{a} (\tau\beta)_{ij} = 0 \text{ for all } j \text{ and } \sum_{j=1}^{b} (\tau\beta)_{ij} = 0 \text{ for all } i. \quad (13.4)$$

It follows that there are $a-1$ independent τ_i's, $b-1$ independent β_j's, and $(a-1)(b-1)$ independent $(\tau\beta)_{ij}$'s. Including the grand mean μ there are

$$1 + (a - 1) + (b - 1) + (a - 1)(b - 1) = ab$$

parameters in this model, the same as the number of μ_{ij}'s in the original model (13.1). This is not surprising, of course, since $\mu + \tau_i + \beta_j + (\tau\beta)_{ij}$ is simply a reparameterization of μ_{ij}.

If all interaction terms, $(\tau\beta)_{ij}$, are equal to zero, then the effect of one factor on the mean response does not depend on the level of the other factor. In other words, the difference in the mean responses for the ith and i'th levels of factor A do not depend on the level of factor B (i.e., $\mu_{ij} - \mu_{i'j}$ is the same for all j; similarly, $\mu_{ij} - \mu_{ij'}$ is the same for all i). Figure 13.1 shows line plots of the μ_{ij} vs. the levels of A for different levels of B when (a) interaction is not present and (b) interaction is present. In case (a) the lines are parallel, while in case (b) they are nonparallel. This plot made for the cell sample means is called the **interaction plot**, which is used to check the presence of interactions.

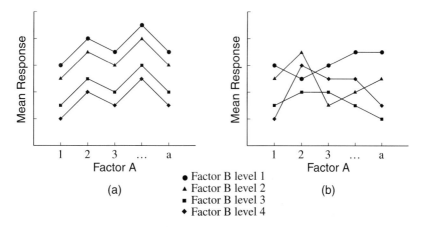

Figure 13.1   Interaction Plots: (a) No AB interaction; (b) AB interaction present

Note that the randomized block (RB) design studied in Section 12.4, is formally a special case of a two-factor experiment[1] with $n = 1$. Interactions are ignored in the model for the RB design, because otherwise the number of parameters in the model would be ab, the same as the total number of observations. Such a model is called a **saturated model**. For a saturated model, the fitted values equal the observed values, the residuals equal zero, and there are no degrees of freedom available for estimating σ^2. To avoid this difficulty, the analysis of the RB design ignores interactions, making the corresponding SS and its degrees of freedom (d.f.) available for estimating σ^2.

Using the dot notation, denote the (i, j)th cell mean by $\bar{y}_{ij\cdot}$, the ith row mean by $\bar{y}_{i\cdot\cdot}$, the jth column mean by $\bar{y}_{\cdot j\cdot}$, and the grand mean by $\bar{y}_{\cdots}$. The **least squares (LS) estimates** of the parameters are the "natural" estimates given by

$$\hat{\mu} = \bar{y}_{\cdots}, \; \hat{\tau}_i = \bar{y}_{i\cdot\cdot} - \bar{y}_{\cdots}, \; \hat{\beta}_j = \bar{y}_{\cdot j\cdot} - \bar{y}_{\cdots}, \; \widehat{(\tau\beta)}_{ij} = \bar{y}_{ij\cdot} - \bar{y}_{i\cdot\cdot} - \bar{y}_{\cdot j\cdot} + \bar{y}_{\cdots} \quad (13.5)$$

It is easy to show that the $\hat{\tau}_i$, $\hat{\beta}_j$, and $\widehat{(\tau\beta)}_{ij}$ satisfy the linear constraints given in (13.4) on the corresponding parameters. Furthermore,

$$\hat{\mu}_{ij} = \hat{\mu} + \hat{\tau}_i + \hat{\beta}_j + \widehat{(\tau\beta)}_{ij} = \bar{y}_{\cdots} + (\bar{y}_{i\cdot\cdot} - \bar{y}_{\cdots}) + (\bar{y}_{\cdot j\cdot} - \bar{y}_{\cdots}) + (\bar{y}_{ij\cdot} - \bar{y}_{i\cdot\cdot} - \bar{y}_{\cdot j\cdot} + \bar{y}_{\cdots}) = \bar{y}_{ij\cdot}.$$

Thus the LS estimate of μ_{ij}, is the corresponding sample mean $\bar{y}_{ij\cdot}$, which is also the **fitted value**, $\hat{y}_{ijk}$, for all observations in the (i, j)th cell.

The **residuals** are given by

$$e_{ijk} = y_{ijk} - \hat{y}_{ijk} = y_{ijk} - \bar{y}_{ij\cdot}. \quad (13.6)$$

The sample variance for the (i, j)th cell is

$$s_{ij}^2 = \frac{\sum_{k=1}^{n}(y_{ijk} - \bar{y}_{ij\cdot})^2}{(n-1)} = \frac{\sum_{k=1}^{n} e_{ijk}^2}{(n-1)}$$

---

[1] However, there is a fundamental difference in how the randomization is carried out in the two designs. In the RB design the treatments are randomized within each block while in a two factor experiment, treatment combinations are completely randomized over all experimental units,

which is an estimate of the error variance σ^2 for that cell. Since the model assumes that σ^2 is common for all cells, the cell sample variances can be averaged together to give a pooled estimate of σ^2. The weights used in averaging are the degrees of freedom (d.f.), which are equal to $n - 1$ for all cells. The resulting pooled estimate of σ^2 is

$$s^2 = \frac{\sum_{i=1}^{a} \sum_{j=1}^{b} (n - 1)s_{ij}^2}{ab(n - 1)} = \frac{\sum_{i=1}^{a} \sum_{j=1}^{b} \sum_{k=1}^{n} e_{ijk}^2}{N - ab}. \tag{13.7}$$

This pooled estimate is based on a total of $ab(n - 1) = N - ab$ d.f.

EXAMPLE 13.1 (BONDING STRENGTH OF CAPACITORS: PARAMETER ESTIMATES)

Capacitors are bonded to a circuit board used in high voltage electronic equipment. Engineers designed and carried out an experiment to study how the mechanical bonding strength of capacitors depends on the the type of substrate (factor A) and the bonding material (factor B). There were three types of substrates: aluminium oxide (Al_2O_3) with bracket, Al_2O_3 without bracket, and beryllium oxide (BeO) without bracket. Four types of bonding material were used: Epoxy I, Epoxy II, Solder I, and Solder II. Four capacitors were tested at each factor level combination. Simulated bonding strength data are given in Table 13.2. Calculate the estimates of the parameters of model (13.3) for these data.

Table 13.2 Bonding Strength of Capacitors (Balanced Data)

Substrate	Bonding Material			
	Epoxy I	Epoxy II	Solder I	Solder II
Al_2O_3	1.51, 1.96	2.62, 2.82	2.96, 2.82	3.67, 3.40
w/o bracket	1.83, 1.98	2.69, 2.93	3.11, 3.11	3.25, 2.90
Al_2O_3	1.63, 1.80	3.12, 2.94	2.91, 2.93	3.48, 3.51
w/ bracket	1.92, 1.71	3.23, 2.99	3.01, 2.93	3.24, 3.45
BeO	3.04, 3.16	1.91, 2.11	3.04, 2.91	3.47, 3.42
	3.09, 3.50	1.78, 2.25	2.48, 2.83	3.31, 3.76

Table 13.3 gives the sample means for cells, rows, and columns. The parameter estimates $\hat{\tau}_i$, $\hat{\beta}_j$, and $\widehat{(\tau\beta)}_{ij}$ can be computed from the sample means; the results are shown in Table 13.4. As an illustration,

$$\hat{\tau}_1 = \bar{y}_{1..} - \bar{y}_{...} = 2.723 - 2.800 = -0.077$$

$$\hat{\beta}_1 = \bar{y}_{.1.} - \bar{y}_{...} = 2.261 - 2.800 = -0.539$$

and

$$\widehat{(\tau\beta)}_{11} = \bar{y}_{11.} - \bar{y}_{1..} - \bar{y}_{.1.} + \bar{y}_{...} = 1.820 - 2.723 - 2.261 + 2.800 = -0.364.$$

The cell sample SD's are as follows:

$$s_{11} = 0.217, \quad s_{12} = 0.138, \quad s_{13} = 0.139, \quad s_{14} = 0.321$$
$$s_{21} = 0.124, \quad s_{22} = 0.131, \quad s_{23} = 0.044, \quad s_{24} = 0.122$$
$$s_{31} = 0.208, \quad s_{32} = 0.209, \quad s_{33} = 0.240, \quad s_{34} = 0.192.$$

The pooled sample variance is the average of all cell variances (because the d.f. are equal for all cells):

$$\frac{(0.217)^2 + \cdots + (0.192)^2}{12} = 0.0349.$$

The pooled sample SD equals $s = \sqrt{0.0349} = 0.187$ with 36 d.f.   ◆

Table 13.3 Sample Means for Capacitor Bonding Strength Data

Substrate	Bonding Material				Row
	Epoxy I	Epoxy II	Solder I	Solder II	mean
Al$_2$O$_3$ w/o bracket	1.820	2.765	3.000	3.305	2.723
Al$_2$O$_3$ w/ bracket	1.765	3.070	2.945	3.420	2.800
BeO	3.198	2.013	2.815	3.490	2.879
Column mean	2.261	2.616	2.920	3.405	2.800

Table 13.4 The Estimates of Model Parameters for Capacitor Bonding Strength Data

Substrate	Bonding Material				Row effects
	Epoxy I	Epoxy II	Solder I	Solder II	
Al$_2$O$_3$ w/o bracket	$\widehat{(\tau\beta)}_{11} = -0.364$	$\widehat{(\tau\beta)}_{12} = 0.226$	$\widehat{(\tau\beta)}_{13} = 0.157$	$\widehat{(\tau\beta)}_{14} = -0.023$	$\hat{\tau}_1 = -0.077$
Al$_2$O$_3$ w/ bracket	$\widehat{(\tau\beta)}_{21} = -0.496$	$\widehat{(\tau\beta)}_{22} = 0.454$	$\widehat{(\tau\beta)}_{23} = 0.025$	$\widehat{(\tau\beta)}_{24} = 0.015$	$\hat{\tau}_2 = 0.000$
BeO	$\widehat{(\tau\beta)}_{31} = 0.858$	$\widehat{(\tau\beta)}_{32} = -0.682$	$\widehat{(\tau\beta)}_{33} = -0.184$	$\widehat{(\tau\beta)}_{34} = 0.006$	$\hat{\tau}_3 = 0.078$
Column effects	$\hat{\beta}_1 = -0.539$	$\hat{\beta}_2 = -0.184$	$\hat{\beta}_3 = 0.120$	$\hat{\beta}_4 = 0.605$	$\hat{\mu} = 2.800$

13.1.2 Analysis of Variance

Define the following sums of squares:

$$\text{SST} = \sum_{i=1}^{a}\sum_{j=1}^{b}\sum_{k=1}^{n}(y_{ijk} - \bar{y}_{...})^2$$

$$\text{SSA} = \sum_{i=1}^{a}\sum_{j=1}^{b}\sum_{k=1}^{n}(\bar{y}_{i..} - \bar{y}_{...})^2 = bn\sum_{i=1}^{a}(\bar{y}_{i..} - \bar{y}_{...})^2 = bn\sum_{i=1}^{a}\hat{\tau}_i^2$$

$$\text{SSB} = \sum_{i=1}^{a}\sum_{j=1}^{b}\sum_{k=1}^{n}(\bar{y}_{.j.} - \bar{y}_{...})^2 = an\sum_{j=1}^{b}(\bar{y}_{.j.} - \bar{y}_{...})^2 = an\sum_{j=1}^{b}\hat{\beta}_j^2$$

$$\text{SSAB} = \sum_{i=1}^{a}\sum_{j=1}^{b}\sum_{k=1}^{n}(\bar{y}_{ij.} - \bar{y}_{i..} - \bar{y}_{.j.} + \bar{y}_{...})^2 = n\sum_{i=1}^{a}\sum_{j=1}^{b}(\bar{y}_{ij.} - \bar{y}_{i..} - \bar{y}_{.j.} + \bar{y}_{...})^2$$

$$= n\sum_{i=1}^{a}\sum_{j=1}^{b}\widehat{(\tau\beta)}_{ij}^2$$

$$\text{SSE} = \sum_{i=1}^{a}\sum_{j=1}^{b}\sum_{k=1}^{n}(y_{ijk} - \bar{y}_{ij.})^2 = \sum_{i=1}^{a}\sum_{j=1}^{b}\sum_{k=1}^{n}e_{ijk}^2.$$

These sums of squares have the usual interpretation: SST is the total sum of squares, SSA is the factor A sum of squares, SSB is the factor B sum of squares, SSAB is the AB interaction sum of squares, and SSE is the error sum of squares. The d.f. associated with these sums of squares are $N-1$, $a-1$, $b-1$, $(a-1)(b-1)$, and $N-ab$, respectively. The following identity can be shown to hold:

$$\text{SST} = \text{SSA} + \text{SSB} + \text{SSAB} + \text{SSE}. \tag{13.8}$$

There is a corresponding decomposition of their d.f.:

$$\underbrace{N-1}_{\text{(Total d.f.)}} = \underbrace{a-1}_{\text{(Main Effect A d.f.)}} + \underbrace{b-1}_{\text{(Main Effect B d.f.)}} + \underbrace{(a-1)(b-1)}_{\text{(Interaction AB d.f.)}} + \underbrace{N-ab}_{\text{(Error d.f.)}}$$

The mean squares are defined as the sums of squares divided by their d.f.:

$$\text{MSA} = \frac{\text{SSA}}{a-1}, \text{MSB} = \frac{\text{SSB}}{b-1}, \text{MSAB} = \frac{\text{SSAB}}{(a-1)(b-1)}, \text{MSE} = \frac{\text{SSE}}{N-ab}.$$

Note that s^2 given by (13.7) is the same as the MSE.

Usually the first step in the analysis is to test the significance of the row and column main effects and row-column interactions. The hypotheses tested are:

$$H_{0A}: \tau_1 = \tau_2 = \cdots = \tau_a = 0 \qquad \text{vs.} \qquad H_{1A}: \text{Not all } \tau_i = 0.$$
$$H_{0B}: \beta_1 = \beta_2 = \cdots = \beta_b = 0 \qquad \text{vs.} \qquad H_{1B}: \text{Not all } \beta_j = 0.$$
$$H_{0AB}: (\tau\beta)_{11} = (\tau\beta)_{12} = \cdots = (\tau\beta)_{ab} = 0 \quad \text{vs.} \quad H_{1AB}: \text{Not all } (\tau\beta)_{ij} = 0.$$

The F-statistics for testing the significance of these hypotheses are computed by taking the ratios of the respective mean squares to the error mean square. The d.f. of the F-statistics correspond to the d.f. of the mean squares which form the ratios. Specifically, the α-level tests of H_{0A}, H_{0B} and H_{0AB} are as follows:

$$\text{Reject } H_{0A} \text{ if } F_A = \frac{\text{MSA}}{\text{MSE}} \quad > \quad f_{a-1,\nu,\alpha}.$$

$$\text{Reject } H_{0B} \text{ if } F_B = \frac{\text{MSB}}{\text{MSE}} \quad > \quad f_{b-1,\nu,\alpha}.$$

$$\text{Reject } H_{0AB} \text{ if } F_{AB} = \frac{\text{MSAB}}{\text{MSE}} \quad > \quad f_{(a-1)(b-1),\nu,\alpha}.$$

The above calculations are conveniently summarized in the ANOVA table shown in Table 13.5.

Table 13.5 ANOVA Table for Crossed Two-Way Layout with Fixed Factors

Source of Variation (Source)	Sum of Squares (SS)	Degrees of Freedom (d.f.)	Mean Square (MS)	F
Main Effects A	$\text{SSA} = bn \sum \hat{\tau}_i^2$	$a-1$	$\text{MSA} = \frac{\text{SSA}}{a-1}$	$F_A = \frac{\text{MSA}}{\text{MSE}}$
Main Effects B	$\text{SSB} = an \sum \hat{\beta}_j^2$	$b-1$	$\text{MSB} = \frac{\text{SSB}}{b-1}$	$F_B = \frac{\text{MSB}}{\text{MSE}}$
Interaction AB	$\text{SSAB} = n \sum \sum \widehat{(\tau\beta)}_{ij}^2$	$(a-1)(b-1)$	$\text{MSAB} = \frac{\text{SSAB}}{(a-1)(b-1)}$	$F_{AB} = \frac{\text{MSAB}}{\text{MSE}}$
Error	$\text{SSE} = \sum \sum \sum e_{ijk}^2$	$N - ab$	$\text{MSE} = \frac{\text{SSE}}{N-ab}$	
Total	$\text{SST} = \sum \sum \sum (y_{ijk} - \bar{y}_{...})^2$	$N - 1$		

One should test the interaction hypothesis H_{0AB} before testing the main effects hypotheses H_{0A} and H_{0B}. The reason is that if there are significant interactions, checking the significance of the main effects becomes moot. After all, the main effects concern the mean responses for the levels of one factor averaged over the levels of the other factor. When interaction is present, it does not follow that the given factor has no effect, even if these averages are the same. It means that the effect of the factor depends on the level of the other factor. For example, consider the means shown in Table 13.6. Note that $\tau_1 = \tau_2 = 0$, since $\bar{\mu}_1 = \bar{\mu}_2 = \bar{\mu}_{..} = 25$. Nevertheless, factor A has an effect, which is equal and opposite at the two levels of B ($\mu_{21} - \mu_{11} = -10$ and $\mu_{22} - \mu_{12} = +10$), so it cancels out on the average.

Table 13.6 Example of Interaction

Factor B

		B_1	B_2	
Factor A	A_1	$\mu_{11} = 20$	$\mu_{12} = 30$	$\bar{\mu}_{1.} = 25$
	A_2	$\mu_{21} = 10$	$\mu_{22} = 40$	$\bar{\mu}_{2.} = 25$
		$\bar{\mu}_{.1} = 15$	$\bar{\mu}_{.2} = 35$	$\bar{\mu}_{..} = 25$

EXAMPLE 13.2 (BONDING STRENGTH OF CAPACITORS: ANALYSIS OF VARIANCE)

Give the ANOVA table for the bonding strength data from Table 13.2. Draw conclusions about the effects of the substrate and bonding material on the bonding strength.

The ANOVA table produced using STATGRAPHICS is shown in Table 13.7. We see that the main effect of bonding material and the interaction between the bonding material and substrate are both highly significant, but the main effect of substrate is not significant at the .05 level. This does not mean, however, that the substrates have no effect on the bonding strength.

These main effects can be displayed graphically in a **main effects plot** shown in Figure 13.2. This is simply a line plot of the row means (for factor A) and column means (for factor B). We see that the substrate main effects plot is rather flat, indicating nonsignificant differences between the row means, while the bonding materials main effects plot shows larger differences between the column means.

Table 13.7 Analysis of Variance for Bonding Strength Data

```
           Analysis of Variance for Strength - Type III Sums of Squares
------------------------------------------------------------------------------
Source of variation   Sum of Squares   d.f.   Mean square   F-ratio  Sig.level
------------------------------------------------------------------------------
MAIN EFFECTS
  A:Substrate            0.1953167        2     0.0976583      2.797    0.0743
  B:Bondmatl             8.4605083        3     2.8201694     80.765    0.0000
INTERACTIONS
  AB                     7.5869167        6     1.2644861     36.213    0.0000
RESIDUAL                 1.2570500       36     0.0349181

------------------------------------------------------------------------------
TOTAL (CORRECTED)       17.499792        47
------------------------------------------------------------------------------
0 missing values have been excluded.
All F-ratios are based on the residual mean square error.
```

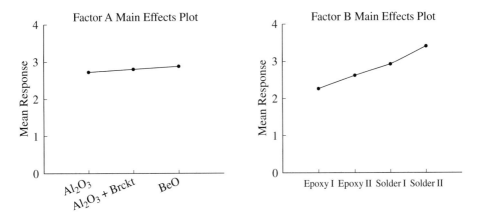

Figure 13.2 Substrate and Bonding Materials Main Effect Plots

The interaction plot for these data is shown in Figure 13.3. Interaction is evident from the crossings of the mean profiles. We see that interaction exists primarily between the type of epoxy (Epoxy I vs. Epoxy II) and the type of substrate (Al_2O_3 vs. BeO). Epoxy I works better with BeO (has a higher bonding strength), while Epoxy II works better with Al_2O_3 (with or without bracket). For each substrate, Solder II works better than Solder I by roughly the same amount. So there is not much interaction between the type of solder and substrate. We can verify these findings by testing the significance of the corresponding **interaction contrasts**.

Type of Substrate vs. Type of Epoxy:

$$\left(\frac{\bar{y}_{11\cdot}+\bar{y}_{21\cdot}}{2}-\bar{y}_{31\cdot}\right)-\left(\frac{\bar{y}_{12\cdot}+\bar{y}_{22\cdot}}{2}-\bar{y}_{32\cdot}\right)=\left(\frac{1.820+1.765}{2}-3.198\right)-\left(\frac{2.765+3.070}{2}-2.013\right)$$

$$= -2.310.$$

Type of Substrate vs. Type of Solder:

$$\left(\frac{\bar{y}_{13\cdot}+\bar{y}_{23\cdot}}{2}-\bar{y}_{33\cdot}\right)-\left(\frac{\bar{y}_{14\cdot}+\bar{y}_{24\cdot}}{2}-\bar{y}_{34\cdot}\right)=\left(\frac{3.000+2.945}{2}-2.815\right)-\left(\frac{3.305+3.420}{2}-3.490\right)$$

$$= 0.285.$$

The variance of both these contrasts is given by

$$2\left\{\frac{1}{4}\left(\frac{\sigma^2}{n}+\frac{\sigma^2}{n}\right)+\frac{\sigma^2}{n}\right\}=\frac{3\sigma^2}{n}.$$

Substituting $s^2 = 0.0349$ as an estimate of σ^2 and $n = 4$, the estimated standard error of both contrasts equals

$$\sqrt{\frac{(3)(0.0349)}{4}} = 0.162.$$

Therefore the t-statistics for the two contrasts are:

$$\text{Type of Substrate vs. Type of Epoxy:}\quad t = \frac{-2.310}{0.162} = -14.259$$

and

$$\text{Type of Substrate vs. Type of Solder:}\quad t = \frac{0.285}{0.162} = 1.759.$$

To determine the significance of these t-statistics we should use a multiple comparison test because these contrasts were not chosen *a priori*, but after we looked at the data. The Scheffé method introduced in Section 12.2.2, may be used here, although it is conservative. We use the critical constant $\sqrt{(a-1)(b-1)f_{(a-1)(b-1),v,\alpha}}$ to test the significance of any interaction contrast selected in light of the data where $(a-1)(b-1)$ is the interaction d.f. This is analogous to the critical constant $\sqrt{(a-1)f_{a-1,v,\alpha}}$ used to test the significance of any contrast among a treatment means with $a-1$ d.f. Thus the t-statistics above are compared with the critical constant $\sqrt{6f_{6,36,.05}} = \sqrt{6 \times 2.37} = 3.771$. The first t- statistic (in absolute value) exceeds this critical constant, while the second does not. Therefore the first contrast is significant, while the second is not.   ◆

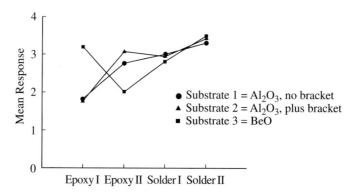

Figure 13.3   Interaction Plot for Bonding Strength Data

*Derivation of the ANOVA Identity and F-Statistics.

We have the following decomposition of each observation:

$$y_{ijk} = \hat{\mu} + \hat{\tau}_i + \hat{\beta}_j + \widehat{(\tau\beta)}_{ij} + e_{ijk}$$

$$= \bar{y}_{...} + (\bar{y}_{i..} - \bar{y}_{...}) + (\bar{y}_{.j.} - \bar{y}_{...}) + (\bar{y}_{ij.} - \bar{y}_{i..} - \bar{y}_{.j.} + \bar{y}_{...}) + (y_{ijk} - \bar{y}_{ij.})$$

or

$$y_{ijk} - \bar{y}_{...} = (\bar{y}_{i..} - \bar{y}_{...}) + (\bar{y}_{.j.} - \bar{y}_{...}) + (\bar{y}_{ij.} - \bar{y}_{i..} - \bar{y}_{.j.} + \bar{y}_{...}) + (y_{ijk} - \bar{y}_{ij.}).$$

Squaring both sides and summing over all i, j, and k, we find that all cross-products sum to zero. For example,

$$\sum_{i=1}^{a}\sum_{j=1}^{b}\sum_{k=1}^{n} \hat{\tau}_i \hat{\beta}_j = n \sum_{i=1}^{a} \hat{\tau}_i \sum_{j=1}^{b} \hat{\beta}_j = 0$$

since $\sum_{i=1}^{a} \hat{\tau}_i = \sum_{j=1}^{b} \hat{\beta}_j = 0$. Therefore

$$\underbrace{\sum_{i=1}^{a}\sum_{j=1}^{b}\sum_{k=1}^{n}(y_{ijk} - \bar{y}_{...})^2}_{\text{SST}} = \sum_{i=1}^{a}\sum_{j=1}^{b}\sum_{k=1}^{n}(\bar{y}_{i..} - \bar{y}_{...})^2 + \sum_{i=1}^{a}\sum_{j=1}^{b}\sum_{k=1}^{n}(\bar{y}_{\cdot j\cdot} - \bar{y}_{...})^2$$

$$+ \sum_{i=1}^{a}\sum_{j=1}^{b}\sum_{k=1}^{n}(\bar{y}_{ij\cdot} - \bar{y}_{i..} - \bar{y}_{\cdot j\cdot} + \bar{y}_{...})^2 + \sum_{i=1}^{a}\sum_{j=1}^{b}\sum_{k=1}^{n}(y_{ijk} - \bar{y}_{ij\cdot})^2$$

$$= \underbrace{bn\sum_{i=1}^{a}\hat{\tau}_i^2}_{\text{SSA}} + \underbrace{an\sum_{j=1}^{b}\hat{\beta}_j^2}_{\text{SSB}} + \underbrace{n\sum_{i=1}^{a}\sum_{j=1}^{b}\widehat{(\tau\beta)}_{ij}^2}_{\text{SSAB}} + \underbrace{\sum_{i=1}^{a}\sum_{j=1}^{b}\sum_{k=1}^{n}e_{ijk}^2}_{\text{SSE}}$$

which is the ANOVA identity (13.8).

The extra sum of squares method can be applied to derive the F-statistic for testing $H_{0A}: \tau_1 = \cdots = \tau_a = 0$ as follows. When a partial model (without the τ_i's), namely,

$$Y_{ijk} = \mu + \beta_j + (\tau\beta)_{ij} + \epsilon_{ijk}$$

is fitted under this hypothesis, the LS estimates of the parameters in this model remain unchanged from the full model estimates. As a result, what would have been the LS estimate of τ_i, namely $\hat{\tau}_i = \bar{y}_{i..} - \bar{y}_{...}$, gets added to e_{ijk}, resulting in the new residual $e'_{ijk} = e_{ijk} + \hat{\tau}_i$. Therefore, the new error sum of squares, SSE$'$, equals

$$\text{SSE}' = \sum_{i=1}^{a}\sum_{j=1}^{b}\sum_{k=1}^{n}(e_{ijk} + \hat{\tau}_i)^2$$

$$= \sum_{i=1}^{a}\sum_{j=1}^{b}\sum_{k=1}^{n}e_{ijk}^2 + \sum_{i=1}^{a}\sum_{j=1}^{b}\sum_{k=1}^{n}\hat{\tau}_i^2 + \underbrace{2\sum_{i=1}^{a}\sum_{j=1}^{b}\sum_{k=1}^{n}\hat{\tau}_i e_{ijk}}_{=0}$$

$$= \text{SSE} + \text{SSA}.$$

The F-statistic is given by

$$F_A = \frac{(\text{SSE}' - \text{SSE})/(a-1)}{\text{SSE}/(N-ab)} = \frac{\text{SSA}/(a-1)}{\text{SSE}/(N-ab)} = \frac{\text{MSA}}{\text{MSE}}.$$

F_A has an F-distribution with $a-1$ and $N-ab$ d.f. when H_{0A} is true. The other F-statistics can be derived similarly.

The decomposition (13.8) of the total sum of squares into SSA, SSB, SSAB, and SSE, which are respectively attributable to the four separate components, τ_i, β_j, $(\tau\beta)_{ij}$, and ϵ_{ijk}, of the model (13.3), is the result of the balanced nature (i.e., equal cell sample sizes) of the design. A related consequence noted above is that the LS estimates of the β_j and the $(\tau\beta)_{ij}$ are the same under the full model and under the partial model, which sets the τ_i equal to zero; the same holds for other parameters. A design having these properties is called an **orthogonal design**.

13.1.3 Model Diagnostics using Residual Plots

The residuals defined in (13.6) (which are simply the differences between the data values and the corresponding cell sample means) are used in the usual way to check the model assumptions. In particular, the plot of residuals against the fitted values (i.e., the corresponding cell sample means) is used to check the constant variance assumption, and the normal plot of the residuals is used to check the normality assumption. A run chart of the residuals is used to check the independence assumption if the time order of data collection is available.

EXAMPLE 13.3 (BONDING STRENGTH OF CAPACITORS: MODEL DIAGNOSTICS)

Check the constant variance and normality assumptions for the bonding strength data from Table 13.2 by making the appropriate residual plots.

The plot of residuals (computed using the cell means from Table 13.3) against the fitted values is shown in Figure 13.4, and the normal plot is shown in Figure 13.5. In the first plot the residuals exhibit a fairly constant dispersion pattern across all fitted values, so the constant variance assumption appears to be valid. The normal plot is linear, indicating that the normality assumption is also valid. ◆

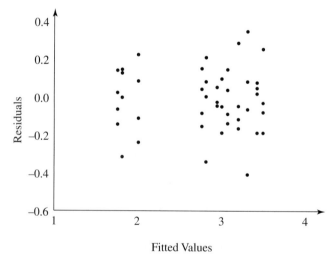

Figure 13.4 Plot of Residuals against Fitted Values for the Bonding Strength Data

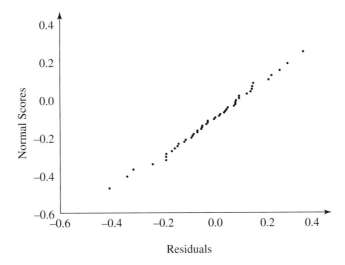

Figure 13.5   Normal Plot of Residuals for the Bonding Strength Data

13.1.4 Multiple Comparisons Between Rows and/or Between Columns

Pairwise comparisons between the row main effects and/or between the column main effects are generally of interest only when the interactions are nonsignificant (H_{0AB} is not rejected). To make comparisons between the rows we can apply the Tukey method to obtain the following $100(1 - \alpha)\%$ simultaneous confidence intervals (SCI's) on the pairwise differences between the row main effects:

$$\bar{y}_{i..} - \bar{y}_{j..} - q_{a,\nu,\alpha}\frac{s}{\sqrt{bn}} \leq \tau_i - \tau_j \leq \bar{y}_{i..} - \bar{y}_{j..} + q_{a,\nu,\alpha}\frac{s}{\sqrt{bn}}$$

where $s = \sqrt{\text{MSE}}$ and $\nu = ab(n-1)$. Similarly, $100(1 - \alpha)\%$ SCI's on the pairwise differences between the column main effects are given by

$$\bar{y}_{.i.} - \bar{y}_{.j.} - q_{b,\nu,\alpha}\frac{s}{\sqrt{an}} \leq \beta_i - \beta_j \leq \bar{y}_{.i.} - \bar{y}_{.j.} + q_{b,\nu,\alpha}\frac{s}{\sqrt{an}}.$$

In the capacitor bonding example, since the interactions are significant, these comparisons between the substrates and/or the bonding materials are not very meaningful.

13.1.5 Unbalanced Two-Way Layouts

The cell sample sizes may be unequal because of missing or bad data in a balanced designed experiment or because of uncontrolled sample sizes in an observational study. Denote the sample size for the (i, j)th cell by n_{ij}. We assume the same model (13.3) for unbalanced data.

How does the analysis of unbalanced data differ from that of balanced data? The LS estimates of the main effects and interactions for unbalanced data are the same as those given for balanced data in (13.5). The necessary sums of squares for testing H_{0A}, H_{0B}, and H_{0AB} can also be computed by applying the extra sum of squares method;

however, they are not given by simple formulas such as those in Table 13.5. Furthermore, the ANOVA identity (13.8) does not hold any more, i.e.,

$$\text{SST} \neq \text{SSA} + \text{SSB} + \text{SSAB} + \text{SSE}.$$

Thus an unbalanced two-way layout is a **nonorthogonal design**.

EXAMPLE 13.4 (BONDING STRENGTH OF CAPACITORS: ANOVA FOR UNBALANCED TWO-WAY LAYOUT)

Consider the capacitor bonding strength data from Table 13.2, but suppose that some of the data values are missing, resulting in an unbalanced two-way layout as shown in Table 13.8. Compute the ANOVA table and carry out the tests of significance of the main effects and interactions for these data.

Table 13.8 Bonding Strength of Capacitors (Unbalanced Data)

Substrate	Bonding Material			
	Epoxy I	Epoxy II	Solder I	Solder II
Al$_2$O$_3$	1.51, 1.96	2.62, 2.82	2.96, 2.82	3.67, 3.40
w/o bracket		2.69	3.11	3.25, 2.90
Al$_2$O$_3$	1.63, 1.80	3.12, 2.94	2.91, 2.93	3.48, 3.51
w/ bracket	1.92, 1.71	3.23, 2.99	3.01	
BeO	3.04, 3.16	1.91, 2.11	3.04, 2.91	3.47, 3.42
	3.09		2.48, 2.83	3.31, 3.76

The ANOVA table obtained using MINITAB is shown in Table 13.9.

Table 13.9 Analysis of Variance for the Unbalanced Bonding Strength Data

```
Analysis of Variance for Strength
Source            DF     Seq SS     Adj SS     Adj MS       F       P
Substrt            2     0.4371     0.1985     0.0993    2.91   0.072
Bondmatl           3     6.9640     7.0349     2.3450   68.73   0.000
Substrt*Bondmatl   6     4.9919     4.9919     0.8320   24.38   0.000
Error             26     0.8871     0.8871     0.0341
Total             37    13.2802
```

We focus on the adjusted sums of squares (also called the type III sum of squares), which are computed using the extra sum of squares method. Notice that the four adjusted sums of squares do not add up to the total sum of squares:

$$\text{SST} = 13.2802 \neq \text{SSA} + \text{SSB} + \text{SSAB} + \text{SSE} = 0.1985 + 7.0349 + 4.9919 + 0.8871 = 13.1124.$$

The F-statistics are computed from the adjusted mean squares. Their P-values are very similar to those obtained from the ANOVA of the balanced data given in Table 13.7. Thus the conclusions regarding the effects of the substrates and bonding materials are unchanged.

The sequential sums of squares (also called the type I sums of squares) listed in the ANOVA table are the changes in the error sum of squares as a result of sequentially adding terms to the model. Denote by SSE[model terms] to be the error sum of squares for the model with the terms listed in square brackets. Thus SSE[constant] = SST and SSE[constant, A, B, AB] = SSE. Then the sequential sums of squares are defined as follows:

$$\begin{aligned}
\text{SSA} &= \text{SSE[constant]} - \text{SSE[constant, A]} \\
\text{SSB} &= \text{SSE[constant, A]} - \text{SSE[constant, A, B]} \\
\text{SSAB} &= \text{SSE[constant, A, B]} - \text{SSE[constant, A, B, AB]} \\
\text{SSE} &= \text{SSE[constant, A, B, AB]}.
\end{aligned}$$

Note that SSA + SSB + SSAB + SSE = SSE[constant] = SST in this case. However, for a nonorthogonal design the sequential SS depend on the order in which the terms are added to the model. Therefore these SS are not appropriate for tests of model effects and do not have a clear interpretation. For orthogonal designs this order is immaterial, and the sequential SS are the same as the adjusted SS. ◆

13.1.6 *Regression Approach to Two-Factor Experiments

A unified approach to the analysis of balanced or unbalanced designs is provided by multiple regression. We have implicitly used this approach when we applied the extra sum of squares method to derive the F-tests of ANOVA. Now we explain it in detail in the context of unbalanced two-way layouts.

Define indicator variables as follows: For $i = 1, \ldots, a - 1$, let

$$u_i = \begin{cases} +1 & \text{if the observation is from the } i\text{th row} \\ -1 & \text{if the observation is from the } a\text{th row} \\ 0 & \text{otherwise.} \end{cases}$$

Similarly, for $j = 1, \ldots, b - 1$, let

$$v_j = \begin{cases} +1 & \text{if the observation is from the } j\text{th column} \\ -1 & \text{if the observation is from the } b\text{th column} \\ 0 & \text{otherwise.} \end{cases}$$

Then the two-way layout model (13.3) can be written as a regression model with the above indicator variables as predictor variables and the τ_i, β_j, and the $(\tau\beta)_{ij}$ as unknown parameters:

$$Y = \mu + \sum_{i=1}^{a-1} \tau_i u_i + \sum_{j=1}^{b-1} \beta_j v_j + \sum_{i=1}^{a-1}\sum_{j=1}^{b-1}(\tau\beta)_{ij} u_i v_j + \epsilon. \qquad (13.9)$$

The equivalence of the models (13.3) and (13.9) is shown at the end of this section.

Any hypotheses regarding the τ_i, β_j, and the $(\tau\beta)_{ij}$ can be tested by using the extra sum of squares method. For example, the hypothesis $H_{0A}: \tau_1 = \tau_2 = \cdots = \tau_a = 0$ is tested by fitting the full model above and the partial model obtained by omitting the predictor variables u_i (but keeping the v_j and $u_i v_j$ terms) from the full model. The difference in the SSE's of the two models gives the sum of squares for testing H_{0A}.

EXAMPLE 13.5 (**BONDING STRENGTH OF CAPACITORS: ANALYSIS USING THE REGRESSION APPROACH FOR UNBALANCED TWO-WAY LAYOUT**)

Compute the adjusted sums of squares shown in Table 13.9 by fitting the appropriate regression models and applying the extra sum of squares method to the data in Table 13.8.

To fit the regression models we first define predictor variables u_1, u_2, v_1, v_2, v_3 as explained above. The fitted models are as follows.

Full Model:

Strength $= 2.784 - 0.105u_1 + 0.0363u_2 - 0.585v_1 - 0.187v_2 + 0.126v_3$

$- 0.358u_1 v_1 + 0.219u_1 v_2 + 0.159u_1 v_3 - 0.470u_2 v_1 + 0.437u_2 v_2 + 0.0043u_2 v_3.$

SSE $= 0.8871.$

Partial Model without Substrate (Factor A) Main Effects:

Strength $= 2.786 - 0.567v_1 - 0.198v_2 + 0.129v_3$

$- 0.332u_1 v_1 + 0.223u_1 v_2 + 0.150u_1 v_3 - 0.479u_2 v_1 + 0.456u_2 v_2 + 0.0008u_2 v_3.$

SSE $= 1.0857.$

Partial Model without Bonding Material (Factor B) Main Effects:

Strength $= 2.802 - 0.0105u_1 - 0.107u_2$

$- 0.217u_1 v_1 + 0.112u_1 v_2 + 0.059u_1 v_3 - 0.513u_2 v_1 + 0.517u_2 v_2 + 0.138u_2 v_3.$

SSE $= 7.9221.$

Partial Model without AB Interactions:

Strength $= 2.806 - 0.099u_1 + 0.001u_2 - 0.615v_1 - 0.081v_2 + 0.084v_3$

SSE $= 5.8791.$

Note that the fitted coefficients are different for different models, which is a result of the nonorthogonal nature of the design. The sums of squares for the main effects and interactions obtained by the extra sum of squares method are:

$$\text{SSA} = 1.0857 - 0.8871 = 0.1986.$$

$$\text{SSB} = 7.9221 - 0.8871 = 7.0350.$$

$$\text{SSAB} = 5.8791 - 0.8871 = 4.9920.$$

These sums of squares are the same as the corresponding adjusted sums of squares in Table 13.9 except for roundoff errors. ◆

*Equivalence of Models (13.3) and (13.9). To see that the two models are equivalent, first consider an observation from cell (i, j) for $i = 1, \ldots, a-1$, $j = 1, \ldots, b-1$. Set $u_i = 1$, $v_j = 1$, $w_{ij} = 1$, and all other u's, v's, and w's equal to zero. Therefore model (13.9) becomes $Y = \mu + \tau_i + \beta_j + (\tau\beta)_{ij} + \epsilon$, which is the same as model (13.3). Next consider an observation from the ath row and the jth column ($j = 1, \ldots, b-1$). We set $u_1 = u_2 = \cdots = u_{a-1} = -1$, $v_j = 1$ and $w_{1j} = w_{2j} = \cdots = w_{a-1,j} = -1$. Therefore model (13.9) becomes

$$Y = \mu - (\tau_1 + \tau_2 + \cdots + \tau_{a-1}) + \beta_j - \{(\tau\beta)_{1j} + (\tau\beta)_{2j} + \cdots + (\tau\beta)_{a-1,j}\} + \epsilon$$

$$= \mu + \tau_a + \beta_j + (\tau\beta)_{aj} + \epsilon \quad \left(\text{since} \ -\sum_{i=1}^{a-1}\tau_i = \tau_a, -\sum_{i=1}^{a-1}(\tau\beta)_{ij} = (\tau\beta)_{aj}\right)$$

which is the same as model (13.3). In the same way, equivalence can be shown for an observation from the ith row ($i = 1, \ldots, a-1$) and the bth column. Finally, for an observation from cell (a, b), we set $u_1 = u_2 = \cdots = u_{a-1} = -1$, $v_1 = v_2 = \cdots = v_{b-1} = -1$, and $w_{ij} = (-1)(-1) = 1$ for $i = 1, \ldots, a-1$, $j = 1, \ldots, b-1$. Therefore model (13.9) becomes

$$Y = \mu - (\tau_1 + \tau_2 + \cdots + \tau_{a-1}) - (\beta_1 + \beta_2 + \cdots + \beta_{b-1}) + \sum_{i=1}^{a-1}\sum_{j=1}^{b-1}(\tau\beta)_{ij} + \epsilon$$

$$= \mu + \tau_a + \beta_b - \sum_{i=1}^{a-1}(\tau\beta)_{ib} + \epsilon \quad \left(\text{since} \ -\sum_{i=1}^{a-1}\tau_i = \tau_a, -\sum_{j=1}^{b-1}\beta_j = \beta_b, \sum_{j=1}^{b-1}(\tau\beta)_{ij} = -(\tau\beta)_{ib}\right)$$

$$= \mu + \tau_a + \beta_b + (\tau\beta)_{ab} + \epsilon \quad \left(\text{since} \ -\sum_{i=1}^{a-1}(\tau\beta)_{ib} = (\tau\beta)_{ab}\right)$$

which is the same as model (13.3).

13.2 2^k **FACTORIAL EXPERIMENTS**

An important class of multifactor experiments consists of designs in which each factor is studied at two levels. If there are k factors, then we have 2^k treatment combinations. It is often the case that only a few factors have large effects on the response variable; the majority have negligible effects ("the vital few, trivial many"). This is referred to as the **effect sparsity** principle. These experiments are used to screen a large number of factors to identify the few **active factors**. Two levels of each factor are used to keep the size of the experiment from becoming too large. Once the few active factors are identified, a detailed experiment involving multiple levels of these factors can be carried out to obtain a more thorough understanding and an accurate empirical model.

13.2.1 Main Effects and Interactions

2^2 **Experiment.**   Consider first a 2^2 experiment with factors A and B, each at two levels, labeled High and Low. A new notation is used to denote the treatment combinations in a 2^2 experiment:

$$ab = \text{(A High, B High)}, \quad a = \text{(A High, B Low)},$$

$$b = \text{(A Low, B High)}, \quad (1) = \text{(A Low, B Low)}.$$

Thus the presence of a lowercase letter in the notation for a treatment combination means that the corresponding factor is at high level, while the absence of the letter means that the factor is at low level; when both factors are at low level, the treatment combination is denoted by (1). This notation extends to more than two treatments in a straightforward manner. Another notation that we will use is to represent the low level of a factor by a $-$ sign and the high level by a $+$ sign.

   We assume a balanced design with n observations for each treatment combination. Denote these observations by y_{ij}, $j = 1, 2, \ldots, n$, where $i = (1), a, b, ab$. A tabular layout of the data is shown in Table 13.10. The corresponding random variables Y_{ij} are assumed to be independent normal with means μ_i and a common variance σ^2:

$$Y_{ij} \sim N(\mu_i, \sigma^2), \quad i = (1), a, b, ab, \ j = 1, 2, \ldots, n.$$

This is the same model that was assumed for the two-way layout design.

Table 13.10 Data from a Balanced 2^2 Design

Factor A	B	Treatment Combination	Data
$-$	$-$	(1)	$y_{(1),1}, \ldots, y_{(1),n}$
$+$	$-$	a	$y_{a,1}, \ldots, y_{a,n}$
$-$	$+$	b	$y_{b,1}, \ldots, y_{b,n}$
$+$	$+$	ab	$y_{ab,1}, \ldots, y_{ab,n}$

We define the **main effect** of factor A (denoted by τ) as the difference in the mean response between the high level of A and the low level of A, averaged over the levels of B. The main effect of B (denoted by β) is defined similarly. Finally we define the **interaction effect** (denoted by $(\tau\beta)$) as the difference between the main effect of A at the high level of B and at the low level of B. Equivalently it can be defined as the difference between the main effect of B at the high level of A and at the low level of A. To summarize,

$$\tau = \frac{(\mu_{ab} - \mu_b) + (\mu_a - \mu_{(1)})}{2} = \frac{\mu_{ab} + \mu_a}{2} - \frac{\mu_b + \mu_{(1)}}{2}$$

$$\beta = \frac{(\mu_{ab} - \mu_a) + (\mu_b - \mu_{(1)})}{2} = \frac{\mu_{ab} + \mu_b}{2} - \frac{\mu_a + \mu_{(1)}}{2}$$

$$(\tau\beta) = \frac{(\mu_{ab} - \mu_b) - (\mu_a - \mu_{(1)})}{2} = \frac{(\mu_{ab} - \mu_a) - (\mu_b - \mu_{(1)})}{2}. \quad (13.10)$$

How are the parameters τ_i, β_j, and $(\tau\beta)_{ij}$ defined in (13.2) related to these three parameters? It is easily shown that

$$\tau_2 = -\tau_1 = \frac{\tau}{2}$$

$$\beta_2 = -\beta_1 = \frac{\beta}{2}$$

$$(\tau\beta)_{22} = -(\tau\beta)_{21} = -(\tau\beta)_{12} = (\tau\beta)_{11} = \frac{(\tau\beta)}{2}.$$

The LS estimates of the main effects and the interaction effect are obtained by replacing the treatment means by the corresponding cell sample means. For convenience, we denote these estimates by A, B, and AB, which are given by

$$\text{Est. Main Effect } A = \hat{\tau} = \frac{(\bar{y}_{ab} - \bar{y}_b) + (\bar{y}_a - \bar{y}_{(1)})}{2}$$

$$\text{Est. Main Effect } B = \hat{\beta} = \frac{(\bar{y}_{ab} - \bar{y}_a) + (\bar{y}_b - \bar{y}_{(1)})}{2}$$

$$\text{Est. Interaction } AB = \widehat{(\tau\beta)} = \frac{(\bar{y}_{ab} - \bar{y}_b) - (\bar{y}_a - \bar{y}_{(1)})}{2}. \quad (13.11)$$

Note that the numerators in the above expressions are simple contrasts (with contrast coefficients ± 1) among the cell sample means. The signs of these coefficients are shown in Table 13.11. The first column in this table is the identity vector I, which represents the grand mean effect, as we shall see in the sequel.

Table 13.11 Contrast Coefficients for Effects in a 2^2 Experiment

Treatment	Effect			
Combination	I	A	B	AB
(1)	$+$	$-$	$-$	$+$
a	$+$	$+$	$-$	$-$
b	$+$	$-$	$+$	$-$
ab	$+$	$+$	$+$	$+$

EXAMPLE 13.6

Calculate the estimated main effects A and B, and the interaction AB, if the cell means are as shown in the following table.

		Factor B	
		Low	High
Factor A	Low	$\bar{y}_{(1)} = 10$	$\bar{y}_b = 15$
	High	$\bar{y}_a = 20$	$\bar{y}_{ab} = 35$

The estimated main effects are

$$A = \frac{(35 - 15) + (20 - 10)}{2} = \frac{35 + 20}{2} - \frac{15 + 10}{2} = 15$$

and

$$B = \frac{(35 - 20) + (15 - 10)}{2} = \frac{35 + 15}{2} - \frac{20 + 10}{2} = 10.$$

The estimated interaction effect is

$$AB = \frac{(35 - 15) - (20 - 10)}{2} = \frac{(35 - 20) - (15 - 10)}{2} = 5. \qquad \blacklozenge$$

It is seen from Table 13.11 that the *dot product* (denoted by $\cdot$) between any two contrast vectors equals zero:

$$A \cdot B = 0, \quad A \cdot AB = 0, \quad B \cdot AB = 0.$$

Thus the contrast vectors for the main effects and interactions are **mutually orthogonal**. An important consequence of this property is that these contrasts are uncorrelated, which together with the normality assumption implies that they are statistically independent.

It is also seen from Table 13.11 that the term-by-term product (denoted by $\times$) of any two contrast vectors yields the third one:

$$A \times B = AB, \quad A \times AB = B, \quad B \times AB = A.$$

For example,

$$A \times B = [(-)(-), (+)(-), (-)(+), (+)(+)] = [+, -, -, +] = AB.$$

This is due to the fact that $A^2 = B^2 = I$, since each term in a contrast vector is ± 1, which when squared yields $+1$. The above result is useful for obtaining contrast vectors of interaction effects for higher order designs ($k > 2$), as we shall see for the 2^3 design discussed next.

2^3 Experiment. Consider three factors: A, B, and C, and assume that n observations are made at each of the $2^3 = 8$ treatment combinations. Using the notation for treatment combinations introduced for 2^2 experiments, the data can be represented in a tabular form as shown in Table 13.12. The corresponding r.v.'s Y_{ij} are assumed to be independent $N(\mu_i, \sigma^2)$ distributed, where i is the index of the treatment combination and $j = 1, 2, \ldots, n$.

Table 13.12 Data from a Balanced 2^3 Design

Factor			Treatment	Data
A	B	C	Combination	
$-$	$-$	$-$	(1)	$y_{(1),1}, \ldots, y_{(1),n}$
$+$	$-$	$-$	a	$y_{a,1}, \ldots, y_{a,n}$
$-$	$+$	$-$	b	$y_{b,1}, \ldots, y_{b,n}$
$+$	$+$	$-$	ab	$y_{ab,1}, \ldots, y_{ab,n}$
$-$	$-$	$+$	c	$y_{c,1}, \ldots, y_{c,n}$
$+$	$-$	$+$	ac	$y_{ac,1}, \ldots, y_{ac,n}$
$-$	$+$	$+$	bc	$y_{bc,1}, \ldots, y_{bc,n}$
$+$	$+$	$+$	abc	$y_{abc,1}, \ldots, y_{abc,n}$

There are three main effects (A, B, and C), three two-factor interaction effects (AB, AC, and BC), and one three-factor interaction effect (ABC) in this case.[2] First, the A main effect can be computed as the difference between the average of the mean responses at the high level of A and at the low level of A. It can also be expressed as the average of four differences, namely, $\bar{y}_{abc} - \bar{y}_{bc}$, $\bar{y}_{ac} - \bar{y}_c$, $\bar{y}_{ab} - \bar{y}_b$, and $\bar{y}_a - \bar{y}_{(1)}$.

---

[2] The population parameters corresponding to these effects can be defined in a manner analogous to the two-factor case. Since the population effects are not used in the ensuing discussion, the "estimated effects" are referred to simply as "effects" from now on.

The B and C main effects are defined similarly. To summarize,

$$A = \frac{\bar{y}_{abc} + \bar{y}_{ac} + \bar{y}_{ab} + \bar{y}_a}{4} - \frac{\bar{y}_{bc} + \bar{y}_c + \bar{y}_b + \bar{y}_{(1)}}{4}$$

$$= \frac{(\bar{y}_{abc} - \bar{y}_{bc}) + (\bar{y}_{ac} - \bar{y}_c) + (\bar{y}_{ab} - \bar{y}_b) + (\bar{y}_a - \bar{y}_{(1)})}{4}.$$

$$B = \frac{\bar{y}_{abc} + \bar{y}_{bc} + \bar{y}_{ab} + \bar{y}_b}{4} - \frac{\bar{y}_{ac} + \bar{y}_c + \bar{y}_a + \bar{y}_{(1)}}{4}$$

$$= \frac{(\bar{y}_{abc} - \bar{y}_{ac}) + (\bar{y}_{bc} - \bar{y}_c) + (\bar{y}_{ab} - \bar{y}_a) + (\bar{y}_b - \bar{y}_{(1)})}{4}.$$

$$C = \frac{\bar{y}_{abc} + \bar{y}_{bc} + \bar{y}_{ac} + \bar{y}_c}{4} - \frac{\bar{y}_{ab} + \bar{y}_b + \bar{y}_a + \bar{y}_{(1)}}{4}$$

$$= \frac{(\bar{y}_{abc} - \bar{y}_{ab}) + (\bar{y}_{bc} - \bar{y}_b) + (\bar{y}_{ac} - \bar{y}_a) + (\bar{y}_c - \bar{y}_{(1)})}{4}.$$

Next we explain how two-factor interaction effects are defined, beginning with the AB interaction. Consider two 2^2 experiments, one with C fixed at high level and the other with C fixed at low level. Using the definition of the AB interaction given for a 2^2 experiment previously, we have the following two expressions:

$$AB = \frac{(\bar{y}_{abc} - \bar{y}_{bc}) - (\bar{y}_{ac} - \bar{y}_c)}{2} \quad \text{for C high,}$$

and

$$AB = \frac{(\bar{y}_{ab} - \bar{y}_b) - (\bar{y}_a - \bar{y}_{(1)})}{2} \quad \text{for C low.}$$

The overall AB interaction is defined as the average of these two. The BC and AC interactions are defined similarly. To summarize,

$$AB = \frac{\{(\bar{y}_{abc} - \bar{y}_{bc}) - (\bar{y}_{ac} - \bar{y}_c)\} + \{(\bar{y}_{ab} - \bar{y}_b) - (\bar{y}_a - \bar{y}_{(1)})\}}{4}.$$

$$BC = \frac{\{(\bar{y}_{abc} - \bar{y}_{ac}) - (\bar{y}_{ab} - \bar{y}_a)\} + \{(\bar{y}_{bc} - \bar{y}_c) - (\bar{y}_b - \bar{y}_{(1)})\}}{4}.$$

$$AC = \frac{\{(\bar{y}_{abc} - \bar{y}_{ab}) - (\bar{y}_{bc} - \bar{y}_b)\} + \{(\bar{y}_{ac} - \bar{y}_a) - (\bar{y}_c - \bar{y}_{(1)})\}}{4}.$$

Finally, the ABC interaction is defined as the difference between the AB interaction at high level of C and the AB interaction at low level of C defined above. Thus,

$$ABC = \frac{\{(\bar{y}_{abc} - \bar{y}_{bc}) - (\bar{y}_{ac} - \bar{y}_c)\} - \{(\bar{y}_{ab} - \bar{y}_b) - (\bar{y}_a - \bar{y}_{(1)})\}}{4}.$$

Note that the same expression is obtained for the ABC interaction if it is defined as the difference between the BC interactions at the high and low levels of A or the difference between the AC interactions at the high and low levels of B.

Table 13.13 Contrast Coefficients for Effects in a 2^3 Experiment

Treatment Combination	Effect							
	I	A	B	AB	C	AC	BC	ABC
(1)	+	−	−	+	−	+	+	−
a	+	+	−	−	−	−	+	+
b	+	−	+	−	−	+	−	+
ab	+	+	+	+	−	−	−	−
c	+	−	−	+	+	−	−	+
ac	+	+	−	−	+	+	−	−
bc	+	−	+	−	+	−	+	−
abc	+	+	+	+	+	+	+	+

The above formulas are summarized in the form of a table of contrast coefficients in Table 13.13. Once again notice that all seven contrasts are mutually orthogonal, i.e., the dot product of any two of them equals zero. The main effect contrasts for any factor have − signs for those treatment combinations in which it is at low level and + signs for those in which it is at high level. Any interaction contrast coefficient vector is obtained by taking the term-by-term product of the main effect contrast coefficient vectors:

$$AB = A \times B, \quad BC = B \times C, \quad AC = A \times C \text{ and}$$

$$ABC = A \times B \times C = AB \times C = BC \times A = AC \times B.$$

The order in which the treatment combinations are listed in Tables 13.12 and 13.13 is called the **standard order**. In this order factor A levels alternate in sign in singletons: $(-, +, -, +, \ldots)$, factor B levels alternate in sign in pairs: $(-, -, +, +, \ldots)$, factor C levels alternate in sign in quadruples: $(-, -, -, -, +, +, +, +, \ldots)$, and so on. Additional factors can be appended to the contrast coefficients table in a straightforward manner by following the standard order. The effects, namely I, A, B, AB, etc., are also listed in the standard order in Table 13.13. It should be emphasized that the order in which the experimental runs are made (the **run order**) should be random, not the standard order. The standard order is mainly useful for the analysis and presentation of results.

Example 13.7 (Bicycle Data: Calculation of the Effects)

Box, Hunter, and Hunter[3] (1978) describe a student project in which the student studied the effects of bicycle seat height, generator use, and tire pressure on the time taken to make a half-block uphill run. The study was done as a 2^3 experiment replicated twice ($n = 2$). The levels of the factors were as follows:

Seat height (Factor A):	26" (−), 30" (+),
Generator (Factor B):	Off (−), On (+),
Tire pressure (Factor C):	40 psi (−), 55 psi (+).

The data are shown in Table 13.14. Calculate all the effects.

Table 13.14 Travel Times from Bicycle Experiment

Factor			Time (Secs.)		
A	B	C	Run 1	Run 2	Mean
−	−	−	51	54	52.5
+	−	−	41	43	42.0
−	+	−	54	60	57.0
+	+	−	44	43	43.5
−	−	+	50	48	49.0
+	−	+	39	39	39.0
−	+	+	53	51	52.0
+	+	+	41	44	42.5

Main Effects:

$$A = \frac{(42.5 - 52.0) + (39.0 - 49.0) + (43.5 - 57.0) + (42.0 - 52.5)}{4} = -10.875.$$

$$B = \frac{(42.5 - 39.0) + (52.0 - 49.0) + (43.5 - 42.0) + (57.0 - 52.5)}{4} = +3.125.$$

$$C = \frac{(42.5 - 43.5) + (52.0 - 57.0) + (39.0 - 42.0) + (49.0 - 52.5)}{4} = -3.125.$$

---

[3] G. E. P. Box, W. G. Hunter, and J. S. Hunter (1978), *Statistics for Experimenters*, New York: Wiley, p. 368.

Interactions:

$$AB = \frac{\{(42.5 - 52.0) - (39.0 - 49.0)\} + \{(43.5 - 57.0) - (42.0 - 52.5)\}}{4} = -0.625.$$

$$AC = \frac{\{(42.5 - 52.0) - (43.5 - 57.0)\} + \{(39.0 - 49.0) - (42.0 - 52.5)\}}{4} = +1.125.$$

$$BC = \frac{\{(42.5 - 39.0) - (43.5 - 42.0)\} + \{(52.0 - 49.0) - (57.0 - 52.5)\}}{4} = +0.125.$$

$$ABC = \frac{\{(42.5 - 52.0) - (39.0 - 49.0)\} - \{(43.5 - 57.0) - (42.0 - 52.5)\}}{4} = +0.875.$$

It appears from the magnitudes of the effects that only the main effects are large; all interactions are small in comparison. The A and C main effects are negative, implying that to reduce the travel time the high levels of these factors (seat height = 30", tire pressure = 55 psi) should be used; the B main effect is positive, implying that to reduce the travel time the low level of B (generator off) should be used. Formal statistical tests will be done in Example 13.8 to confirm these findings. ◆

2^k Experiment.

We now generalize the definitions of the main effects and interactions to $k > 3$ factors. We assume n i.i.d. observations y_{ij} ($j = 1, 2, \ldots, n$) at the ith treatment combination and denote their sample mean by $\bar{y}_i$ ($i = 1, \ldots, 2^k$). Each estimated effect, of which there are $2^k - 1$, is a contrast of the form

$$\text{Est. effect} = \frac{\text{Contrast}}{2^{k-1}} = \frac{\sum_{i=1}^{2^k} c_i \bar{y}_i}{2^{k-1}} \tag{13.12}$$

where each $c_i = \pm 1$. The contrast coefficients for the main effects are given by $c_i = -1$ for the treatment combinations with that factor at low level and $c_i = +1$ for the treatment combinations with that factor at high level. The contrast coefficients for interactions are obtained by taking term-by-term products of the contrast vectors for the corresponding main effects. All contrasts are mutually orthogonal.

13.2.2 Statistical Inference for 2^k Experiments

In this section we discuss how to test hypotheses and calculate confidence intervals based on the estimated main effects and interactions, which are of the general form (13.12).

Each estimated effect is an unbiased estimate of the corresponding population effect. The variance of an estimated effect is given by

$$\text{Var(Est. effect)} = \frac{\sum_{i=1}^{2^k} c_i^2 \text{Var}(\bar{Y}_i)}{(2^{k-1})^2} = \frac{\sum_{i=1}^{2^k} (\pm 1)^2 (\sigma^2/n)}{(2^{k-1})^2} = \frac{(\sigma^2/n)2^k}{2^{2k-2}} = \frac{\sigma^2}{n2^{k-2}}. \tag{13.13}$$

Assuming that $n \geq 2$, we use the MSE to estimate σ^2, where

$$\text{MSE} = s^2 = \frac{\sum_{i=1}^{2^k} \sum_{j=1}^{n} (y_{ij} - \bar{y}_i)^2}{2^k (n - 1)}.$$

The d.f. for this estimate are $\nu = 2^k(n-1)$. Substituting this estimate of σ^2 in (13.13), we get the following formula for the standard error of an estimated effect:

$$\text{SE(Est. effect)} = \frac{s}{\sqrt{n2^{k-2}}}. \tag{13.14}$$

Therefore a $100(1-\alpha)\%$ confidence interval (CI) for any population effect is given by

$$\text{Est. effect} \pm t_{\nu,\alpha/2}\frac{s}{\sqrt{n2^{k-2}}}. \tag{13.15}$$

The t-statistic for testing the significance of any estimated effect is

$$t_{\text{Effect}} = \frac{(\text{Est. effect})}{\text{SE(Est. effect)}} = \frac{\sqrt{n2^{k-2}}(\text{Est. effect})}{s}. \tag{13.16}$$

Equivalently, one can use the following F-statistic to perform the test of significance:

$$F_{\text{Effect}} = t_{\text{Effect}}^2 = \frac{(n2^{k-2})(\text{Est. effect})^2}{s^2}. \tag{13.17}$$

The d.f. of this F-statistic equals 1, and $\nu = 2^k(n-1)$. An estimated effect is deemed significant at level α if

$$|t_{\text{Effect}}| > t_{\nu,\alpha/2} \iff F_{\text{Effect}} > t_{\nu,\alpha/2}^2 = f_{1,\nu,\alpha}.$$

EXAMPLE 13.8 (BICYCLE DATA: TESTS OF SIGNIFICANCE OF EFFECTS)

Test the significance of the individual effects calculated in Example 13.7 at $\alpha = .05$.

We first need to compute the MSE estimate of σ^2. For $n = 2$, the SSE can be calculated by using the fact that

$$\text{SSE} = \sum_{j=1}^{2}(y_{ij} - \bar{y}_i)^2 = \left(y_{i1} - \frac{y_{i1}+y_{i2}}{2}\right)^2 + \left(y_{i2} - \frac{y_{i1}+y_{i2}}{2}\right)^2 = \frac{1}{2}(y_{i1} - y_{i2})^2.$$

Therefore,

$$\begin{aligned}
\text{SSE} &= \sum_{i=1}^{2^k}\sum_{j=1}^{2}(y_{ij} - \bar{y}_i)^2 \\
&= \frac{1}{2}\sum_{i=1}^{8}(y_{i1} - y_{i2})^2 \\
&= \frac{1}{2}\{(51-54)^2 + (41-43)^2 + (54-60)^2 + (44-43)^2 \\
&\quad + (50-48)^2 + (39-39)^2 + (53-51)^2 + (41-44)^2\} \\
&= 33.50.
\end{aligned}$$

The error d.f. equals $2^k(n-1) = 8(2-1) = 8$. Therefore MSE $= 33.50/8 = 4.1875$ and $s = \sqrt{4.1875} = 2.046$. Using (13.14), the common standard error of all effects equals

$$\frac{s}{\sqrt{n2^{k-2}}} = \frac{2.046}{\sqrt{(2)(2)}} = 1.023.$$

The MSE can also be obtained from a one-way ANOVA of the data by regarding the eight factorial combinations as eight nominal treatments. The resulting ANOVA table is shown in Table 13.15.

Table 13.15 One-Way ANOVA of Bicycle Data

Source	Sum of Squares	Degrees of Freedom	Mean Squares	F
Treatments	560.9375	7	80.1339	19.136
Error	33.5000	8	4.1875	
Total	594.4375	15		

For illustration purposes, we will evaluate the significance of the effects by computing their 95% CI's as well as their t and F-statistics. The critical constant required for the 95% CI's and .05-level t-tests is $t_{8,.025} = 2.306$. So the margin of error for all intervals is $\pm(2.306)(1.023) = \pm2.359$. The critical constant for the F-tests is $f_{1,8,.05} = t_{8,.025}^2 = 5.32$. All calculations are summarized in Table 13.16. We see that only the main effects A, B, and C are significant at $\alpha = .05$. ◆

Table 13.16 Confidence Intervals and Test Statistics for Effects from Bicycle Data

Effect	95% CI	t	F
A	-10.875 ± 2.359	-10.628	112.974
B	3.125 ± 2.359	3.054	9.327
AB	-0.625 ± 2.359	-0.610	0.372
C	-3.125 ± 2.359	-3.054	9.327
AC	1.125 ± 2.359	1.098	1.206
BC	0.125 ± 2.359	0.122	0.015
ABC	0.875 ± 2.359	0.855	0.729

Sums of Squares for Effects.   We can write the F-statistic from (13.17) in the form usually expressed as the ratio of two mean squares:

$$F_{\text{Effect}} = \frac{(n2^{k-2})(\text{Est. effect})^2}{s^2} = \frac{\text{MS}_{\text{Effect}}}{\text{MSE}}.$$

Since the numerator d.f. is 1,

$$\text{MS}_{\text{Effect}} = \text{SS}_{\text{Effect}} = (n2^{k-2})(\text{Est. effect})^2. \tag{13.18}$$

The fact that the effects are mutually orthogonal contrasts has the consequence that the sums of squares for all effects add up to the $SS_{\text{Treatments}}$ for the 2^k treatment combinations. If $SS_1, SS_2, \ldots, SS_{2^k-1}$ denote the sums of squares for the $2^k - 1$ effects, then we have

$$SS_{\text{Treatments}} = n \sum_{i=1}^{2^k} (\bar{y}_i - \bar{\bar{y}})^2 = SS_1 + SS_2 + \cdots + SS_{2^k-1}.$$

For example, in a 2^3 experiment $SS_{\text{Treatments}}$ has $2^3 - 1 = 7$ d.f. and can be partitioned into

$$SS_{\text{Treatments}} = SSA + SSB + SSC + SSAB + SSAC + SSBC + SSABC.$$

If the treatment combinations are regarded merely as nominal treatments in a one-way layout, then $SS_{\text{Treatments}}$ with $2^k - 1$ d.f. would be used in the ANOVA of the data. Taking the **factorial structure** of the treatments into account enables us to partition $SS_{\text{Treatments}}$ into single d.f. orthogonal components (each of which corresponds to a main effect or an interaction) and thus do a finer analysis of the data.

EXAMPLE 13.9   (BICYCLE DATA: SUMS OF SQUARES OF THE EFFECTS)

Calculate the sums of squares for the main effects and interactions found in Example 13.7. Check that they add up to the sum of squares for treatments given in Table 13.15.

From (13.18) the formula used for computing the sum of squares of an effect is

$$SS_{\text{Effect}} = 4(\text{Est. effect})^2.$$

The sums of squares produced by the STATGRAPHICS package are listed in Table 13.17, which also gives a detailed ANOVA table. Note that these sums of squares add up to 560.9375, which is the sum of squares for the eight treatment combinations as seen from Table 13.15.   ◆

Table 13.17 ANOVA Table for Bicycle Data Produced by STATGRAPHICS+

Effect	Sum of Squares	DF	Mean Sq.	F-Ratio	P-value
A:A	473.062500	1	473.06250	112.97	0.0000
B:B	39.062500	1	39.06250	9.33	0.0157
C:C	39.062500	1	39.06250	9.33	0.0157
AB	1.562500	1	1.56250	0.37	0.5646
AC	5.062500	1	5.06250	1.21	0.3035
BC	0.062500	1	0.06250	0.01	0.9070
ABC	3.062500	1	3.06250	0.73	0.4262
Total error	33.500000	8	4.18750		
Total (corr.)	594.437500	15			

R-squared = 0.943644   R-squared (adj. for d.f.) = 0.894333

*Yates' Algorithm.   The above calculations can be performed using an algorithm devised by Frank Yates (1902–1994) which exploits the systematic nature of the effect contrasts. The algorithm is best explained through an example.

EXAMPLE 13.10   (BICYCLE DATA: YATES ALGORITHM)

To apply the Yates algorithm, first one must list the $2^k = 8$ treatment combinations and their sample means in the standard order. These are shown in the first two columns of Table 13.18, which also shows all calculations that follow. The $2^{k-1} = 4$ successive pairs of means are first added and then subtracted (subtracting the first mean from the second mean in each pair), and the results are entered in the same order in the column labeled I. Thus the first four and the last four entries in column I are obtained as follows:

$$42.0+52.5=94.5, \quad 43.5+57.0=100.5, \quad 39.0+49.0=88.0, \quad 42.5+52.0=94.5$$
$$42.0-52.5=-10.5, \quad 43.5-57.0=-13.5, \quad 39.0-49.0=-10.0, \quad 42.5-52.0=-9.5.$$

This operation of pairwise addition and subtraction is repeated on column I, and the results are entered in column II. This is continued on each successive column a total of k times. In the present example the operation is repeated $k = 3$ times, resulting in columns I, II, and III. The first entry of column III is simply the total of all means; the remaining entries are the contrasts in treatment means of the effects in the standard order. We divide the first entry in column III by $2^k = 8$ to obtain the grand mean; the remaining entries are divided by $2^{k-1} = 4$ to obtain the effect estimates. The result is shown in the column labeled Estimated Effect. Finally, the last column gives the sums of squares for effects obtained using (13.18), which are the same as those given in Table 13.17.   ◆

Table 13.18 Calculations for the Yates Algorithm for Bicycle Data

Treatment Combination	Treatment Mean	I	II	III	Estimated Effect	SS for Effect
(1)	52.5	94.5	195.0	377.5	$I = 47.1875$	–
a	42.0	100.5	182.5	-43.5	$A = -10.875$	473.0625
b	57.0	88.0	-24.0	12.5	$B = 3.125$	39.0625
ab	43.5	94.5	-19.5	-2.5	$AB = -0.625$	1.5625
c	49.0	-10.5	6.0	-12.5	$C = -3.125$	39.0625
ac	39.0	-13.5	6.5	4.5	$AC = 1.125$	5.0625
bc	52.0	-10.0	-3.0	0.5	$BC = 0.125$	0.0625
abc	42.5	-9.5	0.5	3.5	$ABC = 0.875$	4.1875

13.2.3 Regression Approach to 2^k Experiments

First consider a 2^2 experiment. Define indicator variables x_1 and x_2 to represent the levels of A and B:[4]

$$x_1 = \begin{cases} -1 & \text{if A is low} \\ +1 & \text{if A is high} \end{cases}$$

and

$$x_2 = \begin{cases} -1 & \text{if B is low} \\ +1 & \text{if B is high.} \end{cases}$$

Consider the multiple regression model

$$E(Y) = \gamma_0 + \gamma_1 x_1 + \gamma_2 x_2 + \gamma_{12} x_1 x_2. \tag{13.19}$$

The following is the relation between the parameters in this regression model and the main effects and the interaction effect defined earlier:

$$\gamma_0 = \mu, \quad \gamma_1 = \frac{\tau}{2}, \quad \gamma_2 = \frac{\beta}{2} \quad \text{and} \quad \gamma_{12} = \frac{(\tau\beta)}{2}.$$

It follows that the LS estimates of the main effects and interaction are related to the LS estimates of the regression coefficients in the model (13.19) as follows:

$$\hat{\gamma}_0 = \bar{\bar{y}}, \quad \hat{\gamma}_1 = \frac{\hat{\tau}}{2} = \frac{A}{2}, \quad \hat{\gamma}_2 = \frac{\hat{\beta}}{2} = \frac{B}{2}, \quad \text{and} \quad \hat{\gamma}_{12} = \frac{\widehat{(\tau\beta)}}{2} = \frac{AB}{2}. \tag{13.20}$$

It is straightforward to generalize the regression model (13.19) to $k > 2$. For example, for $k = 3$ the full regression model is

$$E(Y) = \gamma_0 + \gamma_1 x_1 + \gamma_2 x_2 + \gamma_3 x_3 + \gamma_{12} x_1 x_2 + \gamma_{13} x_1 x_3 + \gamma_{23} x_2 x_3 + \gamma_{123} x_1 x_2 x_3 \tag{13.21}$$

where x_1, x_2, and x_3 are indicator variables, taking values -1 and $+1$ for the low and high levels of factors A, B, and C, respectively. The regression coefficients are related to the main effects and interactions in the same way as for the 2^2 experiment model. In particular, the LS fit to the above model is

$$\hat{y} = \bar{\bar{y}} + \frac{A}{2}x_1 + \frac{B}{2}x_2 + \frac{C}{2}x_3 + \frac{AB}{2}x_1 x_2 + \frac{AC}{2}x_1 x_3 + \frac{BC}{2}x_2 x_3 + \frac{ABC}{2}x_1 x_2 x_3.$$

The t-statistics for testing the significance of the regression coefficients in the model (13.21) are the same as the corresponding t-statistics for the estimated effects given by (13.16).

If a reduced model is fitted by dropping some effects from the full model, then the estimates of the remaining effects are unchanged because of the orthogonal nature of the design. Thus if all interactions are dropped from the model, then the new fitted model is

$$\hat{y} = \bar{\bar{y}} + \frac{A}{2}x_1 + \frac{B}{2}x_2 + \frac{C}{2}x_3. \tag{13.22}$$

The sums of squares corresponding to the dropped effects may be pooled together with the pure error sum of squares to form an overall error sum of squares.

---

[4] In Section 13.1.6 we used the notation u_i and v_j to represent the levels of A and B. Here we use the notation x_1 and x_2 for two reasons: (i) Since each factor now has only two levels, we need just one indicator variable to represent the levels of each factor. (ii) This new notation readily extends to any number of factors.

The regression model can be used to predict the responses at specified combinations of the levels of the experimental factors. For a numerical factor, one can linearly interpolate between the low and the high level of the factor.[5] For instance, in the bicycle example the seat height of 28" (midway between the low height of 26" and the high height of 30") corresponds to $x_1 = 0$, and the seat height of 27" corresponds to $x_1 = -0.5$. The interpolation formula is

$$x_i = \frac{\text{Specified level} - \text{Average level}}{\text{Range}/2} = \frac{\text{Specified level} - (\text{High} + \text{Low})/2}{(\text{High} - \text{Low})/2}.$$

For a nominal factor (e.g., generator off or on) it is meaningless to interpolate between the high and low levels. If a full model is fitted, then the predicted response for each cell equals the corresponding cell sample mean. If a reduced model is fitted, then the predicted responses will differ in general from the corresponding cell sample means. The differences between the observed responses and the corresponding predicted (fitted) responses are the residuals, which may be used for model diagnostics, as discussed in the next subsection.

EXAMPLE 13.11 (BICYCLE DATA: THE MAIN EFFECTS MODEL)

Since all interactions were found nonsignificant in Example 13.8, now fit a model that includes only the main effects. Predict the minimum travel time using this model. Also predict the travel time for the following combination: seat height = 27", generator off, and tire pressure = 50 psi. Find the MSE for this model by pooling the sums of squares of the omitted interactions with the pure error sum of squares.

In Example 13.7, the three estimated main effects were calculated to be $A = -10.875$, $B = 3.125$, and $C = -3.125$. Also $\bar{\bar{y}} = 47.1875$. These estimated main effects remain unchanged, even when some or all of the other effects are dropped from the model. So the main effects regression model is

$$\hat{y} = 47.1875 - \frac{10.875}{2}x_1 + \frac{3.125}{2}x_2 - \frac{3.125}{2}x_3 = 47.1875 - 5.4375x_1 + 1.5625x_2 - 1.5625x_3.$$

Since the effects of A (seat height) and C (tire pressure) are negative, while that of B (generator) is positive, the average travel time is minimized when A and C are at set at high level, and B is set at low level. The minimum predicted travel time is

$$\hat{y} = 47.1875 - 5.4375(+1) + 1.5625(-1) - 1.5625(+1) = 38.625 \quad \text{sec.}$$

Similarly the predicted responses at the other seven treatment combinations can be computed. The x_i-values required to calculate the predicted travel time when seat height = 27", generator is off, and tire pressure = 50 psi are as follows:

$$x_1 = \frac{27 - (30 + 26)/2}{(30 - 26)/2} = -0.5, \quad x_2 = -1, \quad x_3 = \frac{50 - (55 + 40)/2}{(55 - 40)/2} = 0.333.$$

The predicted travel time at these settings equals

$$\hat{y} = 47.1875 - 5.4375(-0.5) + 1.5625(-1) - 1.5625(+0.333) = 47.823 \quad \text{sec.}$$

---

[5] Although extrapolation outside the experimental range of a factor is mathematically possible, it is not recommended, because the fitted model may not be valid in that region.

From Example 13.9 we obtain the sums of squares for the omitted interaction terms, which may be pooled as below:

$$\text{SSAB} + \text{SSAC} + \text{SSBC} + \text{SSABC} = 1.5625 + 5.0625 + 0.0625 + 4.1875 = 10.8750$$

with 4 d.f. This may be further pooled with the pure SSE = 33.50 with 8 d.f. to obtain a pooled SSE = 33.50 + 10.875 = 44.375 with $8 + 4 = 12$ d.f. and

$$\text{MSE} = \frac{44.375}{12} = 3.698.$$

This MSE may be used in subsequent statistical inferences.   ◆

13.2.4 Model Diagnostics using Residual Plots

As usual, the residuals are defined by

$$e_{ij} = y_{ij} - \hat{y}_{ij}$$

where the $\hat{y}_{ij}$ are computed from the fitted regression equation such as (13.22). The residuals can be used to check the model assumptions of normality and constant error variance by making the normal plot and the plot against the fitted values. If the time order of data collection is available, then a run chart of the residuals can reveal autocorrelations.

EXAMPLE 13.12   (BICYCLE DATA: MODEL DIAGNOSTICS)

Make residuals plots for the main effects model fitted in Example 13.11 to check the normality and constant variance assumptions.

The data values, the fitted values, and the residuals are shown in Table 13.19. The plot of the residuals against the fitted values is shown in Figure 13.6, and the normal plot of the residuals is shown in Figure 13.7. The dispersion among the residuals appears uneven with respect to the fitted values. The normal plot is satisfactory.   ◆

Table 13.19 The Data Values, Fitted Values, and Residuals from the Main Effects Model for Bicycle Data

Treatment Combination	Data Value Run 1	Data Value Run 2	Fitted Value	Residual Run 1	Residual Run 2
(1)	51	54	52.625	−1.625	1.375
a	41	43	41.750	−0.750	1.250
b	54	60	55.750	−1.750	4.250
ab	44	43	44.875	−0.875	−1.875
c	50	48	49.500	0.500	−1.500
ac	39	39	38.625	0.375	0.375
bc	53	51	52.625	0.375	−1.625
abc	41	44	41.750	−0.750	2.250

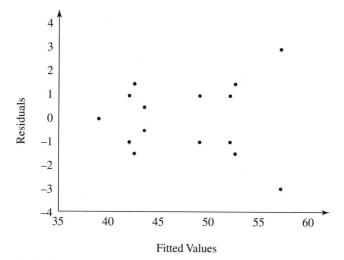

Figure 13.6   Plot of Residuals against Fitted Values from the Main Effects Model for Bicycle Data

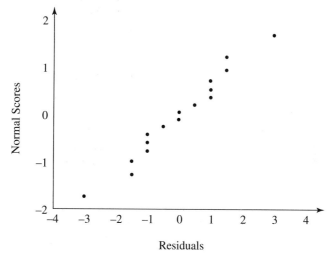

Figure 13.7   Normal Plot of Residuals from the Main Effects Model for Bicycle Data

13.2.5 Single Replicate Case

If a factorial experiment is replicated only once ($n = 1$), then no error d.f. are available to estimate σ^2. As a result, formal tests and confidence intervals given above cannot be used to assess the significance of the estimated effects. A graphical method based on the normal plot is usually employed instead.

When the number of effects is large (e.g., for $k = 4$ there are 15 effects), then, according to the effect sparsity principle, a majority of them are small and can be thought of as having zero mean; only a few are large. Recall that the estimated effects are independent because they are mutually orthogonal, normally distributed, and have a common variance given by (13.13). Therefore a majority of the estimated effects can be thought of as a random sample from a normal distribution with zero mean and a common variance; a few large ones have nonzero means. Therefore, if we make a normal plot of the estimated effects, then most fall roughly along a straight line and the few large ones appear as stragglers. These stragglers are identified as significant effects. (This approach may be used even when $n > 1$.)

Once the few significant effects are identified through a normal plot, one could fit a reduced model retaining only those effects. The sums of squares for the omitted effects can be pooled to form the error sum of squares (SSE). Note, however, that this SSE does not represent the pure error, rather it represents the error due to ignoring negligible effects. Since the sums of squares of the effects are independent, each with 1 d.f., the error d.f. equals the number of effects that are pooled. The resulting MSE can then be calculated by dividing the SSE just obtained by the error d.f., and formal statistical inferences can be carried out about the retained effects. One could also begin by specifying a reduced model (e.g., a model that includes only the main effects and two-factor interactions) and use the sums of squares of the ignored effects to estimate σ^2 and carry out formal inferences.

Example **13.13**

This example is based on a student team project for a quality control class at Northwestern University.[6] The student team analyzed the roller mixer process that makes a paramagnetic microparticles solution used in a immunodiagnostic testing machine for a health care products firm. The purpose was to evaluate which of the following four factors (each studied at two levels) affect the uniformity of the solution.

Factors	Low ($-$)	High ($+$)
Speed (A)	50 ft./min.	150 ft./min.
Bottle size (B)	2 L	50 L
Start % full (C)	20	85
Mix time (D)	10 min.	30 min.

The sixteen factor level combinations were run in a random order. After each run three samples of the microparticle solution were taken from the top, middle, and bottom of the bottle using a pipette and the iron concentration was measured. The uniformity of iron concentration was evaluated as the ratio of the maximum to the minimum concentration. The data are shown in Table 13.20. Note that there is only a single ratio for each treatment combination (which is computed from the three measurements of concentration). Calculate all the effects and evaluate their significance using a normal plot. Pool the negligible effects to form an error sum of squares, and test the significance of the retained effects at $\alpha = .10$.

When dealing with ratios it is usually preferable to analyze their logs. Table 13.20 lists the logs of the ratios (multiplied by 100) of the maximum to the minimum iron concentration. The calculated effects are listed in Table 13.21. The normal plot of these effects is shown in

---

[6] This example is courtesy of Professor Bruce Ankenman, Dept. of Industrial Engineering and Management Sciences, Northwestern University.

Table 13.20 The Iron Concentration Uniformity Data

Treatment Combination	Ratio of Max. to Min. Concentration	$100\log_{10}(\text{Ratio})$
(1)	1.0317	1.3553
a	1.0315	1.3469
b	1.0306	1.3090
ab	1.0491	2.0817
c	1.0275	1.1782
ac	1.0133	0.5738
bc	1.0203	0.8728
abc	1.0095	0.4106
d	1.0377	1.6072
ad	1.0431	1.8326
bd	1.0359	1.5318
abd	1.0542	2.2923
cd	1.0208	0.8941
acd	1.0402	1.7117
bcd	1.0177	0.7620
abcd	1.0393	1.6741

Table 13.21 Effect Estimates for the Iron Concentration Uniformity Data (Using $100\log_{10}(\text{Ratio})$ as Response Variable)

$I = 1.3396$	$A = 0.3017$	$B = 0.0543$	$AB = 0.1941$
$C = -0.6599$	$AC = -0.1359$	$BC = -0.2139$	$ABC = -0.1349$
$D = 0.3972$	$AD = 0.3772$	$BD = -0.0007$	$ABD = -0.0367$
$CD = 0.1044$	$ACD = 0.3218$	$BCD = 0.0754$	$ABCD = 0.0248$

Figure 13.8. From this plot we see that the C main effect is by far the largest. The other large effects are A, D, AD, and ACD. The factor B (bottle size) does not seem to have much effect.

The sums of squares of the 10 negligible effects (B, AB, AC, BC, BD, CD, ABC, ABD, BCD, and $ABCD$) can be computed using the formula $SS_{\text{Effect}} = (n2^{k-2})(\text{Est. effect})^2$ with $n = 1$ and $k = 4$. The pooled sum of squares equals 0.5664, which may be taken as the SSE with 10 d.f. giving MSE = 0.05664 and $s = \sqrt{0.05664} = 0.2380$. Therefore the common standard error for testing the significance of the retained effects (A, C, D, AD, and ACD) equals (from (13.14))

$$\text{SE(Est. effect)} = \frac{s}{\sqrt{n2^{k-2}}} = \frac{0.2380}{\sqrt{(1)(2^2)}} = 0.1190.$$

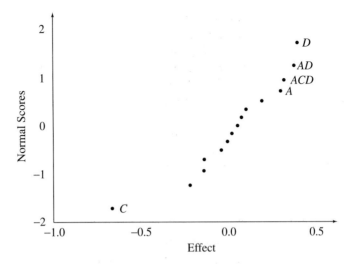

Figure 13.8   Normal Plot of the Effects for the Iron Concentration Data

Thus we obtain the following t-statistics for the retained effects:

Effect	Estimate	t
A	0.3017	2.535
C	−0.6599	−5.545
D	0.3972	3.338
AD	0.3772	3.170
ACD	0.3218	2.704

Comparing the t-statistics with the critical constant $t_{10,.05} = 1.812$, we see that all five effects are significant at the $\alpha = .10$ level (if no adjustment for multiplicity of tests is made).

The final model for predicting the uniformity of iron concentration is

$$\log_{10}(\text{Ratio}) = \bar{\bar{y}} + \frac{A}{2}x_1 + \frac{C}{2}x_3 + \frac{D}{2}x_4 + \frac{AD}{2}x_1x_4 + \frac{ACD}{2}x_1x_3x_4$$

$$= 1.3396 + 0.1508x_1 - 0.3300x_3 + 0.1986x_4 + 0.1886x_1x_4 + 0.1609x_1x_3x_4.$$

We can check that the best combination of the factors to maximize the uniformity (minimize the ratio of the maximum to the minimum concentration) is A High (Speed = 150 ft./min.), C High (Start % full = 85) and D Low (Mix time = 10 min.). The bottle size is unimportant.   ◆

13.3   OTHER SELECTED TYPES OF TWO-FACTOR EXPERIMENTS

13.3.1 Two-Factor Experiments with Crossed and Mixed Factors

Consider a two-factor experiment as in Section 13.1, but now suppose that A is a fixed factor, while B is a random factor. Thus we have a **mixed factors** experiment. Factor

A has a levels, factor B has b levels, and the two are crossed. We assume a balanced design with $n \geq 2$ observations at each of the ab treatment combinations.

For example, consider an experiment to compare three testing laboratories. Material to be tested comes in batches, and several samples from each batch are tested in each laboratory. Here the laboratories are a fixed factor, while the batches are a random factor. The two factors are **crossed**, since samples from each batch are tested in each laboratory.

Let y_{ijk} be the kth observation from the (i, j)th treatment combination and denote the corresponding r.v. by Y_{ijk} ($i = 1, \ldots, a, j = 1, \ldots, b, k = 1, \ldots, n$). To write a probabilistic model for Y_{ijk} we consider any effect involving a random factor as an r.v. Thus the model is

$$Y_{ijk} = \mu + \tau_i + \beta_j + (\tau\beta)_{ij} + \epsilon_{ijk} \tag{13.23}$$

where μ and the τ_i are fixed parameters, while the β_j and the $(\tau\beta)_{ij}$ are random parameters; the ϵ_{ijk} are i.i.d. $N(0, \sigma^2)$ random errors. This is called a **mixed effects model**.

The fixed τ_i represent the main effects of A, which are assumed to sum to zero: $\sum_{i=1}^{a} \tau_i = 0$. The random β_j are the main effects of B, which are assumed to be i.i.d. $N(0, \sigma_B^2)$, where σ_B^2 is called the variance component of the B main effect. Finally, the random $(\tau\beta)_{ij}$ are the AB interactions, which are assumed to be i.i.d. $N(0, \sigma_{AB}^2)$, where σ_{AB}^2 is called the variance component of the AB interaction.[7] The β_j and the $(\tau\beta)_{ij}$ are assumed to be mutually independent and also independent of the ϵ_{ijk}. It follows that

$$\text{Var}(Y_{ijk}) = \sigma_Y^2 = \sigma_B^2 + \sigma_{AB}^2 + \sigma^2. \tag{13.24}$$

This is the **variance components model** corresponding to (13.23).

The decomposition of the total sum of squares (SST) into four independent components, namely, SSA, SSB, SSAB, and SSE, is exactly the same as that given by (13.8) for the fixed-effects model of Section 13.1. To derive the estimates of the variance components and hypothesis tests, we need the expressions for the expected values of the mean squares. These expressions are as follows:

$$E(\text{MSA}) = \sigma^2 + n\sigma_{AB}^2 + \frac{n \sum_{i=1}^{a} \tau_i^2}{a - 1} \tag{13.25}$$

$$E(\text{MSB}) = \sigma^2 + n\sigma_{AB}^2 + an\sigma_B^2$$

$$E(\text{MSAB}) = \sigma^2 + n\sigma_{AB}^2$$

$$E(\text{MSE}) = \sigma^2.$$

---

[7] This model is called the **unrestricted model**. In statistical literature another model, called the **restricted model**, is sometimes employed, which assumes that the $(\tau\beta)_{ij}$ summed over j equal to zero for each $i = 1, \ldots, a$. However, this introduces correlations between the $(\tau\beta)_{ij}$'s, which makes interpretation of the model more difficult.

From these expressions we see that the unbiased estimates of the variance components are as follows:

$$\hat{\sigma}^2 = \text{MSE}, \quad \hat{\sigma}^2_{AB} = \frac{\text{MSAB} - \hat{\sigma}^2}{n} \quad \text{and} \quad \hat{\sigma}^2_B = \frac{\text{MSB} - \hat{\sigma}^2 - n\hat{\sigma}^2_{AB}}{an}. \quad (13.26)$$

The hypotheses usually tested are:

$$H_{0A}: \tau_1 = \ldots = \tau_a = 0 \qquad \text{vs.} \qquad H_{1A}: \text{At least one } \tau_i \neq 0.$$
$$H_{0B}: \sigma^2_B = 0 \qquad \text{vs.} \qquad H_{1B}: \sigma^2_B > 0.$$
$$H_{0AB}: \sigma^2_{AB} = 0 \qquad \text{vs.} \qquad H_{1AB}: \sigma^2_{AB} > 0.$$

The F-statistic to test any null hypothesis is obtained by taking the ratio of two mean squares which have the same expected values under that null hypothesis. This, together with the fact that the mean squares are statistically independent, implies that the ratio of the mean squares has an F-distribution with the numerator and denominator d.f. equal to the d.f. associated with the respective mean squares. For example, if H_{0A} is true, then we have $\sum_{i=1}^{a} \tau_i^2 = 0$, and so $E(\text{MSA}) = E(\text{MSAB})$. Therefore the ratio

$$F_A = \frac{\text{MSA}}{\text{MSAB}} \sim F_{a-1,(a-1)(b-1)}.$$

If H_{1A} is true, then $\sum_{i=1}^{a} \tau_i^2 > 0$ and $E(\text{MSA}) > E(\text{MSAB})$. So we reject H_{0A} for large values of F_A. Similarly tests of H_{0B} and H_{0AB} are derived. The α-level tests of H_{0A}, H_{0B}, and H_{0AB} are summarized below.

$$\text{Reject } H_{0A} \text{ if } F_A = \frac{\text{MSA}}{\text{MSAB}} \qquad > \qquad f_{a-1,(a-1)(b-1),\alpha}.$$

$$\text{Reject } H_{0B} \text{ if } F_B = \frac{\text{MSB}}{\text{MSAB}} \qquad > \qquad f_{b-1,(a-1)(b-1),\alpha}.$$

$$\text{Reject } H_{0AB} \text{ if } F_{AB} = \frac{\text{MSAB}}{\text{MSE}} \qquad > \qquad f_{(a-1)(b-1),\nu,\alpha}.$$

The above calculations are conveniently summarized in the ANOVA table shown in Table 13.22. Notice that the tests of H_{0A} and H_{0B} are different from those given in Section 13.1, where both factors were assumed to be fixed. Specifically, here MSAB is the denominator for F_A and F_B instead of MSE.

EXAMPLE 13.14   (SERVICE TIMES OF DISK DRIVES: ANOVA AND VARIANCE COMPONENT ESTIMATES)

Three types of disk drives were compared in terms of their service times. Five samples of each type of disk drive were repaired by three service technicians.[8] Here the disk drives is a fixed factor and the technicians is a random factor. The data are shown in Table 13.23. Give the ANOVA table for these data. Test if there are significant differences between the three disk drives. Also

---

[8] L. H. Kao and S. Chakraborti (1998), "Nonparametric procedures for comparing treatments with a control in a randomized complete block design," *Communications in Statistics, Ser. A*, **27**, pp. 687–704.

Table 13.22 ANOVA Table for Two-Way Crossed Layout with Mixed Factors

Source of Variation	Sum of Squares, (SS)	Degrees of Freedom, (d.f.)	Mean Square, (MS)	Expected Mean Square, E(MS)	F
Main Effects A	$SSA = bn \sum \hat{\tau}_i^2$	$a-1$	$MSA = \frac{SSA}{a-1}$	$\sigma^2 + n\sigma_{AB}^2 + \frac{n\sum_{i=1}^{a}\tau_i^2}{a-1}$	$\dfrac{MSA}{MSAB}$
Main Effects B	$SSB = an \sum \hat{\beta}_j^2$	$b-1$	$MSB = \frac{SSB}{b-1}$	$\sigma^2 + n\sigma_{AB}^2 + an\sigma_B^2$	$\dfrac{MSB}{MSAB}$
Interaction AB	$SSAB = n \sum \sum \widehat{(\tau\beta)}_{ij}^2$	$(a-1)(b-1)$	$MSAB = \frac{SSAB}{(a-1)(b-1)}$	$\sigma^2 + n\sigma_{AB}^2$	$\dfrac{MSAB}{MSE}$
Error	$SSE = \sum \sum \sum e_{ijk}^2$	$N-ab$	$MSE = \frac{SSE}{N-ab}$	σ^2	
Total	$SST = \sum \sum \sum (y_{ijk} - \bar{y}_{...})^2$	$N-1$			

Table 13.23 Service Times for Disk Drives

Disk	Technician		
Drive	1	2	3
1	51.0, 51.9, 51.8, 49.7, 51.6	61.1, 61.9, 63.0, 63.2, 61.2	70.6, 70.2, 70.8, 69.8, 72.4
2	51.6, 50.4, 49.5, 51.5, 50.3	61.2, 57.6, 59.1, 60.4, 59.7	70.7, 69.0, 71.2, 70.8, 71.7
3	49.5, 46.4, 50.2, 49.3, 50.4	60.0, 59.5, 59.4, 59.5, 58.5	68.0, 67.7, 70.8, 69.5, 69.2

estimate and test the significance of the technician effect and drive × technician interaction. Use $\alpha = .05$ for all tests.

The ANOVA table produced using MINITAB is shown in Table 13.24. We see that there are significant differences between the disk drives ($P = .037$). The differences between the technicians are also very large. The variance component due to technicians is 98.0736, which accounts for almost all the variance of the service time (estimated to be $98.0736 + 0.1717 + 1.2120 = 99.4573$). The interaction is quite nonsignificant. The variance component estimates can be verified using the formulas in (13.26):

$$\hat{\sigma}^2 = MSE = 1.21$$

$$\hat{\sigma}_{AB}^2 = \frac{MSAB - \hat{\sigma}^2}{n} = \frac{2.07 - 1.21}{5} = 0.172$$

$$\hat{\sigma}_B^2 = \frac{MSB - \hat{\sigma}^2 - n\hat{\sigma}_{AB}^2}{an} = \frac{1473.17 - 1.21 - (5)(0.172)}{(3)(5)} = 98.073.$$

These agree with the MINITAB estimates except for roundoff errors.

The conclusion one may draw from this analysis is that, regardless of the technician, the average differences between the service times for the disk drives remain about the same. Drive 1 requires the maximum average service time ($\bar{y}_{1..} = 61.347$), drive 2 the next highest ($\bar{y}_{2..} = 60.313$), and drive 3 the least ($\bar{y}_{3..} = 59.193$). The large variability between the technicians suggests possible differences in their skills levels. More training may be needed to provide the necessary skills to those lacking them. ◆

Table 13.24 ANOVA Table from MINITAB for the Disk Drive Data

```
Analysis of Variance (Balanced Designs)
Factor      Type Levels Values
DRIVE       fixed    3    1    2    3
TECH        random   3    1    2    3

Analysis of Variance for TIME
Source          DF        SS        MS       F       P
DRIVE            2      34.80     17.40     8.40   0.037
TECH             2    2946.35   1473.17   711.49   0.000
DRIVE*TECH       4       8.28      2.07     1.71   0.170
Error           36      43.63      1.21
Total           44    3033.06

Source          Variance Error Expected Mean Square
                component  term (using unrestricted model)
1 DRIVE                     3    (4) + 5(3) + 5Q[1]
2 TECH           98.0736    4    (4) + 5(3) + 15(2)
3 DRIVE*TECH      0.1717    4    (4) + 5(3)
4 Error           1.2120         (4)
```

13.3.2 Two-Factor Experiments with Nested and Mixed Factors

Consider the example from the previous subsection concerning an experiment to compare three testing laboratories, but now suppose that samples from different batches of a material are tested in different laboratories. Since the batches tested in the three laboratories are not the same, we say that the batches are **nested** inside the laboratories. The laboratories are a fixed factor while the batches are a random factor. Thus we have a nested design with mixed factors.

Let A be a fixed factor with a levels. Suppose that for each level of A, b levels of factor B are separately chosen at random. Thus B is a random factor nested under A. At each factor level combination we assume $n \geq 2$ i.i.d. observations $y_{ijk}, i = 1, \ldots, a, j = 1, \ldots, b, k = 1, \ldots, n$.

Because the levels of B for each level of A are different, the "main effects" of B can only be defined separately for each level of A. Furthermore, since we do not have the same combinations of levels of A and B, interactions between A and B are undefined. We denote the main effects of A by τ_i and the main effects of B under the

ith level of A by $\beta_{j(i)}$, and we use the model

$$Y_{ijk} = \mu + \tau_i + \beta_{j(i)} + \epsilon_{ijk} \tag{13.27}$$

where μ and the τ_i are fixed unknown parameters with $\sum_{i=1}^{a} \tau_i = 0$, the $\beta_{j(i)}$ are i.i.d. $N(0, \sigma_{B(A)}^2)$ r.v.'s, and the ϵ_{ijk} are i.i.d. $N(0, \sigma^2)$ random errors. We assume that the $\beta_{j(i)}$ and the ϵ_{ijk} are mutually independent of each other. The variance component model is

$$\text{Var}(Y_{ijk}) = \sigma_Y^2 = \sigma_{B(A)}^2 + \sigma^2$$

where $\sigma_{B(A)}^2$ is the variance component of B nested under A and σ^2 is the error variance.

According to the model (13.27), the total sum of squares (SST) can be partitioned into three components as follows:

$$\underbrace{\sum_{i=1}^{a}\sum_{j=1}^{b}\sum_{k=1}^{n}(y_{ijk} - \bar{y}_{...})^2}_{\text{SST}} = \underbrace{bn\sum_{i=1}^{a}(\bar{y}_{i..} - \bar{y}_{...})^2}_{\text{SSA}} + \underbrace{n\sum_{i=1}^{a}\sum_{j=1}^{b}(\bar{y}_{ij.} - \bar{y}_{i..})^2}_{\text{SSB(A)=SSB+SSAB}}$$

$$+ \underbrace{\sum_{i=1}^{a}\sum_{j=1}^{b}\sum_{k=1}^{n}(y_{ijk} - \bar{y}_{ij.})^2}_{\text{SSE}}.$$

This is the same decomposition as in (13.8) except that the two terms, SSB and SSAB, are now pooled into a single term, which equals $n\sum_{i=1}^{a}\sum_{j=1}^{b}(\bar{y}_{ij.} - \bar{y}_{i..})^2$. This term represents the sum of squares due to the differences between the levels of factor B nested under factor A and is denoted by SSB(A). The other two terms have the same interpretation as before, i.e., the sum of squares due to factor A (SSA) and the error sum of squares (SSE). Thus the above decomposition of SST can be written as the following ANOVA identity:

$$\text{SST} = \text{SSA} + \text{SSB(A)} + \text{SSE}. \tag{13.28}$$

The degrees of freedom (d.f.) for SSB(A) are pooled from the d.f. for SSB and SSAB to yield $(b-1) + (a-1)(b-1) = a(b-1)$; this can also be explained as $b-1$ d.f. due to b levels of B under each of the a levels of A. The d.f. for SSA and SSE are the same as before. Thus we have the following decomposition of the d.f.:

$$\underbrace{N-1}_{\text{(Total d.f.)}} = \underbrace{a-1}_{\text{(Main effect A d.f.)}} + \underbrace{a(b-1)}_{\text{(Main effect B nested under A d.f.)}} + \underbrace{N-ab}_{\text{(Error d.f.)}}$$

The mean squares are computed by dividing the sums of squares by their d.f. The expected values of the mean squares are as follows:

$$E(\text{MSA}) = \sigma^2 + n\sigma^2_{B(A)} + \frac{n\sum_{i=1}^{a}\tau_i^2}{a-1}$$

$$E(\text{MSB(A)}) = \sigma^2 + n\sigma^2_{B(A)}$$

$$E(\text{MSE}) = \sigma^2.$$

The F-statistics to test the hypotheses $H_{0A}: \tau_1 = \cdots = \tau_a = 0$ and $H_{0B(A)}: \sigma^2_{B(A)} = 0$ can be derived by referring to the expected mean squares. The final calculations are summarized in Table 13.25. The variance components $\sigma^2_{B(A)}$ and σ^2 can be estimated as follows:

$$\hat{\sigma}^2 = \text{MSE} \quad \text{and} \quad \hat{\sigma}^2_{B(A)} = \frac{\text{MSB(A)} - \hat{\sigma}^2}{n}.$$

Table 13.25 ANOVA Table for Two-Way Nested Layout with Mixed Factors

Source of Variation (Source)	Sum of Squares SS	Degrees of Freedom d.f.	Mean Square MS	Expected Mean Square E(MS)	F
Main effects A	SSA $=bn\sum(\bar{y}_{i..}-\bar{y}_{...})^2$	$a-1$	$\frac{\text{SSA}}{a-1}$	$\sigma^2 + n\sigma^2_{B(A)} + \frac{n\sum_{i=1}^{a}\tau_i^2}{a-1}$	$\frac{\text{MSA}}{\text{MSB(A)}}$
Main effects B under A	SSB(A) $=n\sum\sum(\bar{y}_{ij.}-\bar{y}_{i..})^2$	$a(b-1)$	$\frac{\text{SSB(A)}}{a(b-1)}$	$\sigma^2 + n\sigma^2_{B(A)}$	$\frac{\text{MSB(A)}}{\text{MSE}}$
Error	SSE $=\sum\sum\sum(y_{ijk}-\bar{y}_{ij.})^2$	$N-ab$	$\frac{\text{SSE}}{N-ab}$	σ^2	
Total	SST $=\sum\sum\sum(y_{ijk}-\bar{y}_{...})^2$	$N-1$			

The two-way nested design represents two stages of nesting. The nesting of B under A is the first stage of nesting, and the observations are nested under AB treatment combinations. More generally, such designs are called **multistage nested designs**. For example, a three-stage nested design has factor B nested under A, factor C nested under each AB combination, and the observations nested under each ABC combination. We can also have a combination of crossed and nested factors. For example, suppose three assay techniques (factor A) are to be tested in two laboratories (factor B). Four technicians (factor C) from each laboratory perform all three assay techniques. In this experiment factors A and B, and A and C, are crossed with each other, while C is nested under B. For the analysis of more complex designs we refer the reader to Montgomery (1997).[9]

---

[9] D. C. Montgomery (1997), *Design and Analysis of Experiments*, 4th ed., New York: Wiley.

13.4 CHAPTER SUMMARY

This chapter discusses **two-factor experiments** with arbitrary numbers of levels per factor and k-factor experiments with two levels per factor (2^k **factorial experiments**). Two-factor experiments are considered for balanced designs (equal number of replicates per treatment combination) and unbalanced designs (unequal number of replicates per treatment combination), while 2^k experiments are considered only for balanced designs.

In a balanced two-factor experiment (with **crossed factors** A and B), the sums of squares for the **main effects** of A and B (SSA and SSB) and the **interaction** AB (SSAB) are statistically independent and have simple closed forms. The total sum of squares (SST) can be decomposed as follows:

$$SST = SSA + SSB + SSAB + SSE$$

where SSE is the error sum of squares. Similarly, the total degrees of freedom (d.f.) can be decomposed into

$$\underbrace{N-1}_{\text{(Total d.f.)}} = \underbrace{a-1}_{\text{(Main effect A d.f.)}} + \underbrace{b-1}_{\text{(Main effect B d.f.)}} + \underbrace{(a-1)(b-1)}_{\text{(Interaction AB d.f.)}} + \underbrace{N-ab.}_{\text{(Error d.f.)}}$$

The mean squares are obtained by dividing the sums of squares by their d.f., e.g., MSA = SSA/$(a-1)$. The F-ratios,

$$F_A = \frac{MSA}{MSE}, \quad F_B = \frac{MSB}{MSE} \quad \text{and} \quad F_{AB} = \frac{MSAB}{MSE}$$

are used to test the significance of A and B main effects, and AB interactions, respectively.

The above ANOVA identity does not hold in an unbalanced two-factor experiment. The **extra sum of squares method** is used to obtain the sums of squares for F-tests of the main effects and interactions, but these sums of squares do not have simple closed forms.

In a 2^k factorial experiment with $n \geq 1$ replicates per treatment we can estimate a total of $2^k - 1$ effects, which consist of k main effects, $\binom{k}{2}$ two-factor interactions, $\binom{k}{3}$ three-factor interactions, etc. These effects are mutually orthogonal contrasts among the treatment means. The standard error of any estimated effect equals $s/\sqrt{n2^{k-2}}$, where $s^2 = $ MSE is an estimate of the experimental error variance with $2^k(n-1)$ d.f. The t-statistic to test the significance of an effect equals (Est. effect)/SE(Effect). These t-statistics cannot be computed when $n = 1$, because no error estimate is available. A normal plot technique is used to judge the significance of the estimated effects in this single replicate case.

A sum of squares $= n2^{k-2}(\text{Est. effect})^2$ can be defined for each effect. Each sum of squares is associated with 1 d.f. Because the contrasts corresponding to the estimated effects are mutually orthogonal, these sums of squares are statistically independent and add up to the treatment sum of squares, which has $2^k - 1$ d.f.

Two other types of two-factor experiments are discussed in the final section. They are **mixed factor experiments** (one factor fixed and the other factor random) and **nested factor experiments**. The focus in these experiments is on estimating the **variance components** associated with **random effects**.

■ **EXERCISES**

Section 13.1

13.1   To study the effects of a cow's age (mature ($\geq$ 5 years old) or young (2 years old)) and breed (Guernsey, Holstein-Fresian, or Jersey) on the percentage of butterfat in milk, ten cows were sampled from each of the six age-breed groups. The group means and standard deviations are given in the table below.[10]

Age		Breed		
		Guernsey	Holstein-Fresian	Jersey
Mature	Mean	4.85	3.72	5.24
	SD	0.503	0.329	0.547
Young	Mean	5.05	3.62	5.34
	SD	0.466	0.166	0.674

(a) Calculate the main effects of age and breed and their interactions.

(b) Calculate the pooled estimate of the error variance (MSE). What are its degrees of freedom?

(c) Calculate the ANOVA table. Test whether there is significant interaction at $\alpha = .05$. Is it meaningful to test for age and breed effects? If so, test for those effects using $\alpha = .05$ and interpret the results.

13.2   ■ The following table[11] gives yields of a chemical process using six different alcohol-base combinations. Four replicate observations were made for each combination.

Percent Yields for Alcohol/Base Combinations

Alcohol	Base			
	1		2	
1	91.3	89.9	87.3	89.4
	90.7	91.4	91.5	88.3
2	89.3	88.1	92.3	91.5
	90.4	91.4	90.6	94.7
3	89.5	87.6	93.1	90.7
	88.3	90.3	91.5	89.8

(a) Make the main effects and interaction plots. What do these plots suggest about the effects of alcohol and base on the percent yield?

---

[10] R. R. Sokal and F. J. Rohlf (1981), *Biometry*, 2nd ed., San Francisco: W. H. Freeman, p. 368. Adapted from data reprinted in *Small Data Sets*, p. 18.

[11] P. R. Nelson (1990), "Design and Analysis of Experiments," Chapter 14 in *Handbook of Statistics for Engineers and Scientists* (ed.: H. M. Wadsworth), New York: McGraw-Hill.

(b) Calculate the ANOVA table. Test for the alcohol and base main effects and inter-action. Use $\alpha = .05$.

(c) Make residual plots to check the normality and constant variance assumptions.

13.3 ◼ A two-factor experiment was conducted to study how the thrust of a small rocket engine is affected by varying altitude cycling (present or absent) and temperature (four levels). Four engines were tested under each factor-level combination. The data are given in the table below.[12]

Altitude	Temperature							
Cycling	\multicolumn{2}{c}{1}	\multicolumn{2}{c}{2}	\multicolumn{2}{c}{3}	\multicolumn{2}{c}{4}
Present	21.60	22.17	11.50	11.32	21.08	20.44	11.72	12.82
	21.86	21.86	9.82	11.18	21.66	20.44	13.03	12.29
Absent	21.60	21.09	11.54	11.14	19.09	19.50	13.11	11.26
	21.60	19.57	11.75	11.69	21.31	20.11	13.72	12.09

(a) Make the main effects and interaction plots. What do these plots suggest about the effects of altitude cycling and temperature on the rocket thrust?

(b) Calculate the ANOVA table. Show that there is no significant altitude cycling by temperature interaction. Test for the main effects of altitude cycling and tempera-ture. Use $\alpha = .05$.

(c) Make residual plots to check the normality and constant variance assumptions.

13.4 ◼ A taste test was conduced by General Foods to determine the palatability resulting from using a high or low amount of liquid and making the texture fine or coarse. The palatability was scored from -3 (terrible) to $+3$ (excellent). Sixteen consumer groups (50 people per group) were given one of the four liquid-texture combinations to score, four groups per combination. The response for each group is the total of their individual palatability scores, which is tabled below.[13]

Low Liquid, Coarse Texture	Low Liquid, Fine Texture	High Liquid, Coarse Texture	High Liquid, Fine Texture
35	104	24	65
39	129	21	94
77	97	39	86
16	84	60	64

(a) Make the main effect and interaction plots. What do these plots suggest about the effects of liquid and texture on the palatability?

(b) Calculate the ANOVA table.

[12] Data adapted from S. R. Wood and D. E. Hartrigsen (1964), "Statistical design and analysis of qualification test program for a small rocket engine," *Industrial Quality Control*, **20**, pp. 14–18.

[13] E. Street and M. G. Carroll (1972), "Preliminary evaluation of a food product," in *Statistics: A Guide to the Unknown*, ed. J. M. Tanur et al, San Francisco: Holden-Day, pp. 220–238.

(c) Test whether there is a significant liquid by texture interaction at $\alpha = .01$. Is it meaningful to test for liquid and texture main effects? If yes, test for the effects and interpret your results; otherwise, explain why not.

(d) Make residual plots to check the normality and constant variance assumptions.

13.5 Refer to the butterfat data of Exercise 13.1. Find 95% simultaneous confidence intervals for pairwise differences in the mean butterfat content of the three breeds. Which breed(s) produces significantly higher amounts of butterfat?

13.6 Refer to the rocket thrust data of Exercise 13.3. Find 95% simultaneous confidence intervals for pairwise differences in the mean rocket thrust at the four temperatures tested. At which temperature(s) does a rocket engine produce significantly greater thrust?

13.7 ◼ An experiment was conducted to investigate the strength of a weld in a steel bar. Two factors were varied: the gauge bar setting (the distance the weld die travels during the automatic weld cycle), which had three settings, and the welding time (total time of the automatic weld cycle), which was fixed at five levels. The weld strength data are shown in the table below.[14]

Gauge Bar	Welding Time									
Setting	1		2		3		4		5	
1	10	12	13	17	21	30	18	16	17	21
2	15	19	14	12	30	38	15	11	14	12
3	10	8	12	9	10	5	14	15	19	11

(a) Make the main effects and interaction plots. What do these plots suggest about the effects of time and setting on the strength of the weld?

(b) Calculate the ANOVA table. Show that there is a significant interaction at $\alpha = .05$. Refer to your interaction plots and cell means to explain the source of interaction. (*Hint*: For each gauge bar setting, note the welding time which produced the greatest average weld strength.)

(c) Make residual plots to check the normality and constant variance assumptions.

13.8 ◼ Refer to the welding strength data of the previous exercise. Fit a regression model to the data. Interpret the parameter estimates from the fitted model.

13.9 ◼ An optical component company had quality problems with their polymer lenses. A cleaning process used in production was not satisfactory. To improve the cleaning step, four different types of detergents, two different temperatures, and two different agitation rates were tested. To keep the analysis simple, the agitation rate factor is ignored here. In each batch $n = 100$ lenses were washed. The following table shows the number of defective lenses from each batch.[15]

[14] V. L. Anderson and R. A. McLean (1984), *Design of Experiments: A Realistic Approach*, New York: Marcel-Dekker.

[15] Data adapted from S. Bisgaard (1997), "Accommodating four-level factors in two-level factorial designs," *Quality Engineering*, **10**, pp. 201–206.

	Detergent							
Temperature	1		2		3		4	
Low	48	55	36	24	45	41	60	63
High	42	54	64	66	57	52	46	50

(a) These data may be assumed to be binomially distributed. To stabilize the variance (see Section 10.4.3) apply the **Freeman-Tukey transformation** (a modification of the arcsin transformation from Exercise 10.25):

$$y = \frac{1}{2}\left[\arcsin\left(\sqrt{\frac{n\hat{p}}{n+1}}\right) + \arcsin\left(\sqrt{\frac{n\hat{p}+1}{n+1}}\right)\right]$$

where $\hat{p}$ is the proportion of defective lenses. Use the transformed data in the following analyses.

(b) Make the main effects and interaction plots. What do these plots suggest about the main effects of detergent and temperature on the proportion of defective lenses produced?

(c) Calculate the ANOVA table. Test for significance of the main effects of detergents and temperatures and their interaction at $\alpha = .05$. Interpret the results.

13.10 Consider a two-factor experiment with $a = 2$ row factor levels and $b = 3$ column factor levels. Write regression models for the six treatment combinations.

13.11 ◨ Refer to the rocket thrust data of Exercise 13.3. Fit a regression model to the data. Interpret the parameter estimates from the fitted model.

13.12 ◨ Refer to the lens data from Exercise 13.9. Fit a regression model to the transformed data. Interpret the parameter estimates from the fitted model.

13.13 ◨ A commonly debated question is the relative effects of heredity and environment on intelligence. The following data[16] give the IQ scores of children with four combinations of the socioeconomic status (SES) of biological and adoptive parents: low biological and low adoptive SES, low biological and high adoptive SES, high biological and low adoptive SES, and high biological and high adoptive SES. Although the design called for ten children in each group, only eight children were obtained in the third group.

(a) Analyze the main effects of the SES for the biological and adoptive parents and their interaction using the analysis of variance. Interpret the results.

(b) Fit separate regression models to obtain the sums of squares for the main effects and interaction. Check that they agree with those obtained in part (a).

---

[16] C. Capron and M. Duyme (1991), "Children's IQs and SES of biological and adoptive parents in a balanced cross-fostering study," *European Bulletin of Cognitive Psychology*, **11**, pp. 323–348. Reprinted in F. L. Ramsey and D. W. Schafer (1997), *The Statistical Sleuth*, Belmont, CA: Duxbury Press.

Biological Parents' SES	Adoptive Parents' SES	IQ Scores of Children									
Low	Low	92	91	98	83	99	68	76	115	86	116
Low	High	94	103	99	125	111	93	101	94	125	91
High	Low	98	99	91	124	100	116	113	119		
High	High	136	99	121	133	125	131	103	115	116	117

13.14 ■ The following table reproduces data from Exercise 13.2 but with some observations missing as indicated. This makes the design unbalanced. Calculate the ANOVA table and do the tests for the main effects and interaction. Compare the results with those previously obtained.

Percent Yields for Alcohol/Base Combinations

Alcohol	Base			
	1		2	
1	91.3	–	87.3	89.4
	90.7	91.4	91.5	88.3
2	–	88.1	92.3	91.5
	90.4	–	–	94.7
3	89.5	87.6	–	–
	88.3	90.3	91.5	89.8

Section 13.2

13.15 The sample means from a 2^2 experiment with 3 observations per treatment combination are as follows:

$$\bar{y}_{(1)} = 5, \qquad \bar{y}_a = 9, \qquad \bar{y}_b = 7, \qquad \bar{y}_{ab} = 15.$$

The SSE was calculated to be 96.

(a) Calculate the main effects A and B and interaction effect AB.

(b) Calculate the MSE. What are the error degrees of freedom?

(c) Which effects are significant at $\alpha = 0.10$?

13.16 ■ An experiment was conducted to study weight gain in rats fed four different diets, distinguished by the source of protein (beef or cereal) and amount of protein (low or high). The data are as follows:[17]

---

[17] G. W. Snedecor and W. G. Cochran (1967), *Statistical Methods*, 6th ed., Ames, IA: Iowa State University Press, p. 347. Reprinted in *Small Data Sets*, p. 7.

Beef	Beef	Cereal	Cereal
Low	High	Low	High
90	73	107	98
76	102	95	74
90	118	97	56
64	104	80	111
86	81	98	95
51	107	74	88
72	100	74	82
90	87	67	77
95	117	89	86
78	111	58	92

(a) Make the main effects and interaction plots. What do these plots tell you about the effects of the source and amount of protein on weight gain?

(b) Analyze the data and draw conclusions about the significance of the differences between the sources and amounts of protein, and the interaction between them.

(c) Make residual plots to check the normality and constant variance assumptions.

13.17 The sample means from a 2^3 experiment are as follows:

$$\bar{y}_{(1)} = 10, \quad \bar{y}_a = 20, \quad \bar{y}_b = 15, \quad \bar{y}_{ab} = 35,$$
$$\bar{y}_c = 15, \quad \bar{y}_{ac} = 15, \quad \bar{y}_{bc} = 20, \quad \bar{y}_{abc} = 30.$$

Calculate the estimated main effects and interactions (using either the contrasts coefficients matrix or the Yates algorithm) and give the corresponding regression equation. What can you say about the effect of factor C?

13.18 Write the contrast coefficients matrix for a 2^4 design.

13.19 ▣ A student group project for a quality control course at Northwestern University studied how the surface finish produced by a milling machine depends on the following three factors:

Factor	Low	High
Drill bit size (A)	0.25"	0.5"
Drill bit rotational speed (B)	500 rpm	2000 rpm
Drill bit feed rate (C)	5 in./min.	10 in./min.

Three parts were produced for each setting of the factors and their surface finish was measured using a profilometer, which drags a diamond pointed stylus over the surface and calculates the average deviation from the mean height of the surface. The data were as follows:

Treatment	Part		
Combination	1	2	3
(1)	297.00	255.67	299.33
a	197.33	190.00	197.00
b	127.00	83.33	91.00
ab	54.00	55.00	47.67
c	243.00	189.00	220.00
ac	323.67	304.00	257.33
bc	178.00	166.33	117.00
abc	69.33	80.67	66.00

(a) Calculate the effect estimates and test their statistical significance at $\alpha = .05$.

(b) Give a detailed ANOVA table that includes separate sums of squares for all effects and the error sum of squares.

(c) Give a regression equation to predict the surface hardness. Include only the significant terms in the equation.

(d) Use the equation to predict the surface hardness for the following settings of the factors: Drill bit size = 0.375", Drill bit rotational speed = 1000 rpm, Drill bit feed rate = 5 in./min.

13.20 An experiment was done to study how the finish of sheet-molded panels of a car grille depends on nine factors, each observed at two levels. To keep the analysis simple, only the following three factors are considered here: the mold temperature (factor A), the mold pressure (factor B), and the priming (factor C). Two grilles were produced for each of eight factor level combinations. The table below gives the number of defects per grille.[18]

Treatment	Defects (d)	
Combination	Grille 1	Grille 2
(1)	4	2
a	2	50
b	0	1
c	56	17
ab	4	3
ac	4	3
bc	12	3
abc	0	0

(a) These data may be assumed to be Poisson distributed. To stabilize the variance (see Section 10.4.3) apply the **Freeman-Tukey transformation** (a modification of

[18] Data adapted from S. Bisgaard and H. T. Fuller (1995), "Analysis of factorial experiments with defects or defectives as the response," *Quality Engineering*, **7**, pp. 429–443.

the square root transformation from Example 10.15):

$$y = \frac{1}{2}[\sqrt{d} + \sqrt{d + 1}]$$

where d is the number of defects per grille. Use the transformed data in the following analyses.

(b) Estimate the main effects and interaction effects.

(c) Calculate the ANOVA table. Which effects are significant at $\alpha = .05$?

(d) Give a regression equation to predict the response. Include only the effects that are significant at $\alpha = .05$ in the equation.

(e) Find the treatment combination that will minimize the average number of defects per grille.

13.21 Write a full regression model for a 2^4 experiment. Interpret the terms in the model.

13.22 ◨ An experiment was done to evaluate the effects of four factors on airflow through a solenoid valve of an air pollution control device for automobiles.[19] The factors were:

Factor	Level	
	Low	High
A = Length of armature	0.595"	0.695"
B = Spring load	70 grams	100 grams
C = Bobbin depth	1.095"	1.105"
D = Tube length	0.500"	0.510"

The table below gives the average of four replicate airflow measurements. (The raw data are not available.)

Treatment Combination	Airflow	Treatment Combination	Airflow
(1)	0.46	d	0.42
a	0.42	ad	028
b	0.57	bd	0.60
ab	0.45	abd	0.29
c	0.73	cd	0.70
ac	0.71	acd	0.71
bc	0.70	bcd	0.72
abc	0.70	abcd	0.72

(a) Estimate the main effects and interaction effects.

(b) Since only a single average airflow measurement is available for each treatment combination, formal tests of significance of the estimated effects are not possible. Make a normal plot of the estimated effects. Which effects appear to be significant?

---

[19] Data adapted from S. Bisgaard and H. T. Fuller (1995), "Reducing variation with two-level factorial experiments," *Quality Engineering*, **8**, pp. 373–377.

(c) Give a regression equation for predicting the airflow. Include only the significant effects in the equation.

(d) Use the equation to predict the airflow for armature length $= 0.610"$, spring load $= 80$ grams, bobbin depth $= 1.10"$, and tube length $= 0.500"$.

13.23 ◼ An experiment was performed to see how gas plasma can be used to make paper more susceptible to ink.[20] The factors studied were A: low and high pressure, B: low and high power, C: low and high gas flow rate and D: the type of gas—oxygen or $SiCl_4$. The response variable was the "wettability" of plasma treated paper, which was measured by placing a water droplet on the paper and estimating the contact angle between the droplet and the paper surface, using a special microscope. Two different types of paper were used, but here the data for only one type are given.

Treatment Combination	Wettability	Treatment Combination	Wettability
(1)	48.6	d	5.0
a	41.2	ad	56.8
b	55.8	bd	25.6
ab	53.5	abd	41.8
c	37.6	cd	13.3
ac	47.2	acd	47.5
bc	47.2	bcd	11.3
abc	48.7	abcd	49.5

(a) Estimate the main effects and interaction effects.

(b) Since only a single wettability measurement is available for each treatment combination, formal tests of significance of the estimated effects are not possible. Make a normal plot of the estimated effects. Which effects appear significant?

(c) Taking into consideration only the significant effects, which combination of factors will maximize wettability?

Section 13.3

13.24 For each of the following two-factor experiments, state whether the factors are crossed or nested, and fixed or random.

(a) The effects of sleep (4, 6, 8, 10 hours) and caffeine (0 mg, 100 mg, 200 mg) on recall are studied using a memorization test by assigning student volunteers randomly to each of twelve sleep/caffeine groups.

(b) A company compares the purity of a chemical purchased from three different suppliers. Four batches are selected at random from each supplier. Samples from each batch are tested for purity.

(c) The effect of morning vs. afternoon math test performance is studied in four randomly selected second grade classes in a school district. Two classes take the test in the morning, while the other two take the test in the afternoon.

---

[20] S. Bisgaard, H. T. Fuller, and E. Barrios (1996), "Two-level factorials run as split plot experiments," *Quality Engineering,* **8,** pp. 705–708.

13.25 For each of the following two-factor experiments, state whether the factors are crossed or nested, and fixed or random.

(a) The effects of two different methods to manage pediatric asthma patients (standard or medical/social work team) are compared in six randomly selected community hospitals. At three hospitals the standard management is used. At the other three hospitals a work team approach is used. At each hospital 20 new asthmatic patients are followed. The response is the number of subsequent readmissions over twelve months.

(b) The type of battery (standard zinc-carbon or alkaline) and storage temperature (0, 20, 40, 80 degrees Celsius) are studied for their effect on voltage. Random samples of standard and alkaline batteries are divided equally into four groups. Each group is stored at the designated temperature for six weeks. The batteries are then tested to determine the maximum voltage.

(c) The effect of three assay methods on the purity of a precipitate is measured in a laboratory. Four randomly selected chemists run assays using the three methods in a random order.

13.26 ▣ An experiment was conducted to measure the breaking strengths of cement test samples. Three different persons prepared cement-water mixtures. Each mixture was divided into 12 samples, which were cast into cubes. The cubes were tested for breaking strength by three different persons, four cubes per person. The breaking strengths (in pounds per square inch) of the sample cubes are given in the following table.[21] Assume that the mixers are fixed, but the breakers are randomly chosen.

	Breaker 1				Breaker 2				Breaker 3			
Mixer 1	5280	5520	4760	5800	4340	4400	5020	6200	4160	5180	5320	4600
Mixer 2	4420	5280	5580	4900	5340	4880	4960	6200	4180	4800	4600	4480
Mixer 3	5360	6160	5680	5500	5720	4760	5620	5560	4460	4930	4680	5600

(a) Calculate the ANOVA table and perform tests for significance of the main effects and interaction.

(b) Estimate the variance components associated with mixers, breakers, and their interaction. Compare the percentage contributions to the total variance from these three sources.

13.27 ▣ Telemarketing is used by an insurance firm to sell life insurance. In order to test three scripts to be read by the callers, each script representing a different sales strategy, a marketing test is done. Three telemarketing companies are randomly chosen for the experiment. The scripts are randomly assigned to 30 callers for each company, each script to 10 callers. The table below shows the average cost per sale for all 90 callers.

---

[21] I. L. Davies and P. L. Goldsmith, eds. (1972), *Statistical Methods in Research and Production*, 4th ed., Edinburgh: Oliver Boyd, p. 154. Reprinted in *Small Data Sets*, p. 25.

Company 1			Company 2			Company 3		
Script A	Script B	Script C	Script A	Script B	Script C	Script A	Script B	Script C
25.00	30.00	20.00	15.00	22.50	27.50	20.00	20.00	17.50
25.00	27.50	145.00	20.00	30.00	27.50	27.50	30.00	30.00
40.00	62.50	112.50	30.00	35.00	62.50	27.50	25.00	22.50
47.50	97.50	150.00	20.00	57.50	147.50	50.00	32.50	37.50
85.00	130.00	160.00	22.50	70.00	125.00	30.00	30.00	25.00
125.00	167.50	167.50	37.50	67.50	100.00	47.50	22.50	80.00
145.00	135.00	162.50	75.00	95.00	85.00	37.50	32.50	70.00
105.00	157.50	172.50	65.00	90.00	102.50	67.50	27.50	85.00
142.50	105.00	180.00	92.50	92.50	92.50	67.50	70.00	82.50
25.00	117.50	165.00	120.00	105.00	127.50	35.00	110.00	125.00

(a) Is the design crossed or nested? Is the script effect fixed or random? Is the company effect fixed or random?

(b) Calculate the ANOVA table. Show that there is a difference in scripts using the $\alpha = .10$ level of signficance. What conclusions can you draw?

(c) Estimate the appropriate variance components.

13.28 ◼ The housing for a pregnancy test kit contains a disposable strip with a hole and a reagent that is jetted onto the strip.[22] When the disposable strip is manufactured, the distance between the alignment hole and a mark on the strip is measured in order to assure visibility of test results when the strip is assembled in the housing. An experiment is done to determine which of three measuring instruments: calipers, an optical comparator, or a coordinate measuring machine (CMM), should be used to measure the distance. The experiment is run by having four randomly selected technicians make three readings with each of the three measuring instruments in a random order. The values of the absolute difference in millimeters between the distance reading and the actual distance are given below.

Instrument	Technician											
	1			2			3			4		
Calipers	.20	.14	.15	.24	.35	.21	.50	.38	.54	.33	.25	.29
Opt. comparator	.26	.25	.30	.20	.19	.28	.14	.15	.17	.13	.15	.16
CMM	.14	.19	.17	.21	.23	.24	.17	.18	.21	.25	.35	.27

(a) Is the design crossed or nested? Is the instrument effect fixed or random? Is the technician effect fixed or random?

(b) Calculate the ANOVA table and perform the tests of significance of effects at $\alpha = .05$. What conclusions can you draw?

(c) Estimate the appropriate variance components.

---

[22] The background for this example was provided by Ted Hanagan of Abbott Laboratories, N. Chicago, IL. The data are simulated.

13.29 ▣ Refer to the previous exercise, but now suppose that a different design was used, in which 12 randomly selected technicians were assigned to the three instruments, four per instrument. The data are rearranged in a different format below to reflect the different design.

Instrument	Calipers				Opt. Comparator				CMM			
Technician	1	2	3	4	5	6	7	8	9	10	11	12
Reading 1	.20	.24	.50	.33	.26	.20	.14	.13	.14	.21	.17	.25
Reading 2	.14	.35	.38	.25	.25	.19	.15	.15	.19	.23	.18	.35
Reading 3	.15	.21	.54	.29	.30	.28	.17	.16	.17	.24	.21	.27

Indicate how the analysis and results differ.

13.30 ▣ A strong risk factor for skin cancer in adults is childhood sun exposure. An educational program using CD-ROM presenting information on sun exposure and skin cancer was developed for children in elementary school. Three interventions were tested: the CD- ROM intervention, regular teacher-led skin health presentations, and control which received no skin health information. Six classes of grade school students, with 20 students per class, were randomly selected to test the interventions. Two classes were assigned to each group. The students' knowledge of skin cancer and the relationship of sun exposure to future skin cancer were tested before the intervention and three months after the intervention. The changes in their test scores are tabled below.[23]

Control				CD-ROM				Teacher Presentation			
Class 1		Class 2		Class 3		Class 4		Class 5		Class 6	
43.75	3.75	38.75	8.75	18.75	2.50	10.00	3.75	72.50	2.50	0.00	32.50
67.50	3.75	53.75	1.25	35.00	11.25	8.75	5.00	81.25	12.50	1.25	37.50
56.25	3.75	45.00	7.50	46.25	0.00	3.75	3.75	80.00	7.50	2.50	55.50
78.75	8.75	43.75	7.50	47.50	10.00	25.00	5.00	93.75	38.75	1.25	67.50
71.25	5.00	56.25	18.75	51.25	16.25	13.75	1.25	81.25	53.75	5.00	70.00
81.25	11.25	60.00	16.25	57.50	21.25	23.75	3.75	75.00	66.25	2.50	75.00
72.50	31.25	43.75	16.25	26.25	31.25	15.00	7.50	82.50	76.25	15.00	77.50
70.00	51.25	62.50	33.75	36.25	27.50	12.50	8.75	91.25	62.50	8.75	77.50
58.75	22.50	78.75	41.25	38.75	27.50	6.25	20.00	88.75	63.75	32.50	75.00
68.75	45.00	67.50	61.25	57.50	40.00	6.25	7.50	80.00	78.75	40.00	81.25

(a) Is the design crossed or nested? Is the intervention effect fixed or random? Is the class effect fixed or random?

(b) Calculate the ANOVA table. Show that there is a difference in interventions using the $\alpha = .01$ level of significance. What conclusions can you draw?

(c) Estimate the appropriate variance components.

---

[23] Data courtesy of Dr. Robin Horning, Department of Preventive Medicine, Northwestern University.

Advanced Exercises

13.31 Consider a balanced two-factor experiment. Sometimes it is suggested that if the interaction AB is not significant, its sum of squares be pooled with the error sum of squares to obtain an error estimate with more d.f. Thus the pooled SSE equals SSE + SSAB and the pooled error d.f. equal $ab(n-1) + (a-1)(b-1)$. However, there is a risk that the AB interaction may in fact be nonnegligible but is not found significant because of lack of power of its F-test; as a result, the pooled MSE may be inflated. Discuss when it might be worthwhile to pool SSAB with SSE by considering two cases: (i) a and b are small, n is large; (ii) a and b are large, n is small.

13.32 Consider a balanced three-factor experiment with crossed and fixed factors A with a levels, B with b levels, and C with c levels, and with $n \geq 2$ observations per factor-level combination. Write the analysis of variance table for this design in analogy with Table 13.5. Also write the regression model for this design.

13.33 Let $\bar{Y}_1, \bar{Y}_2, \ldots, \bar{Y}_p$ be mutually independent sample means, each with variance σ^2/n. (You can think of the $\bar{Y}_i$ as the sample means of n observations at each of $p = 2^k$ treatment combinations from a balanced 2^k experiment.) Let $(c_1, c_2, \ldots, c_p)$ and $(d_1, d_2, \ldots, d_p)$ be orthogonal vectors of contrast coefficients, i.e., $c_1 d_1 + c_2 d_2 + \cdots + c_p d_p = 0$. Show that

$$\text{Cov}\left(\sum_{i=1}^{p} c_i \bar{Y}_i, \sum_{i=1}^{p} d_i \bar{Y}_i\right) = 0.$$

Thus orthogonal contrasts are uncorrelated, and if they are normally distributed then they also are independent.

13.34 ◼ A researcher wanted to study the effects of three factors: A (Heating temperature), B (Heating time) and C (Quench temperature) on the surface hardness (y) of steel. Instead of performing a 2^3 experiment (which would have required 8 runs), he did the following experiment with 12 runs by replicating the four runs: $(-, -, -)$, $(-, +, +)$, $(+, +, -)$, $(+, -, +)$.

Run	A	B	C	y
1	−	−	−	60
2	−	+	+	45
3	−	−	+	52
4	−	+	−	54
5	+	+	−	68
6	+	−	+	83
7	+	−	−	72
8	+	+	+	80
9	−	−	−	64
10	−	+	+	49
11	+	+	−	66
12	+	−	+	85

(a) Check that this is an orthogonal design.

(b) Estimate the main effects A, B, and C.

(c) Use the four replicate observations to estimate the error variance σ^2. What are the error degrees of freedom?

(d) If each observation has variance σ^2, find the common variance formula for each main effect. Use the estimate of σ^2 from part (c) to find the common standard error of each main effect.

(e) Calculate the t-statistics for the three main effects. Which main effects are significant at $\alpha = .01$?

13.35 ■ It is a common practice to augment a 2^k experiment (whose design points can be represented as the vertices of a k-dimensional hypercube) with some replicated runs at the center point. (The center point is defined only when the factors are numerical, in which case it is the factor-level combination, where the level of each factor is the midpoint between its low and high setting.) There are two reasons for this: (i) the replicate runs provide an estimate of the pure error (as opposed to the error estimate obtained by ignoring some model effects), and (ii) the average of the observations at the center point can be compared with the average of the observations at the vertices by a t-test to see if there is a significant curvature in the response function. If the response function is linear, then the two averages should not differ significantly.

Consider the data from the previous exercise, but now suppose that the replicate runs (runs 9–12) are made at the center point.

(a) Analyze the data from this 2^3 design augmented with four replicate runs at the center point. What are the error degrees of freedom?

(b) Derive the t-test for curvature and apply it to these data. Is there a significant curvature in the response function? Use $\alpha = .05$.

CHAPTER 14

NONPARAMETRIC STATISTICAL METHODS

The majority of statistical methods that we have studied thus far have been based on the assumption of normally distributed data. Frequently this assumption is not valid (e.g., income or lifetime data) or the sample sizes may be too small to verify it. Sometimes the data are measured on an ordinal scale, so only their ranks are meaningful—not the actual data values (e.g., letter grades in a course). For analyzing such data we use methods that make very few assumptions about the form of the population distribution from which the data are sampled. These methods, referred to as **nonparametric** or **distribution-free** statistical methods, are the topic of the present chapter.

The outline of the chapter is as follows. Section 14.1 considers the single sample setting and presents methods of inference on the median of the sampled population. These same methods also handle the matched pairs setting. Section 14.2 discusses inferences for comparing two independent samples. Section 14.3 extends the methods for two independent samples to several independent samples. Section 14.4 discusses the problem of comparing several matched samples. Section 14.5 discusses nonparametric measures of correlation. Section 14.6 gives a brief introduction to the **resampling methods**, which draw inferences based on repeated random samples from the observed data, thus using the data to determine the form of the distribution.

14.1 INFERENCES FOR SINGLE SAMPLES

Consider a random sample $x_1, x_2, \ldots, x_n$ from a population with unknown median $\tilde{\mu}$. The median is used as a parameter rather than the mean because, as seen in Chapter 4,

562

the median is a better measure of the center than the mean for nonnormal (especially skewed) distributions. We present two methods for drawing inferences on $\tilde{\mu}$. Throughout we assume that the population distribution is continuous.

14.1.1 Sign Test and Confidence Interval

Sign Test for a Single Sample. Suppose that we want to test the hypotheses

$$H_0: \tilde{\mu} = \tilde{\mu}_0 \text{ vs. } H_1: \tilde{\mu} > \tilde{\mu}_0 \tag{14.1}$$

where $\tilde{\mu}_0$ is a specified value. For example, consider testing whether or not the median household income of a population exceeds \$50,000 based on a random sample $x_1, x_2, \ldots, x_n$ of household incomes from that population.

The sign test compares each x_i with $\tilde{\mu}_0$ and notes whether it is $> \tilde{\mu}_0$ or $< \tilde{\mu}_0$. Initially we will assume no ties, i.e., no $x_i = \tilde{\mu}_0$. The steps in the sign test are as follows:

1. Count the number of x_i's that exceed $\tilde{\mu}_0$. Denote this number by s_+, called the number of plus signs. Let $s_- = n - s_+$, which is the number of minus signs.
2. Reject H_0 if s_+ is large or equivalently if s_- is small.

To determine how large s_+ must be in order to reject H_0 at a given significance level α, we need to know the distribution of the corresponding random variable (r.v.) S_+ when H_0 is true. Denote by X_i and S_- the r.v.'s corresponding to the observed values x_i and s_-, respectively. Let

$$P(X_i > \tilde{\mu}_0) = p \text{ and } P(X_i < \tilde{\mu}_0) = 1 - p.$$

Note that $P(X_i = \tilde{\mu}_0) = 0$, because we assume that the X_i's are continuous r.v.'s. It follows that S_+ has a binomial distribution with sample size n and success probability p. Similarly, S_- has a binomial distribution with sample size n and success probability $1 - p$. Symbolically,

$$S_+ \sim \text{Bin}(n, p) \text{ and } S_- \sim \text{Bin}(n, 1 - p).$$

When H_0 is true, $\tilde{\mu}_0$ is the true median, so by definition $p = 1/2$. When H_1 is true, $p > 1/2$, as can be seen from Figure 14.1. Therefore the hypotheses (14.1) are equivalent to

$$H_0: p = 1/2 \text{ vs. } H_1: p > 1/2.$$

So the sign test is simply a test on a binomial proportion studied in Chapter 9.

When H_0 is true, S_+ (as well as S_-) has a $\text{Bin}(n, 1/2)$ distribution. Denoting this common r.v. by S, the P-value for the sign test is given by

$$P\text{-value} = P\{S \geq s_+\} = \sum_{i=s_+}^{n} \binom{n}{i} \left(\frac{1}{2}\right)^n$$

which by symmetry equals

$$P\text{-value} = P\{S \leq s_-\} = \sum_{i=0}^{s_-} \binom{n}{i} \left(\frac{1}{2}\right)^n.$$

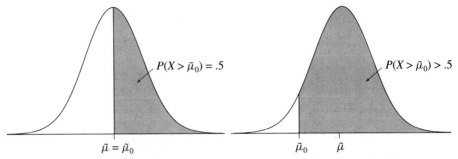

Figure 14.1   The Probability That $X > \tilde{\mu}_0$: (a) Probability under H_0: $\tilde{\mu} = \hat{\mu}_0$; (b) Probability under H_1: $\tilde{\mu} > \tilde{\mu}_0$

The lower tail probabilities of the $\mathrm{Bin}(n, 1/2)$ distribution are listed in Table A.1 for selected values of n.

An α-level test rejects H_0 if P-value $\leq \alpha$. An equivalent way of applying the α-level test is to reject H_0 if

$$s_+ \geq b_{n,\alpha} \text{ or equivalently if } s_- \leq b_{n,1-\alpha}$$

where $b_{n,\alpha}$ is the upper α critical point of the $\mathrm{Bin}(n, 1/2)$ distribution and $b_{n,1-\alpha} = n - b_{n,\alpha}$ is the lower α critical point, i.e.,

$$\sum_{i=b_{n,\alpha}}^{n} \binom{n}{i}\left(\frac{1}{2}\right)^n = \sum_{i=0}^{b_{n,1-\alpha}} \binom{n}{i}\left(\frac{1}{2}\right)^n = \alpha.$$

Note that because of the discreteness of the binomial distribution, only discrete choices of α-values are possible. For example, for $n = 20$ using Table A.1 we find that for $\alpha = .021$ we have $b_{n,1-\alpha} = 5$ and $b_{n,\alpha} = 15$; the next higher value of α is .058, which corresponds to $b_{n,1-\alpha} = 6$ and $b_{n,\alpha} = 14$.

If the sample size is large (≥ 20), then the common distribution of S_+ and S_- can be approximated by a normal distribution with

$$E(S_+) = E(S_-) = \frac{n}{2} \text{ and } \mathrm{Var}(S_+) = \mathrm{Var}(S_-) = \frac{n}{4}.$$

Therefore a large sample z-test (with continuity correction) can be applied as follows. Calculate

$$z = \frac{s_+ - n/2 - 1/2}{\sqrt{n/4}}$$

and reject H_0 if $z \geq z_\alpha$ or equivalently if

$$s_+ \geq \frac{n}{2} + \frac{1}{2} + z_\alpha \sqrt{\frac{n}{4}} \simeq b_{n,\alpha}. \tag{14.2}$$

Sign tests for the lower one-sided alternative (when H_1 is $\tilde{\mu} < \tilde{\mu}_0$ or $p < 1/2$) and the two-sided alternative (when H_1 is $\tilde{\mu} \neq \tilde{\mu}_0$ or $p \neq 1/2$) are performed in an analogous manner. For the two-sided test we use the test statistic $s_{max} = \max(s_+, s_-)$

or $s_{\min} = \min(s_+, s_-)$. The corresponding P-value is computed using

$$P\text{-value} = 2 \sum_{i=s_{\max}}^{n} \binom{n}{i} \left(\frac{1}{2}\right)^n = 2 \sum_{i=0}^{s_{\min}} \binom{n}{i} \left(\frac{1}{2}\right)^n.$$

An α-level test rejects H_0 if P-value $\leq \alpha$ or equivalently if $s_{\max} \geq b_{n,\alpha/2}$. A large sample z-test (with continuity correction) can be based on the statistic

$$z = \frac{s_{\max} - n/2 - 1/2}{\sqrt{n/4}}$$

which rejects H_0 at level α if $z \geq z_{\alpha/2}$.

EXAMPLE 14.1   (THERMOSTAT SETTING: SIGN TEST)

Refer to the thermostat test data reproduced below from Exercise 7.16.

202.2   203.4   200.5   202.5   206.3   198.0   203.7   200.8   201.3   199.0

Perform the sign test to determine if the median setting is different from the design setting of $200°\,$F.

Set up the hypotheses as $H_0: \tilde{\mu} = 200$ vs. $H_1: \tilde{\mu} \neq 200$, where $\tilde{\mu}$ is the median setting of the population of all thermostats. The alternative hypothesis is two-sided, because deviation in either direction from the design setting is critical. On comparing the ten measurements against the design setting of $200°\,$F, we find that $s_+ = 8$ and $s_- = 2$. Therefore the two-sided P-value is obtained from Table A.1 as

$$P\text{-value} = 2 \sum_{i=8}^{10} \binom{10}{i} \left(\frac{1}{2}\right)^{10} = 2 \sum_{i=0}^{2} \binom{10}{i} \left(\frac{1}{2}\right)^{10} = 2(0.055) = 0.110.$$

Thus the difference from the design setting is not significant even at $\alpha = .10$.   ◆

Treatment of Ties.   Although we have assumed that the probability that any X_i equals $\tilde{\mu}_0$ is zero, in practice ties do occur. The question arises as to how to treat tied observations. One solution is to break each tie at random, but this means that two researchers with the same data and using the same test could end up with different results. Another solution is to count each tie as a contribution of 1/2 each toward s_+ and s_-. However, this makes the binomial distribution inapplicable in the calculation of the P-value and critical constants. A simple solution is to ignore the ties and work only with untied observations. This does reduce the effective sample size and hence the power of the test, but the loss is not significant if there are only a few ties.

*Confidence Interval for $\tilde{\mu}$.   Example 5.9 showed that given a random sample $x_1, x_2, \ldots, x_n$ from a continuous distribution, $[x_{\min}, x_{\max}]$ gives a confidence interval (CI) for $\tilde{\mu}$ with confidence level $1 - (1/2)^{n-1}$. In this section we extend that result for general confidence levels $1 - \alpha$. The resulting CI can also be derived by inverting an α-level two-sided sign test on $\tilde{\mu}$.

Let $x_{(1)} \leq x_{(2)} \leq \cdots \leq x_{(n)}$ be the ordered data values. Then a $(1 - \alpha)$-level CI for $\tilde{\mu}$ is given by

$$x_{(b+1)} \leq \tilde{\mu} \leq x_{(n-b)} \tag{14.3}$$

where $b = b_{n,1-\alpha/2}$ is the lower $\alpha/2$ critical point of the $\mathrm{Bin}(n, 1/2)$ distribution. For example, $b = 0$ yields the CI $[x_{(1)}, x_{(n)}] = [x_{\min}, x_{\max}]$ with confidence level $1 - (1/2)^{n-1}$.

EXAMPLE 14.2 (THERMOSTAT SETTING: SIGN CONFIDENCE INTERVAL FOR THE MEDIAN)

Refer to the data from Example 14.1. Find a 95% sign CI for the median $\tilde{\mu}$ of the settings for the population of all thermostats.

Because of the discreteness of the binomial distribution we cannot find an *exact* 95% CI in this case. From Table A.1 we see that for $n = 10$ and $p = 0.5$, the lower 1.1% critical point of the binomial distribution is 1 and by symmetry the upper 1.1% critical point is 9. Setting $\alpha/2 = 0.011$ which gives $1 - \alpha = 1 - 0.022 = 0.978$, we find that $[x_{(2)}, x_{(9)}]$ is a 97.8% CI for $\tilde{\mu}$. From the data given in Example 14.1 we obtain $[x_{(2)}, x_{(9)}] = [199.0, 203.7]$ as a 97.8% CI for $\tilde{\mu}$. Note that this interval includes the design setting of $200°\mathrm{F}$. ◆

*Proof of Confidence Interval (14.3). The coverage probability of the CI (14.3) is given by

$$P\{X_{(b+1)} \leq \tilde{\mu} \leq X_{(n-b)}\} = 1 - P\{X_{(b+1)} > \tilde{\mu}\} - P\{X_{(n-b)} < \tilde{\mu}\}$$

where $b = b_{n,1-\alpha/2}$. Consider $P\{X_{(b+1)} > \tilde{\mu}\}$, which equals the probability that at most b of the X_i's are $< \tilde{\mu}$. Since the probability that any one X_i is $< \tilde{\mu}$ is $1/2$ (because $\tilde{\mu}$ is the median), it follows that

$$P\{X_{(b+1)} > \tilde{\mu}\} = \sum_{i=0}^{b} \binom{n}{i} \left(\frac{1}{2}\right)^n = \alpha/2.$$

By symmetry we have

$$P\{X_{(n-b)} < \tilde{\mu}\} = \sum_{i=n-b}^{n} \binom{n}{i} \left(\frac{1}{2}\right)^n = \alpha/2.$$

Therefore the confidence level equals $1 - \alpha$.

To derive the CI (14.3) by inverting the sign test, consider the set of values of $\tilde{\mu}$ that are "acceptable" using a two-sided α-level sign test discussed above. For a particular value of $\tilde{\mu}$ to be "acceptable" we must have

$$b < s_+ < n - b$$

where $b = b_{n,1-\alpha/2}$ and s_+ is the number of x_i's $> \tilde{\mu}$. Now $s_+ > b$ means that less than $n - b$ of x_i's are $\leq \tilde{\mu}$ or $x_{(n-b)} \geq \tilde{\mu}$. Similarly, $s_+ < n - b$ means that more than b of x_i's are $\leq \tilde{\mu}$ or $x_{(b+1)} \leq \tilde{\mu}$. Thus the CI (14.3) represents the set of "acceptable" values of $\tilde{\mu}$ using an α-level test. ∎

Sign Test for Matched Pairs.   For matched pairs data, the sign test can be applied to test a hypothesis concerning the population median of the differences between the paired observations. Commonly, H_0 postulates that this median equals zero. In that case, s_+ is the number of positive differences and s_- is the number of negative differences. In some applications, for each pair of observations it is only known whether the first or second observation is larger; the actual magnitudes of the observations are not known, e.g., if subjects are asked to simply indicate preference for one of two alternatives. The sign test can be applied to such binary data, while other competing tests (e.g., the matched pairs t-test) cannot.

EXAMPLE 14.3   (COMPARING TWO METHODS OF MEASURING CARDIAC OUTPUT: SIGN TEST)

Consider the cardiac output data from Example 8.6 reproduced in Table 14.1. Perform the sign test to determine if the two methods of measurement differ significantly from each other.

Table 14.1 Cardiac Output (liters/min.) Measured by Methods A and B

No.	Method A	Method B	Difference	No.	Method A	Method B	Difference
i	x_i	y_i	d_i	i	x_i	y_i	d_i
1	6.3	5.2	1.1	14	7.7	7.4	0.3
2	6.3	6.6	−0.3	15	7.4	7.4	0.0
3	3.5	2.3	1.2	16	5.6	4.9	0.7
4	5.1	4.4	0.7	17	6.3	5.4	0.9
5	5.5	4.1	1.4	18	8.4	8.4	0.0
6	7.7	6.4	1.3	19	5.6	5.1	0.5
7	6.3	5.7	0.9	20	4.8	4.4	0.4
8	2.8	2.3	0.5	21	4.3	4.3	0.0
9	3.4	3.2	0.2	22	4.2	4.1	0.1
10	5.7	5.2	0.5	23	3.3	2.2	1.1
11	5.6	4.9	0.7	24	3.8	4.0	−0.2
12	6.2	6.1	0.1	25	5.7	5.8	−0.1
13	6.6	6.3	0.3	26	4.1	4.0	0.1

Dropping the 3 tied pairs, we have net $n = 23$ untied pairs. There are $s_+ = 20$ positive differences and $s_- = 3$ negative differences. The standardized sign statistic equals

$$z = \frac{s_+ - n/2 - 1/2}{\sqrt{n/4}} = \frac{20 - 23/2 - 1/2}{\sqrt{23/4}} = 3.336.$$

The two-sided P-value corresponding to this statistic equals $2[1 - \Phi(3.336)] = 0.0008$, which shows a highly significant difference between the two methods.   ◆

14.1.2 Wilcoxon Signed Rank Test and Confidence Interval

To test the null hypothesis $H_0\colon \tilde{\mu} = \tilde{\mu}_0$, the sign test considers only whether each observation x_i is $> \tilde{\mu}_0$ or $< \tilde{\mu}_0$, but not by how much. The Wilcoxon signed rank test improves on the sign test by taking this extra information into account through the ranks of the ordered magnitudes of the differences $d_i = x_i - \tilde{\mu}_0$. However, it requires the assumption that the population distribution is symmetric. This additional assumption is not required by the sign test.

Return to the hypothesis testing problem (14.1):

$$H_0\colon \tilde{\mu} = \tilde{\mu}_0 \text{ vs. } H_1\colon \tilde{\mu} > \tilde{\mu}_0.$$

Initially assume that there are no ties, by which we mean no d_i equals zero and no $|d_i| = |d_j|$. The steps in the signed rank test are as follows:

1. Rank order the differences d_i in terms of their absolute values. Let r_i be the rank of d_i in this ordering. Since we assume no ties, the ranks r_i are uniquely determined and are a permutation of the integers $1, 2, \ldots, n$.

2. Calculate

$$w_+ = \text{sum of the ranks of the positive differences}$$

and

$$w_- = \text{sum of the ranks of the negative differences.}$$

It follows that

$$w_+ + w_- = r_1 + r_2 + \cdots + r_n = 1 + 2 + \cdots + n = \frac{n(n+1)}{2}.$$

3. Reject H_0 if w_+ is large or equivalently if w_- is small.

To determine how large w_+ or how small w_- must be in order to reject H_0 at a given significance level α, we need to know the distributions of the corresponding r.v.'s W_+ and W_- when H_0 is true. It can be shown that these null distributions are identical and symmetric. This common distribution is discussed later in this section, the upper tail probabilities of this distribution are tabulated in Table A.10. Denoting the common r.v. by W, the P-value is given by

$$P\text{-value} = P\{W \geq w_+\} = P\{W \leq w_-\}.$$

An α-level test rejects H_0 if P-value $\leq \alpha$ or equivalently if $w_+ \geq w_{n,\alpha}$ where $w_{n,\alpha}$ is the upper α critical point of the null distribution of W.

For large n, the null distribution of W can be well-approximated by a normal distribution with mean and variance given by

$$E(W) = \frac{n(n+1)}{4} \text{ and } \text{Var}(W) = \frac{n(n+1)(2n+1)}{24}. \tag{14.4}$$

Exercise 14.43 shows how to derive these formulas. Therefore a large sample z-test (with continuity correction) can be based on the statistic

$$z = \frac{w_+ - n(n+1)/4 - 1/2}{\sqrt{n(n+1)(2n+1)/24}}. \tag{14.5}$$

The test rejects H_0 at level α if $z \geq z_\alpha$ or equivalently if

$$w_+ \geq \frac{n(n+1)}{4} + \frac{1}{2} + z_\alpha \sqrt{\frac{n(n+1)(2n+1)}{24}} \simeq w_{n,\alpha}. \tag{14.6}$$

The Wilcoxon signed rank tests for the lower one-sided alternative (when $H_1: \tilde{\mu} < \tilde{\mu}_0$) and the two-sided alternative (when $H_1: \tilde{\mu} \neq \tilde{\mu}_0$) are performed in an analogous manner. For the two-sided test we use the test statistic $w_{max} = \max(w_+, w_-)$ or $w_{min} = \min(w_+, w_-)$. The two-sided P-value equals

$$P\text{-value} = 2P(W \geq w_{max}) = 2P(W \leq w_{min}).$$

It should be pointed out that while the sign test statistic simply counts the number of signed differences, the signed rank test statistic weights each signed difference by its rank. For example, if the positive differences are larger in magnitude than the negative differences, they get higher ranks, thus contributing to a larger value of w_+. On the one hand, this improves the power of the signed rank test compared to that of the sign test, but on the other hand this also affects its type I error probability if the population distribution is not symmetric. To see this, look at Figure 14.2, which shows a positively skewed population distribution for which $H_0: \tilde{\mu} = \tilde{\mu}_0$ is true. Even though H_0 is true, because of the long right hand tail of the distribution, the positive differences tend to be larger in magnitude than the negative differences, resulting in higher ranks. This inflates the value of the w_+ statistic and hence its type I error probability. The opposite is true for a negatively skewed distribution. Therefore the assumption of a symmetric distribution is required.

EXAMPLE 14.4 (THERMOSTAT SETTING: WILCOXON SIGNED RANK TEST)

Apply the Wilcoxon signed rank test to the thermostat setting data from Example 14.1 to check if the median setting differs from 200° F.

The differences of the measurements from 200° F and their ranks are shown below.

x_i	202.2	203.4	200.5	202.5	206.3	198.0	203.7	200.8	201.3	199.0
$d_i = x_i - 200$	2.2	3.4	0.5	2.5	6.3	−2.0	3.7	0.8	1.3	−1.0
Rank	6	8	1	7	10	5	9	2	4	3

We have

$$w_- = 5 + 3 = 8$$

and

$$w_+ = 6 + 8 + 1 + 7 + 10 + 9 + 2 + 4 = \frac{(10)(11)}{2} - 8 = 47.$$

The two-sided P-value associated with w_+ is obtained from Table A.10 as

$$P\text{-value} = 2P(W \geq 47) = 2P(W \leq 8) = 2 \times 0.024 = 0.048.$$

Thus we find that the population median differs from the design setting of $200°\text{F}$ at $\alpha = .05$. Recall from Example 14.1 that we did not find a significant difference even at $\alpha = .10$ using the sign test. ◆

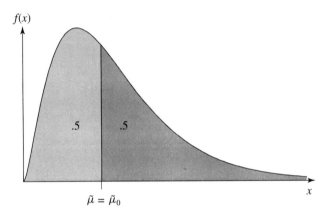

Figure 14.2   A Positively Skewed Distribution When $H_0: \tilde{\mu} = \tilde{\mu}_0$ Is True

*Null Distribution of the Wilcoxon Signed Rank Statistic.

The distribution of the signed rank statistic is obtained by noting that each ranked (in terms of the absolute value) difference, $D_i = X_i - \tilde{\mu}_0$, is equally likely to be positive or negative when H_0 is true. With n observations, there are 2^n possible assignments of signs to the ranks of $|D_i|$ and they are equally likely, each with probability $1/2^n$. Thus the distribution of W_+ can be obtained by enumerating all 2^n sign assignments and calculating the value of W_+ for each. This is illustrated in Table 14.2 for $n = 5$. The distribution of W_+ obtained from this enumeration is tabulated in Table 14.3. The distribution of W_- is the same.

Treatment of Ties.

There are two types of ties. First, some x_i's may be equal to $\tilde{\mu}_0$ and thus the corresponding $d_i = 0$. We choose to drop these observations and retain only the nonzero differences. Second, some of the $|d_i|$'s may be tied for the same rank. In that case we assign average rank (called **midrank**) to them. For example, suppose $d_1 = -1, d_2 = +3, d_3 = -3$, and $d_4 = +5$. Then $r_1 = 1, r_2 = r_3 = (2+3)/2 = 2.5$, and $r_4 = 4$. It should be noted that the distribution given in Table A.10 is based on the assumption of no ties and is not applicable, strictly speaking, when midranks are employed. However, we will ignore this problem and use the same table as if there were no ties. Similarly we will use the same large sample normal approximation, even though the variance of the statistic is slightly smaller in the presence of ties.

Table 14.2 List of All $2^5 = 32$ Assignments of Signs to Ranks

No.	1	2	3	4	5	w_+	No.	1	2	3	4	5	w_+
1	−	−	−	−	−	0	17	+	+	+	−	−	6
2	+	−	−	−	−	1	18	+	+	−	+	−	7
3	−	+	−	−	−	2	19	+	+	−	−	+	8
4	−	−	+	−	−	3	20	+	−	+	+	−	8
5	−	−	−	+	−	4	21	+	−	+	−	+	9
6	−	−	−	−	+	5	22	+	−	−	+	+	10
7	+	+	−	−	−	3	23	−	+	+	+	−	9
8	+	−	+	−	−	4	24	−	+	+	−	+	10
9	+	−	−	+	−	5	25	−	+	−	+	+	11
10	+	−	−	−	+	6	26	−	−	+	+	+	12
11	−	+	+	−	−	5	27	+	+	+	+	−	10
12	−	+	−	+	−	6	28	+	+	+	−	+	11
13	−	+	−	−	+	7	29	+	+	−	+	+	12
14	−	−	+	+	−	7	30	+	−	+	+	+	13
15	−	−	+	−	+	8	31	−	+	+	+	+	14
16	−	−	−	+	+	9	32	+	+	+	+	+	15

Table 14.3 Null Distribution of W_+ for $n = 5$

w_+	$P(W_+ = w_+)$	w_+	$P(W_+ = w_+)$
0	1/32	8	3/32
1	1/32	9	3/32
2	1/32	10	3/32
3	2/32	11	2/32
4	2/32	12	2/32
5	3/32	13	1/32
6	3/32	14	1/32
7	3/32	15	1/32

EXAMPLE 14.5   (COMPARING TWO METHODS OF MEASURING CARDIAC OUTPUT: WILCOXON SIGNED RANK TEST)

Apply the Wilcoxon signed rank test to the cardiac output data in Table 14.1 to determine if there is a significant difference between the two methods of measurement.

We drop the three tied pairs and assign ranks to the remaining paired differences (based on their magnitudes) using the midrank method. For example, the four smallest nonzero paired differences equal 0.1 in magnitude. They are assigned the midrank of $(1 + 2 + 3 + 4)/4 = 2.5$. The complete ranking is shown in the table below.

No.	Difference	Rank	No.	Difference	Rank
1	1.1	19.5	14	0.3	8
2	−0.3	8	15	0.0	–
3	1.2	21	16	0.7	15
4	0.7	15	17	0.9	17.5
5	1.4	23	18	0.0	–
6	1.3	22	19	0.5	12
7	0.9	17.5	20	0.4	10
8	0.5	12	21	0.0	–
9	0.2	5.5	22	0.1	2.5
10	0.5	12	23	1.1	19.5
11	0.7	15	24	−0.2	5.5
12	0.1	2.5	25	−0.1	2.5
13	0.3	8	26	0.1	2.5

We obtain $w_- = 8 + 5.5 + 2.5 = 16$ and $w_+ = (23)(24)/2 - 16 = 260$. The standardized Wilcoxon signed rank statistic equals

$$z = \frac{w_+ - n(n + 1)/4 - 1/2}{\sqrt{n(n + 1)(2n + 1)/24}} = \frac{260 - (23)(24)/4 - 1/2}{\sqrt{(23)(24)(47)/24}} = 3.695.$$

The two-sided P-value corresponding to this statistic equals $2[1 - \Phi(3.695)] = 0.0002$, which shows a highly significant difference between the two methods. ◆

*Signed Rank Confidence Interval for $\tilde{\mu}$. The steps to calculate a $(1 - \alpha)$-level CI for $\tilde{\mu}$ based on the Wilcoxon signed rank test are as follows:

1. Calculate all pairwise averages (called **Walsh averages**) of the data values:

$$\bar{x}_{ij} = \frac{x_i + x_j}{2} \quad (i, j = 1, 2, \ldots, n).$$

There are $N = n(n + 1)/2$ such pairwise averages including $\bar{x}_{ii} = x_i$, $i = 1, 2, \ldots, n$.

2. Order the Walsh averages:

$$\bar{x}_{(1)} \leq \bar{x}_{(2)} \leq \cdots \leq \bar{x}_{(N)}.$$

3. Let $w = w_{n,1-\alpha/2}$ be the lower $\alpha/2$ critical point of the null distribution of W. Then a $(1 - \alpha)$-level CI for $\tilde{\mu}$ is given by

$$\bar{x}_{(w+1)} \leq \tilde{\mu} \leq \bar{x}_{(N-w)}.$$

This CI can be derived by inverting the Wilcoxon signed rank test in the same way as we derived the CI based on the sign test. Since the argument is a little involved, it is omitted.

EXAMPLE 14.6   (THERMOSTAT SETTING: WILCOXON SIGNED RANK CONFIDENCE INTERVAL FOR MEDIAN)

Find a 95% Wilcoxon signed rank CI for the median $\tilde{\mu}$ of the settings for the population of all thermostats using the data from Example 14.1.

Because of the discreteness of the Wilcoxon signed rank statistic distribution we cannot find an *exact* 95% CI in this case. From Table A.10 we see that for $n = 10$, the upper 2.4% critical point of the distribution is 47 and by symmetry the lower 2.4% critical point is $55 - 47 = 8$. Setting $\alpha/2 = 0.024$ and hence $1 - \alpha = 1 - 0.048 = 0.952$, we find that $[\bar{x}_{(9)}, \bar{x}_{(47)}]$ provides a 95.2% CI for $\tilde{\mu}$, where the $\bar{x}_{(i)}$ are the ordered Walsh averages.

The computation and ordering of the Walsh averages can be done on a computer. A hand computation method which is convenient for small data sets ($n \leq 10$) is as follows. Arrange the data values in ascending order along the rows and columns of an array. Let the entries of the array be the averages of the corresponding row and column values, which are just the Walsh averages. Because the data values are ordered along the rows and columns, it is easy to locate the smallest and largest Walsh averages. This method is illustrated in Table 14.4. A common value of 200 is subtracted from all data values for convenience.

Table 14.4 Walsh Averages -200 for Thermostat Setting Data Set

	-2.0	-1.0	$+0.5$	$+0.8$	$+1.3$	$+2.2$	$+2.5$	$+3.4$	$+3.7$	$+6.3$
-2.0	-2.00	-1.50	-0.75	-0.60	-0.35	$+0.10$	$+0.25$	$+0.70$	$+0.85$	$+2.15$
-1.0		-1.00	-0.25	-0.10	$+0.15$	$+0.60$	$+0.75$	$+1.20$	$+1.35$	$+2.65$
$+0.5$			$+0.50$	$+0.65$	$+0.90$	$+1.35$	$+1.50$	$+1.95$	$+2.10$	$+3.40$
$+0.8$				$+0.80$	$+1.05$	$+1.50$	$+1.65$	$+2.10$	$+2.25$	$+3.55$
$+1.3$					$+1.30$	$+1.75$	$+1.90$	$+2.35$	$+2.50$	$+3.80$
$+2.2$						$+2.20$	$+2.35$	$+2.80$	$+2.95$	$+4.25$
$+2.5$							$+2.50$	$+2.95$	$+3.10$	$+4.40$
$+3.4$								$+3.40$	$+3.55$	$+4.85$
$+3.7$									$+3.70$	$+5.00$
$+6.3$										$+6.30$

Counting nine values from the low and high end, we find that $\bar{x}_{(9)} = +0.10$ and $\bar{x}_{(47)} = +3.55$. Thus we obtain $[200.10, 203.55]$ as a 95.2% CI for $\tilde{\mu}$. Since this interval does not include 200, we can reject $H_0\colon \tilde{\mu} = 200$, which agrees with the result from Example 14.4.   ◆

14.2   INFERENCES FOR TWO INDEPENDENT SAMPLES

Often one wants to show that observations from one population *tend* to be larger than those from another population based on independent random samples $x_1, x_2, \ldots, x_{n_1}$ and $y_1, y_2, \ldots, y_{n_2}$ from the two populations. For example, a treated patient tends to live longer than an untreated patient or an equity fund tends to have a higher yield than a bond fund. In this section we study a test due to Wilcoxon, Mann, and Whitney for this purpose.

To make precise the notion of an observation from one population tending to be larger than that from another population, consider two r.v.'s, X and Y, with cumulative distribution functions (c.d.f.'s) F_1 and F_2, respectively. We say that X is **stochastically larger** than Y (denoted by $X \succ Y$) if for all real numbers u,

$$P(X > u) \geq P(Y > u), \text{ that is, } P(X \leq u) = F_1(u) \leq F_2(u) = P(Y \leq u) \quad (14.7)$$

with a strict inequality for at least some u. We will write $F_1 < F_2$ to mean the same thing as $X \succ Y$.

If the distributions of X and Y are identical in shape except that one distribution is shifted from the other, then each distribution can be indexed by a parameter representing its location. This parameter is called the **location parameter**. (A more precise definition is given in a starred section below.) Figure 14.3 displays two distributions that differ only in their location parameters. If θ_1 and θ_2 denote the location parameters of X and Y, respectively, then $X \succ Y$ if $\theta_1 > \theta_2$.

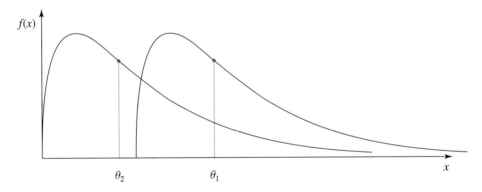

Figure 14.3   Distributions Differing Only in Location

It is easy to show that if $X \succ Y$, then $P(X > Y) > 1/2$; however, the converse is not necessarily true. If X and Y have the same distribution (denoted by $X \sim Y$), then $P(X > Y) = P(X < Y) = 1/2$.

We set up the hypotheses as

$$H_0: F_1 = F_2 \quad (X \sim Y) \text{ vs. } H_1: F_1 < F_2 \quad (X \succ Y). \quad (14.8)$$

The lower one-sided alternative is $H_1: F_1 > F_2$, and the two-sided alternative is $H_1: F_1 < F_2$ or $F_1 > F_2$. Note that the two-sided alternative is not simply stated as $H_1: F_1 \neq F_2$ which admits arbitrary differences between the distributions of X and Y without one r.v. being stochastically larger than the other one. The Wilcoxon-Mann-Whitney test presented below is not sensitive for detecting arbitrary differences between F_1 and F_2.[1] If F_1 and F_2 are distributions differing only in their location parameters,

---

[1] There is a nonparametric test for detecting arbitrary differences between F_1 and F_2, called the **Kolmogorov-Smirnov test**; see E. L. Lehmann (1975), *Nonparametrics: Statistical Methods Based on Ranks*, San Francisco: Holden-Day.

θ_1 and θ_2, respectively, then then the hypotheses (14.8) are equivalent to

$$H_0: \theta_1 = \theta_2 \text{ vs. } H_1: \theta_1 > \theta_2.$$

*Location and Scale Parameter Families.   A class of distributions is said to form a **location and scale parameter family** if the distribution of every r.v. X in the class can be written as

$$P(X \leq x) = F\left(\frac{x - \theta}{\tau}\right) \tag{14.9}$$

where θ is called the **location parameter** and τ is called the **scale parameter**; here F is a distribution function[2] common to all distributions in the class. We can standardize X by defining

$$Z = \frac{X - \theta}{\tau}.$$

Then the location and scale parameters of Z are 0 and 1, respectively, and the c.d.f. of Z is simply $P(Z \leq z) = F(z)$.

The simplest example of a location and scale parameter family is the family of normal distributions. If $X \sim N(\mu, \sigma^2)$, then the c.d.f. of X is given by

$$P(X \leq x) = P\left(Z \leq \frac{x - \mu}{\sigma}\right) = \Phi\left(\frac{x - \mu}{\sigma}\right)$$

where $\Phi(\cdot)$ is the standard normal c.d.f. This distribution is of the form (14.9), where μ is the location parameter and σ is the scale parameter.

14.2.1 Wilcoxon-Mann-Whitney Test

To test the hypotheses in (14.8) two seemingly different nonparametric tests are available: the **Wilcoxon rank sum test** and the **Mann and Whitney U-test**, which are in fact equivalent. We first describe the Wilcoxon rank sum test. Initially assume that there are no ties in the two samples: $x_1, x_2, \ldots, x_{n_1}$ and $y_1, y_2, \ldots, y_{n_2}$. The steps in the test are as follows.

   1. Rank all $N = n_1 + n_2$ observations in ascending order.
   2. Sum the ranks of the x's and y's separately. Denote the sums by w_1 and w_2, respectively. Since the ranks range over the integers $1, 2, \ldots, N$, we have

$$w_1 + w_2 = 1 + 2 + \cdots + N = \frac{N(N + 1)}{2}.$$

   3. Reject H_0 if w_1 is large or equivalently if w_2 is small.

To determine how large w_1 or how small w_2 must be in order to reject H_0 at a given significance level α, we need the null distributions of the corresponding r.v.'s W_1 and W_2. These distributions are not the same if n_1 and n_2 are not equal. The Mann-Whitney test statistic is defined in a symmetric way. The steps in the Mann-Whitney U-test are as follows:

---

[2] That is, $F(-\infty) = 0$, $F(+\infty) = 1$, and F is a nondecreasing function.

1. Compare each x_i with each y_j. Let u_1 be the number of pairs in which $x_i > y_j$ and let u_2 be the number of pairs in which $x_i < y_j$. There are $n_1 n_2$ such comparisons and $u_1 + u_2 = n_1 n_2$.

2. Reject H_0 if u_1 is large or equivalently if u_2 is small.

The Mann-Whitney and the Wilcoxon rank sum statistics are related as follows:

$$u_1 = w_1 - \frac{n_1(n_1 + 1)}{2} \quad \text{and} \quad u_2 = w_2 - \frac{n_2(n_2 + 1)}{2}.$$

The advantage of using the Mann-Whitney form of the test is that the same distribution applies whether we use u_1 or u_2 to carry out the test. The upper tail probabilities of this distribution are tabulated in Table A.11. Notice that this distribution ranges over 0 to $n_1 n_2$ and is symmetric about $n_1 n_2/2$. Denote the common r.v. by U. Then the P-value is given by

$$P\text{-value} = P\{U \geq u_1\} = P\{U \leq u_2\}.$$

An α-level test rejects H_0 if P-value $\leq \alpha$ or equivalently if $u_1 \geq u_{n_1,n_2,\alpha}$, where $u_{n_1,n_2,\alpha}$ is the upper α critical point of the null distribution of U.

For large n_1 and n_2, the null distribution of U can be well approximated by a normal distribution with mean and variance given by

$$E(U) = \frac{n_1 n_2}{2} \quad \text{and} \quad \text{Var}(U) = \frac{n_1 n_2(N + 1)}{12}. \tag{14.10}$$

Therefore a large sample z-test (with continuity correction) can be based on the statistic

$$z = \frac{u_1 - n_1 n_2/2 - 1/2}{\sqrt{\frac{n_1 n_2(N+1)}{12}}}.$$

The test rejects H_0 at level α if $z \geq z_\alpha$ or equivalently if

$$u_1 \geq \frac{n_1 n_2}{2} + \frac{1}{2} + z_\alpha \sqrt{\frac{n_1 n_2(N + 1)}{12}} \simeq u_{n_1,n_2,\alpha}. \tag{14.11}$$

The lower one-sided test and the two-sided tests are done in an analogous manner. For the two-sided test we use the test statistics $u_{\max} = \max(u_1, u_2)$ or $u_{\min} = \min(u_1, u_2)$. The P-value is given by

$$P\text{-value} = 2P\{U \geq u_{\max}\} = 2P\{U \leq u_{\min}\}.$$

EXAMPLE 14.7   (FAILURE TIMES OF CAPACITORS: WILCOXON-MANN-WHITNEY TEST)

Consider the following data[3] on the failure times of 18 capacitors, of which eight were tested under normal operating conditions (control group) and ten under thermally stressed conditions (stressed group). Perform the Wilcoxon-Mann-Whitney test to determine if thermal stress significantly reduces the time to failure of capacitors. Use $\alpha = .05$.

Times to Failure for Two Capacitor Groups

Control Group		Stressed Group	
5.2	17.1	1.1	7.2
8.5	17.9	2.3	9.1
9.8	23.7	3.2	15.2
12.3	29.8	6.3	18.3
		7.0	21.1

Let F_1 be the c.d.f. of the control group and F_2 be the c.d.f. of the stressed group. The hypotheses to be tested are $H_0: F_1 = F_2$ vs. $H_1: F_1 < F_2$. First we assign ranks to observations, as shown in the table below.

Ranks of Times to Failure

Control Group		Stressed Group	
4	13	1	7
8	14	2	9
10	17	3	12
11	18	5	15
		6	16

The rank sums are

$$w_1 = 4 + 8 + 10 + 11 + 13 + 14 + 17 + 18 = 95$$

and

$$w_2 = 1 + 2 + 3 + 5 + 6 + 7 + 9 + 12 + 15 + 16 = 76.$$

Therefore

$$u_1 = w_1 - \frac{n_1(n_1 + 1)}{2} = 95 - \frac{(8)(9)}{2} = 59$$

and

$$u_2 = w_2 - \frac{n_2(n_2 + 1)}{2} = 76 - \frac{(10)(11)}{2} = 21.$$

---

[3] J. D. Gibbons (1990), "Nonparametric Statistics," Chapter 11 in *Handbook of Statistical Methods for Engineers and Scientists* (ed. H. M. Wadsworth), New York: McGraw-Hill.

Check that $u_1 + u_2 = n_1 n_2 = 80$. From Table A.11 we find that the P-value $= .051$. To compare this with the large sample normal approximation, calculate

$$z = \frac{u_1 - n_1 n_2/2 - 1/2}{\sqrt{\frac{n_1 n_2(N+1)}{12}}} = \frac{59 - (8)(10)/2 - 1/2}{\sqrt{\frac{(8)(10)(19)}{12}}} = 1.643$$

which yields the P-value $= 1 - \Phi(1.643) = .0502$.   ◆

Treatment of Ties.   A tie occurs when some x_i equals a y_j. A contribution of 1/2 is counted toward both u_1 and u_2 for a tied pair. This is equivalent to using the midrank method in computing the Wilcoxon rank sum statistic. The exact null distribution is no longer given by Table A.11 in this case, since that table assumes no ties. However, we will still use that table, ignoring any small discrepancies. Similarly we will use the same large sample normal approximation, even though the variance of the statistic is slightly smaller in the presence of ties.

*Null Distribution of the Wilcoxon-Mann-Whitney Test Statistic.   The key point in deriving the distribution of the Wilcoxon rank sum statistic W_1 or the Mann-Whitney statistic U_1 is that under H_0 all $N = n_1 + n_2$ observations are assumed to come from the common distribution $F_1 = F_2$. Therefore all possible orderings of these observations with n_1 coming from F_1 and n_2 coming from F_2 are equally likely. There are

$$\binom{N}{n_1} = \frac{N!}{n_1! n_2!}$$

such orderings. For each ordering we can compute the values of W_1 and U_1, whence their distributions can be generated. We illustrate this for a small example with $n_1 = 2$ and $n_2 = 3$. There are $\binom{5}{2} = 10$ orderings in this case, which are shown in Table 14.5 along with the statistic values w_1 and u_1 for each ordering.

Table 14.5 All Possible Orderings of $n_1 = 2$ x's and $n_2 = 3$ y's, and Associated Values of the Wilcoxon Rank Sum and Mann-Whitney Statistics

Ranks					w_1	u_1	Ranks					w_1	u_1
1	2	3	4	5			1	2	3	4	5		
x	x	y	y	y	3	0	y	x	y	x	y	6	3
x	y	x	y	y	4	1	y	x	y	y	x	7	4
x	y	y	x	y	5	2	y	y	x	x	y	7	4
x	y	y	y	x	6	3	y	y	x	y	x	8	5
y	x	x	y	y	5	2	y	y	y	x	x	9	6

Using the fact that each ordering has 1/10 probability of occurring under H_0, the null distribution of W_1 and U_1 can be obtained, which is given in Table 14.6. Note that the distribution is the same for W_1 and U_1 except that $W_1 = U_1 + n_1(n_1+1)/2 = U_1+3$. The common distribution is symmetric with $E(U_1) = 3$ and $E(W_1) = 6$.

Table 14.6 Null Distribution of W_1 and U_1 for $n_1 = 2$ and $n_2 = 3$

w_1	u_1	$P(W_1 = w_1) = P(U_1 = u_1)$
3	0	0.1
4	1	0.1
5	2	0.2
6	3	0.2
7	4	0.2
8	5	0.1
9	6	0.1

14.2.2 *Wilcoxon-Mann-Whitney Confidence Interval

Suppose that the distributions F_1 and F_2 belong to a location parameter family (i.e., with a common known scale parameter which may be assumed to be 1) with location parameters θ_1 and θ_2, respectively, i.e.,

$$F_1(x) = F(x - \theta_1) \text{ and } F_2(y) = F(y - \theta_2)$$

where F is a common unknown distribution function. Usually we think of θ_1 and θ_2 as the respective population medians. A CI for $\theta_1 - \theta_2$ can be obtained by inverting the Mann-Whitney test. The procedure is as follows:

1. Calculate all $N = n_1 n_2$ pairwise differences $d_{ij} = x_i - y_j$ $(1 \le i \le n_1, 1 \le j \le n_2)$ and rank them:

$$d_{(1)} \le d_{(2)} \le \cdots \le d_{(N)}.$$

2. Let $u = u_{n_1, n_2, 1-\alpha/2}$ be the lower $\alpha/2$ critical point of the null distribution of the U-statistic. Then a $100(1-\alpha)\%$ CI for $\theta_1 - \theta_2$ is given by

$$d_{(u+1)} \le \theta_1 - \theta_2 \le d_{(N-u)}.$$

EXAMPLE 14.8   (FAILURE TIMES OF CAPACITORS: WILCOXON-MANN-WHITNEY CONFIDENCE INTERVAL)

Find a 95% CI for the difference between the median failure times of the control group and thermally stressed group of capacitors for the data from Example 14.7.

Because of the discreteness of the Wilcoxon-Mann-Whitney statistic distribution we cannot find an *exact* 95% CI in this case. From Table A.11 we see that for $n_1 = 8$ and $n_2 = 10$ the lower 2.2% critical point of the distribution of U is 17 and by symmetry the upper 2.2% critical point is $80 - 17 = 63$. Setting $\alpha/2 = 0.022$ and hence $1 - \alpha = 1 - 0.044 = 0.956$, we find that $[d_{(18)}, d_{(63)}]$ provides a 95.6% CI for the difference between the median failure times, where the $d_{(i)}$ are the ordered values of the differences $d_{ij} = x_i - y_j$. These differences are calculated in an array form, as shown in Table 14.7. Counting the 18th ordered difference from the low and high ends, we obtain $[d_{(18)}, d_{(63)}] = [-1.1, 14.7]$ as the 95.6% CI for the difference of two medians. Note that this interval includes zero.   ◆

Table 14.7 Differences $d_{ij} = x_i - y_j$ Between the Failure Times for Control Group and Thermally Stressed Groups of Capacitors

x_i	y_j									
	1.1	2.3	3.2	6.3	7.0	7.2	9.1	15.2	18.3	21.1
5.2	4.1	2.9	2.0	−1.1	−1.8	−2.0	−3.9	−10.0	−13.1	−15.9
8.5	7.4	6.2	5.3	2.2	1.5	1.3	−0.6	−6.7	−9.8	−12.6
9.8	8.7	7.5	6.6	3.5	2.8	2.6	0.7	−5.4	−8.5	−11.3
12.3	11.2	10.0	9.1	6.0	5.3	5.1	3.2	−2.9	−6.0	−8.8
17.1	16.0	14.8	13.9	10.8	10.1	9.9	8.0	1.9	−1.2	−4.0
17.9	16.8	15.6	14.7	11.6	10.9	10.7	8.8	2.7	−0.4	−3.2
23.7	22.6	21.4	20.5	17.4	16.7	16.5	14.6	8.5	5.4	2.6
29.8	28.7	27.5	26.6	23.5	22.8	22.6	20.7	14.6	11.5	8.7

14.3   INFERENCES FOR SEVERAL INDEPENDENT SAMPLES

Consider a **one-way layout** experiment with $a \geq 2$ treatment groups as discussed in Chapter 12. Let n_i be the size of the sample from the ith treatment and let y_{ij} be the jth observation from the ith treatment, $i = 1, 2, \ldots, a; j = 1, 2, \ldots, n_i$.

In Chapter 12 we assumed that the data from different treatments follow normal distributions with different means but a common variance. Here we drop the assumption of normality. Specifically, we assume only that the data on the ith treatment form a random sample from a continuous c.d.f. F_i, $i = 1, 2, \ldots, a$, and the random samples are mutually independent. We may additionally assume that the c.d.f.'s F_i belong to a location parameter family, i.e., the different distributions have the same shape but may differ in their locations. In that case the c.d.f. F_i has the representation $F_i(y) = F(y - \theta_i)$, where θ_i is the location parameter of F_i and F is a common unknown distribution function ($i = 1, 2, \ldots, a$).

Analogous to the null hypothesis of the equality of treatment means tested as part of the analysis of variance (ANOVA) when assuming normality of the data, here we test the following null and alternative hypotheses:

$$H_0: F_1 = F_2 = \cdots = F_a \text{ vs. } H_1: F_i < F_j \text{ for some } i \neq j. \qquad (14.12)$$

Under the location parameter model, the above hypotheses become

$$H_0: \theta_1 = \theta_2 = \cdots = \theta_a \text{ vs. } H_1: \theta_i > \theta_j \text{ for some } i \neq j. \qquad (14.13)$$

Note that the alternative hypothesis in (14.12) postulates that observations from treatment i are stochastically larger than those from treatment j. The Kruskal-Wallis test that we discuss below is not sensitive to detecting arbitrary differences between the distributions of the treatments.

14.3.1 Kruskal-Wallis Test

The Kruskal-Wallis test is a generalization to several independent samples of the Wilcoxon rank sum test for two independent samples in the same way that the F-test of one-way ANOVA is a generalization to several independent samples of the two sample t-test. The steps in the Kruskal-Wallis test are as follows.

1. Rank all $N = \sum_{i=1}^{a} n_i$ observations in ascending order. Assign midranks in case of ties. Let $r_{ij} = \text{rank}(y_{ij})$. Note that the r_{ij} sum to $1+2+\cdots+N = N(N+1)/2$ and the average rank equals $(N+1)/2$.

2. Calculate rank sums $r_i = \sum_{j=1}^{n_i} r_{ij}$ and averages $\bar{r}_i = r_i/n_i, \ i = 1, 2, \ldots, a$.

3. Calculate the Kruskal-Wallis test statistic

$$kw = \frac{12}{N(N+1)} \sum_{i=1}^{a} n_i \left(\bar{r}_i - \frac{N+1}{2} \right)^2 = \frac{12}{N(N+1)} \sum_{i=1}^{a} \frac{r_i^2}{n_i} - 3(N+1).$$

4. Reject H_0 for large values of kw.

Let KW denote the r.v. corresponding to the observed value kw. The exact null distribution of KW can be used to carry out the test. This distribution is obtained by enumerating all possible distinct ways of assigning N ranks to the observations from a treatments and calculating the value of KW in each case. There are

$$\frac{N!}{n_1! n_2! \cdots n_a!}$$

possible assignments, assuming no ties. Under H_0 all of these assignments are equally likely. Unfortunately, the resulting exact distribution of KW depends on the individual sample sizes, $n_1, n_2, \ldots, n_a$, and therefore it is not practical to tabulate it beyond a small number of cases. Therefore we look for an approximation to this distribution.

It can be shown that for large n_i's, the exact null distribution of KW can be approximated by the chi-square distribution with $a - 1$ degrees of freedom (d.f.). This approximation is convenient to use, since it does not depend on the individual sample sizes $n_1, n_2, \ldots, n_a$, and the chi-square distribution is well tabulated. Thus an approximate α-level large sample Kruskal-Wallis test rejects H_0 if

$$kw > \chi^2_{a-1, \alpha}.$$

EXAMPLE 14.9   (COMPARING TEACHING METHODS: KRUSKAL-WALLIS TEST)

Apply the the Kruskal-Wallis test to the following test scores data set from Example 12.10.

Average Test Scores

Teaching Method

Case Method	Formula Method	Equation Method	Unitary Analysis Method
14.59	20.27	27.82	33.16
23.44	26.84	24.92	26.93
25.43	14.71	28.68	30.43
18.15	22.34	23.32	36.43
20.82	19.49	32.85	37.04
14.06	24.92	33.90	29.76
14.26	20.20	23.42	33.88

The ranks of the data values are shown in the following table. Note that two observations = 24.92 are tied for the 14th and 15th rank and are assigned the midrank = (14+15)/2= 14.5.

Ranks of Average Test Scores

Teaching Method

	Case Method	Formula Method	Equation Method	Unitary Analysis Method
	3	8	19	24
	13	17	14.5	18
	16	4	20	22
	5	10	11	27
	9	6	23	28
	1	14.5	26	21
	2	7	12	25
Rank Sum	49	66.5	125.5	165

The value of the Kruskal-Wallis test statistic equals

$$kw = \frac{12}{N(N+1)} \sum_{i=1}^{a} \frac{r_i^2}{n_i} - 3(N+1)$$

$$= \frac{12}{28(29)} \left[\frac{(49)^2}{7} + \frac{(66.5)^2}{7} + \frac{(125.5)^2}{7} + \frac{(165)^2}{7} \right] - 3(29)$$

$$= 18.134.$$

Referring this statistic to the χ_3^2 distribution, we find that it is highly significant. For example, $kw = 18.134 > \chi_{3,.005}^2 = 12.837$, and therefore the P-value $< .005$. Thus there are significant differences among the four teaching methods.   ◆

14.3.2 *Pairwise Comparisons

To determine whether treatment groups i and j differ from each other we can use the difference in their rank averages, $\bar{r}_i - \bar{r}_j$, as a test statistic. If $\bar{R}_i - \bar{R}_j$ denotes the corresponding r.v., then under H_0 it can be shown that

$$E(\bar{R}_i - \bar{R}_j) = 0 \text{ and } \mathrm{Var}(\bar{R}_i - \bar{R}_j) = \frac{N(N+1)}{12}\left(\frac{1}{n_i} + \frac{1}{n_j}\right).$$

Furthermore, for large n_i's, $\bar{R}_i - \bar{R}_j$ is approximately normally distributed. Therefore

$$z_{ij} = \frac{\bar{r}_i - \bar{r}_j}{\sqrt{\frac{N(N+1)}{12}\left(\frac{1}{n_i} + \frac{1}{n_j}\right)}}$$

can be used as an approximately standard normal test statistic. There are $\binom{a}{2}$ such pairwise comparisons between the treatment groups. To control the type I familywise error rate at level α, the $|z_{ij}|$-statistics should be referred to the appropriate Studentized range distribution (tabulated in Table A.7) as in the Tukey method discussed in Chapter 12. The number of treatment groups compared is a, and because of the large sample assumption we take the d.f. $= \infty$. Thus the $|z_{ij}|$-statistics are compared with the critical constant $q_{a,\infty,\alpha}/\sqrt{2}$. Treatments i and j are declared different if

$$|z_{ij}| > \frac{q_{a,\infty,\alpha}}{\sqrt{2}} \text{ or equivalently if } |\bar{r}_i - \bar{r}_j| > \frac{q_{a,\infty,\alpha}}{\sqrt{2}}\sqrt{\frac{N(N+1)}{12}\left(\frac{1}{n_i} + \frac{1}{n_j}\right)}.$$

EXAMPLE 14.10   (COMPARING TEACHING METHODS: PAIRWISE COMPARISONS)

Refer to Example 14.9. Determine which teaching methods differ from each other at an overall significance level $\alpha = .05$.

The critical constant for comparing any pairwise difference $|\bar{r}_i - \bar{r}_j|$ is

$$\frac{q_{4,\infty,.05}}{\sqrt{2}}\sqrt{\frac{N(N+1)}{12}\left(\frac{1}{n_i} + \frac{1}{n_j}\right)} = \frac{3.63}{\sqrt{2}}\sqrt{\frac{(28)(29)}{12}\left(\frac{1}{7} + \frac{1}{7}\right)} = 11.29.$$

The rank averages are $\bar{r}_1 = \frac{49.0}{7} = 7.0, \bar{r}_2 = \frac{66.5}{7} = 9.5, \bar{r}_3 = \frac{125.5}{7} = 17.9,$ and $\bar{r}_4 = \frac{165}{7} = 23.6$. Only $|\bar{r}_1 - \bar{r}_4|$ and $|\bar{r}_2 - \bar{r}_4|$ exceed 11.29. Therefore methods 1 and 2 differ from method 4.   ◆

14.4   INFERENCES FOR SEVERAL MATCHED SAMPLES

As discussed in Chapters 3 and 12, blocking or matching of experimental units results in more precise comparisons between the treatment groups. Consider a **randomized block design** with $a \geq 2$ treatment groups and $b \geq 2$ blocks. Let y_{ij} denote an observation on the ith treatment in the jth block. A distribution-free rank-based test for comparing the treatments in this setting is known as the **Friedman test**, named after the Nobel Laureate economist Milton Friedman who proposed it.

Denote by F_{ij} the c.d.f. of r.v. Y_{ij} corresponding to the observed value y_{ij}. Consider the null hypothesis that the F_{ij} are identical for all treatments i separately for each block j. The alternative hypothesis is that at least one treatment yields stochastically larger observations than does another treatment in all blocks j. Specifically,

$$H_0: F_{1j} = F_{2j} = \cdots = F_{aj} \text{ for all } j \text{ vs. } H_1: F_{ij} < F_{kj} \text{ for some } i \neq k \text{ for all } j.$$
$$(14.14)$$

If we assume that the distributions F_{ij} belong to a location parameter family and there are no treatment $\times$ block interactions, then F_{ij} can be expressed as

$$F_{ij}(y) = F(y - \theta_i - \beta_j)$$

where F is some unknown distribution function, the θ_i are "treatment effects", and the β_j are "block effects." For this model the hypotheses (14.13) can be more simply expressed as

$$H_0: \theta_1 = \theta_2 = \cdots = \theta_a \text{ vs. } H_1: \theta_i > \theta_k \text{ for some } i \neq k. \qquad (14.15)$$

14.4.1 Friedman Test

Since the treatments are blocked, comparisons between them should be made only within each block—not across blocks. The Friedman test assigns ranks accordingly. The steps in the Friedman test are as follows.

1. Rank observations from a treatments separately within each block. Assign midranks in case of ties. Let $r_{ij} = \text{rank}(y_{ij})$.

2. Calculate the rank sums $r_i = \sum_{j=1}^{b} r_{ij}, i = 1, 2, \ldots, a$.

3. Calculate the Friedman statistic

$$fr = \frac{12}{ab(a+1)} \sum_{i=1}^{a} \left\{ r_i - \frac{b(a+1)}{2} \right\}^2 = \frac{12}{ab(a+1)} \sum_{i=1}^{a} r_i^2 - 3b(a+1). \quad (14.16)$$

4. Reject H_0 for large values of fr.

The exact null distribution of the r.v. FR corresponding to the observed value fr can be derived by using the fact that there are $a!$ possible ways of assigning ranks $1, 2, \ldots, a$ to the a observations within each block. There are b blocks, so the total number of possible assignments of ranks is $(a!)^b$, which are equally likely under H_0. These assignments can be enumerated and the value of FR can be calculated for each assignment from which the null distribution of FR can be obtained. As in the case of the Kruskal-Wallis test, this distribution can be well approximated by the χ_{a-1}^2 distribution if the number of blocks b is large. Thus an approximate α-level Friedman test rejects H_0 if

$$fr > \chi_{a-1,\alpha}^2.$$

EXAMPLE 14.11

Reanalyze the meat loaf drip loss data from Example 12.12 (reproduced in Table 14.8 below) using the Friedman test.

   Here the oven positions are treatments and batches are blocks. The ranks of the positions within each batch and the rank sums are shown in Table 14.9.

Table 14.8 Drip Loss in Meat Loaves

Oven	Batch		
Position	1	2	3
1	7.33	8.11	8.06
2	3.22	3.72	4.28
3	3.28	5.11	4.56
4	6.44	5.78	8.61
5	3.83	6.50	7.72
6	3.28	5.11	5.56
7	5.06	5.11	7.83
8	4.44	4.28	6.33

Table 14.9 Ranks of Oven Positions

Oven	Batch			Rank
Position	1	2	3	Sum
1	8	8	7	23
2	1	1	1	3
3	2.5	4	2	8.5
4	7	6	8	21
5	4	7	5	16
6	2.5	4	3	9.5
7	6	4	6	16
8	5	2	4	11

The Friedman statistic equals

$$
\begin{aligned}
fr &= \frac{12}{ab(a+1)} \sum_{i=1}^{a} r_i^2 - 3b(a+1) \\
&= \frac{12}{(8)(3)(9)} [(23)^2 + (3)^2 + (8.5)^2 + (21)^2 + (16)^2 + (9.5)^2 + (16)^2 + (11)^2] - (3)(3)(9) \\
&= 17.583.
\end{aligned}
$$

This value exceeds $\chi^2_{7,.025} = 16.012$. Thus the P-value is less than .025, which indicates significant differences between the oven positions. It should be noted, however, that the number of blocks here is only 3; therefore the large sample chi-square approximation may not be accurate.   ◆

14.4.2 Pairwise Comparisons

To determine which treatment groups differ from each other, we can use the difference in their rank averages, $|\bar{r}_i - \bar{r}_j|$, as a test statistic. Under the null hypothesis H_0 it can be shown that

$$E(\bar{R}_i - \bar{R}_j) = 0 \text{ and } \text{Var}(\bar{R}_i - \bar{R}_j) = \frac{a(a+1)}{6b}.$$

Therefore, as in the case of the Kruskal-Wallis test, treatments i and j can be declared different from each other at the overall significance level α if

$$|\bar{r}_i - \bar{r}_j| > \frac{q_{a,\infty,\alpha}}{\sqrt{2}} \sqrt{\frac{a(a+1)}{6b}}.$$

14.5   RANK CORRELATION METHODS

The Pearson correlation coefficient (discussed in Chapters 4 and 10) measures only the degree of *linear* association between two variables, as has been noted before. Furthermore, as seen in Chapter 10, Section 10.5, inferences on the Pearson correlation coefficient use the assumption of bivariate normality of the two variables. In this section we present two correlation coefficients that take into account only the ranks of the observations and hence can measure the degree of monotone (increasing or decreasing) association between two variables. For example, consider five paired observations:

$$(x, y) = (1, e^1), (2, e^2), (3, e^3), (4, e^4), (5, e^5).$$

There is a perfect positive monotone association between x and y with $y = e^x$. Yet the Pearson correlation coefficient for these data is only 0.886, because the relationship is not linear. The rank correlation coefficients that we consider in this section yield a value of 1 for these data. Also, inferences on the rank correlation coefficients are distribution-free.

14.5.1 Spearman's Rank Correlation Coefficient

Consider two variables, x and y, measured on at least an ordinal scale. Suppose we have n paired observations, $(x_1, y_1), (x_2, y_2), \ldots, (x_n, y_n)$, on these two variables. The Spearman rank correlation coefficient (denoted by r_S) is just the Pearson correlation coefficient computed from the ranks of the x_i's and y_i's. The steps for calculating r_S are as follows.

1. Assign ranks to the x_i's and y_i's separately. In case of ties assign midranks. Let $u_i = \text{rank}(x_i)$ and $v_i = \text{rank}(y_i)$. If there are no ties, then the u_i's and v_i's are some permutations of the integers $1, 2, \ldots, n$.

2. Calculate r_S using the formula (4.8) for the Pearson correlation coefficient, but applied to the ranks:

$$r_S = \frac{\sum_{i=1}^{n}(u_i - \bar{u})(v_i - \bar{v})}{\sqrt{\{\sum_{i=1}^{n}(u_i - \bar{u})^2\}\{\sum_{i=1}^{n}(v_i - \bar{v})^2\}}}. \tag{14.17}$$

If the u_i and v_i are integers, then a more convenient formula for calculating r_S is

$$r_S = 1 - \frac{6\sum_{i=1}^{n} d_i^2}{n(n^2-1)} \tag{14.18}$$

where the $d_i = u_i - v_i$ are the differences in the ranks. This may be used as an approximate formula in case of ties.

Like Pearson's r, Spearman's r_S ranges between -1 and $+1$ with $r_S = -1$ when there is a perfect negative monotone association and $r_S = +1$ when there is a perfect positive monotone association between x and y. The values of r_S for these extreme cases can be checked from the formula (14.18). In case of perfect positive association we have $u_i = v_i$, so $d_i = 0$ for all i, which yields $r_S = +1$. In case of perfect negative association, assuming that the u_i are labeled so that $u_i = i$, we have $v_i = n - i + 1$, e.g., $(u_1 = 1, v_1 = n)$, $(u_2 = 2, v_2 = n-1)$, etc. Then $d_i = i - (n-i+1) = 2i - (n+1)$. Substituting this value in (14.18) and doing some algebra yields $r_S = -1$.

Next we discuss hypothesis testing using r_S. Denote the r.v.'s corresponding to x, y, and r_S by X, Y, and R_S, respectively. Consider the problem of testing

H_0: X and Y are independent vs. H_1: X and Y are positively associated.   (14.19)

The null distribution of R_S can be derived by using the fact that for a fixed ordering of the X_i's, all orderings of the Y_i's are equally likely under H_0. Assuming no ties, corresponding to the ordering $X_1 < X_2 < \cdots < X_n$, there are $n!$ orderings of the Y_i's, each with probability $1/n!$. The value of R_S can be calculated for each ordering, from which its distribution can be obtained. The null distribution of R_S is symmetric about zero. For large n it can be shown that this distribution is well approximated by a normal distribution with mean and variance equal to

$$E(R_S) = 0 \text{ and } \text{Var}(R_S) = \frac{1}{n-1}. \tag{14.20}$$

Therefore

$$z = r_S\sqrt{n-1} \tag{14.21}$$

can be used as a standardized normal test statistic for testing H_0 of (14.19). A table of the exact distribution is available in advanced texts on nonparametric statistics, but we have not given it here, since the large sample normal approximation gives reasonably accurate results for $n \geq 10$.

EXAMPLE 14.12   (WINE CONSUMPTION AND HEART DISEASE DEATHS: SPEARMAN RANK CORRELATION ANALYSIS)

Table 14.10 gives data[4] on the yearly alcohol consumption from wine in liters per person and yearly heart disease deaths per 100,000 people for 19 countries. Test if there is association between these two variables, using Spearman's rank correlation coefficient.

A scatter plot of the data is shown in Figure 14.4. The plot is fairly linear with Pearson's correlation coefficient $r = -0.843$. Because of the linearity of the plot we expect that Spearman's rank correlation coefficient will give a similar result.

[4] D. S. Moore (1997), *The Active Practice of Statistics*, New York: W. H. Freeman, p. 111, Table II.2; originally from *New York Times*, December 28, 1994.

Table 14.10 Wine Consumption and Heart Disease Deaths

Country	Alcohol from Wine (x_i)	Heart Disease Deaths (y_i)	Country	Alcohol from Wine (x_i)	Heart Disease Deaths (y_i)
Australia	2.5	211	Netherlands	1.8	167
Austria	3.9	167	New Zealand	1.9	266
Belgium	2.9	131	Norway	0.8	227
Canada	2.4	191	Spain	6.5	86
Denmark	2.9	220	Sweden	1.6	207
Finland	0.8	297	Switzerland	5.8	115
France	9.1	71	U.K.	1.3	285
Iceland	0.8	211	U.S.	1.2	199
Ireland	0.7	300	W. Germany	2.7	172
Italy	7.9	107			

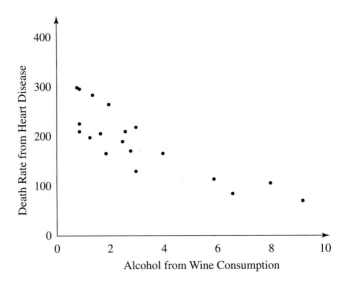

Figure 14.4   Scatter Plot of Heart Disease Deaths vs. Wine Consumption

Table 14.11 gives the ranks u_i and v_i, and the rank differences $d_i = u_i - v_i$. Calculate $\sum_{i=1}^{n} d_i^2 = 2081.5$. Hence, using (14.18), we get

$$r_S = 1 - \frac{(6)(2081.5)}{(19)(360)} = -0.826.$$

To test the significance of r_S, calculate using (14.21)

$$z = -0.826\sqrt{18} = -3.504.$$

This statistic is clearly highly significant with a two-sided P-value = 0.0004. Although this analysis shows significant negative association between wine consumption and heart disease deaths,

Table 14.11 Ranks of Wine Consumption and Heart Disease Deaths

Country i	$u_i =$ rank(x_i)	$v_i =$ rank(y_i)	$d_i = u_i - v_i$	Country i	$u_i =$ rank(x_i)	$v_i =$ rank(y_i)	$d_i = u_i - v_i$
1	11	12.5	−1.5	11	8	6.5	1.5
2	15	6.5	8.5	12	9	16	−7.0
3	13.5	5	−8.5	13	3	15	−12.0
4	10	9	1.0	14	17	2	15.0
5	13.5	14	−0.5	15	7	11	−4.0
6	3	18	−15.0	16	16	4	12.0
7	19	1	18.0	17	6	17	−11.0
8	3	12.5	−9.5	18	5	10	−5.0
9	1	19	−18.0	19	12	8	4.0
10	18	3	15.0				

since the data are observational with many lurking variables, it does not establish a cause-effect relationship between the two variables. ◆

14.5.2 Kendall's Rank Correlation Coefficient

We first introduce the population version of Kendall's rank correlation coefficient. A pair of bivariate r.v.'s: (X_i, Y_i) and (X_j, Y_j) is called a **concordant pair** if $(X_i - X_j)(Y_i - Y_j) > 0$, which holds when $X_i > X_j$ and $Y_i > Y_j$ or $X_i < X_j$ and $Y_i < Y_j$, i.e., X and Y change in the same direction. The pair (X_i, Y_i) and (X_j, Y_j) is called a **discordant pair** if $(X_i - X_j)(Y_i - Y_j) < 0$, which holds when $X_i > X_j$ and $Y_i < Y_j$ or $X_i < X_j$ and $Y_i > Y_j$, i.e., X and Y change in the opposite direction. Finally, the pair (X_i, Y_i) and (X_j, Y_j) is called a **tied pair** if $(X_i - X_j)(Y_i - Y_j) = 0$, which holds when either $X_i = X_j$ or $Y_i = Y_j$ or both. If we assume that the r.v.'s X and Y are continuous, then we can ignore the possibility of a tied pair. Let

$$\pi_c = P\{\text{Concordant pair}\} = P\{(X_i - X_j)(Y_i - Y_j) > 0\}$$

and

$$\pi_d = P\{\text{Discordant pair}\} = P\{(X_i - X_j)(Y_i - Y_j) < 0\}.$$

Because the probability of a tied pair is zero, we have $\pi_c + \pi_d = 1$. Kendall's rank correlation coefficient (denoted by τ and referred to as **Kendall's tau**) is defined as

$$\tau = \pi_c - \pi_d. \tag{14.22}$$

Notice that $-1 \le \tau \le +1$; furthermore, $\tau = -1$ in case of a perfect negative association (when $\pi_c = 0, \pi_d = 1$) and $\tau = +1$ in case of a perfect positive association (when $\pi_c = 1, \pi_d = 0$).

The sample estimate $\hat{\tau}$ of τ can be obtained from the data $(x_1, y_1), (x_2, y_2), \ldots, (x_n, y_n)$ using the relation

$$\hat{\tau} = \hat{\pi}_c - \hat{\pi}_d$$

where $\hat{\pi}_c$ and $\hat{\pi}_d$ are the sample estimates of π_c and π_d, respectively. These estimates can be obtained as the proportions of concordant and discordant pairs in the data. There are $\binom{n}{2} = N$ possible pairwise comparisons among the observations (x_i, y_i), $i = 1, 2, \ldots, n$. Let N_c be the number of concordant pairs and N_d be the number of discordant pairs with $N_c + N_d = N$ (assuming no tied pairs). Then $\hat{\pi}_c = N_c/N$ and $\hat{\pi}_d = N_d/N$, so

$$\hat{\tau} = \frac{N_c - N_d}{N}. \tag{14.23}$$

In case of ties the above formula is modified by effectively subtracting from the denominator of $\hat{\tau}$ the numbers of pairwise comparisons between the tied x_i's and the tied y_i's. Suppose there are g groups of tied x_i's with a_j tied observations in the jth group and h groups of tied y_i's with b_j tied observations in the jth group. The total numbers of tied comparisons between the x_i's and the y_i's are

$$T_x = \sum_{j=1}^{g} \binom{a_j}{2} \quad \text{and} \quad T_y = \sum_{j=1}^{h} \binom{b_j}{2}$$

respectively. As an example, consider five pairs of observations: $(x, y) = (1, 3), (1, 4), (1, 5), (2, 5), (3, 4)$. There is $g = 1$ group of $a_1 = 3$ tied x's equal to 1, and there are $h = 2$ groups of tied y's; group 1 has $b_1 = 2$ tied y's equal to 4 and group 2 has $b_2 = 2$ tied y's equal to 5. Therefore $T_x = \binom{3}{2} = 3$ and $T_y = \binom{2}{2} + \binom{2}{2} = 2$. The formula for $\hat{\tau}$ is modified as

$$\hat{\tau} = \frac{N_c - N_d}{\sqrt{(N - T_x)(N - T_y)}}. \tag{14.24}$$

For small data sets, a systematic method for calculating N_c and N_d by hand is as follows.

1. Relabel the observations so that the x_i's are in ascending order: $x_1 \leq x_2 \leq \cdots \leq x_n$.

2. Count $N_{c1} = \#\{j > 1: x_j > x_1 \text{ and } y_j > y_1\}$ and $N_{d1} = \#\{j > 1: x_j > x_1 \text{ and } y_j < y_1\}$, which are, respectively, the numbers of concordant and discordant pairs relative to the first pair. It is also useful to calculate the number of pairs tied with the first pair: $N_{t1} = \#\{j > 1: x_j = x_1 \text{ or } y_j = y_1\}$.

3. Repeat step 2 for subsequent pairs. Note that we only need to compare a given pair with the pairs that follow it in the order of the x_i's. Thus count $N_{ci} = \#\{j > i: x_j > x_i \text{ and } y_j > y_i\}$, $N_{di} = \#\{j > i: x_j > x_i \text{ and } y_j < y_i\}$ and $N_{ti} = \#\{j > i: x_j = x_i \text{ or } y_j = y_i\}$ for $i = 2, \ldots, n - 1$. Since there are no pairs to be compared with the last pair, we have $N_{cn} = N_{dn} = N_{tn} = 0$.

4. Calculate $N_c = \sum_{i=1}^{n-1} N_{ci}$ and $N_d = \sum_{i=1}^{n-1} N_{di}$. The number of tied pairs is $N_t = \sum_{i=1}^{n-1} N_{ti} = N - (N_c + N_d)$.

The method is illustrated in the example below.

The hypotheses (14.19) can be stated in terms of the population parameter τ as follows:

$$H_0: \tau = 0 \text{ vs. } H_1: \tau > 0. \tag{14.25}$$

The exact distribution of $\hat{\tau}$ under H_0 can be derived by the same method indicated for Spearman's R_S. This distribution is symmetric about zero. A table of this exact distribution is available in advanced texts on nonparametric statistics. We have not given it here, since for large n (≥ 10) the null distribution of $\hat{\tau}$ can be well approximated by a normal distribution with mean and variance equal to

$$E(\hat{\tau}) = 0 \text{ and } \text{Var}(\hat{\tau}) = \frac{2(2n+5)}{9n(n-1)}. \tag{14.26}$$

Therefore

$$z = \hat{\tau}\sqrt{\frac{9n(n-1)}{2(2n+5)}} \tag{14.27}$$

can be used as a standardized normal statistic.

EXAMPLE 14.13   (WINE CONSUMPTION AND HEART DISEASE DEATHS: KENDALL RANK CORRELATION ANALYSIS)

Redo Example 14.12 using Kendall's rank correlation coefficient.

The calculation of the number of concordances and discordances is shown in Table 14.12. We have $N_c = 25$, $N_d = 141$, and $N_t = 5$ for a total of $N = 171$. There are $g = 2$ groups of tied x_i's; the first group has $a_1 = 3$ tied observations (equal to 0.8) and the second group has $a_2 = 2$ tied observations (equal to 2.9). Therefore the number of tied pairs among the x_i's is

$$T_x = \binom{3}{2} + \binom{2}{2} = 3 + 1 = 4.$$

There are $h = 2$ groups of tied y_i's; the first group has $b_1 = 2$ tied observations (equal to 167) and the second group has $b_2 = 2$ tied observations (equal to 211). Therefore the number of tied pairs among the y_i's is

$$T_y = \binom{2}{2} + \binom{2}{2} = 1 + 1 = 2.$$

From (14.24) we get

$$\hat{\tau} = \frac{25 - 141}{\sqrt{(171-4)(171-2)}} = -0.690.$$

Table 14.12 Calculation of N_c and N_d for the Wine Consumption and Heart Disease Deaths Data

i	Country	x_i	y_i	N_{ci}	N_{di}	N_{ti}
1	Ireland	0.7	300	0	18	0
2	Iceland	0.8	211	3	11	3
3	Norway	0.8	227	2	13	1
4	Finland	0.8	297	0	15	0
5	U.S.	1.2	199	5	9	0
6	U.K.	1.3	285	0	13	0
7	Sweden	1.6	207	3	9	0
8	Netherlands	1.8	167	5	5	1
9	New Zealand	1.9	266	0	10	0
10	Canada	2.4	191	2	7	0
11	Australia	2.5	211	1	7	0
12	W. Germany	2.7	172	1	6	0
13	Belgium	2.9	131	2	4	0
14	Denmark	2.9	220	0	5	0
15	Austria	3.9	167	0	4	0
16	Switzerland	5.8	115	0	3	0
17	Spain	6.5	86	1	1	0
18	Italy	7.9	107	0	1	0
19	France	9.1	71	0	0	0
				$N_c = 25$	$N_d = 141$	$N_t = 5$

To test the significance of $\hat{\tau}$, calculate using (14.27)

$$z = -0.690\sqrt{\frac{(9)(19)(18)}{2(43)}} = -4.128,$$

which is clearly highly significant with P-value $< .0001$. ◆

In this example we find that the magnitude of r_S is higher than $\hat{\tau}$. This is typically the case. Since r_S and $\hat{\tau}$ measure correlation in different ways, their scales are not directly comparable. Generally both statistics yield similarly significant results. Kendall's $\hat{\tau}$ has a simpler interpretation (namely, it is the difference between the proportions of concordant and discordant pairs) than Spearman's r_S; it also has a well-defined population parameter associated with it. Therefore $\hat{\tau}$ is preferred to r_s.

14.5.3 *Kendall's Coefficient of Concordance

Kendall's coefficient of concordance is a measure of association between several matched samples. It is closely related to Friedman's test statistic (14.16). To see this relation, think of the a treatments as candidates and the b blocks as judges with each judge ranking the a candidates. If there is perfect agreement between the judges, then each candidate gets the same rank. Assuming the candidates are labeled in the order of their ranking, the rank sum for the ith candidate would be $r_i = ib$. (In the context of the Friedman test this situation corresponds to very large differences between the treatments.) On the other hand, if the judges rank the candidates completely at random ("perfect disagreement"), then the expected rank for each candidate would be $(a + 1)/2$, and the expected value of all rank sums would equal $b(a + 1)/2$. (In the context of the Friedman test this situation corresponds to no differences between the treatments.) The discrepancy of the actual rank sums from their expected values under perfect disagreement as defined by

$$d = \sum_{i=1}^{a} \left\{ r_i - \frac{b(a + 1)}{2} \right\}^2$$

is a measure of agreement between the judges. The maximum value of this measure is attained when there is perfect agreement and is given by

$$d_{\max} = \sum_{i=1}^{a} \left\{ ib - \frac{b(a + 1)}{2} \right\}^2 = \frac{b^2 a(a^2 - 1)}{12}.$$

The ratio of these two is called Kendall's coefficient of concordance (denoted by w):

$$w = \frac{d}{d_{\max}} = \frac{12}{b^2 a(a^2 - 1)} \sum_{i=1}^{a} \left\{ r_i - \frac{b(a + 1)}{2} \right\}^2. \tag{14.28}$$

It follows that $0 \leq w \leq 1$, with small values indicating disagreement and large values indicating agreement.

Comparing this formula with the formula (14.16) for Friedman's statistic, fr, we see that

$$w = \frac{fr}{b(a - 1)}.$$

Thus large values of the Friedman statistic and hence of w demonstrate agreement between the judges and can be used to test the null hypothesis of random assignment of ranks by the judges. As a final note, Spearman's rank correlation coefficient is related to Kendall's coefficient of concordance for $a = 2$ by the formula:

$$r_S = 2w - 1.$$

Example **14.14**

A taste-testing experiment used four tasters to rank eight recipes with the following results. Calculate Kendall's coefficient of concordance between the tasters. Are the tasters in agreement?

Recipe	Taster 1	2	3	4	Rank Sum
1	5	4	5	4	18
2	7	5	7	5	24
3	1	2	1	3	7
4	3	3	2	1	9
5	4	6	4	6	20
6	2	1	3	2	8
7	8	7	8	8	31
8	6	8	6	7	27

The rank sums, r_i, of the recipes are given in the above table. The Friedman statistic equals

$$fr = \frac{12}{(4)(8)(9)}[18^2 + 24^2 + 7^2 + 9^2 + 20^2 + 8^2 + 31^2 + 27^2] - (3)(4)(9) = 24.667.$$

Therefore Kendall's coefficient of concordance equals

$$w = \frac{24.667}{(4)(8)} = 0.881.$$

To test the significance of this coefficient at $\alpha = .05$ we compare $fr = 24.667$ with $\chi^2_{7,.05} = 14.067$. Since fr exceeds this critical value, we conclude that the tasters are in agreement.   ◆

14.6   *RESAMPLING METHODS

To explain the difference between resampling methods and conventional methods, consider the problem of inference from a single sample of size n. Conventional methods are based on the sampling distribution of a statistic computed from the observed sample. The sampling distribution is derived by considering all possible samples of size n (the so-called **sample space**) from the underlying population. Resampling methods, in contrast, generate the sampling distribution of the statistic by drawing repeated random samples from the observed sample itself. This eliminates the need to assume a specific functional form for the population distribution (e.g., normal). Obviously, the sampling distribution thus obtained is only an approximation, since the observed sample is, after all, only a particular realization from the population. Yet, this error could be far less serious than making wrong and often unverifiable assumptions about the population distribution.

The **bootstrap**, due to Bradley Efron,[5] is a computer intensive resampling method which is gaining in popularity. The roots of this method go back to the earlier methods

---

[5] B. Efron (1979), "Bootstrap methods: Another look at the jackknife," *Annals of Statistics*, **7**, pp. 1–26.

of **permutation tests** and **jackknife**. We give a very brief introduction to these methods in this section. For additional details see the books by Efron and Tibshirani[6] and by Davison and Hinkley.[7]

14.6.1 Permutation Tests

The idea behind a permutation test is best explained in the context of the two sample problem. Let $x_1, x_2, \ldots, x_{n_1}$ and $y_1, y_2, \ldots, y_{n_2}$ be independent random samples from distributions F_1 and F_2, respectively. Under $H_0: F_1 = F_2$, all $n_1 + n_2$ observations are assumed to be drawn from the same common distribution. Regard the observations as fixed (instead of random as done in conventional inference methods). If H_0 is true, all assignments of labels x and y to them are equally likely. Under the restriction that n_1 observations must be x's and n_2 observations must be y's, there are $\binom{n_1+n_2}{n_1}$ assignments of labels to the observations, each having equal probability. Each assignment of labels amounts to drawing a simple random sample (SRS) of size n_1 *without replacement* (see Chapter 3, Section 3.3.1) from a total of $n_1 + n_2$ observations and labeling them as x's, the remainder being labeled y's.

We can calculate the value of a suitable test statistic (e.g., $\bar{x} - \bar{y}$ or the t-statistic) for each assignment of labels. The permutation distribution of the statistic is obtained by using the fact that each assignment of labels to the observations has a probability $1/\binom{n_1+n_2}{n_1}$. The actual observed value of the test statistic can be referred to this distribution to find its P-value. The method is illustrated in the following example.

EXAMPLE 14.15   (FAILURE TIMES OF CAPACITORS: PERMUTATION TEST)

Consider the failure time data on capacitors from Example 14.7, but to keep the calculations short consider only the three largest observations from each group:

Control group (x):	17.9	23.7	29.8
Stressed group (y):	15.2	18.3	21.1

Do a permutation test to determine if thermal stress significantly reduces the times to failure of capacitors. Use $\alpha = 0.10$.

We will use $\bar{x} - \bar{y}$ as the test statistic. For our observed data $\bar{x} - \bar{y} = 23.80 - 18.20 = 5.60$. The permutation distribution of the statistic is derived in Table 14.13 by listing all $\binom{6}{3} = 20$ assignments of labels x and y to the observed data values. The assignments are listed in the increasing order of $\bar{x} - \bar{y}$. The permutation distribution is symmetric here because the sample sizes in the two groups are equal, so that for every assignment of labels with an associated value of $\bar{x} - \bar{y}$ there is an assignment with an exchange of the labels x's and y's having the same value of $\bar{x} - \bar{y}$, but with an opposite sign. All $\bar{x} - \bar{y}$ values are distinct, so each has a probability of 1/20 under H_0. There are three assignments with $\bar{x} - \bar{y} \geq$ the observed value 5.60, so the P-value is $3/20 = .15$. Therefore the difference between the two groups of capacitors is not significant at $\alpha = .10$.   ◆

[6] B. Efron and R. J. Tibshirani (1993), *An Introduction to the Bootstrap*, New York: Chapman & Hall.

[7] A. C. Davison and D. V. Hinkley (1997), *Bootstrap Methods and Their Application*, Cambridge, U.K.: Cambridge University Press.

Table 14.13 Permutation Distribution of $\bar{x} - \bar{y}$ for Capacitor Failure Time Data with Three Longest Failure Times from Each Group

| | | | Data Values | | | | |
No.	15.2	17.9	18.3	21.1	23.7	29.8	$\bar{x} - \bar{y}$
1	x	x	x	y	y	y	−7.74
2	x	x	y	x	y	y	−5.86
3	x	y	x	x	y	y	−5.60
4	x	x	y	y	x	y	−4.14
5	x	y	x	y	x	y	−3.86
6	y	x	x	x	y	y	−3.80
7	y	x	x	y	x	y	−2.06
8	x	y	y	x	x	y	−2.00
9	y	x	y	x	y	x	−0.20
10	x	x	y	y	y	x	−0.06
11	y	y	x	x	x	y	0.06
12	x	y	x	y	x	y	0.20
13	y	x	x	y	y	x	2.00
14	x	y	y	x	y	x	2.06
15	x	y	y	y	x	x	3.80
16	y	x	y	x	y	x	3.86
17	y	y	x	x	y	x	4.14
18	y	x	y	y	x	x	5.60
19	y	y	x	y	x	x	5.86
20	y	y	y	x	x	x	7.74

Several points are worth noting about the permutation test.

1. In the Wilcoxon-Mann-Whitney test an identical approach is applied to the ranks of the data values. Therefore the Wilcoxon-Mann-Whitney distribution is independent of the observed data values. On the other hand, the permutation distribution obtained here depends on the observed data values and must be generated separately for each different data set.

2. The idea of a permutation test can be extended to other testing problems—in particular, to the problem of comparing several samples.

3. The number of assignments of labels increases rapidly. For example, for $n_1 = n_2 = 10$, this number equals $\binom{20}{10} = 184,756$. For larger data sets it becomes necessary to *estimate* the permutation distribution via Monte Carlo simulation, even if calculations are done on a computer. Simulations can be performed by drawing a suitably large number of SRS without replacement from the observed

data values. For example, for $n_1 = n_2 = 10$, instead of enumerating all 184,756 assignments, one can draw 10,000 SRS without replacement and estimate the permutation distribution from them.

14.6.2 Bootstrap Method

While the permutation test considers all possible SRS *without replacement* from the set of observed data values, the bootstrap method considers all possible SRS *with replacement* (which means that some of the data values may be repeated in the bootstrap sample). To understand the rationale behind the bootstrap method it is convenient to begin with the problem of finding the standard error of a sample statistic. The standard error may be used to judge the precision of the statistic and/or to calculate a confidence interval for the parameter that the statistic is estimating.

Bootstrap for Estimating Standard Error.   Let $x_1, x_2, \ldots, x_n$ be a random sample from a probability distribution F with mean μ and standard deviation σ. Consider a very simple statistic, namely the sample mean $\bar{x}$, which is an unbiased estimate of μ. We know that the standard error of the mean (SEM) equals

$$\text{SE}(\bar{x}) = \frac{s}{\sqrt{n}} = \sqrt{\frac{\sum_{i=1}^{n}(x_i - \bar{x})^2}{n(n-1)}}. \tag{14.29}$$

So $\text{SE}(\bar{x})$ can be readily calculated and there is no need to estimate it. However, often there are no such simple formulas for more complicated sample statistics, e.g., trimmed mean or sample median, hence the need for the bootstrap method. To explain the method, we will pretend that we do not know the formula for $\text{SE}(\bar{x})$ and we need to estimate it.

One way to estimate $\text{SE}(\bar{x})$ would be to draw a large number of random samples of size n from F, calculate $\bar{x}$ for each sample, and use the standard deviation of these $\bar{x}$ values as the desired estimate. The hitch is that the distribution F is unknown, so we can't sample from it. The bootstrap method uses an estimated distribution $\hat{F}$ to sample from instead of the true distribution F.

The natural estimate $\hat{F}$ is the **sample c.d.f.** defined by

$$\hat{F}(x) = \frac{\sharp\{x_i \leq x\}}{n} = \text{Proportion of the } x_i\text{'s} \leq x$$

which is a step function with a jump of $1/n$ at each ordered x_i. In other words, $\hat{F}$ puts a probability mass of $1/n$ on each x_i. A bootstrap random sample of size n from $\hat{F}$ amounts to drawing an SRS *with replacement* from $x_1, x_2, \ldots, x_n$. It can be shown (see Exercise 14.39) that the distribution of the $\bar{x}$-values computed from all such SRS has the standard deviation

$$\text{BSE}(\bar{x}) = \frac{\sqrt{\sum_{i=1}^{n}(x_i - \bar{x})^2}}{n} \tag{14.30}$$

where BSE stands for the **bootstrap standard error** of $\bar{x}$. Comparing this with (14.29), we see that

$$\text{BSE}(\bar{x}) = \sqrt{\frac{n-1}{n}} \text{SE}(\bar{x}).$$

The bootstrap method estimates $\text{BSE}(\bar{x})$ from a large number, N, of SRS drawn *with replacement* from $x_1, x_2, \ldots, x_n$.

The steps in the **bootstrap algorithm** are as follows:

1. Draw N SRS *with replacement* from $\{x_1, x_2, \ldots, x_n\}$. Denote these bootstrap samples by $\{x_{i1}^*, x_{i2}^*, \ldots, x_{in}^*\}$, $i = 1, 2, \ldots, N$.

2. Calculate the sample mean of each bootstrap sample and the overall sample mean:

$$\bar{x}_i^* = \frac{\sum_{j=1}^{n} x_{ij}^*}{n} \quad \text{and} \quad \bar{\bar{x}}^* = \frac{\sum_{i=1}^{N} \bar{x}_i^*}{N}.$$

3. Calculate

$$\widehat{\text{BSE}}(\bar{x}) = \sqrt{\frac{\sum_{i=1}^{N} (\bar{x}_i^* - \bar{\bar{x}}^*)^2}{N-1}}.$$

It is possible to adjust $\widehat{\text{BSE}}(\bar{x})$ by the factor $\sqrt{\frac{n}{n-1}}$ so that in the limit (as $N \to \infty$) it equals $\text{SE}(\bar{x})$, but this is generally not done.

It is now straightforward to generalize this bootstrap algorithm to estimate the standard errors of more complicated statistics, which is its real focus of application. Let $t = t(x_1, x_2, \ldots, x_n)$ be a sample statistic, which is an estimate of a parameter θ of the distribution F. To estimate $\text{SE}(t)$ we draw N SRS *with replacement* from $\{x_1, x_2, \ldots, x_n\}$ and calculate $t_i^* = t(x_{i1}^*, x_{i2}^*, \ldots, x_{in}^*)$ for the ith sample, $i = 1, 2, \ldots, N$. Let $\bar{t}^* = \sum_{i=1}^{N} t_i^* / N$. Then the bootstrap estimate of $\text{SE}(t)$ is given by

$$\widehat{\text{BSE}}(t) = \sqrt{\frac{\sum_{i=1}^{N} (t_i^* - \bar{t}^*)^2}{N-1}}.$$

Clearly, this algorithm is highly computer intensive, and suitable software is essential to implement it.

To gain an insight into the bootstrap method, write the unknown parameter θ as $\theta(F)$ to make it clear that it depends on F; then $t = \hat{\theta}(F)$. For example, $\mu = \mu(F)$ and $\bar{x} = \hat{\mu}(F)$. The bootstrap method estimates $\text{SE}\{\hat{\theta}(F)\}$ by an estimate of $\text{SE}\{\hat{\theta}(\hat{F})\}$. The accuracy involved in this approximation depends on (i) how accurately $\hat{F}$ estimates F, which depends on the sample size n, and (ii) how large a bootstrap sample N is used to estimate $\text{SE}\{\hat{\theta}(\hat{F})\}$. Although N can be increased, n is fixed and limits the accuracy of the method. Typically, N is at least 100 and may be 1000 or more, although in the examples below we have used $N = 25$ for illustration purposes.

EXAMPLE 14.16 (THERMOSTAT SETTING: BOOTSTRAP ESTIMATES OF STANDARD ERRORS OF MEAN AND MEDIAN)

For the thermostat setting data from Example 14.1 find the bootstrap estimate of the standard errors of mean and median.

We took $N = 25$ SRS of size 10 with replacement from the data set using MINITAB and calculated the sample mean and median for each. The results are shown in Table 14.14. The top row of the table shows the actual data values. The entries in the table show how many times each value was selected in the sample. For example, the first bootstrap sample consisted of 202.2, 203.4, 200.5, 202.5 (repeated twice), 206.3 (repeated twice), and 200.8 (repeated thrice).

Table 14.14 Bootstrap Samples from Thermostat Setting Data and Their Means and Medians

Sample No.	Data Value										Mean	Median
	202.2	203.4	200.5	202.5	206.3	198.0	203.7	200.8	201.3	199.0	$\bar{x}_i^*$	$\tilde{x}_i^*$
1	1	1	1	2	2	0	0	3	0	0	202.61	202.35
2	3	1	0	3	1	0	0	1	0	1	202.36	202.35
3	0	2	0	1	1	0	1	1	1	3	201.84	201.90
4	0	1	0	1	1	1	1	0	2	3	201.35	201.30
5	1	1	0	1	0	1	1	0	2	3	200.94	201.30
6	1	1	0	0	3	1	0	1	2	1	202.49	201.75
7	1	1	1	1	1	1	1	0	2	1	201.82	201.75
8	2	2	2	1	1	1	1	0	0	0	202.27	202.35
9	2	0	1	1	0	1	3	1	1	0	201.86	202.20
10	2	1	2	1	0	1	1	1	0	1	201.28	201.50
11	2	1	1	0	2	0	1	1	1	1	202.57	202.20
12	1	1	1	2	0	1	2	2	0	0	201.81	202.35
13	4	1	1	0	0	1	0	2	1	0	201.36	201.75
14	0	1	1	3	1	1	1	0	1	1	201.97	202.50
15	0	1	1	1	0	2	1	1	2	1	200.85	201.05
16	3	1	0	1	2	0	1	0	0	2	202.68	202.35
17	1	2	0	0	0	1	2	2	2	0	201.86	201.75
18	0	2	1	2	0	0	1	2	1	1	201.79	201.90
19	1	1	2	0	1	1	1	2	0	1	201.52	200.80
20	2	0	1	1	3	0	1	1	1	0	203.21	202.35
21	1	1	1	2	0	1	0	1	3	0	201.38	201.30
22	2	1	1	2	0	1	1	0	2	0	201.76	202.20
23	1	2	1	2	0	3	0	0	0	1	200.75	201.35
24	1	0	3	0	4	2	0	0	0	0	202.49	201.35
25	0	2	1	0	0	2	2	1	0	2	200.95	200.65

From the 25 bootstrap means and medians the estimated standard errors were calculated to be

$$\widehat{\text{BSE}}(\bar{x}) = 0.642 \quad \text{and} \quad \widehat{\text{BSE}}(\tilde{x}) = 0.538.$$

The actual standard error of the mean, $s/\sqrt{n}$, calculated from the data equals 0.760. An approximate standard error of $\tilde{x}$ is $s\sqrt{\pi/2n}$ (assuming that the sample is normally distributed), which equals 0.955 for these data. So the bootstrap standard error estimates are not very accurate in this example, because both n and N are rather small. ◆

The above algorithm extends naturally to statistics calculated from multivariate observations. For example, suppose each observation x_i is a bivariate observation and the sample statistic is the correlation coefficient. There is no simple closed formula for the standard error of the correlation coefficient, but the bootstrap method can provide a reasonable approximation without assuming a specific functional form for the distribution F, e.g., the bivariate normal distribution. See Efron and Gong (1983)[8] for this and more complicated examples of the bootstrap method.

Bootstrap for Hypothesis Testing. Consider again the two sample problem discussed in Section 14.6.1. The bootstrap method for finding the P-value of a test statistic is similar to the permutation test, except that each bootstrap sample is obtained by drawing $n_1 + n_2$ observations *with replacement* from the data set $\{x_1, x_2, \ldots, x_{n_1}; y_1, y_2, \ldots, y_{n_2}\}$ and labeling n_1 of them as x's and n_2 of them as y's.

EXAMPLE 14.17 (FAILURE TIMES OF CAPACITORS: BOOTSTRAP TEST)

Repeat Example 14.15 using the bootstrap test.
Table 14.15 shows $N = 25$ bootstrap samples drawn using S-Plus[9] from the data set

$$\{17.9, 23.7, 29.8, 15.2, 18.3, 21.1\}.$$

As in the permutation test we calculate the statistic $\bar{x}^* - \bar{y}^*$ for each sample. We see that of the 25 samples, only for two samples is the actual observed value of $\bar{x} - \bar{y} = 5.60$ exceeded. Therefore the bootstrap estimate of the P-value is $2/25 = .08$. We find that in this case the result is significant at $\alpha = .10$. ◆

It is apparent that the bootstrap method can be extended to handle more complicated hypothesis tests and other statistical procedures, e.g., fitting a regression model using stepwise regression. All that is required is a scheme for drawing bootstrap samples from the observed data to which a given procedure can be applied. By doing this a large number of times an estimate of the accuracy of the procedure can be obtained.

---

[8] B. Efron and G. Gong (1983), "A leisurely look at the bootstrap, jackknife and cross-validation," *The American Statistician*, **37**, pp. 36–48.

[9] Computations for this example were performed by Professor Edward Malthouse, Northwestern University.

Table 14.15 Bootstrap Samples from Capacitor Data

No.	x_1^*	x_2^*	x_3^*	y_1^*	y_2^*	y_3^*	$\bar{x}^* - \bar{y}^*$
1	21.1	29.8	29.8	15.2	15.2	15.2	11.70
2	15.2	29.8	18.3	15.2	18.3	29.8	0.00
3	18.3	23.7	21.1	18.3	21.1	18.3	1.80
4	21.1	17.9	17.9	23.7	21.1	21.1	−3.00
5	18.3	21.1	17.9	21.1	17.9	23.7	−1.80
6	18.3	21.1	17.9	23.7	21.1	18.3	−1.93
7	17.9	17.9	21.1	21.1	21.1	21.1	−2.13
8	17.9	18.3	21.1	15.2	15.2	15.2	3.90
9	21.1	17.9	18.3	15.2	18.3	21.1	0.90
10	17.9	17.9	15.2	29.8	23.7	23.7	−8.73
11	29.8	15.2	23.7	21.1	21.1	18.3	2.73
12	23.7	17.9	15.2	21.1	18.3	29.8	−4.13
13	23.7	15.2	29.8	17.9	23.7	17.9	3.07
14	18.3	18.3	18.3	21.1	21.1	15.2	−0.83
15	15.2	18.3	21.1	15.2	17.9	29.8	−2.77
16	18.3	23.7	18.3	17.9	23.7	23.7	−1.67
17	23.7	17.9	17.9	29.8	21.1	17.9	−3.10
18	15.2	18.3	18.3	15.2	17.9	29.8	−3.70
19	29.8	29.8	21.1	18.3	29.8	17.9	4.90
20	29.8	29.8	29.8	21.1	18.3	23.7	8.77
21	15.2	17.9	23.7	21.1	29.8	23.7	−5.93
22	17.9	23.7	23.7	15.2	23.7	18.3	2.70
23	23.7	15.2	29.8	21.1	18.3	29.8	−0.17
24	17.9	18.3	18.3	18.3	17.9	23.7	−1.80
25	29.8	15.2	18.3	29.8	15.2	18.3	0.00

In conclusion, the bootstrap method replaces difficult or even impossible analytical solutions to statistical problems with raw computing power. As indicated previously, there are limits to its accuracy. Many of the problems with the bootstrap are not yet fully resolved, and research is ongoing.

14.6.3 Jackknife Method

Consider the problem of estimating the standard error of a statistic $t = t(x_1, x_2, \ldots, x_n)$ calculated based on a random sample from distribution F. In the jackknife method resampling is done by deleting one observation at a time. Thus we calculate n values of the statistic denoted by $t_i^* = t(x_1, x_2, \ldots, x_{i-1}, x_{i+1}, \ldots, x_n)$. Let $\bar{t}^* = \sum_{i=1}^n t_i^*/n$.

Then the jackknife estimate of $SE(t)$ is given by

$$\widehat{JSE}(t) = \sqrt{\frac{n-1}{n} \sum_{i=1}^{n} (t_i^* - \bar{t}^*)^2} = \frac{(n-1)s_{t^*}}{\sqrt{n}} \qquad (14.31)$$

where s_{t^*} is the sample standard deviation of $t_1^*, t_2^*, \ldots, t_n^*$.

This formula is not immediately evident, so let us look at the special case: $t = \bar{x}$. Then

$$t_i^* = \bar{x}_i^* = \frac{1}{n-1} \sum_{j \neq i} x_j = \frac{n\bar{x} - x_i}{n-1} \text{ and } \bar{t}^* = \bar{\bar{x}}^* = \frac{1}{n} \sum_{i=1}^{n} \bar{x}_i^* = \bar{x}.$$

Using simple algebra it can be shown that

$$\widehat{JSE}(\bar{x}) = \sqrt{\frac{n-1}{n} \sum_{i=1}^{n} (\bar{x}_i^* - \bar{\bar{x}}^*)^2} = \sqrt{\frac{\sum_{i=1}^{n} (x_i - \bar{x})^2}{n(n-1)}} = SE(\bar{x}). \qquad (14.32)$$

Thus the jackknife estimate of the standard error (14.31) gives an exact result for $\bar{x}$.

EXAMPLE 14.18 (THERMOSTAT SETTING: JACKKNIFE ESTIMATES OF STANDARD ERRORS OF MEAN AND MEDIAN)

For the thermostat setting data from Example 14.1, find the jackknife estimate of the standard errors of the mean and median.

The 10 jackknife samples along with their means and medians are listed in Table 14.16. The deleted observation in each sample is indicated by 0; the nine included observations are indicated by 1's. The sample standard deviations of the jackknife means, $\bar{x}_i^*$, and medians, $\tilde{x}_i^*$, are calculated to be

$$s_{\bar{x}^*} = 0.267 \text{ and } s_{\tilde{x}^*} = 0.474.$$

Hence the jackknife estimates of the standard errors of the sample mean and sample median are

$$\widehat{JSE}(\bar{x}) = \frac{(n-1)s_{\bar{x}^*}}{\sqrt{n}} = \frac{(9)(0.267)}{\sqrt{10}} = 0.760$$

and

$$\widehat{JSE}(\tilde{x}) = \frac{(n-1)s_{\tilde{x}^*}}{\sqrt{n}} = \frac{(9)(0.474)}{\sqrt{10}} = 1.350.$$

Note that $\widehat{JSE}(\bar{x})$ equals $SE(\bar{x}) = 0.760$. However, $\widehat{JSE}(\tilde{x}) = 1.350$ (as well as $\widehat{BSE}(\tilde{x}) = 0.538$) is an inaccurate estimate of the approximate $SE(\tilde{x}) = 0.955$ calculated assuming that the sample is normally distributed. It can be shown that $\widehat{JSE}(\tilde{x})$ is always an inaccurate estimate of $SE(\tilde{x})$. One reason can be seen in the fact that only two distinct values of the median (201.30 and 202.20) are obtained from the jackknife samples, because each jackknife sample differs from the original sample by just one observation. For many sample statistics, $\widehat{JSE}(t)$ performs worse than $\widehat{BSE}(t)$ but requires less computation.   ◆

Table 14.16 Jackknife Samples from Thermostat Setting Data and Their
Means and Medians

Sample No.	Data Value										Mean	Median
	202.2	203.4	200.5	202.5	206.3	198.0	203.7	200.8	201.3	199.0	$\bar{x}_i^*$	$\tilde{x}_i^*$
1	0	1	1	1	1	1	1	1	1	1	201.72	201.30
2	1	0	1	1	1	1	1	1	1	1	201.59	201.30
3	1	1	0	1	1	1	1	1	1	1	201.91	202.20
4	1	1	1	0	1	1	1	1	1	1	201.69	201.30
5	1	1	1	1	0	1	1	1	1	1	201.27	201.30
6	1	1	1	1	1	0	1	1	1	1	202.19	202.20
7	1	1	1	1	1	1	0	1	1	1	201.56	201.30
8	1	1	1	1	1	1	1	0	1	1	201.88	202.20
9	1	1	1	1	1	1	1	1	0	1	201.82	202.20
10	1	1	1	1	1	1	1	1	1	0	202.08	202.20

14.7   CHAPTER SUMMARY

Nonparametric or distribution-free methods are useful when the data cannot be assumed to follow a specific distribution (e.g., normal). In the single sample case, the nonparametric alternatives to the t-test are the **sign test** and the **Wilcoxon signed rank test**. To test a null hypothesis $H_0\colon \tilde{\mu} = \tilde{\mu}_0$ on the population median $\tilde{\mu}$ based on data $x_1, x_2, \ldots, x_n$ from that population, the sign test takes into account only whether the differences $d_i = x_i - \tilde{\mu}_0 > 0$ or < 0. The test statistics are $s_+ = \sharp(d_i > 0)$ and $s_- = \sharp(d_i < 0) = n - s_+$. Under H_0, both the test statistics have a $\text{Bin}(n, 1/2)$ distribution. The Wilcoxon signed rank test takes into account not only the signs of the d_i but also the ranks of the $|d_i|$. The test statistics are $w_+ =$ sum of the ranks of the positive d_i's and $w_- = n(n + 1)/2 - w_+ =$ sum of the ranks of the negative d_i's. This test is more powerful than the sign test but requires the additional assumption that the population distribution is symmetric. Both these tests can be inverted to obtain a confidence interval for $\tilde{\mu}$. Both methods extend to the paired sample case.

The nonparametric alternative to the two independent samples t-test is the **Wilcoxon-Mann-Whitney test**. Let n_1 and n_2 be the sizes of the two samples. The Wilcoxon test ranks all $N = n_1 + n_2$ observations together and computes rank sums, w_1 and w_2, for the two samples, where $w_1 + w_2 = N(N + 1)/2$. The Mann-Whitney test uses the statistics $u_1 = \sharp(x_i > y_j)$ and $u_2 = \sharp(x_i < y_j) = n_1 n_2 - u_1$. The two tests are equivalent because their test statistics are related: $u_1 = w_1 - n_1(n_1 + 1)/2$ and $u_2 = w_2 - n_2(n_2 + 1)/2$. The null distributions of these statistics are derived using the fact that all $\frac{N!}{n_1! n_2!}$ orderings of the data are equally likely under the null hypothesis that the two populations are identical.

The **Kruskal-Wallis test** is a generalization of the Wilcoxon-Mann-Whitney test for $a \geq 2$ independent samples; it is a nonparametric alternative to the ANOVA F-test for a one-way layout. Let n_i denote the sample size from the ith treatment group. All

$N = \sum_{i=1}^{a} n_i$ observations are ranked together and the rank sums r_i and rank averages $\bar{r}_i = r_i/n_i$ are computed. The test statistic is a weighted sum of squares of the $\bar{r}_i$ around their average, which equals $(N + 1)/2$. The null distribution of the statistic is derived by using the same argument as above, namely that under the null hypothesis of equality of the a population distributions all $\frac{N!}{n_1!n_2!\cdots n_a!}$ orderings of the data are equally likely. Asymptotically (as $n_i \to \infty$ for all i), this null distribution is chi-square with $a - 1$ d.f.

The **Friedman test** is a generalization of the sign test for $a \geq 2$ matched samples; it is a nonparametric alternative to the ANOVA F-test for a randomized block design. Here the rankings are done separately within each of the b sets of matched samples or blocks. The test statistic is similar to the Kruskal-Wallis statistic based on rank averages. The null distribution of the statistic is derived by using the fact that under the null hypothesis of the equality of the a population distributions, all $(a!)^b$ rankings are equally likely. Asymptotically (as $b \to \infty$), this null distribution is chi-square with $a - 1$ d.f.

Two nonparametric alternatives to the Pearson correlation coefficient for n independent pairs of observations, $\{(x_i, y_i) \; i = 1, 2, \ldots, n\}$, are the **Spearman rank correlation coefficient** and the **Kendall rank correlation coefficient**. The Spearman rank correlation coefficient is just the Pearson correlation coefficient applied to the ranks of the x_i's and the y_i's. The Kendall rank correlation coefficient is defined as the difference between the proportions of concordant and discordant pairs, which can also be computed from the ranks. The null distributions (under the hypothesis of independence between the x_i's and the y_i's) of both these rank correlation coefficients are derived by regarding all $n!$ pairings of the ranks as equally likely. Asymptotically (as $n \to \infty$), the null distributions of both the rank correlation coefficients are normal with zero means but different variances.

Resampling methods draw repeated samples from the observed sample itself to generate the sampling distribution of a statistic. The **permutation method** draws samples *without replacement*, while the **bootstrap method** draws samples *with replacement*. The **jackknife method** resamples by deleting one observation at a time. These methods are useful for assessing accuracies (e.g., the bias and standard error) of complex statistics.

■ **EXERCISES**

Section 14.1

14.1   Test whether the median of the population from which the following sample is drawn exceeds 30, i.e., test $H_0: \tilde{\mu} = 30$ vs. $H_1: \tilde{\mu} > 30$:

37   26   31   35   32   32   27   31   34   36.

(a) Find the exact P-value for the sign test and find the normal approximation to it. Is the normal approximation accurate? Can you reject H_0 at $\alpha = .05$?

(b) Repeat part (a) using the Wilcoxon signed rank test.

14.2   In a study of the effect of vitamin B on learning, 12 matched pairs of children were randomly divided into two groups. One child in each pair received a vitamin B tablet (treatment) every day, while the other child received a placebo tablet and served as control. The following table shows the gain in IQ over the six weeks of the study:

Pair	1	2	3	4	5	6	7	8	9	10	11	12
Treated	14	26	2	4	−5	14	3	−1	1	6	3	4
Control	8	18	−7	−1	2	9	0	−4	13	3	3	3

(a) Find the exact P-value for the sign test to determine if vitamin B improves the IQ.

(b) Repeat part (a) using the Wilcoxon signed rank test. Why is a less significant result obtained in this case?

14.3 For the previous exercise calculate 90% sign and Wilcoxon signed rank CI's on the median of the difference in IQ scores of treated vs. control children. Compare the results with those obtained using the corresponding tests.

14.4 Refer to the corneal thickness data of glaucoma patients from Exercise 8.7.

(a) Do the sign test to determine if the corneal thickness differs between an eye affected with glaucoma and an unaffected eye. Use $\alpha = .05$.

(b) Repeat part (a) using the Wilcoxon signed rank test.

14.5 For the previous exercise calculate 95% (or the nearest achievable higher confidence level to be on the conservative side) sign and Wilcoxon signed rank CI's on the median difference in the corneal thickness between an affected and an unaffected eye. Compare the results with those obtained using the corresponding tests.

14.6 Refer to the data from Exercise 8.15 on home heating energy consumption before and after installing insulation.

(a) Do the sign test at $\alpha = .05$ to determine if insulation reduced the energy consumption.

(b) Repeat part (a) using the Wilcoxon signed rank test.

14.7 For the previous exercise calculate 95% (or the nearest achievable higher confidence level to be on the conservative side) sign and Wilcoxon signed rank CI's on the median energy saving due to insulation. Compare the results with those obtained using the corresponding tests.

14.8 Find the null distribution of the Wilcoxon signed rank statistic for $n = 4$ by enumerating all possible assignments of ranks to signed differences as in Table 14.2. Verify that the mean of the distribution equals $n(n+1)/4 = 5$ and variance equals $n(n+1)(2n+1)/24 = 7.5$.

14.9 Many nonparametric test statistics have discrete distributions which impose a lower bound on the P-value (attained when the sample outcome is most favorable for rejecting H_0, e.g., when all signs are plus in the upper one-sided sign test or the Wilcoxon signed rank test) and therefore make it impossible to reject H_0 at an α less than this lower bound.

(a) Show that the lowest attainable P-value using the one-sided sign test or the Wilcoxon signed rank test is $(1/2)^n$.

(b) Is it possible to reject H_0 at $\alpha = .01$ if $n = 6$ using these tests?

(c) What is the smallest sample size required for these tests if rejection of H_0 at $\alpha = .01$ must be possible?

14.10 Check the accuracy of the normal approximation (14.6) to the Wilcoxon signed rank critical constant $w_{n,\alpha}$ by comparing it with the exact constant from Table A.10 for $n = 10$ and $\alpha = .053$.

Section 14.2

14.11 The table below gives the survival times of 16 mice that were randomly assigned to a control group or to a treatment group.[10] Did the treatment prolong survival? Answer using the Wilcoxon-Mann-Whitney test at $\alpha = .10$.

Survival Times of Mice (Days)									
Control Group	52	104	146	10	50	31	40	27	46
Treatment Group	94	197	16	38	99	141	23		

14.12 Consider the dopamine level data from Exercise 4.22. Apply the Wilcoxon-Mann-Whitney test at $\alpha = .05$ to find out if there is a significant difference between the dopamine levels of the psychotic and nonpsychotic patients.

14.13 Consider the data from Exercise 8.11 on the measurement of atomic weight of carbon by two different methods.

    (a) Do the Wilcoxon-Mann-Whitney test at $\alpha = .10$ to determine if there is a significant difference between the two methods.

    (b) Calculate a 90% CI on the median difference between the two methods. Does the result agree with the result of the hypothesis test from part (a)?

14.14 Find the null distribution of the Mann-Whitney statistic (U_1) for $n_1 = n_2 = 3$ by enumerating all possible assignments of ranks to the x's and y's as in Table 14.5. Verify that the mean of the distribution equals $n_1 n_2/2 = 4.5$ and variance equals $n_1 n_2 (N+1)/12 = 5.25$.

14.15 This exercise extends Exercise 14.9 to the Wilcoxon-Mann-Whitney test.

    (a) Show that the lowest attainable P-value using the one-sided Wilcoxon-Mann-Whitney test is $1/\binom{n_1+n_2}{n_1}$, where n_1 and n_2 are the sample sizes of the two groups.

    (b) Is it possible to reject H_0 at $\alpha = .01$ if $n_1 = n_2 = 4$?

    (c) What is the smallest $n_1 = n_2 = n$ required if rejection of H_0 at $\alpha = .01$ must be possible?

14.16 Check the accuracy of the normal approximation (14.11) to the Wilcoxon-Mann-Whitney critical constant $u_{n_1,n_2,\alpha}$ by comparing it with the exact constant from Table A.11 for $n_1 = 8, n_2 = 10$ and $\alpha = .051$.

14.17 Use the formulas (14.10) for the mean and variance of the Mann-Whitney U-statistic to show that the means and variances of the Wilcoxon rank sum statistics are given by

$$E(W_1) = \frac{n_1(N + 1)}{2}, \quad \text{Var}(W_1) = \frac{n_1 n_2(N + 1)}{12}$$

and

$$E(W_2) = \frac{n_2(N + 1)}{2}, \quad \text{Var}(W_2) = \frac{n_1 n_2(N + 1)}{12}.$$

---

[10] B. Efron and R. J. Tibshirani (1993), *An Introduction to the Bootstrap*, New York: Chapman & Hall, p. 11, Table 2.1.

What is the expected rank of any observation under H_0? Use this expected rank to justify the formulas for $E(W_1)$ and $E(W_2)$.

Section 14.3

14.18 How many different assignments of ranks are possible in the Kruskal-Wallis test for a one-way layout with three treatment groups and four observations per group? Assume that there are no ties.

14.19 Sixteen students were randomized to four different educational programs, four students per program. The following are the number of days absent from the program over a period of one academic year.

	Program		
A	B	C	D
17	14	6	11
9	10	8	2
35	21	5	4
20	18	13	7

(a) Perform the Kruskal-Wallis test at $\alpha = .05$ to determine if there are significant differences among the four programs.

(b) Is there a significant difference between the two programs with the most and the least absences? Answer using a multiple comparison test at $\alpha = .05$.

14.20 Refer to the water salinity data from Exercise 12.4. Apply the Kruskal-Wallis test to check if there are significant differences between the salinity levels of water from different sites. If so, apply a nonparametric multiple comparison test to determine which methods differ from each other. Use $\alpha = .01$ for both tests.

14.21 Refer to the sickle cell data from Exercise 12.5. Apply the Kruskal-Wallis test to check if there are significant differences between the hemoglobin levels of patients with different types of sickle cell disease. If so, apply a nonparametric multiple comparison test to determine which disease types differ from each other. Use $\alpha = .05$ for both tests.

Section 14.4

14.22 How many different assignments of ranks are possible in the Friedman test for a randomized block design with three treatment groups and four blocks? Assume that there are no ties.

14.23 Three assembly fixtures were compared using four different workers, with each worker using the three fixtures in a random order. The time (in minutes) taken to complete the assembly is given in the following table.

	Worker			
Fixture	1	2	3	4
1	1.3	1.6	2.0	1.4
2	2.1	1.9	2.2	1.5
3	1.8	1.7	1.2	1.1

(a) Do the Friedman test to determine if there are significant differences between the fixtures in terms of the assembly times required. Use $\alpha = .10$.

(b) If significant differences are found in part (a), determine which fixtures differ from each other using a nonparametric multiple comparison test with $\alpha = .10$.

14.24 Analyze the penicillin yield data from Exercise 12.21 by using the Friedman test to determine if there are significant differences between the methods of manufacture. If so, apply a nonparametric multiple comparison test to determine which methods differ from each other. Use $\alpha = .10$ for both tests.

14.25 Refer to the blood plasma data from Exercise 12.26. Apply the Friedman test to check if there are significant differences between the plasma levels of each person at different times. Use $\alpha = .05$.

Section 14.5

14.26 Consider the following data[11] on the number of rivet holes (x) and the number of minor repairs (y) on sections of an airline fuselage. Test if there is positive association between the two variables using Spearman's and Kendall's rank correlation coefficients. Compare the magnitudes of the two coefficients and their observed levels of significance.

x	38	56	65	43	72	69	64	47	62	44
y	17	36	29	17	40	41	36	13	31	19

14.27 There is a general perception that public apathy in politics is on the rise. Here are the data on voter participation for the last ten Presidential elections since 1960, which was a peak year in recent history. Do a test for a decreasing trend in voter participation using the two rank correlation methods at $\alpha = .05$. What do you conclude?

Year	Voter Participation (%)	Year	Voter Participation (%)
1960	62.8	1980	54.0
1964	61.9	1984	53.1
1968	60.9	1988	50.2
1972	55.2	1992	55.9
1976	53.5	1996	49.0

14.28 Derive the exact null distribution of Spearman's rank correlation coefficient for $n = 3$ by enumerating the 3! distinct permutations of the ranks of x_i's and y_i's. Show that the variance of this distribution equals 1/2, which agrees with the formula $\text{Var}(R_S) = 1/(n-1)$ from (14.20).

14.29 Repeat Exercise 14.28 for Kendall's rank correlation coefficient. Show that the variance of its null distribution equals 11/27, which agrees with the formula $\text{Var}(\hat{\tau}) = \{2(2n+5)\}/\{9n(n-1)\}$ from (14.26).

14.30 Repeat Exercises 14.28 and 14.29 for $n = 4$. Check that the variances of R_S and $\hat{\tau}$ agree with their formulas.

---

[11] J. D. Gibbons (1990), "Nonparametric Statistics," Chapter 11 in *Handbook of Statistical Methods for Engineers and Scientists* (ed. H. M. Wadsworth), New York: McGraw-Hill.

14.31 Derive the computational formula (14.18) for r_S from its definitional formula (14.17). Use the computational formula to show that for perfect negative association between two variables, $r_S = -1$.

14.32 Five candidates were interviewed for a job opening by four interviewers. Each interviewer ranked the candidates from $1 = $ best to $5 = $ worst as follows.

	Interviewer			
Candidate	1	2	3	4
1	3	1	3	5
2	5	3	4	4
3	1	2	2	1
4	2	4	5	3
5	4	5	1	2

   (a) Is there agreement between the interviewers about the relative ranking of the candidates? Test at $\alpha = .10$.

   (b) Does any one candidate clearly stand out as the most agreed upon "best"?

14.33 Kendall's coefficient of concordance can be used as a rank correlation coefficient for multivariate data. Here are the GRE verbal, quantitative, and analytical test scores (out of 800) for 10 students. How well do the three test scores correlate?

Student	GRE-V	GRE-Q	GRE-A
1	560	800	720
2	620	760	710
3	630	750	680
4	590	710	720
5	660	780	710
6	610	680	630
7	690	720	650
8	550	730	710
9	680	730	700
10	600	670	690

Section 14.6

14.34 ◨ Consider a subset of the carbon atomic weight data shown below from Exercise 8.11.

Method 1	12.0129	12.0072	12.0064	12.0054
Method 2	12.0318	12.0246	12.0069	

   Do a two-sided permutation test to compare the two methods of atomic weight determination by listing all $\binom{7}{3} = 35$ assignments of labels x and y to the data values. Use $\alpha = .10$.

14.35 ■ Do a one-sided permutation test on the mouse data from Exercise 14.11 by using a computer package to draw 25 random samples *without replacement*. Enumerate your samples. Estimate the P-value and compare it with that obtained in Exercise 14.11.

14.36 ■ Use a computer package to draw 25 bootstrap samples from the data in Exercise 7.16 on thermostat settings. Enumerate your samples. Estimate the standard error of the sample mean and compare it with the exact value.

14.37 ■ Use the bootstrap samples from Exercise 14.36 to estimate the standard errors of the sample median, sample maximum, and sample minimum.

14.38 ■ Do a bootstrap test on the mouse data from Exercise 14.11 by using a computer package to draw 25 random samples *with replacement* as done in Example 14.7. Enumerate your samples. Estimate the P-value and compare it with that obtained in Exercises 14.11 and 14.35.

14.39 Show the result (14.30) which relates the bootstrap estimate of the standard error of the sample mean to the exact value. You will need to use the following result from **finite population sampling**: Consider a population of N numbers: $\{x_1, x_2, \ldots, x_N\}$ with mean and variance equal to

$$\mu = \frac{\sum_{i=1}^{N} x_i}{N} \quad \text{and} \quad \sigma^2 = \frac{\sum_{i=1}^{N} (x_i - \mu)^2}{N}.$$

If $\bar{X}$ is the sample mean of an SRS of size n *with replacement* from this population, then

$$\text{Var}(\bar{X}) = \frac{\sigma^2}{n} = \frac{\sum_{i=1}^{N} (x_i - \mu)^2}{nN}.$$

14.40 Show the result (14.32) which states that the jackknife estimate of the standard error of the sample mean is exact. Check the result numerically by enumerating the 10 jackknife samples for the data from Exercise 14.1 and calculating the jackknife estimate of the standard error of the sample mean.

Advanced Exercises

14.41 For a random sample $X_1, X_2, \ldots, X_n$ from an $N(\mu, \sigma^2)$ distribution consider testing $H_0: \mu = 0$ vs. $H_1: \mu > 0$ using the sign test. The hypotheses tested by the sign test are $H_0: p = 1/2$ vs. $H_1: p > 1/2$, where $p = P(X_i > 0)$.

(a) Show that the power of the α-level sign test that rejects H_0 when $S_+ = \sharp(X_i > 0) \geq b_{n,\alpha}$ is given by

$$\sum_{i=b_{n,\alpha}}^{n} \binom{n}{i} p^i (1 - p)^{n-i}$$

where $p = \Phi(\mu/\sigma)$.

(b) The power of the corresponding normal theory z-test for testing $H_0: \mu = 0$ vs. $H_1: \mu > 0$ (assuming σ is known) is given by

$$\Phi\left(\frac{\mu\sqrt{n}}{\sigma} - z_\alpha\right)$$

using the results from Chapter 7. Calculate the powers of the sign test and z-test for $n = 10$, $\alpha = .0547$ (in which case $b_{n,\alpha} = 8$ and $z_\alpha = 1.601$) for $\mu/\sigma = 0.5, 1.0,$

and 1.5. (*Hint*: First calculate p for given μ/σ. Then calculate the power of the sign test using the binomial distribution formula.)

(c) Why is the z-test power higher than the sign test power for all values of μ/σ? Do you think that the z-test will be more powerful than the sign test even if the distribution of the X_i's is not normal? Why or why not?

14.42 The sign test is a test on the median or the 50th percentile of a distribution; it is equivalent to a binomial test of $H_0: p = 1/2$, where p is the probability that an observation from the distribution exceeds the median value postulated under H_0.

(a) Generalize the sign test for testing the qth quantile or the $100q$th percentile (denoted by $\tilde{\mu}_q$) of a distribution. State the test procedure. (*Hint*: Define $p = P(X > \tilde{\mu}_q) = 1 - q$.)

(b) Let $\tilde{\mu}_{.75}$ denote the 75th percentile of the distribution of household incomes of a population. Test $H_0: \tilde{\mu}_{.75} = 60\text{K}$ vs. $H_1: \tilde{\mu}_{.75} > 60\text{K}$ at $\alpha = .10$ based on the following incomes (expressed in K$'s) of 15 sample households:

$$75 \ \ 45 \ \ 50 \ \ 62 \ \ 40 \ \ 35 \ \ 80 \ \ 68 \ \ 40 \ \ 38 \ \ 43 \ \ 70 \ \ 55 \ \ 65 \ \ 70.$$

14.43 Derive the formulas (14.4) for the mean and variance of the Wilcoxon signed rank statistic under H_0 by carrying out the steps below.

(a) The ith rank can correspond to a positive sign or a negative sign. Let Z_i be an indicator variable with $Z_i = 1$ if the ith rank corresponds to a positive sign and $Z_i = 0$ if the ith rank corresponds to a negative sign. Show that $W_+ = \sum_{i=1}^{n} i Z_i$.

(b) Note that the Z_i are independent and identically distributed Bernoulli r.v.'s with success probability $p = P(X_i > \tilde{\mu}_0)$. Hence show that

$$E(W_+) = \sum_{i=1}^{n} ip = \frac{pn(n+1)}{2}$$

and

$$\text{Var}(W_+) = \sum_{i=1}^{n} i^2 p(1-p) = \frac{p(1-p)n(n+1)(2n+1)}{6}.$$

Now (14.4) follows by substituting $p = 1/2$ in the above formulas.

14.44 Consider two independent continuous r.v.'s $X \sim F$ and $Y \sim G$. In some applications, an estimate of $p = P(X > Y)$ is required based on independent random samples $X_1, X_2, \ldots, X_{n_1}$ from F and $Y_1, Y_2, \ldots, Y_{n_2}$ from G. For example, a manufacturer may want to know the probability that a part supplied by one vendor will last longer than a part supplied by another vendor based on test data from both. Let U be the Mann-Whitney statistic, $U = \sharp(X_i > Y_j)$.

(a) Show that $\hat{p} = U/n_1 n_2$ is an unbiased estimate of $p = P(X > Y)$.

(b) What is the variance of this estimate when $F = G$, i.e., when $p = 1/2$? Why is this variance different from the binomial variance $\frac{p(1-p)}{n_1 n_2} = \frac{1}{4n_1 n_2}$?

14.45 Consider two independent continuous r.v.'s $X \sim F$ and $Y \sim G$ with density functions f and g, respectively.

(a) Show that

$$p = P(X > Y) = \int G(x)f(x)dx = \int \{1 - F(y)\}g(y)dy,$$

where the integrals are over the ranges of X and Y, respectively. (*Hint*: For the first expression, condition on $X = x$ and then uncondition. For the second expression, condition on $Y = y$ and then uncondition.) Hence show that under $H_0: F = G$, $p = 1/2$.

(b) Show that the exponential distribution with density function $f(x) = \lambda \exp(-\lambda x)$ forms a scale parameter family with $1/\lambda$ as the scale parameter.

(c) Suppose X and Y are exponential r.v.'s with parameters λ_1 and λ_2. Show that X is stochastically larger than Y if $\lambda_1 < \lambda_2$. Explain this result by interpreting X and Y as lifetimes with λ_1 and λ_2 as the respective failure rates or $\mu_1 = 1/\lambda_1$ and $\mu_2 = 1/\lambda_2$ as the respective mean lifetimes.

(d) Use part (a) to show that if X and Y are exponential r.v.'s with parameters λ_1 and λ_2, then

$$p = \frac{\lambda_2}{\lambda_1 + \lambda_2}.$$

14.46 Show that for comparing two independent samples, the Kruskal-Wallis statistic equals the square of the standardized Wilcoxon-Mann-Whitney statistic (without the continuity correction). Specifically, show that for $a = 2$,

$$kw = \frac{12}{N(N+1)} \sum_{i=1}^{a} n_i \left(\bar{r}_i - \frac{N+1}{2} \right)^2 = \left(\frac{w_1 - n_1(N+1)/2}{\sqrt{\frac{n_1 n_2(N+1)}{12}}} \right)^2 = z^2.$$

where $N = n_1 + n_2$, $\bar{r}_1 = w_1/n_1$, and $\bar{r}_2 = w_2/n_2$. Hence show that the large sample Kruskal-Wallis test and the two-sided Wilcoxon-Mann-Whitney test are identical.

14.47 Show that for comparing two matched (paired) samples, the Friedman statistic equals the square of the standardized sign statistic (without the continuity correction). Specifically, show that for $a = 2$ and $b = n$,

$$fr = \frac{12}{an(a+1)} \sum_{i=1}^{a} \left\{ r_i - \frac{n(a+1)}{2} \right\}^2 = \left(\frac{s_+ - n/2}{\sqrt{n/4}} \right)^2 = z^2.$$

Hence show that the large sample Friedman test and the two-sided sign test are identical. (*Hint*: Note that s_+ is the number of paired samples with $r_{1j} = 2$, $r_{2j} = 1$ and s_- is the number of paired samples with $r_{1j} = 1$, $r_{2j} = 2$. Therefore $r_1 = 2s_+ + s_- = s_+ + n$ and $r_2 = 2s_- + s_+ = 2n - s_+$.)

14.48 As shown in the previous exercise, the Friedman test is a generalization of the sign test from two to several matched samples. How can one similarly generalize the Wilcoxon signed rank test? To be able to do that, one must rank observations across blocks, in contrast to the Friedman test which ranks observations only within blocks. However, observations in different blocks cannot be compared unless the block effects are adjusted for. How can this be done?

CHAPTER 15

LIKELIHOOD, BAYESIAN, AND DECISION THEORY METHODS

This chapter introduces three theoretical approaches in statistics: likelihood, Bayesian, and decision theory. The likelihood approach provides theoretical justification for many of the methods given in the previous chapters. The Bayesian and decision theory approaches are two other paradigms used in statistics.

The outline of the chapter is as follows. The first two sections present the likelihood approach. Section 15.1 discusses the maximum likelihood method for estimating unknown parameters. Section 15.2 discusses likelihood ratio tests of hypotheses. Many complex parametric statistical problems can be addressed using these techniques. Section 15.3 introduces the Bayesian approach, which regards a parameter as a random variable (r.v.) having a certain distribution. The data are used to update the distribution of the unknown parameter by employing the Bayes theorem, discussed in Chapter 2. Inferences about the parameter are derived from this updated distribution. Section 15.4 introduces ideas from decision theory, such as the loss function and risk function, which are useful in problems involving decision making under uncertainty.

15.1 MAXIMUM LIKELIHOOD ESTIMATION

Consider the problem of estimating the unknown parameter(s) of a population distribution based on a random sample from that distribution. In previous chapters we used intuitive estimates such as the sample mean for the population mean and the sample median for the population median. While these estimates generally have good properties, it is possible to improve on them for certain distributions. Also, intuitive estimates are not always evident in more complex problems. The method of maximum likelihood proposed by Sir R. A. Fisher (1896–1962) provides a general method which produces good estimates in many situations.

15.1.1 Likelihood Function

Suppose that $X_1, X_2, \ldots, X_n$ are independent and identically distributed (i.i.d.) observations. The sampled population is modeled by a probability distribution which involves an unknown parameter θ. Denote the probability density or mass function (abbreviated as p.d.f. or p.m.f., respectively) of this distribution by $f(x \mid \theta)$. As usual, we denote the observed values of the r.v.'s $X_1, X_2, \ldots, X_n$ by $x_1, x_2, \ldots, x_n$, respectively, and refer to them as a random sample from distribution $f(x \mid \theta)$. The set of all possible values of θ is called the **parameter space**, which is denoted by Θ.

The joint p.d.f. or p.m.f. of $X_1, X_2, \ldots, X_n$ is given by

$$f(x_1, x_2, \ldots, x_n \mid \theta) = f(x_1 \mid \theta) f(x_2 \mid \theta) \cdots f(x_n \mid \theta) = \prod_{i=1}^{n} f(x_i \mid \theta). \quad (15.1)$$

For discrete valued r.v.'s, $f(x_1, x_2, \ldots, x_n \mid \theta) = P(X_1 = x_1, X_2 = x_2, \ldots, X_n = x_n \mid \theta)$. For continuous valued r.v.'s, any probability concerning $X_1, X_2, \ldots, X_n$ can be obtained by integrating $f(x_1, x_2, \ldots, x_n \mid \theta)$ over an appropriate region. In either case, $f(x_1, x_2, \ldots, x_n \mid \theta)$ is viewed as a function of $x_1, x_2, \ldots, x_n$ for given θ. Furthermore, the probability interpretation is valid *before* observing the r.v.'s $X_1, X_2, \ldots, X_n$.

Once the r.v.'s are observed, we can still formally evaluate $f(x_1, x_2, \ldots, x_n \mid \theta)$, although it no longer has a probability interpretation. We call $f(x_1, x_2, \ldots, x_n \mid \theta)$ the **likelihood function** of θ for observed $x_1, x_2, \ldots, x_n$, and denote it by $L(\theta \mid x_1, x_2, \ldots, x_n)$; sometimes we denote it by $L(\theta)$ or simply L for short. Symbolically,

$$L(\theta \mid x_1, x_2, \ldots, x_n) = f(x_1, x_2, \ldots, x_n \mid \theta) = \prod_{i=1}^{n} f(x_i \mid \theta). \quad (15.2)$$

Thus the joint p.d.f. or p.m.f. and the likelihood function are identical quantities but have different interpretations. While the joint p.d.f. or p.m.f. is a function of $x_1, x_2, \ldots, x_n$ for given θ, the likelihood function is a function of θ for given $x_1, x_2, \ldots, x_n$.

EXAMPLE 15.1   (NORMAL DISTRIBUTION: LIKELIHOOD FUNCTION)

Suppose $x_1, x_2, \ldots, x_n$ is a random sample from a normal distribution with p.d.f.

$$f(x \mid \mu, \sigma^2) = \frac{1}{\sigma \sqrt{2\pi}} \exp\left\{ -\frac{(x - \mu)^2}{2\sigma^2} \right\}.$$

Here we have a vector parameter (μ, σ^2). Its likelihood function equals

$$L(\mu, \sigma^2) = \prod_{i=1}^{n} \left[\frac{1}{\sigma \sqrt{2\pi}} \exp\left\{ -\frac{(x_i - \mu)^2}{2\sigma^2} \right\} \right]$$

$$= \left(\frac{1}{\sigma \sqrt{2\pi}} \right)^n \exp\left\{ -\frac{1}{2\sigma^2} \sum_{i=1}^{n} (x_i - \mu)^2 \right\}. \qquad \blacklozenge$$

EXAMPLE 15.2   (UNIFORM DISTRIBUTION: LIKELIHOOD FUNCTION)

Suppose $x_1, x_2, \ldots, x_n$ is a random sample from a uniform distribution over the interval $[0, \theta]$ with p.d.f.

$$f(x \mid \theta) = \begin{cases} \frac{1}{\theta} & \text{if } 0 \leq x \leq \theta \\ 0 & \text{otherwise.} \end{cases}$$

Then assuming that all $x_i \geq 0$, the likelihood function of θ equals

$$L(\theta) = \begin{cases} \left(\frac{1}{\theta}\right)^n & \text{if all } x_i \leq \theta \\ 0 & \text{otherwise.} \end{cases} \qquad \blacklozenge$$

15.1.2 Calculation of Maximum Likelihood Estimators

The **maximum likelihood estimate (MLE)** of a parameter is that value of the parameter which makes the observed data most likely under the assumed probability model. Formally, the MLE of an unknown parameter θ is that value $\hat{\theta} = \hat{\theta}(x_1, x_2, \ldots, x_n)$ which maximizes the likelihood function $L(\theta \mid x_1, x_2, \ldots, x_n)$.

Consider a very simple example. Suppose we make two independent Bernoulli trials with success probability θ. Further suppose that θ is known to be either 1/4 or 1/3; in other words, the parameter space Θ has only two values. Using the binomial distribution formula, the probabilities of observing $x = 0, 1$, or 2 successes can be calculated and are given in the following table:

Probability of Observing x Successes

θ	0	1	2
$\frac{1}{4}$	$\frac{9}{16}$	$\frac{6}{16}$	$\frac{1}{16}$
$\frac{1}{3}$	$\frac{4}{9}$	$\frac{4}{9}$	$\frac{1}{9}$

Now suppose we observe 0 successes. Which estimate should we choose for θ? Since $P(X = 0 \mid \theta = 1/4) = 9/16 > P(X = 0 \mid \theta = 1/3) = 4/9$, the observed value $x = 0$ is more likely if $\theta = 1/4$ than if $\theta = 1/3$. Therefore the MLE of θ (denoted by $\hat{\theta}$) is 1/4 when $x = 0$. For the same reason, the MLE is $\hat{\theta} = 1/3$ when $x = 1$ or 2. The probabilities in the above table are just the likelihoods $L(\theta \mid x)$ for $\theta = 1/4$ and 1/3 for different values of x. The MLE $\hat{\theta}$ is chosen to maximize $L(\theta \mid x)$ for observed x.

If $L(\theta)$ is a differentiable function of θ, then $\hat{\theta}$ can be found by calculus methods, i.e., by setting the derivative of $L(\theta)$ equal to zero and solving for θ. Usually it is more convenient to work with the logarithm of $L(\theta)$, called the **log-likelihood function**. From

(15.2) we see that the MLE of θ can be found by solving the following equation for θ:

$$\frac{d}{d\theta} \ln L(\theta) = \frac{d}{d\theta} \ln \prod_{i=1}^{n} f(x_i \mid \theta) = \sum_{i=1}^{n} \frac{d}{d\theta} \ln f(x_i \mid \theta) = 0. \tag{15.3}$$

In case of a vector parameter $\boldsymbol{\theta} = (\theta_1, \theta_2, \ldots, \theta_k)$, we set the k partial derivatives of $\ln L(\boldsymbol{\theta})$ equal to zero and solve for the k unknown θ_i's. The equations obtained by setting the partial derivatives of $\ln L(\boldsymbol{\theta})$ equal to zero are called the **likelihood equations**. The following points should be noted about this method:

1. A solution to the likelihood equation(s) may not exist. In that case, either the maximum of $\ln L(\theta)$ is not attained over the parameter space Θ or the maximum is attained on the boundary of Θ.

2. Even if a solution exists, it only gives a stationary point of the likelihood function; i.e., it is a local maximum or a local minimum or a saddle point. A check on the second derivatives is necessary to determine the nature of the stationary point.

3. The likelihood equations may have multiple solutions. In that case the individual solutions must be checked to determine which one yields the global maximum. It is possible to have more than one global maximum.[1]

Because of these difficulties, it may be necessary to plot the likelihood function vs. θ to find the MLE. If the likelihood function is not differentiable, then calculus methods cannot be employed, and the MLE must be found by plotting or some other techniques. A useful fact to know is that if $h(\theta)$ is a one-to-one function of θ, then its MLE is $h(\hat{\theta})$. This is called the **invariance property** of the MLE.

EXAMPLE 15.3   (NORMAL DISTRIBUTION: MLE'S OF μ AND σ^2)

To find the MLE's of μ and σ^2, first write the log-likelihood function:

$$\ln L(\mu, \sigma^2) = -n \ln \sqrt{2\pi} - \frac{n}{2} \ln \sigma^2 - \frac{1}{2\sigma^2} \sum_{i=1}^{n} (x_i - \mu)^2.$$

Setting the partial derivatives of $\ln L(\mu, \sigma^2)$ with respect to μ and σ^2 equal to zero yields the equations

$$\frac{\partial \ln L(\mu, \sigma^2)}{\partial \mu} = \frac{1}{\sigma^2} \sum_{i=1}^{n} (x_i - \mu) = 0$$

and

$$\frac{\partial \ln L(\mu, \sigma^2)}{\partial \sigma^2} = -\frac{n}{2\sigma^2} + \frac{1}{2\sigma^4} \sum_{i=1}^{n} (x_i - \mu)^2 = 0.$$

---

[1] For all examples and exercises in this book, the solution to the likelihood equations is unique and yields the global maximum. Therefore it is not necessary to make these checks.

From the first equation we get

$$\sum_{i=1}^{n} x_i - n\mu = 0 \quad \text{or} \quad \hat{\mu} = \frac{\sum_{i=1}^{n} x_i}{n} = \bar{x}.$$

Substituting this value in the second equation and solving for σ^2, we get

$$\hat{\sigma}^2 = \frac{\sum_{i=1}^{n}(x_i - \hat{\mu})^2}{n} = \frac{\sum_{i=1}^{n}(x_i - \bar{x})^2}{n}.$$

Note that the MLE $\hat{\sigma}^2$ uses n as the divisor, while the sample variance s^2 uses $n - 1$.   ◆

EXAMPLE 15.4   (UNIFORM DISTRIBUTION: MLE OF θ)

Assuming that all x_i's are ≥ 0, the likelihood function is

$$L(\theta) = \begin{cases} \left(\frac{1}{\theta}\right)^n & \text{if } x_{\max} \leq \theta \\ 0 & \text{otherwise} \end{cases}$$

since all $x_i \leq \theta$ is equivalent to $x_{\max} \leq \theta$. We see that $L(\theta)$ has a discontinuity at $\theta = x_{\max}$. Therefore calculus methods cannot be employed in this example. If we ignore that the support of $L(\theta)$ (i.e., the θ-values for which $L(\theta) > 0$) depends on the x_i's, we will mistakenly conclude that the MLE is $\hat{\theta} = 0$, since $L(\theta) \to \infty$ as $\theta \to 0$.

To find the maximum of $L(\theta)$ it is helpful to plot it as shown in Figure 15.1. In this figure $x_{\min} = x_{(1)} \leq x_{(2)} \leq \cdots \leq x_{(n)} = x_{\max}$ are the ordered values of the x_i. Note that $L(\theta) = 0$ for all $\theta < x_{\max}$; at $\theta = x_{\max}$ we have $L(\theta) = (1/x_{\max})^n$ and as θ increases further, $L(\theta)$ decreases monotonically to zero as $\theta \to \infty$. Therefore the maximum of $L(\theta)$ is attained at $\hat{\theta} = x_{\max}$, which is the MLE.   ◆

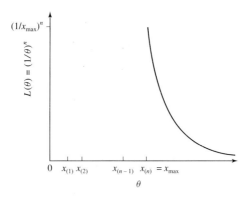

Figure 15.1   Likelihood Function for the Uniform Distribution

EXAMPLE 15.5

Find the MLE's of the cell probabilities of a c-cell multinomial distribution based on a sample size of n resulting in cell counts $x_1, x_2, \ldots, x_c$ with $x_1 + x_2 + \cdots + x_c = n$.

Denote the unknown cell probabilities by $p_1, p_2, \ldots, p_c$. The likelihood function is just the multinomial p.m.f. given by

$$L(p_1, p_2, \ldots, p_c) = \frac{n!}{x_1! x_2! \cdots x_c!} (p_1)^{x_1} (p_2)^{x_2} \cdots (p_c)^{x_c}.$$

To maximize the log-likelihood function it suffices to maximize

$$x_1 \ln p_1 + x_2 \ln p_2 + \cdots + x_c \ln p_c$$

subject to $p_1 + p_2 + \cdots + p_c = 1$. Use of the Lagrangian multiplier λ leads to the objective function to be maximized as

$$Q = \sum_{i=1}^{c} x_i \ln p_i + \lambda \left(\sum_{i=1}^{c} p_i - 1 \right).$$

Setting the partial derivatives of this objective function with respect to the p_i equal to zero results in the equations

$$\frac{\partial Q}{\partial p_i} = \frac{x_i}{p_i} + \lambda = 0 \quad (i = 1, 2, \ldots, c).$$

The solutions $\hat{p}_i$'s to these equations satisfy

$$\frac{\hat{p}_1}{x_1} = \frac{\hat{p}_2}{x_2} = \cdots = \frac{\hat{p}_c}{x_c}.$$

From this it follows that the MLE's are

$$\hat{p}_i = \frac{x_i}{n} \quad (i = 1, 2, \ldots, c). \qquad \blacklozenge$$

Example 15.6   (Linear Regression: ML Estimation)

Consider the simple linear regression model given in Chapter 10. For fixed predictors $x_1, x_2, \ldots, x_n$, let $Y_1, Y_2, \ldots, Y_n$ be independent r.v.'s with $Y_i \sim N(\mu_i, \sigma^2)$, where

$$\mu_i = \beta_0 + \beta_1 x_i \quad (i = 1, 2, \ldots, n),$$

and $\beta_0, \beta_1,$ and σ^2 are unknown parameters. Find the MLE's of the unknown parameters β_0 and β_1.

The likelihood function of β_0 and β_1 for fixed σ^2 is given by the joint p.d.f. of $Y_1, Y_2, \ldots, Y_n$, which is

$$L(\beta_0, \beta_1) = \prod_{i=1}^{n} \left[\frac{1}{\sigma \sqrt{2\pi}} \exp \left\{ -\frac{1}{2\sigma^2} (y_i - \beta_0 - \beta_1 x_i)^2 \right\} \right]$$

$$= \left(\frac{1}{\sigma \sqrt{2\pi}} \right)^n \exp \left\{ -\frac{1}{2\sigma^2} \sum_{i=1}^{n} (y_i - \beta_0 - \beta_1 x_i)^2 \right\}.$$

For fixed σ^2, this likelihood is maximized by minimizing

$$\sum_{i=1}^{n} (y_i - \beta_0 - \beta_1 x_i)^2$$

with respect to β_0, and β_1, which is exactly the least squares (LS) criterion. This result extends in a straightforward way to multiple regression. Therefore the MLE's and the LS estimates of the regression coefficients are identical if the responses Y_i are assumed to be independent and normally distributed with a constant variance. $\qquad \blacklozenge$

EXAMPLE 15.7 (LOGISTIC REGRESSION: ML ESTIMATION)

Consider the logistic regression model introduced in Chapter 11 for a binary response variable Y with a single covariate x:

$$\ln\left[\frac{P(Y = 1\,|\,x)}{P(Y = 0\,|\,x)}\right] = \beta_0 + \beta_1 x.$$

Equivalently,

$$P(Y = 1\,|\,x) = \frac{\exp(\beta_0 + \beta_1 x)}{1 + \exp(\beta_0 + \beta_1 x)} \quad \text{and} \quad P(Y = 0\,|\,x) = \frac{1}{1 + \exp(\beta_0 + \beta_1 x)}.$$

Let $y_1, y_2, \ldots, y_n$ be independent observations on Y for fixed values $x_1, x_2, \ldots, x_n$ of the covariate x, where each $y_i = 0$ or 1. Derive the equations for finding the MLE's of β_0 and β_1.

Denote $P(Y = 1\,|\,x_i)$ by p_i. Then the likelihood function equals

$$L = \prod_{i=1}^{n}[p_i^{y_i}(1 - p_i)^{1-y_i}] = \prod_{i=1}^{n}\left[\frac{\exp(\beta_0 + \beta_1 x_i)}{1 + \exp(\beta_0 + \beta_1 x_i)}\right]^{y_i}$$

$$\times \prod_{i=1}^{n}\left[\frac{1}{1 + \exp(\beta_0 + \beta_1 x_i)}\right]^{1-y_i} = \prod_{i=1}^{n}[\exp(\beta_0 + \beta_1 x_i)]^{y_i}\prod_{i=1}^{n}\left[\frac{1}{1 + \exp(\beta_0 + \beta_1 x_i)}\right].$$

Therefore the log-likelihood function equals

$$\ln L = \sum_{i=1}^{n} y_i(\beta_0 + \beta_1 x_i) - \sum_{i=1}^{n} \ln[1 + \exp(\beta_0 + \beta_1 x_i)]. \tag{15.4}$$

Taking the partial derivatives w.r.t. β_0 and β_1 yields

$$\frac{\partial \ln L}{\partial \beta_0} = \sum_{i=1}^{n} y_i - \sum_{i=1}^{n} \frac{\exp(\beta_0 + \beta_1 x_i)}{1 + \exp(\beta_0 + \beta_1 x_i)} = \sum_{i=1}^{n} y_i - \sum_{i=1}^{n} p_i$$

and

$$\frac{\partial \ln L}{\partial \beta_1} = \sum_{i=1}^{n} x_i y_i - \sum_{i=1}^{n} \frac{x_i \exp(\beta_0 + \beta_1 x_i)}{1 + \exp(\beta_0 + \beta_1 x_i)} = \sum_{i=1}^{n} x_i y_i - \sum_{i=1}^{n} x_i p_i.$$

Setting these partial derivatives equal to zero, we find that the MLE's satisfy the following equations:

$$\sum_{i=1}^{n} \hat{p}_i = \sum_{i=1}^{n} y_i$$

$$\sum_{i=1}^{n} x_i \hat{p}_i = \sum_{i=1}^{n} x_i y_i$$

where $\hat{p}_i$ equals $P(Y = 1\,|\,x_i)$ with β_0 and β_1 replaced by their estimates $\hat{\beta}_0$ and $\hat{\beta}_1$, respectively. These are nonlinear equations without a closed-form solution which need to be solved numerically. ◆

15.1.3 *Properties of Maximum Likelihood Estimators

Now that we know how to calculate the MLE's, it is natural to ask whether they are good estimators and how they can be used to make inferences. The MLE's can be shown to possess certain optimality properties in large samples. In this section we discuss these properties. In the following section we state a result concerning the asymptotic distribution of the MLE's that is useful for making large sample inferences. As a prelude to stating these results, we introduce the concept of **information** due to Fisher.

Fisher Information.   Let X be a continuous r.v. with p.d.f. $f(x|\theta)$. (Discrete r.v.'s can be handled in a similar manner.) We assume that $f(x|\theta)$ satisfies certain regularity conditions. In particular, we assume that $f(x|\theta)$ is at least second order differentiable w.r.t. θ and the limits of the interval of support of $f(x|\theta)$ (i.e., the interval over which $f(x|\theta) > 0$) do not depend on θ. These conditions are needed so that we can exchange the order of differentiation with respect to (w.r.t.) θ and integration w.r.t. x of certain functions of $f(x|\theta)$. As an example, the uniform distribution over the interval $[0, \theta]$ does not satisfy the regularity conditions, because the upper limit of the interval of support depends on θ.

The **Fisher information** is defined as

$$I(\theta) = \int_{-\infty}^{\infty} \left[\frac{d \ln f(x|\theta)}{d\theta} \right]^2 f(x|\theta)dx = E\left\{ \left[\frac{d \ln f(X|\theta)}{d\theta} \right]^2 \right\}. \quad (15.5)$$

Here the right hand side is interpreted as the expected value of the square of the derivative of $\ln f(X|\theta)$, which is an r.v. We shall see through several examples how this measures the information contained in a single observation X about the unknown parameter θ. Before giving these examples we derive a useful identity concerning $I(\theta)$.

We begin with the equation

$$\int_{-\infty}^{\infty} f(x|\theta)dx = 1.$$

Take the derivative w.r.t. θ on both sides of the equation and move the derivative inside the integral sign to get

$$\int_{-\infty}^{\infty} \frac{df(x|\theta)}{d\theta}dx = \frac{d}{d\theta}(1) = 0.$$

However,

$$\int_{-\infty}^{\infty} \frac{df(x|\theta)}{d\theta}dx = \int_{-\infty}^{\infty} \frac{df(x|\theta)}{d\theta} \frac{1}{f(x|\theta)} f(x|\theta)dx$$

$$= \int_{-\infty}^{\infty} \frac{d \ln f(x|\theta)}{d\theta} f(x|\theta)dx$$

$$= E\left\{ \frac{d \ln f(X|\theta)}{d\theta} \right\} \quad (15.6)$$

Therefore,

$$E\left\{\frac{d\ln f(X\,|\,\theta)}{d\theta}\right\} = 0$$

and

$$I(\theta) = E\left\{\left[\frac{d\ln f(X\,|\,\theta)}{d\theta}\right]^2\right\} = \text{Var}\left\{\frac{d\ln f(X\,|\,\theta)}{d\theta}\right\}. \qquad (15.7)$$

Differentiating the second integral expression in (15.6), we get

$$\int_{-\infty}^{\infty}\left[\frac{d^2\ln f(x\,|\,\theta)}{d\theta^2}f(x\,|\,\theta) + \frac{d\ln f(x\,|\,\theta)}{d\theta}\frac{df(x\,|\,\theta)}{d\theta}\right]dx$$

$$= \int_{-\infty}^{\infty}\left[\frac{d^2\ln f(x\,|\,\theta)}{d\theta^2} + \frac{d\ln f(x\,|\,\theta)}{d\theta}\frac{df(x\,|\,\theta)}{d\theta}\frac{1}{f(x\,|\,\theta)}\right]f(x\,|\,\theta)dx$$

$$= \int_{-\infty}^{\infty}\left[\frac{d^2\ln f(x\,|\,\theta)}{d\theta^2} + \left\{\frac{d\ln f(x\,|\,\theta)}{d\theta}\right\}^2\right]f(x\,|\,\theta)dx = 0.$$

Therefore

$$\int_{-\infty}^{\infty}\left[\frac{d\ln f(x\,|\,\theta)}{d\theta}\right]^2 f(x\,|\,\theta)dx = -\int_{-\infty}^{\infty}\left[\frac{d^2\ln f(x\,|\,\theta)}{d\theta^2}\right]f(x\,|\,\theta)dx.$$

From (15.5) we see that the left hand side of the above expression is $I(\theta)$. Therefore we get an alternative expression for $I(\theta)$:

$$I(\theta) = -\int_{-\infty}^{\infty}\left[\frac{d^2\ln f(x\,|\,\theta)}{d\theta^2}\right]f(x\,|\,\theta)dx = -E\left\{\left[\frac{d^2\ln f(X\,|\,\theta)}{d\theta^2}\right]\right\}. \qquad (15.8)$$

Either expression (15.5) or (15.8) may be used, depending on which one is easier to compute.

EXAMPLE 15.8   (NORMAL DISTRIBUTION: FISHER INFORMATION FOR μ)

For the normal p.d.f.

$$f(x\,|\,\mu,\sigma^2) = \frac{1}{\sigma\sqrt{2\pi}}\exp\left\{-\frac{(x-\mu)^2}{2\sigma^2}\right\}$$

assuming σ^2 is known, we have

$$\ln f(x\,|\,\mu) = -\frac{1}{2}\ln(2\pi\sigma^2) - \frac{(x-\mu)^2}{2\sigma^2}.$$

Therefore,

$$\frac{d\ln f(x\,|\,\mu)}{d\mu} = \frac{x-\mu}{\sigma^2}$$

and

$$\frac{d^2\ln f(x\,|\,\mu)}{d\mu^2} = -\frac{1}{\sigma^2}.$$

Using (15.8), it immediately follows that

$$I(\mu) = -E\left\{\frac{d^2 \ln f(X \mid \mu)}{d\mu^2}\right\} = \frac{1}{\sigma^2}.$$

To see that we get the same result using (15.5), note that

$$I(\mu) = E\left\{\left[\frac{d \ln f(X \mid \mu)}{d\mu}\right]^2\right\}$$

$$= E\left\{\frac{(X - \mu)^2}{\sigma^4}\right\}$$

$$= \frac{\text{Var}(X)}{\sigma^4}$$

$$= \frac{\sigma^2}{\sigma^4} = \frac{1}{\sigma^2}.$$

Thus the higher the variance σ^2, the less "information" there is in a single observation X about μ.   ◆

Now let us consider how to define the Fisher information for an i.i.d. sample $X_1, X_2, \ldots, X_n$ from p.d.f. $f(x \mid \theta)$. Denote this information by $I_n(\theta)$. Analogous to the definition (15.8), we can write

$$I_n(\theta) = -E\left\{\frac{d^2 \ln f(X_1, X_2, \ldots, X_n \mid \theta)}{d\theta^2}\right\} \tag{15.9}$$

$$= -E\left\{\frac{d^2}{d\theta^2}[\ln f(X_1 \mid \theta) + \ln f(X_2 \mid \theta) + \cdots + \ln f(X_n \mid \theta)]\right\}$$

$$= -E\left\{\frac{d^2 \ln f(X_1 \mid \theta)}{d\theta^2}\right\} - E\left\{\frac{d^2 \ln f(X_2 \mid \theta)}{d\theta^2}\right\} - \cdots - E\left\{\frac{d^2 \ln f(X_n \mid \theta)}{d\theta^2}\right\}$$

$$= I(\theta) + I(\theta) + \cdots + I(\theta) = nI(\theta).$$

Thus the information is additive if the observations are independent. If the observations are also identically distributed, then the information in n observations is simply n times the information in a single observation. In Example 15.1, $I_n(\mu) = n/\sigma^2$ if we have n i.i.d. observations from an $N(\mu, \sigma^2)$ distribution.

There is a generalization of the Fisher information for the multiparameter case. Suppose that the p.d.f. or the p.m.f. of an r.v. X is $f(x \mid \boldsymbol{\theta})$, where $\boldsymbol{\theta} = (\theta_1, \theta_2, \ldots, \theta_k)$ is a k-dimensional vector parameter. In analogy with (15.5), we define the **information matrix** of $\boldsymbol{\theta}$ as $\boldsymbol{I}(\boldsymbol{\theta})$, where the (i, j)th element of $\boldsymbol{I}(\boldsymbol{\theta})$ is given by

$$I_{ij}(\boldsymbol{\theta}) = E\left\{\left[\frac{\partial \ln f(X \mid \boldsymbol{\theta})}{\partial \theta_i}\right]\left[\frac{\partial \ln f(X \mid \boldsymbol{\theta})}{\partial \theta_j}\right]\right\}. \tag{15.10}$$

In analogy with (15.8), we have the identity

$$I_{ij}(\boldsymbol{\theta}) = -E\left\{\frac{\partial^2 \ln f(X \mid \boldsymbol{\theta})}{\partial \theta_i \partial \theta_j}\right\}. \tag{15.11}$$

As in the scalar parameter case, the information matrix based on n i.i.d. observations from $f(x \mid \boldsymbol{\theta})$ is given by $n\boldsymbol{I}(\boldsymbol{\theta})$.

EXAMPLE 15.9   (NORMAL DISTRIBUTION: INFORMATION MATRIX FOR μ AND σ^2)

Find the information matrix of the unknown parameters μ and σ^2 for a random sample $X_1, X_2, \ldots, X_n$ from an $N(\mu, \sigma^2)$ distribution.

For convenience, denote $\mu = \theta_1$ and $\sigma^2 = \theta_2$. Then

$$\ln f(x \mid \theta_1, \theta_2) = -\frac{1}{2}\ln(2\pi\theta_2) - \frac{(x - \theta_1)^2}{2\theta_2}.$$

It follows that

$$\frac{\partial \ln f(x \mid \theta_1, \theta_2)}{\partial \theta_1} = \frac{(x - \theta_1)}{\theta_2}$$

$$\frac{\partial \ln f(x \mid \theta_1, \theta_2)}{\partial \theta_2} = -\frac{1}{2\theta_2} + \frac{(x - \theta_1)^2}{2\theta_2^2}$$

$$\frac{\partial^2 \ln f(x \mid \theta_1, \theta_2)}{\partial \theta_1^2} = -\frac{1}{\theta_2}$$

$$\frac{\partial^2 \ln f(x \mid \theta_1, \theta_2)}{\partial \theta_1 \partial \theta_2} = -\frac{(x - \theta_1)}{\theta_2^2}$$

$$\frac{\partial^2 \ln f(x \mid \theta_1, \theta_2)}{\partial \theta_2^2} = \frac{1}{2\theta_2^2} - \frac{(x - \theta_1)^2}{\theta_2^3}.$$

Using (15.11), we find that the elements of the information matrix for a single observation are

$$I_{11}(\theta_1, \theta_2) = -E\left\{\frac{\partial^2 \ln f(X \mid \theta_1, \theta_2)}{\partial \theta_1^2}\right\} = \frac{1}{\theta_2}$$

$$I_{12}(\theta_1, \theta_2) = -E\left\{\frac{\partial^2 \ln f(X \mid \theta_1, \theta_2)}{\partial \theta_1 \partial \theta_2}\right\} = E\left\{\frac{(X - \theta_1)}{\theta_2^2}\right\} = 0$$

and

$$I_{22}(\theta_1, \theta_2) = -E\left\{\frac{\partial^2 \ln f(X \mid \theta_1, \theta_2)}{\partial \theta_2^2}\right\} = -\frac{1}{2\theta_2^2} + \frac{E(X - \theta_1)^2}{\theta_2^3} = -\frac{1}{2\theta_2^2} + \frac{\theta_2}{\theta_2^3} = \frac{1}{2\theta_2^2}.$$

Therefore the information matrix of n i.i.d. observations $X_1, X_2, \ldots, X_n$ from an $N(\mu, \sigma^2)$ distribution is (putting $\theta_1 = \mu$ and $\theta_2 = \sigma^2$)

$$n\boldsymbol{I}(\mu, \sigma^2) = \begin{bmatrix} n/\sigma^2 & 0 \\ 0 & n/2\sigma^4 \end{bmatrix}.$$

You may notice that the entries of this matrix are closely related to the variances and covariance of the sample mean and sample variance. This relationship is made explicit in Example 15.12.   ◆

Cramér-Rao Lower Bound.
The Fisher information $I(\theta)$ is related to the lower bound on the variance of any estimator of θ based on a random sample $X_1, X_2, \ldots, X_n$ from the p.d.f. or p.m.f. $f(x \mid \theta)$. Let $\hat{\theta}$ be any estimator of θ with $E(\hat{\theta}) = \theta + B(\theta)$,

where $B(\theta)$ is the bias of $\hat{\theta}$. If $B(\theta)$ is differentiable in θ and if certain regularity conditions hold, then it can be shown that

$$\text{Var}(\hat{\theta}) \geq \frac{[1 + B'(\theta)]^2}{nI(\theta)} \qquad (15.12)$$

where $B'(\theta)$ is the first derivative of $B(\theta)$. This is known as the **Cramér-Rao inequality**. If $\hat{\theta}$ is unbiased, then $B(\theta) = 0$, and the above inequality simplifies to

$$\text{Var}(\hat{\theta}) \geq \frac{1}{nI(\theta)}. \qquad (15.13)$$

The ratio of the lower bound (15.12) to the variance of any estimator (biased or unbiased) of θ is called the **efficiency** of that estimator. An estimator that attains this lower bound (i.e., that has efficiency = 1) is called an **efficient estimator**.

EXAMPLE 15.10

For a random sample of size n from an $N(\mu, \sigma^2)$ distribution, find the efficiency of the sample variance S^2 and of the MLE $\hat{\sigma}^2$ obtained in Example 15.3.

Using the results from Example 15.9, it can be shown that the Cramér-Rao bound on the variance of an unbiased estimator of σ^2 equals

$$\frac{1}{nI(\sigma^2)} = \frac{2\sigma^4}{n}.$$

From Example 6.4 we know that

$$\text{Var}(S^2) = \frac{2\sigma^4}{n-1}.$$

Therefore the efficiency of S^2 equals

$$\frac{2\sigma^4/n}{2\sigma^4/(n-1)} = \frac{n-1}{n}.$$

This ratio approaches 1 as $n \to \infty$, so S^2 is an **asymptotically efficient estimator** of σ^2.

The expected value of the MLE, $\hat{\sigma}^2$, equals

$$E(\hat{\sigma}^2) = \frac{n-1}{n}\sigma^2 = \sigma^2 - \frac{1}{n}\sigma^2.$$

Therefore $B(\sigma^2) = -\sigma^2/n$ and $B'(\sigma^2) = -1/n$. Then the lower bound (15.12) equals

$$\frac{[1 + B'(\sigma^2)]^2}{nI(\sigma^2)} = \frac{(1 - 1/n)^2}{n/2\sigma^4} = \frac{2(n-1)^2\sigma^4}{n^3}.$$

The ratio of this lower bound to

$$\text{Var}(\hat{\sigma}^2) = 2(n-1)\sigma^4/n^2$$

equals $(n-1)/n$, which approaches 1 as $n \to \infty$. Therefore $\hat{\sigma}^2$ is also an asymptotically efficient estimator of σ^2. ◆

15.1.4 Large Sample Inferences Based on the MLE's

Single Parameter.   Large sample inferences based on the MLE's are derived from the following result concerning the asymptotic normality of the MLE's. An outline of the proof of the result is given at the end of this section. It should be noted that all limiting results in this section refer to the sequence $\{\hat{\theta}_n\}$ of the MLE's (which depend on the sample size n) as $n \to \infty$. For the sake of notational simplicity, we have suppressed the dependence of $\hat{\theta}$ on n.

Theorem 15.1.   Under certain regularity conditions on $f(x \mid \theta)$ the MLE $\hat{\theta}$ of θ based on a random sample of size n from $f(x \mid \theta)$ is asymptotically (as $n \to \infty$) normally distributed with mean $= \theta$ and variance $= 1/nI(\theta)$.   ∎

The theorem states that, in addition to being asymptotically normal, $\hat{\theta}$ is asymptotically unbiased (i.e., $E(\hat{\theta}) \to \theta$) and efficient (attains the Cramér-Rao lower bound). In fact, using the Chebyshev inequality (see Chapter 2, Section 2.6) we can show a stronger property that

$$P\{|\hat{\theta} - \theta| > \epsilon\} \to 0$$

as $n \to \infty$ for any $\epsilon > 0$. This is referred to as **convergence in probability** of $\hat{\theta}$ to θ. An estimator having this property is called **consistent**.

To make large sample inferences on the unknown parameter θ, we need to estimate $\text{Var}(\hat{\theta}) = 1/nI(\theta)$. Usually $I(\theta)$ is estimated by

$$I(\hat{\theta}) = -\frac{1}{n} \sum_{i=1}^{n} \left[\frac{d^2 \ln f(x_i \mid \theta)}{d\theta^2} \right]_{\theta = \hat{\theta}}.$$

This estimate does not require evaluation of the expected value and is generally available as a by-product of the numerical maximization of the log-likelihood function; see Exercise 15.40.

An approximate large sample $(1 - \alpha)$-level confidence interval (CI) on θ is given by

$$\hat{\theta} - z_{\alpha/2} \frac{1}{\sqrt{nI(\hat{\theta})}} \leq \theta \leq \hat{\theta} + z_{\alpha/2} \frac{1}{\sqrt{nI(\hat{\theta})}}$$

where $z_{\alpha/2}$ is the upper $\alpha/2$ critical point of the standard normal distribution.

EXAMPLE 15.11

The **Pareto distribution** (see Exercise 2.86) is used to model incomes. If X denotes the scaled income of a person expressed as a multiple of the *known* minimum income (assumed to be positive) in the population, then the p.d.f. of X is

$$f(x \mid \theta) = \frac{\theta}{x^{\theta+1}} \quad \text{for } x > 1$$

and $E(X) = \theta/(\theta - 1)$, where $\theta > 1$. Suppose $x_1, x_2, \ldots, x_n$ are i.i.d. observations from this distribution. The MLE of θ can be shown to be

$$\hat{\theta} = \frac{n}{\sum_{i=1}^{n} \ln x_i}.$$

Use this estimate to find a large sample $(1 - \alpha)$-level CI for θ.

First calculate $I(\theta)$ as follows:

$$\ln f(x \mid \theta) = \ln \theta - (\theta + 1) \ln x$$

$$\frac{d \ln f(x \mid \theta)}{d\theta} = \frac{1}{\theta} - \ln x$$

$$\frac{d^2 \ln f(x \mid \theta)}{d\theta^2} = -\frac{1}{\theta^2}.$$

It follows that $I(\theta) = 1/\theta^2$ and the asymptotic variance of $\hat{\theta}$ is $1/nI(\theta) = \theta^2/n$. (In fact, this is also the exact variance of $\hat{\theta}$. Thus, the MLE $\hat{\theta}$ is efficient.) Therefore a large sample $(1-\alpha)$-level CI for θ is

$$\hat{\theta} - z_{\alpha/2} \frac{\hat{\theta}}{\sqrt{n}} \leq \theta \leq \hat{\theta} + z_{\alpha/2} \frac{\hat{\theta}}{\sqrt{n}}. \qquad \blacklozenge$$

*Multiple Parameters. In the multiparameter case, Theorem 15.1 generalizes as follows: The distribution of the MLE $\hat{\boldsymbol{\theta}}$ of $\boldsymbol{\theta} = (\theta_1, \theta_2, \ldots, \theta_k)$ approaches a k-variate normal distribution (a generalization of the bivariate normal distribution introduced in Section 10.5) with mean vector $\boldsymbol{\theta}$ and covariance matrix $\boldsymbol{I}^{-1}(\boldsymbol{\theta})/n$ as $n \to \infty$. We refer to $\boldsymbol{I}^{-1}(\boldsymbol{\theta})/n$ as the asymptotic covariance matrix of $\hat{\boldsymbol{\theta}}$. Notice that $1/I(\theta)$ for a single parameter is replaced by $\boldsymbol{I}^{-1}(\boldsymbol{\theta})$ for multiple parameters.

EXAMPLE 15.12 (NORMAL DISTRIBUTION: ASYMPTOTIC COVARIANCE MATRIX OF THE MLE'S OF μ AND σ^2)

Find the asymptotic covariance matrix of the MLE's of μ and σ^2 obtained in Example 15.3.

In Example 15.9 we derived the information matrix of μ and σ^2. Inverting that matrix, we get the following as the elements of the asymptotic covariance matrix of the MLE's of μ and σ^2:

$$\text{Var}(\hat{\mu}) = \frac{\sigma^2}{n}, \ \text{Var}(\hat{\sigma}^2) = \frac{2\sigma^4}{n}, \ \text{Cov}(\hat{\mu}, \hat{\sigma}^2) = 0.$$

Notice that the exact small sample $\text{Var}(\hat{\mu})$ and $\text{Cov}(\hat{\mu}, \hat{\sigma}^2)$ equal their asymptotic counterparts. But the exact small sample $\text{Var}(\hat{\sigma}^2) = 2(n-1)\sigma^4/n^2$ (derived in Example 6.4) equals its asymptotic counterpart only in the limit. $\qquad \blacklozenge$

In the multiparameter case we estimate the information matrix by the observed matrix of second partial derivatives (called the **Hessian matrix**):

$$I_{ij}(\hat{\boldsymbol{\theta}}) = -\frac{1}{n} \sum_{\ell=1}^{n} \left[\frac{\partial^2 \ln f(x_\ell \mid \boldsymbol{\theta})}{\partial \theta_i \partial \theta_j} \right]_{\theta = \hat{\theta}} \qquad (1 \leq i \leq j \leq k).$$

The matrix $V(\hat{\boldsymbol{\theta}}) = \boldsymbol{I}^{-1}(\hat{\boldsymbol{\theta}})$ is used to make large sample inferences on the θ_i's. For example, an approximate large sample $(1 - \alpha)$-level CI on θ_i is given by

$$\hat{\theta}_i - z_{\alpha/2}\sqrt{\frac{V_{ii}(\hat{\boldsymbol{\theta}})}{n}} \leq \theta_i \leq \hat{\theta}_i + z_{\alpha/2}\sqrt{\frac{V_{ii}(\hat{\boldsymbol{\theta}})}{n}}$$

where $V_{ii}(\hat{\boldsymbol{\theta}})$ is the ith diagonal element of $V(\hat{\boldsymbol{\theta}})$.

EXAMPLE 15.13 (LOGISTIC REGRESSION: INFORMATION MATRIX)

Refer to Exaple 15.7. Derive the information matrix of β_0 and β_1 in the logistic regression model. The log-likelihood function given by (15.4) is

$$\ln L = - \sum_{i=1}^{n} \ln[1 + \exp(\beta_0 + \beta_1 x_i)] + \sum_{i=1}^{n} y_i(\beta_0 + \beta_1 x_i).$$

The partial derivatives are as follows:

$$\frac{\partial \ln L}{\partial \beta_0} = - \sum_{i=1}^{n} \frac{\exp(\beta_0 + \beta_1 x_i)}{1 + \exp(\beta_0 + \beta_1 x_i)} + \sum_{i=1}^{n} y_i = - \sum_{i=1}^{n} p_i + \sum_{i=1}^{n} y_i$$

$$\frac{\partial \ln L}{\partial \beta_1} = - \sum_{i=1}^{n} \frac{x_i \exp(\beta_0 + \beta_1 x_i)}{1 + \exp(\beta_0 + \beta_1 x_i)} + \sum_{i=1}^{n} x_i y_i = - \sum_{i=1}^{n} x_i p_i + \sum_{i=1}^{n} x_i y_i$$

$$\frac{\partial^2 \ln L}{\partial \beta_0^2} = - \sum_{i=1}^{n} \frac{\exp(\beta_0 + \beta_1 x_i)}{[1 + \exp(\beta_0 + \beta_1 x_i)]^2} = - \sum_{i=1}^{n} p_i(1 - p_i)$$

$$\frac{\partial^2 \ln L}{\partial \beta_0 \partial \beta_1} = - \sum_{i=1}^{n} \frac{x_i \exp(\beta_0 + \beta_1 x_i)}{[1 + \exp(\beta_0 + \beta_1 x_i)]^2} = - \sum_{i=1}^{n} x_i p_i(1 - p_i)$$

$$\frac{\partial^2 \ln L}{\partial \beta_1^2} = - \sum_{i=1}^{n} \frac{x_i^2 \exp(\beta_0 + \beta_1 x_i)}{[1 + \exp(\beta_0 + \beta_1 x_i)]^2} = - \sum_{i=1}^{n} x_i^2 p_i(1 - p_i).$$

Therefore the information matrix is

$$\boldsymbol{I}(\beta_0, \beta_1) = \begin{bmatrix} \sum_{i=1}^{n} p_i(1 - p_i) & \sum_{i=1}^{n} x_i p_i(1 - p_i) \\ \sum_{i=1}^{n} x_i p_i(1 - p_i) & \sum_{i=1}^{n} x_i^2 p_i(1 - p_i) \end{bmatrix}. \tag{15.14}$$

The estimated information matrix is obtained by substituting

$$\hat{p}_i = \frac{\exp(\hat{\beta}_0 + \hat{\beta}_1 x_i)}{1 + \exp(\hat{\beta}_0 + \hat{\beta}_1 x_i)}$$

in place of the p_i in the above matrix. The estimated asymptotic covariance matrix of $\hat{\beta}_0$ and $\hat{\beta}_1$ is obtained by inverting the estimated information matrix. ◆

EXAMPLE 15.14   (LOGISTIC REGRESSION: NUMERICAL EXAMPLE)

Fit the logistic regression model to the following data[2] on the number of days of radiotherapy (x) and response to the treatment (absence (1) or presence (0) of disease after three years) for 24 patients. Find a 95% CI for the coefficient of the number of days of radiotherapy.

Days (x)	Response (y)	Days (x)	Response (y)
21	1	51	1
24	1	55	1
25	1	25	0
26	1	29	0
28	1	43	0
31	1	44	0
33	1	46	0
34	1	46	0
35	1	51	0
37	1	55	0
43	1	56	0
49	1	58	0

The MINITAB output for logistic regression is shown below.

```
Binary Logistic Regression
Link Function:  Logit
Response Information
Variable  Value       Count
y         1              14  (Event)
          0              10
          Total          24
Logistic Regression Table
```

					Odds	95% CI	
Predictor	Coef	StDev	Z	P	Ratio	Lower	Upper
Constant	3.819	1.835	2.08	0.037			
x	-0.08648	0.04322	-2.00	0.045	0.92	0.84	1.00

The MLE's are $\hat{\beta}_0 = 3.819$ and $\hat{\beta}_1 = -0.08648$. Their standard errors are 1.835 and 0.04322, and their z-statistics are 2.08 and −2.00, respectively, both being significant at the .05 level. An approximate 95% CI for β_1 is $-0.08648 \pm (1.960)(0.04322) = [-0.171, -0.002]$. The point estimate of the odds of response for every additional day of therapy is $\exp(-0.0865) = 0.917$. The 95% CI for this coefficient is $[\exp(-0.171), \exp(-0.002)] = [0.843, 0.998]$. The negative

[2] W. M. Mendenhall, J. T. Parsons S. P. Stringer, N. J. Cassissi and R. R. Million (1989), "T2 oral tongue carcinoma treated with radiotherapy: Analysis of local control and complications," *Radiotherapy and Oncology*, **16**, pp. 275–282. Reprinted in M. Tanner (1996), *Tools for Statistical Inference*, 3rd ed., New York: Springer, p. 28.

effect of the number of days of therapy may be surprising, but the explanation is that the total amount of radiation administered is constant and the effect is enhanced if the therapy is completed in fewer days.[3]

The asymptotic standard errors of $\hat{\beta}_0$ and $\hat{\beta}_1$ can be verified via the calculation of the inverse of the information matrix. The estimated response probabilities are tabulated below using the formula

$$\hat{p}_i = \frac{\exp(3.819 - 0.08648x_i)}{1 + \exp(3.819 - 0.08648x_i)}.$$

Days	Response Probability	Days	Response Probability
21	0.8811	51	0.3563
24	0.8511	55	0.2814
25	0.8398	25	0.8398
26	0.8279	29	0.7877
28	0.8018	43	0.5251
31	0.7573	44	0.5035
33	0.7242	46	0.4603
34	0.7065	46	0.4603
35	0.6883	51	0.3563
37	0.6500	55	0.2814
43	0.5251	56	0.2643
49	0.3969	58	0.2320

Substituting these values in (15.14) we get the information matrix of β_0 and β_1 as

$$\begin{bmatrix} 4.723 & 194.127 \\ 194.127 & 8514.89 \end{bmatrix}.$$

By inverting this matrix we obtain the asymptotic covariance matrix of $\hat{\beta}_0$ and $\hat{\beta}_1$ as

$$\begin{bmatrix} 3.367 & -0.0768 \\ -0.0768 & 0.00187 \end{bmatrix}.$$

Therefore $\text{SE}(\hat{\beta}_0) = \sqrt{3.367} = 1.835$ and $\text{SE}(\hat{\beta}_1) = \sqrt{0.00187} = 0.0432.$ ◆

*An Outline of the Proof of Theorem 15.1. A rigorous discussion of the limiting distribution of the MLE's is beyond the scope of this text. The following is a heuristic outline of the proof.

---

[3] Thanks are due to Professor Martin Tanner, Department of Statistics, Northwestern University, for this explanation.

Denote the derivatives of $\ln L(\theta)$ and $\ln f(x \mid \theta)$ evaluated at $\theta = \hat{\theta}$ by $\frac{d \ln L(\hat{\theta})}{d\theta}$ and $\frac{d \ln f(x \mid \hat{\theta})}{d\theta}$, respectively. The MLE $\hat{\theta}$ (regarded as an r.v.) satisfies the equation

$$\frac{d \ln L(\hat{\theta})}{d\theta} = 0.$$

Using the first order Taylor series expansion about θ, we get

$$\frac{d \ln L(\hat{\theta})}{d\theta} \simeq \frac{d \ln L(\theta)}{d\theta} + (\hat{\theta} - \theta)\frac{d^2 \ln L(\theta)}{d\theta^2} \simeq 0. \tag{15.15}$$

Therefore,

$$\hat{\theta} - \theta \simeq \left[\frac{d \ln L(\theta)}{d\theta}\right] \bigg/ \left[-\frac{d^2 \ln L(\theta)}{d\theta^2}\right]. \tag{15.16}$$

Dividing both the numerator and denominator of this ratio by n, we see that the numerator equals

$$\frac{1}{n}\sum_{i=1}^{n}\frac{d \ln f(X_i \mid \theta)}{d\theta}$$

and the denominator equals

$$-\frac{1}{n}\sum_{i=1}^{n}\frac{d^2 \ln f(X_i \mid \hat{\theta})}{d\theta^2}.$$

The numerator is the average of n i.i.d. r.v.'s, each having mean zero (from (15.6)) and variance $I(\theta)$ (from (15.7)). Therefore, by the central limit theorem, the numerator approaches the $N(0, I(\theta)/n)$ distribution. The denominator approaches

$$-E\left\{\frac{d^2 \ln f(X \mid \theta)}{d\theta^2}\right\} = I(\theta).$$

Therefore the ratio (15.16) is asymptotically normal with zero mean and variance equal to

$$\frac{1}{(I(\theta))^2} \times \frac{I(\theta)}{n} = \frac{1}{nI(\theta)}$$

thus proving the theorem. ∎

15.1.5 *Delta Method for Approximating the Variance of an Estimator

Frequently it is of interest to estimate a nonlinear function $h(\theta)$ of θ. We have noted earlier that if $h(\theta)$ is a one-to-one function of θ, then its MLE is $h(\hat{\theta})$, where $\hat{\theta}$ is the MLE of θ. The variance of $h(\hat{\theta})$ can be approximated from the variance of $\hat{\theta}$ by using the first order Taylor series expansion. This method of approximating the variance is called the **delta method**, referred to earlier in Section 10.4.3.

Suppose that $E(\hat{\theta}) \simeq \theta$ and $\text{Var}(\hat{\theta})$ is a known function of θ. Assuming that $h(\theta)$ has at least the first derivative, $h'(\theta)$, expand $h(\hat{\theta})$ around θ using the first order Taylor series to obtain

$$h(\hat{\theta}) \simeq h(\theta) + (\hat{\theta} - \theta)h'(\theta).$$

Using the fact that $E(\hat{\theta} - \theta) \simeq 0$, we have

$$\text{Var}[h(\hat{\theta})] \simeq [h'(\theta)]^2 \text{Var}(\hat{\theta}). \tag{15.17}$$

EXAMPLE 15.15

Let $\hat{p}$ be the sample proportion of successes in n i.i.d. Bernoulli trials with common success probability p. Let $p/(1-p)$ be the odds of success. Find the variance of the sample odds $\hat{p}/(1-\hat{p})$.

Here $h(\hat{p}) = \hat{p}/(1 - \hat{p})$. So

$$\text{Var}\left(\frac{\hat{p}}{1-\hat{p}}\right) \simeq \left[\frac{d}{dp}\left(\frac{p}{1-p}\right)\right]^2 \text{Var}(\hat{p}) = \left[\frac{1}{(1-p)^2}\right]^2 \frac{p(1-p)}{n} = \frac{p}{n(1-p)^3}. \; \blacklozenge$$

15.2   LIKELIHOOD RATIO TESTS

In this section we will study a general method for deriving tests of hypotheses based on the likelihood principle. We will see that the standard z- and t-tests for the mean of a normal population follow from this method.

15.2.1 Neyman-Pearson Lemma

Any hypothesis testing problem involves a tradeoff between the type I and type II error probabilities. The conventional approach controls the type I error probability at a specified level α but does not explicitly consider the type II error probability (or equivalently the power). The α-level tests that we have given in previous chapters are intuitively reasonable tests with good power properties. Yet, since many α-level tests could be possible in any hypothesis testing problem, how do we know whether or not we are using the best possible test? Jerzy Neyman (1894–1981) and Egon Pearson (1895–1980) formulated the problem of finding the **most powerful (MP) test** of level α and showed that in a very simple setting this test is based on comparing the likelihood functions under the null and alternative hypotheses, hence the name **likelihood ratio (LR) test**. The LR test can be generalized to more complex settings, but the resulting tests are not always the most powerful.

Let $x_1, x_2, \ldots, x_n$ be a random sample from a p.d.f. or p.m.f. $f(x \,|\, \theta)$. Suppose we want to test

$$H_0\text{: } \theta = \theta_0 \quad \text{vs.} \quad H_1\text{: } \theta = \theta_1$$

where θ_0 and θ_1 are given. Since θ is the only unknown parameter, each hypothesis specifies a single distribution, namely $f(x \,|\, \theta_0)$ under H_0 and $f(x \,|\, \theta_1)$ under H_1.

If a hypothesis specifies a single distribution, then it is called a **simple hypothesis**. The hypotheses H_0 and H_1 are simple hypotheses. If a hypothesis specifies more than one distribution, then it is called a **composite hypothesis**. For example, for an

$N(\mu, \sigma^2)$ distribution with known σ^2, the hypothesis H_0: $\mu = \mu_0$ is simple, but H_0: $\mu \leq \mu_0$ is composite, since the former hypothesis specifies a single distribution (namely $N(\mu_0, \sigma^2)$), while the latter hypothesis specifies a different distribution for each different value of $\mu \leq \mu_0$. On the other hand, if σ^2 is unknown, then H_0: $\mu = \mu_0$ is also composite, because we have a different $N(\mu_0, \sigma^2)$ distribution for each different value of σ^2.

Neyman and Pearson's solution to finding the most powerful test for a simple vs. simple hypothesis testing problem is summarized in the following lemma.

Neyman-Pearson Lemma: For fixed k ($0 \leq k < \infty$), consider a test that rejects H_0: $\theta = \theta_0$ vs. H_1: $\theta = \theta_1$ when

$$\frac{L(\theta_1 \mid x_1, x_2, \ldots, x_n)}{L(\theta_0 \mid x_1, x_2, \ldots, x_n)} > k. \tag{15.18}$$

Let α be the $P(\text{Type I error}) = P(\text{Reject } H_0 \mid \theta_0)$ of this test. Then it is the most powerful (MP) α-level test, i.e., it maximizes Power $= P(\text{Reject } H_0 \mid \theta_1)$ among all tests with the same level α.   ∎

An intuitive interpretation of the MP test is that it rejects H_0 if the observed data are much more likely when H_1 is true than when H_0 is true. We will not prove this lemma but will illustrate it with several examples.

EXAMPLE 15.16   (TEST ON NORMAL DISTRIBUTION MEAN: MOST POWERFUL TEST)

Derive the most powerful (MP) α-level test of

$$H_0: \mu = \mu_0 \text{ vs. } H_1: \mu = \mu_1$$

where $\mu_0 < \mu_1$ and σ is assumed to be known.

Using the result of Example 15.1, the likelihoods under H_0 and H_1 are, respectively,

$$L(\mu_0 \mid x_1, x_2, \ldots, x_n) = \left(\frac{1}{\sigma\sqrt{2\pi}}\right)^n \exp\left\{-\frac{1}{2\sigma^2}\sum_{i=1}^{n}(x_i - \mu_0)^2\right\}$$

$$= \left(\frac{1}{\sigma\sqrt{2\pi}}\right)^n \exp\left\{-\frac{1}{2\sigma^2}\sum_{i=1}^{n}(x_i - \bar{x})^2 - \frac{n}{2\sigma^2}(\bar{x} - \mu_0)^2\right\}$$

and

$$L(\mu_1 \mid x_1, x_2, \ldots, x_n) = \left(\frac{1}{\sigma\sqrt{2\pi}}\right)^n \exp\left\{-\frac{1}{2\sigma^2}\sum_{i=1}^{n}(x_i - \mu_1)^2\right\}$$

$$= \left(\frac{1}{\sigma\sqrt{2\pi}}\right)^n \exp\left\{-\frac{1}{2\sigma^2}\sum_{i=1}^{n}(x_i - \bar{x})^2 - \frac{n}{2\sigma^2}(\bar{x} - \mu_1)^2\right\}.$$

Taking their ratio and canceling common terms, we get

$$\frac{L(\mu_1 \mid x_1, x_2, \ldots, x_n)}{L(\mu_0 \mid x_1, x_2, \ldots, x_n)} = \frac{\exp\left\{-\frac{n}{2\sigma^2}(\bar{x} - \mu_1)^2\right\}}{\exp\left\{-\frac{n}{2\sigma^2}(\bar{x} - \mu_0)^2\right\}}$$

$$= \exp\left\{\frac{n}{2\sigma^2}[(\bar{x} - \mu_0)^2 - (\bar{x} - \mu_1)^2]\right\}$$

$$= \exp\left\{\frac{n}{2\sigma^2}[2\bar{x} - (\mu_0 + \mu_1)](\mu_1 - \mu_0)\right\}. \qquad (15.19)$$

The MP test rejects H_0 when this likelihood ratio exceeds a constant k. This is equivalent to rejecting H_0 when

$$\bar{x} > \frac{\sigma^2 \ln k}{n(\mu_1 - \mu_0)} + \frac{\mu_0 + \mu_1}{2} = k^* \text{ say,}$$

where in simplifying the inequality we have used the fact that $\mu_1 - \mu_0 > 0$. The exact form of k^* is irrelevant.

To find the MP α-level test of H_0 for specified α, we choose k^* so that

$$P(\bar{X} > k^* \mid \mu = \mu_0) = \alpha.$$

This is just the z-test with

$$k^* = \mu_0 + z_\alpha \frac{\sigma}{\sqrt{n}}.$$

Note that this test is independent of μ_1 as long as $\mu_1 > \mu_0$. Therefore it is the most powerful α-level test for *all* $\mu_1 > \mu_0$. We call such a test a **uniformly most powerful (UMP) test**.   ◆

EXAMPLE 15.17   (UNIFORM DISTRIBUTION: MOST POWERFUL TEST)

Derive the most powerful (MP) α-level test of

$$H_0 \colon \theta = \theta_0 \quad \text{vs.} \quad H_1 \colon ; \theta = \theta_1$$

where $\theta_0 < \theta_1$.

Using the result of Example 15.2, write the likelihood ratio as

$$\frac{L(\theta_1 \mid x_1, x_2, \ldots, x_n)}{L(\theta_0 \mid x_1, x_2, \ldots, x_n)} = \begin{cases} \left(\frac{\theta_0}{\theta_1}\right)^n & \text{if } x_{\max} \leq \theta_0 \\ \infty & \text{if } \theta_0 < x_{\max} \leq \theta_1 \\ \text{undefined} & \text{if } x_{\max} > \theta_1. \end{cases}$$

Since the likelihood ratio takes just two values, only two tests are possible. If $k < (\theta_0/\theta_1)^n$, then the likelihood ratio is always $> k$. Therefore H_0 will be rejected even when it is true; thus $\alpha = 1$. If $k \geq (\theta_0/\theta_1)^n$, then the likelihood ratio is $> k$ only when $x_{\max} > \theta_0$. Therefore H_0 will not be rejected when it is true (since in that case $x_{\max}$ will be $\leq \theta_0$ and hence the likelihood ratio will be $\leq k$); thus $\alpha = 0$.   ◆

15.2.2 *Generalized Likelihood Ratio Test

The Neyman-Pearson lemma shows that the most powerful test for a simple vs. simple hypothesis testing problem is a likelihood ratio test. Unfortunately, this result does not generalize directly to composite hypotheses. One difficulty is that a composite alternative hypothesis specifies more than one distribution, and a single test may not be most powerful for all alternative distributions. In other words, a UMP test may not exist. Still we can generalize the likelihood ratio method for the composite vs. composite hypothesis testing problem, although we cannot make a general claim of its optimality.

Let $x_1, x_2, \ldots, x_n$ be a random sample from a p.d.f. or p.m.f. $f(x \mid \theta)$ with the associated likelihood function

$$L(\theta \mid x_1, x_2, \ldots, x_n) = \prod_{i=1}^{n} f(x_i \mid \theta).$$

Suppose that H_0 specifies that θ is in Θ_0 and H_1 specifies that θ is in Θ_1, where Θ_0 and Θ_1 are disjoint subsets of the parameter space Θ and $\Theta_0 \bigcup \Theta_1 = \Theta$. Symbolically, the hypotheses are

$$H_0: \theta \in \Theta_0 \quad \text{vs.} \quad H_1: \theta \in \Theta_1.$$

The generalized likelihood ratio (GLR) test statistic is defined as

$$\lambda = \lambda(x_1, x_2, \ldots, x_n) = \frac{\max_{\theta \in \Theta_0} L(\theta \mid x_1, x_2, \ldots, x_n)}{\max_{\theta \in \Theta} L(\theta \mid x_1, x_2, \ldots, x_n)} = \frac{L(\hat{\theta}_0 \mid x_1, x_2, \ldots, x_n)}{L(\hat{\theta} \mid x_1, x_2, \ldots, x_n)} \tag{15.20}$$

where the maximum of the likelihood function in the numerator is computed over Θ_0 and that in the denominator is computed over the entire parameter space Θ. Thus $\hat{\theta}_0$ is the restricted MLE of θ (restricted to Θ_0) and $\hat{\theta}$ is the unrestricted MLE. Note that $\lambda \leq 1$. The GLR test rejects H_0 if

$$\lambda = \lambda(x_1, x_2, \ldots, x_n) < k \tag{15.21}$$

where $k < 1$ is a critical constant chosen to make the level of the test equal to specified α. We will now illustrate the GLR test with several examples.

EXAMPLE 15.18   (GLR TEST FOR NORMAL MEAN: KNOWN VARIANCE)

For a random sample $x_1, x_2, \ldots, x_n$ from an $N(\mu, \sigma^2)$ distribution with known σ^2, derive the GLR test for the one-sided testing problem:

$$H_0: \mu \leq \mu_0 \quad \text{vs.} \quad H_1: \mu > \mu_0$$

where μ_0 is specified.

The likelihood function from Example 15.1 is

$$L(\mu \mid x_1, x_2, \ldots, x_n) = \left(\frac{1}{\sigma\sqrt{2\pi}}\right)^n \exp\left\{-\frac{1}{2\sigma^2}\sum_{i=1}^n (x_i - \mu)^2\right\}$$

$$= \left(\frac{1}{\sigma\sqrt{2\pi}}\right)^n \exp\left\{-\frac{1}{2\sigma^2}\sum_{i=1}^n (x_i - \bar{x})^2 - \frac{n}{2\sigma^2}(\bar{x} - \mu)^2\right\}.$$

If $\bar{x} \leq \mu_0$, then the restricted MLE of μ under H_0 is simply $\hat{\mu}_0 = \bar{x}$. If $\bar{x} > \mu_0$, then the restricted MLE of μ under H_0 is $\hat{\mu}_0 = \mu_0$, because in that case the maximum of the likelihood function under H_0 is attained at $\mu = \mu_0$. Thus the numerator of the likelihood ratio (15.20) is

$$\max_{\mu \leq \mu_0} L(\mu \mid x_1, x_2, \ldots, x_n) = \begin{cases} \left(\frac{1}{\sigma\sqrt{2\pi}}\right)^n \exp\left\{-\frac{1}{2\sigma^2}\sum_{i=1}^n (x_i - \bar{x})^2\right\} & \text{if } \bar{x} \leq \mu_0 \\ \left(\frac{1}{\sigma\sqrt{2\pi}}\right)^n \exp\left\{-\frac{1}{2\sigma^2}\sum_{i=1}^n (x_i - \bar{x})^2 - \frac{n}{2\sigma^2}(\bar{x} - \mu_0)^2\right\} & \text{if } \bar{x} > \mu_0. \end{cases}$$

The denominator of the likelihood ratio (15.20) is

$$\max_{\mu} L(\mu \mid x_1, x_2, \ldots, x_n) = \left(\frac{1}{\sigma\sqrt{2\pi}}\right)^n \exp\left\{-\frac{1}{2\sigma^2}\sum_{i=1}^n (x_i - \bar{x})^2\right\}.$$

Taking the ratio of the two and canceling the common terms, we get

$$\lambda = \begin{cases} 1 & \text{if } \bar{x} \leq \mu_0 \\ \exp\left\{-\frac{n}{2\sigma^2}(\bar{x} - \mu_0)^2)\right\} & \text{if } \bar{x} > \mu_0. \end{cases}$$

Clearly, we do not reject H_0 when $\lambda = 1$, i.e., when $\bar{x} \leq \mu_0$. Therefore the condition $\lambda < k$ in (15.21) is equivalent to $(\bar{x} - \mu_0)^2 > k^*$ subject to $\bar{x} > \mu_0$; in other words, reject H_0 if $(\bar{x} - \mu_0)$ is large, which leads to the usual upper one-sided z-test.   ◆

EXAMPLE 15.19   (GLR TEST FOR NORMAL MEAN: UNKNOWN VARIANCE)

For a random sample $x_1, x_2, \ldots, x_n$ from an $N(\mu, \sigma^2)$ distribution with unknown σ^2, derive the GLR test for the two-sided testing problem:

$$H_0\colon \mu = \mu_0 \quad \text{vs.} \quad H_1\colon \mu \neq \mu_0$$

where μ_0 is specified.

Here the restricted MLE's under H_0 are

$$\hat{\mu}_0 = \mu_0 \quad \text{and} \quad \hat{\sigma}_0^2 = \frac{1}{n}\sum_{i=1}^n (x_i - \mu_0)^2$$

and the unrestricted MLE's are

$$\hat{\mu} = \bar{x} \quad \text{and} \quad \hat{\sigma}^2 = \frac{1}{n}\sum_{i=1}^n (x_i - \bar{x})^2.$$

The numerator of the likelihood ratio (15.20) equals

$$
\left(\frac{1}{\sqrt{2\pi}\hat{\sigma}_0}\right)^n \exp\left\{-\frac{1}{2\hat{\sigma}_0^2}\sum_{i=1}^n (x_i - \mu_0)^2\right\} = \left(\frac{1}{\sqrt{2\pi}\hat{\sigma}_0}\right)^n \exp\left(\frac{n\hat{\sigma}_0^2}{2\hat{\sigma}_0^2}\right) = \left(\frac{1}{\sqrt{2\pi}\hat{\sigma}_0}\right)^n \exp\left(-\frac{n}{2}\right)
$$

and the denominator equals

$$
\left(\frac{1}{\sqrt{2\pi}\hat{\sigma}}\right)^n \exp\left\{-\frac{1}{2\hat{\sigma}^2}\sum_{i=1}^n (x_i - \bar{x})^2\right\} = \left(\frac{1}{\sqrt{2\pi}\hat{\sigma}}\right)^n \exp\left(-\frac{n\hat{\sigma}^2}{2\hat{\sigma}^2}\right) = \left(\frac{1}{\sqrt{2\pi}\hat{\sigma}}\right)^n \exp\left(-\frac{n}{2}\right).
$$

Therefore the likelihood ratio equals

$$
\lambda = \left(\frac{\hat{\sigma}_0}{\hat{\sigma}}\right)^{-n}
$$

$$
= \left[\frac{\sum_{i=1}^n (x_i - \mu_0)^2}{\sum_{i=1}^n (x_i - \bar{x})^2}\right]^{-n/2}
$$

$$
= \left[\frac{\sum_{i=1}^n (x_i - \bar{x})^2 + n(\bar{x} - \mu_0)^2}{\sum_{i=1}^n (x_i - \bar{x})^2}\right]^{-n/2}
$$

$$
= \left[1 + \frac{n(\bar{x} - \mu_0)^2}{\sum_{i=1}^n (x_i - \bar{x})^2}\right]^{-n/2}.
$$

Therefore $\lambda < k$ if and only if

$$
\frac{n(\bar{x} - \mu_0)^2}{\sum_{i=1}^n (x_i - \bar{x})^2} = \frac{1}{n-1}\left(\frac{\bar{x} - \mu_0}{s/\sqrt{n}}\right)^2 = \frac{1}{n-1}t^2 > k^* = (k)^{-2/n} - 1
$$

where

$$
s = \sqrt{\frac{\sum_{i=1}^n (x_i - \bar{x})^2}{n-1}}
$$

is the sample SD and t is the usual t-statistic. Thus the GLR test is the usual two-sided t-test.   ◆

In both of the above examples the final statistic used to apply the GLR test has a known null distribution, e.g., the standard normal distribution and Student's t-distribution. In many problems the null distribution of the likelihood ratio statistic cannot be easily obtained. The following result gives an approximation to this null distribution in case of large samples for a general hypothesis testing problem.

Theorem 15.2.   Consider the testing problem

$$
H_0: \theta \in \Theta_0 \quad \text{vs.} \quad H_1: \theta \in \Theta_1
$$

stated at the beginning of this section. Denote by Λ the r.v. corresponding to the GLR test statistic λ defined in (15.20). Then, under certain regularity conditions on $f(x \mid \theta)$, the null distribution of $-2 \ln \Lambda$ is asymptotically (as $n \to \infty$) chi-square with degrees of freedom (d.f.) equal to the difference between the numbers of free parameters in the parameter space Θ and in its restriction Θ_0 under H_0.   ∎

This theorem can be used in the following way to construct a large sample α-level test for a general hypothesis testing problem. Suppose there are p free parameters in Θ and $q < p$ free parameters in Θ_0. In other words, H_0 imposes $r = p-q$ restrictions on the parameter space. Then the large sample approximate α-level GLR test rejects H_0 if $-2 \ln \lambda > \chi^2_{r,\alpha}$. An application of this result is illustrated in the following example.

EXAMPLE 15.20   (GOODNESS OF FIT TEST FOR THE MULTINOMIAL DISTRIBUTION)

Consider a c-cell multinomial distribution for the cell counts $X_1, X_2, \ldots, X_c$ with sample size n:

$$P(X_1 = x_1, X_2 = x_2, \ldots, X_c = x_c) = \frac{n!}{x_1! x_2! \cdots x_c!} (p_1)^{x_1} (p_2)^{x_2} \cdots (p_c)^{x_c}$$

where $p_1, p_2, \ldots, p_c$ are unknown cell probabilities subject to $p_1 + p_2 + \cdots + p_c = 1$ and $x_1 + x_2 + \cdots + x_c = n$. Derive the GLR test of

$$H_0: \ p_1 = p_{10}, p_2 = p_{20}, \ldots, p_c = p_{c0} \quad \text{vs.} \quad H_1: \ \text{At least some } p_i \neq p_{i0}$$

where $p_{10}, p_{20}, \ldots, p_{c0}$ are specified and sum to 1.

Under H_0, the restricted MLE's of the p_i are simply p_{i0}. The unrestricted MLE's are (from Example 15.5) $\hat{p}_i = x_i / n$, $i = 1, 2, \ldots, c$. Therefore the likelihood ratio equals

$$\lambda = \frac{(p_{10})^{x_1} (p_{20})^{x_2} \cdots (p_{c0})^{x_c}}{(\hat{p}_1)^{x_1} (\hat{p}_2)^{x_2} \cdots (\hat{p}_c)^{x_c}}$$

$$= \prod_{i=1}^{c} \left(\frac{n p_{i0}}{x_i} \right)^{x_i}.$$

The log-likelihood ratio statistic equals

$$-2 \ln \lambda = -2 \sum_{i=1}^{c} x_i \ln \left(\frac{n p_{i0}}{x_i} \right)$$

$$= 2 \sum_{i=1}^{c} x_i \ln \left(\frac{x_i}{e_i} \right) \tag{15.22}$$

where the $e_i = n p_{i0}$ are the expected (under H_0) cell counts. Theorem 15.2 tells us that asymptotically (as $n \to \infty$) this statistic has a χ^2-distribution. The number of free parameters in the problem is $c-1$, since the c cell probabilities are subject to one restriction: $p_1 + p_2 + \cdots + p_c = 1$; the number of free parameters under H_0 is 0, since all p_i's are fully specified: $p_1 = p_{10}, p_2 = p_{20}, \ldots, p_c = p_{c0}$. Therefore the d.f. for χ^2 is $c - 1$. Hence the large sample α-level GLR test rejects H_0 when this statistic exceeds $\chi^2_{c-1,\alpha}$.

The statistic derived above in (15.22) is known as the **likelihood ratio statistic**. We will now show that it is asymptotically (as $n \to \infty$) equivalent to the Pearson chi-square statistic from (9.15) in Chapter 9 when H_0 is true. Let $\delta_i = x_i - e_i$, which are the differences (or residuals) between the observed cell counts and expected (under H_0) cell counts. Note that

$$\sum_{i=1}^n \delta_i = \sum_{i=1}^n x_i - \sum_{i=1}^n e_i = n - n = 0.$$

When H_0 is true, $\delta_i \to 0$ as $n \to \infty$.[4] Ignoring the terms of order higher than δ_i^2 in the following series expansion for the logarithm, we get

$$-2 \ln \lambda = 2 \sum_{i=1}^c x_i \ln \left(\frac{x_i}{e_i} \right)$$

$$= 2 \sum_{i=1}^c (\delta_i + e_i) \ln \left(1 + \frac{\delta_i}{e_i} \right)$$

$$= 2 \sum_{i=1}^c (\delta_i + e_i) \left[\frac{\delta_i}{e_i} - \frac{\delta_i^2}{2e_i^2} + \text{ terms of order higher than } \delta_i^2 \right]$$

$$= 2 \underbrace{\sum_{i=1}^c \delta_i}_{=0} + 2 \sum_{i=1}^c \frac{\delta_i^2}{e_i} - 2 \sum_{i=1}^c \frac{\delta_i^2}{2e_i} + \text{ terms of order higher than } \delta_i^2$$

$$\simeq \sum_{i=1}^c \frac{\delta_i^2}{e_i}$$

$$= \sum_{i=1}^c \frac{(x_i - e_i)^2}{e_i}$$

which is the Pearson chi-square statistic.   ◆

15.2.3 *Wald Sequential Probability Ratio Test

So far in all of our discussions of hypothesis tests we have assumed that the sample size is fixed in advance. However, it may be more economical to sample sequentially by taking observations one at a time. After each observation one can make a decision about H_0 (reject or not reject) or decide to take one more observation. Often, such a sequential sampling scheme requires less observations on the average to reach a decision about H_0 than a fixed sampling scheme having the same α- and β-risks does. Sequential sampling is especially practical when the data become available one at a time, e.g., items coming off an assembly line. Abraham Wald (1902–1950) developed the sequential probability ratio test (SPRT) by applying the idea of likelihood ratio testing.

---

[4] This statement needs to be more precise, since the δ_i's are r.v.'s. However, this is beyond the scope of the present text.

Suppose we are sampling from a p.d.f. or p.m.f. $f(x \mid \theta)$. Consider a simple vs. simple hypothesis testing problem:

$$H_0: \theta = \theta_0 \quad \text{vs.} \quad H_1: \theta = \theta_1.$$

Then the likelihood ratio after having taken n observations, $x_1, x_2, \ldots, x_n$, is

$$\lambda_n = \lambda_n(x_1, x_2, \ldots, x_n) = \frac{L_n(\theta_1 \mid x_1, x_2, \ldots, x_n)}{L_n(\theta_0 \mid x_1, x_2, \ldots, x_n)} = \frac{\prod_{i=1}^{n} f(x_i \mid \theta_1)}{\prod_{i=1}^{n} f(x_i \mid \theta_0)}.$$

Choose two constants, $A < 1$ and $B > 1$, and make decisions as follows:

If $\lambda_n(x_1, x_2, \ldots, x_n) \leq A$ stop sampling and decide to not reject H_0 (decision d_0).
If $A < \lambda_n(x_1, x_2, \ldots, x_n) < B$ continue sampling.
If $\lambda_n(x_1, x_2, \ldots, x_n) \geq B$ stop sampling and decide to reject H_0 (decision d_1).

Figure 15.2 shows graphically how the SPRT operates. Sampling stops when the likelihood ratio hits or crosses the boundaries at A or B, which are called the **stopping boundaries**. The region between A and B is called the **continuation region**.

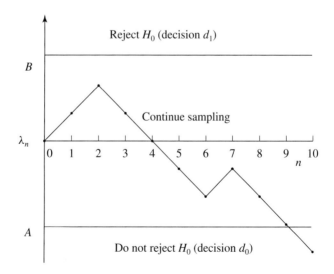

Figure 15.2 Graphical Plot of SPRT

Denote by N the sample size required by the SPRT to stop and decide d_0 or d_1; N is referred to as the **stopping time**. Note that N is an r.v. and could possibly be infinite; i.e., the SPRT could sample indefinitely without reaching a decision. However, it can be shown that N is finite with probability 1. We give expressions for the expected sample size later in this section.

The next question is how to determine A and B. The following theorem gives an answer.

Theorem 15.3. Let α and β be specified with $0 < \alpha < 1 - \beta < 1$. If the constants A and B are chosen so that

$$A = \frac{\beta}{1-\alpha} \quad \text{and} \quad B = \frac{1-\beta}{\alpha} \tag{15.23}$$

then the resulting SPRT has

$$P(\text{Type I error}) = P(d_1 \,|\, \theta_0) \simeq \alpha \quad \text{and} \quad P(\text{Type II error}) = P(d_0 \,|\, \theta_1) \simeq \beta.$$

Proof: The proof assumes that when sampling stops with decision d_0 (do not reject H_0) or d_1 (reject H_0), the likelihood ratio equals approximately A or B, respectively. In other words, we ignore the overshoot of the likelihood ratio past the stopping boundaries. We first derive an approximation for $P(d_0 \,|\, \theta_1)$. All integrals in the expression below are over the subset D_{0n} of the sample space of the observations $x_1, x_2, \ldots, x_n$ where the SPRT makes decisions d_0:

$$P(d_0 \,|\, \theta_1) = \sum_{n=1}^{\infty} \int \cdots \int \prod_{i=1}^{n} f(x_i \,|\, \theta_1) dx_1 \cdots dx_n$$

$$= \sum_{n=1}^{\infty} \int \cdots \int L_n(\theta_1) dx_1 \cdots dx_n$$

$$\simeq \sum_{n=1}^{\infty} \int \cdots \int A L_n(\theta_0) dx_1 \cdots dx_n \quad (\text{since } L_n(\theta_1) \simeq A L_n(\theta_0) \text{ for decision } d_0)$$

$$= A \sum_{n=1}^{\infty} \int \cdots \int L_n(\theta_0) dx_1 \cdots dx_n$$

$$= A \sum_{n=1}^{\infty} \int \cdots \int \prod_{i=1}^{n} f(x_i \,|\, \theta_0) dx_1 \cdots dx_n$$

$$= A P(d_0 \,|\, \theta_0)$$

$$\simeq A(1 - \alpha) = \beta$$

by substituting for A from (15.23). Similarly, we can derive an approximation for $P(d_1 \,|\, \theta_1)$. All integrals in the expression below are over the subset D_{1n} of the sample space of the observations $x_1, x_2, \ldots, x_n$, where the SPRT makes decisions d_1:

$$P(d_1 \mid \theta_1) = \sum_{n=1}^{\infty} \int \cdots \int \prod_{i=1}^{n} f(x_i \mid \theta_1) dx_1 \cdots dx_n$$

$$= \sum_{n=1}^{\infty} \int \cdots \int L_n(\theta_1) dx_1 \cdots dx_n$$

$$\simeq \sum_{n=1}^{\infty} \int \cdots \int B \, L_n(\theta_0) dx_1 \cdots dx_n \quad (\text{since } L_n(\theta_1) \simeq BL_n(\theta_0) \text{ for decision } d_1)$$

$$= B \sum_{n=1}^{\infty} \int \cdots \int L_n(\theta_0) dx_1 \cdots dx_n$$

$$= B \sum_{n=1}^{\infty} \int \cdots \int \prod_{i=1}^{n} f(x_i \mid \theta_0) dx_1 \cdots dx_n$$

$$= B P(d_1 \mid \theta_0)$$

$$\simeq B\alpha = 1 - \beta$$

by substituting for B from (15.23). ∎

It should be noted that the above proof gives the error probabilities of the SPRT only at H_0: $\theta = \theta_0$ and at H_1: $\theta = \theta_1$. An SPRT for composite hypotheses of the type H_0: $\theta \leq \theta_0$ vs. H_1: $\theta \geq \theta_1$ is beyond the scope of this text.

EXAMPLE 15.21   (SPRT FOR NORMAL MEAN: STOPPING RULE)

Suppose we sample from an $N(\mu, \sigma^2)$ distribution where σ^2 is known. Consider the hypothesis testing problem

$$H_0: \mu = \mu_0 \quad \text{vs.} \quad H_1: \mu = \mu_1$$

where $\mu_0 < \mu_1$. To derive the SPRT for this problem we use the expression (15.19) for the likelihood ratio from Example 15.16:

$$\lambda_n = \frac{L_n(\mu_1)}{L_n(\mu_0)} = \exp\left\{ \frac{(\mu_1 - \mu_0) \sum_{i=1}^{n} x_i}{\sigma^2} - \frac{n(\mu_1^2 - \mu_0^2)}{2\sigma^2} \right\}.$$

The continuation region $A < \lambda_n < B$ can be expressed in terms of the sample mean $\bar{x}_n$ as

$$a_n = \frac{\mu_0 + \mu_1}{2} + \frac{\sigma^2}{n(\mu_1 - \mu_0)} \ln A < \bar{x}_n < \frac{\mu_0 + \mu_1}{2} + \frac{\sigma^2}{n(\mu_1 - \mu_0)} \ln B = b_n$$

where A and B are given by (15.23). If $\bar{x}_n \leq a_n$, then sampling stops with decision d_0; if $\bar{x}_n \geq b_n$, then sampling stops with decision d_1. ◆

EXAMPLE 15.22   (SPRT FOR BERNOULLI PARAMETER: STOPPING RULE)

Consider sequential sampling from a Bernoulli distribution with success probability p. The hypotheses to be tested are

$$H_0: \ p = p_0 \quad \text{vs.} \quad H_1: \ p = p_1,$$

where $p_0 < p_1$. For instance, consider the acceptance sampling example from Chapter 6 (Example 6.10) with the difference that here the items are sampled sequentially with each item classified as defective with probability p and nondefective with probability $1 - p$. The hypotheses H_0 and H_1 correspond to declaring the lot being satisfactory or unsatisfactory, respectively. Derive the SPRT for $p_0 = 0.10$, $p_1 = 0.30$, $\alpha = 0.10$, and $\beta = 0.20$.

The observations are $x_i = 1$ or 0. After observing $x_1, x_2, \ldots, x_n$, the likelihood ratio equals

$$\lambda_n = \frac{\prod_{i=1}^{n} \{p_1^{x_i} (1 - p_1)^{1-x_i}\}}{\prod_{i=1}^{n} \{p_0^{x_i} (1 - p_0)^{1-x_i}\}} = \left(\frac{p_1}{p_0}\right)^{s_n} \left(\frac{1 - p_1}{1 - p_0}\right)^{n - s_n}$$

where $s_n = \sum_{i=1}^{n} x_i$ is the number of successes (defectives) in the first n Bernoulli trials. The continuation region $A < \lambda_n < B$ can be expressed in terms of s_n as

$$\ln A \ < \ s_n \ln \left[\frac{p_1(1 - p_0)}{p_0(1 - p_1)}\right] + n \ln \left(\frac{1 - p_1}{1 - p_0}\right) \ < \ \ln B$$

or

$$a_n = \frac{\ln A - n \ln \left(\frac{1-p_1}{1-p_0}\right)}{\ln \left[\frac{p_1(1-p_0)}{p_0(1-p_1)}\right]} \ < \ s_n \ < \ \frac{\ln B - n \ln \left(\frac{1-p_1}{1-p_0}\right)}{\ln \left[\frac{p_1(1-p_0)}{p_0(1-p_1)}\right]} = b_n$$

where A and B are given by (15.23).

For $\alpha = 0.10$ and $\beta = 0.20$, we have

$$\ln A = \ln \left(\frac{\beta}{1 - \alpha}\right) = \ln \left(\frac{0.20}{0.90}\right) = -1.504 \quad \text{and} \quad \ln B = \ln \left(\frac{1 - \beta}{\alpha}\right) = \ln \left(\frac{0.80}{0.10}\right) = 2.079.$$

Next for $p_0 = 0.10$ and $p_1 = 0.30$, we have

$$\ln \left(\frac{p_1}{p_0}\right) = \ln \left(\frac{0.30}{0.10}\right) = 1.099 \quad \text{and} \quad \ln \left(\frac{1 - p_1}{1 - p_0}\right) = \ln \left(\frac{0.70}{0.90}\right) = -0.251.$$

Substituting these values in the expression for the continuation region above, we obtain

$$-1.504 + 0.186n \ < \ s_n \ < \ 1.540 + 0.186n.$$

The different regions of the SPRT are shown in Figure 15.3. For implementation purposes the lower boundary is rounded below and the upper boundary is rounded above. We continue to denote the resulting integer values for the lower boundary by a_n (called the **acceptance numbers**) and those for the upper boundary by b_n (called the **rejection numbers**). Thus sampling continues as long as $a_n < s_n < b_n$. If $s_n \leq a_n$ or $s_n \geq b_n$, then sampling stops; in the former case decision d_0 is made (do not reject H_0 or accept the lot), while in the latter case decision d_1 is made (reject H_0 or reject the lot). Table 15.1 lists these numbers for this example for n up to 20. Note that no acceptance is possible if $a_n < 0$ and no rejection is possible if $b_n > n$. Therefore the corresponding entries are shown by the † signs.   ◆

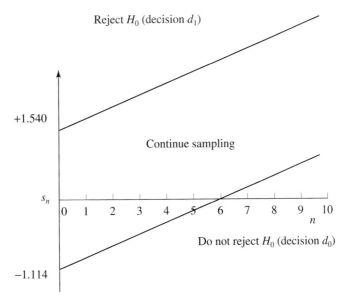

Figure 15.3   Continuation Region of SPRT for Bernoulli Parameter

Table 15.1 Acceptance and Rejection Numbers for a Sequential Sampling Plan ($\alpha = 0.05$, $\beta = 0.10$, $p_0 = 0.10$, $p_1 = 0.30$)

n	a_n	b_n	n	a_n	b_n
1	†	†	11	0	4
2	†	2	12	1	4
3	†	3	13	1	4
4	†	3	14	1	5
5	†	3	15	1	5
6	0	3	16	1	5
7	0	3	17	2	5
8	0	4	18	2	5
9	0	4	19	2	6
10	0	4	20	2	6

Expected Sample Size for SPRT.   To derive a formula for $E(N)$ we use the same approximation that was employed in the derivation of (15.23). Specifically we assume that at the stopping time N, the likelihood ratio $\lambda_N \simeq A$ for decision d_0 and $\lambda_N \simeq B$ for decision d_1. Denote

$$Z_i = \ln\left[\frac{f(X_i \mid \theta_1)}{f(X_i \mid \theta_0)}\right].$$

Then the above approximation yields

$$\ln \lambda_N = \sum_{i=1}^{N} Z_i \simeq \ln A = \ln \left(\frac{\beta}{1 - \alpha} \right) \quad \text{for decision } d_0$$

and

$$\ln \lambda_N = \sum_{i=1}^{N} Z_i \simeq \ln B = \ln \left(\frac{1 - \beta}{\alpha} \right) \quad \text{for decision } d_1.$$

Now, using the facts that $Z_1, Z_2, \ldots$ is a sequence of i.i.d. r.v.'s and that N is an r.v. whose value $N = n$ depends only on the past values $Z_1, Z_2, \ldots, Z_n$ and not on the future values (this is the defining property of a stopping time), the following identity, known as **Wald's identity**, can be shown:

$$E(\sum_{i=1}^{N} Z_i) = E(Z_i)E(N). \tag{15.24}$$

Therefore

$$E(N) = \frac{E(\sum_{i=1}^{N} Z_i)}{E(Z_i)} \simeq \frac{p \ln B + (1 - p) \ln A}{E(Z_i)}$$

where

$$p = P(\text{SPRT rejects } H_0).$$

This yields the following expressions:

$$E(N \mid \theta_0) \simeq \frac{\alpha \ln B + (1 - \alpha) \ln A}{E(Z_i \mid \theta_0)} \quad \text{and} \quad E(N \mid \theta_1) \simeq \frac{(1 - \beta) \ln B + \beta \ln A}{E(Z_i \mid \theta_1)}.$$
$$\tag{15.25}$$

Two remarks are worth noting.

1. The above expressions give $E(N)$ only for $\theta = \theta_0$ and $\theta = \theta_1$. A general expression for $E(N)$ for any θ is beyond the scope of this text.
2. Among all tests (sequential or fixed sample) with

$$P(\text{Type I error}) = P(d_1 \mid \theta_0) \leq \alpha$$

and

$$P(\text{Type II error}) = P(d_0 \mid \theta_1) \leq \beta$$

the SPRT has the smallest values for $E(N \mid \theta_0)$ and $E(N \mid \theta_1)$. Thus the SPRT has the optimality property that it requires the smallest sample sizes on the average under θ_0 and θ_1 among all tests with type I and type II error probabilities less than or equal to α and β, respectively. However, if the true θ is between θ_0, and θ_1, then it is possible for the SPRT to continue sampling for a long time before coming to a decision. Therefore $E(N \mid \theta)$ can exceed the sample size required by the corresponding fixed sample test.

EXAMPLE 15.23   (SPRT FOR NORMAL MEAN: EXPECTED SAMPLE SIZES)

Derive expressions for $E(N \mid \mu_0)$ and $E(N \mid \mu_1)$ for the SPRT from Example 15.21. Compare these expected sample sizes with the fixed sample size, $n = 61$, required by the z-test from Example 7.5, where $\mu_0 = 15$, $\mu_1 = 30$, $\sigma = 40$, $\alpha = 0.05$, and $\beta = 0.10$.

We first need to derive an expression for $E(Z_i)$, where, using (15.19), we have

$$ Z_i = \ln \left[\frac{f(X_i \mid \mu_1)}{f(X_i \mid \mu_0)} \right] = \frac{\mu_1 - \mu_0}{\sigma^2} \left[X_i - \frac{\mu_0 + \mu_1}{2} \right]. $$

Therefore

$$ E(Z_i \mid \mu_0) = \frac{\mu_1 - \mu_0}{\sigma^2} \left[\mu_0 - \frac{\mu_0 + \mu_1}{2} \right] = -\frac{(\mu_1 - \mu_0)^2}{2\sigma^2} $$

and

$$ E(Z_i \mid \mu_1) = \frac{\mu_1 - \mu_0}{\sigma^2} \left[\mu_1 - \frac{\mu_0 + \mu_1}{2} \right] = \frac{(\mu_1 - \mu_0)^2}{2\sigma^2}. $$

Substituting these values in (15.25), we get the following expressions:

$$ E(N \mid \mu_0) \simeq \frac{\alpha \ln B + (1 - \alpha) \ln A}{-(\mu_1 - \mu_0)^2/\sigma^2} \quad \text{and} \quad E(N \mid \mu_1) \simeq \frac{(1 - \beta) \ln B + \beta \ln A}{(\mu_1 - \mu_0)^2/\sigma^2}. $$

For $\alpha = 0.05$ and $\beta = 0.10$ we have

$$ \ln A = \ln \left(\frac{\beta}{1 - \alpha} \right) = \ln \left(\frac{0.10}{0.95} \right) = -2.251 $$

and

$$ \ln B = \ln \left(\frac{1 - \beta}{\alpha} \right) = \ln \left(\frac{0.90}{0.05} \right) = 2.890. $$

Also,

$$ E(Z_i \mid \mu_0) = -\frac{(\mu_1 - \mu_0)^2}{2\sigma^2} = -\frac{(30 - 15)^2}{2(40)^2} = -0.0703 \quad \text{and} \quad E(Z_i \mid \mu_1) = 0.0703. $$

Therefore,

$$ E(N \mid \mu_0) \simeq \frac{(0.05)(2.890) + (0.95)(-2.251)}{-0.0703} = 28.363 $$

and

$$ E(N \mid \mu_1) \simeq \frac{(0.90)(2.890) + (0.10)(-2.251)}{0.0703} = 33.797. $$

Compare these with the fixed sample size of 61 and note the savings due to sequential sampling. ◆

EXAMPLE 15.24   (SPRT FOR BERNOULLI PARAMETER: EXPECTED SAMPLE SIZES)

Calculate the expected sample sizes of the SPRT derived in Example 15.22 for $p_0 = 0.10$, $p_1 = 0.30$, $\alpha = 0.10$, and $\beta = 0.20$.

We first obtain a formula for $E(Z_i)$. Note that

$$Z_i = \ln\left[\frac{f(X_i \mid p_1)}{f(X_i \mid p_0)}\right]$$

$$= \ln\left[\frac{p_1^{X_i}(1 - p_1)^{1-X_i}}{p_0^{X_i}(1 - p_0)^{1-X_i}}\right]$$

$$= X_i \ln\left[\frac{p_1(1 - p_0)}{p_0(1 - p_1)}\right] + \ln\left(\frac{1 - p_1}{1 - p_0}\right).$$

Therefore

$$E(Z_i \mid p) = p \ln\left[\frac{p_1(1 - p_0)}{p_0(1 - p_1)}\right] + \ln\left(\frac{1 - p_1}{1 - p_0}\right).$$

Now compute

$$\ln\left[\frac{p_1(1 - p_0)}{p_0(1 - p_1)}\right] = \ln\left[\frac{(0.30)(0.90)}{(0.10)(0.70)}\right] = 1.350 \quad \text{and} \quad \ln\left(\frac{1 - p_1}{1 - p_0}\right) = \ln\left(\frac{0.70}{0.90}\right) = -0.251.$$

Therefore

$E(Z_i \mid p=0.10)=(0.10)(1.350)-0.251=-0.116$ and $E(Z_i \mid p=0.30)=(0.30)(1.350)-0.251=0.154$.

From Example 15.22 we also have $\ln A = -1.504$ and $\ln B = 2.079$. Substituting these values in the following expressions for $E(N \mid p_0)$ and $E(N \mid p_1)$, we get

$$E(N \mid p = 0.10) \simeq \frac{\alpha \ln B + (1 - \alpha) \ln A}{E(Z_i \mid p = 0.10)} = \frac{(0.10)(2.079) + (0.90)(-1.504)}{-0.116} = 9.877$$

and

$$E(N \mid p = 0.30) \simeq \frac{(1 - \beta) \ln B + \beta \ln A}{E(Z_i \mid p = 0.30)} = \frac{(0.80)(2.079) + (0.20)(-1.504)}{0.154} = 8.847.$$

The sample size for the fixed sample test is given by (9.9) of Chapter 9, which equals

$$n = \left[\frac{z_\alpha \sqrt{p_0 q_0} + z_\beta \sqrt{p_1 q_1}}{\delta}\right]^2 = \left[\frac{(1.282)\sqrt{(0.10)(0.90)} + (0.842)\sqrt{(0.30)(0.70)}}{0.30 - 0.10}\right]^2 = 14.840.$$

Again note the savings due to sequential sampling. ◆

15.3   BAYESIAN INFERENCE

The motivation for the Bayesian approach stems from the premise that in many problems the investigator has some prior knowledge about the unknown parameters. For example, in sampling inspection, the quality engineer has some idea about the true fraction defective rate, θ, of a process from past experience. The Bayesian approach assumes that this prior knowledge can be summarized in the form of a probability distribution on θ, called the **prior distribution**. Effectively, the Bayesian approach treats θ as a random variable. The data are used to update the prior distribution to obtain the **posterior distribution** of θ. Inferences about θ are based on this posterior distribution. This is in contrast to the **frequentist approach** (the likelihood approach being an example of this approach) followed elsewhere in this book, which regards θ as a fixed unknown constant.

Some criticisms of the Bayesian approach should be mentioned here. It is argued by the frequentist school of statisticians that prior knowledge, if any, is often too fuzzy to be quantified in the form of a prior distribution. Also, perceptions of prior knowledge differ from person to person. As a result, inferences from the same data may differ, depending on the specification of the prior distribution.

The philosophical issues dividing the two approaches are deep and have not been fully resolved in statistical literature. Our purpose here is to simply provide an introduction to the Bayesian approach, which offers an alternative paradigm for inference.

15.3.1 Bayesian Estimation

Consider the problem of estimating an unknown parameter θ based on a random sample $x_1, x_2, \ldots, x_n$ from a p.d.f. or p.m.f. $f(x \mid \theta)$. Denote the prior distribution of θ by $\pi(\theta)$. The posterior distribution of θ, denoted by $\pi^*(\theta) = \pi^*(\theta \mid x_1, x_2, \ldots, x_n)$, is defined as the conditional distribution of θ, conditioned on the observed data $x_1, x_2, \ldots, x_n$. By applying the Bayes theorem we obtain

$$\pi^*(\theta) = \frac{f(x_1, x_2, \ldots, x_n \mid \theta)\pi(\theta)}{\int f(x_1, x_2, \ldots, x_n \mid \theta)\pi(\theta)d\theta} = \frac{f(x_1, x_2, \ldots, x_n \mid \theta)\pi(\theta)}{f^*(x_1, x_2, \ldots, x_n)} \quad (15.26)$$

where $f^*(x_1, x_2, \ldots, x_n)$ is the marginal p.d.f. of $X_1, X_2, \ldots, X_n$ (since θ is integrated out). Note that $f^*(x_1, x_2, \ldots, x_n)$ is just a normalizing constant, so that $\pi^*(\theta)$ integrates to 1. The mean and variance of the posterior distribution are referred to as the **posterior mean** and the **posterior variance**, respectively. Inferences about θ are based on this posterior distribution. For example, the posterior mean can be used as a point estimate of θ (called the **Bayes estimate**). Alternatively, the posterior median or the posterior mode can be used as estimates of θ.

The calculation of the posterior distribution is simplified if the prior distribution is chosen to match $f(x \mid \theta)$ so that the posterior distribution is of the same form as the prior distribution (i.e., from the same family of distributions). Such prior distributions have been identified for some standard distributions $f(x \mid \theta)$. They are called **conjugate priors**. If a conjugate prior does not exist then often simulation or other numerical methods must be employed to generate the posterior distribution. The book by Martin Tanner referenced in the footnote in on page 628 is an excellent reference on these methods. The following examples illustrate two conjugate priors.

EXAMPLE 15.25

Let x be an observation from an $N(\mu, \sigma^2)$ distribution where μ is unknown and σ^2 is known. Show that the normal distribution is a conjugate prior on μ.

Consider a normal prior on μ with a specified mean μ_0 and variance σ_0^2. To find the form of the posterior distribution $\pi^*(\mu \mid x)$ using (15.26), we need to focus only on its numerator, because the denominator is just a normalizing factor. The numerator of $\pi^*(\mu \mid x)$ equals

$$f(x \mid \mu)\pi(\mu) = \left[\frac{1}{\sigma\sqrt{2\pi}} \exp\left\{-\frac{(x-\mu)^2}{2\sigma^2}\right\}\right] \times \left[\frac{1}{\sigma_0\sqrt{2\pi}} \exp\left\{-\frac{(\mu-\mu_0)^2}{2\sigma_0^2}\right\}\right]$$

$$= \frac{1}{2\pi\sigma\sigma_0} \exp\left\{-\frac{1}{2\sigma^2\sigma_0^2}[\sigma_0^2(x-\mu)^2 + \sigma^2(\mu-\mu_0)^2]\right\}.$$

We can ignore the factor $1/(2\pi\sigma\sigma_0)$ because it will cancel from both the numerator and denominator of the expression for $\pi^*(\mu \mid x)$. Similarly, any terms not involving μ can be canceled from the numerator and denominator. Thus we see that $\pi^*(\mu \mid x)$ is proportional to

$$\exp\left\{-\left(\frac{\sigma^2+\sigma_0^2}{2\sigma^2\sigma_0^2}\right)[p_0(x-\mu)^2 + q_0(\mu-\mu_0)^2]\right\}$$

$$= \exp\left\{-\left(\frac{\sigma^2+\sigma_0^2}{2\sigma^2\sigma_0^2}\right)[\{\mu-(p_0x+q_0\mu)\}^2 + p_0q_0(x-\mu_0)^2]\right\}$$

where

$$p_0 = \frac{\sigma_0^2}{\sigma^2+\sigma_0^2} \quad \text{and} \quad q_0 = 1 - p_0 = \frac{\sigma^2}{\sigma^2+\sigma_0^2}.$$

Once again, the term $p_0q_0(x-\mu_0)^2$ can be canceled from the numerator and denominator of $\pi^*(\mu \mid x)$. Thus $\pi^*(\mu \mid x)$ is proportional to

$$\exp\left\{-\frac{1}{2\sigma^{*2}}(\mu-\mu^*)^2\right\}$$

where we have put

$$\mu^* = p_0x + q_0\mu_0 \quad \text{and} \quad \sigma^{*2} = \frac{\sigma^2\sigma_0^2}{\sigma^2+\sigma_0^2} = \left(\frac{1}{\sigma^2}+\frac{1}{\sigma_0^2}\right)^{-1}.$$

It follows that $\pi^*(\mu \mid x)$ has the form of the normal distribution. Specifically, $\pi^*(\mu \mid x)$ is the $N(\mu^*, \sigma^{*2})$ distribution (the normalizing constant $1/\sigma^*\sqrt{2\pi}$ comes from the denominator). Note the following remarks.

1. If a single observation x is replaced by the sample mean $\bar{x}$ of n i.i.d. observations from $N(\mu, \sigma^2)$, then the posterior distribution of μ is $N(\mu^*, \sigma^{*2})$ with

$$\mu^* = p_0\bar{x} + q_0\mu_0 \quad \text{and} \quad \sigma^{*2} = \left(\frac{n}{\sigma^2}+\frac{1}{\sigma_0^2}\right)^{-1}$$

where

$$p_0 = \frac{\sigma_0^2}{\sigma^2/n+\sigma_0^2} \quad \text{and} \quad q_0 = 1 - p_0 = \frac{\sigma^2/n}{\sigma^2/n+\sigma_0^2}.$$

2. The posterior mean (Bayes estimate) μ^* is the weighted average of $\bar{x}$ and μ_0, with weights p_0 and q_0 being inversely proportional to their respective variances. If the prior variance $\sigma_0^2 \ll \sigma^2/n$, then the prior dominates the data and μ^* is closer to μ_0. Conversely, if $\sigma_0^2 \gg \sigma^2/n$, then the data dominate the prior and μ^* is closer to $\bar{x}$.

3. The posterior variance σ^{*2} is a harmonic sum of σ^2/n and σ_0^2.   ◆

EXAMPLE 15.26

Let x be the number of successes from n i.i.d. Bernoulli trials with unknown success probability p, i.e., x is an observation from a $\text{Bin}(n, p)$ distribution. Show that the beta distribution is a conjugate prior on p.

Consider a beta prior distribution with parameters a and b (denoted by $\text{Beta}(a, b)$; see Section 2.8.2):

$$\pi(p) = \frac{\Gamma(a + b)}{\Gamma(a)\Gamma(b)} p^{a-1}(1 - p)^{b-1} \quad \text{for } 0 \leq p \leq 1$$

where $a, b > 0$ are specified. Then the posterior $\pi^*(p \,|\, x)$ is proportional to $f(x \,|\, p)\pi(p)$. Keeping only the terms involving p, we obtain that $\pi^*(p \,|\, x)$ is proportional to

$$[p^x(1 - p)^{n-x}] \times [p^{a-1}(1 - p)^{b-1}] = p^{a+x-1}(1 - p)^{b+n-x-1}.$$

This shows that $\pi^*(p \,|\, x)$ has the form of the beta distribution. Specifically, $\pi^*(p \,|\, x)$ is the beta distribution with parameters $a + x$ and $b + n - x$ (the normalizing factor $\Gamma(a + b + n)/\{\Gamma(a + x)\Gamma(b + n - x)\}$ comes from the denominator).

Note the following remarks.

1. The parameters a and b of the prior distribution may be interpreted as prior successes and prior failures, with $m = a + b$ being the total number of prior observations. After actually observing x successes and $n - x$ failures in n i.i.d. Bernoulli trials, these parameters are updated to $a + x$ and $b + n - x$, respectively.

2. The prior and posterior means are, respectively,

$$\frac{a}{m} \quad \text{and} \quad \frac{a + x}{m + n}.$$

    ◆

15.3.2 Bayesian Testing

We will not pursue this topic in any detail here except for the simple vs. simple hypothesis testing problem:

$$H_0 \colon \; \theta = \theta_0 \quad \text{vs.} \quad H_1 \colon \; \theta = \theta_1.$$

Suppose that the prior probabilities of H_0 and H_1 are $\pi_0 = \pi(\theta_0)$ and $\pi_1 = \pi(\theta_1)$, respectively, with $\pi_0 + \pi_1 = 1$. The posterior probabilities of H_0 and H_1 are given by

$$\pi_0^* = \pi^*(\theta_0) = \frac{\pi_0 f(x_1, x_2, \ldots, x_n \,|\, \theta_0)}{\pi_0 f(x_1, x_2, \ldots, x_n \,|\, \theta_0) + \pi_1 f(x_1, x_2, \ldots, x_n \,|\, \theta_1)}$$

and

$$\pi_1^* = \pi^*(\theta_1) = \frac{\pi_1 f(x_1, x_2, \ldots, x_n \,|\, \theta_1)}{\pi_0 f(x_1, x_2, \ldots, x_n \,|\, \theta_0) + \pi_1 f(x_1, x_2, \ldots, x_n \,|\, \theta_1)} = 1 - \pi_0^*.$$

A Bayes test rejects H_0 if

$$\frac{\pi_1^*}{\pi_0^*} > k \tag{15.27}$$

where $k > 0$ is a suitably chosen critical constant. A large value of k corresponds to choosing a small value of the significance level α in conventional testing. If $\pi_0 = \pi_1 = $

$1/2$, i.e., if the a priori chances of H_0 and H_1 being true are equal, then the above test reduces to the Neyman-Pearson likelihood ratio test (15.18).

EXAMPLE 15.27   (TEST ON NORMAL DISTRIBUTION MEAN: BAYES TEST)

Consider the problem of testing

$$H_0: \ \mu = \mu_0 \quad \text{vs.} \quad H_1: \ \mu = \mu_1$$

where $\mu_1 > \mu_0$ based on a random sample $x_1, x_2, \ldots, x_n$ from an $N(\mu, \sigma^2)$ distribution. Derive the Bayes test if the priors on H_0 and H_1 are π_0 and $\pi_1 = 1 - \pi_0$, and a critical constant $k > 0$ is specified.

Using the expression for the likelihood function from Example 15.16 and canceling the common terms, the ratio of the posteriors becomes

$$\frac{\pi_1^*}{\pi_0^*} = \frac{\pi_1 \exp\left\{-\frac{n}{2\sigma^2}(\bar{x} - \mu_1)^2\right\}}{\pi_0 \exp\left\{-\frac{n}{2\sigma^2}(\bar{x} - \mu_0)^2\right\}} = \left(\frac{\pi_1}{\pi_0}\right) \exp\left\{\frac{n(\mu_1 - \mu_0)}{2\sigma^2}[2\bar{x} - (\mu_0 + \mu_1)]\right\}.$$

Therefore $\pi_1^*/\pi_0^* > k$ holds if

$$\exp\left\{\frac{n(\mu_1 - \mu_0)}{2\sigma^2}[2\bar{x} - (\mu_0 + \mu_1)]\right\} > \left(\frac{\pi_0}{\pi_1}\right)k.$$

We see that the Bayes test has the same form as the Neyman-Pearson test derived in Example 15.16, but the critical constant is modified by the ratio of the prior probabilities. ◆

15.4   DECISION THEORY

The subject of statistical decision theory was founded by Abraham Wald (1902–1950). His goal was to provide a unified theoretical framework for diverse problems such as point estimation, confidence interval estimation, and hypothesis testing.

15.4.1 Statistical Decision Problem

The goal in a statistical decision problem is to choose a decision d from a set of possible decisions $\mathcal{D}$, based on a sample outcome (data) x. We refer to $\mathcal{D}$ as the **decision space** and the set of all sample outcomes as the **sample space**, denoted by $\mathcal{X}$. A **decision rule** δ is a function $\delta(x)$ which assigns to every sample outcome $x \in \mathcal{X}$, a decision $d \in \mathcal{D}$. Because the sample outcome is random, a decision chosen by δ is also random. Denote by X the r.v. corresponding to x and the probability distribution of X by $f(x \,|\, \theta)$. This distribution depends on an unknown parameter θ belonging to a **parameter space** Θ. The values of $\theta \in \Theta$ are referred to as the **states of nature**.

Suppose that if one chooses a decision d when the true parameter is θ, a loss of $L(d, \theta)$ is incurred. The function $L(d, \theta)$ is called the **loss function**. The long run performance of the decision rule δ is assessed by evaluating its **expected loss**, called the **risk function**:

$$R(\delta, \theta) = E[L(\delta(X), \theta)] = \int_{\mathcal{X}} L(\delta(x), \theta) f(x \,|\, \theta) dx. \tag{15.28}$$

Note that the risk function of a decision rule δ depends on the unknown parameter θ. The goal of decision theory is to find a "good" decision rule that has low risk over the parameter space Θ.

EXAMPLE 15.28   (POINT ESTIMATION: RISK FUNCTION FOR SQUARED ERROR LOSS)

Consider estimating an unknown parameter $\theta \in \Theta$. A decision d is an estimate $\hat{\theta}$ computed from data x. The decision space $\mathcal{D}$ is the set of all possible estimates. The decision rule δ is the particular function $\hat{\theta}(x)$ which gives an estimate $\hat{\theta}$ for any observed $x \in X$. A common loss function used in point estimation is the **squared error loss function**:

$$L(d, \theta) = (d - \theta)^2 = (\hat{\theta} - \theta)^2.$$

The risk function of a decision rule δ or equivalently of an estimator $\hat{\theta}$ is given by

$$R(\hat{\theta}, \theta) = E(\hat{\theta} - \theta)^2 = \text{Var}(\hat{\theta}) + [\text{Bias}(\hat{\theta})]^2$$

which is the **mean squared error (MSE)** of $\hat{\theta}$ defined in Section 6.1. ◆

EXAMPLE 15.29

Calculate and compare the risk functions for the squared error loss of two estimators of success probability p from n i.i.d. Bernoulli trials. The first is the usual sample proportion of successes and the second is the Bayes estimator from Example 15.26:

$$\hat{p}_1 = \frac{X}{n} \quad \text{and} \quad \hat{p}_2 = \frac{a + X}{m + n}$$

where X is the number of successes, $m = a + b$, and a and b are the parameters of the beta prior on p.

The risk function of $\hat{p}_1$ equals

$$R(\hat{p}_1, p) = \text{MSE}(\hat{p}_1) = \text{Var}(\hat{p}_1) = \frac{p(1 - p)}{n}$$

since $\hat{p}_1$ is unbiased. Next compute

$$\text{Var}(\hat{p}_2) = \text{Var}\left(\frac{a + X}{m + n}\right) = \frac{\text{Var}(X)}{(m + n)^2} = \frac{np(1 - p)}{(m + n)^2}$$

and

$$\text{Bias}(\hat{p}_2) = E\left(\frac{a + X}{m + n}\right) - p = \frac{a + E(X)}{m + n} - p = \frac{a + np}{m + n} - p = \frac{a - mp}{m + n}.$$

Therefore,

$$R(\hat{p}_2, p) = \text{MSE}(\hat{p}_2) = \frac{np(1 - p)}{(m + n)^2} + \frac{(a - mp)^2}{(m + n)^2} = \frac{(m^2 - n)p^2 + (n - 2am)p + a^2}{(m + n)^2}.$$

Suppose $n = 4$, $a = b = 1$, and $m = 2$. Then it can be verified that $R(\hat{p}_1, p) = p(1 - p)/4$ and $R(\hat{p}_2, p) = 1/36$. Notice that the risk function of $\hat{p}_2$ is constant (does not depend on p) in this case. It can also be verified that $R(\hat{p}_1, p) < R(\hat{p}_2, p)$ for $p < 0.1273$ and $p > 0.8727$. The two risk functions are plotted in Figure 15.4. We see that $\hat{p}_1$ would be preferred for $p < 0.1273$ and $p > 0.8727$, and $\hat{p}_2$ would be preferred for $0.1273 \leq p \leq 0.8727$. ◆

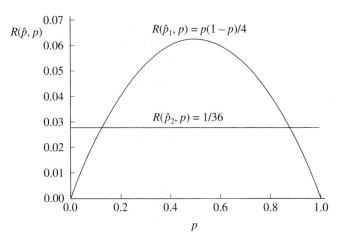

Figure 15.4   Risk Functions of Two Estimators of p

15.4.2 Admissible, Minimax, and Bayes Decision Rules

As seen in the above example, the comparison of different decision rules is complicated by the fact that their risk functions depend on the unknown parameter θ. Often, one decision rule does not have the smallest risk for all values of θ; i.e., there is not a uniformly best rule. However, we can eliminate from consideration at least those decision rules that are dominated by other rules in terms of risk for *all* values of θ. Specifically, given a decision rule δ_1, if there exists another decision rule δ_2 such that

$$R(\delta_1, \theta) \geq R(\delta_2, \theta) \quad \text{for all } \theta \in \Theta$$

with strict inequality for at least some θ, then δ_1 is said to be **inadmissible**. If a rule is not inadmissible, then it is **admissible**. To choose a good decision rule, we may restrict consideration only to admissible decision rules.

To choose among admissible decision rules we need to impose further criteria. Two such criteria are minimax and Bayes. Essentially, both these criteria reduce a risk function to a single number summary.

In the minimax criterion we consider the worst risk performance of each rule and choose the rule that has the least worst performance. Thus a **minimax decision rule** minimizes the maximum risk:

$$\min_{\delta} \left\{ \max_{\theta \in \Theta} R(\delta, \theta) \right\}.$$

In the Bayes criterion, on the other hand, we consider the average risk of each rule with respect to a prior distribution $\pi(\theta)$. This average risk is called the **Bayes risk** and is given by

$$B(\delta) = \int_{\Theta} R(\delta, \theta)\pi(\theta)d\theta = \int_{\Theta} \left[\int_X L(\delta(x), \theta) f(x \mid \theta)dx \right] \pi(\theta)d\theta. \quad (15.29)$$

A **Bayes decision rule** minimizes the Bayes risk.

The minimax criterion is generally conservative because it looks at the worst case scenario, which may not be very likely to occur. The Bayes criterion is not as conservative, but requires specification of a prior.

EXAMPLE 15.30 (ACCEPTANCE SAMPLING: COMPARISON OF TWO DECISION RULES)

A retailer must decide whether to purchase a large lot of items containing an unknown fraction p of defectives. The purchase price is $5 per item. If a purchased item is not defective, then it can be sold at retail for $6, yielding a $1 profit. If an item is defective, then it must be junked. There is also a penalty cost of $2 per item of not being able to meet the demand of a prospective customer. Before making the decision of whether to purchase the lot (decision d_1) or not to purchase the lot (decision d_2), the retailer inspects two items at random from the lot. The retailer wants to evaluate two decision rules given in the following table.

No. Defectives	Decision Rule δ_1	Decision Rule δ_2
x	Decision	Decision
0	d_1	d_1
1	d_2	d_1
2	d_2	d_2

Compare the risk functions of δ_1 and δ_2. Between these two rules, which is minimax? Which rule is Bayes w.r.t. the prior $\pi(p) = 2(1 - p)$ for $0 \le p \le 1$?

If the lot is purchased (decision d_1), then the loss per defective item is the purchase cost + the penalty cost = $5 + $2 = $7, and there is a gain of $1 per nondefective item. If the lot is not purchased (decision d_2), then the loss is just the penalty cost = $2 per item. Therefore the loss function (on a per item basis) is

$$L(d_1, p) = 7p - 1(1 - p) = 8p - 1 \quad \text{and} \quad L(d_2, p) = 2.$$

The risk functions can be calculated as follows:

Decision Rule δ_1:

$$\begin{aligned} R(\delta_1, p) &= L(d_1, p)P(\delta_1 \text{ chooses } d_1 \mid p) + L(d_2, p)P(\delta_1 \text{ chooses } d_2 \mid p) \\ &= (8p - 1)P(X = 0 \mid p) + 2P(X = 1 \text{ or } 2 \mid p) \\ &= (8p - 1)(1 - p)^2 + 2[1 - (1 - p)^2] \\ &= 8p^3 - 19p^2 + 14p - 1. \end{aligned}$$

Decision Rule δ_2:

$$\begin{aligned} R(\delta_2, p) &= L(d_1, p)P(\delta_2 \text{ chooses } d_1 \mid p) + L(d_2, p)P(\delta_2 \text{ chooses } d_2 \mid p) \\ &= (8p - 1)P(X = 0 \text{ or } 1 \mid p) + 2P(X = 2 \mid p) \\ &= (8p - 1)(1 - p^2) + 2p^2 \\ &= -8p^3 + 3p^2 + 8p - 1. \end{aligned}$$

These risk functions are plotted in Figure 15.5. We see that both rules are admissible w.r.t. each other, because neither rule is dominated by the other rule for all values of p. Their risk functions are equal for $p = 0, 3/8$, and 1. For $0 < p < 3/8$, δ_2 is the better rule, while for $3/8 < p < 1$, δ_1 is the better rule.

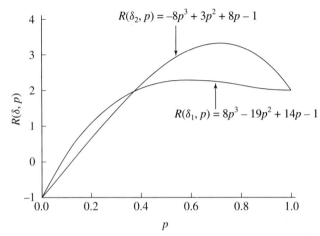

The curves are labeled:
$$R(\delta_2, p) = -8p^3 + 3p^2 + 8p - 1$$
$$R(\delta_1, p) = 8p^3 - 19p^2 + 14p - 1$$

Figure 15.5   Risk Functions of Two Decision Rules for the Acceptance Sampling Problem

The maximum values of the risk functions can be shown to be

$$\max_p R(\delta_1, p) = 2.289, \max_p R(\delta_2, p) = 3.329.$$

Since δ_1 has the smaller maximum risk, it is the minimax rule.

For the given prior $\pi(p)$, the Bayes risks can be computed as follows:

$$B(\delta_1) = \int_0^1 (8p^3 - 19p^2 + 14p - 1)2(1 - p)dp = \frac{39}{30}$$

$$B(\delta_2) = \int_0^1 (-8p^3 + 3p^2 + 8p - 1)2(1 - p)dp = \frac{41}{30}.$$

Since δ_1 has the smaller Bayes risk, it is also the Bayes rule w.r.t. the given prior.   ◆

It is generally not straightforward to compute the minimax rule, and we will not discuss the methods for doing this. The Bayes rule can be computed more easily as follows. Exchange the integrals in the definition (15.29) of the Bayes risk, resulting in

$$B(\delta) = \int_X \left[\int_\Theta L(\delta(x), \theta) f(x \mid \theta)\pi(\theta)d\theta \right] dx = \int_X A(\delta(x), x)dx \qquad (15.30)$$

where

$$A(d, x) = \int_\Theta L(d, \theta) f(x \mid \theta)\pi(\theta)d\theta.$$

Then $B(\delta)$ is minimized by choosing for each $x \in X$ that decision $d = \delta(x)$ which minimizes $A(d, x)$.

In Example 15.30 we showed that decision rule δ_1 has the smaller Bayes risk than decision rule δ_2 for the given prior. Now we will use the method just described to show that δ_1 is in fact Bayes among *all* decision rules for this problem.

Example 15.31 (Acceptance Sampling: Bayes Decision Rule)

Refer to Example 15.30. Find the Bayes decision rule with respect to the prior $\pi(p) = 2(1 - p)$ for $0 \le p \le 1$.

In Example 15.30 we obtained the following loss function:

$$L(d_1, p) = 8p - 1 \quad \text{and} \quad L(d_2, p) = 2.$$

Using the identity

$$\int_0^1 p^a (1 - p)^b \, dp = \frac{a! b!}{(a + b + 1)!}$$

if a and b are nonnegative integers, we can calculate

$$
\begin{aligned}
A(d_1, x) &= \int_0^1 L(d_1, p) f(x \mid p) \pi(p) \, dp \\
&= \int_0^1 (8p - 1) \binom{2}{x} p^x (1 - p)^{2-x} 2(1 - p) \, dp \\
&= \frac{2!2}{x!(2 - x)!} \left[8 \int_0^1 p^{x+1} (1 - p)^{3-x} \, dp - \int_0^1 p^x (1 - p)^{3-x} \, dp \right] \\
&= \frac{4}{x!(2 - x)!} \left[8 \frac{(x + 1)!(3 - x)!}{5!} - \frac{x!(3 - x)!}{4!} \right] \\
&= \frac{(8x + 3)(3 - x)}{30}
\end{aligned}
$$

and

$$
\begin{aligned}
A(d_2, x) &= \int_0^1 L(d_2, p) f(x \mid p) \pi(p) \, dp \\
&= \int_0^1 2 \binom{2}{x} p^x (1 - p)^{2-x} 2(1 - p) \, dp \\
&= \frac{2!4}{x!(2 - x)!} \int_0^1 p^x (1 - p)^{3-x} \, dp \\
&= \frac{8}{x!(2 - x)!} \left[\frac{x!(3 - x)!}{4!} \right] \\
&= \frac{3 - x}{3}.
\end{aligned}
$$

We can now check that for $x = 0$, $A(d_1, x) = 9/30 < A(d_2, x) = 1$, but for $x = 1$, $A(d_1, x) = 22/30 > A(d_2, x) = 2/3$, and for $x = 2$, $A(d_1, x) = 19/30 > A(d_2, x) = 1/3$. Therefore the Bayes rule chooses decision d_1 (purchase the lot) if $x = 0$ and decision d_2 (do not purchase the lot) if $x = 1$ or $x = 2$. This is exactly the decision rule δ_1. Therefore δ_1 is Bayes among all decision rules with respect to the given prior. ◆

EXAMPLE 15.32   (DECISION THEORETIC BAYES TEST)

Consider the simple vs. simple hypothesis testing problem:

$$H_0: \theta = \theta_0 \quad \text{vs.} \quad H_1: \theta = \theta_1,$$

where θ is the unknown parameter in the joint p.d.f. $f(x_1, x_2, \ldots, x_n \mid \theta)$ of the data $x_1, x_2, \ldots, x_n$. Given the prior probabilities $\pi_0 = \pi(\theta_0)$ of H_0 and $\pi_1 = \pi(\theta_1)$ of H_1 with $\pi_0 + \pi_1 = 1$, a Bayes test was derived in (15.27). We now show how that test is related to the decision theoretic Bayes test for the following loss function:

$$L(d_0, \theta_0) = 0, L(d_1, \theta_0) = c_0 \quad \text{and} \quad L(d_0, \theta_1) = c_1, L(d_1, \theta_1) = 0$$

where $c_0, c_1 > 0$, decision d_0 means do not reject H_0, and decision d_1 means reject H_0. Note that c_0 is the cost of a type I error, and c_1 is the cost of a type II error.

We have

$$A(d_0; x_1, x_2, \ldots, x_n) = c_1 \pi_1 f(x_1, x_2, \ldots, x_n \mid \theta_1)$$

and

$$A(d_1; x_1, x_2, \ldots, x_n) = c_0 \pi_0 f(x_1, x_2, \ldots, x_n \mid \theta_0).$$

The Bayes test rejects H_0 (makes decision d_1) if

$$A(d_1; x_1, x_2, \ldots, x_n) < A(d_0; x_1, x_2, \ldots, x_n)$$

which holds if

$$\frac{\pi_1 f(x_1, x_2, \ldots, x_n \mid \theta_1)}{\pi_0 f(x_1, x_2, \ldots, x_n \mid \theta_0)} = \frac{\pi_1^*}{\pi_0^*} > \frac{c_0}{c_1}.$$

Comparing this with the Bayes rule in (15.27), we see that the critical constant k can be interpreted as the ratio of costs of type I and type II errors. If $c_0 \gg c_1$, then k is large, making rejection of H_0 difficult, e.g., by choosing a small value of the level of significance α in classical testing.   ◆

An alternative way of viewing (15.30) is to write

$$f(x \mid \theta)\pi(\theta) = \pi^*(\theta \mid x) f^*(x)$$

where $\pi^*(\theta \mid x)$ is the posterior distribution of θ given the data x and

$$f^*(x) = \int f(x \mid \theta)\pi(\theta)d\theta$$

is the marginal p.d.f. of X which does not depend on θ. Substituting in the above expression for $B(\delta)$, we get

$$B(\delta) = \int_X \left[\int_\Theta L(\delta(x), \theta)\pi^*(\theta \mid x)d\theta \right] f^*(x)dx.$$

The quantity in the square brackets is called the **posterior risk** of decision $\delta(x)$, having observed x. The Bayes rule δ then chooses that decision $\delta(x)$ which minimizes the posterior risk for each $x \in X$.

EXAMPLE 15.33   (POINT ESTIMATION: BAYES ESTIMATOR FOR SQUARED ERROR LOSS)

For the squared error loss function, the posterior risk of an estimator $\hat{\theta} = \hat{\theta}(x)$ is given by

$$\int_{\Theta} [\hat{\theta}(x) - \theta]^2 \pi^*(\theta \,|\, x) d\theta.$$

This is minimized by choosing

$$\hat{\theta}(x) = E(\theta \,|\, x) = \int_{\Theta} \theta \pi^*(\theta \,|\, x) d\theta$$

i.e., the posterior mean of θ. This can be seen as follows. The posterior risk equals

$$\text{Var}(\theta \,|\, x) + [E(\theta \,|\, x) - \hat{\theta}]^2$$

where the variance and expected value of θ (regarded as an r.v.) are computed w.r.t. its posterior distribution $\pi^*(\theta \,|\, x)$. The variance does not depend on $\hat{\theta}$, and the second term is minimized by choosing $\hat{\theta}(x) = E(\theta \,|\, x)$, which makes it equal to 0.

   In conclusion, the Bayes estimator of θ is the posterior mean of θ if one uses the squared error loss function. In Example 15.26 we used the posterior mean of the binomial parameter p without this decision theoretic justification.   ◆

15.5   CHAPTER SUMMARY

This chapter is an introduction to mathematical statistics. The primary focus is on likelihood based inference (estimation and testing). The **likelihood function** is the joint p.d.f. or p.m.f., $\prod_{i=1}^{n} f(x_i \,|\, \theta)$, of i.i.d. observations $x_1, x_2, \ldots, x_n$ from $f(x \,|\, \theta)$; it is regarded as a function of the unknown parameter θ for the given values of the observations. The **maximum likelihood estimate (MLE)** $\hat{\theta}$ of θ maximizes the likelihood function. The **Fisher information** about θ from a single observation X from $f(x \,|\, \theta)$ is defined as

$$I(\theta) = E\left\{ \left[\frac{d \ln f(X \,|\, \theta)}{d\theta} \right]^2 \right\} = -E\left\{ \left[\frac{d^2 \ln f(X \,|\, \theta)}{d\theta^2} \right] \right\}.$$

The information from n i.i.d. observations equals $nI(\theta)$. The **Cramér-Rao lower bound** on the variance of an unbiased estimator of θ is $1/nI(\theta)$. The MLE $\hat{\theta}$ is asymptotically normal with mean $= \theta$ and variance $= 1/nI(\theta)$; i.e., it achieves the Cramér-Rao lower bound asymptotically. Large sample inferences about θ are derived from this distribution.

   The **Neyman-Pearson lemma** shows that the **most powerful (MP) test** of a simple vs. a simple hypothesis uses the ratio of the likelihoods under the two hypotheses as the test statistic. This is called the **likelihood ratio (LR) test**. For the composite vs. composite hypothesis testing problem, the **generalized likelihood ratio (GLR) test** statistic, λ, equals the ratio of the maximum of the likelihood function under H_0 to the overall maximum of the likelihood function. The asymptotic null distribution of the GLR statistic, $-2 \ln \lambda$, is chi-square with d.f. = the number of independent parameters restricted under H_0. The Pearson chi-square test statistic for goodness of fit and contingency tables approximately equals the GLR statistic in large samples.

The **sequential probability ratio test (SPRT)** extends the LR testing principle to sequential sampling. The SPRT uses two fixed **stopping boundaries**. Sampling is continued if the likelihood ratio after a new observation falls within the stopping boundaries. Otherwise sampling is terminated and a decision is made to either accept H_0 or reject H_0, depending on which boundary is crossed. The SPRT for a simple vs. simple hypothesis testing problem requires the smallest expected sample size to reach a decision under both H_0 and H_1 among all tests with specified α- and β-risks.

The **Bayesian approach** regards an unknown parameter θ as a random variable. This differs from the **frequentist approach**, followed elsewhere in the book, which regards θ as a fixed constant. The distribution assumed for θ is called the **prior distribution**. The Bayes formula is used to find the **posterior distribution**, which is the conditional distribution of θ given the data. As an example of Bayesian inference, the mean of the posterior distribution can be used as a point estimate of θ. If the prior and the posterior belong to the same family of distributions, the prior is called a **conjugate prior**.

Decision theory views any statistical problem as a decision problem. A decision problem requires specification of the **decision space** (the possible decisions d), the **parameter space** (the possible true parameter values θ), the **loss function** $L(\theta, d)$ (the loss incurred when the true parameter is θ and decision d is made), and the distribution of the data, X, which depends on the unknown parameter θ. A **decision rule** δ chooses decision $d = \delta(x)$ based on observed data, $X = x$. The **risk function**, $R(\delta, \theta)$, of a decision rule is the expected value of its loss function, given by $R(\delta, \theta) = E[L(\delta(X), \theta)]$, where the expectation is taken with respect to the distribution of X.

Two decision rules, δ_1 and δ_2, can be compared by their risk functions. If $R(\delta_1, \theta) \geq R(\delta_2, \theta)$ for all values of θ with a strict inequality for at least some θ, then δ_1 is said to be **inadmissible**. If a rule is not inadmissible, then it is **admissible**. The choice of a decision rule can be restricted to admissible decision rules. Generally, no rule has the lowest risk function for all values of θ. Therefore some additional criterion must be imposed. One option is the **Bayes criterion**, which bases the choice on $E[R(\delta, \theta)] = B(\delta)$, called the **Bayes risk**, where the expectation is taken with respect to a prior distribution, $\pi(\theta)$, on θ; the resulting rule is called the **Bayes rule**. Another option is the **minimax criterion**, which chooses the decision rule having the minimum value of $\max_\theta R(\delta, \theta)$; the resulting rule is called the **minimax rule**.

■ EXERCISES

Section 15.1

15.1 Suppose x is the number of successes in n i.i.d. Bernoulli trials with success probability p. Show that the MLE of θ equals $\hat{p} = x/n$.

15.2 Suppose x is the number of i.i.d. Bernoulli trials with success probability p required to achieve the first success. Show that the MLE of p equals $\hat{p} = 1/x$.

15.3 Suppose $x_1, x_2, \ldots, x_n$ are i.i.d. observations from an exponential distribution with p.d.f.

$$f(x \mid \theta) = \theta e^{-\theta x} \quad \text{for } x > 0.$$

Find the MLE of the mean $\mu = 1/\theta$.

15.4 Suppose $x_1, x_2, \ldots, x_n$ are i.i.d. observations from a shifted exponential distribution with p.d.f.

$$f(x \mid \theta, \phi) = \theta e^{-\theta(x - \phi)} \quad \text{for } x \geq \phi.$$

Think of the observations as times to failure of n identical items with ϕ as the minimum guaranteed lifetime (the time before which no item will fail) and θ as the failure rate thereafter.

(a) Write the likelihood function of θ and ϕ.

(b) Find the MLE of ϕ, assuming θ is known.

(c) Find the MLE's of θ and ϕ, assuming both parameters are unknown.

15.5 Suppose $x_1, x_2, \ldots, x_n$ are i.i.d. observations from a Poisson distribution with p.m.f.

$$f(x \mid \theta) = \frac{e^{-\theta} \theta^x}{x!} \quad \text{for } x = 0, 1, 2, \ldots$$

Think of them as the number of absent employees on n days in a company.

(a) Find the MLE of θ.

(b) Find the MLE of the probability that there is at least one absent employee.

15.6 Suppose $x_1, x_2, \ldots, x_n$ are i.i.d. observations from a uniform distribution on the interval $[\theta - 1/2, \theta + 1/2]$.

(a) Write the likelihood function of θ.

(b) Show that any θ between $x_{max} - 1/2$ and $x_{min} + 1/2$ maximizes the likelihood function. Usually the MLE is taken to be

$$\hat{\theta} = \frac{x_{min} + x_{max}}{2}$$

which is called the **midrange**.

15.7 Suppose $x_1, x_2, \ldots, x_n$ are i.i.d. observations from a uniform distribution on the interval $[\theta_1, \theta_2]$.

(a) Write the likelihood function of θ_1 and θ_2.

(b) Find the MLE's of θ_1 and θ_2. Hence find the MLE of the mean $\mu = (\theta_1 + \theta_2)/2$.

15.8 Let $x_1, x_2, \ldots, x_{n_1}$ and $y_1, y_2, \ldots, y_{n_2}$ be i.i.d. observations from an $N(\mu_1, \sigma^2)$ and an $N(\mu_2, \sigma^2)$ distribution, respectively.

(a) Write the likelihood function of μ_1, μ_2, and σ^2.

(b) Show that the MLE's are

$$\hat{\mu}_1 = \bar{x}, \hat{\mu}_2 = \bar{y} \quad \text{and} \quad \hat{\sigma}^2 = \frac{\sum(x_i - \bar{x})^2 + \sum(y_i - \bar{y})^2}{n_1 + n_2}.$$

15.9 Suppose $x_1, x_2, \ldots, x_n$ are i.i.d. observations from a **double exponential distribution**

$$f(x \mid \theta) = \frac{1}{2} e^{-|x - \theta|} \quad \text{for } -\infty < x < \infty.$$

Show that for an odd sample size, the MLE of θ is the sample median. (*Hint:* The likelihood function is not differentiable.)

15.10   To estimate the failure rate θ of a given population of items, a random sample of n items is put on test, and the test is terminated at a fixed time t^* (**type II censoring**). Suppose that $m \le n$ items are observed to fail at times $t_1 < t_2 < \cdots < t_m$ before t^* and $n - m$ items are still functional when the test is terminated. Assume that the failure time distribution is exponential as in Exercise 15.3.

(a) Show that conditional on m, the likelihood function of θ is

$$\prod_{i=1}^{m} \{\theta \exp(-\theta t_i)\} \times \{\exp(-\theta t^*)\}^{n-m} = \theta^m \exp\left(-\theta \left[\sum_{i=1}^{m} t_i + (n - m)t^*\right]\right).$$

(b) Find the MLE of the mean time to failure, $\mu = 1/\theta$. Note that it is the same as the estimate from Exercise 6.34 computed from the total time on test.

15.11   Refer to Exercise 15.1. Show that the Cramér-Rao lower bound on the variance of any unbiased estimator of p is $p(1 - p)/n$. Hence the MLE $\hat{p}$ is efficient.

15.12   Refer to Exercise 15.3. Show that the sample mean is an efficient estimator of μ.

15.13   Use the delta method to approximate $\mathrm{Var}(1/\bar{X})$ as a function of $\mathrm{Var}(\bar{X})$, where $\bar{X}$ is the sample mean of n i.i.d. observations from a distribution with mean μ and variance σ^2.

15.14   Refer to Example 15.15. In many problems it is more convenient to work with the log-odds.

(a) Use the delta method to show that

$$\mathrm{Var}\left(\ln\left[\frac{\hat{p}}{1 - \hat{p}}\right]\right) \simeq \frac{1}{np(1 - p)}.$$

(b) Now consider two independent binomial samples of sizes n_1, n_2 and success probabilities p_1, p_2. Let $\hat{p}_1, \hat{p}_2$ be the corresponding sample proportions ($0 < \hat{p}_1, \hat{p}_2 < 1$). Define the sample odds ratio as

$$\hat{\psi} = \frac{\hat{p}_1/(1 - \hat{p}_1)}{\hat{p}_2/(1 - \hat{p}_2)}.$$

Using the result from (a), show that

$$\mathrm{Var}\{\ln(\hat{\psi})\} \simeq \frac{1}{n_1 p_1} + \frac{1}{n_1 q_1} + \frac{1}{n_2 p_2} + \frac{1}{n_2 q_2}$$

where $q_i = 1 - p_i$, $i = 1, 2$. A sample estimate of this is used in the confidence interval formula (9.23) for the log of the odds ratio.

15.15   ▣ Consider two groups of patients (control and treatment, coded as $x = 0$ and $x = 1$) where the response of each patient is a success or a failure.

(a) Suppose that a logistic regression model $\ln[p/(1 - p)] = \beta_0 + \beta_1 x$ where $p = P\,(\text{Success}\,|\,x)$, is fitted to these data. Show that the coefficient β_1 of the indicator variable x for the treatment group in the model equals the logarithm of the odds ratio (log-odds ratio).

(b) Fit the logistic regression model to the leukemia data from Table 9.2. Compare the results with those from Example 9.15. In particular, compare the standard errors of the estimated log-odds ratio from the two analyses. Note that they are the same. Exercise 15.37 shows why.

15.16 This exercise deals with logistic regression for grouped data. Consider k groups of subjects. There are n_i subjects in the i th group, of whom m_i are observed to respond when subjected to a dose level x_i of a certain stimulus; thus the observed proportion of responses at dose x_i is m_i/n_i. For a numerical example of such data, see the following exercise. We want to fit the logistic regression model

$$P(\text{Response} \mid x) = \frac{\exp(\beta_0 + \beta_1 x)}{1 + \exp(\beta_0 + \beta_1 x)}.$$

Modify the equations satisfied by the MLE's of β_0 and β_1 from Example 15.7 for these grouped data.

15.17 ◼ The following table gives data on the number of beetles killed after five hours of exposure to carbon disulphide at various concentrations.[5]

$\log_{10}$(Concentration)	No. of Beetles	No. Killed
1.6907	59	6
1.7242	60	13
1.7552	62	18
1.7842	56	28
1.8113	63	52
1.8369	59	53
1.8610	62	61
1.8839	60	60

Fit a logistic regression model to these data. Interpret the coefficient of $\log_{10}$(Concentration) and find a 95% CI for it.

Section 15.2

15.18 Suppose $x_1, x_2, \ldots, x_n$ are i.i.d. observations from an exponential distribution with p.d.f.

$$f(x \mid \theta) = \theta e^{-\theta x} \quad \text{for } x > 0.$$

Derive the most powerful test of

$$H_0: \ \theta = \theta_0 \quad \text{vs.} \quad H_1: \ \theta = \theta_1$$

where $\theta_0 > \theta_1$. Show how you will find the critical constant for the α-level most powerful test.

15.19 We want to test $H_0: \ p = 1/2$ vs. $H_1: \ p = 3/4$, where p is the common success probability in a sequence of n i.i.d. Bernoulli trials. Suppose that $n = 5$ trials are performed and let x be the number of successes. Then the likelihood functions under H_0 and H_1, calculated using the binomial distribution formula,

$$L(p \mid x) = f(x \mid p) = \binom{5}{x} p^x (1 - p)^{5-x} \quad \text{for } x = 0, 1, \ldots, 5$$

---

[5] C. I. Bliss (1935), "The calculation of dosage-mortality curve," *Annals of Applied Biology*, **22**, 134–167, reproduced in A. J. Dobson (1990), *An Introduction to Generalized Linear Models*, London: Chapman and Hall, Table 8.2, p. 109.

are given in the following table.

Likelihood Function $L(p \mid x)$

p	x					
	0	1	2	3	4	5
1/2	0.0312	0.1562	0.3125	0.3125	0.1562	0.0312
3/4	0.0010	0.0146	0.0879	0.2637	0.3955	0.2373

(a) Compute the likelihood ratios required to derive the most powerful (Neyman-Pearson) test.

(b) Suppose that the critical constant k equals 1 for the Neyman-Pearson test. Give the rejection rule in terms of x. What are the level and the power of this test?

(c) What is the power of the most powerful test of nominal level $\alpha = 0.05$? What is the actual level of this test?

15.20 Refer to Exercise 15.8. Show that the generalized likelihood ratio test of $H_0: \mu_1 = \mu_2$ vs. $H_1: \mu_1 \neq \mu_2$ is equivalent to the usual two independent samples t-test.

15.21 Refer to Exercise 15.8, but now assume that the variances of the two normal populations, denoted by σ_1^2 and σ_2^2, are possibly unequal. Show that the generalized likelihood ratio test of $H_0: \sigma_1^2 = \sigma_2^2$ vs. $H_1: \sigma_1^2 \neq \sigma_2^2$ is equivalent to the F-test for variances from Chapter 8.

15.22 Refer to Examples 15.21 and 15.23.

(a) Find the stopping limits on the sample mean $\bar{x}_n$ of the Wald SPRT for testing $\mu = 0$ vs. $\mu = 1$ based on sequentially observing the values $x_1, x_2, \ldots, x_n$ from an $N(\mu, \sigma^2)$ distribution. Assume $\sigma^2 = 1, \alpha = .01$, and $\beta = .05$.

(b) Calculate the expected sample sizes for the SPRT for $\mu = 0$ and $\mu = 1$. Compare these expected sample sizes with the fixed sample size required by the z-test to guarantee the same error probabilities.

15.23 To decide whether to accept or reject a large lot, items from the lot are sequentially sampled with each item being classified as defective or not defective. Let p be the unknown fraction defective in the lot. The hypotheses are set up as $H_0: p = .05$ (the lot is satisfactory) vs. $H_1: p = .15$ (the lot is unsatisfactory). Let $\alpha = .05$ (the producer's risk) and $\beta = .10$ (the consumer's risk).

(a) Find the acceptance and rejection numbers of the sampling plan for sample sizes up to 25. What are the smallest sample sizes when the acceptance and rejection first become possible?

(b) Calculate the expected sample sizes of this sampling plan for $p = .05$ and for $p = .15$.

Section 15.3

15.24 Refer to Example 15.26 where x is an observation from a $\text{Bin}(n, p)$ distribution. Suppose that the prior on p is uniform over $[0,1]$, which is a special case of the beta distribution for $a = b = 1$. Find the posterior distribution of p. What is the posterior mean? What is the posterior mode (the value of p at which the posterior p.d.f. is maximum)?

15.25 Show that the gamma distribution is a conjugate prior for the exponential distribution. In particular, let $x_1, x_2, \ldots, x_n$ be a random sample from an exponential distribution with p.d.f.

$$f(x \mid \theta) = \theta e^{-\theta x} \quad \text{for } x > 0.$$

Let the prior on θ be a Gamma(α, β) distribution:

$$\pi(\theta) = \frac{1}{\Gamma(\alpha)} \beta^\alpha \theta^{\alpha-1} e^{-\beta\theta}.$$

(a) Show that the posterior distribution of θ is Gamma($\alpha + n, \beta + n\bar{x}$).

(b) Interpret how the Bayes estimate (the posterior mean) of θ,

$$E(\theta \mid x_1, x_2, \ldots, x_n) = \frac{\alpha + n}{\beta + \sum x_i},$$

depends on the prior information and the data. What happens to this estimate as $n \to \infty$?

15.26 Show that the gamma distribution is a conjugate prior for the Poisson distribution. In particular, suppose that $x_1, x_2, \ldots, x_n$ is a random sample from a Poisson distribution:

$$f(x \mid \theta) = \frac{e^{-\theta}\theta^x}{x!} \quad \text{for } x = 0, 1, 2, \ldots$$

and the prior on θ is a Gamma(α, β) distribution given in the previous exercise.

(a) Show that the posterior distribution of θ is Gamma($\alpha + \sum x_i, \beta + n$).

(b) Interpret how the Bayes estimate (the posterior mean) of θ,

$$E(\theta \mid x_1, x_2, \ldots, x_n) = \frac{\alpha + \sum x_i}{\beta + n},$$

depends on the prior information and the data. What happens to this estimate as $n \to \infty$?

Section 15.4

15.27 Refer to Example 15.29. Compare the risk functions of the two estimators of the success probability p using $n = 1$ and $a = b = 1$, i.e, a uniform prior on p.

15.28 Refer to Example 15.30. Show that the Bayes rule with respect to the uniform prior $\pi(p) = 1$ for $0 \le p \le 1$ is the decision rule δ_1.

15.29 Refer to Example 15.30. Show that the Bayes rule with respect to the prior $\pi(p) = 2p$ for $0 \le p \le 1$ decides not to purchase the lot regardless of the sample outcome. Give an intuitive explanation for this rule.

15.30 Refer to Example 15.30. Find a prior on p with respect to which the decision rule δ_2 is Bayes.

15.31 A certain rare disease has a prevalence rate of 1% in the population. The diagnostic test for the disease has a false positive rate of 2% and a false negative rate of 5%. Suppose that the cost of operating on a nondiseased person is $5000 and the cost of operating on a diseased person is −$5000 (i.e., the benefit of operation for a diseased person is $5000). Also, the cost of not operating on a nondiseased person is $0, and the cost of not operating on a diseased person is $10,000.

(a) What are the two states of nature in this problem? Give their prior probabilities.

(b) Think of the outcome of the diagnostic test as the data. Give the distribution of the data under the two states of nature.

(c) What are the two decisions in this problem? Give the loss function for these decisions under the two states of nature.

(d) Show that the Bayes rule decides to operate if and only if the test is positive.

(e) Find a set of prior probabilities and/or loss function values for which the Bayes rule decides to operate regardless of the test result.

(f) Find a set of prior probabilities and/or loss function values for which the Bayes rule decides not to operate regardless of the test result.

15.32 Consider the problem of estimating the parameter θ of the uniform distribution over $[0, \theta]$ based on a single observation X. Assume the squared error loss function and the Gamma$(\alpha = 2, \beta = 1)$ prior on θ:

$$\pi(\theta) = \theta e^{-\theta} \quad \text{for } \theta > 0.$$

(a) Show that the posterior distribution of θ is

$$\pi^*(\theta \mid x) = e^{x-\theta} \quad \text{for } \theta > x$$

and 0 otherwise.

(b) Show that the posterior risk of an estimate $\hat{\theta}$ given $X = x$ is

$$e^x \int_x^\infty (\hat{\theta} - \theta)^2 e^{-\theta} d\theta.$$

(c) Show that the Bayes estimate (which minimizes the above posterior risk) equals

$$\hat{\theta} = x + 1.$$

Advanced Exercises

15.33 To estimate the size of a wildlife population the so-called **capture-recapture method** is employed. As an example, consider estimating the unknown number N of fish in a lake. A random sample of n fish is taken, tagged, and returned to the lake. After these fish have properly mixed with the other fish in the lake, another random sample of m fish is taken and the number of tagged fish in this recapture sample is counted. The probability that the number of tagged fish in the recapture sample equals x is given by the hypergeometric distribution:

$$f(x \mid N) = \frac{\binom{n}{x}\binom{N-n}{m-x}}{\binom{N}{m}}.$$

(a) To find the MLE of N we can use the above probability as the likelihood function $L(N)$ of N. However, because N is integer valued, we cannot find the MLE by calculus methods. Instead consider the following ratio

$$\frac{L(N)}{L(N-1)} = \frac{\binom{n}{x}\binom{N-n}{m-x}}{\binom{N}{m}} \times \frac{\binom{N-1}{m}}{\binom{n}{x}\binom{N-1-n}{m-x}}.$$

Show that this ratio equals

$$\frac{(N-n)(N-m)}{N(N-m-n+x)}.$$

(b) Show that
$$\frac{L(N)}{L(N-1)} > 1 \iff N < \frac{mn}{x}.$$

Thus $L(N)$ is increasing in N for $N < \frac{mn}{x}$ and decreasing in N for $N > \frac{mn}{x}$. Denoting the integer part of mn/x by $[mn/x]$, show that the MLE $\hat{N}$ equals $[mn/x]$ or $[mn/x]+1$, whichever the likelihood function $L(N)$ is larger for.

(c) Give an intuitive explanation of $\hat{N}$. (*Hint:* Note that $\hat{N} \simeq mn/x$ and x/m is the proportion of tagged fish in the recapture sample.)

15.34 Give an alternative proof of the result (15.8) by using the definition (15.5) of the Fisher information in a single observation. (*Hint:* Expand
$$\left[\frac{d \ln f(X_1, X_2, \ldots, X_n \mid \theta)}{d\theta}\right]^2 = \left[\sum_{i=1}^{n}\left(\frac{d \ln f(X_i \mid \theta)}{d\theta}\right)\right]^2$$

and note that the cross-product terms are zero, because from (15.6) we have
$$E\left\{\left(\frac{d \ln f(X_i \mid \theta)}{d\theta}\right)\right\} = 0$$

and the X_i are independent.)

15.35 In Example 15.4 we showed that the MLE of θ for a random sample $X_1, X_2, \ldots, X_n$ from a uniform distribution on $[0, \theta]$ is $\hat{\theta} = X_{\max}$.

(a) Use the result from Exercise 5.44 (b) to show that
$$\frac{n+1}{n}\hat{\theta} = \frac{n+1}{n}X_{\max}$$

is an unbiased estimator of θ.

(b) Show that
$$\text{Var}\left(\frac{n+1}{n}X_{\max}\right) = \frac{\theta^2}{n(n+2)}.$$

(*Hint:* $E(X_{\max}^2) = \frac{n}{n+2}\theta^2$.)

(c) Show that
$$\frac{d \ln f(x \mid \theta)}{d\theta} = -\frac{1}{\theta}.$$

Hence the Cramér-Rao lower bound on the variance of an unbiased estimator of θ is θ^2/n.

(d) Show that the variance obtained in (b) is less than the Cramér-Rao lower bound. Why do you think the lower bound is violated in this case?

15.36 There is an extension of the delta method for nonlinear functions of two or more r.v.'s. In particular, consider two r.v.'s X and Y with means μ_X and μ_Y, variances σ_X^2 and σ_Y^2, and covariance σ_{XY}. Then the variance of a nonlinear function $h(X, Y)$ can be approximated by
$$\text{Var}(h(X, Y)) \simeq \left[\frac{\partial h(\mu_X, \mu_Y)}{\partial x}\right]^2 \sigma_X^2 + \left[\frac{\partial h(\mu_X, \mu_Y)}{\partial y}\right]^2 \sigma_Y^2$$
$$+ 2\left[\frac{\partial h(\mu_X, \mu_Y)}{\partial x}\right]\left[\frac{\partial h(\mu_X, \mu_Y)}{\partial y}\right]\sigma_{XY}$$

where the notation $\partial h(\mu_X, \mu_Y)/\partial x$, etc., means that the corresponding partial derivative of $h(x, y)$ is evaluated at $x = \mu_X, y = \mu_Y$. In many problems it is of interest to estimate the ratio of μ_X and μ_Y based on n i.i.d. bivariate observations (X_i, Y_i), $i = 1, 2, \ldots, n$. Show that the variance of the **ratio estimator** $\bar{X}/\bar{Y}$ can be approximated by

$$\text{Var}\left(\frac{\bar{X}}{\bar{Y}}\right) = \frac{1}{n}\left(\frac{\mu_X}{\mu_Y}\right)^2\left[\frac{\sigma_X^2}{\mu_X^2} + \frac{\sigma_Y^2}{\mu_Y^2} - \frac{2\sigma_{XY}}{\mu_X\mu_Y}\right].$$

15.37 Refer to Exercise 15.15. Let the sample sizes in the treatment and control groups be n_1 and n_2, respectively.

(a) Use (15.14) to show that the information matrix of β_0 and β_1 in the logistic regression model equals

$$I(\beta_0, \beta_1) = \begin{bmatrix} n_1 p_1 q_1 + n_2 p_2 q_2 & n_1 p_1 q_1 \\ n_1 p_1 q_1 & n_1 p_1 q_1 \end{bmatrix}$$

where p_1 and p_2 are the success probabilities for the treatment and control groups, respectively, and $q_i = 1 - p_i$.

(b) Compute the inverse of this matrix and show that the asymptotic variance of the MLE of β_1 equals

$$\frac{1}{n_1 p_1} + \frac{1}{n_1 q_1} + \frac{1}{n_2 p_2} + \frac{1}{n_2 q_2}.$$

Note that this is the same expression as obtained in Exercise 15.14.

15.38 For count response data with covariates, the following **Poisson regression** model is often employed. For fixed covariate values $x_1, x_2, \ldots, x_n$, let $y_1, y_2, \ldots, y_n$ be independent observed counts. Assume that the counts follow the Poisson distributions

$$f(y_i \mid \theta_i) = \frac{e^{-\theta_i}\theta_i^{y_i}}{y_i!}, \quad i = 1, 2, \ldots, n.$$

The Poisson regression model postulates that

$$\ln\theta_i = \beta_0 + \beta_1 x_i, \quad i = 1, 2, \ldots, n.$$

(a) Derive the equations for obtaining the MLE's of β_0 and β_1.

(b) Derive the information matrix of β_0 and β_1.

(c) If x is an indicator variable taking values 0 and 1, interpret the parameter β_1.

15.39 Consider an $r \times c$ contingency table with multinomial sampling (as discussed in Section 9.4.1) with a total sample size of n. Denote the cell counts by x_{ij} and the unknown cell probabilities by p_{ij} $(1 \leq i \leq r, 1 \leq j \leq c)$. The **log-linear model** assumes that

$$\ln p_{ij} = \mu + \tau_i + \beta_j + (\tau\beta)_{ij}$$

for all i, j, where

$$\sum_{i=1}^{r}\tau_i = 0, \sum_{j=1}^{c}\beta_j = 0, \sum_{i=1}^{r}(\tau\beta)_{ij} = 0 \text{ for all } j, \sum_{j=1}^{c}(\tau\beta)_{ij} = 0 \text{ for all } i.$$

(a) Derive the equations for obtaining the MLE's of all unknown parameters in the log-linear model.

(b) Show that the independence hypothesis corresponds to testing that the $(\tau\beta)_{ij} = 0$ for all i, j. Derive the equations for obtaining the MLE's of the remaining parameters under this hypothesis.

(c) Derive the generalized likelihood ratio test of the independence hypothesis and show that asymptotically it is equivalent to the Pearson chi-square test.

15.40 ■ A numerical recursive algorithm to calculate the MLE $\hat{\theta}$ is obtained as follows from the first order Taylor series expansion given in (15.15). Begin with an initial guess $\hat{\theta}^{(1)}$ and let $\hat{\theta}^{(r)}$ denote the estimate value for the rth iteration. Then

$$\frac{d \ln L(\hat{\theta})}{d\theta} \simeq \frac{d \ln L(\hat{\theta}^{(r)})}{d\theta} + (\hat{\theta} - \hat{\theta}^{(r)})\frac{d^2 \ln L(\hat{\theta}^{(r)})}{d\theta^2}$$

where the derivatives on the right hand side are evaluated at $\theta = \hat{\theta}^{(r)}$. Setting the above equal to zero and solving for $\hat{\theta}$ yields the following value for the $(r+1)$st iteration:

$$\hat{\theta}^{(r+1)} = \hat{\theta}^{(r)} - \left[\frac{d^2 \ln L(\hat{\theta}^{(r)})}{d\theta^2}\right]^{-1} \frac{d \ln L(\hat{\theta}^{(r)})}{d\theta} = \hat{\theta}^{(r)} + [I(\hat{\theta}^{(r)})]^{-1}\frac{d \ln L(\hat{\theta}^{(r)})}{d\theta}$$

where $I(\hat{\theta}^{(r)})$ is the observed Fisher information evaluated at $\theta = \hat{\theta}^{(r)}$. This is known as the **Newton-Raphson algorithm**. Note that the algorithm yields an estimate of the asymptotic variance, $1/I(\hat{\theta})$, as a by-product.

A genetic linkage model[6] postulates that four types of species of an animal occur according to the following probabilities:

$$p_1 = \frac{1}{2} + \frac{\theta}{4}, p_2 = \frac{1}{4}(1 - \theta), p_3 = \frac{1}{4}(1 - \theta), p_4 = \frac{\theta}{4}.$$

(a) Suppose that in a random sample of n animals, the numbers in the four species are x_1, x_2, x_3, and x_4. Derive the Newton-Raphson recursion for finding the MLE of θ. Program this recursion.

(b) Use your program to compute the MLE for the following data: $x_1 = 125, x_2 = 18, x_3 = 20, x_4 = 34$, and $n = 197$. Use the estimate obtained from x_4 as an initial guess, namely, $\hat{\theta}^{(1)} = 4(34)/197 = 0.69$.

15.41 Consider the one-way layout setting with $a \geq 2$ independent random samples, $y_{i1}, y_{i2}, \ldots, y_{in_i}$, from $N(\mu_i, \sigma_i^2)$ distributions for $i = 1, 2, \ldots, a$.

(a) Assuming that the σ_i^2's are equal to a common unknown value σ^2, show that the GLR test of

$$H_0: \mu_1 = \mu_2 = \cdots = \mu_a \quad \text{vs.} \quad H_1: \mu_i \neq \mu_j \text{ for some } i \neq j$$

is the usual F-test.

(b) Derive the GLR test of

$$H_0: \sigma_1^2 = \sigma_2^2 = \ldots = \sigma_a^2 \text{ vs. } H_1: \sigma_i^2 \neq \sigma_j^2 \text{ for some } i \neq j.$$

The **Bartlett test for homogeneity of variances** is based on the GLR test statistic $-2 \ln \lambda$ with a correction factor to obtain a closer approximation to the asymptotic χ^2_{a-1} distribution.

---

[6] M. Tanner (1996), *op. cit.*, p. 66. Originally from C. R. Rao (1973), *Linear Statistical Inference and Its Applications*, New York: Wiley.

APPENDIX A

TABLES

Table A.1 Cumulative Binomial Probabilities

a. $n = 5$

		| 0.01	0.05	0.10	0.20	0.25	0.30	0.40	p 0.50	0.60	0.70	0.75	0.80	0.90	0.95	0.99
	0	.951	.774	.590	.328	.237	.168	.078	.031	.010	.002	.001	.000	.000	.000	.000
	1	.999	.977	.919	.737	.633	.528	.337	.188	.087	.031	.016	.007	.000	.000	.000
x	2	1.000	.999	.991	.942	.896	.837	.683	.500	.317	.163	.104	.058	.009	.001	.000
	3	1.000	1.000	1.000	.993	.984	.969	.913	.812	.663	.472	.367	.263	.081	.023	.001
	4	1.000	1.000	1.000	1.000	.999	.998	.990	.969	.922	.832	.763	.672	.410	.226	.049

b. $n = 10$

		| 0.01	0.05	0.10	0.20	0.25	0.30	0.40	p 0.50	0.60	0.70	0.75	0.80	0.90	0.95	0.99
	0	.904	.599	.349	.107	.056	.028	.006	.001	.000	.000	.000	.000	.000	.000	.000
	1	.996	.914	.736	.376	.244	.149	.046	.011	.002	.000	.000	.000	.000	.000	.000
	2	1.000	.988	.930	.678	.526	.383	.167	.055	.012	.002	.000	.000	.000	.000	.000
	3	1.000	.999	.987	.879	.776	.650	.382	.172	.055	.011	.004	.001	.000	.000	.000
x	4	1.000	1.000	.998	.967	.922	.850	.633	.377	.166	.047	.020	.006	.000	.000	.000
	5	1.000	1.000	1.000	.994	.980	.953	.834	.623	.367	.150	.078	.033	.002	.000	.000
	6	1.000	1.000	1.000	.999	.996	.989	.945	.828	.618	.350	.224	.121	.013	.001	.000
	7	1.000	1.000	1.000	1.000	1.000	.998	.988	.945	.833	.617	.474	.322	.070	.012	.000
	8	1.000	1.000	1.000	1.000	1.000	1.000	.998	.989	.954	.851	.756	.624	.264	.086	.004
	9	1.000	1.000	1.000	1.000	1.000	1.000	1.000	.999	.994	.972	.944	.893	.651	.401	.096

Table A.1 Cumulative Binomial Probabilities (*cont.*)

c. $n = 15$

								p							
	0.01	0.05	0.10	0.20	0.25	0.30	0.40	0.50	0.60	0.70	0.75	0.80	0.90	0.95	0.99
0	0.860	.463	.206	.035	.013	.005	.000	.000	.000	.000	.000	.000	.000	.000	.000
1	.990	.829	.549	.167	.080	.035	.005	.000	.000	.000	.000	.000	.000	.000	.000
2	1.000	.964	.816	.398	.236	.127	.027	.004	.000	.000	.000	.000	.000	.000	.000
3	1.000	.995	.944	.648	.461	.297	.091	.018	.002	.000	.000	.000	.000	.000	.000
4	1.000	.999	.987	.836	.686	.515	.217	.059	.009	.001	.000	.000	.000	.000	.000
5	1.000	1.000	.998	.939	.852	.722	.403	.151	.034	.004	.001	.000	.000	.000	.000
6	1.000	1.000	1.000	.982	.943	.869	.610	.304	.095	.015	.004	.001	.000	.000	.000
x 7	1.000	1.000	1.000	.996	.983	.950	.787	.500	.213	.050	.017	.004	.000	.000	.000
8	1.000	1.000	1.000	.999	.996	.985	.905	.696	.390	.131	.057	.018	.000	.000	.000
9	1.000	1.000	1.000	1.000	.999	.996	.966	.849	.597	.278	.148	.061	.002	.000	.000
10	1.000	1.000	1.000	1.000	1.000	.999	.991	.941	.783	.485	.314	.164	.013	.001	.000
11	1.000	1.000	1.000	1.000	1.000	1.000	.998	.982	.909	.703	.539	.352	.056	.005	.000
12	1.000	1.000	1.000	1.000	1.000	1.000	1.000	.996	.973	.873	.764	.602	.184	.036	.000
13	1.000	1.000	1.000	1.000	1.000	1.000	1.000	1.000	.995	.965	.920	.833	.451	.171	.010
14	1.000	1.000	1.000	1.000	1.000	1.000	1.000	1.000	1.000	.995	.987	.965	.794	.537	.140

d. $n = 20$

								p							
	0.01	0.05	0.10	0.20	0.25	0.30	0.40	0.50	0.60	0.70	0.75	0.80	0.90	0.95	0.99
0	.818	.358	.122	.012	.003	.001	.000	.000	.000	.000	.000	.000	.000	.000	.000
1	.983	.736	.392	.069	.024	.008	.001	.000	.000	.000	.000	.000	.000	.000	.000
2	.999	.925	.677	.206	.091	.035	.004	.000	.000	.000	.000	.000	.000	.000	.000
3	1.000	.984	.867	.411	.225	.107	.016	.001	.000	.000	.000	.000	.000	.000	.000
4	1.000	.998	.957	.630	.415	.238	.051	.006	.000	.000	.000	.000	.000	.000	.000
5	1.000	1.000	.989	.804	.617	.416	.126	.021	.002	.000	.000	.000	.000	.000	.000
6	1.000	1.000	.998	.913	.786	.608	.250	.058	.006	.000	.000	.000	.000	.000	.000
7	1.000	1.000	1.000	.968	.898	.772	.416	.132	.021	.001	.000	.000	.000	.000	.000
8	1.000	1.000	1.000	.990	.959	.887	.596	.252	.057	.005	.001	.000	.000	.000	.000
9	1.000	1.000	1.000	.997	.986	.952	.755	.412	.128	.017	.004	.001	.000	.000	.000
x 10	1.000	1.000	1.000	.999	.996	.983	.872	.588	.245	.048	.014	.003	.000	.000	.000
11	1.000	1.000	1.000	1.000	.999	.995	.943	.748	.404	.113	.041	.010	.000	.000	.000
12	1.000	1.000	1.000	1.000	1.000	.999	.979	.868	.584	.228	.102	.032	.000	.000	.000
13	1.000	1.000	1.000	1.000	1.000	1.000	.994	.942	.750	.392	.214	.087	.002	.000	.000
14	1.000	1.000	1.000	1.000	1.000	1.000	.998	.979	.874	.584	.383	.196	.011	.000	.000
15	1.000	1.000	1.000	1.000	1.000	1.000	1.000	.994	.949	.762	.585	.370	.043	.003	.000
16	1.000	1.000	1.000	1.000	1.000	1.000	1.000	.999	.984	.893	.775	.589	.133	.016	.000
17	1.000	1.000	1.000	1.000	1.000	1.000	1.000	1.000	.996	.965	.909	.794	.323	.075	.001
18	1.000	1.000	1.000	1.000	1.000	1.000	1.000	1.000	.999	.992	.976	.931	.608	.264	.017
19	1.000	1.000	1.000	1.000	1.000	1.000	1.000	1.000	1.000	.999	.997	.988	.878	.642	.182

Table A.1 Cumulative Binomial Probabilities (*cont.*)

e. $n = 25$

								p							
	0.01	0.05	0.10	0.20	0.25	0.30	0.40	0.50	0.60	0.70	0.75	0.80	0.90	0.95	0.99
0	.778	.277	.072	.004	.001	.000	.000	.000	.000	.000	.000	.000	.000	.000	.000
1	.974	.642	.271	.027	.007	.002	.000	.000	.000	.000	.000	.000	.000	.000	.000
2	.998	.873	.537	.098	.032	.009	.000	.000	.000	.000	.000	.000	.000	.000	.000
3	1.000	.966	.764	.234	.096	.033	.000	.000	.000	.000	.000	.000	.000	.000	.000
4	1.000	.993	.902	.421	.214	.090	.009	.000	.000	.000	.000	.000	.000	.000	.000
5	1.000	.999	.967	.617	.378	.193	.029	.002	.000	.000	.000	.000	.000	.000	.000
6	1.000	1.000	.991	.780	.561	.341	.074	.007	.000	.000	.000	.000	.000	.000	.000
7	1.000	1.000	.998	.891	.727	.512	.154	.022	.001	.000	.000	.000	.000	.000	.000
8	1.000	1.000	1.000	.953	.851	.677	.274	.054	.004	.000	.000	.000	.000	.000	.000
9	1.000	1.000	1.000	.983	.929	.811	.425	.115	.013	.000	.000	.000	.000	.000	.000
10	1.000	1.000	1.000	.994	.970	.902	.586	.212	.034	.002	.000	.000	.000	.000	.000
11	1.000	1.000	1.000	.998	.980	.956	.732	.345	.078	.006	.001	.000	.000	.000	.000
x 12	1.000	1.000	1.000	1.000	.997	.983	.846	.500	.154	.017	.003	.000	.000	.000	.000
13	1.000	1.000	1.000	1.000	.999	.994	.922	.655	.268	.044	.020	.002	.000	.000	.000
14	1.000	1.000	1.000	1.000	1.000	.998	.966	.788	.414	.098	.030	.006	.000	.000	.000
15	1.000	1.000	1.000	1.000	1.000	1.000	.987	.885	.575	.189	.071	.017	.000	.000	.000
16	1.000	1.000	1.000	1.000	1.000	1.000	.996	.946	.726	.323	.149	.047	.000	.000	.000
17	1.000	1.000	1.000	1.000	1.000	1.000	.999	.978	.846	.488	.273	.109	.002	.000	.000
18	1.000	1.000	1.000	1.000	1.000	1.000	1.000	.993	.926	.659	.439	.220	.009	.000	.000
19	1.000	1.000	1.000	1.000	1.000	1.000	1.000	.998	.971	.807	.622	.383	.033	.001	.000
20	1.000	1.000	1.000	1.000	1.000	1.000	1.000	1.000	.991	.910	.786	.579	.098	.007	.000
21	1.000	1.000	1.000	1.000	1.000	1.000	1.000	1.000	.998	.967	.904	.766	.236	.034	.000
22	1.000	1.000	1.000	1.000	1.000	1.000	1.000	1.000	1.000	.991	.968	.902	.463	.127	.002
23	1.000	1.000	1.000	1.000	1.000	1.000	1.000	1.000	1.000	.998	.993	.973	.729	.358	.026
24	1.000	1.000	1.000	1.000	1.000	1.000	1.000	1.000	1.000	1.000	.999	.996	.928	.723	.222

SOURCE: Adapted from L. L. Chao (1980), *Statistics for Management*, Wadsworth, Inc.

Table A.2 Cumulative Poisson Probabilities

					λ					
	.1	.2	.3	.4	.5	.6	.7	.8	0.9	1.0
0	.905	.819	.741	.670	.607	.549	.497	.449	.407	.368
1	.995	.982	.963	.938	.910	.878	.844	.809	.772	.736
2	1.000	.999	.996	.992	.986	.977	.966	.953	.937	.920
x 3		1.000	1.000	.999	.998	.997	.994	.991	.987	.981
4				1.000	1.000	1.000	.999	.999	.998	.996
5							1.000	1.000	1.000	.999
6										1.000

Table A.2 Cumulative Poisson Probabilities (*cont.*)

	λ										
	2.0	3.0	4.0	5.0	6.0	7.0	8.0	9.0	10.0	15.0	20.0
0	.135	.050	.018	.007	.002	.001	.000	.000	.000	.000	.000
1	.406	.199	.092	.040	.017	.007	.003	.001	.000	.000	.000
2	.677	.423	.238	.125	.062	.030	.014	.006	.003	.000	.000
3	.857	.647	.433	.265	.151	.082	.042	.021	.010	.000	.000
4	.947	.815	.629	.440	.285	.173	.100	.055	.029	.001	.000
5	.983	.916	.785	.616	.446	.301	.191	.116	.067	.003	.000
6	.995	.966	.889	.762	.606	.450	.313	.207	.130	.008	.000
7	.999	.988	.949	.867	.744	.599	.453	.324	.220	.018	.001
8	1.000	.996	.979	.932	.847	.729	.593	.456	.333	.037	.002
9		.999	.992	.968	.916	.830	.717	.587	.458	.070	.005
10		1.000	.997	.986	.957	.901	.816	.706	.583	.118	.011
11			.999	.995	.980	.947	.888	.803	.697	.185	.021
12			1.000	.998	.991	.973	.936	.876	.792	.268	.039
13				.999	.996	.987	.966	.926	.864	.363	.066
14				1.000	.999	.994	.983	.959	.917	.466	.105
15					.999	.998	.992	.978	.951	.568	.157
16					1.000	.999	.996	.989	.973	.664	.221
17						.999	.998	.995	.986	.749	.297
18						1.000	.999	.998	.993	.819	.381
19							1.000	.998	.997	.875	.470
20								1.000	.998	.917	.559
21									.999	.947	.644
22									1.000	.967	.721
23										.981	.787
24										.989	.843
25										.994	.888
26										.997	.922
27										.998	.948
28										.999	.966
29										1.000	.978
30											.987
31											.992
32											.995
33											.997
34											.999
35											.999
36											1.000

SOURCE: L. L. Chao (1974), *Statistics: Methods and Analysis*, 2nd ed. New York: McGraw-Hill.

Table A.3 Standard Normal Curve Areas $\Phi(z) = P(Z \leq z)$

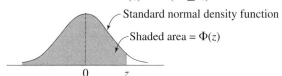

z	0.00	0.01	0.02	0.03	0.04	0.05	0.06	0.07	0.08	0.09
−3.4	0.0003	0.0003	0.0003	0.0003	0.0003	0.0003	0.0003	0.0003	0.0003	0.0002
−3.3	0.0005	0.0005	0.0005	0.0004	0.0004	0.0004	0.0004	0.0004	0.0004	0.0003
−3.2	0.0007	0.0007	0.0006	0.0006	0.0006	0.0006	0.0006	0.0005	0.0005	0.0005
−3.1	0.0010	0.0009	0.0009	0.0009	0.0008	0.0008	0.0008	0.0008	0.0007	0.0007
−3.0	0.0013	0.0013	0.0013	0.0012	0.0012	0.0011	0.0011	0.0011	0.0010	0.0010
−2.9	0.0019	0.0018	0.0017	0.0017	0.0016	0.0016	0.0015	0.0015	0.0014	0.0014
−2.8	0.0026	0.0025	0.0024	0.0023	0.0023	0.0022	0.0021	0.0021	0.0020	0.0019
−2.7	0.0035	0.0034	0.0033	0.0032	0.0031	0.0030	0.0029	0.0028	0.0027	0.0026
−2.6	0.0047	0.0045	0.0044	0.0043	0.0041	0.0040	0.0039	0.0038	0.0037	0.0036
−2.5	0.0062	0.0060	0.0059	0.0057	0.0055	0.0054	0.0052	0.0051	0.0049	0.0048
−2.4	0.0082	0.0080	0.0078	0.0075	0.0073	0.0071	0.0069	0.0068	0.0066	0.0064
−2.3	0.0107	0.0104	0.0102	0.0099	0.0096	0.0094	0.0091	0.0089	0.0087	0.0084
−2.2	0.0139	0.0136	0.0132	0.0129	0.0125	0.0122	0.0119	0.0116	0.0113	0.0110
−2.1	0.0179	0.0174	0.0170	0.0166	0.0162	0.0158	0.0154	0.0150	0.0146	0.0143
−2.0	0.0228	0.0222	0.0217	0.0212	0.0207	0.0202	0.0197	0.0192	0.0188	0.0183
−1.9	0.0287	0.0281	0.0274	0.0268	0.0262	0.0256	0.0250	0.0244	0.0239	0.0233
−1.8	0.0359	0.0352	0.0344	0.0336	0.0329	0.0322	0.0314	0.0307	0.0301	0.0294
−1.7	0.0446	0.0436	0.0427	0.0418	0.0409	0.0401	0.0392	0.0394	0.0375	0.0367
−1.6	0.0548	0.0537	0.0526	0.0516	0.0505	0.0495	0.0485	0.0475	0.0465	0.0455
−1.5	0.0668	0.0655	0.0643	0.0630	0.0618	0.0606	0.0594	0.0582	0.0571	0.0559
−1.4	0.0808	0.0793	0.0778	0.0764	0.0749	0.0735	0.0722	0.0708	0.0694	0.0681
−1.3	0.0968	0.0951	0.0934	0.0918	0.0901	0.0885	0.0869	0.0853	0.0838	0.0823
−1.2	0.1151	0.1131	0.1112	0.1093	0.1075	0.1056	0.1038	0.1020	0.1003	0.0985
−1.1	0.1357	0.1335	0.1314	0.1292	0.1271	0.1251	0.1230	0.1210	0.1190	0.1170
−1.0	0.1587	0.1562	0.1539	0.1515	0.1492	0.1469	0.1446	0.1423	0.1401	0.1379
−0.9	0.1841	0.1814	0.1788	0.1762	0.1736	0.1711	0.1685	0.1660	0.1635	0.1611
−0.8	0.2119	0.2090	0.2061	0.2033	0.2005	0.1977	0.1949	0.1922	0.1894	0.1867
−0.7	0.2420	0.2389	0.2358	0.2327	0.2296	0.2266	0.2236	0.2206	0.2177	0.2148
−0.6	0.2743	0.2709	0.2676	0.2643	0.2611	0.2578	0.2546	0.2514	0.2483	0.2451
−0.5	0.3085	0.3050	0.3015	0.2981	0.2946	0.2912	0.2877	0.2843	0.2810	0.2776
−0.4	0.3446	0.3409	0.3372	0.3336	0.3300	0.3264	0.3228	0.3192	0.3156	0.3121
−0.3	0.3821	0.3783	0.3745	0.3707	0.3669	0.3632	0.3594	0.3557	0.3520	0.3483
−0.2	0.4207	0.4168	0.4129	0.4090	0.4052	0.4013	0.3974	0.3936	0.3897	0.3859
−0.1	0.4602	0.4562	0.4522	0.4483	0.4443	0.4404	0.4364	0.4325	0.4286	0.4247
−0.0	0.5000	0.4960	0.4920	0.4880	0.4840	0.4801	0.4761	0.4721	0.4681	0.4641

Table A.3 Standard Normal Curve Areas $\Phi(z) = P(Z \leq z)$ *(cont.)*

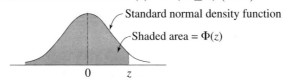

z	0.00	0.01	0.02	0.03	0.04	0.05	0.06	0.07	0.08	0.09
0.0	0.5000	0.5040	0.5080	0.5120	0.5160	0.5199	0.5239	0.5279	0.5319	0.5359
0.1	0.5398	0.5438	0.5478	0.5517	0.5557	0.5596	0.5636	0.5675	0.5714	0.5753
0.2	0.5793	0.5832	0.5871	0.5910	0.5948	0.5987	0.6026	0.6064	0.6103	0.6141
0.3	0.6179	0.6217	0.6255	0.6293	0.6331	0.6368	0.6406	0.6443	0.6480	0.6517
0,4	0.6554	0.6591	0.6628	0.6664	0.6700	0.6736	0.6772	0.6808	0.6844	0.6879
0.5	0.6915	0.6950	0.6985	0.7019	0.7054	0.7088	0.7123	0.7157	0.7190	0.7224
0.6	0.7257	0.7291	0.7324	0.7357	0.7389	0.7422	0.7454	0.7486	0.7517	0.7549
0.7	0.7580	0.7611	0.7642	0.7673	0.7704	0.7734	0.7764	0.7794	0.7823	0.7852
0.8	0.7881	0.7910	0.7939	0.7967	0.7995	0.8023	0.8051	0.8078	0.8106	0.8133
0.9	0.8159	0.8186	0.8212	0.8238	0.8264	0.8289	0.8315	0.8340	0.8365	0.8389
1.0	0.8413	0.8438	0.8461	0.8485	0.8508	0.8531	0.8554	0.8577	0.8599	0.8621
1.1	0.8643	0.8665	0.8686	0.8708	0.8729	0.8749	0.8770	0.8790	0.8810	0.8830
1.2	0.8849	0.8869	0.8888	0.8907	0.8925	0.8944	0.8962	0.8980	0.8997	0.9015
1.3	0.9032	0.9049	0.9066	0.9082	0.9099	0.9115	0.9131	0.9147	0.9162	0.9177
1.4	0.9192	0.9207	0.9222	0.9236	0.9251	0.9265	0.9278	0.9292	0.9306	0.9319
1.5	0.9332	0.9345	0.9357	0.9370	0.9382	0.9394	0.9406	0.9418	0.9429	0.9441
1.6	0.9452	0.9463	0.9474	0.9484	0.9495	0.9505	0.9515	0.9525	0.9535	0.9545
1,7	0.9554	0.9564	0.9573	0.9582	0.9591	0.9599	0.9608	0.9616	0.9625	0.9633
1.8	0.9641	0.9649	0.9656	0.9664	0.9671	0.9678	0.9686	0.9693	0.9699	0.9706
1.9	0.9713	0.9719	0.9726	0.9732	0.9738	0.9744	0.9750	0.9756	0.9761	0.9767
2.0	0.9772	0.9778	0.9783	0.9788	0.9793	0.9798	0.9803	0.9808	0.9812	0.9817
2.1	0.9821	0.9826	0.9830	0.9834	0.9838	0.9842	0.9846	0.9850	0.9854	0.9857
2.2	0.9861	0.9864	0.9868	0.9871	0.9875	0.9878	0.9881	0.9884	0.9887	0.9890
2.3	0.9893	0.9896	0.9898	0.9901	0.9904	0.9906	0.9909	0.9911	0.9913	0.9916
2.4	0.9918	0.9920	0.9922	0.9925	0.9927	0.9929	0.9931	0.9932	0.9934	0.9936
2.5	0.9938	0.9940	0.9941	0.9943	0.9945	0.9946	0.9948	0.9949	0.9951	0.9952
2.6	0.9953	0.9955	0.9956	0.9957	0.9959	0.9960	0.9961	0.9962	0.9963	0.9964
2.7	0.9965	0.9966	0.9967	0.9968	0.9969	0.9970	0.9971	0.9972	0.9973	0.9974
2.8	0.9974	0.9975	0.9976	0.9977	0.9977	0.9978	0.9979	0.9979	0.9980	0.9981
2.9	0.9981	0.9982	0.9982	0.9983	0.9984	0.9984	0.9985	0.9985	0.9986	0.9986
3.0	0.9987	0.9987	0.9987	0.9988	0.9988	0.9989	0.9989	0.9989	0.9990	0.9990
3.1	0.9990	0.9991	0.9991	0.9991	0.9992	0.9992	0.9992	0.9992	0.9993	0.9993
3.2	0.9993	0.9993	0.9994	0.9994	0.9994	0.9994	0.9994	0.9995	0.9995	0.9995
3.3	0.9995	0.9995	0.9995	0.9996	0.9996	0.9996	0.9996	0.9996	0.9996	0.9997
3.4	0.9997	0.9997	0.9997	0.9997	0.9997	0.9997	0.9997	0.9997	0.9997	0.9998

Table A.4 Critical Values $t_{v,\alpha}$ for the t-Distribution

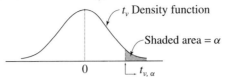

t_v Density function

Shaded area $= \alpha$

0          $t_{v,\alpha}$

v	α						
	.10	.05	.025	.01	.005	.001	.0005
1	3.078	6.314	12.706	31.821	63.657	318.31	636.62
2	1.886	2.920	4.303	6.965	9.925	22.326	31.598
3	1.638	2.353	3.182	4.541	5.841	10.213	12.924
4	1.533	2.132	2.776	3.747	4.604	7.173	8.610
5	1.476	2.015	2.571	3.365	4.032	5.893	6.869
6	1.440	1.943	2.447	3.143	3.707	5.208	5.959
7	1.415	1.895	2.365	2.998	3.499	4.785	5.408
8	1.397	1.860	2.306	2.896	3.355	4.501	5.041
9	1.383	1.833	2.262	2.821	3.250	4.297	4.781
10	1.372	1.812	2.228	2.764	3.169	4.144	4.587
11	1.363	1.796	2.201	2.718	3.106	4.025	4.437
12	1.356	1.782	2.179	2.681	3.055	3.930	4.318
13	1.350	1.771	2.160	2.650	3.012	3.852	4.221
14	1.345	1.761	2.145	2.624	2.977	3.787	4.140
15	1.341	1.753	2.131	2.602	2.947	3.733	4.073
16	1.337	1.746	2.120	2.583	2.921	3.686	4.015
17	1.333	1.740	2.110	2.567	2.898	3.646	3.965
18	1.330	1.734	2.101	2.552	2.878	3.610	3.922
19	1.328	1.729	2.093	2.539	2.861	3.579	3.883
20	1.325	1.725	2.086	2.528	2.845	3.552	3.850
21	1.323	1.721	2.080	2.518	2.831	3.527	3.819
22	1.321	1.717	2.074	2.508	2.819	3.505	3.792
23	1.319	1.714	2.069	2.500	2.807	3.485	3.767
24	1.318	1.711	2.064	2.492	2.797	3.467	3.745
25	1.316	1.708	2.060	2.485	2.787	3.450	3.725
26	1.315	1.706	2.056	2.479	2.779	3.435	3.707
27	1.314	1.703	2.052	2.473	2.771	3.421	3.690
28	1.313	1.701	2.048	2.467	2.763	3.408	3.674
29	1.311	1.699	2.045	1.462	2.756	3.396	3.659
30	1.310	1.697	2.042	2.457	2.750	3.385	3.646
40	1.303	1.684	2.021	2.423	2.704	3.307	3.551
60	1.296	1.671	2.000	2.390	2.660	3.232	3.460
120	1.289	1.658	1.980	2.358	2.617	3.160	3.373
∞	1.282	1.645	1.960	2.326	2.576	3.090	3.291

SOURCE: This table is produced with the kind permission of
the Trustees of Biometrika from E. S. Pearson and H. O. Hartly
(eds.) *The Biometrika Tables for Statisticians*, vol. 1, 3rd ed.
(1966) Biometrika.

Table A.5 Critical Values $\chi^2_{v,\alpha}$ for the Chi-square Distribution

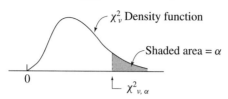

χ^2_v Density function

Shaded area = α

0

$\chi^2_{v,\alpha}$

v	.995	.99	.975	.95	.90	.10	.05	.025	.01	.005
1	0.000	0.000	0.001	0.004	0.016	2.706	3.843	5.025	6.637	7.882
2	0.010	0.020	0.051	0.103	0.211	4.605	5.992	7.378	9.210	10.597
3	0.072	0.115	0.216	0.352	0.584	6.251	7.815	9.348	11.344	12.837
4	0.207	0.297	0.484	0.711	1.064	7.779	9.488	11.143	13.277	14.860
5	0.412	0.554	0.831	1.145	1.610	9.236	11.070	12.832	15.085	16.748
6	0.676	0.872	1.237	1.635	2.204	10.645	12.592	14.440	16.812	18.548
7	0.989	1.239	1.690	2.167	2.833	12.017	14.067	16.012	18.474	20.276
8	1.344	1.646	2.180	2.733	3.490	13.362	15.507	17.534	20.090	21.954
9	1.735	2.088	2.700	3.325	4.168	14.684	16.919	19.022	21.665	23.587
10	2.156	2.558	3.247	3.940	4.865	15.987	18.307	20.483	23.209	25.188
11	2.603	3.053	3.816	4.575	5.578	17.275	19.675	21.920	24.724	26.755
12	3.074	3.571	4.404	5.226	6.304	18.549	21.026	23.337	26.217	28.300
13	3.565	4.107	5.009	5.892	7.041	19.812	22.362	24.735	27.687	29.817
14	4.075	4.660	5.629	6.571	7.790	21.064	23.685	26.119	29.141	31.319
15	4.600	5.229	6.262	7.261	8.547	22.307	24.996	27.488	30.577	32.799
16	5.142	5.812	6.908	7.962	9.312	23.542	26.296	28.845	32.000	34.267
17	5.697	6.407	7.564	8.682	10.085	24.769	27.587	30.190	33.408	35.716
18	6.265	7.015	8.231	9.390	10.865	25.989	28.869	31.526	34.805	37.156
19	6.843	7.632	8.906	10.117	11.651	27.203	30.143	32.852	36.190	38.580
20	7.434	8.260	9.591	10.851	12.443	28.412	31.410	34.170	37.566	39.997
21	8.033	8.897	10.283	11.591	13.240	29.615	32.670	35.478	38.930	41.399
22	8.643	9.542	10.982	12.338	14.042	30.813	33.924	36.781	40.289	42.796
23	9.260	10.195	11.688	13.090	14.848	32.007	35.172	38.075	41.637	44.179
24	9.886	10.856	12.401	13.848	15.659	33.196	36.415	39.364	42.980	45.558
25	10.519	11.523	13.120	14.611	16.473	34.381	37.652	40.646	44.313	46.925
26	11.160	12.198	13.844	15.379	17.292	35.563	38.885	41.923	45.642	48.290
27	11.807	12.878	14.573	16.151	18.114	36.741	40.113	43.194	46.962	49.642
28	12.461	13.565	15.308	16.928	18.939	37.916	41.337	44.461	48.278	50.993
29	13.120	14.256	16.147	17.708	19.768	39.087	42.557	45.772	49.586	52.333
30	13.787	14.954	16.791	18.493	20.599	40.256	43.773	46.979	50.892	53.672
31	14.457	15.655	17.538	19.280	21.433	41.422	44.985	48.231	52.190	55.000
32	15.134	16.362	18.291	20.072	22.271	42.585	46.194	49.480	53.486	56.328
33	15.814	17.073	19.046	20.866	23.110	43.745	47.400	50.724	54.774	57.646
34	16.501	17.789	19.806	21.664	23.952	44.903	48.602	51.966	56.061	58.964
35	17.191	18.508	20.569	22.465	24.796	46.059	49.802	53.203	57.340	60.272
36	17.887	19.233	21.336	23.269	25.643	47.212	50.998	54.437	58.619	61.581
37	18.584	19.960	22.105	24.075	26.492	48.363	52.192	55.667	59.891	62.880
38	19.289	20.691	22.878	24.884	27.343	49.513	53.384	56.896	61.162	64.181
39	19.994	21.425	23.654	Z5.695	28.196	50.660	54.572	58.119	62.420	65.473
40*	20.706	22.164	24.433	26.509	29.050	51.805	55.758	59.342	63.691	66.766

* For $v > 40$, $x^2_{v,\alpha} \simeq \left(1 - \frac{2}{9v} + z_\alpha \sqrt{\frac{2}{9v}}\right)^3$.

SOURCE: This table is produced with the kind permission of the Trustees of Biometrika from E. S. Pearson and H. O. Hartly (eds.) *The Biometrika Tables for Statisticians*, vol. 1, 3rd ed. (1966) Biometrika.

Table A.6 Critical Values $f_{v_1, v_2, \alpha}$ for the F-Distribution ($\alpha = .01$)

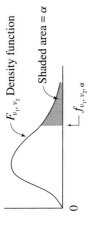

F_{v_1, v_2} Density function

Shaded area = α

$f_{v_1, v_2, \alpha}$

	Degrees of freedom for the numerator (v_1)																		
v_2	1	2	3	4	5	6	7	8	9	10	12	15	20	24	30	40	60	120	∞
1	4052.0	4999.5	5403.0	5625.0	5764.0	5859.0	5928.0	5982.0	6022.0	6056.0	6106.0	6157.0	6209.0	6235.0	6261.0	6287.0	6311.0	6339.0	6366.0
2	98.50	99.00	99.17	99.25	99.30	99.33	99.36	99.37	99.39	99.40	99.42	99.43	99.45	99.46	99.47	99.47	99.48	99.49	99.50
3	34.12	30.82	29.46	28.71	28.24	27.91	27.67	27.49	27.35	27.23	27.05	26.87	26.69	26.60	26.50	26.41	26.32	26.22	26.13
4	21.20	18.00	16.69	15.98	15.52	15.21	14.98	14.80	14.66	14.55	14.37	14.20	14.02	13.93	13.84	13.75	13.65	13.56	13.46
5	16.26	13.27	12.06	11.39	10.97	10.67	10.46	10.29	10.16	10.05	9.89	9.72	9.55	9.47	9.38	9.29	9.20	9.11	9.02
6	13.75	10.92	9.78	9.15	8.75	8.47	8.26	8.10	7.98	7.87	7.72	7.56	7.40	7.31	7.23	7.14	7.06	6.97	6.88
7	12.25	9.55	8.45	7.85	7.46	7.19	6.99	6.84	6.72	6.62	6.47	6.31	6.16	6.07	5.99	5.91	5.82	5.74	5.65
8	11.26	8.65	7.59	7.01	6.63	6.37	6.18	6.03	5.91	5.81	5.67	5.52	5.36	5.28	5.20	5.12	5.03	4.95	4.86
9	10.56	8.02	6.99	6.42	6.06	5.80	5.61	5.47	5.35	5.26	5.11	4.96	4.81	4.73	4.65	4.57	4.48	4.40	4.31
10	10.04	7.56	6.55	5.99	5.64	5.39	5.20	5.06	4.94	4.85	4.71	4.56	4.41	4.33	4.25	4.17	4.08	4.00	3.91
11	9.65	7.21	6.22	5.67	5.32	5.07	4.89	4.74	4.63	4.54	4.40	4.25	4.10	4.02	3.94	3.86	3.78	3.69	3.60
12	9.33	6.93	5.95	5.41	5.06	4.82	4.64	4.50	4.39	4.30	4.16	4.01	3.86	3.78	3.70	3.62	3.54	3.45	3.36
13	9.07	6.70	5.74	5.21	4.86	4.62	4.44	4.30	4.19	4.10	3.96	3.82	3.66	3.59	3.51	3.43	3.34	3.25	3.17
14	8.86	6.51	5.56	5.04	4.69	4.46	4.28	4.14	4.03	3.94	3.80	3.66	3.51	3.43	3.35	3.27	3.18	3.09	3.00
15	8.68	6.36	5.42	4.89	4.56	4.32	4.14	4.00	3.89	3.80	3.67	3.52	3.37	3.29	3.21	3.13	3.05	2.96	2.87
16	8.53	6.23	5.29	4.77	4.44	4.20	4.03	3.89	3.78	3.69	3.55	3.41	3.26	3.18	3.10	3.02	2.93	2.84	2.75
17	8.40	6.11	5.18	4.67	4.34	4.10	3.93	3.79	3.68	3.59	3.46	3.31	3.16	3.08	3.00	2.92	2.83	2.75	2.65
18	8.29	6.01	5.09	4.58	4.25	4.01	3.84	3.71	3.60	3.51	3.37	3.23	3.08	3.00	2.92	2.84	2.75	2.66	2.57
19	8.18	5.93	5.01	4.50	4.17	3.94	3.77	3.63	3.52	3.43	3.30	3.15	3.00	2.92	2.84	2.76	2.67	2.58	2.49
20	8.10	5.85	4.94	4.43	4.10	3.87	3.70	3.56	3.46	3.37	3.23	3.09	2.94	2.86	2.78	2.69	2.61	2.52	2.42
21	8.02	5.78	4.87	4.37	4.04	3.81	3.64	3.51	3.40	3.31	3.17	3.03	2.88	2.80	2.72	2.64	2.55	2.46	2.36
22	7.95	5.72	4.82	4.31	3.99	3.76	3.59	3.45	3.35	3.26	3.12	2.98	2.83	2.75	2.67	2.58	2.50	2.40	2.31
23	7.88	5.66	4.76	4.26	3.94	3.71	3.54	3.41	3.30	3.21	3.07	2.93	2.78	2.70	2.62	2.54	2.45	2.35	2.26
24	7.82	5.61	4.72	4.22	3.90	3.67	3.50	3.36	3.26	3.17	3.03	2.89	2.74	2.66	2.58	2.49	2.40	2.31	2.21
25	7.77	5.57	4.68	4.18	3.85	3.63	3.46	3.32	3.22	3.13	2.99	2.85	2.70	2.62	2.54	2.45	2.36	2.27	2.17
26	7.72	5.53	4.64	4.14	3.82	3.59	3.42	3.29	3.18	3.09	2.96	2.81	2.66	2.58	2.50	2.42	2.33	2.23	2.13
27	7.68	5.49	4.60	4.11	3.78	3.56	3.39	3.26	3.15	3.06	2.93	2.78	2.63	2.55	2.47	2.38	2.29	2.20	2.10
28	7.64	5.45	4.57	4.07	3.75	3.53	3.36	3.23	3.12	3.03	2.90	2.75	2.60	2.52	2.44	2.35	2.26	2.17	2.06
29	7.60	5.42	4.54	4.04	3.73	3.50	3.33	3.20	3.09	3.00	2.87	2.73	2.57	2.49	2.41	2.33	2.23	2.14	2.03
30	7.56	5.39	4.51	4.02	3.70	3.47	3.30	3.17	3.07	2.98	2.84	2.70	2.55	2.47	2.39	2.30	2.21	2.11	2.01
40	7.31	5.18	4.31	3.83	3.51	3.29	3.12	2.99	2.89	2.80	2.66	2.52	2.37	2.29	2.20	2.11	2.02	1.92	1.80
60	7.08	4.98	4.13	3.65	3.34	3.12	2.95	2.82	2.72	2.63	2.50	2.35	2.20	2.12	2.03	1.94	1.84	1.73	1.60
120	6.85	4.79	3.95	3.48	3.17	2.96	2.79	2.66	2.56	2.47	2.34	2.19	2.03	1.95	1.86	1.76	1.66	1.53	1.38
∞	6.63	4.61	3.78	3.32	3.02	2.80	2.64	2.51	2.41	2.32	2.18	2.04	1.88	1.79	1.70	1.59	1.47	1.32	1.00

Degrees of freedom for the denominator (v_2)

Table A.6 Critical Values $f_{v_1,v_2,\alpha}$ for the F-Distribution ($\alpha = .05$) (cont.)

F_{v_1,v_2} Density function

Shaded area $= \alpha$

$0 \qquad f_{v_1,v_2,\alpha}$

	\multicolumn{19}{c}{Degrees of freedom for the numerator (v_1)}
v_2	1	2	3	4	5	6	7	8	9	10	12	15	20	24	30	40	60	120	∞
1	161.4	199.5	215.7	224.6	230.2	234.0	236.8	238.8	240.5	241.9	243.9	245.9	248.0	249.1	250.1	251.1	252.2	253.3	254.3
2	18.51	19.00	19.16	19.25	19.30	19.33	19.35	19.37	19.38	19.40	19.41	19.43	19.45	19.45	19.46	19.47	19.48	19.49	19.50
3	10.13	9.55	9.28	9.12	9.01	8.94	8.89	8.85	8.81	8.79	8.74	8.70	8.66	8.64	8.62	8.59	8.57	8.55	8.53
4	7.71	6.94	6.59	6.39	6.26	6.16	6.09	6.04	6.00	5.96	5.91	5.86	5.80	5.77	5.75	5.72	5.69	5.66	5.63
5	6.61	5.79	5.41	5.19	5.05	4.95	4.88	4.82	4.77	4.74	4.68	4.62	4.56	4.53	4.50	4.46	4.43	4.40	4.36
6	5.99	5.14	4.76	4.53	4.39	4.28	4.21	4.15	4.10	4.06	4.00	3.94	3.87	3.84	3.81	3.77	3.74	3.70	3.67
7	5.59	4.74	4.35	4.12	3.97	3.87	3.79	3.73	3.68	3.64	3.57	3.51	3.44	3.41	3.38	3.34	3.30	3.27	3.23
8	5.32	4.46	4.07	3.84	3.69	3.58	3.50	3.44	3.39	3.35	3.28	3.22	3.15	3.12	3.08	3.04	3.01	2.97	2.93
9	5.12	4.26	3.86	3.63	3.48	3.37	3.29	3.23	3.18	3.14	3.07	3.01	2.94	2.90	2.86	2.83	2.79	2.75	2.71
10	4.96	4.10	3.71	3.48	3.33	3.22	3.14	3.07	3.02	2.98	2.91	2.85	2.77	2.74	2.70	2.66	2.62	2.58	2.54
11	4.84	3.98	3.59	3.36	3.20	3.09	3.01	2.95	2.90	2.85	2.79	2.72	2.65	2.61	2.57	2.53	2.49	2.45	2.40
12	4.75	3.89	3.49	3.26	3.11	3.00	2.91	2.85	2.80	2.75	2.69	2.62	2.54	2.51	2.47	2.43	2.38	2.34	2.30
13	4.67	3.81	3.41	3.18	3.03	2.92	2.83	2.77	2.71	2.67	2.60	2.53	2.46	2.42	2.38	2.34	2.30	2.25	2.21
14	4.60	3.74	3.34	3.11	2.96	2.85	2.76	2.70	2.65	2.60	2.53	2.46	2.39	2.35	2.31	2.27	2.22	2.18	2.13
15	4.54	3.68	3.29	3.06	2.90	2.79	2.71	2.64	2.59	2.54	2.48	2.40	2.33	2.29	2.25	2.20	2.16	2.11	2.07
16	4.49	3.63	3.24	3.01	2.85	2.74	2.66	2.59	2.54	2.49	2.42	2.35	2.28	2.24	2.19	2.15	2.11	2.06	2.01
17	4.45	3.59	3.20	2.96	2.81	2.69	2.61	2.55	2.49	2.45	2.38	2.31	2.23	2.19	2.15	2.10	2.06	2.01	1.96
18	4.41	3.55	3.16	2.93	2.77	2.66	2.58	2.51	2.46	2.41	2.34	2.27	2.19	2.15	2.11	2.06	2.02	1.97	1.92
19	4.38	3.52	3.13	2.90	2.74	2.63	2.54	2.48	2.42	2.38	2.31	2.23	2.16	2.11	2.07	2.03	1.98	1.93	1.88
20	4.35	3.49	3.10	2.87	2.71	2.60	2.51	2.45	2.39	2.35	2.28	2.20	2.12	2.08	2.04	1.99	1.95	1.90	1.84
21	4.32	3.47	3.07	2.84	2.68	2.57	2.49	2.42	2.37	2.32	2.25	2.18	2.10	2.05	2.01	1.96	1.92	1.87	1.81
22	4.30	3.44	3.05	2.82	2.66	2.55	2.46	2.40	2.34	2.30	2.23	2.15	2.07	2.03	1.98	1.94	1.89	1.84	1.78
23	4.28	3.42	3.03	2.80	2.64	2.53	2.44	2.37	2.32	2.27	2.20	2.13	2.05	2.01	1.96	1.91	1.86	1.81	1.76
24	4.26	3.40	3.01	2.78	2.62	2.51	2.42	2.36	2.30	2.25	2.18	2.11	2.03	1.98	1.94	1.89	1.84	1.79	1.73
25	4.24	3.39	2.99	2.76	2.60	2.49	2.40	2.34	2.28	2.24	2.16	2.09	2.01	1.96	1.92	1.87	1.82	1.77	1.71
26	4.23	3.37	2.98	2.74	2.59	2.47	2.39	2.32	2.27	2.22	2.15	2.07	1.99	1.95	1.90	1.85	1.80	1.75	1.69
27	4.21	3.35	2.96	2.73	2.57	2.46	2.37	2.31	2.25	2.20	2.13	2.06	1.97	1.93	1.88	1.84	1.79	1.73	1.67
28	4.20	3.34	2.95	2.71	2.56	2.45	2.36	2.29	2.24	2.19	2.12	2.04	1.96	1.91	1.87	1.82	1.77	1.71	1.65
29	4.18	3.33	2.93	2.70	2.55	2.43	2.35	2.28	2.22	2.18	2.10	2.03	1.94	1.90	1.85	1.81	1.75	1.70	1.64
30	4.17	3.32	2.92	2.69	2.53	2.42	2.33	2.27	2.21	2.16	2.09	2.01	1.93	1.89	1.84	1.79	1.74	1.68	1.62
40	4.08	3.23	2.84	2.61	2.45	2.34	2.25	2.18	2.12	2.08	2.00	1.92	1.84	1.79	1.74	1.69	1.64	1.58	1.51
60	4.00	3.15	2.76	2.53	2.37	2.25	2.17	2.10	2.04	1.99	1.92	1.84	1.75	1.70	1.65	1.59	1.53	1.47	1.39
120	3.92	3.07	2.68	2.45	2.29	2.17	2.09	2.02	1.96	1.91	1.83	1.75	1.66	1.61	1.55	1.50	1.43	1.35	1.25
∞	3.84	3.00	2.60	2.37	2.21	2.10	2.01	1.94	1.88	1.83	1.75	1.67	1.57	1.52	1.46	1.39	1.32	1.22	1.00

Degrees of freedom for the denominator (v_2)

Table A.6 Critical Values $f_{v_1,v_2,\alpha}$ for the F-Distribution ($\alpha = .10$) (cont.)

F_{v_1,v_2} Density function

Shaded area = α

$f_{v_1,v_2,\alpha}$

Degrees of freedom for the numerator (v_1)

v_2	1	2	3	4	5	6	7	8	9	10	12	15	20	24	30	40	60	120	∞
1	39.86	49.50	53.59	55.83	57.24	58.20	58.91	59.44	59.86	60.19	60.71	61.22	61.74	62.00	62.26	62.53	62.79	63.06	63.33
2	8.53	9.00	9.16	9.24	9.29	9.33	9.35	9.37	9.38	9.39	9.41	9.42	9.44	9.45	9.46	9.47	9.47	9.48	9.49
3	5.54	5.46	5.39	5.34	5.31	5.28	5.27	5.25	5.24	5.23	5.22	5.20	5.18	5.18	5.17	5.16	5.15	5.14	5.13
4	4.54	4.32	4.19	4.11	4.05	4.01	3.98	3.95	3.94	3.92	3.90	3.87	3.84	3.83	3.82	3.80	3.79	3.78	3.76
5	4.06	3.78	3.62	3.52	3.45	3.40	3.37	3.34	3.32	3.30	3.27	3.24	3.21	3.19	3.17	3.16	3.14	3.12	3.10
6	3.78	3.46	3.29	3.18	3.11	3.05	3.01	2.98	2.96	2.94	2.90	2.87	2.84	2.82	2.80	2.78	2.76	2.74	2.72
7	3.59	3.26	3.07	2.96	2.88	2.83	2.78	2.75	2.72	2.70	2.67	2.63	2.59	2.58	2.56	2.54	2.51	2.49	2.47
8	3.46	3.11	2.92	2.81	2.73	2.67	2.62	2.59	2.56	2.54	2.50	2.46	2.42	2.40	2.38	2.36	2.34	2.32	2.29
9	3.36	3.01	2.81	2.69	2.61	2.55	2.51	2.47	2.44	2.42	2.38	2.34	2.30	2.28	2.25	2.23	2.21	2.18	2.16
10	3.29	2.92	2.73	2.61	2.52	2.46	2.41	2.38	2.35	2.32	2.28	2.24	2.20	2.18	2.16	2.13	2.11	2.08	2.06
11	3.23	2.86	2.66	2.54	2.45	2.39	2.34	2.30	2.27	2.25	2.21	2.17	2.12	2.10	2.08	2.05	2.03	2.00	1.97
12	3.18	2.81	2.61	2.48	2.39	2.33	2.28	2.24	2.21	2.19	2.15	2.10	2.06	2.04	2.01	1.99	1.96	1.93	1.90
13	3.14	2.76	2.56	2.43	2.35	2.28	2.23	2.20	2.16	2.14	2.10	2.05	2.01	1.98	1.96	1.93	1.90	1.88	1.85
14	3.10	2.73	2.52	2.39	2.31	2.24	2.19	2.15	2.12	2.10	2.05	2.01	1.96	1.94	1.91	1.89	1.86	1.83	1.80
15	3.07	2.70	2.49	2.36	2.27	2.21	2.16	2.12	2.09	2.06	2.02	1.97	1.92	1.90	1.87	1.85	1.82	1.79	1.76
16	3.05	2.67	2.46	2.33	2.24	2.18	2.13	2.09	2.06	2.03	1.99	1.94	1.89	1.87	1.84	1.81	1.78	1.75	1.72
17	3.03	2.64	2.44	2.31	2.22	2.15	2.10	2.06	2.03	2.00	1.96	1.91	1.86	1.84	1.81	1.78	1.75	1.72	1.69
18	3.01	2.62	2.42	2.29	2.20	2.13	2.08	2.04	2.00	1.98	1.93	1.89	1.84	1.81	1.78	1.75	1.72	1.69	1.66
19	2.99	2.61	2.40	2.27	2.18	2.11	2.06	2.02	1.98	1.96	1.91	1.86	1.81	1.79	1.76	1.73	1.70	1.67	1.63
20	2.97	2.59	2.38	2.25	2.16	2.09	2.04	2.00	1.96	1.94	1.89	1.84	1.79	1.77	1.74	1.71	1.68	1.64	1.61
21	2.96	2.57	2.36	2.23	2.14	2.08	2.02	1.98	1.95	1.92	1.87	1.83	1.78	1.75	1.72	1.69	1.66	1.62	1.59
22	2.95	2.56	2.35	2.22	2.13	2.06	2.01	1.97	1.93	1.90	1.86	1.81	1.76	1.73	1.70	1.67	1.64	1.60	1.57
23	2.94	2.55	2.34	2.21	2.11	2.05	1.99	1.95	1.92	1.89	1.84	1.80	1.74	1.72	1.69	1.66	1.62	1.59	1.55
24	2.93	2.54	2.33	2.19	2.10	2.04	1.98	1.94	1.91	1.88	1.83	1.78	1.73	1.70	1.67	1.64	1.61	1.57	1.53
25	2.92	2.53	2.32	2.18	2.09	2.02	1.97	1.93	1.89	1.87	1.82	1.77	1.72	1.69	1.66	1.63	1.59	1.56	1.52
26	2.91	2.52	2.31	2.17	2.08	2.01	1.96	1.92	1.88	1.86	1.81	1.76	1.71	1.68	1.65	1.61	1.58	1.54	1.50
27	2.90	2.51	2.30	2.17	2.07	2.00	1.95	1.91	1.87	1.85	1.80	1.75	1.70	1.67	1.64	1.60	1.57	1.53	1.49
28	2.89	2.50	2.29	2.16	2.06	2.00	1.94	1.90	1.87	1.84	1.79	1.74	1.69	1.66	1.63	1.59	1.56	1.52	1.48
29	2.89	2.50	2.28	2.15	2.06	1.99	1.93	1.89	1.86	1.83	1.78	1.73	1.68	1.65	1.62	1.58	1.55	1.51	1.47
30	2.88	2.49	2.28	2.14	2.03	1.98	1.93	1.88	1.85	1.82	1.77	1.72	1.67	1.64	1.61	1.57	1.54	1.50	1.46
40	2.84	2.44	2.23	2.09	2.00	1.93	1.87	1.83	1.79	1.76	1.71	1.66	1.61	1.57	1.54	1.51	1.47	1.42	1.38
60	2.79	2.39	2.18	2.04	1.95	1.87	1.82	1.77	1.74	1.71	1.66	1.60	1.54	1.51	1.48	1.44	1.40	1.35	1.29
120	2.75	2.35	2.13	1.99	1.90	1.82	1.77	1.72	1.68	1.65	1.60	1.55	1.48	1.45	1.41	1.37	1.32	1.26	1.19
∞	2.71	2.30	2.08	1.94	1.85	1.77	1.72	1.67	1.63	1.60	1.55	1.49	1.42	1.38	1.34	1.30	1.24	1.17	1.00

Degrees of freedom for the denominator (v_2)

SOURCE: This table is produced with the kind permission of the Trustees of Biometrika from E. S. Pearson and H. O. Hartly (eds.) *The Biometrika Tables for Statisticians*, vol. 1, 3rd ed. (1966) Biometrika.

Table A.7 Critical Values $q_{a,v,\alpha}$ for the Studentized Range Distribution

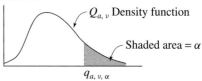

v	α	\multicolumn{9}{c}{a}
		2	3	4	5	6	7	8	9	10
5	.01	5.70	6.98	7.80	8.42	8.91	9.32	9.67	9.97	10.24
	.05	3.64	4.60	5.22	5.67	6.03	6.33	6.58	6.80	6.99
	.10	2.09	3.72	4.26	4.66	4.98	5.24	5.46	5.65	5.82
8	.01	4.75	5.64	6.20	6.62	6.96	7.24	7.47	7.68	7.86
	.05	3.26	4.04	4.53	4.89	5.17	5.40	5.60	5.77	5.92
	.10	1.98	3.37	3.83	4.17	4.43	4.65	4.83	4.99	5.13
10	.01	4.48	5.27	5.77	6.14	6.43	6.67	6.87	7.05	7.21
	.05	3.15	3.88	4.33	4.65	4.91	5.12	5.30	5.46	5.60
	.10	1.94	3.27	3.70	4.02	4.26	4.47	4.64	4.78	4.91
12	.01	4.32	5.05	5.50	5.84	6.10	6.32	6.51	6.67	6.81
	.05	3.08	3.77	4.20	4.51	4.75	4.95	5.12	5.27	5.39
	.10	1.92	3.20	3.62	3.92	4.16	4.35	4.51	4.65	4.78
14	.01	4.21	4.89	5.32	5.63	5.88	6.08	6.26	6.41	6.54
	.05	3.03	3.70	4.11	4.41	4.64	4.83	4.99	5.13	5.25
	.10	1.90	3.16	3.56	3.85	4.08	4.27	4.42	4.56	4.68
16	.01	4.13	4.79	5.19	5.49	5.72	5.92	6.08	6.22	6.35
	.05	3.00	3.65	4.05	4.33	4.56	4.74	4.90	5.03	5.15
	.10	1.89	3.12	3.52	3.80	4.03	4.21	4.36	4.49	4.61
18	.01	4.07	4.70	5.09	5.38	5.60	5.79	5.94	6.08	6.20
	.05	2.97	3.61	4.00	4.28	4.49	4.67	4.82	4.96	5.07
	.10	1.88	3.10	3.49	3.77	3.98	4.17	4.31	4.44	4.55
20	.01	4.02	4.64	5.02	5.29	5.51	5.69	5.84	5.97	6.09
	.05	2.95	3.58	3.96	4.23	4.45	4.62	4.77	4.90	5.01
	.10	1.87	3.08	3.46	3.74	3.95	4.13	4.27	4.40	4.51
24	.01	3.96	4.55	4.91	5.17	5.37	5.54	5.69	5.81	5.92
	.05	2.92	3.53	3.90	4.17	4.37	4.54	4.68	4.81	4.92
	.10	1.86	3.05	3.42	3.69	3.90	4.07	4.21	4.34	4.45
30	.01	3.89	4.45	4.80	5.05	5.24	5.40	5.54	5.65	5.76
	.05	2.89	3.49	3.85	4.10	4.30	4.46	4.60	4.72	4.82
	.10	1.85	3.02	3.39	3.65	3.85	4.02	4.16	4.28	4.38
40	.01	3.82	4.37	4.70	4.93	5.11	5.26	5.39	5.50	5.60
	.05	2.86	3.44	3.79	4.04	4.23	4.39	4.52	4.63	4.73
	.10	1.84	2.99	3.35	3.61	3.80	3.97	4.10	4.22	4.32
60	.01	3.76	4.28	4.59	4.82	4.99	5.13	5.25	5.36	5.45
	.05	2.83	3.40	3.74	3.98	4.16	4.31	4.44	4.55	4.65
	.10	1.83	2.96	3.31	3.56	3.76	3.92	4.04	4.16	4.25
120	.01	3.70	4.20	4.50	4.71	4.87	5.01	5.12	5.21	5.30
	.05	2.80	3.36	3.68	3.92	4.10	4.24	4.36	4.47	4.56
	.10	1.82	2.93	3.28	3.52	3.71	3.86	3.99	4.10	4.19
∞	.01	3.64	4.12	4.40	4.60	4.76	4.88	4.99	5.08	5.16
	.05	2.77	3.31	3.63	3.86	4.03	4.17	4.29	4.39	4.47
	.10	1.81	2.90	3.24	3.48	3.66	3.81	3.93	4.04	4.13

Table A.8 One-Sided Multivariate t Critical Points $t_{k,\nu,\alpha}$ for Common Correlation $\rho = 0.5$

ν	α	k								
		2	3	4	5	6	7	8	9	10
5	.01	3.900	4.211	4.429	4.597	4.733	4.846	4.944	5.030	5.106
	.05	2.440	2.681	2.848	2.976	3.078	3.163	3.236	3.300	3.356
	.10	1.873	2.094	2.245	2.359	2.451	2.527	2.592	2.649	2.699
10	.01	3.115	3.314	3.453	3.559	3.644	3.715	3.777	3.830	3.878
	.05	2.151	2.338	2.466	2.562	2.640	2.704	2.759	2.807	2.849
	.10	1.713	1.899	2.024	2.119	2.194	2.256	2.309	2.355	2.396
15	.01	2.908	3.080	3.198	3.289	3.362	3.422	3.474	3.520	3.560
	.05	2.067	2.239	2.356	2.444	2.515	2.573	2.623	2.667	2.705
	.10	1.665	1.840	1.959	2.047	2.118	2.716	2.225	2.268	2.306
20	.01	2.813	2.972	3.082	3.166	3.233	3.289	3.337	3.378	3.416
	.05	2.027	2.192	2.304	2.389	2.456	2.512	2.559	2.601	2.637
	.10	1.642	1.813	1.927	2.013	2.081	2.137	2.185	2.227	2.263
25	.01	2.758	2.911	3.016	3.095	3.159	3.212	3.258	3.298	3.333
	.05	2.004	2.165	2.274	2.356	2.422	2.476	2.522	2.562	2.598
	.10	1.629	1.796	1.909	1.993	2.060	2.115	2.162	2.202	2.238
30	.01	2.723	2.871	2.973	3.050	3.111	3.163	3.207	3.245	3.279
	.05	1.989	2.147	2.255	2.335	2.399	2.453	2.498	2.537	2.572
	.10	1.620	1.786	1.897	1.980	2.046	2.100	2.146	2.186	2.222
35	.01	2.698	2.843	2.942	3.018	3.078	3.128	3.171	3.209	3.242
	.05	1.978	2.135	2.241	2.320	2.384	2.436	2.481	2.519	2.554
	.10	1.614	1.778	1.888	1.971	2.036	2.090	2.135	2.175	2.210
40	.01	2.680	2.822	2.920	2.994	3.053	3.103	3.145	3.181	3.214
	.05	1.970	2.125	2.230	2.309	2.372	2.424	2.468	2.506	2.540
	.10	1.609	1.772	1.882	1.964	2.028	2.082	2.127	2.167	2.201
50	.01	2.655	2.794	2.889	2.962	3.019	3.068	3.109	3.145	3.176
	.05	1.959	2.112	2.216	2.294	2.356	2.407	2.450	2.488	2.521
	.10	1.603	1.764	1.873	1.954	2.018	2.071	2.116	2.155	2.189
100	.01	2.0605	2.738	2.829	2.898	2.953	2.999	3.038	3.072	3.102
	.05	1.938	2.087	2.188	2.263	2.324	2.373	2.415	2.452	2.484
	.10	1.590	1.749	1.885	1.935	1.998	2.050	2.094	2.132	2.166
200	.01	2.581	2.711	2.800	2.867	2.921	2.966	3.004	3.037	3.006
	.05	1.927	2.074	2.174	2.249	2.308	2.357	2.398	2.434	2.466
	.10	1.583	1.741	1.847	1.926	1.988	2.039	2.083	2.121	2.154
∞	.01	2.558	2.685	2.772	2.837	2.889	2.933	2.970	3.002	3.031
	.05	1.916	2.062	2.160	2.234	2.292	2.340	2.381	2.417	2.448
	.10	1.577	1.734	1.838	1.916	1.978	2.029	2.072	2.109	2.148

SOURCE: Adapted from R. E. Bechhofer and C. W. Dunnett (1988), "Percentage points of multivariate t-distribution," Selected Tables in Mathematical Statistics, **11**, Providence, RI: American Mathematical Society.

Table A.9 Two-Sided Multivariate t Critical Points $|t|_{k,v,\alpha}$ for Common Correlation $\rho = 0.5$

v	α	k								
		2	3	4	5	6	7	8	9	10
5	.01	4.627	4.975	5.219	5.406	5.557	5.683	5.792	5.887	5.971
	.05	3.030	3.293	3.476	3.615	3.727	3.821	3.900	3.970	4.032
	.10	2.433	2.669	2.832	2.956	3.055	3.137	3.207	3.268	3.322
10	.01	3.531	3.739	3.883	3.994	4.084	4.159	4.223	4.279	4.329
	.05	2.568	2.759	2.890	2.990	3.070	3.137	3.194	3.244	3.288
	.10	2.149	2.335	2.463	2.559	2.636	2.700	2.755	2.802	2.844
15	.01	3.253	3.426	3.547	3.639	3.713	3.776	3.829	3.875	3.917
	.05	2.439	2.610	2.727	2.816	2.887	2.946	2.997	3.041	3.080
	.10	2.066	2.238	2.355	2.443	2.514	2.572	2.622	2.665	2.703
20	.01	3.127	3.285	3.395	3.479	3.547	3.603	3.651	3.694	3.731
	.05	2.379	2.540	2.651	2.735	2.802	2.857	2.905	2.946	2.983
	.10	2.027	2.192	2.304	2.388	2.455	2.511	2.559	2.600	2.636
25	.01	3.055	3.205	3.309	3.388	3.452	3.505	3.551	3.591	3.626
	.05	2.344	2.500	2.607	2.688	2.752	2.806	2.852	2.891	2.927
	.10	2.004	2.165	2.274	2.356	2.421	2.476	2.522	2.562	2.597
30	.01	3.009	3.154	3.254	3.330	3.391	3.442	3.486	3.524	3.558
	.05	2.321	2.474	2.578	2.657	2.720	2.772	2.817	2.856	2.890
	.10	1.989	2.147	2.254	2.335	2.399	2.452	2.498	2.537	2.572
35	.01	2.976	3.118	3.215	3.289	3.349	3.398	3.441	3.478	3.511
	.05	2.305	2.455	2.558	2.635	2.697	2.748	2.792	2.830	2.864
	.10	1.978	2.135	2.240	2.320	2.383	2.436	2.480	2.519	2.553
40	.01	2.952	3.091	3.186	3.259	3.317	3.366	3.408	3.444	3.476
	.05	2.293	2.441	2.543	2.619	2.680	2.731	2.774	2.812	2.845
	.10	1.970	2.125	2.230	2.309	2.372	2.424	2.468	2.506	2.540
50	.01	2.920	3.054	3.147	3.218	3.274	3.321	3.362	3.397	3.428
	.05	2.276	2.422	2.522	2.597	2.657	2.707	2.749	2.786	2.819
	.10	1.959	2.112	2.216	2.294	2.355	2.407	2.450	2.488	2.521
100	.01	2.856	2.983	3.071	3.137	3.191	3.235	3.273	3.306	3.335
	.05	2.244	2.385	2.481	2.554	2.611	2.659	2.700	2.735	2.767
	.10	1.938	2.087	2.188	2.263	2.323	2.373	2.415	2.452	2.484
200	.01	2.825	2.949	3.034	3.098	3.150	3.193	3.230	3.262	3.291
	.05	2.228	2.367	2.461	2.532	2.589	2.636	2.676	2.711	2.741
	.10	1.927	2.074	2.174	2.249	2.308	2.357	2.398	2.434	2.466
∞	.01	2.794	2.915	2.998	3.060	3.110	3.152	3.188	3.219	3.246
	.05	2.212	2.349	2.442	2.511	2.567	2.613	2.652	2.686	2.716
	.10	1.916	2.062	2.160	2.234	2.292	2.340	2.381	2.417	2.488

SOURCE: Adapted from Bechhofer and Dunnett, *op. cit.*

Table A.10 Upper-Tail Probabilities of the Null Distribution of the Wilcoxon
Signed Rank Statistic

n	w	$P(W \geq w \mid H_0)$	n	w	$P(W \geq w \mid H_0)$
3	6	0.125		78	0.011
4	9	0.125		79	0.009
	10	0.062		81	0.005
5	13	0.094	14	73	0.108
	14	0.062		74	0.097
	15	0.031		79	0.052
6	17	0.109		84	0.025
	19	0.047		89	0.010
	20	0.031		92	0.005
	21	0.016	15	83	0.104
7	22	0.109		84	0.094
	24	0.055		89	0.053
	26	0.023		90	0.047
	28	0.008		95	0.024
8	28	0.098		100	0.011
	30	0.055		101	0.009
	32	0.027		104	0.005
	34	0.012	16	93	0.106
	35	0.008		94	0.096
	36	0.004		100	0.052
9	34	0.102		106	0.025
	37	0.049		112	0.011
	39	0.027		113	0.009
	42	0.010		116	0.005
	44	0.004	17	104	0.103
10	41	0.097		105	0.095
	44	0.053		112	0.049
	47	0.024		118	0.005
	50	0.010		125	0.010
	52	0.005		129	0.005
11	48	0.103	18	116	0.098
	52	0.051		124	0.049
	55	0.027		131	0.024
	59	0.009		138	0.010
	61	0.005		143	0.005
12	56	0.102	19	128	0.098
	60	0.055		136	0.052
	61	0.046		137	0.048
	64	0.026		144	0.025
	68	0.010		152	0.010
	71	0.005		157	0.005
13	64	0.108	20	140	0.101
	65	0.095		150	0.049
	69	0.055		158	0.024
	70	0.047		167	0.010
	74	0.024		172	0.005

SOURCE: Adapted from W. J. Dixon and F. J. Massey, Jr. (1969), *Introduction to Statistical Methods*, 3rd ed. New York: McGraw-Hill.

Table A.11 Upper-Tail Probabilities of the Null Distribution of the Wilcoxon-Mann-Whitney Statistic

n_1	n_2	w_1	u_1	$P(W \geq w_1)$ $=$ $P(U \geq u_1)$	n_1	n_2	w_1	u_1	$P(W \geq w_1)$ $=$ $P(U \geq u_1)$	n_1	n_2	w_1	u_1	$P(W \geq w_1)$ $=$ $P(U \geq u_1)$
3	3	15	9	0.050	4	9	44	34	0.006	6	10	66	45	0.059
	4	17	11	0.057		10	42	32	0.053		10	69	48	0.028
	4	18	12	0.029		10	44	34	0.027		10	72	51	0.011
	5	20	14	0.036		10	46	36	0.012		10	74	53	0.005
	5	21	15	0.018		10	47	37	0.007	7	7	66	38	0.049
	6	22	16	0.048	5	5	36	21	0.048		7	68	40	0.027
	6	23	17	0.024		5	37	22	0.028		7	71	43	0.009
	6	24	18	0.012		5	39	24	0.008		7	72	44	0.006
	7	24	18	0.058		5	40	25	0.004		8	71	43	0.047
	7	26	20	0.017		6	40	25	0.041		8	73	45	0.027
	7	27	21	0.008		6	41	26	0.026		8	76	48	0.010
	8	27	21	0.042		6	43	28	0.009		8	78	50	0.005
	8	28	22	0.024		6	44	29	0.004		9	75	47	0.057
	8	29	23	0.012		7	43	28	0.053		9	78	50	0.027
	8	30	24	0.006		7	45	30	0.024		9	81	53	0.011
	9	29	23	0.050		7	47	32	0.009		9	83	55	0.006
	9	31	25	0.018		7	48	33	0.005		10	80	52	0.054
	9	32	26	0.009		8	47	32	0.047		10	83	55	0.028
	9	33	27	0.005		8	49	34	0.023		10	87	59	0.009
	10	31	25	0.056		8	51	36	0.009		10	89	61	0.005
	10	33	27	0.024		8	52	37	0.005	8	8	84	48	0.052
	10	34	28	0.007		9	50	35	0.056		8	87	51	0.025
	10	35	29	0.003		9	53	38	0.021		8	90	54	0.010
4	4	24	14	0.057		9	55	40	0.009		8	92	56	0.005
	4	25	15	0.029		9	56	41	0.006		9	89	53	0.057
	4	26	16	0.014		10	54	39	0.050		9	93	57	0.023
	5	27	17	0.056		10	56	41	0.027		9	96	60	0.010
	5	28	18	0.032		10	59	44	0.010		9	98	62	0.006
	5	29	19	0.016		10	60	45	0.006		10	95	59	0.051
	5	30	20	0.008	6	6	50	29	0.047		10	98	62	0.027
	6	30	20	0.057		6	52	31	0.021		10	102	66	0.010
	6	32	22	0.019		6	54	33	0.008		10	104	68	0.006
	6	33	23	0.010		6	55	34	0.004	9	9	104	59	0.057
	6	34	24	0.005		7	54	33	0.051		9	108	63	0.025
	7	33	23	0.055		7	56	35	0.026		9	111	66	0.012
	7	35	25	0.021		7	58	37	0.011		9	114	69	0.005
	7	36	26	0.012		7	60	39	0.004		10	110	65	0.056
	7	37	27	0.006		8	58	37	0.054		10	114	69	0.027
	8	36	26	0.055		8	61	40	0.021		10	118	73	0.011
	8	38	28	0.024		8	63	42	0.010		10	121	76	0.005
	8	40	30	0.008		8	65	44	0.004	10	10	127	72	0.053
	8	41	31	0.004		9	62	41	0.057		10	131	76	0.026
	9	39	29	0.053		9	65	44	0.025		10	135	80	0.012
	9	41	31	0.025		9	68	47	0.009		10	138	83	0.006
	9	43	33	0.010		9	70	49	0.004					

SOURCE: Adapted from M. Hollander and D. A. Wolfe (1972), *Nonparametric Statistical Methods*, New York: Wiley, Table A.5

Table A.12 Critical Values for Tolerance Intervals

$1-\alpha$	0.90			0.95			0.99		
$1-\gamma$	0.90	0.95	0.99	0.90	0.95	0.99	0.90	0.95	0.99
n									
6	3.131	3.723	4.870	3.712	4.414	5.775	5.337	6.345	8.301
7	2.902	3.452	4.521	3.369	4.007	5.248	4.612	5.488	7.182
8	2.743	3.264	4.278	3.136	3.732	4.891	4.147	4.936	6.468
9	2.626	3.125	4.098	2.967	3.532	4.631	3.822	4.550	5.966
10	2.535	3.018	3.959	2.839	3.379	4.433	3.582	4.265	5.594
11	2.463	2.933	3.849	2.737	3.259	4.277	3.397	4.045	5.308
12	2.404	2.863	3.758	2.665	3.162	4.150	3.250	3.870	5.079
13	2.355	2.805	3.682	2.587	3.081	4.044	3.130	3.727	4.893
14	2.314	2.756	3.618	2.529	3.012	3.955	3.029	3.608	4.737
15	2.278	2.713	3.562	2.480	2.954	3.878	2.945	3.507	4.605
16	2.246	2.676	3.514	2.437	2.903	3.812	2.872	3.421	4.492
17	2.219	2.643	3.471	2.400	2.858	3.754	2.808	3.345	4.393
18	2.194	2.614	3.433	2.366	2.819	3.702	2.753	3.279	4.307
19	2.172	2.588	3.399	2.337	2.784	3.656	2.703	3.221	4.230
20	2.152	2.564	3.368	2.310	2.752	3.615	2.659	3.168	4.161
21	2.135	2.543	3.340	2.286	2.723	3.577	2.620	3.121	4.100
22	2.118	2.524	3.315	2.264	2.697	3.543	2.584	3.078	4.004
23	2.103	2.506	3.292	2.244	2.673	3.512	2.551	3.040	3.993
24	2.089	2.489	3.270	2.225	2.651	3.483	2.522	3.004	3.947
25	2.077	2.474	3.251	2.208	2.631	3.457	2.494	2.972	3.904
26	2.065	2.460	3.232	2.193	2.612	3.432	2.469	2.941	3.865
27	2.054	2.447	3.215	2.178	2.595	3.409	2.446	2.914	3.828
28	2.044	2.435	3.199	2.164	2.579	3.388	2.424	2.888	3.794
29	2.034	2.424	3.184	2.152	2.554	3.368	2.404	2.864	3.763
30	2.025	2.413	3.170	2.140	2.549	3.350	2.385	2.841	3.733
31	2.017	2.403	3.157	2.129	2.536	3.332	2.367	2.820	3.706
32	2.009	2.393	3.145	2.118	2.524	3.316	2.351	2.801	3.680
33	2.001	2.385	3.133	2.108	2.512	3.300	2.335	2.782	3.655
34	1.994	2.376	3.122	2.099	2.501	3.328	2.320	2.764	3.632
35	1.988	2.368	3.112	2.090	2.490	3.272	2.306	2.748	3.611
36	1.981	2.361	3.102	2.081	2.479	3.258	2.293	2.732	3.590
37	1.975	2.353	3.092	2.073	2.470	3.246	2.281	2.717	3.571
38	1.969	2.346	3.083	2.068	2.464	3.237	2.269	2.703	3.552
39	1.964	2.340	3.075	2.060	2.455	3.226	2.257	2.690	3.534
40	1.959	2.334	3.066	2.052	2.445	3.213	2.247	2.677	3.518
41	1.954	2.328	3.059	2.045	2.437	3.202	2.236	2.665	3.502
42	1.949	2.322	3.051	2.039	2.429	3.192	2.227	2.653	3.486
43	1.944	2.316	3.044	2.033	2.422	3.183	2.217	2.642	3.472
44	1.940	2.311	3.037	2.027	2.415	3.173	2.208	2.631	3.458
45	1.935	2.306	3.030	2.021	2.408	3.165	2.200	2.621	3.444
46	1.931	2.301	3.024	2.016	2.402	3.156	2.192	2.611	3.431
47	1.927	2.297	3.018	2.011	2.396	3.148	2.184	2.609	3.419
48	1.924	2.292	3.012	2.006	2.390	3.140	2.176	2.593	3.407
49	1.920	2.288	3.006	2.001	2.384	3.133	2.169	2.584	3.396
50	1.916	2.284	3.001	1.969	2.379	3.126	2.162	2.576	3.385

SOURCE: Adapted from Table 8.3 of A. H. Bowker and G. J. Lieberman (1972), *Engineering Statistics*, 2nd ed., Upper Saddle River, NJ: Prentice Hall.

APPENDIX B

ABBREVIATED ANSWERS TO SELECTED ODD-NUMBERED EXERCISES

Chapter 2

2.1 **(a)**

Die Result	Coin(s) Result	Number of Outcomes
1	$\{(H), (T)\}$	2
2	$\{(H, H), \ldots, (T, T)\}$	4
3	$\{(H, H, H), \ldots, (T, T, T)\}$	8
4	$\{(H, H, H, H), \ldots, (T, T, T, T)\}$	16
5	$\{(H, H, H, H, H), \ldots, (T, T, T, T, T)\}$	32
6	$\{(H, H, H, H, H, H), \ldots, (T, T, T, T, T, T)\}$	64

There are a total of 126 outcomes.

(b)

Die Result	Number of Heads	Number of Outcomes
1	$\{(0), (1)\}$	2
2	$\{(0), (1), (2)\}$	3
3	$\{(0), (1), \ldots, (3)\}$	4
4	$\{(0), (1), \ldots, (4)\}$	5
5	$\{(0), (1), \ldots, (5)\}$	6
6	$\{(0), (1), \ldots, (6)\}$	7

There are a total of 27 outcomes.

2.5 **(a)** $\binom{52}{2} = 1326$. **(b)** $\binom{4}{2} = 6$. **(c)** $\binom{4}{1}\binom{48}{1} + \binom{4}{2} = 198$.

2.7 $\binom{m+n}{m}$.

2.11 **(a)** $\frac{\binom{12}{3}}{\binom{34}{3}} = \frac{220}{5984}$. **(b)** $\frac{\binom{2}{2}\binom{32}{1}}{\binom{34}{3}} = \frac{32}{5984}$. **(c)** $\frac{\binom{2}{2}\binom{32}{1}}{\binom{34}{3}} + \frac{\binom{12}{2}\binom{22}{1}}{\binom{34}{3}} + \frac{\binom{20}{2}\binom{14}{1}}{\binom{34}{3}} = \frac{4144}{5984}$.

(d) $\frac{\binom{2}{2}\binom{32}{1}}{\binom{34}{3}} + \frac{\binom{12}{2}\binom{22}{1}}{\binom{34}{3}} + \frac{\binom{20}{2}\binom{14}{1}}{\binom{34}{3}} + \frac{\binom{12}{3}\binom{22}{0}}{\binom{34}{3}} + \frac{\binom{20}{3}\binom{14}{0}}{\binom{34}{3}} = \frac{5504}{5984}$.

2.13   (a) $P(T \cap N^c) = 0.32$. (b) $P((T \cup R)^c) = 0.05$. (c) $P((T \cup R \cup N)^c) = 0.02$.

2.15 $\dfrac{\binom{4}{1}\binom{13}{2}\binom{13}{1}\binom{13}{1}\binom{13}{1}}{\binom{52}{5}} = \dfrac{685,464}{25,827,165}$.

2.17   (a) $p = 0.4$. (b) $p = 2/3$.

2.19   (a) $P(E_1 \cap F_1) = 0.15$. (b) $P(F_1) = 0.167$. (c) $P(F_2 \cap E_2) = 0.15$.

2.23   Using $p = 0.9$, for $n = 2$ the reliability is 0.99, for $n = 3$ the reliability is 0.999, and for $n = 4$ the reliability is 0.9999. As n gets larger, the reliability approaches 1.

2.25   (a) $P(B \cap D) = 0.0296$. (b) $P(D) = 0.0548$. (c) $P(B|D) = 0.5401$.

2.27   (a) $P(D|+) = 0.846$.

(b) $P(ND|-) = 0.999$. The diagnostic test appears pretty reliable, although it is less reliable in identifying true positives than true negatives.

(c) $P(D|+) = 0.047$.

(d) For rare diseases, too many false positives would appear in the screening program, and it would not be very effective in identifying people with the disease.

2.29   (a)

x	$f(x)$	$F(y)$, for $x \le y < x+1$
0	6/36	6/36
1	10/36	16/36
2	8/36	24/36
3	6/36	30/36
4	4/36	34/36
5	2/36	1

(b) $P(0 < x \le 3) = 24/36$ and $P(1 \le x < 3) = 18/36$.

2.33   (a) Continuous. (b) $P(1 \le X \le 3) = 0.4$. (c) $P(X \ge 1) = 0.6$.

2.35   (a) The p.m.f. is

$$f(x) = \begin{cases} \frac{1}{N} & \text{if } x = 1, 2, \ldots, N \\ = 0 & \text{otherwise.} \end{cases}$$

(c) $E(X) = 7/2 = 3.5$ and $\text{Var}(X) = (7)(5)/12 = 2.917$.

2.37   (a) Estimate N by $\hat{N} = \frac{x(n+1)}{n} - 1$.

2.39   (a) $E(X) = 6.19$.

(b) If $X \le n$ then Profit $= 1.5X - n$. If $X > n$ then Profit $= 1.25n - 0.75X$.

(c) For $n = 5$, $E(\text{Profit}) = 0.798$. For $n = 6$, $E(\text{Profit}) = 1.26$. For $n = 7$, $E(\text{Profit}) = 1.205$. $n = 6$ maximizes the expected profit.

2.41   (a) The c.d.f. is

$$F(x) = \begin{cases} 0 & \text{if } x < 1 \\ 1 - x^{-2} & \text{if } x \ge 1 \end{cases}$$

(b) $\theta_p = \sqrt{\frac{1}{1-p}}$. $\theta_{0.5} = 1.414$. (c) $E(X) = 2$. $\text{Var}(X) = \infty$.

2.53   (a) $E(X) = 280$. $\sigma_X = 240$.

(b) $E(Y) = 260$. $\sigma_Y = 120$.

(c)

u	$f(u)$	v	$f(v)$
-300	0.02	-500	0.18
100	0.18	-100	0.02
300	0.08	100	0.72
700	0.72	500	0.08

(d) $E(U) = 540$. $\sigma_U = 268.328$. $E(V) = 20$. $\sigma_V = 268.328$.

(e) $E(U) = 280 + 260 = 540$. $E(V) = 280 - 260 = 20$. $\sigma_U = \sigma_V = \sqrt{(240)^2 + (120)^2} = 268.328$.

2.55   (a) $f_X(x) = 4x - 4x^3$. $f_Y(y) = 4y^3$. Since $f(x, y) \neq f_X(x)f_Y(y)$, X and Y are not independent.

(b) $f(y|x) = \frac{2y}{1-x^2}$.   (c) $\text{Cov}(X, Y) = 0.017$.

2.57   (a) $P(|\bar{X} - \mu| \leq c) \geq 1 - \frac{1}{nc^2}$.

(b) For $c = 0.1$, n must be 2000. For $c = 1.0$, n must be 20. For $c = 2.0$, n must be 5.

2.59   (a) Let X be the number of occupied lanes, then $P(X \leq 9) = 0.944$.

(b) $E(X) = 7.5$ and $\sigma_X = 1.369$.

2.61   (a) $P(X \leq 2) = 0.958$.   (b) $P(X \leq 2) \approx 0.949$. The approximation is fairly accurate.

2.63   (a) Let X be the number of emissions in a week. Then $P(X \geq 1) = 0.221$.

(b) Let Y be the number of emissions in a year. Then $P(Y \geq 1) = 1.000$.

2.65   (a) $P(X > 10) = 0.014$.   (b) $f(x) = \frac{e^{-5}5^x}{x!}\frac{1}{0.986}$. $E(X) = 4.910$.

2.67   (a) Let X_1, X_2, and X_3 be the numbers of low, middle, and upper income people surveyed out of 4, respectively. Then $P(X_1 = 1, X_2 = 1, X_3 = 2) = \frac{4!}{1!1!2!}(0.3)^1(0.45)^1(0.25)^2 = 0.101$.

(b) $P(X_1 = 0, X_2 = 4, X_3 = 0) = \frac{4!}{0!4!0!}(0.3)^0(0.45)^4(0.25)^0 = 0.041$.

(c) $P(X_3 = 0) = \binom{4}{0}(0.25)^0(1 - 0.25)^4$.

2.71   (a) $P(90 \leq X \leq 100) = 0.333$.   (b) $\theta_{0.9} = 97$.

2.73   (a) $\theta_p = -10\ln(1 - p)$. $\theta_{0.5} = 6.931$. $\theta_{0.75} = 13.863$.

(b) $P(\text{No jobs in 15 minutes}) = P(X > 15) = 0.223$.

2.75 $T \sim \text{Gamma}(\lambda = 1/10000, \ r = 5)$. $E(T) = 50{,}000$ and $\text{Var}(T) = 500{,}000{,}000$.

2.77 $E(T) = 92.5$. $\text{Var}(T) = 33.75$.

2.79   (a) $z_{.3} = 0.525$, $z_{.15} = 1.04$, and $z_{.075} = 1.44$.

(b) $x_{.3} = 5.575$, $x_{.15} = 7.12$, and $x_{.075} = 8.32$.

2.81   (a) W has a normal distribution.   (b) $E(W) = 40$ and $\text{Var}(W) = 1525$.

(c) $P(U - V > 50) = 0.398$.

2.83   (a) $\bar{X}$ has a normal distribution with mean $\mu = 90$ and SD $= \sigma/\sqrt{n} = 20/\sqrt{25} = 4$.

(b) $P(\bar{X} > 100) = 0.0062$.   (c) $x_{.10} = 95.12$ dollars.

2.87   (a) The p.d.f. is $g(y_1, y_2) = \frac{y_2}{2\pi}\exp\left\{-\frac{y_2^2}{2}(1 + y_1^2)\right\}$.   (b) $f(y_1) = \frac{1}{\pi(1+y_1^2)}$ for $-\infty < y_1 < \infty$.

Chapter 3

3.1   (a) (i) Observational. (ii) Descriptive.

(b) (i) Observational. (ii) Comparative. (iii) Response: Baby's birthweight. Explanatory: Mother's weight gain during pregnancy.

(c) (i) Experimental. (ii) Comparative. (iii) Response: Occurrence of heart disease. Explanatory: Amount of fiber in diet.

(d) (i) Observational. (ii) Comparative. (iii) Response: Annual rate of return. Explanatory: Group of mutual fund.

3.3   **(a)** The lower death rate may be due to heightened awareness of the staff to heart patients, a change in patient mix over time, or changes in medical treatments, and not the new screening procedure.

(b) Proofreading accuracy may decrease over amount of time spent proofreading. Also, a high error rate in the beginning may motivate readers to be more vigilant in the later part of the document. For each person, one should randomize the order of the low or high error rate sections of text to avoid this confounding.

3.5   Response: Mortality rates among heart attack survivors. Explanatory: Exercise. Confounding factors: Diet, weight, and age could all be correlated with willingness to join the exercise program, and could affect mortality. The control group is inappropriate because: i) Physician disapproved of exercise program could be becase of other health concerns, and ii) Lack of interest in exercise program could reflect a lack of motivation to control diet and take medication reliably.

3.7   **(a)** (i) Survey. (ii) Descriptive.

(b) (i) Retrospective Study. (ii) Comparative. (iii) Response: Term of pregnancy. Explanatory: Mother's smoking habits.

(c) (i) Survey. (ii) Descriptive.

(d) (i) Survey. (ii) Descriptive.

3.9   Most listeners are people with regular working hour jobs, creating a convenience sample of employed, more affluent adults. Also, in call-in polls, people who feel strongly for or against a particular issue are more likely to voice their opinion.

3.11   People with more education are more likely to have access to, or even recognize the need to consult, a medical specialist. This gives a selection bias of people with AD that is related to education level.

3.17   A 2-stage stratified sample: Create 4 strata of 100 male managers, 50 female managers, 1900 male employees, and 1450 female employees. Since the sample size relative to the population size is $700/3500 = 1/5$, from each strata sample 1/5 of the people. This sample will reflect the proportion of males and females in management.

3.19   Response: Fabric strength (loss in fabric weight). Treatments: Chemical agent, wash times. Blocks: Martindale wear tester batches and bolts of fabric.

3.21   Response: Mileage. Treatments: Gasoline additive, Concentrations. Blocks: Make of car.

3.23   **(a)** Let A = method 1, B = method 2, and C = method 3. Then one CR design is

$$\{A,B,B,C,A,A,B,C,B\}.$$

(b) One randomized block design is

$$\{ \underbrace{A,C,B}_{\text{Person 1}} , \underbrace{B,A,C}_{\text{Person 2}} , \underbrace{B,C,A}_{\text{Person 3}} \}.$$

3.25   **(a)** Let A = aerobic, S = strengthening, and C = control. Then one CR design is

$$\{A,C,C,S,A,A,C,A,A,C,S,S,S,C,A,C,S,S,C,S,A,S,A,C\}.$$

(b) One possible randomized block design is

$$\{\underbrace{A,C,S,S,C,C,A,S,C,A,S,A}_{65\text{--}79} , \underbrace{S,A,C,C,A,A,S,C,A,C,S,S}_{80 \text{ and older}}\}.$$

Chapter 4

4.1   **(a)** Categorical (Ordinal). **(b)** Categorical (Nominal). **(d)** Numerical (Practically Continuous). **(e)** Categorical (Nominal).

4.3   **(a)** Enrollment: Numerical (Practically Continuous).
Required Entrance Tests: Categorical (Nominal).
Annual Tuition: Numerical (Practically Continuous).
Fields of Study: Categorical (Nominal).
Selectivity: Categorical (Ordinal).
Percent of Applicants Selected: Numerical (Continuous).

(b) Enrollment: Ratio scale.
Annual Tuition: Ratio scale.
Percent of Applicants Selected: Ratio scale.

4.5   Pareto Charts: E(45%), C(25%), and B(15%) account for more than 80% of all complaints.

4.7   **(a)** The number of doctorate degrees awarded to women were: 916 in physical sciences, 453 in engineering, 2674 in life sciences, 3027 in social sciences, 1904 in humanities, 3717 in education, and 836 in other professional fields. The number of doctorate degrees awarded to men were: 5360 in physical sciences, 4759 in engineering, 4254 in life sciences, 3100 in social sciences, 2190 in humanities, 2680 in education, and 1581 in other professional fields.

(b) The degrees awarded most to men and women are different. Men are more likely to earn degrees in physical sciences, engineering, and life sciences, while women are more likely to earn degrees in life sciences, social sciences, humanities, and education.

4.9   **(a)** The median will be larger because the long left tail will shift the mean left.

(b) The sample skewness will be negative.

(c) One would expect Q_1 to be farther from the median because the long left tail will shift the first quartile farther to the left.

4.11   **(a)** $\bar{x} = 98.563$, $Q_2 = 98.6$, $s = 0.751$, $Q_1 = 98.125$, and $Q_3 = 99.125$.

(b) There are no outliers, since no observations fall outside the fences (LF $= 96.625$ and UF $= 100.625$).

(c) Histogram: The shape is unimodal with no outliers or skew.

4.13   **(a)** Stem-and-Leaf Plot: The shape is right-skewed and unimodal, with one outlier.

(b) Boxplot: The fences are LF $= -480.5$ and UF $= 3067.5$. So only one observation, 3830, falls outside the fences and is an outlier.

(c) Normal plot: This looks like a right-skewed distribution.

4.15   **(a)** Stem-and-Leaf Plot: The shape is left-skewed and trimodal, with two possible outliers.

(b) Boxplot: The fences are LF $= 5.438$ and UF $= 7.458$. So two observations, 2.86 and 2.92, fall outside the fences and are outliers.

(c) Normal Plot: This looks like a left-skewed distribution.

4.17   **(a)** Stem-and-Leaf Plot: The shape is approximately symmetric and bimodal, with one outlier.

(b) Boxplot: The fences are LF $= -2$ and UF $= 70$. So only one observation, 94, falls outside the fences and is an outlier.

(c) Normal Plot: This looks like a normal distribution.

4.19   **(a)** Stem-and-Leaf Plot: The shape is approximately symmetric and unimodal, with one apparent outlier.

(b) Boxplot: The fences are LF = 2 and UF = 36. So only two observations, 37 and 46, fall outside the fences and are outliers.

4.21   **(a)** Histogram: The shape is skewed right and unimodal, with one outlier.

(b) Boxplot: The fences are LF = 23.625 and UF = 1572.625. So only one observation, 1800, falls outside the fences and is an outlier.

4.23   **(a)**

Data	4.7	7.3	9.8	12.5	14.4	18.0	20.1	26.6	36.2
Normal scores	−1.282	−0.842	−0.524	−0.253	0	0.253	0.524	0.842	1.282

(b) Normal Plot: Probably close enough to a normal distribution.

4.25   Normal Plots: The control group cost looks right-skewed. The log cost looks normally distributed.

4.27   **(a)** Normal Plot: The distribution looks right-skewed.

(b) $\sqrt{\text{HPT}}$: Looks heavy-tailed or right-skewed. log HPT: Looks heavy-tailed. 1/HPT: Looks like a normal distribution with an outlier. The inverse transformation 1/HPT gives the most nearly normal distribution.

4.29   **(a)** False. **(b)** False. **(c)** True. **(d)** False.

4.31   **(a)**

	Black		White	
Gender	Graduated	Did not Graduate	Graduated	Did not Graduate
Female	54	89	498	298
Male	197	463	878	747

(b) For blacks, 38% of females graduated compared to 30% of males. For whites, 63% of females graduated compared to 54% of males. In both ethnic groups, women had a higher graduation rate by about 8–9%.

(c)

Gender	Graduated	Did not Graduate
Female	552	387
Male	1075	1210

The graduation rate for women is 59% compared to 47% for men. This disparity among graduation rates, similar to that found in (b), indicates that graduation rate is not independent of gender.

4.33   **(a)** For low risk patients, hospital A's success rate is 80% while hospital B's success rate is 60%. For high risk patients, hospital A's success rate is 20% while hospital B's success rate is 10%. Hospital A is better.

(b) Hospital A's overall success rate is 43%, while hospital B's overall success rate is 46%. Hospital B has the higher success rate.

(c) This is an example of Simpson's Paradox. While Hospital A has a higher success rate for both risk groups, it has a larger percentage of high risk patients than hospital B. Since the high risk patients have a lower success rate, this descrepancy brings hospital A's overall success rate below hospital B.

4.35   **(a)** The midpoints are 7.5, 22.5, 37.5, 52.5, 67.5, and 82.5. The scatterplot indicates a positive linear trend in the number of goals scored.

(b) The correlation coefficient is 0.975. Yes, it does correspond to the linear relationship on the scatterplot.

4.37   **(a)** The scatterplot indicates a decreasing relationship between city mileage and fuel costs. However, it appears to be curved, and not quite linear.

   (b) The correlation coefficient is -0.865. Yes, it does match the decreasing but not linear relationship indicated by the scatterplot.

4.39   The person would be predicted to spend 0.9 standard deviations shorter than the average time spent with the family. The person's predicted family time is 42 minutes.

4.41   **(a)** The scatterplot indicates an increasing relationship between year and math scores, although it does not look linear.

   (b) The least squares line is $y = 514.207 + 2.454x$.

   (c) The scatterplot indicates a curved relationship between year and verbal scores, first decreasing, and then increasing. The least squares line is $y = 463.034 + 0.798x$.

   (d) The math scores follow a more linear trend than the verbal scores. The verbal scores seem to go down for the first 5–6 years before finally going up, which is not very well described by a linear regression line.

4.43   **(a)** Time Series Plot: This series appears stationary, except for possibly a decreasing trend in sales.

   (b) The mean absolute percent error (MAPE) is 13.9%.

   (c) The mean absolute percent error (MAPE) is 18.2%.

   (d) $r_1 = 0.818$, $r_2 = 0.535$, and $r_3 = 0.190$. These coefficients indicate that sales in successive years are positively correlated, but that this correlation decreases as the lag between years increases.

4.45   **(a)** Time Series Plot: This series is not stationary, since there is a steadily increasing trend in the composite index of leading indicators.

   (b) $w = 0.4$ gives the smallest MAPE ($=0.4\%$).

4.47   **(a)** The overall average SAT score is 1210. The overall average "loss" is 40 points.

   (b) The reason for this larger overall "loss" is that a higher number of students are accepting offers at school B, which has the lower average SAT score. This brings down the average more than the expected 30 points.

Chapter 5

5.1   **(a)** The population is the uniform distribution over integers 1 to 5. The mean and variance of the population are $\mu = 3$ and $\sigma^2 = 2$.

   (c)

$\bar{x}$	1.0	1.5	2.0	2.5	3.0	3.5	4.0	4.5	5.0
$f(\bar{x})$	$\frac{1}{25}$	$\frac{2}{25}$	$\frac{3}{25}$	$\frac{4}{25}$	$\frac{5}{25}$	$\frac{4}{25}$	$\frac{3}{25}$	$\frac{2}{25}$	$\frac{1}{25}$

   (d) $E(\bar{X}) = 3$. $\text{Var}(\bar{X}) = 1$. These equal μ and $\sigma^2/2$, respectively.

5.3   **(a)** Bar Chart: The empirical distribution is fairly close to the theoretical distribution.

   (b) From the simulation, the mean is 3.49 and the variance is $(0.54)^2 = 0.2916$. These are reasonably close to the true values, except for some sampling error.

   (c) The bar chart for the average of 10 dice looks more normal, and has a smaller variance, than the one for the average of two dice.

5.5   **(a)** U is approximately normal with mean $\mu = 40$ and SD $= 2.121$. V is approximately normal with mean $\mu = 40$ and SD $= 1.5$.

   (b) $P(35 \leq V \leq 45)$ should be larger.

   (c) $P(35 \leq U \leq 45) \approx 0.9818$. $P(35 \leq V \leq 45) \approx 0.9992$.

5.7   **(a)** $\bar{X} \sim$ Gamma(5, 25). $E(\bar{X}) = 5$. Var$(\bar{X}) = 1$.

(b) The straight line pattern in the normal plot suggests that the sample means are approximately normal.

(c) $P(4.5 \leq \bar{X} \leq 5.5) = 0.3830$.

5.9   **(a)** $P(X \leq 10) = 0.586$.   **(b)** $P(X \leq 10) \approx 0.5$.   **(c)** $P(X \leq 10.5) \approx 0.5793$.

5.11   **(a)** $P(\text{Accept Lot}) = 0.736$.   **(b)** $P(\text{Accept Lot}) \approx 0.736$.   **(c)** $P(\text{Accept Lot}) \approx 0.697$.

(d) The Poisson approximation gives the better result because $np = 1 \leq 10$, so n is not large enough for the normal approximation.

5.13   **(a)** $P(X \geq 6) = 0.85$.

(b) $P(X \geq 26) = 0.9976$. Since $n(1 - p) = 15 \geq 10$, the normal approximation will be accurate ($P(X \geq 26) \approx 0.9983$).

5.15   **(b)**

s^2	0.0	0.5	2.0	4.5	8.0
$f(s^2)$	$\frac{5}{25}$	$\frac{8}{25}$	$\frac{6}{25}$	$\frac{4}{25}$	$\frac{2}{25}$

(c) $E(S^2) = 2$. This equals $\sigma^2 = 2$ calculated in exercise 5.1.

5.17   **(a)** $E(\chi_8^2) = 8$ and Var$(\chi_8^2) = 2 \times 8 = 16$.

(b) $a = 15.507$, $b = 1.646$, $c = 13.362$, $d = 2.180$, $e = 17.534$.

(c) $a = \chi_{8,0.05}^2$, $b = \chi_{8,0.99}^2$, $c = \chi_{8,0.10}^2$, $d = \chi_{8,0.975}^2$, and $e = \chi_{8,0.025}^2$.

5.21   **(a)** From the simulation, $\chi_{4,0.25}^2 = 1.676$, $\chi_{4,0.5}^2 = 3.187$, and $\chi_{4,0.90}^2 = 6.734$. The exact values are $\chi_{4,0.25}^2 = 1.923$, $\chi_{4,0.50}^2 = 3.357$, and $\chi_{4,0.90}^2 = 7.779$.

5.23   **(a)** $c = 1.197$.   **(b)** Since $s = 7.5 > 5c = 5.983$, the engineer would conclude that $\sigma > 5$.

5.25   **(a)** $a = 1.812$, $b = -2.764$, $c = 1.372$, $d = 2.228$.

(b) $a = t_{10,0.05}$, $b = t_{10,0.99} = -t_{10,0.01}$, $c = t_{10,0.10}$, $d = t_{10,0.025}$.

5.27   **(a)** From the simulation, $t_{4,0.25} = -0.656$, $t_{4,0.5} = 0.081$, and $t_{4,0.90} = 2.065$. The exact values are $t_{4,0.25} = -0.741$, $t_{4,0.5} = 0$, and $t_{4,0.90} = 1.533$.

5.29 $f_{10,10,0.025} = 3.72$, $f_{10,10,0.975} = 1/3.72 = 0.27$, $f_{5,10,0.10} = 2.52$, $f_{5,10,0.90} = 1/f_{10,5,0.10} = 0.30$, and $f_{10,5,0.90} = 1/2.52 = 0.40$.

5.33   For $(n_1 = 7, n_2 = 5)$, $P\left(\frac{S_1^2}{S_2^2} > 4\right) \approx 0.05$. For $(n_1 = 13, n_2 = 7)$, $P\left(\frac{S_1^2}{S_2^2} > 4\right) \approx 0.01$. For $(n_1 = 9, n_2 = 16)$, $P\left(\frac{S_1^2}{S_2^2} > 4\right) \approx 0.10$.

5.35 $f_{(1)}(x) = 0.90e^{-0.90x}$, $f_{(9)}(x) = 0.90\left(1 - e^{-0.10x}\right)^8 e^{-0.10x}$, $f_{(5)}(x) = \frac{9!}{4!4!}0.1\left(1 - e^{-0.10x}\right)^4 e^{-0.50x}$.

5.37   **(a)** $\mu = 1.15$. $\sigma = 1.492$.

(b) From the simulation, the mean is 1.18 and the SD is 0.69.

(c) The histogram in (b) looks a little skewed. The new histogram looks less skewed.

(d) The mean and SD in (b) are both very close to their true values, $\mu = 1.15$ and $\sigma/\sqrt{5} = 0.667$.

5.39   **(b)** 25th percentile: simulated value = 2.160, exact value = 1.923. 50th percentile: simulated value = 3.603, exact value = 3.357. 90th percentile: simulated value = 7.763, exact value = 7.779.

Chapter 6

6.1   **(a) 3** is a parameter, **0** is a statistic.   **(b) 63** is a statistic.

  (d) 48% is a statistic, **52%** is a parameter.

6.3   **(a)** $\text{Bias}(X_{\max}) = \frac{-1}{n+1}\theta$.   **(b)** $\text{Bias}(X_{\max} + X_{\min}) = 0$.

6.5   **(a)** $E(\hat{p}_1) = p$, $E(\hat{p}_2) = 1/2$, $\text{Bias}(\hat{p}_1) = 0$, and $\text{Bias}(\hat{p}_2) = 1/2 - p$.

  (b) $\text{Var}(\hat{p}_1) = \frac{p(1-p)}{n}$ and $\text{Var}(\hat{p}_2) = 0$. $\hat{p}_2$ has the lower variance.

  (c) $\text{MSE}(\hat{p}_1) = \frac{p(1-p)}{n}$ and $\text{MSE}(\hat{p}_2) = (1/2 - p)^2$. Plot against p: $\hat{p}_1$ is generally a flatter curve, meaning there is less downside risk. However, $\hat{p}_2$ has a lower MSE for p near 0.5, so $\hat{p}_1$ is not always a better estimator.

6.7   SEM $= 0.15$.

6.9 $\hat{\theta}_1 = \frac{\hat{\mu}}{\hat{\sigma}^2}$ and $\hat{\theta}_2 = \frac{\hat{\mu}^2}{\hat{\sigma}^2}$.

6.11   **(a)** Since $P(-1.645 \le Z \le +1.645) = .90$, a 90% CI for μ is $[\bar{X} - 1.645\frac{\sigma}{\sqrt{n}}, \bar{X} + 1.645\frac{\sigma}{\sqrt{n}}]$.

  (b) 90% CI $= [28.355, 31.645]$.   **(c)** The probability is either 0 or 1 (not .90).

6.13   **(a)** You would expect $100 \times 0.95 = 95$ intervals to contain the true mean 70.

  (b) X $\sim$ Bin(100,0.95).

6.15   **(a)** A 95% CI for μ is $[108.64, 112.36]$. Since this interval falls completely within the specification limits of $[107.5, 112.5]$, we can conclude that the specifications are met.

  (b) A lower 95% confidence bound is 108.94. Since this exceeds 107.5, the lower specification limit is met.

  (c) An upper 95% confidence bound is 112.06. Since this is smaller than 112.5, the upper specification limit is met.

6.17   **(a)** $H_0: p = 0.54$ vs. $H_1: p \neq 0.54$, where p is the actual proportion of voters who favor the congressman.

  (b) $H_0: p = 0.05$ vs. $H_1: p < 0.05$, where p is the true proportion of overdue books.

  (c) $H_0: p = 0.40$ vs. $H_1: p < 0.40$, where p is the true scrap rate.

  (d) $H_0: p = \frac{1}{2}$ vs. $H_1: p \neq \frac{1}{2}$, where $p = P(\text{prefer Gatorade})$.

6.19   **(a)** H_0 : It is not safe in the amount normally consumed vs. H_1 : It is safe.

  (b) H_0 : It is not effective vs. H_1 : It is effective.

  (c) H_0 : It is not equivalent vs. H_1 : It is equivalent.

  (d) H_0 : It is not effective vs. H_1 : It is effective.

6.21 $OC(p) = \sum_{i=0}^{2} \binom{50}{i} p^i (1-p)^{50-i}$. $\alpha = 0.078$, $\beta = 0.112$, and Power$(0.15) = 0.986$.

6.23   **(a)** $\alpha = 0.05$ and $\beta = 0.087$.

  (b) In a simulation, $\alpha = 0.05$ and $\beta = 0.05$.

6.25 $OC(\mu) = P\left(Z \le \frac{10{,}500 - \mu}{1000/\sqrt{10}}\right)$.

6.27   **(a)** $H_0: \mu = 10$ minutes vs. $H_1: \mu < 10$ minutes.

  (b) $z = -2.517$. Since $z < -z_{.05} = -1.645$, our conclusion is to reject H_0. There is significant evidence that the average time, μ, has been reduced.

  (c) Power $= 0.8962$.

6.29   **(a)** The control limits are $[15.888, 16.112]$. $\alpha = 0.0124$.

  (b) For the 2.5 σ chart, $\beta = 0.604$. For the 3 σ chart, $\beta = 0.776$. The 3 σ charts have a much higher β risk, while the α risk is not substantially lower.

6.31   (i) For $n = 100$, P-value $= 0.159$. (ii) For $n = 400$, P-value $= 0.023$. (iii) For $n = 900$, P-value $= 0.001$. As the sample size gets large, the P-value gets small, implying that even small differences from the hypothesized mean will be found to be significant if the sample size is large enough.

Chapter 7

7.1   (a) $n = 55.41$ or 56 fish.

    (b) If $n = 100$, then $E = 0.0037$. The new margin of error is 74% of the old.

7.3   (a) $n = 96.04$ or 97 employee files.   (b) A 90% CI for μ is [5.391, 7.209].

7.5   (a) The appropriate hypotheses are $H_0: \mu = 120$ vs. $H_1: \mu \neq 120$.

    (b) $z = 2.545$. Since the P-value is $P = 0.0108$, do not reject H_0 at level $\alpha = 0.01$ (although it is on the borderline). The mean yield for Illinois does not appear to differ from the national average.

    (c) The assumption that the 50 farmers are a random sample is far more important, since the sample mean of a random sample is approximately normal regardless of the original distribution.

7.7   (a) $z = 2.021$. Since the P-value is $P = 0.022$, do not reject H_0 at level $\alpha = 0.01$. The new tread design does not appear to differ from the national average.

    (b) If $\mu = 61,000$, $\pi(61,000) = 0.633$.   (c) $n = 29.29$ or 30 tires.

7.9   (a) Since the consumer watchdog group suspects that the mean fat content exceeds 98% (or 3.4 grams per yogurt cup), the appropriate hypotheses are $H_0: \mu = 3.4$ vs. $H_1: \mu > 3.4$.

    (b) $z = 2.0$. Since the P-value is $P = 0.023$, do not reject H_0 at level $\alpha = 0.01$. The fat content does not appear to be higher than advertised.

    (c) If $\mu = 3.7$, $\pi(3.7) = 0.75$. To assure 95% power, $n = 43.80$ or 44 yogurt cups.

7.11   (a) You would expect 95 of the 95% z-intervals to contain the true mean $\mu = 12$.

    (b) We still expect 95 of the 95% t-intervals to contain the true mean.

7.13   (a) A lower 95% confidence bound is 87.195. Since this lower confidence bound exceeds 87, we would conclude that the mean octane rating exceeds 87.

    (b) The hypotheses are $H_0: \mu \leq 87$ vs. $H_1: \mu > 87$. $t = 3.413$. Since $t_{19,0.005} = 2.861 < t < 3.579 = t_{19,0.001}$, the P-value lies between 0.005 and 0.001. Therefore this result would be significant at $\alpha = 0.005$ but not at $\alpha = 0.001$.

7.15   (a) μ refers to the true average proportion of students using the food service.

    (b) $t = 5.77$. Since $|t| > t_{20-1,.01} = 2.539$, we reject H_0 at level $\alpha = 0.01$. There is sufficient evidence that the mean usage of the food service has increased.

    (c) The appropriate hypotheses are $H_0: \mu \leq 70$ vs. $H_1: \mu > 70$.

    (d) $t = -1.007$. Since $t < t_{20-1,.10} = 1.328$, we do not reject H_0 at level $\alpha = 0.10$. There is not sufficient evidence that the food service has met its goal.

7.17   (a) Normal Plot: Indicates that the data follow a normal distribution.

    (b) $\chi^2 = 9.226$. Since $\chi^2 < \chi^2_{25-1,0.10} = 15.659$, we reject the null hypothesis. The new device appears to be more precise.

    (c) An upper confidence bound for σ is 7.676. Since this is less than $\sigma_0 = 10$, we reject H_0.

7.19   (a) The appropriate hypotheses are $H_0: \sigma = 3500$ vs. $H_1: \sigma \neq 3500$.

    (b) A 95% CI for σ is [3651, 6505]. A 99% CI for σ is [3394, 7286]. Since the 95% CI includes $\sigma_0 = 3500$ but the 99% CI does not, we reject H_0 at $\alpha = 0.05$ but not at $\alpha = 0.01$.

7.21   (a) A 95% CI is [476.03, 476.77].

(b) A 95% PI is [474.86, 477.94].   (c) A 95% TI is [474.368, 478.432]. Since the tolerance interval does not fall within the specification limits of [475,477], the variability of the new filling machine is unacceptable.

Chapter 8

8.1   (a) Matched pairs.   (b) Independent samples.   (c) Matched pairs.   (d) Independent samples.

8.3   (a) Matched pairs.   (b) Matched pairs.   (c) Independent samples.   (d) Independent samples.

8.5   (a) The clouds in each group are not matched to one another on some characteristic.

(b) Q-Q Plot. Seeded cloud rainfalls tend to be larger than unseeded cloud rainfalls.

8.7   (a) The two different types of eyes belong to the same person.

(b) Scatterplot. The pairs tend to lie pretty close to the 45 degree line through the origin. Eyes with glaucoma do not appear to have thicker corneas than unaffected eyes.

8.9   (a) A 95% CI is [0.376, 2.625]. There is a significant difference at $\alpha = 0.05$, since the CI does not contain 0.

(b) Using $\nu = 34.845 \approx 35$, a 95% CI is [0.392, 2.608]. The results are similar.

8.11   (a) $t = -2.162$. Since $|t| > t_{10+5-2,0.025} = 2.16$, we reject H_0 at level $\alpha = 0.05$.

(b) $t = -1.817$, $\nu = 5.481 \approx 5$. Since $t < t_{5,.025} = 2.571$, we do not reject H_0 at $\alpha = 0.05$. This is the opposite conclusion as that obtained from assuming equal variances.

8.13   (a) A 95% CI for $\mu_1 - \mu_2$ is [−0.556, 0.132]. No significant difference at $\alpha = 0.05$.

(b) Using $\nu = 15.809 \approx 16$, a 95% CI is [−0.560, 0.136]. The results are similar.

8.15   (a) $H_0: \mu_B - \mu_A = 0$ vs. $H_1: \mu_B - \mu_A > 0$. $t = 1.681$. Since $t > t_{10-1,0.10} = 1.383$, we reject H_0 at level $\alpha = 0.10$.

(b) Temperature: A warmer second winter could confound the insulation effect. Thermostat setting: If different settings are used, then the results could be affected.

8.17   (a) $t = 2.625$. Since $t > t_{8-1,0.025} = 2.365$, we reject H_0 at level $\alpha = 0.05$.

(b) A 95% CI is [0.397, 7.603].

8.19   A 95% CI for σ_1^2/σ_2^2 is [0.471, 2.344]. Since this interval contains 1, we can recommend using the pooled variance t-test.

8.21   A 90% CI for σ_1^2/σ_2^2 is [0.060, 1.308]. Since this interval contains 1, we can conclude that the variances are not significantly different and recommend using the pooled variance t-test.

8.23   (a) A 95% CI is [−0.459, 0.419]. Treating the data as independent samples, the high and low fiber diets are not significantly different.

(b) A 95% CI is [−0.207, 0.167]. Although the CI is narrower, the high and low fiber diets are still not significantly different.

(c) A 95% CI is [0.173, 0.547]. There is a significant difference between high fiber diets and baseline diets.

(d) High/low fiber diets have a significant effect at $\alpha = 0.05$ of reducing the total cholesterol levels from baseline, but there is no significant difference between high and low fiber diets.

8.25   (a) The salary boxplots are right-skewed with numerous outliers. The $\log_e$(salary) boxplots are more symmetric with fewer outliers. The log transformed data would work better because the skewness and outliers inflate the variance and would make a difference in the means harder to detect.

(b) $t = -2.129$. Since $|t| > t_{72+72-2,0.025} = 1.98$, reject H_0 at level $\alpha = 0.05$, and conclude that the two groups are significantly different.

(c) $t = -2.418$. Since $|t| > t_{72+72-2,0.025} = 1.98$, reject H_0 at level $\alpha = 0.05$, and conclude that the two groups are significantly different.

(d) The conclusions are the same for $\alpha = 0.05$. However, note that the t-statistic is larger for the log-transformed data. Using log-transformed data yields a more significant result.

8.27 $\pi(c^2) = 1 - G\left(\frac{f_{n_1-1,n_2-1,\alpha}}{c^2}\right)$, where G is the cdf of the F distribution with $n_1 - 1$ and $n_2 - 1$ degrees of freedom. Using $\alpha = 0.05$, $n_1 = n_2 = 16$, and $c = 2.40$, $\pi(c^2) = 0.95$.

Chapter 9

9.1   **(a)** $n = 663.062$ or 664. **(b)** $n = 556.972$ or 557.

(c) $N = 1392.5$ or 1393. Such a nonresponse rate may cause a bias in the results if the non-response rate is related to the proportion of interest; i.e., subscribers with income above \$100,000 may be less likely to respond to the survey.

9.3   **(a)** A 95% CI, using formula 9.1 is [0.027,0.133]. A 95% CI, using formula 9.3 is [0.041,0.150]. The second confidence interval is shifted higher than the first by about 0.015.

(b) Do not reject H_0 at $\alpha = 0.05$, so continue monitoring the trainee at the same rate.

9.5   **(a)** $H_0: p = .465$ vs. $H_1: p > .465$. One-sided because the quarterback is interested in *improvement* of his pass completion percentage.

(b) $z = 1.923$. P-value $= 0.0274$. Reject H_0 at $\alpha = 0.05$, conclude that there is significant improvement.

(c) 82.23 or 83 completed passes.

9.7   **(a)** $H_0: p = .8$ vs. $H_1: p > .8$.

(b) $z = 2.121$. P-value $= .017$. Reject H_0 at $\alpha = 0.05$, conclude that the new method is significantly more accurate.

9.9 $n = 4897.6$ or 4898. If 2500 voters are sampled, $\pi(0.52) = .516$.

9.11 $z = -1.674$. Since the P-value $= 0.095$, we reject H_0 at $\alpha = 0.10$. A two-sided alternative is appropriate here because we are interested in detecting a change, but we do not have any prior knowledge of the direction of that change.

9.13 **(a)** $H_0: p_1 = p_2$ vs. $H_1: p_1 \neq p_2$. Use Fisher's exact test.

(b) P-value $= 0.168$. Do not reject H_0 at $\alpha = 0.05$, conclude that there is no significant difference in the proportions of male and female Ph.D.'s.

9.15 **(a)** $H_0: p_1 = p_2$ vs. $H_1: p_1 \neq p_2$. Use McNemar's test.

(b) P-value $= 0.021$. Reject H_0 at $\alpha = 0.05$, conclude that drugs are significantly different.

9.17 $H_0: p_1 = p_2 = \cdots = p_8 = 1/8$ vs. H_1: Not H_0. $\chi^2 = 16.333$. Since $\chi^2 > \chi^2_{8-1,0.05} = 14.067$, reject H_0 at $\alpha = 0.05$ and conclude that chances of winning are not the same for each starting gate.

9.19 **(a)** $H_0: p_i = \binom{7}{i}(.5)^7$ vs. H_1: Not H_0. $\chi^2 = 6.278$. Since $\chi^2 < \chi^2_{6-1,.10} = 9.236$, do not reject H_0 and conclude that this is a plausible distribution.

(b) $H_0: p_i$ is binomial vs. H_1: Not H_0. $\chi^2 = 3.223$. Since $\chi^2 < \chi^2_{6-2,.10} = 7.779$, do not reject H_0. This agrees with (a), since $\hat{p} = .531 \approx .5$.

9.21 $\chi^2 = 0.960$. Since $\chi^2 < \chi^2_{6-2,0.05} = 9.488$, do not reject H_0 and conclude that the Poisson distribution is a plausible model.

9.25 **(a)** Multinomial sampling. $H_0: p_{ij} = p_i \cdot p_{\cdot j}$ for all i, j, where i refers to religious affiliation and j refers to political party affiliation.

(b) Product Multinomial sampling. $H_0: p_{ij} = p_j$ for all i, j, where i refers to the type of mutual fund and j refers to the return classification.

9.27 **(a)** Product Multinomial sampling.

(b) $\chi^2 = 101.494$. Since $\chi^2 > \chi^2_{(2-1)(13-1),0.01} = 26.217$, reject H_0 and conclude that the Q.C.S. letters do not match Mark Twain's word length patterns.

9.29 **(a)** Multinomial sampling.

(b) $H_0: p_{ij} = p_i \cdot p_{\cdot j}$ for all i, j, where i refers to gender and j refers to height above ground.

(c) $\chi^2 = 4.593$. Since $\chi^2 > \chi^2_{(2-1)(2-1),0.05} = 3.841$, reject H_0 and conclude that gender and trap height are not independent.

9.31 **(a)**

		Cholesterol Level	
		≤ 250	> 250
Personality Type	A	12	8
	B	17	3

(b) $H_0: p_{ij} = p_i \cdot p_{\cdot j}$ for all i, j, where i refers to the personality type and j refers to the cholesterol level. $\chi^2 = 3.135$. Since $\chi^2 > \chi^2_{(2-1)(2-1),0.10} = 2.706$, reject H_0 and conclude that personality type and cholesterol level are not independent

9.33 **(a)** $H_0: p_{ij} = p_i \cdot p_{\cdot j}$ for all i, j where i refers to the opinion on full evacuation and j refers to the distance from Three Mile Island.

(b) $\chi^2 = 0.449$. Since $\chi^2 < \chi^2_{(6-1)(2-1),0.10} = 9.236$, do not reject H_0 and conclude that there is no association between distance from site and evacuation attitudes.

9.35 **(a)** $H_0: p_{ij} = p_i \cdot p_{\cdot j}$ for all i, j, where i refers to the age at diagnosis of breast cancer and j refers to the frequency of breast self-exam.

(b) $\chi^2 = 25.086$. Since $\chi^2 > \chi^2_{(3-1)(3-1),0.10} = 7.779$, reject H_0 and conclude that there is an association between age at diagnosis and frequency of self-exam.

9.37 $\hat{\psi} = 0.265$. A 90% CI for ψ is $[0.074, 0.947]$. Since this is below 1, type A personalities have higher odds of having higher cholesterol levels than do type B personalities.

9.41 **(a)**

Defendant's	Death Penalty		Row
Race	Yes	No	Total
White	19	141	160
Black	17	149	166

$z = 0.470$. P-value $= 0.638$. Do not reject H_0 and conclude that there is no racial difference between black and white defendants.

(b) White victims: $z = -0.888$, P-value $= 0.374$. Do not reject H_0 and conclude that there is no racial difference between black and white defendants when the victim is white.
Black victims: $z = -2.50$, P-value $= 0.012$. Reject H_0 and conclude that there is a racial difference between black and white defendants when the victim is black.

(c) Black defendants are more likely to receive the death penalty than whites when the victim is black, but not when the victim is white.

Chapter 10

10.1 (a) Theoretical, deterministic. (b) Empirical, probabilistic. (c) Empirical, probabilistic.

10.3 Experimental Study: Chemical reaction, where the temperature is controlled at various settings to determine its effect on yield.
Observational Study: Model income as a function of years of education for a sample of workers.

10.5 (a) The scatterplot shows a positive approximately linear relationship.
(b) $\hat{y} = -62.312 + 0.040x$. (c) MSE $= 0.104$, and $\hat{\sigma} = 0.322$.

10.7 (a) The scatterplot shows a negative approximately linear relationship.
(b) $\hat{y} = 774.012 - 0.359x$. (c) MSE $= 1.728$, and $\hat{\sigma} = 1.315$.

10.9 (a) $t = 16.312$. Since $t > t_{21-2, 0.05} = 1.729$, we reject H_0 and conclude that there is a significant increasing linear trend.
(b) A 95% PI is $[17.714, 19.208]$. This is unreliable because we are extrapolating beyond the domain of the data. A 95% CI for the winning jump does not have a meaningful interpretation because there will only be one winning jump in 1996.

10.11 (a) 95% PI: $[47.238, 73.529]$. (b) 95% CI: $[57.510, 63.257]$. This is narrower than the PI.
(c) 95% PI: $[26.330, 55.276]$. We would not expect this PI to be reliable because it extrapolates beyond the domain of the data.

10.13 (a) The average rate of decrease was -0.270. $t = 2.212$. Since $t > t_{10-2, 0.05} = 1.860$, we reject H_0 and conclude that the U.S. IMR was significantly less than the rest of the Western world.
(b) Predicted IMR for 1995 is 7.95. A 95% PI is $[7.525, 8.375]$.

10.15 $h(p) = \log_e \left(\frac{p}{1-p} \right)$.

10.17 (a) The scatterplot of the transformed data shows a negative linear relationship.
(b) $\hat{p} = 0.846 - 0.079 \log_e t$. For 50% retention, $t = 79.818$.

10.19 The appropriate transformation is $h(\text{speed}) = \frac{1}{\text{speed}^2}$.

10.21 (a) The original data appears curved, but after using a reciprocal transformation of wind velocity, the scatterplot appears linear. The regression equation is
DC Output $= 2.98 - 6.93 \times \frac{1}{\text{Wind Velocity}}$.
(b) No unusual patterns or uneven spreads in the residual plots.
(c) The predicted DC Output for a wind velocity of 8 mph would be 2.112.

10.23 (a) $\beta_0 = \log_e a$ and $\beta_1 = \log_e b$.
(b) The scatterplot of the transformed data shows a positive approximately linear relationship.
(c) $\hat{y} = 5.279 + 0.010w$. (d) For a weight of 1.2 kg, $\hat{t} = 198.600$.

10.27 $\text{Var}(Y) = \mu^4$.

10.29 (a) The scatterplot shows a very strong linear relationship, so the correlation is probably close to 1.
(b) $r = 0.971$. A 95% CI for ρ is $[0.897, 0.992]$.

10.31 (a) The scatterplot shows a moderately strong negative linear relationship, so the correlation is probably around -0.6 to -0.8.
(b) $r = -0.702$. A 95% CI for ρ is $[-0.848, -0.457]$. $z = -0.020$. Since the p-value is 0.492, accept H_0 and conclude that ρ is not significantly higher than 0.7 in absolute value.

10.37 $F = 0.02$. Since $F < f_{5-2, 10-5, 0.05} = 5.409$, we accept H_0 and conclude that the linearized model fits the data sufficiently well.

Chapter 11

11.1   The normal equations are

$$\sum y_i = n\beta_0 + \beta_1 \sum x_i + \beta_2 \sum x_i^2,$$

$$\sum x_i y_i = \beta_0 \sum x_i + \beta_1 \sum x_i^2 + \beta_2 \sum x_i^3,$$

$$\sum x_i^2 y_i = \beta_0 \sum x_i^2 + \beta_1 \sum x_i^3 + \beta_2 \sum x_i^4.$$

11.3 $\hat{y} = 111.354 + 2.060x_1 - 2.732x_2 + 0.000x_3$. $R^2 = 0.295$, so 29.5% of the variability in PIQ is accounted for by the brain size, height, and weight of a person.

11.5

$$y = \begin{bmatrix} 11 \\ 18 \\ 18 \\ 10 \\ 7 \\ -2 \\ -13 \end{bmatrix}, X = \begin{bmatrix} 1 & 3 \\ 1 & 2 \\ 1 & 1 \\ 1 & 0 \\ 1 & -1 \\ 1 & -2 \\ 1 & -3 \end{bmatrix}, X'X = \begin{bmatrix} 7 & 0 \\ 0 & 28 \end{bmatrix}, (X'X)^{-1} = \begin{bmatrix} 0.143 & 0 \\ 0 & 0.036 \end{bmatrix}$$

$$X'y = \begin{bmatrix} 49 \\ 123 \end{bmatrix}, \hat{\beta} = \begin{bmatrix} 7 \\ 4.393 \end{bmatrix}, \text{ and } e = \begin{bmatrix} -9.179 \\ 2.214 \\ 6.607 \\ 3.000 \\ 4.393 \\ -0.214 \\ -6.821 \end{bmatrix}.$$

11.7   **(a)**

$$X = \begin{bmatrix} x_1 \\ x_2 \\ \vdots \\ x_n \end{bmatrix}, X'X = [\sum x_i^2], (X'X)^{-1} = \left[\frac{1}{\sum x_i^2} \right].$$

(b) $\hat{\beta} = \frac{\sum x_i y_i}{\sum x_i^2}$. **(c)** $\text{Var}(\hat{\beta}) = \frac{\sigma^2}{\sum x_i^2}$.

11.9   **(a)**

$$X = \begin{bmatrix} 1 & x_1 - \bar{x} \\ 1 & x_2 - \bar{x} \\ \vdots & \vdots \\ 1 & x_n - \bar{x} \end{bmatrix}, X'X = \begin{bmatrix} n & 0 \\ 0 & \sum(x_i - \bar{x})^2 \end{bmatrix}, (X'X)^{-1} = \begin{bmatrix} \frac{1}{n} & 0 \\ 0 & \frac{1}{\sum(x_i - \bar{x})^2} \end{bmatrix}.$$

(b)

$$\hat{\beta} = \begin{bmatrix} \bar{y} \\ \frac{\sum(x_i - \bar{x})y_i}{\sum(x_i - \bar{x})^2} \end{bmatrix}.$$

$\hat{\beta}_1$ of Exercises 11.8 and 11.9 are the same, but $\hat{\beta}_0$ from Exercise 11.8 equals $\hat{\beta}_0 + \hat{\beta}_1 \bar{x}$ from Exercise 11.9.

(c) $\text{Var}(\hat{\beta}_0) = \frac{\sigma^2}{n}$ and $\text{Var}(\hat{\beta}_1) = \frac{\sigma^2}{\sum (x_i - \bar{x})^2}$. **(d)** $\hat{\beta}_0$ and $\hat{\beta}_1$ are uncorrelated.

11.11

Source	SS	d.f.	MS	F
Regression	37.70	3	12.567	2.084
Error	180.90	30	6.03	
Total	218.60	33		

Since $F < f_{3,30,0.05} = 2.922$, do not reject H_0 and conclude that the regression is not significant.

11.13 $t_1 = 1.2$, $t_2 = 2.067$, and $t_3 = 5.909$. Compare these to $t_{32-4,0.025} = 2.048$ and conclude that β_2 and β_3 are significant. Only x_1 should be removed from the model.

11.15 (a) $\hat{y} = 53.967 + 0.408t - 0.002t^2$.

(b) $t = -2.953$. $P = 0.032$. Since $P > \alpha = 0.01$, do not reject H_0 and conclude that β_2 is not significant and the quadratic term can be dropped from the model.

(c) $\hat{y} = 55.108 + 0.615t - 0.004t^2$. $t = -5.935$. $P = 0.002$. Since $P > \alpha$, reject H_0 and conclude that β_2 is significant and the quadratic term should be retained in the model.

11.17 $F = 45.65$. Since $F > f_{3,34,0.05} = 2.92$, we reject H_0 and conclude that the quadratic fit is significantly better.

11.19 (a) A 95% CI for the coefficient of log(Alkalinity) is $[-0.699, -0.219]$. A 95% CI for the coefficient of log(Calcium) is $[-0.062, 0.356]$. A 95% CI for the coefficient of pH is $[-0.289, 0.129]$. Both log(Calcium) and pH should be excluded from the model, since their CI's include 0.

(b) After refitting the model, excluding log(Calcium) and pH, $r^2 = 0.579$, so 57.9% of the variability is accounted for. Previously, 60.7% was accounted for, so excluding log(Calcium) and pH does not substantially affect the goodness of fit of the model.

11.23 (a) The scatterplot indicates an increasing trend in the men's SAT scores.

(b) $\hat{y} = 493.399 + 0.592t$.

(c) The residuals tend to be negative for low values of t and positive for high values of t.

(d)

t_i	0	5	7	8	9	10	11	12	13	14	15
e_i^*	-0.157	-1.683	-1.354	-0.123	-0.599	0.206	1.438	0.962	0.059	0.864	0.387

Since none of the standardized residuals are > 2, there do not appear to be any outliers.

(e) An observation is influential if $h_{ii} > 0.364$. Only $t = 0$ (1980) satisfies this condition. It is influential because it is farther to the left on the t axis than the other observations.

11.25 (a) Both residual plots exhibit a curved pattern with negative residuals at the extremes and positive residuals in the middle, suggesting a quadratic model.

(b) There are no longer any patterns in the residuals, except that the variance increases as the predicted value increases.

11.27 (a) The refitted model is $\widehat{\log y} = 7.205 - 0.508 \log x_1 + 0.136 \log x_2$. Residual plots: Except for the large outlier, the variances appear stable and there are no unusual patterns in the residual plots against the predictors or the fitted values.

(b) There is no unusual pattern in this residual plot against the omitted predictor, pH. There is no reason that pH should be included in the model, as it contributes little to the fit of the model, nor is it strongly associated with the residuals of the fit.

11.29 The rate of change is $\beta_1 + 2\beta_2 t$. β_2 represents how the rate of change in cigarette consumption is changing over time. If β_2 is negative, then cigarette consumption is flattening out.

11.31 $\hat{\beta}_1^* = 0.596$ and $\hat{\beta}_2^* = 0.637$. SAT-M has a slightly larger effect on GPA than does SAT-V.

11.33 $\hat{\beta}_{\log x_1}^* = -0.878$, $\hat{\beta}_{\log x_2}^* = 0.275$, and $\hat{\beta}_{x_3}^* = -0.013$. Log(Alkalinity) has the largest effect on predicting mercury content, followed by log(calcium).

11.35 $\text{VIF}_{\log x_1} = 4.410$, $\text{VIF}_{\log x_2} = 3.227$, and $\text{VIF}_{x_3} = 2.771$. These are all less than 10 and are therefore acceptable. There does not appear to be high multicollinearity.

11.37 **(a)** $\hat{y} = 4271.026 + 379.510t - 5269.407z + 549.918tz$. $r^2 = 0.998$ compared to 0.940 before, so this model improves the amount of variation explained by about 6%.

(b) $F = 242.264$. Since $F > f_{2,16,0.05} = 3.634$, we reject H_0 and conclude that the z terms improve the fit of the model.

(c) The final model is $\hat{y} = 4271.026 + 379.510t - 5269.407z + 549.918tz$. For younger children, the model is $\hat{y} = 4271.026 + 379.510t$. For older children the model is $\hat{y} = -998.381 + 929.428t$.

11.39 **(a)** The coding 1–2–3 implies that a drug stock has twice the effect on the P/E ratio than an oil stock, and a computer stock has three times the effect. This is nonsense because the type of industry is a purely nominal variable.

(b) After recoding industry as two dummy variables, OIL and DRUG, with Computers/Electronics as the baseline, the fitted model is $\hat{y} = 6.704 + 0.183\,\text{PROFIT} + 0.213\,\text{GROWTH} + 0.835\,\text{OIL} + 3.819\,\text{DRUG}$. Only DRUG is significant at $\alpha = 0.05$

(c) If we choose the drug/healthcare industry as the baseline, then we would instead have an indicator COMPUTER. The new model would be $\hat{y} = 10.523 + 0.183\,\text{PROFIT} + 0.213\,\text{GROWTH} - 2.984\,\text{OIL} - 3.819\,\text{COMPUTER}$

11.41 **(a)** $r_{yx_1} = 0.378$, $r_{yx_2} = -0.093$, and $r_{yx_3} = 0.003$. x_1 would enter first.

(b) $r_{yx_2|x_1} = 0.421$ and $r_{yx_3|x_1} = 0.241$.

(c) $F_2 = 7.556$ and $F_3 = 2.156$. Height(x_2) is the better predictor given that brain size is included in the model.

11.45 **(a)** Using the C_p criterion, the model with only $\log x_1$ has the lowest $C_p (= 2.4)$. This is the same model that was selected in Exercise 11.19. The fitted model is $\log \hat{y} = 7.21 - 0.398 \log x_1$, where $\hat{\beta}_{\log x_1}$ was highly significant (P-value ≈ 0.000).

11.49 **(a)**

e_{yx_2}									
−0.489	−0.202	−0.118	0.491	0.918	−0.062	−1.329	−0.132	0.666	0.309

(b)

$e_{x_1 x_2}$									
−3.655	−1.480	0.620	0.845	4.020	1.520	−3.655	−2.730	1.720	3.295

(c) The correlation between the two sets of residuals is $r_{yx_1|x_2} = 0.834$.

11.51 **(a)** $r_{x_1 x_2} = 0.224$, $r_{x_1 x_3} = -0.958$, and $r_{x_2 x_3} = -0.240$. Only $r_{x_1 x_3}$ is large, indicating a multicollinearity problem.

(b)

Predictor	x_1	x_2	x_3	x_{12}	x_{13}	x_{23}	x_1^2	x_2^2	x_3^2
VIF	2,856,749	10,956	2,017,162	9803	1,428,092	240	2,501,945	66	12,667

There is a serious multicollinearity problem, since all of the VIF values are much larger than 10. This is due to the introduction of additional interaction and quadratic terms that are highly correlated with each other and the main effects, as well as the strong correlation between x_1 and x_3 mentioned in (a).

(c)

Centered Predictor	x_1	x_2	x_3	x_{12}	x_{13}	x_{23}	x_1^2	x_2^2	x_3^2
VIF	375	2	680	31	6563	36	1763	3	1157

Centering improves the VIF values, but they are still large. Centering helps remove the multicollinearity from the interaction terms and quadratic terms, but it cannot fix the correlation between x_1 and x_3.

(d) The LS fit of the above model will not give reliable results because of the high degree of multicollinearity remaining even after centering the data. Small perturbations to the data will dramatically change the regression coefficients.

Chapter 12

12.1 (a) Sugar: The 95% CI's are: Shelf 1: [3.906,5.694], Shelf 2: [8.956,10.744], Shelf 3: [5.206,6.994]. Fiber: The 95% CI's are: Shelf 1: [1.142,2.218], Shelf 2: [0.412,1.488], Shelf 3: [1.632,2.708]. Shelf 2 cereals are higher in sugar content than shelves 1 and 3, since the CI for shelf 2 is above those of shelves 1 and 3. Similarly, the shelf 2 fiber content CI is below that of shelf 3. So in general, shelf 2 cereals are higher in sugar and lower in fiber.

(b) Sugar:

Source	SS	d.f.	MS	F
Shelves	275.03	2	137.5	34.41
Error	227.80	57	3.996	
Total	502.83	59		

Since $F > f_{2,57,0.05} = 3.15$, there do appear to be significant differences among the shelves in terms of sugar content.

Fiber:

Source	SS	d.f.	MS	F
Shelves	15.08	2	7.54	5.21
Error	82.47	57	1.447	
Total	97.55	59		

Since $F > f_{2,57,0.05} = 3.15$, there do appear to be significant differences among the shelves in terms of fiber content.

(c) The grocery store strategy is to place high sugar/low fiber cereals at the eye height of school children where they can easily see them.

12.3 (a) The box plots indicate that the control is higher than the two treatments in the average number of eggs laid.

(b)

Source	SS	d.f.	MS	F
Genetic types	1362.2	2	681.106	8.666
Error	5659.0	72	78.598	
Total	7021.2	74		

Since $F > f_{2,72,0.05} = 3.11$, there do appear to be significant differences in the numbers of eggs laid per day between the different genetic types of fruit flies.

(c) From the plot of the residuals against the predicted values, the constant variance assumption appears satisfied. From the normal plot of the residuals, the residuals appear to follow the normal distribution.

12.5 **(a)** The box plots indicate that HBSC has the highest average hemoglobin level, followed by HBS, and then HBSS.

(b)

Source	SS	d.f.	MS	F
Disease type	99.889	2	49.945	49.999
Error	37.959	38	0.999	
Total	137.848	40		

Since $F > f_{2,38,0.05} = 3.23$, there do appear to be significant differences in the hemoglobin levels between patients with different types of sickle cell disease.

(c) From the plot of the residuals against the predicted values, the constant variance assumption appears satisfied. From the normal plot of the residuals, the residuals appear to follow the normal distribution.

12.7 **(a)** The side-by-side boxplots of the pre-treatment weights overlap quite a bit and don't indicate large differences among the groups.

(b)

Source	SS	d.f.	MS	F
Treatment	31.2	2	15.6	0.50
Error	1503.5	48	31.0	
Total	1534.7	50		

Since $F < f_{2,48,0.05} = 3.19$, the pre-treatment weights are not significantly different among the different treatment groups.

(c) In these boxplots, the differences among the treatment groups are more pronounced. The family group appears to be different than the other two, but it is hard to tell if the differences are significant.

(d)

Source	SS	d.f.	MS	F
Treatment	479.3	2	239.7	3.85
Error	2990.6	48	62.3	
Total	3469.9	50		

Since $F > f_{2,48,0.05} = 3.19$, the weight differences are significantly different among the different treatment groups.

12.9 $t_{12} = 11.277$, $t_{13} = 6.8$, and $t_{23} = 4.712$. The Tukey critical point is $q_{3,27,0.05}/\sqrt{2} = 2.482$. Since all t statistics are above both critical points, conclude that all group means are different using the Tukey method. For the Ryan method, first compare t_{12} to 2.482 and reject H_0. Then compare t_{13} and t_{23} to 2.051. Since these are both significant, conclude that all group means are different using the Ryan method, the same conclusion as with the as with the Tukey method.

12.11 The 90% Tukey CI's are : For $\mu_{T1} - \mu_{T2}$: [-2.875,0.875]. For $\mu_{T1} - \mu_{B1}$: [-3.457,-0.169]. For $\mu_{T1} - \mu_{B2}$: [-4.262,-0.698]. For $\mu_{T2} - \mu_{B1}$: [-2.457,0.831]. For $\mu_{T2} - \mu_{B2}$: [-3.262,0.302]. For $\mu_{B1} - \mu_{B2}$: [-2.024,0.971].

12.13 **(a)** $t_{12} = 3.237$, $t_{13} = 3.886$, and $t_{23} = 0.649$. The Tukey critical point is $q_{3,72,0.05}/\sqrt{2} = 2.39$. Since t_{12} and t_{13} are both above the critical point, we conclude that group 1 (Control) is significantly different than both groups 2(Resistant) and 3(Susceptible), but groups 2 and 3 are not significantly different.

(b) The Dunnett critical value is $|t|_{2,72,0.05} = 2.26$. The conclusion is the same as in (a).

(c) The Tukey method is inefficient because it adjusts for comparisons that we are not interested in doing; i.e., those that don't involve the control. This results in a lower power for detecting the differences of interest.

12.15 s.e. $= 4.378$.

12.17 **(a)**

Player	Rodman	Kukoc	Longley	Harper
l_i	-13.092	-2.362	-6.912	-5.822
u_i	0	5.822	1.272	2.362

Since no player has $l_i = 0$, there is no clear second best shooter. However, since Rodman has $u_i = 0$, he is not a candidate.

(b)

Player	Jordan	Kukoc	Longley	Harper
l_i	-1.549	-4.539	-2.989	-3.989
u_i	2.989	0	1.549	0.549

Since no player has $l_i = 0$, there is no clear second best rebounder. However, since Kukoc has $u_i = 0$, he is not a candidate.

(c)

Player	Jordan	Rodman	Kukoc	Longley	Harper
l_i	-3.948	-4.938	0	-4.398	-4.668
u_i	0	0	3.948	0	0

Since Kukoc is the only player with $l_i = 0$, he does appear to have the most assists.

12.19 **(b)** The control limits are [29.624,39.284]. Since all of the batch means fall within these limits, the process is under control.

12.21 **(a)** $\hat{\tau}_1 = -2$, $\hat{\tau}_2 = -1$, $\hat{\tau}_3 = 3$, and $\hat{\tau}_4 = 0$. $\hat{\beta}_1 = 6$, $\hat{\beta}_2 = -3$, $\hat{\beta}_3 = -1$, $\hat{\beta}_4 = 2$, and $\hat{\beta}_5 = -4$.

(b)

Source	SS	d.f.	MS	F
Blend	264	4	66.000	3.504
Method	70	3	23.333	1.239
Error	226	12	18.833	
Total	560	19		

For method, $F < f_{3,12,0.05} = 3.49$, so there do not appear to be significant differences between methods. For blend, $F > f_{4,12,0.05} = 3.26$, so there do appear to be significant differences between blends.

(c) The residual plots show that there is possibly a decreasing variance with increasing yield, but this is unclear because there are also less observations at higher yields, so the distribution is less likely to be filled out. From the normal plot of the residuals, the residuals appear to follow the normal distribution.

12.23 $t = -3.578$. Since $|t| > t_{10,0.025} = 2.228$, conclude that there is a significant difference between domed stadiums and outdoor stadiums.

12.25 The direction means are, in increasing order, West (45.179), East (46.179), South (49.679), and North (50.536). Using the Tukey method, West is significantly different than South and North, and East is significantly different from North only. Using the Ryan or the Newman-Keuls method, West and East are both significantly different form South and North.

12.27 **(a)** The profile plot indicates that the new parks generally have a higher HR/G ratio than the unchanged parks.

(b)

Source	SS	d.f.	MS	F
Park	0.170	1	0.170	14.130
Year	1.064	7	0.152	12.627
Error	0.084	7	0.012	
Total	1.319	15		

Since $F_{\text{Park}} > f_{1,7,0.05} = 5.59$, there do appear to be significant differences between new and unchanged parks in their HR/G ratios.

12.29

Variety	A	B	C	D	E	F	G
l_i	-32.242	-10.642	-14.242	-20.342	-10.442	-23.742	-20.842
u_i	0	10.442	6.842	0.742	10.642	0	0.242

Varieties A and F are definitely nonbest varieties and all others are candidates for best variety. There is no clearly best variety, since none have $l_i = 0$.

Chapter 13

13.1   **(a)**

Age	Breed			Row
	Guernsey	Holstein-Fresian	Jersey	Effects
Mature	$\widehat{(\tau\beta)}_{11} = -0.067$	$\widehat{(\tau\beta)}_{12} = 0.083$	$\widehat{(\tau\beta)}_{13} = -0.017$	$\hat{\tau}_1 = -0.033$
Young	$\widehat{(\tau\beta)}_{21} = 0.067$	$\widehat{(\tau\beta)}_{22} = -0.083$	$\widehat{(\tau\beta)}_{23} = 0.017$	$\hat{\tau}_2 = 0.033$
Column Effects	$\hat{\beta}_1 = 0.313$	$\hat{\beta}_2 = -0.967$	$\hat{\beta}_3 = 0.653$	

(b) MSE $= 0.227$, with 54 degrees of freedom.

(c)

Source	SS	d.f.	MS	F	Sig.
Age	0.067	1	0.067	0.294	0.590
Breed	29.189	2	14.595	64.414	0.000
Interaction	0.233	2	0.117	0.515	0.600
Error	12.235	54	0.227		
Total	41.724	59			

There is no significant interaction effect. Breed is the only significant main effect.

13.3   **(a)** Main effect plots show that the means for cycling do not vary much, and cycling does not have a large main effect. However, the means for temperature vary substantially, and this effect is probably large. On the interaction plot, the lines are parallel, and almost identical, indication that the interaction effect is negligible.

(b)

Source	SS	d.f.	MS	F	Sig.
Cycling	0.667	1	0.667	1.199	0.284
Temperature	667.132	3	222.377	399.634	0.000
Interaction	3.283	3	1.094	1.967	0.146
Error	13.355	24	0.556		
Total	684.437	31			

There is no significant interaction effect. Temperature is the only significant main effect.

(c) The plot of the residuals against the fitted values appears random and with the same spread, so the equal variance assumption is reasonable. The normal plot looks linear, so the assumption of normality is reasonable.

13.5   A 95% CI for $\mu_1 - \mu_2$ is $[0.914, 1.646]$. A 95% CI for $\mu_1 - \mu_3$ is $[-0.706, 0.026]$. A 95% CI for $\mu_2 - \mu_3$ is $[-1.986, -1.254]$. Groups 1 and 3 (Guernsey and Jersey) produce significantly higher amounts of butterfat.

13.7   **(a)** Main effect plots show that both factors have a sizeable effect on the means. On the interaction plot, the lines are parallel except for time 3, where bar 3 moves in a different direction than 1 and 2. This suggests that there is a significant interaction effect.

(b)

Source	SS	d.f.	MS	F	Sig.
Bar	278.600	2	139.300	12.741	0.001
Time	385.533	4	96.383	8.816	0.001
Interaction	597.067	8	74.633	6.826	0.001
Error	164.000	15	10.933		
Total	1425.200	29			

The interaction effect is significant. For bar settings 1 and 2, the time of greatest weld strength is 3, while for bar setting 3, the time of greatest weld strength is 4 or 5.

(c) The plot of the residuals against the fitted values appears random and evenly spread, so the assumption of constant variance is valid. The normal plot appears linear, so the assumption of normality is reasonable.

13.9　**(a)** The transformed data are:

Temperature	Detergent							
	1		2		3		4	
Low	0.766	0.835	0.645	0.515	0.736	0.696	0.885	0.916
High	0.825	0.706	0.947	0.926	0.855	0.805	0.746	0.785

(b) Main effect plots show that both factors appear to have a sizeable effect on the means. On the interaction plot, since the two lines cross, the interaction effect appears to be significant.

(c)

Source	SS	d.f.	MS	F	Sig.
Temperature	0.0226	1	0.0226	8.440	0.020
Detergent	0.0127	3	0.0042	1.571	0.270
Interaction	0.1370	3	0.0456	16.988	0.001
Error	0.0215	8	0.0027		
Total	0.1930	15			

The main effect of temperature and the interaction effect are significant.

13.11　Thrust $= 16.405 - 0.144u_1 + 5.014v_1 - 5.163v_2 + 4.049v_3 - 0.309u_1v_1 + 0.432u_1v_2 - 0.307u_1v_3$. These parameter estimates are different than the effect estimates because they use the last group as a baseline, rather than the mean.

13.13　**(a)**

Source	SS	d.f.	MS	F	Sig.
Biological	2275.8	1	2275.8	13.02	0.001
Adoptive	1277.4	1	1277.4	7.31	0.011
Biol*Adopt	1.9	1	1.9	0.01	0.917
Error	5941.2	34	174.7		
Total	9712.2	37			

The interaction effect is nonsignificant. All main effects are significant.

(b) From Minitab, $SSE_{full} = 5941.2$, $SSE_{w/o\ biol} = 8217.0$, $SSE_{w/o\ adopt} = 7218.6$, and $SSE_{w/o\ interact} = 5943.1$. Then $SSE_{biol} = 8217.0 - 5941.2 = 2275.8$, $SSE_{adopt} = 7218.6 - 5941.2 = 1277.4$, $SSE_{interact} = 5943.1 - 5941.2 = 1.9$. These match the adjusted SS from part (a).

13.15　**(a)** $A = 6$, $B = 4$, and $AB = 2$.　**(b)** $MSE = 12$ with 8 degrees of freedom.

(c) $F_A = 9$, $F_B = 4$, and $F_{AB} = 1$. Compare to $f_{1,8,0.10} = 3.46$, and conclude that the interaction is not significant, but both main effects are significant.

13.17 $A = 10, B = 10, AB = 5, C = 0, AC = -5, BC = 0,$ and $ABC = 0.$ The regression equation is $\hat{y} = 20 + 5x_1 + 5x_2 + 2.5x_1x_2 - 2.5x_1x_3.$ C is only active as an interaction with $A.$

13.19   **(a)** $A = -35.388, B = -153.167, AB = -29.610, C = 26.667, AC = 33.333, BC = 9.888,$ and $ABC = -50.112.$

   (b)

Source	SS	d.f.	MS	F	Sig.
A	7514	1	7514	14.371	0.009
B	140,760	1	140,760	269.217	0.000
AB	5261	1	5261	10.061	0.019
C	4267	1	4267	8.160	0.029
AC	6667	1	6667	12.751	0.012
BC	587	1	587	1.122	0.330
ABC	15,067	1	15067	28.817	0.002
Error	8368	16	523		
Total	188,487	23			

   BC is the only nonsignificant main effect or interaction.

   (c) $\hat{y} = 171.2 - 17.694x_1 - 76.583x_2 - 14.805x_1x_2 + 13.333x_3 + 16.667x_1x_3 - 25.056x_1x_2x_3.$

   (d) $x_1 = 0, x_2 = -1/3, x_3 = -1,$ and $\hat{y} = 183.4.$

13.21

$$\hat{y} = \bar{y}.. + \frac{A}{2}x_1 + \frac{B}{2}x_2 + \frac{C}{2}x_3 + \frac{D}{2}x_4$$

$$+ \frac{AB}{2}x_1x_2 + \frac{AC}{2}x_1x_3 + \frac{AD}{2}x_1x_4 + \frac{BC}{2}x_2x_3 + \frac{BD}{2}x_2x_4 + \frac{CD}{2}x_3x_4$$

$$+ \frac{ABC}{2}x_1x_2x_3 + \frac{ABD}{2}x_1x_2x_4 + \frac{BCD}{2}x_2x_3x_4 + \frac{ABCD}{2}x_1x_2x_3x_4.$$

13.23   **(a)** $A = 17.725, B = 4.525, AB = -4.325, C = -3.250, AC = 3.150, BC = -1.750,$ $ABC = 3.300, D = -16.125, AD = 17.375, BD = -3.125, ABD = -3.575, CD = 1.350, ACD = -2.050, BCD = 0.350,$ and $ABCD = 6.600.$

   (b) From the normal plot, $A, D,$ and the AD interaction all appear significant.

   (c) Using only the significant factors, the regression equation is $\hat{y} = 39.4 + \frac{17.7}{2}x_1 - \frac{16.1}{2}x_4 + \frac{17.4}{2}x_1x_4.$ Therefore, $x_1 = +1$ and $x_4 = +1$ (high A and high D) will maximize wettability.

13.25   **(a)** Method is nested within hospital. Method is fixed, hospital is random.

   (b) Type and temperature are crossed and are both fixed.

   (c) Chemist and assay method are crossed. Chemist is random, method is fixed.

13.27   **(a)** The design is crossed. The script effect is fixed, the company effect is random.

   (b)

Source	SS	d.f.	MS	F	Sig.
Script	14,326	2	7163	5.718	0.067
Company	83,822	2	41,911	33.456	0.003
Script*Company	5011	4	1253	0.882	0.479
Error	115,101	81	1421		
Total	218,260	89			

   The interaction is not significant. Script is not a significant factor at $\alpha = 0.05.$ The company effect is significant, so we conclude that the variance component due to different companies is nonzero.

   (c) $\hat{\sigma}^2 = 1421, \hat{\sigma}^2_{AB} = 0$ (adjusted from -16.820), and $\hat{\sigma}^2_B = 1349.66.$

13.29 Technician is now nested within instrument, so SSB and SSAB get combined into SSB(A) = 0.206. This is highly significant (P-value = 0.000). The denominator of F_A changes to $MS_{B(A)}$, but the significance is almost unchanged (P-value = 0.271). The conclusion is that technician is significant as a nested factor, but instrument is still not significant as a main effect.

13.31 If a and b are small and n is large, then the d.f.= $ab(n-1)$ is still large. Not much is gained by pooling since the extra d.f.= $(a-1)(b-1)$ is small. The opposite conclusion is true for case (ii).

13.35 (a)

Source	SS	d.f.	MS	F	Sig.
A	801.2	1	801.2	4.840	0.115
B	38.1	1	38.1	0.230	0.665
AB	3.2	1	3.2	0.020	0.895
C	3.2	1	3.2	0.020	0.895
AC	152.6	1	152.6	0.922	0.409
BC	0.0	1	0.0	0.0	1.000
ABC	0.4	1	0.4	0.003	0.965
Error	662.0	4	165.5		
Total	1666.8	11			

No factors or interactions are significant.

(b) $t = -0.194$. Since $|t| < t_{3,0.025} = 3.182$, we do not reject H_0 and conclude that there is no significant curvature.

Chapter 14

14.1 (a) Exact P-value: 0.055, Approx. P-value: 0.0571, do not reject H_0, although it is close.

(b) Exact P-value: 0.053, Approx. P-value: 0.057, do not reject H_0, although it is close.

14.3 A 93.4% Sign CI for $\tilde{\mu}$ is $[1, 6]$. A 91.7% Wilcoxon Signed Rank CI for $\tilde{\mu}$ is $[-2, 5.5]$. These confidence intervals agree with the results of the hypothesis test.

14.5 A 98.44% Sign CI for $\tilde{\mu}$ is $[-12, 18]$. A 95.32% Wilcoxon Signed Rank CI for $\tilde{\mu}$ is $[-8, 16]$. These confidence intervals agree with the results of the hypothesis test.

14.7 A 97.86% Sign CI for $\tilde{\mu}$ is $[0.1, 1.2]$. A 95.12% Wilcoxon Signed Rank CI for $\tilde{\mu}$ is $[-0.1, 1.35]$. Both confidence intervals are consistent with a two-sided hypothesis test.

14.9 (b) Since $(0.5)^6 = 0.016$, it is not possible to reject H_0.

(c) Since $(0.5)^7 < 0.01$, need $n = 7$.

14.11 $u_1 = 27, u_2 = 36$. Since the P-value is 0.340, do not reject H_0 and conclude that treatment does not prolong survival.

14.13 (a) $u_1 = 12, u_2 = 38$. Since the P-value is 0.129, do not reject H_0 and conclude that the methods are not significantly different.

(b) A 90.08% CI for $\tilde{\mu}_2 - \tilde{\mu}_1$ is $[-0.0002, 0.0241]$. This CI contains 0 and therefore agrees with the hypothesis test in (a).

14.15 (b) It is not possible to reject H_0 since the smallest P-value is 0.014.

(c) $n_1 = n_2 = 5$, which yields a minimum P-value of 0.004.

14.19 (a) $kw = 8.868$. Since $kw > \chi^2_{4-1,0.05} = 7.815$, we reject H_0 and conclude that there are significant differences among the 4 programs.

(b) $q_{4,\infty,0.05} = 3.63$, so the critical point is $\frac{q_{4,\infty,0.05}}{\sqrt{2}}\sqrt{\frac{N(N+1)}{12}\frac{2}{n}} = 8.641$. Since $\bar{r}_A - \bar{r}_D = 8 < 8.641$, we conclude that the programs with the most and least absences are not significantly different.

14.21 $kw = 28.473$. Since $kw > \chi^2_{3-1,0.05} = 5.991$, we reject H_0 and conclude that there are significant differences among the types of disease. $z_{12} = 2.559$, $z_{13} = 5.328$, and $z_{23} = 2.164$. The critical point is $q_{3,\infty,0.05}/\sqrt{2} = 3.31/\sqrt{2} = 2.341$. Conclude that groups 1 and 3 are significantly different from one another.

14.23 (a) $fr = 6$. Since $fr > \chi^2_{3-1,0.10} = 4.605$, reject H_0 and conclude that there are significant differences among fixtures.

   (b) $q_{3,\infty,0.10} = 2.90$, so the critical point is $\frac{q_{3,\infty,0.10}}{\sqrt{2}}\sqrt{\frac{a(a+1)}{6b}} = 1.45$. $\bar{r}_1 = \bar{r}_3 = 1.5$, and $\bar{r}_2 = 3$. Conclude that fixtures 1 and 2 and fixtures 2 and 3 are significantly different from one another.

14.25 $fr = 12.54$. Since $fr > \chi^2_{5-1,0.05} = 9.488$, conclude that there are significant differences between the plasma levels at different times.

14.27 $r_s = -0.806$, $z_s = -2.418$, with P-value 0.0078. $\hat{\tau} = -0.733$, $z_\tau = -2.950$, with P-value 0.0016. In both cases, conclude that voter participation has declined.

14.29

$\hat{\tau}$	-1	$-1/3$	$1/3$	1
$f(\hat{\tau})$	1/6	2/6	2/6	1/6

14.33 $fr = 9.073$, $w = 0.336$. Since $fr < \chi^2_{10-1,0.05} = 16.919$, conclude that there is no significant association between the three GRE scores.

14.35 The 25 permutation samples are given below:

Sample	Control (x)									Treatment (y)							$\bar{y}-\bar{x}$
	52	104	146	10	50	31	40	27	46	94	197	16	38	99	141	23	30.6
1	40	46	197	10	38	141	31	146	23	27	52	99	50	104	16	94	−11.5
2	146	27	94	31	104	40	10	50	23	197	38	46	16	99	52	141	25.8
3	104	40	52	38	50	46	23	27	99	197	16	31	10	146	94	141	37.5
4	27	23	50	146	99	104	10	197	16	38	52	40	31	46	141	94	−11.5
5	52	40	94	141	16	27	197	146	99	23	38	50	104	10	31	46	−47.1
6	52	99	27	146	104	16	46	197	141	23	10	40	31	50	94	38	−51.1
7	40	23	27	146	38	52	94	16	99	197	10	31	141	46	50	104	23.3
8	99	141	104	52	40	27	197	38	23	46	31	50	16	94	146	10	−24.0
9	23	141	146	31	52	38	46	50	16	94	197	40	27	10	99	104	21.2
10	146	94	50	40	16	46	141	197	23	104	31	99	10	27	52	38	−32.1
11	99	146	16	38	10	141	23	104	40	94	197	46	50	31	52	27	2.4
12	104	99	38	50	31	10	16	197	52	23	40	27	146	141	46	94	7.5
13	50	38	31	46	94	10	16	23	99	27	52	104	141	40	146	197	55.8
14	141	27	197	94	104	31	16	99	40	46	38	10	146	23	50	52	−31.1
15	197	141	94	46	52	40	23	104	27	146	50	38	16	10	99	31	−24.7
16	104	27	50	31	141	146	16	10	52	197	46	38	40	99	23	94	12.6
17	38	40	52	94	16	10	31	23	50	141	197	146	104	99	27	46	69.2
18	99	38	31	141	40	27	197	16	23	104	46	50	146	10	52	94	3.7
19	10	23	38	46	146	31	50	197	27	16	52	40	141	104	94	99	14.9
20	31	94	38	46	27	23	10	50	141	99	104	146	52	40	16	197	42.3
21	141	99	31	52	146	104	38	27	23	10	94	50	16	40	197	46	−8.7
22	31	16	10	146	50	40	197	23	141	104	38	27	46	94	99	52	−7.0
23	99	40	197	141	46	50	10	27	146	52	38	16	23	104	94	31	−32.9
24	23	16	50	31	46	197	94	99	146	10	52	40	27	141	104	38	−19.1
25	141	94	99	40	197	38	146	16	27	50	10	46	23	52	104	31	−43.5

Since only 4 of these permutation samples exceed the critical value of $\bar{y} - \bar{x} = 30.6$, the permutation resampling P-value is $4/25 = 0.16$. The exact P-value using the Wilcoxon-Mann-Whitney test is 0.3403.

14.37 Using the above samples, the bootstrap medians, maximums, and minimums follow:

	Median	Min	Max
Sample	201.75	198	206.3
1	202.2	200.5	206.3
2	202.35	198	206.3
3	202.95	198	203.7
4	201.75	198	206.3
5	202.95	198	206.3
6	201.3	198	203.4
7	202.2	198	206.3
8	203.4	198	203.7
9	200.8	198	206.3
10	202.35	199	206.3
11	201.9	198	206.3
12	201.75	198	203.7
13	201.75	199	206.3
14	202.35	199	206.3
15	201.3	198	206.3
16	201.75	199	203.4
17	202.35	200.5	206.3
18	202.35	199	203.7
19	202.5	199	206.3
20	201.5	198	203.7
21	202.8	198	206.3
22	201.05	198	206.3
23	202.2	198	206.3
24	202.35	199	206.3
25	201.3	198	206.3
Estimate	202.058	198.48	205.548
SE(Estimate)	0.637	0.757	1.233

From these bootstrap samples, the standard error of the sample median is 0.637, the standard error of the sample minimum is 0.757, and the standard error of the sample maximum is 1.233.

Chapter 15

15.3 $\hat{\mu} = \bar{x}$.

15.5   **(a)** $\hat{\theta} = \bar{x}$.   **(b)** $P(\text{At least one absent employee}) = 1 - e^{-\theta}$, so the MLE is $1 - e^{-\bar{x}}$.

15.7   **(a)** $L(\theta_1, \theta_2) = \begin{cases} \left(\frac{1}{\theta_2 - \theta_1}\right)^n & \text{if } x_{min} \geq \theta_1 \text{ and } x_{max} \leq \theta_2 \\ 0 & \text{if } \theta_1 > x_{min} \text{ or } \theta_2 < x_{max} \end{cases}$

(b) $\hat{\theta}_1 = x_{min}$, $\hat{\theta}_2 = x_{max}$, and $\hat{\mu} = \frac{x_{min} + x_{max}}{2}$.

15.13   Since $h(\mu) = 1/\mu$, $V(1/\bar{X}) = \sigma^2/(n\mu^4)$.

15.15   **(b)**

Predictor	Coeff	StDev	Z	P	Odds Ratio	95% CI Lower	Upper
Constant	3.809	1.149	3.32	0.001			
Control	-1.558	0.700	-2.22	0.026	0.21	0.05	0.83

The results are identical to the analysis from Example 9.15.

15.17

Logistic Regression Table

Predictor	Coef	StDev	Z	P	Odds Ratio	95% CI Lower	Upper
Constant	-60.717	5.181	-11.72	0.000			
Dose	34.270	2.912	11.77	0.000	7.65E+14	2.54E+12	2.30E+17

Then a 95% CI for β_1 is $[28.562, 39.978]$. $\exp\{\beta_1\}$ represents the change in the odds ratio of death to survival associated with a unit change in $\log_{10}$ dose concentration.

15.19 **(a)**

Likelihood Ratios

x	0	1	2	3	4	5
LR	0.032	0.093	0.281	0.844	2.532	7.606

(b) LR $> k \iff x > 3$(i.e., $x = 4, 5$). The level of this test is 0.1874, and the power is 0.6328.

(c) If $\alpha = 0.05$, then the critical region only includes $x = 5$. The power of this test is 0.2373, and the actual level is $0.0312 < 0.05$.

15.23 **(a)** The stopping boundaries are $A = 0.1053$ and $B = 18$. The rejection numbers based on $s_n = \sum x_i$ are $a_n = -1.861 + 0.092n$ and $b_n = 2.389 + 0.092n$. For acceptance to be possible, $n \geq 20.228$ or 21. For rejection to be possible, $n \geq 2.602$ or 3.

(b) The expected sample sizes for the SPRT are $E(N|p_0) = 39.327$ and $E(N|p_1) = 33.825$.

15.27 The risk functions are $R(\hat{p}_1, p) = p(1-p)$ and $R(\hat{p}_2, p) = \frac{3p^2 - 3p + 1}{9}$. The Bayes estimator p_2 is preferred over p_1 for $0.091 < p < 0.909$.

15.31 **(a)** Denote the state of nature by D, where $D = 1$ means that the person has the disease, and $D = 0$ means that the person does not have the disease. Then $P(D = 1) = 0.01$ and $P(D = 0) = 0.99$.

(b) Denote the outcome by X, where $X = 1$ means that the person tests positive for the disease, and $X = 0$ means that the person tests negative for the disease. Then $X|D = 1 \sim$ Bernoulli(0.95) and $X|D = 0 \sim$ Bernoulli(0.02).

(c) The two decisions are d_1: operate, and d_2: do not operate. The loss functions are $L(d_1, D) = 5000 - 10,000D$ and $L(d_2, D) = 10,000D$.

(d) If $x = 1$ (test is positive), then $A(d_1, d) = 51.5$ and $A(d_2, D) = 95$. If $x = 0$ (test is negative), then $A(d_1, d) = 4848.5$ and $A(d_2, D) = 5$. Hence, the Bayes rule selects d_1 (to operate) if $x = 1$ (test is positive) and selects d_2 (not to operate) if $x = 0$ (test is negative).

(e) If the cost of the operation was $500 instead of $5000, and the prior probabilities were $P(D = 1) = 0.5$, then the Bayes rule would always select d_1, to operate.

(f) If the prior prevalence rate was 0.1%, then the Bayes rule would always select d_2, not to operate.

INDEX

A

α-level test, 216, 228, 287
α- and β-risks, 212
Acceptance numbers, 642
Acceptance region, 210
Acceptance sampling, 86
  See also Examples
Active factors, 522
Additive model, 491
Adjusted r_p^2-criterion, 433
Adjusted (standardized) rates, 132
Admissible decision rule, 652, 658
Alternative hypothesis, 208–10
Analysis of variance (ANOVA) identity, 463–65, 486
Analysis of variance (ANOVA) F-statistic and F-test, 463–65
Analysis of variance (ANOVA) table, 360–61, 409, 463–64
Analytical studies, *See* Comparative study
arcsin transformation, 395
arctan hyperbolic transformation, 396
Asymmetric distribution, 113
Asymptotically efficient estimator, 624
Autocorrelation, 369

Autocorrelation coefficients, 147–49
Axiomatic approach to probability, 8, 62
Axioms of probability, 10–11

B

Balanced design, 458
Balanced two-way layout, 505
Banach, Stefan, 79
Banach's Matchbox Problem, 79
Bar chart, 109, 148
Bartlett test for homogeneity of variances, 667
Bayes, Rev. Thomas, 19
Bayes' theorem, 19–20, 62
Bayesian inference, 646–50
  Bayes decision rule, 652–53, 655
  Bayes risk, 658
  Bayesian estimation, 647–49
  Bayesian testing, 649–50
  posterior distribution, 647, 658
  prior distribution, 646–47, 658
Bernoulli, James, 7
Bernoulli distribution, 42–43, 59
Bernoulli proportions, comparing, 329–30
Bernoulli random variable, 42–43, 63

Bernoulli trial, 42, 44–45
Best linear unbiased estimator (BLUE), 454
Best subsets regression, 431–37, 440
  optimality criteria, 432–36
Beta distribution, 52, 59, 63
Bias:
  in estimation, 198–201
  in sampling, 88
Bimodal distribution, 120
Binomial coefficient, 14–15
Binomial distribution, 43–44, 59, 63
  normal approximation to, 172–74
  Poisson approximation to, 46
Birthday Problem, 13–14
Bivariate data:
  correlation coefficient, 135–38
  scatter plot, 132–34, 149
  Simpson's paradox, 131–32, 149
  straight line regression, 139–40, 149
  summarizing, 128–42
  two-way table, 129–31, 149
Bivariate distribution, 39
Bivariate normal distribution, 379–80, 386

Blocking factor, 96, 101, 270
Blocks, 96, 482–3
Bonferroni inequality, 11
Bonferroni method, 227, 468, 491
Bootstrap method, 597–601
  bootstrap for estimating standard error, 597–600
  bootstrap for hypothesis testing, 600
  bootstrap standard error (BSE), 598
Box-Müller transformation, 62
Box and whiskers (Box) plot, 121–22, 148
  side-by-side box plots, 122, 271, 459

C

C_p-criterion, 434
Calibration, 363
Capture-recapture method, 664
Case-control studies, 90–91
Categorical data:
  summarizing bivariate data, 129–32
  summarizing univariate data, 109
  types of, 108
Cauchy distribution, 78, 195
Cavendish, Henry, 250
Cell counts and probabilities, 314
Censored data, 166
  type I censoring, 235
  type II censoring, 236, 660
Census, 86
Centering, 418
Central limit theorem (CLT), 170–72, 187, 208, 237, 269, 273
Central moment, 27
Chebyshev, Pafnuty, 40
Chebyshev's inequality, 40–41
Chi-square distribution, 176–78, 187–88
Chi-square goodness of fit test, 318–21, 330
Chi-square statistic, 256, 330
Chi-square test, for two-way tables, 326–27
Classical approach to probability, 7–8
Class intervals, 119
Coefficient of concordance (Kendall), 592–94
Coefficient of determination, 354, 385
Coefficient of multiple determination, 404
Coefficient of variation (CV), 116

Cohort studies, 90–91
Combinations, 14
Comparative studies, 83, 100
  importance of control group in, 84–85
Complement, of an event, 9
Completely randomized (CR) design, 97–98, 101, 457–67, 490
  analysis of variance (ANOVA), 462–65
  model diagnostics using residual plots, 466–67
  Kruskal-Wallis test, 581–82
  model/estimates of parameters, 460–62
  multiple comparisons of means, 467–479
  random effects model, 480
Composite hypothesis, 214, 631–32
Compound Poisson distribution, 81
Concordant pair, 589
Concurrent control group, 85
Conditional distribution, 33–35, 62
Conditional expectation (mean), 34, 348
Conditional probability, 15–16, 62
Conditional variance, 35
Confidence interval estimation, 197, 203–8
  confidence level, 203
  confidence limits, 203
  one-sided confidence intervals, 206–8
  two-sided confidence intervals, 203–6
Confounding, 83, 96, 100
Confounding variables, 83–84
Conjugate prior, 647, 658
Consumer's risk, 213
Contingency table, 330
Continuation region, 639
Continuity correction, 174–75, 187
Continuous distributions, 49–52
Continuous random variables, 22–24
Continuous variable, 108–9
Contrast, 473–74, 491
Control chart, 222–23
Control group, 84, 100–101, 269–70
Convenience sampling, 91
Convergence in probability, 625
Cook's distance, 456
Correlation analysis:
  bivariate normal distribution, 379–80
  correlation and causation, 138
  correlation coefficient, population, 38–39, 63

correlation coefficient, sample, 135–38, 149, 385
  pitfalls of, 384–85
  inference on the correlation coefficient, 380–84
Correlation coefficient, 38–39, 63, 135–38, 149, 385
Correlation matrix, 40, 417, 423–4
Counting process, 46
Covariance:
  covariance matrix, 40
  population, 36–38, 62
  sample, 135
Covariates, 96
Cramér-Rao inequality, 623–24, 659
Critical constants, 210
Crossed factor experiments, 504, 541, 547
Cross-over design, 99, 295
Cross-validation, 438, 440
Cumulative distribution function (c.d.f.), 21, 23, 62

D

Data, 82, 107
  types of, 107–9
Data collection, 2, 6, 82–106
  basic experimental designs, 97–99
  basic sampling designs, 91–94
  comparative studies, 83, 100
  experimental studies, 83, 95–100
  noncomparative studies, 83
  observational studies, 83–84
  statistical studies, types of, 83–85
Decision rule, 650, 658, 659
Decision space, 650, 658
Decision theory, 650–58
Degrees of freedom:
  blocks, 486, 491
  error, 360, 408, 463, 486, 490–91, 530, 545, 547
  interaction, 510, 532, 543, 547
  main effects, 510, 543, 545, 547
  regression, 360, 409
  of sampling distributions, 176, 180, 182
  total, 360, 409, 490–91, 510, 531, 543, 545
  treatments, 462, 490–91, 532
Delta method, 377–78, 630–31
Deming, Edward, 120
De Moivre, Abraham, 7, 52
De Morgan, Augustus, 9
De Morgan's law, 9–10
Dependent variables, 346
Descriptive studies, 83, 100

Design:
  balanced, 458
  completely randomized (CR),
    97–98, 101, 457–67, 490
  cross-over, 99, 295
  independent samples, 269–71
  matched pairs, 99, 270–71, 289
  multistage nested, 546
  orthogonal, 516
  pretest only, 84
  pretest–posttest, 84
  randomized block (RBD),
    98–99, 101
  sampling, 91–94
  unbalanced, 458
Discordant pair, 589
Discrete distributions, 42–49, 59,
    62, *See also* Distributions
Discrete random variables,
    21–22
Discrete variable, 108–9, 148
Disjoint events, 9
Distribution-free statistical meth-
    ods, *See* Nonparametric
    statistical methods
Distributions:
  Bernoulli, 42
  beta, 52
  binomial, 43–44, 59, 63
  Cauchy, 78, 195
  chi-square, 176–8
  double exponential, 78, 659
  Erlang, 51
  exponential, 24, 50–51, 59, 63
  gamma, 51
  Gaussian, 52
  geometric, 35–36, 46–47, 59, 63
  hypergeometric, 44–45, 59, 63
  logistic, 77
  lognormal, 57, 59
  multivariate t, 475
  multinomial, 48–49, 63
  negative binomial, 59, 75
  normal, 52–59, 63
  Pareto, 78
  Poisson, 3, 45–46, 59, 63
    compound Poisson, 81
    truncated Poisson, 75
  Snedecor-Fisher's F, 181–2
  Studentized range, 469
  Student's t, 179–80, 188
  table of distributions, 59
  uniform, 49, 59, 63
    continuous, 49, 59, 63
    discrete, 59
  Weibull, 165–66
Double blind study, 85, 295
Double exponential distribution,
    78, 659
Dummy predictor variables,
    419–22
Dunnett method for comparisons
    with a control, 475–77

E

Effect sparsity principle, 522
Empirical model, 346
Erlang distribution, 51
Estimated standard error (SE),
    201
Estimation, 196
  Bayes, 647
  confidence interval, 203
  least squares (LS), 350, 385, 439
  maximum likelihood, 613–31,
    657
  method of moments, 202–3
  point, 197–203
Estimator, 197, 227
  best linear unbiased (BLUE),
    454
  consistent, 625
  efficient, 624
  unbiased, 198
Events, 8–10, 62
  event algebra, 9–10
EWMA, *See* Exponentially
    weighted moving averages
    (EWMA)
Examples:
  acceptance sampling, 45, 209–10,
    217, 219, 653–55
  airline revenues, 204–06, 207–08,
    239
  bicycle data, 528–29, 530–33, 536
  Birthday Problem, 13–14
  bonding strength of capacitors,
    508–09, 512–14, 516, 518
  cardiac output, 132–33, 139–140,
    567, 571–72
  cement data, 416–17, 431–32,
    436–37
  chemical impurities, 221–22
  chemical process yield, 98–99
  control chart, 222–3, 246, 249
  drip loss in meat loaves,
    484–85, 487–89, 584–85
  failure times of capacitors,
    577–79, 598, 600
  genetic experiment using garden
    peas, 316–17
  heat treatment of steel, 95
  hospitalization costs, 271,
    276–78, 280–83
  industrial sales, 424–25, 428–29
  Literary Digest poll, 88–89
  leukemia therapies comparison,
    309, 312, 325, 328
  logistic regression, numerical
    example, 628–29
  memory experiment, 98, 99
  Monte Hall Problem, 20
  1970 draft lottery, 92–93
  pizza tasting, 305–6
  plastic container weights,
    458–59, 461–63, 466–67,
    469–70, 472–74, 477–78

Pólya's urn scheme, 18–19
probability and statistics grades,
    33, 34, 37–38
radioactive decay of polonium,
    319–21
random digits, testing uniformity
    of, 316
rolling two dice, 16, 21, 26, 41,
    168, 175
Salk polio vaccine trial, 210, 309
SAT coaching, 209–11, 215–19,
    223–24, 244, 248
series-parallel system reliability,
    17
service times of disk drives,
    542–44
soda can sales, 420–22
teaching methods comparison,
    581–83
tear strength of rubber, 251–53,
    259–60
test instrument correlation,
    382, 384
thermometer precision, 256–57
thermostat setting, 565–66,
    569–70, 573, 599–600,
    602–3
tire wear data, 349, 353–56, 358,
    362–63, 365–67, 373–74,
    404–7, 410–12
tooth cavities, 43–44, 46
Traveling Salesman Problem,
    13
wine consumption and heart
    disease deaths, 587–89,
    591–92
Expected loss, 650
Expected value, 24–25, 62
Experimental errors, 101
  strategy to reduce, 95–96
Experimental studies, 83, 95–100
  basic concepts and terminology,
    95
  basic designs, 97–99
    completely randomized design
      (CRD), 97–98, 101
    randomized block design
      (RBD), 98–99, 101
  blocking, 96, 101
  experimental errors, 101
    strategy to reduce, 95–96
  experimental units, 95, 100–101
  iterative nature of experimenta-
    tion, 100
  levels, of a factor, 95
  nuisance (noise) factors, 95–97,
    100
  randomization, 97, 101
  repeat measurements, 95, 101
  replication, 95, 101
  run, 95
  treatments, 95, 100
Experimental units, 95, 100–101

Explanatory variables, 83, 346
Exploratory data analysis, 2
   See also Summarizing data
Exponential distribution, 24, 50–51
   double, 78, 659
   memoryless property, 50
   moment generating function,
      29
   moments, 27–28
   percentiles, 30
Exponentially weighted moving
      averages (EWMA),
      144–47, 149
Exponential plot, 165
Exponential smoothing, *See*
      Exponentially weighted
      moving averages
      (EWMA)
Exponential spacings, 195, 235
Extrapolation, 363
Extra sum of squares method,
      410–11, 439–50

F

Factorial experiments, 504
False alarm probability, 223
False negative, 212
False positive, 212
Familywise error rate (FWE),
      467, 491
F-distribution, *See*
      Snedecor-Fisher's
      F-distribution
F-test:
   of analysis of variance, 463–65
   for comparing variances,
      287
Fences, box plot, 121
Fermat, Pierre, 7
Finite population, 87
   sampling, 610
Fisher, Sir Ronald, 181
Fisher information, 620–23, 657
Fisher's exact test, 310, 312
Fisher's protected LSD method,
      468
Fitted values, 353, 385, 404
Fitted vector, 439
Five number summary, 114, 148
Fixed effects model, 480, 491
Fixed factor, 480
Forecast error, 143
Forward stepping algorithm,
      430
Frequency table, 109, 148
Frequentist approach, 7, 167, 647,
      658
Friedman test, 583, 584–85, 604
   pairwise comparisons, 586

G

Galton, Francis, 140
Gambler's ruin problem, 79
Gamma distribution, 51, 59, 63
Gauss, Karl, 7, 52
Gaussian distribution, 52
Gauss–Markov Theorem, 454
Generalized likelihood ratio
      (GLR) tests, 634–38, 657
Geometric distribution, 35–36,
      46–47, 59, 63
Goodness of fit test:
   chi-square, 318–21
   GLR test for multinomial
      distribution, 637–38
   of Poisson distribution, 319–21
Gosset, William (Student), 179

H

Haphazard sampling, 91
Hardy-Weinberg law, 66
Hat matrix, 413, 440
Hessian matrix, 626–27
High leverage points, 370–71
Hinges, box plot, 121, 152
Histogram, 119–20, 148
   class intervals, 119
Historical control group, 85
Historical data, 83
Homogeneity hypothesis, 323, 330,
      462
Hsu method for comparisons with
      the best, 478–79
Hypergeometric distribution,
      44–45, 59, 63
Hypothesis:
   alternative, 208–10
   composite, 214
   of homogeneity, 323, 330, 462
   of independence, 323
   null, 208–10
   simple, 214, 631
Hypothesis tests:
   α- and β-risks, 212
   acceptance region, 210
   critical constants, 210
   formulation of as two-decision
      problem, 211
   level of significance, 216–19
      observed (P-value), 219
   one-sided vs. two-sided, 224
   operating characteristic (OC)
      function, 214–16
   power, 212
   rejection region, 210
   significance test, 211
   test statistics, 210
   type I and type II errors,
      211
   type I and type II error
      probabilities, 211–14
   use and misuse of, 227–29

I

Inadmissible decision rule, 652,
      658
Inclusion–exclusion principle,
      11
Independence hypothesis, 330
Independent events, 16–17, 62
Independent and identically
      distributed (i.i.d.)
      observations, 168
Independent random variables,
      32–33, 62
Independent samples design,
      269–71, 289
   comparing two means, 272–78
      graphical methods, 271–72
      inferences for large samples,
         272–75
      inferences for small samples,
         275–82
   comparing two proportions,
      307–12
      inferences for large samples,
         307–10
      inferences for small samples,
         310–12
   comparing two variances,
      286–89
Independent variables, 346
Inference, 196–236
   confidence interval estimation,
      203–8
   hypothesis tests, 196, 208–27
   point estimation, 197–203
   prediction intervals, 257–58
   tolerance intervals, 258–60
   See also Bayesian inference;
      Inferences for count data;
      Inferences on mean;
      Inferences on proportion;
      Inferences for single samples;
      Inferences for two samples;
      Inferences on variance
Inferences for count data:
   One-way, 314–21
      chi-square goodness of fit test,
         318–21
      test for multinomial
         distribution, 314–18
   two-way, 321–29
      hypothesis tests, 322–27
      odds ratio as a measure of
         association, 327–29
      sampling models, 321–22
Inferences on proportion, 299–345
   comparing two proportions,
      307–14
      independent samples design,
         307–12
      matched pairs design, 312–14
   large sample inferences, 299–306
   power calculation, 305–6

Inferences on proportion
(*continued*)
sample size determination,
301–2, 305–6
small sample inferences, 306
Inferences for single samples (on
mean): 237–54
for large samples, 237–49
confidence intervals on mean,
238–39
hypothesis tests on mean,
239–49
for small samples, 249–54
confidence intervals on mean,
249–52
hypothesis tests on mean,
252–54
robustness of inference methods
for mean, 254
Inferences for single samples (on
variance), 254–57
confidence intervals on variance,
255–56
hypothesis tests on variance,
256–57
Inferences for two samples,
269–98
comparing means of two
populations, 272–86
independent samples design,
270–71, 272–78
matched pairs design, 270–71,
283–86
comparing variances of two
populations, 286–89
graphical methods for comparing
two samples, 271–72
Infinite population, 87
Influential observations, 370, 386,
413, 440
Information matrix, 622–23
Interaction contrasts, 512
Interaction effect, 523
Interaction plot, 506–7
Interaction(s), 418, 483, 506, 547
Interquartile range (IQR), 115
Intersection, of events, 9
Interval variable, 109
Invariance property, of MLE,
616
Inverse probability, 19–20
Inverse regression, 363
Inverse transformation, 396

J

Jackknife method, 595, 601–3, 604
Jacobian of transformation,
61, 63
Jointly distributed random
variables, 30–40
conditional distribution, 33–35,
62
correlation coefficient, 38–39, 63

independent random variables,
32–33
marginal distribution, 31–32,
39–40, 62
Joint probability distribution,
30–31, 62
Judgment sampling, 91

K

Kendall's coefficient of concordance, 592–94
Kendall's rank correlation
coefficient (tau), 589–92,
604
Kolmogorov, Andre, 10
Kruskal-Wallis test, 581–82, 603–4
pairwise comparisons, 583
Kurtosis, 27–28, 118

L

Labeled scatter plot, 134
Lack of fit test, 399–400
Lag, 147
Laplace, Pierre, 7, 52
Law of total probability, 187–89
Law of large numbers, 41
Least significant difference (LSD)
method, 467–68, 491
Least squares (LS) estimates,
350, 385, 439
sampling distribution, 358–360,
408
Least squares (LS) estimation,
202, 348–53, 403–4
Least squares (LS) fitted line,
352–55
Left skewed distribution, 113
Levels of a factor, in experimental
studies, 95
Level of significance, 216–19, 228
choice of, 218–19
observed (*P*-value), 219
Leverage, 370–71
Likelihood function, 614–15, 657
Likelihood ratio (LR) tests,
631–38, 657
generalized, 634–38
Neyman-Pearson lemma,
631–33, 657
Likelihood ratio statistic, 638
Linear regression, 347
ML estimation, 618
multiple, 401–56
simple, 346–400
See also Multiple linear
regression; Simple linear
regression
Location parameter, 574, 575
Logarithmic transformation,
378
Logistic distribution, 77
Logistic function, 391

Logistic regression:
information matrix, 627
maximum likelihood estimation,
619
model, 426
numerical example, 628–29
Logistic transform, 426
Log-likelihood function, 615–16
Log-linear model, 666
Lognormal distribution, 57, 59
Loss function, 58, 658
Lower confidence bound, 206
Lower one-sided test, 220
Lurking variables, 83–84, 131, 149,
385

M

McNemar's test, 313
MA (moving average) forecast,
143
Main effects, 506, 523, 547
Main effects plot, 512
Mann and Whitney U-test,
575
Marginal distributions, 31–32,
39–40, 62
Margin of error, 238, 301
Matched pairs design, 99, 270–71,
289
comparing two means, 283–86
comparing two proportions,
312–14
Matching Game problem, 78
Maximum likelihood estimation,
202, 613–31, 657, 658
likelihood function, 614–15, 657
Maximum likelihood estimator
(MLE):
calculation of, 615–19
efficiency of, 624
invariance property of, 616
large sample inferences based
on, 625–30
multiple parameters, 626–30
single parameter, 625–26
outline of proof of limiting
distribution of, 629–30
properties of, 620–24
Mean, 24–25, 62, 111–13, 148
conditional, 34
confidence intervals (CIs) on,
238–39, 249–52
hypothesis tests on, 239–49,
252–54
population (expected value),
24
robustness of inference methods
for, 254
sample, 111
standard error of the mean
(SEM), 201
Mean absolute percent error
(MAPE), 143

Mean square, 360, 490
Mean squared error (MSE),
198–201, 227, 360, 651
Mean time between failures
(MTBF), 268
Measurement bias, 88
Measurement errors, 96, 101
Measures of dispersion, 113–17
coefficient of variation (CV),
116
five number summary, 114, 148
interquartile range, 115
percentiles, 114–15
quartiles, 114–15, 148
range, 115
standard deviation (SD) and
variance, 115–16
Measures of location, 111–13
mean, 111–13
median, 111–13
resistant (robust) measure of
center, 113
trimmed mean, 113
Median, 29–30, 62, 111–13, 148
population, 29–30
sample, 112
Memoryless property:
exponential distribution, 50
geometric distribution, 47
Mendel, Gregor, 316
Method of moments, 202–3
Midrange, 197, 659
Midrank, 570
Minimax criterion, 658
Minimax decision rule, 652, 658
Mixed effects model, 490, 541
Mixed factor experiments, 540–44,
547
Mixture distribution, 79
MLE, *See* Maximum likelihood
estimator, Maximum
likelihood estimation
Moment generating function
(m.g.f.), 28–29
of sum of independent random
variables, 33
Monte Hall Problem, 20
Most powerful (MP) test, 631,
632–33, 657
Moving averages (MA), 143–44,
149
MSE$_p$ criterion, 433
Multicollinearity, 415–17, 440
measures of, 417
Multifactor experiments:
Two-factor experiments:
with crossed and fixed factors,
505–21
with crossed and mixed
factors, 540–44
with nested and mixed factors,
544–46

2^k factorial experiments,
522–40
Multinomial coefficient, 15
Multinomial distribution, 48–49, 63
Multinomial sampling model,
322
Multiple comparisons of means,
467–479
Bonferroni method, 227, 468,
491
Dunnett method for comparisons
with a control, 475–77
Hsu method for comparisons
with the best, 478–79
Scheffé method for general
contrasts, 477–78
stepwise methods, 470–72
Tukey method for pairwise
comparisons, 469, 491
Multiple comparisons problem,
226–27
Multiple correlation coefficient,
404, 439
Multiple linear regression, 401–56
dummy predictor variables,
419–22
extra sum of squares method,
410–11
least squares (LS) fit, 403–5
multicollinearity, 415–17
multiple regression model:
in basic form, 402–3
in matrix notation, 405–7
strategy for building, 437–39
polynomial regression, 418
prediction of future observations,
412
regression diagnostics, 413–15
standardized regression
coefficients, 423–25
statistical inference for, 407–12
variable selection methods,
427–37
best subsets regression,
431–37
stepwise regression, 427–31
Multiplication Rule, 12
Multistage cluster sampling,
94, 100
Multistage nested designs, 546
Multivariate data, 129, 149
Multivariate distributions, 39–40
t-distribution, 475
Mutually exclusive events, 9
Mutually independent random
variables, 40

N

Negative binomial distribution,
59, 75
Negatively skewed distribution,
113

Nested factor experiments,
504, 544–46, 547
Newsboy problem, 70
Newton-Raphson algorithm,
667
Neyman, Jerzy, 631
Neyman-Pearson lemma, 631–33,
657
Noise factors, 95
Nominal variable, 108, 148
Noncentrality parameter, 254
Noncentral t-distribution, 254
Noncomparative studies, 83, 100
Nonlinear models, 415, 426
Nonparametric statistical methods,
562–612
inferences for several
independent samples,
580–83
Kruskal-Wallis test, 581–82
inferences for several matched
samples, 583–86
Friedman test, 584–85
inferences for single samples,
562–73
sign test and confidence
interval, 563–67
Wilcoxon signed rank test
and confidence interval,
568–73
inferences for two independent
samples, 573–80
Wilcoxon-Mann-Whitney test,
575–79
rank correlation methods,
586–94
Kendall's coefficient of
concordance, 592–94
Kendall's rank correlation
coefficient, 589–92
Spearman's rank correlation
coefficient, 586–89
resampling methods, 594–603
bootstrap method, 597–601
jackknife method, 601–3
permutation tests, 595–97
Nonsampling errors, 88, 100
Normal approximation to binomial,
172–74
Normal distribution, 52–59, 63
linear combinations of normal
r.v.'s, 57–58
percentiles of, 55–57
standard, 53–55
Normal equations, 351, 403
Normal plots, 123–25, 148
Normal scores, 123
Normalizing transformation,
125–28
Nuisance factors, 95–97, 100
Null hypothesis, 208–10

Numerical data, 148
  box and whiskers plot, 121–22
  histogram, 119–20, 148
  measures of dispersion, 113–17
  measures of location, 111–13
  normal plot, 123–25, 148
  run chart, 128
  sample kurtosis, 118
  sample skewness, 118
  stem and leaf plot, 120–21, 148
Numerical variable, 108

O

Observational studies, 83–91
  prospective study, 86, 90–91, 100
  retrospective study, 86, 90–91,
    100
  sample surveys, 85–89, 100
Observed level of significance,
    219
OC curve, 215
Odds ratio, 307, 327–29
One-sided confidence intervals,
    206–8
One-sided tests, 220–21
One-way layout, 458, 580 *See also*
    Completely randomized
    design
Operating characteristic (OC)
    function, 214–16, 228
Order statistics, 112, 184–88
  sampling distributions of,
    184–87
Ordinal variable, 108–9, 148
Ordinary least squares (OLS),
    453–54
Orthogonal contrasts, 527, 529
Orthogonal design, 516
Outcome variables, 83, 346
Outliers, 112, 148, 386, 414, 440
  checking for, 117, 121, 369–70
  dealing with, 372–73

P

Paired t-test, 284, 290
Pairwise comparisons, *See* Multiple
    comparisons of means
  for Friedman test, 586
  for Kruskal-Wallis test, 583
Parameters, 3, 24, 62, 86, 100
Parameter space, 614, 650, 658
Pareto chart, 109, 148
Pareto distribution, 78, 625–26
Partial correlation coefficients,
    428, 440
Partial F-test, 427–28, 440
Pascal, Blaise, 7
Pascal's triangle, 64
p-chart, 302–3
Pearson, Egon, 211
Pearson, Karl, 140

Pearson chi-square statistic,
    318
Percentiles, 29–30, 114–15
Permutation, 12–13, 604
Permutation tests, 595–97
Personal approach to probability,
    8
Pie chart, 109
Pivotal r.v., 205, 260–61
Placebo effect, 85
Point estimation, 197–203
  Bayes estimator, 657
  bias, 198–201
  expected squared error loss,
    198, 651
  mean square error (MSE),
    198–201
  methods of estimation, 202–3
  standard error (SE), 201, 227
  unbiased estimator, 198
  variance, 198–201
Poisson approximation to binomial,
    46
Poisson distribution, 3, 45–46, 59,
    63
  compound, 81
  truncated, 75
Poisson process, 46
Poisson regression, 666
Poisson, Simeon, 7
Pólya, George, 18
Pólya's urn scheme, 18–19
Polynomial regression, 418
Population, 3, 86–88, 100
Positively skewed distribution,
    113
Posterior distribution, 647, 658
Posterior mean, 647
Posterior probability, 19–20
Posterior risk, 656
Posterior variance, 647
Power, of hypothesis test, 212, 228
Power function, 214–16
Prediction error sum of squares
    (PRESS), 436
Prediction interval (PI), 257–58,
    362, 386, 412
Predictive model, 437
Predictor variables, 83, 346
PRESS$_p$ criterion, 435–36
Pretest only design, 84
Pretest–posttest design, 84
Prior distribution, 646–47, 658
Prior probability, 19–20
Probability, 7–81
  axiomatic approach, 8, 62
  axioms of, 10–11
  Bayes' theorem, 19–20, 62
  Bonferroni inequality, 11
  central limit theorem, 170–72
  Chebyshev's inequality, 40–41
  classical approach, 7–8
  conditional, 15–16, 62

  continuous distributions, 49–52
  convergence in, 625
  correlation coefficient, 38, 63
  counting formulas, 12
  covariance, 36–38, 62
  cumulative distribution function
    (c.d.f.), 21, 23, 62
  discrete distributions, 42–49, 59
  distributions, 62
  event algebra, 8–10
  expected value (mean), 24–25,
    62
  frequentist approach, 7
  inclusion–exclusion principle,
    11
  jointly distributed random
    variables, 30–40
  law of total probability, 187–89
  law of large numbers, 42
  moment generating function
    (m.g.f.), 28–29, 33
  multiplication rule, 12
  normal distribution, 52–59, 63
  personal approach, 8
  posterior, 19–20
  prior, 19–20
  probability density function
    (p.d.f), 22–23, 62
  probability mass function
    (p.m.f.), 21, 62
  random variables, 20–24, 62
  sample spaces, 8–10, 12
  statistics, relation to, 2–4
  subjective approach, 8
Probability density function (p.d.f.),
    22–23, 62
Probability histograms, 172
Probability integral transform,
    195
Probability mass function (p.m.f.),
    21, 62
Probability proportional to
    size (PPS) sampling,
    94
Producer's risk, 213
Product multinomial sampling
    model, 322
Proportion(s):
  confidence interval for, large
    sample, 299–302
  inferences for comparing two
    proportions, 307–14
  independent samples design,
    307–12
  matched pairs design, 312–14
  large sample hypothesis tests on,
    302–6
  power calculation/sample
    size determination for,
    304–6
  small sample hypothesis tests on,
    306
Prospective study, 86, 90–91, 100

Pure error estimate, 399
P-value, 219, 222, 228

Q

Qualitative variable, 108
Quantile-quantile plot, 271, 289
Quantiles, 29–30, 114
Quantitative variable, 108
Quartiles, 114–15, 148
Quota sampling, 91

R

r_p^2-criterion, 432–33
Random allocation, 84
Random component, time series, 142
Random effects model, 480, 491
Random errors, 347, 403, 547
Random experiments, 8
Random factor, 480
Randomization, 97, 101
Randomized block (RB) design, 98–99, 101, 482–90, 583
    analysis of variance (ANOVA), 485–87
    fixed-effects model, 483
    Friedman test, 583–585
    Mixed effects model for, 489–90
    model diagnostics using residual plots, 487–88
    multiple comparisons of treatment effects, 489
Randomized response, 235
Random sample, 168
Random variables, 20–24, 62
    continuous, 22–24
    discrete, 21–22
    independent, 32–33, 62
    jointly distributed, 30–40
    mutually independent, 40
    transformations of, 58–62
Range, 115
Rank correlation methods, 586–94
    Kendall's coefficient of concordance, 592–94
    Kendall's rank correlation coefficient, 589–92
    Spearman's rank correlation coefficient, 586–89
Ratio variable, 109
Ratio estimator, 666
RB design, See Randomized block (RB) design
Redundancy, 17
Regression analysis, See Regression modeling
Regression diagnostics, 365–79, 413–15
Regression fallacy, 141–42
Regression function, 34, 348
Regression line, 149, 347

Regression modeling:
    dummy predictor variables, 419–22
    interactions, 419, 438–39
    logistic regression, 426, 619, 627–29
    multiple linear regression, 415–26
    polynomial regression, 418
    simple linear regression, 346–79
    strategy for, 437–39
Regression sum of squares (SSR), 354, 404, 439
Regression toward the mean, 140–42, 149
Rejection numbers, 642
Rejection region, 210
Relative frequency, 109
Relative risk, 307
Reliability, 17
Repeat measurements, 95, 101
Replication, 95, 101, 505
Representative sample, 89, 91, 100
Resampling methods, 594–603, 604
    bootstrap method, 597–601
    jackknife method, 601–3
    permutation tests, 595–97
Residual analysis, 365–79, 413–14, 466, 487–88, 516–17
Residual plots, See Residual analysis
Residuals, 353, 385
    standardized, 369, 413–14
Residual vector, 439
Response bias, 88
Response variables, 83, 100, 346
Restricted model, 541
Retrospective study, 86, 90–91, 100
Right skewed distribution, 113
Risk function, 650–51, 658, 659
Run, 95
Run chart, 128, 142
Run order, 527

S

Sample, 3, 86–88, 100
Sample c.d.f., 597
Sample correlation coefficient, 353–54
Sample covariance, 135
Sampled population, 87
Sample mean, 111
    sampling distributions of, 168–75
Sample median, 112
Sample size determination:
    for a confidence interval on proportion, 301–2
    for a large sample test on proportion, 304–6
    for a matched pairs t-test, 285–86

for an independent samples t-test, 282–83
    for a single sample t-test, 253–54
    for a z-interval, 238–39
    for a z-test, 246–49
Sample spaces, 8–10, 594, 650
Sample surveys, 85–89, 100
Sample variance, sampling distributions of, 175–79
Sampling designs, 91–94
    convenience sampling, 91
    haphazard sampling, 91
    judgment sampling, 91
    multistage cluster sampling, 94, 100
    quota sampling, 91
    simple random sampling (SRS), 91–93, 100
    stratified random sampling, 93–94, 100
    systematic sampling, 94
Sampling distributions, 167–95
    central limit theorem (CLT), 170–72, 187
    chi-square distribution, 176–78, 187–88
    of order statistics, 184–88
    of sample mean, 168–75
    of sample variance, 175–79
    Snedecor-Fisher's F-distribution, 181–84, 188
    Student's t-distribution, 179–80, 188
Sampling errors, 4, 88, 100, 167, 187
Sampling fraction (rate), 92
Sampling frame, 87
Sampling with/without replacement, 44, 194
Sampling units, 86
Saturated model, 507
Scale parameter, 575
Scatter plot, 132–34, 149, 289, 348–49
Scheffé method for general contrasts, 477–78
Screening experiments, 504
Seasonal component, time series, 142
Self-selection bias, 88
Sensitivity, of a diagnostic test, 67
Sequential probability ratio test (SPRT), 638–46, 658
    for Bernoulli parameter:
        expected sample sizes, 645–46
        stopping rule, 642
    continuation region, 639
    expected sample size for, 643–46

Sequential probability ratio test
  (SPRT) (*continued*)
  for normal mean:
    expected sample sizes,
      645
    stopping rule, 641
    stopping boundaries, 639, 658
    stopping time, 639–40
Serial correlation, 147, 369
Side-by-side box plot, 271, 276,
  289, 458–59
Significance level, *See* Level of
  significance
Significance test, 211
Sign test, 563–67, 603
  confidence interval, 565–67
  for matched pairs, 567
  for a single sample, 563–65
Simple hypothesis, 214, 631
Simple linear regression:
  analysis of variance for, 360–61
  calibration (inverse regression),
    363
  checking model assumptions,
    365–69
  data transformations, 373–79
  influential observations, 370–73
  least squares (LS) fit, 348–53
  outliers, 369–73
  prediction of future observations,
    361–65
  probabilistic model for, 347–48
  regression diagnostics, 365–7
  sampling distribution of
    regression coefficients,
    358–61
  statistical inference for, 356–65
Simple random sampling (SRS),
  91–93, 100
Simpson's paradox, 131–32, 149
Simultaneous confidence intervals
  (SCIs), 468
Simultaneous confidence level
  (SCL), 468
Single blind study, 85
Single factor experiments, 457–503
  completely randomized (CR)
    design, 457–67
  multiple comparisons of means,
    467–79, 491
  random effects model for
    one-way layout, 480–82,
    491
  randomized block (RB) design,
    482–90
Skewed distribution, 113, 148
Skewness, 27–28, 118
Smoothing constant for EWMA,
  145
Snedecor-Fisher's F-distribution,
  181–84, 188
Snedecor, George, 181

Spearman's rank correlation
  coefficient, 586–89, 604
Specificity, of a diagnostic test,
  67
SPRT, *See* Sequential probability
  ratio test (SPRT)
Squared error loss function,
  198, 651
Square root transformation,
  379
Stable component, time series,
  142
Standard deviation (SD), 25–26,
  115–16
Standard error of the mean
  (SEM), 201
Standard error (SE), 201, 227
Standardized rates, 132
Standardized regression
  coefficients, 423–25
Standardized residuals, 369,
  413–14, 440
Standardized z-scores, 117
Standardizing, 53, 418
Standard normal distribution,
  53–55, 63
Standard order, 527
Stationary time series, 143
Statistical decision problem,
  650–52
Statistical studies, 83–85
Statistics, 86
  Bayesian, 19
  descriptive, 2
  exploratory, 2, 6
  inferential, 2
  and probability, 2–4
Stem and leaf plot, 120–21, 148
Stepwise regression, 427–31
Stirling's approximation, 195
Stochastically larger, use of term,
  574
Stopping boundaries, 639, 658
Stopping time, 639–40
Straight line regression, 139–40,
  149
Strata, 93
Stratified random sampling,
  93–94, 100
Strong Law of Large Numbers
  (SLLN), 41
Studentized range distribution,
  469
Student's t-distribution, 179–80,
  188
Subjective approach to probability,
  8
Sum of Squares:
  blocks, 485–86, 491
  effects, 531
  error, 353, 404, 439, 463, 486,
    490–91, 530, 545, 547
  interaction, 510, 532, 543, 547

  main effects, 510, 543, 545, 547
  regression, 354, 404, 439
  total, 354, 404, 439, 463, 485,
    490–91, 510, 531, 543,
    545, 547
  treatments, 462, 485, 490–91, 532
Summarizing data, 107–66
  bivariate data, 128–42, 149
  categorical data, 109
  numerical data, 109–28
  time-series data, 142–48
Symmetric distribution, 112
Systematic errors, 96, 101
Systematic sampling, 94, 100

T

Tau, Kendall's, 589
t-distribution:
  multivariate, 475
  noncentral, 254
  Student's (central), 179–80, 188
Tests of hypotheses, *See* hypothesis
  tests
Test set, 438, 440
Test statistics, 210
Three-sigma control limits, 222
Tied pair, 589
Time-series data, 128
  autocorrelation coefficients,
    147–49
  components, 142, 149
  data smoothing and forecasting
    techniques, 142–47
  exponentially weighted moving
    averages (EWMA),
    144–47, 149
  moving averages (MA), 143–44,
    149
  run chart, 142
  stationary time-series, 143
  summarizing, 142–48
  time-series plot, 142
t-interval, 261
Tolerance interval (TI), 258–60
Total probability, law of, 187–89
Total time on test (TTT), 236
Training set, 438
Transformations of Data, 373–79
  arcsin, 395
  arctan hyperbolic, 396
  inverse, 396
  linearizing, 373–77
  logarithmic, 378
  logistic, 426
  normalizing, 125–28
  square root, 379
  variance stabilizing, 377–79
Transformations of random
  variables, 58–62
Traveling salesman problem,
  13
Treatments, 84, 95, 100, 490, 504,
  532

Treatment combinations, 504
Treatment effect, 247, 460, 483, 490
Treatment factors, 95, 100, 270
Trend component, time series, 142
Trimmed mean, 113
Truncated Poisson distribution, 75
t-tests, 252, 261
  paired, 284, 290
  power calculation and sample size determination for, 253–54
Tukey method, 469, 491
2^k experiments, 522–40
  active factors, 522
  effect sparsity principle, 522
  main effects and interactions, 522–29
  model diagnostics using residual plots, 536–37
  regression approach to, 533–36
  single replicate case, 537–40
  statistical inference for, 529–33
Two-decision problem, 211
Two-factor experiments:
  with crossed and fixed factors, 505–21
  with crossed and mixed factors, 540–44
  with nested and mixed factors, 544–46
Two-sided confidence interval, 203–6
Two-sided tests, 220–24
Two-stage test, 267
Two-way layout, balanced, 505
Two-way tables, 129–31, 149
  chi-square test for, 326–27
Type I censoring, 203–8, 236

Type I error and error probability, 211, 228
Type II censoring, 236, 660
Type II error and error probability, 211, 228

U

Unbalanced design, 458
Unbiased estimator, 198, 227
Uniform distribution:
  continuous, 49, 59, 63, 617
  discrete, 59
Uniformly most powerful (UMP) test, 633
Unimodal distribution, 120
Union, of events, 9, 11
Unit exponential scores, 165
Units, 3, 86
  experimental, 95, 100–101
  sampling, 86
Unrestricted model, 541
Upper confidence bound, 206

V

Variables, 82, 107–9
Variable selection methods:
  best subsets regression, 431–37
  stepwise regression, 427–31
Variance, 24–26, 62, 115, 227
Variance components, 547
Variance components model, 480, 491, 541
Variance-covariance matrix, 40
Variance inflation factors (VIF), 417
Variance stabilizing transformation, 377–79, 466
Venn diagram, 9–10

W

Waiting time distribution, 46, 50
Wald, Abraham, 638
Wald sequential probability ratio test, 638–46
Wald's identity, 644
Walsh averages, 572
Weak Law of Large Numbers (WLLN), 41–42
Weibull distribution, 165–66
Weibull plot, 165
Weighted least squares (WLS) estimation, 454
Welch-Satterthwaite method, 280–81
Whiskers, of box plot, 121
Wilcoxon-Mann-Whitney test, 575–79, 596, 603
  confidence interval, 579–80
Wilcoxon rank sum test, 575
Wilcoxon signed rank test, 568–73
  confidence interval, 572–73
Window for moving average, 143

X

$\bar{X}$-control chart, 222–23

Y

Yates, Frank, 533
Yates algorithm, 533

Z

z-intervals, 205, 238, 260
z-score, 117
z-tests, 242–48